THE PRESS OF IDEAS

*Readings for Writers
on Print Culture
and the Information Age*

THE PRESS OF IDEAS

*Readings for Writers
on Print Culture
and the Information Age*

EDITED BY

Julie Bates Dock

BEDFORD BOOKS OF ST. MARTIN'S PRESS
Boston

For Bedford Books

President and Publisher: Charles H. Christensen
General Manager and Associate Publisher: Joan E. Feinberg
Managing Editor: Elizabeth M. Schaaf
Developmental Editor: Steve Scipione
Editorial Assistants: Mark Reimold, Alanya Harter
Production Editor: Ann Sweeney
Production Assistant: Bill McKenna
Copyeditors: Carol Blumentritt, Kathy Smith
Text Design: Anna Post George
Cover Design: Night & Day Design
Cover Art: *Writer's Collage.* Copyright © Rei Taka, 1995. Courtesy of Yancey
Richardson Gallery, New York.
Library of Congress Catalog Card Number: 95–80792

0   9   8   7   6
f   e   d   c   b   a

For information, write: St. Martin's Press, Inc.
175 Fifth Avenue, New York, NY 10010

Editorial Offices: Bedford Books *of* St. Martin's Press
75 Arlington Street, Boston, MA 02116

ISBN: 0–312–13319–7

ACKNOWLEDGMENTS

PREFACE
FOR INSTRUCTORS

WHY THIS BOOK? PRINT CULTURE, CRITICAL THINKING, AND STUDENT WRITING

The Press of Ideas begins from the premise that our culture has not, as some would have us believe, abandoned text-based communication for the image-based communication of television and film. Instead, *The Press of Ideas* assumes that printed texts still govern our understanding of our world, even as we are barraged by images. Images have captured our attention because new media and new techniques have continually demanded new decoding methods. But print acts on us in equally complex ways as it is actively decoded by readers.

Our interactions with printed materials have become so habitual that we no longer pay attention to them. Reading print in its many forms has become a transparent activity, one we scarcely notice that we are doing. *The Press of Ideas* aims to make the invisible visible once more. It focuses attention on the act of reading print, an act we perform thousands of times a day. It highlights the materiality of print—the physical properties of books, magazines, flyers, newspapers, and contracts—in ways that allow us to scrutinize how form and content cooperate to impart meaning.

What could be more central to becoming a strong writer than understanding the interactions between writers and readers that take place through printed texts? This book's approach gives students a framework for examining texts and analyzing their own assumptions. Students can learn critical thinking skills as they analyze the documents of their culture. They can develop a critical perspective on everything they read as they increase their understanding of how and why they read as they do. They can grow as writers by examining the varieties of discourse in these pages, and responding in writing to the assignments.

WHY THIS APPROACH? PRINT CULTURE STUDIES

The approach of this book derives from the field of print culture studies, or "history of the book." As the latter phrase implies, an awareness of the past is vital to our understanding of how printed texts work. However, print culture studies extends to include electronic communication as well. This book emphasizes the continuities between the concrete world of print and the virtual world of cyberspace. It looks at how processes long established persist and how they are changed as technology influences the flow of information.

Encompassing many disciplines and types of discourse, print culture studies continually probes the relations of literacy, knowledge, technology, and power. It seeks to uncover the connections between reading, writing, and behavior that profoundly affect every member of literate society. The topics addressed by the book are both timely and timeless. Each chapter offers a historic perspective on an essential aspect of print culture while simultaneously connecting that issue to our present and future lives.

WHY THESE READINGS? THE RANGE OF PRINT CULTURE

The sixty-four readings represent a broad cross-section of printed culture. They include generous samplings from the world of belles-lettres, from *Harper's*, the *Atlantic Monthly* (both today and a century ago), and *The New Yorker*. Right alongside those works are pieces from popular magazines such as *Details*, *Time*, *Newsweek*, and *Ms.*, and newspaper journalism from the *Los Angeles Times* and the *New York Times*. Some selections come from the in-house magazines of political advocacy groups, such as STAT [Stop Teenage Addiction to Tobacco] and FAIR [Fairness and Accuracy in Reporting]. Others come from professional journals addressed to publishers, librarians, or teachers. The *Utne Reader* and the fan 'zine *h2so4* give students a glimpse of the alternative press. And finally, each chapter includes at least one selection originally published by and for scholars, since college students must master the style and techniques of academic discourse, both as readers and writers, even though they often find such discourse bewildering.

Similarly, students may know contemporary culture most thoroughly and feel uncomfortable with older idioms and ways of thinking. But printed culture goes back five hundred years, and it's important to assess historical continuities. Therefore, this book includes eighteenth-century writings by Benjamin Franklin and Samuel Johnson, and nineteenth-century memoirs by Frederick Douglass and Zitkala-Ša, placed side by side with modern pieces. An excerpt from Louisa May Alcott's *Little Women* is juxtaposed with one from the novelization of the 1994 movie by Laurie Lawlor, so students can compare how authors from different centuries address an audience of adolescents.

Diversity of publications is matched by diversity in genres. In these pages students will read memoirs and fiction, as well as memoranda, letters, and extracts from a concentration camp diary. Two of the selections are transcriptions of dialogues, though they differ from each other dramatically: One is a conversation among lawyers Catharine MacKinnon, Floyd Abrams, and Anthony Lewis held in the august offices of the *New York Times*; the other is an online "chat" among computer hackers that spanned eleven days and included twenty participants, known by such names as Acid Phreak, Phiber Optik, and Eddie Joe Homeboy.

The world of print has more pluralities than can be explored in one anthology, but this book has tried to bring students into contact with as many forms and voices as possible. People from many cultures and perspectives come together within the covers of this book.

HOW DOES IT WORK? THE ORGANIZATION AND EDITORIAL APPARATUS

The book is comprised of a general introduction, six chapters, and reading selections. The general introduction lays the conceptual groundwork for the topics that follow, giving students a context from which to approach the readings. Each of the chapters is organized around a key question in print culture studies; chapter introductions explore various ramifications of the organizing questions. Headnotes to each selection provide contextual information about the author(s), the issues, and the original site of publication.

Each reading selection is followed by two sets of questions labeled "Consider the Source" and "Consider the Implications." Consider the Source questions guide students to fuller comprehension of the selection, asking them to identify key concepts, define important terms, assess the author's use of evidence, and articulate the main ideas of the piece. They also ask students to evaluate how the selection was targeted to its original audience, either by looking within the text for the author's appeals to particular kinds of readers or by looking at the appendix entry for clues to the original publication's readership.

Consider the Implications questions prompt students for class discussion, journal entries, research and analytical writing. They ask students to make connections among readings in various chapters, as well as connections to the world outside of this book. Many of the assignments involve research, which may mean flipping to the appendix, browsing in bookstores, conducting online searches, or interviewing faculty or peers.

Following the readings is the appendix, "Who Publishes What?," where you and your students will find thumbnail sketches of the original publishers of every selection. These concise histories provide opportunities for further discussion, writing, and research as students rediscover the target audiences and marketing strategies that the original writing enjoyed.

Finally, the *Editor's Notes on Teaching THE PRESS OF IDEAS* provides an overview of print culture studies and an annotated bibliography of readings in this field, suggestions for organizing your syllabus and using collaborative journals, discussions of each selection, and ideas for building research assignments from the appendix.

WHO HELPED? ACKNOWLEDGMENTS

As this book continually emphasizes, every product of print culture depends on the collaboration of many minds and many hands. *The Press of Ideas* is no exception.

The extensive involvement on the part of Bedford Books surprised me, even though I was prepared for it in principle. I am grateful to Chuck Christensen and Joan Feinberg for taking a chance with this unusual material and encouraging the project to go forward. Elizabeth Schaaf and Ann Sweeney skillfully steered the manuscript through the press with the help of Kathy Smith, Bill McKenna, and Carol Blumentritt; Mark Reimold ran the review program; Kim Chabot and Karen Rose tracked down obscure information; Alanya Harter assisted in countless ways. The appendix was the work of Joyce Hinnefeld, from whose careful research I learned a lot. To all of them, my thanks. But my greatest debt goes to Steve Scipione, who guided the development of the book from first to last. His innumerable phone calls, faxes, and FedEx packages kept my mind working and my spirits high.

I also thank the many reviewers of the manuscript whose suggestions helped shape the final contents of the book: J. D. Applen, University of California, Santa Barbara; Donna Dunbar-Odom, East Texas State University; Russel Durst, University of Cincinnati; Barbara Sloan, Santa Fe Community College; and Irwin Weiser, Purdue University. Lee Heller of Hampshire College contributed her expertise in print culture and made valuable recommendations of articles. I was especially fortunate to have the advice of Sonia Maasik, UCLA Writing Programs. Her thoughtful suggestions sharpened the focus of the editorial apparatus and helped the book reach its potential audience.

Friends and colleagues who helped in diverse ways include Dorothy Goldbart Clark, who was there when this all began; Bill Gilmore and the participants in the American Antiquarian Society's summer seminar in "Regional Cultures of the Book"; and the members of the Society for the History of Authorship, Reading and Publishing (SHARP) who responded to my e-mail queries with valuable tips, especially E. Jennifer Monaghan, Priscilla Coit Murphy, and Joan Shelley Rubin. Roger Daniels, Sue Kunitomi Embrey, and Harry Honda gave me invaluable leads on Japanese internment camps. June License supplied examples of prison literature. Janet and Charles Payne, my kindly neighbors, lent vital technical support.

At Loyola Marymount University I had the support and assistance of Dean Mary Milligan; Linda Bannister, Chair of the Department of English; Angie Guzman; Steve Thacker and Karen Schatz of Interlibrary Loan; and the many reference librarians who helped me track down obscure information and sources. Lori Jane Gloyd did yeoman's service garnering all the permissions for the book. Most importantly, I had the advice and feedback of my many students, both in freshman writing and in my Book in Society course.

My family's constant support has never been more important to me. My husband Charles and daughter Abigail have been especially patient through all the deadlines and crises, never failing to encourage me and always helping to recharge my intellectual batteries.

I dedicate this book to Lester A. Beaurline, who first introduced me to book history, and to the memory of my grandmother, Rose Lowenstein, a regular sojourner in the world of books.

CONTENTS

3   WHAT DO YOU THINK? Print and Opinion Making   *203*

THE PRESS OF IDEAS

Readings for Writers
on Print Culture
and the Information Age

INTRODUCTION

Reading test scores decline year after year while sales of video games skyrocket. Television invades our homes on more than a hundred channels. Music videos broadcast a jumble of images, several dozen per minute. Popular wisdom tells us that our country is no longer a nation of readers. Instead, we are told that we belong to a visual culture, an image-based culture. Perhaps you've even heard today's college students characterized as illiterate, or "postliterate."

Is this true? Are we really nonreaders? You can't step out of bed in the morning without being assaulted by writing clamoring to be read: the label on the coffee can, the instructions on the frozen waffles, the directions for making the orange juice, the texts that tell you which carton contains creamer and which holds buttermilk, not to mention the brand name on the refrigerator that you opened to get at those cartons. All these messages confront you even before you find the funnies in the morning paper. When you get in your car, writing on the dashboard tells you "Fasten Seatbelts" or warns you to check your brakes. While driving down the street, you read stop signs and merge signs, street names, and freeway directions. You might even need to read a map with all its written messages, just to get where you're going. When you go shopping, you read price tags and size labels, washing instructions and sale signs, along with the brand names and slogans that lured you into the stores in the first place. Then, there are the newspapers, magazines, and advertisements that you routinely read without stopping to think about it. And if you are truly a nonreader, why are those direct marketing companies always bombarding you with junk mail?

Print saturates our culture. The problem is not so much that we read images better than we read words on a page; rather, we're so used to reading that we no longer notice that we're doing it. You and I are so thoroughly immersed in print on a day-to-day basis that we don't pay attention to it, even though it routinely instructs us, informs us, and shapes our views of the world and of ourselves. From the survival reading that we do just to get around in our world to the "real" reading that we associate with books, our brains are busy processing print-based information all day long.

The Press of Ideas grows out of the belief that instead of tuning out print, we should be tuning it in if we're going to understand how it affects our opinions and behavior. The book's perspective comes from the emerging discipline of the history of the book—also known as print culture studies—an interdisciplinary field that explores how print-based knowledge is produced, distributed, and absorbed by readers.

This book is designed to help you explore and establish your own place in our print-dominated culture. You're already an experienced reader, having decoded millions of words by the time you reached college. As a student in a writing class, you'll now be asked to produce texts of your own instead of just reading texts written by others. If you've come to college straight from high school, your writing experience may be limited. You may have written papers for school assignments or even worked on the school newspaper. Perhaps you've written letters to friends or family. If you've had experience in the workplace, you'll have done other kinds of writing, such as memos, reports, and business letters. But your writing pace will probably accelerate now that you're in college. You'll be asked to write more papers, more often, for more different types of courses than ever before. You'll be writing for an audience of students and teachers at the college level, and your success will depend not only on what you have to say, but on how astutely you gauge that audience's interests and purposes.

This book will focus your attention on the ways that print influences readers and will make you a more savvy consumer of print. The same analytical skills that will help you as a reader will also help you become a more effective writer, producing texts shaped for a variety of critical readers. Before we examine various methods of analyzing print, a little historical background will help clarify how revolutionary print has been in our culture. Perhaps the best way to measure how profoundly print has affected the way we view the world is to look back to the time before the invention of the printing press.

THE WORLD BEFORE THE PRINTING PRESS

In a world where scribes laboriously copied each book or document by hand, books were rare and, therefore, highly prized. Few people could read, and fewer still could write. Such skills were largely restricted to the nobility, the clergy, and the occasional merchant. Knowledge of the written word was intimately associated with power—the king's power to govern through edicts and proclamations, the court's power to summon you to trial by means of a writ, the landlord's power to serve you with an eviction order, not to mention the power of God embodied in the Bible and the prayer book. Our circumstances may be different today, but knowledge and power are still closely linked, as we shall see.

Most people in medieval Europe didn't need to read, since commerce and culture were largely oral. News was delivered by word of mouth, often through the songs of traveling minstrels. Literature took the form of stories and songs recited before groups, or plays enacted in public squares. Legal and business transactions also relied on oral delivery, and our present-day language still reflects this oral world. We talk about a *hearing* in court or an *audit* (from the Latin verb "*to hear*") of accounts, terms that are holdovers from the world before the printing press.

This world changed irrevocably about A.D. 1450 when a German goldsmith named Johannes Gutenberg invented a method of printing from movable type. He figured out how to cast individual letters from lead and then arrange those pieces of lead type into words, sentences, and paragraphs that could be printed quickly in multiple copies. Once the copies were printed, the lead type could be rearranged and used again to print a different document. Now, instead of the months or even years that scribes needed to produce a single copy of a book, printers could churn out hundreds of identical copies in a fraction of the time.

In the thousand years before the invention of the printing press, scribes may have produced, according to some estimates, about eight million books in all of Europe. By comparison, in the first fifty years after Gutenberg, about twenty million books were printed. Clearly, the printing press caught on fast.

Many people opposed the new invention, claiming that it would destroy people's memories. According to the Greek philosopher Plato, his teacher Socrates had had the same complaint about the spread of writing, some eighteen centuries before print. Writing, Socrates feared, would weaken the mind by making people dependent on written words as a crutch for recalling information. Furthermore, it would distance words from the person who spoke them, making them lifeless and dehumanized. Now, print was charged with weakening the memory. Who needed to memorize anything if a handy reference book was available? By the same token, who needed a sage or wise man if the same information could be had by looking in a book? Printing democratized knowledge by making it accessible to everyone.

Or, almost everyone. As the oral culture became increasingly literate, controlling who could read and what could be read became a means to influence behavior. Slaves were prohibited from learning to read; women were channeled into only certain kinds of reading; controversial or disruptive books were burned, banned, or limited to particular audiences. Exclusion from full participation in the world of literacy quickly meant exclusion from the corridors of power.

KNOWLEDGE AND POWER

This crucial connection between knowledge and power is explored throughout *The Press of Ideas*. Each chapter asks a fundamental question about reading and the world of print, but all the questions address some aspect of the power of printed information. The first chapter, "How Do We Read?" considers how readers make meaning from printed works. Books are not always read the same way by everyone; therefore, it is important to look at how and why different readers approach the same text. It is equally important to see how print enhances the status of an idea. A major phone company recently built an entire ad campaign on the belief that the written word intrinsically possesses greater value than the spoken word. "Put it in writing," AT&T admonished MCI, tapping into our assumption that print carries the cachet of truth.

But what if writing cannot be read, or if ideas never get printed in the first place? Chapter 2, "Who Reads?" looks at how access to print has been denied or limited to certain groups, and the consequent value that literacy has for these groups. We'll look at various kinds of literacy, and who gets to participate in them. Because our knowledge of the world is so often shaped by what we read, print profoundly affects our opinions, as we'll see in chapter 3, "What Do You Think?" Representations of minorities, women, social trends, and foreign affairs are filtered for us through print. Human minds and motives determine what gets printed and, perhaps more importantly, what does not get printed.

Have you read a good book lately? It's likely you immediately thought of literary works in order to answer that question. Did you include or exclude that trashy novel you read over summer vacation or the latest thriller from Stephen King or Tom Clancy? How about Harlequin romances or detective stories? Are they "good books"? The real question here is, "Who decides what constitutes culture?" Print has the power to establish and lend authority to "culture." Popular culture often gets dismissed when it isn't in the pantheon of print. Even when it is in print, it may not be the right sort of print. Chapter 4, "What Should You Read?" will look at how print helps determine which cultural products are validated and which are scorned.

Since knowledge and power have been forever connected, there have always been a variety of forces that try to restrict the flow of information. Chapter 5, "What Shouldn't You Read?" examines some of the many forms of censorship. We'll hear voices raised in protest over books that have been printed, others protesting the suppression of books. We'll see how the First Amendment protects authors and publishers, and how it is being challenged in the cause of protecting society. We'll also look at the people and ideologies that have shaped your textbooks from the time you learned to read.

Finally, chapter 6, "What's Next?" addresses communication in the electronic era. With the advent of computers, many people are predicting the demise of the book and the decline of literacy. Computers, they say, will replace books as the vehicles for information and entertainment. To some extent, this may be true. We like to think that computers are ushering in a new age, but many of the concerns that arose from the spread of print still apply in cyberspace, though in different forms. As we enter the information age, we'll need to be conscious of the mechanisms that are used to control the flow of electronic information, and how those same mechanisms were handled in the print era. Which students will have computer access to the information superhighway? Who decides? What are the consequences if you're not connected to the latest technogoodies?

All of the readings in these chapters are designed to let you explore the many aspects of print that affect you. Throughout the book, you'll be invited to go outside the book and think about your own reading choices and about the impact print has on your life. I think you'll discover that you know a great deal about the world of print, for you have lived your whole life swimming in a virtual sea of ink.

As you read and think critically about printed texts, you'll also learn to think critically about your own writing. Print culture studies offers strategies for examining written communication, both printed and digital, published and unpublished. It asks how and why people read or write. What purposes guide the writer? What interests or assumptions guide the reader? How do readers differ? What effect do physical format and reading habits have on how the book or article is understood? How can the author have the greatest impact on the reader? These and many other questions arise each time an author tries to reach a reader through written communication.

SIFTING THROUGH TEXTS

Just as our brains constantly evaluate the millions of sensory signals that bombard our nervous systems each moment, filtering out the extraneous ones, so we have developed ways to sift through hundreds of printed messages to select only a few to attend to. This ability was not needed in the days before the printing press, but it has become essential for survival in a print-based culture. With thirteen thousand magazines and fifty thousand different books published every year—in addition to the ads, signs, letters, and other printed matter that surrounds us—we need to be highly selective about what we read.

What texts do you pay attention to? Why? How do you value them once you've selected them?

Situation certainly helps determine which messages you choose to read. When you put on a shirt in the morning, you're probably more concerned with the designer label or the slogan on the front than with the washing instructions sewn to the inside. But later, when you're doing laundry, your priorities will be reversed. Similarly, with survival reading such as road signs, maps, and coffee-making instructions, you pay attention only to those messages that give you information you need at the moment. You ignore all the others. Your selection process is virtually automatic. The main criterion here is the reader's *purpose*. You read what you need to read to get the results or information that you want. You filter out what doesn't serve your immediate needs.

All of us use certain criteria and assumptions to evaluate print, to decide what to read and how to read it. Most of the time, these evaluations take place automatically, without any conscious awareness that we're making them. But if we stop and think about what our criteria might be, we'll be in a better position to judge their validity. That is, we'll be able to assess our evaluations to see if they make sense.

Here are some of the ways you might judge the worth of a piece of printed matter:

— What kind of print is it? A book, a magazine article, a flyer?
— How long is it? Is it a blurb that you can skim, or will it take a substantial chunk of your time?
— Who wrote it? Have you heard of the author? Is the author credible? Is the author on a crusade?
— Who published it? Is it from a reputable press or something more like the *National Enquirer?*
— What does it look like? Is it professional or trashy?
— How many other people might read this? Is it part of the mainstream press or is it an underground publication?

What other criteria can you think of? What features of a book or magazine are important to you?

Once you've articulated your criteria, you can look at them critically to see if they are trustworthy bases for judgments. Take quantity, for instance. One of the printing press's essential powers is its ability to make a lot of copies of anything. Yet, it's easy to be fooled by numbers. Just because many copies of a falsehood exist doesn't bring the falsehood any closer to the truth. A glossy, full-color magazine that reaches millions may seem more trustworthy than a local newsletter done on a photocopy machine. We've come to assume that numbers carry the weight of authority, but millions of copies do not necessarily guarantee accuracy or trustworthiness. The way we evaluate material may not always be justifiable, or even prudent, but it does shape our responses to printed texts.

THE MEDIUM IS THE MESSAGE

When describing how various technologies have extended human consciousness, communications theorist Marshall McLuhan told the world more than thirty years ago that "the medium is the message." That dictum easily applies within the world of print, for our responses to texts are influenced by the formal properties of the print that embodies them. How the message is presented—its physical form—is a vital part of the message's meaning. If it's true that we take reading for granted, it's even more true that we take for granted the materiality of books and other printed objects. Print culture studies focuses on the medium, not just on the message, to see what effect the physical form might have on a publication's readers.

The medium for all these messages is, of course, print. But what kind of print? Not all print is the same. One glance confirms that the *National Enquirer* and the *Washington Post* differ widely in their journalistic standards: One has a sober front page filled with orderly columns of newsprint and a few grainy photos; the other carries banner headlines (called "screamers" in the news business) along with a front-page picture of a two-headed space alien hugging Madonna. Which format inspires more trust? Similarly, an article on skin care printed in the *Journal of Dermatology* and illustrated with scientific graphs, charts, and microscope images will score differently on your credibility meter than one that shows up in *Elle,* right next to a slick ad for the product the article raves about.

To give you a feel for the diversity of print, the selections in this book have been chosen from across the spectrum of print. Some come from daily newspapers such as the *New York Times,* others from weekly newsmagazines such as *Time* and *Newsweek.* Articles are included from popular magazines such as *Details, Harper's, Ms.,* and *The New Yorker,* each with its own look and style for its own audience. Excerpts from scholarly books and articles are also included, which carry with them the authority of university presses and the weight of academic journals such as *Publishing Research Quarterly* and the *Wilson Library Bulletin.* Along with these academic readings, you'll find pieces from alternative publications such as the *Utne Reader* and fan 'zines such as *h2so4.*

But how can you evaluate the medium in a textbook like this, where all the pages look pretty much the same? They are printed on the same paper, using the same typeface and the same number of words per page. There are no glossy ads to distract the reader, no money-saving coupons, no subscription cards to fall onto the floor, no heavily per-fumed inserts. The uniform appearance of this book's pages can easily make you forget that publications differ widely in their look and feel.

This book tries to bring its diversity of sources back into view. Be-cause the site of publication is such an important feature of print culture studies, this book includes an appendix, "Who Publishes What?" For each essay or excerpt from a book, you'll find information about its orig-inal publisher in the appendix—information that will help you assess the source of the message. Additionally, many of the assignments will send you to copies of the magazine or newspaper that the readings came from to see what they looked or felt like in their original forms.

Although there is a uniform feel to the readings as they are pre-sented in the book you hold in your hand, remember as you read that this collection has been constructed with its own purposes and editorial priorities in mind. Those purposes may not always be immediately ap-parent. Print culture studies gives you tools to examine the array of in-terests that shape each publication's production and reception, allowing you to determine how you are being influenced by what you read.

AUTHORS DON'T WRITE BOOKS

When it comes to books and articles, you might think that the au-thors' purposes are the only ones that we need to consider. It's not that simple. Contrary to popular belief, authors do not write books; they string together words that are eventually transformed into books. Books are products, commodities, pieces of material culture. An author was somewhere behind the book that you read last summer, but there was also an editor, a publisher, a printer, an ad agency, and a bookseller. In fact, there was an army of people involved in the production and distri-bution of that book. Those people helped shape the book you read, not just in its material form, but in its content as well. Authors write what we might call "texts," but "books" are produced by committee, as it were. Historians of the book also study this aspect of printed objects: How do texts get turned into books and transmitted from the writer to the reader?

Whose purposes and decisions guided this book? If you look at the title page, you'll see the name of the editor/author who selected the readings for the book and wrote the introductions, headnotes, questions, and assignments that accompany each selection. But was the author alone in that effort? Turn over the title page and read the list of other people who contributed on behalf of the publisher. How was each per-son involved? Can you tell how much they influenced the final shape of the book? Did they influence the contents? Did they determine what this book would look like? You bet they did. Some, of course, contributed more than others, but to some extent all those people had a say in shaping the book you hold.

Since writers don't work in isolation, it's not a bad idea to see who influenced a book, article, or report. That way, you may know in advance what approach the author will take or what school of thought he or she is from. You may, for example, find out that your instructor or your boss had a major role in shaping what you're about to read; if that's the case, you'll want to criticize it more diplomatically than you might otherwise. One way to find out who influenced a book is to read the author's acknowledgments; that's where the author thanks everyone who helped the book along its way from conception to realization. You'll usually find acknowledgments at the beginning of a book, either as a separate section or within an introduction or preface. (In this book, they're at the end of the Preface for Instructors.)

Just what do all those "editors" do? How much did the author "edit" the pieces you'll be reading? Quite a lot in some cases, not at all in others. And you'll never know by looking at the pages of this book. That's the beauty of the printing press. It can create a seamless new text out of a messy cut and paste editing job. The material form of these readings has been changed many times by many people since the author first typed words onto the screen of a word processor.

IMAGINED AUDIENCES

Just as it's naive to assume that authors are solely responsible for the books we read, it's equally dubious to believe that readers do not influence the authors in what they write. Every author writes with an audience in mind. That audience may be a projection of him- or herself for the diary writer; it may be the recipient of a letter or a small coterie of like-thinking friends for those who write for limited circulation; or it may be the public at large for the author of a mass-circulation book or article. What audience the author imagines will help determine the tone, the level of language, the set of references, the whole approach of the piece of writing. Students of print culture examine who each publication is aimed at, and why it presents the information it does.

When you pick up an article, you may have some idea what your purposes and interests are as a reader, but do you know the agendas of the author, the editor, the publisher, the distributor? Who did they imagine you would be? That is to say, what audience was this article written for? What assumptions did they make about the reader? Are you the audience they had in mind? If not, how do you differ? What ideas and interests do you bring to the text as you begin to make mean-ing from the words on the page?

Consciously or unconsciously, you ask similar questions about your reader every time you write. You may not think of yourself as a profes-sional writer, but you already write with an eye to your audience and not just for self-expression. Admit it. You would probably write differ-ently if you knew your paper would be read aloud to your classmates or published in the school newspaper than if you thought only your teacher would see it.

As you become increasingly aware of the projected audiences that shape other people's writing, you'll also become more attuned to your own audience when you sit down to write. Just as the questions related to each reading selection will ask you to pay attention to the author's imagined audience, the writing suggestions will focus your attention on your audience and let you consciously shape your words for particular readers.

WHY THIS BOOK?

Consider why your instructor chose this book. What purposes guided the selection process? What material considerations influenced it? After all, there are plenty of other textbooks on the market. Why this one instead of some other one? What does it have to offer?

First, let's look at *The Press of Ideas* as a printed artifact. It's just as much a product of print culture as any other, and as such, it comes with its own assumptions and marketing strategies. Perhaps your teacher read some promotional literature that prompted the selection of this book. In all likelihood, he or she received a free examination copy of this book to compare to the many other writing textbooks lining the office shelves. Take another look at the book and imagine yourself in your in-structor's shoes. What features would help you evaluate the book with-out reading it from cover to cover? Would you pick it up at all if it had a plain white cover? How does the outside of the book help lure you into the inside? Scan the table of contents. It's more than a bare list of authors and titles. How do the chapter headings and the annotations about each selection help you evaluate this book? Are there any other structural fea-tures that might influence your selection?

Now let's examine the actual content of the book. You've already read something about the general topics covered in each chapter. The in-troductions to the chapters present specific issues in more detail and give you things to think about as you read the individual essays. Each essay has a headnote that tells you about the author and offers you a context for thinking about the essay. It also lets you know where the piece was originally published so you can assess what audience the au-thor was writing for.

Following each essay you'll find two sets of questions. The first set, labeled "Consider the Source," sends you back into the reading to grasp key concepts and to analyze how the author conveyed them. The second set, "Consider the Implications," prompts connections with other readings, with your life, and with the world outside the confines of the reading. The questions ask you to analyze how different authors treat the same topic and to assess what the ramifications of an author's argument might be. You'll be invited to explore your own experience as a reader and consumer of print and to engage with your peers through discussion and with the authors through writing. You might be asked to write a letter, design a new publication, hold a debate, or dramatize an argument.

The questions also ask you to conduct research, but they won't always send you to the library, as you might expect. Research comes in many forms, and you've already done a lot of it.

The process can be as simple as interviewing people and analyzing their remarks. You do research like this every time you ask your friends their opinion of a movie that you are thinking about seeing. Before you pay for a ticket, you ask questions, solicit answers, and then bring your critical judgment to bear on those answers. That is, you evaluate evidence. One friend may be notorious for liking Sylvester Stallone movies—even the real stinkers. You'll treat his or her judgments of Sly's latest film with some skepticism. Another may oppose all films containing scenes more violent than a broken heart—again, you'll weigh that in your decision. The research suggestions in this book include interviews with fellow students, with faculty or with school librarians, as well as with people outside of the college environment.

Research in print culture studies also includes examination of printed materials as products. You'll therefore find research assignments that don't require you to read the books and magazines for their ideas. You can just look at them as objects and still count it as research, for you will be evaluating cover design, marketing strategies, placement of ads, or ratio of ads to editorial content. Or, you'll be asked to flip to the appendix to learn more about a publisher and apply that information to the readings.

Because computer technology is an important subject of this book, you'll also be asked to do research online. You may be sent out into cyberspace to cruise the Internet. You may "chat" with others online or interact with a multimedia CD-ROM "book." You may explore the complexities of hypertext or write in your own online journal.

In short, the varied assignments will ask you to conduct all kinds of field research in addition to traditional library research. You'll be gathering evidence, questioning it, evaluating it, and then presenting your findings to your own reader in an organized and persuasive manner. If you can perform that process for an analysis of the covers of Harlequin romances, you can apply the same principles to any other kind of research.

CRITICAL READING AND CRITICAL WRITING

All your life you have been acted on by writers and publishers. Now it's your turn. You are entering into a world of ideas transmitted largely through print, and you need to be attuned to the forces that lie behind what you read and how you write. Becoming more conscious of the processes involved in the exchanges between readers and writers will make you a more critical reader and a more effective writer.

It's no accident that each chapter of this book begins with a question, for the book as a whole continually invites you to question what you read, how you read, and why you read. It asks you, in short, to take nothing for granted when you approach a printed text. By training your mind to analyze the print that assails you, you'll be in a better position to decide whether to believe or act on what you read.

That sort of critical reading is a step along the way to good writing. If you question everything you read, you'll learn what kind of evidence is persuasive and what isn't. You can turn that knowledge to your advantage when you try to persuade others through your own writing. By the same token, if you can make explicit some of your implicit assumptions about your audience and your own intent, you'll be better able to tailor your message for effective communication.

The issues addressed by print culture studies are not incidental to your concerns as you learn to become a better writer. They're central.

CHAPTER

1

HOW DO WE READ?
Interacting with Print

W hen you were a young child, you deciphered an ancient and mysterious code. At first you struggled to interpret individual swirls and markings, connecting them to specific sounds. Then you began to recognize a word or two. Finally, one day, you did it! You cracked the code and opened up the secrets of the written word.

You may not remember how or when you learned to read, and it may not have seemed as exciting as cracking codes with a Spiderman Decoder Ring. Nevertheless, the process was much the same, for written language is a powerful system of coded messages. The signs on the page require decoding by individual readers if they are to have any meaning.

Even though our everyday immersion in books, newspapers, magazines, and junk mail may make reading seem an easy, natural activity, our interaction with the printed word is anything but simple. Psychologists and sociologists have written scores of books about how children learn to read and what environmental factors encourage or inhibit the development of literacy. Physiologists have mapped the brain's electrical activity to understand where comprehension takes place. Linguists have examined the patterns that language forms and the ways those patterns convey meaning.

All these fields of study—these academic disciplines—face the difficult task of trying to understand a process that leaves few physical traces, one that occurs differently in every person yet in its largest outlines remains fundamentally the same for everyone. Since this book is designed for a writing class, the aspects of reading that are most important are those that shed light on the writing process, those that highlight the interaction between authors and readers. Therefore, we'll leave the scientists and linguists to their research and focus on the ways that English teachers and historians of print culture approach the subject of reading.

Common sense tells us that reading involves two main participants: author and reader. It is a process that depends as much on the originator of the coded message as it does on the person deciphering that message. When you read, you are subtly aware of the source of the words you are decoding, whether that source is Stephen King, the editors of *Car & Driver*, the makers of Coca-Cola, or your college's registrar. On some level, you are also aware of yourself as the reader and interpreter of the messages.

Print culture studies adds a third component to the mix. It examines the interaction of three elements of the reading experience: the text that the author writes; the reader who decodes the marks on the page; and the printed page or the book that carries that text to the reader. Without the participation of all three elements, no "reading" is possible. Let's look closely at each of these elements, thinking of them as points on a triangle.

TEXT, READER, AND BOOK

As we have already seen in the introduction (p. 8), authors don't write books. They write texts that are turned into books by editors, typesetters, and printers. This point in the triangle—the text that the author writes in a manuscript (or, these days, composes on a word processor)—has no meaning in and of itself. It has only the potential for meaning. It must be decoded by a reader in order for any meaning to come into being. (This is rather like the old conundrum of the tree falling in a forest: Does it make a sound if nobody is there to hear it?)

The reader plays a major role in determining the meaning of any text, for the reader actualizes the potential meaning. You don't have to think too long about this before you realize that readers will vary dramatically. Forrest Gump and Albert Einstein can't possibly read the *New York Times* in exactly the same way. Clearly, variations in reading ability must affect how we derive meaning from a text. In addition to literacy level, other variations among readers influence the process, including gender, cultural expectations, reasons for reading, and ways of interpreting. We'll return to this second element in a moment.

The final point in the triangle is the book, the printed pages that carry the text to the reader. Without it reading could not occur. Whether it's the *National Enquirer* or the *Encyclopedia Britannica*, *Sassy* or *The New Yorker*, the Cheerios box or the letter telling you that you may already have won the Publishers' Clearinghouse Sweepstakes, all of these printed pages fulfill the same role: They bring readers and text messages together.

These three elements—text, reader, and book—must interact in order for reading to happen. A variation in any one of the three elements will affect the meaning that results from the reading experience. This will become clearer if we look at some possible permutations.

It's easy to see what happens when the text and the book remain the same, but the reader changes. You encounter this situation whenever you and a friend or classmate disagree about something you've both read. A change in readers could also arise from a lapse of time, as when you read a book that was written in the eighteenth century. Say you get your hands on a first edition of Jonathan Swift's *Gulliver's Travels,* printed in 1726. You are likely to handle that 270-year-old volume with greater care and reverence than its original purchaser (not least because some rare-book librarian will be breathing down your neck, making sure you don't damage a book worth thousands of dollars). More importantly, you'll bring to that book a different set of cultural references and attitudes than its original audience brought to it. For one thing, the pot shots that Swift took at political figures of his day will be incomprehensible to you without the explanatory footnotes of a modern edition. Understanding of current events can't help but be one of the conditions for reading the book. In *The Order of Books* scholar Roger Chartier has described the effect of time with the following paradox: "A book changes by the fact that it does not change when the world changes." On the other hand, you'll bring to Swift's book your knowledge that *Gulliver's Travels* is considered a "classic." Its original readers would have regarded it as just another new book. Your attitude toward Swift's masterpiece will undoubtedly influence the way you read and will affect the meaning you derive from the reading experience, even though the text and the book have not changed.

Now let's alter a different point on the triangle. Imagine that the reader and the book remain the same, but the text varies. How is this possible? The production of a printed book involves many stages, many people, and many occasions for error or variation. For example, when Shakespeare's plays were first collected in one grand volume—the First Folio of 1623—the printers often stopped the press to correct a typographical error that someone had just caught. They would change the troublesome word or phrase and then continue printing. With paper so expensive in those days, the earlier sheets containing the erroneous reading would not be destroyed. Instead, they would be treated like all the other pages and would eventually be bound into a completed book. This means that two copies of the same book could contain different texts. For instance, in *Julius Caesar,* Cato asks Brutus to note whether Titinius "have crown'd dead Cassius" in some copies of the First Folio, but other copies claim that he "have *not* crown'd" him (V.iv.97). As you can see, even slight differences can affect interpretation.

A more common alteration in our "print triangle" occurs when the text and the reader stay the same, but the book varies. That is, the same text is presented in a different physical form. This happens whenever an article is reprinted. The type style and paper quality of the two articles will differ, as will the visual arrangement of the words on the page. Every article in the book you're holding has undergone such a transformation, which will undoubtedly affect how you read the selections. You will read the works differently than if you had encountered them in their original forms and contexts. Even if each essay had been reproduced photographically, so that you could see it in its original type style and layout on the page, the fact that the essay was in an anthology instead of in, say, *Rolling Stone* or *Details* would affect the meaning of the text. Your purpose in reading is simply not the same when you scan the pages of your favorite magazine as it is when you read a selection assigned by your instructor. Reader and text may remain stable in this instance, but the change in the book will have important consequences for the reading.

Usually more than one element of the triad will change at a time. A hardcover novel comes out in a less expensive paperback version and reaches a new set of readers. A celebrity's private diary is made public and printed in the local newspaper. A new edition of *The Bridges of Madison County* comes out with photographs of Clint Eastwood and Meryl Streep on the cover. The relationship between text, book, and reader can vary in countless ways. It's important to remain attentive to all three elements in order to understand how we read.

COMMUNITIES OF READERS

While it's interesting and valuable to appreciate that all readers are different, what's more useful is to understand the similarities among readers. The ways that you as a reader align with other readers can shed light on how texts and books affect you. Moreover, as a writer you'll need to have a clear idea of the groups of readers you want your text to reach in order to make sure you send the right signals to those groups.

Individuals may read in solitude, but they don't read alone. They read as members of communities of readers. Those communities can be constructed along various lines. You're probably reading this introduction as a member of your writing class, but you are also a member of a larger community: people in college at a certain age in a certain place. You also read as a member of your particular race and class. You read as a male or as a female. You read as a person with particular interests and political opinions. Your "communities" may be abstract entities instead of physical ones. Moreover, not all members of an identifiable community will read the same way. Nonetheless, the communities that you belong to influence your reading and contribute to the meaning that you derive from what you read.

The abstractness of reading communities is one of the crucial differences between our literate culture and the oral culture that existed before writing and print. In an oral culture, words could only reach those who were physically close enough to hear them. You might remember Monty Python's famous rendition of Jesus' Sermon on the Mount from the movie *Life of Brian* (1979). As Jesus spoke to his listeners, the moviegoing audience experienced the speech from the vantage point of people at the very back of the crowd, almost but not quite beyond earshot. Jesus' memorable blessing of the "peacemakers" was construed by the Python characters as "blessed are the cheesemakers." After yelling back to Jesus for clarification, they try to make sense of this nonsensical message on their own. Finally, they decide it's a mercantile image that "refers to any manufacturers of dairy products." This may be a silly example, but it neatly demonstrates the limitations of orality. The audience for oral communication is physically present, allowing the speaker to see his or her listeners and even permitting them to respond to the message. However, the message can spread no further than the sound of the human voice, and then it is easily garbled.

In a literate culture, by contrast, writing carries words far beyond any immediate audience. The words are disembodied, disconnected from the writer. They can float through time and space to reach innumerable unknown readers in the exact same form. The writer cannot predict with certainty who will read the text and, therefore, cannot control interpretation. This was precisely what made passing notes during class so perilous when you were in school: If your teacher or the wrong student got your note, the consequences could be humiliating, at the very least. Published works face the same problem magnified many hundreds of times. Print also denies the reader the ability to respond directly to the author for instant clarification, the way the characters in the Python episode tried to do. In this century, radio and television have given oral messages these same characteristics of disembodiment. As Walter Ong will discuss in his essay, in this chapter, such technology produces "secondary orality," since it arises out of a literate culture.

As students of print culture who are trying to understand how a community of readers interacts with a particular printed work, we look at the testimony of individual readers to determine their habitual reading practices. How was the book read? That is, what was the situation of its reading? Was it read hesitantly or fluently? Was it read aloud or silently? In company or alone? At school or work or home? Some books are read casually, others voraciously.

We also need to know *why* the book was read. Readers can be examined in terms of their purposes. That is, we can look at the uses readers make of their reading, the role reading plays in their lives. Is reading a means of self-improvement? Is it a duty or a pleasure? Does it offer instruction or role models? Does it provide escape from everyday reality or does it bring imaginary worlds into the concrete realm of day-to-day lives?

BOOKS AS COMMODITIES

It's nice to idealize books as part of our intellectual life, but they're also part of our consumer culture. They are concrete objects made of paper and ink, and those materials cost money. Books exist to be read, but also to be sold—at least in such quantities that they'll compensate the publisher for the costs of production. The same holds true for any printed matter. *USA Today, Ebony, Sports Illustrated, Elle*—all of these publications justify their existence by their ability to sell copies.

In the competition for your dollars, publishers try to package their products so that you'll buy, buy, buy. Quite often this means that as much care goes into devising the form of a book as the author puts into crafting the text of the book. Cover design and illustration, type style, layout, catchy title, author's photo, blurbs of critical praise—these are likely to be important factors in your decision to pull one book off the shelves of the bookstore instead of another.

But the material considerations that help a book, magazine, or newspaper sell also affect how the printed work will be interpreted. The feel of the object in your hand—the heft of a book, the glossy slickness of a magazine—contributes subtly but importantly to your reading experience. Even the way the type appears on the page will matter in your construction of meaning.

The earliest books were written by hand in a time when paper was scarce and therefore precious. Words were written close together to save paper. Paragraphs were unheard of. When a new section of text occurred, the scribe might indicate it by writing the first word in red instead of black, but that was about it. One glance at a hand copied Bible, for instance, will show you a virtually solid page of text: no breaks, no verses, hardly any white space whatsoever.

The competition for readers in a print culture changed all that. It put the reader in the driver's seat. Books and magazines that offered greatest readability found the greatest number of readers. Early printers quickly developed type styles that were easier to read than the Gothic lettering of medieval manuscripts. They broke up long treatises into chapters and subsections of chapters. By the eighteenth century, pages of type were divided into shorter and shorter chunks, corresponding to the logic of the prose and gradually creating paragraphs as we use them today.

The appeal to readers continues to affect the way our printed materials look. *USA Today* changed the face of this country's newspapers when it appeared in the mid-1980s with its easy-to-read graphs, polls, and diagrams. Other newspapers followed suit, trying to win readers with "factoids" that offered bite-sized morsels of information. Just look at your local paper and count how many full-length articles it has, as compared to blurbs and news-at-a-glance features.

By paying attention to printed works as material objects, we can bring written discourse down from the lofty heights of some abstract world of ideas and ground it in the day-to-day motives of authors and publishers, readers and consumers. This not only makes for greater understanding of printed works, but it also allows a glimpse into the practice of writing that will help you when you sit down to write.

PARTICIPATING IN PRINT CULTURE

Without a doubt, you are a consumer of print culture. But you are also a producer of it. If you think that your writing doesn't yet fall into the arena of print culture studies, you underestimate yourself.

No less than that of a professional writer, your writing is grounded in considerations of audience and concrete form. You may think that your audience for essays in this class is your instructor, but he or she really only stands in for a larger audience of educated readers. Even if you really were writing for one particular individual, that person belongs to several communities of readers, as we have described them. Moreover, that person's ways of reading have been conditioned by the world of print. Even though your instructor is a captive audience—someone who has to read your essays because of the circumstances of the classroom— the look of your words on the page will have important consequences. Your printed product will be received based on expectations that your reader has for material in this realm of discourse. Those expectations will include, at the very least, easy-to-read copy typed on good paper, with few or no typographical errors. A material product that fails to meet these expectations will influence your audience's appreciation for your message.

How we decipher the signs on the page and what use we make of them is the chief focus of this chapter. But keep in mind that you are working on improving your ability not just to decode signs, but to produce them as well. Keep asking questions of the reading process. How do we take in texts? What do we do with books? What conditions affect reading? What effects do books have on us? How does the printing process affect the messages it carries?

THE READINGS

Sven Birkerts begins this chapter with his recollections of the sheer joy of reading. Books allowed him to escape into a private world where he could try on fictional identities as he tried to discover his identity as a writer in the real world. Benjamin Franklin then explains how he used books to educate himself and raise his position in society. Larzer Ziff then uses the example of Franklin to explore how print functioned in the early years of the American republic. Linking Franklin's activity as a printer and publisher with his ideas about the relationship between public and private life, Ziff demonstrates print's ability to create a "representation" of Franklin, while leaving the real Franklin concealed. Walter Ong adds to Ziff's discussion of the impact of print, as he analyzes the effects that the shift from the oral world to the literate has had on our ways of thinking, knowing, and organizing information.

The next four selections form a cluster concerning Louisa May Alcott's *Little Women*. After a selection from Alcott, Barbara Sicherman's feminist study examines the functions Alcott's classic novel has fulfilled for various reading communities, focusing on readings of the character of Jo March. Caryn James provides a counterpoint to Sicherman, using the release of the 1994 movie version to reveal her deep, dark secret: Instead of emulating the tomboy author Jo, she always aspired to be the pampered princess, Jo's sister Amy. Finally, Laurie Lawlor's novelization of the recent movie offers an opportunity to see how a twentieth-century sensibility reinterprets Alcott's nineteenth-century world. The three selections that close the chapter cluster around a vastly different cultural icon: the *Star Trek* series. Richard Zoglin and Erik Davis provide overviews of the *Star Trek* phenomenon as it has moved from television to fanzines, to books and movies, and on into the lives of its most avid fans, the Trekkers. The chapter closes with Franz Joseph's imaginative correspondence justifying the existence on twentieth-century Earth of the *Star Fleet Technical Manual*. These selections provide an opportunity to see what happens when cultural productions that arose in the video world cross over into the world of print.

SVEN BIRKERTS

The Paper Chase

Book reviewer, essayist, and literary critic, Sven Birkerts (b. 1951) has had a lifelong love affair with the printed page. Here he reflects on his early attachment to books and his path toward becoming a writer. He describes reading as an enthralling activity, with each book allowing a magical entry into a private realm of wonder. Birkerts has channeled his passion for books into a productive career, making a living and a reputation as a book reviewer. His essays have appeared in such prominent literary magazines as The Atlantic, Harper's, The New Republic, *and* The New York Times Book Review. *His work as a reviewer was recognized by his peers in the National Book Critics Circle when they awarded him the Citation for Excellence in Reviewing. This essay comes from his most recent book,* The Gutenberg Elegies: The Fate of Reading in an Electronic Age *(1994), which explores the impact of technology on the experience of reading.*

Many years ago, when I was still in college and affecting paperbacks in my back pockets and dreaming of the great novels I would one day produce, I went to hear Anthony Burgess[1] speak on "The Writer's Life." The man was, as one might expect, a charming raconteur, and he carried on with great authority about the perils and perquisites of literary careers. I have forgotten most of what was said, but I do remember that at one point Burgess joked about his experiences as a book reviewer. Every day, he said, the postman would bring him parcels of bright new review copies. These he would pile neatly in the hallway by his front door until he had a tall stack, at which point he would cart them down to the local bookseller and "flog" them for pocket money. I didn't know the slang idiom "flog" then, but it had a raffish ring to it and I thought, "Yes, that's quite a racket." And for a long time I thought nothing more about it.

I thought no more about it because I had bigger fish to fry. I was incubating important creative works and all other writing endeavors seemed insignificant in comparison. Besides, I knew that book reviewing was not a vocation that one aspired to; rather, one did it with the left hand while doing worthier things with the right.

I can almost see myself as I was then. Stubbled, slouching, eager above all else to be perceived as different—in the crowd but not of it, a

---

From *The Gutenberg Elegies: The Fate of Reading in an Electronic Age* (Boston: Faber and Faber, 1994), pp. 33–41.

1. **Anthony Burgess** (1917–1993): Erudite British author, best known for his novel *A Clockwork Orange* (1962).—ED.

young writer not about to waste his time on the lower part of the mountain. And if I pick that afternoon lecture as a place to start from it is because I am now that thing I so confidently scorned, a book reviewer. It has taken me almost twenty years to free myself of the idea that writing about novels represents the defeat of the would-be novelist. And even now I'm not completely liberated. When people ask me what I do, I usually say I'm an essayist or a critic. More honorable terms, both, and they mostly fit. They almost conceal the fact that the greater part of what I do is read and write about books.

There is a path, then, from A to B, from disaffected renegade to reviewer, though of course it neither begins right at A nor ends obligingly at B. As paths go it is a meandering thing, with many twists and divagations, each describing some choice made at a crucial moment. Back then, when the whole idea of a path was hazy, I did not think of myself as following or making any sort of track. I wandered to and fro in the realm of the immediate, moving toward what I liked and striking out against whatever displeased me. Retrospect alters everything. Looking through the aperture of time is like watching a movement from a great altitude. What felt like blundering starts to look like a fate.

That stubbled poseur, that angry and no-doubt-irritating nineteen year old—where did he get the idea that he wanted to write? Why that and not filmmaking or professing law or practicing psychotherapy? To ask this is naturally to initiate a regress, to scramble all the way back to the psyche in formation. Why words on a page, why a desire to write fiction?

There is one obvious answer: that the urge was a direct outgrowth of a love of reading, a determination to master the source of that pleasure—but this answer hardly exhausts the matter. Why did I become such a reader in the first place? What made me so susceptible to the figments I coaxed from the printed page? Was it something innate in my disposition (both grandparents on my father's side had been literary people back in Latvia), or some fortuitous early exposure (the fact that my mother delighted in reading me stories)? Or were the influences of greater psychological complexity, having to do with the fact that our family spoke another language (Latvian) at home, a fact that marked my childhood deeply and filled me with a sense of being different? Or was reading just my way of blocking out family tensions—my father's strictness, the unpredictable flaring of his temper? I would have to circle all of the above.

But to list determinants in this way, even to think of them as factors in isolation, must misrepresent the experience. True, these were all things that pushed me toward books—toward an "other" place away from my immediate surroundings—but what made me a reader were the experiences I got from the books themselves. An obvious assertion, but a true one. It is easy enough in retrospect to see a book as a screen, a shield, an escape, but at the time there was just the magic—the startling and renewable discovery that a page covered with black markings could, with a slight mental exertion, be converted into an environment, an inward depth populated with characters and animated by diverse excitements. A world inside the world, secret and concealable. A world that I could carry about as a private resonance, a daydream, even when I was not reading. A moveable feast.

From the time of earliest childhood, I was enthralled by books. First just by their material mysteries. I studied pages of print and illustrations, stared myself into the wells of fantasy that are the hallmark of the awakening inner life. Mostly there was pleasure, but not always. I remember a true paralytic terror brought on by the cartoon dalmations pictured on the endpapers of my Golden Books. For a time I refused to be alone in the room with the books, even when the covers were safely closed. Ascribing power to likeness, I thought the dogs would slip free of their confinement and come baying after me.

But that was the exception. Dreamy sensuousness generally prevailed. A page was a field studded with tantalizing signs and a book was a vast play structure riddled with openings and crevices I could get inside. This notion of hiding, secreting myself in a text was important to me—it underlies to this day my sense of a book as a refuge. That I could not yet translate the letters into words and meanings only added to the grave mysteriousness of the artifact. On the far side of that plane of scrambled markings was a complete other world. And then one day the path came clear. I was in the first grade. I went over and around and suddenly *through* the enormous letter shapes of Kipling's *Jungle Book.*[2] The first sentence, that is. I read! And from that moment on, the look of a word became a window onto its meaningful depths.

Once I got underway, I was an interested, eager, but not terribly 10 precocious reader—I was no Susan Sontag[3] knocking back nutritive classics while still in grade school. I was a dreamer and books were my tools for dreaming. I read the ones that were more or less suited to my age and did so devotedly. Books about Indian chiefs, explorers, and dogs; biographies of inventors and athletes; the pasteurized versions of London and Poe that came via the Scholastic Book Club.[4] I had the first real thrill of ownership in second or third grade, when the teacher broke open the first shipment and handed each of us in the class the books we had ordered. Later it was the Hardy Boys, with their illustrated covers and crisp blue spines; then James Bond, the slim little pocketbooks reeking of sexual innuendo and high-class gadgetry. Not until I was in ju-

---

2. Rudyard **Kipling** (1865–1936): British novelist whose children's story *Jungle Book* (1894) has become a classic.—ED.

3. **Susan Sontag** (b. 1933): Prolific novelist and critic.—ED.

4. Jack **London** (1876–1916) and Edgar Allan **Poe** (1809–1849): These American authors' short stories of adventure and mystery are staples of such mail-order suppliers of juvenile literature as the **Scholastic Book Club.**—ED.

nior high did I begin to make contact with some of the so-called better books—by Salinger, Wolfe, Steinbeck, and others. But even then I had no idea of bettering myself. I was simply looking for novels with characters whose lives could absorb mine for a few hours.

That demand has not changed much over the years. What have changed are my empathic capacities. I have gradually grown interested in lives that are utterly different from my own. I find that I have little difficulty now slipping into the skin of emperor Hadrian or Clarissa Dalloway[5] or anyone else, provided the narrative is psychologically compelling and credible. But when I was ten or twelve or fourteen I needed to hear what other young men, my age or a few years older, had to say about things. I looked to Tom Sawyer, later to Holden Caulfield and Eugene Gant and the heroes of William Goldman's novels.[6] I prowled the aisles of Readmore Books, the local temple to the mass market paperback, searching for books with a certain kind of cover—usually a rendering of a moody-looking young man with some suggestion of meditated rebellion in his stance. Interestingly enough, there were quite a few books that fit the bill, from William Goldman's *Temple of Gold* to Romain Gary's *Ski Bum* to Harold Robbins's *Stone for Danny Fisher*. The approach of the late-1960s counterculture could have been discerned here by anyone with a grasp of how images translated into collective attitudes, and vice versa. Although I did not know it then, I was on the cusp of my own rebellion, slowly readying myself for a major bout of acting out. When the time came, two or three years later, my guides would be Jack Kerouac, Ken Kesey, Richard Fariña, Kurt Vonnegut, Norman Mailer, Henry Miller, and others.

The reading I did in late boyhood and early adolescence was passionate and private, carried on at high heat. When I went to my room and opened a book, it was to seal myself off as fully as possible in another place. I was not reading, as now, with only one part of the self. I was there body and soul, living vicariously. When Finney died at the end of John Knowles's *Separate Peace* I cried scalding tears, unable to believe that the whole world did not grind to a sorrowful halt. That was then. Books no longer tap my emotions quite so directly; I am rarely brought to tears or fury. But what I have not lost is a churning anxiety, an almost intolerable sensation that sometimes has me drawing breaths to steady myself. There is something about the reading act that cuts through the sheath of distractedness that usually envelops me. It is as if I

---

5. **Emperor Hadrian** and **Clarissa Dalloway:** Main characters of Marguerite Yourcenar's novel *Memoirs of Hadrian* (1954) and Virginia Woolf's *Mrs. Dalloway* (1922).—ED.

6. **Tom Sawyer, Holden Caulfield, Eugene Gant**: These characters—created by Mark Twain, J. D. Salinger, and Thomas Wolfe, respectively—are all boys who struggle to come to terms with mainstream American society, as do the heroes in the works that Birkerts mentions in the next several paragraphs.—ED.

can suddenly feel the pure flow of time behind the stationary letters. Vertigo is not a comfortable sensation, but I keep seeking it out, taking it as an inoculation against what a Latin poet called *lacrimae rerum*, "the tears of things."

I remember so clearly the shock I would feel whenever I looked up from the vortex of the page and faced the strangely immobile world around me. My room, the trees outside the window—everything seemed so dense, so saturated with itself. Never since have I known it so intensely, this colliding of realities, the current of mystery leaping the gap between them. In affording this dissociation, reading was like a drug. I knew even then, in my early teen years, that what I did in my privacy was in some way a betrayal of the dominant order of things, an excitement slightly suspect at its core.

This last is a complex business, intensified for me by my father's attitudes. In my childhood, my father was a stern man with a quick temper and an impatient disdain for anything that smacked of reverie or private absorption, almost as if these states in some way challenged his authority. I find his attitude strange, the more so since he idolized his mother, who was one of the most bookish people I have ever known. Indeed, when we first traveled to Riga to visit her, when I first stepped through the door into her apartment, I was stunned. I suddenly understood a great deal about my own genetic inheritance. As I took in the walls of books, the piles of journals and papers on every available surface, I saw the signs of a mania I knew all too well.

But my father was nothing like his mother in this respect. He was a 15 man out in the world, a problem-solver. He had the idea that a boy should be outside in the fresh air, playing, doing chores, whatever. For him there was something against nature in the sight of a healthy individual sitting by himself with a book in his lap. This shouldn't surprise anyone—it is the prevalent bias in our culture. Doing is prized over being or thinking. Reading is something you do because it has been assigned in school, or because all other options have been exhausted—no more chores to do, all other games and activities put away.

It says a great deal about the dynamics of our family that my mother was—and remains—a devoted reader. She read for pleasure, for company, and for escape. Novels, biographies, popular histories—there was never a time when she did not have at least one book going. My father had long since given up any idea he might have had of reforming her (into what?), but to this day he continues to mock what he considers to be her absorption in secondhand experience.

Naturally books became something of a battleground—although no one ever admitted this directly. When I read I was, in my father's understanding of things, siding not only with my mother but with the feminine principle itself, never mind that I might have been reading Hemingway or Thomas Wolfe or Ian Fleming. And whenever the jibes began ("What are you doing on the couch in the middle of the day? You need something to do? *I'll* give you something to do."), my mother, no doubt recognizing a sidelong swipe at herself, would rush to my defense. At which point I had to recognize that I was being caught up in what looked like a traditional "mama's boy" scenario. And I did *not* want to be seen by anyone, especially my father, as a mama's boy.

I therefore began to be more careful about my reading. Although I could still be spotted with a book in my hand, my real reading life, the main current of it, flowed on behind closed doors. If that life was not secret, it was private. I read when my parents were away; I read late into the night. Befitting my usual pattern, I was outwardly yielding to my father while inwardly rebelling. By cultivating a hidden reading life I was, in one sense, acceding to his view that there was something not altogether savory about the way I was using the best energies of my youth. But I was also thereby giving the act a more privileged place in my life; I was investing it with some of the cachet of the prohibited. If reading was worth guarding and being secretive about, there had to be genuine power in it.

So I read. I moved into the space of reading as into a dazzling counterworld. I loved just thinking about books, their wonderful ciphering of thought and sensation. I was pleased by the fact that from a distance, even from a nearby but disinterested vantage, every page looked more or less the same. A piano roll waiting for its sprockets. But for the devoted user of the code that same page was experience itself. I understood that this was something almost completely beyond legislation. No one, not even another reader reading the same words, could know what those signs created once they traveled up the eyebeam.

And the connection of all this to the writing urge? Again, the precise 20 origins are hard to trace. The roots extend back into earliest childhood where only the faintest hints of inclination are ever discernible. Certainly both the desire and the ability to write are closely bound up with the love of the word. Love? Wouldn't it be more accurate to speak in terms of pleasure, of sensuousness, of finding joy in the making and hearing of meaningful sounds? My situation was complicated and no doubt intensified by my relation to the words, by the fact that my first language was Latvian, the language of home, and that immersion in English only came once I was old enough to play with the neighborhood kids and start school.

I don't have any clear memories of learning English or of making some difficult transition from native to adopted tongue. I don't recall stammering or looking for words I didn't have, or suffering ridicule from my preschool peers. But I do know that for a long time, for much of my childhood, I felt that English was not mine, that it belonged to *them.* The fact that I traded in one language for another as soon as I set foot in our house underscored what I knew from the start: We were different. I envied the slangy ease of others, envied it in the basic way that all kids envy the looks or toys of their more fortunate playmates. I heard, or I imagined, how they were at home in their speech, and I wanted it.

By the time I was in second grade I could mimic them perfectly, saying "betcha" and "wanna" without a betraying flicker. But deep down I knew that my possession of the idioms of the kid world was secondhand. Unlike them, I could step back from myself and experience what W.E.B. Du Bois in another context called "double consciousness."[7] I watched myself playing the role of the normal American kid.

Did this sharpen my sense of English? How could it not? I was bent upon blending in, upon never giving away what I knew to be my outsider status. Looking back now it seems a small issue, but then it was my life. Everything depended upon acceptance by others. I became, in my way, a student of inflection, a scholar of offhand delivery. And I managed it well. Still, I had my private agonies. Whenever either of my parents came in contact with my friends, even with other adults, I winced at their accents. Both spoke English in a way that called attention to the fact that they were foreigners. Every fumble they made, every syntactical misstep, threatened the edifice I was building for myself. And yet, the odd thing is, I don't remember any of my friends making cracks or comments about the way my parents spoke—I inflicted all the lashes myself.

The drive to write declared itself only gradually. Just as I was not a devourer of classics at a young age, so too I was not one of those gifted children who are forever making up stories or creating little books. I did take a real interest in writing school reports and papers, but of course I concealed it. Like everyone else, I groaned when a new writing assignment was announced. But behind the mask I was glad. I liked my handwriting and quite enjoyed the physical transcription of materials for reports. I was also compulsive. I prized neatness and if a handwritten page did not look right I would tear it up and start again. I remember toiling over vast projects on the human body, the Olympics, and my state of choice, Oregon. I copied out far more information than I had to. I had discovered something gratifying in the act of inscribing signs on a page in an orderly way. The basic warps of character are there from the start and we do not outgrow them easily; drafting these words into a spiral notebook, I find that both the compulsiveness and pleasure remain.

The more purposeful, creative kind of writing became important to me once I started junior high school. In response to a class assignment for English—write a description of someone you know—I produced an utterly fictitious portrait of my grandfather, my mother's father, endow-

---

7. **W.E.B. Du Bois** (1868–1963): African American editor, author, and social reformer, who described the "double consciousness" with reference to African Americans' position in a white-dominated society.—ED.

ing him with a white beard, a pipe, and a fund of stories about faraway places he had explored. In fact, he was clean-shaven, nonsmoking, and quite private about his past experiences. My teacher entered the sketch in a citywide writing contest and stunned me one day by announcing before the whole class that I had won a gold key. How little encouragement it sometimes takes. From that day on, I have thought of myself as a writer.

▪ **CONSIDER THE SOURCE**

1. Explain what Birkerts means when he says "doing is prized over being or thinking." Where does reading fit into this spectrum of activity?

2. How does secrecy figure in Birkerts's recollections of reading? What is the effect of such secrecy?

3. What assumptions does Birkerts make about his audience's attitude toward books? What authors does he assume his reader is familiar with?

4. List the authors and titles Birkerts claims influenced him. What kinds of books dominate the list? What does the list tell you about Birkerts? What does it tell you about his family?

▪ **CONSIDER THE IMPLICATIONS**

5. Compare the books Birkerts mentions to those described by Benjamin Franklin in "A Bookish Inclination" (the next selection). What purposes seem to guide each man's selection of reading material? Which uses of books most closely match your own?

6. In a journal entry, list the books that you found influential or memorable in your own life. What does that list tell you about yourself? How has your reading shaped your self-image?

7. Compare Birkerts's description of the private world of the reader to the descriptions offered by the romance readers in Janice Radway's essay "The Act of Reading the Romance" (pp. 388–404). Write an essay in which you support or challenge the value of reading as a private occupation.

8. Birkerts describes his early scorn for book reviewing as a profession. After reading Joseph Deitch's "Portrait of a Book Reviewer: Christopher Lehmann-Haupt" (pp. 304–311) and Katharine Weber's "The Reviewer's Experience" (pp. 311–314), analyze the role of the book reviewer in the literary world. Write an essay supporting, refuting, or modifying Birkerts's view of the reviewer as a drudge "wast[ing] his time on the lower part of the mountain."

9. Going against proverbial wisdom, Birkerts judged books by their covers when he selected reading material as a teenager. Visit a bookstore and look closely at different types of books—romances, mysteries, sports biographies, computer manuals, thrillers. See if you can spot any patterns among the book jackets of one category that interests you. Present your

findings in an essay that describes and evaluates important cover features of that category.

10. Birkerts's selection ends by connecting his reading activity to his "drive to write." In small groups, list the ways that Birkerts connects reading to writing. Drawing on your own recollections, add to that list other ways you have linked the two activities. Share your list with the class.

▪ ▪ ▪ ▪ ▪ ▪

BENJAMIN FRANKLIN

A Bookish Inclination

One of the great promises American culture holds out to its people is the opportunity to better their position in life. Books can be a powerful tool in that quest for self-improvement and social mobility, as Benjamin Franklin (1706–1790) shows in this selection from The Autobiography of Benjamin Franklin. *Written in several parts, beginning in 1771, this autobiography has come to stand as a model for the story of the self-made man. Franklin carefully describes those aspects of his life that would serve as examples of conduct for young men, such as his son, to whom he nominally addresses his text. In this excerpt, Franklin tells of his training when he was bound in an apprenticeship to his brother James, printer of* The New-England Courant, *one of America's earliest newspapers. You'll notice an older style of spelling and punctuating some words—a reminder that conventions of rendering language into print change over time.*

From a child I was fond of reading, and all the little money that came into my hands was ever laid out in books. Pleased with the *Pilgrim's Progress,* my first collection was of John Bunyan's works in separate little volumes. I afterward sold them to enable me to buy R. Burton's *Historical Collections;* they were small chapmen's books, and cheap, forty or fifty in all. My father's little library consisted chiefly of books in polemic divinity, most of which I read, and have since often regretted that, at a time when I had such a thirst for knowledge, more proper books had not fallen in my way, since it was now resolved I should not be a clergyman. Plutarch's *Lives* there was in which I read abundantly, and I still think that time spent to great advantage. There was also a book of De Foe's, called an *Essay on Projects,* and another of Dr. Mather's,

---

From *The Works of Benjamin Franklin* (New York: G. P. Putnam's Sons, 1901), vol. 1, pp. 47–60.

called *Essays to do Good,* which perhaps gave me a turn of thinking that had an influence on some of the principal future events of my life.

This bookish inclination at length determined my father to make me a printer, though he had already one son (James) of that profession. In 1717 my brother James returned from England with a press and letters to set up his business in Boston. I liked it much better than that of my father, but still had a hankering for the sea. To prevent the apprehended effect of such an inclination, my father was impatient to have me bound to my brother. I stood out some time, but at last was persuaded, and signed the indentures when I was yet but twelve years old. I was to serve as an apprentice till I was twenty-one years of age, only I was to be allowed journeyman's wages during the last year. In a little time I made great proficiency in the business, and became a useful hand to my brother. I now had access to better books. An acquaintance with the apprentices of booksellers enabled me sometimes to borrow a small one, which I was careful to return soon and clean. Often I sat up in my room reading the greatest part of the night, when the book was borrowed in the evening and to be returned early in the morning, lest it should be missed or wanted.

And after some time an ingenious tradesman, Mr. Matthew Adams, who had a pretty collection of books, and who frequented our printing-house, took notice of me, invited me to his library, and very kindly lent me such books as I chose to read. I now took a fancy to poetry, and made some little pieces; my brother, thinking it might turn to account, encouraged me, and put me on composing occasional ballads. One was called *The Lighthouse Tragedy,* and contained an account of the drowning of Captain Worthilake, with his two daughters; the other was a sailor's song, on the taking of *Teach* (or Blackbeard) the pirate. They were wretched stuff, in the Grub-street-ballad style;[1] and when they were printed he sent me about the town to sell them. The first sold wonderfully; the event, being recent, having made a great noise. This flattered my vanity; but my father discouraged me by ridiculing my performances, and telling me verse-makers were generally beggars. So I escaped being a poet, most probably a very bad one; but as prose writing has been of great use to me in the course of my life, and was a principal means of my advancement, I shall tell you how, in such a situation, I acquired what little ability I have in that way.

There was another bookish lad in the town, John Collins by name, with whom I was intimately acquainted. We sometimes disputed, and very fond we were of argument, and very desirous of confuting one another, which disputatious turn, by the way, is apt to become a very bad

---

1. **Grub-street-ballad style**: During the eighteenth century, London's Grub Street was inhabited by hack writers who sold hastily written and cheaply printed ballads on topics of current interest, such as scandals, hangings, or shipwrecks.— ED.

habit, making people often extremely disagreeable in company by the contradiction that is necessary to bring it into practice; and thence, besides souring and spoiling the conversation, is productive of disgusts and, perhaps, enmities where you may have occasion for friendship. I had caught it by reading my father's books of dispute about religion. Persons of good sense, I have since observed, seldom fall into it, except lawyers, university men, and men of all sorts that have been bred at Edinborough.

A question was once, somehow or other, started between Collins and me, of the propriety of educating the female sex in learning, and their abilities for study. He was of opinion that it was improper, and that they were naturally unequal to it. I took the contrary side, perhaps a little for dispute's sake. He was naturally more eloquent, had a ready plenty of words, and sometimes, as I thought, bore me down more by his fluency than by the strength of his reasons. As we parted without settling the point, and were not to see one another again for some time, I sat down to put my arguments in writing, which I copied fair and sent to him. He answered, and I replied. Three or four letters of a side had passed, when my father happened to find my papers and read them. Without entering into the discussion, he took occasion to talk to me about the manner of my writing; observed that, though I had the advantage of my antagonist in correct spelling and pointing[2] (which I ow'd to the printing-house), I fell far short in elegance of expression, in method and in perspicuity, of which he convinced me by several instances. I saw the justice of his remarks, and thence grew more attentive to the manner in writing, and determined to endeavor at improvement.

About this time I met with an odd volume of the *Spectator*.[3] It was the third. I had never before seen any of them. I bought it, read it over and over, and was much delighted with it. I thought the writing excellent, and wished, if possible, to imitate it. With this view I took some of the papers, and, making short hints of the sentiment in each sentence, laid them by a few days, and then, without looking at the book, try'd to complete the papers again, by expressing each hinted sentiment at length, and as fully as it had been expressed before, in any suitable words that should come to hand. Then I compared my *Spectator* with the original, discovered some of my faults, and corrected them. But I found I wanted a stock of words, or a readiness in recollecting and using them, which I thought I should have acquired before that time if I had gone on making verses; since the continual occasion for words of the same import, but of different length, to suit the measure, or of different sound for the rhyme, would have laid me under a constant necessity of search-

---

2. **pointing**: Punctuation.—ED.

3. *Spectator*: A magazine of manners, morals, and literature published by Richard Steele and Joseph Addison from 1711–1712.—ED.

ing for variety, and also have tended to fix that variety in my mind, and make me master of it. Therefore I took some of the tales and turned them into verse; and, after a time, when I had pretty well forgotten the prose, turned them back again. I also sometimes jumbled my collections of hints into confusion, and after some weeks endeavored to reduce them into the best order, before I began to form the full sentences and complete the paper. This was to teach me method in the arrangement of thoughts. By comparing my work afterwards with the original, I discovered my faults and amended them; but I sometimes had the pleasure of fancying that, in certain particulars of small import, I had been lucky enough to improve the method or the language, and this encouraged me to think I might possibly in time come to be a tolerable English writer, of which I was extremely ambitious. My time for these exercises and for reading was at night, after work or before it began in the morning, or on Sundays, when I contrived to be in the printing-house alone, evading as much as I could the common attendance on public worship which my father used to exact of me when I was under his care, and which indeed I still thought a duty, though I could not, as it seemed to me, afford time to practice it.

When about sixteen years of age I happened to meet with a book, written by one Tryon, recommending a vegetable diet. I determined to go into it. My brother, being yet unmarried, did not keep house, but boarded himself and his apprentices in another family. My refusing to eat flesh occasioned an inconveniency, and I was frequently chid for my singularity. I made myself acquainted with Tryon's manner of preparing some of his dishes, such as boiling potatoes or rice, making hasty pudding, and a few others, and then proposed to my brother, that if he would give me, weekly, half the money he paid for my board, I would board myself. He instantly agreed to it, and I presently found that I could save half what he paid me. This was an additional fund for buying books. But I had another advantage in it. My brother and the rest going from the printing-house to their meals, I remained there alone, and, despatching presently my light repast, which often was no more than a biscuit or a slice of bread, a handful of raisins, or a tart from the pastry-cook's, and a glass of water, had the rest of the time, till their return, for study, in which I made the greater progress, from that greater clearness of head and quicker apprehension which usually attend temperance in eating and drinking.

And now it was that, being on some occasion made asham'd of my ignorance in figures, which I had twice failed in learning when at school, I took Cocker's book of Arithmetick, and went through the whole by myself with great ease. I also read Seller's and Shermy's books of Navigation, and became acquainted with the little geometry they contain; but never proceeded far in that science. And I read about this time Locke *On Human Understanding*, and the *Art of Thinking*, by Messrs. du Port Royal.

While I was intent on improving my language, I met with an English grammar (I think it was Greenwood's), at the end of which there were two little sketches of the arts of rhetoric and logic, the latter finishing with a specimen of a dispute in the Socratic method, and soon after I procur'd Xenophon's *Memorable Things of Socrates,* wherein there are many instances of the same method. I was charm'd with it, adopted it, dropt my abrupt contradiction and positive argumentation, and put on the humble inquirer and doubter. And being then, from reading Shaftesbury and Collins,[4] become a real doubter in many points of our religious doctrine, I found this method safest for myself, and very embarrassing to those against whom I used it; therefore I took a delight in it, practis'd it continually, and grew very artful and expert in drawing people, even of superior knowledge, into concessions, the consequences of which they did not foresee, entangling them in difficulties out of which they could not extricate themselves, and so obtaining victories that neither myself nor my cause always deserved. I continu'd this method some few years, but gradually left it, retaining only the habit of expressing myself in terms of modest diffidence, never using, when I advanced any thing that may possibly be disputed, the words *certainly, undoubtedly,* or any others that give the air of positiveness to an opinion, but rather say, I conceive or apprehend a thing to be so and so; it appears to me, or *I should think it so or so,* for such and such reasons; or *I imagine it to be so;* or *it is so, if I am not mistaken.* This habit, I believe, has been of great advantage to me when I have had occasion to inculcate my opinions, and persuade men into measures that I have been from time to time engag'd in promoting; and, as the chief ends of conversation are to *inform* or to be *informed,* to *please* or to *persuade,* I wish well-meaning, sensible men would not lessen their power of doing good by a positive, assuming manner, that seldom fails to disgust, tends to create opposition, and to defeat every one of those purposes for which speech was given to us,—to wit, giving or receiving information or pleasure. For, if you would inform, a positive and dogmatical manner in advancing your sentiments may provoke contradiction and prevent a candid attention. If you wish information and improvement from the knowledge of others, and yet at the same time express yourself as firmly fix'd in your present opinions, modest, sensible men, who do not love disputation, will probably leave you undisturbed in the possession of your error. And by such a manner, you can seldom hope to recommend yourself in *pleasing* your hearers, or to persuade those whose concurrence you desire. Pope[5] says, judiciously:

---

4. **Shaftesbury and Collins**: Anthony Ashley Cooper, third earl of Shaftesbury (1671–1713), and Anthony Collins (1676–1729) wrote liberal theological treatises examining religion in the light of reason.—ED.

5. Alexander **Pope** (1688–1744): British poet and satirist.—ED.

> Men should be taught as if you taught them not,
> And things unknown propos'd as things forgot;

farther recommending to us

> To speak, tho' sure, with seeming diffidence.

And he might have coupled with this line that which he has coupled with another, I think, less properly:

> For want of modesty is want of sense.

If you ask, Why less properly? I must repeat the lines:

> Immodest words admit of no defense,
> For want of modesty is want of sense.

Now, is not *want of sense* (where a man is so unfortunate as to want it) some apology for his *want of modesty?* and would not the lines stand more justly thus?

> Immodest words admit *but* this defense,
> That want of modesty is want of sense.

This, however, I should submit to better judgments.

My brother had, in 1720 or 1721, begun to print a newspaper. It was 10 the second that appeared in America, and was called the *New-England Courant.* The only one before it was the *Boston News-Letter.* I remember his being dissuaded by some of his friends from the undertaking, as not likely to succeed, one newspaper being, in their judgment, enough for America. At this time [1771] there are not less than five-and-twenty. He went on, however, with the undertaking, and after having worked in composing the types and printing off the sheets, I was employed to carry the papers thro' the streets to the customers.

He had some ingenious men among his friends, who amus'd themselves by writing little pieces for this paper, which gain'd it credit and made it more in demand, and these gentlemen often visited us. Hearing their conversations, and their accounts of the approbation their papers were received with, I was excited to try my hand among them; but, being still a boy, and suspecting that my brother would object to printing any thing of mine in his paper if he knew it to be mine, I contrived to disguise my hand, and, writing an anonymous paper, I put it in at night, under the door of the printing-house. It was found in the morning, and communicated to his writing friends when they call'd in as usual. They read it, commented on it in my hearing, and I had the exquisite pleasure of finding it met with their approbation, and that, in their different guesses at the author, none were named but men of some character among us for learning and ingenuity. I suppose now that I was rather lucky in my judges, and that perhaps they were not really so very good ones as I then esteem'd them.

Encourag'd, however, by this, I wrote and convey'd in the same way to the press several more papers, which were equally approv'd; and I kept my secret till my small fund of sense for such performances was pretty well exhausted, and then I discovered it, when I began to be considered a little more by my brother's acquaintance, and in a manner that did not quite please him, as he thought, probably with reason, that it tended to make me too vain. And, perhaps, this might be one occasion of the differences that we began to have about this time. Though a brother, he considered himself as my master, and me as his apprentice, and, accordingly, expected the same services from me as he would from another, while I thought he demean'd me too much in some he requir'd of me, who from a brother expected more indulgence. Our disputes were often brought before our father, and I fancy I was either generally in the right, or else a better pleader, because the judgment was generally in my favor. But my brother was passionate, and had often beaten me, which I took extremely amiss; and, thinking my apprenticeship very tedious, I was continually wishing for some opportunity of shortening it, which at length offered in a manner unexpected.

One of the pieces in our newspaper on some political point, which I have now forgotten, gave offense to the Assembly. He was taken up, censur'd, and imprison'd for a month, by the Speaker's warrant, I suppose, because he would not discover his author. I too was taken up and examin'd before the council; but, tho' I did not give them any satisfaction, they content'd themselves with admonishing me, and dismissed me, considering me, perhaps, as an apprentice, who was bound to keep his master's secrets.

During my brother's confinement, which I resented a good deal, notwithstanding our private differences, I had the management of the paper; and I made bold to give our rulers some rubs in it, which my brother took very kindly, while others began to consider me in an unfavorable light, as a young genius that had a turn for libelling and satyr. My brother's discharge was accompany'd with an order of the House (a very odd one), that *"James Franklin should no longer print the paper called the New-England Courant."*

There was a consultation held in our printing-house among his friends, what he should do in this case. Some proposed to evade the order by changing the name of the paper; but my brother, seeing inconveniences in that, it was finally concluded on as a better way, to let it be printed for the future under the name of BENJAMIN FRANKLIN; and to avoid the censure of the Assembly, that might fall on him as still printing it by his apprentice, the contrivance was that my old indenture should be return'd to me, with a full discharge on the back of it, to be shown on occasion, but to secure to him the benefit of my service, I was to sign new indentures for the remainder of the term, which were to be kept private. A very flimsy scheme it was; however, it was immediately executed and the paper went on accordingly, under my name for several months.

At length, a fresh difference arising between my brother and me, I took upon me to assert my freedom, presuming that he would not venture to produce the new indentures. It was not fair in me to take this advantage, and this I therefore reckon one of the first errata of my life; but the unfairness of it weighed little with me, when under the impressions of resentment for the blows his passion too often urged him to bestow upon me, though he was otherwise not an ill-natur'd man: Perhaps I was too saucy and provoking.

When he found I would leave him, he took care to prevent my getting employment in any other printing-house of the town, by going round and speaking to every master, who accordingly refus'd to give me work. I then thought of going to New York, as the nearest place where there was a printer; and I was rather inclin'd to leave Boston when I reflected that I had already made myself a little obnoxious to the governing party, and, from the arbitrary proceedings of the Assembly in my brother's case, it was likely it might, if I stay'd, soon bring myself into scrapes; and farther, that my indiscrete disputations about religion began to make me pointed at with horror by good people as an infidel or atheist. I determin'd on the point, but my father now siding with my brother, I was sensible that, if I attempted to go openly, means would be used to prevent me. My friend Collins, therefore, undertook to manage a little for me. He agreed with the captain of a New York sloop for my passage, under the notion of my being a young acquaintance of his that had got a naughty girl with child, whose friends would compel me to marry her, and therefore I could not appear or come away publicly. So I sold some of my books to raise a little money, was taken on board privately, and as we had a fair wind, in three days I found myself in New York, near three hundred miles from home, a boy of but seventeen, without the least recommendation to or knowledge of, any person in the place, and with very little money in my pocket.

▪ **CONSIDER THE SOURCE**

1. How did Franklin's apprenticeship as a printer help him satisfy his "passion" for reading?

2. Locate at least two places in the selection where Franklin explicitly addresses his reader. What purposes do such direct addresses serve? How does his tone throughout the essay contribute to those same purposes?

3. Franklin compares two modes of argumentation: "positive argumentation" and "the humble enquirer." Which does he decide is preferable and why? Do you agree?

4. Trace the various ways that Franklin links the activities of reading and writing in this excerpt.

▪ **CONSIDER THE IMPLICATIONS**

5. What are some of the functions of reading for Franklin? Are these the same reasons that you read? As a class, list all the reasons for reading that you can think of and compare them to how Franklin uses books.

6. In "Writing for Print" (the next selection), Larzer Ziff claims that "secrecy and deception were conditions of life" for Franklin. Do you see examples of secrecy and deception in this selection from the *Autobiography*? How do printing and books figure in the secrets and deceptions? In your journal, describe any secret reading or writing you might have done and analyze why secrecy was necessary.

7. Franklin describes how he imitated the style of others as a way to develop his writing skills. Write a brief description of what you did yesterday, imitating Franklin's style as closely as possible.

8. Franklin describes for his son many books that influenced and instructed him in his early years. Make a list of books (and items from other media) that have contributed similarly to your education. Writing as if to your son or daughter, describe how those items influenced you and explain why they were important.

9. Find an editorial from your local newspaper that adopts what Franklin describes as a "positive, dogmatical manner." Rewrite the editorial using Franklin's stance of "humble enquirer." Which version is more persuasive?

▪ ▪ ▪ ▪ ▪ ▪

LARZER ZIFF

Writing for Print

Benjamin Franklin presents himself for public view in his autobiography, and we know him best from that work. Or at least we know the Franklin that he wanted us to know. As Larzer Ziff (b. 1927) points out, Franklin understood and exploited the printing press's ability to publish an idea and reinforce it through multiple repetitions; he used the press to craft a public image that has lasted for two centuries. In the following essay from Writing in the New Nation: Prose, Print, and Politics in the Early United States *(1991), literary scholar and historian Ziff analyzes the con-*

From *Writing in the New Nation: Prose, Print, and Politics in the Early United States* (New Haven: Yale University Press, 1991), pp. 83–94, and 100–106.

*sequences and implications of Franklin's use of print. He addresses the is-
sues of fame and reputation, credibility and authority, and intellectual
property and plagiarism. Finally, Ziff develops a connection between the
printing press and the American system of government, each offering to
represent the voice of the people in a public forum. Ziff currently chairs the
English Department at Johns Hopkins University. In addition to his books,*
The American 1890s *(1966),* Puritanism in America *(1973), and* Literary Democracy *(1981), Ziff has edited works by Franklin, Nathaniel
Hawthorne, and Ralph Waldo Emerson.*

Examining the notorious chart of virtues in Benjamin Franklin's *Autobiography*, Max Weber comments, "According to Franklin those virtues,
like all others, are only in so far virtues as they are actually useful to the
individual, and the surrogate of mere appearance is always sufficient
when it accomplishes the end in view."[1]

His point is well taken, but, then, Franklin made no attempt to disguise his sense of the matter. A virtue such as temperance was indispensable for worldly success because intemperance led to wasteful expenditure and undermined efficiency on the job. The mere appearance
of temperance, therefore, would not suffice because even if others regarded the individual as temperate, intemperance itself would have
deleterious consequences. On the other hand, humility was necessary
only because others are apt to be persuaded by and trust an individual
whom they regard as modest more than one who appears arrogant. In
this case, then, Franklin admitted, appearance will serve: "I cannot boast
of much Success in acquiring the *Reality* of this Virtue, but I had a good
deal with regard to the *Appearance* of it."[2]

At the core of Franklin's use of the terms *appearance* and *reality* was
his concern with the distinction between the public and the private life.
Convinced that both personal success and the welfare of society depend upon the public conduct of individuals, he insisted upon the private development of virtues such as temperance that had an inevitable
effect upon public behavior, while he fully admitted that other
virtues—humility, for example—were in the keeping of the observer
rather than the observed and need not necessarily arise from private
character.

To recognize this is to appreciate that to a degree unmatched by any

---

1. **Max Weber** (1864–1920): German political economist who pioneered the
field of sociology with such works as *Theory of Social and Economic Organization*
(1947) and *Methodology of the Social Sciences* (1949). This remark is from his best-
known work, *The Protestant Ethic and the Spirit of Capitalism*, trans. Talcott Parsons
(New York, 1958), p. 52.—ED.

2. Benjamin Franklin, *Autobiography*, in *Writings* (New York, 1987), p. 1,393.
Subsequent citations in the text are to this edition.

other leader of the new nation, Franklin was formed by the city, by the conditions of trade and the circumstances of daily intercourse with a range of his fellow citizens. Shaped by the city, he was also its shaper, founding the institutions of modern urban life—such as hospitals, schools, fire companies, sanitation agencies, and streetlighting facilities— and advocating patterns of conduct that ensured the advancement of both the individual and society, which, he believed, went hand in hand.

Franklin was raised in Boston where, famously, his father took him 5 on visits to the various tradesmen and craftsmen of the town in order to prepare his mind for the choice of a vocation, and where his apprentice- ship to his brother, printer of an intensely political newspaper, gave him daily glimpses into the crucial importance of acting in association with others rather than individually. At the age of sixteen he took this knowl- edge to Philadelphia, America's largest and the British empire's second largest city, and his developing genius was further shaped by urban conditions when he worked in the empire's largest city, London, in his nineteenth and twentieth years.

The range of experience thus acquired resulted in a conviction of the inseparability of the individual and society, the dependence of private character upon public perception, and the need to associate if one were to succeed. By the standard of the Puritan patriarchs of his native Boston, such a merging of the private and the public was heretical, an obliteration of the central condition of identity, the soul's relation to and dependence upon God. And even those who had drifted from such or- thodoxy nevertheless clung to notions of individual identity as ulti- mately independent of social circumstances. For them, America was a nation of yeoman farmers where the immanent self was formed by daily contact with nature and nature's god; the individual brought such an identity to society and there retained its core inviolable.

Another circumstance related to his urban experience also differen- tiated Franklin's development from that of his celebrated peers. He had arrived in both Philadelphia and London as a stranger and, accordingly, fashioned himself in terms of what those cities required of young men. For want of other credentials he had to give an account of himself in words and deeds, and the account he gave was what he became. To the moment of his death at the age of eighty-four, when he was renowned throughout the Western world, Franklin was still giving an account of himself. Dictating the final part of his *Autobiography* from his sickbed, he was fashioning the narrative that he thought should stand for—should be—Benjamin Franklin. Although from his day to ours corrections, sup- plements, and refutations of the details in that narrative have been un- dertaken on the basis of evidence external to it, still the Franklin of the *Autobiography* is the Franklin of persisting significance because that Franklin incorporates his central perception of the public nature of pri- vate character.

The success story that is the core fable of the *Autobiography* is designedly there. With his view of the interdependence of public and private, Franklin's account of himself had also to be an account of his country, not so much of the great public events in which he participated as of the reflexive relationship that existed between his career and the opportunities presented by his homeland. As such, his story has for generations rightly been taken as a manual for success, the best single model of how to achieve wealth and honor. That pattern requires no further rehearsing. But two of the themes that accompany Franklin's rise from runaway apprentice to internationally renowned sage are worthy of greater attention because they figure largely in his success and yet— amply and frankly present as they are in the *Autobiography*—Franklin does not point to them as he points to many a less significant motif when, from time to time, he generalizes his experience into maxims for those who would benefit from it.

The first theme is the way in which secrecy, sometimes carrying over into duplicity, formed an essential part of his world and played an important role at crucial stages of his career. When, for example, his brother James, to whom he was apprenticed, was forbidden by legal order to print the *New-England Courant,* that paper was continued under the name of Benjamin Franklin, printer, a legalistic maneuver bordering on deceit since the James Franklin who was prohibited from publishing the paper continued to do so by using his apprentice as the nominal publisher. In order to cover the maneuver, James publicly dissolved the apprenticeship while secretly retaining the document that still bound Benjamin to him. When, therefore, Benjamin decided his apprenticeship was intolerable, he fled from it knowing that his brother could not retain him without publicly revealing his evasion of the legal order against his printing the *Courant.* Benjamin took advantage of one deception to practice another.

In Philadelphia the runaway found that Bradford, the printer, had no need for an additional hand, but Bradford's father, on a visit to his son from New York where he too was a printer, volunteered to take the young man to the town's other printer, Keimer, who threatened to be a dangerous commercial rival to his son. The elder Bradford posed as a well-wisher who was bringing Keimer a needed assistant and in this guise drew Keimer out about his plans to surpass Bradford in the Philadelphia market, the young and knowing Ben Franklin meanwhile standing by in silence.

Encouraged by Governor William Keith to set up in rivalry to both Bradford and Keimer, Franklin against his father's advice embarked on the venture and so literally embarked for London to purchase supplies for the new printing establishment. He had no resources for this other than those promised by Keith as forthcoming, but the one letter that he found in the ship's post bag that might possibly have been the promised letter of credit from Keith proved, when he presented it to the royal stationer to whom it was addressed, to have been written by a crony of Keith's who wished to involve the stationer in a political plot against the plans of Andrew Hamilton, a distinguished Philadelphia politician then in London. Contemptuous of the letter's sender, the stationer handed the paper back to Franklin in an abrupt dismissal. Thus abandoned in London, Franklin carried the letter to Hamilton, thereby aiding Hamilton in his plans and establishing an acquaintanceship that eventually led to his benefitting commercially from Hamilton's wide influence. (This betrayal of correspondence foreshadowed the notorious publication of the confidential Hutchinson-Oliver letters years later in London, an incident that does not figure in the *Autobiography*.)

Back in Philadelphia and again employed by Keimer, Franklin entered into an agreement with a fellow employee, Hugh Meredith, to set up a printing establishment financed by Meredith's father. They sent to London for the necessary equipment and meanwhile remained in Keimer's employ, keeping secret the fact that they would soon be his competitors.

Other examples occur, but the foregoing sufficiently reflect that in the commercial and political world in which young Franklin began to advance his career, secrecy and deception were conditions of life; one employed them in order to advance oneself and, almost inevitably, worst others, and one expected that others were employing them against oneself. Franklin draws no general maxims from this in the *Autobiography*; he does not explicitly advise that the world being a treacherous place one must be prepared to do as he is done by (although Poor Richard's proverbs frequently imply this).[3] But since duplicity is a given in the world of the *Autobiography*, if its practice is not recommended neither is it condemned. It is simply a morally neutral fact of life, and Franklin treats it neither rancorously when it operates against him nor gleefully when it operates for him. Keith deceived him, but then, he shrugs, Keith having nothing else to give gave expectations. Franklin wastes no energy in preaching against Keith's practice; he simply turns around and betrays a private letter into the hands of Keith's enemies. The prominence of secrecy in the affairs of Franklin's world is especially noteworthy in view of the fact that he was a printer and so a publisher by trade, that is, one whose business it is to make things public, and the relation between the secret and the printed will receive attention farther along in the discussion.

The second prominent theme of the success story in the *Autobiography* that is never elevated into an explicit maxim is the *social* advantages that adhere to the possession and reading of books. The narrative abounds in examples of the practical part played by reading in self-improvement: through it Franklin learned how to write, how to dispute, and even how to plan his meals. And reading, of course, educated him

---

3. **Poor Richard's proverbs**: Written and published by Benjamin Franklin from 1733–1758, Poor Richard's Almanack was famous for its witty proverbs and shrewd observations about how to succeed.—ED.

into the many fields his genius mastered. But in addition, books were his passport to social and thence to commercial and political advancement. He received an early indication of this when as a runaway of suspicious appearance he stopped at an inn in New Jersey and there began a lifelong friendship with its owner, Dr. Brown, when the older man discovered that the youth owned and read books. On a return journey to Boston, Franklin, still an unknown, was summoned to the home of Governor Burnet of New York because the governor had heard from the captain of the ship on which Franklin arrived that there was a young man aboard who owned a number of books. "The Governor treated me with great Civility," Franklin wrote, "show'd me his Library, which was a very large one, & we had a good deal of Conversation about Books & Authors" (p. 1,336). When Keimer received the commission to print New Jersey's paper currency, he and Franklin went to Burlington and in a three-month stay there executed the job under the close supervision of members of the colony's legislature. "My mind having been more improv'd by Reading than Keimer's," Franklin wrote, "I suppose it was for that Reason my Conversation seem'd to be more valu'd. They had me to their Houses, introduc'd me to their Friends and show'd me much Civility.... These Friends were afterwards of great Use to me" (p. 1,358). When his rise in Philadelphia was substantially forwarded by his appointment as printer to the Pennsylvania Assembly, Franklin learned that a new member of that body who promised to be influential was opposed to his continuing as printer. He therefore set out to win him over: "Having heard that he had in his Library a certain very scarce & curious Book, I wrote a Note to him expressing my Desire of perusing that Book, and requesting he would do me the Favour of lending it to me for a few Days. He sent it immediately, and I return'd it in about a Week, with another Note expressing strongly my sense of the Favour" (p. 1,403). Thus began another lifelong and politically profitable friendship.

Franklin's interest in books and his conversion of private reading 15 into a body of knowledge superior to any university education available in America were not matters of calculated social climbing, although the mere fact of being familiar with books certainly gained him access to a higher social circle. He reached beyond this to establish the emerging class of ambitious, self-taught trades- and craftsmen as the deciding cultural and political force in American society. In a world in which money to acquire and leisure to read books were marks of the elite class he was displacing, Franklin had to avoid the appearance of leisure appropriate to that class—"a Book, indeed, sometimes debauch'd me from my Work; but this was seldom, snug, & gave no Scandal" (p. 1,369)—even as he benefited from the entry into the company of the influential that his reading afforded him.

Yet further still, books engaged his imagination in excess of any goal. The manuscript of the *Autobiography* consists of four parts. The first was written in England in 1771, the second in France in 1784, and the last two in Philadelphia in 1788, part four consisting of only three final paragraphs. Neither when he resumed his narrative in France after a lapse of thirteen years nor when he resumed it again in Philadelphia after a lapse of four years did Franklin have the previous parts before him. His memory of what he had written earlier had to suffice, and it is therefore striking that as he rummaged in his mind for the points at which to resume, in both instances, uncertain of whether or not he was repeating himself, he decided upon books as the topic that was the most important to be included if, by chance, he had omitted it, or the least annoying to repeat if, by chance, he had already mentioned it. The first part closes with an account of how his friends and he founded the first subscription library in North America, and the second part commences with a similar account. Stirring his imagination to generate the third part, Franklin again turned to books and commenced with "Observations on my Reading History in Library."

Viewed objectively, the two ungeneralized yet encompassing themes of the *Autobiography*, secrecy and books, are not any more closely related to each other than they are to other features of Franklin's world. But viewed subjectively, as phenomena integrated by his life, they cohere into the essence of his character. Franklin was a printer, and beyond others of his day, even fellow printers, he comprehended the cultural revolution that print was effecting. To publish is to make public in a multitude of identical copies that have the effect of depersonalizing discourse and transferring authority from the speaker to the spoken. To replicate in print is to translate self into the general. Printing, to be sure, had been established centuries before Franklin took up the trade, but his America was contemporary with, and to a marked extent the consequence of, the spread of print from centers of learning or population into the countryside of towns and villages. Print was put to an increasing number of uses as a growing proportion of the population relied upon reading for instruction and amusement, and the printing press followed the flow of settlement, becoming an institution of daily life. Clearly, the democratization of print both promoted and was promoted by the democratization of society.

Although many writers were slow to grasp the fact, there was a difference between a written piece that was later printed and a piece written deliberately to be printed. They proceeded from the assumption that the writer—because of his rank, learning, or office—was in a position of authority relative to his readership and that that readership was a determinate body of interested persons. To the extent that such assumptions operated, the literate culture which had replaced oral culture was still not yet print culture.

But Franklin did grasp the features that distinguished modern print culture. He saw that print's capacity to diffuse information, thought, and sentiment beyond the limits of place and moment meant that it need not address an audience conceived of as a determinate group, such as the members of a religious denomination, occupation, or social class, but could cross such boundaries in constructing its readership. The new group constituted by a readership was indeterminate because [it was] made up of individuals who, by and large, neither knew nor lived in proximity to one another, yet it possessed the power of its numbers and could be made to weigh as heavily as more determinate groups.

From his perception of the implications of print for written dis- 20 course, Franklin twitted the two groups, clergymen and lawyers, who dominated written discourse but failed to grasp the nature of print. Targeting the sermon, the preeminent oral performance of his day, Franklin lampooned its format once it was viewed in cold print, saying of the publishing preachers:

> Let them have the Liberty of repeating the same Sentence in other Words; let them put an Adjective to every Substantive, and double every Substantive with a Synonima, for this is more agreeable than hauking, spitting, taking Snuff, or other Means of concealing Hesitation. Let them multiply Definitions, Comparisons, Similitudes, and Examples. Permit them to make a Detail of Causes and Effects, enumerate all the Consequences, and express one Half by Metaphor and Circumlocution. Nay, allow the Preacher to tell us whatever a Thing is negatively, before he begins to tell what it is affirmatively; and suffer him to divide and subdivide as far as *Two and fiftiethly.*[4]

But when a discourse is to be printed, "bound down upon Paper," as Franklin puts it, then the brief, the perspicuous, and the direct are called for because the discourse must stand without the aid of the speaker's presence.

Similarly, Franklin lampooned the verbosity of legal writings in a day when print made them available to common readers: "You must abridge the Performances to understand them; and when you find how little there is in a Writing of vast Bulk, you will be as much supriz'd as a Stranger at the opening of a Pumpkin."[5] In short, Franklin knew that print meant a readership for sermons that was not to be treated as if they were sitting unquestioningly under the minister's gaze and a readership for legal matters larger than and distinct from those familiar with the professional jargon. The principle could be extended into almost all areas of knowledge.

Franklin's first published writings were designed for his brother's *New-England Courant,* and throughout his career he shaped his writing for an assumed audience of intelligent, busy people who had the ability to understand even technical subjects if they were presented in a clear and simple—even homely—style within the relatively brief compass of

---

4. Benjamin Franklin, "On Literary Style," *Papers* (New Haven, 1959–), 1:330.

5. "On Amplification," *Papers,* 2:146.

the usual journal article. Each of his pieces proceeds from the pen of a persona; none presumes to be written by an individual whose reputation having gone before him establishes the authority of what he says. Each piece must take its independent chance, deriving its effect from what it can work in the reader. Franklin's acknowledged masters, the great English essayists of the early century such as Addison and Swift,[6] had taught him technique. But in one respect at least he went beyond them. Influenced by American conditions he accepted the indeterminate nature of his readership—neither learned nor ignorant; interested in the weather and interested in statistics; alert to personal profit and sympathetic to schemes of social benevolence—and he called forth the audience that from his day to this exists substantially yet elusively under the title of the common reader.

The American world of print that Franklin's mastery shaped is put into relief by the notes of a young scholar who had been formed by it. Studying in Göttingen in 1819, the Massachusetts-born George Bancroft marveled at what he called the "democracy" of German literary culture. America had not prepared him for a land in which a class of men could earn their living by learning and publishing regardless of their birth. In his homeland democratic opportunity extended to economic and social mobility but did not encourage learning as a trade; in Germany, Bancroft noted, "much knowledge is collected that one may have a chance of selling himself at a higher price." There was also, however, a price to be paid. Whereas in America similar knowledge was purveyed to the public by Franklinesque writers whose articles and books were outgrowths of occupations and concerns broader if shallower than those of professional scholars, in Germany, "the learned write for the learned." As a result, while the products of the American press were received as matters of public consequence, in Germany, "the literary class had little or no influence on the people."[7]

The way writing entered into the daily life of the people in the United States may be glimpsed in a range of personal narratives. Recalling his youth in Connecticut at the turn of the century, for example, Samuel Goodrich said that at that time books and newspapers "were read respectfully, as if they were grave matters, demanding thought and attention. They were not . . . hastily dismissed, like waste paper. . . . Even the young approached a book with reverence, and a newspaper with awe."[8] And an exasperated Stephen Burroughs reported on how his efforts to give a true account of himself were thwarted by those who

---

6. Joseph **Addison** (1672–1719) and Jonathan **Swift** (1667–1745): Regular contributors to London literary journals of the early eighteenth century, such as *The Tatler* and the *Spectator*, with which Franklin was familiar.—ED.

7. Bancroft, as quoted in Orie William Long, *Literary Pioneers* (Cambridge, Mass., 1935), p. 122.

8. Samuel Goodrich, *Recollections of a Lifetime* (New York, 1856), 1:86.

claimed to know better because they had read about him in a newspaper and for them the printed word was far more authoritative than any oral testimony. . . .

John Adams contemplated Franklin's phenomenal fame with a mix-   25
ture of bafflement, outrage, and envy, yet also with a degree of shrewd penetration. He could not quite put the pieces together. He sensed that that fame was something new in the world of letters because, although it resulted from Franklin's writings, still, unlike the reputation of other men of letters, say of John Locke,[9] it was not confined to readers. "His name was familiar to government and people," Adams said, "to kings, courtiers, nobility, clergy, and philosophers, as well as plebians, to such a degree that there was scarcely a peasant or a citizen, a *valet de chambre*,[10] coachman or footman, a lady's chambermaid or a scullion in a kitchen, who was not familiar with it, and who did not consider him as a friend to human kind." But as he puzzled over why this was so, Adams was too readily attracted to an answer that hinted at conspiracy:

> He had been educated a printer, and had practiced his art in Boston, Philadelphia, and London for many years, where he not only learned the full power of the press to exalt and spread a man's fame, but acquired the intimacy and the correspondence of many men of that profession with all their editors and many of their correspondents. This whole tribe became enamored and proud of Mr. Franklin as a member of their body, and were consequently always ready and eager to publish any panegyric upon him that they could procure. Throughout his whole life he courted and was courted by the printers, editors, and correspondents of reviews, magazines, journals, and pamphleteers, and those little busy meddling scribblers that are always buzzing about the press in America, England, France, and Holland.[11]

To be sure, Franklin enjoyed excellent relations with the whole "tribe" connected with printing, but the reasons for his great reputation extended beyond the puffing he thus received. Adams held the key to a better answer when he noted: "His rigorous taciturnity was very favorable to this singular felicity. He conversed only with individuals, and freely only with confidential friends. In company he was totally silent" (Lemay and Zall, p. 246). Blinded by the way in which his own reputation had suffered from the press, Adams left the point unanalyzed and fixed on the more obvious circumstance of Franklin's standing in the fraternity of printers.

---

9. **John Locke** (1632–1704): Religious and political philosopher, best known for his *Essay Concerning Human Understanding* (1690) and his two *Treatises of Government* (1690).—ED.

10. *valet de chambre*: A man's personal servant.—ED.

11. *Benjamin Franklin's Autobiography*, ed. J. A. Leo Lemay and P. M. Zall (New York, 1986), pp. 245, 246.

Franklin's celebrated silence seems, indeed, to be at the root of the matter. Even in deliberative assemblies he spoke infrequently and then only briefly—never more than "ten minutes at a time, nor to any but the main point," Jefferson recalled.[12] He acted from a conviction so deeply held that it was an essential trait of character rather than an idea, a conviction that speech was fittest for private moments and print for public. Since the deliberations in which he participated as a representative were to eventuate in public documents, he aimed at the shaping of those documents rather than the display of his personal views and reserved his force for the closed-door conferences and committees concerned with drafting.

The ideological context of Franklin's outlook is acutely identified in the work of Michael Warner: "Social authority, like truth, holds validity not in persons but despite them; it is located not in the virtuous citizen nor in God nor in the king but in the light of day, in the scopic vision of publicity itself. Thus print—not speech—is the ideal and idealized guardian of civic liberty, as print discourse exposes corruption in its lurking holes but does so without occupying a lurking hole of its own."[13] And Warner amplifies his perception thus: "Developed in practices of literacy that included the production and consumption of newspapers, broadsides, pamphlets, legal documents, and books, the republican ideology of print arranged the values of generality over those of the personal. In this cognitive vocabulary the social diffusion of printed artifacts took on the investment of the disinterested virtues of the public orientation, as opposed to the corrupting interests and passions of particular and local persons."[14]

Presenting his generalized self replicated in print time and again, Franklin exemplifies the ideology that disembodied him. The personal self was not to be written and was not even to be spoken in public. Indeed, so guarded was personality that for Franklin to write was, in effect, to publish even if print were not the goal, and he regarded all writing as public property.

Thus, in justifying the publication of some confidential letters written by Governor Thomas Hutchinson that he had obtained, Franklin coolly stated, "It is in vain to say, this would be betraying private Correspondence, since if the Truth only was written, no Man need be ashamed or afraid of its being known; and if Falsehoods have been maliciously covered under the Cloak of Confidence, 'tis perfectly just the incendiary Writers should be exposed and punished."[15] There may well be more than a touch of sophistry in this argument that nothing should

30

---

12. Thomas Jefferson, *The Life and Selected Writings,* ed. Adrienne Koch and William Peden (New York, 1944), p. 61.

13. Michael Warner, "Franklin and the Letters of the Republic," *Representations* 16 (Fall, 1986): 116.

14. Michael Warner, "Textuality and Legitimacy in the Printed Constitution," *Proceedings of the American Antiquarian Society,* vol. 97, part 1 (1987), p. 74.

15. Benjamin Franklin, "On the Hutchinson Letters," *Writings,* p. 687.

be written, even in confidence, unless it can bear public exposure; that, in effect, there is no such thing as private correspondence. The contention reminds us that Franklin was the First American printer of *Pamela*,[16] the work that set the style for the age's popular epistolary novels, revelations, as it were, of private correspondence, and it also leads to second thoughts about the way Franklin may have viewed the opportunities he received as postmaster. For him, to write was to publish.

Carried to a logical extreme, such a contention means that there is no such thing as intellectual property. Once a person commits ideas to writing they become the legitimate possession of all who can read. Franklin's scientific career proceeded from this premise as he exchanged theories of electricity with his correspondents or declined to patent his stove because it was designed for all who could read about its merits. He even, notoriously, applied it to dismiss plagiarism in a manner that must have warmed the heart of Stephen Burroughs if he learned of it. Disdainful of the doctrinal preaching of his day as socially inconsequential at best and socially divisive at worst, Franklin remained apart from sectarian controversy, a Presbyterian in name and a Deist[17] in belief. But when Samuel Hemphill, a Presbyterian minister from Ireland, appeared in Philadelphia, Franklin, impressed by his "most excellent discourses," became his zealous partisan in the controversy that arose after Hemphill's moral preachings were accused of heterodoxy because they stressed good works rather than piety. To the chagrin of the Hemphill party, however, the case against their man was suddenly strengthened beyond appeal by the discovery that without acknowledging the fact he had preached sermons by others that he had memorized. Although the Hemphill party disintegrated as a result, Franklin wrote, "I stuck by him, however, as I rather approv'd his giving us good Sermons compos'd by others, than bad ones of his own Manufacture."[18] For him ideas were general property and their consequences rather than their origins were what counted.

The argument that maintains the publicity of writing implies the legitimacy of secrecy in all matters kept from print. Conduct that is not on public display and speech that is not overheard have no obligation to be consistent with what comes under public view. The taciturnity of the personal is, for Franklin, the logical complement of the publicity of the general.

"Oratory in this age?" Adams exclaimed in disgust at its decline. "Secrecy! Cunning! Silence! *Voila les grandes sciences des temps modernes.*[19]

---

16. *Pamela* (1740): A novel by Samuel Richardson (1689–1761) narrated as a series of private letters from the novel's heroine.—ED.

17. **Deist**: A believer in Deism, or "natural religion," which held that a supreme being created the universe, but thereafter assumed no control, exerted no influence on the course of events, and gave no supernatural revelations.—ED.

18. Franklin, *Autobiography*, p. 1,400.

19. *Voila les grandes sciences des temps modernes* (French): "Behold the great science of modern times!"—ED.

Washington! Franklin! Eternal silence! impenetrable secrecy! deep cunning! These are the talents and virtues which are triumphant in these days." And he thought he knew the reason:

> Silence is most commonly design and intrigue. In Franklin it was very remarkable, because he was naturally a great talker. I have conversed with him frequently in his garrulous humors, and his grandson, Billy, has told me that he never knew a greater talker than his grandfather. But at other times he was silent as midnight, and often upon occasions and in relation to subjects on which it was his duty to speak. Arthur Lee told me he had known him to sit whole evenings in London, without uttering a word, in company with the first men for science and literature, when the conversation had turned upon subjects on which he was supposed to be well informed.
>
> Whether the age of oratory will ever return I know not. At present it seems to be of little use, for every man in our public assemblies will vote with his party, and his nose is counted before his seat.[20]

While the rise of parties diminished the consequences of oratory in legislative assemblies, it augmented the consequences of print because of the press's role in influencing voters to elect members of one or another party. Thomas Green Fessenden,[21] the feisty poet of Federalist doggerel, scolded his party for "not taking pains to circulate anti-Jacobin newspapers, and other periodicals, as antidotes to the poison of the Aurora, the Democratic Press, the Chronicle &c. It is folly to say that exertions of that kind will have no effect. Our adversaries ought to have taught us better. Their maxim is command the press and we command the union."[22] Fessenden, however, underestimated the avidity with which his party seized the lesson. As Gordon Wood demonstrates, the Federalists not only counterattacked in presses they controlled but did so with maxims about representational government and the popular character of the Constitution that were similar in kind to the slogans of their opposition. "By using the most popular and democratic rhetoric available to explain and justify their aristocratic system," Wood observes, "the Federalists helped to foreclose the development of an American intellectual tradition in which differing ideas of politics would be intimately and genuinely related to differing social interests." The result was the creation of "that encompassing liberal tradition which has mitigated and often obscured the real social antagonisms of American politics."[23]

---

20. *The Spur of Fame: Dialogues of John Adams and Benjamin Rush, 1805–1813*, ed. John A. Schatz and Douglas Adair (San Marino, 1966), pp. 59, 64.

21. **Thomas Green Fessenden** (1771–1837): Using the pseudonym Christopher Caustic, he satirized Thomas Jefferson and the Democrats in *Democracy Unveiled* (1805).—ED.

22. Thomas Green Fessenden, *Pills, Poetical, Political and Philosophical* (Philadelphia, 1809), p. vi.

23. Gordon Wood, *The Creation of the American Republic, 1776–1787* (New York, 1972), p. 562.

The establishment of the United States and the spread of print went   35
hand in hand. The Constitution itself was a printed document;[24] written
by "We the people, it was authored by no particular person but anchored
in the fiction of the general made possible by print, and it was not signed
by individuals in their own right but by representatives of the people of
each state. The press's role in influencing elections compelled both parties
to employ similar rhetorical appeals in their effort to attract the voters.
The "liberal tradition" which Wood identifies was not the result of a liberal press but of the fact that the press by its very nature shaped itself to
the widest possible audience and, therefore, regardless of party repeated
the catchwords that had emerged as icons in the Revolution.

As the spread of the press was linked to both the spread of personal
as opposed to real property and the shift from immanence to representation in commercial transactions, so it was linked to the issue of political
representation. Even the stoutest patriotic opponents of the argument
that the American colonists were virtually represented by Parliament
came, after the Revolution, to see that the notion of literal representation—of the body of representatives being a replication of the body of
the people—was a greater fiction than that of virtual representation.
Women and the propertyless, for example, were not replicated in the republic's assemblies; if represented at all they were represented virtually.
Replicated representation, however, was the lifeblood of the press
which kept the ideology alive by claiming to be the voice of the people
even as it promoted the notion that the people were one.

Cathy N. Davidson has argued that the American novels of the period represent the concerns of precisely those people who were not literally represented politically, particularly women.[25] This contention, however, needs to be located within the larger circumstance that even those
who were represented politically were dependent upon literary representation for their sense of their common identity. Print made Americans who were separated by geographical distances, who belonged to
different churches, and who came from contrasting social backgrounds
aware of the size and nature of the invisible political community to
which they belonged, aware, that is, of their power. As Franklin's career
illustrates in the strongest light, the immanent world of secrecy could be
mastered by the represented world of print.

▪ CONSIDER THE SOURCE

1. According to Ziff, what relationship does Franklin see between private
character and public perception? Which is more important for success

---

24. See Warner, "Textuality and Legitimacy," for an excellent exposition of the
matter.

25. This is a major thesis of Davidson's *Revolution and the Word* (New York,
1986).

and why? How does the urban setting contribute to Franklin's views about the divided self?

2. Ziff argues that "to replicate in print is to translate self into the general." What does Ziff mean when he refers to Franklin's "generalized self"? How does it differ from his "personal self"?

3. Trace the argument that the audience for print differs from the audience for oratory, such as sermons. What are the most important differences?

4. What connection does Ziff see between the spread of print and the establishment of the U.S. system of representative government?

■ **CONSIDER THE IMPLICATIONS**

5. Franklin's knowledge and ownership of books opened doors for him as a young man making his way in the world. Do books still function this way? Brainstorm in class about possessions that offer social advantages. In your journal, discuss one type of possession that you feel helps you gain access to a particular segment of society.

6. The distance that print puts between author and reader requires that an author establish credibility for his or her words. In class discussion, examine how Franklin establishes his credibility in the *Autobiography* (p. 29). What techniques does Ziff use to make his words believable? How does each author's purpose and audience govern his choice of techniques? Which strategies do you find most effective?

7. Ziff describes the powerful connection between print and fame in Franklin's time. In our era, is the printed word still "far more authoritative than any oral testimony"? Write an essay in which you argue for or against the thesis that the printed word has more authority in establishing fame and reputation than the spoken word.

8. Research how a current public figure—an actor, a writer, a politician, or a musician, for instance—uses various media to convey or control his or her public image. Compare print coverage in magazines and newspapers to other media, such as television and radio talk shows. Write an essay that evaluates how the different media shape our perceptions of the person you've researched.

9. Compare Franklin's belief that committing ideas to writing and/or print makes them common property with Walter Ong's discussion of how "print created a new sense of the private ownership of words" (p. 58). Hold a class debate on the issue of intellectual property, with one group taking Franklin's position that published ideas belong to everyone, and the other arguing for the rights of individuals to own the products of their intellectual labor.

Walter J. Ong

Print, Space, and Closure

Try to imagine what it was like when you were two or three years old, unable to read and unconscious of written language. Communication with others at that stage depended on your ears more than your eyes. Once we learn to read, writing and print organize our consciousness, and we quickly forget what life was like when spoken language was the only way that words reached us. In Orality and Literacy *(1982), from which this selection is taken, Walter J. Ong (b. 1912) tries to rediscover the distinctions between the oral and the literate worlds. He explores how the shift from a spoken culture to a written (and then printed) culture has affected human understanding and identity. He extends his discussion to consider the difference between "primary orality"—the state of society before written language—and "secondary orality"—the "orality of telephones, radio, and television, which depends on writing and print for its existence." Ong, now retired from Saint Louis University, has written several important books on other aspects of this topic, notably* The Presence of the Word *(1967),* Rhetoric, Romance, and Technology *(1971), and* Interfaces of the Word *(1977). His most recent book is* Faith and Contexts *(1992), a series of studies on religion and the social order. Ong writes from an academic frame of reference, and he addresses primarily a scholarly audience. However, once you get beyond his specialized and often difficult vocabulary, you'll find that the ideas he presents are not beyond your grasp. Print's encouragement of re-reading works to your advantage here.*

For thousands of years human beings have been printing designs from variously carved surfaces, and since the seventh or eighth century, Chinese, Koreans, and Japanese have been printing verbal texts, at first from wood blocks engraved in relief (Carter 1955). But the crucial development in the global history of printing was the invention of alphabetic letterpress print in fifteenth-century Europe. Alphabetic writing had broken the word up into spatial equivalents of phonemic units (in principle, though the letters never quite worked out as totally phonemic indicators). But the letters used in writing do not exist before the text in which they occur. With alphabetic letterpress print it is otherwise. Words are made out of units (types) which preexist as units before the words which they will constitute. Print suggests that words are things far more than writing ever did.

Like the alphabet, alphabetic letterpress print was a nonce invention

From *Orality and Literacy: The Technologizing of the Word* (New York: Methuen, 1982), pp. 118–138.

(Ong 1967, and references there cited). The Chinese had had movable type, but no alphabet, only characters, basically pictographic. Before the mid-1400s the Koreans and Uigur Turks had both the alphabet and movable type, but the movable types bore not separate letters but whole words. Alphabet letterpress printing, in which each letter was cast on a separate piece of metal, or type, marked a psychological breakthrough of the first order. It embedded the word itself deeply in the manufacturing process and made it into a kind of commodity. The first assembly line, a manufacturing technique in which a series of steps produces identical complex objects made up of replaceable parts, was not one which produced stoves or shoes or weaponry but one which produced the printed book. In the late 1700s, the Industrial Revolution applied to other manufacturing the replaceable-part techniques which printers had worked with for three hundred years. Despite the assumptions of many semiotic structuralists, it was print, not writing, that effectively reified the word, and, with it, noetic activity[1] (Ong 1958, pp. 306–318).

Hearing rather than sight had dominated the older noetic world in significant ways, even long after writing was deeply interiorized. Manuscript culture in the West remained always marginally oral. Ambrose of Milan caught the earlier mood in his *Commentary on Luke* (iv. 5): "Sight is often deceived, hearing serves as guarantee." In the West through the Renaissance, the oration was the most taught of all verbal productions and remained implicitly the basic paradigm for all discourse, written as well as oral. Written material was subsidiary to hearing in ways which strike us today as bizarre. Writing served largely to recycle knowledge back into the oral world, as in medieval university disputations, in the reading of literary and other texts to groups (Crosby 1936; Ahern 1982; Nelson 1976–1977), and in reading aloud even when reading to oneself. At least as late as the twelfth century in England, checking even written financial accounts was still done aurally, by having them read aloud. Clanchy (1979, pp. 215, 183) describes the practice and draws attention to the fact that it still registers in our vocabulary: Even today, we speak of "auditing," that is, "hearing" account books, though what an accountant actually does today is examine them by sight. Earlier, residually oral folk could understand even figures better by listening than by looking.

Manuscript cultures remained largely oral-aural even in retrieval of material preserved in texts. Manuscripts were not easy to read, by later typographic standards, and what readers found in manuscripts they tended to commit at least somewhat to memory. Relocating material in a manuscript was not always easy. Memorization was encouraged and facilitated also by the fact that in highly oral manuscript cultures, the verbalization one encountered even in written texts often continued the oral mnemonic patterning that made for ready recall. Moreover, readers

---

1. **noetic activity**: Ong uses the phrase to indicate purely intellectual activity.—ED.

commonly vocalized, read slowly aloud or *sotto voce*,[2] even when reading alone, and this also helped fix matter in the memory.

Well after printing was developed, auditory processing continued for some time to dominate the visible, printed text, though it was eventually eroded away by print. Auditory dominance can be seen strikingly in such things as early printed title pages, which often seem to us crazily erratic in their inattention to visual word units. Sixteenth-century title pages very commonly divide even major words, including the author's name, with hyphens, presenting the first part of a word in one line in large type and the latter part in smaller type, as in the edition of Sir Thomas Elyot's *The Boke Named the Gouernour* published in London by Thomas Berthelet in 1534 (Figure 1 here; see Steinberg 1974, p. 154). Inconsequential words may be set in huge typefaces: On the title page shown here the initial "THE" is by far the most prominent word of all. The result is often aesthetically pleasing as a visual design, but it plays havoc with our present sense of textuality. Yet this practice, not our practice, is the original practice from which our present practice has deviated. Our attitudes are the ones that have changed, and thus that need to be explained. Why does the original, presumably more "natural" procedure seem wrong to us? Because we feel the printed words before us as visual units (even though we sound them at least in the imagination when we read). Evidently, in processing text for meaning, the sixteenth century was concentrating less on the sight of the word and more on its sound than we do. All text involves sight and sound. But whereas we feel reading as a visual activity cueing in sounds for us, the early age of print still felt it as primarily a listening process, simply set in motion by sight. If you felt yourself as reader to be listening to words, what difference did it make if the visible text went its own visually aesthetic way? It will be recalled that pre-print manuscripts commonly ran words together or kept spaces between them minimal.

Eventually, however, print replaced the lingering hearing-dominance in the world of thought and expression with the sight-dominance which had its beginnings with writing but could not flourish with the support of writing alone. Print situates words in space more relentlessly than writing ever did. Writing moves words from the sound world to a world of visual space, but print locks words into position in this space. Control of position is everything in print. "Composing" type by hand (the original form of typesetting) consists in positioning by hand preformed letter types, which, after use, are carefully repositioned, redistributed for future use into their proper compartments in the case (capitals or "uppercase" letters in the upper compartments, small or "lowercase" letters in the lower compartments). Composing on the linotype consists in using a machine to position the separate matrices for individual lines so that a line of type can be cast from the properly positioned matrices. Composing on a computer terminal or word processor

---

2. *sotto voce:* Italian for "under the voice," that is, in an undertone.—ED.

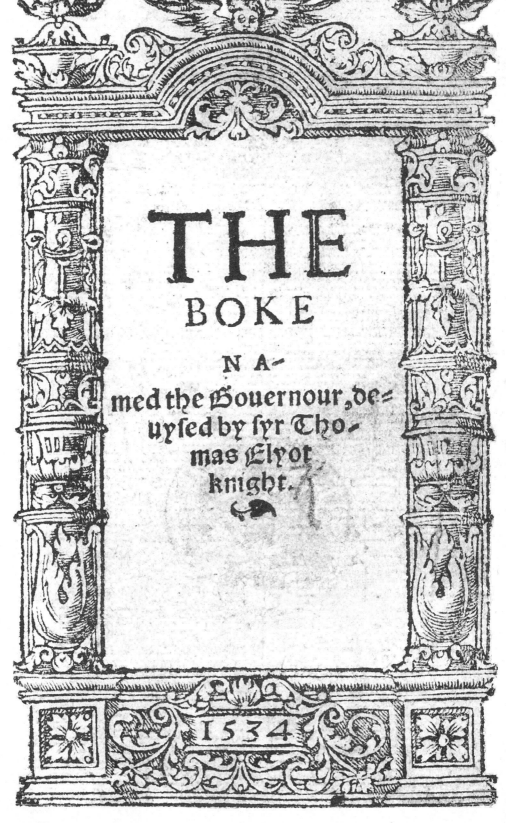

THE
BOKE

N A-
med the Gouernour, de-
uysed by syr Tho-
mas Elyot
knight.

1534

Figure 1.

positions electronic patterns (letters) previously programmed into the computer. Printing from "hot metal" type (that is, from cast type—the older and still widely used process) calls for locking up the type in an absolutely rigid position in the chase, locking the chase firmly onto a press, affixing and clamping down the makeready, and squeezing the form of type with great pressure onto the paper printing surface in contact with the platen.[3]

Most readers are of course not consciously aware of all this locomotion that has produced the printed text confronting them. Nevertheless, from the appearance of the printed text they pick up a sense of the word-in-space quite different from that conveyed by writing. Printed texts look machine-made, as they are. Chirographic[4] control of space tends to be ornamental, ornate, as in calligraphy. Typographic control typically impresses more by its tidiness and inevitability: the lines perfectly regular, all justified on the right side, everything coming out even visually, and without the aid of the guidelines or ruled borders that often occur in manuscripts. This is an insistent world of cold, nonhuman, facts. "That's the way it is"—Walter Cronkite's television signature comes from the world of print that underlies the secondary orality of television (Ong 1971, pp. 284–303).[5]

By and large, printed texts are far easier to read than manuscript texts. The effects of the greater legibility of print are massive. The greater legibility ultimately makes for rapid, silent reading. Such reading in turn makes for a different relationship between the reader and the authorial voice in the text and calls for different styles of writing. Print involves many persons besides the author in the production of a work—publishers, literary agents, publishers' readers, copyeditors, and others. Before as well as after scrutiny by such persons, writing for print often calls for painstaking revisions by the author of an order of magnitude virtually unknown in a manuscript culture. Few lengthy prose works from manuscript cultures could pass editorial scrutiny as original works today: They are not organized for rapid assimilation from a printed page. Manuscript culture is producer-oriented, since every individual copy of a work represents great expenditure of an individual copyist's time. Medieval manuscripts are turgid with abbreviations, which favor the copyist although they inconvenience the reader. Print is consumer-

---

3. **chase, makeready, form, platen**: These terms come from the world of the handpress. The *chase* was the metal frame that held pages of set type ready for printing; the locked-in type, called a *form*, was placed on the press; backing sheets, or *makeready*, were positioned on the press to ensure that the inked type would hit the paper properly when it was pressed against the *platen*, the heavy block of wood or metal that actually pressed type against paper.—ED.

4. **Chirographic**: Handwritten.—ED.

5. **Walter Cronkite's television signature**: From 1962–1981, news anchor Cronkite concluded the *CBS Evening News* by proclaiming, "And that's the way it is."—ED.

oriented, since the individual copies of a work represent a much smaller investment of time: A few hours spent in producing a more readable text will immediately improve thousands upon thousands of copies. The effects of print on thought and style have yet to be assessed fully. The journal *Visible Language* (formerly called the *Journal of Typographic Research*) publishes many articles contributory to such an assessment. . . .

Print eventually removed the ancient art of (orally based) rhetoric from the center of academic education. It encouraged and made possible on a large scale the quantification of knowledge, both through the use of mathematical analysis and through the use of diagrams and charts. Print eventually reduced the appeal of iconography[6] in the management of knowledge, despite the fact that the early ages of print put iconographic illustrations into circulation as they had never been before. Iconographic figures are akin to the "heavy" or type characters of oral discourse and they are associated with rhetoric and with the arts of memory that oral management of knowledge needs (Yates 1966).

Print produced exhaustive dictionaries and fostered the desire to legislate for "correctness" in language. This desire in great part grew out of a sense of language based on the study of Learned Latin. Learned tongues textualize the idea of language, making it seem at root something written. Print reinforces the sense of language as essentially textual. The printed text, not the written text, is the text in its fullest, paradigmatic form.

Print established the climate in which dictionaries grew. From their origins in the eighteenth century until the past few decades, dictionaries of English have commonly taken as their norm for language only the usage of writers producing text for print (and not quite all of them). The usage of all others, if it deviates from this typographic usage, has been regarded as "corrupt." *Webster's Third New International Dictionary* (1961) was the first major lexicographical work to break cleanly with this old typographical convention and to cite as sources for usage persons not writing for print—and of course many persons, formed in the old ideology, immediately wrote off this impressive lexicographical achievement (Dykema 1963) as a betrayal of the "true" or "pure" language.

Print was also a major factor in the development of the sense of personal privacy that marks modern society. It produced books smaller and more portable than those common in a manuscript culture, setting the stage psychologically for solo reading in a quiet corner, and eventually for completely silent reading. In manuscript culture and hence in early print culture, reading had tended to be a social activity, one person reading to others in a group. As Steiner (1967, p. 383) has suggested, private reading demands a home spacious enough to provide for individual isolation and

10

---

6. **iconography**: Pictorial illustration of a given subject, used as a means of knowing or understanding that subject in all its parts.—ED.

quiet. (Teachers of children from poverty areas today are acutely aware that often the major reason for poor performance is that there is nowhere in a crowded house where a boy or girl can study effectively.)

Print created a new sense of the private ownership of words. Persons in a primary oral culture can entertain some sense of proprietary rights to a poem, but such a sense is rare and ordinarily enfeebled by the common share of lore, formulas, and themes on which everyone draws. With writing, resentment at plagiarism begins to develop. The ancient Latin poet Martial uses the word *plagiarius,* a torturer, plunderer, oppressor, for someone who appropriates another's writing. But there is no special Latin word with the exclusive meaning of plagiarist or plagiarism. The oral commonplace tradition was still strong. In the very early days of print, however, a royal decree or *privilegium* was often secured forbidding the reprinting of a printed book by others than the original publisher. Richard Pynson secured such a *privilegium* in 1518 from Henry VIII. In 1557 the Stationers' Company was incorporated in London to oversee authors' and printers' or printer-publishers' rights, and by the eighteenth century modern copyright laws were shaping up over western Europe. Typography had made the word into a commodity. The old communal oral world had split up into privately claimed freeholdings. The drift in human consciousness toward greater individualism had been served well by print. Of course, words were not quite private property. They were still shared property to a degree. Printed books did echo one another, willy-nilly. At the onset of the electronic age, Joyce faced up to the anxieties of influence squarely and in *Ulysses* and *Finnegans Wake* undertook to echo everybody on purpose.[7]

By removing words from the world of sound where they had first had their origin in active human interchange and relegating them definitively to visual surface, and by otherwise exploiting visual space for the management of knowledge, print encouraged human beings to think of their own interior conscious and unconscious resources as more and more thing-like, impersonal, and religiously neutral. Print encouraged the mind to sense that its possessions were held in some sort of inert mental space.

PRINT AND CLOSURE: INTERTEXTUALITY

Print encourages a sense of closure, a sense that what is found in a   15
text has been finalized, has reached a state of completion. This sense affects literary creations and it affects analytic philosophical or scientific work.

---

7. James **Joyce** (1882–1941): Irish novelist whose masterpieces *Ulysses* (1922) and *Finnegans Wake* (1939) are densely textured with allusions to hundreds of other works.—ED.

Before print, writing itself encouraged some sense of noetic closure. By isolating thought on a written surface, detached from any interlocutor, making utterance in this sense autonomous and indifferent to attack, writing presents utterance and thought as uninvolved with all else, somehow self-contained, complete. Print in the same way situates utterance and thought on a surface disengaged from everything else, but it also goes farther in suggesting self-containment. Print encloses thought in thousands of copies of a work of exactly the same visual and physical consistency. Verbal correspondence of copies of the same printing can be checked with no resort to sound at all but simply by sight: A Hinman collator will superimpose corresponding pages of two copies of a text and signal variations to the viewer with a blinking light.[8]

The printed text is supposed to represent the words of an author in definitive or "final" form. For print is comfortable only with finality. Once a letterpress form is closed, locked up, or a photolithographic plate is made, and the sheet printed, the text does not accommodate changes (erasures, insertions) so readily as do written texts. By contrast, manuscripts, with their glosses or marginal comments (which often got worked into the text in subsequent copies) were in dialogue with the world outside their own borders. They remained closer to the give-and-take of oral expression. The readers of manuscripts are less closed off from the author, less absent, than are the readers of those writing for print. The sense of closure or completeness enforced by print is at times grossly physical. A newspaper's pages are normally all filled—certain kinds of printed material are called "fillers"—just as its lines of type are normally all justified (i.e., all exactly the same width). Print is curiously intolerant of physical incompleteness. It can convey the impression, unintentionally and subtly, but very really, that the material the text deals with is similarly complete or self-consistent.

Print makes for more tightly closed verbal art forms, especially in narrative. Until print, the only linearly plotted lengthy story line was that of the drama, which from antiquity had been controlled by writing. Euripides' tragedies[9] were texts composed in writing and then memorized verbatim to be presented orally. With print, tight plotting is extended to the lengthy narrative, in the novel from Jane Austen's[10] time on, and reaches its peak in the detective story. . . .

---

8. **Hinman collator**: Originally used to compare before and after photographs of bombing targets in World War II, the collator was adapted by Charlton Hinman for use in textual studies. It is now used to compare copies of the same printed work to detect slight textual variations that may have occurred as the work was being printed.—ED.

9. **Euripides** (480–406 B.C.): Along with Aeschylus and Sophocles, one of the three great tragedians of ancient Greece.—ED.

10. **Jane Austen** (1775–1817): British author best known for her novels *Emma* (1816) and *Pride and Prejudice* (1813).—ED.

Print ultimately gives rise to the modern issue of intertextuality, which is so central a concern in phenomenological and critical circles today (Hawkes 1977, p. 144). Intertextuality refers to a literary and psychological commonplace: A text cannot be created simply out of lived experience. A novelist writes a novel because he or she is familiar with this kind of textual organization of experience.

Manuscript culture had taken intertextuality for granted. Still tied to the commonplace tradition of the old oral world, it deliberately created texts out of other texts, borrowing, adapting, sharing the common, originally oral, formulas and themes, even though it worked them up into fresh literary forms impossible without writing. Print culture of itself has a different mind-set. It tends to feel a work as "closed," set off from other works, a unit in itself. Print culture gave birth to the romantic notions of "originality" and "creativity," which set apart an individual work from other works even more, seeing its origins and meaning as independent of outside influence, at least ideally. When in the past few decades doctrines of intertextuality arose to counteract the isolationist aesthetics of a romantic print culture, they came as a kind of shock. They were all the more disquieting because modern writers, agonizingly aware of literary history and of the *de facto* intertextuality of their own works, are concerned that they may be producing nothing really new or fresh at all, that they may be totally under the "influence" of others' texts. Harold Bloom's work *The Anxiety of Influence* (1973) treats this modern writer's anguish. Manuscript cultures had few if any anxieties about influence to plague them, and oral cultures had virtually none.

Print creates a sense of closure not only in literary works but also in analytic philosophical and scientific works. With print came the catechism and the "textbook," less discursive and less disputatious than most previous presentations of a given academic subject. Catechisms and textbooks presented "facts" or their equivalents: memorizable, flat statements that told straightforwardly and inclusively how matters stood in a given field. By contrast, the memorable statements of oral cultures and of residually oral manuscript cultures tended to be of a proverbial sort, presenting not "facts" but rather reflections, often of a gnomic kind, inviting further reflection by the paradoxes they involved.

Peter Ramus (1515–1572) produced the paradigms of the textbook genre: textbooks for virtually all arts subjects (dialectic or logic, rhetoric, grammar, arithmetic, etc.) that proceeded by cold-blooded definitions and divisions leading to still further definitions and more divisions, until every last particle of the subject had been dissected and disposed of. A Ramist textbook on a given subject had no acknowledged interchange with anything outside itself. Not even any difficulties or "adversaries" appeared. A curriculum subject or "art," if presented properly according to Ramist method, involved no difficulties at all (so Ramists maintained): If you defined and divided in the proper way, everything in the art was completely self-evident and the art itself was complete and self-contained. Ramus relegated difficulties and refutations of adversaries to separate "lectures" (*scholae*) on dialectic, rhetoric, grammar, arithmetic, and all the rest. These lectures lay outside the self-enclosed "art." Moreover, the material in each of the Ramist textbooks could be presented in printed dichotomized outlines or charts that showed exactly how the material was organized spatially in itself and in the mind. Every art was in itself completely separate from every other, as houses with intervening open spaces are separate from one another, though the arts were mingled in "use"—that is to say, in working up a given passage of discourse, one used simultaneously logic, grammar, rhetoric, and possible other arts as well (Ong 1958, pp. 30–31, 225–69, 280).

A correlative of the sense of closure fostered by print was the fixed point of view, which as Marshall McLuhan has pointed out (1962, pp. 126–127, 135–136), came into being with print. With the fixed point of view, a fixed tone could now be preserved through the whole of a lengthy prose composition. The fixed point of view and fixed tone showed in one way a greater distance between writer and reader and in another way a greater tacit understanding. The writer could go his or her own way confidently (greater distance, lack of concern). There was no need to make everything a kind of Menippean satire,[11] a mixture of various points of view and tone for various sensibilities. The writer could be confident that the reader would adjust (greater understanding). At this point, the "reading public" came into existence—a sizable clientele of readers unknown personally to the author but able to deal with certain more or less established points of view.

POST-TYPOGRAPHY: ELECTRONICS

The electronic transformation of verbal expression has both deepened the commitment of the word to space initiated by writing and intensified by print and has brought consciousness to a new age of secondary orality. Although the full relationship of the electronically processed word to the orality-literacy polarity with which this book concerns itself is too vast a subject to be considered in its totality here, some few points need to be made.

Despite what is sometimes said, electronic devices are not eliminating printed books but are actually producing more of them. Electronically taped interviews produce "talked" books and articles by the thousands, which would never have seen print before taping was possible. The new medium here reinforces the old, but of course transforms it because it fosters a new, self-consciously informal style, since typographic folk believe that oral exchange should normally be informal (oral folk

---

11. **Menippean satire**: Though the works of Menippus (3rd century B.C.) are now lost, his distinctive mixture of prose and verse was imitated by other satirists, notably Marcus Terentius Varro (116–27 B.C.) in his *Saturae Menippeae*.—ED.

believe it should normally be formal—Ong 1971, pp. 82–91). Moreover, as earlier noted, composition on computer terminals is replacing older forms of typographic composition, so that virtually all printing will soon be done in one way or another with the aid of electronic equipment. And of course information of all sorts electronically gathered and/or processed makes its way into print to swell the typographic output. Finally, the sequential processing and spatializing of the word, initiated by writing and raised to a new order of intensity by print, is further intensified by the computer, which maximizes commitment of the word to space and to (electronic) local motion and optimizes analytic sequentiality by making it virtually instantaneous.

At the same time, with telephone, radio, television, and various kinds of sound tape, electronic technology has brought us into the age of "secondary orality." This new orality has striking resemblances to the old in its participatory mystique, its fostering of a communal sense, its concentration on the present moment, and even its use of formulas (Ong 1971, pp. 284–303; 1977, pp. 16–49, 305–341). But it is essentially a more deliberate and self-conscious orality, based permanently on the use of writing and print, which are essential for the manufacture and operation of the equipment and for its use as well.

Secondary orality is both remarkably like and remarkably unlike primary orality. Like primary orality, secondary orality has generated a strong group sense, for listening to spoken words forms hearers into a group, a true audience, just as reading written or printed texts turns individuals in on themselves. But secondary orality generates a sense for groups immeasurably larger than those of primary oral culture—McLuhan's "global village." Moreover, before writing, oral folk were group-minded because no feasible alternative had presented itself. In our age of secondary orality, we are group-minded self-consciously and programmatically. The individual feels that he or she, as an individual, must be socially sensitive. Unlike members of a primary oral culture, who are turned outward because they have had little occasion to turn inward, we are turned outward because we have turned inward. In a like vein, where primary orality promotes spontaneity because the analytic reflectiveness implemented by writing is unavailable, secondary orality promotes spontaneity because through analytic reflection we have decided that spontaneity is a good thing. We plan our happenings carefully to be sure that they are thoroughly spontaneous.

The contrast between oratory in the past and in today's world well highlights the contrast between primary and secondary orality. Radio and television have brought major political figures as public speakers to a larger public than was ever possible before modern electronic developments. Thus in a sense orality has come into its own more than ever before. But it is not the old orality. The old-style oratory coming from primary orality is gone forever. In the Lincoln-Douglas debates of 1858, the combatants—for that is what they clearly and truly were—faced one another often in the scorching Illinois summer sun outdoors, before wildly responsive audiences of as many as twelve thousand or fifteen thousand persons (at Ottawa and Freeport, Illinois, respectively— Sparks 1908, pp. 137–138, 189–190), speaking for an hour and a half each. The first speaker had one hour of rebuttal—all this with no amplifying equipment. Primary orality made itself felt in the additive, redundant, carefully balanced, highly agonistic style, and the intense interplay between speaker and audience. The debaters were hoarse and physically exhausted at the end of each bout. Presidential debates on television today are completely out of this older oral world. The audience is absent, invisible, inaudible. The candidates are ensconced in tight little booths, make short presentations, and engage in crisp little conversations with each other in which any agonistic edge is deliberately kept dull. Electronic media do not tolerate a show of open antagonism. Despite their cultivated air of spontaneity, these media are totally dominated by a sense of closure which is the heritage of print: A show of hostility might break open the closure, the tight control. Candidates accommodate themselves to the psychology of the media. Genteel, literate domesticity is rampant. Only quite elderly persons today can remember what oratory was like when it was still in living contact with its primary oral roots. Others perhaps hear more oratory, or at least more talk, from major public figures than people commonly heard a century ago. But what they hear will give them very little idea of the old oratory reaching back from pre-electronic times through two millennia and far beyond, or of the oral lifestyle and oral thought structures out of which such oratory grew.

▪ WORKS CITED

Ahern, John (1982) "Singing the Book: Orality in the Reception of Dante's *Comedy*," *Annals of Scholarship* (in press).

Carter, Thomas Francis (1955) *The Invention of Printing in China and Its Spread Westward*, rev. by L. Carrington Goodrich, 2nd ed. (New York: Ronald Press).

Clanchy, M. T. (1979) *From Memory to Written Record: England, 1066–1307* (Cambridge, Mass.: Harvard University Press).

Crosby, Ruth (1936) "Oral Delivery in the Middle Ages," *Speculum*, 11, 88–110.

Dykema, Karl (1963) "Cultural Lag and Reviewers of *Webster III*," *AAUP Bulletin* 49, 364–69.

Hawkes, Terence (1977) *Structuralism and Semiotics* (Berkeley and Los Angeles: University of California Press; London: Methuen).

McLuhan, Marshall (1962) *The Gutenberg Galaxy: The Making of Typographic Man* (Toronto: University of Toronto Press).

Nelson, William (1976–1977) "From 'Listen, Lordings' to 'Dear Reader'," *University of Toronto Quarterly*, 46, 111–24.

Ong, Walter J. (1958) *Ramus, Method, and the Decay of Dialogue* (Cambridge, Mass.: Harvard University Press).

———— (1967) *The Presence of the Word* (New Haven and London: Yale University Press).

———— (1971) *Rhetoric, Romance, and Technology* (Ithaca and London: Cornell University Press).

———— (1977) *Interfaces of the Word* (Ithaca and London: Cornell University Press).

Sparks, Edwin Erle (ed.) (1908) *The Lincoln-Douglas Debates of 1858,* Collections of the Illinois State Historical Library, vol. III, Lincoln Series, vol. I (Springfield, Ill.: Illinois State Historical Society Library).

Steinberg, S. H. (1974) *Five Hundred Years of Printing,* 3rd ed. rev. by James Moran (Harmondsworth, England: Penguin Books).

Steiner, George (1967) *Language and Silence: Essays on Language, Literature, and the Inhuman* (New York: Athenaeum).

Yates, Frances A. (1966) *The Art of Memory* (Chicago: University of Chicago Press).

▪ CONSIDER THE SOURCE

1. Trace the key points of Ong's argument that hearing-dominance has given way to sight-dominance.

2. Explain the difference between "producer-oriented" and "consumer-oriented" texts. What role does the audience play in consumer-oriented texts?

3. How does print encourage a "sense of closure"? What does Ong mean by "intertextuality"? How does it relate to closure?

4. How does print reduce what Ong calls the "give-and-take of oral expression"? How did the shift from scribal to print culture affect the relationship between author and reader?

5. What does Ong mean by "secondary orality" and "primary orality"? How do the two concepts differ? In what ways are they alike?

▪ CONSIDER THE IMPLICATIONS

6. Compare the title page of this book with the title page of Thomas Elyot's *The Boke Named the Gouernour* discussed by Ong (p. 54). How does the arrangement of type signal the relative importance of the different pieces of information being conveyed? Working in groups, examine the title pages of a variety of other books—best-selling fiction, children's books, how-to, or cookbooks, for instance. How do they vary? What can you learn about the intended audience for the book from the way the title page looks?

7. Neatly type a page of your journal or print it out from a word processor with justified margins. Now copy a paragraph of this book by hand. Compare the handwritten texts with the printed texts. How does print lend authority or, as Ong says, "inevitability" to the words? Does the change in format affect your understanding of the words? Does it alter your attitude toward the message?

8. In your journal discuss how modern textbooks resemble or differ from those of Peter Ramus, described by Ong. To what extent is the modern textbook "disputatious"? Compare, for example, your biology or economics textbook with this book, which is an anthology of readings. How is

"closure" encouraged or discouraged in each type of book? How much involvement does each type of book expect from the reader?

9. Write a paper applying Ong's notion of "secondary orality" to today's radio talk shows. How does the talk show foster a sense of community in its audience? What roles do spontaneity and analytical reflection play in the world of talk radio?

10. Compare Ong's discussion of plagiarism and "the private ownership of words" with Benjamin Franklin's attitudes toward intellectual property, as Larzer Ziff describes them (pp. 47–48). Which of these attitudes seems most prevalent today? Write an essay supporting or challenging private ownership of words or proposing some compromise position.

■ ■ ■ ■ ■ ■
┊┈┈┈┈┈┈┈┈┈
┊
┊   LOUISA MAY ALCOTT
┊
┊   *Literary Lessons*
┊

In her early career, author Louisa May Alcott (1832–1888) wrote gothic thrillers—lurid stories filled with seductions, murders, and elopements. Later, she wrote Moods *(1864) and* Work *(1873), novels for adults about serious issues confronting women. But Alcott's most enduring fame came from* Little Women *(1869), one of the best-loved works of American literature. This novel chronicles the daily lives of four sisters, Meg, Jo, Beth, and Amy March, and their best friend Laurie, the boy next door. The eldest sisters try to alleviate the family's genteel poverty, but few avenues of employment are open to women of their day. Meg works as a governess, while Jo is paid to be a companion to a crabby but wealthy aunt. In this selection Jo learns that she can make money from her literary talents, once she discovers what kind of writing readers and publishers will pay for. Like Jo, Alcott wrote several kinds of fiction, but she found her most profitable niche writing books for adolescents about the March family (there were several sequels). In the past two decades, feminist literary critics have increasingly turned their attention to the whole range of Alcott's work for the light it sheds on nineteenth-century images of women.*

Fortune suddenly smiled upon Jo, and dropped a good-luck penny in her path. Not a golden penny, exactly, but I doubt if half a million would have given more real happiness than did the little sum that came to her in this wise.

From *Little Women* (Boston: Roberts Brothers, 1868–1869), vol. II pp. 44–50.

Every few weeks she would shut herself up in her room, put on her scribbling suit, and "fall into a vortex," as she expressed it, writing away at her novel with all her heart and soul, for till that was finished she could find no peace. Her "scribbling suit" consisted of a black woolen pinafore on which she could wipe her pen at will, and a cap of the same material, adorned with a cheerful red bow, into which she bundled her hair when the decks were cleared for action. This cap was a beacon to the inquiring eyes of her family, who during these periods kept their distance, merely popping in their heads semioccasionally to ask with interest, "Does genius burn, Jo?" They did not always venture even to ask this question, but took an observation of the cap and judged accordingly. If this expressive article of dress was drawn low upon the forehead, it was a sign that hard work was going on; in exciting moments it was pushed rakishly askew; and when despair seized the author it was plucked wholly off, and cast upon the floor. At such times the intruder silently withdrew, and not until the red bow was seen gaily erect upon the gifted brow did anyone dare address Jo.

She did not think herself a genius by any means; but when the writing fit came on, she gave herself up to it with entire abandon, and led a blissful life, unconscious of want, care, or bad weather while she sat safe and happy in an imaginary world full of friends almost as real and dear to her as any in the flesh. Sleep forsook her eyes, meals stood untasted, day and night were all too short to enjoy the happiness which blessed her only at such times, and made these hours worth living, even if they bore no other fruit. The divine afflatus usually lasted a week or two, and then she emerged from her "vortex" hungry, sleepy, cross, or despondent.

She was just recovering from one of these attacks when she was prevailed upon to escort Miss Crocker to a lecture, and in return for her virtue was rewarded with a new idea. It was a People's Course, the lecture on the Pyramids, and Jo rather wondered at the choice of such a subject for such an audience, but took it for granted that some great social evil would be remedied or some great want supplied by unfolding the glories of the Pharaohs to an audience whose thoughts were busy with the price of coal and flour, and whose lives were spent in trying to solve harder riddles than that of the Sphinx.

They were early, and while Miss Crocker set the heel of her stocking   5
Jo amused herself by examining the faces of the people who occupied the seat with them. On her left were two matrons with massive foreheads, and bonnets to match, discussing Woman's Rights and making tatting. Beyond sat a pair of humble lovers artlessly holding each other by the hand, a somber spinster eating peppermints out of a paper bag, and an old gentleman taking his preparatory nap behind a yellow bandanna. On her right, her only neighbor was a studious-looking lad absorbed in a newspaper.

It was a pictorial sheet, and Jo examined the work of art nearest her, idly wondering what unfortuitous concatenation of circumstances needed the melodramatic illustration of an Indian in full war costume tumbling over a precipice with a wolf at his throat while two infuriated young gentlemen, with unnaturally small feet and big eyes, were stabbing each other close by, and a disheveled female was flying away in the background with her mouth wide-open. Pausing to turn a page, the lad saw her looking, and with boyish good nature offered half his paper, saying bluntly:

"Want to read it? That's a first-rate story."

Jo accepted it with a smile, for she had never outgrown her liking for lads, and soon found herself involved in the usual labyrinth of love, mystery, and murder, for the story belonged to that class of light literature in which the passions have a holiday, and when the author's invention fails, a grand catastrophe clears the stage of one half the dramatis personae, leaving the other half to exult over their downfall.

"Prime, isn't it?" asked the boy as her eye went down the last paragraph of her portion.

"I think you and I could do as well as that if we tried," returned Jo, amused at his admiration of the trash.

"I should think I was a pretty lucky chap if I could. She makes a good living out of such stories, they say," and he pointed to the name of Mrs. S.L.A.N.G. Northbury[1] under the title of the tale.

"Do you know her?" asked Jo, with sudden interest.

"No, but I read all her pieces, and I know a fellow who works in the office where this paper is printed."

"Do you say she makes a good living out of stories like this?" And Jo looked more respectfully at the agitated group and thickly sprinkled exclamation points that adorned the page.

"Guess she does! She knows just what folks like, and gets paid well for writing it."

Here the lecture began, but Jo heard very little of it, for while Professor Sands was prosing away about Belzoni, Cheops, scarabei, and hieroglyphics, she was covertly taking down the address of the paper, and boldly resolving to try for the hundred-dollar prize offered in its columns for a sensational story. By the time the lecture ended and the audience awoke, she had built up a splendid fortune for herself (not the first founded upon paper), and was already deep in the concoction of her story, being unable to decide whether the duel should come before the elopement or after the murder.

She said nothing of her plan at home, but fell to work next day, much to the disquiet of her mother, who always looked a little anxious when "genius took to burning." Jo had never tried this style before, con-

---

1. **S.L.A.N.G. Northbury:** Alcott is parodying the name of a famous writer of melodramatic fiction, E.D.E.N. Southworth (1819–1899), author of such works as *The Curse of Clifton* (1853) and *The Hidden Hand* (1888).—ED.

tenting herself with very mild romances for the *Spread Eagle*. Her theatrical experience and miscellaneous reading were of service now, for they gave her some idea of dramatic effect, and supplied plot, language, and costumes. Her story was as full of desperation and despair as her limited acquaintance with those uncomfortable emotions enabled her to make it and, having located it in Lisbon, she wound up with an earthquake, as a striking and appropriate denouement. The manuscript was privately dispatched, accompanied by a note modestly saying that if the tale didn't get the prize, which the writer hardly dared expect, she would be very glad to receive any sum it might be considered worth.

Six weeks is a long time to wait, and a still longer time for a girl to keep a secret. But Jo did both, and was just beginning to give up all hope of ever seeing her manuscript again when a letter arrived which almost took her breath away; for on opening it, a check for a hundred dollars fell into her lap. For a minute she stared at it as if it had been a snake, then she read her letter and began to cry. If the amiable gentleman who wrote that kindly note could have known what intense happiness he was giving a fellow creature, I think he would devote his leisure hours, if he has any, to that amusement; for Jo valued the letter more than the money, because it was encouraging, and after years of effort it was so pleasant to find that she had learned to do something, though it was only to write a sensation story.

A prouder young woman was seldom seen than she when, having composed herself, she electrified the family by appearing before them with the letter in one hand, the check in the other, announcing that she had won the prize. Of course there was a great jubilee, and when the story came everyone read and praised it; though after her father had told her that the language was good, the romance fresh and hearty, and the tragedy quite thrilling, he shook his head, and said in his unworldly way:

"You can do better than this, Jo. Aim at the highest, and never mind the money." 20

"*I* think the money is the best part of it. What *will* you do with such a fortune?" asked Amy.

"Send Beth and Mother to the seaside for a month or two," answered Jo promptly.

"Oh, how splendid! No, I can't do it, dear, it would be so selfish," cried Beth, who had clapped her thin hands, and taken a long breath, as if pining for fresh ocean breezes, then stopped herself and motioned away the check which her sister waved before her.

"Ah, but you shall go, I've set my heart on it. That's what I tried for, and that's why I succeeded. I never get on when I think of myself alone, so it will help me to work for you, don't you see? Besides, Marmee needs the change, and she won't leave you, so you *must* go. Won't it be fun to see you come home plump and rosy again? Hurrah for Dr. Jo, who always cures her patients!"

To the seaside they went, after much discussion; and though Beth   25
didn't come home as plump and rosy as could be desired, she was much
better, while Mrs. March declared she felt ten years younger. So Jo was
satisfied with the investment of her prize money, and fell to work with a
cheery spirit, bent on earning more of those delightful checks. She did
earn several that year, and began to feel herself a power in the house; for
by the magic of a pen, her "rubbish" turned into comforts for them all.
"The Duke's Daughter" paid the butcher's bill, "A Phantom Hand" put
down a new carpet, and "The Curse of the Coventrys" proved the blessing of the Marches in the way of groceries and gowns. . . .

▪ **CONSIDER THE SOURCE**

1. How does Alcott describe Jo as a writer? Where does she present Jo's
   writing ambitions seriously? Where does she present them comically?

2. What distinctions among types of writing do the characters in the story
   make? What constitutes "trash"?

3. Look at Alcott's discussion of the audience for the lecture Jo attends.
   What kind of people attend the lecture, and why are they there? Why
   does Jo feel the subject is inappropriate for them? What would make the
   subject appropriate?

▪ **CONSIDER THE IMPLICATIONS**

4. Alcott's description of Jo falling "into a vortex" when she writes sounds
   very much like the "vortex of the page" that Birkerts (pp. 24–25) encountered as a reader. In a journal entry, explore the qualities of absorption
   that Alcott and Birkerts describe. What sorts of texts trigger such a response in you, and why? Which don't? Which other activities (that you
   could discuss in class) grant you the self-forgetfulness that these authors
   cherish?

5. Examine Alcott's description of Jo's scribbling suit and her writing
   processes. In small groups, discuss your own writing habits: Do you have
   favorite writing attire? A particular work area? A lucky pen? Do you
   "scribble" by hand or type at a computer? Do you require silence or do
   you prefer music while you write? Explain how your practices promote
   the writing process.

6. Which category would S.L.A.N.G. Northbury's works fall into among
   those offered by Thomas Roberts in "On Low Taste" (pp. 360–371)? What
   contemporary works would you consider "trash" and why? Write an
   essay defending your designation of a particular work as "trash," or defending a favorite work against someone else's condemnation of it.

7. Jo initially displays contempt for the popular fiction printed in the newspaper, until she learns that the author "makes a good living out of such
   stories." In class discussion, explore the connection between writing and
   money. Do popularity and sales necessarily cheapen the writing? What
   kind of writing sells best in today's market?

what else set for em?   more →
(e.s. help Mamee + Beth)   pay bills

8. Write an essay analyzing how Jo's status as a woman relates to her writing. What opportunities does writing offer her? How does her writing relate to her life? What role do men play in encouraging or discouraging her efforts?

▪ ▪ ▪ ▪ ▪ ▪

BARBARA SICHERMAN

Reading Little Women:
The Many Lives of a Text

If beauty is in the eye of the beholder, a book's meaning is in the mind of the reader—at least partially. The same book can be interpreted differently by diverse readers, depending upon the background and needs that they bring to the text. Historian Barbara Sicherman (b. 1934) investigates the varying uses that different audiences have made of a single text, Louisa May Alcott's Little Women *(1869). She looks at more than a century of readers, from Alcott's contemporaries to ours. But Sicherman also demonstrates that historical context isn't the only factor that influences how we read: Social class and cultural background play equally vital roles in shaping readers' responses to a text. Sicherman's article originally appeared in a collection entitled* U.S. History as Women's History: New Feminist Essays *(1995). In addition to several scholarly books on women's history, she is the coeditor of* Notable American Women: The Modern Period *(1980) and is writing a new book entitled* Gender and the Culture of Reading in Late-Victorian America. *Sicherman is the Kenan Professor of American Institutions and Values in the History Department of Trinity College in Hartford, Connecticut.*

"I have read and reread 'Little Women' and *it* never seems to grow old," fifteen-year-old Jane Addams[1] confided to a friend. Writing in 1876, Addams did not say why she liked *Little Women*. But her partiality was by no means unusual among women, and even some men, of her

From *U.S. History as Women's History: New Feminist Essays,* ed. Linda Kerber, et al. (Chapel Hill: University of North Carolina Press, 1995), pp. 245–266. Citations from the Little, Brown and Co. Papers (*87M-113) and the Alcott Family Papers (bMS Am 1130.8 and bMS Am 800.23) are by permission of the Houghton Library, Harvard University.

1. **Jane Addams** (1860–1935): Sociologist and reformer who founded Hull House, a Chicago settlement house dedicated to improving life in slum communities.—ED.

generation. Louisa May Alcott's tale of growing up female was an unexpected success when it appeared in the fall of 1868. Already a classic when Addams wrote, the book has been called "the most popular girls' story in American literature"; a century and a quarter after publication, there are twenty editions in print.

The early history of this publishing phenomenon is full of ironies. Not the least of them is the author's expressed distaste for the project. When Thomas Niles Jr., literary editor of the respected Boston firm of Roberts Brothers, asked Alcott to write a *"girls' story,"* the author tartly observed in her journal: "I plod away, though I don't enjoy this sort of thing. Never liked girls or knew many, except my sisters, but our queer plays and experiences may prove interesting, though I doubt it." After delivering twelve chapters in June 1868, she claimed that both she and her editor found them *"dull."* Niles assured her that he was "pleased—I ought to be more emphatic and say delighted,—so *please* do consider 'judgment' as favorable"; the following month he predicted that the book would "'hit.'"[2] Influenced perhaps by the verdict of "some girls" who had pronounced the manuscript "'splendid!'" Alcott reconsidered while correcting proof: "It reads better than I expected. Not a bit sensational, but simple and true, for we really lived most of it." Of the youngsters who liked it, she observed: "As it is for them, they are the best critics, so I should be satisfied."

The informal "readers' report" was right on target. Published in early October 1868, the first printing (two thousand copies) of *Little Women, or, Meg, Jo, Beth and Amy* sold out within the month. A sequel appeared the following April, with only the designation *Part Second* differentiating it from the original. By the end of the year some thirty-eight thousand copies (of both parts) were in print, with another thirty-two thousand in 1870. Nearly two-hundred thousand copies had been printed by Roberts Brothers by January 1888, two months before Alcott's death.[3] Like it or

---

2. Niles to [Louisa May] Alcott, June 16, 1868 (#1) and July 25, 1868 (#2), bMS Am 1130.8, Alcott Family Papers, Houghton Library, Harvard University (all citations from Niles's letters are from this collection). On Alcott's publishing history, see Raymond L. Kilgour, *Messrs. Roberts Brothers Publishers* (Ann Arbor: University of Michigan Press, 1952), and Daniel Lester Shealy, "The Author-Publisher Relationships of Louisa May Alcott" (Ph.D. diss., University of South Carolina, 1985). I am grateful to Michael Winship for the last reference.

3. For an account of Alcott's sales through 1909, by which time nearly 598,000 copies of *Little Women* had been printed by Roberts Brothers, see Joel Myerson and Daniel Shealy, "The Sales of Louisa May Alcott's Books," *Harvard Library Bulletin,* n.s., I (Spring 1990), esp. pp. 69–71, 86. I am grateful to Michael Winship for this reference. See also Roberts Brothers Cost Book D, [i], *87M-113, Little, Brown and Co. Papers, Houghton Library, Harvard University (hereafter cited as Little, Brown Papers). These figures do not include foreign sales. Although *Little Women* was not published in a single volume until 1880, I will refer to it in the singular except when one volume is specifically intended.

Sales figures are unreliable for the twentieth century, in part because of foreign sales and the proliferation of editions after the expiration of copyright.

not, with this book Alcott established her niche in the expanding market for juvenile literature.

Perhaps even more remarkable than *Little Women*'s initial success has been its longevity. It topped a list of forty books compiled by the Federal Bureau of Education in 1925 that "all children should read before they are sixteen." Two years later—in response to the question "What book has influenced you most?"—high school students ranked it first, ahead of the Bible and *Pilgrim's Progress*. On a bicentennial list of the best eleven American children's books, *Little Women, The Adventures of Tom Sawyer,* and *The Adventures of Huckleberry Finn* were the only nineteenth-century titles. Like most iconic works, *Little Women* has been transmuted into other media, into song and opera, theater, radio, and film. A comic strip even surfaced briefly in 1988 in the revamped *Ms.*

Polls and statistics do not begin to do justice to the *Little Women* phe-   5 nomenon. Reading the book has been a rite of passage for generations of adolescent and preadolescent females of the comfortable classes. It still elicits powerful narratives of love and passion. In a 1982 essay on how she became a writer, Cynthia Ozick declared: "I read *Little Women* a thousand times. Ten thousand. I am no longer incognito, not even to myself. I am Jo in her 'vortex'; not Jo exactly, but some Jo-of-the-future. I am under an enchantment: Who I truly am must be deferred, waited for and waited for." Ozick's avowal encapsulates recurrent themes in readers' accounts: the deep, almost inexplicable emotions engendered by the novel; the passionate identification with Jo March, the feisty tomboy heroine who publishes stories in her teens; and—allowing for exaggeration—a pattern of multiple readings. Numerous women who grew up in the 1940s and 1950s report that they read the book yearly or more during their teens or earlier; some confide that they continue to read it as adults, though less frequently. Presumably for them, as for Jane Addams, the story did not grow old.

One of many intriguing questions about *Little Women* is how and why the "dull" book, the girls' story by a woman who claimed she never liked girls, captivated so many readers. An added irony is that Alcott, the product of an unconventional upbringing, whose eccentric Transcendentalist father self-consciously tested his child-rearing theories on

---

Dorothea Lawrence Mann, "When the Alcott Books Were New," *Publishers' Weekly* 116 (September 28, 1929): 1619, claimed sales of nearly three million. According to an account published three years later, Little, Brown and Co., which had absorbed Roberts Brothers, reported that over 1.5 million copies of *Little Women* had been sold in the United States. "Louisa M Alcott Centenary Year," *Publishers' Weekly* 122 (July 2, 1932): 23–24. Charles A. Madison, *Book Publishing in America* (New York: McGraw-Hill, 1966), p. 134, cites sales of 3 million but gives no sources.

Sales, of course, are only part of the story: Library use was high at the outset and remained so. Niles to Alcott (#18), undated fragment [1870? but probably about August 1869] and "Popularity of *Little Women*," December 22, 1912, "Press [illegible] Albany," in bMS Am 800.23 (newspaper clippings, reviews, and articles about Louisa May Alcott and her family), Alcott Family Papers.

his daughters, took them to live in a commune, and failed utterly as a breadwinner, should write what many contemporaries considered the definitive story of American family life.

My concern here, however, is with *Little Women* as a cultural phenomenon and what it can tell us about the relationship between reading and female identity. A cultural profile of the book and its readers casts light on *Little Women's* emergence as the classic story of American girlhood and why, in the words of a recent critic, it has remained "a kind of miracle of preservation" when most other works of its era have long since disappeared from the juvenile canon. Building on recent work in cultural criticism and history, this study also examines the "cultural work" *Little Women* performed for diverse reading communities.[4] Such an approach challenges traditional assumptions about the universality of texts. It also demonstrates the importance of reading for construction of female identity.

Little Women was commissioned because the publisher believed a market existed for a "girls' story," a relatively new genre still in the process of being defined. The book's success suggests that this assumption was correct, although there is also evidence that its readership extended beyond the targeted group. Two unusual features affected the book's production and early reception. First, its two-stage publication gave readers unusual influence in constructing the plot, an important element in its long-term appeal. Second, the book was marketed in ways that elicited reader identification with author as well as heroine, an author, moreover, who was not only astonishingly successful but whose connections with Ralph Waldo Emerson (her intellectual mentor) and Nathaniel Hawthorne (her neighbor) were widely known. Enjoying considerable popularity from the outset, *Little Women* became part of the prescribed reading of an American girlhood, as did Alcott's own life.

Knowing how a book is promoted is not the same as knowing how it is read, however. *Little Women* has been interpreted in many ways, by ordinary readers as well as critics.[5] Initially praised by readers and reviewers as a realistic story of family life, by the time of its successful

---

4. On cultural work, see Jane Tompkins, *Sensational Designs: The Cultural Work of American Fiction 1790–1860* (New York: Oxford University Press, 1985). Two theoretically sophisticated, historically based studies of readers are Janice A. Radway, *Reading the Romance: Women, Patriarchy, and Popular Literature* (1984; reprint, with a new introduction by the author, Chapel Hill: University of North Carolina Press, 1991), and Roger Chartier, "Texts, Printing, Readings," in *The New Cultural History*, edited by Lynn Hunt (Berkeley: University of California Press, 1989), pp. 154–175.

5. The critical literature on *Little Women* is immense and growing. Useful starting points are Madeleine B. Stern, ed., *Critical Essays on Louisa May Alcott* (Boston: G. K. Hall, 1984); Alma J. Payne, *Louisa May Alcott: A Reference Guide* (Boston: G. K. Hall, 1980); and Judith C. Ullom, *Louisa May Alcott: A Centennial for* Little Women: *An Annotated Selected Bibliography* (Washington, D.C.: Library of Congress, 1969).

stage adaptation in 1912–1914 it seemed "quaint" to some.[6] In the twentieth century, Jo, always the most admired sister, was for many the only one who mattered.

With its origin as a girls' story—by definition a domestic story—and a plot in which the sisters overcome their personal failings as they move from adolescence to womanhood, *Little Women* has been viewed by some recent critics as exacting discipline from its readers as well as its heroines. This interpretative line recognizes only one way of reading the story—a conservative one. Feminist explications have for the most part focused on Jo, who has been variously read as "the one young woman in nineteenth-century fiction who maintains her individual independence, who gives up no part of her autonomy as payment for being born a woman—and who gets away with it" and as a character who is betrayed and even murdered by her creator, who allows her to be tamed and married.

Whether they discern negative or positive messages, critics agree on the importance of the story. *Little Women* has been called "*the* American female myth," Jo "the most influential figure of the independent and creative American woman."[7] To read the book in this way, even as a failed bildungsroman,[8] as do critics who view Jo's marriage as a surrender of autonomy and a capitulation to traditional femininity, assumes an individualistic outlook on the part of readers, a belief that a woman could aspire to and even attain personal success outside the family claim.

The formulation of *Little Women* as "*the* American female myth" is a distinctly middle-class reading, one that assumes both a universality of female experience and a single mode of reading Alcott's text that transcends class, race, ethnicity, and historical era. While adolescents from diverse backgrounds *can* interpret *Little Women* as a search for personal autonomy—and have in fact done so—this is by no means a universal reading. The female quest plot is inflected by class and culture as well as gender. The story has appealed primarily to an audience that is white and middle class. Historical evidence from working-class sources is scarce and is often filtered through middle-class observers. What we have suggests that working-class women did not necessarily have access

10

---

6. For nineteenth- and early-twentieth-century reviews, mainly in newspapers, see bMS Am 800.23, Alcott Family Papers, and Janet S. Zehr, "The Response of Nineteenth-Century Audiences to Louisa May Alcott's Fiction," *American Transcendental Quarterly*, n.s., 1 (December 1987): 323–342, which draws on this mostly undated collection.

7. Madelon Bedell, "Introduction," *Little Women* (New York: Modern Library, 1983), p. xi, and Elaine Showalter, "*Little Women:* The American Female Myth," chap. 3 in *Sister's Choice: Tradition and Change in Women's Writing* (Oxford: Clarendon Press, 1991), p. 42. All quotations from *Little Women* are from the Modern Library edition, which is taken from 1869 printings of parts one and two.

8. **bildungsroman:** A novel of education.—ED.

to "the simple, every-day classics that the school-boy and -girl are supposed to have read," among them *Little Women*, and that many had a penchant for less "realistic" fiction of the sort usually dismissed as "escapist."[9] For some Jewish working-class immigrant women early in the twentieth century, Alcott's story provided a model for becoming American and middle-class rather than for removing themselves from women's domestic lot, as was the case with the native-born writers and intellectuals to whom *Little Women*'s appeal is better known. In this reading, *Little Women* was still a success story—but of a different kind.

Dissimilar though they are, in both interpretations women readers found in *Little Women* a sense of future possibility. Gerda Lerner has demonstrated that access to learning has been central to the creation of feminist consciousness over the centuries. I would add that literature in general and fiction in particular have been critically important in the construction of female identity, although not always a feminist one. The scarcity in life of models for nontraditional womanhood has prompted women more often than men to turn to fiction for self-authorization.[10]

Little Women's long-lived popularity permits examination of the ways in which adolescent girls of diverse class, culture, and historical era have read the text. Where critics have debated the meaning of the novel, in particular whether Jo is a symbol of independent or resigned womanhood, I hope to show that meaning resides in the social location, interpretive conventions, and perceived needs of disparate communities of readers.[11] But the story of *Little Women* is one of continuity as well as difference, particularly in the common interpretive stance of white, middle-class women readers for more than a century. This persistence can perhaps best be understood as a consequence of the snail-like pace

---

9. Dorothy Richardson, *The Long Day: The Story of a New York Working Girl as Told by Herself* (1905; reprint, New York: Quadrangle Books, 1972), pp. 84–85. Alcott's juvenile fiction did not appear in the story papers most likely to be found in working-class homes; nor was it available in the Sunday school libraries to which some poor children had access. The latter might encounter Alcott in middle-class sites. In the late 1880s, for example, she was one of the three most popular authors at the reading room for "deprived" girls run by the United Workers and Woman's Exchange in Hartford; the others were Mrs. A. D. T. Whitney and Edgar Allan Poe. *Annual Report* 1 (1888): 8.

10. Lewis M. Terman and Margaret Lima, *Children's Reading: A Guide for Parents and Teachers*, 2d ed. (New York: Appleton, 1931), pp. 68–84, found that "at every age girls read more than boys" (p. 68) and read more fiction. Half the adult female respondents in one study named *Little Women* as one of ten books read in childhood that they could recall most easily. Men's choices were far more varied.

11. By reading communities, I adopt the definition proposed by Janice Radway for those who, without necessarily constituting a formal group, "share certain assumptions about reading as well as preferences for reading material" based on their social location or, I would add, the position to which they aspired. "Interpretive Communities and Variable Literacies: The Functions of Romance Reading," *Daedalus* 113 (Summer 1984): 54.

of change for women and the dearth of models for such a quest—in fiction and in life. In this context, Jo March was unique.

EARLY PUBLISHING AND MARKETING HISTORY

Alcott claimed that she kept on with *Little Women* because "lively, 15 simple books are very much needed for girls, and perhaps I can supply the need." She subsequently redirected her energies as a writer away from adult fiction—some of it considered sensational and published anonymously or pseudonymously—to become not only a successful author of "juveniles," but one of the most popular writers of the era. Alcott may have regretted being channeled into one type of literature, but she was extremely well paid for her efforts, a source of considerable pride to a woman whose father was so feckless about money.

Juvenile literature was entering a new phase in the 1860s at the very time Alcott was refashioning her career. This literature was more secular and on the whole less pietistic than its antebellum precursors, the characterizations more apt; children, even "bad boys," might be basically good, whatever mischievous stages they went through. An expanding middle class, eager to provide its young with cultural as well as moral training, underwrote the new juvenile market that included genteel literary magazines paralleling those read by adults. So seriously was this literature taken that even journals that embraced "high culture" devoted as much space to reviewing children's as adult fiction; thus the seeming anomaly of a review of Alcott's *Eight Cousins* in the *Nation* by the young Henry James.[12]

In contrast to the overtly religious antebellum stories, in which both sexes were expected to be good and domesticated, the new juvenile market was becoming increasingly segmented by gender. An exciting new adventure literature for boys developed after 1850, featuring escape from domesticity and female authority. Seeking to tap into a new market, Niles asked Alcott to write a "girls' story" after he observed the hefty sales of boys' adventure stories by "Oliver Optic," pseudonym of William Taylor Adams. Since prevailing gender ideology defined tales for girls as domestic, it is understandable why Alcott, who idolized her Concord mentor Emerson, adored Goethe, and loved to run with boys, would be disinclined to write one. The designation "girls' story" connoted classification by age as well as gender. Although people of all ages and both sexes read *Little Women*, the book evolved for the emerging female youth market, the "young adults" in the transitional period between childhood and adulthood that would soon be labeled adolescence.

---

12. **Henry James** (1843–1916): American novelist whose sophisticated realistic fiction typically chronicled life among the upper classes.—ED.

These readers had an unusual say in determining Jo's fate. Eager to capitalize on his experiment, Niles urged Alcott to add a chapter "in which allusions might be made to something in the future."[13] Employing a metaphor well suited to a writer who engaged in theatrical performances most of her life, the volume concludes: "So grouped the curtain falls upon Meg, Jo, Beth, and Amy. Whether it ever rises again, depends upon the reception given to the first act of the domestic drama, called 'LITTLE WOMEN.'" Reader response to Alcott's floater was positive but complicated her task. Reluctant to depart from autobiography, Alcott insisted that by rights Jo should remain a "literary spinster." But she felt pressured by readers to imagine a different fate for her heroine. The day she began work on the sequel, she observed: "Girls write to ask who the little women marry, as if that was the only end and aim of a woman's life. I *won't* marry Jo to Laurie to please anyone." To foil her readers, she created a "funny match" for Jo—the middle-aged, bumbling German professor, Friedrich Bhaer.

The aspect of the book that has frustrated generations of readers— the foreclosing of marriage between Jo and Laurie—thus represents a compromise between Alcott and her initial audience. Paradoxically, this seeming misstep has probably been a major factor in the story's enduring success. If Jo had remained a spinster, as Alcott wished, or if she had married the attractive and wealthy hero, as readers hoped, it is unlikely that the book would have had such a wide appeal. Rather, the problematic ending contributed to *Little Women*'s popularity, the lack of satisfying closure helping to keep the story alive, something to ponder, return to, reread, perhaps with the hope of a different resolution. Alcott's refusal of the conventionally happy ending represented by a pairing of Jo and Laurie and her insistence on a "funny match" to the rumpled and much older professor effectively subvert adolescent romantic ideals. The absence of a compelling love plot has also made it easier for generations of readers to ignore the novel's ending when Jo becomes Mother Bhaer and to retain the image of Jo as the questing teenage tomboy.

At the same time, an adolescent reader, struggling with her appear- 20 ance and unruly impulses while contemplating the burdens of future womanhood, might find it reassuring that her fictional counterpart emerges happily, if not perhaps ideally, from similar circumstances. For Jo is loved. And she has choices. She turns down the charming but erratic hero, who consoles himself by marrying her pretty and vain younger sister, Amy. Professor Bhaer is no schoolgirl's hero, but Jo believes that he is better suited to her than Laurie. The crucial point is that the choice is hers, its quirkiness another sign of her much-prized individuality. Jo gives up writing sensation stories because her prospective

13. Niles to Alcott, July 25, 1868 (#2).

husband considers them unworthy, but she makes it clear that she intends to contribute to the support of their future family.

By marrying off the sisters in the second part, Alcott bowed to young women's interest in romance. The addition of the marriage to the quest plot enabled *Little Women* to touch the essential bases for middle-class female readers in the late nineteenth century. In this regard, it was unusual for its time. In adult fiction, marriage and quest plots were rarely combined; success in the former precluded attainment of the latter. The inclusion of a marriage plot in a book for a nonadult audience was also unusual. Even though critics noted the need for literature for the in-between stage, variously designated as eight to eighteen and fourteen to twenty, *Harper's New Monthly Magazine* judged the sequel "a rather mature book for the little women, but a capital one for their elders." The conjunction of quest and marriage plots helps to account for the book's staying power: It is difficult to imagine large numbers of adolescent female readers in the twentieth century gravitating to a book in which the heroine remained single. . . .

JO AS A LITERARY AND INTELLECTUAL MODEL

. . . Readers' explanations of their fondness for Alcott constitute a trope for personal preferences. Not all of Alcott's early readers focused on Jo; some were taken with the saga of the entire March family, which invited comparisons with their own. Charlotte Perkins Gilman, for example, who grew up in genteel poverty after her father abandoned the family, liked the fact that in Alcott, as in Whitney, "the heroes and heroines were almost always poor, and good, while the rich people were generally bad." S. Josephine Baker, for her part, considered Alcott "the unattainable ideal of a great woman." A tomboy who became a prominent physician and wore ties to downplay her gender, "Jo" Baker not only claimed Jo March as her "favorite character in all fiction" but pointedly dissociated herself from Elsie Dinsmore.[14] . . .

With its secular recasting of *Pilgrim's Progress*, *Little Women* transforms Christian's allegorical search for the Celestial City into the quintessential female quest plot. In a chapter entitled "Castles in the Air," each of the March sisters reveals her deepest ambition. In its loving de-

---

14. **Charlotte Perkins Gilman** (1860–1935): American reformer, lecturer, and writer, whose *Women and Economics* (1898) has become a classic of feminist social criticism; Mrs. A. D. T. **Whitney** (1824–1906): Wrote books for children that were often compared to Alcott's, especially *Faith Gartney's Girlhood* (1863); **S. Josephine Baker** (1873–1945): Physician and public health administrator who pioneered efforts to improve the health of infants and children through preventive medicine; **Elsie Dinsmore**: Pious and long-suffering heroine of twenty-eight novels for children by Martha Finley (1828–1909).—ED.

pictions of the sisters' struggles to attain their goals (Jo to be a famous writer, Amy an artist, and Meg mistress of a lovely house), *Little Women* succeeds in authorizing female vocation and individuality. Nor did Alcott rule out the possibility of future artistic creativity: Although married and managing a large household and school, Jo has not entirely given up her literary dreams, nor Amy her artistic ones. Beth, who has no ambition other than "to stay at home safe with father and mother, and help take care of the family," dies because she can find no way of growing up; her mysterious illness may be read as a failure of imagination, her inability to build castles in the air.

In Jo, Alcott creates a portrait of female creativity that was not traditionally available to women:

> Every few weeks she would shut herself up in her room, put on her scribbling suit, and "fall into a vortex," as she expressed it, writing away at her novel with all her heart and soul, for till that was finished she could find no peace. . . .
> She did not think herself a genius by any means; but when the writing fit came on, she gave herself up to it with entire abandon, and led a blissful life, unconscious of want, care, or bad weather, while she sat safe and happy in an imaginary world, full of friends almost as real and dear to her any in the flesh. Sleep forsook her eyes, meals stood untasted, day and night were all too short to enjoy the happiness which blessed her only at such times, and made these hours worth living, even if they bore no other fruit. The divine afflatus usually lasted a week or two, and then she emerged from her "vortex" hungry, sleepy, cross, or despondent.

Alcott's portrait of concentrated purpose—which describes her own creative practice—is as far removed as it could be from the ordinary lot of women, at least any adult woman. Jo not only has a room of her own; she also has the leisure—and the license—to remove herself from all obligation to others. Jo was important to young women . . . because there were so few of her—in literature or in life. One need only recall the example of Margaret Fuller,[15] a generation older than Alcott, who suffered nightmares and delirium from her hothouse education and often felt isolated as the exceptional woman. By contrast, Jo is enmeshed in a family that constitutes a sustaining community of women.

More conventional readers of [the 1870s] could find in *Little Women* 25 practical advice on two subjects of growing concern to women: economic opportunities and marriage. Alcott was well qualified to advise on the former because of her long years of struggle in the marketplace. Though portrayed more starkly in *Work* (1873), an autobiographical novel for the adult market, middle-class women's need to be able to

---

15. **Margaret Fuller** (1810–1850): A critic, social reformer, and journalist, she belonged to the circle of Transcendentalist thinkers in Concord that included Alcott's father, Bronson Alcott. Her *Woman in the Nineteenth Century* (1845) is regarded as the first major feminist document published in America.—ED.

earn a living is a central motif in *Little Women,* as it was in Alcott's life. The novel can be read as a defining text on this subject, at a time when even conservative critics were beginning to concede the point. Mr. March's economic setback, like Bronson Alcott's, forces his daughters into the labor market. Their jobs (as governess and companion) are depicted as mainly unrewarding, although Jo's literary career is described with loving particularity. As we have seen, to please her readers, Alcott compromised her belief that "liberty [was] a better husband." But although the March sisters marry, Marmee March, who wishes no greater joy for her daughters than a happy marriage, declares that it is better to remain single than to marry without love. Opportunities for self-respecting singlehood and women's employment went hand in hand, as Alcott knew.

If Alcott articulated issues highly pertinent to young women of her era, Jo's continued appeal suggests not only the dearth of fictional heroines to foster dreams of glory but the continued absence of real-life models. Perhaps that is why Simone de Beauvoir[16] was so attracted to *Little Women,* in which she thought she "caught a glimpse of my future self":

> I identified passionately with Jo, the intellectual. . . . She wrote: In order to imitate her more completely, I composed two or three short stories. . . . [T]he relationship between Jo and Laurie touched me to the heart. Later, I had no doubt, they would marry one another; so it was possible for maturity to bring the promises made in childhood to fruition instead of denying them: This thought filled me with renewed hope. But the thing that delighted me most of all was the marked partiality which Louisa Alcott manifested for Jo. . . . [I]n *Little Women* Jo was superior to her sisters, who were either more virtuous or more beautiful than she, because of her passion for knowledge and the vigor of her thinking; her superiority was as outstanding as that of certain adults, and guaranteed that she would have an unusual life: She was marked by fate. I, too, felt I was entitled to consider my taste in reading and my scholastic success as tokens of a personal superiority which would be borne out by the future. I became in my own eyes a character out of a novel.[17]

De Beauvoir found in Jo a model of authentic selfhood, someone she could emulate in the present and through whom she could read—and invent—her own destiny. It was a future full of possibility, open rather than closed, intellectual and literary rather than domestic. By fictionalizing her own life, de Beauvoir could more readily contemplate a career as a writer and an intellectual, no matter how improbable such an outcome seemed to her family. She could also rationalize her sense of superiority

---

16. **Simone de Beauvoir** (1908–1986): French feminist and existentialist whose most famous work, *The Second Sex* (1952), was a rallying cry for the modern feminist movement.—ED.

17. Simone de Beauvoir, *Memoirs of a Dutiful Daughter.* Translated by James Kirkup. (1949; reprint, Cleveland, World Publishing Co., 1959), pp. 94–95.

to her environment and to her own sister. Although de Beauvoir later claimed that she first learned from *Little Women* that "marriage was not necessary," she responded to the romance as well as the quest plot. Far from interfering with her enjoyment, her disappointment that Jo did not marry Laurie prompted her to rework the story to her own satisfaction. Her conviction that Jo and Laurie would marry some day and the "renewed hope" this belief gave her suggest the power of wish fulfillment and the reader's capacity to create her own text. There is no textual basis for this belief: Jo and Laurie each marry someone else; each is a parent by the end of the story. De Beauvoir's reading is therefore not just a matter of filling in gaps but of rewriting the text. Her powerful commentary suggests the creativity of the reading experience and the permeability of boundaries between life and art: Lives can be fictionalized, texts can be rewritten, art can become life and life art. . . .

INFLECTIONS OF CLASS AND CULTURE

Not everyone has access to the same cultural resources, wishes to engage the same texts, or interprets them in identical ways. Although class is by no means the sole determinant of what or how much is read, it is a critical variable in determining basic literacy and educational levels. These in turn, in conjunction with the aspirations of group, family, or individual, influence reading practices and preferences.

For African American women, in the nineteenth century at least, class rather than race was probably the primary determinant of reading practices. Both Mary Church Terrell, a graduate of Oberlin College, and Ida B. Wells, the slave-born daughter of a carpenter and "a famous cook" who became a journalist and reformer, read Alcott. Terrell claimed that her books "were received with an acclaim among the young people of this country which has rarely if ever been equaled and never surpassed," while Wells observed: "I had formed my ideals on the best of Dickens's stories, Louisa May Alcott's, Mrs. A.D.T. Whitney's, and Charlotte Brontë's books, and Oliver Optic's stories for boys." Neither singled out *Little Women;* both seem to have read Alcott as part of the standard fare of an American middle-class childhood.

For African American writer Ann Petry, now in her eighties, *Little Women* was much more than that. On the occasion of her induction into the Connecticut Women's Hall of Fame, she noted her admiration for women writers who had preceded and set the stage for her—"Think of Louisa May Alcott." *Little Women* was the first book Petry "read on her own as a child." Her comments are reminiscent of those of de Beauvoir and other writers: "I couldn't stop reading because I had encountered Jo March. I felt as though I was part of Jo and she was part of me. I, too, was a tomboy and a misfit and kept a secret diary. . . . She said things like 'I wish I was a horse, then I could run for miles in this splendid air and not lose my breath.' I found myself wishing the same thing whenever I ran for the sheer joy of running. She was a would-be writer—and so was I."[18]

Two contrasting responses to *Little Women* from up and down the class ladder suggest the essentially middle-class and perhaps also middle-brow nature of the book's appeal. Edith Wharton,[19] who drops the names of famous books and authors in an autobiography dominated by upper-class and high-culture values, noted that her mother would not let her read popular American children's books because "the children spoke bad English *without the author's knowing it.*" She claimed that when she was finally permitted to read *Little Women* and *Little Men* because everyone else did, "[M]y ears, trained to the fresh racy English of *Alice in Wonderland, The Water Babies,* and *The Princess and the Goblin,* were exasperated by the laxities of the great Louisa."[20]

Like Wharton, though for different reasons, some working-class women also found *Little Women* too banal. Dorothy Richardson, a journalist, suggests as much in the *The Long Day,* an account of her life among the working class. In an arresting episode, Richardson ridicules the reading preferences of her fellow workers in a paper box factory. The plot of a favorite novel, Laura Jean Libbey's *Little Rosebud's Lovers; or, A Cruel Revenge,* is recounted by one of the workers as a tale of a woman's triumph over all sorts of adversity, including abductions and a false marriage to one of the villains. When Richardson summarizes *Little Women,* a co-worker dismisses it: "'[T]hat's no story—that's just everyday happenings. I don't see what's the use of putting things like that in books. I'll bet any money that lady what wrote it knew all them boys and girls. They just sound like real, live people; and when you was telling about them I could just see them as plain as plain could be. . . . I

---

18. *The Middletown Press,* June 1, 1994, p. B1, and Ann Petry to author, letter postmarked July 23, 1994; I am grateful to Farah Jasmine Griffin for the *Middletown Press* reference. *Little Women* continues to play an important role in the lives of some young black women. A high school student in Jamaica, for example, rewrote the story to fit a local setting. And a young, African American academic felt so strongly about *Little Women* that, on learning about my project, she contended with some heat that Aunt March was unfair in taking Amy rather than Jo to Europe; she seemed to be picking up a conversation she had just left off. Comments like these and Petry's suggest the need for research on the interaction between race and class in African American women's reading practices. A conversation with James A. Miller was helpful on this point.

19. **Edith Wharton** (1862–1937): American novelist and member of a distinguished New York family.—ED.

20. Edith Wharton, *A Backward Glance* (New York: Appleton-Century, 1934), p. 51. Annie Nathan Meyer, a member of New York's German-Jewish elite who describes the authors in the family library as "impeccable," claims that Alcott was the only writer of children's books she could "endure." Meyer, *It's Been Fun: An Autobiography* (New York: Henry Schuman, 1951), pp. 32–33.

suppose farmer folks likes them kind of stories. . . . They ain't used to the same styles of anything that us city folks are.'"[21]

The box makers found the characters in *Little Women* "real"—an interesting point in itself—but did not care to enter its narrative framework. Though they were not class conscious in a political sense, their awareness of their class position may account at least in part for their disinterest in a story whose heroines, despite economic reverses, had the leisure to pursue their interests in art, music, and literature and could expect to live in suburban cottages, conditions out of reach for most working-class women. Since *their* "everyday happenings" were poverty and exhausting work, the attraction of fictions about working girls who preserved their virtue and came into great wealth, either through marriage or disclosure of their middle- or upper-class origins, is understandable. Such denouements would have seemed just as likely—or unlikely—as a future in a suburban cottage. In the absence, in story or in life, of a female success tradition of moving up the occupational ladder, the "Cinderella tale" of marrying up was the nearest thing to a Horatio Alger story for working-class women.[22]

Reading practices depend on cultural as well as class location. It is a telling commentary on class in America that some Jewish immigrant women, who would be defined as working class on the basis of family income and occupation, not only enjoyed *Little Women* but also found in it a vehicle for envisioning a new and higher status.[23] For them, Alcott's classic provided a model for transcending their status as ethnic out-

---

21. Dorothy Richardson, *The Long Day*, pp. 75–86 (quotations, p. 86); I am grateful to Michael Denning for pointing out this episode. *The Long Day*, which purports to be the story of an educated woman forced by circumstances to do manual labor, must be used with caution. It was initially published anonymously, and many scenes read like sensational fiction. Leonora O'Reilly, a feminist trade unionist, was so outraged at the book's condescension and its insinuations that working-class women were immoral that she drafted a blazing indictment. Leonora O'Reilly Papers, edited by Edward T. James, *Papers of the Women's Trade Union League and Its Principal Leaders* (Woodbridge, Conn.: Research Publications, 1981), reel 9.

22. Michael Denning, *Mechanic Accents: Dime Novels and Working-Class Culture in America* (London: Verso, 1987), pp. 197–200, analyzes *Little Rosebud's Lovers* as a "Cinderella tale." He suggests that stories read by the middle class tended to depict working-class women as victims (of seduction and poverty) rather than as triumphant. Joyce Shaw Peterson, "Working Girls and Millionaires: The Melodramatic Romances of Laura Jean Libbey," *American Studies* 24 (Spring 1983): 19–35, also views Libbey's stories as a "success myth for women." There were other sorts of female working-class traditions than the one suggested here, particularly among the politically aware. These included reading circles, some with a particular political or philosophical slant, and various efforts at "self-improvement." See, e.g., n. 19. **Horatio Alger** (1832–1899): Wrote more than 120 immensely popular novels for boys all based on a virtuous hero's rise from rags to riches.—ED.

23. I have discussed Jewish immigrants at some length because of the abundance of evidence, not because I view them as the only model for an alternative reading of *Little Women*.

siders and for gaining access to American life and culture. . . . These immigrants found the book liberating and read it as a success story—but of a different kind.

In *My Mother and I*,[24] Elizabeth G. Stern (1889–1954) charts the cultural distance a Jewish immigrant woman traveled from Russia and a midwestern urban ghetto to the American mainstream: She graduates from college, studies social work, marries a professional man, and becomes a social worker and writer. *Little Women* occupies a crucial place in the story. After the narrator comes across it in a stack of newspapers in a rag shop, the book utterly engrosses her: "I sat in the dim light of the rag shop and read the browned pages of that ragged copy of *Little Women*. . . . [N]o book I have opened has meant as much to me as did that small volume telling in simple words such as I myself spoke, the story of an American childhood in New England. I had found a new literature, the literature of childhood." She had also found the literature of America: "I no longer read the little paper-bound Yiddish novelettes which father then sold. In the old rag shop loft I devoured the English magazines and newspapers." Of the books her teachers brought her from the public library, she writes:

> Far more marvellous than the fairy stories were to me in the ghetto street the stories of American child life, all the Alcott and the Pepper books. The pretty mothers, the childish ideals, the open gardens, the homes of many rooms were as unreal to me as the fairy stories. But reading of them made my aspirations beautiful.
>
> My books were doors that gave me entrance into another world. Often I think that I did not grow up in the ghetto but in the books I read as a child in the ghetto. The life in Soho passed me by and did not touch me, once I began to read.

Stern's testimony to the importance of reading in reconfiguring aspiration is not unlike de Beauvoir's, although the context is entirely different, as is the nature of the desire elicited by her reading. In American books, the ghetto fell away and the protagonist discovered both childhood and beauty. Far from being realistic, *Little Women* was an American fairy tale. Indeed, some of the narrator's "precocious" thirteen-year-old school friends "scoffingly averred that there were 'no such peoples like Jo and Beth.'" As she climbs the educational ladder, she discovers that such people do exist and that a life of beauty is possible, even for those of humble origin. With its emphasis on middle-class domesticity, *My Mother and I* is a story of Americanization with a female twist.

Stern was not unique in reading *Little Women* as a vehicle for assimilation into American middle-class life or in conflating "American" and "middle class." More than half a century later, a Jewish male writer explored the novel's appeal as an "American" book:

---

24. Elizabeth G. Stern, *My Mother and I* (New York: Macmillan, 1917).

[T]o me, a first generation American, raised in an Orthodox Jewish house-hold where more Yiddish was spoken than English, everything about *Little Women* was exotic. It was all so American, so full of a life I did not know but desperately hoped to be part of, an America full of promises, hopes, optimisms, an America where everyone had a chance to become somebody wonderful like Jo March—Louisa May Alcott who (I had dis-covered that the Marches and the Alcotts were almost identical) did be-come, with this story book that I adored, world famous.

What had been realistic to the early middle- and upper-middle-class WASP readers of *Little Women* was "exotic" to Jewish immigrants a gen-eration or two later. Could there be a better illustration of the impor-tance of historical location in determining meaning?

Teachers, librarians, and other cultural mediators encouraged Jew-ish immigrant women to read what many viewed as the archetypal American female story. Book and author became enshrined in popular legend, especially after publication of *Louisa May Alcott: Her Life, Letters, and Journals* (1889), the year after the author's death, by her friend Ednah Dow Cheney. Interest in Alcott remained high in the early twentieth century. There was a 1909 biography by Belle Moses and a dramatiza-tion in 1912 that received rave reviews and toured the country. Alcott's books were sometimes assigned in public schools. Jews themselves often served as cultural intermediaries between native and immigrant com-munities. When Rose Cohen, an immigrant affiliated with the Nurses' (later Henry Street) Settlement, found *Julius Caesar* too difficult, she asked the librarian at the Educational Alliance, a Jewish agency that as-sisted recent Eastern European immigrants, for a book "any book—like for a child. She brought me *Little Women*."

Cohen was offered *Little Women* as a less taxing vehicle for learning English than Shakespeare. But Alcott was often prescribed as a safe and even salutary writer. Librarians had long debated the effects of reading on those who were young, female, and impressionable. They were echoed by some members of the working class, including Rose Pastor Stokes, an immigrant from Eastern Europe via England. Contending that "*all* girls are what they read," Stokes, writing as "Zelda" for the English page of the *Yiddishes Tageblatt,* admonished her readers to avoid "crazy phantasies from the imbecile brains" of writers like Laura Jean Libbey. She urged those sixteen and under to read Alcott, a writer known for her "excellent teachings" and one from whom "discriminat-ing or indiscriminating" readers alike derived pleasure. Zelda also rec-ommended Cheney, claiming that "the biographies of some writers are far more interesting, even, than the stories they have written."

One of the Jewish immigrants for whom Alcott's success proved in-spiring was Mary Antin, a fervent advocate of assimilation into Ameri-can life. Alcott's were the children's books she "remember[ed] with the greatest delight" (followed by boys' adventure books, especially Alger's). Antin, who published poems in English in her teens and con- 40 templated a literary career, lingered over the biographical entries she found in an encyclopedia. She "could not resist the temptation to study out the exact place . . . where my name would belong. I saw that it would come not far from 'Alcott, Louisa M.'; and I covered my face with my hands, to hide the silly, baseless joy in it." We have come full circle. Eager to assimilate, Antin responded in ways reminiscent of Alcott's early native-born and middle-class readers who admired her success as an author. Antin, too, could imagine a sucessful American career for herself, a career for which Alcott was still the model.

CONCLUSION

Not all readers of *Little Women* read the same text. This is literally the case, since the story went through many editions. Not until 1880 did it appear in one volume, illustrated in this case and purged of some of its slang. Since then there have been numerous editions and many publishers. I have been concerned here with the changing meaning of the story for different audiences and with historical continuities as well. For many middle-class readers, early and later, *Little Women* provided a model of womanhood that deviated from conventional gender norms, a continuity that suggests how little these norms changed in their essentials from the late 1860s to the 1960s. Reading individualistically, they viewed Jo as an intellectual and a writer, the liberated woman they sought to become. No matter that Jo marries and raises a family; such readers remember the young Jo, the teenager who is far from beautiful, struggles with her temper, is both a bookworm and the center of action, and dreams of literary glory while helping to support her family with her pen. These readers for the most part took for granted their right to a long and privileged childhood, largely exempt from the labor market. Jewish women who immigrated to the United States in their youth could not assume such a childhood. Nor were those raised in Orthodox Jewish households brought up on an individualistic philosophy. Their school experiences and reading— American books like *Little Women*—made them aware of different standards of decorum and material life that we tend to associate with class, but that are cultural as well. For some of these readers, *Little Women* offered a fascinating glimpse into an American world. Of course we know, as they did not, that the world Alcott depicted was vanishing, even as she wrote. Nevertheless, that fictional world, along with their school encounters, provided a vision of what life, American life, could be.

Can readers do whatever they like with texts? Yes and no. As we have seen, *Little Women* has been read in may ways, depending not only on when and by whom it was read but also on readers' experiences and aspirations. It has been read as a romance or as a quest, or both. It has been read as a family drama that validates virtue over wealth. It has been read as a how-to manual by immigrants who wanted to assimilate into American, middle-class life and as a means of escaping that life by women who knew its gender constraints too well. For many, especially in the early years, *Little Women* was read through the life of the author, whose literary success exceeded that of her fictional persona.

At the same time, both the passion *Little Women* has engendered in diverse readers and its ability to survive its era and transcend its genre point to a text of unusual permeability. The compromise Alcott effected with her readers in constructing a more problematic plot than is usual in fiction for the young has enhanced the story's appeal. If *Little Women* is not exactly a "problem novel," it is a work that lingers in readers' minds in ways that allow for imaginative elaboration. The frequent rereadings reported by women in their fifties also hint at nostalgia for lost youth and for a past that seems more secure than the present, perhaps even an imagined re-creation of idealized love between mothers and daughters. Most important, readers' testimony in the nineteenth and twentieth centuries points to *Little Women* as a text that opens up possibilities rather than foreclosing them. With its multiple reference points and voices (four sisters, each distinct and recognizable), its depictions of joy as well as sorrow, its fresh and unlabored speech, Alcott's classic has something for almost everyone. For readers on the threshold of adulthood, the text's authorizing of female ambition has been a significant counterweight to more habitual gender prescriptions. . . .

▪ CONSIDER THE SOURCE

1. Summarize what Sicherman means by the "female quest plot," and explain how *Little Women* fits that pattern.

2. List all the "communities of readers" that Sicherman examines. What groups does she omit? How does her selection contribute to her argument?

3. Explain in your own words how the novel helped its adolescent readers construct a female identity.

4. What kinds of evidence does Sicherman use to support her argument about how different readers interpreted the novel?

▪ CONSIDER THE IMPLICATIONS

5. Sicherman describes the "cultural work" that *Little Women* performed for various readers. Compare their ways of using the novel with the varying uses of romance novels described by the women interviewed by Janice Radway in "The Act of Reading the Romance" (pp. 388–40). In your journal, explore what "cultural work" a specific novel has performed for you.

6. Sicherman claims that *Little Women* provided immigrant Jewish women with a model of "American life and culture" to which they could aspire in the late nineteenth century. In small groups, select one current book, one television show, and one movie that can model contemporary American

life for today's immigrants. Share your list with the class and be prepared to justify your selections.

7. In class, list on the blackboard novels or tales that you consider "girls'" books and "boys'" books. What patterns emerge from your list? What do your lists reveal about American attitudes toward girls and boys, at least as far as those attitudes are represented by the publishing industry?

8. Is there a particular book that many of your peers have been reading lately? Interview your friends about how they read the book and assess how their interpretations differ from one another. Which characters did they empathize with? Which provided role models? Why? Summarize your findings in an essay that draws on the evidence of your interviews.

9. Reread the excerpt from *Little Women* (pp. 65–69) that describes Jo's literary success. Using examples from that passage, write an essay supporting or refuting Sicherman's contention that the novel "succeeds in authorizing female vocation and individuality."

10. Alcott's novel struck a chord with generations of girls in their early teens. Today's publishers offer the same target audience dozens of books in a single series: the Sweet Valley High books. Write an essay comparing the constructions of female identity promoted by Alcott and the current novels for early adolescents. What conclusions can you draw about the similarities or differences in women's position in society in the 1860s and 1990s?

11. Read all of Alcott's *Little Women,* or the sequel *Little Men* (1871), paying close attention to the male characters. Write an essay analyzing how Alcott constructs male identity. Consider, for instance, how Laurie or Professor Bhaer find ways to fit into society. What obstacles must the characters overcome? What assumptions does Alcott make about male roles?

▪ ▪ ▪ ▪ ▪ ▪

CARYN JAMES

Amy Had Golden Curls; Jo Had a Rat. Who Would You Rather Be?

In this frank and funny essay, Caryn James confesses her guilty secret about Little Women: *She never aspired to be the literary tomboy Jo; instead, she wanted to be Amy, the "pampered princess." James, a film critic for the* New York Times *and former editor of* The New York Times Book Review, *analyzes her childhood response to Alcott's famous book*

From *The New York Times Book Review* (25 December 1994), pp. 3, 17.

and then brings the discussion into the present with a comparison of the various movie versions of the novel. The occasion for this piece in The New York Times Book Review *was the opening of Hollywood's latest take on Alcott's classic, the 1994 film starring Winona Ryder and Susan Sarandon.*

Was there ever a more passive-aggressive trio than those whiny little March sisters, Meg, Jo, and Beth? Meg, the dutiful oldest, sighing as she tosses off her frequent complaint that it is dreadful to be poor, but she can bear it; Jo such a martyr she lops off her hair to sell for quick cash, when she could easily have borrowed the money from her aunt; Beth wasting away and not once snarling about it. Only Amy, the spoiled baby of the family, refuses to beg for attention. She simply accepts it as her due. The pretty one who marries the handsome boy next door, Amy is the pampered princess of *Little Women*. That's what I liked about her.

Among female readers and especially writers, there is no more sacred a cow in all of literature than *Little Women*. We are all supposed to have worshiped Jo, identified with her, found in her a role model for our writing lives. Louisa May Alcott clearly adored Jo, her idealized self, and generations of readers have fallen in line behind her.

In 1968, one hundred years after the book first appeared, Elizabeth Janeway praised the independent Jo in *The New York Times Book Review*, calling her "the tomboy dream come true" and a "New Woman." In 1977, Carolyn Heilbrun wrote, "Jo was a miracle," a role model for "girls dreaming beyond the confines of a constricted family destiny." And more recently both Perri Klass and Anna Quindlen have cited Jo as a model who inspired them as professional writers.

You can't argue with other people's childhood memories. But *my* girlhood memory is that books were usually about fantasies, not career plans, and I wanted to be Amy. The idea of New Womanhood hadn't trickled down to me yet. Amy had golden curls; Jo had a pet rat. Who would you rather be?

For years this was my guilty secret. Then the new film version of *Little Women* approached . . . promising Winona Ryder as a Jo for the 1990s. The March sisters became a topic of conversation and I discovered a group of secret-sharers who had always found Jo to be actively annoying. She was loud, imperious, altogether obnoxious. The cult of Jo has conspired to make her a protofeminist saint and *Little Women* a tract, but a great deal of that comes from cultural hindsight. The novel admits many more ambiguous readings and imaginative possibilities.

As a girl, I read *Little Women* the way I read fairy tales. I wanted to be the princess in *Cinderella*, too, but I didn't think I'd grow up to be royal (at least not until I heard about Grace Kelly and Wallis Simpson).[1] It never occurred to me that Amy was a pathetic weakling or that *Cinderella* should have come with a warning label: "This story contains a woman who depends on a man. It may be dangerous to your economic self-sufficiency later on."

Part of the enduring charm of *Little Women* is that each March sister still has her followers, and the anti-Jo's haven't turned out any the worse for it. Some of my best friends say they wanted to be Beth; these are women who, as Alcott might have put it, now earn their livings by their pens. Being Beth was a sure-fire way to get attention, but dying seemed a little extreme to me. I identified with the responsible Meg, but the character you long to be is never the one you most resemble. Amy went to Europe, traipsed through the Palais-Royal, and fell in love with the dashing Laurie; then she married him. Jo moved to a boarding house in New York, where the bearish Professor Bhaer scolded her for writing sensational stories; then she married him anyway. Choosing Amy as a heroine was, as Alcott would *not* have put it, a no-brainer.

I wasn't the only one who wanted to be Amy. Louisa May Alcott envied her, too.

In a journal entry written a few years before *Little Women,* Alcott notes that her youngest sister, May, the real-life model for Amy, was being sent to art school by a magnanimous neighbor. With the pity-me tone that would soon creep into the Marches, Alcott wrote about her sister: "She is a fortunate girl, and always finds someone to help her as she wants to be helped. Wish I could do the same, but suppose as I never do that it is best for me to work and wait and do all for myself."

A common theme in biographies of Alcott is her complicated relationship with May. Part lavish love and part reined-in resentment, it is copiously documented in Louisa Alcott's journals. Louisa paid for her sister to go to Europe to study art, but she was always keenly aware of her self-sacrifice. In 1873, she described a day: "Cold and dull; but the thought of May free and happy was my comfort as I messed about." 10

It's not much of a jump from there to *Little Women,* especially when Jo learns that Aunt March will be taking Amy to Europe in her place: "'Amy has all the fun and I have all the work. It isn't fair, oh, it isn't fair!' cried Jo passionately." Then Jo turns on Amy and says, "You hate hard work, and you'll marry some rich man, and come home to sit in the lap of luxury all your days." Jo means those words as a curse, not a compliment, but a little girl reading them could certainly reach a different conclusion.

---

1. **Grace Kelly** (1929–1982) and **Wallis Simpson** (1896–1986): Both of these American women married European royalty. Kelly, an actress, became Princess Grace of Monaco after her marriage to Prince Rainier in 1956; Edward VIII abdicated the throne of England in 1936 in order to marry Simpson, a divorcée, who then became the Duchess of Windsor.—ED.

And when college boys come to visit the March sisters, whose side should we be on when Alcott writes: "They all liked Jo immensely, but never fell in love with her, though very few escaped without paying the tribute of a sentimental sigh or two at Amy's shrine"? In many ways Amy was the sister Louisa longed to be, though not the one she most resembled.

There were many trade-offs and see-saw changes in the sisters' life-long competition. Amy was a mediocre artist in *Little Women* (as an adult, I hardly remembered that she painted at all), a judgment that turned out to be prophetic. May illustrated the first edition of *Little Women,* and critics faulted her lifeless drawings when they noticed them at all.

With Louisa a public success, it seemed only fair that May should have the upper hand in private life. When she was thirty-seven and spending more time in Europe than in Concord, May married a man fifteen years younger than she was. This left her spinster sister looking to the afterlife for comfort. "How different our lives are just now!" Louisa wrote in her journal. "I so lonely, sad, and sick; she so happy, well, and blessed. She always had the cream of things, and deserved it. My time is yet to come somewhere else, when I am ready for it."

They both arrived somewhere else far sooner than they expected. 15 Within two years of her marriage, May gave birth to a child and died weeks later. "Of all the trials in my life I never felt any so keenly as this," Louisa wrote of May's death. Yet even then there were compensations. May left her daughter, named Louisa May, in the care of her sister Louisa, who raised the child until she herself died eight years later, only fifty-five.

In the 1990s, grown-up readers of *Little Women* tend to see both Alcott and Jo as flawlessly strong, shining heroines, forgetting how much Alcott improved her life in her fiction. Jo sold her hair as a heroic gesture because she was too proud to beg Aunt March for money. In real life, Alcott lost her precious three and a half feet of brown hair helplessly. She caught typhoid pneumonia while nursing soldiers during the Civil War, and while she was delirious doctors ordered her hair cut off. *Little Women* transforms Louisa the victim into Jo the willful.

If some people can't tell Jo from Louisa, even more believe that Jo is Katharine Hepburn. The Jo cultists may not like to admit it, but they get a lot of mileage from Ms. Hepburn's performance in the 1933 movie. From then on, Jo's image mingled with that of the typical Hepburn heroine. She is smart, spirited, confident—though in a heavily made-up, movie-star way. She even looks glamorous when her hair is cropped. Ms. Hepburn's Jo is a vast improvement over Alcott's, and the George Cukor film more quaintly enjoyable than the 1949 remake.

Yet June Allyson, in the 1949 version, seems truer to my sense of Alcott's Jo. She is loud and abrasive, a stumblebum foolishly grinning at her own clumsiness. Amy, on the other hand, is Elizabeth Taylor, preserved forever in her stunningly beautiful youth. (Joan Bennett was never very convincing as the baby Amy in 1933, possibly because Ms. Bennett was expecting a baby of her own. By the end of filming, Amy was conspicuously pregnant, Cukor was reportedly shooting her from the waist up, and the costume designers were grateful for nineteenth-century pinafores.)

The novel and the old movies of *Little Women* haven't held up as well as you might think. It's surprising to look back and realize that the book is crammed with preachy, do-good lessons from Marmee. The earlier films pared down the sermons, yet kept a cloying, saccharine tone.

The latest movie version, in keeping with the image of Jo as saint, 20 runs wild with Alcott's moralism. A humorless Marmee (Susan Sarandon) preaches about the evils of corsets and the value of women's education. In New York, Jo takes part in a conversation decrying sexism and racism. All these concerns were important in the abolitionist, suffragist, temperance-minded Alcott family, but dragging them into the movie clumsily and without historical context simply reveals how the film strains to make this nineteenth-century novel relevant today.

Ms. Ryder's character lives through the same events as the previous Jo's. But her tomboy ways (not a pair of clean white gloves to her name!) no longer matter. Stereotypes of girls and boys have broken down so much in the past few decades that Jo seems no more or less than an ordinary girl. She does grow up to be an unfortunately pedantic one, though. "Do you know the word 'Transcendentalist?'" she asks Professor Bhaer.

In the midst of this misguided *Little Women*, it is Professor Bhaer who carries on a tradition, though it is a Hollywood tradition. With each film version, the professor gets better looking. Alcott made it clear that Jo, that sexless martyr, married an older, unattractive man because she found in him a soul mate and intellectual equal. Faithfully, Ms. Hepburn's Jo married the grizzly Paul Lukas. But June Allyson's Jo got the romantic (if distinctly non-Germanic) Rossano Brazzi. And the latest Jo is luckiest of all. Her Professor Bhaer is Gabriel Byrne, who hasn't looked so handsome or romantic since he played Byron in Ken Russell's *Gothic*. He apologizes for being harsh in his criticism of Jo's writing; he takes her to the opera, where they sit in the wings and he kisses her. This sentimental courtship is an extreme perversion of the novel, of course. But the fairy tale romance is the most appealing part of a movie that labors to make Alcott seem more modern than she really is.

Louisa May Alcott, in her heavenly "somewhere else," may be tearing out her hair in grief at this latest version of her story. Or maybe not. Perhaps this is her revenge. Finally, Jo is pretty and marries the handsome man in the room next door. He even knows the word "Transcendentalist." Finally, Jo is more like Amy.

Meanwhile, the latest movie Amy (played as a girl by Kirsten Dunst and as a woman by Samantha Mathis) is a pallid blonde who carries on a pallid romance with Laurie. Some people have always seen her this way, but I say: Jo has all the fun and Amy gets second-best. It isn't fair, oh, it isn't fair!

Little Women was never my favorite Louisa May Alcott novel, any- 25 way. The one I loved was *Eight Cousins* (tossed off in 1875, when Alcott was a literary star, much in demand). It's the story of a thirteen-year-old orphan named Rose, who lives in a big house with her kind maiden aunts, Peace and Plenty. Her rich guardian, Uncle Alec, is a seafaring doctor who brings her rainbow-colored scarves and beautiful embroidered jackets from Asia. The family has a maid about Rose's age who becomes her best friend—which means her best friend has to clean up after her! Best of all, she has seven male cousins, all of whom live nearby, all of whom adore her, in the days when you could marry your cousin. Now that was a fantasy worth having. That book was worthy of the Amy I know.

▪ CONSIDER THE SOURCE

1. Describe James's attitude toward the feminist reading of *Little Women*. What words and phrases contribute most to your sense of her tone?

2. What evidence does James use to support her thesis that Louisa May Alcott envied Amy?

3. Why do you suppose this piece appeared in *The New York Times Book Review*? Would you categorize it as a book review, a film review, or something else entirely?

4. What trends does James see in Hollywood's rendering of Alcott's novel?

▪ CONSIDER THE IMPLICATIONS

5. Barbara Sicherman (pp. 70–87) and Caryn James offer dramatically different views of Alcott's relation to her characters. Discuss in class which author's arguments are more convincing and why. Write an essay in which you support or refute their points of view, or offer a compromise between them.

6. According to James, "The character you long to be is never the one you most resemble." In your journal, explore how this applies to your own childhood aspirations. Which fictional character did you long to be? Which character did you most resemble? You may wish to draw on characters in movies or television instead of limiting yourself to those in literature.

7. Drawing on the previous journal entry, write an essay that argues for or against the thesis that fiction helps readers (or viewers) construct their own identities.

8. Write a response to Barbara Sicherman in the voice of Caryn James, in which you challenge her thesis that readers used the character of Jo to help them construct a female identity.

9. Sicherman contends that Alcott refused the conventionally romantic marriage for Jo, preferring to make a "funny match" for her. James suggests that Alcott secretly wanted Jo to marry the handsome hero. Write a letter from Louisa May Alcott to the casting director for the current film, praising or condemning the choice of Gabriel Byrne as Jo's future husband, Professor Bhaer.

10. Watch at least two of the movie versions of *Little Women* that James describes (1933, 1949, and 1994). Write a comparison of the films in which you explore how movies or television shows based on other sources (books or real life) function as "readings" in the context of print culture studies.

▪ ▪ ▪ ▪ ▪ ▪
....

LAURIE LAWLOR

Miss March, the Famous American Authoress

Hollywood has made three different movies based on Louisa May Alcott's Little Women, *but the 1994 film was the first to be accompanied by a "novelization." After Robin Swicord prepared a screenplay from Alcott's novel, children's author Laurie Lawlor (b. 1953) was hired to turn that screenplay back into a novel. Her version of the novel is only one-sixth the length of Alcott's original, and so she necessarily condenses episodes and omits many scenes. According to Lawlor, she hopes her version will allow middle grade readers to enter the historical time period without extra plot lines. Lawlor has also published a picture book version of* Little Women *for younger readers, illustrated with color stills from the movie, as well as several other children's books, including* Addie across the Prairie *(1986) and* Addie's Dakota Winter *(1989). In the following selection from Lawlor's* Little Women, *Jo submits her first stories for publication in the* Concord Eagle.*

When spring finally arrived, it seemed to Jo as if all the world had come back to life. Fiddlehead ferns poked up through the soil in the se-

---

From the novelization of Robin Swicord's screenplay of *Little Women* (New York: Pocket Books, 1994), pp. 62–66.

cret places in the woods where purple violets and white trillium bloomed. Jo listened to the flutelike song of the wood thrush and wondered what secrets he was singing.

With so much growing and budding and singing and winging all around her, Jo felt as if she might explode with ideas for stories. Every night she spent hunched over her desk in her writing cap, creating new exotic worlds for her characters. Sometimes she read what she wrote aloud in a grand, dramatic voice for the mice who lived in the attic.

Jo was so busy, she did not mind when Meg was invited by Aunt March to visit the Moffat family in Boston and attend countless teas, balls, and parties. What could be worse than listening to Aunt March's numerous opinions on such a long carriage ride? Jo thought.

Even before their journey began, Aunt March was busy giving Marmee advice. "I shake my head at the way you are managing Margaret," Aunt March scolded. "How is she to be married without a proper debut? Your family's only hope is for Margaret to marry well, although I don't know who marries governesses."

The trip to Boston did not improve Meg's strange behavior. When 5 she returned, she seemed more lovesick than ever. I won't worry about Meg today, Jo told herself. I've more important things to do.

Stealthily Jo hurried to the attic, where she found her finished manuscripts. She folded and tied these with a ribbon. Then she slipped on her hat and coat. With her work safely stowed in her pocket, she slid open the rear attic window and lowered herself onto the back porch roof.

As she had done many times before, she tied her skirt around her waist and shimmied down the gutter pipe. Once she dropped into the yard, she hurried away from the house before Hannah noticed her from the kitchen window.

The merry, mysterious expression on Jo's face changed as soon as she reached Concord's[1] dusty Main Street. As she shuffled along the boardwalk, she began to wonder. Should she go forward with her plan? Or should she give up while there was still time?

Jo walked past Hastings Dry Goods to the building with a sign that said *Dentist* and *The Eagle*. She took a deep breath, opened the door, and climbed the steps. To her utter amazement, it was not nearly so difficult to leave her stories as she had thought. She ran down the stairs with the editor's "Thank you, Miss March" ringing in her ears. Did that mean he would buy the stories?

Jo was so busy wondering that she did not notice that someone had 10 fallen into step beside her.

"Hello, Mysterious," a familiar voice said, making her jump.

"Laurie! What are you doing?"

---

1. **Concord,** Massachusetts: Alcott's hometown, but she did not explicitly set *Little Women* there.—ED.

"You tell me your secret first. I saw where you went. Did you get a tooth pulled?"

Jo nodded but looked away because she knew she couldn't lie to Laurie.

"You're up to mischief, I can tell, Miss March. Tell me your secret 15 and I'll tell you mine."

Jo began to walk even faster down the street, dodging around a horse trough, an ice wagon, and a stray dog. "Does your secret have something to do with going to Harvard in the fall?" she demanded.

"Not at all!" Laurie laughed so loudly that two women turned and looked at him in surprise.

"I know you're going to come home so brilliant, you'll find me utterly impossible to talk to or share secrets with, for that matter," Jo told him.

Laurie slowed his pace. "Nothing's going to change. I'll still be the same old Laurie. You'll still be the same old Jo."

"I wish I could go to college," she replied thoughtfully. She paused 20 for a moment, then she gave Laurie a playful jab in the ribs. "I'll tell you my secret. Then you tell me yours." She held her hand to Laurie's ear and whispered, "I've left two stories with a newspaperman, and he's to give his answer next week."

Laurie threw his hat in the air and caught it. "Hurrah for Miss March, the famous American authoress!". . .

▪ CONSIDER THE SOURCE

1. Compare Lawlor's version of *Little Women* with the corresponding passages from Alcott's original *Little Women* (pp. 65–69)? What details and characters does Lawlor omit? What does she add? What effect do the changes have on how you envision the story's characters and interpret the events?

2. How is Jo portrayed in Lawlor's narrative? What details contribute to your sense of her character?

▪ CONSIDER THE IMPLICATIONS

3. In class discussion, explore the image of American society that Lawlor's text conveys. What are the opportunities for women? What activities are they expected to engage in? What are the restrictions on their behavior?

4. Caryn James contends that "the film strains to make this nineteenth-century novel relevant today" (p. 92). What evidence to support her assertion do you find in this excerpt from the movie's novelization?

5. Jo is clearly the heroine of Lawlor's version, as she is in Swicord's screenplay. Watch the 1994 movie and then explore in your journal how the movie constitutes a "reading" of the original novel, especially with regard

to the portrayal of Jo. You may wish to reread Barbara Sicherman's account of the various interpretations of Jo's character ("Reading *Little Women:* The Many Lives of a Text," pp. 70–88).

6. Like Alcott, Lawlor aims her version of *Little Women* at an audience of early adolescent readers. Based on the differences you see between Lawlor's version and Alcott's original (pp. 65–69), what assumptions would you say Lawlor makes about her readers? Write an essay evaluating the validity of her assumptions.

▪ ▪ ▪ ▪ ▪ ▪

RICHARD ZOGLIN

Trekking Onward

On November 28, 1994, a photograph of actors William Shatner and Patrick Stewart filled the cover of Time *magazine. That same issue of the magazine also included an "exclusive memoir" from Nelson Mandela on his years in a South African prison. Why were images of the captains of an imaginary spaceship featured on a national newsmagazine instead of the face of a world-famous political prisoner? Richard Zoglin uncovers part of the reason in this feature article on the* Star Trek *phenomenon: Trek sells. Zoglin, a senior writer and television critic for* Time *since 1984, surveys the history of the 1960s TV show and its many spinoffs and discovers a multimillion dollar industry catering to millions of avid consumers. From fan magazines and novelizations of episodes, to encyclopedias and technical manuals, to biographies of the actors and news stories about the phenomenon, the original television experience has been solidified and enlarged by print. Zoglin not only analyzes the remarkable spread of* Star Trek's *popularity, he contributes to that process. As the editors of* Time *magazine certainly know, Captains Kirk and Picard can sell more magazines than Nelson Mandela. Live long and prosper.*

For *Star Trek* fans, the memory still hurts. It was a *Saturday Night Live* sketch eight years ago, and William Shatner—the indomitable Captain James Tiberius Kirk from the original TV series—was playing himself making a guest appearance at a *Star Trek* convention. After fielding a few dumb questions from the nerdy, trivia-obsessed fans, he suddenly

From *Time* (28 November 1994), pp. 72–79.

exploded: "I'd just like to say . . . Get a life, will you, people?! I mean, for crying out loud, it was just a TV show!"

No matter that Shatner, in the sketch, quickly recanted, telling the crestfallen Trekkies that his outburst was, of course, a re-creation of "the evil Captain Kirk" from Episode 37. The put-down was like a phaser to the heart. Trekkies (or Trekkers, as many prefer to be called these days) have always existed in something of a parallel universe of TV viewing. They're the ones who can debate for hours the merits of the episode in which Mr. Spock mind-melded with a bloblike alien called the Horta, or the one where Captain Kirk time-traveled back to the Great Depression and fell in love with Joan Collins. They know the scientific properties of dilithium crystals, they have memorized the floor plan of the Starship *Enterprise,* and they can say, "Surrender or die!" in the Klingon language. They have immersed themselves, with a fervor matched by few devotees of any religious sect, in a fully imagined future world, where harmony and humanism have triumphed and the shackles of time and space can be cast aside almost at will. Trekkies are true-believing optimists, and a few of them may be nuts.

They are also the custodians of perhaps the most enduring and all-embracing pop-culture phenomenon of our time. Consider the industry that has grown out of a quirky TV series that ran for three years in the late 1960s, only to be canceled because of low ratings. Two decades later, a second series, *Star Trek: The Next Generation,* ran for seven seasons and became the highest-rated syndicated show in TV history. A third *Trek* series, *Deep Space Nine,* if not quite as big a hit, is currently the number-one-rated drama in syndication. Six *Star Trek* movies have earned a total of nearly five hundred million dollars at the box office. Videocassettes (of every series episode, as well as the movies) are so popular that most video stores devote an entire section to them. *Star Trek* is seen around the world in seventy-five countries, and *Trek* mania has hit many of them; the official *Star Trek* fan club in Britain has eighteen thousand members. *Trek*-related merchandise, ranging from T-shirts and backpacks to a $2,200 brass replica of the *Enterprise,* has exploded in the past five years, with total revenues topping one billion dollars. More than sixty-three million *Star Trek* books are in print, and new titles—from tell-alls by former cast members to novelizations of *Trek* episodes—are appearing at the rate of more than thirty a year.

And the *Trek* phenomenon is bursting again like a fresh supernova. A seventh feature film, *Star Trek: Generations* . . . brings together for the first time the two *Enterprise* big shots: Shatner as the heroic, headstrong Captain Kirk of the original series and of every movie until now; and Patrick Stewart, the baldpated Brit who succeeded him as the more cerebral Captain Picard in *The Next Generation.* The new film, a smashingly entertaining mix of outer-space adventure and spaced-out metaphysics, almost certainly marks the last movie appearance of the classic *Trek* crew (Kirk, in a secret no one seems able to keep, dies at the end of the film) and launches what promises to be a new string of movies featuring Stewart and his *Next Generation* gang. With *Deep Space Nine* continuing, and yet another TV series, *Star Trek: Voyager,* debuting in January [1995], the pump is primed for more TV-to-movie transfers in the future. The mother ship of all TV cult hits seems poised to boldly go where none has gone before: into eternity.

For all that, *Star Trek* has never won much respect. In the realm of long-running entertainment phenoms, Sherlock Holmes has more history; James Bond, more class; *Star Wars* and Indiana Jones, more cinematic cachet. And while no one sneers at the Baker Street Irregulars,[1] noninitiates consider Trekkies to be pretty odd: Trekkies like Pete Mohney, a computer programmer in Birmingham, Alabama, who leads a double life as captain of his local Starfleet "ship," the *Hephaestus NC-2004,* and publisher of a forty-page Trekkie newsletter; or Jerry Murphy, a Sugar Grove, Illinois, business manager and father of two, who is commander of a local Klingon club and frequently dresses up as one of the big-browed aliens for charity events. "Nobody messes with Klingons," he says. "We're the bikers of the *Star Trek* world."

After all, you have to wonder about people who would pore over *The Star Trek Encyclopedia,* with five thousand entries on every character, planet, gadget, or concept ever mentioned in the series, from *gagh* ("serpent worms, a Klingon culinary delicacy") to *Pollux V* ("planet in the Beta Geminorum system that registered with no intelligent life forms when the *Enterprise* investigated that area of space on Stardate 3468"). Gene Roddenberry, *Star Trek*'s late creator and guiding spirit, once got a letter from a group of scientists who complained about a scene in which Captain Picard visited France and looked up at the night sky. By their calculations, they said, the stars could not have been in that position in France in the twenty-fourth century.

Yet *Star Trek* has legions of more temperate fans too. General Colin Powell is a watcher; so are Robin Williams, Mel Brooks, and Stephen Hawking, the best-selling physicist (*A Brief History of Time*) who made a guest appearance in an episode of *The Next Generation,* playing poker with holographic re-creations of Albert Einstein and Sir Isaac Newton. Rachelle Chong, a member of the Federal Communications Commission [FCC], has decorated her office with *Trek* paraphernalia and dressed up as Captain Picard for Halloween. "I like the show because it shows me tomorrow," she says. And sometimes today: The cellular phone-like communicators used by the *Trek* crew back in the 1960s are almost exact precursors of the personal-communication systems the FCC has just begun issuing licenses for.

---

1. **Baker Street Irregulars:** This name applies within the Sherlock Holmes books to the street children who occasionally assist Holmes in his various criminal investigations; it has come subsequently to apply to superfans of the Holmes stories.

According to Paramount TV research, *Star Trek's* regular weekly audience of more than twenty million includes more high-income, college-educated viewers (as well as more men) than the average TV show. Even at the better than two hundred Trekkie conventions held each year, the clientele is more likely to be middle-aged couples with kids in tow than computer geeks sporting Vulcan ears. "In the early days, everyone had a shirt and a costume," says Mary Warren, who was selling *Trek* apparel at a recent convention in Tucson, Arizona. "Now you get all these normal people in here." Among the two thousand who attended was Elaine Koste, who came with her husband David and five-year-old daughter Karessa. "I use *Star Trek* as a tool to educate my daughter," said Koste. "It's good for her to see the characters deal with other races and teach good values."

"People have not gotten a real sense of what *Star Trek* fandom is really all about," says Leonard Nimoy, who played Mr. Spock, the super-rational, pointy-eared Vulcan on the original series. "I talk to people in various professions all the time who say, 'I went to college to study this or that because of *Star Trek.*'" Jonathan Frakes, Commander Riker on *The Next Generation,* concurs: "If you go in looking for geeks and nerds, then yeah, you'll find some. But this is a show that doesn't insult the audience. It is intelligent, literate, and filled with messages and morals—and that's what most of the people who watch are interested in."

Star Trek has evolved over the years from the brash, sometimes campy original series, with its Day-Glo colors and dimestore special effects, to the more meditative, slickly produced *Next Generation,* to the relatively conventional action-flick pleasures of the feature films. In all its incarnations, however, *Star Trek* conveys Roddenberry's optimistic view of the future. Sinister forces and evil aliens might lurk behind every star cluster, but on the bridge of the *Enterprise,* people of various races, cultures, and planets work in utopian harmony. Their adventures, in the early days, were often allegories for earthbound problems like race relations and Vietnam—problems that were solved with reason. A key concept of the show, which began during the Vietnam War, was the Prime Directive. It stated that the *Enterprise* crew must not interfere with the normal course of development of any civilization they might encounter.

The comforting ethos of the series was expressed not merely in the amity of the crew—who never fought amongst themselves except when one or another had been taken over by aliens, which seemed to happen about every third episode. Beyond that, the freewheeling way the starship broke the constraints of time and space was a testament to unlimited human possibilities. Hundreds of light-years could be traversed in minutes (just accelerate to "warp factor"); crew members could be transported from place to place in an instant ("Beam me up, Scotty"). Time travel was a particular *Star Trek* favorite; characters were often shuttling back and forth to the past, trying to rectify mistakes of history and avoid disasters of the future. Talk about power trips!

Despite its techno-talk, *Star Trek* and *The Next Generation* were, at bottom, shows about the nature and meaning of being human. The endless parade of evil aliens and perverted civilizations—from the bellicose Klingons to the pernicious Borg, with their hivelike collective consciousness—was always contrasted to the civilized humans on board the *Enterprise*. The most popular characters were the nonhuman ones—Spock, the "logical" Vulcan, and Data, the soulless android—precisely because they were constantly being confronted with the human qualities they lacked: the emotions they either scorned (in Spock's case) or craved (in Data's).

Star Trek: Generations (directed by David Carson, who did several episodes of the series) continues the exploration of this theme. Data (Brent Spiner) has an "emotion chip" implanted in his brain, then suddenly has to deal with unfamiliar feelings like fear, remorse, and giggly irresponsibility. Captain Picard, meanwhile, must overcome the siren-like lure of the Nexus, a timeless zone of pure joy that is being sought by the villainous Dr. Soran (Malcolm McDowell). The Nexus is a personalized fantasyland, where Picard experiences the idyllic home life he never had. Captain Kirk is there too, going through his own homey fantasy, but both must reject the Nexus and return to the real world to help defeat Soran. Responsibility, caring for others, recognizing your mortality—these things too are part of being human.

Star Trek's optimistic morality plays were especially appealing when the show first went on the air in 1966. "It seemed like there was a hell of a lot of trouble in the world," says D. C. Fontana, a writer on the original show, "and it was a time there might not be a whole lot of hope in America. And here comes this series that says mankind is better than we might think." Says Ian Spelling, who publishes a weekly *Star Trek* newspaper column: "It's a story of a positive future in which people are getting along. And if they're not, they're trying to work things out."

The multicultural *Star Trek* crew—a Russian, a Japanese, a black 15 woman, a Vulcan (make that multiplanetary)—was of symbolic importance to many viewers. "As a teen, I was a fan," says Whoopi Goldberg, who had a recurring role in *The Next Generation*. "I recognized the multicultural, multiracial aspects, and different people getting together for a better world. Racial issues have been solved. Male-female problems have been solved. The show is about genuine equality."

Star Trek has won praise from many science-fiction writers. Ray Bradbury, a close friend of Roddenberry's until the latter's death in 1991, finds the show's popularity unsurprising: "We're living in a science-fiction time. We're swimming in an ocean of technology, and that's why *Star Trek*, *Star Wars*, and 90 percent of the most successful films of the last ten years are science fiction." Indeed, *Star Trek* has helped spark a revival of science fiction on TV, including such shows as *Babylon 5* and *SeaQuest DSV* and an entire cable network, the Sci-Fi Channel.

Many scientists too admire the show for its faithfulness to the scientific method, if not to factual science. "They have a respect for the way science and engineering work," says Louis Friedman, a former programs director at Pasadena's Jet Propulsion Laboratory. "For example, when you make measurements of a planet and try to determine its atmosphere, then get into the transporter . . . well, if you had a transporter that's probably how you'd do it. They make it believable because they go through a reasonable process."

Others attribute *Star Trek*'s popularity less to its science than to its dramatic and mythic qualities. Richard Slotkin, professor of English at Wesleyan University, says the show echoes the pioneer stories that dominate American history and literature. "What's so appealing about *Star Trek* is that it takes the old frontier myth and crosses it with a platoon movie," Slotkin says. "Instead of the whites against the Indians, you have a multiethnic crew against the Romulans and Klingons."

Star Trek has always had its literary pretensions; allusions to Shakespeare abound, and it has often been compared to *The Odyssey*. "There was something heroic and epic to the underlying themes," says Patrick Stewart, a member of the Royal Shakespeare Company. "In terms of its ambition, the stage on which it was set was Homeric." Says Shatner: "I think there is a need for the culture to have a myth, like the Greeks had. We don't have any. So I think people look to *Star Trek* to set up a leader and a hearty band of followers. It's Greek classical storytelling." Not that the stars buy all the highfalutin analyses of their work. Kirk has been described as a classic Kennedyesque cold warrior. "That's too esoteric for me," says Shatner. "All I wanted to do was come up with a good character. I always played Kirk close to myself, mostly because of fatigue."

Shatner wouldn't have played Kirk at all if the original pilot for the 20 series had pleased NBC. The show, which Roddenberry produced in 1964, starred Jeffrey Hunter as the captain. But NBC wanted changes, and by the time a new pilot was done, Hunter had dropped out. One actor who remained from the first pilot was Nimoy as Mr. Spock—though only after Roddenberry persuaded NBC not to drop the character. The network had other alarming suggestions: At one point, Roddenberry recalled, NBC executives suggested that Spock smoke a space cigarette, to please a tobacco-company sponsor.

The original *Star Trek* never drew much of an audience, and it was saved from cancellation after two seasons only with the help of a letter-writing campaign from fans. But in its third season, NBC moved the show to a weak time slot, on Fridays at 10 P.M., and cut its budget by nine thousand dollars an episode, putting a further crimp in the already bargain-basement special effects. The show was gone after that season.

But three seasons and seventy-nine episodes were just enough to put the show's reruns into syndication, and there they were an enormous hit. By the end of the seventies, the success of *Star Wars* and *Close Encounters of the Third Kind* had prompted Paramount to give its TV space crew a crack at the big screen. *Star Trek: The Motion Picture* displeased hard-core fans. But it made a sturdy $82 million at the box office and launched a series of films that peaked in 1986 with *Star Trek IV: The Voyage Home,* which grossed $110 million. Only Roddenberry felt left out. Though listed as executive consultant on all the films, he was largely supplanted by other producers. "He was pretty bitter about the films," recalls writer Tracy Tormé. "He really felt like they took the films away from him."

Yet Roddenberry got a second chance on TV, when *Star Trek: The Next Generation* debuted in 1987. The show, set eighty years after the original, introduced a new *Enterprise* crew and had a much bigger budget. But still there was turmoil: Roddenberry's insistence on rewriting scripts alienated many of the writers. Things settled down when Rick Berman, Roddenberry's second-in-command, and coexecutive producer Michael Piller took control. The show soon hit its stride, with an accomplished cast, better special effects, and some of the most imaginative sci-fi writing ever for TV. The series was ended last May, at the height of its popularity, because Paramount wanted to switch it to the big screen exclusively.

Deep Space Nine is a drearier show, set in a kind of outer-space bus stop, where another imposing commander (Avery Brooks) presides over a melting pot of alien riffraff. The upcoming series, *Voyager,* aims to return to the exploration theme of the earlier series. Its premise: A Starfleet ship, chasing a band of rebels who oppose a Federation peace treaty, is transported (through a pesky space-time anomaly) to a distant part of the universe. The Starfleet crew and the rebel band must then join forces to find their way back home. The new show also responds to one long-time complaint about the *Star Trek* series: the lack of prominent roles for women. The captain of this Starfleet ship is played by Kate Mulgrew (replacing Genevieve Bujold, who quit the show after two days of shooting).

The *Star Trek* mystique has grown big enough that there's money to be made in debunking it. Two cast members from the original show, Nichelle Nichols (Uhura) and George Takei (Sulu), have written books in which they describe Shatner as an egomaniac on the set. Shatner has given his side in two volumes of *Trek* reminiscences, and some ex-colleagues charge that he has exaggerated his creative role. "The only thing that surprises me about Bill's [first] book," says Majel Barrett Roddenberry, who played Nurse Chapel in the original series and later married Roddenberry, "is that he managed to get it in the nonfiction category."

Bruised egos also resulted, not surprisingly, from the effort to combine the two TV casts for a passing of the torch in the new movie. Nimoy declined a role after he saw how small his part would be. "I told them," he says, "'The lines that you've written to be spoken by somebody named Spock can be easily distributed to any of the other characters on the screen.'" Which is what happened: Captain Kirk appears with two lesser members of the old crew: chief engineer "Scotty" (James Doohan) and Ensign Chekov (Walter Koenig). Several members of the *Next Generation* cast, meanwhile, were less than thrilled with their relatively small amount of screen time. Says LeVar Burton, who plays Geordi: "Hopefully, if we do another one of these, we will have an opportunity to spread the wealth more."

Then there was the film's controversial ending. As originally shot, Captain Kirk was killed by a phaser in the back. But test audiences were reportedly dissatisfied, and the scene was reshot just weeks before the film opened. Kirk now has a more action-packed, though considerably lower-tech demise; *Trek* fans are already grumbling.

None of which will matter much if the film is, as expected, a big hit. Then all that Paramount will have to worry about is trying not to squeeze too much out of its cash cow. The studio plans to produce a new feature film every two years, while keeping two TV shows running simultaneously. "*Star Trek* will do fine if they don't kill the goose," says Barrett Roddenberry. Berman acknowledges the danger: "There's always the question about taking too many trips to the well, and one of the tasks Roddenberry left me with was at least to try to prevent that from happening."

Yet Roddenberry's old optimism seems to be prevailing. "Gene Roddenberry had a point of view that space is infinite as far as we know, and therefore the possibilities for stories are infinite," says Brent Spiner, with Data-like precision. "In the original series, I think they had explored some 18 percent of the universe. We [*The Next Generation*] went into another 15 percent. So that leaves 67 percent of the universe left to explore." Which, by our calculations, should carry the show well into the twenty-first century, and that's not even traveling at warp speed.

—*Reported by Dan Cray and Martha Smilgis/Los Angeles, Suneel Ratan/New York, Mark Shuman/Chicago, and Scott Norvell/Atlanta*

▪ **CONSIDER THE SOURCE**

1. How does Zoglin describe the typical audience for *Star Trek?* What community of viewers does the show appeal to, and why?

2. What are the humanistic values that Zoglin claims explain *Star Trek's* popularity? What examples does he use to demonstrate how those values are manifested in the original show and in the sequels?

3. Trace the different ways that viewers of *Star Trek* have helped to shape the cultural phenomenon that the show has become. What forms does audience interaction with the show take?

4. Who is Zoglin writing for? What assumptions does he make about *Time* magazine's readers? How does his article exemplify the magazine's practice of "group journalism," discussed in the appendix (p. 664)?

5. Examine Zoglin's use of the terms *Trekkie* and *Trekker*. How does his choice of terms convey his attitude toward his subject? Does he seem sympathetic or critical toward them? What other ways does he characterize *Star Trek* fans?

■ **CONSIDER THE IMPLICATIONS**

6. In your journal, explore how *Star Trek* has figured in your life. What words or phrases in your vocabulary originated in the series? Are you an avid or occasional viewer of the television show and/or movies? Have you ever owned any *Star Trek* products—books, action figures, lunchboxes, or other paraphernalia? What is the show's appeal for you?

7. Frequently, groups are labeled one way by outsiders but claim different labels for themselves. In class, list on the blackboard examples of groups with two or more labels. What patterns can you find in your lists? What labels are most often chosen by the newsmedia to describe the groups? How does the choice of label affect your perceptions of a given group?

8. Zoglin begins and ends his essay with information about the amount of money *Star Trek* movies, TV shows, books, and other products generate. How does this data help him to justify the cultural phenomenon? Hold a class debate on whether the money to be made from popular culture gives it more value or less.

9. Compare Jo March's attitude toward best-selling popular culture with Zoglin's. Write a letter from Jo March to her loyal readers, explaining why she has stopped writing sensational fiction and begun to write science fiction. Alternatively, explain why she will continue to write gothic thrillers instead of following market trends and switching to sci-fi.

10. In your library, survey a full year of *Time* magazine cover stories. Categorize the topics that are featured on the cover. Are they political events, international crises, or important social concerns? How often does popular culture appear on the cover of *Time*? Summarize your research in an essay that helps your reader assess the importance of *Time* magazine's cover story on *Star Trek*.

11. Examine one of the many print manifestations of *Star Trek*—a novelization of an episode, a *Trek* encyclopedia, the Klingon dictionary, for instance—and write an essay analyzing the shift from screen to print. How does print alter the *Star Trek* phenomenon? In what ways is the experience of reading *Star Trek* different from viewing it? How well does the image-based medium of television or movies translate into print? What advantages or disadvantages does each medium offer?

ERIK DAVIS

True Believers

Every week, TV Guide *promotes the medium of television and provides viewers with such information as viewing schedules, star profiles, and programming trends. For most TV shows, the magazine's format offers enough space to satisfy readers' curiosity and Hollywood's marketing goals. But* Star Trek *has become so huge that in Spring 1995 it spilled over the confines of the weekly magazine; it rated a special "Collector's Edition" of* TV Guide—*a glossy, oversized, full-color publication devoted exclusively to "Star Trek: Four Generations." Free-lance writer Erik Davis (b. 1967) contributed the following article on the world of* Trek *fandom to that special issue. Described as "a fan of fandom," Davis seeks to go beyond the stereotypes of fans as oddball cultists who use their fantasy world to compensate for their own lack of "real lives." Davis writes on the social impacts of technology for such publications as the* Village Voice, Spin, The Nation, *and* Wired. *He has just begun his first novel, which he describes as a story about "the cultural interface of spirituality and information technology."*

A young woman in an aquamarine Starfleet uniform guards the door at a New York City *Star Trek* convention. Running down her neck is a trail of brown Magic Marker spots that provide an essential clue to her identity. *Aha,* any savvy Trekker would think—she's impersonating Dax, the Trill science officer played by Terry Farrell on *Star Trek: Deep Space Nine.* But things are rarely so straightforward in this particular world of fandom. The young woman insists that she is a not a Trill at all, but Q the Omnipotent, a visitor from the Q Continuum who has taken over a Trill symbiont. She also asserts that she is 1,201 years old and by no means human. "Terrans are nasty," says Q with a grin.

Q is just one of an intriguing crew of hardcore *Star Trek* fans hired by the event's sponsor, Creation Entertainment, to perform security functions here at the Pennsylvania Hotel. Q and her cohorts—a Romulan, a Klingon, and several members of the renegade Maquis—monitor folks streaming into the dealers' hall: a girl clutching a tribble; a woman carrying a deadly Klingon bat'telh blade. "If you don't have a hand-stamp, you will be subject to Jem' Hadar war testing," Q threatens the crowd.

They're familiar stereotypes, perhaps, dismissed by non-Trekkers as obsessive cybernerds and/or cult members who clutter their lives and

---

From *Star Trek: Four Generations.* Collector's Edition TV Guide. (Radnor, Pa.: News America Publications, Spring 1995), pp. 78–82.

their imaginations with the minutiae of a fantasy world. Even William Shatner—who owes his career to these folks—once berated Trekkers on *Saturday Night Live* with his infamous suggestion that they "get a life." What many critics of the Trekker subculture fail to understand, however, is that beyond the oddball surface of the conventions and the cult, there's a rich and complex world of camaraderie and creativity. More than that, in fact. It can be argued that in their avid participation in a prime-time produced fantasy, *Star Trek* superfans defy the popular notion of TV as an inherently passive act. For Trekkers, watching TV is a truly active experience.

Some comb through episodes for subtle shifts in characterization, obscure references and tiny plot points. Others invest in state-of-the-art VCRs just so they can hit the freeze-frame button and decode the information on the computer screens in Engineering. Still others are inspired to design costumes, write stories, build models, and paint tableaux of their favorite scenes. And because fans love to communicate with other fans, the often isolated act of watching television gives rise to an intensely social community that comes together in the pages of countless fanzines, online discussion groups, and—especially—at *Star Trek* conventions, or *cons,* as they're known to those who frequent them.

For many fans, *Star Trek* conventions offer a place to unwind, to   5 meet faraway friends, to slip into a "weekend world" that is more imaginative, hopeful, and accepting than the one outside the hotel doors. For Peter Koester, a fan whose business card reads "Director of the Institute of Federation Science and Technology," fandom is "an alternate reality." Koester is no slacker—shortly after this convention he is scheduled to become a sonar technician on a naval submarine. But for him, fandom is more than a simple hobby. "Sometimes I like to believe this life is more real than the mundane one in which I have to make a living."

The goods fans buy at a con aren't simply merchandise—they're a way to bring the alternate reality of *Star Trek* a little closer to this one. Bajoran earrings, Starfleet uniforms, badges, T-shirts, cutlery, posters, photos, key chains, mugs: They are all physical manifestations of the connection between viewer and show. There's more to fandom than amassing collectibles, however. At one booth, travel agents hand out fliers for Cruise Trek '95, an ocean-liner trip to Bermuda that includes *Trek* series actors as fellow passengers. But the items that best exemplify the unique relationship between *Star Trek* and its fans are those created by fan artisans—items such as Klingon weapons and models of Federation and Romulan starships. Technically, selling these goods without a license is illegal, but Paramount tolerates the trade on a small level. "If they went after every hobbyist, they'd be tied up in court for a thousand years," says George, a thirty-seven-year-old computer software publisher who is selling his hand-crafted array of phasers, tricorders, and medical equipment. He's asking around $130 for a beautiful type-2 phaser with light and sound, but confides that he keeps his best models for his own collection.

Below the dealer floor, hundreds of fans crowd a convention hall to watch videos, listen to special-effects experts, and grill Paramount representatives about *Star Trek: Voyager.* But primarily, they've gathered to see the stars. This afternoon, it's—take note, Omnipotent Q—Terry Farrell, *DS9*'s sexy Trill science officer. Led to the stage by bodyguards, Farrell appears strangely plain without her wig or extraterrestrial markings. As fans hand her flowers and gifts, she begins fielding questions. A longhaired guy in a tie-dye T-shirt asks her if she was a science-fiction freak before starring on *DS9*. "Do I look like a science-fiction freak?" the exmodel responds, setting off laughter in the crowd. "I mean, look at your neighbor!" Though clearly not in character, Farrell is still directed questions as if she were, in fact, Dax. "How far do your spots go down?" a heavyset man inquires. It is a measure of the extent to which both star and fan buy into the separate reality of the *Trek* cult that she answers matter-of-factly, "All the way to my toes."

Glitzy touches, such as the presence of *Trek* stars, are not uncommon at the larger events organized by Creation Entertainment, a Glendale, California-based company. But a network of much smaller fan-run cons has also evolved. With much less emphasis on vending, these smaller cons—the Shore Leave and the Farpoint series, for example—make up in grass-roots vitality what they may lack in polish, and allow the fan community to really come alive. Fans convene for panel discussions, stage fashion shows, throw marathon video sessions, hold art competitions, and play out the constantly shifting alliances between different fan organizations. Amateur publishers swap fanzines stuffed with drawings and original fiction—including "slash" stories, a rather risqué genre that feature Kirk and Spock as lovers. Other Trekkers show homemade videos that splice together *Trek* episodes and set them to popular songs—often revealing hidden meanings in the process. Some rooms are devoted to bardic circles of "filk" singers, who set usually funny lyrics about *Star Trek* and fandom to well-known folk, rock, and TV theme songs.

It's all very arcane and cabalistic, but really a logical extension of the fandom that almost immediately sprang up around *Star Trek* during the first series' original run in the 1960s. Loosely organized during the show's first season, the fandom consolidated into a nationwide force in reaction to NBC's threat in 1968 to cancel *Trek* after two seasons of mediocre ratings. The now famous letter-writing campaign not only saved the show, it established the Trekkers' proprietary attitude toward the program. *Star Trek* wasn't just any prime-time adventure; it was *theirs.*

That possessiveness and protectiveness immediately distinguished the *Star Trek* fan as a different animal from the era's other science fiction aficionados. And there were plenty of them. The well populated sci-fi scene of the day traced its origins back forty years to pulp magazines like *Amazing Stories,* published by the legendary Hugo Gernsback.[1] Enthusiasts began writing and trading their own amateur publications (the first "fanzines"), which they packed with fiction, criticism, letters, and science articles. Eventually, this movement reached a new threshold with the first World Science Fiction Convention, held in New York in 1939.

In the three decades separating that convention from the arrival of *Trek,* science-fiction gatherings grew in number and size. The typical participant, however, tended to be a reserved intellectual attracted by the genre's literary potential. The events themselves were rather like elaborate seminars. For these more "serious" aficionados, *Star Trek* was a decent TV series which sometimes attracted real talent like Harlan Ellison and Theodore Sturgeon.[2] But Trekkers were another breed entirely. They just couldn't get enough of their show, enjoying everything from *Enterprise* technical specs to blooper reels to making fun of lousy episodes like "Spock's Brain." After the series was canceled, fandom continued to grow, and when the first official *Star Trek*-only con met in 1972, it drew more than three thousand people.

Through the seventies and eighties, fandom and the *Star Trek* industry developed together symbiotically, and the cartoon series, the *Star Trek* movies, and a new series were born. Today Paramount writers and producers track the pulse of fandom (probably even lifting some ideas), while some Trekkers specialize in studio gossip, leaked scripts, and Hollywood's byzantine power plays. A select number of fans even end up making *Star Trek* their profession.

One thing links them all, however: their fierce devotion to the Roddenberry vision. Of course, there are as many interpretations of the specifics of that vision as there are Trekkers. Some older fans reject the syndicated sequels in favor of the original series (call them the "Classicists"). And Trekkers always leaven their love with strong criticism and mockery (countless *TNG* fans bonded around their shared hatred of Wesley Crusher).

But as is evident at the con today, Trekkers all make a sincere effort to live the principals the show embodied, perhaps best summarized in the IDIC: the Vulcan philosophy of Infinite Diversity in Infinite Combinations. If Gene Roddenberry had a creed, IDIC was it, and fandom exuberantly makes this ideal real. Trekkers come from all ranks of society—

---

1. **Hugo Gernsback** (1884–1967): A major science fiction writer and one of the founding publishers of *Amazing Stories,* Gernsback is remembered annually by the science fiction community when they present their award for best science fiction book, the Hugo Award.

2. **Harlan Ellison** (b. 1934) and **Theodore Sturgeon** (1918–1985): Groundbreaking and influential science fiction writers most active during the 1940s, 1950s, and 1960s.

cops and plumbers, librarians and NASA officials, secretaries and rave musicians. Born-again Christians, atheist scientists, and neopagan witches are all attracted to Roddenberry's cosmos. While men dominate science-fiction fandom, women have an equal share of the *Trek* world, and even dominate fanzine writing. In our sadly fragmented society, *Trek* cons are some of the few social zones that bring together blacks and whites, Asians and Hispanics, men and women, toddlers and grandmothers (many young Trekkers are second-generation fans). People with disabilities feel at home in fandom, as do others who do not fit into our society's cookie-cutter standards of beauty and social grace. A Klingon I met told me about a blind man who came to cons wearing a Geordi visor.

In the small room Creation Entertainment has set aside for fan clubs   15
and fanzine vendors, George Petrusha sits proudly behind a two-foot-long model of the USS *Nimitz*, NCC 90125 (he lifted the numbers from the title of the 1983 Yes album). The commanding officer of the ship, Petrusha has recently been elevated to the position of Rear Admiral within the hierarchy of the IDIC Alliance, his fan club. Run out of a mansion in Erie, Pennsylvania, the IDIC Alliance is no joke—with over three thousand members scattered from here to Japan, it's one of a number of large Trekker organizations that serve as umbrella groups for the more volatile world of local fan clubs.

A big, balding guy in a red command uniform, Petrusha works as a plant engineer at a hospital. Now thirty-seven, he's been active in fandom for years, but traces his enthusiasm back to the first moment he saw the show as a kid. "It was like a calling. I knew I would have something to do with that show." Like some fans, Petrusha feels like he has benefited from identifying with the characters and the positive outlook of the show. "*Star Trek* teaches us how to overcome our own nature. Kirk is very dear to me. When he died in the movie, a piece of me died as well."

At the table next to Petrusha sit two big Klingons. Anton S. Kirchenko, twenty-five, wears a homemade version of Klingon garb—a silvery sash, thick eyebrows, and white sneakers. As Kirch zantai Ta 'Dich, he serves as chief of special operations for KLAW, the Klingon Legion of Assault Warriors—which is another way of saying that he's the fan club's treasurer. Sitting beside Kirchenko is his admiral, an impressive, no-nonsense African American woman named Ines Peek, who goes by the name Ka'Hil zantai Dok'Marr and who has the most convincing forehead ridges of any Klingon I've seen at the con.

But though these two pay homage to the marauding Vikings of the *Star Trek* universe, what attracts both of them to the show is its optimism about the future.

"There's no racism, no massive sexism, no poverty," Kirchenko says, pointing out that you don't see people here dressed up like *Blade Runner* replicants or the monsters from *Alien*. "I've worn the videotape out by watching those movies. But I'm glad I don't live there."

"We want that hopeful future to come about," Peek says in her com- 20
manding voice. "Everyone here tries to bring it alive now. We're not
black or white or handicapped. We're *Star Trek* fans."

▪ CONSIDER THE SOURCE

1. Explain how Davis's language signals his assumptions about his readers'
   familiarity with the various *Star Trek* shows.
2. What value does Davis find in the Trekker subculture?
3. How do *Trek* merchandise and conventions function for the fan, according to Davis?

▪ CONSIDER THE IMPLICATIONS

4. Compare Davis's stance toward *Star Trek* fans with that of Richard Zoglin
   ("Trekking Onward," pp. 97–105). What features of the typical fan does
   each author describe?
5. *Star Trek* is not the only cultural product to have a thriving fan scene.
   How do *Trek* fans differ from fans of baseball or football, rock stars or
   movie stars, soap operas or rap artists? How do they resemble Sven Birkerts (pp. 21–29) or the women Janice Radway describes (pp. 388–404),
   who could be called "fans" of reading? In class discussion, compare various types of fans and decide what, if anything, sets Trekkers apart.
6. Attend a *Star Trek* convention (or recollect your prior experience with
   one) or log onto one of the many *Trek*-related discussion groups on computer networks. Drawing on your experiences, write an essay analyzing
   Trekkers and their subculture. Use your own observations to support, refute, or modify the views of Davis and/or Zoglin.
7. By insisting that watching TV is not a passive activity for Trekkers, Erik
   Davis bears out Sven Birkerts's claim that in our culture "Doing is prized
   over being or thinking" (pp. 21–29). In your journal, explore this cultural
   assumption. How has the bias toward activity affected your choices of
   leisure pursuits? Which ones do you find you have to justify to yourself
   or to others? Which need no justification? Why?
8. Working in small groups, place various media interactions on a continuum from most passive to most active. Include such activities as reading a
   novel or a cookbook, watching a movie, reading the newspaper, watching
   baseball on television, viewing a TV game show, playing video games, listening to radio talk shows, or surfing the Internet. Which activities encourage consumer passivity? How and why do others encourage interaction?
9. Compare the "community of readers" that Barbara Sicherman has described for *Little Women* (pp. 70–87) with the "community of viewers" for
   Star Trek. What "cultural work" does each of these cultural products perform for its community? How does the book, movie, or television show
   create an identifiable community? How does each one contribute to its
   audience's creation of identity? Write an essay applying Sicherman's
   strategies to *Star Trek* and analyzing Trekkers as a community.

FRANZ JOSEPH

Communications from
Star Fleet Command

Every crew member of a Federation Starship must have had to go through basic training, and if the twenty-third century runs its institutions anything like we do, those space cadets would certainly need a training manual. Hence the existence of the Star Fleet Technical Manual, *issued in 1975 by Star Fleet Academy in an official Version for Cadets from United Nations, Earth, Sol System. The handbook, compiled by Franz Joseph, includes schematic diagrams of every class of spaceship from the original* Star Trek *series, specifications for weaponry, uniforms, and flags, and even scale diagrams of a Vulcan lyrette and instructions for playing tridimensional chess.*

In order not to disrupt the Trekkers' imaginary world, Joseph published the following letters to explain how Terrans in the twentieth century got their hands on a book from the future. Elsewhere, he addresses whether a future "manual" would even exist in book form. It seems that Star Fleet cadets only rely on a "print-out version" of the manual until they learn how to operate the "data read-out stations" at headquarters. Moreover, the technical data banks of Star Fleet Command could never be printed because "if [they] were to be published in 'book' form, the sum total would amount to more books than you now have stored in your 'libraries.'"

From *Star Trek Star Fleet Technical Manual* (New York: Ballantine Books, 1975), pp. 3–6.

FOREWORD I

PHOTOCOPY

UNITED STATES MILITARY FORCES
GENERAL STAFF HEADQUARTERS
WASHINGTON, D.C., U.S.A.

```
memorandum to: Franz Joseph Designs

from:          Col. Robert Argon, Director Security

               Control/MFHQ

date:          15 April 1973

subject:       MF Security Docket #075140

enclosure:     one (1) copy of subject docket
```

1. Pursuant to your inquiry we are enclosing one (1) copy of
   subject docket without restrictions. The security
classification has been removed, and there is no longer any
official interest in the matter.

2. The printed 'message' was: "ALERT.....ALERT.....UNITED
   FEDERATION FLEET HEADQUARTERS MASTER LIBRARY COMPUTER.....
TO.....LIBRARY COMPUTER.....ALL FEDERATION STARSHIPS ON SPECIAL
SERVICE.....STARDATE 3113.....SUBJECT.....TRANSMISSION OF
UPDATED TECHNICAL MANUAL MASTER DATA SECTIONS.....00:00:00
.....00:00:00.....BEGIN TRANSMISSION....."

3. The message and the "data sheets" which followed were found in
   the memory banks of the master computer at Security Control,
Omaha MFB, and were accidentally discovered in 1970 during a
print-out run, while the computer was being interrogated for
another reason. A top security lid was immediately clamped on the
matter while an investigation was launched to attempt to identify
the source of the unusual transmission. Neither the message nor
the data could be traced to any known country, or alliance, in
the World. All of the terminology, uniforms, weaponry, and other
material was completely foreign to the terminology, uniforms,
weaponry, and other material known to be in existence at that
time.

4. The investigation was terminated with a final determination
   that the whole affair had been a hoax. That the "unusual"
material had been inserted into the computer as a prank. And the
file was closed, while a search was initiated to find the person,
or persons, responsible for this breach of Security Control. To
date this effort has been fruitless.

FOREWORD II

PHOTOCOPY

OFFICIAL USE ONLY
O MARK O R5PC
STAR FLEET COMMAND
STAR FLEET HEADQUARTERS
UNITED FEDERATION OF PLANETS

SIDRE AEL SARDELAS, DIRECTOR
MILITARY STAFF COMMITTEE   STARDATE 3150.10

                    to: All Divisions concerned
                        Star Fleet Command

1. Pursuant to the matter of the unauthorized transmission of SFAF
material (viz: SFHQ/Mastercom Computer Data) into the Master
Computer at Security Control, Omaha MFB, Earth, Sol System as of
stardate 3113, the Special Review Board examined the following
pertinent documentation:

    (a) report of Capt. James T. Kirk, commanding, U.S.S. Enterprise;
    (b) report of Lt. Cmdr. Spock, First Officer, U.S.S. Enterprise;
    (c) report of the ivestigation by the Special Review Commission;
    (d) report of the historical events sequential review of the
        data banks of Mastercom/SFHQ;

2. The Special Review Board has now concluded its determination.
It finds: (1) that both Capt. James T. Kirk and Lt. Cmdr. Spock
cannot be faulted for the matter since it occurred in the routine
computer-to-computer transmission, which operates independently of
the SFAF Communications Systems or human supervision; and: (2)
that it occurred as the result of an unpredicted, and unforeseen
gravitational space-warp which is now known to be a natural
phenomenon within the galaxy; and (3) that it was a purely random
matter which occurred without human intervention and therefore is
considered to be a natural accidental occurrence in the sequential
train of historical events.

3. The Special Review Board further finds that in the event the
material now stored in the data banks of the Master Computer at
Security Control, Omaha MFB, should become known in that time
period, it would be advisable to review whatever material is
included in that storage to: (a) delete any technology which is
not known to Earth's technology in that time period, in order to
preserve the Prime Directive's doctrine of nonintervention; and:
(b) to correct any material which is determined to be "safe" but
which was distorted in the transmission.

4. Therefore, the Planetary Relations Division of Star Fleet
Command is hereby assigned the task of this final determination in
the event it should become necessary, and all Divisions shall
support this effort as required. The Planetary Relations Division
shall also prepare a final report upon the conclusion of any
actions they may take, for submission to the Federation Council.

▪ CONSIDER THE SOURCE

1. How do the type style and format of the memos contribute to the imaginary world that Franz Joseph evokes?

2. Why is the *Technical Manual* as printed on Earth in 1975 incomplete?

3. Describe the tone of the two memos. Does the tone enhance or reduce the credibility of the correspondence?

▪ CONSIDER THE IMPLICATIONS

4. Explore in class discussion how successfully these memos justify the existence of the *Technical Manual*. What explanation do they provide for the manual's appearance on Earth in 1975?

5. Consider how the *Technical Manual* serves its audience. What use might a Trekker make of a book like this? How does the book assist or disrupt the fantasy of the Trekker? How do such texts affect or extend the community of *Star Trek* fans?

6. Examine a copy of the *Star Fleet Technical Manual* or one of its successors. Then read or review Walter Ong's discussion of typography and closure in "Print, Space, and Closure" (pp. 52–65). Applying Ong's ideas, analyze the *Technical Manual* as a printed object. How does the printed text make the imaginary world concrete? How does the book give the impression of completeness?

7. Print plays a major role in spreading and sustaining the *Star Trek* phenomenon. Write an essay analyzing how such printed works as Joseph's technical manual or the essays by Richard Zoglin and Erik Davis contribute to this process. Be sure to consider the readers of such writings. Explore the impact that these printed artifacts might have on both Trekkers and non-Trekkers.

CHAPTER

2

WHO READS?

Access to Print

The skill that you are demonstrating this very minute—the ability to read—once would have granted you an exemption from the death penalty. In medieval times, someone who was *litteratus* (literate) could read Latin and, therefore, was likely to be a member of the clergy, who were not subject to capital punishment. In order to prove literacy and avoid the executioner, a prisoner had to read a passage from the Psalter, the book of Psalms. By the time printing was invented in the fifteenth century, English court records show that a wide variety of people were claiming the privilege of the learned clergy by proving their literacy: grocers, carpenters, barbers, tailors—all were reading enough to escape the hangman's noose. Reading literally meant the difference between life and death.

Okay, so maybe the ability to read this book won't save you from a hangman's noose. But the value of literacy in a print-driven culture such as ours is certainly high. If you can't read, you can scarcely find or hold a job; you can't understand your bills or your rental agreement; you can't even look up when *Melrose Place* is on TV. In short, you're shut out of most areas of our society.

But what if you *can* read. How much literacy is enough? What do we mean by *literacy*? Is access to print guaranteed by the ability to decode written signs? This chapter will explore various kinds of literacy and show how certain writers have valued their access to the printed word. First, however, we need to look at what constitutes a literate person.

DEFINING AND MEASURING LITERACY

Any historical survey of literacy immediately runs into problems when it tries to determine how many people were literate in a given era because literacy has traditionally been gauged by whether people could *write*, not whether they could read. The ability to sign your name instead of making an X or some other mark indicated that you were "literate." But the connection between reading and writing is by no means clear. Plenty of people could sign their names but couldn't read or write anything else. Others could read but never learned to write or sign, especially since reading instruction generally preceded writing instruction.

The 1840 U.S. Census offered the first assessment of literacy across the nation. While it revealed some predictable trends—men were more literate than women, wealthier people were more literate than poor people—the census-takers only asked about "white persons in your family over twenty years of age." Those who were not white, not family members (such as servants), or not adults were not counted. You can see how such statistics might be misleading.

By 1870, census-takers counted everyone over ten years old, and they defined literacy as the ability to write in any language, not just in English. Measured this way, literacy rates climbed from 80 percent in 1870 to 95 percent by 1930. During World War II, the standard of measurement shifted from writing to reading ability. Functional literacy was defined as the ability to read well enough to fulfill basic duties as a soldier. After the war it was decided that a fifth-grade education should be the standard for literacy, and the U.S. literacy rate stood at about 98 percent through 1960. Then, the yardstick changed once again. Census reports from 1970, counting people fifteen and older, determined that 99 percent could read, even if 4 percent of those people did not have at least a fifth-grade education. By 1980, that number was up to 99.5 percent, implying that we're a nation with nearly universal literacy!

The problem with these statistics is that the definition of literacy keeps changing. There's virtually no way to compare literacy rates from one era to the next. So the next time you hear someone moaning about how literacy rates have declined, ask how those rates were measured. Our great literacy crisis may not be due to declining numbers of people who can read. Instead, it may have more to do with an increase in what we feel is a necessary level of reading competence.

Think about it. How well did you read and write in fifth grade? Could you make it in today's world with just that much education? Of course you couldn't. As society's complexity has increased in the past forty years, so has the standard for functional literacy.

But functional literacy isn't the only game in town. As we'll see, there are several definitions of literacy—functional, critical, cultural, to name a few—each with its own agenda behind it. We also have to contend with the technological advancements of our age, making math literacy, science literacy, and computer literacy part of our educational objectives. Society has upped the ante on us, requiring more and more skills and competencies. It's hard to keep up under the best of circumstances and harder still when there are limitations or restrictions that have to be overcome.

INCENTIVES AND ROADBLOCKS

The playing field in the game of literacy is not level. What's more, it never has been in Western society.

The ability to read and write was initially limited to the elite classes: the aristocracy and the clergy. They would pass along verbally anything that they felt the peasants needed to know. This system remained the norm for hundreds of years, although some literacy did trickle down to the merchant class. With the Protestant Reformation, things changed. In the belief that each person should have unmediated contact with the word of God, Protestant reformers agitated for broader education so that everyone would be able to read the Bible. Missionary zeal continued to be a strong motivation for literacy education, and it provided many slaves and Native Americans their only opportunity to learn reading and writing.

In the United States, literacy boomed after the Revolution. Every citizen needed to be educated in order to participate intelligently in the democratic system of government. Unfortunately, "citizen" had a very narrow definition: white, male, property-owner. Since women couldn't vote, the reasoning went, they didn't need to read or write (but, as Linda Kerber demonstrates) they got involved by being "Republican Mothers" who needed those skills in order to raise children who would grow up to become citizens. Slaves and Native Americans were specifically excluded from the privileges of citizenship, so of course, they didn't need to read or write either. In fact, educating slaves was against the law in many places until the end of the Civil War.

Many people have been locked out of the world of print. Others have been locked *in* to particular corners of that world. Given access only to certain kinds of printed material, they receive a distorted picture of their position in educated society. Do you remember the uproar a few years ago, when Talking Barbie uttered "Math is hard"? Barbie and her creators tapped into a familiar bias in women's education: Girls were supposed to leave "hard" subjects such as math and science to the boys, while they concentrated on "easy" subjects such as English and art. After vocal protests from women's groups, Barbie was redesigned to burble "Math is cool."

What we read or don't read directly affects our behavior because it influences the way we view the world. Chapter 3 will explore this issue in greater detail, examining who controls the presses and for what purpose. For now, it's enough to consider how print gives us images of ourselves and our possibilities.

ACCESS AND POWER

One of the most common images used to describe the effect of learning to read is that of the prison. Time and again authors recollect how reading liberated them and broadened their horizons, even from within the walls of actual prisons. Reading unlocked the gates.

If you think about it, it's sort of like learning to ride a bike. At first you spent all your time around your own block. Then, acquiring a simple skill suddenly freed you to explore broader territory. You could zip off to the park, to the mall, to your friends' houses. You could see the world—at least a bigger chunk of the world than before. You had access, and access meant power.

Access is a twofold concept. On the one hand, we've been using it to describe the ability to acquire and decode printed materials. If you can read reasonably well and can get your hands on *Rolling Stone, USA Today,* or John Grisham's latest thriller, you can become a consumer of print. However, it's not enough just to decode the material that others print. Real power comes from printing your own material so that you can be read and recognized by others. The ability to produce print may be as important as the ability to consume it. Print lets us express and define ourselves. It can even help build a community.

Reading gives us the words and images to describe our feelings, our fears, our hopes. It allows us to understand who we are or to re-create ourselves imaginatively. Writing and publishing allow us to control how others perceive us. As you know, if you've ever belonged to a club, having a publication confers status. A newsletter, a magazine, a photocopied flyer—any sort of print helps establish recognition for your group. Control of the press gives you control over other people's minds and imaginations. You can define yourself on your own terms or counteract the images of your group that others have purveyed. After all, it was a printed book, Douglas Coupland's novel *Generation X: Tales for an Accelerated Culture* (1991), that first defined "Generation X," after which a legion of magazine articles and books expanded on and propagated the definition. It will take a lot of ink to wash away the powerful images that those printed materials established. Without access to print, your generation will have to sit passively while it is defined by others.

THE READINGS

C. H. Knoblauch initiates our discussion by surveying several types of literacy and inviting us to look behind the definitions to see the political agendas that motivate different types of literacy education. Former slave Frederick Douglass then describes what it meant to be shut out from basic literacy and how learning to read showed him the road to freedom. Women who had "functional literacy" were channeled into certain kinds of reading, as Linda Kerber demonstrates in her study of women's education in the nineteenth century. Their images of themselves and their place in society were conditioned by restrictions on their education. When Zitkala-Ša left the oral world of her Sioux tribe to enter the print-dominated world of white society, she found that literacy defined who was "civilized." Charles Kikuchi chronicles the role that a newspaper played in a camp where Japanese Americans were interned during World War II. Malcolm X's reading while he was in prison gave him a clear picture of how the history of mankind had been "whitened" by the exclusion or misrepresentation of blacks by white historians. His reading gave him fuel for his political struggle to create a more powerful sense of black community. Mike Rose's reading, on the other hand, allowed him to escape his impoverished community and imagine a different world and a different self. Other children of poverty are in danger of losing the facilities that enable such empowering fantasies, according to Helena Maria Viramontes, who penned eloquent pleas for keeping a community library open. Jimmy Santiago Baca explains how access to books opened the doors to the language of poetry and allowed him to journey deep inside himself. Seeing Chicanos represented in print confirmed his sense of his own identity, a function that Mark Thompson describes as crucial to the mission of *The Advocate*, one of the nation's foremost gay and lesbian publications. Finally, LynNell Hancock reminds us that all these issues of access persist in the world of computer literacy.

C. H. KNOBLAUCH

Literacy and the Politics of Education

*The term "literacy" does not simply denote the ability to read, as C. H.
Knoblauch (b. 1945) shows in this essay from a collection of papers presented at the 1988 Right to Literacy Conference. Literary means many
things to many people. Knoblauch surveys the different uses of the concept
and shows how even the definition of literacy is politicized. Knoblauch is a
professor of English at the State University of New York at Albany, where
he specializes in rhetoric. His books include* Rhetorical Traditions and
the Teaching of Writing *(1984) and* Critical Teaching and the Idea of
Literacy *(1993), both coauthored with Lil Brannon.*

Literacy is one of those mischievous concepts, like virtuousness and
craftsmanship, that appear to denote capacities but that actually convey
value judgments. It is rightly viewed, Linda Brodkey has noted, "as a social trope" and its sundry definitions "as cultural Rorschachs" (47). The
labels *literate* and *illiterate* almost always imply more than a degree or
deficiency of skill. They are, grossly or subtly, sociocultural judgments
laden with approbation, disapproval, or pity about the character and
place, the worthiness and prospects, of persons and groups. A revealing
exercise would be to catalog the definitions of literacy that lie explicit or
implicit in the pages of this collection, definitions that motivate judgments, political no less than scholarly, about which people belong in literate and illiterate categories; the numbers in each group; why and in
what ways literacy is important; what should be done for or about those
who are not literate or are less literate than others; and who has the
power to say so. It would be quickly apparent that there is no uniformity of view, since the values that surround reading and writing abilities differ from argument to argument. Instead, there are competing
views, responsive to the agendas of those who characterize the ideal. Invariably, definitions of literacy are also rationalizations of its importance. Furthermore, they are invariably offered by the literate, constituting, therefore, implicit rationalizations of the importance of literate
people, who are powerful (the reasoning goes) because they are literate
and, as such, deserving of power.

The concept of literacy is embedded, then, in the ideological disposi-
tions of those who use the concept, those who profit from it, and those
who have the standing and motivation to enforce it as a social requirement. It is obviously not a cultural value in all times and places; when

---

From *The Right to Literacy,* ed. Andrea A. Lunsford, Helene Moglen, and James
Slevin (New York: Modern Language Association of America, 1990), pp. 74–80.

Sequoya brought his syllabic writing system to the Cherokee,[1] their first inclination was to put him to death for dabbling in an evil magic. The majority of the world's languages have lacked alphabets, though they have nonetheless articulated rich oral traditions in societies that have also produced many other varieties of cultural achievement. To be sure, there is ready agreement, at least among the literate, about the necessity of literacy in the so-called modern world; this agreement is reinforced by explanations that typically imply a more developed mode of existence among literate people. I. J. Gelb has written, for instance: "As language distinguishes man from animal, so writing distinguishes civilized man from barbarian," going on to point out that "an illiterate person cannot expect to participate successfully in human progress, and what is true of individuals is also true of any group of individuals, social strata, or ethnic units" (221–222). This argument offers a common and pernicious half-truth, representing the importance of literacy, which is unquestionable, in absolutist and ethnocentric terms.

However, if literacy today is perceived as a compelling value, the reason lies not in such self-interested justifications but in its continuing association with forms of social reality that depend on its primacy. During the Middle Ages, clerks were trained to read and write so that they could keep accounts for landowners, merchants, and government officials. Bureaucratic documentation was not conceived so that people could acquire literacy. Christian missionaries in nineteenth-century Africa spread literacy so that people could read the Bible; they did not teach the Bible so that the illiterate could become readers and writers. There is no question that literacy is necessary to survival and success in the contemporary world—a world where the literate claim authority to set the terms of survival and success, a world that reading and writing abilities have significantly shaped in the first place. But it is important to regard that necessity in the context of political conditions that account for it, or else we sacrifice the humanizing understanding that life can be otherwise than the way we happen to know it and that people who are measured positively by the yardstick of literacy enjoy their privileges because of their power to choose and apply that instrument on their own behalf, not because of their point of development or other innate worthiness. Possessing that understanding, educators in particular but other citizens as well may advance their agendas for literacy with somewhat less likelihood of being blinded by the light of their own benevolence to the imperial designs that may lurk in the midst of their compassion.

In the United States today, several arguments about the nature and importance of literacy vie for power in political and educational life.

---

1. **Sequoya** (c. 1773–1843): Created a syllabic writing system, approved by tribal elders in 1821, that enabled the Cherokee language to be reproduced in printed form.—ED.

Sketching the more popular arguments may remind us of the extent to which definitions of the concept incorporate the social agendas of the definers, serving the needs of the nonliterate only through the mediation of someone's vision of the way the world should be. Literacy never stands alone in these perspectives as a neutral denoting of skills; it is always literacy for something—for professional competence in a technological world, for civic responsibility and the preservation of heritage, for personal growth and self-fulfilment, for social and political change. The struggle of any one definition to dominate the others entails no merely casual or arbitrary choice of values, nor does it allow for a conflating of alternatives in some grand compromise or list of cumulative benefits. At stake are fundamentally different perceptions of social reality; the nature of language and discourse; the importance of culture, history, and tradition; the functions of schools, as well as other commitments, few of which are regarded as negotiable. At the same time, since no definition achieves transcendent authority, their dialectical interaction offers a context of choices within which continually changing educational and other social policies find their justification. The process of choosing is visible every day, for better and worse, in legislative assemblies, television talk shows, newspaper editorials, and classrooms throughout the country.

The most familiar literacy argument comes from the functionalist 5 perspective, with its appealingly pragmatic emphasis on readying people for the necessities of daily life—writing checks, reading sets of instructions—as well as for the professional tasks of a complex technological society. Language abilities in this view are often represented by the metaphors of information theory: Language is a code that enables the sending of messages and the processing of information. The concern of a functionalist perspective is the efficient transmission of useful messages in a value-neutral medium. Basic-skill and technical-writing programs in schools, many on-the-job training programs in business and industry, and the training programs of the United States military—all typically find their rationalization in the argument for functional literacy, in each case presuming that the ultimate value of language lies in its utilitarian capacity to pass information back and forth for economic or other material gain.

The functionalist argument has the advantage of tying literacy to concrete needs, appearing to promise socioeconomic benefit to anyone who can achieve the appropriate minimal competency. But it has a more hidden advantage as well, at least from the standpoint of those whose literacy is more than minimal: It safeguards the socioeconomic status quo. Whatever the rhetoric of its advocates concerning the "self-determined objectives" (Hunter and Harman 7) of people seeking to acquire skills, functionalism serves the world as it is, inviting outsiders to enter that world on the terms of its insiders by fitting themselves to roles that they are superficially free to choose but that have been prepared as a range of acceptable alternatives. Soldiers will know how to repair an MX missile by reading the field manual but will not question the use of such weapons because of their reading of antimilitarist philosophers; clerks will be able to fill out and file their order forms but will not therefore be qualified for positions in higher management. Functionalist arguments presume that a given social order is right simply because it exists, and their advocates are content to recommend the training of persons to take narrowly beneficial places in that society. The rhetoric of technological progressivism is often leavened with a mixture of fear and patriotism (as in *A Nation at Risk*)[2] in order to defend a social program that maintains managerial classes—whose members are always more than just functionally literate—in their customary places while outfitting workers with the minimal reading and writing skills needed for usefulness to the modern information economy.

Cultural literacy offers another common argument about the importance of reading and writing, one frequently mounted by traditionalist educators but sustained in populist versions as well, especially among people who feel insecure about their own standing and their future prospects when confronted by the volatile mix of ethnic heritages and socioeconomic interests that make up contemporary American life. The argument for cultural literacy moves beyond a mechanist conception of basic skills and toward an affirmation of supposedly stable and timeless cultural values inscribed in the verbal memory—in particular, the canonical literature of Western European society. Its reasoning is that true literacy entails more than technical proficiency, a minimal ability to make one's way in the world; that literacy also includes an awareness of cultural heritage, a capacity for higher-order thinking, even some aesthetic discernment—faculties not automatically available to the encoders and decoders of the functionalist perspective. Language is no mere tool in this view but is, rather, a repository of cultural values and to that extent a source of social cohesion. To guard the vitality of the language, the advocates of cultural literacy say, citizens must learn to speak and write decorously, as well as functionally, and must also read great books, where the culture is enshrined. In some popular versions of cultural literacy, English is regarded as the only truly American language and is, therefore, the appropriate medium of commerce and government. The economic self-interest that pervades the functionalist perspective frequently gives way here to jingoistic protectionism; cultural literacy advocates presume that the salvation of some set of favored cultural norms or language practices lies necessarily in the marginalizing or even extinction of others.

The argument for cultural literacy often presents itself within a

---

2. *A Nation at Risk:* This 1983 report by the National Commission on Excellence in Education couched many of its criticisms and recommendations in terms of the present and future position of the United States as a world leader.—ED.

myth of the fall from grace: Language and, by extension, culture once enjoyed an Edenlike existence but are currently degenerating because of internal decay and sundry forces of barbarism. People no longer read, write, or think with the strength of insight of which they were once capable. They no longer remember and, therefore, no longer venerate. The age of high culture has passed; minds and characters have been weakened by television or rock music or the 1960s. The reasons vary, but the message is clear: Unless heritage is protected, the former purity of language reconstituted, the past life of art and philosophy retrieved, we risk imminent cultural decay. However extravagant such predictions appear to unbelievers, there is no mistaking the melancholy energy of contemporary proponents of cultural literacy or, if we are to judge from the recent best-seller lists, the number of solemn citizens—anxious perhaps about recent influxes of Mexicans, Vietnamese, and other aliens—who take their warnings to heart.

Arguments for cultural and functional literacy plainly dominate the American imagination at the moment and for obvious reasons. They articulate the needs, hopes, anxieties, and frustrations of the conservative temper. They reveal in different ways the means of using an ideal of literacy to preserve and advance the world as it is, a world in which the interests of traditionally privileged groups dominate the interests of the traditionally less privileged. Schools reflect such conservatism to the extent that they view themselves as agencies for preserving established institutions and values, not to mention the hierarchical requirements of the American economy. But still other arguments, if not quite so popular, reflect the priorities and the agendas of liberal and even radical ideologies struggling to project their altered visions of social reality, seeking their own power over others under the banner of literacy. The liberal argument, for instance, emphasizes literacy for personal growth, finding voice in the process-writing movement in American high schools or in the various practices of personalized learning. The liberal argument has been successful, up to a point, in schools because it borrows from long-hallowed American myths of expressive freedom and boundless individual opportunity, romantic values to which schools are obliged to pay at least lip service even when otherwise promoting more authoritarian curricula.

The assumption of a literacy-for-personal-growth argument is that 10 language expresses the power of the individual imagination, so that nurturing a person's reading and writing abilities enables the development of that power, thereby promoting the progress of society through the progress of the individual learner. The political agenda behind this liberalism tends to be educational and other social change; its concern for personal learning draws attention to school practices that supposedly thwart the needs of individual students or that disenfranchise some groups of students in the interest of maintaining the values of the status quo. The kinds of change that the personal-growth argument recommends are, on the whole, socially tolerable because they are moderate in character: Let students read enjoyable novels, instead of basal reader selections; let young women and young Hispanics find images of themselves in schoolwork, not just images of white males. Using the rhetoric of moral sincerity, the personal-growth argument speaks compassionately on behalf of the disadvantaged. Meanwhile, it avoids, for the most part, the suggestion of any fundamental restructuring of institutions, believing that the essential generosity and fair-mindedness of American citizens will accommodate some liberalization of outmoded curricula and an improved quality of life for the less privileged as long as fundamental political and economic interests are not jeopardized. Frequently, Americans do hear such appeals, though always in the context of an implicit agreement that nothing important is going to change. Accordingly, advocates of expressive writing, personalized reading programs, whole-language curricula, and open classrooms have been permitted to carry out their educational programs, with politicians and school officials quick to realize the ultimate gain in administrative control that comes from allowing such modest symbols of self-determination to release built-up pressures of dissatisfaction.

A fourth argument, substantially to the left of the personal-growth advocates, is one for what Henry Giroux, among others, calls critical literacy (226). Critical literacy is a radical perspective whose adherents, notably Paulo Freire,[3] have been influential primarily in the Third World, especially Latin America. Strongly influenced by marxist philosophical premises, critical literacy is not a welcome perspective in this country, and it finds voice currently in only a few academic enclaves, where it exists more as a facsimile of oppositional culture than as a practice, and in an even smaller number of community-based literacy projects, which are typically concerned with adult learners. Its agenda is to identify reading and writing abilities with a critical consciousness of the social conditions in which people find themselves, recognizing the extent to which language practices objectify and rationalize these conditions and the extent to which people with authority to name the world dominate others whose voices they have been able to suppress. Literacy, therefore, constitutes a means to power, a way to seek political enfranchisement— not with the naive expectation that merely being literate is sufficient to change the distribution of prerogatives but with the belief that the ability to speak alone enables entrance to the arena in which power is contested. At stake, from this point of view, is, in principle, the eventual reconstituting of the class structure of American life, specifically a change of those capitalist economic practices that assist the dominance of particular groups.

For that reason, if for no other, such a view of literacy will remain

---

3. **Paulo Freire** (b. 1921): Author of *The Politics of Education: Culture, Power, and Liberation* (1985) and *Pedagogy of the Oppressed* (1970).—ED.

suspect as a theoretical enterprise and will be considered dangerous, perhaps to the point of illegality, in proportion to its American adherents' attempts to implement it practically in schools and elsewhere. The scholarly Right has signaled this institutional hostility in aggressive attacks on Jonathan Kozol's *Illiterate America,* the most popular American rendering of critical-literacy arguments, for its supposedly inaccurate statistics about illiteracy and in calculatedly patronizing Kozol's enthusiasm for radical change. Meanwhile, although critical literacy is trendy in some academic circles, those who commend it also draw their wages from the capitalist economy it is designed to challenge. Whether its advocates will take Kozol's risks in bringing so volatile a practice into community schools is open to doubt. Whether something important would change if they did take the risks is also doubtful. Whether, if successful, they would still approve a world in which their own privileges were withheld may be more doubtful still. In any case, one can hardly imagine NCTE or the MLA,[4] let alone the Department of Education, formally sanctioning such a fundamental assault on their own institutional perquisites.

Definitions of literacy could be multiplied far beyond these popular arguments. But enumerating others would only belabor my point, which is that no definition tells, with ontological or objective reliability, what literacy is; definitions only tell what some person or group—motivated by political commitments—wants or needs literacy to be. What makes any such perspective powerful is the ability of its adherents to make it invisible or, at least, transparent—a window on the world, revealing simple and stable truths—so that the only problem still needing to be addressed is one of implementation: how best to make the world—other people—conform to that prevailing vision. At the same time, what makes any ideology visible as such and, therefore, properly limited in its power to compel unconscious assent is critical scrutiny, the only safeguard people have if they are to be free of the designs of others. To the extent that literacy advocates of one stripe or another remain unconscious of or too comfortable with those designs, their offerings of skills constitute a form of colonizing, a benign but no less mischievous paternalism that rationalizes the control of others by representing it as a means of liberation. To the extent that the nonliterate allow themselves to be objects of someone else's "kindness," they will find no power in literacy, however it is defined, but only altered terms of dispossession. When, for instance, the memberships of U.S. English and English First,[5]

---

4. The **NCTE** (National Council of Teachers of English) and the **MLA** (Modern Language Association): The two largest professional associations of English teachers in the country.—ED.

5. **U.S. English** and **English First:** Active in the 1980s, the political organizations English First, a project of the Committee to Protect the Family, and U.S. English petitioned for a constitutional amendment to make English the official language of the United States.—ED.

totaling around half a million citizens, argue for compulsory English, they may well intend the enfranchisement of those whose lack of English-language abilities has depressed their economic opportunities. But they also intend the extinction of cultural values inscribed in languages other than their own and held to be worthwhile by people different from themselves. In this or any other position on literacy, its advocates, no less than its intended beneficiaries, need to hear—for all our sakes—a critique of whatever assumptions and beliefs are fueling their passionate benevolence.

▪ **WORKS CITED**

Brodkey, Linda. "Tropics of Literacy." *Journal of Education* 168 (1986):47–54.

Commission on Excellence in Education. *A Nation at Risk: The Imperative for Educational Reform.* Washington: GPO, 1983.

Gelb, I. J. *A Study of Writing.* Chicago: U of Chicago P, 1963

Giroux, Henry A. *Theory and Resistance in Education: A Pedagogy for the Opposition.* South Hadley: Bergin, 1983.

Hunter, Carman St. John, and David Harman. *Adult Literacy in the United States.* New York: McGraw, 1979.

Kozol, Jonathan. *Illiterate America.* New York: Anchor, 1985.

▪ **CONSIDER THE SOURCE**

1. Explain what Knoblauch means when he asserts that "imperial designs . . . may lurk in the midst of [educators'] benevolence."

2. Summarize the four types of literacy that Knoblauch discusses and locate them on the political spectrum from conservative to liberal.

3. Knoblauch's essay originally appeared in a collection of essays on *The Right to Literacy,* published by the Modern Language Association (MLA), an association of educators. What relationship does he establish between himself and his intended audience? Between himself and the other authors in the collection? How does that relationship help or hinder his argument's effectiveness?

▪ **CONSIDER THE IMPLICATIONS**

4. Knoblauch contends that the labels *literate* and *illiterate* are "sociocultural judgments laden with approbation, disapproval, or pity." In your journal, explore these labels and Knoblauch's assertion. How would you characterize someone you regard as "illiterate"? Can you envision that person in neutral terms, without any value judgments? Are there other labels that would be less value laden?

5. There has been talk in recent years about other kinds of literacy, such as "science literacy" and "computer literacy." In class discussion, examine whether such terms contain political implications similar to those

Knoblauch describes. What are the agendas behind these literacy movements?

6. Knoblauch refers to "recent best-seller lists" filled with books about the crisis in American literacy. In your library, look up the *New York Times* nonfiction best-seller lists of 1988–1989, when Knoblauch would have been writing his essay. What books might he be referring to? Read some reviews of the books to understand the position the authors take on this issue. Based on your research, write an essay that supports or refutes Knoblauch's characterization of these "proponents of cultural literacy."

7. Working in small groups, compare the education you received from kindergarten through high school. What type of literacy did your schools promote? How was illiteracy defined and measured? Discuss the political implications of your education in terms of Knoblauch's essay.

8. Of the four kinds of literacy Knoblauch discusses, which do you think is most important and why? Write a letter to the head of your hometown's board of education in which you define literacy and argue that the public schools should address the literacy problem based on your definition. Mention what should be taught along with how and why it should be taught.

▪ ▪ ▪ ▪ ▪ ▪

FREDERICK DOUGLASS

Learning Reading, Learning Freedom

Until the end of the Civil War, it was against the law in many southern states to teach slaves to read and write. Although the laws were unevenly enforced, they carried a symbolic power to prohibit literacy that was recognized by slaves and masters alike. Slaves who did learn to read usually did so secretly, either from other slaves or from sympathetic whites. In the following selection, former slave Frederick Douglass (1817?–1895) narrates his struggle to teach himself to read after his master Hugh Auld forbade his wife, Sophia Auld, to continue teaching twelve-year-old Frederick his alphabet. After escaping slavery, Douglass went on to become a powerful orator and a prolific writer. He founded and edited a weekly abolitionist newspaper and wrote voluminous speeches, editorials, letters, and magazine articles, in addition to three autobiographies: The Narrative of the Life of Frederick Douglass *(1845),* My Bondage and My Freedom

From *Narrative of the Life of Frederick Douglass, An American Slave,* ed. Benjamin Quarles (Cambridge, Mass.: Belknap Press of Harvard University Press, 1960), pp. 57–59 and 63–68; originally published in 1845 in Boston by the Anti-Slavery Office.

(1855), and Life and Times of Frederick Douglass *(1881). The earliest of those autobiographies, from which this excerpt was taken, sold out its first printing in just four months; by the end of its first five years it had sold thirty thousand copies, a huge number for its day.*

   My new mistress proved to be all she appeared when I first met her at the door,—a woman of the kindest heart and finest feelings. She had never had a slave under her control previously to myself, and prior to her marriage she had been dependent upon her own industry for a living. She was by trade a weaver; and by constant application to her business, she had been in a good degree preserved from the blighting and dehumanizing effects of slavery. I was utterly astonished at her goodness. I scarcely knew how to behave towards her. She was entirely unlike any other white woman I had ever seen. I could not approach her as I was accustomed to approach other white ladies. My early instruction was all out of place. The crouching servility, usually so acceptable a quality in a slave, did not answer when manifested toward her. Her favor was not gained by it; she seemed to be disturbed by it. She did not deem it impudent or unmannerly for a slave to look her in the face. The meanest slave was put fully at ease in her presence, and none left without feeling better for having seen her. Her face was made of heavenly smiles, and her voice of tranquil music.

   But, alas! this kind heart had but a short time to remain such. The fatal poison of irresponsible power was already in her hands, and soon commenced its infernal work. That cheerful eye, under the influence of slavery, soon became red with rage; that voice, made all of sweet accord, changed to one of harsh and horrid discord; and that angelic face gave place to that of a demon.

   Very soon after I went to live with Mr. and Mrs. Auld, she very kindly commenced to teach me the A, B, C. After I had learned this, she assisted me in learning to spell words of three or four letters. Just at this point of my progress, Mr. Auld found out what was going on, and at once forbade Mrs. Auld to instruct me further, telling her, among other things, that it was unlawful, as well as unsafe, to teach a slave to read. To use his own words, further, he said, "If you give a nigger an inch, he will take an ell.[1] A nigger should know nothing but to obey his master— to do as he is told to do. Learning would *spoil* the best nigger in the world. Now," said he, "if you teach that nigger (speaking of myself) how to read, there would be no keeping him. It would forever unfit him to be a slave. He would at once become unmanageable, and of no value to his master. As to himself, it could do him no good, but a great deal of harm. It would make him discontented and unhappy." These words sank deep into my heart, stirred up sentiments within that lay slumber-

---

1. **ell:** An obsolete unit of linear measurement, equal to 45 inches.—ED.

ing, and called into existence an entirely new train of thought. It was a new and special revelation, explaining dark and mysterious things, with which my youthful understanding had struggled, but struggled in vain. I now understood what had been to me a most perplexing difficulty—to wit, the white man's power to enslave the black man. It was a grand achievement, and I prized it highly. From that moment, I understood the pathway from slavery to freedom. It was just what I wanted, and I got it at a time when I the least expected it. Whilst I was saddened by the thought of losing the aid of my kind mistress, I was gladdened by the invaluable instruction which, by the merest accident, I had gained from my master. Though conscious of the difficulty of learning without a teacher, I set out with high hope, and a fixed purpose, at whatever cost of trouble, to learn how to read. The very decided manner with which he spoke, and strove to impress his wife with the evil consequences of giving me instruction, served to convince me that he was deeply sensible of the truths he was uttering. It gave me the best assurance that I might rely with the utmost confidence on the results which, he said, would flow from teaching me to read. What he most dreaded, that I most desired. What he most loved, that I most hated. That which to him was a great evil, to be carefully shunned, was to me a great good, to be diligently sought; and the argument which he so warmly urged, against my learning to read, only served to inspire me with a desire and determination to learn. In learning to read, I owe almost as much to the bitter opposition of my master, as to the kindly aid of my mistress. I acknowledge the benefit of both. . . .

   I lived in Master Hugh's family about seven years. During this time, I succeeded in learning to read and write. In accomplishing this, I was compelled to resort to various stratagems. I had no regular teacher. My mistress, who had kindly commenced to instruct me, had, in compliance with the advice and direction of her husband, not only ceased to instruct, but had set her face against my being instructed by any one else. It is due, however, to my mistress to say of her, that she did not adopt this course of treatment immediately. She at first lacked the depravity indispensable to shutting me up in mental darkness. It was at least necessary for her to have some training in the exercise of irresponsible power, to make her equal to the task of treating me as though I were a brute.

   My mistress was, as I have said, a kind and tender-hearted woman; 5 and in the simplicity of her soul she commenced, when I first went to live with her, to treat me as she supposed one human being ought to treat another. In entering upon the duties of a slaveholder, she did not seem to perceive that I sustained to her the relation of a mere chattel, and that for her to treat me as a human being was not only wrong, but dangerously so. Slavery proved as injurious to her as it did to me. When I went there, she was a pious, warm, and tender-hearted woman. There was no sorrow or suffering for which she had not a tear. She had bread for the hungry, clothes for the naked, and comfort for every mourner that came within her reach. Slavery soon proved its ability to divest her of these heavenly qualities. Under its influence, the tender heart became stone, and the lamblike disposition gave way to one of tiger-like fierceness. The first step in her downward course was in her ceasing to instruct me. She now commenced to practice her husband's precepts. She finally became even more violent in her opposition than her husband himself. She was not satisfied with simply doing as well as he had commanded; she seemed anxious to do better. Nothing seemed to make her more angry than to see me with a newspaper. She seemed to think that here lay the danger. I have had her rush at me with a face made all up of fury, and snatch from me a newspaper, in a manner that fully revealed her apprehension. She was an apt woman; and a little experience soon demonstrated, to her satisfaction, that education and slavery were incompatible with each other.

From this time I was most narrowly watched. If I was in a separate room any considerable length of time, I was sure to be suspected of having a book, and was at once called to give an account of myself. All this, however, was too late. The first step had been taken. Mistress, in teaching me the alphabet, had given me the *inch*, and no precaution could prevent me from taking the *ell*.

The plan which I adopted, and the one by which I was most successful, was that of making friends of all the little white boys whom I met in the street. As many of these as I could, I converted into teachers. With their kindly aid, obtained at different times and in different places, I finally succeeded in learning to read. When I was sent of errands, I always took my book with me, and by going one part of my errand quickly, I found time to get a lesson before my return. I used also to carry bread with me, enough of which was always in the house, and to which I was always welcome; for I was much better off in this regard than many of the poor white children in our neighborhood. This bread I used to bestow upon the hungry little urchins, who, in return, would give me that more valuable bread of knowledge. I am strongly tempted to give the names of two or three of those little boys, as a testimonial of the gratitude and affection I bear them; but prudence forbids—not that it would injure me, but it might embarrass them; for it is almost an unpardonable offense to teach slaves to read in this Christian country. It is enough to say of the dear little fellows, that they lived on Philpot Street, very near Durgin and Bailey's shipyard. I used to talk this matter of slavery over with them. I would sometimes say to them, I wished I could be as free as they would be when they got to be men. "You will be free as soon as you are twenty-one, *but I am a slave for life!* Have not I as good a right to be free as you have?" These words used to trouble them; they would express for me the liveliest sympathy, and console me with the hope that something would occur by which I might be free.

I was now about twelve years old, and the thought of being *a slave for life* began to bear heavily upon my heart. Just about this time, I got hold of a book entitled *The Columbian Orator*.[2] Every opportunity I got, I used to read this book. Among much of other interesting matter, I found in it a dialogue between a master and his slave. The slave was represented as having run away from his master three times. The dialogue represented the conversation which took place between them, when the slave was retaken the third time. In this dialogue, the whole argument in behalf of slavery was brought forward by the master, all of which was disposed of by the slave. The slave was made to say some very smart as well as impressive things in reply to his master—things which had the desired though unexpected effect; for the conversation resulted in the voluntary emancipation of the slave on the part of the master.

In the same book, I met with one of Sheridan's mighty speeches on and in behalf of Catholic emancipation.[3] These were choice documents to me. I read them over and over again with unabated interest. They gave tongue to interesting thoughts of my own soul, which had frequently flashed through my mind, and died away for want of utterance. The moral which I gained from the dialogue was the power of truth over the conscience of even a slaveholder. What I got from Sheridan was a bold denunciation of slavery, and a powerful vindication of human rights. The reading of these documents enabled me to utter my thoughts, and to meet the arguments brought forward to sustain slavery; but while they relieved me of one difficulty, they brought on another even more painful than the one of which I was relieved. The more I read, the more I was led to abhor and detest my enslavers. I could regard them in no other light than a band of successful robbers, who had left their homes, and gone to Africa, and stolen us from our homes, and in a strange land reduced us to slavery. I loathed them as being the meanest as well as the most wicked of men. As I read and contemplated the subject, behold! that very discontentment which Master Hugh had predicted would follow my learning to read had already come, to torment and sting my soul to unutterable anguish. As I writhed under it, I would at times feel that learning to read had been a curse rather than a blessing. It had given me a view of my wretched condition, without the remedy. It opened my eyes to the horrible pit, but to no ladder upon

---

2. *The Columbian Orator:* This popular collection of speeches, compiled by Caleb Bingham (1757–1817), was designed to instruct young people in the "art of eloquence." First published in 1797, it remained in print until 1860.—ED.

3. Parallels were frequently drawn between the abolitionist cause in the United States and the Catholic emancipation movement, the effort to repeal anti-Catholic laws in the British Isles that dated back to the sixteenth century. Charles Francis Sheridan (1750–1806) included a discussion of Catholicism in Ireland in his frequently reprinted "Essay on the true principles of civil liberty, and of free government" (1793).—ED.

which to get out. In moments of agony, I envied my fellow slaves for their stupidity. I have often wished myself a beast. I preferred the condition of the meanest reptile to my own. Any thing, no matter what, to get rid of thinking! It was this everlasting thinking of my condition that tormented me. There was no getting rid of it. It was pressed upon me by every object within sight or hearing, animate or inanimate. The silver trump of freedom had roused my soul to eternal wakefulness. Freedom now appeared, to disappear no more forever. It was heard in every sound, and seen in every thing. It was ever present to torment me with a sense of my wretched condition. I saw nothing without seeing it, I heard nothing without hearing it, and felt nothing without feeling it. It looked from every star, it smiled in every calm, breathed in every wind, and moved in every storm. . . .

▪ CONSIDER THE SOURCE

1. Why did Hugh Auld think it "unsafe" to educate slaves? To whom did he believe such education was most dangerous?

2. Explain the relationship Douglass sees between literacy and freedom.

3. Douglass's *Narrative* was published in the North in 1845. What attitudes and interests do you think he assumed on the part of his audience?

4. Describe Douglass's tone when he writes about Sophia Auld. What words most clearly convey his attitude toward her? Why does he say that the effects of slavery were as "injurious" to her as they were to him?

▪ CONSIDER THE IMPLICATIONS

5. Douglass claims that his reading of *The Columbian Orator* and the emancipation speeches of Sheridan "gave tongue" to thoughts that had previously "died away for want of utterance." In your journal, explore Douglass's use of these documents. What powers does he attribute to literacy?

6. Compare Douglass's use of reading with that of Benjamin Franklin (pp. 29–37), Malcolm X (pp. 164–171), or Jimmy Santiago Baca (pp. 180–187). Working in groups, discuss how literacy affected each writer's freedom and social mobility. How did initial literacy education prompt discontent and stimulate further education in each man? Has your education ever prompted similar discontent?

7. Douglass's determination to learn to read was fueled, he says, by the opposition of his master. In your journal, explore this notion that the value of an activity is increased by its prohibition.

8. Using Frederick Douglass's experience as your chief example, write an essay supporting or rejecting Paulo Freire's notion of critical literacy, as described by C. H. Knoblauch (p. 127).

9. Read or review Knoblauch's discussion of the political aims of "functional literacy" (pp. 124–29). How does Frederick Douglass's experience refute Knoblauch's claim that functional literacy fits people for a limited range

of roles? Write a letter from Frederick Douglass to Knoblauch defending instruction in functional literacy or complicating Knoblauch's thesis that functional literacy "safeguards the socioeconomic status quo."

■ ■ ■ ■ ■

LINDA K. KERBER

Why Should Girls Be Learned or Wise?

Even when education was not forbidden, as it was for Frederick Douglass and his fellow slaves, it could be severely limited. In this selection from her scholarly study Women of the Republic: Intellect and Ideology in Revolutionary America *(1980), Linda Kerber (b. 1940) shows that women's education, or lack of it, prepared them to fulfill prescribed roles in American society. As the Revolution altered those roles, women's education changed and broadened, but not without substantial resistance from those who considered an educated woman a freak of nature. Kerber, a professor of liberal arts and history at the University of Iowa, is the coeditor of* Women's America: Refocusing the Past *(1995) and* U.S. History as Women's History: New Feminist Essays *(1995). She is currently completing a book entitled* A Right to Be Ladies: American Women and the Obligations of Citizenship.

And why should girls be learnd or wise,
Books only serve to spoil their eyes.
The studious eye but faintly twinkles
And reading paves the way to wrinkles.
                                    —JOHN TRUMBULL[1]

"I expect to see our young women forming a new era in female history," wrote Judith Sargent Murray in 1798.[2] Her optimism was part of a general sense that in the post-Revolutionary world all possibilities were open; as Benjamin Rush[3] put it, the first act of the republican drama had

---

From *Women of the Republic: Intellect and Ideology in Revolutionary America* (Chapel Hill: University of North Carolina Press, 1980), pp. 187–218.

1. **John Trumbull** (1750–1831): Wrote a satirical poem about college education, published as *The Progress of Dulness* (1772–1773).—ED.

2. Judith Sargent Murray, *The Gleaner* (Boston, 1798), III, 189.

3. **Benjamin Rush** (1745–1813): A prominent and influential medical scientist, he was a signer of the Declaration of Independence and surgeon general of the Continental army.—ED.

only begun. The experience of war had given words like *independence* and *self-reliance* personal as well as political overtones. Ordinary folk had learned that the world could, as the song played at Yorktown had it, turn upside down: The rich could quickly become poor, wives might suddenly have to manage the family economy. Women might even, as the famous Deborah Gannett had done, shoulder a gun.[4] Revolutionary experience taught that it was useful to be prepared for a wide range of unusual possibilities; political theory taught that republics rested on the virtue and intelligence of their citizens. The stability and competence on which republican government relied required a highly literate and politically sophisticated constituency. Maintaining the Republic was an educational challenge as well as a political one.

The years immediately after the Revolution witnessed a great expansion of educational opportunity, an expansion sustained by the belief that the success of the republican experiment demanded a well-educated citizenry. Listing reading, writing, measurement and arithmetic, geography, and history as the subjects that ought to be taught in primary schools, Thomas Jefferson said the purpose of these institutions was to "instruct the mass of our citizens in these their rights, interests, and duties, as men and citizens."[5] Interest in formal education was also encouraged by industrial developments that put a premium on certain basic intellectual skills. The self-sufficient farmer might manage without literacy, but any boy expecting to run a small artisan's shop or to work in a business enterprise of some sort would need to be able to read, to write orders, and to keep accounts. Schemes for educating the "rising generation" proliferated. The need for literate workers would translate into heightened economic, as well as intellectual, opportunity for teachers, who found their skills in demand. "The Spirit for Academy making is vigorous," Ezra Stiles wrote joyfully in 1786. In Connecticut alone, Stiles counted twelve private academies, established by the subscriptions of philanthropic citizens in the previous five years.[6]

Institutions for boys' education seemed to flourish in the early Republic. But what of institutions for girls? "Schools and academies there are, intended for training up boys, and young gentlemen, in sundry branches of useful learning," mused Samuel Magaw in 1787, "but female instruction hath been left, as it were, to chance. . . . As if of trivial

---

4. **Deborah Sampson Gannett** (1760–1827): Enlisted in the Continental army under the alias Robert Shurtleff. She served from May 1782 until October 1783, when she was hospitalized with fever and doctors discovered she was a woman.— ED.

5. Quoted in Fred M. and Grace Hechinger, *Growing Up in America* (New York, 1975), 41.

6. Nov. 17, 1786, Dexter, ed., *Literary Diary of Ezra Stiles*, III, 247–248. For an extensive treatment of chartered private boys' academies, see James McLachlan, *American Boarding Schools: A Historical Study* (New York, 1970).

moment; no great deal hath been said about it, and still less accomplished."[7]

The reasons for this disparity reached far back into the history of Western thought. Deeply rooted in each of the colonists' native cultures was the assumption that women's energies were properly fully devoted to the service of their families. If learning was intended to prepare young men for active roles in the public sector and for service to the state, the shelter of coverture seemed to make sophisticated learning of little use to a woman. The first European academic institutions had been church related, intended to prepare men for the clerical life; the colleges at Oxford, Cambridge, Paris, and Bologna, which developed and fixed the definition of classical education, were male preserves. In schools that prepared boys for college, as Walter J. Ong has suggested, the teaching of Latin functioned as a "puberty rite" by which young men were introduced into an exclusively male world of scholarly learning. By contrast, the cultural world that women inhabited was practical, technical, and vernacular. A woman could not enter the academy, because it offered not disembodied knowledge but a classical curriculum designed to prepare young men for survival in a political world, a curriculum in which the requisite skills ranged from polemics and oratory to the making of war.[8] Academic study, a meritorious male pursuit, seemed self-indulgent when found among women. Americans inherited the image of the learned woman as an unenviable anomaly and kept alive the notion that the woman who developed her mind did so at her own risk.

Educational options for girls were far more limited than they were for boys. "How many female minds, rich with native genius and noble sentiment, have been lost to the world, and all their mental treasures

---

7. Samuel Magaw, "An Address delivered in the Young Ladies Academy, at Philadelphia, on February 8th, 1787, at the close of a Public Examination," *Am. Museum*, III (1788), 25–28.

8. Walter J. Ong, *The Presence of the Word: Some Prolegomena for Cultural and Religious History* (New Haven, Conn., 1967), 245–255. Ong suggests that "romanticism gave the final blow to polemic Latin-sustained oralism" (*ibid.*, 252). The change is symbolized by a shift in the definition of artistic inspiration from the muses ("strongly feminine figures ... obviously the projections of the male psyche") to romantic creativity, which produces "something out of nothing, like God's act of creation," and (though Ong does not say so) like women's act of childbearing. The romantic version makes the sources of creativity available to women also, who flourished as romantic writers. Ong maintains that the art of oratory was inaccessible to women because "without artificial amplification, the normal woman's voice simply cannot reach the thousands who found themselves enthralled by the bellowing of the old-line male orator" (*ibid.*, 249–250). However, voice projection is an acquired, not a natural, skill; great actresses of the premechanized theater, from Susannah Cibber to Katharine Hepburn, have shown that women can become excellent orators.

buried in oblivion?" asked the *Royal American Magazine* shortly before the war. "I regret the trifling narrow contracted Education of the Females of my own country," Abigail Adams wrote to her husband in 1778. "You need not be told how much female Education is neglected, nor how fashionable it has been to ridicule Female learning."[9]

That some well-known couples, like John and Abigail Adams, were equally facile with words has perhaps camouflaged the extent to which they were exceptional in their generation. There was more likely to be severe disparity in the verbal fluency of husband and wife, brother and sister. Other pairs may be more representative than the Adamses: Benjamin Franklin is an instructive contrast to his nearly illiterate—though nonetheless intelligent and shrewd—wife, Deborah. Elbridge Gerry courted a young woman who was, though the daughter of a state legislator, so illiterate she could not read his love letters.[10]. . .

These disparities in literacy—from the basic ability to sign one's name and to read simple prose to the sophisticated ability to read difficult or theoretical prose, foreign languages, and the classics—have enormous implications for the history of the relations between the sexes. One of the most important measures of modernization in a society may well be the degree to which print replaces oral communication. To the extent that female culture had relied on the spoken word, it was premodern at a time when male culture was increasing its dependence on written communication.[11] Literacy, after all, is more than a technical skill. It makes possible certain kinds of competencies. It makes practical the maintenance of a communication network wider than one's own locality. It may promote skepticism about local opin-

---

9. Clio [pseud.], "Thoughts on Female Education," *Royal American Magazine* (Jan. 1774), 9–10; Abigail Adams to John Adams, June 30, 1778, *Adams Family Correspondence*, III, 52.

10. Compare also the prose of Philip Van Cortlandt with that of his sister Cornelia Van Cortlandt Beckman as it appears in Jacob Judd, ed., *Correspondence of the Van Cortlandt Family of Cortlandt Manor, 1748–1800*, II (Tarrytown, N.Y., 1976), 27–29. Elbridge Gerry courted, but did not marry, a young woman who was not taught to read and write because her grandfather had insisted that all girls needed to learn was to "make a shirt and a pudding." See Abigail Adams to John Adams, Aug. 14, 1776, *Adams Family Correspondence*, II, 94–95,95n. Anne Firor Scott has written a subtle interpretation of Jane Franklin Mecom's life in "Self-Portraits: Three Women," in Richard Bushman et al., eds., *Uprooted Americans: Essays to Honor Oscar Handlin* (Boston, 1979), 46–55.

11. Harry Stout has suggested, for example, that the religious revivals of the early nineteenth century may represent the temporary revitalization of an older form of transmitting information, challenging the modern reliance on print ("Culture, Structure, and the 'New' History: A Critique and an Agenda," *Computers and the Humanities*, IX [1975], 213–230, esp. 223–224).

ions by promoting access to other viewpoints. Increased dependence on writing rather than on oral communication would ultimately help to bridge the gap between male and female experience, since the spoken word—depending as it does on the physical presence of the speaker—conveys the speaker's gender in a way that the written word cannot.[12]

The closing of the literacy gap between American men and women cannot yet be precisely dated. It occurred sometime between 1780—the year Kenneth Lockridge estimates that New England women's sign literacy was half that of men's—and 1850, when the first federal census that measured basic literacy reported little difference between the numbers of northeastern men and women who could read and write. Since the old people, who had been educated before and during the Revolution, accounted for most of the illiterates in 1850, we can assume that major improvements in female education took place between 1790 and 1830 or so. The literacy gap between men and women persisted longer in the South than in the North, and it persisted in technical competencies long after it had been bridged for simple reading and writing.[13] No social change in the early Republic affected women more emphatically than the improvement of schooling, which opened the way into the modern world.

Those who wished to improve educational opportunity for women had to work against a pervasive skepticism. Abigail Adams had been right to note that female education was ridiculed when it was not ne-

---

12. See Jack Goody and Ian Watt, "The Consequences of Literacy," *Comparative Studies in Society and History*, V (1962), 334: "The mere size of the literate repertoire means that the proportion of the whole which any one individual knows must be infinitesimal in comparison with what obtains in oral culture. Literate society, merely by having no system of elimination, no 'structural amnesia,' prevents the individual from participating fully in the total cultural tradition to anything like the extent possible in nonliterate society." Margaret Mead remarked that "primitive education was a process by which continuity was maintained between parents and children. . . . Modern education includes a heavy emphasis upon the function of education to create discontinuities" ("Our Educational Emphases in Primitive Perspective," *American Journal of Sociology*, XLVIII [1943], 637).

13. Kenneth Lockridge, *Literacy in Colonial New England: An Enquiry into the Social Context of Literacy in the Early Modern West* (New York, 1974), 38–44 and *passim;* Daniel Calhoun, *The Intelligence of a People* (Princeton, N.J., 1973), 76 and *passim.* In 1929 Thomas Woody commented on the substantial disparity in literacy between colonial men and women; his call for additional study in this area has only begun to be answered (*A History of Women's Education in the United States,* I [New York, 1929], 159). Woody's book remains the basic survey history, but it is diffuse and often anecdotal at the expense of analysis. A new appraisal remains to be written. For a recent case study, see Linda Auwers, "The Social Meaning of Female Literacy: Windsor, Connecticut, 1660–1775," Newberry Library Papers in Family and Community History, No. 77–4A, Newberry Library, Chicago. Even in 1980, it is generally agreed that women are less likely than men to be well educated in mathematics and science.

glected. "Deluded maid! thy claim forego," began a poem "To a Lady, Who Expressed a Desire of Seeing An University Established for Women."[14] It was not only Latin, but all serious learning, that was an exclusively male puberty rite. Those who would add scholarly indoctrination to female adolescent experiences were inventing a ritual and an institution that threatened the woman's traditional life pattern of unremitting physical toil and unremitting social subservience. "Tell me," the Philadelphian Gertrude Meredith wrote angrily, "do you imagine, from your knowledge of the young men in this city, that ladies are valued according to their mental acquirements? I can assure you that they are not, and I am very confident that they never will be, while men indulge themselves in expressions of contempt for one because she has a *bare elbow*, for another because she . . . never made a *good pun, nor smart repartee.* . . . [Would they] not titter . . . at her expense, if a woman made a Latin quotation, or spoke with enthusiasm of Classical learning?"[15]. . .

Improvements in women's education, although impeded by criti- 10 cisms like these, did come. Between 1790 and 1830 facilities for girls' education expanded and improved, especially in the North, making possible the closing of the literacy gap. The reasons for this are related both to the political revolution and to the industrial revolution. The political revolution had been an act of faith. Believing as they did that republics rested on the virtue of their citizens, Revolutionary leaders had to believe not only that Americans of their own generation displayed that virtue, but that Americans of subsequent generations would continue to display the moral character that a republic required. The role of guarantor of civic virtue, however, could not be assigned to a formal branch of government. Instead it was hoped that other agencies—churches, schools, families—would fulfill that function.[16] And within families, the crucial role was thought to be the mother's: the mother who trained her children, taught them their early lessons, shaped their moral choices. To determine to what extent this role was assigned to women or to what extent they claimed it themselves requires a calculus too precise for the historian. But it is clear that women integrated these expectations into their own understanding of what a mother ought to do. Motherhood was discussed almost as if it were a fourth branch of government, a device that ensured social control in the gentlest possible way. If the Republic indeed rested on responsible motherhood, prospective mothers needed to be well informed and decently educated. The industrial revolution, occurring at the same time, reinforced the need for improved ed-

---

14. *Am. Museum,* XI (1792), Pt. i, app. 1, 3. See also *Burlington Advertiser* (Burlington, N.J.), Dec. 6, 1791.

15. Letter signed M. G., "American Lounger," *Port Folio* (Apr. 7, 1804), 106.

16. See Linda K. Kerber, *Federalists in Dissent: Imagery and Ideology in Jeffersonian America* (Ithaca, N.Y., 1970), 206–212.

ucation. As the postwar world became more print-oriented, and as it became harder to function in it as an illiterate, interest in the improvement of girls' schooling increased.[17]

An important shift in public expectation was marked by the change in wording of the Massachusetts school law of 1789. As Kathryn Kish Sklar has pointed out, this law for the first time spoke of schoolmistresses as well as of schoolmasters. It probably validated an increasingly frequent practice, rather than initiated a new one.[18]

There was an enormous amount of variation in the educational opportunities open to girls in the late eighteenth century. Quakers and Moravians had early established coeducational schools or pairs of schools (one for boys and a matching one for girls). In New England, girls and younger children of both sexes began to attend schools in special summer sessions, when boys were working in the fields. (Girls' major contributions to the family economy were likely to be indoor winter activities: spinning, dyeing, sewing, preserving foods.) Education costs were low during these months, for schoolhouses did not need to be heated, and teachers were young women paid substantially less than their male counterparts. . . .

These schools were often defended on the grounds that they would serve a new purpose. The education of young women had traditionally been an education for marriage—if at all possible, an upwardly mobile marriage. Girls were said to need a new kind of education because their traditional training had been superficial and their resulting behavior shallow. How, it was asked, can women's minds be free if they are

---

17. These developments are discussed in detail in Cott, *Bonds of Womanhood,* esp. chap. 3. Cott correctly links changes in education to changes in the domestic economy. Her book provides the most subtle analysis yet of the intrusion of the industrial revolution into household production. Daughters, for example, had contributed to the family economy by carding, spinning, dyeing, and weaving. In between their tasks, they had also taught younger siblings and neighbor children the rudiments of reading, writing, and household skills. In the course of a generation their roles were usurped by steam-powered factories. Daughters were left without their traditional work, but with a continuing obligation to contribute to the family economy. Many followed their work to the mills; others extended their informal teaching to work as paid teachers in new schools. In Cott's analysis, these changes do not connect with politics until a later generation of young women—Grimkes and Stanton—develop an explicitly feminist ideology in the 1830s.

18. In 1778, for example, Groton had begun to count girls in its school census: "Voted, that the children be numbered through the town; males unmarried from four years old to twenty-one; females unmarried from four years old to eighteen" (Caleb Butler, *History of the Town of Groton . . .* [Boston, 1848], 221). See also Mary Eastman, "The Education of Woman in the Eastern States," in Annie Nathan Meyer, ed., *Woman's Work in America* (New York, 1891), 3–53; Cott, *Bonds of Womanhood: "Women's Sphere" in New England, 1780–1835* (New Haven, Conn.: Yale Univ. Press, 1977), 30, 102–103, 112–114; and Kathryn Kish Sklar, "Growing Up Female in Eighteenth-Century Massachusetts" (paper delivered at the University of Michigan, 1977).

taught that their sphere is limited to fashion, music, and needlework? Fashion became an emblem of superficiality and dependence. It was distasteful in a wife, inappropriate in a republic. The Philadelphia *Lady's Magazine* criticized a father who prepared his daughters for the marriage market: "You boast of having given your daughters an education which will enable them 'to shine in the first circles.' . . . They sing indifferently; they play the harpsichord indifferently; they are mistresses of every common game at cards . . . ; they . . . have just as much knowledge of dress as to deform their persons by an awkward imitation of every new fashion which appears. . . . Placed in a situation of difficulty, they have neither a head to dictate, nor a hand to help in any domestic concern."[19] Teaching young girls to dress well was part of the larger message that their primary lifetime goal must be marriage; fashion was a feature of sexual politics. "I have sometimes been led," remarked Benjamin Rush, "to ascribe the invention of ridiculous and expensive fashions in female dress entirely to the gentlemen in order to divert the ladies from improving their minds and thereby to secure a more arbitrary and unlimited authority over them."[20]

In the marriage market, beauty, flirtatiousness, and charm were at a premium; intelligence, good judgment, and competence (in short, the republican virtues) were at a discount. Because it seemed appropriate for women in a republic to have greater control over their own lives, "the *dependence* for which women are uniformly educated" was deplored. The Republic did not need fashion plates; it needed citizens—women as well as men—of self-discipline and of strong mind. The contradiction between the counsel given to young women and their own self-interest, as well as the best interests of the Republic, seemed obvious. In theory the marriage market undercut the Republic.[21]

The idea that political independence should be the catalyst for a 15 new female self-reliance that would free women from the constraints of the marriage market and prepare them to be economically independent

---

19. *Lady's Mag.* (Aug. 1792), 121–123.

20. Benjamin Rush, "Thoughts upon Female Education, Accommodated to the Present State of Society, Manners and Government in the United States of America" (Philadelphia, 1787), in Frederick Rudolph, ed., *Essays on Education in the Early Republic* (Cambridge, Mass., 1965), 39.

21. "The greater proportion of young women are trained up by thoughtless parents, in ease and luxury, with no other dependence for their future support than the precarious chance of establishing themselves by marriage: for this purpose (the men best know why) elaborate attention is paid to external attractions and accomplishments, to the neglect of the more useful and solid acquirements. . . . [Marriage is the] *sole* method of procuring for themselves an establishment" (*New York Magazine* [Aug. 1779], 406). For comment on the marriage market, see letter signed "A Matrimonial Republican," *Lady's Mag.* (July 1792), 64–67, and "Legal Prostitution, Or Modern Marriage," *Independent Chronicle* (Boston), Oct. 28, 1793. For criticism of fashion, see *Am. Mag.* (Dec. 1787), 39; *ibid.* (July 1788), 594; *Am. Museum* (Aug. 1788), 119; and *Massachusetts Mercury* (Boston), Aug. 16, 1793, Jan. 16, 1795.

appears in its most developed form in the work of Judith Sargent Murray. In 1784 she published a prescient argument calling for the strengthening of what she called "Self-Complacency in Female Bosoms." Lacking a strong and positive sense of their own identity, she complained, young women had no personal resources with which to resist the marriage market, and so they rushed into marriages to establish their social status.[22] Eight years later, widowed and remarried to the Universalist minister John Murray, she developed this theme at great length in a series of essays, which were published in the *Massachusetts Magazine* between 1792 and 1794 and collected under the title of *The Gleaner* in 1798. In these essays, Murray insisted that instruction in a manual trade was especially appropriate in a republic, and she decried the antiegalitarian habit of assuming that a genteel and impractical education was superior to a vocational one. She was critical of fathers who permitted their sons to grow up without a useful skill and was even more critical of parents who "pointed their daughters" toward marriage and dependence. This direction made girls' education contingent on a single event. It offered young women a single vision of the future. "Our girls, in general, are bred up with one particular view, with one monopolizing consideration, which seems to absorb every other plan that reason might point out as worthy [of] their attention: An establishment by marriage; this is the goal to which they are constantly pointed, the great ultimatum of every arrangement: *An old maid,* they are from infancy taught, at least indirectly, to consider as a contemptible being; and they have no other means of advancing themselves but in the matrimonial line.". . .

Even were it granted that girls ought to be educated for the Republic, what ought that education to comprise? Ought it to be the same as boys' schooling? Ought the goal of the Republic to be a generation of learned ladies? Was the "Lady" who wrote a long imitation of Alexander Pope[23] for the *American Museum* correct in her claim that women might even share that distinctly masculine passion, ambition?

> In either sex the appetite's the same,
> For love of pow'r is still the love of fame.
> . . . .
>
> In education all the diff'rence lies;
> Women, if taught, wou'd be as learn'd and wise
> As haughty man, improv'd by arts and rules . . .[24]

---

22. "Desultory Thoughts Upon the Utility of Encouraging a Degree of Self-Complacency, Especially in FEMALE BOSOMS," *Gentlemen and Ladies Town and Country Magazine* (Oct. 1784), 251–252.

23. **Alexander Pope** (1688–1744): Wrote many satires, including *The Dunciad* (1728), which included viciously witty portraits of leading writers of Pope's day.— ED.

24. "On Pope's Characters of Women," By A Lady, *Am. Museum*, XI (1792), app. I, 13–15.

As these verses suggest, opinions on women's education were inextricably tangled with opinions about the capacity of women's minds; educational policy was dependent on assumptions about the female intellect. At one end of the spectrum of reforming opinion was the "Female Advocate," who indulged in a proposal—only half in jest—that the tables be turned. "What would be the consequence," she asked, "if the doors of our seminaries were as effectually shut against the gentlemen, as they now are against the other sex; and colleges and superior schools of scientific improvement, were appropriately thrown open to the benefit of the female world . . . ?" At the other end was Samuel Harrison Smith, who began the essay that won the American Philosophical Society's 1797 prize for the best plan for a national system of education by proposing "that every male child, without exception, be educated." He said nothing about female children.[25]

The founders of the new girls' schools were striking out on new terrain. Since women were not being prepared for the traditional professions—law, medicine, the clergy—teachers could not easily assume that girls ought to have the same studies as did boys. Indeed teachers were forced to confront the question, For what profession were girls being prepared? With near unanimity they answered that girls were being prepared to be wiser wives and better mothers. Domesticity was treated as a vocation, motherhood a profession.[26] Devising a curriculum for girls was an exercise in answering the question, What does a woman need to know?

Judith Sargent Murray recommended a course of study that could be taught at home by mothers. A woman, she thought, should be able to write and converse elegantly and correctly, pronounce French, read history, comprehend some simple geography and astronomy. All these a mother would teach to her children.[27] Perhaps the best-known proposal for a new female curriculum was prepared by Benjamin Rush, who prescribed reading, grammar, penmanship, "figures and bookkeeping," and geography. He added "the first principles of natural philosophy," vocal music to soothe cares and exercise the lungs (but not instrumental

---

25. *Female Advocate,* 29; Samuel Harrison Smith, "Remarks on Education: Illustrating the Close Connection between Virtue and Wisdom" (Philadelphia, 1798), in Rudolph, ed., *Essays on Education,* 211. Smith did acknowledge that female instruction was important, but concepts of its makeup seemed so varied that he feared to make any proposals and despaired of including women in his scheme. "It is sufficient, perhaps, for the present, that the improvement of women is marked by a rapid progress and that a prospect opens equal to their most ambitious desires" (*ibid.,* 217). The other prizewinner, Samuel Knox, proposed to admit girls to the primary schools, but not to the academies or colleges. Knox's "An Essay on the Best System of Liberal Education" is reprinted in Rudolph, ed., *Essays on Education,* 271–372. See also Charles E. Cunningham, *Timothy Dwight, 1752–1817: A Biography* (New York, 1942), 154–163, and Nov. 17, 1786, Dexter, ed., *Literary Diary of Ezra Stiles,* III, 247–248.

26. Cott, *Bonds of Womanhood,* chap. 2, esp. 70–74.

27. Murray, *The Gleaner,* I, No. 7, 68–71.

music, which seemed to him a waste of valuable time for all but the most talented), and history as an antidote to novel reading.

Rush offered his model curriculum in a speech to the Board of Visitors of the Young Ladies' Academy of Philadelphia, later published and widely reprinted under the title "Thoughts Upon Female Education, Accommodated to the Present State of Society, Manners and Government in the United States of America." The academy claimed to be the first female academy chartered in the United States. When Rush spoke on July 28, 1787, he was offering practical advice to a new school, which he linked to the greater cause of demonstrating the possibilities of women's minds. Those who were skeptical of education for women, Rush declared, were the same who opposed "the general diffusion of knowledge among the citizens of our republics." Rush argued that "female education should be accommodated to the state of society, manners, and government of the country in which it is conducted." An appropriate education for American women would be condensed, because they married earlier than their European counterparts. It would include bookkeeping, because American women could expect to be "the stewards and guardians of their husbands' property" and executrices of their husbands' wills. It would qualify them for "a general intercourse with the world" by an acquaintance with geography and chronology. If education is preparation for life, then American women required a newly tailored educational program.[28]

The curriculum of the Young Ladies' Academy (which one of the school's Board of Visitors called "abundantly sufficient to complete the female mind") included reading, writing, arithmetic, English grammar, composition, rhetoric, and geography. It did not include the natural philosophy Rush hoped for (although Rush did deliver a dozen vaguely scientific lectures), advanced mathematics, or the classics. Most significantly, needlework was not a part of the curriculum. . . .

The curriculum of the Young Ladies' Academy could also be found, with moderate variations, at female branches of town academies and at female boarding schools, where needlework, music, and dancing were often additional subjects. It became common practice for schools to require each student to keep a journal of the day's lessons and sermons;

---

28. Rush, "Thoughts Upon Female Education," in Rudolph, ed., *Essays on Education*, 25–40. Rush seems to have partially overstated his assertion that American conditions demanded more mathematical and economic sophistication of women than did European. According to Daniel Scott Smith, "Inheritance and the Position and Orientation of Colonial Women" (paper delivered at Berkshire Conference of Women Historians, 1974, Schlesinger Library, Radcliffe College, Cambridge, Mass.), Rush's female contemporaries seem to have been *less* likely to be named executrices than their ancestors; when they were, a male heir was more likely to be named as a partner. It is not yet established to what extent the exclusion of women was an aspect of the modernization of finance and the economy.

these journals show the extensive reliance on rote learning and on working one's way slowly, lesson-by-lesson, chapter-by-chapter, through a text—a technique common in boys' schools as well. The informal comments added to the journal entries make them a window into the girls' schools, a rich source of insight into the quality of daily life there.

Nevertheless, these journals must not be read as private diaries (though they often masquerade as such). They originated as school exercises and were regularly reviewed by teachers. At the Newark Academy in New Jersey, keeping a journal was an explicit part of the curriculum, "a happy expedient for giving" the students "a facility of expression," according to Principal Timothy Alden. Sarah Pierce set a formal quota for her girls: "sixty lines of good writing every week." Some years later, a perceptive girl in Margaret Fuller's Providence, Rhode Island, school described the dynamics of the assignment accurately. "It appears to me," she remarked, "that these Journals must be very nice keys—by which, the teachers, can unlock the hearts, the characters, and as it were read the very thoughts of their scholars."[29]

The new women's seminaries of the post-Revolutionary era, with their grammar books, their translations from the classics, their "Ladies' Libraries," can be seen as efforts to absorb women into a modern culture that increasingly relied on print. The common practice of requiring a school journal was in part a device for monitoring a pupil's studies, but it also may have been a mode of forcing her to give a written, rather than an oral, account of her experiences. The journal writer must transfer her private feelings into written words for public scrutiny; through her entries the adult can monitor the development of the self-conscious use of the public medium.

Less inhibited by traditional assumptions about what had "always been done," the curriculum of the new girls' schools could be imaginative, even adventurous. This feature of the schools is not often recognized. Because the usual textbooks were "so dry & devoid of interest that children" were "disgusted by them," the founders of girls' academies were often driven to prepare their own collections or to write their own teaching materials. Finding "from long experience . . . that children and youth imbibe ideas most easily, when placed in the form of question and answer," Sarah Pierce wrote a world history in dialogue form for

---

29. *Quarterly Catalogue of the names of the young ladies, who belong to the Newark academy, under the instruction Rev. Timothy Alden* (Newark, N.J., 1811), 38; Journal of Mary C. Camp [at Sarah Pierce's School], July 1818, Conn. State Lib., Hartford; Journal of Anna D. Gale [at Margaret Fuller's School], Feb. 15, 1838, Gale Family Papers, Am. Antq. Soc., Worcester, Mass. See also Mary Chester to Edwin Chester, May 29, 1819, Emily Noyes Vanderpoel, *Chronicles of a Pioneer School, from 1792 to 1833: Being the History of Miss Sarah Pierce and Her Litchfield School* (Cambridge, Mass., 1903), 191: "My time is wholly taken up. I have to keep a journal and write compositions which with other studies occupy all the time of a moderate genius."

her students.[30] Some of the first American history and geography text-books were written by Emma Willard, who objected to the usual practice of beginning the study of history with the ancient world. She believed that young women needed to know the history of their own country more than they needed to know about Greece and Rome, and when she found no texts that suited her, she wrote some good ones herself. Indeed, Willard's teaching methods, as Anne Firor Scott has shown, encouraged active, not passive, learning and anticipated the approach of John Dewey and other progressive educators of the twentieth century. "Each individual is to himself the center of his own world," Willard observed, "and the more intimately he connects his knowledge with himself, the better will it be remembered." In her geography classes, the first assignment was to draw a map of one's hometown.[31] Acting was introduced; instead of pompous graduation orations, girls read poetry or presented dramatic skits.[32]

Perhaps the most far-reaching reform was the wholesale elimination of the classics from the curriculum. Classics were already coming to be regarded as a decorative accomplishment for men. They had never been part of the education of lower-class boys and were on their way to becoming a vestigial part of the training of all except prospective lawyers and doctors at the close of the eighteenth century. A very few individuals did try to bridge the intellectual gap between men and women by introducing women to the classics, but most who did so tutored their daughters at home and risked the label of eccentricity. Aaron Burr,[33] for example, made certain that his daughter, Theodosia, learned Latin and Greek. He insisted that her tutor demand much of her and scribbled for her a mock journal entry that suggests his high expectations: "Learnt 230 lines which finished Horace. heigh ho. for Terence & the Greek Grammar Tomorrow. . . . Began Gibbon this evening—I find he requires as much study as Horace."[34] But in his educational standards, as in so

30. Vanderpoel, *Chronicles of a Pioneer School*, 82, 81.

31. Emma Willard, *History of the United States, or Republic of America* (New York, 1828–1849), v–vi; Anne Firor Scott, "What, Then, is the American: This New Woman?" *JAH*, LXV (1978), 689–691.

32. Several examples are published in Vanderpoel, *Chronicles of a Pioneer School*, 84–145. Sally Ripley's diary includes the full texts of two one-act plays.

33. **Aaron Burr** (1756–1836): A politician and lawyer, he served as a senator (1791–1797), vice president under Thomas Jefferson, and second president of the College of New Jersey, which later became Princeton University.— ED.

34. Aaron Burr to Theodosia Burr, Dec. 16, 1793, Burr Papers, Microfilm, Reel 3, 430, N.-Y. Hist. Soc., New York City; Aaron Burr to Theodosia Burr, Feb. 13, 1794, Matthew L. Davis, ed., *Memoirs of Aaron Burr with Miscellaneous Selections from His Correspondence* (New York, 1836). I, 376. See other letters on the subject in Davis, ed., *Memoirs of Burr*, I, 364, 369–370, 373, 376, 378, 380–387, 392–393, and Herbert S. Parmet and Marie B. Hecht, *Aaron Burr: Portrait of an Ambitious Man* (New York, 1967), 89–90. See also Harriott Pinckney to Mrs. Favell, Mar. 1763, Pinckney Papers.

much else, Burr is a poor guide to things of which his contemporaries approved.

Benjamin Rush is a better guide. Rush thought of the classics as remnants of aristocratic education unsuited to a republican nation and an industrial economy. He had no patience at all with the Latin quotations that dotted the oratory and philosophical writings of his day. "Do not men use Latin and Greek as scuttlefish emit their ink," he bitterly asked John Adams, "on purpose to conceal themselves from an intercourse with the common people?"[35]. . .

■ **CONSIDER THE SOURCE**

1. According to Kerber, what purpose did education serve for men and women in the young Republic? How did women's education correspond to their role(s) in society?

2. What does Kerber mean by the term *marriage market*? How did the marriage market affect women's education? How did it "undercut the Republic"?

3. Describe the curriculum of a typical women's academy. Which subjects were thought appropriate for women? Which were not? Why?

4. What evidence does Kerber draw on to substantiate her claims? How do her sources lend credibility to her argument?

■ **CONSIDER THE IMPLICATIONS**

5. In class discussion, brainstorm about images of women in today's society and compare them with the society Kerber describes. What positive and negative characteristics do you associate with politically active or intellectually accomplished women? How are those women portrayed by the media? To what extent are the biases against women's education that Kerber outlines still in effect today?

6. Kerber describes how the gap in basic literacy between men and women closed during the nineteenth century. In your journal, explore similar gaps that may persist in today's society. In what subjects do men and women differ in their degree of "literacy"? How might such literacy gaps affect employment, political empowerment, conception of one's role in society?

7. The first colleges for women opened their doors in the nineteenth century to provide the new kind of education Kerber describes. In the past twenty years, most of these colleges have become coeducational. In 1990, Mills College in Oakland, California, decided to abandon its women-only policy but rescinded that decision after student protest and heated public debate. Research accounts of the debate in newspapers and magazines. Once you understand the specific issues involved, write a letter to the

---

35. Benjamin Rush to John Adams, July 21, 1789, Butterfield, ed., *Letters of Rush,* I, 524.

president of Mills College, defending or challenging the college's decision to remain an all-women's school.

8. Assuming that the success of America still demands the "well-educated citizenry" Kerber describes, how should that education be defined? In small groups, list the subjects that you believe are essential for today's American citizen and those that you think would be desirable. Compare your list to those of other groups. Write a proposal detailing the model education for the model American citizen, making sure to explain your reasons for the curriculum you propose.

9. Kerber cites at least one author who challenged the common assumption that "a genteel and impractical education was superior to a vocational one." In class, debate the value of these two sorts of education. Which does your college offer? Why did you choose that type of education?

10. Read or review C. H. Knoblauch's essay (pp. 122–30) on the political implications of various types of literacy and extend his argument to the split between genteel and vocational education. Write an essay that argues for one or the other type of education or that modifies the dichotomy between them.

11. Frederick Douglass (pp. 130–35) recalls his slave master telling him that education would "unfit him to be a slave" and would make him "discontented and unhappy." Write an essay comparing the reasons Kerber cites for restricting women's education with the reasons for keeping slaves illiterate. What consequences did opponents of education for these groups fear? What benefits did women and slaves anticipate from greater education?

▪ ▪ ▪ ▪ ▪ ▪
....

Zitkala-Ša (Gertrude Bonnin)

The Civilizing Machine

Zitkala-Ša or Gertrude Bonnin (1876–1938), a Yankton Sioux, achieved literacy in accordance with the U.S. educational policy toward Native Americans. Believing that Indian children would assimilate into American society more rapidly if they were taken away from their reservations, the Bureau of Indian Affairs encouraged the establishment of boarding schools in the East. At age eight, Zitkala-Ša boarded a train to Indiana, where she spent the next three years at a Quaker school. She described her traumatic dislocation between her oral tribal culture and the alien white school in memoirs published in the Atlantic Monthly, *"Impressions of an Indian*

From "The School Days of an Indian Girl," *Atlantic Monthly,* February 1900, 189–192.

Childhood" (1900) and "The School Days of an Indian Girl" (1900), from which this selection is taken. Though she published a few original short stories and poems, along with Old Indian Legends *(1901), a collection of traditional oral tales, most of her writing was done in her capacity as an Indian rights activist. She was an officer of the Society of the American Indian, before founding the National Council of American Indians and serving as its president from 1926 to 1938.*

THE DEVIL

Among the legends the old warriors used to tell me were many stories of evil spirits. But I was taught to fear them no more than those who stalked about in material guise. I never knew there was an insolent chieftain among the bad spirits, who dared to array his forces against the Great Spirit, until I heard this white man's legend from a paleface woman.

Out of a large book she showed me a picture of the white man's devil. I looked in horror upon the strong claws that grew out of his fur-covered fingers. His feet were like his hands. Trailing at his heels was a scaly tail tipped with a serpent's open jaws. His face was a patchwork: He had bearded cheeks, like some I had seen palefaces wear; his nose was an eagle's bill, and his sharp-pointed ears were pricked up like those of a sly fox. Above them a pair of cow's horns curved upward. I trembled with awe, and my heart throbbed in my throat, as I looked at the king of evil spirits. Then I heard the paleface woman say that this terrible creature roamed loose in the world, and that little girls who disobeyed school regulations were to be tortured by him.

That night I dreamt about this evil divinity. Once again I seemed to be in my mother's cottage. An Indian woman had come to visit my mother. On opposite sides of the kitchen stove, which stood in the center of the small house, my mother and her guest were seated in straight-backed chairs. I played with a train of empty spools hitched together on a string. It was night, and the wick burned feebly. Suddenly I heard someone turn our doorknob from without.

My mother and the woman hushed their talk, and both looked toward the door. It opened gradually. I waited behind the stove. The hinges squeaked as the door was slowly, very slowly pushed inward.

Then in rushed the devil! He was tall! He looked exactly like the picture I had seen of him in the white man's papers. He did not speak to my mother, because he did not know the Indian language, but his glittering yellow eyes were fastened upon me. He took long strides around the stove, passing behind the woman's chair. I threw down my spools, and ran to my mother. He did not fear her, but followed closely after me. Then I ran round and round the stove, crying aloud for help. But my mother and the woman seemed not to know my danger. They sat still, looking quietly upon the devil's chase after me. At last I grew dizzy. My head revolved as on a hidden pivot. My knees became numb, and doubled under my weight like a pair of knife blades without a spring. Beside my mother's chair I fell in a heap. Just as the devil stooped over me with outstretched claws my mother awoke from her quiet indifference, and lifted me on her lap. Whereupon the devil vanished, and I was awake.

On the following morning I took my revenge upon the devil. Stealing into the room where a wall of shelves was filled with books, I drew forth *The Stories of the Bible.* With a broken slate pencil I carried in my apron pocket, I began by scratching out his wicked eyes. A few moments later, when I was ready to leave the room, there was a ragged hole in the page where the picture of the devil had once been.

Iron Routine

A loud-clamoring bell awakened us at half past six in the cold winter mornings. From happy dreams of Western rolling lands and unlassoed freedom we tumbled out upon chilly bare floors back again into a paleface day. We had short time to jump into our shoes and clothes, and wet our eyes with icy water, before a small hand bell was vigorously rung for roll call.

There were too many drowsy children and too numerous orders for the day to waste a moment in any apology to nature for giving her children such a shock in the early morning. We rushed downstairs, bounding over two high steps at a time, to land in the assembly room.

A paleface woman, with a yellow-covered roll book open on her arm and a gnawed pencil in her hand, appeared at the door. Her small, tired face was coldly lighted with a pair of large gray eyes.

She stood still in a halo of authority, while over the rim of her spec- 10 tacles her eyes pried nervously about the room. Having glanced at her long list of names and called out the first one, she tossed up her chin and peered through the crystals of her spectacles to make sure of the answer "Here."

Relentlessly her pencil black-marked our daily records if we were not present to respond to our names, and no chum of ours had done it successfully for us. No matter if a dull headache or the painful cough of slow consumption had delayed the absentee, there was only time enough to mark the tardiness. It was next to impossible to leave the iron routine after the civilizing machine had once begun its day's buzzing; and as it was inbred in me to suffer in silence rather than to appeal to the ears of one whose open eyes could not see my pain, I have many times trudged in the day's harness heavy-footed, like a dumb sick brute.

Once I lost a dear classmate. I remember well how she used to mope along at my side, until one morning she could not raise her head from her pillow. At her deathbed I stood weeping, as the paleface woman sat near her moistening the dry lips. Among the folds of the bedclothes I saw the open pages of the white man's Bible. The dying Indian girl talked disconnectedly of Jesus the Christ and the paleface who was cooling her swollen hands and feet.

I grew bitter, and censured the woman for cruel neglect of our physical ills. I despised the pencils that moved automatically, and the one teaspoon which dealt out, from a large bottle, healing to a row of variously ailing Indian children. I blamed the hard-working, well-meaning, ignorant woman who was inculcating in our hearts her superstitious ideas. Though I was sullen in all my little troubles, as soon as I felt better I was ready again to smile upon the cruel woman. Within a week I was again actively testing the chains which tightly bound my individuality like a mummy for burial.

The melancholy of those black days has left so long a shadow that it darkens the path of years that have since gone by. These sad memories rise above those of smoothly grinding school days. Perhaps my Indian nature is the moaning wind which stirs them now for their present record. But, however tempestuous this is within me, it comes out as the low voice of a curiously colored seashell, which is only for those ears that are bent with compassion to hear it.

FOUR STRANGE SUMMERS

After my first three years of school, I roamed again in the Western 15 country through four strange summers.

During this time I seemed to hang in the heart of chaos, beyond the touch or voice of human aid. My brother, being almost ten years my senior, did not quite understand my feelings. My mother had never gone inside of a schoolhouse, and so she was not capable of comforting her daughter who could read and write. Even nature seemed to have no place for me. I was neither a wee girl nor a tall one; neither a wild Indian nor a tame one. This deplorable situation was the effect of my brief course in the East, and the unsatisfactory "teenth" in a girl's years.

It was under these trying conditions that, one bright afternoon, as I sat restless and unhappy in my mother's cabin, I caught the sound of the spirited step of my brother's pony on the road which passed by our dwelling. Soon I heard the wheels of a light buckboard, and Dawee's familiar "Ho!" to his pony. He alighted upon the bare ground in front of our house. Tying his pony to one of the projecting corner logs of the low-roofed cottage, he stepped upon the wooden doorstep.

I met him there with a hurried greeting, and, as I passed by, he looked a quiet "What?" into my eyes.

When he began talking with my mother, I slipped the rope from the pony's bridle. Seizing the reins and bracing my feet against the dashboard, I wheeled around in an instant. The pony was ever ready to try his speed. Looking backward, I saw Dawee waving his hand to me. I turned with the curve in the road and disappeared. I followed the winding road which crawled upward between the bases of little hillocks. Deep waterworn ditches ran parallel on either side. A strong wind blew against my cheeks and fluttered my sleeves. The pony reached the top of the highest hill, and began an even race on the level lands. There was nothing moving within that great circular horizon of the Dakota prairies save the tall grasses, over which the wind blew and rolled off in long, shadowy waves.

Within this vast wigwam of blue and green I rode reckless and insignificant. It satisfied my small consciousness to see the white foam fly from the pony's mouth.   20

Suddenly, out of the earth a coyote came forth at a swinging trot that was taking the cunning thief toward the hills and the village beyond. Upon the moment's impulse, I gave him a long chase and a wholesome fright. As I turned away to go back to the village, the wolf sank down upon his haunches for rest, for it was a hot summer day; and as I drove slowly homeward, I saw his sharp nose still pointed at me, until I vanished below the margin of the hilltops.

In a little while I came in sight of my mother's house. Dawee stood in the yard, laughing at an old warrior who was pointing his forefinger, and again waving his whole hand, toward the hills. With his blanket drawn over one shoulder, he talked and motioned excitedly. Dawee turned the old man by the shoulder and pointed me out to him.

"Oh han!" (Oh yes) the warrior muttered, and went his way. He had climbed the top of his favorite barren hill to survey the surrounding prairies, when he spied my chase after the coyote. His keen eyes recognized the pony and driver. At once uneasy for my safety, he had come running to my mother's cabin to give her warning. I did not appreciate his kindly interest, for there was an unrest gnawing at my heart.

As soon as he went away, I asked Dawee about something else.

"No, my baby sister, I cannot take you with me to the party   25
tonight," he replied. Though I was not far from fifteen, and I felt that before long I should enjoy all the privileges of my tall cousin, Dawee persisted in calling me his baby sister.

That moonlight night, I cried in my mother's presence when I heard the jolly young people pass by our cottage. They were no more young braves in blankets and eagle plumes, nor Indian maids with prettily painted cheeks. They had gone three years to school in the East, and had become civilized. The young men wore the white man's coat and trousers, with bright neckties. The girls wore tight muslin dresses, with ribbons at neck and waist. At these gatherings they talked English. I could speak English almost as well as my brother, but I was not properly dressed to be taken along. I had no hat, no ribbons, and no close-fitting gown. Since my return from school I had thrown away my shoes, and wore again the soft moccasins.

While Dawee was busily preparing to go I controlled my tears. But when I heard him bounding away on his pony, I buried my face in my arms and cried hot tears.

My mother was troubled by my unhappiness. Coming to my side, she offered me the only printed matter we had in our home. It was an Indian Bible, given her some years ago by a missionary. She tried to console me. "Here, my child, are the white man's papers. Read a little from them," she said most piously.

I took it from her hand, for her sake; but my enraged spirit felt more like burning the book, which afforded me no help, and was a perfect delusion to my mother. I did not read it, but laid it unopened on the floor, where I sat on my feet. The dim yellow light of the braided muslin burning in a small vessel of oil flickered and sizzled in the awful silent storm which followed my rejection of the Bible.

Now my wrath against the fates consumed my tears before they 30 reached my eyes. I sat stony, with a bowed head. My mother threw a shawl over her head and shoulders, and stepped out into the night.

After an uncertain solitude, I was suddenly aroused by a loud cry piercing the night. It was my mother's voice wailing among the barren hills which held the bones of buried warriors. She called aloud for her brothers' spirits to support her in her helpless misery. My fingers grew icy cold, as I realized that my unrestrained tears had betrayed my suffering to her, and she was grieving for me.

Before she returned, though I knew she was on her way, for she had ceased her weeping, I extinguished the light, and leaned my head on the window sill.

Many schemes of running away from my surroundings hovered about in my mind. A few more moons of such a turmoil drove me away to the Eastern school. I rode on the white man's iron steed, thinking it would bring me back to my mother in a few winters, when I should be grown tall, and there would be congenial friends awaiting me.

■ **CONSIDER THE SOURCE**

1. Summarize how printed material is used to control the behavior of Zitkala-Ša and her classmates.

2. Compare the images Zitkala-Ša uses to describe her life at school and her life back home.

3. How do the tone and point of view contribute to the message Zitkala-Ša sends to her audience?

4. What role does literacy play in Zitkala-Ša's dream of the devil? Explain how literacy alienates Zitkala-Ša from her mother.

▪ **CONSIDER THE IMPLICATIONS**

5. In the final paragraph of the section "Iron Routine," the author uses an oral metaphor to describe her written record of the past and the audience who can understand it. In class discussion, explore how orality and literacy function in this memoir. Where and how is each one valued? How do speakers and writers differ in their impact on their audience?

6. Zitkala-Ša describes her education as a "civilizing machine." In your journal, compare her education to your own. What aspects of education did you find machinelike, and why? How did school "civilize" you?

7. This essay was originally published in the *Atlantic Monthly*. Read the description of the *Atlantic* in the appendix (p. 632) and write an essay explaining how Zitkala-Ša shapes her memoir to appeal to her audience.

8. Read or review Frederick Douglass's account of his education (pp. 130–136). Compare Douglass's "discontentment" with Zitkala-Ša's "unrest." What role does education play in each person's discontent? What do they feel is the remedy for their unhappiness?

9. The Christian Bible appears in all three of these sections from Zitkala-Ša's memoirs. Write an essay analyzing how the Bible functions in each section.

▪ ▪ ▪ ▪ ▪ ▪

CHARLES KIKUCHI

Tanforan, 1942: Chronicle from an American Concentration Camp

After the bombing of Pearl Harbor in December 1941, Japanese Americans were viewed by many as a threat to national security. On March 2, 1942, the entire Pacific Coast was declared a military area, from which the evacuation of all Japanese—regardless of their status as American citizens— would be necessary. Charles Kikuchi (b. 1916), an American-born Japanese, was twenty-six years old at the time and a student at the School of Social Welfare, University of California at Berkeley. Along with some eight thousand others, Kikuchi and his family were taken from their home to a

From *Kikuchi Diary: Chronicle from an American Concentration Camp*, ed. John Modell (Urbana: Univ. of Illinois Press, 1973).

makeshift camp at the Tanforan race track just south of San Francisco before they were ultimately transferred to camps in Arizona and Utah. Kikuchi helped to found the camp newspaper, the Tanforan Totalizer, *a mimeographed paper that published nineteen issues for the English-speaking Japanese internees. During the five months that Kikuchi spent in stable 10, stall 5, at Tanforan, he also kept a remarkable diary of the daily activities in camp, from which these excerpts are taken.*

MAY 3, 1942   SUNDAY

We are planning to get the paper underway as soon as possible. It is needed now as a "morale raiser" and also for the information service that it could render. With four thousand more people coming in next week, the confusion may grow greater.

MAY 4, 1942   MONDAY

About twenty of us met tonight to really get the Camp paper going because we really do need some source of information. Most of the group were represented and they are all behind the movement. Taro Katayama was elected Temporary Editor so that the policy setting will at least be liberal and outspoken. We plan to distribute the papers through the mail service. All the Nisei[1] lads want to be postmen because they feel that it will be a good opportunity to get to know the girls. . . .

MAY 5, 1942   TUESDAY

We got approval to go ahead with the paper and the boys are working hard in order to get the first issue out by Saturday.

MAY 14, 1942   THURSDAY

The first baby was born in camp last Monday. I wonder what it will be named. We got the news too late to headline it in the paper so had to box it in one corner. Taro certainly is having a headache with the paper. Everything has to be read and "okayed" by the front office. They are cautious to the nth degree. (By a consensus of opinion the paper was

---

1. **Nisei:** The name for second-generation Japanese Americans, in contrast to the Issei, who were born in Japan and then immigrated to the United States.—ED.

named the *Tanforan Totalizer,* a racing theme. I got a front page story on the post office, edited by Jimmy.) K. says that the administration is very sensitive about radicalism or unfavorable publicity; I think that he has pretty good information that a sample of the outgoing mail is censored, but I hardly think that this is true. There are bound to be mistakes made, but they shouldn't be afraid of that as long as they are sincere. W. H. and some others write directly to WRA[2] with their complaints and they seem to think that they get immediate action. It would be much better if they were frank with the administration here and took their problems to them; I'm sure that they would give it consideration—if they had time. Notice was issued today that no notice could be placed on any bulletin board without an official "OK." Reason??

MAY 27, 1942 WEDNESDAY

Busy all morning sending out exchange copies of our camp paper   5
to the fifteen other Assembly and Relocation Centers. A copy goes to the Library of Congress, U. C. Library, and California State Library. Mr. Greene[3] provides a secretary to do the actual work of sending it out. We are trying to get the third issue out by Saturday morning so that we can have a special feature for Memorial Day. Taro is really not aggressive enough. He should push the paper a little more. Although there is a tight censorship and a lot of red tape, there are ways in which we can at least have some sort of policy. I haven't talked to Greene about social work for a couple of days, but I think I am continually getting in his and Mr. Davis's[4] hair with all my requests for the paper. Wrote a little piece about the coming special elections in S. F. and told the Nisei how to obtain the absentee ballot. Then I asked Davis if they would provide an officer with a seal for the ballot marking. Davis was not very cooperative, and he said that they would do this if there were not too many Nisei who came with the ballots to his office. It's very likely that a lot of the Nisei will not even bother to vote. Even if they don't think it means much they should keep in the habit. This is one time that they should be on guard and fight for their civil rights or else the disfranchisement movement will get stronger. Mr. Davis scoffed at this and said that only a short notice in the paper was necessary without any elaboration on the wider issues. Warren calls me "The Power behind the throne," because I boss Taro around on what should be done for the good of the paper. One of these days he might get sore, but he seems to depend on

---

2. **WRA**: The War Relocation Authority, established in March 1942, administered the removal of Japanese Americans from the Pacific Coast.—ED.

3. **Mr. Greene**: An employment officer in the Tanforan Assembly Center.—ED.

4. **Mr. Davis**: Apparently, the chief administrator of the camp.—ED.

me a lot right now and willingly follows any suggestions that we may make.

JUNE 2, 1942 TUESDAY

Our newspaper office is getting to be a very popular place. A lot of people were up today. It will be interesting to note what they talk about. The big fuss today was over the coming elections.[5] . . .

JUNE 16, 1942 TUESDAY 11:45

Had a very busy day running around to get election information for the newspaper. As if there is nothing else of concern in the world! It's funny how isolation can cut one off from the realities of the great outside. We seem to get so wound up in our little camp affairs. In a sense this may be a little bad; but on the other hand a positive interest by the residents towards camp life is a healthy sign. It indicates that they are not contented in a wholly passive role. This energy can be guided into useful channels if we could develop the right sort of leadership among the Nisei.

JUNE 17, 1942 WEDNESDAY

Censorship note: Ran a statement for the paper about how the Nisei could get the complete Tolan Reports[6] and where to send for it. Mc-Queen[7] sent it back censored completely and gave no reason. We were all pretty burnt up, but what can you do except protest? Taro suggests that we all quit and get into education. The paper is not worth that much trouble. It is now checked and double checked. . . .

The administration makes the mimeographing of the paper hard because of the lack of cooperation. Yet they take about two hundred copies to send out. We were not able to get the complete election results. . . . Because of the close votes, Davis would make no official statement for us. He sealed the ballot boxes up and will wait for demands for a recount before issuing a statement. This means that we

---

5. **coming elections**: Interned Japanese were allowed to elect their own governance council, but the elected body had virtually no power to affect camp life.—ED.

6. **Tolan Reports**: The House of Representatives established a Select Committee Investigating National Defense Migration, which held hearings in early 1942. Chaired by Representative John H. Tolan, the committee issued a report on the relocation in June 1942.—ED.

7. **McQueen:** Official censor for the Wartime Civil Control Administration.—ED.

will not get a lot of statistics in for this week's issue. I went to the two losing candidates and both Tosh Suzuki and Dave Tatsuno said that they were perfectly satisfied with the results and would not contest it. But Davis was "too busy" to let us get at the returns today. On top of this, the sentry at the gate is balking at keeping our copy for McQueen to pick up because he claims that he is too busy. Besides, I don't like the idea of putting out a paper all "sweetocated" as if everything is running smoothly.

JUNE 20, 1942   SATURDAY

Most of the rumors these days concern the time and place for the next move.[8] Everyone feels that it will be before fall and a great deal of speculation goes on as to the exact date. Two weeks ago the rumors were chiefly about food and crime. The way that rumors spread like wildfire also indicates the lack of news for the Issei. Most of them can't read the *Totalizer* so they don't know what is going on. From now on, it will be almost impossible to put bulletins out in Japanese. No reading matter in Japanese at all is available for them. Without authentic news they seize every piece of gossip as gospel truth and are too eager to believe it. Most of the Issei don't know what is going on around here and many don't want to move again now that they are settled down here for the duration. They have a lot of free time to go around and pass the gossip on. The stories get bigger and better as they are tossed around [one] barrack to another. . . .

JUNE 22, 1942   MONDAY

The Army photographers disrupted our day by taking a moving picture of our pressroom in action. These official documentary films will probably be used to show the "bigwigs" how well off we are and they will also be kept for the record of the "greatest mass migration in American history." We can't write about it in the *Totalizer*, the sergeant says. Anyway we were excited about being in the movies. They put the huge klieg lights in and it made us sweat like hell. I had on Jack's Hawaiian shirt and typed out a letter while they took some shots. The director made us go through the motions of being busy. Bob Tsuda kept his back to the camera except when he turned around and asked for a cigarette. Yuki and Emiko posed under our office American flag to lend inspiration to the scene. . . .

---

8. **next move**: The Tanforan Assembly Center was only a temporary holding facility. Residents were relocated to more permanent camps farther east, and the center was closed in October 1942.—ED.

JULY 1, 1942 WEDNESDAY 1:45

My news note on Kochiyama got in the *Berkeley Gazette* via the *Totalizer*. First time we have hit the daily metropolitan press. Taro and I went to see Greene and argued him into letting us increase up to ten pages. No doubt that we rank among the best among center papers. Administration thinks highly of it; no wonder, we paint a bright picture of things inadvertently. As long as I get my plugs on Americanism in, it suits me. Had to run around like hell to get news to fill the extra page. I slop the stuff in and let Jimmy rewrite and polish it up if necessary. I hate to stay cooped up there writing when I can be out and around. Bill covers sport and recreation, Jim and I education, Ben odds and ends, and administrative news has been piling up on me. Swiped some occupational survey figures, copied them, and returned the original. Gunder will throw a fit since he doesn't want to release anything until after completion, but we can't wait that long and I'm unscrupulous anyway.[9] Have got fair contacts with most of the administration and Taro makes me do most of the dirty work, but it inflates my ego to hear them say that they have to depend on me for the news.

JULY 4, 1942 SATURDAY INDEPENDENCE DAY 11:00

I was talking to Mr. Besig, Fred Korematsu, Mitch, and C. H. when I saw Mr. Gunder rush up to the administration office. "Oh! Oh!" says I, "he is going to raise verbal thunder, that Gunder!" And then Nobby rushes down and tells us that Davis ordered that all copies of the *Totalizer* had to be collected at once. Taro was called up by Davis and given hell, but he wouldn't tell him what was wrong with the paper. I surmised that it was the employment story since I had obtained the figures by devious methods. And the Constitution story was a little doubtful. We had distributed the paper without getting the double check. The staff was lined up and told to see the house managers and get all the papers back in an hour. I spotted Mitzi going home for lunch so I temporarily lost interest in the proceedings and walked her home. The rest of them rushed around excitedly getting the copies back. The whole camp got in an uproar and they hastily read the paper to find out what was wrong. The house managers did not know what it was so they collected them very seriously. It will probably be the only time that the *Totalizer* got such a careful reading (Gonzales thinks it is the greatest morale builder in camp). Everyone was mystified. I met a few people on the way back from lunch and they asked me the reason so I told them that the army and Davis were cracking down because of one of the arti-

---

9. Gunder, Kikuchi remembers, "was some sort of a guard for the WCCA."

cles and from there the rumors began to grow. Some thought it was the lend-lease articles about goods intended for China ending up here. We finally found out from Davis that he objected to a part of the Constitution story and the scrip book item, which had to be changed. He said that he had marked it out, but we told him that there was no initial on the copy so we ran it as it was. Greene came up and he was very sympathetic. He even helped us unstaple. In order to stop rumors we decided to get the copy out as soon as possible and so spent most of the afternoon unstapling twenty-four hundred copies. About three hundred copies were not turned in.

From now on the paper has to be triple checked. I saw Toby and asked him to bring up the matter of freedom of the press, within limits, and he will do so Monday. Davis allowed the occupational story to go through, but Gunder is still in an uproar about the whole thing. The two pages have to be run over tomorrow, on our decision. We haven't much to make an issue out of it and this was not the time to quit. The three articles in question were mine but Taro had to take the verbal lashing for it. Told Pop I was going to jail for the crime and they got excited for a while.

JULY 31, 1942   FRIDAY   12:30

The paper has come along to its peak. We have to fight for every 15 inch and never have received much cooperation from the administration. We take the censorship in stride, feeling that there is not much use in trying to buck Davis and McQueen with their fascist ideas. The work has fallen into a routine and some of the old zip is gone. I wanted to get it up to twelve pages, but Taro and the others absolutely refuse to expend more energy under the present setup. And I hardly blame them. We have sort of developed a policy of subtle Americanization and avoid loud protestations of loyalty, of waving the flag. We minimize things Japanese. I notice that the other center papers play up such things as *Bon Odori* and *Sumo*.[10] We did not even mention the repatriation[11] business. The *Totalizer* gives much space to all educational activities and minimizes sports, which is usually given double and triple the space in other center papers. We are the only one to have regular features and the paper is planned out in magazine style, the chief credit going to Bob and Taro. Standards of writing are kept up by them, plus Jimmy and Lillian. I get the stories in and they all take turns giving it a thorough going over. I don't mind since it makes our paper more polished. Bill H. is

---

10. ***Bon Odori***: A Japanese festival honoring the spirits of the dead; the popular Japanese sport of ***Sumo*** wrestling drew large crowds within the camp.—ED.

11. The possibility of repatriation to Japan became a subject of very great appeal, to whites who hated the Japanese, to many of the oppressed Issei, and ultimately, to some Nisei.

much worse than I am. He uses typical H. S. style. With our limitation on space we thought that it would be better not to develop a straight news style. My "Your Opinion" column is getting on to a higher level, but then I run into difficulties because there is always the uncertainty of censorship on a controversial subject. . . .

AUGUST 4, 1942 TUESDAY 11:07

There are no such things as freedom of the press or speech around here. Everything has to have the "approval" of the Administration. I realize that they have a heavy responsibility, but why can't they start from the assumption that we are average Americans and give us a decent chance instead of being so suspicious about everything that we do. Chas., you are getting excited over something you cannot control!

I didn't do a damn thing on the paper today either. Suddenly, the paper is unimportant. I can feel what Taro has been saying for the past couple of weeks now. It's such a waste of time struggling to get the news for the people, yet there is morale-raising value in it, that can't be denied. Most of the Nisei are just starved for news and almost all that I have talked to say that they read the *Totalizer* from cover to cover. This proves that time hangs heavy on their hands!

[*Editor's Note:* On September 1, 1942, Charles Kikuchi was transferred to Gila River (Arizona) Relocation Center. The *Tanforan Totalizer* published its final issue on September 28, 1942.]

■ **CONSIDER THE SOURCE**

1. Describe the various functions that Kikuchi claims the *Tanforan Totalizer* served within the camp. What function did the newspaper serve for the mainstream American community outside the camp?

2. How does this selection's status as a diary affect the way you read the text? What authority do you grant to the writer?

3. What subjects did the newspaper cover? What features of a regular newspaper did it include? What was excluded?

4. Why does Kikuchi claim "there are no such things as freedom of the press or speech around here"? How does his diary support or refute his assertion?

■ **CONSIDER THE IMPLICATIONS**

5. Discuss Kikuchi's objections to publishing a "sweetocated" newspaper. How does the paper represent camp life? In what ways does it misrepresent camp life? How does Kikuchi contribute to either representation?

6. What role should a free press have within a concentration camp? If you were Davis, what criteria would you use to decide which stories to permit and which to censor?

7. Read or review Erwin Knoll's discussion of "prior restraint" (pp. 437–440). Does Kikuchi's experience with the *Tanforan Totalizer* constitute prior restraint? How were the writers' and editors' decisions influenced by Davis and other army overseers? Write a letter to camp officials in the voice of Erwin Knoll, arguing that government censorship created an atmosphere of restraint that violated Kikuchi's First Amendment rights to free speech. Alternatively, adopt the position of Davis and write a letter to the *Totalizer's* editor, justifying the scrutiny of the publication.

8. Working in groups, plan a newspaper to serve a limited community, such as a small college or organization, a single dormitory, or a fraternity or sorority. Decide what purpose your newspaper should serve and then describe the newspaper. What would be in it? What would you exclude? Why?

9. Compare the *Tanforan Totalizer* with *The Advocate* as described by Mark Thompson (pp. 188–97). Write an essay analyzing how each publication reflects and serves its community.

10. Kikuchi wrote not just for himself but for others. He intended to hand on his diary to Berkeley sociologist Dorothy Swaine Thomas for her Japanese Evacuation and Relocation Study. In your journal, describe the various audiences you write for. How do they differ? How does your sense of audience affect what and how you write?

▪ ▪ ▪ ▪ ▪
....

MALCOLM X

A Homemade Education

Born Malcolm Little, Malcolm X (1925–1965) was a brilliant natural orator but found when he was imprisoned in 1946 that the spoken word would not suffice to get his message across. Frustrated by his inability to use written language, he determined to educate himself using the books in the Norfolk Prison Colony (Massachusetts) library. Malcolm X's painstaking efforts to learn to read provide impressive testimony to the power of literacy and to the connection between reading and writing. In his memoir, he lists many of the books that influenced him and shaped his political views. After his release from prison in 1952, he became one of the most articulate

From *The Autobiography of Malcolm X*. With the assistance of Alex Haley. (New York: Ballantine Books, 1965), pp. 171–179. (See entry under Random House in appendix.)

spokesmen for the cause of black separatism. Drawing on his wide reading in history, he urged African Americans to sever their ties with white America, which he believed had historically done nothing but oppress and enslave the black man. In collaboration with Alex Haley, he published The Autobiography of Malcolm X *in 1965, the same year he was assassinated.*

It was because of my letters that I happened to stumble upon starting to acquire some kind of a homemade education.

I became increasingly frustrated at not being able to express what I wanted to convey in letters that I wrote, especially those to Mr. Elijah Muhammad.[1] In the street, I had been the most articulate hustler out there—I had commanded attention when I said something. But now, trying to write simple English, I not only wasn't articulate, I wasn't even functional. How would I sound writing in slang, the way I would *say* it, something such as, "Look, daddy, let me pull your coat about a cat, Elijah Muhammad—."

Many who today hear me somewhere in person, or on television, or those who read something I've said, will think I went to school far beyond the eighth grade. This impression is due entirely to my prison studies.

It had really begun back in the Charlestown Prison, when Bimbi first made me feel envy of his stock of knowledge. Bimbi had always taken charge of any conversation he was in, and I had tried to emulate him. But every book I picked up had few sentences which didn't contain anywhere from one to nearly all of the words that might as well have been in Chinese. When I just skipped those words, of course, I really ended up with little idea of what the book said. So I had come to the Norfolk Prison Colony still going through only book-reading motions. Pretty soon, I would have quit even these motions, unless I had received the motivation that I did.

I saw that the best thing I could do was get hold of a dictionary—to study, to learn some words. I was lucky enough to reason also that I should try to improve my penmanship. It was sad. I couldn't even write in a straight line. It was both ideas together that moved me to request a dictionary along with some tablets and pencils from the Norfolk Prison Colony school.

I spent two days just riffling uncertainly through the dictionary's pages. I'd never realized so many words existed! I didn't know *which* words I needed to learn. Finally, just to start some kind of action, I began copying.

In my slow, painstaking, ragged handwriting, I copied into my

5

---

1. **Mr. Elijah Muhammad** (1897–1975): Leader of the Nation of Islam, a militant Muslim organization committed to the idea of black nationalism.—ED.

tablet everything printed on that first page, down to the punctuation marks.

I believe it took me a day. Then, aloud, I read back, to myself, everything I'd written on the tablet. Over and over, aloud, to myself, I read my own handwriting.

I woke up the next morning, thinking about those words—immensely proud to realize that not only had I written so much at one time, but I'd written words that I never knew were in the world. Moreover, with a little effort, I also could remember what many of these words meant. I reviewed the words whose meanings I didn't remember. Funny thing, from the dictionary first page right now, that "aardvark" springs to my mind The dictionary had a picture of it, a long-tailed, long-eared, burrowing African mammal, which lives off termites caught by sticking out its tongue as an anteater does for ants.

I was so fascinated that I went on—I copied the dictionary's next page. And the same experience came when I studied that. With every succeeding page, I also learned of people and places and events from history. Actually the dictionary is like a miniature encyclopedia. Finally the dictionary's A section had filled a whole tablet—and I went on into the B's. That was the way I started copying what eventually became the entire dictionary. It went a lot faster after so much practice helped me to pick up handwriting speed. Between what I wrote in my tablet, and writing letters, during the rest of my time in prison I would guess I wrote a million words.

I suppose it was inevitable that as my word-base broadened, I could for the first time pick up a book and read and now begin to understand what the book was saying. Anyone who has read a great deal can imagine the new world that opened. Let me tell you something: From then until I left that prison, in every free moment I had, if I was not reading in the library, I was reading on my bunk. You couldn't have gotten me out of books with a wedge. Between Mr. Muhammad's teachings, my correspondence, my visitors—usually Ella and Reginald—and my reading of books, months passed without my even thinking about being imprisoned. In fact, up to then, I never had been so truly free in my life.

The Norfolk Prison Colony's library was in the school building. A variety of classes was taught there by instructors who came from such places as Harvard and Boston universities. The weekly debates between inmate teams were also held in the school building. You would be astonished to know how worked up convict debaters and audiences would get over subjects like "Should Babies Be Fed Milk?"

Available on the prison library's shelves were books on just about every general subject. Much of the big private collection that Parkhurst[2] had willed to the prison was still in crates and boxes in the back of the li-

---

2. Charles Henry **Parkhurst** (1842–1933): American reformer and president of the Society for the Prevention of Crime.—ED.

brary—thousands of old books. Some of them looked ancient: covers faded, old-time parchment-looking binding. Parkhurst, I've mentioned, seemed to have been principally interested in history and religion. He had the money and the special interest to have a lot of books that you wouldn't have in general circulation. Any college library would have been lucky to get that collection.

As you can imagine, especially in a prison where there was heavy emphasis on rehabilitation, an inmate was smiled upon if he demonstrated an unusually intense interest in books. There was a sizable number of well-read inmates, especially the popular debaters. Some were said by many to be practically walking encyclopedias. They were almost celebrities. No university would ask any student to devour literature as I did when this new world opened to me, of being able to read and *understand*.

I read more in my room than in the library itself. An inmate who   15
was known to read a lot could check out more than the permitted maximum number of books. I preferred reading in the total isolation of my own room.

When I had progressed to really serious reading, every night at about 10:00 P.M. I would be outraged with the "lights out." It always seemed to catch me right in the middle of something engrossing.

Fortunately, right outside my door was a corridor light that cast a glow into my room. The glow was enough to read by, once my eyes adjusted to it. So when "lights out" came, I would sit on the floor where I could continue reading in that glow.

At one-hour intervals the night guards paced past every room. Each time I heard the approaching footsteps, I jumped into bed and feigned sleep. And as soon as the guard passed, I got back out of bed onto the floor area of that light-glow, where I would read for another fifty-eight minutes—until the guard approached again. That went on until three or four every morning. Three or four hours of sleep a night was enough for me. Often in the years in the streets I had slept less than that.

The teachings of Mr. Muhammad stressed how history had been "whitened"—when white men had written history books, the black man simply had been left out. Mr. Muhammad couldn't have said anything that would have struck me much harder. I had never forgotten how when my class, me and all of those whites, had studied seventh-grade United States history back in Mason, the history of the Negro had been covered in one paragraph, and the teacher had gotten a big laugh with his joke, "Negroes' feet are so big that when they walk, they leave a hole in the ground."

This is one reason why Mr. Muhammad's teachings spread so   20
swiftly all over the United States, among *all* Negroes, whether or not they became followers of Mr. Muhammad. The teachings ring true—to every Negro. You can hardly show me a black adult in America—or a

white one, for that matter—who knows from the history books anything like the truth about the black man's role. In my own case, once I heard of the "glorious history of the black man," I took special pains to hunt in the library for books that would inform me on details about black history.

I can remember accurately the very first set of books that really impressed me. I have since bought that set of books and have it at home for my children to read as they grow up. It's called *Wonders of the World*. It's full of pictures of archaeological finds, statues that depict, usually, non-European people.

I found books like Will Durant's *Story of Civilization*. I read H. G. Wells's *Outline of History*. *Souls of Black Folk* by W.E.B. Du Bois gave me a glimpse into the black people's history before they came to this country. Carter G. Woodson's *Negro History* opened my eyes about black empires before the black slave was brought to the United States, and the early Negro struggles for freedom.[3]

J. A. Rogers's three volumes of *Sex and Race*[4] told about race-mixing before Christ's time; about Aesop being a black man who told fables; about Egypt's Pharaohs; about the great Coptic Christian Empires; about Ethiopia, the earth's oldest continuous black civilization, as China is the oldest continuous civilization.

Mr. Muhammad's teaching about how the white man had been created led me to *Findings in Genetics* by Gregor Mendel.[5] (The dictionary's G section was where I had learned what "genetics" meant.) I really studied this book by the Austrian monk. Reading it over and over, especially certain sections, helped me to understand that if you started with a black man, a white man could be produced; but starting with a white man, you never could produce a black man—because the white chromosome is recessive. And since no one disputes that there was but one Original Man, the conclusion is clear.

During the last year or so, in the *New York Times*, Arnold Toynbee[6]   25

---

3. **Will Durant** (1885–1981): A popular historian whose eleven-volume *Story of Civilization* (1935–1975), coauthored with his wife Ariel, has been described as a "biography of mankind"'; **H. G. Wells** (1866–1946): British author of *Outline of History: Being a Plain History of Life and Mankind* (1920); **W.E.B. Du Bois** (1868–1963): Pioneering black historian and activist, whose *Souls of Black Folk* (1903) ranks as one of the most influential works on racism in America; **Carter G. Woodson** (1875–1950): Author of *The Negro in Our History* (1922), Woodson is considered the father of black history.—ED.

4. **Joel Augustus Rogers** (1883–1965): His three-volume *Sex and Race* (1940) was subtitled "Negro-Caucasian Mixing in All Ages and All Lands."—ED.

5. **Gregor Mendel** (1822–1884): Pioneering Austrian botanist and geneticist. He published his theories of dominant and recessive genes in a scientific journal in the 1860s, but his work remained unknown until the twentieth century.—ED.

6. **Arnold Toynbee** (1889–1975): English historian, author of the twelve-volume *A Study of History* (1934–1961), which described history in terms of the cyclical development and decline of civilizations.—ED.

used the word "bleached" in describing the white man. (His words were: "White (i.e., bleached) human beings of North European origin. . . .") Toynbee also referred to the European geographic area as only a peninsula of Asia. He said there is no such thing as Europe. And if you look at the globe, you will see for yourself that America is only an extension of Asia. (But at the same time Toynbee is among those who have helped to bleach history. He has written that Africa was the only continent that produced no history. He won't write that again. Every day now, the truth is coming to light.)

I never will forget how shocked I was when I began reading about slavery's total horror. It made such an impact upon me that it later became one of my favorite subjects when I became a minister of Mr. Muhammad's. The world's most monstrous crime, the sin and the blood on the white man's hands, are almost impossible to believe. Books like the one by Frederick Olmstead[7] opened my eyes to the horrors suffered when the slave was landed in the United States. The European woman, Fannie Kimball,[8] who had married a Southern white slaveowner, described how human beings were degraded. Of course I read *Uncle Tom's Cabin*.[9] In fact, I believe that's the only novel I have ever read since I started serious reading.

Parkhurst's collection also contained some bound pamphlets of the Abolitionist Anti-Slavery Society of New England. I read descriptions of atrocities, saw those illustrations of black slave women tied up and flogged with whips; of black mothers watching their babies being dragged off, never to be seen by their mothers again; of dogs after slaves, and of the fugitive slave catchers, evil white men with whips and clubs and chains and guns. I read about the slave preacher Nat Turner,[10] who put the fear of God into the white slavemaster. Nat Turner wasn't going around preaching pie-in-the-sky and "nonviolent" freedom for the black man. There in Virginia one night in 1831, Nat and seven other slaves started out at his master's home and through the night they went from one plantation "big house" to the next, killing, until by the next morning fifty-seven white people were dead and Nat had about seventy slaves following him. White people, terrified for their lives, fled from their homes, locked themselves up in public buildings, hid in the woods,

---

7. **Frederick Olmstead** (*sic*) (1822–1903): Frederick Law Olmsted, a founder of landscape architecture in the United States, was also a social critic and reformer. His criticisms of slavery were published as *The Cotton Kingdom* (1861).—ED.

8. **Fannie Kimball** (*sic*): Frances (Fanny) Kemble (1809–1893) was a noted British actress and abolitionist who recounted her experiences in the South in *Journal of a Residence on a Georgia Plantation* (1863).—ED.

9. **Uncle Tom's Cabin** (1852): An antislavery novel by Harriet Beecher Stowe (1811–1896), often cited as one of the causes of the Civil War.—ED.

10. **Nat Turner** (1800–1831): Led the bloodiest slave revolt in U.S. history. His four-day revolt in August 1831 left fifty-seven whites dead and led to the retaliatory killings of many innocent slaves.—ED.

and some even left the state. A small army of soldiers took two months to catch and hang Nat Turner. Somewhere I have read where Nat Turner's example is said to have inspired John Brown[11] to invade Virginia and attack Harpers Ferry nearly thirty years later, with thirteen white men and five Negroes.

I read Herodotus, "the father of History,"[12] or, rather, I read about him. And I read the histories of various nations, which opened my eyes gradually, then wider and wider, to how the whole world's white men had indeed acted like devils, pillaging and raping and bleeding and draining the whole world's nonwhite people. I remember, for instance, books such as Will Durant's story of Oriental civilization, and Mahatma Gandhi's[13] accounts of the struggle to drive the British out of India.

Book after book showed me how the white man had brought upon the world's black, brown, red, and yellow peoples every variety of the sufferings of exploitation. I saw how since the sixteenth century, the so-called "Christian trader" white man began to ply the seas in his lust for Asian and African empires, and plunder, and power. I read, I saw how the white man never has gone among the nonwhite peoples bearing the Cross in the true manner and spirit of Christ's teachings—meek, humble, and Christ-like.

I perceived, as I read, how the collective white man had been actu- 30 ally nothing but a piratical opportunist who used Faustian machinations to make his own Christianity his initial wedge in criminal conquests. First, always "religiously," he branded "heathen" and "pagan" labels upon ancient nonwhite cultures and civilizations. The stage thus set, he then turned upon his nonwhite victims his weapons of war.

I read how, entering India—half a *billion* deeply religious brown people—the British white man, by 1759, through promises, trickery, and manipulations, controlled much of India through Great Britain's East India Company.[14] The parasitical British administration kept tentacling out to half of the subcontinent. In 1857, some of the desperate people of India finally mutinied—and, excepting the African slave trade, nowhere has history recorded any more unnecessary bestial and

---

11. **John Brown** (1800–1859): In 1859 Brown and his followers attacked the arsenal at Harpers Ferry, intending to arm the slaves and encourage them to rise up in rebellion against their masters.—ED.

12. **Herodotus** (484?–425? B.C.): Greek historian whose account of the Persian Wars was the first narrative history in the Western world.—ED.

13. **Mahatma Gandhi**: Mohandas K. Gandhi (1869–1948), dubbed "Mahatma" or "Great-Souled," advocated nonviolence in the fight for Indian independence from British rule.—ED.

14. The British **East India Company**: Chartered by Elizabeth I in 1600, this association of merchants was given rights to develop the colonies of the British Empire on the Indian subcontinent.—ED.

ruthless human carnage than the British suppression of the nonwhite Indian people.

Over 115 million African blacks—close to the 1930s population of the United States—were murdered or enslaved during the slave trade. And I read how when the slave market was glutted, the cannibalistic white powers of Europe next carved up, as their colonies, the richest areas of the black continent. And Europe's chancelleries for the next century played a chess game of naked exploitation and power from Cape Horn to Cairo.

Ten guards and the warden couldn't have torn me out of those books. Not even Elijah Muhammad could have been more eloquent than those books were in providing indisputable proof that the collective white man had acted like a devil in virtually every contact he had with the world's collective nonwhite man. . . .

Mr. Muhammad, to whom I was writing daily, had no idea of what a new world had opened up to me through my efforts to document his teachings in books.

When I discovered philosophy, I tried to touch all the landmarks of philosophical development. Gradually, I read most of the old philosophers, Occidental and Oriental. The Oriental philosophers were the ones I came to prefer; finally, my impression was that most Occidental philosophy had largely been borrowed from the Oriental thinkers. Socrates, for instance, traveled in Egypt. Some sources even say that Socrates was initiated into some of the Egyptian mysteries. Obviously Socrates got some of his wisdom among the East's wise men.

I have often reflected upon the new vistas that reading opened to me. I knew right there in prison that reading had changed forever the course of my life. As I see it today, the ability to read awoke inside me some long dormant craving to be mentally alive. I certainly wasn't seeking any degree, the way a college confers a status symbol upon its students. My homemade education gave me, with every additional book that I read, a little bit more sensitivity to the deafness, dumbness, and blindness that was afflicting the black race in America. Not long ago, an English writer telephoned me from London, asking questions. One was, "What's your alma mater?" I told him, "Books."

▪ **CONSIDER THE SOURCE**

1. Summarize the stages of Malcolm X's homemade education.

2. Explain Malcolm X's assertion that "up to then, I never had been so truly free in my life." What constitutes freedom for him?

3. How, according to Malcolm X, has history been "whitened"? What examples does he give to support this assertion?

4. Why does Malcolm X want his children to read *Wonders of the World*? What do you think impressed him when he read it?

▪ **CONSIDER THE IMPLICATIONS**

5. Compare the self-educating programs of Malcolm X and Benjamin Franklin ("A Bookish Inclination," pp. 29–36). What prompts each man's education? What use do they make of their reading? How does the physical act of copying texts serve their purposes?

6. Both Malcolm X and Jimmy Santiago Baca (pp. 180–87) discovered literacy in prison. Citing at least these two examples, write a letter to your senator or congressional representative arguing for increased funding for literacy programs in federal and state prisons.

7. Read or review the discussions of school textbooks by Joan DelFattore (pp. 440–449) and William Noble (pp. 449–456). Analyze Malcolm X's account of the "whitening" of American history in terms of the controversies that DelFattore and Noble examine. What role does print play in promoting or authorizing views of history? To what extent do new-style textbooks remedy the problem Malcolm X describes?

8. Bring into class a book that surveys American history. In small groups, compare several books in their treatment of non-Europeans. How much space does each book give to the contributions of minorities to American culture and development? Can you see any difference between textbooks published before and after the 1980s?

9. Watch Spike Lee's 1992 movie *Malcolm X* and observe how Lee depicts Malcolm X's prison education. In your journal, compare the movie's treatment with that of the book. How effective is the film in rendering the private experience of reading that Malcolm X describes? How might you have done it differently if you were the director?

▪ ▪ ▪ ▪ ▪

MIKE ROSE

Reading My Way Out of South L.A.

Mike Rose (b. 1944) grew up in South Los Angeles, an area populated by working-class immigrants like his Italian parents. Early in his schooling he was channeled into "vocational education," and school became a place of boredom, frustration, and very little learning. He was eventually reclassified as "college material" and suddenly found himself at Loyola University, without the background and learning skills expected of a college student. Rose went on to become a poet, a teacher, and associate director of UCLA

From *Lives on the Boundary: The Struggles and Achievements of America's Underprepared* (New York: The Free Press, 1989), pp. 18–22.

Writing Programs; he is currently a professor of education at UCLA. He has won awards from the National Academy of Education, the National Council of Teachers of English (NCTE), and the John Simon Guggen-heim Memorial Foundation. His works include textbooks, two books on writer's block, Perspectives on Literacy *(1988), and* Lives on the Boundary: The Struggles and Achievements of America's Under-prepared *(1989), a widely acclaimed account of disadvantaged students. In this excerpt from* Lives on the Boundary, *Rose describes how his reading outside of the classroom enriched his life and provided fodder for his fantasies.*

Some people who manage to write their way out of the working class describe the classroom as an oasis of possibility. It became their intellectual playground, their competitive arena. Given the richness of my memories of this time, it's funny how scant are my recollections of school. I remember the red brick building of St. Regina's itself, and the topography of the playground: the swings and basketball courts and peeling benches. There are images of a few students: Erwin Petschaur, a muscular German boy with a strong accent; Dave Sanchez, who was good in math; and Sheila Wilkes, everyone's curly-haired heartthrob. And there are two nuns: Sister Monica, the third-grade teacher with beautiful hands for whom I carried a candle and who, to my dismay, had wedded herself to Christ; and Sister Beatrice, a woman truly crazed, who would sweep into class, eyes wide, to tell us about the Apocalypse.

All the hours in class tend to blend into one long, vague stretch of time. What I remember best, strangely enough, are the two things I couldn't understand and over the years grew to hate: grammar lessons and mathematics. I would sit there watching a teacher draw her long horizontal line and her short, oblique lines and break up sentences and put adjectives here and adverbs there and just not get it, couldn't see the reason for it, turned off to it. I would hide by slumping down in my seat and page through my reader, carried along by the flow of sentences in a story. She would test us, and I would dread that, for I always got Cs and Ds. Mathematics was a bit different. For whatever reasons, I didn't learn early math very well, so when it came time for more complicated opera-tions, I couldn't keep up and started daydreaming to avoid my inade-quacy. This was a strategy I would rely on as I grew older. I fell further and further behind. A memory: The teacher is faceless and seems very far away. The voice is faint and is discussing an equation written on the board. It is raining, and I am watching the streams of water form pat-terns on the windows.

I realize now how consistently I defended myself against the lessons I couldn't understand and the people and events of South L.A. that were too strange to view head-on. I got very good at watching a blackboard with minimum awareness. And I drifted more and more into a variety of protective fantasies. I was lucky in that although my parents didn't read or write very much and had no more than a few books around the house, they never debunked my pursuits. And when they could, they bought me what I needed to spin my web.

One early Christmas they got me a small chemistry set. My father brought home an old card table from the secondhand store, and on that table I spread out my test tubes, my beaker, my Erlenmeyer flask, and my gas-generating apparatus. The set came equipped with chemicals, minerals, and various treated papers—all in little square bottles. You could send away to someplace in Maryland for more, and I did, saving pennies and nickels to get the substances that were too exotic for my set, the Junior Chemcraft: Congo red paper, azurite, glycerine, chrome alum, cochineal—this from female insects!—tartaric acid, chameleon paper, logwood. I would sit before my laboratory and play for hours. My father rested on the purple couch in front of me watching wrestling or *Gunsmoke* while I measured powders or heated crystals or blew into solutions that my breath would turn red or pink. I was taken by the blends of names and by the colors that swirled through the beaker. My equations were visual and phonetic. I would hold a flask up to the hall light, imagining the veils of a million atoms dancing. Sulfur and alcohol hung in the air. I wanted to shake down the house.

One day my mother came home from Coffee Dan's with an awful story. The teenage brother of one of her waitress friends was in the hospital. He had been fooling around with explosives in his garage "where his mother couldn't see him," and something happened, and "he blew away part of his throat. For God's sake, be careful," my mother said. "Remember poor Ada's brother." Wow! I thought. How neat! Why couldn't my experiments be that dangerous? I really lost heart when I realized that you could probably eat the chemicals spread across my table.

I knew what I had to do. I saved my money for a week and then walked with firm resolve past Walt's Malts, past the brake shop, across Ninetieth Street, and into Palazolla's market. I bought a little bottle of Alka-Seltzer and ran home. I chipped up the wafers and mixed them into a jar of white crystals. When my mother came home, dog tired, and sat down on the edge of the couch to tell me and Dad about her day, I gravely poured my concoction into a beaker of water, cried something about the unexpected, and ran out from behind my table. The beaker foamed ominously. My father swore in Italian. The second time I tried it, I got something milder—in English. And by my third near-miss with death, my parents were calling my behavior cute. Cute! Who wanted cute? I wanted to toy with the disaster that befell Ada Pendleton's brother. I wanted all those wonderful colors to collide in ways that could blow your voice box right off.

But I was limited by the real. The best I could do was create a toxic antacid. I loved my chemistry set—its glassware and its intriguing labels—but it wouldn't allow me to do the things I wanted to do. St. Regina's had an all-purpose room, one wall of which was lined with old books—and one of those shelves held a row of plastic-covered space novels. The sheen of their covers was gone, and their futuristic portraits were dotted with erasures and grease spots like a meteor shower of the everyday. I remember the rockets best. Long cylinders outfitted at the base with three slick fins, tapering at the other end to a perfect conical point, ready to pierce out of the stratosphere and into my imagination: X-fifteens and Mach 1, the dark side of the moon, the Red Planet, Jupiter's Great Red Spot, Saturn's rings—and beyond the solar system to swirling wisps of galaxies, to stardust.

I would check out my books two at a time and take them home to curl up with a blanket on my chaise lounge, reading, sometimes, through the weekend, my back aching, my thoughts lost between galaxies. I became the hero of a thousand adventures, all with intricate plots and the triumph of good over evil, all many dimensions removed from the dim walls of the living room. We were given time to draw in school, so, before long, all this worked itself onto paper. The stories I was reading were reshaping themselves into pictures. My father got me some butcher paper from Palazolla's, and I continued to draw at home. My collected works rendered the Horsehead Nebula, goofy space cruisers, robots, and Saturn. Each had its crayon, a particular waxy pencil with mood and meaning: rust and burnt sienna for Mars, yellow for the Sun, lime and rose for Saturn's rings, and bright red for the Jovian spot. I had a little sharpener to keep the points just right. I didn't write any stories; I just read and drew. I wouldn't care much about writing until late in high school.

The summer before the sixth grade, I got a couple of jobs. The first was at a pet store a block or so away from my house. Since I was still small, I could maneuver around in breeder cages, scraping the heaps of parakeet crap from the tin floor, cleaning the water troughs and seed trays. It was pretty awful. I would go home after work and fill the tub and soak until all the fleas and bird mites came floating to the surface, little Xs in their multiple eyes. When I heard about a job selling strawberries door-to-door, I jumped at it. I went to work for a white-haired Chicano named Frank. He would carry four or five kids and dozens of crates of strawberries in his ramshackle truck up and down the avenues of the better neighborhoods: houses with mowed lawns and petunia beds. We'd work all day for seventy-five cents, Frank dropping pairs of us off with two crates each, then picking us up at preassigned corners. We spent lots of time together, bouncing around on the truck bed redolent with strawberries or sitting on a corner, cold, listening for the sputter of Frank's muffler. I started telling the other kids about my books, and soon it was my job to fill up that time with stories.

Reading opened up the world. There I was, a skinny bookworm ₁₀ drawing the attention of street kids who, in any other circumstances, would have had me for breakfast. Like an epic tale-teller, I developed the stories as I went along, relying on a flexible plot line and a repository of heroic events. I had a great time. I sketched out trajectories with my finger on Frank's dusty truck bed. And I stretched out each story's climax, creating cliff-hangers like the ones I saw in the Saturday serials. These stories created for me a temporary community.

It was around this time that fiction started leading me circuitously to a child's version of science. In addition to the space novels, St. Regina's library also had half a dozen books on astronomy—*The Golden Book of the Planets* and stuff like that—so I checked out a few of them. I liked what I read and wheedled enough change out of my father to enable me to take the bus to the public library. I discovered star maps, maps of lunar seas, charts upon charts of the solar system and the planetary moons: Rhea, Europa, Callisto, Miranda, Io. I didn't know that most of these moons were named for women—I didn't know classical mythology—but I would say their names to myself as though they had a woman's power to protect: Europa, Miranda, Io . . . The distances between stars fascinated me, as did the sizes of the big telescopes. I sent away for catalogs. Then prices fascinated me too. I wanted to drape my arm over a thousand-dollar scope and hear its motor drive whirr. I conjured a twelve-year-old's life of the astronomer: sitting up all night with potato chips and the stars, tracking the sky for supernovas, humming "Earth Angel" with the Penguins. What was my mother to do but save her tips and buy me a telescope?!

It was a little reflecting job, and I solemnly used to carry it out to the front of the house on warm summer nights, to find Venus or Alpha Centauri or trace the stars in Orion or lock onto the moon. I would lay out my star maps on the concrete, more for their magic than anything else, for I had trouble figuring them out. I was no geometer of the constellations; I was their balladeer. Those nights were very peaceful. I was far enough away from the front door and up enough from the sidewalk to make it seem as if I rested on a mound of dark silence, a mountain in Arizona, perhaps, watching the sky alive with points of light. Poor Freddie, toothless Lester whispering promises about making me feel good, the flat days, the gang fights—all this receded, for it was now me, the star child, lost in an eyepiece focused on a reflecting mirror that cradled, in its center, a shimmering moon.

▪ **CONSIDER THE SOURCE**

1. Compare Rose's classroom memories with his recollections of his chemistry experiments at home. How do specific details contribute to his descriptions?

2. Explain what Rose means when he says, "I was limited by the real." How does reading free him from the "real"?

3. What kind of reading does Rose indulge in? Why do you suppose he selected the books he chose?

4. List the various characterizations Rose gives of himself. Which ones come
   from books?

■ **CONSIDER THE IMPLICATIONS**

5. Compare Rose's memoir with Sven Birkerts's recollections of his early
   reading (pp. 21–29). What do books provide each boy? How are their
   reading environments similar? What role do their parents play in their
   reading?

6. In your journal, describe your first experience reading a book that completely absorbed you. What book was it? Why did it capture your imagination? What fantasies did it enable you to indulge in?

7. Rose lovingly describes the heroic fantasies generated by the books he
   read. Discuss how print enables such fantasies. How does print compare
   with other media, such as radio, television, or movies in this regard? How
   about computer games? Which ones "open up the world" and which ones
   restrict it?

8. Rose's book *Lives on the Boundary,* mixes autobiographical recollections like
   this one with expository prose directed toward an audience of teachers
   and others concerned with the state of American education. Using details
   from Rose's memoir, rewrite this selection as an argumentative essay.

■ ■ ■ ■ ■ ■

HELENA MARÍA VIRAMONTES

An Island of Flight in the Barrio

— *When there are no books to read, mere literacy is not enough. Chicana fiction writer Helena María Viramontes (b. 1954) grew up in the East Los
Angeles barrio in a household with eleven people and no books. Her only
contact with the written word came from the many hours she spent in the
public library. Therefore, when news reached her that an adjunct library in
the barrio was about to close its doors, Viramontes proposed a letter-*
— *writing campaign to encourage the city of Orange, California, to keep the
library open. Her open letter to friends of the library is preceded here by a
brief history that she wrote for this book. Viramontes is the author of* The
Moths and Other Stories *(1985) and coeditor of* Chicana Creativity
and Criticism *(1988). Her first novel,* Under the Feet of Jesus *(1995),
concerns migrant farm workers. She currently teaches creative writing at
Cornell University.*

HISTORY

Back in 1992, I was invited by Anthony Garcia, the librarian of "The Friendly Stop" Library, to come and do a reading. When I went, the trailer was packed with teens, mostly Chicana/o-Latina/os, who after school found refuge and help and books and friendship. Here, in the middle of the barrio, was an island of flight. Here, the teens were introduced to Latino/a books, something they didn't have access to in their respective schools. Here, they were safe. Here, they read. See, what people didn't understand, was here was a whole group of teens who felt at home surrounded by books and the infinity of wonder and the possibility that it belonged to them, too. I was so impressed that then and there I became an advocate, donating books and time.

When Anthony told me about the possible closing of "The Friendly Stop," I became increasingly angry. How dare the city do this? It was/is always the argument of "budget cuts," and "cutting costs," and I thought, don't they have any idea that it would cost a thousand times more in violence and tears and anger? Why close something that works so effectively? The right to read is as basic as the right to shelter, the right to breathe clean air, and the right to exercise imagination. Where else but in a library can this be done? It was then I realized that perhaps it was indicative of a growing climate of hate: We were growing in numbers and growing in strength through literacy and that could pose a danger to the powers of the status quo. Sometimes I think I carry this thought too far, while others don't think I carry it far enough. The accumulation of this climate exploded in the passing of Prop. 187.[1] Who is the target? These very students who came to "The Friendly Stop," who were becoming increasingly empowered by the books they read.

I was right in the middle of my graduate work at the time, but in good conscience, could not stand by and let them do this, at least not without a good fight. So I wrote the letter and sent it out to everyone I knew.

The response was overwhelming. Coupled with organized community protests, "The Friendly Stop" at least temporarily was kept open. But the ground that it sits on is as shaky as an earthquake. Too shaky for me to comfort myself. Too shaky.

January 12, 1993

Dear friends, writers, scholars, camaradas, y those of you interested: 5

Several weeks ago I was informed that a branch library in the city of Orange, appropriately called "The Friendly Stop/La Parada De Amistad," is in the process of being shut down. This deeply concerns me. I have been involved with the library, which is a trailer situated in the barrio of West-Central Orange. The one-room library is constantly vis-

---

1. **Prop. 187**: A controversial ballot measure passed in California in 1994 that barred illegal aliens from receiving education or medical benefits.—ED.

ited by Latina/os primarily, mostly teens, who have found the library a comfortable reprieve from the streets. They read, receive homework assistance, or become involved in the many bilingual activities the library has to offer. Take my word for it, it's a wonderful place. One of their most recent activities was "Books in the Hood: Promoting Reading to Youth." The concept of the event was created by Phil Yeh as a response to the riots in Los Angeles. Yeh writes: "There is simply too much violence and drugs going on in our streets and we have to become as passionate about pushing books as pushers are about pushing drugs."

We must keep the library open.

How many of us Chicana/o-Latina/o writers grew up in bookless homes? How many of us found solace and rapture in being able to attend the library, sit in a quiet place and read or have the right to exercise our imaginations? I, for one, made an office of a library chair and piece of table where I would sit for hours and read, conduct meetings, write in my journal, dream, even nap. In a house with eleven people, this library space was my private heaven. It was a space filled with floating answers, infinite questions, and the quiet time for meditation. It was a space for me like no other and we simply can't sit by and let this experience be ripped away from our youth who so very much need it AND want it.

That is why I am calling on all of my friends, and those interested in accelerating literacy among us. We know how important literacy is in the struggle against a system that maintains our oppression, keeps us out, or locks us up. We know how important a library in the heart of a barrio is. We all know how important it is to read.

So I'm calling for a chain letter campaign. . . .   10

Let's show them that we will not stand by and let them close a place that has proven time and time again to be a sacred place for us all. Next time you pick a book up, ready to enjoy the flight of a good story, think hard of the library about to close its doors.

All my love to you. I trust you will respond promptly as time is running out.

Que viva el libro y la palabra.[2]

Helena María Viramontes
Fiction Writer, Editor, Parent

[*Editor's note:* The Friendly Stop closed its doors in June 1994, when funding from federal and local grants ran out.]

■ **CONSIDER THE SOURCE**

1. What "costs" does Viramontes foresee from closing The Friendly Stop?
2. How, according to Viramontes, does literacy pose a threat to the status quo?

---

2. **Que viva el libro y la palabra**: "Long live the book and the word."—ED.

3. What effect does Viramontes's mixture of English and Spanish have on the reader? Who does it suggest she envisions as her audience?

■ **CONSIDER THE IMPLICATIONS**

4. Discuss the connection that Viramontes notes between literacy and political activism. How would C. H. Knoblauch (pp. 122–129) explain that connection? What type of literacy does Viramontes seem to be describing?

5. Several authors have described how and where they read books. Compare the reading environments described by Sven Birkerts (p. 21), Malcolm X (p. 164), and Mike Rose (p. 172) with the library that Viramontes recalls from her girlhood. What characteristics do they have in common? How does each facilitate reading?

6. In your journal, describe your recollections of a library or other refuge. What made the place special? What activities did that place permit that other places inhibit?

7. Libraries all over the country have felt the pinch of budget cuts. Investigate the library system in your community to see how it has changed in the last ten years. Are the libraries expanding or declining? What hours are they open? Do they offer any special programs for children, teens, seniors? Is there an adult literacy program? Write about your findings.

8. Write an essay in which you defend or refute Viramontes's thesis that reading is a "right."

9. Write a letter to city administrators of Orange, California, urging them to reopen The Friendly Stop. Alternatively, write a letter from a city official to Viramontes, explaining why The Friendly Stop was closed and suggesting that patrons visit the library's main branch.

▪ ▪ ▪ ▪ ▪ ▪

JIMMY SANTIAGO BACA

Coming into Language

Like Malcolm X, Jimmy Santiago Baca (b. 1952) "came into language" in prison, while he was serving time for drug possession. Much of that time was spent in solitary confinement where he was sent when he refused to work unless prison officials allowed him the opportunity to study for his high school diploma. Born into a poor Chicano family in New Mexico, Baca lived in an orphanage until he ran away at age ten. After that, he alternated between life on the streets and life in prison for minor offenses. In

From *Working in the Dark: Reflections of a Poet of the Barrio* (Santa Fe, N.M.: Red Crane Books, 1992), pp. 3–11.

this opening selection from his autobiographical Working in the Dark: Reflections of a Poet of the Barrio *(1992), he vividly describes the frustrating incoherence of illiteracy. Baca has won several awards for his poetry, including the Wallace Stevens Yale Poetry Fellowship, the 1989 International Hispanic Heritage Award, and the Before Columbus Foundation American Book Award. His works include* Immigrants in Our Own Land *(1978) and* Black Mesa Poems *(1989).*

On weekend graveyard shifts at St. Joseph's Hospital I worked the emergency room, mopping up pools of blood and carting plastic bags stuffed with arms, legs, and hands to the outdoor incinerator. I enjoyed the quiet, away from the screams of shotgunned, knifed, and mangled kids writhing on gurneys outside the operating rooms. Ambulance sirens shrieked and squad car lights reddened the cool nights, flashing against the hospital walls: gray—red, gray—red. On slow nights I would lock the door of the administration office, search the reference library for a book on female anatomy and, with my feet propped on the desk, leaf through the illustrations, smoking my cigarette. I was seventeen.

One night my eye was caught by a familiar-looking word on the spine of a book. The title was *450 Years of Chicano History in Pictures*. On the cover were black-and-white photos: Padre Hidalgo exhorting Mexican peasants to revolt against the Spanish dictators; Anglo vigilantes hanging two Mexicans from a tree; a young Mexican woman with rifle and ammunition belts crisscrossing her breast; César Chávez[1] and field workers marching for fair wages; Chicano railroad workers laying creosote ties; Chicanas laboring at machines in textile factories; Chicanas picketing and hoisting boycott signs.

From the time I was seven, teachers had been punishing me for not knowing my lessons by making me stick my nose in a circle chalked on the blackboard. Ashamed of not understanding and fearful of asking questions, I dropped out of school in the ninth grade. At seventeen I still didn't know how to read, but those pictures confirmed my identity. I stole the book that night, stashing it for safety under the slop sink until I got off work. Back at my boardinghouse, I showed the book to friends. All of us were amazed; this book told us we were alive. We, too, had defended ourselves with our fists against hostile Anglos, gasping for breath in fights with the policemen who outnumbered us. The book reflected back to us our struggle in a way that made us proud.

---

1. **Padre Hidalgo:** Father Miguel Hidalgo y Costilla (1753–1811) began the Mexican independence movement when he led an 1810 revolt against Spanish forces in Mexico; **César Chávez** (1927–1993): Founder of the United Farm Workers of America, a labor union representing the interests of the largely Hispanic population of migrant workers.—ED.

Most of my life I felt like a target in the cross hairs of a hunter's rifle. When strangers and outsiders questioned me I felt the hang-rope tighten around my neck and the trapdoor creak beneath my feet. There was nothing so humiliating as being unable to express myself, and my inarticulateness increased my sense of jeopardy, of being endangered. I felt intimidated and vulnerable, ridiculed and scorned. Behind a mask of humility, I seethed with mute rebellion.

Before I was eighteen, I was arrested on suspicion of murder after refusing to explain a deep cut on my forearm. With shocking speed I found myself handcuffed to a chain gang of inmates and bused to a holding facility to await trial. There I met men, prisoners, who read aloud to each other the works of Neruda, Paz, Sabines, Nemerov, and Hemingway.[2] Never had I felt such freedom as in that dormitory. Listening to the words of these writers, I felt that invisible threat from without lessen—my sense of teetering on a rotting plank over swamp water where famished alligators clapped their horny snouts for my blood. While I listened to the words of the poets, the alligators slumbered powerless in their lairs. Their language was the magic that could liberate me from myself, transform me into another person, transport me to other places far away.

And when they closed the books, these Chicanos, and went into their own Chicano language, they made barrio life come alive for me in the fullness of its vitality. I began to learn my own language, the bilingual words and phrases explaining to me my place in the universe. Every day I felt like the paper boy taking delivery of the latest news of the day.

Months later I was released, as I had suspected I would be. I had been guilty of nothing but shattering the windshield of my girlfriend's car in a fit of rage.

Two years passed. I was twenty now, and behind bars again. The federal marshals had failed to provide convincing evidence to extradite me to Arizona on a drug charge, but still I was being held. They had ninety days to prove I was guilty. The only evidence against me was that my girlfriend had been at the scene of the crime with my driver's license in her purse. They had to come up with something else. But there was nothing else. Eventually they negotiated a deal with the actual drug dealer, who took the stand against me. When the judge hit me with a million-dollar bail, I emptied my pockets on his booking desk: twenty-six cents.

One night in my third month in the county jail, I was mopping the floor in front of the booking desk. Some detectives had kneed an old

---

2. Pablo **Neruda** (1904–1973): Chilean poet; Octavio **Paz** (b. 1914): Mexican poet and Nobel laureate; Jaime **Sabines** (b. 1926): Contemporary Mexican poet; Howard **Nemerov** (1920–1991): Pulitzer Prize winner and poet laureate of the United States; Ernest **Hemingway** (1899–1961): American novelist.— ED.

drunk and handcuffed him to the booking bars. His shrill screams raked my nerves like a hacksaw on bone, the desperate protest of his dignity against their inhumanity. But the detectives just laughed as he tried to rise and kicked him to his knees. When they went to the bathroom to pee and the desk attendant walked to the file cabinet to pull the arrest record, I shot my arm through the bars, grabbed one of the attendant's university textbooks, and tucked it in my overalls. It was the only way I had of protesting.

It was late when I returned to my cell. Under my blanket I switched 10 on a pen flashlight and opened the thick book at random, scanning the pages. I could hear the jailer making his rounds on the other tiers. The jangle of his keys and the sharp click of his boot heels intensified my solitude. Slowly I enunciated the words . . . p-o-n-d, ri-pple. It scared me that I had been reduced to this to find comfort. I always had thought reading a waste of time, that nothing could be gained by it. Only by action, by moving out into the world and confronting and challenging the obstacles, could one learn anything worth knowing.

Even as I tried to convince myself that I was merely curious, I became so absorbed in how the sounds created music in me and happiness, I forgot where I was. Memories began to quiver in me, glowing with a strange but familiar intimacy in which I found refuge. For a while, a deep sadness overcame me, as if I had chanced on a long-lost friend and mourned the years of separation. But soon the heartache of having missed so much of life, that had numbed me since I was a child, gave way, as if a grave illness lifted itself from me and I was cured, innocently believing in the beauty of life again. I stumblingly repeated the author's name as I fell asleep, saying it over and over in the dark: Words-worth, Words-worth.[3]

Before long my sister came to visit me, and I joked about taking her to a place called Kubla Khan and getting her a blind date with this *vato* named Coleridge[4] who lived on the seacoast and was *malías* on morphine. When I asked her to make a trip into enemy territory to buy me a grammar book, she said she couldn't. Bookstores intimidated her, because she, too, could neither read nor write.

Days later, with a stub pencil I whittled sharp with my teeth, I propped a Red Chief notebook on my knees and wrote my first words. From that moment, a hunger for poetry possessed me.

Until then, I had felt as if I had been born into a raging ocean where I swam relentlessly, flailing my arms in hope of rescue, of reaching a shoreline I never sighted. Never solid ground beneath me, never a resting place. I had lived with only the desperate hope to stay afloat; that and nothing more.

---

3. William **Wordsworth** (1770–1850): English Romantic poet.—ED.

4. Samuel Taylor **Coleridge** (1772–1834): Author of the poem "Kubla Khan," said to have been inspired by an opium dream.—ED.

But when at last I wrote my first words on the page, I felt an island 15 rising beneath my feet like the back of a whale. As more and more words emerged, I could finally rest: I had a place to stand for the first time in my life. The island grew, with each page, into a continent inhabited by people I knew and mapped with the life I lived.

I wrote about it all—about people I had loved or hated, about the brutalities and ecstasies of my life. And, for the first time, the child in me who had witnessed and endured unspeakable terrors cried out not just in impotent despair, but with the power of language. Suddenly, through language, through writing, my grief and my joy could be shared with anyone who would listen. And I could do this all alone; I could do it anywhere. I was no longer a captive of demons eating away at me, no longer a victim of other people's mockery and loathing, that had made me clench my fist white with rage and grit my teeth to silence. Words now pleaded back with the bleak lucidity of hurt. They were wrong, those others, and now I could say it.

Through language I was free. I could respond, escape, indulge; embrace or reject earth or the cosmos. I was launched on an endless journey without boundaries or rules, in which I could salvage the floating fragments of my past, or be born anew in the spontaneous ignition of understanding some heretofore concealed aspect of myself. Each word steamed with the hot lava juices of my primordial making, and I crawled out of stanzas dripping with birth-blood, reborn and freed from the chaos of my life. The child in the dark room of my heart, that had never been able to find or reach the light switch, flicked it on now; and I found in the room a stranger, myself, who had waited so many years to speak again. My words struck in me lightning crackles of elation and thunderhead storms of grief.

When I had been in the county jail longer than anyone else, I was made a trustee. One morning, after a fistfight, I went to the unlocked and unoccupied office used for lawyer-client meetings, to think. The bare white room with its fluorescent tube lighting seemed to expose and illuminate my dark and worthless life. And yet, for the first time, I had something to lose—my chance to read, to write; a way to live with dignity and meaning, that had opened for me when I stole that scuffed, secondhand book about the Romantic poets. In prison, the abscess had been lanced.

"I will never do any work in this prison system as long as I am not allowed to get my G.E.D."[5] That's what I told the reclassification panel. The captain flicked off the tape recorder. He looked at me hard and said, "You'll never walk outta here alive. Oh, you'll work, put a copper penny on that, you'll work."

---

5. **G.E.D.**: General Equivalency Diploma, a high-school equivalency certificate.—ED.

After that interview I was confined to deadlock maximum security [20] in a subterranean dungeon, with ground-level chicken-wired windows painted gray. Twenty-three hours a day I was in that cell. I kept sane by borrowing books from the other cons on the tier. Then, just before Christmas, I received a letter from Harry, a charity house samaritan who doled out hot soup to the homeless in Phoenix. He had picked my name from a list of cons who had no one to write to them. I wrote back asking for a grammar book, and a week later received one of Mary Baker Eddy's[6] treatises on salvation and redemption, with Spanish and English on opposing pages. Pacing my cell all day and most of each night, I grappled with grammar until I was able to write a long true-romance confession for a con to send to his pen pal. He paid me with a pack of smokes. Soon I had a thriving barter business, exchanging my poems and letters for novels, commissary pencils, and writing tablets.

One day I tore two flaps from the cardboard box that held all my belongings and punctured holes along the edge of each flap and along the border of a ream of state-issue paper. After I had aligned them to form a spine, I threaded the holes with a shoestring, and sketched on the cover a hummingbird fluttering above a rose. This was my first journal.

Whole afternoons I wrote, unconscious of passing time or whether it was day or night. Sunbursts exploded from the lead tip of my pencil, words that grafted me into awareness of who I was; peeled back to a burning core of bleak terror, an embryo floating in the image of water, I cracked out of the shell wide-eyed and insane. Trees grew out of the palms of my hands, the threatening otherness of life dissolved, and I became one with the air and sky, the dirt and the iron and concrete. There was no longer any distinction between the other and I. Language made bridges of fire between me and everything I saw. I entered into the blade of grass, the basketball, the con's eye, and child's soul.

At night I flew. I conversed with floating heads in my cell, and visited strange houses where lonely women brewed tea and rocked in wicker rocking chairs listening to sad Joni Mitchell songs.

Before long I was frayed like a rope carrying too much weight, that suddenly snaps. I quit talking. Bars, walls, steel bunk, and floor bristled with millions of poem-making sparks. My face was no longer familiar to me. The only reality was the swirling cornucopia of images in my mind, the voices in the air. Mid-air a cactus blossom would appear, a snake-flame in blinding dance around it, stunning me like a guard's fist striking my neck from behind.

The prison administrators tried several tactics to get me to work. [25] For six months, after the next monthly prison board review, they sent cons to my cell to hassle me. When the guard would open my cell door to let one of them in, I'd leap out and fight him—and get sent to thirty-

---

6. **Mary Baker Eddy** (1821–1910): Founder of the Church of Christ, Scientist.— ED.

day isolation. I did a lot of isolation time. But I honed my image-making talents in that sensory-deprived solitude. Finally they moved me to death row, and after that to "nut-run," the tier that housed the mentally disturbed.

As the months passed, I became more and more sluggish. My eyelids were heavy, I could no longer write or read. I slept all the time.

One day a guard took me out to the exercise field. For the first time in years I felt grass and earth under my feet. It was spring. The sun warmed my face as I sat on the bleachers watching the cons box and run, hit the handball, lift weights. Some of them stopped to ask how I was, but I found it impossible to utter a syllable. My tongue would not move, saliva drooled from the corners of my mouth. I had been so heavily medicated I could not summon the slightest gesture. Yet inside me a small voice cried out, I am fine! I am hurt now but I will come back! I am fine!

Back in my cell, for weeks I refused to eat. Styrofoam cups of urine and hot water were hurled at me. Other things happened. There were beatings, shock therapy, intimidation.

Later, I regained some clarity of mind. But there was a place in my heart where I had died. My life had compressed itself into an unbearable dread of being. The strain had been too much. I had stepped over that line where a human being has lost more than he can bear, where the pain is too intense, and he knows he is changed forever. I was now capable of killing, coldly and without feeling. I was empty, as I have never, before or since, known emptiness. I had no connection to this life.

But then, the encroaching darkness that began to envelop me forced ₃₀ me to re-form and give birth to myself again in the chaos. I withdrew even deeper into the world of language, cleaving the diamonds of verbs and nouns, plunging into the brilliant light of poetry's regenerative mystery. Words gave off rings of white energy, radar signals from powers beyond me that infused me with truth. I believed what I wrote, because I wrote what was true. My words did not come from books or textual formulas, but from a deep faith in the voice of my heart.

I had been steeped in self-loathing and rejected by everyone and everything—society, family, cons, God, and demons. But now I had become as the burning ember floating in darkness that descends on a dry leaf and sets flame to forests. The word was the ember and the forest was my life.

I was born a poet one noon, gazing at weeds and creosoted grass at the base of a telephone pole outside my grilled cell window. The words I wrote then sailed me out of myself, and I was transported and metamorphosed into the images they made. From the dirty brown blades of grass came bolts of electrical light that jolted loose my old self; through the top of my head that self was released and reshaped in the clump of scrawny grass. Through language I became the grass, speaking its language and feeling its green feelings and black root sensations. Earth was my mother and I bathed in sunshine. Minuscule speckles of sunlight passed through my green skin and metabolized in my blood.

Writing bridged my divided life of prisoner and free man. I wrote of the emotional butchery of prisons, and of my acute gratitude for poetry. Where my blind doubt and spontaneous trust in life met, I discovered empathy and compassion. The power to express myself was a welcome storm rasping at tendril roots, flooding my soul's cracked dirt. Writing was water that cleansed the wound and fed the parched root of my heart.

I wrote to sublimate my rage, from a place where all hope is gone, from a madness of having been damaged too much, from a silence of killing rage. I wrote to avenge the betrayals of a lifetime, to purge the bitterness of injustice. I wrote with a deep groan of doom in my blood, bewildered and dumbstruck; from an indestructible love of life, to affirm breath and laughter and the abiding innocence of things. I wrote the way I wept, and danced, and made love.

■ **CONSIDER THE SOURCE**

1. Explain the effect on Baca of the *Chicano History* book he finds in the hospital library.

2. What relationship does Baca see between his illiteracy and his "sense of jeopardy"?

3. How does writing empower Baca? How does it silence him?

4. Trace Baca's use of figurative language over the course of the essay. What images does he use, and why?

■ **CONSIDER THE IMPLICATIONS**

5. Jimmy Baca claims that "through language I was free." Writing was a powerful tool that allowed him to "respond, escape, indulge; embrace or reject earth or the cosmos." In your journal, explore how you use the powers of language. Why do you write? What type of writing gives you most pleasure. Why?

6. Find some of Baca's books in your school library and read his poetry. What issues seem to concern him? Write an essay analyzing how his poems connect to the sense of identity he discovered in prison.

7. How would C. H. Knoblauch (pp. 122–30) categorize the type of literacy that Baca describes? What function does reading and writing serve for Baca? To what extent is that function political?

8. In class discussion, compare Baca's reaction to *450 Years of Chicano History* with Malcolm X's response to books about African American history (pp. 164–72). How does each man use books about his own race or ethnicity? What effect do such books have on their sense of identity?

9. Examine how Baca describes the reasons for his imprisonment and the be-

havior of prison officials. How does his point of view color your interpretation of his memoir? What community of readers is he writing for? Write an essay comparing Baca's approach to his audience with that of Zitkala-Ša (pp. 150–56) or Malcolm X (pp. 164–72).

10. Contact a nearby prison and inquire about literacy programs available to the prisoners. What sort of educational opportunities do prisoners have? How many prisoners attend classes? How extensive are library privileges? Are there any restrictions on reading and writing? If so, why? Present your findings in a report.

▪ ▪ ▪ ▪ ▪ ▪
....

MARK THOMPSON

The Evolution of The Advocate

For many groups of people, the problem of access is not one of illiteracy or the inability to acquire publications. Instead, the problem consists in the absence of publications to acquire. When no printed material exists to represent your group, you can feel invisible. As Mark Thompson explains in his introduction to Long Road to Freedom: *The Advocate* History of the Gay and Lesbian Movement *(1994), a newspaper or magazine functions as a "mouthpiece" for the community it serves. It represents that community to itself and to the mainstream. Thompson joined the staff of* The Advocate *in 1976 as a writer and assistant to the publication's designer; he wrote this overview of the magazine's history in his capacity as senior editor. He is also the author of* Gay Spirit: Myth and Meaning *(1987) and editor of* Leatherfolk: Radical Sex, People, Politics, and Practice *(1991).*

Few publications in American life have had a more intimate relationship with their readers than *The Advocate*. From its modest, homespun beginnings twenty-six years ago to its preeminence today as the largest gay and lesbian newsmagazine in the world, *The Advocate* has recorded the story of a remarkable community-in-the-making with proximity, verve, and a dedication not often found in the nation's press.

The swift growth of the gay and lesbian movement in the latter half of the twentieth century can arguably be counted as among the most significant social events of our time. Yet few outside the movement's

---

From the Introduction to *Long Road to Freedom:* The Advocate *History of the Gay and Lesbian Movement* (New York: St. Martin's Press, 1994), pp. xvii–xxvi.

ranks have contributed impartial witness to the emergence of this new, previously unrecognized class of people. Our rise to visibility, then to community, and, finally, to a full-fledged identity has remained to most of society a frightening, incomprehensible development of postmodern life, just one more rift in an increasingly anxious age. *The Advocate* has done its best to stand on both sides of this great divide; fueling the birth of a shame-free consciousness for the homosexual minority by offering principled reportage and positive imagery, while at the same time justifying the love that dare not speak its name to a prejudiced majority, which the novelist Christopher Isherwood[1] sharply referred to as "the heterosexual dictatorship."

Like any intimate union, the relationship between *The Advocate* and its readers is richly complex. The publication initially came into existence to bolster confidence and instill pride where before there had been precious little. In short order, as this overview of *The Advocate*'s evolution will show, it grew from being primarily a catalyst for social change to a critical voice within its own community. The pitch could range from sage to shrill, and later, some claimed, to curmudgeonly and somber, out of touch and asleep even to the sound of its own noise.

But over the years the publication has displayed a rare capacity for self-reinvention, much like the people it serves. It has been almost a case where the news—the facts of the day, the truth to be told—was simply *too* much, too much for *The Advocate* not to go a tad somnambulistic from time to time. From a period when homosexuals were regarded as second-class citizens, if regarded humanistically at all, to countless brutal assaults and numbing assassinations, to the mounting horrors of the plague, *The Advocate* has had to make sense of the senseless, take stock of outrageous injustices unfamiliar to the mainstream.

At its most awake, the tiny newsletter now grown to sleek news- 5 magazine stands as a hopeful beacon, holistic in its concern for a people previously broken, adamant in its conviction that the pieces stay mended together. "*The Advocate* was for many of us the first exposure we'd had to the idea that what we are is not bad," says one longtime reader, speaking for many. "It was a light in the dark by which we could navigate."

Not surprisingly, the publication itself germinated and took root in the darkness that so much of gay life inhabited a quarter of a century ago. This first issue, dated September 1967, was clandestinely printed in the basement of ABC Television's Los Angeles headquarters by gay men working there. Five hundred copies of the crudely composed twelve-page paper were quietly passed out for twenty-five cents each, mainly from behind the counters of the city's gay bars. In retrospect, from a basement duplicating machine to a half-lit bar was not an inappropriate

---

1. **Christopher Isherwood** (1904–1986): British novelist, activist, and icon of contemporary gay culture.— ED.

route for the paper; in 1967, most of gay life, if it was lived at all, was carried out underground, hidden and disguised by any means available.

Unrest and Uprising

Before *The Advocate* came secretly rolling out of the Silver Lake mailroom of one of America's largest media conglomerates, it had existed in an even more humble form as the newsletter of PRIDE, a local homophile organization whose acronym stood for Personal Rights in Defense and Education. The group was started in May 1966 by Steve Ginsberg, a local activist, and others concerned over mounting police harassment of Los Angeles homosexuals. . . . The particularly brutal Los Angeles Police Department raid on the Black Cat bar in the first hour of 1967. . . put the players in motion. Police swept into the Black Cat shortly into the New Year, severely beating an employee and arresting others there and at another nearby Silver Lake gay bar. A few weeks later, PRIDE organized its largest public protest ever in response to the attack, two and a half years before another police raid on the Stonewall Inn in New York City would similarly ignite gay men and lesbians on the East Coast.

The Los Angeles gay community was galvanized, and PRIDE swelled with new members. Among the recruits was Dick Michaels, a professional writer who had attended several meetings and PRIDE-sponsored dances the previous fall with his lover, Bill Rand, but who had nevertheless kept a reserved distance. The Black Cat raid and subsequent demonstration changed all that. The group needed every volunteer it could attract, and Michaels seized upon the task of revitalizing the group's struggling newsletter. "It soon became apparent that the gay community needed something more," he would later comment. "It needed something that had a chance to grow into a real newspaper; it needed a publication with widespread circulation, some way to get the word out about what was happening."

The almost nonexistent coverage of gay news by the *Los Angeles* 10 *Times* and the blatant homophobia of the *Hollywood Citizen-News* made the need for a regular gay newspaper all the more urgent. Michaels spent the summer of 1967 mulling over his idea for expanding the PRIDE newsletter, enlisting the help of Rand and their friend Sam Winston, a talented artist and cartoonist with an offbeat sense of humor who chaired PRIDE's publications committee. "We formulated a crude plan, which depended more on guts than sense," recalled Michaels, yet the trio persisted. They settled on a name, the *Los Angeles Advocate*, and decided to fill the new publication with as many features of a regular newspaper as they could: news, editorials, cartoons, letters, reviews, and classified ads. Their only investment was a used IBM typewriter bought for $175, which they used to laboriously type out each column with justified margins. Headlines were rubbed down one letter at a time from sheets of transfer type. The whole thing was composed at Michaels and Rand's small Wilshire district apartment and then reproduced in the mailroom where Rand and another PRIDE member worked.

By Michaels's own admission, the contents of the first issue were "hardly breathtaking." The incendiary front-page banner, U.S. CAPITAL TURNS ON TO GAY POWER, was actually the heading for a rather plodding piece about the Third National Planning Conference of Homophile Organizations (NACHO) held in Washington, D.C. Elsewhere in the eight-and-a-half-by-eleven sheet was a notice about *ONE's*[2] fifteenth anniversary, an editorial promising not "to be dull," news about the Black Cat court case, travel tips, and a review of *Queer Path* ("To say that this book emphasizes the darker, sadder side of homosexual life is putting it mildly"). Still, a claim had been staked.

The paper grew rapidly in content during the following months even though PRIDE disintegrated, a victim of internal squabbling and piled-up legal bills. Undaunted, *The Advocate's* founding trio bought the rights to the publication from the organization for one dollar and kept meeting their deadlines. By July 1968 the newspaper had a telephone and its first paid employee; the next month saw a completely typeset issue. On the first anniversary of its creation, fifty-five hundred copies of a professionally printed thirty-two-page *Advocate* were circulated throughout California's southland.

The local gay community seemed ready to embrace its new mouthpiece. In October, the Reverend Troy Perry placed a paid ad announcing the formation of the Metropolitan Community Church. Gay bars, restaurants, and other area businesses decided it was also time to take the wraps off gay life and be publicly affirmative. The paper was now tabloid size and sold openly in coin machines around the city. By June of 1969, the month the Stonewall Riots took place, the newspaper had acquired a national distributor and dropped the words "Los Angeles" from its name.

The Advocate had moved from a cramped apartment to a second-story suite of offices over a bar on Western Avenue. In due time, it would expand again to a roomy bungalow nearby. . . . [Jim] Kepner, who by then had joined the fledgling staff as an all-round reporter, remembers not only the grueling pace but the responsibility of seriously covering such a far-ranging field. "We were very concerned about staying in touch and giving representation to the various factions of the community," he says. "We knew the gay community was diverse, but we had no idea *how* diverse. We were also militant, which scared a lot of people."

There were other problems to attend to beside deadlines, payrolls, 15

---

2. *ONE:* Founded in 1953, it was the nation's first publicly sold gay publication.—Ed.

advertisers' demands, and the host of dilemmas any struggling publication must face—there was the matter of editorial control. Under Michaels's firm hand, there was little allowance for journalistic leeway. The paper was filled with news—all the minutiae one could possibly want to read about a movement then taking hold of a new generation of activists across the nation. Gay Liberation Fronts were springing up in city after city like exotic blooms after a rare desert rain. A new leadership was taking charge, too, spouting radical slogans of militancy that made older activists pale. Still, the journalism in *The Advocate* was seldom colorful, interpretive, or wide in scope. "He was straitlaced and not inclined toward the 'new journalism' of the underground press," says Kepner. "Michaels often rewrote things and argued with staff members who wanted a more free style."

The paper's regular editorial pages were filled with opinion, but often it seemed a case of one voice trying to outshout the other. Women's issues and the progress of other burgeoning liberation movements were given scant coverage. *The Advocate* was an important achievement—all the more so considering how far it had gone in such a short time—but it seemed insular, oddly cut off from the rest of the world. Given society's horrendous attitudes about homosexuality and the mainstream media's virtual blackout of gay concerns, Michaels's tact is understandable. Still, *The Advocate*'s first editor-in-chief covered his one neighborhood to the exclusion of others. But soon, all of that was to change.

GREAT EXPECTATIONS

By 1974, *The Advocate* had grown in stature and size to the point where it could justify its claim of being the "newspaper of America's homophile community." Even though the bulk of its coverage and readers were still based in Southern California, the periodical's print run had steadily increased to forty thousand copies per issue, and its pages included news accounts and columnists from other large cities, where *The Advocate* was available for purchase at select locations.

The movement's ambitions had grown dramatically as well; the social and political agenda set forth by gay and lesbian leaders, while not always precisely delineated, was at least well vocalized. The American Psychiatric Association's classification of homosexuality as a mental disorder had just come crashing down, thanks to the persistent efforts of activists, and municipal gay-rights ordinances were being proposed and state sodomy laws were being challenged nationwide. Job discrimination in government and private sectors, child custody, and legal reform were all on the front lines. Most important, men and women in previously unimagined numbers were coming out in small towns and big cities everywhere.

Among the swelling tide of immigrants to gay liberation was David

B. Goodstein, a millionaire investment banker from New York who had moved to San Francisco in the early seventies at the behest of his firm. Goodstein had barely arrived, however, when he learned that the bank was letting him go because it had discovered he was homosexual. Rather than sue for damages, Goodstein decided to stay in the Bay Area and become involved in gay liberation. . . . It was at the urging of a recent acquaintance, artist-editor Dennis Forbes, that Goodstein turned an eye toward *The Advocate*. . . . Nothing seemed to spring from his suggestion, though, until one day early in December 1974 when Forbes received a call. It was Goodstein, who excitedly announced that he had just purchased *The Advocate* with the intention of turning it into a truly national biweekly gay newsmagazine. He offered Forbes any job he wanted on the soon-to-be reconfigured staff except for the position of editor, which he had filled with John Preston, a young journalist based in New York.

As Goodstein not only wanted the content of the new *Advocate* to 20
read "more professionally" but its layout to be upgraded as well, Forbes signed aboard as the publication's designer. At the beginning of the new year, Forbes, Preston, and Goodstein's business manager traveled to Los Angeles, where they spent a month as "flies on the wall," says Forbes, observing the staff at work. Their presence was met with coolness and clear disapproval, as the old regime of reporters and editors nervously wondered what the outsiders had in mind. They had little time to ponder, however, since in short order the newly hired trio set about remaking *The Advocate* to Goodstein's mandate.

THIS ISSUE BEGINS NEW ERA FOR GAY PEOPLE, the cover banner on the January 29, 1975, edition grandiosely proclaimed beneath a full-page photograph of openly gay actor Cal Culver. Gone was the jumbled newspaper format with its endless columns of dull type; readers now held a graphically sophisticated tabloid-style magazine on newsprint. Gone, too, were many of the bylines and features of the old *Advocate*. Local gay activists were furious. Goodstein was sweeping *The Advocate* clean not only of previous journalistic ways, but of a whole school of Los Angeles activists who had once had unlimited access to the publication's pages.

"He wanted to work from within the power structure and work for change inside, rather than storming the barricades," explains Forbes about Goodstein's motives. "He saw *The Advocate* as the only serious voice in the gay movement, and as a result of that attitude there was a lot of negative reaction from people who were closed out." The new publisher had other changes in mind, too. To further shift emphasis from Southern California, he moved the paper's offices to a suburban office complex in San Mateo, about twenty-five miles south of San Francisco. Most of the old staff was let go or chose not to make the trek north. Those few contributors who did decide to weather the upheaval, like Jim Kepner, who remained in Southern California filing news reports for another year, found they frequently clashed with the policies of the opinionated new owner.

Goodstein was determined to make his $350,000 investment pay off, and he set out to make over not just *The Advocate* but the face of the gay movement as well. A. J. Liebling's[3] acerbic line "The freedom of the press belongs to him who owns one" had never been truer. Some movement spokespeople, especially adversaries of the powerful businessman, now simply ceased to exist in print, consigned to a gulag of unmentionable names. New personalities and voices were actively promoted and recruited. I was part of this fresh infusion, invited to contribute to the recast newsmagazine by Goodstein himself.

[By early 1976] Preston had left the publication and in his place was Robert I. McQueen, a darkly handsome and discerning man who had previously worked with the *Salt Lake Tribune* and the University of Utah. Key to McQueen's spirit of activism was his thorny relationship with the Mormon Church, which regarded his prominent role as the new editor of *The Advocate* with considerable dismay. Try as they might, they could not convince McQueen to return to the fold, so church elders, armed with an impressive document, showed up at *Advocate* headquarters one day and excommunicated their wayward son on the spot. McQueen was not afraid to write about his troubles with the Mormons, nor to publish articles about the struggles of other gay men and lesbians with organized religion. In fact, he was fearless about most matters of importance to his readers, and ushered in a new era of incisive journalism and lively coverage on a wide range of topics.

McQueen was a composer and poet during his off-hours, and so put a high emphasis on cultural reporting. Articles on opera appeared as frequently as pieces on disco, and believing above all else that reading mattered, he devoted numerous pages to the coverage of authors and their books. Famous names from all areas of the arts consented to be interviewed: Gore Vidal and Christopher Isherwood (in the first of their many *Advocate* profiles), Bette Midler and Lily Tomlin (both interviewed by Vito Russo near the beginning of their—and his—enterprising careers), and a surprising parade of others, from Beverly Sills to Timothy Leary.[4] Political analysis and news writing were also greatly improved; Randy Shilts began a series of ground-breaking pieces about health problems then troubling the gay community, and Sasha Gregory-Lewis[5]

25

3. **A. J. Liebling** (1904–1963): Essayist for *The New Yorker.*—ED.

4. **Gore Vidal** (b. 1925) wrote *Myra Breckenridge* (1968), a novel about a transsexual; **Vito Russo** (1946–1990) Activist and film historian who examined Hollywood's portrayal of homosexuality in his book *The Celluloid Closet* (1981); **Beverly Sills** (b. 1929) Opera singer; **Timothy Leary** (b. 1920) Psychologist often regarded as a spokesman for the 1960s counterculture.— ED.

5. **Randy Shilts** (1951–1995): His award-winning book *And the Band Played On* (1987) chronicles the political impact of the AIDS epidemic; **Sasha Gregory-Lewis** (b. 1947) An investigative journalist and author of *Sunday's Women: A Report on Lesbian Life Today* (1979) and *Slave Trade Today: American Exploitation of Illegal Aliens* (1979).—ED.

expanded coverage of women's issues and zealously delved into investigating the New Right's homophobic agenda.

The mainstream media began to take notice at last. HOMOSEXUAL PERIODICALS ARE PROLIFERATING, the *New York Times* announced in an August 1978 piece about *The Advocate* and other gay magazines such as *Christopher Street* and *Blueboy*. Articles in the *Chicago Tribune*, the *Wall Street Journal, Los Angeles Times, Time,* and *Newsweek* similarly reported on the expanding gay press, usually concentrating on the high-profile *Advocate*, and more often than not dwelling on readers' mobile lifestyles and expendable incomes rather than on their struggle for civil rights.

The mass coming-out and sudden ascendancy of the gay Boomers—the post-Stonewall generation who had come of age in the late sixties and early seventies—had infused fresh vitality into the movement, but not, it seemed, to *The Advocate*'s subscription list. Many former readers had dropped away with Goodstein's dramatic retooling, and it was argued that young urban readers had less need of a strictly gay publication than might have been foreseen. . . .

The main strength of the magazine seemed to be in those areas of the United States where gays were isolated and felt inhibited, due to employment or family ties, from living fully open lives. Advertising was problematic as well, with very few national accounts, aside from an occasional liquor or record company willing to take the plunge. Many used the excuse of *The Advocate*'s sexually explicit pull-out classifieds section (dubbed the "Pink Pages" after the color of the paper it was printed on) to keep from committing their advertising dollars. But Goodstein, like McQueen, remained adamantly sex-positive, and refused to let thinly veiled prejudice sway his conviction that the classifieds—many gay men's only sexual outlet—not be sacrificed for ready cash.

In truth, it was Goodstein's deep pockets that kept the publication going through the next several years, a period of rising backlash fueled by the antigay campaigns of Anita Bryant and John Briggs and the assassination of Harvey Milk,[6] who had finally achieved public office as a San Francisco city supervisor. With McQueen's astute hand on editorial content, Goodstein continued slowly to build the publication; a new generation of readers eventually replaced the old, and improvements such as better paper stock and four-color covers were incrementally added. Fresh talent, like associate editor Brent Harris and art director

---

6. **Anita Bryant** (b. 1940): Former Miss America and advertising spokesperson for the Florida orange growers, she formed the Save Our Children group to lobby against a Florida gay-rights ordinance in 1977; **John Briggs** (b. 1930) California member of Congress who drafted the unsuccessful Briggs Amendment in 1978, which tried to ban gays from teaching in the public schools; **Harvey Milk** (1930–1978) A symbol of gay participation in the mainstream political process, he was assassinated along with San Francisco mayor George Moscone in 1978.

Ray Larson (who had been friends of McQueen from his Salt Lake City days), were also brought on staff, adding their keen abilities to producing an ambitious publication with limited resources every two weeks.

Pat Califia was another addition to the staff during this time, contributing insightful essays about the nation's rising tide of "new puritanism" and stemming the flood the best she could with her widely read "Advisor" column in which readers' intimate queries about sex and relationships were candidly answered. Califia is one of the many writers and editors over the years for whom *The Advocate* has served as a springboard to a larger career.[7] 30

Taking potshots at Goodstein, and by extension *The Advocate*, had by the early eighties become a favorite sport of wags and critics within the community. The magazine seemed like a slow-moving target, the old "gray lady" of gay media, which by then had exploded into dozens of local publications; some large cities even had more than one gay newspaper, and the National Gay Press Association could count hundreds of attendees at its annual conventions. Upstart papers like the *New York Native* seemed feisty and daring when compared to *The Advocate*'s more cautious and reserved tone, especially when it came to reporting news about the spread of a mysterious new disease called GRID.[8] But if *Advocate* editors did not exactly leap on every new theory-of-the-week, neither did they shirk their considerable job of providing a comprehensive national picture on what was shaping gay and lesbian lives—for better or worse. And all on a budget that would make others in the profession blush.

Maintaining a balance between editorial objectivity and impassioned advocacy has not always been an easy task for the nation's gay journal of record. That the publication has appeared less than sure of itself over the years is evident; its reach exceeded its grasp at times, and it seems unfocused on certain issues. Perhaps it is enough to say that *The Advocate* has always been there; a fresh edition without fail every two weeks. Certainly, that is accomplishment enough during a time when every survival is worthy of note. But, of course, there are reasons beyond longevity alone to commemorate the ground-breaking trail—however vertiginous—*The Advocate* has blazed through our lives.

▪ **CONSIDER THE SOURCE**

1. Summarize the various functions that *The Advocate* tried to fulfill for its readership. How did those functions change over time?

2. Which "features of a regular newspaper" did the *Los Angeles Advocate* include? Why do you think the editors chose to include them?

---

7. **Pat Califia** (b. 1954): Lesbian essayist, editor, and fiction writer.—ED.

8. **GRID:** An acronym for Gay-Related Immunodeficiency, it was the first name of the disease now known as AIDS.—ED.

3. Describe the evolution of *The Advocate*'s physical appearance. How do the changes in format reflect changes in editorial direction? What changes does Thompson chart in the gay community during this period? How do the format changes of *The Advocate* relate to the "community-in-the-making" that he describes?

■ **CONSIDER THE IMPLICATIONS**

4. Scan the magazine and newspaper racks at your area's largest newsstand and survey the variety of physical formats that the publications use. Which publications look "professional" and which look amateur? Why? In your journal, analyze how the format of magazines affects your attitude toward the publications.

5. Examine a current issue of *The Advocate*. Where is it sold? How do bookstores market this publication? What magazines is it alongside? What publications does it most resemble? Who advertises in the magazine? What features does it include? What stories does is cover? Write an incisive portrait of the "gay journal of record."

6. Compare *The Advocate* with another publication targeted to the gay and lesbian community. What topics does each publication assume will interest readers? How do they differ in their conception of their gay/lesbian audience?

7. Thompson claims that *The Advocate* was "a catalyst for social change" in the gay community. In class, list other publications that serve particular segments of the reading public. What patterns can you discern in your list? How do those magazines and newspapers foster a sense of community among their readers? How do they establish political recognition for their readership? Why do the groups they serve require separate publications? Compare your list with the publications described by Laurie Ouellette in "'Zines: Notes from the Underground" (pp. 413–418).

8. Interview the editors of your campus's various publications, including the small club and organizational newsletters. What role do they feel their publications play on campus? What constituency do they serve? What difficulties do these editors face? What do they feel is the most pressing problem for their publications? Write an essay summarizing your findings.

9. Working in small groups, draft a proposal for a new publication that will serve an underrepresented segment of your school's population. Addressing your remarks to whoever controls the budget, justify the need for this publication and describe the benefits you foresee.

10. Using examples from the selections in this chapter, support or refute A. J. Liebling's statement that "freedom of the press belongs to him who owns one."

LynNell Hancock

Computer Gap:
The Haves and the Have-Nots

In spite of the hype about how the Information Highway will democratize knowledge, the problem of access remains as acute in the information age as it has ever been. In fact, disparities in access may prove more consequential in the future, as LynNell Hancock points out in this article from a 1995 Newsweek *cover story on "Technomania." Hancock, an education writer and general editor at* Newsweek, *has written about education for the New York* Daily News *and the* Village Voice *and taught in Columbia University's Graduate School of Journalism. Here she assesses the consequences of the "computer gap" that currently afflicts our nation's schools. Jobs and lifestyles will depend increasingly on "computer literacy," according to the experts, but many of today's students are already at a disadvantage. How about you? Will you be one of the haves or the have-nots in the information society?*

Aaron Smith is a teenager on the techno track. In America's breathless race to achieve information nirvana, the senior from Issaqua, a middle-class district east of Seattle, has the hardware and hookups to run the route. Aaron and six hundred of his fellow students at Liberty High School have their own electronic-mail addresses. They can log on to the Internet every day, joining only about 15 percent of America's schoolchildren who can now forage on their own for documents in European libraries or chat with experts around the world. At home, the eighteen-year-old e-mails his teachers, when he is not prowling the World Wide Web to track down snowboarding conditions on his favorite Cascade Mountain passes. "We have the newest, greatest thing," Aaron says.

On the opposite coast, in Boston's South End, Marilee Colon scoots a mouse along a grimy Apple pad, playing a Kid Pix game on an old black-and-white terminal. It's Wednesday at a neighborhood center, Marilee's only chance to poke around on a computer. Her mom, a secretary at the center, can't afford one for their home. Marilee's public-school classroom doesn't have any either. The ten-year-old from Roxbury depends on the United South End Settlement Center and its less than state-of-the-art Macs and IBMs perched on mismatched desks. Marilee has never heard of the Internet. She is thrilled to double-click on the stick of dynamite and watch her teddy-bear creation fly off the

From *Newsweek* (27 February 1995), pp. 50–53.

screen. "It's fun blowing it up," says the delicate fifth grader, twisting a brown ponytail around her finger.

Certainly Aaron was born with a stack of statistical advantages over Marilee. He is white and middle class and lives with two working parents who both have higher degrees. Economists say the swift pace of high-tech advances will only drive a further wedge between these youngsters. To have an edge in America's job search, it used to be enough to be well educated. Now, say the experts, it's critical to be digital. Employees who are adept at technology "earn roughly 10 to 15 percent higher pay," according to Alan Krueger, chief economist for the U.S. Labor Department. Some argue that this pay gap has less to do with technology than with industries' efforts to streamline their workforces during the recession. Still, nearly every American business from Wall Street to McDonald's requires some computer knowledge. Taco Bell is modeling its cash registers after Nintendo controls, according to Rosabeth Moss Kanter. The "haves," says the Harvard Business School professor, will be able to communicate around the globe. The "have-nots" will be consigned to the "rural backwater of the information society."

Like it or not, America is a land of inequities. And technology, despite its potential to level the social landscape, is not yet blind to race, wealth, and age. The richer the family, the more likely it is to own and use a computer, according to 1993 census data. White families are three times as likely as blacks or Hispanics to have computers at home. Seventy-four percent of Americans making more than $75,000 own at least one terminal, but not even one third of all Americans own computers. A small fraction—only about 7 percent—of students' families subscribe to online services that transform the plastic terminal into a telecommunications port.

At least in public schools, the computer gap is closing. More than half the students have some kind of computer, even if it's obsolete. But schools with the biggest concentration of poor children have the least equipment, according to Jeanne Hayes of Quality Education Data. Ten years ago schools had one computer for every 125 children, according to Hayes. Today the figure is one for twelve.

Though the gap is slowly closing, technology is advancing so fast, and at such huge costs, that it's nearly impossible for cash-strapped municipalities to catch up. Seattle is taking bids for one company to wire each ZIP code with fiber optics, so everyone—rich or poor—can hook up to video, audio, and other multimedia services. Estimated cost: $500 million. Prosperous Montgomery County, Maryland, has an $81 million plan to put every classroom online. Next door, the District of Columbia public schools have the same ambitious plan but less than $1 million in the budget to accomplish it.

New ideas—and demands—for the schools are announced every week. The Nineties populist slogan is no longer "A chicken in every pot" but "A computer on every desk." Vice President Al Gore has appealed to the telecommunications industry to cut costs and wire all schools, a task Education Secretary Richard Riley estimates will cost $10 billion. House Speaker Newt Gingrich stumbled into the discussion with a suggestion that every poor family get a laptop from Uncle Sam. Representative Ed Markey wants a computer sitting on every school desk within ten years. "The opportunities are enormous," Markey says.

Enormous, yes, but who is going to pay for them? Some successful school projects have relied heavily on the kindness of strangers. In Union City, New Jersey, school officials renovated the guts of a one hundred-year-old building five years ago, overhauling the curriculum and wiring every classroom in Christopher Columbus Middle School for high tech. Bell Atlantic provided wiring free and agreed to give each student in last year's seventh-grade class a computer to take home. Even parents, most of whom are South American immigrants, can use their children's computers to e-mail the principal in Spanish. He uses translation software and answers them electronically. The results have shown up in test scores. In a school where 80 percent of the children are poor, reading, math, attendance, and writing scores are now the best in the district. "We believe that technology will improve our everyday life," says principal Bob Fazio. "And that other schools will piggyback and learn from us."

Still, for every Christopher Columbus, there are far more schools like Jordan High School in South Central Los Angeles. Only thirty computers in the school's lab, most of them twelve to fifteen years old, are available for Jordan's two thousand students, many of whom live in the nearby Jordan Downs housing project. "I am teaching these kids on a system that will do them no good in the real world when they get out there," says Robert Doornbos, Jordan's computer-science instructor. "The school system has not made these kids' getting on the Information Highway a priority."

DONKEY KONG

Having enough terminals to go around is one problem. But another 10 important question is what the equipment is used for. Not much beyond rote drills and word processing, according to Linda Roberts, a technology consultant for the U.S. Department of Education. A 1992 National Assessment of Education Progress survey found that most fourth-grade math students were using computers to play games, "like Donkey Kong." By the eighth grade, most math students weren't using them at all.

Many school officials think that access to the Internet could become the most effective equalizer in the educational lives of students. With a modem attached, even most ancient terminals can connect children in rural Mississippi to universities in Asia. A Department of Education report released [in February 1995] found that 35 percent of schools have at least one computer with a modem. But only half the schools let students use it. Apparently administrators and teachers are hogging the Info Highway for themselves.

There is another gap to be considered. Not just between rich and poor, but between the young and the used-to-be-young. Of the one hundred million Americans who use computers at home, school, or work, nearly 60 percent are seventeen or younger, according to the census. Children, for the most part, rule cyberspace, leaving the over-forty set to browse through the almanac.

The gap between the generations may be the most important, says MIT guru Nicholas Negroponte, author of the new book *Being Digital*. Adults are the true "digitally homeless, the needy," he says. In other words, adults like Debbie Needleman, forty-three, an office manager at Wallpaper Warehouse in Natick, Massachusetts, are wary of the digital age. "I really don't mind that the rest of the world passes me by as long as I can still earn a living," she says.

These aging choose-nots become a more serious issue when they are teachers in schools. Even if schools manage to acquire state-of-the-art equipment, there is no guarantee that trained adults will be available to understand them. This is something that tries Aaron Smith's patience. "A lot of my teachers are quite illiterate," says Aaron, the fully equipped Issaqua teenager. "You have to explain it to them real slow to make sure they understand everything." Fast or slow, Marilee Colon, Roxbury's fifth-grade computer lover, would like her chance to understand everything too.

—*LynNell Hancock with Pat Wingert in Washington, Patricia King in San Francisco, Debra Rosenberg in Boston, and Allison Samuels in New York*

■ **CONSIDER THE SOURCE**

1. What "gaps" does Hancock describe? What causes does she assign to the disparities among computer users?

2. Describe the tone that Hancock uses in her article. How do her juxtapositions of examples contribute to that tone?

3. Who is Hancock's audience? What age group does she address? What income level? How do you know?

■ **CONSIDER THE IMPLICATIONS**

4. In small groups, compare the computer availability and usage in your various high schools. How many computers did your school have? How old were they? How were they used in classroom instruction? What factors seem to have determined the level of computer literacy you were offered?

5. Describe in your journal your own relationship with information technol-

ogy. Do you consider yourself "computer literate"? What was your first contact with computers? How do you use computers? Have you logged onto the Internet? The World Wide Web? Are you a have, a have-not, or a choose-not?

6. Read or review Linda Kerber's essay about women's education, (pp. 136–50), and M. Kadi's article "The Internet Is Four Inches Tall" (pp. 598–608). Have you witnessed or experienced any gender bias when it comes to instruction in computers or sciences? Conduct a class debate about whether women's and men's educations prepare them equally for the challenges of the computer age. Use examples from your own experience to defend your position.

7. Visit a local computer store and observe the sales personnel discussing the purchase of a new personal computer system with a variety of customers. Pay attention to how each customer is treated. What assumptions did the sales staff make on the basis of gender, age, economic status, or any of the other criteria Hancock describes? How were those assumptions manifested in the staff's behavior? Describe and analyze your observations in an essay, giving specific examples to support your assertions.

CHAPTER

3

WHAT DO YOU THINK?

Print and Opinion Making

What do you think the United States should do about the conflict in Bosnia? What movie should win the Academy Award for best picture? Which proposal to balance the budget is more fiscally responsible, the Republican or the Democratic one? Whose books are better, Stephen King's or John Grisham's?

Chances are, you have personal opinions about some of these questions. You know exactly what you think and can probably defend your position with facts and examples. About other questions, you're clueless. You need more information in order to form an opinion. If you stop and think about it, most of your "personal" opinions have been formed on the basis of information you received from other people.

You might decide the question about Best Picture by going to see the nominated films for yourself. And you can read King and Grisham to compare the two writers. But you probably don't have the time or inclination to visit Bosnia personally in order to form an opinion about U.S. foreign policy. And nobody who doesn't absolutely have to do it is likely to read the entire budget proposal of either political party. Our world is just too large and complex to permit firsthand evaluation of everything. We rely on others to sift through such information and pass on to us what we need to know.

As we've already seen, knowledge and power go hand in hand. Knowledge of current events and public policies guides the power of the electorate. Knowledge of brands and products translates into the power of the dollar. Because we're so dependent on secondhand sources for our knowledge, we need to learn to evaluate those sources carefully to see how they shape our views.

The information that shapes your attitudes is likely to come from a variety of sources, principally newspapers, magazines, television, and radio. Even if you don't regularly read a newspaper or magazine, the information you get from other sources will have been heavily influenced by the print media. Just think about how often a television news story will begin by saying "The *Wall Street Journal* today reported . . ." or "According to a report in this week's *New England Journal of Medicine. . . .*" But who decides what gets covered by those media and how it gets covered? More importantly, who decides what *doesn't* get covered, what information you don't get to evaluate? As this chapter's readings will demonstrate, many forces guide the media's output of information and imagery. These guiding forces may be political, whether from the left, the right, or the center. They may be the forces of the status quo, trying to maintain existing power structures or resisting the admission of new groups to power and influence. Just as frequently in our advertising-saturated culture, the forces that shape our opinions are commercial. Whatever the case, your challenge is to evaluate carefully all the information you receive and to recognize when your views are being unduly influenced.

MIRRORS AND GATES

One of the most cherished notions that we associate with the free press is "journalistic objectivity." Reporters don't act on behalf of the government, nor do they insert their own opinions into news stories. They act as neutral observers, passing on "just the facts, ma'am," as Sergeant Friday from *Dragnet* would say. Those facts come from direct observation or from documents and records that substantiate a reporter's story. Thirty years ago, CBS President Frank Stanton characterized the media this way: "What the media do is to hold a mirror up to society and try to report it as faithfully as possible." The press supplies us with reliable, verifiable, unbiased information that impartially reflects the society we live in.

Is this true? Is it even possible? The ace reporter can try to be impartial by presenting both sides of every story. He or she can present facts and let the reader interpret them. After deciding which facts should be presented, the reporter draws conclusions and inferences from facts, creating coherent patterns from disparate bits of information. Inevitably, human judgment informs the process of selecting and arranging information. Look back for a moment at LynNell Hancock's report in our last chapter on the computer gap between rich and poor (pp. 198–202). How would her story be different if she began it with the portrait of poor little Marilee Colon instead of rich cybersurfer Aaron Smith? What if she eliminated these portraits entirely and gave "just the facts"? By selecting and arranging the information into a "story," Hancock has helped you form an opinion about the facts she chooses to present.

Counteracting the mirror metaphor, some analysts of the media prefer the image of journalists as "gatekeepers" who control the flow of information to the reader or viewer. The gatekeepers select some things as newsworthy and not others, according to a number of factors. Typically, these include the following:

— Unusualness—does it interrupt life's routine?
— Impact—does it affect a lot of people?
— Prominence—does it involve important people?
— Timeliness—is it "new" or recent?
— Proximity—is it geographically or psychologically close to the audience?

The reporter decides what story to pursue and what to include in that story; an editor or producer decides how much of each story to run and what to cut out; someone else determines which stories to highlight on the front page or at the top of television news shows. Over and over, human judgment filters information before it gets to you, the reader or viewer. The gatekeepers' values and attitudes necessarily complicate (if not invalidate) the ideal of objectivity.

Moreover, the nature of language works against the impartiality we expect of the press. Words don't just "denote" explicit meanings. They also "connote" implicit associations. They call up suggestions, impressions, images. *U.S. News and World Report* might run a story on "pro-life demonstrations," while *Time* magazine calls them "anti-abortion protests." One historian writes of Columbus's "discovery" of America; another speaks of the "encounter" between Europeans and Native Americans; a third details how Columbus "conquered" self-governing indigenous peoples. The "facts" are the same, but the impressions they give differ dramatically. Language and labels shape our past, our present, and our future as we act on the knowledge we receive through words.

Journalists may not be able to be wholly objective, but they can strive for credibility. Giving the illusion of bias-free reporting, relying on verifiable facts, and eliminating unnecessarily loaded language are tactics that help make an author's words believable. Additional credibility can be gained by the appeal to authority, the use of experts. A reporter may not be an expert biologist, but may add credibility to a report on environmental policy by quoting people who devote their lives to the study of wetland ecosystems. Another reporter can beef up a story on arts funding by interviewing the head of the National Endowment for the Arts. However, as we all know from watching courtroom dramas, experts disagree. One expert may say that DNA testing is 99.5 percent accurate. Another expert will focus on that half-percent margin of error.

So what's the beleaguered reader or viewer to do? How can we figure out when we're being manipulated? How do we know what the truth is? Putting aside philosophical speculations as to the existence of absolute truth, shrewd consumers of information can weigh evidence by bringing a healthy skepticism to bear on anything that they read or view.

THE PAGE AND THE SCREEN

The first step in developing that skepticism is to assess the nature of the media that supply the information that shapes our opinions. The two media that concern us most in this regard are television and print. Let's begin with television, since that's increasingly where people get their news.

Television presents vivid, often unforgettable images. The moving pictures and sound present the illusion of reality, unmediated and unfiltered. "Seeing is believing," we often say, and so television seems highly believable. But what information do television's images communicate? Quite often, what people remember most from a TV news broadcast, for example, are the images, not the verbal content that accompanied them. Think back to last night's news. What do you recall? You may remember pictures of a war zone, but what part of the world was it in? Who was fighting? Which side were we supporting? The powerful visual content tends to overwhelm the story content.

Print reverses the balance, relying almost exclusively on verbal instead of visual content. The words may be supplemented by images, but the text takes precedence. Because the printed page sits tangibly before the reader, print easily offers a feature that television lacks: Printed words can be reread. If you miss something in a story, you can glance back a paragraph or two and review what was written. You can look for supporting evidence when an assertion sounds dubious. You can compare today's paper with yesterday's to see how a story has changed. You can even read the stories in any order you want. You can follow your own interests, lingering over stories that intrigue you, skimming those that don't.

Television exists in the continuous stream of time. Words float by quickly so it's hard to go back and check up on a TV story. Of course, VCR technology makes it possible to review television, but most of us don't routinely videotape the news for later study. Print requires no such technological maneuvering. It's fixed, easy to check, simple to reread. Television may be more "believable," but print is more "reliable" because it can so easily be held accountable.

Another key difference between spoken and written information is how we perceive the amount of reflection and deliberation that goes into each. Spoken words are usually spontaneous. They may be more susceptible to error because of this, but they simultaneously seem more truthful because they represent gut responses. In fact, you may have noticed the recent trend among local news shows to highlight this feature of oral discourse by encouraging "dialogue" between news anchors and reporters in the field. These "conversations," of course, are carefully scripted, and anything but spontaneous. Yet they convey the immediacy and intimacy that we associate with spoken words.

Printed words, by contrast, can be revised and polished. They may not be spontaneous, but they are carefully considered. Clarity of thought benefits from the kind of revision that print affords. Of course, writing doesn't guarantee clarity or accuracy. We often think it does, and so we grant printed words greater authority than spoken ones. "Put it in writing," we say, as if that were some sort of guarantee of truthfulness or accountability.

Finally, print and television offer different degrees of closure or finality. Television news is typically open-ended these days. Walter Cronkite may have summed up his broadcasts of the 1960s by pronouncing, "That's the way it is," but today's news shows are more likely to end with a plug for the late-night news: "Tune in at eleven o'clock for more on this breaking story." Most of the stories are so short and cursory that there is always more to tell. Print gives the opposite impression. Just look at the daily paper. The entire page is filled with stories and ads, top to bottom, left to right. The layout gives the illusion of completeness. The coverage is also deeper, or at least it's presumed to be, since any story usually takes longer to read than the thirty seconds that television news might allot to the same story.

Television exists as if on a stage. The actors in the foreground are highlighted, but we always know there's a background we're not seeing. Most of us are familiar enough with the staginess of TV to be skeptical of its claims, however much we "believe" what we see on some immediate level. Print does not seem staged in the way that television does. It foregrounds some stories, but it can also give the deep background—related stories fill in history, details, full texts of speeches.

As an example, look at Kato Kaelin, the unemployed actor who became an instant celebrity by virtue of living in O. J. Simpson's guest house. Once he was catapulted into the public eye, he spent months telling his story. He told it on the witness stand, on *Oprah,* on *Donahue,* on *Geraldo,* and on every television and radio talk show that would have him. After a year of saturating the airwaves, Kaelin (and ghost writer Mark Elliott) produced a book, *Kato Kaelin: The Whole Truth.* We can assume that Kaelin wrote it (and HarperCollins published it) to make money, but why should anyone need to pay twenty dollars to read it? What does the book offer that hasn't already been said? The book promises the "whole" story, as if the others were somehow manipulated, truncated, or partial because of the medium of television. Unlike the many hours of Kato Kaelin live, print gives his story authenticity. Whether or not consumers buy it for its truth value or its entertainment value, the book is marketed as a product that presents the complete story, the carefully deliberated story, the story that can be held accountable.

Readers, it would seem, can move back and forth between background and foreground to get the whole picture in a way that viewers cannot. But that's an illusion, too. There's a lot left out of the print account by players in the background whom we never see. Then, too, print can manipulate our emotions and bias our judgments, even as it seems to offer full disclosure. Just how personal our "personal opinions" will be depends on how wary we are as consumers of secondhand information.

THE READINGS

The selections in this chapter focus on the various ways that information gleaned from print can shape the views that we consider to be uniquely ours. Patricia Nelson Limerick provides historical perspective with her essay on how "verbal activity" formed—and continues to form—our images of the American West. She calls attention to newspapers, treaties, and contracts as documents that we must read with a critical eye if we want to avoid being "suckered" by the motives of those who created the texts. The remaining essays in the chapter concern three overlapping topics: news reporting, advertising, and book reviewing. Jeff Cohen arrestingly characterizes our contemporary free press as a propaganda vehicle for middle-of-the-road ideology, while Farai Chideya demonstrates how the scarcity of black journalists makes the press the voice of the white mainstream. The interplay between Michael Massing, A. M. Rosenthal, and the editors of the *Wall Street Journal* gives us an opportunity to scrutinize the background players who so often shape our news, but who so rarely appear to do so. Susan Faludi and Christina Hoff Sommers debate whether larger societal forces conspire to influence how news is presented—specifically news about American women. Joe Tye has no doubt that commercial interests affect the press's dissemination of information: He offers evidence to show that cigarette advertisers have directly influenced coverage of smoking-related health news in recent years. Separated by a distance of more than two centuries, Samuel Johnson and Gloria Steinem offer remarkably similar critiques of how ads affect the news stories that sit next to them on the page. Steinem also shows us the editorial obstacles advertisers present to women's magazines. Finally, Joseph Deitch and Katharine Weber offer an inside look at the world of book reviewing: how books are chosen for review, how publishers market their books to reviewers, and how reviewers influence consumers.

PATRICIA NELSON LIMERICK

Making the Most of Words: Verbal Activity and Western America

No territory of the United States has prompted a bigger flood of words than the American West, however you define it. Print proliferated stories of the untamed frontier, brave pioneers, and noble or ignoble savages. The western novels of Louis L'Amour continue to spread images of the Wild West, long after Holiday Inn, air conditioning, and cable TV have "civilized" such places as Tombstone and Deadwood. Historian Patricia Nelson Limerick (b. 1951) studies the "verbal activity" that has profoundly shaped our views of the West: She looks at languages, newspapers, and legal documents to see what role words played in how the West was and is imagined. Her essay comes from Under an Open Sky: Rethinking America's Western Past *(1992), a collection of essays by a new generation of western historians. Limerick, who teaches history at the University of Colorado, Boulder, has written* Desert Passages *(1985),* Legacy of Conquest: The Unbroken Past of the American West *(1987), and several essays to accompany books of photographs of the western landscape; she is also the co-editor of* Trails: Toward a New Western History *(1991).*

In 1849 Kit Carson[1] set out to rescue a white woman, providentially named Mrs. White, who had been taken captive by the Jicarilla Apaches. When the search party caught up with the Indians, it was too late; Mrs. White had just been killed. But Kit Carson came upon a surprising souvenir. "We found a book in the camp," he reported, "the first of the kind I had ever seen, in which I was represented as a great hero, slaying Indians by the hundreds."[2]

It could pass as a moment in postmodernist fiction:[3] Kit Carson, in the midst of an adventure, comes upon a printed and bound history of the adventures of Kit Carson. In experimental fiction Carson's course of action would be clear: Look up "White, Mrs., failed rescue of" in the index, and check to see what happened next. Surreal options aside, this incident highlights the complicated connection between words and actions in western American history. Much of western expansion had, of

---

From *Under an Open Sky: Rethinking America's Western Past,* ed. William Cronon, George Miles, and Jay Gitlin (New York: Norton, 1992), pp. 167–84.

1. **Kit Carson** (1809–1868): Legendary frontiersman and scout.—ED.

2. Milo Milton Quaife, ed., *Kit Carson's Autobiography* (Lincoln: University of Nebraska Press, 1966), p. 135.

3. **postmodernist fiction:** A style of writing notable for its discontinuities and experiments with literary forms and conventions.—ED.

necessity, a kind of heightened self-consciousness about it, as written words framed and shaped experiences, sometimes even before the experience had occurred. In 1849 the universe did indeed seem to be asking Kit Carson to reflect on the relationship between printed words and western actuality. Carson took a stab at the question: "I have often thought that Mrs. White must have read it [the book], and knowing that I lived nearby, must have prayed for my appearance in order that she might be saved."[4] But Carson, in life, was not the omnipotent, individualistic hero of the printed text. If Mrs. White did indeed read it, the book would only have given her false hopes. And in that case she would then represent a widespread pattern in the relationship between printed words about the West and their readers. That pattern is one of betrayal, and the critical question in any individual instance is this: Did the reader, unlike Mrs. White, live long enough to discover how much he or she had been deceived?

Writing and thinking about western history today, we have by no means escaped the treachery of words. We do not, to put it in the simplest terms, want to be suckers. Yet we know that western history is virtually the P. T. Barnum[5] of historical fields, providing opportunities galore for suckers to confuse literal fact with literary fact. Simply quoting from Kit Carson's ostensible autobiography raises one aspect of the problem. While Carson clearly did not write the autobiography, he did, apparently, dictate it. But whose words, exactly, appear on the page? How reliable was the transcriber? How reliable was Carson's own memory? These are questions we more often associate with the problems of Indian history: fitting oral traditions into written history; appraising and filtering written records of spoken words. But even a society devoted to recording the world in written words relies on oral transactions in the vast majority of its daily activities.[6] In dealing with print or speech, the words of the nonliterate or the words of the overliterate, one simply

---

4. Ibid., 135.

5. **P. T. Barnum** (1810–1891): Circus owner and showman famous for his dictum that "there's a sucker born every minute."—ED.

6. In an earlier draft of this paper I overstated the differences between print cultures and oral cultures; my understanding of the continued predominance of oral experience was much deepened by Professor Steven Siporin at Utah State, who provided me with assigned readings in western folklore, and by Professor Rolena Adorno at the University of Michigan, who called my attention to the illuminating collection "Selections from the Symposium on 'Literacy, Reading, and Power,'" *Yale University Journal of Criticism* 2:1 (1988) and to the work of Jack Goody, especially *The Interface between the Written and the Oral* (Cambridge, England: Cambridge University Press, 1987). Goody lists three aspects of the written-oral interface: "There is the meeting of cultures with and without writing, historically and geographically. There is the interface of written and oral traditions in societies that employ writing to varying degrees in various contexts. And there is the interface between the use of writing and speech in the linguistic life of any individual" (ix). Goody's work on these aspects is perfectly set up for applications to western America.

must learn to live with uncertainty, applying measured doses of skepticism and trust, incredulity, and confidence, as circumstances warrant.

The obligation to read words critically rests heavily on historians in any field, but it lands with particular weight on western American historians for three principal reasons. First, western historians inherit a long and sometimes embarrassing legacy from predecessors who did not keep a critical distance between themselves and the written words of the pioneers; this earlier breed of western historians adopted the terms, the point of view, and the assumptions of the people they studied. Their dependence on words like "civilization," "savagery," "frontier," and "progress" left western scholars echoing, not analyzing, the thinking of Anglo-American colonizers.

Second, the process of invasion, conquest, and colonization was the kind of activity that provoked shiftiness in verbal behavior. Filled with people using written words to justify, promote, sell, entice, cover up, evade, defend, deny, congratulate, persuade, and reassure, western history puts a premium on the critical evaluation of written words. In most settings, colonization was preceded by a torrent of words exaggerating the future and was followed by a torrent of words exaggerating the past, leaving western actuality sandwiched between romances of prospect and retrospect.

Third, the slipperiness of the essential term "West" leaves the field of western American history in a constant crisis of definition. If "the West" is sometimes in Massachusetts, sometimes in Florida, sometimes in Kentucky, sometimes in Illinois, sometimes in California, sometimes in Colorado, then what on earth is a "western American historian"? However one solves this conundrum, a western American historian had better be the sort of person who can comfortably cope with the shifting meanings of key words, the sort of person who is more challenged than irritated by questions of terminology, such as that endless refrain "What is the West?"

In this essay that question receives a simple answer: "the trans-Mississippi West." While I am, here and elsewhere, committed to a regional definition, I recognize that Anglo-Americans once thought of other regions of the United States as the West. It is, of course, essential to compare the history of conquest and colonization in the trans-Mississippi West with parallel events in other parts of the nation and the planet. Although I will not focus here on the colonial West, the trans-Appalachian West, the Old Southwest, or the Old Northwest, my examination of verbal behavior in the trans-Mississippi West may well be of some comparative interest to specialists in those other regions that briefly wore the label "West."

More important than a regional definition of "the West," this essay rests on an expansion and exploration of that phrase "verbal activity."[7]

---

7. Reading a first draft of this essay, my colleague at the University of Colorado Phillip Tompkins pointed out that I had unknowingly adopted a key term, "verbal behavior," from B. F. Skinner. Since I did not intend the essay to carry any "behaviorist" implications, I have accordingly shifted to the word "activity."

Most readers easing into an essay on words and the West might well expect reflections on the image of the West in literature, especially in fiction. I myself first took on the topic with a resigned feeling that I was off to the literary wars, off to the trenches to reread Cooper's *Leatherstocking Tales* and to keep track of the plots of dime novels.[8] This topic seemed to me, in other words, to give marching orders that directed me to the periphery, away from the daylight zone of political, economic, and social behavior and off to the twilight zone of myth and symbol. The phrase "verbal activity" proved to be my ticket out of this methodological despair. It is my hope that it can provide a similar service for other western historians, providing a category of analysis that permits cross-cultural comparisons, bridges the gap between oral and literate cultures, and squarely addresses the significance of the human relationship to words.

In substituting the study of verbal activity for the usual categories of "myth and symbol interpretation," or "literary history," one looks directly at what westerners have done to and with words and what words have done to and with westerners.[9] Just as one writes the history of the western environment by looking at what westerners have done to nature and what nature has done to westerners, so one approaches the history of verbal activity with an eye out for concrete and visible consequences. One looks, especially, for behavior that has become repeated, ritualized, and formulaic. This often entails returning to the turf of what used to be "myth and symbol" studies, but now one asks, much more concretely and literally, "What are the functions and consequences of

---

8. James Fenimore **Cooper** (1789–1851): Author of the **Leatherstocking Tales**, a series of five romantic novels of frontier life that includes *The Last of the Mohicans* (1826) and *The Deerslayer* (1841); **dime novels:** Cheaply printed thrillers, often set on the frontier.—ED.

9. Much of my approach here was inspired by my reading, fifteen years ago, the works of Kenneth Burke, especially *A Grammar of Motives* (1945; reprinted, Berkeley: University of California Press, 1969) and *A Rhetoric of Motives* (1950; reprinted, Berkeley: University of California Press, 1969). Phillip Tompkins and George Cheney of the University of Colorado reminded me of my debt to Burke by calling my attention to Burke's essays "Definition of Man" and "Terministic Screens," in *Language as Symbolic Action: Essays on Life, Literature, and Method* (Berkeley: University of California Press, 1966). Susanne K. Langer, *Philosophy in a New Key: A Study in the Symbolism of Reason, Rite, and Art* (1942; reprinted, Cambridge: Harvard University Press, 1976) was another useful source of ways of thinking about language. The work of folklorists is also an inspiration in ways of analyzing verbal activity; see Barre Toelken's essays "Northwest Regional Folklore" in *Northwest Perspectives: Essays on the Culture of the Pacific Northwest*, edited by Edwin R. Bingham and Glen A. Love (Seattle: University of Washington Press, 1979), pp. 21–42, and "Folklore in the American West," in *A Literary History of the American West* (Fort Worth: Texas Christian University Press, 1987), pp. 29–67. Also worth noting is J. Sanford Rikoon, "The Narrative of 'Chief Bigfoot': A Study in Folklore, History and World View," in *Idaho Folklife: Homesteads to Headstones*, edited by Louis W. Attebery (Salt Lake City: University of Utah Press, 1985), pp. 199–215.

this patterned human behavior toward particular words?" This approach does not simply recast the old territory of myths and symbols; it adds new subject matter that in turn refreshes our interpretation of the old material. . . .

ON THE BEACH: "BABEL" IN CALIFORNIA

. . . .Curing hides in Southern California in the 1830s, [Richard 10 Henry] Dana[10] took a great leap forward in the analysis of western history. What he saw taking shape on the San Diego beach was no Turnerian[11] wave of Anglo-Americans relentlessly pushing a frontier line westward. Instead, Dana observed an amiable, haphazard colony of men from "almost every nation under the sun." Convivial evenings bridged the cultural gaps. "[A]mid the Babel of English, Spanish, French, Indian, and Kanaka," Dana remembered, "we found some words that we could understand in common."[12]

In this passage, Dana captured a central fact of western American life that many later writers on the West barely noticed. As one of the great meeting grounds of the planet, the trans-Mississippi West played host to a remarkable convergence of languages. Dana's list is, of course, only the beginning. Add the whole array of Indian languages, the range of European languages beyond Dana's "English, Spanish, [and] French," and Asian languages from Chinese and Japanese through Vietnamese and Hmong, and "Babel" becomes a mild term for the flurry of words echoing through western America.

In episode after episode of cultural conflict, when different groups acted "as if" they were speaking different languages, they sometimes were. Conflicts over property, trade, or social behavior were often compounded by the failure to find a common language. When one speaks to people with a limited command of one's own native language, it is all too easy to slip into speaking as if the audience were childlike or stupid, an impression apparently confirmed by their struggles to speak in what is to them an alien language. Novitiates fumbling with new languages have a way of sounding simpleminded. Might it be that much of the

---

10. **Richard Henry Dana, Jr.** (1815–1882): His narrative of a sea voyage to California in 1834, published as *Two Years Before the Mast* (1840), presented Eastern readers with realistic accounts of life on the Pacific coast in the days of the fur traders.—ED.

11. **Turnerian**: Western historian Frederick Jackson Turner (1861–1932) delivered an address in 1893 on "The Significance of the Frontier in American History," claiming that the movement of European settlers from east to west across the continent was a dominant factor in creating the American national character.—ED.

12. Richard Henry Dana, Jr., *Two Years before the Mast* (New York: New American Library, 1964), pp. 151, 142–43.

Anglo-American belief in the inferiority of Indian, Hispanic, or Asian people emerged from this dynamic—from English speakers meeting non-English speakers and constructing judgments of the intrinsic character of "others" based on this mismatch in speech? Surely the English speakers would not have come out of these encounters looking much more impressive themselves. Apache people now have a standard set of teasing rituals concluding with the punch line "White men are stupid." Some of the inspiration for these jokes and others like them must have come from white people's fumblings with non-European languages.[13] Nonetheless, in studies of cultural contact and conflict the role played by language has gotten short shrift.

Despite the variety of speech and culture on the San Diego beach, Dana remembered, "We found some words that we could understand in common." That memorable sentence fixes our attention on the remarkable peacefulness of the nineteenth-century West, encapsulated in the fact that western people talked with each other far more than they shot at each other. And with the challenge of these linguistic differences, to talk with each other often required spirited intellectual effort. Sometimes that effort was anonymous and collective, as in the creation of the Pacific Northwest's Chinook jargon, combining Indian, English, and French words into a trading patois.[14] Sometimes it involved individuals working together in the quietest setting, as in Washington Territory during the 1850s when an old Indian man would join Phoebe Judson's family on social evenings and try "to instruct us in his language, by giving the names of different objects, while we, in turn, gave him the 'Boston' names." Judson realized that this exchange only scratched the surface: "As I listened to the legends and superstitions told in the limited Chinook jargon, of which I could understand only enough to make me long to know more, how I wished I could understand [the Indians] in their native tongue, as it flowed so fluently and softly from their lips; but the jargon and signs were our only method of communication."[15] She was quite right; communication by Chinook jargon was always limited. But it was also a considerable advance over silence and an even greater advance over hostile misunderstanding. Like Dana and his fellow hide curers, Judson and her Indian acquaintance "found some words that we could understand in common."

The professionals at providing these words were the interpreters who played essential roles in transaction after transaction—in trade, land

---

13. Keith H. Basso, *Portraits of "The Whiteman": Linguistic Play and Cultural Symbols among the Western Apache* (Cambridge, England: Cambridge University Press, 1979).

14. George Gibbs, *Dictionary of the Chinook Jargon, or Trade Language of Oregon* (New York: Cramoisy Press, 1863).

15. Phoebe Goodell Judson, *A Pioneer's Search for an Ideal Home* (Lincoln: University of Nebraska Press, 1984), p. 111.

acquisition, labor negotiation, and the acceleration and resolution of conflicts. The diversity of languages in use in the West made the translator a crucial mediator. Of necessity, the broad stream of relations between groups contracted to fit the narrow channel of the interpreters' words. The serious consequences of the interpreters' role appear in the records of every treaty-negotiating session. They appear more dramatically in instances like the Grattan Massacre of 1854, when an inept interpreter bungled the exchange between Lieutenant John L. Grattan and a group of Sioux, triggering the killing of Grattan's party and opening the Plains Wars. Interpreters were crucial players in western history, yet in a misallocation of energy symbolic of the problems of the field, we ended up with hundreds of studies of miners, cattlemen, cowboys, and farmers and with no systematic, book-length studies of interpreters and translators.[16]

Dana's passage raises one final issue: the relationship of power, dominance, and language. Neither temperament nor status inclined Dana to see the diversity of western languages as a problem in need of correction. As a common sailor, he did not have the authority to make others meet him on his linguistic homeground. Moreover, as a man who had already studied classical languages, he evidently found more pleasure than injury in the necessity of learning new words. But in his delight in languages, Dana did not represent all Anglo-Americans. The counterpoint to the intellectual curiosity and flexibility of Dana and Judson was the intolerance of Indian school officials who forbade the use of native languages or the irritability of more recent campaigners in the cause of making English the official language of various western states. In the midst of "all manner of languages," Richard Henry Dana wrote, "Spanish was the common ground upon which we all met; for everyone knew more or less of that."[17] One cannot help wishing that California historical preservation officials could secure a special provision, exempting the plot of land that housed Dana's beach "Babel" from the current "official English" law and establishing a museum on the site to explore both historical patterns: the celebration as well as the condemnation of western linguistic diversity.

OFF THE PRESS: THE NECESSITY FOR NEWSPAPERS

In newly created western towns, where one expects every ounce of energy would have gone to more practical concerns, newspapers were an almost immediate crop. It was, indeed, peculiar that Anglo-

---

16. I have found Kenneth Haltman's Yale seminar paper "'Sober and Obedient': Preliminary Notes to a Biographical Index of Nineteenth Century Indian-White Linguistic Interpreters on the North American Frontier" to be very useful; Haltman plans a book-length study in the future.

17. Dana, *Two Years*, p. 151.

Americans would leap with such urgency into the production of paper with printed words. But it was another example of the compulsion to write and to read demonstrated in many episodes of Anglo-American colonization. With dutifully recorded diary entries, anxious trips to check the mail and carefully packed editions of the Bible or of Frémont's reports,[18] westerners showed their dependence on the written word as a device to hold things together when the process of expansion threatened to pull them apart. Yet for all the centrality of literacy as a mechanism of cultural (and personal) cohesion, we do not yet have studies of western literacy that are in any degree comparable with the studies of literacy in the colonies and early republic.

Newspapers are, of course, prime sources for the study of verbal activity in the American West.[19] They embody the community's compulsion to put words to immediate and permanent use. They show editors and writers as active and practical wordsmiths, trying to hold the town together and to advance its fortunes (and their own) with their words. They record the self-consciousness and, often enough, self-dramatization of western settlements, targeting audiences at home and elsewhere with the message of the town's possible prosperity. Newspapers give us an excellent opportunity to study the booster mind at work, hovering between knowing misrepresentation and sincere self-deception and exhibiting a remarkable uniformity of expression, regardless of era, location, or local enterprise. Consider, for instance, the archetypal (if also unusually frank) thinking of a Southern California booster in the 1880s: "In fact, we may say that San Diego has a population of 150,000, only they are not all here yet."[20] Using a ritualized language, boosters constructed what they hoped would be self-fulfilling prophecies, spinning virtual incantations to bewitch the future into following their hopes.[21]

---

18. **Frémont's reports**: John Charles Frémont (1813–1890) led several expeditions to map the western territories. His *Report of the Exploring Expedition to the Rocky Mountains* (1843) and *Report of the Exploring Expedition to Oregon and North California* (1845) quickly became handbooks for western adventurers.—ED.

19. See David Fridtjof Halaas, *Boom Town Newspapers: Journalism on the Rocky Mountain Mining Frontier, 1850–1881* (Albuquerque: University of New Mexico Press, 1981). Charles Rankin, the editor of *Montana—The Magazine of Western History,* is presently completing a very insightful, comprehensive study of western journalism.

20. Quoted in Glenn S. Dumke, *The Boom of the Eighties in Southern California* (San Marino, Calif.: Huntington Library, 1944), p. 138.

21. See David Emmons, *Garden in the Grasslands: Boomer Literature of the Central Great Plains* (Lincoln: University of Nebraska Press, 1971) and Jan Blodgett, *Land of Bright Promise: Advertising and the Texas Panhandle and South Plains, 1870–1917* (Austin: University of Texas Press, 1988).

Newspapers reveal patterns of social change. When, if ever, did western newspapers go beyond boosterism, and what changes in their surroundings made that possible? The historian Charles Rankin points out one unfortunate symptom of a locale's "maturation": Newly founded western newspapers had more room for humor, whether in the play of the editor's personality or in the inclusion of hoaxes and spoofs, a trait that faded with the passage of time.[22] Newspapers provide case studies in cultural replication and regional distinctiveness: How did western newspapers resemble or differ from eastern newspapers? Newspapers reveal, as well, the workings of power. "Ruling elites," as Rankin puts it, made "the press a filter, rather than a conveyor of information," a case made dramatic by the Anaconda Copper Company's control of "almost three-fourths of the newspaper circulation" in Montana for "more than half a century."[23] Finally, newspapers provide us with opportunities for cross-cultural comparisons, returning us to an awareness of the West's language diversity. The region ended up stocked with newspapers in a variety of languages, serving various ethnic communities, American Indian, Chinese, Japanese, German, Norwegian, Swedish, Spanish, and Basque, to name a few.

Western history shows us repeatedly that we make a mistake when we take for granted any people's behavior toward written words. As compulsively literate sorts ourselves, historians have an obligation to step back in astonishment from a demonstration of white people's compulsive literacy like the one provided by the overlander William Swain. On the Humboldt River in 1849, preparing for the last, difficult crossing of desert and mountains, Swain made this diary entry:

> This forenoon the committee on which I am chosen and whose business is to report to the company upon the reports of the Agents and Directors met and spent the forenoon in examining its papers and making out its report. We recommend a reception of J. D. Potts', James Pratt's, H. Ladd's and F. Cook's reports, and a rejection of Thomas Rawson's and R. Hobart's reports and of the report of the Directors, for reasons set forth in our report.[24]

Here and elsewhere, Swain and his people seemed to be one step short of calling a halt to the journey while they ordered in a printing press to

---

22. Rankin points out additional aspects of change "from pioneer to modern journalism": "replacement of informal fraternity" among editors "with more formal professionalism"; "the transition from overt political dependence to increased political independence"; "economic consolidation"; "increased divisions of labor." Letter to the author, December 4, 1989.

23. Ibid.

24. J. S. Holliday, *The World Rushed In: The California Gold Rush Experience* (New York: Simon & Schuster, 1981), pp. 239–40.

ensure all these reports their necessary permanence. Compulsive literacy and ritualized language, shown in the struggles that produced thousands of western reports and newspapers, demand an ethnohistorical analysis. What did the use of words mean to these people, and why did their need for written language sometimes take precedence over what might have seemed to be more urgent matters of life and death?

IN THE COURTS: THE LAW AS LITERATURE

Mark Twain led the way in recognizing the West's rich potential as   20
a site for literary mining. He knew how central newspapers were to boomtown life and saw in legal language another variety of literature that could outdo James Fenimore Cooper in romantic expectations of an ideal West and Mark Twain himself in comedy. Taking office as the Nevada territorial secretary, Twain's brother had "sworn to obey his volume of written 'instructions.'" It quickly became clear, however, how utterly inappropriate those words were for the Nevada setting. Putting his brother's "instructions" to their proper use, Twain reported, "We used to read a chapter from them every morning, as intellectual gymnastics, and a couple of chapters in Sunday school every Sabbath, for they treated of all subjects under the sun and had much valuable religious material in them along with the other statistics."[25]

Along with metal pots and firearms, Bibles and plows, Euroamericans imported into the West cartloads of legal words—from territorial instructions to lawbooks. Western expansion produced its own flood of legal words: treaties; town, county, territorial, and state laws and regulations; judicial decisions, and precedents. Along with the words, and quite in line with Twain's allusion to religion, came the priesthood—a subpopulation of lawyers and judges and officials devoted to interpreting those words. Indeed, most of the central struggles over power, property, and profit in the West came to a focus in legislatures and courtrooms, with much of western history hinging on the question, Who could most effectively cite, interpret, or rewrite legal words to support their (or their clients') interests? The practicality of the outcome may have caused us to forget that litigation, in both written and oral argument, is finally a literary exercise.

Probably the most effective way to add solidity and consequence to the study of western words is to add words with legal status to the usual list of items that qualify as literature.[26] To poems, novels, autobiogra-

---

25. Mark Twain, *Roughing It* (New York: New American Library, 1962), pp. 148–49.

26. James Boyd White, *When Words Lose Their Meaning: Constitutions and Recon-*

phies, letters, diaries, and speeches, add "laws, treaties, executive orders, and instructions." And to the more conventional interpreters of words, add legislators, lawyers, judges, and officials charged with applying and enforcing statutes. With these additions, no one can claim to be mystified by the proposition that words and their interpretation carry consequence.[27]

To drive this point home, consider a set of words that have been more puzzled and pored over than anything ever written by a poet. According to the treaties of the 1850s, the Indians of the Pacific Northwest have the right "to fish at all their usual and accustomed places in common with the settlers." "Usual and accustomed places"? Do those words take precedence over any drawing of official reservation boundaries? Does "in common with" mean "some part of the catch"? If it does, then *which* part of the catch? A third of the catch? Half the catch? "Usual and accustomed," "in common with"—the words are evocative, maybe even poetic. They are certainly susceptible to multiple interpretations, as that unacknowledged literary critic Judge George H. Boldt surely knew when he handed down his controversial ruling in the 1970s, restoring fishing rights to Indian peoples in the Northwest.[28]

Western history is full of other examples of words consulted and puzzled over as if they were Scripture. When mining law awarded ownership of all the "angles, dips, spurs, and variations" of a vein to the person who claims the "apex" of that vein, lawyers took on the trying task of translating a verbal construction into a geological reality. The keepers of the national parks are charged with providing for the "enjoyment" of the parks "in such manner and by such means as will leave them unimpaired for the enjoyment of future generations," adding "enjoyment" and "unimpaired" to the list of words to be puzzled over and weighed, defended, and contested. Perhaps the culmination of the literary history we have more conventionally known as the law came with recent environmentalism, when forests and rivers, antelope and coyotes, found themselves well represented by lawyers. When inarticulate nature

stitution's of Language, Character, and Community (Chicago: University of Chicago Press, 1984) is a key book for the study of law and literature and, indeed, for the study of verbal activity altogether. White's definition of rhetoric asks to be applied to western history: "The study of the ways in which character and community—and motive, value, reason, social structure, everything, in short, that makes a culture—are defined and made real in performances of language" (xi).

27. Western legal history is presently thriving. See, for instance, the special issue ("Law in the West," edited by David Langum) of *Journal of the West* XXIV:1 (January 1985), and the newly created journal *Western Legal History* (first issue Winter–Spring 1988).

28. Alvin Josephy, *Now That the Buffalo's Gone: A Study of Today's Indians* (New York: Alfred A. Knopf, 1982), chap. 6.

found a voice in legal proceedings, the world of words had reached its peak of inclusiveness.[29]

As do newspapers, legal words provide abundant opportunities for cross-cultural comparisons. The prevailing trend in western legal history leads naturally in that direction; following John Phillip Reid and David Langum, western legal historians have been looking at "legal culture," at the whole complex of behavior by which people of different groups reveal their legal assumptions.[30] Written or oral, legal tradition is transmitted in words, by which power and influence flow toward the appointed custodians and interpreters of those words. The study of law and verbal behavior also provides important information on intergroup relations in the West.[31] Anglo-American efforts to prohibit Indians, blacks, or Asians from testifying in court give the most concrete demonstration possible that the key to keeping a group powerless is to keep it speechless, to deny it access to the formal record of conflict. By the same token, the training of Indian lawyers and the emergence of groups such as the Native American Rights Fund show the proposition in reverse, as Indian-initiated litigation revives the words of forgotten treaties and restores the voices of Indian tribes.[32] Once again, in the study of behavior toward words the divide between oral cultures and print cultures dissolves. With its combination of oral argument and written briefs and decisions, legal behavior itself falls right on the border.

▪ **CONSIDER THE SOURCE**

1. Summarize in your own words the three reasons that western historians in particular must read words critically, according to Limerick. Explain what she means by the "treachery of words."

2. Limerick looks at three kinds of "verbal activity" to discover "what westerners have done to and with words and what words have done to and with westerners." How does she believe differences in languages affected

---

29. Rodman Wilson Paul, *Mining Frontiers of the Far West, 1848–1880* (Albuquerque: University of New Mexico Press, 1963), pp. 173–75; Alfred Runte, *National Parks: The American Experience* (Lincoln: University of Nebraska Press, 1979) p. 104; and Christopher Stone, *Should Trees Have Standing? Toward Legal Rights for Natural Objects* (New York: Avon Books, 1974).

30. John Phillip Reid, *Law for the Elephant: Property and Social Behavior on the Overland Trail* (San Marino: Huntington Library, 1980) and David J. Langum, *Law and Community on the Mexican California Frontier: Anglo-American Expatriates and the Clash of Legal Traditions, 1821–1846* (Norman: University of Oklahoma Press, 1987).

31. John R. Wunder's work on the standing of the Chinese in western American law is on the forefront of ethnic and legal history; see his "Chinese in Trouble: Criminal Law and Race on the Trans-Mississippi West Frontier," *Western Historical Quarterly* XVII:1 (January 1986), pp. 25–41.

32. Charles Wilkinson, *American Indians, Time, and the Law: Native Societies in a Modern Constitutional Democracy* (New Haven: Yale University Press, 1986).

westerners? What role did newspapers play in creating the West? How do legal documents reveal the cultural assumptions of westerners?

3. What does Limerick mean by calling litigation a "literary exercise"? How do her examples help reinforce her argument?

4. How does Limerick target her essay to her audience of historians? What fields besides history does she rely on in her study of the American West?

■ **CONSIDER THE IMPLICATIONS**

5. In class make a list of historical events, facts, and images that you associate with "the West." Try to trace them back to their sources. Did they come from history books? Movies? Television shows? What cultural products generated the imagery?

6. Limerick claims that people "fumbling with new languages have a way of sounding simpleminded." Test this claim by examining how American media portray non-English-speaking people. Which groups or languages are most commonly depicted? How are they characterized? Do you see differences between representations in printed newspapers and magazines and those in movies and television?

7. In light of Limerick's characterization of the West as "one of the great meeting grounds of the planet," debate the merits of proposals that would designate English as the "official language" of the United States. You might wish to revisit C. H. Knoblauch's views on this issue (pp. 122–30).

8. Compare the urgency to establish newspapers that Limerick notes among westerners with the reasons given by Mark Thompson (pp. 188–97), and Charles Kikuchi (pp. 156–64), for their respective publications. What functions do the newspapers serve? Who are their target audiences?

9. Examine a small, local newspaper or your campus newspaper. Does the paper demonstrate Limerick's claims that newspapers show us "the booster mind at work" and also reveal "the workings of power"? To what extent does "boosterism" play a role in the content of the paper? Does the paper contain criticism of the "ruling elite"? Write an analysis of the paper.

10. Like Benjamin Franklin (pp. 29–37), Mark Twain lampoons legal language for its inappropriateness to everyday situations, as Limerick points out; both critics call attention to the ways audiences respond to such language. In your journal, articulate your response to the legal language found in a product warranty, a rental agreement, a disclaimer, or a similar text. Who does the language empower? What effect does it have on you as a reader?

11. Bring to class examples of contracts or other legal documents and analyze them in small groups. To what extent do the documents validate Limerick's claim that legal language is "susceptible to multiple interpretations"? How does the language empower those who interpret the words, the "legislators, lawyers, judges, and officials charged with applying and enforcing statutes"? As a group, write a paraphrase of one document in language that could be understood by nonlawyers. What are the advantages and disadvantages of each version?

JEFF COHEN

Propaganda from the Middle of the Road: The Centrist Ideology of the News Media

Like blackmail, propaganda *is an ugly word, calling up images of repressive governments, muzzled journalists, and uninformed citizens. That sort of thing doesn't happen in the United States . . . or does it? According to Jeff Cohen (b. 1951), our mainstream news media feed us a steady diet of propaganda dished up to look like news. This sort of propaganda, he argues, is designed to support the status quo. It repeatedly reassures American readers that our system, though sometimes flawed, invariably works for peace, democracy, and human rights. Cohen's essay was adapted from a keynote speech he delivered to the "Propaganda and Postmodernism" conference sponsored by the journal* Propaganda Review. *Cohen is the executive director of FAIR (Fairness and Accuracy in Reporting), a national media watchdog group based in New York. He has recently published* Adventures in Medialand: Behind the News, Beyond the Pundits *(1993) with Norman Solomon.*

When mainstream journalists tell me during debates that "our news doesn't reflect bias of the left or the right," I ask them if they therefore admit to reflecting bias of the center. Journalists react as if I've uttered an absurdity: "Bias of the center! What's that?"

The question to put to these journalists is a simple one: "While you're busy weeding out propaganda of the left and the right, who's protecting us from propaganda of the center—which is most of what the press dishes out every day?"

It is a strange concept to many in the media. They can accept that conservatism or rightism is an ideology that carries with it certain values and opinions, beliefs about the past, goals for the future. They can accept that leftism carries with it values, opinions, beliefs. But being in the center—being a centrist—is somehow not having an ideology at all. Somehow centrism is not an "ism" carrying with it values, opinions, and beliefs.

When we talk of the journalistic center or m-o-r[1] news media, we mean network TV news; *MacNeil/Lehrer;* "newspapers of record" such as the *New York Times* and *Washington Post* and the dozens of dailies offering similar news; AP and UPI; *Time; Newsweek;* etc.

The journalistic center is not inert. It moves. It shifted slightly left- 5

From *Extra!* (November 1989), pp. 12–14.

1. **m-o-r:** "Middle-of-the-road"—ED.

ward in the mid-seventies in the wake of Watergate[2] when reporters were allowed greater latitude for independent inquiry. In the eighties the journalistic center has veered strongly rightward.

The two main establishment papers—the *New York Times* and the *Washington Post*—are the primary propaganda organs of the center, though editorially they've tilted rightward throughout the eighties. As soon as Reagan was inaugurated, both papers began promoting White House charges that the Soviets were the primary source of terrorism in the world. The *Times* opposed the nuclear freeze, while the *Post* labeled two women's groups in the freeze movement as "Soviet stooge groups" (and later retracted the charge). Both papers vehemently opposed the nuclear weapons test halt initiated by Gorbachev.[3] The *Times* backed the neutron bomb.

The *Post* supported the Grenada invasion. Both supported the bombing of Libya.[4] The *Times* sided with Reagan against the Democratic Party leadership in supporting military aid to the contras in 1986. Both consistently backed so-called humanitarian aid to the contras. On the homefront, both papers increasingly opposed organized labor. Despite these conservative positions, the two papers are best seen as organs of the (corporate) center. . . .

But instead of belaboring the point that the centrist media are presently tilting rightward, I'd like to address some elements of centrist news propaganda that are somewhat constant.

If, for simplicity's sake, we define the left as seeking substantial social reform toward a more equitable distribution of wealth and power . . . and we define the right as seeking to undo social reform and regulation toward a free marketplace that allows wide disparities in wealth and power . . . then we can define the political center as seeking to preserve the status quo, tinkering with the system only very prudently to work out what are seen as minor glitches, problems, or inequities.

How do these three positions play out journalistically? Unlike left- 10 wing or right-wing publications, which are often on the attack, centrist propaganda emphasizes system supporting news, frequently speaking

---

2. **Watergate:** In June of 1972, then-President Richard Nixon authorized a break-in of Democratic Party offices in the Watergate building in order to obtain information that could aid him in the upcoming presidential election. *Washington Post* reporters Carl Bernstein and Bob Woodward exposed the crime and Nixon's subsequent cover-up attempts.

3. Mikhail **Gorbachev** (b. 1931): President of the Soviet Union from 1988 to 1991.—ED.

4. **Grenada invasion:** President Ronald Reagan ordered U.S. troops to invade the tiny West Indian island of Grenada in October 1983, allegedly to protect some 1,000 American citizens from the Cuban military personnel on the island; **bombing of Libya:** Reagan also authorized an airstrike on Tripoli in April 1986, in retaliation for Libya's continued support of terrorism.—ED.

in euphemisms. If scandals come to light, centrist propaganda often focuses less on the scandal than on how well "the system works" in fixing it. (This was the editorial drumbeat in the papers of record following both Watergate and Iran-contra.)[5] When it comes to foreign policy, centrist propaganda sometimes questions this or that tactic, but it never doubts that the goal of policy is anything other than promoting democracy, peace, and human rights. Other countries may subvert, destabilize or support terrorism. The United States just wages peace.

If propaganda from the center only emphasized the upbeat, pointing so much to silver linings that it never acknowledged the existence of clouds, there'd be a credibility problem. The public wouldn't believe such bland, euphemistic reporting. So, in selective cases, centrist propaganda does talk tough about government tyrants . . . especially if they're foreign tyrants or U.S. officials already deposed. (J. Edgar Hoover[6] was one such tyrant whose fifty-year reign at the FBI was rigorously scrutinized by the mainstream media only after he was dead and buried.) And centrist propaganda can take a tough look at a social problem . . . especially if it's deemed fixed or on its way to being fixed. Centrist propaganda can also make systemic critiques of a social system . . . as long as it's someone else's system.

Euphemisms in the centrist press (putting a good news gloss on bad news) can be quite comical. Prime examples are found in headlines that miscapsulize the news. A *New York Times* article after the Moscow summit (June 2, 1988) quoted Margaret Thatcher[7] commenting on Ronald Reagan: "Poor dear, there's nothing between his ears." The article's headline: "Thatcher Salute to Reagan Years." . . .

Centrist propaganda can sometimes contain blunt, social criticism—especially of someone else's system. A news story in the *New York Times* (July 23, 1989) on political discontent in Japan carried this headline: "Trembling at the Top: Japan's Ruling Elite Faces a Fed-up People." The *Times,* which has little trouble identifying a "ruling elite" in Japan, has never been able to discern such an elite in the United States in all its voluminous reporting on our political-economic system.

According to centrist propaganda, not only is the United States without a "ruling elite," the United States is also without an "empire"—unlike other countries. Lowly Vietnam has an empire. Big bad Soviet Union has an empire; the June *Christian Science Monitor World Magazine*

---

5. **Iran-contra:** In 1986, the press disclosed that the Reagan administration had secretly sold arms to Iran and channeled the profits to the Nicaraguan contra rebels in express violation of Congress's ban on aid to the contras.—ED.

6. **J. Edgar Hoover** (1895–1972): Headed the Federal Bureau of Investigation from 1924 until his death.—ED.

7. **Margaret Thatcher** (b. 1925): Conservative British prime minister from 1979 to 1990.—ED.

ran this subhead on its cover: "How Hungary's Quiet Revolution Is Eroding Moscow's Empire." In the thousands of mainstream news stories we've seen on the Nicaraguan revolution, never once has it been counterposed to "Washington's Empire." In the *Times*, "U.S. imperialism" is one of those dubious concepts that only appears between quote marks.

Is narrowing concentration of media ownership a grave problem in the United States? You wouldn't know it from the *New York Times*, which covered the Time/Warner merger[8] as just another business story, hardly mentioning threats to pluralism and the First Amendment. One of the few *Times* articles questioning the Time/Warner merger—"Time Deal Worrying Competitors" (March 7, 1989)—featured the complaints of Robert Wright, president of little ole NBC, owned by GE.

But you shouldn't conclude that the *Times* is unconcerned about media concentration. The *Times* is concerned . . . at least in Italy. "Newspaper Deal in Italy Stirs Debate Over Press Freedom" *(NYT*, April 24, 1989) probed the handful of firms that owns Italy's press. The candid article cited complaints of Italian reporters that "concentration produces bland journalism, especially on economic matters and political issues close to their owners' hearts or pocketbooks." The *Times* quoted one journalist saying his boss doesn't have to interfere in the newsroom "because there's total self-censorship." If only the *Times* paid as much attention to owner influences and self-censorship at home.

Is there a wide disparity in living conditions between America's rich and America's poor—between, for example, those who own or manage America's coal mines and the miners who work in them? Such contrasts could be graphically shown on TV and would probably attract big ratings. U.S. television is obsessed with *Lifestyles of the Rich and Famous* but not in juxtaposing the wealth of the rich against the poverty of, say, Donald Trump's kitchen workers or Lawrence Tisch's field hands.[9]

This didn't stop ABC's Rick Inderfurth *(World News Tonight,* July 21, 1989) who boldly took a film crew inside the ramshackle homes of striking coal miners and vividly contrasted that with the relative wealth of the mine managers. There's a catch: ABC's flirtation with Marxist agitprop[10] dealt not with conditions in Virginia but in the Soviet Union. (The militant strike against the Pittston coal company in Virginia—occurring at the same time as the Soviet strike—has been sparsely covered; the evening network newscasts devoted thirty-six minutes to the Soviet

---

8. **Time/Warner merger:** Time Incorporated Magazine Company merged with Warner Communications in March 1989, forming a huge conglomerate that straddles the communications and entertainment industries.—ED.

9. **Donald Trump** (b. 1946): Flamboyant American real estate tycoon; **Lawrence Tisch** (b. 1923): Became chair and CEO of CBS in 1990.—ED.

10. **agit-prop:** Derived from the Russian word *Agitpropbyuro, agit-prop* refers to agitation and propaganda, especially in Marxist causes.—ED.

miners in eight days, twice the coverage of the U.S. strike over four months.) One wonders if a TV reporter doing the same video class analysis of U.S. coal fields would have been fired for leftist bias.

In foreign coverage, the key signature of centrist propaganda is the portrayal of the United States as mediator or peacemaker. If rightist propaganda sees the United States caving in to communism and terrorism around the world . . . and leftist propaganda sees the United States subverting governments and Third World movements in the interests of a corporate elite and blind anti-communism . . . then centrist propaganda sees the United States going around the world doing good, mediating in the cause of peace. . . .

In Central America, the United States consistently worked to disrupt 20 the peace process, and the *Times* just as consistently portrayed U.S. policy as supporting it. The key element of the Esquipulas ("Arias") peace accord signed by the five Central American presidents on August 7, 1987, was the cessation of aid to the contras and other guerrilla groups in the region. The accord asked the United States by name to end all aid, even financial, to the contras. Despite U.S. subversion of the accord by continuing to finance and equip the contras, week after week for two years the *Times* told its readers that the United States supported the accord, e.g. (August 5, 1989): "The Bush administration supports the Arias plan but says the contras should not be disbanded until after the elections."

Another hallmark of centrist propaganda is to affirm, no matter what the evidence, that U.S. foreign policy is geared toward promoting democracy. Journalists are not unaware that the United States helped overthrow democratic governments, for example, in Guatemala in '54, Brazil in '64, Chile in '73, but these cases are considered ancient history no longer relevant.[11] (In centrist ideology, since the system is constantly fixing and renewing itself, U.S. abuses—even against democracy—become distant past overnight.)

Mainstream journalists respond to such criticism by explaining that articles for the daily press are not history texts and cannot include everything. That's true, but centrist propaganda finds space for certain histories and not others. Many, if not most, of the reports on Hungary this summer [1989] traced human rights abuses to the Soviet suppression of the Hungarian uprising in 1956. By contrast, reports on Guatemala's current human rights situation rarely traced events to the U.S.-sponsored coup of 1954. . . .

---

11. **U.S. helped overthrow . . . Chile in '73:** A conservative takeover of the government of Guatemala in 1954 owed its success to U.S. military intervention; Juscelino Kubitschek, elected president of Brazil in 1955, was overthrown by a rightist military coup in 1964, and Brazil did not return to a democratically elected leadership until 1989; Chilean general Augusto Pinochet overthrew and killed Socialist president Salvador Allende.—ED.

Besides consistently promoting peace and democracy overseas, according to centrist propaganda, the U.S. also consistently supports the good guys abroad. Not surprisingly, the good guys are always "centrists" on the political spectrum. At least that's what the media makes them out to be. And there's another media cliché one hears about our good guys, the centrists: they are perpetually hemmed in by the bad guys of left and right.

For years as El Salvador's armed forces and allied-death squads murdered thousands of civilians, media pundits told us that massive U.S. aid to Salvador's military was needed to bolster "centrists" such as José Napoleon Duarte.[12] In the media mantra of the time, Duarte was "hemmed in by death squads of the right and guerrillas on the left." In using that cliché, centrist media chose to promote a dubious State Department line, while ignoring groups such as Americas Watch and Amnesty International[13] who had documented that the security forces of the Duarte government worked hand in glove with the death squads. . . .

Perhaps the most graphic component of foreign policy coverage in 25 centrist media is the inordinate number of (often unnamed) government sources: White House, State, Pentagon, U.S. intelligence, etc. Some reporters act more like stenographers for those in power than journalists. When discussing these reporters, the phrase "centrist propaganda" misses the mark. "State propaganda" is a more apt description.

▪ CONSIDER THE SOURCE

1. What does Cohen mean by "ideology"? According to Cohen, how is centrism an ideology?

2. How does Cohen define the positions of the left, the right, and the center? Do you agree with his definitions?

3. How would you characterize Cohen's position on the political spectrum? What audience does he seem to be addressing?

▪ CONSIDER THE IMPLICATIONS

4. Follow the coverage of a foreign affairs story for several weeks in the mainstream press, such as *Time, Newsweek,* the *New York Times,* the *Washington Post,* the network TV news broadcasts, or other sources scrutinized in Cohen's essay. To what extent do Cohen's claims hold up? Do you see signs of the media clichés Cohen cites, such as the propping up of "cen-

---

12. **José Napolean Duarte** (1925–1990): Duarte was declared president of El Salvador by the military junta in 1980, but was forced from office in 1982. He was elected president in 1984 in a controversial election boycotted by the left.—ED.

13. **Americas Watch** (founded 1981) and **Amnesty International** (founded 1961): Organizations that monitor human rights violations and campaign against the detention of political prisoners.—ED.

trist" leaders, hemmed in by left and right? Do reporters rely heavily on unnamed sources?

5. Cohen offers several examples of newspaper headlines that "miscapsulize the news." Study a mainstream newspaper to see how accurately the headlines summarize the stories. What expectations do the headlines prompt in you as a reader? Do the stories fulfill those expectations? What impression of the day's events would you have if you only read the headlines?

6. Compile a list of euphemisms from watching the network TV news or reading one of the newspapers or other middle-of-the-road publications Cohen cites. Share your list with the class and discuss what these euphemisms are covering up.

7. Are you a leftist, a rightist, or a centrist? In your journal explore which characterization most accurately reflects your political beliefs. How do those beliefs affect your responses to news stories? Does the press customarily represent your view of American society? Or, does it usually reflect a different political slant? Give examples from recent events that support your views of the press.

8. Cohen's 1989 article discussed the "narrowing concentration of media ownership." Recently, Congress paved the way for even more consolidated ownership of media sources, permitting single corporations or individuals to own additional newspapers, magazines, and television and radio stations in the same market. Research the debate surrounding the Telecommunications Act of 1995. How do media analysts believe news coverage might be influenced by such ownership? What are the advantages and disadvantages of loosening restrictions on ownership? What mergers and changes in ownership were precipitated by the act? Write an essay assessing whether the issue is "just another business story" or constitutes a "[threat] to pluralism and the First Amendment."

▪ ▪ ▪ ▪ ▪ ▪

FARAI CHIDEYA

Who's Making What News?

"All the news that's fit to print"—that's been the slogan of the New York Times *throughout the twentieth century. But who decides what's "fit"? Who determines what constitutes "news"? Farai Chideya (b. 1969) looks at the racial make-up of America's news media and argues that the interests of white society largely control what makes news and how it gets cov-*

From *Don't Believe the Hype: Fighting Cultural Misinformation about African-Americans* (New York: Plume, 1995), pp. 241–53.

ered. The underrepresentation of minorities in the ranks of reporters, columnists, editors, and managers skews the way the media present non-white groups. Chideya worked as a reporter for Newsweek's Washington bureau from 1990 to 1993, where she won a National Education Reporting Award and a Unity Award for her stories. Here she focuses on African Americans, but her remarks apply as well to Hispanic Americans, Asian Americans, Native Americans, and women. Since 1994, Chideya has been an assignment editor at MTV News, where she combines her interests in hard news and popular culture.

News is what is exceptional. To a white in a dominant white society, being black is unusual. Having a black mayor is unusual. . . . [R]ace is the basis for deciding what is unusual, and what is, therefore, news.

> – Ohio State University journalism
> professors LEE B. BECKER, THOMAS A.
> SCHWARTZ, and SHARON C. WEST[1]

Washington Post magazine editor Jay Lovinger, interviewing black writer Jill Nelson for a job in 1986: "The Metro editors . . . were intrigued by your perspective."
   Nelson's mental reply: "I'm not surprised. Two white males running the Metropolitan desk in a 70 percent black city that is also the nation's capital are probably in a constant state of intrigue."

> – paraphrased from JILL NELSON's book on
> her experiences as a black writer at the *Post*
> magazine, *Volunteer Slavery: My Authentic
> Negro Experience*[2]

In August 1993, two thousand black reporters gathered to hear recalled Clinton civil rights nominee Lani Guinier[3] speak during the annual conference of the National Association of Black Journalists. Guinier analyzed how her views were consistently misconstrued and sensationalized in the media, then, quoting another author, chided journalists for being "stenographers to power." Rather than become offended by that statement—after all, it was a jab at the chosen career of almost everyone gathered—the audience greeted it with fervent clapping. Either it was a moment of unquestioning humility, or, despite their positions, the black

---

1. "Notable and Quotable" column, *Wall Street Journal* (April 17, 1984).

2. Jill Nelson, *Volunteer Slavery: My Authentic Negro Experience* (Chicago: The Noble Press, 1993).

3. **Lani Guinier** (b. 1950): A law professor at the University of Pennsylvania, Guinier was nominated in May 1993 for the position of Assistant Attorney General in charge of Civil Rights. Her nomination was withdrawn after opponents criticized her outspoken views on antidiscrimination policies.—ED.

journalists gathered were clapping heartily because they did not consider themselves part of "the media" being criticized.

Black journalists weren't the only ones at the NABJ conference. White managers, editors, and writers showed up to look for fresh talent (or, as some black journalists suspect, to look like they were looking). Among the recruiters was a *Washington Post* staff writer, Richard Leiby, who recounted his time as a minority-majority in a column titled "White Like Me." Sitting in a seminar, he wrote: "I suddenly feel blonder, paler, and more thin-lipped than I ever have in my life." His solution? To blend in. "And so you start dropping the '*gs*' on your 'ing'-verbs in a phony jive," he continued, ". . . 'like I was sayin' to him'—and even trying out 'dis' and maybe even 'yo.'" When a colleague tried to introduce Leiby at a dinner by telling everyone he'd written a story on Bob Marley,[4] he bristled. "I think I might have been patronized," he fretted. But before long, the conference was over, and everything was right again. "Flying back to Washington, I'm in first class, courtesy of my employer," he concluded. "There are a dozen white faces in first class, one black. I settle comfortably into my seat. For some reason, I feel like I'm already home."[5]

Events like the NABJ conference make clear just how deep the rift between African Americans and that perceived monolith "the mainstream media" is. Only five percent of reporters in the United States are black, making journalism one of this country's most segregated professions. That's a shameful statistic in and of itself—but just as important is how it affects the news. The dearth of black journalists is one of the key reasons why the media consistently overreports the violence and weaknesses of the black community and underreports black everyday life and its strengths. The body of overwhelmingly white reporters don't seem willing or able to locate hardworking African Americans but are able to hone in on urban deprivation, which they at least know where to go to find. The media's constant attention to certain stories—like crime—in the black community borders on obsession; the trend of ignoring others—like black community watch groups and self-help—borders on true pathology. And too often, news organizations are smug about their strengths, blind to their weaknesses, and surly when these weaknesses are pointed out.

OVERVIEW: BLACK REPRESENTATION IN THE MEDIA

Looking at the many African American television anchors on local stations and reading the strong black columnists who have joined media's comfortable upper ranks, it would be difficult at first to see just

---

4. **Bob Marley** (1945–1981): One of the leading figures in Jamaican reggae music.—ED.

5. Richard Leiby, "White Like Me," *Washington Post* (August 1, 1993).

how skimpy the African American presence in the media is. The reality? Although progress has been made, television and print media are still unwilling or unable to hire and retain black journalists—and are especially bad on promoting people into positions where they actually can influence the news America sees and reads. Here is an overview of the present and past of African Americans in the broadcast and print industries.

Broadcast

In the broadcast industry, only 6 percent of management jobs are held by African Americans.[6] Although most major cities now have at least one black news anchor, without black counterpart producers and managers, they too often have little control over the tone and content of the news.

Just three decades ago, the picture for black broadcasters and black viewers was grim. During integration, for example, WLBT-TV in Jackson, Mississippi, was so blatantly antiblack that it was rebuked by the Federal Communications Commission in 1965. In 1969, the station's license was revoked.[7] And at the 1965 convention of the National Association of Educational Broadcasters only five of the 1,600 attendees were black.[8]

Black broadcasters made great strides in the 1970s and early 1980s, when, for example, the late Max Robinson became the first African American to co-anchor a nightly national newscast. But during the Reagan years, the picture for black broadcasters dimmed some. Carole Simpson anchors ABC's weekend broadcasts, sometimes sits in for weekly anchor Peter Jennings, and also hosted one of the 1992 presidential debates. In the 1980s, Simpson summed up the disappearing opportunities by stating, "We're not voguish anymore."[9]

Even in areas which would seem "naturals" for black representation, like sports broadcasting, African Americans are underrepresented. In 1989, for example, of the sixty sports producers and directors at ABC, NBC, and CBS only one was black.[10]

---

6. 1992 Federal Communications Commission employment survey.

7. Jannette L. Dates and William Barlow, eds., *Split Image: African Americans in the Mass Media,* Second edition (Howard University Press, 1993), 421.

8. Dave Berkman, "Is Educational Broadcasting Segregated?" *NAEB Journal* (January/February 1966): 67–70.

9. Michael Massing, "Blackout in Television," *Columbia Journalism Review* (November/December 1982); and Robert Entman, "Representation and Reality in the Portrayal of Blacks on Network Television News," unpublished draft of article forthcoming in *Journalism Quarterly* (Northwestern University Department of Communications, 1993).

10. Norman Chad, "Balance of Power Affects Balance of Color," *Washington Post* (June 22, 1989).

Today, black anchors and co-anchors are standard on the nightly newscasts in most cities, but there are no regular black anchors on network nightly news.

Newspapers and Magazines

According to the American Society of Newspaper Editors, only 5 percent of newspaper reporters are black. Only 3.1 percent of newspaper managers are black.[11] 10

Forty-five percent of all newspapers do not employ *any* nonwhite reporters. And even major metropolitan dailies often employ shockingly few reporters of color. For example, only 15 percent of the staff of the *New York Times* is nonwhite, though the city is "majority-minority." Only 19 percent of the *Washington Post*'s staff is nonwhite, though the District of Columbia is 66 percent black. Both of these prominent papers are national in distribution and scope. But their small rosters of nonwhite journalists contribute to the alienation of many readers in the cities in which they're based.[12]

Many prominent newspapers are family-owned and run, which limits the chances that outsiders will reach top management ranks. The *New York Times,* for example, is owned by the Sulzbergers; the *Washington Post* Company (which also owns *Newsweek*) by the Grahams. Not only are the very top management positions passed from one generation to the next, but the broader group of people at the highest levels are picked to "fit in" at the organization, and are often selected in part because of personal referrals and recommendations.

In the magazine industry, which is both smaller than the newspaper industry and even more reliant on word of mouth and connections, only 2 percent of the senior ranks were African American.[13] Media giant Time Warner, which owns a stable of thirty magazines, including *Time* and *Sports Illustrated,* had no black top publishing executives in its magazine division until 1993. That year, Keith Clinkscales became president of the newly published hip-hop magazine *Vibe,* a joint venture between Time Inc. and musician/producer Quincy Jones.

Black reporters and writers were generally confined to black publications until the urban unrest of the 1960s. By the mid-seventies, about one hundred black journalists were working in mainstream publications. By the mid-eighties, that number had jumped to three thousand.[14] For example, in the 1950s, pioneering black journalist Bob Maynard got nearly three hundred letters of rejection because of his race. When he

---

11. "Newsroom minorities top 10 percent, ASNE 1993 survey shows," news release from the American Society of Newspaper Editors (March 30, 1993).

12. *Minority Employment Survey.* American Society of Newspaper Editors, 1994.

13. 1992 National Association of Minority Media Executives survey.

14. Dates and Barlow, *Split Image: African Americans in the Mass Media,* 392.

deleted all references to race in his inquiry letters, he would get interviews. But when he showed up for those interviews, he was dismissed
out of hand. In 1983, he became editor and publisher of the *Oakland Tribune,* the first time an African American had owned a "mainstream"
newspaper.[15] Before his death in 1993, financial difficulties forced him to
relinquish control of the paper.

Despite the checkered opportunities available to black journalists, 15
many have succeeded spectacularly. Well over twenty African Americans have won Pulitzer Prizes in the past decade, including Les Payne of
Newsday for International Reporting (1992), and two-time photography
winner Michel duCille of the *Miami Herald* (1986 and 1988). Photographer Moneta Sleet of Johnson Publications was the first African American to win a Pulitzer, in 1969.[16] Among those African Americans in
prominent positions in the newspaper and magazine industry are Jay
Harris, editor of the *San Jose Mercury News,* and Joel Dreyfuss, editor of
Information Week (and former editor of *PC* magazine).[17]

Race in the Newsroom

Many African American journalists struggle with the "inside-out-
sider" status the job confers. In the "White Like Me" column, Leiby
speaks of attending a book signing for Jill Nelson's *Volunteer Slavery.*
"Many whites at the *Post* view the book as mean-spirited, one-sided,
even paranoid. Can race possibly be so transcendent a factor in one's job
experience? Why is she so angry?"

"Why are they so angry?" is a common managerial chant about
African American reporters, who, it is not so secretly believed, should
be deeply grateful for the opportunities white editors give them. Less
well-explored is the anger of white reporters who've lashed out at the
"special preference" they imagine black reporters have. At the *Boston
Globe* in 1991, white reporter Peter Howe acted as a "deep throat"[18] for a
column in the rival daily on white *Globe* reporters' anger over "special
treatment" for blacks. Among those specifically skewered was African
American journalist Fred Biddle, who was promoted to the state
house—the same beat as Howe—after being courted by the *Washington
Post.* Biddle pointed out that no one complained when *Globe* sportswrit-
ers won higher salaries after being courted by the (now-defunct) sports
daily *The National.* And no one pointed out that Howe was hardly an objective observer—at the same time he was venting about an "alleged

---

15. Ibid., 392–93.

16. Ibid., 397.

17. The National Association of Black Journalists, *NABJ Journal,* vol. 2, no. 4
(December 1993/January 1994).

18. **"deep throat":** The nickname that Bob Woodward and Carl Bernstein gave
to their undisclosed source of information on the Watergate conspiracy.—ED.

double standard," he may have been feeling the pressure on his own beat.[19]

During the Los Angeles riots in 1992, black *Los Angeles Times* editor Linda Williams was quoted as stating that the paper was "bussing minority journalists into the city to use as cannon fodder."[20] Lower-ranking reporters and trainees, including the minorities Williams was speaking about, often get their start in suburban bureaus; if there's "urban unrest," they get to make a guest appearance on the choicer Metro beat. The 1992 riots were an ironic statement on how little things change. Three decades earlier, during the Watts riots, black copy boys were instantly promoted to reporters to fit the media's needs.

A 1993 study by the National Association of Black Journalists found widespread disagreement between blacks and white managers on career opportunities. Among the findings: Only half of black journalists thought their news organization made a serious effort to recruit black journalists; 91 percent of managers thought they did. Just under one-third of black journalists thought that bringing up racial issues damaged their chances for advancement. In July 1994, the National Association of Black Journalists hosted the first-ever joint meeting of African American, Hispanic American, Asian American and Native American journalists. Each of the four journalism groups has expressed a belief that race-based reporting in some way helps stereotype their communities and a desire to increase the representation of minority reporters at America's newspapers, magazines, and television stations.[21]

MYTHS OF BLACK MEDIA INFLUENCE

Time and time again, journalists (usually African American ones) have documented pervasive trends of biased coverage in the media. Yet, dishearteningly, the industry seems to have changed little in recent years.

In 1990, David Shaw did an extensive series on race and the media for the *Los Angeles Times*, criticizing coverage by his own and other papers. As he pointed out, "[A]part from truly major stories—a big election or earthquake . . . what's newsworthy is largely an arbitrary decision made by mostly white editors."[22]

20

---

19. Howard Kurtz, "Raises & Racism," *Washington Post* (November 2, 1991); and Kurtz, "Source of Leak Tracked Down at *Boston Globe*" (November 28, 1991).

20. Howard Kurtz, "Diverse Views of the News," *Washington Post* (March 2, 1993).

21. David G. Savage, "Minority Journalists Assail Crime Stories," *Los Angeles Times* (July 29, 1994).

22. David Shaw, "Newspapers Struggling to Raise Minority Coverage," *Los Angeles Times* (December 12, 1990).

Myth: *Even if African Americans aren't heavily represented among members of the media, black viewpoints are represented—if anything, overrepresented.*

Reality: Black viewpoints are consistently underrepresented in the mainstream media, and sometimes journalists are shockingly honest about their perceptions.

Said *60 Minutes* executive producer Don Hewitt at a speech at the University of California, Berkeley: "Listen, you got a whole section of America that talks sort of blackspeak that white America doesn't understand . . . even when they don't say 'Ax!' they say, 'Hey, man!' And if no one understands it, you can't tell it very well."[23] *60 Minutes,* of course, is considered one of America's more evenhanded media outlets.

The lack of African American journalists and African Americans as sources in the media has a profound effect on coverage of black issues. On April 6, 1990, the Associated Press ran a story titled "Bush Foresees Black as President." The body of the story was far different: it focused on how angry black leaders were about Bush's attempts to gut civil rights legislation.

Another example: On March 27, 1987, public television aired "Street Cop," a documentary on drug crime in Boston. They only aired footage from black neighborhoods, showing black dealers and users. [24] The reality of drugs in America is far different. The commander of the Boston Police Department's Drug Control unit admits: "We've arrested people from every town in the metropolitan area for buying drugs in the city. The majority are fully employed white males in their thirties."[25] The *Frontline* documentary ignored drug crime in white areas and, most important, the white suburban consumers who drive into the city for their fixes and keep the trade alive. America rarely sees these white users, even on public television.

Myth: *News about African Americans is not disproportionately "negative." Journalists would be "going out of their way" if they tried to publish more "positive" stories.*

Wrote *Washington Post* columnist Bob Levy: "Should visible columnists . . . go out of their way to publish positive news about black people, and should they label black news as such? I say heavens, no."[26]

---

23. Mark Zingarelli, "Ya Wanna Be a *60 Minutes* Producer, Eh?" *Mother Jones* (September/October 1993).

24. Kirk A. Johnson, "Can We Talk About Race," *Extra! Focus on Racism in the Media* (July/August 1992).

25. Holly Sklar, "Young and Guilty by Stereotype" *Z Magazine* (July/August 1993).

26. Bob Levy, "Bob Levy's Washington—A Need for Positive Black News?" *Washington Post* (September 17, 1990).

Reality: For most columnists, the vast majority of whom are white, black America *is* out of their way. Columns are powerful and incisive because they tend to be personal and anecdotal—but they are limited for the same reasons. Journalists, as might be expected (but is usually not acknowledged), tend to write what they know. To provide better coverage of African Americans would not be a matter of "going out of their way"—it would be a matter of journalists knowing their weak spots.

Despite the presence of columnists like the *Washington Post*'s 30 Pulitzer Prize-winning William Raspberry, the vast majority of newspapers do not give African American journalists the power and latitude of top editorial positions. Until 1993, when the paper hired Bob Herbert, the *New York Times* did not have a regular black editorial columnist.[27]

Mainstream media misses big stories as well as small ones. Nelson Mandela[28] finally gave his approval to ending economic sanctions against South Africa in October 1993; at the time he was in New York City and gave a press conference with David Dinkins.[29] Yet neither the *New York Post, Daily News,* nor *Newsday* thought it front-page news. And when the commandant of the Marine Corps said on national television that blacks and other minority officers were less proficient than whites, it was conveniently excised from the media. On the October 31, 1993, episode of *60 Minutes,* General Carl Mundy was asked why blacks make up nearly a third of Armed Forces enlistees but only about 10 percent of officers. Mundy said that "in the military skills, we find that the minority officers . . . don't do as well." Yet the vast majority of national newspapers did not pick up on his comments, allowing them to stand virtually unchallenged.[30]

CASE STUDY: SOME PICTURES ARE WORTH A THOUSAND WRONG WORDS

On March 1, 1993, the nationwide newspaper *USA Today* took the bold step of apologizing for misrepresenting members of the African American community. In this instance, the offending medium was largely pictorial—photographs of Los Angeles gang members. The young men were told they would appear in a story on exchanging their guns for jobs but instead appeared in a front-page, all-too-stereotypic story titled "Gangs Put L.A. on Edge."[31] It didn't mention the guns-for-

---

27. Pat Guy, "Columnist Keeps Style at 'Times,'" *USA Today* (July 19, 1993).

28. **Nelson Mandela** (b. 1918): Released from prison in 1990 after twenty-six years, Mandela became South Africa's first black president in 1994.—ED.

29. **David Dinkins** (b. 1927): Became the first African American mayor of New York City in 1990.—ED.

30. Howard Kurtz, "The Shot Not Heard Round the World," *Washington Post* (November 12, 1993).

31. Richard Price, "Gangs Put L.A. on Edge," *USA Today* (February 16, 1993).

jobs program, but rather speculated about the possibility of rioting after the second trial of the officers who beat Rodney King. It was a case of the facts being bent to fit the "news." In fact, when one of the young men showed up without a gun, the reporter, Richard Price, took the unusual and possibly unethical step of driving him to his mother's house to pick up his shotgun.

USA Today tried to play down the controversy at first. Two days after the article ran, the paper printed a one-sentence "clarification" at the bottom of a box on page one.[32] But eventually the paper was forced to bring the story out into the open. Los Angeles community activist CaShears, who arranged the guns-for-jobs photo op, was given the opportunity to write a long column on the aftermath. When he told the young men what had happened, CaShears wrote, he took "verbal abuse from my own people for bringing white guys into the projects to 'use and take advantage' of them again. . . . Yes, they were angry, but I saw more pain, hurt, and disappointment than anything else. Their trust had been betrayed. . . . I think you've done a disservice to my people who are very sensitive about a media portrayal of black males across America," he wrote in conclusion. "I feel that you've fanned the fires of racism, hatred, and division."[33]

While it was certainly admirable for the newspaper to print CaShears's statement, there were signs that the editors were not quite ready to consider all of the implications of this case. "On its own, the photograph was accurate," wrote an editor in a parallel column to CaShears's. "None of the subjects in the photo have denied being gang members or having access to guns."[34] That statement ignores the story's other failings: that its premise was sensationalistic and misguided. Using black gangs as the pivot of a story on the riots doesn't mesh with the fact that the vast majority of those who rioted were not gang members, nor were the majority of those arrested even African American. The constant emphasis on black potential for violence only heightens racial tensions and white fears.

THE BIG PICTURE

The positive side to the misrepresentations of African Americans in the media is that they spur more and more Americans to be critical of what we see and read. For example, a 1993 article in *Newsweek* about a brutal multisuspect Houston murder was accompanied by a stereotypic   35

---

32. Howard Kurtz, "Why the Press Is Always Right," *Columbia Journalism Review* (May/June 1993).

33. CaShears, "Activist: 'Paper Has Done Disservice,'" *USA Today* (March 1, 1993).

34. Joe Urschel, "*USA Today*: Here's How It Happened," *USA Today* (March 1, 1993).

picture of a menacing, scowling black man. In a subsequent issue, a reader wrote in: "Since five of the six defendants in the Houston rape/murder case were Hispanic, why did your accompanying photo picture only the African American defendant? That doesn't seem to give a very representative portrait."[35] At the 1993 National Association of Black Journalists convention, actor Tim Reid put the need for monitoring media coverage in succinct terms. "If you don't react then shut up!" he said.[36] In fact, millions of Americans are deeply concerned that the media's failings are helping to drive the races apart. A 1994 Gallup poll found that over 40 percent of both blacks and whites felt that news coverage *worsened* American race relations. (Smaller numbers of Asian and Hispanic Americans felt the same way.) Only 21 percent of whites and 19 percent of blacks felt news coverage helped improve race relations.[37] Refusing to talk about racial issues, particularly in the media, will not change things for the better. It's only if we take a stand and make our presence known that we can fight the hype.

Three decades ago, following the Watts Riots, Lyndon Johnson's Kerner Commission lambasted news organizations for being "shockingly backward" in not hiring, training, and promoting more African Americans: "For if the media are to comprehend and then to project the Negro community, they must have the help of Negroes. If the media are to report with understanding, wisdom, sympathy on the problems of the black man—for the two are increasingly intertwined—they must employ, promote, and listen to Negro journalists."[38] Those words were prophetic when they were first written, and are still crucially important now. Unfortunately, it seems that the media will only show us the real face of black America when we compel it to do so.

▪ CONSIDER THE SOURCE

1. What link does Chideya see between the number of black journalists and the way black communities are characterized in the media?

2. In your own words, summarize the "myths of black media influence" that Chideya tries to counteract. What tactics does she use to oppose those myths? Do you find Chideya's depictions of "reality" persuasive? How do her headings "myth" and "reality" affect you as a reader?

---

35. Sally Campbell of Houston, TX, letter printed in the August 9, 1993 issue of *Newsweek*, referring to the July 19, 1993 issue.

36. *The NABJ Monitor*, a publication of the National Association of Black Journalists' convention (July 22, 1993).

37. *USA Today* (no byline), "Racial, Ethnic Groups Give Mixed Reviews to Media," (July 26, 1994).

38. "The News Media and Disorders," *Report of the National Advisory Commission on Civil Disorders* (1968): 362–86

3. What solutions does Chideya see to the problem of media misrepresentation of minorities?

■ **CONSIDER THE IMPLICATIONS**

4. In your journal, explore your reactions to Chideya's charge that "the media consistently overreports the violence and weaknesses of the black community and underreports black everyday life and its strengths." How does media coverage affect your views of the black community? How well has your own experience of minority communities coincided with their portrayal in the press?

5. Scan the Sunday edition of your regional newspaper and make note of any stories by or about minorities. How were nonwhite communities portrayed? What was considered newsworthy by the paper's editors? Was there a difference in the coverage of African Americans, Asian Americans, Hispanic Americans, and Native Americans?

6. Dividing your class into groups, each one responsible for a different television network, observe the reporters and anchors on television during a single news day—include morning news shows, late afternoon, prime time nightly news, and late night news. What stories are covered? How are minorities portrayed? How many onscreen personnel are nonwhite? Which news events do they cover? Report your findings to the class and compare them with those of other groups. Were there any notable differences between networks?

7. How would Jeff Cohen (pp. 222–28) explain the coverage of black issues that Chideya notes? Write a concise statement of the "centrist" view of race in America, relying on the journalistic clichés that Cohen says help "preserve the status quo."

8. Compare two major daily newspapers' coverage of the same day's events. Which stories made the front page? What did editors think was of greatest concern to their readers? Write an analysis of the day's news from Chideya's perspective.

9. Write a letter to Chideya arguing for or against her thesis that news coverage is worsening race relations in America.

MICHAEL MASSING

Bringing the Truth Commission Back Home

The forces that determine what news we read usually remain hidden. But occasionally, the public is allowed to peek behind the veil of journalistic objectivity and catch a glimpse of editors, managers, and reporters squabbling over what news to present. The drama surrounding reporter Raymond Bonner's departure from the New York Times *presents just such an opportunity.*

Bonner (b. 1942) wrote a January 1982 story about a military massacre of unarmed civilians in El Mozote, El Salvador. His report was denied at the time by U.S. State Department officials concerned with supporting the Salvadoran military, and Bonner was later reassigned to the Times's *New York offices. A. M. Rosenthal (b. 1922), then managing editor of the* Times, *was accused of removing Bonner from the El Salvador beat in response to pressure from U.S. officials. Michael Massing (b. 1952) wrote a 1983 article in the* Columbia Journalism Review, *which claimed that Bonner's removal had a chilling effect on subsequent press coverage of events in El Salvador. When Bonner's original story was corroborated in March 1993 by the United Nations "Truth Commission," the editors of the* Wall Street Journal, *who had criticized Bonner and the* Times *in 1982 for running the El Mozote story, now chastised Rosenthal for removing Bonner. This prompted Rosenthal to write a letter to the editor of the* Wall Street Journal, *which he claimed would "set the record straight." Three months after Rosenthal's letter was printed,* Harper's *magazine allowed Massing the opportunity to annotate Rosenthal's letter with his own commentary. You be the judge: How much objectivity do any of these journalists display, and where does the truth reside?*

Massing, a freelance writer based in New York, has contributed to the New York Times Magazine, *the* Atlantic Monthly, The New Yorker, *and* The New York Times Book Review. *He served as executive editor of the* Columbia Journalism Review *from 1979 until 1982, and published several articles in the early 1990s about media coverage of the Persian Gulf War. Massing cofounded the Committee to Protect Journalists, which monitors human rights abuses against reporters across the globe. He received a MacArthur Fellowship in 1992 and is currently writing a book on the drug wars. Raymond Bonner wrote occasional political commentaries for the* New York Times *through December of 1992. In August 1993 he rejoined the paper as a foreign correspondent, filing regular reports from Rwanda, the former Yugoslavia, and the republics of the former Soviet Union.*

From *Harper's Magazine* (July 1993), pp. 64–67.

Letters to the Editor
Let's Set the Record Straight

In your March 19 editorial "On Credulity," you state that you did not fire Raymond Bonner, the former Times correspondent in El Salvador—"The *New York Times* did." You amend that slightly by saying that as the then-managing editor I "pulled Mr. Bonner off the beat" and that then he left.

You add if the *Times* thinks that the recent confirmation of Mr. Bonner's stories about the massacre by El Salvadoran government troops vindicates him then the Times should "rehire him."

Thus the *Wall Street Journal*, in its criticism of Mr. Bonner, picks up and repeats two lies. One is that Mr. Bonner was fired or pushed out of the *Times*, the other that such a step was taken in connection with Mr. Bonner's reporting on the massacre.

You wrote that editorial without any attempt to ask me if the parts pertaining to me were true. Your violation of elementary journalistic ethics does astonish me.

But I believe that the failure to get in

On April 22, A. M. Rosenthal's distinctive prose showed up in the Wall Street Journal: *His reputation was on his mind. For more than ten years, Rosenthal—the former executive editor of the* New York Times *and now a columnist for the paper— has been dogged by charges that at the height of U.S. involvement in El Salvador he withdrew the paper's correspondent there, Raymond Bonner, for political reasons. The episode had a profound effect on press coverage of Central America in the 1980s. Until Bonner's recall, in August 1982, correspondents reported extensively on the dismal human-rights situation in El Salvador. This greatly complicated the Reagan administration's efforts to prop up the Salvadoran military and "draw the line" against leftist forces in the region. Bonner's sudden recall to New York, however, cast a deep chill over correspondents in Central America. It also raised a number of troubling questions that have yet to be answered: Did the* Times *bow to pressure from the government? When does official criticism of a reporter amount to a threat? What happens to a reporter when his or her interpretation of events contradicts that of the powers that be?*

The Journal's *editorial page, with its strong rightward slant, would have seemed the last place in which to find Rosenthal accused of recalling Bonner. For years, in fact, the Right took gleeful credit for having persuaded the* Times *to pull the correspondent. In an editorial published on March 19 of this year, however, the* Journal *joined in the finger-pointing. "Et tu?"[1] seems to be Rosenthal's startled response.*

The El Mozote massacre was perhaps the single most controversial story of the entire Salvadoran saga. On January 27, 1982, Ray Bonner, in a front-page story for the Times, *reported that "it is clear that a massacre of major proportions" took place in El Mozote, a village located in rebel-held territory. Bonner, who had been led to the site by guerrillas, cited estimates that between 733 and*

---

1. **Et tu?:** "Also you?", the dying Julius Caesar asks his friend Brutus in Shakespeare's play, after Brutus has joined conspirators to overthrow Caesar.—ED.

926 *unarmed men, women, and children had been killed. Based on interviews with people living in the area, including one survivor, Bonner concluded that Salvadoran soldiers had probably been responsible. A similar story, by Alma Guillermo-prieto, appeared on the same day in the* Washington Post. *The articles caused a firestorm of protest against administration policy in El Salvador. Bonner came under withering attack from the State Department and from commentators on the Right, with the* Journal *leading the way. In a blistering editorial covering two full columns, the paper called Bonner "overly credulous" and dismissed his story as a "propaganda exercise." The* Journal *suggested that Bonner and the* Times *would bear some of the blame if El Salvador went the way of Cuba. Seven months later, Bonner received a call from the* Times *foreign desk ordering him back to New York. He was replaced by a young reporter from the business section who had virtually no overseas experience.*

For more than a decade the truth about the massacre remained a matter of dispute. Then, in the fall of 1992, with the Salvadoran conflict at an end, a team of forensic anthropologists began digging in El Mozote. They unearthed scores of skeletons, most of which belonged to children who clearly had been murdered. On October 22, 1992, the Times—*now under the stewardship of Rosenthal's successor, Max Frankel—reported in a front-page article that "nearly eleven years after American-trained soldiers were said to have torn through El Mozote and surrounding hamlets on a rampage in which at least 794 people were killed, the bones have emerged as stark evidence that the claims of peasant survivors and the reports of a couple of American journalists were true." Further corroboration came in mid-March 1993, when a United Nations-sponsored "Truth Commission," concluding an investigation into human-rights abuses in El Salvador, stated that "it was fully proven" that a massacre took place at El Mozote, and that U.S.-trained infantry battalions were responsible.*

For years, Rosenthal has attempted to discredit the Columbia Journalism Review *(CJR) article, see-*

touch with me was an aberration on the part of a newspaper I respect. Therefore I am writing this letter, one of very few I have written to any newspaper. I thought you and your readers would be interested in knowing the truth about the journalistic and political falsehoods you helped spread.

It will also set the record straight for journalists who have seen your editorial or will come across it in the future—or have seen one of the variations of these falsehoods in other, less admirable, journals, over the past decade.

In 1983 the *Columbia Journalism Review* richly fulfilled its reputation of the time for politicized amateurism by printing a piece hinting and implying but of course never presenting the slightest proof that Mr. Bonner was withdrawn by the *Times* because the U.S. government put pressure on me and the *New York Times*.

The *Review's* fairy tale was picked up by other sloppy or politically motivated journalists and sometimes embellished until just about everybody even forgot where it originated. But until you came along doing the same thing I never replied because I did not see it in any newspaper for which I had any respect.

So now I want to say that that story about the *Times*, or any variant, that Mr. Bonner was taken out of El Salvador because of pressure from the U.S. government, or pressure of any kind whatsoever, or because of his reporting on the massacre, is a lie.

Is that clear enough?

This kind of conspiratorial myth making—another way of saying lie—fascinates me. The reason is that the myths and the process of inventing them so often reflect the character of those who create or spread them. These people are really holding up a mirror to themselves and do not even realize it.

They know that if they had been put under any pressure by a government agency or anybody with power, why they would just crumble. So they assume the editor of the *Times* would crumble too. That is one of the many excellent reasons that people like that do not become editors of the *Times*. They do not have the guts for it.

If the CIA or any other agency or official had tried to pressure the *Times* into removing Mr. Bonner, as far as I am concerned he would have been there still, or at least as long as it

ing it as the source of all his woes. Titled "About-face on El Salvador," the piece—which I wrote—was based on interviews with more than a dozen correspondents, plus several Times *editors (including Rosenthal). The article described the government's attacks on Bonner and the widespread impression among his colleagues that he was recalled because of them. Reviewing a year's worth of articles appearing in the* Times *and other papers, I concluded in my CJR piece—and believe no less today—that the press's coverage of death squads, land reform, and the Salvadoran military notably softened after Bonner's departure.*

With Bonner vindicated, the Journal *came under attack. CBS's 60 Minutes, National Public Radio, and the* Times *itself, in an editorial, all chided the* Journal *for having smeared Bonner. Thus the paper's March 19 editorial, in which it attempted to shift the blame to Rosenthal. The* Times *editor, it stated, had "pulled Mr. Bonner off the beat and back to New York, where he left the paper. If the* Times *thinks Mr. Bonner has been vindicated, it should stop carping at us and rehire him forthwith."*

A decade earlier, when the Journal *attacked Bonner, Rosenthal wrote not a single word in his defense. Now, with his own reputation at stake, he weighs in with more than twelve hundred.*

A red herring. No account of the incident has ever attributed any role to the CIA. In mentioning the agency, Rosenthal is apparently attempting to impute Oliver Stone-like tendencies[2] to his critics.

In spring 1982, Rosenthal traveled to El Salvador, where he had lunch with the U.S. ambassador, Deane Hinton. According to a U.S. Embassy official I interviewed in 1983, Hinton made clear to Rosenthal his displeasure over Bonner's reporting. Certainly Hinton's views were no secret. At a breakfast with reporters in Washington

---

2. **Oliver Stone** (b. 1946): Movie producer and director whose 1991 film *JFK* gave credence to conspiracy theories about the assassination of President John F. Kennedy. —Ed.

in June 1982, for instance, he called Bonner an "advocate journalist"—i.e., a guerrilla sympathizer. In addition, Thomas Enders, the assistant secretary of state for inter-American affairs, had attacked the Mozote-massacre stories in testimony before Congress. Stating that the U.S. Embassy had sent two officials to the village to investigate the incident, Enders asserted that "there is no evidence at all to confirm that government forces systematically massacred civilians in the operations zone."

Last March the State Department acknowledged that, based on newly available evidence, the reporting by Bonner and Guillermoprieto was accurate. As recent news reports have made clear, the two embassy officials sent to investigate the massacre never actually reached El Mozote; rather, they had to rely on interviews with refugees from the area. Even then, one of the officials had concluded that large numbers of civilians had probably been killed. This information was conveyed to Deane Hinton. Rather than investigate further, though, the ambassador focused his fury on the messenger—i.e., Bonner.

It's nice to learn that the notoriously thin-skinned Rosenthal was so open to people's complaints, and that he paid them all equal attention. No doubt a letter from Joe Citizen would have received as much of his attention as a phone call from an ambassador or assistant secretary of state. Rosenthal's notion of threats is interesting as well. Certainly few officials would be so crass as to make them. In those politically charged times, a member of the Reagan Administration had only to "complain" about a story to cast doubts about its author's patriotism—and about a newspaper's continued access to government officials for quotes, "background" interviews, and the like.

What went through Rosenthal's mind when he ordered Bonner out of El Salvador is, of course, anybody's guess. Given Rosenthal's well-known political views, he may not have needed much prodding from the government. He has freely admitted that when he was executive editor he believed the Times had gotten too liberal. Not long after Bonner's re-

took to teach the agency and government what the Times is all about.

But it never happened. As a matter of fact, I do not recall any U.S. official, in El Salvador or in the United States, making any complaint to me about him. The U.S. government did make public its unhappiness with Mr. Bonner and we took note of that in our news columns.

Now the government has gotten around to confirming one of Mr. Bonner's major stories that it once called false —the massacre of villagers by the military. If that vindicates Mr. Bonner's coverage of that story, which it does, it also vindicates the Times for printing it.

If the U.S. officials had complained to me, I would have listened as I tried to listen to everybody with a complaint. Complaints are perfectly legitimate as long as not accompanied by threats, a point the conspiracy-minded myth makers are incapable of grasping. No pressure was ever put on me by any government agency to remove or punish Mr. Bonner or any other correspondent, never during my long editorship at the Times. This fact will upset many of the conspiracy theorists and government haters inside and outside of journalism and doubtless they will ignore it—but there it is.

Now, as for your own participation in myth making, Mr. Bonner was not pushed out or fired out or "pulled out," and at no time was his transfer to New York at all involved with the massacre story.

He was asked to return to New York after he had been in El Salvador a substantial amount of time. The reason is simple, having to do with training and staff development, prosaic things, not plots and pressures.

Mr. Bonner was not an experienced journalist at all when he began working for the *Times*.

But Mr. Bonner was on the spot, became our stringer and performed bravely and fruitfully. As a matter of fact, he was promoted to staff, a step taken rarely with stringers.

But after some time the feeling began to grow among some editors who handled his copy daily that in a sense we were exploiting Mr. Bonner, demanding a great deal without giving him the journalistic training most other *Times* reporters had acquired on or off the *Times* before they went into a foreign assignment for us.

At the *Times*, re-

call from El Salvador, the paper ran several articles by conservative journalist Claire Sterling asserting that the Soviet bloc was behind the assassination attempt on the pope. And, in 1985, Rosenthal hired Shirley Christian, a Miami Herald correspondent known for her vehemently anti-Sandinista views. To many, the shift from Bonner to Christian summed up the Times's ideological journey under Rosenthal.

Bonner did have an unusual résumé for a reporter. A lawyer by training, he had spent three years in the Marine Corps, including a year in Vietnam. He had also worked as a litigator for Ralph Nader[3] in Washington and as a lawyer in the district attorney's office in San Francisco. Tiring of law, Bonner went to South America in 1979 and began "stringing" for news organizations. By December 1980 he had made his way to El Salvador, where he began a trial with the Times. With the violence there escalating, the paper soon made him a full-time correspondent.

Bonner's reporting was not without flaws. In January 1982, for instance, he wrote an article maintaining that a group of U.S. Army advisers had sat in on two torture sessions conducted by Salvadoran soldiers. Based on the statements of a single self-proclaimed defector, the story turned out to be false.

In fact, Bonner had already been back to New York for such training. He had returned in January 1981, soon after being hired, and had spent most of the next ten months on the metro desk. By the time he was sent back to El Salvador, in the fall of 1981, Bonner was thoroughly familiar with Times procedures.

---

3. **Ralph Nader** (b. 1934): Leading consumer advocate and founder of the Center for the Study of Responsive Law.—ED.

Hardly the whole story. On his return to New York, Bonner was assigned to the Times*'s business desk. When the Anne Burford scandal erupted at the Environmental Protection Agency, he was sent to Washington, where he scored several scoops on the issue. He also broke stories about secret Pentagon spying operations in Central America and on Reagan Administration plans to build a military base in Honduras. The Washington bureau wanted to keep Bonner in the capital to cover U.S. policy in Central America. The deal was all but done when New York made clear its opposition. Discouraged, Bonner took some time off in the summer of 1983 to write a book about El Salvador. Rejoining the paper in the fall, he was reassigned to the business section but was told he would eventually end up on metro—clearly a demotion. With his days at the* Times *numbered, Bonner in July 1984 reluctantly left the paper. He went on to write a book about U.S. policy in the Philippines, then accepted a position as a writer with* The New Yorker, *where he remained until late last year.*[4]

In a way, the whole episode comes down to who duped whom. In its March 19 editorial, the Journal *claimed that its editorial of eleven years earlier had "never denied that there was a massacre at El Mozote." In fact, the paper had unquestioningly accepted Enders's denials about the massacre. The whole point of its attack on Bonner was to discredit his El Mozote report and pave the way for U.S. aid to El Salvador. As the Truth Commission report now makes clear, it was the* Wall Street Journal, *and not Ray Bonner, that was duped. As for Rosenthal, he, too, seems to have been taken in.*

porters are almost never sent abroad without experience at the home office. And reporters hired abroad are almost always asked to work in New York for a while, the length depending on experience. The idea is to make the reporter familiar with the ways of the paper and its staff, part of the *Times* journalistic family, not an outsider on the payroll.

So we asked Mr. Bonner to return—not to punish him but to equip him further for an assignment anyplace. Apparently, he did not like working in New York or preferred to be abroad, because after a time he resigned. At no time did Mr. Bonner indicate to me any belief that he had been pulled, pushed, or fired out.

But when he left, the conspiracy-minded went to work concocting the myth of the *Times* crumbling under government pressure. That is the way their minds work and what their mirrors show them about themselves.

That is no great matter. Myth making about the *Times* is a journalistic industry. Sometimes they are just gossip-myths. Sometimes, like this one, they are largely politically inspired.

Their only signifi-

---

4. Bonner's *Weakness and Deceit: U.S. Policy and El Salvador* (1984) and *Waltzing with a Dictator: The Marcoses and the Making of American Policy* (1987) were both published by Times Books.—ED.

cance comes when they are repeated and spread so often
that they become accepted as
reality by journalists who
allow themselves to be duped
or fail to check through ordinary journalistic techniques. I
am sorry that in this case, for
one of my favorite newspapers, both shoes fit. But I know
you have many much better
pairs. Wear them well.

— A. M. ROSENTHAL
New York

■   **CONSIDER THE SOURCE**

1. Summarize the various versions of the "truth" about El Mozote.

2. Summarize the various versions of the "truth" about Bonner's tenure
   with the *New York Times.*

3. How does Rosenthal define "elementary journalistic ethics"? What procedures do he and Massing believe help guarantee accuracy in reporting?

4. How does Massing characterize Rosenthal? Do his language and tone
   support or undermine his own position?

5. What concessions does Rosenthal make to his audience? How does he attempt to keep his reader's goodwill?

■   **CONSIDER THE IMPLICATIONS**

6. Massing raises the issue of "reputation," with reference to Rosenthal. Divide into four groups, each taking the part of one of the key players: Bonner, Rosenthal, Massing, and the *Wall Street Journal.* Discuss how your
   player's reputation and motives are challenged. Hold a class forum in
   which each group defends the "truth" of its position.

7. Examine Massing's claim that "Bonner's sudden recall to New York . . . cast
   a deep chill over correspondents in Central America." What evidence does
   he give to support this claim? How "sudden" was that recall?

8. Write a letter from A. M. Rosenthal to the editors of *Harper's Magazine* regarding their publication of Massing's annotations. What role do they
   play in "setting the record straight"?

9. Analyze this coverage of Bonner's departure from the *Times* from the position of Jeff Cohen (pp. 222–28). What ideologies would he say are being
   served by the various publications involved? Does this coverage invoke
   any of the journalistic clichés Cohen describes?

10. Read closely several reports of a recent world event from different news
    sources. Which do you believe most? Why? What evidence do you find
    persuasive? Do you detect any biases in the reporting, any of what Mass-
    ing refers to as "advocacy journalism"? Summarize your findings in an
    essay that analyzes the various reports.

11. In your journal, analyze the experience of reading Massing's annotations of Rosenthal's letter. How did moving back and forth between the two parts of the text add to or detract from your reading experience? Compare reading Massing/Rosenthal with reading a heavily footnoted article, such as those by Barbara Sicherman (pp. 70–87), Linda Kerber (pp. 136–49), or Patricia Nelson Limerick (pp. 209–220).

▪ ▪ ▪ ▪ ▪ ▪

SUSAN FALUDI

The Media and the Backlash

The mainstream press undoubtedly influences our views of foreign and domestic politics. Less obvious, perhaps, but at least as important is the press's ability to mold our self-images. In 1991, a best-selling book by Susan Faludi (b. 1958), Backlash: The Undeclared War Against American Women *claimed that national attitudes toward feminism and women's roles had shifted in the 1980s. She argues that the news media, movies, television, and the fashion industry contributed to the backlash against feminism by peddling "news" and images of women trading the independence and equality won during the 1970s for a return to traditional roles. Such reports were inaccurate, Faludi claims, but they changed women's images of themselves nonetheless. In this excerpt from her chapter on the press, Faludi exposes the news behind some of the "news," tracing the process of trend reporting and scrutinizing the statistics used to support media claims. Faludi has since left her position as a reporter for the* Wall Street Journal *to spend a year on a Knight Journalism Fellowship at Stanford. She is now writing a book on American masculinity, along with freelance articles for* Newsweek, The New Yorker, Ms. *and* Esquire, *among other magazines.*

"What has happened to American women?" ABC asked with much consternation in its 1986 special report. The show's host Peter Jennings promptly answered, "The gains for women sometimes come at a formidable cost to them."[1] *Newsweek* raised the same question in its 1986 story on the "new problem with no name." And it offered the same diagnosis: "The emotional fallout of feminism" was damaging women; an "emphasis on equality" had robbed them of their romantic and maternal rights

---

From *Backlash: The Undeclared War Against American Women* (New York: Crown Publishers, 1991), pp. 75–111.

1. "After the Sexual Revolution," *ABC News Closeup,* July 30, 1986.

and forced them to make "sacrifices."[2] The magazine advised: "'When the gods wish to punish us, they answer our prayers,' Oscar Wilde wrote.[3] So it would seem to many of the women who looked forward to 'having it all.'" (This happens to be the same verdict *Newsweek* reached when it last investigated female discontent—at the height of the feminine-mystique backlash. "American women's unhappiness is merely the most recently won of women's rights," the magazine reported then.)[4]

The press might have looked for the source of women's unhappiness in other places. It could have investigated and exposed the buried roots of the backlash in the New Right and a misogynistic White House, in a chilly business community and intransigent social and religious institutions. But the press chose to peddle the backlash rather than probe it.

The media's role as backlash collaborator and publicist is a familiar one in American history. The first article sneering at a "Superwoman" appeared not in the 1980s press but in an American newspaper headline at the turn of the century. Feminists, according to the late Victorian press, were "a herd of hysterical and irrational she-revolutionaries," "fussy, interfering, faddists, fanatics," "shrieking cockatoos," and "unpardonably ridiculous." Feminists had laid waste to the American female population; any sign of female distress was surely another "fatal symptom" of the feminist disease, the periodicals reported. "Why Are We Women Not Happy?" the male-edited *Ladies' Home Journal* asked in 1901—and answered that the women's rights movement was debilitating its beneficiaries.[5]

As American studies scholar Cynthia Kinnard observed in her bibliography of American antifeminist literature, journalistic broadsides against women's rights "grew in intensity during the late nineteenth century and reached regular peaks with each new suffrage campaign." The arguments were always the same: Equal education would make women spinsters, equal employment would make women sterile, equal rights would make women bad mothers. With each new historical cycle, the threats were simply updated and sanitized, and new "experts" enlisted. The Victorian periodical press turned to clergymen to support its brief against feminism; in the eighties, the press relied on therapists.

The 1986 *Newsweek* backlash article, "Feminism's Identity Crisis," 5

---

2. Eloise Salholz, "Feminism's Identity Crisis," *Newsweek*, March 31, 1986, p. 58.

3. **Oscar Wilde** (1854–1900): Irish writer and witty satirist.—ED.

4. *Newsweek*, March 7, 1960, cited in Betty Friedan, *The Feminine Mystique* (New York: A Laurel Book/Dell, 1983 ed.), pp. 19–20.

5. "Superwoman," *Independent*, Feb. 21, 1907, cited in Cynthia D. Kinnard, ed. *Antifeminism in American Thought: An Annotated Bibliography* (Boston: G. K. Hall & Co., 1986), pp. xiii–ix, 55–61, 214.

quoted many experts on women's condition—sociologists, political scientists, psychologists—but none of the many women supposedly suffering from this crisis. The closest the magazine came was two drawings of a mythical feminist victim: A dour executive with cropped hair is pictured first at her desk, grimly pondering an empty family-picture frame, and then at home, clutching a clock and studying the hands—poised at five minutes to midnight.

The absence of real women in a news account that is allegedly about real women is a hallmark of eighties backlash journalism. The press delivered the backlash to the public through a series of "trend stories," articles that claimed to divine sweeping shifts in female social behavior while providing little in the way of evidence to support their generalizations. The trend story, which may go down as late-twentieth-century journalism's prime contribution to its craft, professes to offer "news" of changing mores, yet prescribes more than it observes. Claiming to mirror public sentiment, its reflections of the human landscapes are strangely depopulated. Pretending to take the public's pulse, it monitors only its own heartbeat—and its advertisers'.

Trend journalism attains authority not through actual reporting but through the power of repetition. Said enough times, anything can be made to seem true. A trend declared in one publication sets off a chain reaction, as the rest of the media scramble to get the story, too. The lightning speed at which these messages spread has less to do with the accuracy of the trend than with journalists' propensity to repeat one another. And repetition became especially hard to avoid in the eighties, as the "independent" press fell into a very few corporate hands.[6]

Fear was also driving the media's need to dictate trends and determine social attitudes in the eighties, as print and broadcast audiences, especially female audiences, turned to other news sources and advertising plunged—eventually falling to its lowest level in twenty years.[7] Anxiety-ridden media managements became preoccupied with conducting market research studies and "managing" the fleeing reader, now renamed "the customer" by such news corporations as Knight-Ridder.[8]

---

6. In 1982, fifty corporations controlled over half the media business; by the end of 1987, the number was down to twenty-six. See Ben H. Bagdikian, *The Media Monopoly* (Boston: Beacon Press, 1990), pp. xix, 3–4; *Media Report to Women*, Sept. 1987, p. 4.

7. After 1985, profit margins fell steadily at papers owned by publicly traded communications companies. Women, who make up the majority of newspaper readers and network news viewers, were turning to specialty publications and cable news programs in mass numbers, taking mass advertising dollars with them. See Alex S. Jones, "Rethinking Newspapers," *New York Times*, Jan. 6, 1991, III, p. 1; "Marketing Newspapers to Women," *Women Scope Surveys of Women*, 2, no. 7 (April 1989), pp. 1–2.

8. In a typical media strategy of the decade, Knight-Ridder Newspapers launched a "customer-obsession" campaign to give readers what management imagined they wanted, rather than what was simply news.

And their preoccupations eventually turned up in the way the media covered the news. "News organizations are moving on to the same ground as political institutions that mold public opinion and seek to direct it," Bill Kovach, former editor of the *Atlanta Journal-Constitution* and the Nieman Foundation's curator,[9] observed. "Such a powerful tool for shaping public opinion in the hands of journalists accustomed to handling fact is like a scalpel in a child's hands: it is capable of great damage."[10]

Journalists first applied this scalpel to American women. While eighties trend stories occasionally considered the changing habits of men, these articles tended to involve men's latest hobbies and whimsies—fly fishing, beepers, and the return of the white shirt. The eighties female trends, by contrast, were the failure to find husbands, get pregnant, or properly bond with their children. NBC, for instance, devoted an entire evening news special to the pseudotrend of "bad girls,"[11] yet ignored the real trend of bad boys: The crime rate among boys was climbing twice as fast as for girls. (In New York City, right in the network's backyard, rape arrests of young boys had jumped 200 percent in two years.) Female trends with a more flattering veneer surfaced in women's magazines and newspaper "Style" pages in the decade, each bearing, beneath new-and-improved packaging, the return-to-gender trademark: "the New Abstinence," "the New Femininity," "the New High Monogamy," "the New Morality," "the New Madonnas," "the Return of the Good Girl." While anxiety over AIDS has surely helped fuel promotion of these "new" trends, that's not the whole story. While in the eighties AIDS remained largely a male affliction, these media directives were aimed almost exclusively at women. In each case, women were reminded to re-embrace "traditional" sex roles—or suffer the consequences. For women, the trend story was no news report; it was a moral reproach.

The trends for women always came in instructional pairs—the trend 10 that women were advised to flee and the trend that they were pushed to join. For this reason, the paired trends tended to contradict each other. As one woman writer observed wryly in an *Advertising Age* column, "The media are having a swell time telling us, on the one hand, that marriage is 'in' and, on the other hand, that women's chances of marrying are slim. So maybe marriage is 'in' because it's so hard to do, like coal-walking was 'in' a year ago."[12] Three contradictory trend pairs, concerning work, marriage, and motherhood, formed the backlash

9. **Nieman Foundation** (founded 1938): Awards annual fellowships to journalists to expand their intellectual horizons by studying at Harvard University.—ED.

10. Bill Kovach, "Too Much Opinion, at the Expense of Fact," *New York Times*, Sept. 13, 1989, p. A31.

11. "Bad Girls," *NBC News*, August 30, 1989.

12. "The Next Trend: Here Comes the Bribe," *Advertising Age*, June 16, 1986, p. 40.

media's triptych: Superwoman "burnout" versus New Traditionalist "cocooning"; "the spinster boom" versus "the return of marriage"; and "the infertility epidemic" versus "the baby boomlet."

Finally, in female trend stories fact and forecast traded places. These articles weren't chronicling a retreat among women that was already taking place; they were compelling one to happen. The "marriage panic," as we have seen, didn't show up in the polls until after the press's promotion of the Harvard-Yale study.[13] In the mid-eighties, the press deluged readers with stories about how mothers were afraid to leave their children in "dangerous" day care centers. In 1988, this "trend" surfaced in the national polls: Suddenly, almost 40 percent of mothers reported feeling fearful about leaving their children in day care; their confidence in day care fell to 64 percent, from 76 percent just a year earlier—the first time the figure had fallen below 70 percent since the survey began asking that question four years earlier. Again, in 1986 the press declared a "new celibacy" trend—and by 1987 the polls showed that the proportion of single women who believed that premarital sex was acceptable had suddenly dropped 6 percentage points in a year; for the first time in four years, fewer than half of all women said they felt premarital sex was okay.[14]

Finally, throughout the eighties the media insisted that women were fleeing the work force to devote themselves to "better" mother-hood. But it wasn't until 1990 that this alleged development made a dent—a very small one—in the labor charts, as the percentage of women in the work force between twenty and forty-four dropped a tiny 0.5 per-cent, the first dip since the early sixties.[15] Mostly, the media's advocacy of such a female exodus created more guilt than flight: In 1990, a poll of working women by Yankelovich Clancy Shulman found almost 30 per-cent of them believed that "wanting to put more energy into being a good homemaker and mother" was cause to consider quitting work al-together—an 11 percent increase from just a year earlier and the highest proportion in two decades.

The trend story is not always labeled as such, but certain character-istics give it away: an absence of factual evidence or hard numbers; a tendency to cite only three or four women, typically anonymously, to es-tablish the trend; the use of vague qualifiers like "there is a sense that" or "more and more"; a reliance on the predictive future tense ("Increas-ingly, mothers will stay home to spend more time with their families"); and the invocation of "authorities" such as consumer researchers and

---

13. "Women's Views Survey: Women's Changing Hopes, Fears, Loves," *Glam-our*, Jan. 1988, p. 142.

14. Mark Clements Research, Women's Views Survey, 1988.

15. Amy Saltzman, "Trouble at the Top," *U.S. News & World Report*, June 17, 1991, p. 40.

psychologists, who often support their assertions by citing other media trend stories. . . .

COCOONERS, NEW TRADITIONALISTS, AND MOMMY TRACKERS

"Many Young Women Now Say They'd Pick Family over Career," the front page of the *New York Times* announced in 1980.[16] Actually, the "many" women were a few dozen Ivy League undergraduates who, despite their protestations, were heading to medical school and fellowships at Oxford. The *Times* story managed to set off a brief round of similar back-to-the-home stories in the press. But with no authority to bless the trend, return-to-nesting's future looked doubtful. Then, midway through the decade, a media expert surfaced spectacularly in the press. Her name, which soon became a household word, was Faith Popcorn.

A former advertising executive (with the former name of Faith 15 Plotkin), Popcorn had reinvented herself as a "leading consumer authority" and launched her own market research firm, BrainReserve, which had one specialty: "trend identification."[17] Popcorn even maintained a "Trend Bank," whose deposits she loaned to clients at a charge of $75,000 to $600,000. Claiming a 95 percent accuracy rate, Popcorn promised to identify not only "major trend directions in the nation today" but also "upcoming TIPs (trends-in-progress)."

The information in Popcorn's Trend Bank was hardly proprietary. While she did have a group of consumers that she polled, she derived her predictions mainly from popular TV shows, best-sellers, and "lifestyle" magazines. "*People* is my bible," Popcorn said.[18] She also checked out movies and fashion from the last backlash, on the theory that styles repeat every thirty years. In spite of this rather elementary method of data collection, she managed to attract hundreds of corporate clients, including some of the biggest Fortune 500 names in the packaged food and household goods industries. Popcorn's clients, fretting over sluggish consumerism and the failure of more than 80 percent of new products introduced in the contemporary marketplace, were most interested in her promise of "brand renewal." Rather than coming up with new products that appealed to shoppers, they could rely on Pop-

16. Dena Kleiman, "Many Young Women Now Say They'd Pick Family over Career," *New York Times,* Dec. 28, 1980, p. 1. See also "I'm Sick of Work: The Back to the Home Movement," *Ladies' Home Journal,* cover story, Sept. 1984.

17. "The BrainReserve Mission Statement," press packet, and promotional literature, 1988; "Her Ideas on Tomorrow Pop Up Today," *USA Today,* Oct. 5, 1987, p. 1; Tim Golden, "In, Out and Over: Looking Back at the '90s," *New York Times,* Jan. 16, 1990, p. B1.

18. Gary Hanauer, "Faith Popcorn: Kernels of Truth," *American Way,* July 1, 1987.

corn's promotion of retrotrends to get their has-been goods flying off the shelves again. As Popcorn promised, "Even if people don't move to the country, they will buy L. L. Bean's stuff."[19] Campbell Soup Company turned to BrainReserve to sprinkle nostalgic stardust on moribund chicken potpies. Quaker Oats hired Popcorn to revive American appetites for porridge.

In 1986, Faith Popcorn managed to please the media trend writers and her corporate clients at the same time with the coining of a single word, "cocooning." The word "just popped into my head" in the middle of an interview with the *Wall Street Journal,* Popcorn recalls. "It was a prediction. . . . It hadn't happened." But that wasn't quite how she marketed it to the media at the time.[20]

Cocooning was *the* national trend for the eighties, she told the press. "We're becoming a nation of nesters. . . . We like to stay home and cocoon. Mom foods, like meat loaf and chicken potpie, are very big right now."[21] Her foodmaker clients were more than happy to back her up on that. As one enthusiastic spokesman for Pillsbury told *Newsweek,* "I believe in cocooning."[22]

The press evidently did, too. In the next year alone Popcorn and her cocoon theories were featured in, to mention just a few publications, *Newsweek* (five times), the *Wall Street Journal* (four times), *USA Today* (twice), the *Atlantic, U.S. News & World Report,* the *Los Angeles Times, Boardroom Reports, Success!,* and, of course, *People.* "Is Faith Popcorn the *ur* of our era," a bemused writer wondered in *The New Yorker.* "Is she the oversoul incarnate?"[23] Faith Popcorn is "one of the most interviewed women on the planet," grumbled *Newsweek* in 1987, which, despite its irritation, allotted her another two pages.[24]

"Cocooning" was no gender-neutral concept; from the start, it was a female trend. Popcorn defined cocooning not as *people* coming home but as *women* abandoning the office. As she put it to the press, "Fewer women will work. They will spend their time at home concentrating on their families." The press feminized this trend even further, envisioning not only cocooning but the cocoon itself as female. "Little in-home wombs," was how the *Los Angeles Times* described these shells to which women were supposed to be retreating.[25]

Female cocooning might have shown up on Popcorn's trend meter

---

19. Personal interview with Faith Popcorn, Nov. 1989.

20. Ibid.

21. Hanauer, "Faith Popcorn."

22. "Putting Faith in Trends," *Newsweek,* June 15, 1987, pp. 46–47.

23. "Eager," *The New Yorker,* July 7, 1985, p. 22.

24. "Putting Faith," p. 46.

25. Elizabeth Mehren, "Life Style in the '90s, According to Popcorn," *Los Angeles Times,* Jan. 16, 1987, p. 1.

but it had yet to make a blip on U.S. Bureau of Labor Statistics charts. Women steadily increased their representation in the work force in the eighties—from 51 to 57 percent for all women, and to more than 70 percent for women between twenty-five and forty-four. And the increase in working mothers was the steepest.[26] Opinion polls didn't support her theory either: They showed adult women increasingly more determined to have a career with a family (63 percent versus 52 percent a decade earlier) and less interested in having a family with no career (26 percent versus 38 percent a decade earlier). And 42 percent of the women who weren't working said they would if there were more day care centers in the vicinity.[27]

What made Popcorn think that "cocooning" was a trend among women? In the press, she cited the following evidence: the improving sales of "mom foods," the popularity of "big comfortable chairs," the ratings of the *Cosby* show, and one statistic—"a third of all the female MBAs of 197[6] have already returned home."[28] But the sales spurt in "mom foods" was the consequence, not the cause, of her relentless "cocooning" promotions; if it had been the other way around, Campbell Soup wouldn't have needed her services. And while people might well be sinking into BarcaLoungers or tuning in the Huxtables on *Cosby,* that hardly meant real women were flocking home. Only the last statistic had anything remotely to do with gauging women's actual behavior— and that statistic, as it happened, was highly dubious.

Popcorn borrowed the MBA figure from what was, at the time, a celebrated trend article—a 1986 *Fortune* cover story entitled "Why Women Are Bailing Out."[29] The article, about businesswomen trained at elite schools fleeing the corporate suite, inspired similar "bailing out" articles in *Forbes, USA Today,* and *U.S. News & World Report,* among others.[30]

The *Fortune* story left an especially deep and troubling impression on young women aspiring to business and management careers; after all, it seemed to have hard data. A year later at Stanford University's Graduate School of Business, women were still talking about the article and the effect it had had on them.[31] Phyllis Strong, a Stanford MBA can-

---

26. *The American Woman 1990–91: A Status Report,* ed. Sara E. Rix (W. W. Norton & Co., 1990), Table 14, p. 376.

27. Louis Harris, *Inside America* (New York: Vintage Books, 1987), pp. 94, 96

28. See, for example, William E. Geist, "One Step Ahead of Us: Trend Expert's View," *New York Times,* Oct. 15, 1986, p. B4.

29. Alex Taylor III, "Why Women Are Bailing Out," *Fortune,* August 18, 1986, p. 16.

30. *USA Today*'s story was, in fact, a report on the *Fortune* "findings": "1 in 3 Management Women Drop Out," *USA Today,* July 31, 1986, p. 1.

31. Personal interviews with a group of female Stanford MBA students, Summer 1988.

didate, said she now planned to look for a less demanding career, after reading how "you give up too much" and "you lose that sense of bonding and family ties" when you take on a challenging business job. Marcia Walley, another MBA candidate, said that she now understood "how impossible it is to have a successful career and a good family life. You can't have it all and you have to choose." A group of women at the business school even wrote a musical number on this theme for the senior play. Set to the tune of Paul Simon's "You Can Call Me Al," the bitter little anthem provoked tears from young women in the audience:

> When I was at B-school, they said . . .
> Girl, you can have it all. But I
> Didn't think I'd lose so much.
> Didn't want such long hours.
> Who'd think my only boyfriend
> Would be a blow-up doll? . . .
> Where are my old boyfriends now?
> Nesting, nesting,
> Getting on with their lives,
> Living with women who get off at five.

The year after *Fortune* launched the "bailing out" trend, the proportion of women applying to business schools suddenly began to shrink—for the first time in a decade.[32]

Fortune's 1986 cover photo featured Janie Witham, former IBM systems engineer, seated in her kitchen with her two-year-old daughter on her lap. Witham is "happier at home," *Fortune*'s cover announced. She has time now to "bake bread." She is one of "many women, including some of the best educated and most highly motivated," wrote the article's author, *Fortune* senior writer Alex Taylor III, who are making "a similar choice" to quit work. "These women were supposed to lead the charge into the corridors of corporate power," he wrote. "If the MBAs cannot find gratification there [in the work force], can *any* [his italics] women?"[33]

The *Fortune* story originated from some cocktail chatter at a *Fortune* editor's class reunion. While mingling with Harvard Business School classmates, Taylor's editor heard a couple of alumnae say they were staying home with their newborns. Suspecting a trend, he assigned the story to Taylor. "He had this anecdotal evidence but no statistics," Taylor recalls.[34] So the reporter went hunting for numbers.

Taylor called Mary Anne Devanna, research coordinator at Columbia Business School's Center for Research in Career Development. She

---

32. Laurie Baum, "For Women, the Bloom Might Be Off the MBA," *Business Week*, March 14, 1988, p. 30.

33. Taylor, "Bailing Out," pp. 16–23.

34. Personal interview with Alex Taylor III, 1988.

had been monitoring MBA women's progress for years—and she saw no such trend. "I told him, 'I don't believe your anecdotes are right,'" she recalls. "'We have no evidence that women are dropping out in larger numbers.' And he said, 'Well, what would convince you?'" She suggested he ask *Fortune* to commission a study of its own. "Well, *Fortune* apparently said a study would cost $36,000 so they didn't want to do one," she says, "but they ended up running the story anyway."[35]

Instead of a study, Taylor took a look at alumni records for the Class of '76 from seventeen top business schools. But these numbers did not support the trend either: In 1976, the same proportion of women as men went to work for large corporations or professional firms, and ten years later virtually the same proportion of women and men were still working for these employers.

Nonetheless, the story that Taylor wrote stated, "After ten years, significantly more women than men dropped off the management track." As evidence, Taylor cited this figure: "Fully 30 percent of the 1,039 women from the Class of '76 reported they are either self-employed or unemployed, or they listed no occupation." That would seem newsworthy but for one inconvenient fact: 21 percent of the *men* from the same class also were self-employed or unemployed. So the "trend" boiled down to a 9 percentage-point difference. Given that working women still bear primary responsibility for child care and still face job discrimination, the real news was that the gap was so *small*.

"The evidence is rather narrow," Taylor concedes later. "The drop-out rates of men and women are roughly the same."[36] Why then did he claim that women were fleeing the work force in "disquieting" numbers? Taylor did not actually talk to any of the women in the story. "A [female] researcher did all the interviews," Taylor says. "I just went out and talked to the deep thinkers, like the corporate heads and social scientists." One woman whom Taylor presumably did talk to, but whose example he did not include, is his own wife. She is a director of corporate communications and, although the Taylors have two children, three years old and six months old at the time of the interview, she's still working. "She didn't quit, it's true," Taylor says. "But I'm struck by the strength of her maternal ties."

The *Fortune* article passed lightly over political forces discouraging businesswomen in the eighties and concluded that women flee the work force because they simply would "rather" stay home. Taylor says he personally subscribes to this view: "I think motherhood, not discrimination, is the overwhelming reason women are dropping out." Yet, even the ex-IBM manager featured on the cover didn't quit because she wanted to stay home. She left because IBM refused to give her the flex-

---

35. Personal interview with Mary Anne Devanna, 1988.

36. Personal interview with Taylor, 1988. (Subsequent quotes are from personal interview with Taylor unless otherwise noted.)

worked out," Witham told the magazine's interviewer. "I would like to go back."

Three months later, *Fortune* was back with more of the same. "A woman who wants marriage and children," the magazine warned, "realizes that her Salomon Brothers job probably represents a choice to forgo both."[37] But *Fortune* editors still couldn't find any numbers to support their retreat-of-the-businesswoman trend. In fact, in 1987, when they finally did conduct a survey on business managers who seek to scale back career for family life, they found an even smaller 6 percent gender gap, and 4 percent *more* men than women said they had refused a job or transfer because it would mean less family time.[38] The national pollsters were no help either: They couldn't find a gap at all; while 30 percent of working women said they might quit if they could afford it, 30 percent of the men said that too. And contrary to the press about "the best and brightest" burning out, the women who were well educated and well paid were the least likely to say they yearned to go home.[39] In fact, a 1989 survey of twelve hundred Stanford business-school graduates found that among couples who both hold MBAs and work, the husbands "display more anxiety."[40]

Finally *Fortune* just turned its back on these recalcitrant career women and devoted its cover instead to the triumph of the "trophy wife," the young and doting second helpmate who "make[s] the fifty- and sixty-year-old CEOs feel they can compete"—unlike that selfish first wife who failed to make her husband "the focus of her life" and "in the process loses touch with him and his concerns."[41] *Fortune* wasn't the only publication to resort to this strategy. *Esquire*, a periodical much given to screeds against the modern woman, devoted its entire June 1990 issue to a dewy tribute to "the American Wife," the traditional kind

---

37. Stratford P. Sherman, "The Party May Be Ending," *Fortune,* Nov. 24, 1986, p. 29.

38. F. S. Chapman, "Executive Guilt: Who's Taking Care of the Children?" *Fortune,* Feb. 16, 1987. A later review of the alumni records at Columbia University's Graduate School of Business for the class of '76 (the same class that Taylor's story focused on) found no significant female defection from the corporate world and no differences in the proportion of men and women leaving to start their own businesses. See Mary Anne Devanna, "Women in Management: Progress and Promise," *Human Resource Management,* 26, no. 4 (Winter 1987): 469.

39. The 1986 Virginia Slims Opinion Poll; Doris L. Walsh, "What Women Want," *American Demographics,* June 1986, p. 60. A survey conducted jointly by *Working Woman* and *Success* magazines also found that men were more concerned about family life than women and less concerned about career success than women. See Carol Sonenklar, "Women and Their Magazines,"p. 44.

40. Margaret King, "An Alumni Survey Dispels Some Popular Myths About MBA Graduates," *Stanford Business School Magazine,* March 1989, p. 23.

41. Julie Connelly, "The CEO's Second Wife," *Fortune,* Aug. 28, 1989, p. 52.

only.[42] In one memorable full-page photo, a model homemaker was featured on her knees, happily scrubbing a toilet bowl.

While women in business management received the most pressure to abandon their careers—the corporate boardroom being the most closely guarded male preserve—the media flashed its return-to-the-nest sign at all working women. "A growing number of professional women have deliberately stepped off the fast track," *Newsweek* asserted in 1988, an assertion once again not supported by federal labor statistics. Women who give up career aspirations, the magazine said, are "much happier," offering the examples of only three women (two of whom were actually complaining of self-esteem problems because they weren't working full time).[43] More professional career women are "choosing" to be "something they never imagined they would be—stay-at-home mothers," a *New York Times Magazine* article announced. It maneuvered around the lack of data to back its claim by saying, "No one knows how many career women each year leave jobs to be with their children."[44] A *Savvy* article weighed in with an even more unlikely scenario: "More and more women," the magazine maintained, are actually "turning down" promotions, top titles, and high salaries—because they have realized "the importance of a balanced life."[45] . . .

The media jumped when Felice Schwartz, the founder of Catalyst— a consulting firm to corporations on women's careers—claimed that "most" women are "willing to trade some career growth and compensation for freedom from the constant pressure to work long hours and weekends."[46] Not only was Schwartz a bona fide expert, she was taking her stand in the esteemed *Harvard Business Review.*

The "mommy-tracking" trend, as the media immediately coined it, became front-page news; Schwartz personally fielded seventy-five interviews in the first month and her words inspired more than a thousand articles.[47] It wasn't as dramatic as women "bailing out" of the work force altogether, but it was better than nothing. "Across the country, fe-

---

42. "The Secret Life of the American Wife," Special Issue, *Esquire,* June 1990.

43. Barbara Kantrowitz, "Moms Move to Part-time Careers," *Newsweek,* Aug. 15, 1988, p. 64. In fact, the polls were finding that more women wanted to work full time rather than stay home, and the proportion of women who regarded a full-time job outside the home as "an integral part" of their ideal lifestyle had been sharply increasing since 1975. See The Gallup Poll, 1982, p. 186.

44. Barbara Basler, "Putting a Career on Hold," *The New York Times Magazine,* Dec. 7, 1986, p. 152.

45. Carol Cox Smith, "Thanks But No Thanks," *Savvy,* March 1988, p. 22.

46. Felice N. Schwartz, "Management Women and the New Facts of Life," *Harvard Business Review,* Jan.–Feb. 1989, pp. 65–76.

47. The *New York Times,* not Schwartz, came up with the phrase. The interview count comes from a personal interview with Schwartz's media relations director, Vivian Todini, Nov. 1989.

male managers and professionals with young families are leaving the fast track for the mommy track," *Business Week* proclaimed in a cover story. Their numbers are "multiplying."[48] It offered no actual numbers, only a few pictures of women holding children's books and stuffed animals, and quotes from four part-time workers. The woman on the cover was even a mommy-tracking employee from Faith Popcorn's client and retrotrend booster, Quaker Oats. (In another photo inside, she was posed next to three different Quaker Oats products.)

If the media had no evidence that the mommy trackers were multiplying, neither did Felice Schwartz. She merely speculated that the majority of women, whom she called "career-and-family women," were "willing" and "satisfied" to give up higher pay and promotions. Corporations should somehow identify these women and treat them differently from "career-primary" women, allotting them fewer hours, bonuses, and opportunities for advancement. That this would amount to discrimination didn't seem to occur to Schwartz. In fact, at a conference sponsored by traditional women's magazines, she proposed that young women ignore Title VII of the Civil Rights Act[49] and review their child-rearing plans with prospective employers; women need to move beyond "insistence on the rights women achieved in an era when we weren't valued," she told her audience.[50]

Women with this mommy-track mind-set were, in reality, vastly in the minority in the workplace: in the 1984 *Newsweek* Research Report on Women Who Work, for example, more than 70 percent of women interviewed said they would rather have high-pressure jobs in which advancement was possible than low-pressure jobs with no advancement.[51] And a year after Schwartz's article was published, when the 1990 Virginia Slims poll specifically asked women about "mommy tracking," 70 percent of the women called it discriminatory and "just an excuse for paying women less than men."[52]

Corporations, Schwartz asserted, had cause to be impatient with female employees; as she put it in the first sentence of her *Harvard Business Review* article, "The cost of employing women in management is greater than the cost of employing men." As evidence she vaguely alluded to two studies, neither published, conducted by two corporations which

---

48. Elizabeth Ehrlich, "The Mommy Track," *Business Week,* March 20, 1989, p. 126.

49. **Title VII**: The equal employment opportunity provision of the Civil Rights Act of 1964. It prohibits discrimination in hiring, business practice, or conduct in the workplace on the basis of race, creed, color, gender, or age.—ED.

50. Ellen Hopkins, "Who Is Felice Schwartz?" *Working Woman,* Oct. 1990, p. 116.

51. *The Newsweek Research Report on Women Who Work: A National Survey* (Princeton, N.J.: Mathematica Policy Research, 1984), p. 32.

52. The 1990 Virginia Slims Opinion Poll, pp. 79–81.

she refused to identify. One of them, a "multinational corporation," claimed its rate of turnover in management positions was two and a half times higher among top-performing women than men. That company, Schwartz reveals in a later interview, is Mobil Corporation—and its women managers were fleeing not because they were mommy tracking but because "until the last few years, it was a company that was not responsive to women."[53] Only in 1989 did Mobil even get around to modifying its leave-of-absence policy to allow its employees to work a reduced workweek temporarily to care for sick children or elderly parents, Mobil's employee policy manager Derek Harvey concedes. But, Harvey maintains, Mobil is very accommodating of its women: "We're a very paternalistic company."[54]

■ **CONSIDER THE SOURCE**

1. What are the hallmarks of the "trend story," in Faludi's view?

2. According to Faludi, how have economic pressures on newspapers and magazines changed the way news is reported?

3. Summarize Faludi's argument about media reporting of the cocooning and mommy-tracking trends. How well does it exemplify her definition of "trend journalism"? What evidence does she draw on to refute these trends?

4. What relationship does Faludi see between Faith Popcorn's contracts with advertisers and her predictions of national trends? How does Faludi establish the connection?

■ **CONSIDER THE IMPLICATIONS**

5. Discuss the journalistic practices condemned and condoned in Faludi's article and in the selections from Massing and Rosenthal, (pp. 240–48), and Jeff Cohen, (pp. 222–28). As a class, prepare a code of journalistic ethics.

6. Look at the language used to label various trends: "mommy track," "cocooning," "bailing out." In your journal, make a list of the images that each of these labels evokes and then analyze your list. How would those images change if the press referred to these trends as "the family values track," "hibernating," or "scaling back"?

---

53. Personal interview with Felice Schwartz, Nov. 1989. Apparently Schwartz was no model employer in this regard either. While Schwartz claimed to be "totally flexible about pregnancy," a Catalyst employee who had had a complicated and difficult pregnancy told *Working Woman* that when she came back to work, she discovered that her job was no longer available. Schwartz's explanation to *Working Woman*'s reporter: The woman "absolutely refused to keep me posted on whether she was coming in or not," she said, and that was "a ridiculous imposition on Catalyst." See Hopkins, "Felice Schwartz," p. 148.

54. Personal interview with Derek Harvey, June 1991.

7. Research the trends that have been predicted or defined for your generation. Did the trends come in pairs? Where did you see them reported? Were the stories targeted at your generation or at a different audience? What evidence was given to support the predictions? Summarize your findings in an essay.

8. Identify a trend story that appears in several mainstream magazines and newspapers. You'll usually find such stories in the "Living" or "Lifestyle" sections of newspapers, where feature articles regularly appear. Write an essay comparing different journalists' coverage of the same story. What sources do the reporters cite? Do they build on the same evidence? Do they build on each other's stories? How does the story change as it passes from one publication to another?

9. Write a letter to Faludi in which you support or refute her implied thesis that the press should objectively chronicle the news instead of trying to shape public opinion.

▪ ▪ ▪ ▪ ▪ ▪

CHRISTINA HOFF SOMMERS

The Backlash Myth

After Susan Faludi described a media backlash against women in general, her book Backlash *prompted some media lashing of her in particular. One of the loudest voices raised against Faludi's analysis of our culture was that of Christina Hoff Sommers (b. 1950). In the following selection from her book,* Who Stole Feminism? How Women Have Betrayed Women *(1994), Sommers directly rebuts the arguments made by Faludi in "The Media and the Backlash" (pp. 248–62). She builds on several magazine reviews critical of Faludi's book and counters Faludi's experts with her own authorities, claim by claim. Sommers both relies on and exemplifies print's function as a medium for disputation, where one's published words can be reread, checked for accuracy, and then publicly challenged. An associate professor of philosophy at Clark University, Sommers is the editor of two textbooks on ethics. Her articles on feminism have appeared in* The New Republic, *the* Wall Street Journal, USA Today, *and* The National Review.

When regard for truth has been broken down or even
slightly weakened, all things will remain doubtful.
— ST. AUGUSTINE

From *Who Stole Feminism? How Women Have Betrayed Women* (New York: Simon & Schuster, 1994), pp. 227–54.

A couple of years ago, American publishing was enlivened by the release of Susan Faludi's *Backlash* and Naomi Wolf's *The Beauty Myth*, two impassioned feminist screeds uncovering and denouncing the schemes that have prevented women from enjoying the fruits of the women's movement.[1] For our purposes, what these books have in common is more interesting and important than what distinguishes them. Both reported a widespread conspiracy against women. In both, the putative conspiracy has the same goal: to prevent today's women from making use of their hard-won freedoms—to punish them, in other words, for liberating themselves. As Ms. Wolf informs us: "After the success of the women's movement's second wave, the beauty myth was perfected to checkmate power at every level in individual women's lives."[2]

Conspiracy theories are always popular, but in this case the authors, writing primarily for middle-class readers, faced a tricky problem. No reasonable person in this day and age could be expected to believe that somewhere in America a group of male "elders" has sat down to plot ways to perpetuate the subjugation of women. How, then, could they persuade anyone of the existence of a widespread effort to control women for the good of men?

The solution that they hit upon made it possible for them to have their conspiracy while disavowing it. Faludi and Wolf argued that the conspiracy against women is being carried out by malevolent but invisible backlash forces or beauty-myth forces that act in purposeful ways. The forces in question are subtle, powerful, and insidiously efficient, and women are largely unconscious of them. What is more, the primary enforcers of the conspiracy are not a group of sequestered males plotting and planning their next backlash maneuvers: it is women themselves who "internalize" the aims of the backlash, who, unwittingly, do its bidding. In other words, the backlash is Us. Or, as Wolf puts it, "many women internalize Big Brother's eye."[3]

Faludi's scope is wider than Wolf's; she argues that the media and the political system have been co-opted by the backlash, as well:

> The backlash is not a conspiracy, with a council dispatching agents from some central control room, nor are the people who serve its ends often aware of their role; some even consider themselves feminists. For the most part, its workings are encoded and internalized, diffuse and chameleonic . . . generated by a culture machine that is always scrounging for a "fresh" angle. Taken as a whole, however, these codes and cajolings,

1. Susan Faludi, *Backlash: The Undeclared War Against American Women* (New York: Crown, 1991); Naomi Wolf, *The Beauty Myth: How Images of Beauty Are Used against Women* (New York: Doubleday, 1992).

2. Wolf, *The Beauty Myth*, p. 19.

3. Ibid., p. 99; **Big Brother's eye**: In George Orwell's novel *1984*, the government, personified as "Big Brother," constantly observes people in their homes.—ED.

these whispers and threats and myths, move overwhelmingly in one direction: they try to push women back into their "acceptable" roles.[4] ...

Faludi's approach is that of the muckraking reporter bent on saving [5] women by exposing the lies, half-truths, and deceits that the male-oriented media have created to demoralize women and keep them out of the workplace. Her readers might naturally assume that she herself has taken care to be truthful. However, not a few astonished reviewers discovered that *Backlash* relies for its impact on many untruths—some far more serious than any it exposes. In her *New York Times* review, the journalist and feminist Ellen Goodman gently chastised Faludi for overlooking evidence that did not fit her puzzle. But Goodman's tone was so enthusiastic—she praised the book for its "sharp style" and thoroughness—that few heeded her criticisms.[5] Within weeks *Backlash* jumped to the top of the best-seller lists, becoming the hottest feminist book in decades. Faludi was in demand—on the lecture circuit, on talk shows, in book stores, and in print. The more serious criticism came a few months later.

In a letter to *The New York Times Book Review,* Barbara Lovenheim, author of *Beating the Marriage Odds,* reported that she had looked into some of Faludi's major claims and found them to be erroneous. Her letter presented some egregious examples and concluded that Faludi "skews data, misquotes primary sources, and makes serious errors of omission."[6] Although Lovenheim is a respected and responsible journalist, the review editors of the *Times* have a policy of fact-checking controversial material, and they asked Lovenheim to provide detailed proof that her criticisms of Faludi were well grounded. She complied, and the *Times* devoted half a page to the publication of Lovenheim's letter. Here is a portion of Lovenheim's argument and findings.

Faludi had written: "Women under thirty-five now give birth to children with Down's syndrome at a higher rate than women over thirty-five."[7] That claim fits well with Faludi's central thesis that the backlash is particularly aimed at professionally successful single women. By propagating false reports that women over thirty-five are at a higher risk of bearing a child with birth defects, the backlash seeks to discourage women and to harm their careers by causing them to worry about their decision to delay childbirth.

But, says Ms. Lovenheim, the deplorable truth is that age *sharply* increases a woman's chance of having a baby with Down's syndrome. The

---

4. Faludi, *Backlash,* p. xxii.

5. Ellen Goodman, "'The Man Shortage' and Other Big Lies," *The New York Times Book Review,* October 27, 1991, p. 1.

6. Barbara Lovenheim, letter to *The New York Times Book Review,* February 9, 1992.

7. Faludi, *Backlash,* p. 30.

chances are one in one thousand under age twenty-five, one in four hundred at thirty-five, one in one hundred at forty, and one in thirty-five at forty-four.[8] Lovenheim points out that, in making her false claim, Faludi misrepresents her own source, *Working Woman* (August 1990). For *Working Woman* had warned its readers that a variety of abnormalities are associated with maternal age, among them that older women "are more likely to conceive fetuses with chromosomal defects such as Down's syndrome."[9]

One of Faludi's more sensational claims—it opens her book—is that there is a concerted effort under way to demoralize successful women by spooking them about a man shortage. Faludi denies that there is a shortage, but Lovenheim shows that the facts do not support her. Though there is no man shortage for women in their twenties and early thirties, things change by the time women reach their mid-thirties. The census data indicate that between the ages of thirty-five and forty-four, there are eighty-four single men for every hundred women.[10] There are as many as one million more single women than single men between ages thirty-five and fifty-four. Lovenheim points out that Faludi made it look otherwise by leaving out all divorced and widowed singles.

Faludi responded to Lovenheim's letter two weeks later. She said she "welcomed" attempts to correct "minor inaccuracies." But she could not "help wondering at the possible motives of the letter writer, who is the author of a book called *Beating the Marriage Odds*." She made an attempt to explain her bizarre claim that older women have a lower incidence of Down's births. The claim was poorly worded, she conceded: She really meant to say that since women over thirty-five tend to be screened for birth defects, many abort their defective fetuses, lowering their rate of live births to babies with this abnormality. She neglected to add that this concession undercuts her larger argument.

After Lovenheim's letter was published, reviewers in several journals began to turn up other serious errors in Faludi's arguments. She had cited, for example, a 1986 article in *Fortune* magazine reporting that many successful women were finding demanding careers unsatisfying and were "bailing out" to accommodate marriage and children. According to Faludi, "The *Fortune* story left an especially deep and troubled impression on young women aspiring to business and management careers. . . . The year after *Fortune* launched the 'bailing out' trend, the proportion of women applying to business schools suddenly began to shrink—for the first time in a decade."

---

8. "Facts About Down Syndrome for Women over 35" (Washington D.C.: National Institute of Health, 1979), p. 9.

9. Lovenheim, ibid., p. 30.

10. Bureau of Census, Current Population Reports, Series P 23, no. 162, June 1989. Cited in Barbara Lovenheim, *Beating the Marriage Odds* (New York: William Morrow, 1990), p. 34.

In a review, Gretchen Morgenson of *Forbes* magazine called this thesis "interesting but wrong." She wrote, "There was no shrinkage following the *Fortune* story. According to the American Assembly of Collegiate Schools of Business, which reports on business school graduates, the proportion of women graduates increased every year from 1967 through 1989, the most recent figures available."[11]

Morgenson also deflated Faludi's claim that in the eighties, "women were pouring into many low-paid female work ghettos." United States Bureau of Labor statistics, she pointed out, show that "the percentage of women executives, administrators, and managers among all managers in the American work force has risen from 32.4 percent in 1983 to 41 percent in 1991." Morgenson judged Faludi's book "a labyrinth of nonsense followed by eighty pages of footnotes."[12]

Time magazine, which was preparing an article on Faludi, found other glaring inconsistencies, primarily in Faludi's economic reckonings, which apparently led them to modify the ebullient tone of their story with the admonition that Faludi "rightly slams journalists who distort data in order to promote what they view as a larger truth; but in a number of instances, she can be accused of the same tactics."[13] *Time* reporter Nancy Gibbs looked into some of Faludi's complaints about the way the media have dealt with the economic effects of divorce on women:

> Faludi demonstrates that the studies on the impact of divorce greatly exaggerate the fall in the average woman's living standard in the year after she leaves her husband. But she adds that five years after divorce, most women's standard of living has actually improved. She relegates to a footnote the fact that this is because most have remarried.[14]

Faludi is especially critical of anyone in the media who finds fault 15 with current day-care arrangements. She treats a 1984 *Newsweek* story as a diatribe against day care that glorifies women who give up careers to raise their kids. But Cathy Young, the reviewer from *Reason* magazine, points out that Faludi carefully refrained from mentioning that the author of the article called for quality day care and considered it to be "a basic family need."[15] To make her general case for a media backlash, Faludi assiduously collected media stories that question the joys of single life or the wisdom of a mother with small children choosing to work. Young observed that Faludi nowhere mentions the numerous articles that *encourage* women in these choices, nor those that celebrate

---

11. Gretchen Morgenson, "A Whiner's Bible," *Forbes,* March 16, 1992, p. 153.

12. Ibid., p. 152.

13. Nancy Gibbs, "The War Against Feminism," *Time,* March 9, 1992, p. 52.

14. Ibid.

15. Cathy Young, "Phony War," *Reason,* November 1991, p. 57.

"the new fatherhood, the benefits for girls of having working mothers, women in business and nontraditional jobs." Throughout her long book, Faludi gives the clear impression that the slant of coverage in major newspapers and magazines is distinctly antifeminist. According to Ms. Young, the opposite is true.

In a review for *Working Woman* magazine, Carol Pogash finds that Faludi "misconstrues statistics to suit her view that American women are no longer very anxious to wed."[16] Faludi interprets a 1990 Virginia Slims poll as finding that women placed the quest for a husband way at the bottom of their list of concerns. "Perhaps," says Ms. Pogash, "that's because 62 percent of the women in the sample were already married, a fact [Faludi] doesn't mention."[17] Ms. Pogash notes that Faludi also misstated the results of another Virginia Slims poll as showing that "70 percent of women believed they could have a 'happy and complete life' without a wedding ring." In fact the question was, "Do you think it is possible for a woman to have a complete and happy life if she is single?"—not whether the respondent herself could be happy as a single woman.

Faludi talks about "the wages of the backlash," and her most insistent theme is that women are being severely punished economically for the social and civic progress they had made prior to the eighties. How a feminist reacts to data about gender gaps in salaries and economic opportunities is an excellent indication of the kind of feminist she is. In general, the equity feminist points with pride to the many gains women have made toward achieving parity in the workplace. By contrast, the gender feminist makes it a point to disparage these gains and to speak of backlash. It disturbs her that the public may be lulled into thinking that women are doing well and that men are allowing it. The gender feminist insists that any so-called progress is illusory.

■ **CONSIDER THE SOURCE**

1. How does the opening quotation from St. Augustine relate to Sommers's critique of Susan Faludi's claims?

2. What sort of evidence does Sommers use to refute Faludi? What sources does she rely on?

3. According to Sommers, what differentiates the two categories of feminists that she describes?

4. Look closely at Sommers's refutation of Faludi's claim about a decline in applications to business school. Does Sommers's source provide information that directly contradicts Faludi?

---

16. *Working Woman,* April 1992, p. 104.
17. Ibid.

▪ **CONSIDER THE IMPLICATIONS**

5. How "egregious" are the "untruths" that Sommers reveals? How seriously do they undermine Faludi's arguments? Hold a class discussion comparing the credibility of Faludi and Sommers. Which author do you believe and why?

6. To support her claim about declining applications to business school, Faludi cites an article by Laurie Baum, while Sommers's refutation quotes Gretchen Morgenson. Research Sommers's and Faludi's claims by comparing their essays to the sources they cite. Do the authors accurately represent their sources? How trustworthy do the original sources seem? What is the basis for your impressions?

7. Examine the labels that Sommers applies to the two types of feminists she describes: "equity feminists" and "gender feminists." In your journal, explore how the labels affect your assessments of the two groups. What other labels might you apply to the same groups?

8. Read at least six reviews of Faludi's book. How do the reviewers evaluate Faludi's use of sources? Do they characterize her book in the same way that Sommers does? Are the reviews largely positive or negative? Summarize your findings and compare them to Sommers's assessment.

9. Read at least six reviews of Sommers's book. How do the reviewers characterize her approach to feminism? What objections do they raise? Are the reviews largely positive or negative? How does each review reflect the position of the publication it appeared in?

10. Read Gloria Steinem's essay (pp. 277–303) and decide whether Sommers would categorize Steinem as an "equity feminist" or a "gender feminist." Study the appendix entry on Simon & Schuster and discuss why the same publisher would have published both Steinem's and Sommers's books. What other books on women's issues does Simon & Schuster publish?

▪ ▪ ▪ ▪ ▪ ▪

JOE TYE

Buying Silence: Self-Censorship of Smoking and Health in National Newsweeklies

Our nation's press corps zealously guards its freedom to report all the news without interference from governmental forces or political pressures. But what about economic pressure? In order to meet the high costs of production and distribution, most newspapers and magazines today

From *Tobacco-Free Youth Reporter*, 4:1 (Spring 1989), p. 14.

depend on advertising revenues, not subscription dollars. This can leave editors and publishers at the mercy of their advertisers, as Joe Tye (b. 1951) indicates in this survey of the impact of cigarette advertising on three national newsmagazines. Tye's article originally appeared in Tobacco-Free Youth Reporter, *the quarterly publication of Stop Teenage Addiction to Tobacco (STAT), an organization devoted to coverage of the tobacco industry's efforts to hook teens on cigarettes. The magazine offered the editors of the three newsweeklies the opportunity to reply to Tye's article, but none responded. Joe Tye was the administrator of Baystate Medical Center in Springfield, Massachusetts until 1992. He has coauthored several articles on smoking and children for the* Journal of the American Medical Association. *Now a professional writer and speaker, Tye is the author of* Never Fear, Never Quit: A Story of Courage and Perseverance *(1995) and* Staying on Top When the World's Upside Down *(1995).*

The media's self-censorship on smoking and health may well be contributing to the occurrence of avoidable illnesses and premature deaths among tens of thousands of Americans.
– KENNETH E. WARNER, PhD
New England Journal of Medicine, 1985

Quite likely, publishers will feel increasing moral pressure to drop cigarette ads.
– Time, 1969

On December 18, 1953, John C. Whitaker, then-chairman of the RJ Reynolds tobacco company, was infuriated by an article in the *Charlotte Observer* which stated that lung cancer deaths in South Carolina were up 25 percent in the past six years, and that "recent medical reports have indicated smoking may be connected with lung cancer." He grabbed his pen and scrawled across the page: "Carolina *contacts:* Can't such outbursts as the attached be silenced?"

The tobacco industry was well experienced at using its contacts to prevent the media from reporting on smoking and health issues. As reported by Thomas Whiteside in his landmark 1971 book, *Selling Death,* results of the 1954 Hammond & Horn study on smoking and lung cancer "made the front pages of the press in this country but were virtually ignored on network television news shows—which, as it happened, were nearly all sponsored by cigarette companies."

On January 1, 1971, cigarette commercials were outlawed on television and radio, and tobacco companies transferred hundreds of millions of dollars in advertising to the print media. As the national newsweeklies began to depend on cigarette advertising revenues, one would expect to see a significant decline in their coverage of smoking and health issues.

To test this conclusion, STAT (Stop Teenage Addiction to Tobacco) researchers examined coverage of smoking and tobacco issues in *Time, Newsweek,* and *U.S. News & World Report* from 1950 to 1985. Each article listed in the *Reader's Guide to Periodical Literature* under "tobacco," "cigarettes," and "smoking" was examined.

As shown in the charts (below), a clear drop in coverage of smoking   5 and health topics by all three newsweeklies followed the elimination of broadcast cigarette advertising in 1971.

The 63 percent decline in the number and length of articles between 1960–1969 and 1970–1979 substantially understates the reduction in coverage of smoking and health issues. During the 1950s and 1960s most articles were about smoking and lung cancer or other diseases, but after 1970, most focused on business or political matters.

In defending *Time* magazine's acceptance of cigarette advertising, then-publisher Ralph P. Davidson said, "In our Medicine section, we take special care to report fully on any statistical and laboratory evidence which may link smoking with cancer and heart and respiratory disease." (*Business and Society Review,* Winter 1977–1978.)

However, we were unable to find a single article on statistical or laboratory evidence linking smoking with any of these diseases in *Time* magazine from 1971 until that statement was made. During all of the 1970s, in fact, *Time* ran only seventeen articles on smoking, one-third of which concerned business issues and were unrelated to health.

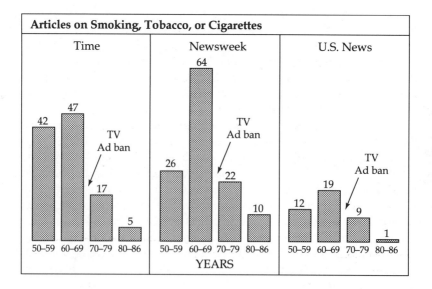

Articles on Smoking, Tobacco, or Cigarettes

A SMOKE SCREEN?

Perhaps more important than the reduction in the number of articles is the exclusion of smoking from articles about diseases caused by smoking. A study by the American Council on Science and Health showed that from 1981 to 1986, *U.S. News & World Report* did not mention smoking in eighteen stories about cancer and mentioned it only once in nineteen stories about heart disease. During the same period, *Time* mentioned smoking only once in twenty-two stories about heart disease and not at all in five articles about cancer.

In 1979, *Newsweek* carried a two-page article about the boom in smokeless tobacco use but did not hint that adverse health consequences might be associated with the product. A *Newsweek* cover story in August 1988 on the "Medical Mystery of Miscarriages" did not mention maternal cigarette smoking, although this has been identified as a major cause of miscarriage and spontaneous abortion.

Evidence suggests that the ignoring of smoking and health issues by these magazines is a direct result of publishers not wishing to offend cigarette advertisers. For example, in October 1984, *Time* included a personal health supplement written by the American Academy of Family Physicians. According to the academy, all references to smoking and health were excised by *Time* without the academy's approval. The only reference to smoking was a statement that smoking in bed should be avoided.

In November 1983, *Newsweek* ran a sixteen-page special supplement written by the American Medical Association [AMA], which virtually ignored smoking and health, although the original AMA manuscript included information on the subject. According to the AMA science editor, *Newsweek* "resisted any mention of cigarettes." That issue of *Newsweek* had twelve full-page cigarette advertisements.

The following October, *Newsweek* ran another personal health supplement written by the AMA. This one had a brief but hard-hitting section on smoking and health. That issue had only four cigarette ads. Evidently, the publishers got the message because in September 1985, a third personal health supplement said only that heavy smokers should see their physicians before exercising, and it downplayed the role of smoking and lung cancer in women's cancer mortality.

The publishers and editors of magazines justify their acceptance of cigarette advertising on the grounds that they are able to maintain a "Chinese Wall" between editorial policy and advertising policy.

This study supports earlier work concluding that this separation is more of a Japanese paper house wall and that from the beginning of the broadcast ban on cigarette ads until 1985, the major national newsweeklies systematically failed to accurately and completely report on smoking and health issues.

Although this study does not cover the period since 1985, these three newsweeklies appear to have increased their coverage of smoking and health issues during the past several years.

IGNORING THE ISSUES

No editor ever acknowledges that many cigarette ads are deceptive. Many do not even meet the minimal standards of the tobacco industry's own code of advertising ethics which prohibits depiction of vigorous athletic activity and of smoking as essential to social or sexual success. Nor will editors comment on the implicit health claims made in many cigarette ads which are unproven, false, and deceptive.

Nowhere could we find any article or editorial critical of the efforts of the tobacco industry to promote smoking or offering an alternative point of view. On the other hand, a number of editorials criticized "self-righteous" nonsmokers' rights advocates, and, not surprisingly, opposed any restrictions on tobacco advertising on freedom-of-speech grounds.

In 1985, when the AMA called for a total ban on all advertising and promotion of tobacco, marking a reversal of a decades-long hands-off position, the action should have been a major news story. The three newsweeklies, however, did not even cover the proposal. Also absent have been articles and editorial condemnation about the tobacco industry's efforts to develop cigarette markets in lesser developed nations.

Although the publishers and editors of *Time, Newsweek,* and *U.S. News & World Report* claim that their editorial policies are totally uncompromised by the acceptance of cigarette ads, evidence suggests that receiving millions of dollars in tobacco advertising fees every year has resulted in a systematic self-censorship on the issue of smoking and disease. 20

Articles on the nation's leading cause of preventable death have averaged less than two per year per magazine, which contrasts sharply with the coverage given AIDS, drugs, cholesterol, and other health-related issues. When cancer, heart disease, complications of pregnancy, and other diseases are covered, the role of smoking is minimized or eliminated.

A conflict of interest has prevented the major newsweeklies from appropriately covering the worldwide epidemic of cigarette-caused diseases. So long as these publications benefit from tobacco industry advertising revenues, it is unlikely that the public will be adequately informed of all important smoking and health and public policy issues.

▪ **CONSIDER THE SOURCE**

1. According to Tye, how did outlawing cigarette advertising on television and radio affect the print media?

2. Summarize the different ways that Tye demonstrates cigarette advertis-

ing's effect on reporting about smoking. Which of his examples is most persuasive? Why?

3. Who does Tye hold responsible for the decline in magazine coverage of the dangers of smoking?

▪ **CONSIDER THE IMPLICATIONS**

4. Using Tye's methodology, update his study in a group project. Scan the *Reader's Guide to Periodical Literature* or an online bibliography and locate all articles on "cigarettes," "smoking," and "tobacco" published in *Time, Newsweek,* and *U.S. News & World Report* in the past two years. How many articles in that time discuss the risks or adverse medical consequences of smoking? What other subjects do the articles treat? How many cigarette ads, on average, did you find in each magazine?

5. Compare the number and type of cigarette ads in several different types of magazines: a major newsweekly, a women's magazine (such as *Vogue, Mademoiselle,* or *Cosmopolitan*), a men's magazine (such as *Esquire, GQ,* or *Playboy*), and a sports magazine (*Sports Illustrated, Surfer, Hot Rod, Skiing,* or *Tennis*). Which audience is most heavily targeted by cigarette companies? What images do the ads associate with smoking? Do those images vary by audience?

6. Analyze several cigarette ads in terms of the "industry's own code of advertising ethics" that Tye describes.

7. In your journal, explore how your own attitudes toward smoking may have been affected by advertising. Do you remember any particular ads? What brands were considered the coolest in high school? Why?

8. Consider other types of advertising, such as those mentioned by Gloria Steinem (pp. 277–303). How might liquor distributors, automobile companies, or airlines, for instance, affect the news coverage that magazines offer us? Look back to some big stories of the past few years that portrayed those industries in a negative way. Count the number of ads from the affected industries in each issue that contained a story critical of the industry.

9. *JAMA: The Journal of the American Medical Association* periodically publishes a list of magazines that refuse to accept tobacco advertising. Study the list that appeared in the February 23, 1994, issue (reprinted here on pp. 571–76) and sort them into categories. What subject areas do these magazines cover? What are the publications' target audiences? How might these factors relate to their advertising policy?

10. Write a letter to the editor of the magazine of your choice, outlining your views on the magazine's advertising policies. Give specific examples to support your opinions.

11. In class discussion, explore the effect of advertisers' dollars on editorial policy. Could the journalistic trend that Tye outlines have resulted from a form of censorship? Compare the "self-censorship" Tye describes to what Erwin Knoll calls "prior restraint" (pp. 437–439).

DR. SAMUEL JOHNSON

On the Art of Advertising

Advertisers continually devise cleverer and subtler ways of hooking the ever-savvier consumer. They have honed their persuasive strategies until it seems that they couldn't possibly get any sharper. Yet many of the strategies they use are as old as advertising itself. In 1759, Dr. Samuel Johnson (1709–1784) criticized advertisers of his day for "abuses" that seem remarkably similar to the common practices of our present-day advertisers. He zeros in on the rhetoric that ads rely on to catch the attention of busy and inattentive readers. The comments of this British poet and critic appeared in a series of essays between 1758 and 1760, which were later collected in a publication called The Idler *(1761).*

The practice of appending to the narratives of public transactions more minute and domestic intelligence, and filling the newspapers with advertisements, has grown up by slow degrees to its present state.

Genius is shown only by invention. The man who first took advantage of the general curiosity that was excited by a siege or battle, to betray the readers of news into the knowledge of the shop where the best puffs and powder were to be sold, was undoubtedly a man of great sagacity and profound skill in the nature of man. But when he had once shown the way, it was easy to follow him; and every man now knows a ready method of informing the public of all that he desires to buy or sell, whether his wares be material or intellectual; whether he makes clothes, or teaches the mathematics; whether he be a tutor that wants a pupil, or a pupil that wants a tutor.

Whatever is common is despised. Advertisements are now so numerous that they are very negligently perused, and it is therefore become necessary to gain attention by magnificence of promises, and by eloquence sometimes sublime and sometimes pathetic.

Promise, large promise, is the soul of an advertisement. I remember a *wash-ball* that had a quality truly wonderful—it gave *an exquisite edge to the razor.* And there are now to be sold, *for ready money only,* some *duvets for bed-coverings of down, beyond comparison, superior to what is called otterdown,* and indeed such, that its *many excellences cannot be here set forth.* With one excellence we are made acquainted—*it is warmer than four or five blankets, and lighter than one.*

There are some, however, that know the prejudice of mankind in 5 favor of modest sincerity. The vender of the *beautifying fluid* sells a lotion that repels pimples, washes away freckles, smooths the skin, and

---

From *The Idler* (1761).

plumps the flesh, and yet, with a generous abhorrence of ostentation, confesses that it will not *restore the bloom of fifteen to a lady of fifty.*

The true pathos of advertisements must have sunk deep into the heart of every man that remembers the zeal shown by the seller of the *anodyne necklace,* for the ease and safety of *poor teething infants,* and the affection with which he warned every mother that *she would never forgive herself* if her infant should perish without a necklace.

I cannot but remark to the celebrated author who gave, in his notifications of the camel and dromedary, so may specimens of the genuine sublime, that there is now arrived another subject yet more worthy of his pen. *A famous Mohawk Indian warrior, who took Dieskaw, the French General prisoner, dressed in the same manner with the native Indians when they go to war, with his face and body painted, with his scalping-knife, tom-axe, and all other implements of war! a sight worthy the curiosity of every true Briton!* This is a very powerful description; but a critic of great refinement would say that it conveys rather *horror* than *terror.* An Indian, dressed as he goes to war, may bring company together; but if he carries the scalping knife and tom-ax, there are many true Britons that will never be persuaded to see him but through a grate.

It has been remarked by the severer judges that the salutary sorrow of tragic scenes is too soon effaced by the merriment of the epilogue; the same inconvenience arises from the improper disposition of advertisements. The noblest objects may be so associated as to be made ridiculous. The camel and dromedary themselves might have lost much of their dignity between *the true flour of mustard* and the *original Daffy's elixir;* and I could not but feel some indignation when I found this illustrious Indian warrior immediately succeeded by a *fresh parcel of Dublin butter.*

The trade of advertising is now so near to perfection, that it is not easy to propose any improvement. But as every art ought to be exercised in due subordination to the public good, I cannot but propose it as a moral question to these masters of the public ear, whether they do not sometimes play too wantonly with our passions, as when the registrar of lottery tickets invites us to his shop by an account of the prizes which he sold last year; and whether the advertising controvertists do not indulge asperity of language without any adequate provocation; as in the dispute about *straps for razors,* now happily subsided, and in the altercation which at present subsists concerning *eau de luce?*

In an advertisement it is allowed to every man to speak well of him- 10 self, but I know not why he should assume the privilege of censuring his neighbour. He may proclaim his own virtue or skill, but ought not to exclude others from the same pretensions.

Every man that advertises his own excellence should write with some consciousness of a character which dares to call the attention of the public. He should remember that his name is to stand in the same paper with those of the King of Prussia and the Emperor of Germany, and endeavour to make himself worthy of such association.

Some regard is likewise to be paid to posterity. There are men of diligence and curiosity who treasure up the papers of the day merely because others neglect them, and in time they will be scarce. When these collections shall be read in another century, how will numberless contradictions be reconciled; and how shall fame be possibly distributed among the tailors and bodice-makers of the present age?

Surely these things deserve consideration. It is enough for me to have hinted my desire that these abuses may be rectified; but such is the state of nature, that what all have the right of doing, many will attempt without sufficient care or due qualifications.

■ **CONSIDER THE SOURCE**

1. What is Johnson's attitude toward the "art of advertising"? What language best conveys his point of view?

2. Explain what Johnson means by "sublime" and "pathetic." What examples does he give of each sort of eloquence?

3. List the "abuses" of advertising that Johnson feels should be corrected.

4. In your own words, paraphrase Johnson's arguments in paragraphs 11 and 12. What status does publication in a newspaper confer? Why should advertisers care about posterity?

5. Compare Johnson's writing style with that of his contemporary, Benjamin Franklin (pp. 29–37 and 431–436). How long are their sentences? What sort of language do they use? What audience(s) do they seem to be targeting?

■ **CONSIDER THE IMPLICATIONS**

6. In small groups, study the ads in a current magazine or newspaper. To what extent do current advertisers rely on the "large promise," "modest sincerity," "pathos," or "asperity of language" that Johnson describes? What additional strategies do today's advertisers use?

7. Compare Johnson's remarks about how the location of ads affects the editorial copy with Steinem's discussion of advertisers' "insertion orders" (pp. 295–297). What effect do Johnson and Steinem believe ads have on the credibility of editorial content? How do advertisers seem to view the relationship between ads and editorial copy?

8. Examine a current magazine or newspaper to see how and where ads are placed in relation to copy. What patterns can you discover? How does placement enhance or diminish the impact of either the ads or the articles? Summarize your findings in an essay that analyzes the relationship between ads and magazine content.

9. In your library, locate copies of newspapers of an earlier era, either on microfilm or in their original printed form. How do they differ from papers of today? Where are the ads placed? How much space is devoted to news as compared to advertising? How closely do the advertisers' appeals resemble those of current advertisers?

GLORIA STEINEM

Sex, Lies, and Advertising

Gloria Steinem (b. 1934) remains one of the best-known figures of the women's movement. She helped organize the Women's Political Caucus in 1971 and a year later became the founding editor of Ms. *magazine, where she fought for twenty years to change how American women viewed themselves and how corporations approached women consumers. When* Ms. *reinvented itself as a reader-supported, advertising-free publication, Steinem was finally able to go public with the inside story you are about to read about how advertisers use economic leverage to influence the content of women's magazines. In the 1991 version of her exposé, Steinem recalls that she "put on paper the ad policies that had been punishing* Ms. *for all the years of its nonconforming life and still were turning more conventional media, especially (but not only) those directed at women, into a dumping ground for fluff." Response to that article came from all over. While editors and writers for other women's magazines offered "additional horror stories," advertising executives justified their policies and blamed* Ms. *for being too controversial. Readers wrote hundreds of letters expressing outrage at how their access to news stories had been manipulated by advertisers. Steinem's article has been reprinted in dozens of textbooks like this one, allowing college students to take a hard look at the publications that provide the "images that shape our dreams." This updated version of the article comes from Steinem's most recent book,* Moving Beyond Words *(1994). Her other books include* Outrageous Acts and Everyday Rebellions *(1983), and* Revolution from Within: A Book of Self-Esteem *(1992).*

Toward the end of the 1980s, when glasnost was beginning and *Ms.* magazine seemed to be ending, I was invited to a press lunch for a Soviet official. He entertained us with anecdotes about the new problems of democracy in his country; for instance, local Communist leaders who were being criticized by their own media for the first time, and were angry.

"So I'll have to ask my American friends," he finished pointedly, "how more subtly to control the press."

In the silence that followed, I said: "Advertising."

The reporters laughed, but later one of them took me aside angrily: How dare I suggest that freedom of the press was limited in this country? How dare I imply that *his* newsmagazine could be influenced by ads?

From *Moving Beyond Words* (New York: Simon & Schuster, 1994), pp. 125–68. (See listing under *Ms.* in appendix.)

I explained that I wasn't trying to lay blame, but to point out ad-   5
vertising's media-wide influence. We can all recite examples of "soft"
cover stories that newsmagazines use to sell ads, and self-censorship
in articles that should have taken advertised products to task for, say,
safety or pollution. Even television news goes "soft" in ratings wars,
and other TV shows don't get on the air without advertiser support.
But I really had been thinking about women's magazines. There, it
isn't just a little content that's designed to attract ads; it's almost all of
it. That's why advertisers—not readers—had always been the problem
for *Ms.* As the only women's magazine that didn't offer what the
ad world euphemistically describes as "supportive editorial atmosphere" or "complementary copy" (for instance, articles that praise
food/fashion/beauty subjects in order to "support" and "complement" food/fashion/beauty ads), *Ms.* could never attract enough ads
to break even.

"Oh, *women's* magazines," the journalist said with contempt.
"Everybody knows they're catalogs—but who cares? They have nothing
to do with journalism."

I can't tell you how many times I've had this argument since I
started writing for magazines in the early 1960s, and especially since
the current women's movement began. Except as moneymaking machines—"cash cows," as they are so elegantly called in the trade—
women's magazines are usually placed beyond the realm of serious
consideration. Though societal changes being forged by women have
been called more far-reaching than the industrial revolution by such
nonfeminist sources as the *Wall Street Journal*—and though women's
magazine editors often try hard to reflect these changes in the few
pages left after all the ad-related subjects are covered—the magazines
serving the female half of this country are still far below the journalistic
and ethical standards of news and general-interest counterparts. Most
depressing of all, this fact is so taken for granted that it doesn't even
rate an exposé.

For instance: If *Time* and *Newsweek,* in order to get automotive and
GM ads, had to lavish editorial praise on cars and credit photographs in
which newsmakers were driving, say, a Buick from General Motors,
there would be a scandal—maybe even a criminal investigation. When
women's magazines from *Seventeen* to *Lear's* publish articles lavishing
praise on beauty and fashion products, and crediting in text describing
cover and other supposedly editorial photographs a particular makeup
from Revlon or a dress from Calvin Klein because those companies also
advertise, it's just business as usual.

When *Ms.* began, we didn't consider *not* taking ads. The most important reason was to keep the price of a feminist magazine low enough
for most women to afford. But the second and almost equal reason was

to provide a forum where women and advertisers could talk to each other and experiment with nonstereotyped, informative, imaginative ads. After all, advertising was (and is) as potent a source of information in this country as news or TV or movies. It's where we get not only a big part of our information but also images that shape our dreams.

We decided to proceed in two stages. First, we would convince makers of "people products" that their ads should be placed in a women's magazine: cars, credit cards, insurance, sound equipment, financial services—everything that's used by both men and women but was then advertised only to men. Since those advertisers were accustomed to the division between editorial pages and ads that news and general-interest magazines at least try to maintain, such products would allow our editorial content to be free and diverse. Furthermore, if *Ms.* could prove that women were important purchasers of "people products," just as men were, those advertisers would support other women's magazines, too, and subsidize some pages for articles about something other than the hothouse worlds of food/fashion/beauty. Only in the second phase would we add examples of the best ads for whatever traditional "women's products" (clothes, shampoo, fragrance, food, and so on) that subscriber surveys showed *Ms.* readers actually used. But we would ask those advertisers to come in *without* the usual quid pro quo of editorial features praising their product area; that is, the dreaded "complementary copy."

From the beginning, we knew the second step might be even harder than the first. Clothing advertisers like to be surrounded by editorial fashion spreads (preferably ones that credit their particular labels and designers); food advertisers have always expected women's magazines to publish recipes and articles on entertaining (preferably ones that require their products); and shampoo, fragrance, and beauty products in general insist on positive editorial coverage of beauty aids—a "beauty atmosphere," as they put it—plus photo credits for particular products and nothing too depressing; no bad news. That's why women's magazines look the way they do: saccharine, smiley-faced and product-heavy, with even serious articles presented in a slick and sanitized way.

But if *Ms.* could break this link between ads and editorial content, then we should add "women's products" too. For one thing, publishing ads only for gender-neutral products would give the impression that women have to become "like men" in order to succeed (an impression that *Ms.* ad pages sometimes *did* give when we were still in the first stage). For another, presenting a full circle of products that readers actually need and use would allow us to select the best examples of each category and keep ads from being lost in a sea of similar products. By being part of this realistic but unprecedented mix, products formerly advertised only to men would reach a growth market of women, and good ads for women's products would have a new visibility.

Given the intelligence and leadership of *Ms.* readers, both kinds of products would have unique access to a universe of smart consultants whose response would help them create more effective ads for other media too. Aside from the advertisers themselves, there's nobody who cares as much about the imagery in advertising as those who find themselves stereotyped or rendered invisible by it. And they often have great suggestions for making it better.

As you can see, we had all our energy, optimism, and arguments in good working order.

I thought at the time that our main problem would be getting ads with good "creative," as the imagery and text are collectively known. That was where the women's movement had been focusing its efforts, for instance, the National Organization for Women's awards to the best ads, and its "Barefoot and Pregnant" awards for the worst. Needless to say, there were plenty of candidates for the second group. Carmakers were still draping blondes in evening gowns over the hoods like ornaments that could be bought with the car (thus also making clear that car ads weren't directed at women). Even in ads for products that only women used, the authority figures were almost always male, and voice-overs for women's products on television were usually male too. Sadistic, he-man campaigns were winning industry praise; for example, *Advertising Age* hailed the infamous Silva Thin cigarette theme, "How to Get a Woman's Attention: Ignore Her," as "brilliant." Even in medical journals, ads for tranquilizers showed depressed housewives standing next to piles of dirty dishes and promised to get them back to work. As for women's magazines, they seemed to have few guidelines; at least none that excluded even the ads for the fraudulent breast-enlargement or thigh-thinning products for which their back pages were famous.

Obviously, *Ms.* would have to avoid such offensive imagery and seek out the best ads, but this didn't seem impossible. *The New Yorker* had been screening ads for aesthetic reasons for years, a practice that advertisers accepted at the time. *Ebony* and *Essence* were asking for ads with positive black images, and though their struggle was hard, their requests weren't seen as unreasonable. . . .

Let me take you through some of our experiences—greatly condensed, but just as they happened. . . .

— Cheered on by early support from Volkswagen and one or two other car companies, we finally scrape together time and money to put on a major reception in Detroit. U.S. carmakers firmly believe that women choose the upholstery color, not the car, but we are armed with statistics and reader mail to prove the contrary: A car is an important purchase for women, one that is such a symbol of mobility and freedom that many women will spend a greater percentage of income for a car than will counterpart men.

15

But almost nobody comes. We are left with many pounds of shrimp on the table, and quite a lot of egg on our face. Assuming this near-total boycott is partly because there was a baseball pennant play-off the same day, we blame ourselves for not foreseeing the problem. Executives go out of their way to explain that they wouldn't have come anyway. It's a dramatic beginning for ten years of knocking on resistant or hostile doors, presenting endless documentation of women as car buyers, and hiring a full-time saleswoman in Detroit—all necessary before *Ms.* gets any real results.

This long saga has a semi-happy ending: Foreign carmakers understood better than Detroit that women buy cars, and advertised in *Ms.;* also years of research on the women's market plus door-knocking began to pay off. Eventually, cars became one of our top sources of ad revenue. Even Detroit began to take the women's market seriously enough to put car ads in other women's magazines too, thus freeing a few more of their pages from the food/fashion/beauty hothouse.

But long after figures showed that a third, even half, of many car models were being bought by women, U.S. makers continued to be uncomfortable addressing female buyers. Unlike many foreign carmakers, Detroit never quite learned the secret of creating intelligent ads that exclude no one and then placing them in media that overcome past exclusion. Just as an African American reader may feel more invited by a resort that placed an ad in *Ebony* or *Essence,* even though the same ad appeared in *Newsweek,* women of all races may need to see ads for cars, computers, and other historically "masculine" products in media that are clearly directed at them. Once inclusive ads are well placed, however, there's interest and even gratitude from women. *Ms.* readers were so delighted to be addressed as intelligent consumers by a routine Honda ad with text about rack-and-pinion steering, for example, that they sent fan mail. But even now, Detroit continues to ask: "Should we make special ads for women?" That's probably one reason why foreign cars still have a greater share of the women's market in the United States than of the men's.

— In the *Ms.* Gazette, we do a brief report on a congressional hearing into coal tar derivatives used in hair dyes that are absorbed through the skin and may be carcinogenic. This seems like news of importance: Newspapers and newsmagazines are reporting it too. But Clairol, a Bristol-Myers subsidiary that makes dozens of products, a few of which have just come into our pages as ads *without* the usual quid pro quo of articles on hair and beauty, is outraged. Not at newspapers or newsmagazines, just at us. It's bad enough that *Ms.* is the only women's magazine refusing to provide "supportive editorial" praising beauty products, but to criticize one of their product

categories on top of it, however generically or even accurately—
well, *that* is going too far.

We offer to publish a letter from Clairol telling its side of the
story. In an excess of solicitousness, we even put this letter in the
Gazette, not in Letters to the Editors, where it belongs. Eventually,
Clairol even changes its hair-coloring formula, apparently in response to those same hearings. But in spite of surveys that show *Ms.*
readers to be active women who use more of almost everything
Clairol makes than do the readers of other women's magazines, *Ms.*
gets almost no ads for those dozens of products for the rest of its
natural life.

— Women of color read *Ms.* in disproportionate numbers. This is a
source of pride to *Ms.* staffers, who are also more racially representative than the editors of other women's magazines (which may include some beautiful black models but almost no black decisionmakers; Pat Carbine hired the first black editor at *McCall's,* but she
left when Pat did). Nonetheless, the reality of *Ms.'s* staff and readership is obscured by ads filled with enough white women to make
the casual reader assume *Ms.* is directed at only one part of the population, no matter what the editorial content is.

When Pat Carbine requests African American, Latina, Asian,
and other diverse images (which exist, if at all, in ads created for
"special media"), she remembers mostly "astonishment." Marcia
Ann Gillespie, then a *Ms.* contributing editor and previously editor
in chief of *Essence,* is witnessing ad bias a second time around: Having tried for *Essence* to get white advertisers to use black images
(Revlon did so eventually, but L'Oréal, Lauder, Chanel, and other
companies never came through during her tenure), she now sees
similar problems getting racially diverse ads for a racially diverse
magazine. In an exact parallel of the fear that marketing a product
to females will endanger its appeal to males, the agency response is
often: "But your [white] readers won't identify."

In fact, those few ads we are able to get that feature women of 25
color—for instance, one made by Max Factor for *Essence* and *Ebony*
that Linda Wachner gives us while she is president of Max Factor—
are greeted with praise and relief by white readers, too, and make
us feel that more inclusive ads should win out in the long run. But
there are pathetically few such images. Advertising "creative" also
excludes women who are not young, not thin, not conventionally
pretty, well-to-do, able-bodied, or heterosexual—which is a hell of a
lot of women.

— Our intrepid saleswomen set out early to attract ads for the product
category known as consumer electronics: sound equipment, computers, calculators, VCRs, and the like. We know that *Ms.* readers
are determined to be part of this technological revolution, not to be

left out as women have been in the past. We also know from surveys that readers are buying this kind of stuff in numbers as high as those of readers of magazines like *Playboy* and the "male eighteen to thirty-four" market, prime targets of the industry. Moreover, unlike traditional women's products that our readers buy but don't want to read articles about, these are subjects they like to see demystified in our pages. There actually *is* a supportive editorial atmosphere.

"But women don't understand technology," say ad and electronics executives at the end of our presentations. "Maybe not," we respond, "but neither do men—and we all buy it."

"If women *do* buy it," counter the decisionmakers, "it's because they're asking their husbands and boyfriends what to buy first." We produce letters from *Ms.* readers saying how turned off they are when salesmen say things like "Let me know when your husband can come in."

Then the argument turns to why there aren't more women's names sent back on warranties (those much-contested certificates promising repair or replacement if anything goes wrong). We explain that the husband's name may be on the warranty, even if the wife made the purchase. But it's also true that women are experienced enough as consumers to know that such promises are valid only if the item is returned in its original box at midnight in Hong Kong. Sure enough, when we check out hair dryers, curling irons, and other stuff women clearly buy, women don't return those warranties very often either. It isn't the women who are the problem, it's the meaningless warranties.

After several years of this, we get a few ads from companies like   30 JVC and Pioneer for compact sound systems—on the grounds that women can understand compacts, but not sophisticated components. Harry Elias, vice president of JVC, is actually trying to convince his Japanese bosses that there is something called a woman's market. At his invitation, I find myself speaking at trade shows in Chicago and Las Vegas trying to persuade JVC dealers that electronics showrooms don't have to be locker rooms. But as becomes apparent, however, the trade shows are part of the problem. In Las Vegas, the only women working at technology displays are seminude models serving champagne. In Chicago, the big attraction is Marilyn Chambers, a porn star who followed Linda Lovelace of *Deep Throat* fame as Chuck Traynor's captive and/or employee, whose pornographic movies are being used to demonstrate VCRs.

In the end, we get ads for a car stereo now and then, but no VCRs; a welcome breakthrough of some IBM personal computers, but no Apple or no Japanese-made ones. Furthermore, we notice that *Working Woman* and *Savvy*, which are focused on office work, don't benefit as much as they should from ads for office equipment either.

In the mind's eye of the electronics world, females and technology don't mix, even in the designing of children's video games. Electronics is further behind than Detroit. Finally, I threaten to hire male ad reps for a magazine called *Mr.*, send them out with all the same readership statistics, and reveal only at the end of the presentation that these consumer dollars are coming from women. But I'm not sure even that would do the trick. As long as advertisers keep feeding "women" into the computer, "not our target audience" will keep coming out. The trick is to feed in "people" instead—but that isn't what happens. Even newsstands are gender segregated: *Ms.* gets placed with women's magazines—where our readers are less likely to browse and where we look odd anyway—instead of with *Time, Newsweek, Rolling Stone,* and other things our readers buy. It's still an upside-down world, with genitalia placed above heads or hearts. . . .

When *Ms.* began, the staff decided not to accept ads for feminine hygiene sprays and cigarettes on the same basis: they are damaging to many women's health but carry no appropriate warnings. We don't think we should tell our readers what to do—if marijuana were legal, for instance, we would carry ads for it along with those for beer and wine—but we should provide facts so readers can decide for themselves. Since we've received letters saying that feminine sprays actually kill cockroaches and take the rust off metal, we give up on those. But antismoking groups have been pressuring for health warnings on cigarette ads as well as packages, so we decide we will accept advertising if the tobacco industry complies.

Philip Morris is among the first to do so. One of its brands, Virginia Slims, is also sponsoring women's tennis tournaments and women's public opinion polls that are historic "firsts." On the other hand, the Virginia Slims theme, "You've come a long way, baby," has more than a "baby" problem. It gives the impression that for women, smoking is a sign of progress.

We explain to the Philip Morris people that this slogan won't do well in our pages. They are convinced that its success with *some* women means it will work with *all* women. No amount of saying that we, like men, are a segmented market, that we don't all think alike, does any good. Finally, we agree to publish a small ad for a Virginia Slims calendar as a test, and to abide by the response of our readers.

The letters from readers are both critical and smart. For instance: Would you show a photo of a black man picking cotton next to one of an African American man in a Cardin suit, and symbolize progress from slavery to civil rights by smoking? Of course not. So why do it for women? But instead of honoring test results, the executives seem angry to have been proved wrong. We refuse Virginia Slims ads, thus annoying tennis players like Billie Jean King as well as incurring a new level of wrath: Philip Morris takes away ads for *all* its many products, costing *Ms.* about $250,000 in the first year. After five years, the damage is so great we can no longer keep track.

Occasionally, a new set of Philip Morris executives listens to *Ms.* saleswomen, or laughs when Pat Carbine points out that even Nixon got pardoned. I also appeal directly to the chairman of the board, who agrees it is unfair, sends me to another executive—and *he* says no. Because we won't take Virginia Slims, not one other Philip Morris product returns to our pages for the next sixteen years.

Gradually, we also realize our naivete in thinking we could refuse all cigarette ads, with or without a health warning. They became a disproportionate source of revenue for print media the moment television banned them, and few magazines can compete or survive without them; certainly not *Ms.*, which lacks the support of so many other categories. Though cigarette ads actually inhibit editorial freedom less than ads for food, fashion, and the like—cigarette companies want only to be distant from coverage on the dangers of smoking, and don't require affirmative praise or photo credits of their product—it is still a growing source of sorrow that they are there at all. By the 1980s, when statistics show that women's rate of lung cancer is approaching men's, the necessity of taking cigarette ads has become a kind of prison. . . .

— We hear that women in the (then) Soviet Union have been producing feminist samizdat (underground, self-published books) and circulating them throughout the country. Through feminists in Paris, we get one such samizdat, which has been smuggled out and translated into French: a diverse, brave, tough-minded, and lyrical collection of essays called *Mother Russia.* Soon, we also hear that four of the main organizers and writers have been exiled—given a choice between Siberia and exile, they chose with sadness to leave their country—and so are free to talk for the first time. Though *Ms.* is operating on its usual shoestring, we solicit contributions for plane fare and send Robin Morgan to interview them in Vienna.

The result is an exclusive cover story; a rare grassroots, bottom-up view of Russian life in general and the lives of Russian women in particular. The interview also includes the first news of a populist peace movement against the Soviet occupation of Afghanistan, and prediction of glasnost to come. From the popular media to women's studies and political science courses, the response is great. The story wins a Front Page award. 40

Nonetheless, this journalistic coup undermines years of hard work trying to get an ad schedule from Revlon. Why? Because the Soviet women on our cover *are not wearing makeup.*

— General Mills, Pillsbury, Carnation, Del Monte, Dole, Kraft, Stouffer, Hormel, Nabisco: You name the food giant, we try to get its ads. But no matter how desirable the *Ms.* readership, our lack of editorial recipes and traditional homemaking articles proves lethal.

We explain that women flooding into the paid labor force have changed the way this country eats; certainly, the boom in convenience foods proves that. We also explain that placing food ads *only* next to recipes and how-to-entertain articles is actually a negative for many women. It associates food with work—in a way that says only women have to cook—or with guilt over *not* cooking and entertaining. Why not advertise food in diverse media that don't always include recipes (thus reaching more men, who have become a third of all supermarket shoppers anyway) and add the recipe interest with specialty magazines like *Gourmet* (a third of whose readers are men)?

These arguments elicit intellectual interest but no ads. No advertising executive wants to be the first to say to a powerful client, "Guess what, I *didn't* get you complementary copy." Except for an occasional hard-won ad for instant coffee, diet drinks, yogurt, or such extras as avocados and almonds, the whole category of food, a mainstay of the publishing industry, remains unavailable to us. Period.

Traditionally, wines and liquors didn't advertise to women: Their 45 makers were convinced that even though the wife might do the buying, the husband chose the brand. After alcoholic beverages (other than beer and wine) were forbidden to advertise on television, women's magazines were at a continual disadvantage.

But with the leadership of Michel Roux of Carillon Importers (distributor of Grand Marnier, Absolut vodka, and other brands), that begins to change. With a Frenchman's assumption that food and drink have no gender, and with ads that use good artists, he begins to lead the category out of its men's club. Meanwhile, diligent *Ms.* saleswomen have carried their studies on brand choice and entertaining from one ad agency to the next, like cross-pollinating bees. By the 1980s, Drummond Bell, president of National Distillers and self-described as "to the right of Genghis Khan," has discovered that feminism is actually about fair play, something he understands as a self-made man; and Ernest Gallo, once so angry at *Ms.*'s coverage of Cesar Chavez and the United Farm Workers that he said he would put wine ads in *Ms.* "only after *Pravda*," now also comes into our pages.

As a result of countless such efforts, this category of ads supports a lot of good fiction, investigative journalism, feminist theory, humor, and art in *Ms.*

Of course, there are exceptions. Beermakers keep right on selling masculinity. Though they know college women drink beer, they assume this ends with graduation. Besides, they believe beer is "masculine," and showing women in the ads as customers, not just ornaments, will devalue it as "feminine." (Sort of like the old "Negro retainers" shown serving elegant "white" drinks on a silver tray but certainly never drinking them. The sex/race parallel rarely fails.) It takes *Ms.* eight years to get even one beer ad: Michelob Light.

But in general, liquor as a "people product" is less pushy editorially and less condescending in the creative content of its ads. When there *are* problems with an ad campaign (for instance, "After she cooks a great dinner, pay tribute to it with Grand Marnier"), there's also more willingness to change ("After a great dinner, . . ." a deletion of two words that got praise). When the "Hit Me with a Club" campaign of Heublein's Club Cocktail got letters from *Ms.* readers because it trivialized violence (it showed a smiling woman with a black eye, and some versions showed a man), the whole multimillion-dollar campaign was changed nationally, and Heublein published a letter in *Ms.* to thank readers for their responsiveness and help.

But given the underrepresentation of other categories in *Ms.,* 50 these very facts tend to create a disproportionate number of ads for alcoholic beverages. This in turn dismays readers who are worried about women and alcoholism.

— Four years of research and presentations go into convincing airlines that women make their own travel choices and business trips. United, the first airline to advertise in *Ms.,* is so impressed with the response from our readers that one of its executives agrees to be filmed giving us a testimonial so we can use it as an ad presentation. As usual, good ads get great results.

But we have other problems. Because flight attendants for American Airlines include among their union demands a request to have their last names preceded by "Ms." on their name tags—a revolt against the standard "I am your pilot, Captain Rothgart, and this is your flight attendant, Cindy Sue"—American officials think the magazine is partly responsible for this uppity behavior. We get no ads.

At Eastern there is a different disaster. Thousands of subscriptions keep *Ms.* on hundreds of Eastern flights: part of our circulation guarantee to advertisers. Suddenly, they are canceled. Why? Because the vice president in charge of putting magazines on planes is offended by *Ms.* classified ads for lesbian poetry journals; at least, that's what he gives us as an example. As he explains to me coldly on the phone, "a family airline has to draw the line somewhere."

Obviously, *Ms.* can't exclude lesbians and serve women. That's been clear ever since our first issue, when we were warned not to include anything by or about lesbians—and so, of course, published a major article that was both. Letters from readers, both gay and straight, were appreciative: All nonconforming women can be stopped by the word "lesbian" until it becomes as honorable as any other. But Suzanne Braun Levine, our main editor, and I were lectured by such media heavy hitters as Ed Kosner, then editor of *Newsweek* (now editor of *Esquire,* and perhaps in a different state of consciousness), who insisted that *Ms.* should "position" itself as the feminist magazine *against* lesbians. In Eastern's case, the same message came with economic clout. Ad rates are based on reaching a certain number of readers, and soliciting new subscriptions to replace the canceled ones would cost $150,000 (which we don't have), plus rebating money to advertisers in the meantime.

Like most experiences with the ad world, this presents a Kafkaesque organizing problem. After days of unsuccessful searching for a sympathetic ear on the Eastern board of directors, Frank Thomas, president of the Ford Foundation, kindly offers to call Roswell Gilpatric, who is an Eastern director. I talk with Mr. Gilpatric, who kindly offers to call Frank Borman, then the president of Eastern. Frank Borman calls me to say his airline is not in the business of censoring magazines. *Ms.* will be returned to Eastern flights.

I have one more conversation with the vice president, who is angry at having been overruled—I hope he has no blunt instruments—but we're fine. Except that we've wasted three weeks of energy and ingenuity, which could have been used to move forward. Too much of our lives corresponds to the "lost-wallet" theory of life. You lose something, spend a long time finding it, and then feel grateful to be back where you started. . . .

— By the end of 1986, magazine production costs have skyrocketed and postal rates have increased 400 percent. Ad income is flat for the whole magazine industry. The result is more competition, with other magazines offering such "extras" as free golf trips for advertisers or programs for "sampling" their products at parties and other events arranged by the magazine for desirable consumers. We try to compete with the latter by "sampling" at what we certainly have enough of: movement benefits. Thus, little fragrance bottles turn up next to the dinner plates of California women lawyers (who are delighted), or wine samples lower the costs at a reception for political women. A good organizing tactic comes out of this. We hold feminist seminars in shopping centers. They may be to the women's movement what churches were to the civil rights movement in the South—that is, *where people are.* Anyway, shopping center seminars are a great success. Too great. We have to stop doing them in Bloomingdale's up and down the East Coast, because meeting space in the stores is too limited, and too many women are left lined up outside stores. We go on giving out fancy little liquor bottles at store openings, which makes the advertisers happy—but not us.

Mostly, however, we can't compete in this game of "value-added" (the code word for giving the advertisers extras in return for their ads). Neither can many of the other independent magazines. Deep-pocketed corporate parents can offer such extras as reduced rates for ad schedules in a group of magazines, free tie-in spots on radio stations they also own, or vacation junkets on corporate planes.

Meanwhile, higher costs and lowered income have caused the *Ms.* 60/40 preponderance of edit over ads—something we promised to readers—to become 50/50: still a lot better than most women's magazines' goal of 30/70, but not good enough. Children's stories, most poetry, and some fiction are casualties of reduced space. In order to get variety into more limited pages, the length (and sometimes the depth) of articles suffers. Though we don't solicit or accept ads that would look like a parody in our pages, we get so worn down that some slip through. Moreover, we always have the problem of working just as hard to get a single ad as another magazine might for a whole year's schedule of ads.

Still, readers keep right on performing miracles. Though we haven't been able to afford a subscription mailing in two years, they maintain our guaranteed circulation of 450,000 by word of mouth. Some of them also help to make up the advertising deficit by giving *Ms.* a birthday present of fifteen dollars on its fifteenth anniversary, or contributing one thousand dollars for a lifetime subscription—even those who can ill afford it.

What's almost as angering as these struggles, however, is the way the media reports them. Our financial problems are attributed to lack of reader interest, not an advertising double standard. In the Reagan-Bush era, when "feminism-is-dead" becomes one key on the typewriter, our problems are used to prepare a grave for the whole movement. Clearly, the myth that advertisers go where the readers are—thus, if we had readers, we would have advertisers—is deeply embedded. Even industry reporters rarely mention the editorial demands made by ads for women's products, and if they do, they assume advertisers must be right and *Ms.* must be wrong; we must be too controversial, outrageous, even scatological to support. In fact, there's nothing in our pages that couldn't be published in *Time, Esquire,* or *Rolling Stone*—providing those magazines devoted major space to women—but the media myth often wins out. Though comparable magazines our size (say, *Vanity Fair* or the *Atlantic*) are losing more money in a single year than *Ms.* has lost in sixteen years, *Ms.* is held to a different standard. No matter how much never-to-be-recovered cash is poured into starting a magazine or keeping it going, appearances seem to be all that matter. (Which is why we haven't been able to explain our fragile state in public. Nothing causes ad flight like the smell of nonsuccess.)

My healthy response is anger, but my not-so-healthy one is depression, worry, and an obsession with finding one more rescue. There is hardly a night when I don't wake up with sweaty palms and pounding heart, scared that we won't be able to pay the printer or the post office; scared most of all that closing our doors will be blamed on a lack of readers and thus the movement, instead of the real cause. ("Feminism couldn't even support one magazine," I can hear them saying.)

Out of chutzpah and desperation, I spend weeks trying to schedule a lunch with Leonard Lauder, president of Estée Lauder, whose ads we've spent years pursuing. With the exception of Clinique (the brainchild of Carol Phillips, a line of skin products whose appeal is more purity than glamour), none of Lauder's brands has advertised in *Ms.* A year's schedule for just a few of his hundreds of products would make all the difference. Indeed, as the scion of a family-owned company whose ad practices influence those of the whole industry, he is one of the few people who could liberate many pages in all women's magazines just by changing his mind about "complementary copy."

Over a fancy lunch that costs more than we can pay for some articles, I explain how much we need his leadership. I also lay out the record of *Ms.:* more literary and journalistic prizes won, more new ideas introduced to the country, more new writers discovered, and more impact on society than any other magazine; more articles that became books, stories that became movies, ideas that became television series; and, most important for him, a unique place for his ads to reach women who are, to use the advertising word, "trendsetters," and just aren't reachable any other way. They don't read other women's magazines regularly or have time for television. But whether it's waiting until later to have first babies, or pioneering PABA in skin products as protection against skin cancer, *whatever* these readers are doing today, a third to half of American women will be doing three to five years from now. It's never failed. Moreover, he will be reaching a constantly "refreshed" readership, to use the advertising term, because the median age has remained in the early thirties for more than a decade, so we know younger readers are constantly arriving.

But, he says, *Ms.* readers are not *our* women. They're not interested 65 in things like fragrance, moisturizer, and blush. If they were, *Ms.* would be writing articles about them.

On the contrary, I explain, *Ms.* readers are more likely to buy such things than are the readers of, say, *Cosmopolitan* or *Vogue.* We're out in the world more and need several sets of everything: for home, work, purse, travel, gym, and so on. But what we don't need is articles about fragrance, moisturizer, and blush. After all, would men's magazines be expected to publish monthly features on how to shave as the price of getting ads for shaving products from Aramis (his line of men's skin products)?

He concedes that beauty features are often concocted more for advertisers than for readers. But *Ms.* isn't appropriate for his ads anyway. Why? Because Estée Lauder is selling "a kept-woman mentality."

I can't quite believe this. Sixty percent of the women who use his products are salaried and greatly resemble the profile of *Ms.* readers. Besides, unlike Revlon and most others, his company has the appeal of being founded by a creative and hardworking woman, his mother, Estée Lauder.

That doesn't matter, he says. He knows his customers, and they would *like* to be kept women. That's why he will never advertise in *Ms.*

Perhaps feeling sorry for me by now, he gives me advice on getting *other* advertisers. For instance, I should borrow the apartment of a mutual friend who is rich, hold dinner parties there, and invite a lot of celebrities—plus just one advertiser. (If you invite two, he warns, each may feel demeaned by the presence of the other.) He himself often does this with department store executives and other people he needs for business. In his art-filled apartment, he hosts dinner parties, with one business target plus distinguished guests and celebrities. Why? Because if you enable executives to say in the office tomorrow, "As Henry Kissinger said to me last night . . . ," they'll do anything for you.

On my way back to the office to report this debacle to the waiting staff, I feel a terrible empathy for everybody in this crazy system—including Leonard Lauder (who, incidentally, still stoutly insists this conversation never took place). We're all being flattened by a velvet steamroller. The only difference is that at *Ms.*, we keep standing up again.

Ms. has been getting thinner and thinner and having more and more harrowing escapes from death. In November 1987, by vote of the Ms. Foundation for Education and Communication (*Ms.*'s owner and publisher, the media subsidiary of the Ms. Foundation for Women), *Ms.* is sold to Fairfax, an Australian company whose officers, Australian feminists Sandra Yates and Anne Summers, have persuaded its board to come up with the money, and who have already started *Sassy*, a U.S. version of an Australian magazine for teenage women. It's very sad— but also better than being bought for our subscription list and folded into a traditional magazine. These are two good women who want to do their best to keep *Ms.*'s feminist spirit.

In their two-year tenure, circulation goes up to 550,000 because of investment in subscription mailings, but they fall afoul of the ad world in a different way. They give in a bit to its pressures, and, to the dismay of some readers, clothes, new products, more celebrities, gardening, and other editorial features are added. Nonetheless, *Ms.* is still far from the commercial habits of other magazines, and ad pages fall below previous levels. In addition, *Sassy*, whose fresh voice and sexual frankness started out as an unprecedented success among young readers, is targeted for an ad boycott by two mothers from Indiana who began, as one of them put it, "calling every Christian organization I could think of." In re- sponse to letters from organizations like the American Family Associa- tion in Tupelo, Mississippi, at least nine major advertisers pull back. Though *Sassy* doesn't give in completely, a preboycott spirit that in- cluded reader letters about incest and such titles as "The Truth About Boys' Bodies" turns into a postboycott atmosphere with such articles as "Virgins Are Cool."

This kind of link between ads and editorial was a problem in Aus- tralia, too, but to a lesser degree. "Our readers pay two times more for their magazines," Anne Summers explained, "so advertisers have less power to threaten a magazine's viability."

"I was shocked," said Sandra Yates with characteristic directness. 75 "In Australia, we think you have freedom of the press here—but you don't."

After Fairfax gets into financial problems of its own, Anne and San- dra bravely find new investors, but they don't control their destiny as we did—which is why we could choose to keep going for so long on a shoestring. When they are unable to meet their budget's projections for ad revenue, they are forced to sell. In October 1989, *Ms.* and *Sassy* are taken over by Dale Lang, owner of *Working Mother, Working Woman,* and one of the few independent publishing companies left among the con- glomerates. In response to a request from those of us on the original *Ms.* staff—as well as to reader letters urging *Ms.* to continue, plus his own belief that *Ms.*'s existence benefits his other women's magazines by blaz- ing a trail—Lang agrees to publish *Ms.*, with the staff retaining editorial control, and to experiment with a new ad-free format supported entirely by newsstand sales and subscriptions.

The idea of having no ads at all is regarded as total folly by the mag- azine industry. Readers are accustomed to paying full cost of books but never magazines, readers really like the ads—there are all kinds of in- dustry arguments against this. Nonetheless, checks come rolling in for subscriptions that cost nearly 300 percent more now that they're ad- free. . . .

I would like to tell you that industry reporters are saying, "We were wrong, advertising was the problem all along"—but they're not. *Ms.* has found a new way of publishing by proving that readers will pay for what they really want, but we're regarded mostly as an oddity. So far, the old way is still in place—especially for publications aimed at women.

At the time of *Ms.*'s sale to Fairfax in 1987, I gave a farewell speech to the American Association of Advertising Agencies. The audience in- cluded many creative and caring people, a few of whom had gone out on a limb to help *Ms.*, and I hoped some of them would consider the possibility—I would say the fact—that insisting on "complementary" editorial actually penalizes advertisers too. For one thing, there is no re- search proving that an ad placed next to a similar article is more effective than the same ad next to, say, a good piece of fiction or investigative reporting. According to Joseph Smith of Oxtoby-Smith, Inc., a consumer research firm: "Broadly speaking, there is no persuasive evidence that the editorial context of an ad matters." For another thing, there is research that shows just the opposite: Such links damage *everybody's* credibility. A 1987 survey by the *Journal of Advertising Research* concluded that the "higher the rating of editorial believability, the higher the rating of the advertising."

So I screw up my courage, give many examples, tap-dance my heart out, and try for a big finish. "*Ms.* won reader support and jeopardized traditional advertiser support for exactly the same reason—the editorial content wasn't dictated by the ads." In a voice shaking with sixteen years of work and emotion, I say as forcefully as I can: "*There's something wrong in a world in which women readers—and advertisers trying to reach them—don't want the same thing.*"

There is polite applause. Then they all go out to play golf. The velvet steamroller goes right on.

If we're going to have diverse and free sources of information, we have to understand how deep this tradition of ad influence goes, and how wide it spreads.

Ever since *Ladies' Magazine* debuted in Boston in 1828, editorial copy directed to women has been informed by something other than their interests. There were no ads then, but in an age when married women were legal minors, with no right to their own money to pay for subscriptions, there was another controlling revenue source: husbands. "Husbands may rest assured," wrote editor Sarah Josepha Hale, "that nothing found in these pages shall cause [their wives] to be less assiduous in preparing for his reception or encourage her to 'usurp station' or encroach upon prerogatives of men."

Hale went on to become the editor of *Godey's Lady's Book*, a magazine featuring "fashion plates": engravings of dresses to be copied by one's seamstress or by readers themselves. Gradually, Hale added the "how to" articles that were to set the social tone of women's service magazines—how to write politely, how to avoid sunburn of one's ladylike skin, and, in no fewer than 1,200 words, how to maintain a goose quill pen. She also advocated women's education, but not to the point of controversy. Just as most women's magazines now praise socially approved ways of living, suggest individual solutions to what really are political problems, and avoid taking editorial stands on controversial issues like abortion (even if their own polls show that an overwhelming majority of their readers support them), Hale made sure that *Godey's* avoided the hot topics of its day: slavery, abolition, and female suffrage.

What turned women's magazines into catalogs, however, were two events: Ellen Butterick's invention of the clothing pattern in 1863, and the mass manufacture of patent medicines that contained anything from harmless colored water to small amounts of cocaine. For the first time, readers could purchase what a magazine had encouraged them to want. As the sale of such products made these magazines more profitable and they were able to pay better salaries, they also began to attract male editors. (Indeed, men continued to be the top editors of most women's magazines until the current feminist revolt launched protests like the 1970 sit-in at *Ladies' Home Journal*.) Edward Bok, who became the *Ladies' Home Journal* editor in 1889, inadvertently discovered the power of advertisers when he rejected patent medicines as useless or worse, and other advertisers canceled their ads in retribution. By the early twentieth century, *Good Housekeeping* had started a special institute to "test and approve" products. Its Seal of Approval became the grandfather of all "value-added" programs that offer public relations and merchandising to advertisers.

Generations of suffragist struggle finally won women the vote in 1920, but women's magazines were in no position to help them use it. The magazines' main function was to create a desire for products, instruct in the use of products, and make products a crucial part of gaining social approval, catching a husband, pleasing a husband, and performing as a homemaker. A few short stories and unrelated articles might be included to persuade women to buy what otherwise would have been given away as a catalog—and some of them offered women a voice and sense of community within these pages that came into their own homes. But even those articles were rarely critical from a consumerist point of view or rebellious in other ways. Fiction, too, usually had a formula: If a woman had an affair outside marriage, she must come to a bad end. If she hadn't been chaste before marriage, she could only hope to find an unusually glamorous man who would forgive her—and to whom she would be forever grateful.

Helen Gurley Brown at *Cosmopolitan* began to change that formula in the 1960s by bringing the "sexual revolution" into a women's magazine—but in an ad-oriented way. Sex outside marriage became OK for women too, which was a major and welcome departure. Nonetheless, as the "Cosmo Girl" made clear, attracting multiple men required even more products.

In response to women who flooded the workforce in the 1970s, traditional women's magazines—that is, trade magazines for women who work at home (or, as antifeminists would say, "women who don't work")—were joined by *New Woman* (then a collection of reprints), *Savvy, Working Woman,* and other trade magazines for women who work outside the home (though they mostly portrayed these jobs as white-collar; since advertisers weren't interested in low-salaried blue-collar workers, or lower-salaried pink-collar ones in fields where most women work, neither were these magazines). By continuing to publish the fashion/beauty/entertaining articles necessary to get traditional ads and then adding a few career articles on top of that, these new magazines inadvertently helped to create the antifeminist stereotype of Superwoman. (They may also have contributed to their own demise in some cases, for Superwoman made women tired just to read about her.) This male-imitative, dress-for-success woman carrying a briefcase—as well as raising perfect children, cooking gourmet meals, having multiple orgasms, and entertaining beautifully—became the media image of a woman worker. Though women at a real briefcase-carrying level are statistically rare and the glorified secretarial jobs that occupy most women in offices pay less than blue-collar women often earn, advertisers continued to believe that a prime female target must be like her male executive counterpart—only cook, have children, and be sexy besides. Needless to say, dress-for-success women were also thin, white, and beautiful. The majority of women in the workforce might see their family work in traditional women's magazines, but they rarely see their paid work as secretaries, salesclerks, teachers, and nurses.

Do you think, as I once did, that advertisers make decisions based on rational and uniform criteria? Well, think again. There is clearly a double standard. The same food companies that insist on recipes in women's magazines place ads in *People* where there are no recipes. Cosmetics companies support *The New Yorker*, which has no regular beauty columns, and newspaper pages that have no "beauty atmosphere."

Meanwhile, advertisers' control over the editorial content of women's magazines has become so institutionalized that it is sometimes written into "insertion orders" or dictated to ad salespeople as official policy—whether by the agency, the client, or both. The following are orders given to women's magazines effective in 1990. Try to imagine them being applied to *Time* or *Newsweek*. 90

– Dow's Cleaning Products stipulated that ads for its Vivid and Spray 'n Wash products should be adjacent to "children or fashion editorial"; ads for bathroom cleaner should be next to "home furnishing/family" features; with similar requirements for other brands. "If a magazine fails for half the brands or more," the Dow order warned, "it will be omitted from further consideration."

– Bristol-Myers, the parent of Clairol, Windex, Drano, Bufferin, and much more, stipulated that ads be placed next to "a full page of compatible editorial."

– S. C. Johnson & Son, makers of Johnson Wax, lawn and laundry products, insect sprays, hair sprays, and so on, insisted that its ads "*should not be opposite extremely controversial features or material antithetical to the nature/copy of the advertised product.*" (Italics theirs.)

– Maidenform, manufacturer of bras and other women's apparel, left a blank for the particular product and stated in its instructions: "The creative concept of the _____ campaign, and the very nature of the product itself appeal to the positive emotions of the reader/consumer. Therefore, it is imperative that all editorial adjacencies reflect that same positive tone. The editorial must not be negative in content or lend itself contrary to the _____ product imagery/message (e.g., *editorial relating to illness, disillusionment, large size fashion, etc.*)." (Italics mine.)

— The De Beers diamond company, a big seller of engagement rings, ₉₅ prohibited magazines from placing its ads with "adjacencies to hard news or antilove/romance themed editorial."

— Procter & Gamble, one of this country's most powerful and diversified advertisers, stood out in the memory of Anne Summers and Sandra Yates (no mean feat in this context) because its products were not to be placed in *any* issue that included *any* material on gun control, abortion, the occult, cults, or the disparagement of religion. Caution was also demanded in any issue that included articles on sex or drugs, even for educational purposes.

When I went back to see if these orders were still in effect, my ad agency source said that giving out such information would "breach our contract" with clients, so you'll have to make your own judgment by looking at those ads and their surroundings in current magazines. But here are three insertion orders given to a national women's magazine in 1993.

— Kraft/General Foods, a giant with many brands, sent this message with an Instant Pudding ad: "urgently request upbeat parent/child activity editorial, mandatory positioning requirements—opposite full page of positive editorial—right hand page essential for creative— minimum six page competitive separation (i.e., all sugar-based or sugar-free gelatins, puddings, mousses, creames [sic] and pie filling)—Do not back with clippable material. Avoid: controversial/negative topics and any narrow targeted subjects."

— An American Tobacco Company order for a Misty Slims ad noted that the U.S. government warning must be included, but also that there must be: "no adjacency to editorial relating to health, medicine, religion, or death."

— Lorillard's Newport cigarette ad came with similar instructions, ₁₀₀ plus: "Please be aware that the Nicotine Patch products are competitors. The minimum six-page separation is required."

Quite apart from anything else, you can imagine the logistical nightmare this creates when putting a women's magazine together, but the greatest casualty is editorial freedom. Though the ratio of advertising to editorial pages in women's magazines is only about 5 percent more than in *Time* or *Newsweek*, that nothing-to-read feeling comes from all the supposedly editorial pages that are extensions of ads. To find out what we're really getting when we pay our money, I picked up a variety of women's magazines for February 1994, and counted the number of pages in each one (even including table of contents, letters to the editors, horoscopes, and the like) that were not ads and/or copy complementary to ads. Then I compared that number to the total pages. Out of 184 pages, *McCall's* had 49 that were non-ad or ad-related. Of 202, *Elle* gave readers 48. *Seventeen* provided its young readers with only 51 non-ad or ad-related pages out of 226. *Vogue* had 62 out of 292. *Mirabella* offered readers 45 pages out of a total of 158. *Good Housekeeping* came out on top, though only at about a third, with 60 out of 176 pages. *Martha Stewart Living* offered the least. Even counting her letter to readers, a page devoted to her personal calendar, and another one to a turnip, only seven out of 136 pages had no ads, products, or product mentions. . . .

Sometimes, advertisers invade editorial pages—literally—by plunging odd-shaped ads into the text, no matter how that increases the difficulty of reading. When Ellen Levine was editor of *Woman's Day*, for instance, a magazine originally founded by a supermarket chain, she admitted, "The day the copy had to rag around a chicken leg was not a happy one."

The question of ad positioning is also decided by important advertisers, a rule that's ignored at a magazine's peril. When Revlon wasn't given the place of the first beauty ad in one Hearst magazine, for instance, it pulled its ads from *all* Hearst magazines. In 1990 Ruth Whitney, editor in chief of *Glamour*, attributed some of this pushiness to "ad agencies wanting to prove to a client that they've squeezed the last drop of blood out of a magazine." She was also "sick and tired of hearing that women's magazines are controlled by cigarette ads." Relatively speaking, she was right. To be as controlling as most advertisers of women's products, tobacco companies would have to demand articles in flat-out praise of smoking, and editorial photos of models smoking a credited brand. As it is, they ask only to be forewarned so they don't advertise in the same issue with an article about the dangers of smoking. But for a magazine like *Essence*, the only national magazine for African American women, even taking them out of one issue may be financially difficult, because other advertisers might neglect its readers. In 1993, a group called Women and Girls Against Tobacco, funded by the California Department of Health Services, prepared an ad headlined "Cigarettes Made Them History." It pictured three black singers—Mary Wells, Eddie Kendricks, and Sarah Vaughan—who died of tobacco-related diseases. *Essence* president Clarence Smith didn't turn the ad down, but he didn't accept it either. When I talked with him in 1994, he said with pain, "the black female market just isn't considered at parity with the white female market; there are too many other categories we don't get."

That's in spite of the fact that *Essence* does all the traditional food-fashion-beauty editorial expected by advertisers. According to California statistics, African American women are more addicted to smoking than the female population at large, with all the attendant health problems.[1]

Alexandra Penney, editor of *Self* magazine, feels she has been able to include smoking facts in health articles by warning cigarette advertisers in advance (though smoking is still being advertised in this fitness magazine). On the other hand, up to this writing in 1994, no advertiser has been willing to appear opposite a single-page feature called "Outrage," which is reserved for important controversies, and is very popular with readers. Another women's magazine publisher told me that to this day Campbell's Soup refuses to advertise because of an article that unfavorably compared the nutritional value of canned food to that of fresh food—fifteen years ago.

I don't mean to imply that the editors I quote here share my objections to ad demands and/or expectations. Many assume that the women's magazines at which they work have to be the way they are. Others are justifiably proud of getting an independent article in under the advertising radar, for instance, articles on family violence in *Family Circle* or a series on child sexual abuse and the family courts in *McCall's*. A few insist they would publish exactly the same editorial, even if there were no ads. But it's also true that it's hard to be honest while you're still in the job. "Most of the pressure came in the form of direct product mentions," explained Sey Chassler, who was editor in chief of *Redbook* from the sixties to the eighties and is now out of the game. "We got threats from the big guys, the Revlons, blackmail threats. They wouldn't run ads unless we credited them.

"But it's not fair to single out the beauty advertisers, because these pressures came from everybody. Advertisers want to know two things: What are you going to charge me? What *else* are you going to do for me? It's a holdup. For instance, management felt that fiction took up too much space. They couldn't put any advertising in that. Over the last years, the number of fiction entries into the National Magazine Awards has declined.

"And pressures are getting worse. More magazines are more bottom-line oriented, because they have been taken over by companies with no interest in publishing.

"I also think advertisers do this to women's magazines specially," he concluded, "because of the general disrespect they have for women."

Even media experts who don't give a damn about women's magazines are alarmed by the spread of this ad-edit linkage to other media. As the *Wall Street Journal* headlined: "Hurt by Ad Downturn, More Mag-

---

1. Jan Ferris, "BUTT OUT: Publishers and Their Tobacco Habit," *Columbia Journalism Review*, January/February 1994, pp. 16–18.

azines Use Favorable Articles to Woo Sponsors."[2] Women's products are increasingly able to take their practices with them wherever they go. For instance, newsweeklies publish uncritical stories on fashion and fitness to court ads. *Vanity Fair* published a profile of Ralph Lauren, a major advertiser, illustrated by the same photographer who does his ads, and turned the lifestyle of another, Calvin Klein, into a cover story. At *Longevity*, the editor-in-chief quit because publisher Bob Guccione (who invented *Penthouse*) insisted on running a Nuprin ad featuring tennis star Jimmy Connors right next to a Connors interview, with a photo a lot like the ad.[3] Even the outrageous *Spy* has gotten tamer since it began to seek fashion ads.

Newspapers seem to give in more often, too. *The New York Times* 110 *Magazine* recently ran an article on "firming creams," complete with mentions of advertisers. Toward the end of 1993, it ran an eight-page article and fashion spread photographed in Vietnam—the same crowded streets and poor countryside we remember from the war. Only now, the Vietnamese were modeling $3,000 Chanel dresses, or clothes from Ralph Lauren, Armani, and other advertisers, all available in New York department stores. ("Eastern dress is subtly sexy," we are told, "Indo-chic" clothes and "frog closures are like erotic flash points.")[4] As for women's pages in general, now often called the "Style" or "Living" section, they were originally invented to report on social events given by wives of prominent citizens, often the president of the local supermarket chain or other advertisers. Even now, the commercialism on some of those pages might cause a scandal if transferred to the front page.

Some advertisers of "people products" are also feeling emboldened even when dealing with serious media. Columbia Pictures (part of the Sony empire) recently threatened to withhold ads from the *Los Angeles Times* as punishment for a scathing review of a Schwarzenegger movie (though it's rumored that the *Times* got even by reporting a prostitution scandal involving Columbia executives). Graef Crystal, a former columnist for *Financial World* who did investigative reporting that helped make excessive corporate salaries a national issue, feels he was fired because of pressure from corporate advertisers, and NBC offered to feature advertisers in a sports program if they would purchase commercials during its breaks.[5] "Many journalists, who are paid to see trends," reported the *Wall Street Journal*, "think they see an alarming one in their

---

2. Joanne Lipman, *Wall Street Journal*, July 30, 1991.

3. Jon Swan, "The Crumbling Wall," *Columbia Journalism Review*, May/June 1992, p. 23.

4. Text by Philip Shenon, produced by Polly Hamilton, photographs by Marie Laure De Decker, "The Mist of Perfume River," *The New York Times Magazine*, November 21, 1993.

5. Jon Swan, "The Crumbling Wall," p. 23.

own industry. With newspapers facing tough times financially, they see an increase in the tendency of newspapers to cater to advertisers or pull their punches when it comes to criticizing advertisers in print."[6]

And just to make us really worry, films and books, the last media to go directly to the public without having to pass through the minds of advertisers first, are seeing some inroads, too. Producers are beginning to depend on fees paid for displaying products in movies. Books, the chief refuge of in-depth investigative reporting, have been commissioned by companies like Federal Express.

But women's products—in or out of women's magazines—have never been the subjects of much serious reporting anyway. Even news and general-interest publications write about food and clothing as "cooking" and "fashion," though male-oriented banking and financial services wouldn't be reported with such a cheerful and uncritical eye. Food products are almost never evaluated by brand name and rarely by category. Though chemical additives, pesticides, and animal fats are major health risks in the United States (for instance, as contributors to the one-in-eight incidence of breast cancer, and one-in-three rate for all cancers combined), they don't get a fraction of the investigative attention lavished on one political campaign. Clothes take up more of our consumer dollars than cars, but their shoddiness, sweatshop production, and durability are mostly ignored in favor of uncritical fashion stories that would be a Ralph Nader-level scandal if applied to Detroit. The ingredients in beauty products are usually overlooked, too, though they're absorbed into our bodies through our skins, and also have profit margins that would make a loan shark blush.

The truth is that individuals are fair game for the media and corporations are not—individuals don't advertise.

What could women's magazines be like if they were as editorially 115 free as good books? As realistic as the best newspaper articles? As creative as poetry and films? As diverse as women's lives? What if we as women—who are psychic immigrants in a public world rarely constructed by or for us—had the same kind of watchful, smart, supportive publications on our side that other immigrant groups have often had?

We'll find out only if we take the media directed at us seriously. If readers were to act in concert in large numbers for a few years to change the traditional practices of *all* women's magazines and the marketing of *all* women's products, we could do it. After all, they depend on our consumer dollars—money we now are more likely to control. If we include all the shopping we do for families and spouses, women make 85 percent of purchases at point of sale. You and I could:

---

6. G. Pascal Zachary, *Wall Street Journal,* February 6, 1992.

- Refuse to buy products whose ads have clearly dictated their surroundings, and write to tell the manufacturers why.

- Write to editors and publishers (with copies to advertisers) to tell them that we're willing to pay *more* for magazines with editorial independence, but will *not* continue to pay for those that are editorial extensions of ads.

- Write to advertisers (with copies to editors and publishers) to tell them that we want fiction, political reporting, consumer reporting, strong opinion, humor, and health coverage that doesn't pull punches, praising them when their ads support this and criticizing them when they don't.

- Put as much energy and protest into breaking advertising's control over what's around it as we put into changing the images within it or protesting harmful products like cigarettes.

- Support only those women's magazines and products that take us seriously as readers and consumers.

- Investigate new laws and regulations to support freedom from advertising influence. The Center for the Study of Commercialism, a group founded in 1990 to educate and advocate against "ubiquitous product marketing," recommends whistle-blower laws that protect any members of the media who disclose advertiser and other commercial conflicts of interest, laws that require advertiser influence to be disclosed, Federal Trade Commission involvement, and denial of income tax exemptions for advertising that isn't clearly identified— as well as conferences, citizen watchdog groups, and a national clearinghouse where examples of private censorship can be reported.[7]

Those of us in the magazine world can also use this carrot-and-stick technique. The stick: If magazines were a regulated medium like television, the editorial quid pro quo demanded by advertising would be against the rules of the FCC, and payola and extortion would be penalized. As it is, there are potential illegalities to pursue. For example: A magazine's postal rates are determined by the ratio of ad pages to editorial pages, with the ads being charged at a higher rate than the editorial. Counting up all the pages that are *really* ads could make an interesting legal action. There could be consumer fraud cases lurking in subscriptions that are solicited for a magazine but deliver a catalog.

The carrot is just as important. In twenty years, for instance, I've found no independent, nonproprietary research showing that an ad for, say, fragrance is any more effective placed next to an article about fra-

---

7. For membership and publications, contact Center for the Study of Commercialism, 1875 Connecticut Avenue N.W., Suite 300, Washington, D.C. 20009–5278. Telephone: 202–797–7080; FAX 202–265–4954.

grance than it would be when placed next to a good piece of fiction or reporting. As we've seen, there are studies showing that the greatest factor in determining an ad's effectiveness is the credibility and independence of its surroundings. An airtight wall between ads and edit would also shield corporations and agencies from pressures from both ends of the political spectrum and from dozens of pressure groups. Editors would be the only ones responsible for editorial content—which is exactly as it should be.

Unfortunately, few agencies or clients hear such arguments. Editors 125 often maintain the artificial purity of refusing to talk to the people who actually control their lives. Instead, advertisers see salespeople who know little about editorial, are trained in business as usual, and are usually paid on commission. To take on special controversy editors might also band together. That happened once when all the major women's magazines did articles in the same month on the Equal Rights Amendment. It could happen again—and regularly.

Meanwhile, we seem to have a system in which everybody is losing. The reader loses diversity, strong opinion, honest information, access to the arts, and much more. The editor loses pride of work, independence, and freedom from worry about what brand names or other critical words some sincere freelancer is going to come up with. The advertiser loses credibility right along with the ad's surroundings, and gets more and more lost in a sea of similar ads and interchangeable media.

But that's also the good news. Because where there is mutual interest, there is the beginning of change.

If you need one more motive for making it, consider the impact of U.S. media on the rest of the world. The ad policies we tolerate here are invading the lives of women in other cultures—through both the content of U.S. media and the ad practices of multinational corporations imposed on other countries. Look at our women's magazines. Is this what we want to export?

▪ **CONSIDER THE SOURCE**

1. In your own words, describe the direct and indirect methods by which advertising inhibits freedom of the press, according to Steinem.

2. Explain what Steinem means by the "double-standard" that afflicts women's magazines.

3. What does Steinem say would be gained by breaking advertisers' control over editorial copy? What would be the advantages to consumers, editors, and advertisers?

4. How does Steinem characterize *Ms.*'s readers? Why does she feel they are an ideal target audience for advertisers of "people products" as well as "women's products"? What distinguishes these two kinds of products?

▪ CONSIDER THE IMPLICATIONS

5. Study a newsstand or bookstore display of magazines. In your journal, analyze how the various publications are arranged and marketed. What categories do they seem to fall into? Are the genders and races separated? Can you locate the category of "women's magazines" that Steinem writes about? What features identify such publications?

6. How would Susan Faludi explain the media coverage of *Ms.* magazine and other women's magazines that Steinem describes on page 289?

7. Bring your favorite "women's" and "men's" magazines into class and compare them in small groups. What proportion of ads to editorial copy do you find? Do the women's magazines establish a "beauty atmosphere"? How would you describe the atmosphere of the men's magazines? How much "supportive copy" do you find in each type of magazine?

8. Review Farai Chideya's analysis of how the scarcity of African American journalists affects the press's portrayal of blacks (pp. 228–39). Compare Chideya's findings with Steinem's discussion of women in the magazine and advertising industries. Write an essay arguing for or against the proposition that racial and gender inequities in media hiring influence public perceptions of women and minorities.

9. Write a letter to Samuel Johnson updating him on what has happened to advertising since he wrote his essay "On the Art of Advertising" in 1759 (pp. 274–76). How has it changed? How is it the same?

10. Read or review Joan DelFattore's essay on efforts by religious fundamentalists to censor school textbooks (pp. 440–449). Write a letter to the editors of *Sassy* magazine arguing for or against their decision to change the tone of their magazine in response to pressure from these groups.

11. Steinem claims that advertisers' influence inhibits "diverse and free sources of information," while Joe Tye (pp. 268–73) describes editors' failed attempts to keep a "Chinese Wall" of separation between advertising and editorial content. Write one of the letters Steinem suggests on page 301, either to an advertiser or to an editor, arguing that current advertising practices constitute a serious restraint of freedom of the press. Alternatively, write a letter to Steinem or Tye from an advertiser, supporting current policy in the interests of free trade.

JOSEPH DEITCH

Portrait of a Book Reviewer: Christopher Lehmann-Haupt

Have you ever wondered how a certain book becomes a best-seller? What makes so many people buy one book instead of another? One answer: reviews. In this interview with Joseph Deitch, influential New York Times *book critic Christopher Lehmann-Haupt (b. 1934) describes how he chooses, reads, and writes about the select few books that make it into his column "Books of the* Times." *He also discusses the power that reviewers have to make or break a book. Interviewer Joseph Deitch has contributed many articles about and interviews with figures in the publishing and library world to* Publishers Weekly, *the* Wilson Library Bulletin, *and* Editor and Publisher.

An avid baseball fan who is an insatiable reader once spent a year in search of his sport's gods. He ended up with a bat in his hands facing Goose Gossage, the fireball pitcher for the New York Yankees. The confrontation took place on a late afternoon in Yankee Stadium. Shaking in fear, the fan waited for the pitch. It and others came with blinding speed and, much to his surprise, he connected each time. His saga concludes: "Gossage throws again, and this time I put some muscle in my swing. The crack of the bat feels sweet. The ball is rising in the night sky. Lara [Yankee batting coach] is whistling. [Manager Billy] Martin steps onto the field. Somebody is even cheering."

None of this happened, of course. The batter was, of all people, Christopher Lehmann-Haupt, the senior daily book critic of the *New York Times*. His adventures and misadventures and daydreamed encounter with Gossage are recalled in *Me and DiMaggio*, published last year by Simon & Schuster.

Lehmann-Haupt's chief baseball divinity is "Joltin' Joe," also called DiMaggio, who, in addition to superb fielding, hit safely in fifty-six consecutive games, including three fan-hysterical home runs in one game. For the first time, the man who had written reviews of two thousand books was himself reviewed last year. If anything, *Me and DiMaggio* enabled him to feel what a couple of thousand other authors felt as they awaited verdicts from one of the most influential book critics in the country.

In an interview at his home in the Riverdale section of the Bronx, Lehmann-Haupt seemed content with the book's critical reception. It received a good number of favorable reviews and a few bad ones.

From *Wilson Library Bulletin* (December 1987), pp. 61–63.

"What I missed was an intelligent bad review from someone who knew what I was trying to do," he said. "Many of the good reviews understood this. I did not mind the bad reviews, but most of them were stupid."

Book reviewing is done with widely assorted degrees of responsibility, seriousness, and competence in thousands of newspapers, magazines, professional journals, and in broadcasting. It is becoming recognized that a book—or play, opera, pianist, dancer, actor, TV show, painter, monologist, or zitherist—may get rave notices elsewhere, but if the *New York Times* doesn't like the way these cultural commodities are handled, the customers are apt to stay away in droves. Especially if it is books.

A kind word about a book from the *Times* alone may get it on somebody's best-seller list. An adverse, or bad, review could consign it to oblivion, even though other papers praised the book. Aware of its influence, the *Times* takes the quality of its criticism and its critical standards most seriously.

For many, *Times* criticism—in authority, experience, and objectivity—is about the best in world journalism. Much of it can give the best academic criticism a run for its money. What, I recently wondered, goes on behind the scenes for a *Times* daily book review—for "Books of the *Times*," as this column is titled? Do Lehmann-Haupt and his daily-reviewer colleagues, John Gross and Michiko Kakutani, arrive in the morning, put their feet up on desks, and start reading, break for lunch, return, put their feet up on desks again and read till five, come in next morning and tap out their reviews—then repeat the process for the next books?

The reviewing procedure for Lehmann-Haupt (probably much the same way for his colleagues) is carried out in two-day cycles, working at home. It begins, of course, with picking books for review. Lehmann-Haupt receives about five thousand books a year—those sold in bookstores for off-the-street trade; no textbooks. Books come to his desk for review at the rate of a hundred or so a week—more at the height of the publishing seasons in spring and fall.

He opens the book packages himself. By doing so, he weeds out 90 percent of what comes in. He can tell by the titles which books do not belong in "Books of the *Times*." Immediately rejected are books on specialized subjects and most cookbooks. Books that seem to deserve review go into his study. "I have been doing this for so long, it is hard to articulate, anymore, why I choose among these for review." In general, the criteria are that books have to do with the news—directly, like the new Bob Woodward book, *Veil: The Secret Wars of the CIA 1981–87.* New books by prominent writers constitute news of this kind.

Lehmann-Haupt often works under deadlines. *Veil* was an example. He had to produce his review for publication the same day, September 30, 1987, as a *Times* news story on the book out of Washington.

Lehmann-Haupt got the book at 4:30 P.M. on September 28. His deadline was 4 P.M. the next day. He met that deadline by reading the 543-page book and writing his approximately one thousand-word review in less than twenty-four hours.

Another type of major book news, in contrast to books whose contents make news, is the sale of a paperback for millions of dollars. "People become curious about what such a book is like, and buy it," Lehmann-Haupt said. Asked if the new book by John Kenneth Galbraith, *Economics in Perspective*, might be reviewed for news value, he said the author's name and reputation and his role in economic history for fifty years would warrant attention in "Books of the *Times*."

Even from the ten out of a hundred books that become candidates for the column every week, the *Times* senior reviewer has to "pick and choose before admitting two of them to my column every week." Great care goes into selection "because I only do two reviews a week for the thousands of books we receive—only," he added with some irony, as if those two reading, judging, and writing chores were enough.

Although he gets some books a month or so before publication dates, he does not read ahead, he said. "If I do, I tend to forget what I read in advance by the time I get around to giving the book full attention."

He would normally start reading the Woodward book on Sunday night—Lehmann-Haupt was interviewed on Saturday afternoon. The book was not available until Monday, which meant that he would have to read "very fast" for a Wednesday morning appearance in "Books of the *Times*" in conjunction with the *Times* Washington bureau story on newsworthy revelations in the book. Usually, his reviews are due late Tuesday night or Wednesday morning. But the need to read a book in a day or less does not come up often.

Why the occasional need for speed?   15

The paper wants to be among the first to report on a book with news potential, and the review itself becomes a kind of news story, with evaluation of content. The *Times* had assigned someone to search the book for news. "My job is to report what *Veil* is like as a book: Is it an interesting story? The question on everybody's mind is, What did Woodward discover that is worth 543 pages?" A lot of newsworthy stories but much else, according to Lehmann-Haupt's review, that was "irrelevant," "morally neutral," "lacking in narrative punch," "a great deal taken on faith," and failure to identify most of the 250 people Woodward said he interviewed.

"'Books of the *Times*' is supposed to come out with the first reviews of books, but it isn't always first by any means," Lehmann-Haupt said. It competes, most of all, with Sunday's *Times Book Review*, which has much more space. As preparation for his reviews and as a professional reader and critic, Lehmann-Haupt takes extensive notes and makes marginal notes for his eight hundred- to one thousand-word critiques.

After finishing a book, he goes over his notes and underlines, in red, the high points, which he has already "asterisked." Then he draws a line down the middle of an 8½-by-11-inch sheet of paper. On the left side of the line, he makes a list of points he wants to include in the review. On the right side, he outlines the review—the most difficult and creative part of the process, he said. He adheres "pretty strictly" to the outline.

You might think that Lehmann-Haupt and other professional readers and book critics must be among the world's fastest readers. Lehmann-Haupt is not a particularly fast reader. He can read speedily if he has to. His normal rate is rather slow. He likes to savor what he reads and to "exercise his imagination." By imagination, he means the link between words and the pictures they conjure up. It takes slower reading to form pictures, he said.

He waits for a book to impact on him and even to justify its existence. He does not do research on a book's subject. He might check to see what the author's earlier books were about and how the new book fits in. Beyond that, he does not delve deeply into a book's subject in advance or while reading it. "There just isn't time on a daily paper," he said. "I take the background for it out of my head"—a reference library of world affairs, events, and people, drawn on as needed. 20

He added: "In reading and reviewing the Galbraith book, I did not fancy myself an economist who could say that he is wrong about this and right about that. The two things I had to tell was first, the satisfaction of getting a sense of everything in its place. The other was to convey the clarification I got—after reading about it over and over again, like the ideas of classical economists—about the book's governing principle. This was the notion of perspective that allowed the author to select only what he thinks is important and to be critical of ideas he does not agree with from his perspective."

Lehmann-Haupt made a distinction between reviewing and criticism. To begin with, the daily *New York Times* reports the news. The Sunday edition, including the "Book Review," has more time and space to reflect on the news. Many books reviewed by Lehmann-Haupt are in the context of the day's news or of the recent past.

"Sunday book critics are presumably experts on their subjects, and the three of us who do 'Books of the *Times*' are not," Lehmann-Haupt said. The daily reviews are often part of each day's news mainstream.

"We are intelligent ombudsmen[1] for the reader who is going to tell other people what the experience of reading a book is like. The Sunday reviewer comes along and says the book may be fun to read, as the daily reviewer has already said, but adds his own perspectives. Ideally, the reader reads the two reviews back to back and learns one thing from the daily and something else from the Sunday review."

---

1. **ombudsmen:** An ombudsman investigates consumer complaints and helps to obtain fair settlements from producers or government agencies.—ED.

Lehmann-Haupt reads as fast as the book demands. Where the writ- 25
ing and content are important, he reads slowly, he said. Where a book
conveys a lot of information, he will read it faster. "If you have been
around books, professionally, long enough, you know how to read
them. You know where you can skim or will have to read every word.
The first will give you a better sense of a book's structure. If you have to
skim, chapter headings, bibliography—even the rhythm of the prose
and sentence structure—can more quickly help determine the author's
main points. But this is a matter of experience.

"So my advice is that the more you read, the better you get at it."

Letters from readers praise, criticize, or offer information and insight. Generally, they get a form response—"there isn't time to do more,
except for letters from distinguished people in their fields from whom I
learn something. They get personal letters."

Authors who complain, in print, about bad reviews given them in
The New York Times Book Review and in other book sections play a risky
game. Below their usually long letters to the editor wondering, for example, if the reviewer really read their books, the reviewers are given a
chance to respond. Reviewers are apt to reply that they reread the complaining author's book and not only stand by their initial criticisms but
found the book even worse on a second reading.

The *Times*'s senior book critic got a complaining letter sent to Arthur
Gelb, one of the paper's news executives. It was from Joan Peyser, author of a biography of Leonard Bernstein, the conductor. Lehmann-
Haupt did not like the book. The letter noted that he had once been a
tenant of hers in a building she owned and that he should not have been
allowed to review a book by his former landlord.

"She said it was not fair, implying that the experience of being a ten- 30
ant would dispose me not to like her book," Lehmann-Haupt said. "She
also said that I had snatched the book from another reviewer to get revenge on her [by panning her book]." All this happened some twenty
years ago, at about the time he went to work for the *Times*.

"The irony is that I never disliked her at all. In fact, she always
treated me as if she was dying for me to review her. It was amusing, to
us, that she turned everything around after she got the negative review."

Lehmann-Haupt did a hitch in the army and trained as an artillery-
man at Fort Sill, Oklahoma. He played a lot of golf at the fort's links,
"where enlisted men and officers were equal." He holds a master's degree from the Yale University Drama School. Married, he has two children, Rachel and Noah, to whom—with Natalie, his wife—he dedicated
Me and DiMaggio. They "cheered," the dedicatory note says.

His venture into fantasy in the book's last chapter—Billy Martin
leaves the Yankee dugout to see who hit that long fly ball—displays a
gift for fiction. He is, in fact, writing a novel, which led me to ask, "As a
book critic, what do you expect of a novel?"

He has no rules, "except that it engage me at some level of intellect or emotion and that it do something to me. It doesn't have to be a story, which is often totally lacking in modern fiction, yet, through some magic, you are moved to feel or think. I try hard to review novels on their own terms: What is it trying to do and does it succeed?"

Lehmann-Haupt tends not to use sweeping adjectives, pro or con. About as far as he has gone on the favorable end was to call Philip Roth's *Portnoy's Complaint* a "technical masterpiece" and "tour de force," but he uses these terms very sparingly, he said. 35

Doesn't all reviewing boil down to letting readers know whether they should buy or, in any case, read a book?

"No. Many readers merely want to know about the book so they don't have to buy or read it. They want to be able to talk about it at cocktail parties. Reviews enable them to do that.

"There's only so much time we can give to reading these days. Even I read half of what I should read. I would like people to get from my reviews a sense of what a book is about and where to put it in their minds."

Does he tire of the endless stream of "definitive" biographies—of Thomas Wolfe, Faulkner, Hemingway, H. G. Wells, Dostoyevski, among others? "You mean the bios that, in Hemingway's case, minutely describe every duck he shot and every bottle of wine he drank," Lehmann-Haupt said. "Their value is that they enable more selective writers to winnow through them for everything they might want to know for their biographies."

This and a publishing incident in Wolfe's *Of Time and the River* that I mentioned reminded Lehmann-Haupt of the publisher he worked for who appeared not to read manuscripts but "rippled through them to make sure there was print on each page and then said, 'Yes, we'll publish this.'" 40

The greater a book's challenge, the greater the excitement for the *Times*'s senior book critic. One of the most challenging in several years was Allan Bloom's *The Closing of the American Mind*, "an outstanding book that hits," he said, quoting an ad for the book, "with the approximate effect of electric shock therapy."

The great British critic George Saintsbury called book reviewing the "difficult art." "Any art is difficult: difficult to do well," Lehmann-Haupt said. "Even after doing it for twenty years, I can hit only one out of ten, and I am being generous to myself. Only one book in ten isn't routine. And it doesn't matter whether it is, as you say, quite a good book. It is the one that not only compels you to write a good review of it, but it transcends itself not only by saying something worthwhile about its subject but about life.

"That's where reviewing becomes art—everything comes together for the review, like a batter focusing himself to hit a baseball. Even so, he will hit a home run in maybe seven or eight times at bat."

The failure of such twentieth-century literary titans as Proust, Henry James, James Joyce, and Nabokov to win Nobel Prizes greatly lessened Lehmann-Haupt's respect for that award. The Pulitzer Prize for fiction "invariably goes to a mediocre book," he said.

Sitting at ease in his living room amid family pictures, it seemed, for 45 a moment, hard to reconcile Lehmann-Haupt with the power and influence he could wield as the *Times* senior book reviewer. A word or two from the *Times,* or so popular perception might indicate, could make or break a book. "Not really," he said. Book critics "are not as powerful as *Times*'s theater criticism, which can close down a show. Fortunately, we are not as powerful as that." But the *Times* does better, more convincing criticism—"Perhaps more influential; I am not sure about better.

"I try not to be conscious of 'power.' Any review sort of legitimizes a book in a way that an unreviewed book is not. Certain reviews are capable of selling large numbers of books and, in certain cases, negative reviews hurt books." Suggestions of power and influence "are not relevant to reading and reviewing. What you try to do is your job."

▪ **CONSIDER THE SOURCE**

1. Describe the process Christopher Lehmann-Haupt uses to decide which books he'll review. What are his selection criteria? How does the process favor established writers over new ones?

2. Explain the distinction Lehmann-Haupt makes between reviewing and criticism.

3. What is Joseph Deitch's attitude toward Lehmann-Haupt, whom he calls "one of the most influential book critics in the country"?

▪ **CONSIDER THE IMPLICATIONS**

4. Examine the process that Lehmann-Haupt uses to read a book and then to write about it. In your journal, compare his methods with your own. Try writing a review of a new book using his techniques.

5. In small groups, make a list of the reasons why you might read a review, whether of a book, movie, or concert. What do you look for in a review? How does a good or bad review influence you? Does it matter who the reviewer is or where the review was published?

6. Explore Lehmann-Haupt's statement that "any review sort of legitimizes a book." How are reviews used to market books? How are reviews used to market other products, such as movies, cars, or computer software?

7. Examine the link that Deitch describes between the book review and the "news" story about Woodward's *Veil.* What function does the review serve for the paper? What function does the news story serve? In class, discuss how well this practice serves the interests of the newspaper's reader.

8. Study a recent book review from your local or regional paper. How does

the reviewer establish credibility and authority? What features of the book does the reviewer describe? Does the review evaluate or merely summarize the book? How does the review help you decide whether to buy the book? Write an evaluative review of the review, noting its strengths and weaknesses.

9. Evaluate several reviews of a book you've recently read (or a movie, television show, play, or concert you've watched). How do the reviewers' opinions compare to your own evaluation? To what extent do the reviewers' experiences differ from yours? How do you account for the differences?

▪ ▪ ▪ ▪ ▪ ▪

KATHARINE WEBER

The Reviewer's Experience

If book reviewing is an art, as British critic George Saintsbury claimed, it is also a vital part of the commerce of publishing. Every publisher hopes to have some juicy words of praise to plaster onto the back of a book, some "blurb" that will help sell the book to a consumer already overwhelmed with choices. Therefore, advance copies are sent to reviewers so that they can begin drumming up interest in books that haven't even hit the stores. Katharine Weber (b. 1955) gives us a glimpse of what it's like to receive books in their unfinished state, accompanied by mountains of sales material from the publisher's publicity department. In the following essay from Publishers Weekly, *a trade magazine for the book industry, she describes her tactics for negotiating the conflicting interests of the publisher and her readers. Weber writes reviews and interviews for* Publishers Weekly *and* The New York Times Book Review. *She has also published short fiction in* The New Yorker, *along with a recent novel* Objects in Mirror Are Closer than They Appear *(1995).*

As a steady fiction reviewer for the past five years, I've read a lot of books. They come to me in the form of what most of us call "galleys,"[1] though they are technically not galleys but bound page proofs. Usually,

From *Publishers Weekly* (15 February 1993), p. 248.

1. **galleys:** In the days of handset type, galleys were metal trays that held long columns of type ready for proofreading. *Galley proofs* were the first and roughest form of a printed book, while *page proofs* showed what the book would look like once it was divided into pages.—ED.

the only thing that distinguishes one galley from another is the choice of color for the outside cover.

This year there seems to be a predominance of baby blue and red. (Who chooses these colors? Is it a random thing, or are these cardboard hues subtly calculated by expensive demographic studies, or are they an editorial assistant's favorite color? . . .)

Sometimes there will be a rough representation of finished cover art or typography printed on the front of the reading copy, and some publishers offer a color reproduction of the jacket art. It is actually useful to know what the book is going to look like when it hits the bookstores; the books I read haven't been reviewed anywhere else and I like to have a feel for what the physical book is going to be like.

That's because the cover art and flap copy provide clues about how the publisher intends to market the book to the reading public, as opposed to the way the book is being presented to me as a reviewer.

At times, I get the feeling that I read books more carefully than most   5 publicity departments. You might think that a publisher would spend a lot of time and money to avoid sending out reading copies with missing pages. But it happens all the time. They do it to debut novelists, and they do it to Nadine Gordimer.[2]

Every now and then the pages in a galley are printed so badly that each page has broken type and resembles a fiftieth-generation photocopy. This does not make a reviewer want to linger over the pages of even the best of books.

Of course, every now and then a reading copy comes through all gussied up with a slick cover looking like a finished book. This is one of the ways publishers get the message to reviewers and editors that this is an Important Book worthy of much (preferably positive) attention. Erica Jong's[3] books tend to look better than most mass market paperbacks when they are still in the galley stage.

My reaction to a fancied-up reading copy can be the opposite of what the publisher intended. I bristle at all the lavish presentation and take it as a flung gauntlet. So, this novel is the greatest thing since sliced bread and oughta sell a million copies? *I'll* be the judge of that! But it's not always the case. I've penned my share of rave reviews of books that have been figuratively shoved in my face.

Publishers send reading copies to reviewers with a wad of documentation. This assortment of biographical material—author photos, rave quotes from past reviews, rave quotes about the book at hand (some of them from the author's cronies or the author's agent's other clients) and a blurb from the publicity department—has a name, in

---

2. **Nadine Gordimer** (b. 1923): Nobel Prize-winning South African novelist. —ED.

3. **Erica Jong** (b. 1942): Poet and author of *Fear of Flying* (1973) and other popular novels.—ED.

British publishing circles if not in American ones. They call it *bumph*. Bumph is a derogatory term for papers, documents. It is also a term used to describe lavatory paper, which explains the derivation—it's an abbreviation of *bum-fodder*.

Bumph can be enormously helpful, providing as it does some 10 knowledge about the author and the context of the book at hand within the author's oeuvre. Author photos can be distracting, but interesting. (Why does Richard Bausch wear that silly hat? Is Larry Woiwode always so grubby?) Knowing that Philip Roth admired the author's last novel does impress me.[4] Quotes from promiscuous quote-givers are less inspiring.

But that which can be gleaned from the actual book can transmit some bits of information that probably influence my expectations as well. Any book dedicated to William Shawn,[5] for instance, raises my hopes for quality. Acknowledgments that include various outfits like the Guggenheim Foundation or the MacDowell Colony[6] tell me something. (Although I suppose nothing would stop an author from thanking William Shawn *and* the MacArthur Foundation,[7] say, even if neither had ever heard of him.)

Dedications and acknowledgments, like bumph, can also have a negative impact. Gushing thanks to long lists of people "who believed in the brilliance of my work when I didn't see it" turn me off. An acknowledgment to a psychoanalyst for "relieving me of such handicapping neurotic debris of infancy and childhood as ambivalence, penis envy, and a too-strict superego" was a show-stopper in a university press biography a couple of years ago.

But getting back to bumph. Inaccuracies abound. Plot summaries that get names and relationships and plot descriptions *wrong* are less than useful. Or are they intended as traps for lazy reviewers who only skim? Bumph that makes extravagant claims for a book or author does not serve the author or the publisher well. Comparing a new writer to Hemingway, for instance, seems immodest at best and foolishly destructive at worst. Maybe I'll agree, but more likely I'll think, "Yeah, right. Hemingway. In your dreams."

I want to like books. I want to write reviews that are analytical and

4. **Richard Bausch, Larry Woiwode,** and **Philip Roth:** Contemporary novelists.—ED.

5. **William Shawn** (1907–1992): Editor of *The New Yorker* magazine for forty years.—ED.

6. The John Simon **Guggenheim Foundation** (incorporated 1925): Offers fellowships to further development of the arts; the **MacDowell Colony:** A retreat for artists, writers, and composers, founded in Peterborough, New Hampshire, by the widow of American composer Edward Alexander MacDowell (1861–1908).—ED.

7. The John D. and Catherine T. **MacArthur Foundation** (incorporated 1970): Annually awards its "genius grants" to promising individuals in all fields.—ED.

useful and interesting to read, and good books are a pleasure to write about. *Why Bad Bumph Happens to Good Books* is a publishing industry book waiting to be written.

▪ **CONSIDER THE SOURCE**

1. What is *bumph* and how is it used by publishers, according to Weber? How do reviewers use it?

2. List the factors that influence Weber's expectations as a reviewer. Which have a positive effect and which exert negative influence?

3. How does Weber tailor her remarks to her audience of book industry professionals? What does she hope to convey to the readers of *Publishers Weekly?* Why?

▪ **CONSIDER THE IMPLICATIONS**

4. Examine a display of new books at a local bookstore. Look at the glossy dust jackets, the poster-sized photos of the author, and any other aspects of the display that are intended to attract consumers. Which books are most prominent? Where is the display placed in the store? Why? What audience does the publisher seem to be targeting for each new book? What authorities are quoted on the book or elsewhere? Write an analysis of the consumer equivalent to *bumph.*

5. Weber describes her reactions to the physical properties of the books she reviews. Take your journal to a bookstore and jot down notes about books as you browse. Try to determine what you look for in a book. What attracts your attention? What turns you off? Why?

6. In small groups, analyze the advertisements for new books in *The New York Review of Books* or the Sunday book review section of a major newspaper, such as the *New York Times, Washington Post,* or *Los Angeles Times.* What authority is granted to reviewers? How are their comments used? Which reviewers or reviewing publications are given prominence?

7. Review a new book for your school newspaper. Consider why the book might or might not appeal to your paper's readers. What will your audience want to know about the book? How much background information do you need in order to write the review? How much information will your readers need in order to understand your assessment of the book?

CHAPTER

4

WHAT SHOULD YOU READ?

Popular versus Official Culture

There are two kinds of people in the world: those who divide the world into two kinds of people, and those who don't.

This joke may be silly, but it points out an important feature of the human mind: the need to categorize. The capacity to distinguish likeness and difference seems to be part of our basic intellectual make-up. We're always dividing things into groups, making distinctions, separating, sorting. This activity can have obvious social consequences if we sort by race or gender. When the sorting takes place along cultural lines, it can be just as consequential, for it can determine who has power and who doesn't.

People continually make reference to "good" and "bad" art. They divide taste into "highbrow," "lowbrow," and the inevitable compromise category, "middlebrow." They speak of "serious" music as opposed to "popular" music, or the "legitimate" theater as opposed to—what?—the illegitimate theater? These are not the morally neutral distinctions that scientific taxonomy makes between, for instance, vertebrates and invertebrates; scientists make such distinctions among animals solely on the basis of the presence or absence of a backbone, without implying that having a backbone makes a sturgeon morally superior to a squid. Cultural distinctions, on the other hand, convey value judgments by their labels: high, low, serious.

The distinctions we make are important, not necessarily for anything they tell us about the items in each category, but rather for the use we make of them. They allow us to include some people and exclude others on the basis of their cultural preferences. If you believe jazz is superior to all other forms of music, you can immediately exclude Barry Manilow fans from your list of acquaintances, and seek out Charlie Parker devotees. You may think that you'd never judge people so superficially, but you do it all the time. You seek out people with similar interests—people whose tastes are compatible with yours. You rank interests and tastes according to some hierarchy, and you use that ranking to judge others. Granted, you may judge them according to a complicated set of criteria, and not just their taste in music, but those criteria may be equally arbitrary.

Similarly, you use your taste barometer to judge yourself against existing images. From your years of consuming popular culture, you've absorbed stereotypes of what's considered refined and sophisticated: "Cultured" people attend the opera, enjoy productions of Shakespeare or the ballet, and wear clothes by French designers. You also know what "cool" people do: They listen to grunge music, hip-hop, rap (or whatever is "cool" by the time you read this); they go to movies (not films) and rock concerts; they wear the latest look in teen clothing, whether it's the baggy pants of gangsta rappers or retro sixties tie-dye. All of us have a list of such stereotypes, ranked in order of desirability. You may aspire to be cooler than cool, or you may wish to project the suave refinement of James Bond. Whatever category you choose to identify yourself with reflects your taste and your self-image. We all want to be included in categories that we rank high on the cultural ladder. That makes us feel good about ourselves, and it allows us to position ourselves in relation to others.

This chapter addresses those hierarchies of value, primarily as they are reflected in our attitudes toward the printed works that form such an enormous part of our culture. Two of the main questions that the readings in this chapter will address are the following:

— Who decides what has cultural value?

— On what bases do we judge value?

These questions overlap, and neither lends itself to any simple answer, but let's look at them briefly to survey the ground they'll cover.

WHO DECIDES?

Hundreds of thousands of books and magazines are out there waiting to be read, and nobody can possibly read them all. Which ones should you read in order to consider yourself "well read"? As soon as you start discussing great books, someone will mention Shakespeare's plays. They're always on the list. And then maybe John Milton's *Paradise Lost.* Perhaps Herman Melville's *Moby-Dick* will get a nod. There may be some debate about Mark Twain's *Huckleberry Finn* (as we'll see in chapter 5), but most people will agree that these authors and works are "classics." What arbiter of taste gave them the seal of approval?

One group we've always looked to for evaluations of literature is the "literati." You may recall from chapter 2 that this word originally designated anybody who could read—not a bad group to turn to for judgments on reading material. Typically, literati were clerics or nobles, the elite classes who had access to books and education. The word still refers to the elite, even though literacy extends much further down the social ladder. Today, literati are the distinguished writers and scholars—the intellectual elite. Those who spend their lives in the world of books are accorded the privilege of judging the world of books.

Academics and critics deliver most of the formal judgments on books, and they do it by means of several print mechanisms. In the book reviews that appear in every sizeable newspaper and magazine in the country, reviewers pass judgment on books. They let the rest of us know something about the book and generally tell us whether we should spend our time and money on that particular book. They sort through the dross to locate the gold on our behalf. Literary scholars go one step further. They study the works and write learned papers about them. If a work can stand up to their scrutiny, it gets the label of "serious" literature. Both reviewers and academic critics use print to validate more print.

Academics aren't alone in determining which books have stature. Just as the *meaning* of a book owes much to the act of reading (as we saw in chapter 1), the *value* of a book comes from readers as well—the consumers of the cultural artifacts. The publishing industry avidly tallies book buyers' purchases, and then generates lists of best-sellers to let everyone know what everybody else is reading. Here the focus is not on how they interpret the book, but simply on how many readers a book has. The word *best-seller* attached to John Grisham's latest title instantly tells people that others have found the book valuable. It matters little if those others are the "literati." Sheer volume at the cash register connotes value.

Paradoxically, numbers can also diminish the perceived value of a book, especially in the eyes of the literati. When a book has sold too many copies, it can find itself in the dreaded category of "popular" books. The implication, of course, is that the general population doesn't know what a good book is. If a book appeals to the masses, therefore, it must pander to lower, more vulgar tastes than we associate with the "best" books. A book that sells very few copies is clearly no good, but one that sells millions must not be any good either, by this reasoning. It's not exactly clear where the cutoff number is. How many copies is too many?

The irony inherent in our methods of assigning value is apparent if we look at the "classics." Milton appealed to the elite, learned class, but

Shakespeare's work was—dare we say it—popular entertainment. His work appealed to all classes, though now it has been enshrined as one of our most solid symbols of elite taste. Then there's Herman Melville. Though he began as a writer of popular sea adventures, his 1851 masterpiece *Moby-Dick* languished virtually unread, even by his former fans, until the 1920s. *Huckleberry Finn* has had mixed reviews ever since it appeared in 1885. It enjoyed widespread popularity but was simultaneously criticized by many in the elite literary establishment for its depiction of society's riff-raff. By the same token, many works that earlier generations deemed literary gems now seem lusterless to us.

CRITERIA FOR VALUE

Surely the assignment of value can't depend only on how many people read a book or whether the "right" people read it. There must be some solid criteria that reviewers and consumers use to determine what's good and what's not.

One of the criteria that's often used to determine whether a book will stand the test of time is its universality. A classic, this logic says, addresses the human condition, the great conflicts and crises that every man or woman will face. Everyone can find some wisdom and inspiration in such a classic. All of us recognize something of ourselves in the ambitious Macbeth pursuing power, the grieving Hamlet seeking justice, or the unfortunate lovers, Romeo and Juliet. The problem with this line of reasoning is that many nonclassics address the "human condition," too. Grisham's books are all about power, detective stories deal with justice, and Harlequin romances have just about cornered the market on love.

Another problem, as we'll see in Laura Bohannan's essay on *Hamlet* (pp. 342–52), is that what we think is universal may be culturally mediated. "Universality" may turn out to be a measure of personal taste. It may be just another way of saying, "This work appeals to me and therefore it should appeal to everyone who has the good sense to be like me." Classics have self-perpetuating reputations. Once *Hamlet* is established as a yardstick by which we measure a person's literary taste, those who appreciate *Hamlet* have a stake in keeping it on the list. Its continued high status confirms their continued good taste. Those who don't appreciate *Hamlet* don't have good taste, according to this line of thinking and, therefore, can't be trusted to determine what other works should be regarded as classics. The canon—the body of acknowledged classics of a culture—turns out to be a very conservative force. It's hard to dislodge works that have been there for decades (if not centuries), and it's equally hard to add new works, though it can be done.

Not everyone likes to read "classics." Perhaps you'd rather read magazines, or what is called genre fiction—books that follow recognizable and familiar formulas, such as romances, Westerns, mysteries, thrillers, sci-fi, or fantasy works. Does this mean that you have no taste? Does it mean that your reading is valueless? Not necessarily.

Another way that people frequently assign value to reading material is according to its capacity to convey information. Because our culture promotes self-improvement and education, we point to the instructional content of books and magazines as a way to justify primarily the time we spend on them—even if we read them for escape or titillation. You may feel that a particular Louis L'Amour story taught you a lot about life in the Old West or that Tom Clancy's *The Hunt for Red October* gave you an insider's look at Cold War politics. You may think that your powers of deduction and logical reasoning improve every time you read another Sue Grafton mystery or that your encyclopedic knowledge of English manners and costumes of the Regency period would not be possible without the Candlelight romances.

This educational function of reading has helped solidify the "how-to" book as a perennial best-seller. It also powers the magazine industry. In addition to the thousands of books that peddle advice on diets, relationships, childrearing, or self-realization, hundreds of thousands of magazine articles do the same thing on a smaller scale. The versatile "how-to" feature story has become a magazine mainstay. It adapts to any hobby or field of interest and so can fit into every speciality magazine on the market. *Forbes* has investment "how-to" stories, *Golf Digest* gives tips on putting, while *Elle* tells readers how to apply make-up or style their hair. For only a few bucks per copy, you can get advice on anything you want from real, honest-to-goodness professionals.

"Professionals," of course, only publish in professional-looking publications. That's another way we assign value to our reading choices. We look at how they're packaged. We judge books, magazines, newspapers, and club newsletters by their covers, not necessarily by their content. The conventions of print have habituated us to certain design features and physical formats that we now associate with higher or lower positions in the print culture hierarchy. A hardcover book, for instance, usually carries more weight—conceptually as well as physically—than a paperback. A glossy, high-concept magazine with lots of colorful ads gets more respect than one printed on dull paper, with only black-and-white print and a few ads.

When we judge a printed object on its appearance we're really assessing how well the object conforms to other things that we already grant value to. Does it look like something that we have already determined is valuable? Companies such as the Franklin Mint capitalize on this method of judging with their deluxe editions of literary classics. They offer copies of books that tradition has said are worth reading, such as *Moby-Dick* and *Gulliver's Travels*, and they offer them in a format that has traditionally connoted value: Each book is bound in leather and gilt-edged, with gold lettering on the spine, just like the fine editions that aristocrats bought in the early days of printing. These books look so handsome on a bookshelf that we can't help but glow with pride in our own sense of being "cultured"—even if we've never opened a single volume. But wouldn't we be just as cultured, if not more so, if we had copies of all those books in mismatched dog-eared paperback editions and had read all of them?

Our orientation toward the written word is so ingrained that the mere fact that something is printed conveys value. It signals "real" time-less culture, as opposed to transitory oral culture. Popular culture ranks lower in conventional estimates of value because it so often exists in nonprinted formats, such as movies or television, or in the ephemeral print of fan magazines and concert posters. Even traditions that are cen-turies old get little notice if they are not inscribed in the printed record that we use to determine official culture. Thus, the highly developed oral cultures of native Americans or of Africans brought to the Americas as slaves could be dismissed as "primitive" or "uncivilized" by literate Europeans. In a print culture, print authorizes culture.

THE READINGS

The selections in this chapter explore the many ways our culture values or devalues printed texts. We begin with Bernard Berelson's sur-vey of American reading habits, which seems remarkably timely even though it was written nearly half a century ago. Many of the assump-tions about American readers that he debunked in 1951 still get circu-lated as truths today. Especially tenacious is the belief that Americans no longer read "good" books, which leads E. D. Hirsch Jr. to analyze how national cultures are formed and what role they play in making a diverse population cohere into a unified country. In trying to explain *Hamlet* to the nonliterate Tiv of West Africa, anthropologist Laura Bo-hannan gives a new view of how well the universal classics of our cul-ture translate into other cultures. Henry Louis Gates Jr. treats a similar issue from the opposite perspective: He examines how Africans, coming from exclusively oral cultures, had to represent themselves in print in order to be regarded as humans by the print-centered Western cultures that enslaved them. Thomas J. Roberts's analysis of "low taste" begins a series of readings that explore how good taste is judged and dissemi-nated. John P. Dessauer decries the book world's bias in favor of high culture over popular culture, while Joan Shelley Rubin shows us how a "middlebrow" culture was promoted and diffused by the shrewd ad-vertising and marketing techniques of the Book-of-the-Month Club. The last four selections examine types of publications that usually are not considered part of official culture. Janice A. Radway reports on how a group of women uses romance novels and how they justify reading books often regarded as "trash." Self-help books catch the attention of

Steven Starker, who assesses the principal reasons for their success among bookbuyers and questions whether Americans rely on them too heavily. Finally, Laurie Ouellette and Gridley Minima look at the 'zine scene, the ever-expanding world of underground, self-published magazines that occupy narrowly defined niches in pop culture.

BERNARD BERELSON

Who Reads What, and Why?

Writing at the dawn of the television age, sociologist and communications specialist Bernard Berelson (1912–1979) offered an assessment of the state of "popular reading" in the United States. When Berelson penned this essay for the Saturday Review of Literature *in 1951, America's intellectual landscape was very different than it is today. College education was still comparatively rare, with only about 430,000 college degrees conferred every year, three-fourths of which went to men. (Compare that with the 1.1 million bachelors' degrees given in 1995, more than half to women.) Television was the new kid on the mass communications block, and radio remained an important outlet for drama, news, and political debate. Berelson organizes his essay by listing several popular assumptions about America's reading habits, each of which he examines in order to refute it or suggest a more subtle way of evaluating the evidence. Among Berelson's many books are* What Reading Does to People *(1940),* The People's Choice: How the Voter Makes Up His Mind in a Presidential Campaign *(1968), and* Reader in Public Opinion and Communication *(1966).*

Who reads what books and why?

The answer to this general question is by no means easy to give. The state of popular reading is complex and changing: Different kinds of people are reading different amounts and kinds of books for different reasons. Mrs. Jones down the street is reading light fiction "to pass the time" and books on childrearing because she wants to do well by her children and to hold her own with other mothers. Her husband reads an occasional mystery story and a technical book on his occupation. The people next door don't read books at all because "they don't have time," although they manage to spend four hours a day with radio and television. The people on the other side read classical novels, modern poetry, and the latest serious books on political affairs. And so it goes: The variety is so extensive that any reasonable ordering of the data is bound to violate some aspects of the overall picture.

And yet some ordering is necessary if we are to secure a systematic answer to the question. In recent years, with the development of communication research in industry and in the universities, a body of data has been assembled which presents a reasonably coherent picture of the state of book reading in this country today. We can by no means answer all—or even very many—of the questions we would like to ask about book reading, but we can answer some. Unfortunately, definite answers

From *Saturday Review of Literature* (12 May 1951), pp. 7–8, 30–31.

cannot be given without a great deal of careful (and costly) research, much of which has not yet been done. In some cases technical problems have not been solved. In this connection we know a good deal more about magazine reading and radio listening than about book reading. At the same time, however, the studies done to date, utilizing social science techniques for collecting and analyzing empirical data, have provided valid and reliable data on questions which previously were largely subject to literary impression, historical speculation, or commercial preference. Conclusions based upon these methods have not infrequently mistaken the particular for the general, the familiar for the typical, the dramatic for the general, or the preferred for the actual. The business of the social scientist, if I may say so, is to see book reading steadily and to see it whole—and, while he cannot claim to have done the job, it is fair to say that he has made a start.

What, then, is the state of adult (nonspecialized) book reading today? Let us review the major facts (or best guesses) by organizing them around some assumptions held by various people and encountered here and there, explicitly or implicitly, in popular writing on the subject.

Assumption: That "the American people" read many books or, al- 5 *ternately, that they don't read them.* This assumption comes both ways, depending upon whether the writer is in a mood to praise or blame—or perhaps depending upon the point he wants to make at the time. Many librarians, especially when writing their annual reports, like to think that people *do* read books; many critics stress the latter part of the assumption, especially when writing for the "little" magazines.[1] Actually, of course, the statement is so undifferentiated that, like many statements about "the American public" or "the people of this country" or "we," it doesn't make much sense anyway. The obvious fact is that some Americans read books frequently, some read them occasionally, some seldom, and some not at all.

If by "book reader" we mean anyone who reads at least one book every six months then about half the adult population would qualify. If the definition requires the reading of at least one book a month—the usual definition in the field—the figure becomes 25 to 30 percent; and if it requires at least one book a week then only 6 to 8 percent of the adult population are "book readers." By a reasonable definition, then, only from one-quarter to one-third of the adults qualify as "book readers." This makes the actual audience for books the smallest among the major media of communication; radio-television, newspapers, magazines, and motion pictures all attract much larger numbers than books. Although the evidence on this point is not definitive, there are some data which

---

1. **"little" magazines:** Small circulation literary journals that generally cater to a sophisticated readership.—ED.

suggest that there is less book reading in the United States than in such countries as Britain, Denmark, Sweden, Norway, and Holland.

More than that: the so-called concentration of the audience is higher for book reading than for the other media. About 10 percent of the adult population does 70 percent of the book reading. Within the book-reading group itself (as defined) 20 percent of the readers do 70 percent of the reading. Thus a relatively small group of people accounts for a large share of the reading. Nor does the tremendous sale of quarter books[2] contradict this point: 10 percent of the buyers are responsible for 80 percent of the sales. The reading of books is certainly not evenly distributed throughout society.

Assumption: That the book reading public is representative of the total population. Not only does the frequency of book reading vary markedly; it is also unevenly distributed among the constituent groups of the community. For a variety of reasons some kinds of people read a great deal and some not much. The major factor which differentiates readers from nonreaders in research to date is education—in the limited sense of number of years of formal schooling. The more years of schooling the individual has the more likely he is to read books. In one national survey only 12 percent of the college-educated had not read a book in the preceding year as against 74 percent of those with only some grammar-school education or less.

Now this might mean several things. It might mean that additional schooling has improved the individual's basic reading skills or that it has developed his reading habits or that it has produced in him the types of interests which are ordinarily satisfied by books or even that the people who go on to further schooling already have a reading disposition which formal education only reinforces. Research has not yet settled the matter, any more than it can say now why *some* college graduates do not read or why *some* people with little schooling read not only a great deal but well. There are numerous hypotheses but few data. But research *has* demonstrated the high relationship between formal education and the practice of book reading, and it seems quite likely that the schools have progressively developed book readers.

Other personal characteristics also affect the amount of book reading. Contrary to the popular conception, men read just about as much as women, although they tend to read differently. Young adults read more than their elders, but that is directly traceable to their greater degree of formal education; among people on the same educational level the older people more than hold their own. The sharpest and most dramatic drop in book reading comes at the school-leaving age—whatever that may imply about the educational system. Wealthier people read more than

10

---

2. **quarter books:** The successor to the dime novels, quarter books were cheap paperback fiction that sold for a quarter.—ED.

poorer people, again largely—though apparently not exclusively—because of their greater education. This means that the "higher" occupations provide more book readers than the "lower"; there are relatively fewer readers among the working class. Finally, because of the availability of sources (and again the educational level) urban residents read more than rural.

In sum, then, college-educated, better-off, middle-aged people living in the city (a description of the modal *SRL* reader?) are most likely to be book readers in this country today. And people combining the opposite characteristics are the least likely. Thus it is clear that book readers as a group are far from representative of the total population. They live differently from the population as a whole, they have different attitudes and interests, they have different tastes. In short, projecting the book readers as "America" is apt to be just plain wrong.

Assumption: That the amount and/or the quality of book reading in this country has fallen off in recent years. It is not hard to find writers who are Alarmed about the Deplorable State of popular reading. In 1949 Clifton Fadiman,[3] regretting in this journal "the decline of attention," concluded that the "mainstream [of our culture] is composed largely of men and women whose faculty of attention is in process either of decay or displacement." Another writer at about the same time asserted that "never before have there been so few good readers—so few who have retained anything or profited from what they read." Fadiman himself quoted Cyril Connolly[4] to the effect that "we must accustom ourselves to a reading public which is both too slothful and too restless to read until a sense of values is restored to it." And, what is more, he noted that Henry James had done the same job of deploring fifty years earlier and Wordsworth a century before that—without drawing therefrom what seems to be an obvious inference.[5]

The point is that this kind of Viewing with Alarm the state of popular culture is by no means limited to our day; it is characteristic of the intellectuals of every period since popular education began to create what might be called a mass audience. Today they hearken back to the good old days of a century ago when "the people" were reading *Walden.*[6] A

---

3. **Clifton Fadiman** (b. 1904): Book critic for *The New Yorker* (1933–1943) and member of the Book-of-the-Month Club review board (1944–1994), Fadiman also hosted the radio quiz show "Information, Please!" (1938–1948).—ED.

4. **Cyril Connolly** (1903–1974): English critic whose literary reviews in the *Observer* and the *Sunday Times* influenced a wide audience of British and American readers.—ED.

5. **Henry James** (1843–1916): American novelist and critic; William Wordsworth (1770–1850) English Romantic poet.—ED.

6. *Walden* (1854): Philosophical narrative by Henry David Thoreau (1817–1862).—ED.

century ago, however, Hawthorne was fulminating against the "mob of scribbling women. . . . I should have no chance of success while the public taste is occupied with their trash."[7]

In this sense the good old days probably never did exist; that is, there probably never was a *mass* audience for good books. Almost certainly there are more book readers today than ever before. It may be that the average quality of *all* the book reading done today is lower than the average quality decades or a few centuries ago—although this is far from certain. We tend to forget the poorer books of 1850 that were widely read (for example, *The Lamplighter*)[8] and remember only the better ones that were not, then or since (except in the schools). At best all we can do is to compare the book reading of a highly selected group totaling less than 5 percent of the population with a public five or six times larger today. Despite the general and pervasive impact of mass culture today, it is altogether likely that there is just as large and hard a core of serious readers today as there ever was. I personally believe it is larger and that it will grow with increases in popular education.

Assumption: That the competition of the mass media of communi- 15
cation is crowding out the book.   Now that the book business has survived price cutting, book clubs, quarter books, and high manufacturing costs the new menace is television. A generation ago it was radio. Here again the broad assumption is too gross to fit the facts. In some ways the different media are in competition, in other ways not. In the first place book readers are more active users of the other media (except perhaps radio-television) than the nonreaders. They read more newspapers, they see more films, they read more magazines. Secondly, the kind of person who is attracted to serious reading is not ordinarily the kind distracted by the nature of much of the mass media content. Third, there is a considerable amount of intermedia stimulation—some people read the book after they have seen the film adapted from it or have read a magazine condensation. Fourth, in general intermedia relations show a supplementary rather than complementary pattern; people who read books about, say, politics are also likely to listen to discussions of politics on the air and read about it in magazines and newspapers. Or again: the readers of better books are likely to be listeners to serious radio. Finally, there is a sort of reverse competition in operation, in that book readers are found relatively often among the critics of the other media. They are more likely than nonreaders to be dissatisfied with the radio or with the movies or with their newspapers. Not only is their better education re-

---

7. Nathaniel **Hawthorne** (1804–1864): American novelist whose works, now considered must-read classics, originally appealed to a relatively small and elite audience.—ED.

8. *The Lamplighter* (1854): Sentimental novel by Maria Cummins (1827–1866), one of the best-selling books of the mid-nineteenth century.—ED.

sponsible for this tendency; their book reading probably helps to sustain their critical faculties against the flood.

A word on the effect of TV. It is too early, in my judgment, to say anything definitive about the impact of television on book reading. Most studies to date do show that television owners read fewer books than nonowners. It is not completely clear, however, that this is altogether due to television itself; they may have read less or differently before. More important, it is not clear yet just how book reading will be affected over a long period by the kind of television content that is now available. Once the novelty wears off, assuming that the content remains at the present level, television may affect book reading as little as radio does. And, of course, we do not yet know what will happen to the book reading of a generation raised on television. If television content improves considerably it may affect book reading rather more. So far it does seem to have cut down the gross amount of book reading, though probably it will not affect the reading of quality books.

Assumption: That "the American public" reads poor books or, alternately, that it reads good books.   This assumption also comes both ways. For example, at the same time Henry Seidel Canby[9] was claiming to have discovered that "the intelligent interest of the American public had been grossly underestimated by publishers and advertisers," Edmund Wilson[10] concluded that the popularity of Lloyd Douglas "is something to give pause to anyone who may have supposed that the generation of Mencken had lifted the taste of the American public above the level of Gene Stratton Porter and Harold Bell Wright."[11] Again, it is necessary to point out that the substance of both these observations may be true for different groups of readers or even for the same people at different times, although neither statement is correct as it stands. At the risk of being tiresome one must insist upon differentiating within "the American public," upon recognizing the complexity of the actual reading picture.

This particular question is further complicated by lack of agreement upon the standards by which quality is to be judged. If by "poor books" we mean light fiction of the adventure, Western, romance, and mystery type, then at least 60 percent of adult book reading qualifies as "poor"

---

9. **Henry Seidel Canby** (1878–1961): Editor, literary critic, and original member of the Book-of-the-Month Club's review board.—ED.

10. **Edmund Wilson** (1895–1972): Preeminent American critic and literary historian whose essays appeared in *The New Yorker, Vanity Fair,* and *The New Republic.* In his hundreds of book reviews, Wilson tried to distinguish "the first-rate from the second-rate" for his readers.—ED.

11. H. L. **Mencken** (1880–1956): Acerbic columnist who frequently criticized the complacent middle class; **Lloyd Douglas** (1877–1951), **Gene Stratton Porter** (1863–1924), and **Harold Bell Wright** (1872–1944): Wrote immensely popular historical novels during the first half of the twentieth century.—ED.

(although the data on this are not too clear). If by "good books" we mean recognized classics and highly regarded contemporary writing of a serious sort then perhaps 10 to 15 percent of book reading is "good." A couple of years ago a well-known librarian claimed for the ALA's[12] list of "Notable Books" that it was "representative of what people the country over are reading." The list included such titles as Bush's *Modern Arms and Free Men*, Bemis's *John Quincy Adams and the Foundation of American Foreign Policy*, Kluckhohn's *Mirror for Man*, and Welty's *Golden Apples;* the best-sellers for that year included such titles as Douglas's *The Big Fisherman*, Waltari's *The Egyptian*, Keyes's *Dinner at Antoine's*, a Costain, a Yerby, and the Zoo and Canasta books.[13]

Put it this way: Book reading in this country varies in quality as widely as do the books themselves. Much of the reading involves books whose quality does not justify any particular consideration just because the pages are bound inside a hard cover. More fiction is read than nonfiction (especially by women) and more "light" fiction than "heavy." There is a substantial core of "good readers." And the more formal education, the more likely one is to be a good reader.

Assumption: That people read what interests them. Of course 20 subject interest is a major factor in the selection of reading matter, especially if other things are equal. However, they are not always equal or not often so, and thus other influences come into play. Notable among them is the factor of accessibility, which determines some of what all of us read (*The National Geographic* in the dentist's waiting room) and a great deal of what some people read. Books that are handy are read more frequently than those even a little hard to get, especially for that large group of people who "just want something interesting." Books that are delivered to the house, for example, have a better chance to be read than books that have to be brought from the library or the bookstore. People who live close to a public library read more books than people who live some blocks away. Books that are easily accessible within a library—for example, on the "interesting books" shelf—are read more than books not so easily accessible—for example, on the bottom shelf of a dark stack. Books the public or rental librarian "pushes" are read more than others.

Another factor is readability. Experts tell us that for many people there simply are no readable books on subjects of interest to them. Then

---

12. **ALA:** The American Library Association.—ED.

13. Vannevar **Bush** (1890–1974), Samuel Flagg **Bemis** (1891–1973), Frank L. **Kluckhohn** (1907–1970) and Eudora **Welty** (b. 1909) wrote intellectually respectable works of history, politics, or literature, in contrast to the pseudohistorical and sensational novels of Lloyd **Douglas** (1877–1951), Mika **Waltari** (1908–1979), Frances Parkinson **Keyes** (1885–1970), Thomas B. **Costain** (1885–1965), and Frank **Yerby** (1916–1991).—ED.

there is the great effect of social pressure, felt even when not articulated. People read what other people around them are reading; in a sense they are "forced" to read certain books in order to be up-to-date in bookish conversations. If everybody around you is reading *The Disenchanted* or *The Far Side of Paradise* you don't have to be particularly interested in F. Scott Fitzgerald[14] to read them, too—you "have to" read them as a matter of self-protection, if nothing else. Sometimes the social pressure generates interest, but even when it does not it can stimulate the reading of particular titles. In any case the motives for reading are extremely complex and in many instances interest is not the determining factor.

There are other assumptions commonly made about book reading, particularly about their effects upon individuals and the society, but we cannot go into them here. For example, there is the assumption that "reading maketh the full man"—which is probably true only for a very few readers since the rest read rather narrowly in terms of subject or form. Or there is the assumption that book reading makes people into good citizens by informing them about current affairs—which is probably true only for a minority of the readers of political books, since most readers are deliberately reinforcing their own political viewpoints. Or there is the assumption that books have had great effects directly upon large classes of readers, as in Mark Twain's charge that the state of the South was attributable to the reading of Walter Scott[15] or in Archibald MacLeish's[16] assertion that the "distrustful" state of mind of a whole generation could be laid at the door of the World War I novelists. Actually "the books that have changed our minds" (of the Freud-Marx-Darwin variety) have their major effects in an indirect and remote fashion upon people who have never read them and often hardly heard of them.

The general moral of this tale, then, is that the state of popular reading is complicated, uneven, shifting, sometimes obscure. The broad generalizations in terms of which the subject is usually discussed are simply not appropriate to a serious, realistic view of it. Although it is more fun that way, it is more correct to pay some respect to the accumulated evidence, such as it is, and hence to take account of the actual differentiation which characterizes the state of popular reading today.

---

14. *The Disenchanted* (1950) by Budd Schulberg and *The Far Side of Paradise* (1951) by Arthur Mizener: Works based on the life of jazz-age novelist F. Scott Fitzgerald (1896–1940).—ED.

15. **Walter Scott:** Twain frequently lampooned the Southern passion for the historical romances of English novelist Sir Walter Scott (1771–1832).—ED.

16. **Archibald MacLeish** (1892–1982): Pulitzer Prize-winning American poet.—ED.

▪ CONSIDER THE SOURCE

1. How does Berelson define "book readers"? Which definition do you think would be most appropriate today?

2. What does Berelson say is the relation between educational level and book reading? What other factors contribute to the book-reading habit?

3. To what extent do books and television compete with one another, according to Berelson?

4. What cultural assumptions does Berelson make? Who are the "American people" he seems to envision? What does he mean by "better books" and "serious reading"?

▪ CONSIDER THE IMPLICATIONS

5. Read the description of the *Saturday Review of Literature (SRL)* in the appendix (p. 662). How closely does Berelson's description of the average book reader resemble "the modal *SRL* reader"? Would that reader be likely to approve or disapprove of Berelson's conclusion that "book readers are far from representative of the total population"? Why?

6. As a class, draw up a list of your assumptions about book reading in today's culture, keeping in mind the book readers whose essays you read in chapter 2. How closely does your list resemble Berelson's assumptions of forty-five years ago?

7. Berelson offers a brief and highly conditional assessment of the effect television is likely to have on book-reading habits. From your vantage point as a member of "a generation raised on television," write a letter to Berelson, letting him know what impact television has had on you as a reader.

8. In your journal, make a list of why you read the books or magazines that you do. What roles do "interest," "accessibility," "readability," and "self-protection" play in your reading choices? Are there other factors Berelson does not mention?

9. Focusing on an activity you know well, generate a set of broad popular assumptions about the pastime and the people who engage in it. You might think about people who listen to rap music, surf, collect baseball cards, or watch soap operas. Begin by describing the stereotypical participant and then list the assumptions that undergird the stereotype. For instance, the stereotypical surfer may be the blond dude who spends all his time at the beach; the underlying assumption is that he ditches all his classes and probably isn't very bright. Write an essay in which you refute or elaborate on those assumptions, offering evidence to support your views.

E. D. HIRSCH JR.

The Formation of Modern National Cultures

The practice that Bernard Berelson dubbed "Viewing with Alarm the state of popular culture" began over a century ago and continues unabated in our own day. One of the most highly respected figures to expound on the problems with American literacy in recent years is E. D. Hirsch Jr. (b. 1928). His book Cultural Literacy: What Every American Needs to Know *(1987) prompted a national debate on the core texts, authors, and ideals of American culture. Translated into Japanese (1988) and Chinese (1989), the book spawned several guides to American culture that Hirsch co-authored:* The Dictionary of Cultural Literacy *(1988) tells adults all they'll need to know, while a whole series of books, beginning with* What Your First Grader Needs to Know *(1993), provides the same service for grade-school children through sixth grade. Hirsch is the William R. Kenan Professor of English at the University of Virginia. Before he became a spokesman for cultural literacy, he authored several books and articles about the British Romantic poets and wrote two influential books about the theory of literary criticism.*

Every national culture is . . . contrived: It . . . transcends dialect, region, and social class and is partly a conscious construct. National cultures were formed on many of the same principles as national languages, and for many of the same reasons, as Ernest Gellner observes:

> The cultural shreds and patches used by nationalism are often arbitrary historical inventions. Any old shred or patch would have served as well. But in no way does it follow that the principle of nationalism itself, as opposed to the avatars it happens to pick up for its incarnations, is in the least contingent and accidental. Nothing could be further from the truth than such a supposition. Nationalism is not what it seems, and above all, not what it seems to itself. The cultures it claims to defend and revive are often its own inventions, or are modified out of all recognition.[1]

Gellner shows that nation builders use a patchwork of scholarly folk materials, old songs, obscure dances, and historical legends, all apparently quaint and local, but in reality selected and reinterpreted by intellectuals to create a culture upon which the life of the nation can rest.

> If the nationalism prospers it eliminates the alien high culture, but it does not then replace it by the old local low culture; it revives, or invents, a

---

From *Cultural Literacy: What Every American Needs to Know* (Boston: Houghton Mifflin, 1987), pp. 82–93.

1. Ernest Gellner, *Nations and Nationalism* (Ithaca, N.Y.: Cornell University Press, 1983), p. 56.

local high (literate, specialist-transmitted) culture of its own, though admittedly one which will have some links with the earlier folk styles and dialects. But it was the great ladies at the Budapest Opera who really went to town in peasant dresses, or dresses claimed to be such.[2]

Because language making has been studied more than culture making, the historical process of creating a national culture is perhaps less well understood. But the need for a culture in building a nation is really just another dimension of the need for a language. A nation's language can be regarded as a part of its culture, or conversely, its culture can be regarded as the totality of its language. The American legend about Lincoln in his log cabin can be conceived either as part of our culture, or, with equal justification, as part of our shared language. Americans need to learn not just the grammar of their language but also their national vocabulary. They need to learn not just the associations of such words as *to run* but also the associations of such terms as *Teddy Roosevelt, DNA,* and *Hamlet.*

For nation builders, fixing the vocabulary of a national culture is analogous to fixing a standard grammar, spelling, and pronunciation. When culture makers begin their task in the early days of a nation, they are limited, as are language normalizers, by the range of materials that history has made available to them, but the choices made from those possibilities are not always inevitable.[3] Abraham Lincoln was certain to become a central figure in our culture, but Betsy Ross was not. The candidates for her position of legendary Revolutionary War heroine were potentially many. But Martha Crabtree, Sarah Smith, and Janet Blair were weighed in the balance and found wanting. Such choices are no more inevitable than the spelling *monk* instead of *munk.*[4]

In addition to using dictionaries that transmit the national language to all parts of the nation, national systems of education use textbooks and readers that carry the national culture to outlying provinces. After Napoleon's time, it used to be said that on a particular day in France each child in the fifth grade would be reading the same page of the same textbook. The British, like the Americans, used more subtle means for achieving the same uniformity. Textbooks were not prepared by the central government but by the provinces. The effect, however, was the same.

The story of one such provincial textbook, Blair's *Rhetoric,* is instruc- 5

---

2. Ibid., 57.

3. On the arbitrariness of the early prescriptive orthographers in English, see R. L. Venezky, *The Structure of English Orthography* (The Hague: Mouton, 1970), as well as E. J. Dobson, *English Pronunciation 1500–1700,* 2d ed., 2 vols. (Oxford: Oxford University Press, 1968), and Henry Bradley, *On the Relations between Spoken and Written Language, with Special Reference to English* (Oxford: Oxford University Press, 1919).

4. For *monk* see Dobson, *English Pronunciation,* 953.

tive. In 1762, seven years after the publication of Johnson's dictionary,[5] the first professorship of English was established, and significantly, it was created in the provinces—in Scotland—where instruction in English national culture was felt to be needed. The new chair was the Regius Professorship of Rhetoric and Belles Lettres (i.e., composition and literature) at the University of Edinburgh. The first holder of the chair, Hugh Blair, was a Scot. In 1783 he delivered the fruit of twenty years of teaching, his *Lectures on Rhetoric and Belles Lettres,* to an eager public that had already been using pirated versions of his *Rhetoric* based on notes from his university lectures.

Blair's book became one of the most influential textbooks ever issued in Great Britain or the United States. Between 1783 and 1911 it went through 130 editions.[6] Throughout the nineteenth century the *Rhetoric* remained in the college and school curriculum on both sides of the Atlantic. Its authority in the United States persisted long after the Civil War. Designed as a college text, it was condensed and adapted for use in schools, and it influenced the contents of other school readers and spellers.

What did Blair's book contain? Its index includes not one mention of a Scottish poet, despite the distinction of Blair's fellow Scotsmen William Dunbar and Robert Henryson.[7] Blair and his public implicitly understood that his job was to introduce his students and readers to the specific tradition that they needed to know if they were to read and write well in English. He was thus an early, perhaps the first, definer of cultural literacy for the English national language. He gathered and codified for the Scots materials that literate Englishmen had absorbed through the pores. The clarity and authority of his book made it nearly as influential in fixing the cultural content of the language as Johnson's dictionary was in fixing its forms. Blair created, in effect, a dictionary of cultural literacy for those who had not been born to English literate culture, for use by provincials like the Scots and colonials like the Americans. His book would later be used to educate native-born Englishmen as well.

The literate tradition that Blair thus rendered explicit, which largely persists to the present day, was by no means simply English in its origins. It contained material from Greece and Rome and from Europe. The index to his *Rhetoric* reads like a sampling from the pre-nineteenth-

---

5. **Johnson's dictionary:** Written by Samuel Johnson (1709–1784), the *Dictionary of the English Language* (1755) attempted to preserve the "purity" of the English language.—ED.

6. See David Potter, Preface, in Hugh Blair, *Lectures on Rhetoric and Belles Lettres,* ed. Harold F. Harding, 2 vols. (Carbondale: Southern Illinois University Press, 1965), vol. 2, p. 435.

7. **William Dunbar** (1465?–1530?) **and Robert Henryson** (1430?–1506): Scotland's most famous poets of the late Middle Ages.—ED.

century part of a current index to American cultural literacy. Some items are:

Achilles	Dr. Johnson
Adam	Juvenal
Addison	Livy
Aeneid	Locke
Aeschylus	Longinus
Aetna	Lucretius
Arabian Nights	Machiavelli
Aristophanes	Milton
Aristotle	Molière
Bacon	Odyssey
Berkeley	Oedipus
Caesar	Paradise Lost
Cicero	Pericles
Corneille	Pindar
King David	Plato
Dido	Pope
Dryden	Racine
Euripedes	Robinson Crusoe
Eve	Rousseau
Fielding	Satan
Helen	Shakespeare
Herodotus	Solomon
Homer	Sophocles
Horace	Swift
Iliad	Tacitus
Isaiah	Thucydides
Jeremiah	Virgil
Job	Voltaire

For each of these items, and for many more, Blair conveyed the attitudes and associations that make up the lore of the literate tradition. For example, this is how he gave his readers the traditional range of views about Achilles:

> Homer has been blamed for making his hero Achilles of too brutal and inamiable a character. But I am inclined to think that injustice is commonly done to Achilles, upon the credit of two lines of Horace, who has certainly overloaded his character.
>
> Impiger, iracundus, inexorabilis, acer,
> Jura negat sibi nata; nihil non arrogat armis.
>
> [Energetic, angry, inexorable, fierce, / He spurns the law, and respects only arms.]
> Achilles is passionate indeed to a great degree; but he is far from being a contemner of laws and justice. . . . Besides his wonderful bravery and contempt of death, he has several other qualities of a Hero. He is

open and sincere. He loves his subjects and respects the Gods. He is distinguished by strong friendships and attachments.[8]

And so on through two volumes and more than a thousand pages, each sentence of which conveyed commonly shared information that aspiring readers, writers, and speakers would do well to remember.

By the early twentieth century Blair was obsolete, not because of any defect in his presentation but because essential new elements not found in his book had come into literate culture during the nineteenth century, and some names had drifted into oblivion. Dickens and Hawthorne came in, Fenelon and Dr. Pitcairn went out.[9] A reconstituted Blair could have served anywhere English was written and read. Yet no one in the United States created a revised Blair, because such a book would still have lacked the national dimension of cultural literacy.

In the nineteenth century we began to replace Blair with textbooks that attempted to create and transmit the mythology and values of the new country. In a study of American school materials of the nineteenth century, Ruth Miller Elson found an almost complete unanimity of values and emphases in our schoolbooks from 1790 to 1900.[10] They consistently contrasted virtuous and natural Americans with corrupt and decadent Europeans; they unanimously stressed love of country, love of God, obedience to parents, thrift, honesty, and hard work; and they continually insisted upon the perfection of the United States, the guardian of liberty and the destined redeemer of a sinful Europe.

Among the militant and self-conscious writers of these schoolbooks, the jingoistic Noah Webster[11] was as typical as he was important. But although his spellers, readers, and dictionaries enjoyed uniquely large sales, they were not unique in any other respect. In fact, as Elson has shown, the contents of American schoolbooks of the nineteenth century were so similar and interchangeable that their creators might seem to have participated in a conspiracy to indoctrinate young Americans with commonly shared attitudes, including a fierce national loyalty and pride.[12]

---

8. Ibid.

9. Charles **Dickens** (1812–1870) and Nathaniel **Hawthorne** (1804–1864): The preeminent nineteenth-century novelists of England and the United States, respectively; François de **Fenelon** (1651–1715) French theologian whose writings influenced Enlightenment theories of politics and education; **Dr.** Archibald **Pitcairn** (1652–1713) British physician and poet.—ED.

10. Ruth Miller Elson, *Guardians of Tradition: American Schoolbooks of the Nineteenth Century* (Lincoln: University of Nebraska Press, 1964), 337–42.

11. **Noah Webster** (1758–1843): His *American Dictionary of the English Language* (1828) was the first dictionary to distinguish American language usage from conventional British usage.—ED.

12. Elson, *Guardians of Tradition*, 186–220.

One American culture maker who was driven by the aim of doing well by doing good was Mason Weems, the author of numerous popular works, including an edition of Franklin's *Autobiography* expanded by anecdotes, a "romanticized" life of General Francis Marion, and many popular tracts in support of virtuous living, early marriage, and the avoidance of strong drink. His chef-d'oeuvre and main contribution to the American tradition was his biography of George Washington, wherein could be found the original legend of the cherry tree.

We have more significant stories about Washington—for instance, the winter at Valley Forge—and more important traditions of national life. But the story of the cherry tree is a useful illustration of the way our national culture was formed. What were Weems's motivations in creating that durable piece of American folklore? His letters suggest that he was not consciously helping to form part of the tradition needed to weld Americans into a nation. He assumed that George Washington had already become part of American lore by virtue of the great offices he had held. He had been glorified unceasingly up and down the land in many a published oration and eulogy. Weems felt that these outpourings of official praise had turned Washington into an intimidating, distant personage, because they presented his life entirely in terms of generalship and statesmanship. No ordinary boy or girl could identify with such a demigod.

But since Americans had an infinite appetite for Washingtonian hagiography,[13] and since no one had yet humanized Washington, Weems detected a market opportunity. As an itinerant book salesman, he knew that the public wanted a Washington who, while still mythic, was nonetheless human and private. Weems deduced that the public needed a domesticated Everyman whose life would serve as a model for American youth. He confided as much in the first pages of his biography. 15

> However glorious, I say, all this [bravery and statesmanship] may have been to himself, or instructive to future generals and presidents, yet does it but *little* concern our *children*. For who among us can hope that his son shall ever be called, like Washington, to direct the storm of war, or to ravish the ears of deeply listening Senates? . . . Oh no! give us his *private* virtues! In *these* every youth is interested, because in these every youth may become a Washington—a Washington in piety and patriotism,—in industry and honor—and consequently a Washington in what alone deserves the name, SELF-ESTEEM and UNIVERSAL RESPECT.[14]

Characteristically, some of the most persistent elements of our national lore owe their longevity to human universality rather than conscious political design: Lincoln in his log cabin, Washington in his fa-

---

13. **hagiography:** Originally the biography of a saint, a hagiography can refer to any idealizing, worshipful biography.—ED.

14. Mason L. Weems, *The Life of George Washington* (1809), ed. Marcus Cunliffe (Cambridge: Harvard University Press, 1962), 4–5.

ther's garden. The stories of Weems have outlived those of Webster. There could hardly be a more attractive tale than the one which portrays for the delight of children a parent who happily forgives a wayward child (for what child does not feel wayward?) and for parents a model who, in the most charming possible way, persuades young people to tell the truth.

> George, said his father, *do you know who killed that beautiful little cherry tree yonder in the garden?* This was a *tough question;* and George staggered under it for a moment; but quickly recovered himself: and looking at his father, with the sweet face of youth brightened with the inexpressible charm of all-conquering truth, he bravely cried out, *I can't tell a lie, Pa; you know I can't tell a lie. I did cut it with my hatchet.*[15]

If this legend had been left to languish in Weems's book, it might have been forgotten. For the sober later biographers of Washington, anxious to discriminate between fact and what Weems openly called romance, were successful in discrediting Weems's book, the popularity of which waned greatly in the later nineteenth century. But with a sure instinct, the compilers of textbooks took up the Weems stories. McGuffey included a sterner version of the cherry tree episode in his *Second Eclectic Reader*[16] and thus assured it a place in many other readers, and in our permanent lore.

Abraham Lincoln relates in his *Autobiography* how he educated himself by carefully reading and rereading a few books . . . Weems's *Life of Washington,* the Bible, *Robinson Crusoe, Pilgrim's Progress,* the *Autobiography* of Benjamin Franklin (possibly the expanded version by Weems), Paine's *Age of Reason,* and Volney's *Ruins.*[17] This typical frontier education itself became part of American national mythology after Lincoln's assassination. In the Lincoln story, as narrated inside and outside the school, Americans continued an ideal of a peculiarly American education, in which the reading of a few central books could yield virtue, patriotism, and prudence. As Lawrence A. Cremin notes,

---

15. Ibid., 12–13.

16. **McGuffey's** *Second Eclectic Reader*: Part of a best-selling series of readers (1836–1857) by American educator William Holmes McGuffey (1800–1873) that provided moral education along with reading instruction and was used well into the twentieth century.—ED.

17. Abraham Lincoln, "Autobiography Written for John L. Scripps" [June 1860], in *The Collected Works of Abraham Lincoln,* ed. Roy B. Basler, 8 vols. (New Brunswick, N.J.: Rutgers University Press, 1953), vol. 4, 62. Volney's *Ruins,* now forgotten but an influential book of the Enlightenment, was subtitled *Meditations on the Revolutions of Empires.* A translation from the French was begun by Thomas Jefferson, a friend of Volney's, and finished by Joel Barlow. See Constantin C. Volney, *A New Translation of Volney's Ruins in Two Volumes,* ed. Robert D. Richardson, Jr. (New York: Garland, 1979).

The Lincoln of folklore had a significance even beyond the Lincoln of actuality. For the Lincoln of folklore embodied what ordinary inarticulate Americans cherished as ideals. Put otherwise, if the Lincoln of actuality imbibed the American *paideia* [i.e., our traditional scheme of education], the Lincoln of folklore personified it, and in reflecting it back on education writ large, helped transmit it to successive generations of Americans.[18]

The Washington and Lincoln legends might have developed differently, just as the spelling of the word *doubt* might have. In the early stages of a nation's life, its traditions are in flux. But with the passage of time, traditions that have been recorded in a nation's printed books and transmitted in its education system become fixed in the national memory. They become known by so many people over so long a time that they enter the oral and written tradition, where they tend to remain through generations. Consequently, these early traditions are not easy to change. Important legends, names, and events become fixed by constant usage, just as spellings do.

But the analogy with spelling and grammar is only partial. Our national culture resembles a vocabulary more than a system of grammar and spelling. And the vocabulary of a culture, like that of a language, is open to change. All languages are linguistically progressive. That is, they tend to shorten words that are used frequently. For instance, *TV* will probably slowly supplant *television,* and *phone, telephone.*[19] Coinages come into the cultural lexicon, and old words drop out or get expelled. Sometimes entirely new objects or events must be named. Occasionally it is possible to change our vocabulary by acts of common will, as we are changing it to remove racism and sexism in language. 20

But the occurrence, and more rarely the introduction, of specific change into our vocabulary has led some to believe, erroneously, that our culture can be remade on a large scale by an act of common will. This is a false and damaging myth. Rapid, large-scale change is no more possible in the sphere of national culture than in the sphere of national language. It is no more desirable or practicable to drop biblical and legendary allusions from our culture than to drop the letter *s* from the third person singular.

---

18. Lawrence A. Cremin, *American Education: The National Experience 1783–1876* (New York: Harper and Row, 1980), 499.

19. The tendency for frequently used words to become shortened is one of the few universals of language and has been well studied since the path-breaking work of G. K. Zipf, "Relative Frequency as a Determinant of Phonetic Change," *Harvard Studies in Classical Philology* 40 (1929): 1–95. See also A. Martinet, *A Functional View of Language* (Oxford: Oxford University Press, 1962). Martinet gives numerous examples and observes: "The unmistakable existence of an inverse relationship between frequency and linguistic complexity is a most precious discovery" (144).

The traditional materials of national culture can be learned by all citizens only if the materials are taught in a nation's schools. But to teach them, the schools must have access to books that explain them—dictionaries like Johnson's and indexes to cultural literacy like Blair's. Because such compendia help outsiders enter mainstream literate culture, works like Blair's and Johnson's are socially progressive instruments, despite the fact that they contain traditional materials. Like everything that helps to spread literate language and culture, a nation's dictionaries, including those of cultural literacy, have helped to overcome class distinctions and barriers to opportunity. Historically, they have had a liberalizing and democratic effect.

But these benefits of national literate culture will be lost if we take our cultural traditions and national language too much for granted. It is all too easy for us to make this mistake, because of our history. When our nation began, we did not experience the bloody animosities and social dislocations that followed the imposition of national languages in France, Spain, and Britain and that are now following the same process in Russia. Fortunately, we inherited a standard written language that by 1776 had become normalized in grammar, spelling, and pronunciation. Our ancient charters, the Declaration of Independence and the Constitution, were written in a language that is current more than two hundred years later—a remarkable fact that we too easily take for granted when we read them. We remain happily unaware of the political struggles that usually accompanied the establishment of a national language. The Scots and Irish and Welsh did not begin to speak English because they believed it to be superior to their own language. The work of standardizing our language had been done for us long ago in such bloody, faraway battles as Flodden, Worcester, and Drogheda[20] and in numerous decades of work by English scholars and schoolmasters.

Our only experience of civil strife over the language was a tempest in a teapot called the war of the dictionaries. Joseph Worcester of Massachusetts and Noah Webster of Connecticut argued over such towering questions as whether the *a* in *grass* should be pronounced like the "*grahs* of a British lawn or the *grass* of the boundless prairies," or whether the word for honest work should be spelled *labour* as in Britain or *labor* as befits the land of opportunity and equality. Worcester, the conservative, wanted to follow British practice in everything. Webster, representing the spirit of national pride and independence, wanted to introduce an American flavor into pronunciation and spelling. Worcester's loyalty to Britain in these matters was unpopular and found acceptance only in a

---

20. The defeats of the Scots at the battles of **Flodden** (1513) and **Worcester** (1651) and the Irish at **Drogheda** (1649) effectively established English supremacy throughout the British Isles.—ED.

few places, notably Harvard and the University of Virginia; elsewhere in the land, Noah Webster's dictionary was victorious.[21]

Our fortunate inexperience of bloodshed over language may explain   25 why some of us look with equanimity upon recent proposals favoring multilingualism in our country. Defenders of linguistic pluralism invite us to look to Switzerland, not realizing that Switzerland has achieved multi*literacy* (as distinct from multilingualism) through a small, intensive, centralized educational system that, coupled with universal military service, enables the Swiss to communicate with one another despite their linguistic handicaps. Moreover, they have achieved this only after hundreds of years of bloody conflict between the Swiss cantons. In fact, there are good reasons why no large nation has been able to imitate Switzerland. The examples of Belgium and Canada are not encouraging.

In America the reality is that we have not yet properly achieved *mono*literacy, much less multiliteracy.[22] Because of the demands created by technology we need effective monoliteracy more than ever. Linguistic pluralism would make sense for us only on the questionable assumption that our civil peace and national effectiveness could survive multilingualism. But in fact, multilingualism enormously increases cultural fragmentation, civil antagonism, illiteracy, and economic-technological ineffectualness. These are the very disabilities the Chinese are attempting to overcome.

National languages are not ethnic media. Each one is an elaborate composite contrived to overcome local and ethnic dialectal variations inside a large nation.[23] It is contrary to the purpose and essence of a national language, whether English or German or Spanish or French, that a modern nation should deliberately encourage more than one to flourish within its borders. Once a national language is permanently fixed in grammars, schoolbooks, and dictionaries, and used in millions of books, magazines, and newspapers, it becomes, except for its vocabulary, an immovable, almost unchanging substance. When two great standard literate languages like English and Spanish, or English and French, coexist inside a nation, neither can yield to the other except by strife or vigorous intervention in the educational system.

In considering bilingualism in America, we should therefore understand that well-meaning linguistic pluralism, which would encourage

---

21. See the article "Webster, Noah" in James D. Hart, ed., *The Oxford Companion to American Literature* (New York: Oxford University Press, 1956).

22. The term *bilingualism* is sometimes used with deliberate vagueness, and in a quite misleading way, to capitalize on our positive valuation of people who know more than one language. For those who really mean the word in this positive sense, I suggest the term *biliteracy*. In current discussions, *bilingualism* is often used to describe people who are literate in no language.

23. See Otto Jespersen, *Mankind, Nation and Individual from a Linguistic Point of View* (Bloomington: Indiana University Press, 1964).

rather than discourage competing languages within our borders, is much different from Jeffersonian pluralism, which has encouraged a diversity of traditions, values, and opinions. Toleration of diversity is at the root of our society, but encouragement of multilingualism is contrary to our traditions and extremely unrealistic. Defenders of multilingualism should not assume that our Union has been preserved once and for all by the Civil War, and that we can afford to disdain the cultural and educational vigilance exercised by other modern nations. To think so complacently is to show a fundamental misunderstanding of the role of national literacy in creating and sustaining modern civilization.

This book is not, of course, directly concerned with the question of bilingualism. But I know that well-meaning bilingualism could unwittingly erect serious barriers to cultural literacy among our young people and therefore create serious barriers to universal literacy at a mature level. I am opposed neither to bi*literacy* nor to the learning of foreign languages. I am strongly in favor of both. In the best of worlds, all Americans would be multiliterate. But surely the first step in that direction must be for all of us to become literate in our own national language and culture.

▪ CONSIDER THE SOURCE

1. Explain what Hirsch means when he says, "Every national culture is contrived." Who constructs national culture? What are the materials that go into it?

2. Trace Hirsch's analogy between linguistic and cultural systems. How are cultural elements part of a "national vocabulary"? Does Hirsch believe it's possible to change that vocabulary? Why or why not?

3. Summarize the process by which the legend of Washington and the cherry tree became inscribed in our national mythology. What role did printed books play in the process?

4. How does Hirsch differentiate multiliteracy and multilingualism? Why is the distinction important to his argument?

▪ CONSIDER THE IMPLICATIONS

5. Did you know the story of Washington and the cherry tree? If so, explore in your journal when and how you were introduced to this element of our national mythology. Was it formalized in a textbook? How did you interpret the story's message?

6. Read or review C. H. Knoblauch's essay on the political implications of different kinds of literacy (pp. 122–30). Do you agree with Knoblauch's assessment of the politics behind Hirsch's "cultural literacy"? How might Hirsch respond to Knoblauch's argument?

7. Consider Hirsch's claim that books that codify cultural literacy are "socially progressive instruments, despite the fact that they contain tradi-

tional materials." Hold a class debate on whether schools should emphasize Western tradition or open the curriculum up to non-Western cultural
materials.

8. Like Blair in his eighteenth-century *Rhetoric,* Hirsch has compiled a *Dictionary of Cultural Literacy* to convey "commonly shared information that
aspiring readers, writers, and speakers would do well to remember." In
small groups, list the names and concepts that you would include in a dictionary designed to "transmit the mythology and values" of contemporary culture. Compare your list with those of other groups. Which features of today's culture did you emphasize?

9. Write an essay exploring the viability of the notion of "national culture"
in the United States of the 1990s.

10. How might Patricia Nelson Limerick (pp. 209–21) respond to Hirsch's arguments for "monolingualism"?

11. As an appendix to *Cultural Literacy,* Hirsch provides a list of "What Literate Americans Know." Louisa May Alcott and *Little Women* both make it
onto Hirsch's list. Review the cluster of readings on *Little Women* in chapter 1 and discuss how Alcott's novel fits Hirsch's criteria for elements of
"national literate culture."

▪▪▪▪▪▪

LAURA BOHANNAN

Shakespeare in the Bush

*One of the justifications for promoting the classics of high culture has al-
ways been that they are "universal"; they address fundamental human
concerns that can be understood the same way by everyone. Anthropologist Laura Bohannan (b. 1922) provides amusing evidence that this may
not necessarily be true. "Human nature is pretty much the same the
whole world over," she claimed before setting off to live among the Tiv
tribe in West Africa. But that was before she tried to explain Shakespeare's* Hamlet *to the Tiv. As she narrates the story of one of her country's "things of long ago," her African audience continually interrupts to
question, debate, and correct her interpretation, casting serious doubt on
her assumptions about human nature. Bohannan has served as editor of*
American Anthropologist, *a scholarly journal. With Paul Bohannan,
she has co-authored two books on the African tribe she writes about here:*
The Tiv of Central Nigeria *(1953) and* Tiv Economy *(1968), which
won the 1968 Herskovits award for best book on Africa. This essay originally appeared in the journal* Natural History *in 1966.*

From *Natural History* (August–September, 1966), pp. 28–33.

Just before I left Oxford for the Tiv in West Africa, conversation turned to the season at Stratford.[1] "You Americans," said a friend, "often have difficulty with Shakespeare. He was, after all, a very English poet, and one can easily misinterpret the universal by misunderstanding the particular."

I protested that human nature is pretty much the same the whole world over; at least the general plot and motivation of the greater tragedies would always be clear—everywhere—although some details of custom might have to be explained and difficulties of translation might produce other slight changes. To end an argument we could not conclude, my friend gave me a copy of *Hamlet* to study in the African bush: It would, he hoped, lift my mind above its primitive surroundings, and possibly I might, by prolonged meditation, achieve the grace of correct interpretation.

It was my second field trip to that African tribe, and I thought myself ready to live in one of its remote sections—an area difficult to cross even on foot. I eventually settled on the hillock of a very knowledgeable old man, the head of a homestead of some 140 people, all of whom were either his close relatives or their wives and children. Like the other elders of the vicinity, the old man spent most of his time performing ceremonies seldom seen these days in the more accessible parts of the tribe. I was delighted. Soon there would be three months of enforced isolation and leisure, between the harvest that takes place just before the rising of the swamps and the clearing of new farms when the water goes down. Then, I thought, they would have even more time to perform ceremonies and explain them to me.

I was quite mistaken. Most of the ceremonies demanded the presence of elders from several homesteads. As the swamps rose, the old men found it too difficult to walk from one homestead to the next, and the ceremonies gradually ceased. As the swamps rose even higher, all activities but one came to an end. The women brewed beer from maize and millet. Men, women, and children sat on their hillocks and drank it.

People began to drink at dawn. By midmorning the whole homestead was singing, dancing, and drumming. When it rained, people had to sit inside their huts: There they drank and sang or they drank and told stories. In any case, by noon or before, I either had to join the party or retire to my own hut and my books. "One does not discuss serious matters when there is beer. Come, drink with us." Since I lacked their capacity for the thick native beer, I spent more and more time with *Hamlet*. Before the end of the second month, grace descended on me. I was quite sure that *Hamlet* had only one possible interpretation, and that one universally obvious. 5

---

1. **season at Stratford**: The Royal Shakespeare Company (established 1960) annually presents a summer season of drama at Stratford-upon-Avon, Shakespeare's birthplace.—ED.

Early every morning, in the hope of having some serious talk before the beer party, I used to call on the old man at his reception hut—a circle of posts supporting a thatched roof above a low mud wall to keep out wind and rain. One day I crawled through the low doorway and found most of the men of the homestead sitting huddled in their ragged cloths on stools, low plank beds, and reclining chairs, warming themselves against the chill of the rain around a smoky fire. In the center were three pots of beer. The party had started.

The old man greeted me cordially. "Sit down and drink." I accepted a large calabash full of beer, poured some into a small drinking gourd, and tossed it down. Then I poured some more into the same gourd for the man second in seniority to my host before I handed my calabash over to a young man for further distribution. Important people shouldn't ladle beer themselves.

"It is better like this," the old man said, looking at me approvingly and plucking at the thatch that had caught in my hair. "You should sit and drink with us more often. Your servants tell me that when you are not with us, you sit inside your hut looking at a paper."

The old man was acquainted with four kinds of "papers": tax receipts, bride price receipts, court fee receipts, and letters. The messenger who brought him letters from the chief used them mainly as a badge of office, for he always knew what was in them and told the old man. Personal letters for the few who had relatives in the government or mission stations were kept until someone went to a large market where there was a letter writer and reader. Since my arrival, letters were brought to me to be read. A few men also brought me bride price receipts, privately, with requests to change the figures to a higher sum. I found moral arguments were of no avail, since in-laws are fair game, and the technical hazards of forgery difficult to explain to an illiterate people. I did not wish them to think me silly enough to look at any such papers for days on end, and I hastily explained that my "paper" was one of the "things of long ago" of my country.

"Ah," said the old man. "Tell us."   10

I protested that I was not a storyteller. Storytelling is a skilled art among them; their standards are high, and the audiences critical—and vocal in their criticism. I protested in vain. This morning they wanted to hear a story while they drank. They threatened to tell me no more stories until I told them one of mine. Finally, the old man promised that no one would criticize my style "for we know you are struggling with our language." "But," put in one of the elders, "you must explain what we do not understand, as we do when we tell you our stories." Realizing that here was my chance to prove *Hamlet* universally intelligible, I agreed.

The old man handed me some more beer to help me on with my storytelling. Men filled their long wooden pipes and knocked coals from the fire to place in the pipe bowls; then, puffing contentedly, they sat back to listen. I began in the proper style, "Not yesterday, not yesterday, but long ago, a thing occurred. One night three men were keeping watch outside the homestead of the great chief, when suddenly they saw the former chief approach them."

"Why was he no longer their chief?"

"He was dead," I explained. "That is why they were troubled and afraid when they saw him."

"Impossible," began one of the elders, handing his pipe on to his 15 neighbor, who interrupted, "Of course it wasn't the dead chief. It was an omen sent by a witch. Go on."

Slightly shaken, I continued. "One of these three was a man who knew things"—the closest translation for scholar, but unfortunately it also meant witch. The second elder looked triumphantly at the first. "So he spoke to the dead chief saying, 'Tell us what we must do so you may rest in your grave,' but the dead chief did not answer. He vanished, and they could see him no more. Then the man who knew things—his name was Horatio—said this event was the affair of the dead chief's son, Hamlet."

There was a general shaking of heads round the circle. "Had the dead chief no living brothers? Or was this son the chief?"

"No," I replied. "That is, he had one living brother who became the chief when the elder brother died."

The old men muttered: Such omens were matters for chiefs and elders, not for youngsters; no good could come of going behind a chief's back; clearly Horatio was not a man who knew things.

"Yes, he was," I insisted, shooing a chicken away from my beer. "In 20 our country the son is next to the father. The dead chief's younger brother had become the great chief. He had also married his elder brother's widow only about a month after the funeral."

"He did well," the old man beamed and announced to the others, "I told you that if we knew more about Europeans, we would find they really were very like us. In our country also," he added to me, "the younger brother marries the elder brother's widow and becomes the father of his children. Now, if your uncle, who married your widowed mother, is your father's full brother, then he will be a real father to you. Did Hamlet's father and uncle have one mother?"

His question barely penetrated my mind; I was too upset and thrown too far off balance by having one of the most important elements of *Hamlet* knocked straight out of the picture. Rather uncertainly I said that I thought they had the same mother, but I wasn't sure—the story didn't say. The old man told me severely that these genealogical details made all the difference and that when I got home I must ask the elders about it. He shouted out the door to one of his younger wives to bring his goatskin bag.

Determined to save what I could of the mother motif, I took a deep breath and began again. "The son Hamlet was very sad because his mother had married again so quickly. There was no need for her to do so, and it is our custom for a widow not to go to her next husband until she has mourned for two years."

"Two years is too long," objected the wife, who had appeared with the old man's battered goatskin bag. "Who will hoe your farms for you while you have no husband?"

"Hamlet," I retorted without thinking, "was old enough to hoe his mother's farms himself. There was no need for her to remarry." No one looked convinced. I gave up. "His mother and the great chief told Hamlet not to be sad, for the great chief himself would be a father to Hamlet. Furthermore, Hamlet would be the next chief: therefore he must stay to learn the things of a chief. Hamlet agreed to remain, and all the rest went off to drink beer." 25

While I paused, perplexed at how to render Hamlet's disgusted soliloquy to an audience convinced that Claudius and Gertrude had behaved in the best possible manner, one of the younger men asked me who had married the other wives of the dead chief.

"He had no other wives," I told him.

"But a chief must have many wives! How else can he brew beer and prepare food for all his guests?"

I said firmly that in our country even chiefs had only one wife, that they had servants to do their work, and that they paid them from tax money.

It was better, they returned, for a chief to have many wives and sons 30 who would help him hoe his farms and feed his people; then everyone loved the chief who gave much and took nothing—taxes were a bad thing.

I agreed with the last comment, but for the rest fell back on their favorite way of fobbing off my questions: "That is the way it is done, so that is how we do it."

I decided to skip the soliloquy. Even if Claudius was here thought quite right to marry his brother's widow, there remained the poison motif, and I knew they would disapprove of fratricide. More hopefully I resumed, "That night Hamlet kept watch with the three who had seen his dead father. The dead chief again appeared, and although the others were afraid, Hamlet followed his dead father off to one side. When they were alone, Hamlet's dead father spoke."

"Omens can't talk!" The old man was emphatic.

"Hamlet's dead father wasn't an omen. Seeing him might have been an omen, but he was not." My audience looked as confused as I sounded. "It *was* Hamlet's dead father. It was a thing we call a 'ghost.'" I had to use the English word, for unlike many of the neighboring tribes, these people didn't believe in the survival after death of any individuating part of the personality.

"What is a 'ghost?' An omen?" 35

"No, a 'ghost' is someone who is dead but who walks around and can talk, and people can hear him and see him but not touch him."

They objected. "One can touch zombis."

"No, no! It was not a dead body the witches had animated to sacrifice and eat. No one else made Hamlet's dead father walk. He did it himself."

"Dead men can't walk," protested my audience as one man.

I was quite willing to compromise. "A 'ghost' is the dead man's shadow." 40

But again they objected. "Dead men cast no shadows."

"They do in my country," I snapped.

The old man quelled the babble of disbelief that arose immediately and told me with that insincere, but courteous, agreement one extends to the fancies of the young, ignorant, and superstitious, "No doubt in your country the dead can also walk without being zombis." From the depths of his bag he produced a withered fragment of kola nut, bit off one end to show it wasn't poisoned, and handed me the rest as a peace offering.

"Anyhow," I resumed, "Hamlet's dead father said that his own brother, the one who became chief, had poisoned him. He wanted Hamlet to avenge him. Hamlet believed this in his heart, for he did not like his father's brother." I took another swallow of beer. "In the country of the great chief, living in the same homestead, for it was a very large one, was an important elder who was often with the chief to advise and help him. His name was Polonius. Hamlet was courting his daughter, but her father and her brother . . . [I cast hastily about for some tribal analogy] warned her not to let Hamlet visit her when she was alone on her farm, for he would be a great chief and so could not marry her."

"Why not?" asked the wife, who had settled down on the edge of 45
the old man's chair. He frowned at her for asking stupid questions and growled, "They lived in the same homestead."

"That was not the reason," I informed them. "Polonius was a stranger who lived in the homestead because he helped the chief, not because he was a relative."

"Then why couldn't Hamlet marry her?"

"He could have," I explained, "but Polonius didn't think he would. After all, Hamlet was a man of great importance who ought to marry a chief's daughter, for in his country a man could have only one wife. Polonius was afraid that if Hamlet made love to his daughter, then no one else would give a high price for her."

"That might be true," remarked one of the shrewder elders, "but a chief's son would give his mistress's father enough presents and patronage to more than make up the difference. Polonius sounds like a fool to me."

"Many people think he was," I agreed. "Meanwhile Polonius sent 50 his son Laertes off to Paris to learn the things of that country, for it was the homestead of a very great chief indeed. Because he was afraid that Laertes might waste a lot of money on beer and women and gambling, or get into trouble by fighting, he sent one of his servants to Paris secretly, to spy out what Laertes was doing. One day Hamlet came upon Polonius's daughter Ophelia. He behaved so oddly he frightened her. Indeed"—I was fumbling for words to express the dubious quality of Hamlet's madness—"the chief and many others had also noticed that when Hamlet talked one could understand the words but not what they meant. Many people thought that he had become mad." My audience suddenly became much more attentive. "The great chief wanted to know what was wrong with Hamlet, so he sent for two of Hamlet's age mates [schoolfriends would have taken long explanation] to talk to Hamlet and find out what troubled his heart. Hamlet, seeing that they had been bribed by the chief to betray him, told them nothing. Polonius, however, insisted that Hamlet was mad because he had been forbidden to see Ophelia, whom he loved."

"Why," inquired a bewildered voice, "should anyone bewitch Hamlet on that account?"

"Bewitch him?"

"Yes, only witchcraft can make anyone mad, unless, of course, one sees the beings that lurk in the forest."

I stopped being a storyteller, took out my notebook and demanded to be told more about these two causes of madness. Even while they spoke and I jotted notes, I tried to calculate the effect of this new factor on the plot. Hamlet had not been exposed to the beings that lurk in the forests. Only his relatives in the male line could bewitch him. Barring relatives not mentioned by Shakespeare, it had to be Claudius who was attempting to harm him. And, of course, it was.

For the moment I staved off questions by saying that the great chief 55 also refused to believe that Hamlet was mad for the love of Ophelia and nothing else. "He was sure that something much more important was troubling Hamlet's heart."

"Now Hamlet's age mates," I continued, "had brought with them a famous storyteller. Hamlet decided to have this man tell the chief and all his homestead a story about a man who had poisoned his brother because he desired his brother's wife and wished to be chief himself. Hamlet was sure the great chief could not hear the story without making a sign if he was indeed guilty, and then he would discover whether his dead father had told him the truth."

The old man interrupted, with deep cunning, "Why should a father lie to his son?" he asked.

I hedged: "Hamlet wasn't sure that it really was his dead father." It was impossible to say anything, in that language, about devil-inspired visions.

"You mean," he said, "it actually was an omen, and he knew

witches sometimes send false ones. Hamlet was a fool not to go to one skilled in reading omens and divining the truth in the first place. A man-who-sees-the-truth could have told him how his father died, if he really had been poisoned, and if there was witchcraft in it; then Hamlet could have called the elders to settle the matter."

The shrewd elder ventured to disagree. "Because his father's brother was a great chief, one-who-sees-the-truth might therefore have been afraid to tell it. I think it was for that reason that a friend of Hamlet's father—a witch and an elder—sent an omen so his friend's son would know. Was the omen true?" 60

"Yes," I said, abandoning ghosts and the devil; a witch-sent omen it would have to be. "It was true, for when the storyteller was telling his tale before all the homestead, the great chief rose in fear. Afraid that Hamlet knew his secret he planned to have him killed."

The stage set of the next bit presented some difficulties of translation. I began cautiously. "The great chief told Hamlet's mother to find out from her son what he knew. But because a woman's children are always first in her heart, he had the important elder Polonius hide behind a cloth that hung against the wall of Hamlet's mother's sleeping hut. Hamlet started to scold his mother for what she had done."

There was a shocked murmur from everyone. A man should never scold his mother.

"She called out in fear, and Polonius moved behind the cloth. Shouting, 'A rat!' Hamlet took his machete and slashed through the cloth." I paused for dramatic effect. "He had killed Polonius!"

The old men looked at each other in supreme disgust. "That Polonius truly was a fool and a man who knew nothing! What child would not know enough to shout, 'It's me!' " With a pang, I remembered that these people are ardent hunters, always armed with bow, arrow, and machete; at the first rustle in the grass an arrow is aimed and ready, and the hunter shouts "Game!" If no human voice answers immediately, the arrow speeds on its way. Like a good hunter Hamlet had shouted, "A rat!" 65

I rushed in to save Polonius's reputation. "Polonius did speak. Hamlet heard him. But he thought it was the chief and wished to kill him to avenge his father. He had meant to kill him earlier that evening. . . ." I broke down, unable to describe to these pagans, who had no belief in individual afterlife, the difference between dying at one's prayers and dying "unhousell'd, disappointed, unaneled."

This time I had shocked my audience seriously. "For a man to raise his hand against his father's brother and the one who has become his father—that is a terrible thing. The elders ought to let such a man be bewitched."

I nibbled at my kola nut in some perplexity, then pointed out that after all the man had killed Hamlet's father.

"No," pronounced the old man, speaking less to me than to the young men sitting behind the elders. "If your father's brother has killed your father, you must appeal to your father's age mates; *they* may avenge him. No man may use violence against his senior relatives." Another thought struck him. "But if his father's brother had indeed been wicked enough to bewitch Hamlet and make him mad that would be a good story indeed, for it would be his fault that Hamlet, being mad, no longer had any sense and thus was ready to kill his father's brother."

There was a murmur of applause. *Hamlet* was again a good story to 70 them, but it no longer seemed quite the same story to me. As I thought over the coming complications of plot and motive, I lost courage and decided to skim over dangerous ground quickly.

"The great chief," I went on, "was not sorry that Hamlet had killed Polonius. It gave him a reason to send Hamlet away, with his two treacherous age mates, with letters to a chief of a far country, saying that Hamlet should be killed. But Hamlet changed the writing on their papers, so that the chief killed his age mates instead." I encountered a reproachful glare from one of the men whom I had told undetectable forgery was not merely immoral but beyond human skill. I looked the other way.

"Before Hamlet could return, Laertes came back for his father's funeral. The great chief told him Hamlet had killed Polonius. Laertes swore to kill Hamlet because of this, and because his sister Ophelia, hearing her father had been killed by the man she loved, went mad and drowned in the river."

"Have you already forgotten what we told you?" The old man was reproachful. "One cannot take vengeance on a madman; Hamlet killed Polonius in his madness. As for the girl, she not only went mad, she was drowned. Only witches can make people drown. Water itself can't hurt anything. It is merely something one drinks and bathes in."

I began to get cross. "If you don't like the story, I'll stop."

The old man made soothing noises and himself poured me some 75 more beer. "You tell the story well, and we are listening. But it is clear that the elders of your country have never told you what the story really means. No, don't interrupt! We believe you when you say your marriage customs are different, or your clothes and weapons. But people are the same everywhere; therefore, there are always witches and it is we, the elders, who know how witches work. We told you it was the great chief who wished to kill Hamlet, and now your own words have proved us right. Who were Ophelia's male relatives?"

"There were only her father and her brother." Hamlet was clearly out of my hands.

"There must have been many more; this also you must ask of your elders when you get back to your country. From what you tell us, since Polonius was dead, it must have been Laertes who killed Ophelia, although I do not see the reason for it."

We had emptied one pot of beer, and the old men argued the point with slightly tipsy interest. Finally one of them demanded of me, "What did the servant of Polonius say on his return?"

With difficulty I recollected Reynaldo and his mission. "I don't think he did return before Polonius was killed."

"Listen," said the elder, "and I will tell you how it was and how your story will go, then you may tell me if I am right. Polonius knew his son would get into trouble, and so he did. He had many fines to pay for fighting, and debts from gambling. But he had only two ways of getting money quickly. One was to marry off his sister at once, but it is difficult to find a man who will marry a woman desired by the son of a chief. For if the chief's heir commits adultery with your wife, what can you do? Only a fool calls a case against a man who will someday be his judge. Therefore Laertes had to take the second way: He killed his sister by witchcraft, drowning her so he could secretly sell her body to the witches."

I raised an objection. "They found her body and buried it. Indeed Laertes jumped into the grave to see his sister once more—so, you see, the body was truly there. Hamlet, who had just come back, jumped in after him."

"What did I tell you?" The elder appealed to the others. "Laertes was up to no good with his sister's body. Hamlet prevented him, because the chief's heir, like a chief, does not wish any other man to grow rich and powerful. Laertes would be angry, because he would have killed his sister without benefit to himself. In our country he would try to kill Hamlet for that reason. Is this not what happened?"

"More or less," I admitted. "When the great chief found Hamlet was still alive, he encouraged Laertes to try to kill Hamlet and arranged a fight with machetes between them. In the fight both the young men were wounded to death. Hamlet's mother drank the poisoned beer that the chief meant for Hamlet in case he won the fight. When he saw his mother die of poison, Hamlet, dying, managed to kill his father's brother with his machete."

"You see, I was right!" exclaimed the elder.

"That was a very good story," added the old man, "and you told it with very few mistakes. There was just one more error, at the very end. The poison Hamlet's mother drank was obviously meant for the survivor of the fight, whichever it was. If Laertes had won, the great chief would have poisoned him, for no one would know that he arranged Hamlet's death. Then, too, he need not fear Laertes' witchcraft; it takes a strong heart to kill one's only sister by witchcraft.

"Sometime," concluded the old man, gathering his ragged toga about him, "you must tell us some more stories of your country. We, who are elders, will instruct you in their true meaning, so that when you return to your own land your elders will see that you have not been sitting in the bush, but among those who know things and who have taught you wisdom."

▪ **CONSIDER THE SOURCE**

1. How does Bohannan characterize the Tiv? Trace how her attitude toward them changes through the course of the story.

2. How does Bohannan portray herself? How does she envision her role as an anthropologist? Where does she poke fun at herself?

3. What functions does the written word have in the Tiv's oral culture? How does storytelling compare to reading and writing?

4. Chart the differences between Western and Tiv interpretations of *Hamlet*. How do customs influence each group's understanding?

▪ **CONSIDER THE IMPLICATIONS**

5. Rank the various cultures that are invoked in Bohannan's essay according to their degree of "civilization." Which culture ranks the highest according to Bohannan's Oxford friend? Does Bohannan agree with that ranking? On what basis do Bohannan and the Tiv rank each other's cultures? How does one's understanding of *Hamlet* determine cultural rankings?

6. Adopting Bohannan's point of view, write a letter to E. D. Hirsch ("The Formation of Modern National Cultures," pp. 331–42) supporting, refuting, or complicating his claim that "the most persistent elements of our national lore owe their longevity to human universality."

7. Using evidence from Bohannan's experience and E. D. Hirsch's essay (pp. 331-42), hold a class debate on the proposition that all college students should be required to read *Hamlet*.

8. In your journal, explore how familiarity or unfamiliarity with *Hamlet* affects your conception of your own position in "literate" society. How would E. D. Hirsch explain the function of Shakespeare's play in our national culture?

9. Read Henry Louis Gates Jr. on the intersection of the African oral tradition with the Western literate tradition ("The Trope of the Talking Book," pp. 353-59). How would Gates explain Bohannan's experience with the Tiv? What Western cultural assumptions does Bohannan exhibit?

■ ■ ■ ■ ■ ■

HENRY LOUIS GATES JR.

The Trope of the Talking Book

As a civilization becomes increasingly literate, being literate increasingly becomes the proof that one is "civilized." Literate people often perceive members of predominantly oral cultures as "inferior," as was the case with Africans brought into Western culture as slaves, according to literary scholar Henry Louis Gates Jr. (b. 1950). The way slaves could prove their status as humans was to master the world of print. However, their vernacular tradition of everyday speech did not give way entirely to the literate tradition of formal written prose. Instead, Gates argues, black writers folded their oral voices into their written texts by using what he calls the trope of the talking book: The figurative image of a book speaking words to those who are able to understand it. African American writers combined the traditions by "making the white written text speak with a black voice." The Signifying Monkey: A Theory of Afro-American Literary Criticism *(1988), from which this selection is taken, won a National Book Award in 1989. Gates, W.E.B. Du Bois Professor of the Humanities at Harvard University, has edited many collections of works by African American writers and has contributed articles on race relations and popular culture to* Harper's, The New Yorker, *and the* Village Voice, *among other magazines. His publications include* Loose Canons: Notes on the Culture Wars *(1992), a memoir,* Colored People *(1993), and* Figures in Black: Words, Signs, and the Racial Self *(1987). Most recently, he co-edited* The Dictionary of Global Culture *(1995), a compendium of "cultural literacy" that takes a worldwide focus in response to E. D. Hirsch's* Dictionary of Cultural Literacy.

The literature of the slave, published in English between 1760 and 1865, is the most obvious site to excavate the origins of the Afro-American literary tradition. Whether our definition of *tradition* is based on the rather narrow lines of race or nationality of authors, upon shared themes and narrated stances, or upon repeated and revised tropes, it is to the literature of the black slave that the critic must turn to identify the beginning of the Afro-American literary tradition.

"The literature of the slave" is an ironic phrase, at the very least, and is an oxymoron at its most literal level of meaning. "Literature," as Samuel Johnson used the term,[1] denoted an "acquaintance with 'letters'

From *The Signifying Monkey: A Theory of Afro-American Literary Criticism* (New York: Oxford University Press, 1988), pp. 127–32.

1. **as Samuel Johnson used the term**: Samuel Johnson (1709–1784), author of the *Dictionary of the English Language* (1755) attempted to record precisely how words were used in his day.—ED.

or books," according to the *Oxford English Dictionary*. It also connoted "polite or humane learning" and "literary culture." While it is self-evident that the exslave who managed (as Frederick Douglass put it)[2] to "steal" some learning from his or her master and the master's texts, was bent on demonstrating to a skeptical public an acquaintance with letters or books, we cannot honestly conclude that slave literature was meant to exemplify either polite or humane learning or the presence in the author of literary culture. Indeed, it is more accurate to argue that the literature of the slave consisted of texts that represent impolite learning and that these texts collectively railed against the arbitrary and inhumane learning which masters foisted upon slaves to reinforce a perverse fiction of the "natural" order of things. The slave, by definition, possessed at most a liminal status within the human community.[3] To read and to write was to transgress this nebulous realm of liminality. The slave's texts, then, could not be taken as specimens of black literary culture. Rather, the texts of the slave could only be read as testimony of defilement: The slave's *representation* and reversal of the master's attempt to transform a human being into a commodity, and the slave's simultaneous verbal witness of the possession of a humanity shared in common with Europeans. . . . The slave wrote not primarily to demonstrate humane letters, but to demonstrate his or her own membership in the human community.

This intention cannot be disregarded as a force extraneous to the production of a text, a common text that I like to think of as the text of blackness. If we recall Ralph Ellison's[4] apt phrase by which he defines what I am calling tradition, "a sharing of that 'concord of sensibilities' which the group *expresses*," then what I wish to suggest by the text of blackness is perhaps clearer. Black writers to a remarkable extent have created texts that express the broad "concord of sensibilities" shared by persons of African descent in the Western hemisphere. Texts written over two centuries ago address what we might think of as common subjects of condition that continue to be strangely resonant, and relevant, as we approach the twenty-first century. Just as there are remarkably few literary traditions whose first century's existence is determined by texts created by slaves, so too are there few traditions that claim such an ap-

---

2. **Frederick Douglass** (1817–1895): Former slave who recounted in his autobiographies how he "stole" lessons in reading and writing from white boys in defiance of laws forbidding slaves to learn literacy.—ED.

3. My understanding of *liminality* arises from Robert D. Pelton's usages in *The Trickster in West Africa* (Los Angeles: University of California Press, 1980) and from Houston A. Baker's novel usage as taken from Victor Turner's work. See Houston A. Baker's *Blues, Ideology, and Afro-American Literature: A Vernacular Theory* (Chicago: University of Chicago Press, 1985).

4. **Ralph Ellison** (1914–1994): African American author best known for his novel *Invisible Man* (1952) and a collection of essays *Shadow and Act* (1964).—ED.

parent unity from a fundamental political condition represented for over two hundred years in such strikingly similar patterns and details.

Has a common experience, or, more accurately, the shared sense of a common experience, been largely responsible for the sharing of this text of blackness? It would be foolish to say no. Nevertheless, shared experience of black people vis-à-vis white racism is not sufficient evidence upon which to argue that black writers have shared patterns of representation of their common subject for two centuries—unless one wishes to argue for a genetic theory of literature, which the biological sciences do not support. Rather, shared modes of figuration result only when writers read each other's texts and seize upon topoi and tropes[5] to revise in their own texts. This form of revision is a process of grounding and has served to create curious formal lines of continuity between the texts that together comprise the shared text of blackness, the discrete chapters of which scholars are still establishing.

What seems clear upon reading the texts created by black writers in English or the critical texts that responded to these black writings is that the production of literature was taken to be the central arena in which persons of African descent could, or could not, establish and redefine their status within the human community. Black people, the evidence suggests, had to represent themselves as "speaking subjects" before they could even begin to destroy their status as objects, as commodities, within Western culture. In addition to all of the myriad reasons for which human beings write books, this particular reason seems to have been paramount for the black slave. At least since 1600, Europeans had wondered aloud whether or not the African "species of men," as they most commonly put it, could ever create formal literature, could ever master the arts and sciences. If they could, then, the argument ran, the African variety of humanity and the European variety were fundamentally related. If not, then it seemed clear that the African was destined by nature to be a slave.

Determined to discover the answer to this crucial quandary, several Europeans and Americans undertook experiments in which young African slaves were tutored and trained along with white children. Phillis Wheatley[6] was merely one result of such an experiment. Francis Williams, a Jamaican who took the B.A. at Cambridge before 1750; Jacobus Capitein, who earned several degrees in Holland; Wilhelm Amo, who took the doctorate degree in philosophy at Halle; and Ignatius Sancho, who became a friend of Laurence Sterne's[7] and who published a

5. **topoi** (plural of the Greek *topos,* meaning "a commonplace"): Recurrent poetic formulas or concepts; **trope:** Figurative use of a word or expression that noticably alters the standard literal meaning of the phrase.—ED.

6. **Phillis Wheatley** (1753?–1784): Poet who was one of the first African American authors to receive recognition from white readers.—ED.

7. **Laurence Sterne** (1713–1768): British author of *Tristram Shandy* (1760–1767).—ED.

volume of *Letters* in 1782, are just a few of the black subjects of such experiments. The published writings of these black men and one woman, who wrote in Latin, Dutch, German, and English, were seized upon both by pro- and antislavery proponents as proof that their arguments were sound.

So widespread was the debate over "the nature of the African" between 1730 and 1830 that not until the Harlem Renaissance[8] would the work of black writers be as extensively reviewed as it was in the eighteenth century. Phillis Wheatley's list of reviewers includes Voltaire, Thomas Jefferson, George Washington, Samuel Rush, and James Beatty, to list only a few. Francis Williams's work was analyzed by no less than David Hume and Immanuel Kant. Hegel, writing in the *Philosophy of History* in 1813, used the absence of writing of Africans as the sign of their innate inferiority. The list of commentators is extensive, amounting to a "Who's Who" of the French, English, and American Enlightenment.

Why was the creative writing of the African of such importance to the eighteenth century's debate over slavery? I can briefly outline one thesis. After Descartes,[9] reason was privileged, or valorized, over all other human characteristics. Writing, especially after the printing press became so widespread, was taken to be the visible sign of reason. Blacks were reasonable, and hence "men," if—and only if—they demonstrated mastery of "the arts and sciences," the eighteenth century's formula for writing. So, while the Enlightenment is famous for establishing its existence upon man's ability to reason, it simultaneously used the absence and presence of reason to delimit and circumscribe the very humanity of the cultures and people of color which Europeans had been "discovering" since the Renaissance. The urge toward the systematization of all human knowledge, by which we characterize the Enlightenment, in other words led directly to the relegation of black people to a lower rung on the Great Chain of Being, an eighteenth-century metaphor that arranged all of creation on the vertical scale from animals and plants and insects through man to the angels and God himself. By 1750, the chain had become individualized; the human scale rose from "the lowliest Hottentot" (black South Africans) to "glorious Milton and Newton." If blacks could write and publish imaginative literature, then they could, in effect, take a few giant steps up the Chain of Being, in a pernicious game of "Mother, May I?" The Rev. James W. C. Pennington, an ex-slave who wrote a slave narrative and who was a prominent black abolitionist, summarized this curious idea in his prefatory note to Ann Plato's

---

8. **Harlem Renaissance**: The name given to the outpouring of literary work in the 1920s by such authors as Langston Hughes, Jean Toomer, Countee Cullen, Gwendolyn Bennett and Zora Neale Hurston.—ED.

9. René **Descartes** (1596–1650): French physicist, mathematician, and philosopher.—ED.

1841 book of essays, biographies, and poems: "The history of the arts and sciences is the history of individuals, of individual nations." Only by publishing books such as Plato's, he argues, can blacks demonstrate "the fallacy of that stupid theory, *that nature has done nothing but fit us for slaves, and that art cannot unfit us for slavery!*"[10]

Not a lot changed, then, between Phillis Wheatley's 1773 publication of her *Poems* (complete with a prefatory letter of authenticity signed by eighteen of "the most respectable characters in Boston") and Ann Plato's, except that by 1841 Plato's attestation was supplied by a black person. What we might think of as the black text's mode of being, however, remained pretty much the same during these sixty-eight years. What remained consistent was that black people could become speaking subjects only by inscribing their voices in the written word. If this matter of recording an authentic black voice in the text of Western letters was of widespread concern in the eighteenth century, then how did it affect the production of black texts, if indeed it affected them at all? It is not enough simply to trace a line of shared argument as context to show that blacks regarded this matter as crucial to their tasks; rather, evidence for such a direct relationship of text to context must be found in the black texts themselves.

The most salient indication that this idea informed the writing of black texts is found in a topos that appears in five black texts published in English by 1815. This topos assumed such a central place in the black use of figurative language that we can call it a trope. It is the trope of the Talking Book, which first occurred in a 1770 slave narrative and was then revised in other slave narratives published in 1785, 1787, 1789, and 1815. Rebecca Jackson refigures this trope in her autobiographical writings, written between 1830 and 1832 but not published until 1981. Jackson's usage serves as a critique of her black male antecedents' usages because she refigures the trope in terms of male domination of a female's voice and her quest for literacy. . . . Not only does this shared but revised trope argue forcefully that blacks were intent on placing their individual and collective voices in the text of Western letters, but also that even the earliest writers of the Anglo-African tradition read each other's texts and grounded these texts in what soon became a tradition. . . .

The explication of the trope of the Talking Book enables us to witness the extent of intertextuality[11] and presupposition at work in the first discrete period in Afro-American literary history. But it also reveals, rather surprisingly, that the curious tension between the black

---

10. James W. C. Pennington, "To the Reader," in Ann Plato, *Essays; Including Biographies and Miscellaneous Pieces, in Prose and Poetry* (Hartford: for the author, 1841), pp. xviii, xx.

11. **intertextuality**: In literary theory, this term refers to the ways that a given literary text is inseparably related to other texts.—ED.

vernacular and the literate white text, between the spoken and the written word, between the oral and the printed forms of literary discourse, has been represented and thematized in black letters at least since slaves and ex-slaves met the challenge of the Enlightenment to their humanity by literally writing themselves into being through carefully crafted representations in language of the black self.

Literacy, the very literacy of the printed book, stood as the ultimate parameter by which to measure the humanity of authors struggling to define an African self in Western letters. It was to establish a collective black voice through the sublime example of an individual text, and thereby to register a black presence in letters, that most clearly motivated black writers, from the Augustan Age to the Harlem Renaissance. Voice and presence, silence and absence, then, have been the resonating terms of a four-part homology in our literary tradition for well over two hundred years.

The trope of the Talking Book became the first repeated and revised trope of the tradition, the first trope to be Signified upon. The paradox of representing, of containing somehow, the oral within the written, precisely when oral black culture was transforming itself into a written culture, proved to be of sufficient concern for five of the earliest black autobiographers to repeat the same figure of the Talking Book that fails to speak, appropriating the figure accordingly with embellished rhetorical differences. Whereas James Gronniosaw, John Marrant, and John Jea employ the figure as an element of plot, Ottobah Cugoano and Olaudah Equiano, with an impressive sense of their own relation to these earlier texts, bracket the tale in ways that direct attention to its status as a figure. The tension between the spoken and the written voice, for Cugoano and Equiano, is a matter they problematize as a rhetorical gesture, included in the text for its own sake, voicing, as it were, for the black literary tradition a problematic of speaking and writing. . . .

This general question of the voice in the text is compounded in any literature, such as the Afro-American literary tradition, in which the oral and the written literary traditions comprise separate and distinct discursive universes which, on occasion, overlap, but often do not. Precisely because successive Western cultures have privileged written art over oral or musical forms, the writing of black people in Western languages has, at all points, remained political, implicitly or explicitly, regardless of its intent or its subject. Then, too, since blacks began to publish books they have been engaged in one form of direct political dialogue or another, consistently up to the present. The very proliferation of black written voices, and the concomitant political import of them, led fairly rapidly in our literary history to demands both for the coming of a "black Shakespeare or Dante," as one critic put it in 1925, and for an authentic black printed voice of deliverance, whose presence would, by definition, put an end to all claims of the black person's subhumanity. In the black tradition, writing became the visible sign, the commodity of exchange, the text and technology of reason.

■ CONSIDER THE SOURCE

1. In your own words, explain why Gates considers "the literature of the slave" to be "an ironic phrase."

2. According to Gates, how are writing and reason connected in the debate over the status of Africans?

3. What does Gates claim was the primary motivation behind early African American literature?

4. What does Gates mean by the "text of blackness"? What two reasons does he give for the existence of this common text among African American writers?

5. How does Gates shape his essay for an academic audience? What expectations of academic writing does he fulfill?

■ CONSIDER THE IMPLICATIONS

6. With their permission, tape a brief conversation among your friends. Write a paraphrase of their discussion in your own words and then transcribe the tape word for word. Compare the two versions and analyze how written and oral discourse differ. What are the advantages and disadvantages of each rendition?

7. Read or review Zitkala-Ša's narrative about her transition from an oral to a literate culture (pp. 150–56). What recurrent patterns in her essay could be likened to Gates's "trope of the Talking Book"? How did her culture "voice" itself in her writing?

8. If writing is the way to become recognized in literate society, what place does nonwritten culture have in that society? Consider, for instance, various forms of popular culture that exist in the oral realm, such as rap music or playing the dozens. Write an essay justifying the inclusion or exclusion of nonwritten materials in a college course on contemporary American culture.

9. Write an essay defending, refuting, or modifying Gates's assertion that "Western cultures have privileged written art over oral or musical forms."

10. Gates claims that the slave wrote "to demonstrate his or her own membership in the human community." Review the discussions of literacy in chapter 2 and discuss in class how the experiences described by such authors as Malcolm X (pp. 164–72), Jimmy Santiago Baca (pp. 180–88), or Zitkala-Ša (pp. 150–56) extend Gates's argument beyond the slave community. How did the publication projects described by Charles Kikuchi (pp. 156–64) and Mark Thompson (pp. 188–97) fulfill the same function of demonstrating membership in the human community?

Thomas J. Roberts

On Low Taste

What's a good book? We can debate that question all day, but finally it all boils down to the personal matter of taste. And who's to say that one person's taste is any better than another's? In the following excerpt from his book An Aesthetics of Junk Fiction *(1990), Thomas J. Roberts (b. 1925) takes a look at "low" taste, "high" taste, and the people whose taste in fiction straddles both low and high. Roberts looks most closely at the kind of reader who takes public pleasure in the novels of James Joyce and Henry James but secretly dips into the pulp novels of Ian Fleming or John D. MacDonald. Roberts sees this "taste incoherence" as a form of "bilingualism," or biculturalism, that complicates the literary critics' impulse to dismiss paperback genre fiction as "trash." Roberts, a professor of English at the University of Connecticut, Storrs, has also written* When Is Something Fiction? *(1972) and several scholarly articles on critics' assessments of fiction.*

Traditionally, we have divided readers of the novel into three types. There are the discriminating few—the *serious readers,* who include the reading of certain novels among the most important experiences in their lives; there are the many—the *plain readers,* who seem to read only what everyone else is reading; and there are the millions—the *paperback readers,* who sometimes seem to be browsing on novels rather than reading them. None of these readers feels anyone really understands him, but none would object to the labels we are using.

We all see that this division is inexact; for one thing, the three bookscapes in which the serious, plain, and paperback readers are supposed to be leading separate reading lives overlap. Still, the division is everywhere accepted, and readers do seem to identify themselves as principally one or another of these three types. Some of the differences we recognize are shown in the table.[1]

Some of the difficulties we encounter when making charts of this type—however useful they may be—are evident in the item "Writers' rewards." All writers want fame, money, and love, of course; but the serious writer usually has to settle for fame alone; the plain writer, for money alone; and the writer of junk fiction, for love alone. (The large financial rewards come only to writers who are successful with plain read-

From *An Aesthetics of Junk Fiction* (Athens: University of Georgia Press, 1990), pp. 31–51.

1. Some of the observations on the serious reader have been taken from C. S. Lewis's *Experiment in Criticism* (1965, 1–5), and some of those on the plain reader from the chapter on the best-selling social melodrama in John G. Cawelti's *Adventure, Mystery, and Romance* (1976, 260–95).

	SERIOUS READER	PLAIN READER	PAPERBACK READER
Orientation	Reads by author	Reads by book	Reads by genre
Paradigmatic work	*Ulysses*	*The Godfather*	*I, the Jury*
Favored form	Experimental novel	Social melo-drama	Thriller
Admired author	Italo Calvino	Sidney Sheldon	John D. MacDonald
Socializing	Writes about books	Chats about books	Reads alone
Expectations	Originality	Information	Gratification
Stimulus to read	A good review	Book club	Titles, covers
Writers' rewards	Fame	Money	Love

ers.) The standard objection to this sort of charting of differences is that it is difficult to locate any person who is purely and only either a serious reader or a plain reader or a paperback reader, however. We certainly do find people talking as though they were one of these types, however, and as though they were implacably opposed to every other. Here, for instance, is Benjamin Walker writing in a cold rage about the sorts of degenerates who swell the ranks of the readers of serious fiction. "There is also the higher class of degenerate. Young men and women of this category win scholarships and fill the universities. The chief faculty of the higher degenerate is the excessive development of the speech centers in the cerebral cortex that gives them an extraordinary facility with words. But though remarkably articulate they seldom have anything original to say" (57). Walker is apparently so mistrustful of these higher degenerates that he would be equally mistrustful of the sorts of stories they prefer: He would not, perhaps, be patient enough to learn how to read them.

We cannot always be certain that people who condemn other reading types mean everything they seem to be implying. Here, for example, is Anthony Burgess[2] writing of the inadequacies of science-fiction writers and, by implication, their readers: "Certainly, in respect of the techniques and insights of modernism, they cherish a peculiar blindness: There is not one SF [science fiction] writer whom we would read for freshness or originality of his style" ("Apocalypse" 256). Burgess goes on to insist that "fiction is not about what happens to the world but what happens to a select group of human souls, with crisis or catastrophe as the mere pretext for an exquisitely painful probing, as in James, of personal agonies and elations." We infer from this essay that Burgess disapproves sharply of paperback fiction; but a year later (1984) we find him putting together his own selection of the best novels of the modern era and confessing that he does not confine his reading to serious fiction.

---

2. **Anthony Burgess** (1917–1993): British novelist and critic.—ED.

He reads best-sellers and paperback fiction, too. "When I say that I have read a great number of novels for sheer pleasure, as opposed to cold-eyed professional assessment, I have to admit that some of these novels never stood a chance of being placed on my list. I am an avid reader of Irving Wallace, Arthur Hailey, Frederick Forsyth, Ken Follett, and other practitioners of well-wrought sensational fiction" ("Modern Novels"). Burgess's distinction between his reading "for sheer pleasure" and his reading with "cold-eyed professional assessment" is curious. Presumably, the sentence was hastily struck off; it certainly encourages the inference that we do not read the best novels for pleasure—a suggestion that serious readers (and Burgess himself) would dismiss immediately.

In Burgess's personal acceptance of both a body of serious fiction   5
and a body of popular fiction, we see a familiar incoherence in operational aesthetics: Although we believe we know which is the better, we nevertheless choose what we believe is the worse. The people who read one of the three strands of fiction but refuse to read either of the others are intriguing in their own right, and we shall look at this sort of reading allergy in a later chapter. The people who feel one of these strands is better than the others but still do read the others are more interesting. The fact that readers as sophisticated as Burgess also read paperback fiction is a continuing warning against the oversimple explanation of its appeal.

TASTE INCOHERENCE

It is 1775, and Sheridan's Lydia Languish in *The Rivals*[3] is preparing to entertain certain sharp-eyed visitors.

> LYDIA. Here, my dear Lucy, hide these books. Quick, quick! Fling *Peregrine Pickle* under the toilet—throw *Roderick Random* into the closet—put *The Innocent Adultery* into *The Whole Duty of Man*—thrust *Lord Aimworth* under the sofa—cram *Ovid* behind the bolster—there—put *The Man of Feeling* into your pocket—so, so—now lay *Mrs. Chapone* in sight, and leave *Fordyce's Sermons* open on the table.
> LUCY. O burn it, Ma'am! the hair-dresser has torn away as far as *Proper Pride.*
> LYDIA. Never mind—open at *Sobriety.* Fling me *Lord Chesterfield's Letters.* Now for 'em.

Lydia, alas, had low taste: She read novels. Or, at least, her contemporaries felt she had low taste. Sometimes low taste successfully redefines itself as good taste over time; twentieth-century Lydia Languishes are more likely to hide *Fordyce's Sermons* and put *Roderick Random* on display. They would certainly rather be caught reading Smollett's novel than, say, a romance by Barbara Cartland.

---

3. Richard Brinsley **Sheridan** (1751–1816): English dramatist whose play *The Rivals* (1775) pokes fun at fashionable eighteenth-century society.—ED.

It is tiresome for us always to be returning to the Greeks when we begin asking ourselves fundamental questions about good and bad, high and low taste; but they formulated our kinds of questions with a directness that allows us to see the problem clearly. Plato turned his mind to the question of differences in response in book 2 of his *Laws*. He asked himself the question we still have not answered, "Are beautiful things not the same to us all, or are they the same in themselves, but not in our opinion of them?" He spoke about his contemporaries' different responses to the dance. "Choric movements are imitations of manners, and the performers range over all the various actions and changes of life with characterization and mimicry; and those to whom the words, or songs, or dances are suited either by nature or habit or both, cannot help feeling pleasure in them and applauding them, and calling them beautiful. But those whose natures or ways, or habits are unsuited to them, cannot delight in them or applaud them, and they call them base." We cannot prevent ourselves taking pleasure in some dances (or books) and so we applaud them; we cannot find a way to take pleasure in others and so we dismiss them. Whether it is nurture, nature, or both that have made us what we are, these responses are unselfconscious, immediate. "There are others, again, whose natures are right and their habits wrong, or whose habits are right and their natures wrong, and they praise one thing, but are pleased at another. For they say that all these imitations are pleasant, but not good. And in the presence of those whom they think wise, they are ashamed of dancing and singing in the baser manner, in a way which would indicate deliberate approval; and yet, they have a secret pleasure in them" (220–21). Well, we recognize those others. They are the aesthetic pretenders. They secretly like one thing but praise something that gives them no pleasure. And they know better: They are embarrassed when those they think wise find them enjoying themselves in the baser manner.

We are not shocked when we see others praising one kind of book and taking secret pleasure in another, for we are all experienced in the observation of hypocrisy. We do become confused when we uncover it in ourselves, when we hear ourselves giving public approval to books in which we have little interest and public disapproval to books that please us greatly, or when we find ourselves reaching past the book we know is good for the book we know is poorer. We will all generously admit to being complex; we deny we are hypocritical. Are we hypocritical if we allow others to suppose we enjoy reading Milton when the truth is that we prefer reading Ian Fleming's James Bond stories? Are we aesthetically confused if we do thoroughly enjoy Milton but enjoy the Westerns of Louis L'Amour also?

How unusual is the serious reader who deeply enjoys pulp fiction as well? Whenever and wherever there has been a division recognized between serious and popular culture, the serious reader has probably always participated quietly but deeply in popular culture. . . .

The Middle Ages was familiar with the duality of serious/unserious 10 taste to which Anthony Burgess confessed. In *Popular Culture in Early Modern Europe,* Peter Burke shows that medieval participants in the learned traditions also participated in the unlearned traditions.

> There were two cultural traditions in early modern Europe, but they did not correspond symmetrically to the two main social groups, the elite and the common people. The elite participated in the little tradition, but the common people did not participate in the great tradition. This asymmetry came about because the two traditions were transmitted in different ways. The great tradition was transmitted formally at grammar schools and at universities. It was a closed tradition in the sense that people who had not attended these institutions, which were not open to all, were excluded. In a quite literal sense, they did not speak the language. The little tradition, on the other hand, was transmitted informally. It was open to all, like the church, the tavern and the market-place, where so many of the performances occurred.
>
> Thus the crucial cultural difference in early modern Europe (I want to argue) was that between the majority, for whom popular culture was the only culture, and the minority, who had access to the great tradition but participated in the little tradition as a second culture. They were amphibious, bicultural, and also bilingual. Where the majority of people spoke their regional dialect and nothing else, the elite spoke or wrote Latin or a literary form of the vernacular, while remaining able to speak in dialect as a second or third language. (28)

We are perhaps not so very different. There are traditions we learn in the schools and others we learn informally, by word of mouth, by example. (We would want to be a bit cautious about using the words *little* and *great*, though. American jazz in the early twentieth century was transmitted informally, but it was not in any diminishing sense a "little" tradition.) We still find the learned participating in the unlearned traditions. At Christmas festivities, at the great national horse race (the Grand National, the Kentucky Derby), at the World Cup or World Series, at the Indianapolis 500, the learned are not always smallest of voice and dimmest of eye.

The awareness of popular culture appears incidentally in serious reflection. Here is Clive James in the *New York Review of Books* on the editors of a fine scholarly study of the photographer Eugene Atget: "Together, they have performed prodigies of research, but one expects no less. Less predictable was the way Szarkowski, while diving around among all this visual wealth like Scrooge McDuck in Money Barn No. 64, has managed to keep his critical balance, something that a man with his capacity for enthusiasm does not always find easy." James's reference to Carl Barks's delightful *Donald Duck* comic books gives precisely the simile needed, suggesting the visual arts, hoarded treasure, an apparently methodless porpoising—and with just enough humor in that slant analogy to save the reviewer's own enthusiasm from lapsing into uncritical awe. And here is Michael Roaf, Research Fellow at Wolfson College, Oxford, commenting in the *Times Literary Supplement* on a report of archaeological excavation: "The illusion of being in the realm of science fiction is increased by the melodramatic names of the places that Helms has coined—the Black Desert, *bilad ash-shaytan* (the country of the devil), the Road of the Rising Sun—and by the occasional Arabic words and place-names which bring Frank Herbert's *Dune* to mind." Neither reviewer felt their serious readers required a gloss on their references to popular fiction.

Of course! we say. Who makes any fuss today about the distinctions between high culture and low culture? Some do still keep what they no doubt perceive as the Faith. Not all publishers are ready to submit their authors—even the dead ones—to the humiliation of having their work mentioned by purveyors of pulp fiction. A science-fiction story written by Dean McLaughlin for the magazine *Analog* included a quotation from Hemingway's "Snows of Kilimanjaro" as an epigraph. McLaughlin requested permission from Hemingway's publishers, Charles Scribner's Sons, to use the passage. In a letter to *Locus* in March 1981, McLaughlin says that the editor of *Analog* announced that "Scribner's rights department had phoned him to assert that they did not want a quotation from Hemingway to appear 'in a science fiction magazine.'" Apparently, while McLaughlin reads Hemingway, the people entrusted with Hemingway's fragile reputation do not read science fiction. . . .

THE BADNESS OF THE WRITING

One explanation for the serious reader's interest in this or that strain of pulp fiction suggests itself: that the ultimate preoccupations of paperbacks are indistinguishable from the ultimate preoccupations of canonical and serious fiction.

Here are the five themes that the MLA (Modern Language Association) identified in 1984 in its "Trends of Scholarly Publishing" as the themes on which scholars who specialize in canonical literature are most often writing. I attach the names of paperback genres that the themes bring to mind.

death	the detective story
nature	the Western
religion	fantasy
love	the romance
time	science fiction

Such matchings are sometimes useful. The Western is more resonant to the theme of man in nature than is the detective story; science fiction, more resonant to speculations on time than is the romance; and so on. A Western that concerns itself with love (Wister's *Virginian* has a love story) is an antinomy, however welcome. So—the argument would continue—the paperbacks attract serious readers because their thematic burdens are those that have always attracted thoughtful people. This claim cannot satisfy us, however, for people do not have to turn to the paperbacks for these themes: Best-sellers and serious fiction concern themselves with those five major themes, too.

If we choose our books carefully (or luckily), a second answer will suggest itself. As stories like *The Last Unicorn* and *The Einstein Intersection*[4] demonstrate, paperback fiction is much, much better than we have supposed it is. Some of the stories equal the best that serious writers give us. This claim is made by each genre's enthusiasts and especially by those passionate few who read in that genre exclusively. This second defense is very attractive, but it is based on an error—a subtle and dangerous error. It is predicated on a false assumption about the reading focus of a genre's followers—a matter I shall go into in a later chapter. The claim that the stories are excellent is also denied by the readers we are considering at the moment. The people who read both serious fiction and popular fiction say that the stories that come from the popular tradition are poorer.

And the writers of those books have a poorer opinion of those readers. As Binyon's impatience with the academic reader of the tale of detection suggests, some paperback writers lash out at serious and academic readers before the latter have a chance to be rude to them—preemptive insults, as it were. The writers of paperbacks are confident that serious readers despise them: As we saw in our brief consideration of "Ghost Writer," the story about a future in which some men and women are recovering the lost works of Swift and Shakespeare by sending their psyches backward in time, popular writers find it easy to suppose that originality can bring upon them the wrath of the critical establishment. The detective story—or at least the kind that calls itself the tale of detection—likes academics; but most paperback fiction mistrusts them and anyone else who reads serious fiction. For serious readers, to read in these traditions is rather like maintaining a cordial relationship with people who are always making it plain that they dislike you.

The stories really do not measure up to the standards that serious readers set for the other fiction they read. People who do not read in the paperback genres sometimes wonder whether readers who are faithful to them see how badly written the stories in these genres are. They do, of course. Paperback readers love to compare their inadvertently gathered collections of clumsiness and staleness of invention in their favorite genres. There is so much that serious readers find unintentionally funny

15

---

4. Peter Beagle's *The Last Unicorn* (1968) and Samuel R. Delaney's *The Einstein Intersection* (1967): Fantasy and science fiction works that allude to many works of mainstream literary culture that the authors assume their readers will recognize.—ED.

and it is so much a part of reading these stories—and not just for the more sophisticated readers—that we shall be looking into the matter of clownish writing in the next chapter. Here, in anticipation, is John Sladek's long inventory of science-fiction clichés from Peter Nichols's *Science Fiction Encyclopedia*.

> SF cliché plots and plot devices are so numerous that any list must be incomplete. We have the feeble old nightwatchman left to guard the smouldering meteorite crater overnight ("I'll be all right, yessirree"); the doomed society of lotus-eaters; civilization's future depending upon the outcome of a chess game, the answer to a riddle, or the discovery of a simple formula ("a one-in-a-million chance, but so crazy, it just might work!"); the shape-shifting aliens ("One of us aboard this ship is not human"); invincible aliens ("the billion-megaton blast had no more effect than the bite of a Sirian flea"); alien invaders finally stopped by ordinary water (as in the films of both *The Day of the Triffids* and *The Wizard of Oz*); the android spouse who cuts a finger and bleeds machine oil; the spouse possessed or hypnotized by aliens ("Darling, you've been acting so strangely since your trip to Ganymede"); disguised alien sniffed out by "his" pet dog, who never acted this way before; destruction of giant computer brain by a simple paradox ("When is a door not a door?"); robot rebellion ("Yes, 'Master' "); a doppelgänger[5] in the corridors of time ("It was—himself!"); Montagues and Capulets[6] living in parallel universes; the evil Master of the World stops to smirk before killing hero; everyone is controlled by alien mind-rays *except one man*; Oedipus kills great-great-grandad; world is saved by instant technology ("It may have looked like just a hunk of breadboard, a few widgets and wires—but wow!"); a youth-elixir—but at what terrible price?; thickheaded scientist tampers unwittingly with elemental forces better left in the hands of the Deity; immortality tempts Nature to a terrible revenge; monster destroys its creator; dying alien race must breed with earthling models and actresses; superior aliens step in to save mankind from self-destruction (through H-bombs, pollution, fluoridation, decadence); Dr. X's laboratory (island, planet) goes up in flames. . . .
> Pulp can always be recycled. (124)

(A small but excellent collection of inept and clichéd sentences from the detective story appears in Barzun and Taylor's *Catalogue of Crime*: [1971] see pages 450, 622, 700, and 722.) People who fiercely dislike any of the popular genres find in a catalog of the genre's clownishness definitive confirmation of their worst imaginings and may suppose that the compilers of those catalogs share their feelings about that genre. We saw Sladek himself end his list of clichés with a dismissive remark: "Pulp can always be recycled." That genre's followers are not angry, however.

---

5. **doppelgänger:** A living person's exact double, usually of supernatural origin.—Ed.

6. **Montagues and Capulets**: The feuding families in Shakespeare's *Romeo and Juliet.*—Ed.

They know that none of us is born with the knowledge of what is and what is not a cliché: We earn that knowledge. They know that no one can parody a genre so well as one of its devoted followers, that a good catalog of clichés is the precipitate of dozens, scores, hundreds, of stories. Anyone who puts together a useful list of clichés has been reading steadily in that genre. They may be wincing at every cliché, but they are reading onward, ever onward, nevertheless. . . .

The interest that cultured readers manifest in what they themselves think of as throwaway materials denies us certain conveniently belittling explanations: that, say, paperbacks appeal only to the unintelligent or only to those who do not know of better books or only to the young or the neurotic. Pulp fiction appeals to readers of whom none of these claims is true. It appeals to intelligent, educated, and well-informed readers who are mature and who are as healthy as those of us who find their behavior interesting. If some of its readers are unintelligent or uneducated or young or neurotic, the fact that cultivated people are reading shoulder to shoulder with them is a continuing reminder that inexperience, distress, and the like is irrelevant.

The kinds of readers we have been considering in this chapter are reading poorer stories when they have better stories available. That is the anomaly, the puzzle, in its simplest form, but no sentence that talks about books and uses words like *better* and *poorer* (or *good* and *bad, high* and *low*) is simple, and especially not now, when none of us is quite certain how anyone else is using the words. Here, though, there should be no difficulty. Questions of absolute and relative literary value are not at issue, for we are not concerned with whether one novel is, or can be, intrinsically superior to another. What interests us, rather, is that readers who do feel that some novels are better than others do continue to read those others. When they have finished Calvino's *Invisible Cities* or Jane Austen's *Emma,* they confess that they admire those novels more highly than they do Mickey Spillane's *I, the Jury* or Louis L'Amour's *Heller with a Gun* but go on to read more Spillane and L'Amour anyway—even when there are Austen and Calvino novels yet to read.

These are the people Plato described. They praise one thing but are also pleased by another; they agree that while many stories are pleasant, only some of them are good; in the presence of the wise they are ashamed of their reading but find in it a secret pleasure. Not all are ashamed, of course, nor even most of them, perhaps; but they all know that there are others who think they should be ashamed. Betty Rosenberg's *Genre-flecting,* a bibliography of paperback fiction, begins with characteristic bravado: "This book is the fruit of a blissfully squandered reading life" (15). Anyone can translate that sentence: "I refuse to be ashamed of the behavior that I think is shameful."

How many of the learned follow fictions inside the world of pulp culture? An intriguing question, one not easily answered. It is not always easy to find out about others. It is not always easy to be sure about oneself.

For his now-classic study of the interaction of social structure and speech pattern, *The Social Stratification of English in New York City,* William Labov found a way to expose the linguistic insecurity of New Yorkers. When Labov had his subjects pronounce a word and then afterward asked them how they had pronounced it, he uncovered "a systematic tendency to report their own speech inaccurately. Most of the respondents seemed to perceive their own speech in terms of the norms at which they were aiming rather than the sound actually produced" (479–80). Apparently, it is not what we have done but what we think we should—and therefore must—have done that distinguishes us.

In his *Sociology of Literature,* the French scholar Robert Escarpit comments on a difficulty facing people investigating the kinds of reading habits that interest us here.

> While the confession of one's sexual peculiarities may flatter a latent exhibitionist, the avowal of literary or antiliterary tastes (whether too undiscriminating or too refined) which lower one's position in society can only be painful. Most people find great difficulty in confessing to themselves the nature of their taste.
>
> The comparison of data obtained by direct and systematic observation of the cultural comportment of one person with data which he himself supplies, even in good faith, enables one to understand the extreme difficulty of using subjective information. He who cites Stendhal or Malraux as customary reading and who confides that he sometimes reads a detective novel or two to relax, will hardly admit that the time he devotes to detective novels is several times greater than the time he gives his "bedside" books. If he mentions newspapers, he will forget the few minutes he spends looking at the comic strips which, accumulated, represent an appreciable period of time. Similarly, the reading one does in waiting rooms or the reading of books borrowed from children's libraries goes by unnoticed. Who will ever be able to completely appreciate the enormous importance of such a book as the *Sapeur Camember* or *Tintin*[7] in the reading of a cultivated French adult? (16–17)

We all do seem to have the capacity to disregard the facts when they threaten to cloud those deeper truths about ourselves that we prefer.

When the matter of pulp fiction and its consumers comes up, we seem to map ourselves and our tastes against a usably simple grid we have inherited from the past. Two groups read pulp fiction, we say. The people in its primary readership may be brilliant in business, in politics, or in some other realm, but when they turn to books it is always and only to pulp fiction that they turn. It is this primary readership that publishers, editors, and writers have in mind when they market their wares.

---

7. *Sapeur Camember* by Christophe (Georges Colomb) and *Tintin* by Hergé (Georges Rémi): Immensely popular French comic strips.—ED.

We have been taught to say that these people may have other qualities any of us might envy, but they do have low taste. Pulp fiction does find other readers as well, for it has long been recognized that a secondary readership comes to it occasionally from the study of literature and reads alongside that primary readership now and then. These people have good taste—for they take unselfconscious pleasure in literature—but they also have low taste. If they did not have a taste for the low, they would not be taking unselfconscious pleasure from the Mickey Spillanes and Louis L'Amours and Adam Halls of the paperback bookscape.

This is the question with which we began: How many of the people 25 who are at home in those learned bookscapes also make regular visits to pulp fiction? I suggest that all of them do.

It may be that there are readers who have only low taste, but there are no readers who have only good taste. Even the most sensitive readers of literature enjoyably read, watch, or listen to some form of vernacular fiction as well. Today, pulp materials are coming at us from every direction within our culture and at every moment (Roberts, 1978). If the taste of our most cultivated sensibilities were too refined for them to find something rewarding in some form of pulp fiction—some television, some movies, some paperbacks, some jokes, some comic monologues—they would not be able to remain in contact with the rest of us. If only in self-defense, our psyches find ways of turning what seems dross to gold. If our psyches cannot do that, we withdraw from the human conversation.

▪ **WORKS CITED**

Barzun, Jacques, and Wendell Hertig Taylor (1971) *A Catalogue of Crime* (New York: Harper).

Burgess, Anthony (1983) "The Apocalypse and After," rev. of *Terminal Visions: The Literature of Last Things* by W. Warren Wagar. *Times Literary Supplement* 18 Mar.: 256.

———— (1984) "Modern Novels: The 99 Best." *New York Times Books Review*. 5 Feb., 1+.

Burke, Peter (1978) *Popular Culture in Early Modern Europe* (New York: Harper).

Cawelti, John G. (1976) *Adventure, Mystery, and Romance: Formula Stories as Art and Popular Culture* (Chicago: University of Chicago Press).

Escarpit, Robert (1965) *Sociology of Literature,* trans. Ernest Pick. Lake Erie College Studies 4 (Painesville, Ohio: Lake Erie College Press).

Labov, William (1966) *The Social Stratification of English in New York City* (Washington, D.C.: Center for Applied Linguistics).

Lewis, C. S. (1961) *An Experiment in Criticism* (Cambridge: Cambridge University Press, reprint, 1965).

Plato, Laws, vol. 5 of *The Dialogues of Plato Translated into English*. Trans. B. Jowett. 3d ed. 5 vols. (New York: Macmillan, 1982).

Roberts, Thomas J. (1978) "Fiction Outside Literature." *Literary Review* 22.1, 5–21.

Rosenberg, Betty (1992) *Genreflecting: A Guide to Reading Interests in Genre Fiction* (Littleton, Colo.: Libraries Unlimited).

Sladek, John (1979) "Clichés." *The Science Fiction Encyclopedia.* Ed. Peter Nicholls (Garden City, N.Y.: Dolphin).

Walker, Benjamin (1978) *Encyclopedia of Metaphysical Medicine* (London: Routledge).

▪ **CONSIDER THE SOURCE**

1. Summarize in your own words the three categories of readers that Roberts describes. Which category most interests Roberts and why?

2. What relationship does Roberts see between pulp writers and serious readers? How does each regard the other?

3. Why does Roberts think that "there are no readers who have only good taste"? What purpose does mixed taste serve?

▪ **CONSIDER THE IMPLICATIONS**

4. Are you an "aesthetic pretender"? Have you ever claimed to enjoy a book, a movie, or other cultural product because you thought you ought to? In your journal, explore such an incident, making careful note of who your audience was and what purpose was served by pretending.

5. Examine the division among readers that Roberts says is "everywhere accepted." Do you agree with his description of the serious, plain, and paperback readers? Discuss Roberts's distinctions in class and argue for or against the validity of his table.

6. In small groups, list five books that would appeal to each category of readers: serious, plain, and paperback. Which have you read? Which would you rather not admit to having read? What motivated you to read them?

7. In class, brainstorm a list of clichés for a genre modeled after the list Roberts offers for science fiction. You might select detective stories, horror stories, Westerns, or romances, for example. What does the list tell you about the genre's appeal to readers? Why do the clichés continue to be recycled?

8. How has your education changed your sense of which books you should like? In your journal, explore where and how taste "education" takes place. What kinds of literature are you taught to value? Which are you encouraged to avoid?

9. Analyze E. D. Hirsch's essay on "The Formation of Modern National Cultures" (pp. 331–42) from Roberts's point of view. If Roberts is correct about serious readers' indulgence in pulp fiction, what "commonly shared information" would he argue forms a part of our national culture?

10. Conduct an informal poll on campus to test Roberts's claim that "there are no readers who have only good taste." Ask several "serious readers" if they ever (or even regularly) read what Roberts describes as "vernacular fiction." What kinds of books do they read? How often? How much embarrassment do they show when asked to name such books? Report your findings to the class.

JOHN P. DESSAUER

Cultural Pluralism and the Book World

For the past several decades, our country's laws have increasingly barred discrimination on the basis of race, religion, gender, ethnicity, and other characteristics that make people who and what they are. But what about cultural discrimination? Publisher John P. Dessauer (b. 1924) looks at the book world and finds rampant discrimination on the basis of taste. In this 1986 article from Book Research Quarterly *he claims that the prejudices of an elite segment of society—those who went to the "right" schools and read the "right" books—govern how cultural products are evaluated and disseminated. Dessauer has worked in publishing since 1943, and he's familiar with both popular and academic presses. He has been a sales manager for Ballantine Books and Barnes & Noble, associate director of Indiana University Press, and director of the University Press of Kansas, as well as a contributing editor of the industry trade magazine* Publishers Weekly. *His own books include* A Manual on Bookselling *(1974) and* Book Publishing: What It Is, What It Does *(1974).*

Most Americans are accustomed to complying with the demands of a pluralistic society. They recognize that the indulgence of prejudices against people of other races and beliefs is not only immoral but intolerable if civil concord is to be maintained. They are persuaded that their acceptance of diversity in others will help guarantee to them the free exercise of their own individuality.

Thus, we have come to terms with racial, ethnic, linguistic, religious, and political pluralism as inevitable conditions of our national life. Indeed, our view of history prompts us to perceive our diversity as a glorious heritage that has consistently enriched our past. Our sense of fair play demands that we approach others with the same openness and respect we hope they will accord to us, while our civic and religious traditions prompt us to reach out to them with genuine regard.

But if most of us have therefore accepted the reality of social and political pluralism, few of us have attuned ourselves to the cultural pluralism that also confronts us. In fact, very few have even given thought to the existence of a cultural pluralism and its implications. Yet, like other forms of discrimination, cultural prejudices can be deeply destructive, inflicting great psychic injury on their victims. They can inhibit social development, retard aesthetic fulfillment, diminish artistic growth, and effectively prevent cultural communities, like the book world, from playing their destined roles.

From *Book Research Quarterly* 2 (Fall 1986), pp. 3–6.

How do I define cultural pluralism? As the social reality whereby the aesthetic tastes and interests of individuals vary greatly from one to the next. Thus some people love classical music while others prefer jazz, some like "easy listening" whereas others are soft- or hard-rock fans, some enjoy every musical style while still others are indifferent to all music. Some individuals admire Italian Renaissance painting yet cannot abide abstract art, others are put off by any work earlier than the Impressionists'. Some find all art satisfying while many more rarely set foot in a museum and are content with the images they encounter in their everyday experience. Some people read only literary fiction and poetry while others pursue only serious nonfiction; some enjoy only genre fiction while still others will read only how-to books, or perhaps no book whatever.

Personality makeup, home and educational background, and life ex-   5
periences work together to shape our interests and aesthetic preferences. Their shape never becomes permanently fixed, for, like our moral character, our intellectual and aesthetic self is always growing—or regressing. No matter what its disposition or sophistication, however, the intellectual and aesthetic self represents an integral aspect of our identity, a vital dimension of our souls. One cannot affirm or deny its value without, to a significant extent, affirming or denying our value as human beings.

This is why cultural pluralism, like other forms of pluralism in a free society, demands that we respect persuasions with which we differ. Just as I may disagree profoundly with your religious convictions but respect them because you, a neighbor and fellow human, hold them, so might I find your artistic and literary tastes incompatible with mine yet still respect them and you for the humanity they manifest. Even if I believe my cultural attainments to be superior to yours I cannot deny you my respect for, in justice, I recognize that my "superiority" is largely due to circumstances beyond my control—native gifts, a favorable home environment, a good education—and cannot claim that you would not have achieved a great deal more than I if you had enjoyed my advantages.

Yet cultural prejudice is rampant in American society. That simple respect, which acknowledges the dignity of every individual and which most of us prize supremely in our relations with others, is often denied by those who fancy themselves culturally superior to fellow citizens who haven't attended the "right" kind of school, worked at the "right" kind of job, or read the "right" kind of books. At the very least, such snobbery inflicts deep psychic wounds on its victims; at its worst, when it denies well-earned opportunities to otherwise qualified individuals, it can damage or even destroy lives.

However, here we are concerned more with the cultural consequences of such prejudices, particularly with their effects in the world of books. It is well known that many book people—authors, editors, booksellers, reviewers, librarians, and educators—believe that of all books published only literary fiction and poetry are of real value and that all else can be justified only insofar as it contributes to the creation of and is "redeemed" by fiction and poetry. This attitude is based on conviction that artistic/literary creation constitutes the ultimate achievement and therefore the goal of life, an idea which in turn grows out of the "art for art's sake" persuasion of the modernist movement.

As a child, I was exposed to this philosophy. My father, a Viennese art critic and painter, believed that the entire universe had been created only so that an occasional Michelangelo or del Sarto[1] might emerge from it. I loved my father, but I was discriminating enough to conclude that his conviction was inspired more by his unbounded enthusiasm for art than by sound judgment. Even at the age of eight or nine I was persuaded that God made me and the many people I knew and loved—parents, relatives, servants, and kindly storekeepers—for our own sake, not merely as stepping stones to a Raphael or da Vinci.

And that touches the heart of the matter, does it not? For ultimately a book, like any work of art or artifact from the most sublime creation to the humblest tool, derives its civilized value from the human service it is capable of performing, be that to enrapture or to enlighten, to inspire or to entertain. Human creation, including literature and art, is a *social* endeavor; it lacks meaning and fulfillment without an audience; it justifies its existence by contributing to the welfare of that audience. That at their best books of all descriptions contribute to the welfare of their readers is obvious. Therefore the claim that out of tens of thousands of educational texts, legal, medical, technical, and business handbooks, and general titles of instruction, information, inspiration, practical guidance, and diversion only a handful of literary novels and verses contribute sufficiently to our benefit to warrant genuine admiration and support betokens a cultural bias of monumental proportions.

Significantly, most literary elitists do not even take the educational, professional, and scholarly provinces into account when they discuss the state of the book world. So preoccupied are they with fiction and poetry that they focus their attention only on the consumer sector, where such titles are actually distributed, as though the role of books in education and scholarship were of no consequence for cultural phenomena, including the public's interest in literary writing. But even their view of the consumer book segment is distorted by preconceptions. For them, best-selling books are automatically suspect. Behind that suspicion lurks the persuasion that most book buyers are insensitive and undiscriminating, that to be popular a book must have a coarse and vulgar appeal. A comparable view in the political realm would hold that American voters have so little good sense and judgment that the greater the popularity of

10

---

1. Andrea **del Sarto** (1486–1531): Florentine artist known as the "faultless painter."—ED.

a candidate or issue, the less their worth. Most people in a democratic society would reject such a notion as arrogant and absurd.

The elitists complain that popular books, notably popular fiction, are badly written. On examination it develops that they make no distinction between truly bad writing and writing that merely fails to conform to their preferred style or manner, and so very often their dislike is less a product of discriminating judgment than of the familiar bias. Furthermore, they themselves must shoulder responsibility for much of the bad writing and mediocrity in the popular book field. How can they expect other publishers to accord such material the respect and care it deserves when they themselves doubt its value and have contempt for its audience? Their cynicism in justifying the publication of worthless trash so long as it helps pay for the launching of literary creations is an encouragement to others to do likewise for greed alone, while to the betrayed public it matters little for what reasons the integrity of popular material is being sacrificed.

The literary elitists in the critical community share this responsibility. Because of the excessive emphasis given to literary material by some general review media, the critical praise that should encourage worthwhile popular writing and the censure that should be meted out to the mediocre have often been lacking. Yet constructive criticism could play a significant role in raising the quality of popular literature to levels consonant with its maturing readership.

A publication purporting to serve the general public whose book coverage is limited largely to literary material should certainly ask itself how it can justify serving only a very small segment of its book-reading audience. Not that I would advocate a quota system as an alternative. Important books, literary or otherwise, deserve critical priority and in making cultural judgments we can never be guided solely by numerical popularity. On the other hand, a general medium cannot totally ignore its responsibility to popular books and to the popular audience in discharging its cultural obligation.

Some elitist booksellers stock and promote not the titles their customers most want to read, but only books they themselves admire. Because their economic base is therefore weak, they are vulnerable to competition from more pluralistically oriented chain and independent stores and sometimes are forced out of business. When such an event occurs elitist critics usually cite it as proof that "good" bookstores cannot survive in the present, "hostile" environment.

Similarly, librarians and educators who insist on guiding readers by elitist preferences, rather than allowing them to follow their own bent in selecting material, usually succeed only in creating boredom where there might have been satisfaction and, very often, in encouraging a reader to abandon an incipient reading habit altogether.

During the past forty years the acceptance of books by American consumers has grown dramatically, and today books play a role in almost every facet of national life. As they became "democratized," the number of books sold, as well as the number of publishers and bookstores in the United States, increased substantially. But the growth occurred largely in the educational, professional, and popular sectors of the field, especially among consumers who in earlier decades would not have bought books at all. Expectably the markets for literary fiction and poetry grew at a much slower pace.

Elitists, alarmed at their shrinking influence, have bemoaned the entire development, complaining of a decline in public tastes and vulgarization of the book world. But those who value all sorts of people and all kinds of books have witnessed the exploding popularity of books with gratitude and pride. For my part, I wish that the elitists would match their literary sensitivity with humanity and civic spirit and accept the inevitability of cultural democracy in America.

▪ CONSIDER THE SOURCE

1. What does Dessauer mean by "cultural pluralism"? How is it like other forms of pluralism?

2. What evidence does Dessauer offer to support his thesis that "cultural prejudice is rampant in American society"?

3. How does a book justify its existence, according to Dessauer?

4. Who are the "literary elitists" that Dessauer criticizes? Does his identification of them by category instead of by name strengthen or weaken his argument? How?

5. Using the appendix (p. 658) as your guide, consider how the audience Dessauer addresses might react to this essay from *Book Research Quarterly*.

▪ CONSIDER THE IMPLICATIONS

6. Have you ever been a victim or witness of the cultural snobbery Dessauer condemns? In your journal describe the incident and analyze the effects of such cultural prejudice.

7. In class, hold a debate on the subject of cultural pluralism, with some students supporting Dessauer's position and others defending E. D. Hirsch's arguments about monoliteracy (pp. 331–42). To what extent are the two positions opposed? Can they be reconciled? If so, how?

8. Study all of the cultural reviews printed in a major metropolitan newspaper in a single week. Compare the book reviews with reviews of other forms of culture, such as movies, television shows, plays, or concerts. Do you detect equal levels of "elitism" in the coverage of all cultural forms? If so, write a letter to the editor arguing for broader coverage of all forms or commending the paper's review policies. If not, write a letter proposing a broadening of coverage for cultural arenas that are too elite in your view

or arguing for narrower coverage of areas that descend too far into popular culture.

9. Debate the connection that Dessauer makes between commerce and culture. Is popularity always the death knell of "serious" art? Can you name an example of serious art that is also popular? Can you name popular art that is also serious?

10. Read Joseph Deitch's description of how Christopher Lehmann-Haupt, the senior book critic for the *New York Times*, selects which books to review (pp. 304–11). Write a letter from Dessauer to Lehmann-Haupt, proposing a set of criteria to use when making such decisions in the future. What sorts of cultural products does Dessauer think deserve more respect from reviewers?

▪ ▪ ▪ ▪ ▪ ▪
⋮⋯⋯⋯⋯⋯⋯

Joan Shelley Rubin

Why Do You Disappoint Yourself? The Early History of the Book-of-the-Month Club

Hundreds of new book titles roll off the presses every week on every subject imaginable. Which ones are worth reading? Which can you ignore? Who can you turn to for help? In the 1920s, this dilemma was solved by the Book-of-the-Month Club, which is still going strong seven decades later. Joan Shelley Rubin (b. 1947) examines the club's origins in Progressive Era advertising and marketing in this excerpt from her book-length historical study The Making of Middlebrow Culture *(1992). She finds that overwhelmed consumers gratefully turned to experts who would select the "right" books and to a delivery system that would bring the books straight to their doors. By freeing the reader from the burden of choice, the club helped construct a "middlebrow culture," according to Rubin. It appealed to the person that Thomas J. Roberts dubbed the "plain reader," the one whose taste ran neither to the avant-garde nor to the trashy. Rubin, a professor of American Studies and History at the State University of New York (SUNY), Brockport, focuses her research on "the values and anxieties Americans have expressed in literature and the arts." She is currently doing research on books and readers in modern America.*

From *The Making of Middlebrow Culture* (Chapel Hill: University of North Carolina Press, 1992), pp. 94–103.

THE CREATION OF THE BOOK-OF-THE-MONTH CLUB

When Harry Scherman, a New York advertising man, started the Book-of-the-Month Club in 1926, he did so on the assumption that the nation's bookstores were not meeting the American reader's desire for new books. Scherman's savvy appraisal of the market reflected his long experience with both literature and commerce. Born in Montreal in 1887, he grew up in Philadelphia, briefly attended business and law school after college, and settled in 1907 on a career as a writer. For five years he covered cultural and political affairs for the weekly *American Hebrew,* while trying his hand at fiction and dabbling in advertising copywriting. Scherman shelved his literary ambitions in 1913 and began working full-time for the Ruthrauff and Ryan advertising firm, where he concentrated on direct-mail circulars. The following year he joined the mail-order department of the J. Walter Thompson agency. Even so, he remained connected to a group of artists and intellectuals, counting among his friends Walter Lippmann, Irita Van Doren's brother-in-law Charles Boni, and Charles's brother Albert.[1]

In 1916 Charles Boni happened to show him a publishing gimmick—a miniature leather-bound edition of Shakespeare. Scherman decided a set of such classics had merchandising potential and convinced the manufacturers of Whitman's chocolates to include a volume in each candy box. To oversee production, he resigned his job and, with the Boni brothers, established the Little Leather Library Corporation. Joining them as partner was Maxwell Sackheim, another Thompson copywriter whose highly effective campaign on behalf of a correspondence school ("Do You Make These Mistakes in English?") became a model of selling technique.

The enterprise prospered. To augment the Whitman's order, Scherman and his associates printed additional titles, which Woolworth's sold at ten cents apiece. The Little Leather Library later issued a set of "Thirty World's Greatest Masterpieces," capitalizing on the same clamor for access to liberal culture that the "Five-Foot Shelf"[2] exploited. It even offered the shelf itself. That is—anticipating a theme of Book-of-the-Month Club promotion—it enabled purchasers to display their refine-

---

1. **Walter Lippman** (1889–1974): Influential American journalist whose syndicated column "Today and Tomorrow" shaped public opinion on politics, economics, philosophy, and culture; **Irita Van Doren** (1891–1966): Literary editor of *The Nation* in the 1920s, and later associate editor of the *New York Herald Tribune's Books* magazine; **Charles** and **Albert Boni**: Founders of the publishing company Boni and Liveright.—ED.

2. **"Five-Foot-Shelf"**: Charles W. Eliot (1834–1926), president of Harvard University, claimed that a "five-foot shelf of books" could provide a complete liberal education for those who could not attend college. The Harvard Classics series that he began editing in 1909 was an attempt to fill that shelf.—ED.

ment by giving away "a handsome quartered-oak bookrack which will ornament any library table." Scherman did have to deal with one disaster, now a comical part of Book-of-the-Month Club lore: As leather prices rose, the publishers switched to synthetic bindings which, it turned out, smelled bad in hot weather. Despite that setback, however, by 1920 the Little Leather Library had marketed over twenty-five million volumes, many of them by mail.[3]

Thereafter, the Bonis sold their interest in the concern and went on to other undertakings, including the founding of the Modern Library, initially a reprint series intended to bring avant-garde fiction to American readers. Scherman and Sackheim sold out as well a few years later. In the meantime, though, they formed their own advertising agency and tried to apply the lessons they had learned about book distribution to further projects. Although Scherman recognized that he had tapped a profitable wellspring of customers by operating outside retail outlets, he also realized that he could not make money unless, following their first purchase, buyers were hooked into returning for additional ones. After some false starts, he devised a plan that combined the use of the mails with a subscription feature that ensured the necessary "repeat business." This time, instead of the classics, Scherman tendered newly published works. The Book-of-the-Month Club, a child of advertising, was born.[4]

Aside from Scherman's own prior activities, the club was not entirely unprecedented: German book societies, which printed cheap editions for sale directly to the public, had entailed a similar arrangement since 1919, and Samuel Craig had conceived of what eventually became the Literary Guild as early as 1921. Scherman's inventiveness, however, lay in the fact that he, Sackheim, and the venture's first president, Robert K. Haas, were the first club organizers to act as distributors rather than publishers, to rely heavily on mail-order techniques, and to employ a board of expert judges to win the confidence of consumers.

Under the terms of the club's initial contract, subscribers agreed to buy one new book per month for a year, at full retail price plus postage, with no book costing more than three dollars. For their money, they also received the guidance of the Selecting Committee, or Board of Judges, comprised of five of America's most famous writers and critics: Henry Seidel Canby, Dorothy Canfield Fisher, Christopher Morley, Heywood

3. Charles Lee, *The Hidden Public: The Story of the Book-of-the-Month Club* (Garden City, N.Y.: Doubleday, 1958), pp. 20–23. Lee's book is a useful, though virtually in-house, business history of the club. See also "The Reminiscences of Harry Scherman," interview by Louis M. Starr, 1955, Columbia University Oral History Collection, Butler Library, Columbia University, New York, N.Y., pp. 1–38 (hereafter cited as Scherman, COHC).

4. Scherman, COHC, p. 38.

Broun, and William Allen White.[5] The committee identified the "book of the month," furnished comments about it for a monthly newsletter called the *Book-of-the-Month Club News*, and generated a list of alternate selections from which subscribers could order if, after examining the judges' choice, they wished to exchange it for another volume.

Within a year, that formula had earned the club over sixty thousand members. Subsequently, Scherman and his partners modified the contract to require the purchase of only four books per year and replaced the exchange policy with the "privilege" of substituting an alternate selection in advance of the shipping date. The result was a rise in membership to 110,588 in 1929 and steadily increasing returns for the club's investors. Those trends, except during the worst years of the Depression, continued through 1946. Three innovations in the early 1930s gave the club essentially the structure it has today: the manufacture of special Book-of-the-Month Club editions, the occasional (and now routine) cutting of prices, and the implementation of the "book dividend" plan, which provided free books to members on the principle of stock dividends. All contributed to making the Book-of-the-Month Club an enduring feature of the cultural landscape and the progenitor of dozens more book clubs and other "of-the-month" marketing devices.[6]

If the public's response to the enterprise was enthusiastic, however, the attitude of the literary community was far more ambivalent. Part of the animus toward the club derived simply from the fact that it competed with publishers and booksellers. The publishing industry and Scherman initially enjoyed a brief honeymoon, allied against the Literary Guild, which began underselling both retailers and the Book-of-the-Month Club early in 1927.[7] In the spring of 1929, however, the Book-of-the-Month Club and the Literary Guild together incurred a vehement denunciation from the American Booksellers Association—and particularly from Dutton's John Macrae. The provocation for the attack was the

---

5. **Henry Seidel Canby** (1878–1961): Editor and literary critic who helped found and later edited the *Saturday Review of Literature*; **Dorothy Canfield Fisher** (1879–1958): Popular American novelist of the period between the two world wars; **Christopher Morley** (1890–1957): Prolific writer of fiction, nonfiction, and poetry, and editor of the *Saturday Review of Literature* from 1924 to 1941; **Heywood Broun** (1888–1939): Newspaper columnist, drama critic, and humorist, whose column "It Seems to Me" in the *New York World* and *Telegram* examined American political and cultural life from an independent vantage point that was unusual for its day; **William Allen White** (1868–1944): Writer, editor, and publisher whose Kansas newspaper the *Emporia Gazette* became a model for small-town newspapers.—ED.

6. R. L. Duffus, *Books: Their Place in a Democracy* (Boston: Houghton Mifflin, 1930), pp. 85–89; Lehmann-Haupt, Helmut, Lawrence C. Wroth, and Rollo G. Silver, *The Book in America: A History of the Making and Selling of Books in the United States.* (New York: R. R. Bowker, 1951), pp. 381–83; Lee, *Hidden Public*, pp. 14–18, 30–43.

7. The Literary Guild was the Book-of-the-Month Club's chief competitor, although the club remained the larger of the two operations until World War II.

club's designation as the March book of the month Joan Lowell's *Cradle of the Deep*, a sensational "autobiography" later revealed as a hoax. Macrae and the booksellers seized the occasion not only to ridicule the selection but to argue that the idea of a "best book of the month" was an "intellectual sham." Deploring the unwarranted advertising club selections received as "detrimental to the sale of scores of other books in the same field," the booksellers and publishers barely concealed beneath a plea for noncommercialism their desire to protect their own pocketbooks.

Yet Macrae's contention that the book clubs foreshadowed the "mechanization of the American mind" echoed the concerns of more disinterested observers. The "cultural effect," the *Commonweal* argued, "is to standardize American reading, precisely because the selection is buttressed by authority. . . . Moreover, a similarity of tone pervades almost all the selections made, so that eventually a certain kind of literature becomes the vogue." An anonymous writer in the *Bookman* for April 1927 likewise asked, "Has America a Literary Dictatorship?" Answering in the affirmative, he condemned associates of book clubs as "clever publicists and literary boosters, advocates of standardization and self advocated boards of authoritative criticism" who had promoted passivity and a decline in taste among the reading public.[8] . . .

SYMPTOMS AND CURE

When Scherman and Sackheim turned their copywriting talents to- 10 ward promoting their new project, they targeted what they called the "average intelligent reader." As Canby explained, the phrase denoted someone "who has passed through the usual formal education in literature, who reads books as well as newspapers and magazines, who, without calling himself a litterateur,[9] would be willing to assert that he was

---

More willing to emphasize bargains and less flexible about exchanges, the Literary Guild nevertheless at first resembled the club in structure and in general approach. Carl Van Doren initially presided over its selecting committee. In 1934, however, Nelson Doubleday purchased all the Guild's stock and started screening publishers' submissions for the judges; three years later the Guild eliminated judges altogether and began concentrating on selling popular fiction to an audience presumed to be less sophisticated than the club's. Robert E. Spiller, et al., *Literary History of the United States*, 3rd ed. (New York: Macmillan, 1963), pp. 1267–68; Charles A. Madison, *Book Publishing in America* (New York: McGraw-Hill, 1960), pp. 289–90; Duffus, *Books*, pp. 90–91.

8. "New Battle of the Books," *Literary Digest*, June 1, 1929, pp. 27–28; Lee, *Hidden Public*, pp. 45–59; "Daniel Among the Lions," *Commonweal*, Apr. 3, 1929, p. 615; "Has America a Literary Dictatorship?" *Bookman*, Apr. 1927, pp. 191–99; Leon Whipple, "Books on the Belt," *Nation*, Feb. 13, 1929, pp. 182–83.

9. **litterateur:** A man or woman of letters, i.e., a writer or critic.—ED.

fairly well read and reasonably fond of good reading. Your doctor, your lawyer, the president of your bank, and any educated businessman who has not turned his brain into a machine, will fit my case."[10] Hence, in contrast to Eliot, who envisioned the "Five-Foot Shelf of Books" as a liberal education for the workingman, the Book-of-the-Month Club aimed from the start at well-heeled college graduates. The first "test" list was the New York Social Register, with profitable results, and university alumni lists were fruitful later on.[11]

If potential subscribers had money and academic degrees, however, the club's advertising strategy implied that they had other difficulties. In accordance with Sackheim's first principle of mail-order copywriting, the advertisements identified "symptoms" and provided a "cure."[12] That technique, beautifully epitomizing the link between the therapeutic outlook and consumption, was a common one by the early twentieth century. What is striking, however, is that the particular ailment club membership promised to heal was the same one Lears and Susman detected at the center of campaigns for home furnishings and soap: the modern anxiety about the self.[13] The use of that approach in conjunction with the marketing of books thus illustrates both the versatility of the technique—its disconnection from the nature of the product advertised—and the extent to which such anxiety permeated American culture by the mid-1920s.

The early Book-of-the-Month Club advertisements, the model for the club's circulars into the 1950s,[14] created a persona who sets out to choose books but instead commits a series of self-betrayals. The shortcoming to which the copy referred most explicitly was the failure to carry out one's intentions. "Think over the last few years," the first ad-

---

10. Henry Seidel Canby, *Definitions: Essays in Contemporary Criticism;* (New York: Harcourt, Brace, 1922), p. 227.

11. Lee, *Hidden Public,* pp. 138, 149. The club did not develop sophisticated analyses of its audience until the late 1930s, when George Gallup conducted his first survey of the membership. (Gallup later became a director of the club.) Scherman's impression, in the club's early period, was that the "most representative type" of member was a middle-aged, married college graduate who had drifted away from intellectual pursuits. He also singled out a "good-sized proportion" of "girls, secretaries, career girls," who, Scherman added, were "awfully good readers." By the 1940s women outnumbered male subscribers two to one, although women sometimes registered subscriptions for the entire family. Scherman, COHC, pp. 118–19; William K. Zinsser, *Revolution in American Reading,* (New York: Book-of-the-Month Club, 1966), p. 12.

12. Maxwell Sackheim, *My First Sixty Years in Advertising,* (Englewood Cliffs, N.J.: Prentice-Hall, 1970), pp. 54, 78.

13. T. J. Jackson Lears, "From Salvation to Self-Realization," in *The Culture of Consumption: Critical Essays in American History, 1880–1980,* edited by Richard Wightman Fox and T.J. Jackson Lears (New York: Pantheon, 1983), pp. 1–38.

14. Lee, *Hidden Public,* p. 134.

vertisement for the enterprise began. "How often have outstanding books appeared, widely discussed and widely recommended, books you were really anxious to read and fully intended to read when you 'got around to it,' but which nevertheless you *missed*! Why is it you disappoint yourself so frequently in this way?" That pitch, which Scherman summarized as an appeal to the fear of "backsliding," was especially successful at arousing guilt among (and producing subscriptions from) male college graduates who, convinced of the value of culture, had nevertheless subordinated reading to business.[15] But the question "Why is it you disappoint yourself?"—which might have served as the modern American's motto—had greater resonances: It suggested the powerlessness of a self in conflict, one half vainly trying to prevent the other from spinning off in its own direction.

The answer the advertisements provided to that unsettling question only made matters worse, since it pinned the blame on the individual incapable of ordering his or her experience. The first advertisements typically alluded to the expansion of the book market and the resulting confusion about the "best." As an advertisement in *The New York Times Book Review* in January 1927 observed, "You know that, out of the thousands of books published, there are only a few you are interested in. You want the outstanding ones. But what are they?"[16] Yet Scherman and Sackheim did more than capitalize on a general perception of intellectual chaos; they enhanced the discomfort by implying that consumers were responsible for their own sense of disarray. "Occasionally, at haphazard and almost altogether by chance," the club's 1927 direct-mail brochure explained, the booklover "reads an advertisement or review of a book that engages his interest. . . . He says to himself, 'I must read that.'. . . Unfortunately, his memory is not always good. He stops and thinks: 'What *was* that book I wanted to read?' He cannot remember; he hasn't the time to search among the hundreds of books on the counters. . . . Perhaps afterward, in a group of bookish people, again he hears the book recommended. He confesses sadly that he had 'never got around to reading it.'"[17] In that scenario, the reader's "confession" amounts to much more than a statement about the vicissitudes of book selection; as the phrases "at haphazard" and "by chance" underscore, it is an admission that he has, through his own negligence, lost control of his will, his memory, and a good part of his world. In particular, he is victimized by time, his shortage of which is both a source and a reflection of his disorganization.

---

15. Reprinted in Sackheim, *My First Sixty Years,* p. 118; Scherman, COHC, pp. 117–18, 120.

16. Advertisement for the Book-of-the-Month Club, *The New York Times Book Review,* Jan. 30, 1927, p. 19.

17. "The Book-of-the-Month Club," pp. 2–3, 5 (hereafter cited as BOMC, 1927 brochure).

That hapless condition could in turn lead to one more self-betrayal: the inability to project to others the image of being au courant.[18] Copy for the Literary Guild, the *Elbert Hubbard Scrapbook*, or, as noted, the "Five-Foot Shelf" was much more blatant in this regard than that for the club. Yet the presumption of a disappointed audience—the accusatory "You didn't say a single word all evening" (as one Hubbard advertisement put it)—infiltrated Book-of-the-Month Club appeals as well. "What a deprivation it is to miss reading an important new book at a time everyone else is reading and discussing it," the club's 1927 brochure announced, reminding potential subscribers that neglect of the latest books meant loss of "fine camaraderie." Other blurbs wailed, "He is Always Saying Apologetically: 'I Just Can't Find Any Time to Read Books!'" or "I'm Sorry I Haven't Read the Book Yet!"[19]

The cure for that array of symptoms, all of which might be sub- 15 sumed under the heading "loss of mastery," was an "ingenious, but quite simple, system" with two major components: the imposition of time management and the use of experts. Both of those innovations made dependence on others the remedy for the ailing self. Yet, given American culture in the 1920s, Scherman's solution was just what the doctor ordered: That is, it accepted and reinforced the values of a mass consumer society while alleviating some of the distress the expansion of that society had engendered. This capaciousness functioned in several ways.

First, after 1927 members surrendered to the club's "automatic"— that is, externally controlled—schedule of distribution: One book parceled out each month, arriving unless the subscriber took the initiative of canceling it. This arrangement, perhaps Sackheim and Scherman's greatest brainstorm, was the key to the business's profits, yet it was presented to consumers as an altruistically administered prescription for the distracted reader. As Charles Lee observed, the frequently used slogan "Handed to You by the Postman—the New Books You Intend to Read" was "shrewdly directed, not only to the customer's sense of comfort, but also to his sense of intellectual fulfillment."[20] The club's newsletter, enclosed with the book, likewise furnished a victory over the inexorable flow of print, the knowledge of the next month's choice literally placing subscribers ahead of time.

Similarly, the use of expert judges appended book promotion to the areas in which the Progressive faith in bureaucracy as an antidote to disorder asserted itself. The club's 1927 brochure included full-page pho-

---

18. **au courant**: French phrase meaning "up to date" or "in the know."—ED.

19. BOMC, 1927 brochure, p. 2; Lee, *Hidden Public*, p. 136; advertisement for *The Elbert Hubbard Scrap Book*, *The New York Times Book Review*, Jan. 23, 1927, p. 32.

20. Lee, *Hidden Public*, pp. 28, 37, 135; Sackheim, *My First Sixty Years*, pp. 119–20.

tographs of each member of the Selecting Committee, with captions listing their credentials, a format that made the judges into larger-than-life exemplars of mastery. Pictures of the judges routinely appeared in magazine advertisements from 1926 to 1933 and occasionally thereafter. The club's advertising assured prospective subscribers that the experts assigned to the task of "culling out of the best books from the hundreds that are published" had no financial connection (other than a salary) with the business end of the club; thus, they were free to perform in an entirely "disinterested" manner the intellectual triage the bewildered bookbuyer required. The vehicle for communicating their decision, the *News*, was depicted in the same terms. Drawing on well-worn Progressive language (one is reminded of Jane Addams's pronouncements about "carefully collected" facts), the promotional brochure specified the contents of that "simple and sensible" newsletter: "a very careful description of the next chosen 'book-of-the-month,' *explaining exactly the type of book it is*, why the judges selected it, and something about the author." Protected by such "clear and unbiased reports," readers need not fear that they would unwittingly succumb to an alluring—but bad—book.[21]

By the 1920s Scherman was hardly alone in basing a marketing campaign on what Roland Marchand has called "a public demand for broad guidance" in the face of "proliferating choices."[22] (As noted previously, *Books* capitalized on something of the same appeal.) To some observers, however, Scherman's invention of the Selecting Committee went too far in applying to book promotion strategies apparently acceptable for selling pharmaceuticals and hosiery. In a sense, the expert board was merely extending the genteel critic's insistence on diffusing awareness of the "best." Yet, as the anonymous *Bookman* writer cited earlier implied, the manner in which they did so forced the issue of passivity out into the open. The result was that, of all its features, the committee loomed largest in the attacks the club incurred during its first few years. By agreeing to identify the book of the month, the club's assailants charged, not only had the experts sold their souls to commercial interests, they had also conspired to prevent readers from actively assaying the competing judgments of reviewers. Said the *Bookman:* "The reason by which the judges arrived at their decision are [*sic*] not discussed in open court; only the result and not the process by which the conclusion is arrived at is known to those who accept the decision; the matter must in the final analysis rest on the authority of the judges alone." As Janice Radway has concluded in a rich essay informed by literary and social theory, the "transgression" of the club was to unmask this exercise of

---

21. BOMC, 1927 brochure, pp. 11, 16.

22. Roland Marchand, *Advertising the American Dream: Making Way for Modernity, 1920–40* (Berkeley, Calif.: University of California Press, 1985), pp. 341–47.

power, instead of perpetuating the fiction of what the *Bookman* author called "free critical inquiry."[23]

Nevertheless, the actual form in which the committee or board rendered its verdicts—the *News*—argues that the club's "transgressions" in the service of supplying order also included the opposite sin: the withholding, or underexercise, of critical authority. Edited by Scherman himself, the monthly mailing featured a lead article about the main selection which integrated background about the book with excerpts from the judges' comments. (Beginning in the early 1930s, Scherman merely introduced a "review" signed by a member of the board.) Briefer notices of alternate choices followed for around ten pages. While those reports made culture accessible, they also tended to substitute narrative for evaluation, information for aesthetics. The title *Book-of-the-Month Club News* makes the point most economically. The reportorial emphasis was underscored, however, by several additions to the publication (some longer-lived than others) in the 1930s and 1940s: a section of frankly "informational, not critical" summaries for books of "sectional or special" appeal; the segregation of works "For the More Serious-Minded"; a "Panorama of New Books" consisting of single-paragraph plot descriptions interspersed with illustrations; and, accompanying the glossier look the brochure acquired in the early 1940s, a collection of anecdotes about authors compiled by Scherman's wife, Bernadine Kielty.[24]

Furthermore, all news was good news, since the judges included only the books they recommended, a feature of the club's operation that Scherman defended as necessary to business. "After all," he mused, "the publishers send in books to us, go to considerable trouble, and to damn their books. . . ." Clifton Fadiman, appointed to the board in 1944, was even more candid on this score. The articles in the *News*, he observed, "are pretty largely sales talks. We're trying to be fair, but at the same time we are trying to put the book in the best possible light so that people will like it as well as we did. In that sense, the reviews are not truly judgmatical." As was true for Stuart Sherman's *Books* audience, some club patrons reacted to that practice by demanding more, not less, mediation by the Selecting Committee. In Scherman's words, "In the beginning we were pretty severely criticized by subscribers themselves for what they called favorable reviews—'All the reviews are favorable reviews.' Well, obviously they were favorable; they were recommended." That discontent might be construed simply as a sign that confident readers wished more opportunity to weigh good books against bad on their own. Yet it also suggests a desire for even greater relief from the anxiety

---

23. "Has America a Literary Dictatorship?," pp. 195–96; Janice Radway, "The Scandal of the Middlebrow: The Book-of-the-Month Club, Class Fracture, and Cultural Authority," *South Atlantic Quarterly* 89 (Fall 1990): 703–36.

24. Lee, *Hidden Public*, p. 57. For features of the *Book-of-the-Month Club News*, see, for example, Dec. 1943, Mar. 1936, June 1940, Jan. 1944.

about the ineffectual self—about making wrong decisions in a chaotic world—that reliance on experts could palliate.[25]

■ **CONSIDER THE SOURCE**

1. Explain Rubin's characterization of the Book-of-the-Month Club as "a child of advertising."

2. What "symptom" was the club designed to "cure," according to Rubin? How does that symptom manifest itself?

3. In your own words, describe the "average intelligent reader" that club founders originally targeted.

4. Summarize the advantages and disadvantages that Rubin ascribes to the use of a panel of experts to select books for the club.

■ **CONSIDER THE IMPLICATIONS**

5. Compare the audience targeted by the Book-of-the-Month Club's founders in 1926 with the average book reader described by Bernard Berelson twenty-five years later. What features do they have in common? What difference, if any, did the lapse of a quarter of a century make? How would you define the target audience today?

6. Rubin claims that Book-of-the-Month Club founders tapped into people's desire to "project to others the image of being au courant." In your journal, explore that desire in yourself. In what subject areas do you feel most strongly the necessity to appear up to date? How do you keep current in the subject? How do you project the image of being current, even if you have not kept up on the subject?

7. Are you a member of any club with monthly selections, such as Columbia House? If so, how do its marketing strategies compare with those Rubin describes? What service do you feel it provides you? Write an analysis of the club using the same techniques Rubin used to explore the Book-of-the-Month Club.

8. Critics charged that the club's panel of experts rendered the book reader too passive in his or her selection of books. Using your own experiences as readers of reviews, discuss in class the extent to which this is true for all sorts of reviewing. What degree of "free critical inquiry" does the practice of reviewing—whether books, movies, or whatever—encourage?

9. Reread the essays by Joseph Deitch (pp. 304–11), and Katharine Weber (pp. 311–14), to see what role some reviewers think they play in the general public's acquisition of culture. Compare their conception of the reviewer's role with your own practical use of reviews. How often do you read full reviews or the excerpts from them quoted in ads? What authority do you assign to reviewers? How do you evaluate their comments?

---

25. Scherman, COHC, pp. 100–101; "The Reminiscences of Clifton Fadiman," interview by Louis M. Starr, 1955, Columbia University Oral History Collection, Butler Library, Columbia University, New York, N.Y., pp. 33–34.

10. Examine some recent ads for the Book-of-the-Month Club. (You're likely to find them in *The New York Times Book Review, New York Review of Books,* or other "bookish" publications.) Would John Dessauer (pp. 372–77), approve or disapprove of the Book-of-the-Month Club as it currently exists? Why or why not?

11. Summarize the motives for reading that Rubin attributes to club members. How would Bernard Berelson (pp. 322–30) describe those motives? To what extent do they resemble the motives for reading offered by Sven Birkerts (pp. 21–29), Jimmy Santiago Baca (pp. 180–88), Malcolm X (pp. 164–72), or Benjamin Franklin (pp. 29–37)? What accounts for the differences?

▪ ▪ ▪ ▪ ▪ ▪
....

JANICE A. RADWAY

The Act of Reading the Romance

Next time you pass a rack of Harlequin or Silhouette romances in your local grocery store, consider the fact that those cheap, formulaic stories account for more than a third of all paperback mass-market book sales. In 1980 literary historian Janice Radway (b. 1949) set out to study why millions of women read these romances so devotedly, in spite of the scorn such books receive from critics and other arbiters of taste. She conducted sixty hours of interviews in June 1980 and February 1981 with sixteen customers of a bookstore employee who regularly advised women which romances to buy. Along with a questionnaire Radway administered to forty-two romance readers, the interviews with "Dot Evans" and her customers in "Smithton" form the basis of this literary anthropologist's study. In this section of the resulting academic study Reading the Romance: Women, Patriarchy, and Popular Literature *(1984), Radway examines what the act of reading this genre of fiction does for these women. They repeatedly mention two main functions of the romance: escape and instruction. In the course of explaining their attraction to romances, they raise important issues about the function of reading in general and the justifications for reading that are acceptable in today's culture. Radway is a professor of literature at Duke University. Like Joan Shelley Rubin, (pp. 377–88), she is interested in the Book-of-the Month Club and its influence on shaping middlebrow culture. She is currently working on a book-length study of the club.*

From *Reading the Romance: Women, Patriarchy, and Popular Literature* (Chapel Hill: University of North Carolina Press, 1984), pp. 86–118.

By the end of my first full day with Dorothy Evans and her customers, I had come to realize that although the Smithton women are not accustomed to thinking about what it is in the romance that gives them so much pleasure, they know perfectly well why they like to read. I understood this only when their remarkably consistent comments forced me to relinquish my inadvertent but continuing preoccupation with the text. Because the women always responded to my query about their reasons for reading with comments about the pleasures of the act itself rather than about their liking for the particulars of the romantic plot, I soon realized I would have to give up my obsession with textual features and narrative details if I wanted to understand their view of romance reading. Once I recognized this it became clear that romance reading was important to the Smithton women first because the simple event of picking up a book enabled them to deal with the particular pressures and tensions encountered in their daily round of activities. Although I learned later that certain aspects of the romance's story do help to make this event especially meaningful, the early interviews were interesting because they focused so resolutely on the significance of the *act of romance reading* rather than on the meaning of the romance.

The extent of the connection between romance reading and my informants' understanding of their roles as wives and mothers was impressed upon me first by Dot herself during our first two-hour interview which took place before I had seen her customers' responses to the pilot questionnaire. In posing the question, "What do romances do better than other novels today?," I expected her to concern herself in her answer with the characteristics of the plot and the manner in which the story evolved. To my surprise, Dot took my query about "doing" as a transitive question about the *effects* of romances on the people who read them. She responded to my question with a long and puzzling answer that I found difficult to interpret at this early stage of our discussions. It seems wise to let Dot speak for herself here because her response introduced a number of themes that appeared again and again in my subsequent talks with other readers. My question prompted the following careful meditation:

> It's an innocuous thing. If it had to be . . . pills or drinks, this is harmful. They're very aware of this. Most of the women are mothers. And they're aware of that kind of thing. And reading is something they would like to generate in their children also. Seeing the parents reading is . . . just something that I feel they think the children should see them doing. . . . I've got a woman ·with teenage boys here who says "you've got books like . . . you've just got oodles of da . . . da . . . da . . . [counting an imaginary stack of books]." She says, "Now when you ask Mother to buy you something, you don't stop and think how many things you have. So this is Mother's and it is my money." Very, almost defensive. But I think they get that from their fathers. I think they heard their fathers sometime or other saying, "Hey, you're spending an awful lot of money on books

aren't you?" You know for a long time, my ladies hid 'em. They would hide their books; literally hide their books. And they'd say, "Oh, if my husband [we have distinctive blue sacks], if my husband sees this blue sack coming in the house...." And you know, I'd say, "Well really, you're a big girl. Do you really feel like you have to be very defensive?" A while ago, I would not have thought that way. I would have thought, "Oh, Dan is going to hit the ceiling." For a while Dan was not thrilled that I was reading a lot. Because I think men do feel threatened. They want their wife to be in the room with them. And I think my body is in the room but the rest of me is not (when I am reading).[1]

Only when Dot arrived at her last observation about reading and its ability to transport her out of her living room did I begin to understand that the real answer to my question, which she never mentioned and which was the link between reading, pills, and drinks, was actually the single word, "escape," a word that would later appear on so many of the questionnaires. She subsequently explained that romance novels provide escape just as Darvon and alcohol do for other women. Whereas the latter are harmful to both women and their families, Dot believes romance reading is "an innocuous thing." As she commented to me in another interview, romance reading is a habit that is not very different from "an addiction."

Although some of the other Smithton women expressed uneasiness about the suitability of the addiction analogy, as did Dot in another interview, nearly all of the original sixteen who participated in lengthy conversations agreed that one of their principal goals in reading was their desire to do something *different* from their daily routine. That claim was borne out by their answers to the open-ended question about the functions of romance reading. At this point, it seems worth quoting a few of those fourteen replies that expressly volunteered the ideas of escape and release. The Smithton readers explained the power of the romance in the following way:

> They are light reading—escape literature—I can put down and pick up effortlessly.

> Everyone is always under so much pressure. They like books that let them escape.

> Escapism.

---

1. All spoken quotations have been taken directly from taped interviews. Nearly all of the comments were transcribed verbatim, although in a few cases repeated false starts were excised and marked with ellipses. Pauses in a speaker's commentary have been marked with dashes. I have paragraphed lengthy speeches only when the informant clearly seemed to conclude one topic or train of thought in order to open another deliberately. Lack of paragraphing, then, indicates that the speaker's comments continued apace without significant rest or pause.

I guess I feel there is enough "reality" in the world and reading is a means of escape for me.

Because it is an Escape [*sic*], and we can dream and pretend that it is our life.

I'm able to escape the harsh world for a few hours a day.

They always seem an escape and they usually turn out the way you wish life really was.

The response of the Smithton women is apparently not an unusual one. Indeed, the advertising campaigns of three of the houses that have conducted extensive market-research studies all emphasize the themes of relaxation and escape. Potential readers of Coventry Romances, for example, have been told in coupon ads that "month after month Coventry Romances offer you a beautiful new escape route into historical times when love and honor ruled the heart and mind."[2] Similarly, the Silhouette television advertisements featuring Ricardo Montalban asserted that "the beautiful ending makes you feel so good" and that romances "soothe away the tensions of the day." Montalban also touted the value of "escaping" into faraway places and exotic locales. Harlequin once mounted a travel sweepstakes campaign offering as prizes "escape vacations" to romantic places. In addition, they included within the books themselves an advertising page that described Harlequins as "the books that let you escape into the wonderful world of romance! Trips to exotic places . . . interesting places . . . meeting memorable people . . . the excitement of love. . . . These are integral parts of Harlequin Romances—the heartwarming novels read by women everywhere."[3] Fawcett, too, seems to have discovered the escape function of romance fiction, for Daisy Maryles has reported that the company found in in-depth interviewing that "romances were read for relaxation and to enable [women] to better cope with the routine aspects of life."[4]

Reading to escape the present is neither a new behavior nor one peculiar to women who read romances. In fact, as Richard Hoggart demonstrated in 1957, English working-class people have long "regarded art as escape, as something enjoyed but not assumed to have much connection with the matter of daily life."[5] Within this sort of aesthetic, he continues, art is conceived as "marginal, as 'fun,'" as some-

---

2. These coupon ads appeared sporadically in national newspapers throughout the spring and summer of 1980.

3. Betty Neels, *Cruise to a Wedding,* (Toronto: Harlequin Books, Harlequin Salutes Edition, 1980), p. 190.

4. Daisy Maryles, "Fawcett Launches Romance Imprint with Brand Marketing Techniques," *Publishers Weekly,* 3 Sept. 1979, p. 70.

5. Richard Hoggart, *The Uses of Literacy: Changing Patterns in English Mass Culture,* (Fair Lawn, N.J.: Essential Books, 1957), p. 196.

thing "for you to *use*." In further elaborating on this notion of fictional escape, D. W. Harding has made the related observation that the word is most often used in criticism as a term of disparagement to refer to an activity that the evaluator believes has no merit in and of itself. "If its intrinsic appeal is high," he remarks, "in relation to its compensatory appeal or the mere relief it promises, then the term escape is not generally used."[6] Harding argues, moreover, on the basis of studies conducted in the 1930s, that "the compensatory appeal predominates mainly in states of depression or irritation, whether they arise from work or other causes."[7] It is interesting to note that the explanations employed by Dot and her women to interpret their romance reading for themselves are thus representative in a general way of a form of behavior common in an industrialized society where work is clearly distinguished from and more highly valued than leisure despite the fact that individual labor is often routinized, regimented, and minimally challenging.[8] It is equally essential to add, however, that although the women will use the word "escape" to explain their reading behavior, if given another comparable choice that does not carry the connotations of disparagement, they will choose the more favorable sounding explanation. To understand why, it will be helpful to follow Dot's comments more closely.

In returning to her definition of the appeal of romance fiction—a definition that is a highly condensed version of a commonly experienced process of explanation, doubt, and defensive justification—it becomes clear that romance novels perform this compensatory function for women because they use them to diversify the pace and character of their habitual existence. Dot makes it clear, however, that the women are also troubled about the propriety of indulging in such an obviously pleasurable activity. Their doubts are often cultivated into a full-grown feeling of guilt by husbands and children who object to this activity because it draws the women's attention away from the immediate family circle. As Dot later noted, although some women can explain to their families that a desire for a new toy or gadget is no different from a desire to read a new romantic novel, a far greater number of them have found it necessary to hide the evidence of their self-indulgence. In an effort to combat both the resentment of others and their own feelings of shame about their "hedonistic" behavior, the women have worked out a complex rationalization for romance reading that not only asserts their

6. D. W. Harding, "The Notion of 'Escape' in Fiction and Entertainment," *Oxford Review* 4 (Hilary 1967): p. 24.

7. Ibid., p. 25.

8. For discussions of the growth of the reading public and the popular press, see Raymond Williams, *The Long Revolution* (New York: Columbia University Press, 1961), pp. 156–213, and Richard Altick, *The English Common Reader: A Social History of the Mass Reading Public, 1800–1900* (Chicago: University of Chicago Press, 1957), passim.

equal right to pleasure but also legitimates the books by linking them with values more widely approved within American culture. Before turning to the pattern, however, I want to elaborate on the concept of escape itself and the reasons for its ability to produce such resentment and guilt in the first place.

Both the escape response and the relaxation response on the second questionnaire immediately raise other questions. Relaxation implies a reduction in the state of tension produced by prior conditions, whereas escape obviously suggests flight from one state of being to another more desirable one.[9] To understand the sense of the romance experience, then, as it is enjoyed by those who consider it a welcome change in their day-to-day existence, it becomes necessary to situate it within a larger temporal context and to specify precisely how the act of reading manages to create that feeling of change and differentiation so highly valued by these readers.

In attending to the women's comments about the worth of romance reading, I was particularly struck by the fact that they tended to use the word escape in two distinct ways. On the one hand, they used the term literally to describe the act of denying the present, which they believe they accomplish each time they begin to read a book and are drawn into its story. On the other hand, they used the word in a more figurative fashion to give substance to the somewhat vague but nonetheless intense sense of relief they experience by identifying with a heroine whose life does not resemble their own in certain crucial aspects. I think it important to reproduce this subtle distinction as accurately as possible because it indicates that romance reading releases women from their present pressing concerns in two different but related ways.

Dot, for example, went on to elaborate more fully in the conversation quoted above about why so many husbands seem to feel threatened by their wives' reading activities. After declaring with delight that when she reads her body is in the room but she herself is not, she said, "I think this is the case with the other women." She continued, "I think men cannot do that unless they themselves are readers. I don't think men are *ever* a part of anything even if it's television." "They are never really out of their body either," she added. "I don't care if it's a football game; I think they are always consciously aware of where they are." Her triumphant conclusion, "but I think a woman in a book isn't," indicates that Dot is aware that reading not only demands a high level of attention but also draws the individual *into* the book because it requires her participation. Although she is not sure what it is about the book that prompts this absorption, she is quite sure that television viewing and film watching are dif-

---

9. As Robert Escarpit has observed in *The Sociology of Literature*, trans. Ernest Pick (Painesville, Ohio: Lake Erie College Press, 1965), p. 91, "there are a thousand ways to escape and it is essential to know from what and towards what we are escaping."

ferent. In adding immediately that "for some reason, a lot of men feel threatened by this, very, very much threatened," Dot suggested that the men's resentment has little to do with the kinds of books their wives are reading and more to do with the simple fact of the activity itself and its capacity to absorb the participants' entire attention.

These tentative observations were later corroborated in the conversations I had with other readers. Ellen, for instance, a former airline stewardess, now married and taking care of her home, indicated that she also reads for "entertainment and escape." However, she added, her husband sometimes objects to her reading because he wants her to watch the same television show he has selected. She "hates" this, she said, because she does not like the kinds of programs on television today. She is delighted when he gets a business call in the evening because her husband's preoccupation with his caller permits her to go back to her book.

Penny, another housewife in her middle thirties, also indicated that her husband "resents it" if she reads too much. "He feels shut out," she explained, "but there is nothing on TV I enjoy." Like Ellen's husband, Penny's spouse also wants her to watch television with him. Susan, a woman in her fifties, also "read[s] to escape" and related with almost no bitterness that her husband will not permit her to continue reading when he is ready to go to sleep. She seems to regret rather than resent this only because it limits the amount of time she can spend in an activity she finds enjoyable. Indeed, she went on in our conversation to explain that she occasionally gives herself "a very special treat" when she is "tired of housework." "I take the whole day off," she said, "to read."

This theme of romance reading as a special gift a woman gives herself dominated most of the interviews. The Smithton women stressed the privacy of the act and the fact that it enables them to focus their attention on a single object that can provide pleasure for themselves alone. Interestingly enough, Robert Escarpit has noted in related fashion that reading is at once "social and asocial" because "it temporarily suppresses the individual's relations with his [sic] universe to construct new ones with the universe of the work."[10] Unlike television viewing, which

---

10. Ibid., p. 88. Although Dot's observations are not couched in academic language, they are really no different from Escarpit's similar observation that "reading is the supreme solitary occupation." He continues that "the man [sic] who reads does not speak, does not act, cuts himself away from society, isolates himself from the world which surrounds him. . . . Reading allows the senses no margin of liberty. It absorbs the entire conscious mind, making the reader powerless to act" (p. 88). The significance of this last effect of the act of reading to the Smithton women will be discussed later in this chapter. For a detailed discussion of the different demands made upon an individual by reading and radio listening, see Paul F. Lazarsfeld, *Radio and the Printed Page: An Introduction to the Study of Radio and Its Role in the Communication of Ideas,* (New York: Duell, Sloan, and Pearce, 1940), pp. 170–79.

is a very social activity undertaken in the presence of others and which permits simultaneous conversation and personal interaction, silent reading requires the reader to block out the surrounding world and to give consideration to other people and to another time. It might be said, then, that the characters and events of romance fiction populate the woman's consciousness even as she withdraws from the familiar social scene of her daily ministrations.

I use the word ministrations deliberately here because the Smithton women explained to me that they are not trying to escape their husbands and children "per se" when they read. Rather, what reading takes them away from, they believe, is the psychologically demanding and emotionally draining task of attending to the physical and affective needs of their families, a task that is solely and peculiarly theirs. In other words, these women, who have been educated to believe that females are especially and naturally attuned to the emotional requirements of others and who are very proud of their abilities to communicate with and to serve the members of their families, value reading precisely because it is an intensely private act. Not only is the activity private, however, but it also enables them to suspend temporarily those familial relationships and to throw up a screen between themselves and the arena where they are required to do most of their relating to others. . . .

It seems highly probable that in repetitively reading and writing romances, these women are participating in a collectively elaborated female fantasy that unfailingly ends at the precise moment when the heroine is gathered into the arms of the hero who declares his intention to protect her forever because of his desperate love and need for her. These women are telling themselves a story whose central vision is one of total surrender where all danger has been expunged, thus permitting the heroine to relinquish self-control. Passivity *is* at the heart of the romance experience in the sense that the final goal of each narrative is the creation of that perfect union where the ideal male, who is masculine and strong yet nurturant too, finally recognizes the intrinsic worth of the heroine. Thereafter, she is required to do nothing more than *exist* as the center of this paragon's attention. Romantic escape is, therefore, a temporary but literal denial of the demands women recognize as an integral part of their roles as nurturing wives and mothers. It is also a figurative journey to a utopian state of total receptiveness where the reader, as a result of her identification with the heroine, feels herself the *object* of someone else's attention and solicitude. Ultimately, the romance permits its reader the experience of feeling cared for and the sense of having been reconstituted affectively, even if both are lived only vicariously.

Dot's readers openly admit that parts of the romantic universe little resemble the world as they know it. When asked by the questionnaire how closely the fictional characters resemble the people they meet in real life, twenty-two answered "they are not at all similar," eighteen checked "they are somewhat similar," and two asserted that "they are very similar." None of Dot's customers believed that romantic characters are "almost identical" to those they meet daily.[11] In a related set of responses, twenty-three revealed that they consider the events in romances to be "not at all similar" to those occurring in real life. An additional eighteen said that the two sets of events are "somewhat similar," while only one checked "very similar."

It is interesting to note, however, that when the questionnaire asked them to compare the heroine's reactions and feelings with their own, only thirteen saw no resemblance whatsoever, while twenty-two believed that the heroine's feelings "are somewhat like mine." Five women did not answer the question. The general shift from perceptions of no similarity to detection of some resemblance suggests that Dot's readers believe that the heroine is more realistically portrayed than other characters. At the very least, they recognize something of themselves in her feelings and responses. Thus while the lack of similarity between events in the fantasy realm and those in the real world seems to guarantee a reading experience that is "escapist," emotional identification with the central character also ensures that the experience will be an affectively significant one for the reader.

These conclusions are supported by comments about the nature of escape reading culled from the interviews. Jill, a very young mother of two, who had also begun to write her own romance, commented, for example, that "we read books so we won't cry." When asked to elaborate, she responded only that romances portray the world as "I would like it to be, not as it really is." In discussing why she preferred historicals to contemporary romances, Susan explained that "the characters shouldn't be like now because then you couldn't read to escape." "I don't want to read about people who have all the problems of today's world," she added. Her sentiments were echoed by Joy who mentioned in her discussion of "bad romances" that while "perfection's not the main thing," she still hates to see an author "dwelling on handicaps or disfigurements." "I find that distasteful and depressing," she explained. This sort of desire to encounter only idealized images is carried over even into meetings with romance authors. Several told of their disappointment at meeting a favorite writer at an autograph session who was neither pretty nor attractively dressed. All agreed, however, that Kathleen Woodiwiss is the ideal romance author because she is pretty, petite, feminine, and always elegantly turned out.

When I pursued this unwillingness to read about ugliness, despair, or serious human problems with Dot, she indignantly responded, "Why

---

11. It is important to point out here that certain behaviors of the Smithton readers indicate that they actually hold contradictory attitudes about the realism of the romance. Although they admit the stories are unreal, they also claim that they learn about history and geography from their reading.

should we read depressing stuff when we have so much responsibility?" Ann made a similar remark, mentioning that she particularly dislikes books that attribute the hero's "nastiness" toward the heroine to a bad love affair that soured him on other women. When I asked her for her reasons, she said, "because *we've* been through it, we've been ditched, and it didn't sour us!" This comment led immediately to the further observation, "Optimistic! That's what I like in a book. An optimistic plot. I get sick of pessimism all the time."

Her distinction between optimistic and pessimistic stories recurred 20 during several of the interviews, especially during discussions of the difference between romances and other books. At least four of the women mentioned Colleen McCullough's best-selling novel, *The Thorn Birds,* as a good example of a tale that technically qualified as a romance but that all disliked because it was too "depressing." When urged to specify what made the story pessimistic, none cited specific events in the plot or the death of the hero. Rather, they referred to the general tenor of the story and to the fact that the characters were poor. "Too much suffering," one reader concluded. In similarly discussing a writer whose books she never enjoys, Dot also mentioned the problem of the depressing romance and elaborated on her usual response to such a story. She described her typical argument with herself as follows:

> "Well, Dorothy, you were absolutely, physically exhausted, mentally exhausted because everything was down—it was depressing." And I'd get through it and it was excellently written but everyone worked in the coal mines. They were poor as church mice. They couldn't make ends meet. Somebody was raped, an illegitimate kid. By the time I got through, I said, "What am I reading this for? This is dumb." So I quit.

Dot's sentiments were echoed by Ann when she volunteered the information that she dislikes historical romances set in Ireland, "because they always mention the potato famine" and "I tend to get depressed about that."

In a related discussion, Dot's daughter, Kit, observed that an unhappy ending is the most depressing thing that can happen in a romance. She believes, in fact, as does nearly everyone else, that an unhappy ending excludes a novel that is otherwise a romantic love story from the romance category. Kit is only one of the many who insist on reading the endings of the stories *before* they buy them to insure that they will not be saddened by emotionally investing in the tale of a heroine only to discover that events do not resolve themselves as they should. Although this latter kind of intolerance for ambiguity and unhappiness is particularly extreme, it is indicative of a tendency among Dot's customers to avoid any kind of reading matter that does not conform to their rigid requirements for "optimism" and escapist stories. Romances are valuable to them in proportion to their lack of resemblance to the real world. They choose their romances carefully in an attempt to assure themselves of a reading experience that will make them feel happy and hold out the promise of utopian bliss, a state they willingly acknowledge to be rare in the real world but one, nevertheless, that they do not want to relinquish as a conceptual possibility. . . .

In embarking for Smithton, I was prepared to engage in detailed conversations about the connections between love and sex, the differences between romance and pornography, and the continued validity of traditional definitions of femininity. I was not, however, prepared to spend as much time as I did conversing about the encyclopedic nature of romance fiction. When I questioned Dot and her customers about why they like romances, I was surprised to find that immediately after extolling their benefits as an "escape," nearly every reader informed me that the novels teach them about faraway places and times and instruct them in the customs of other cultures. As Dot herself explained in our first formal interview, "These women [the authors] research the tar out of them. They go to great lengths. You don't feel like you've got a history lesson, but somewhere in there you have."

Throughout my stay, readers consistently referred to the "facts" and "truths" contained in the novels. Indeed, the tapes and transcripts of the interviews confirm that we spent more time discussing this aspect of romance reading than any other topic except its escape function and the nature of the romantic fantasy. Yet when these same women later filled out the extended questionnaire and rank ordered several sentences best explaining their reasons for reading romances, only nineteen checked the response "to learn about faraway places and times." Of those nineteen, only six selected this as their primary reason for reading. As I noted earlier, nineteen claimed that above all else they read romances to relax, eight answered "because reading is just for me—it is my time," and five said they read to escape their daily problems.

It seems necessary to explain this discrepancy between orally reported motives and those singled out as most significant under the guarantee of anonymity promised by the questionnaire form.[12] I think it likely that the "reading for instruction" explanation is a secondary justification for repetitive romance consumption that has been articulated by the women to convince skeptical husbands, friends, and interviewers that the novels are not merely frothy, purposeless entertainment but possess a certain intrinsic value that can be transferred to the reader. According to their

---

12. The difficulty of eliciting honest answers from readers about their literary preferences and tastes is well known. As Escarpit has wryly observed, "The likelihood of lucid and sincere answers is extremely reduced as soon as someone's reading habits are examined. While the confession of one's sexual peculiarities may flatter a latent exhibitionist, the avowal of literary or anti-literary tastes . . . which lower one's position in society can only be painful" (*The Sociology of Literature,* p. 16). Indeed it was for this very reason that I decided to do some of my interviewing in groups. Because I knew beforehand that many women are afraid to admit their

theory, the value of the romance novel is a function of the information it is thought to *contain*. Because this information, which is a highly valued commodity in the advanced industrial society of which they are a part, can be imparted to these readers, their reading activity is transformed into a worthwhile pursuit precisely because its successful completion leaves them with something to show for their investment of time and money. When the reader can demonstrate to her husband or to an interviewer that an *exchange* has taken place, that she has acquired something in the process of reading, then her activity is defined retroactively as goal-directed work, as labor with a purpose, which is itself desirable in cultural terms.

In thus claiming that romance reading teaches them about the world, the Smithton women associate themselves with the long-standing, middle-class belief that education is closely connected with success and status. To read a romance, their informal theory implies, is to act deliberately to better one's self and thus, indirectly, one's social position. I might add that it is also an implicit declaration of faith in the ideologies of progress and democracy. Knowledge is not only the prerogative of the rich who can afford expensive educations, but it can be purchased by anyone in the form of a paperback book.

Dot's cryptic comment from that first interview should now make sense. When she responded to my question about what romances "do better than other reading matter available today" with a few apparently disconnected sentences, she was providing me with a glimpse of a quite logical thought process common among romance readers that moves from honest explanation to self-doubt to a more acceptable form of justification. It will be worthwhile to look briefly at her comments once again: "It's an innocuous thing. If it had to be pills or drinks—this is harmful. They're very aware of this. Most of the women are mothers. And they're aware of that kind of thing. And reading is something they would like to generate in their children also." At first, Dot contends that romance reading is an innocuous form of escape. It performs the same function as pills or drink but, unlike them, it is not harmful. She abruptly shifts, however, from the themes of escape reading and "addiction" to the thought that the women also want their children to see them reading, evidently because the activity itself is considered valuable. In Dot's case, it is clear that she has indeed conveyed this idea about reading to her children. Kit commented later in a discussion about the differences between reading and other forms of escape, that she, too, reads for "escape and entertainment." How-

---

preference for romantic novels for fear of being scorned as illiterate or immoral, I suspected that the strength of numbers might make my informants less reluctant about discussing their obsession. The strategy seemed to work, for as the shyer women saw that I did not react negatively when others volunteered information, they too began to participate in the discussions. Group interviewing, of course, creates the possibility that one individual will influence the others, thus falsifying the results. I do not think this happened to any great extent because the answers to the questionnaires generally bear out what I discovered through the interviews.

ever, her very next statement indicated that she is not content with giving this as her only reason for romance reading. She continued, "The TV doesn't really have that much to offer—nothing that's intellectually stimulating—I mean—at least you learn something when you're reading books." Romance reading is "better" than other forms of escape in Kit's mind because, in addition to the enjoyment the activity gives her, it also provides her with information she would otherwise miss.

Dot and Kit are not unique in their tendency to resort to this kind of logic to justify their expenditures of time, money, and energy on romances. All of the Smithton women cited the educational value of romances in discussion as other readers apparently have when questioned by researchers for Harlequin, Fawcett, and Silhouette. Romance editors are all very aware of the romance reader's penchant for geographical and historical accuracy despite the usual restriction of information about audiences to the houses' marketing departments. When she was an editor at Dell, Vivien Stephens showed me the extensive research library she had compiled on the English Regency to help her check the accuracy of the manuscripts submitted to her for Dell's planned Candlelight series.[13] Her knowledge of reader preferences had come from letters written to authors as well as from the authors themselves who understand that instruction is one of the principal functions books can perform for their readers.

If it seems curious that the very same readers who willingly admit that romances are fairy tales or fantasies also insist that they contain accurate information about the real world, it should be noted that the contradictory assertions seem to result from a separation of plot and setting. When the Smithton women declare that romantic fiction is escapist because it isn't like real life, they are usually referring to their belief that reality is neither as just nor as happy as the romances would have it. Rewards do not always accrue to the good nor are events consistently resolved without ambiguity in the real world. A romance is a fantasy, they believe, because it portrays people who are happier and better than real individuals and because events occur as the women wish they would in day-to-day existence.

The fact that the story is fantastic, however, does not compromise the accuracy of the portrayal of the physical environment within which the idealized characters move. Even though the Smithton women know the stories are improbable, they also assume that the world that serves as the backdrop for those stories is exactly congruent with their own. Indeed, they believe so strongly in the autonomous reality of the fictional world that they are positively indignant if book covers inaccurately portray the heroine or the hero. A good cover, according to the Smithton readers, is one that implicitly confirms the validity of the

---

13. Personal interview with Vivien Stephens, New York, 12 April 1979. Stephens is now an editor with Harlequin Books.

imaginary universe by giving concrete form to that world *designated* by the book's language. As Ann patiently explained, a good cover is dependent on the artist's "having read the book and at least if you're going to draw the characters, have the right color hair." Favorite covers include several "factual" vignettes, again because these portrayals give credence to the separate, real existence of the fictive universe. That this belief in a parallel world is important to the women can also be seen in their commonly stated wish that more authors would write sequels to stories in order to follow the lives of particularly striking minor characters. The technique again continues the illusion that the romantic world is as real as the readers' world and that the characters' lives continue just as theirs do. As a consequence of this assumption about the congruence of the two worlds, anything the readers learn about the fictional universe is automatically coded as "fact" or "information" and mentally filed for later use as knowledge applicable to the world of day-to-day existence. . . .

My conversations with Dot's customers confirmed her claim in our ₃₀ first interview that although husbands usually object to their wives' reading at first, they generally change their minds if the women persist long enough. She has a theory, she tells her women, "that if you can hang in there for three years, [the fact that they are threatened] goes away as such." When she recounted her theory, she added, "it's true. It is weird. And before long, they get to the point where they're thinking, 'Oh well, you know my wife reads x amount of books a week.' And they're braggin' about it." If they can shift perspectives, in other words, and rather than see romance reading as a pointless activity with no utilitarian purpose, consider the ability to read many books both an achievement in itself and a way to learn, they can then justify their wives' book expenses. Some of these men can even be persuaded that the form is interesting if their wives decide to try their hand at romance writing themselves. Dot observed, "Here we have some of these women who have decided, 'Well, I can write a book.' And now these very same husbands are so supportive that they are almost pushy. 'Well, get that book done. That's a good book. I've been reading it.' So you see, it can be a change if they just kind of push it in place." Romance reading can be justified to others, then, if the reader learns to stress the books' educational function, if she can demonstrate the extraordinary adeptness and speed with which she reads, or if she can turn the whole process around and write her own romance to be read and, of course, bought by others.

In maintaining that the "reading for instruction" argument helps to legitimate an activity that would otherwise be seen as self-indulgent and frivolous because it does not immediately appear to accomplish anything useful, I do not mean to imply that the Smithton women are being dishonest when they say they want to learn. Nor am I questioning whether they do, in fact, learn anything of value. I think it important to emphasize here that a genuine craving for knowledge of the world beyond the doors of their suburban homes is an important motivating factor in their decision to read rather than watch television, participate in craft activities, or involve themselves in physical recreation. They are cognizant that their lives have been limited by the need to stay close to home to care for children and to provide a supportive environment for their husbands. A common refrain in all of the conversations centered about the value of a book as a provider of "adult conversation" which they missed as a result of their confinement within their homes as the principal provider and companion for small children.

In summary, romances can be termed compensatory fiction because the act of reading them fulfills certain basic psychological needs for women that have been induced by the culture and its social structures but that often remain unmet in day-to-day existence as the result of concomitant restrictions on female activity. From the Smithton readers' experiences, in particular, it can be concluded that romance reading compensates women in two distinct ways. Most important, it provides vicarious emotional nurturance by prompting identification between the reader and a fictional heroine whose identity as a woman is always confirmed by the romantic and sexual attentions of an ideal male. When she successfully imagines herself in the heroine's position, the typical romance reader can relax momentarily and permit herself to wallow in the rapture of being the center of a powerful and important individual's attention. This attention not only provides her with the sensations evoked by emotional nurturance and physical satisfaction, but, equally significantly, reinforces her sense of self because in offering his care and attention to the woman with whom she identifies, the hero implicitly regards that woman and, by implication, the reader, as worthy of his concern. This fictional character thus teaches both his narrative counterpart and the reader to recognize the value they doubted they possessed.

Romance fiction is compensatory in a second sense because it fills a woman's mental world with the varied details of simulated travel and permits her to converse imaginatively with adults from a broad spectrum of social space. Moreover, the world-creating and instructional functions of romances provide the woman who believes in the value of individual achievement with the opportunity to feel that education has not ceased for her nor has the capacity to succeed in culturally approved terms been erased by her acceptance of the less-valued domestic roles. Because romance reading is coded as an instructional activity even as it is acknowledged to be entertaining, a woman can indulge herself by engaging in an activity that makes her feel good and simultaneously congratulate herself for acting to improve her awareness of the world by learning through books. Romance reading compensates, then, for a certain kind of emotional deprivation just as it creates the illusion of movement or change achieved through informal acquisition of factual "knowledge."

In populating her imagination with the attractive and exotically employed individuals found in romances, the woman whose intercourse with the community has been restricted in favor of her family widens her range of acquaintances and vicariously enriches the social space she inhabits. Like an individual prevented from dreaming who then begins to hallucinate in waking life to compensate for the reduction in symbolic activity, a woman who has been restricted by her relative isolation within the home turns to romances for the wealth of objects, people, and places they enable her to construct *within* her own imagination. The fact that she is reading, and therefore learning, functions for the romance reader as an assurance that she is not an example of that much-maligned cultural stereotype, the simpleminded housewife who can manage little more than to feed her children, iron a few shirts, and watch the afternoon soap operas. The Smithton women are all acutely aware that American culture does not value the role they perform and they indignantly protest that their employment as mothers and housewives does not mean that they are necessarily stupid. Their reading, finally, serves to confirm their image of themselves as intelligent individuals who are yet deserving of occasional pleasure and escape from responsibilities that are willingly accepted and dutifully performed. . . .

▪ **CONSIDER THE SOURCE**

1. Explain how romances provide "escape" for the readers Radway interviewed. Escape from what? To what?

2. What did the women cite as the main objections to romance reading? Who raised the objections? Why?

3. In what ways are romances fantasies, according to Radway and the women she interviewed? In what ways are they "congruent" with the real world?

4. What three justifications for romance reading does Radway say women offer to others? How and why do these differ from the reasons women offer to themselves?

5. Summarize in your own words the "compensatory" functions of romances that Radway notes.

▪ **CONSIDER THE IMPLICATIONS**

6. Compare the escapist function of romances with the uses of reading noted by Sven Birkerts, (pp. 21–29), Barbara Sicherman (pp. 70–88), and Caryn James (pp. 88–94). How does a reader's identification with a novel's character contribute to that function? In your journal describe a book or movie that you used for "escape" and explore the degree to which you identified with a main character.

7. Radway's observation that a person reads to "better one's self and thus, indirectly, one's social position" can be compared to Benjamin Franklin's discussion of his uses of very different books (pp. 29–37). Write a letter

from Franklin to Dot Evans, supporting or condemning her choice of books and her use of that reading material.

8. Dot Evans claims that men and women differ in their capacity to be absorbed in a book or television show (pp. 393–94). Based on your own experience, hold a class debate on the validity of her claim. Is gender the only factor that determines "absorption" ability?

9. Do any of your family members or friends regularly read "genre" fiction, such as romances, Westerns, mysteries, science fiction, horror, or suspense novels? Interview one such reader and analyze, as Radway did, what the act of reading those books does for the reader. Why does the reader choose that particular genre over others? Does gender play a role in selecting genres? If so, why?

10. Analyze the covers of some romances displayed in a bookstore or grocery store. What features do they share? Which seem to portray the "factual vignettes" that the Smithton women valued? What do the covers tell you about the marketing techniques the publisher is using?

11. Read a Harlequin or similar romance. Then write an essay defending or refuting one romance reader's assertion that "romance reading is 'better' than other forms of escape . . . because, in addition to the enjoyment the activity gives [the reader], it also provides her with information she would otherwise miss."

12. What role do romances play in the "national culture" envisioned by E. D. Hirsch (pp. 331–42)? How highly would Thomas Roberts (pp. 360–71) or John P. Dessauer (pp. 372–77) value them? Why?

13. List on the board all the kinds of evidence used by Radway, Barbara Sicherman (p. 70–88), Linda K. Kerber (pp. 136–50), and Joan Shelley Rubin (pp. 377–88) in their studies of book reading. How do these academic writers use their varied sources to support their arguments? What practices do they have in common? Draft a set of guidelines for academic writers based on your analysis of these authors' techniques.

▪ ▪ ▪ ▪ ▪ ▪

STEVEN STARKER

The New Oracle: Self-Help Books in American Culture

Best-selling books come in all varieties, but typically they have been listed in two large categories, fiction and nonfiction. However, in 1983, the venerable New York Times Book Review *created a third list: "Advice, How-to, and Miscellaneous" recognizes the top sellers in an extremely lucrative area of publishing. The self-help book now reaches an audience of*

From *Book Research Quarterly* 4 (Summer 1988), 26–32. (See entry under Transaction Publishers in appendix.)

millions, dispensing advice on every aspect of modern life and becoming "a highly visible and powerful force in American society," says Steven Starker (b. 1942). Yet the popular instruction manual is the Rodney Dangerfield of the book world: It gets no respect from reviewers, critics, or scholars who traditionally advise the reading public on what books to buy. In this 1988 article from Book Research Quarterly, *Starker surveys self-help books as a publishing phenomenon, isolating several factors that contribute to their success in the marketplace. He has written several books on the role of popular psychology in American culture, including* Oracle at the Supermarket *(1988) and* Evil Influences: Crusades against the Mass Media *(1989). Presently, he is chief of Psychology Service with the Veteran's Administration Medical Center in Portland, Oregon.*

The quest for enlightenment is a ubiquitous and noble part of human culture, calling to mind images of ancient scrolls, arduous pilgrimages, blind soothsayers, bearded prophets, Indian gurus, encounters with the oracle of Delphi,[1] and a certain forbidden, but inescapably tempting, apple. In contemporary Western society, mention of the quest also stimulates images of vast university campuses, laboratories brimming with electronic apparatus, esoteric professional journals, cavernous libraries, and computers offering gigabytes of stored information.

For millions of Americans, however, the individual search for practical, moral, and spiritual instruction has taken a drastically altered form, one requiring a new set of images. For these seekers after truth, Delphi, ivy-covered library, and supercomputer have given way to the bookracks of the neighborhood supermarket or bookstore. Prophet, sage, oracle, and scroll have grown pale and insignificant in comparison with a new, more powerful icon: the self-help book. The search for the Holy Grail, for spiritual renewal and hope, no longer requires a heroic trip into the distant corners of the kingdom; the object of the quest may be found conveniently in paperback, at the grocery, to the left of the chocolate milk.

The self-help book, particularly in its inexpensive, omnipresent paperback edition, has become a highly visible and powerful force in American society. In bookstores and supermarkets, potential readers are confronted by a vast accumulation of apparent expertise on topics medical, psychological, spiritual, financial, and otherwise. *Eat to Win,* suggests one best-selling title concerned with diet and nutrition for fitness and sports; *Go For It,* advises another, and become a winner at work, love, and play; *Thin Thighs in Thirty Days* promises a major blockbuster to those whose difficulties are of the fleshy variety.

Television talk shows parade for their viewers the authors of the latest such volumes, persons in the process of becoming nationally ac-

---

1. **oracle of Delphi**: In ancient Greece an oracle was a priestess who could convey the gods' replies to human questions. The Delphic oracle was the most powerful.—ED.

claimed authorities and celebrities. At informal social gatherings, guests are likely to argue the relative merits of various published approaches to diet, exercise, success, relationships, personal growth, and so on. The self-help book, with its attendant mystique, has come to occupy a very central niche in American popular culture, dispensing advice on virtually all aspects of living and achieving a huge audience.

Many phenomena of popular or mass culture fail to attract or long retain the attention of social scientists. There have been, for example, few dissertations on the hula hoop or pet rock, and we have yet to witness the birth of the *Journal of Cabbage Patchology*. It is easy to accord self-help books the usual pop culture treatment: the shake of the head, momentary sneer, superior smile, and benign neglect. In fact, taking seriously the ephemeral productions of pop culture may even entail some degree of academic risk, as colleagues sitting on review committees ponder and debate whether a faculty member has sold out intellectually, "gone pop," and ought therefore to be disenfranchised.

Nevertheless, the self-help book is a firm part of the fabric of American culture, too pervasive and influential to be ignored or lightly dismissed, and certainly worthy of investigation. Along with television and the motion picture, the self-help book is, at the very least, an important reflection of enduring human concerns and changing social needs. Unlike these other media, however, it is also an explicit instruction manual for achieving health, wealth, and happiness. What is it saying to our children, our neighbors, our parents, our spouses, and why are they willing to listen? What do we really know about this new oracle at the supermarket?

THE PROLIFERATION OF ADVICE

Books in Print, 1983–84 lists approximately 3,700 titles beginning with the words "How to." This figure, already large, is a gross underestimate of the self-help volumes available, inasmuch as authors are not constrained as to title. Among the offerings near the beginning of the list:

— *How to Achieve Security, Confidence, and Peace;*
— *How to Achieve Total Success;*
— *How to Avoid Stress Before It Kills You;*
— *How to Be a Better Parent;*
— *How to Be a Winner at Love;*
— *How to Be More Creative;*
— *How to Be Slimmer, Trimmer, and Happier;*
— *How to Beat Death*

Expert "how-to" advice seems available in all areas of endeavor. In a 1978 article in the *American Psychologist,* Clarke-Stewart reported counting some two hundred popularized books, then in print, on child care alone; she noted also that this was clearly an underestimate. Among the titles found were such mainstream works as *Baby and Child Care* (Spock, 1946), *Between Parent and Child* (Ginott, 1965), and *Infants and Mothers* (Brazelton, 1969), but also a sizable group of books described as "more exotic and esoteric,"[2] including *Hypnosis and Your Child* (Alexandroff, 1972), *Sun and Daughter Signs: An Astrological Guide to Child Care* (Wagman, 1974), and *Toilet Training in Less than a Day* (Azrin and Foxx, 1974). Based on the sales figures revealed in her survey of publishers, the number of child care books sold in the United States during the five-year period studied was about twenty-three million. In an extensive investigation in the Chicago area, based on personal interviews, Clarke-Stewart found more than 44 percent of the mothers of two-to-four year-olds had read more than five child care/parenting books.

Diet books, today among the most popular of self-help works, are written and published with astounding regularity. Elaine Fitzpatrick, author and self-confessed "perpetual dieter," in 1982 published a volume entitled *Diets, Diets, Diets: A Digest for Dieters,* providing a brief summary of over a hundred popular diet books published during the preceding decade. Having read "countless diet books," she selected these for presentation because they were "interesting, generally popular, and readily available."[3] "Anyone—even persons without an iota of nutritional training can design, develop, publish, and promote a diet. . . . All it takes is an idea and the ability to string some words together."[4]

Approaching the self-help literature from another vantage point, psychologists Glasgow and Rosen identified those publications that offered specific behavior therapy treatments addressed to certain clinical problems: phobia, obesity, smoking, sexual dysfunction, assertiveness, child behavior, and physical fitness. Even using these stringent criteria, the investigators were able to locate eighty-six self-administered behavioral programs.[5] Moreover, in a related publication, dated only one year later, they noted that an "unprecedented proliferation of do-it-yourself advice books" had occurred in the brief interim between studies.[6]

10

---

2. K. Alison Clarke-Stewart, "Popular Primers for Parents," *American Psychologist* 33(1978): 360.

3. Elaine Fitzpatrick, *Diets, Diets, Diets: A Digest for Dieters* (San Diego: Atea Press, 1982), preface.

4. Frederick J. Stare and Elizabeth M. Whelan, "Warning: Fad Diets Can Be Dangerous!" *Readers Digest,* March 1983, 49.

5. Russell E. Glasgow and Gerald M. Rosen, "Behavioral Bibliotherapy," *Psychological Bulletin* 85 (1978): 1–23.

6. Russell E. Glasgow and Gerald M. Rosen, "Self-Help Behavior Therapy Manuals: Recent Developments and Clinical Usage," *Clinical Behavior Therapy Review.* 1 (1979): 1.

The subject guide to *Books in Print, 1983–84* reveals many volumes concerned with the psychological aspects of self-improvement and growth. The editors, moreover, somehow managed to break down the topic into a variety of related subheadings: Self-Acceptance (14 titles), Self-Actualization (95), Self-Control (27), Self-Realization (61), Self-Reliance (18), Self-Respect (54). (Most of us, I suspect, would have difficulty knowing whether we had actualized, realized, or merely accepted ourselves.) Once again, the 269 books counted represent an underestimate of the total available volumes because of the many other related categories under which these might appear.

Looking at the data from still another perspective, that of market impact, a single self-help author, Samm Sinclair Baker, is credited with twenty-eight self-help books on subjects including psychology, physical fitness, and diet. One of these, written with a prominent "diet doctor" and titled *The Doctor's Quick Weight Loss Diet,* has sold over ten million copies. Even this profoundly successful effort cannot approach the accomplishment of Dr. Benjamin Spock's landmark book on *Baby and Child Care* (1946), which is said to have sold thirty-six million copies with translations into twenty-six languages, and is ranked second only to the Bible in its popularity with Americans. Regarding the speed with which self-help information may be disseminated, *Thin Thighs in Thirty Days,* a runaway success in 1982, was released in June and by year's end had been distributed to the tune of 1,233,000 copies.

According to Dwight Macdonald, in a 1954 *New Yorker* essay on "Howtoism," "Howto writers are to other writers as frogs are to mammals; their books are not born, they are spawned. A Howtoer with only three or four books to his credit is looked upon as sterile."[7] R. D. Rosen, author and critic of the popular psychology scene, noted in his 1977 book on *Psychobabble* that "the number of psychobabble books offered to the public with a solemnity formerly reserved for great works is astounding."[8]

Unlike drugs, which are subjected to lengthy research trials prior to their general availability, or professional research articles, which are scrutinized by knowledgeable reviewers prior to acceptance for publication, self-help books are totally unregulated except for the limitations imposed by production and distribution schedules, profit margins, and supply/demand ratios. A new diet, treatment for phobia, approach to child care, exercise program, or technique of mind-expansion can sweep the country in only a few months. It may be the work of a well-known medical or psychological authority, but it is as likely to be an idea created by a publishing house or "book packager," or originated and promoted by a television or movie personality. (*Jane Fonda's Workout Book,*

---

7. Dwight Macdonald, "Howtoism," *The New Yorker,* 22 May 1954, 82.

8. Richard D. Rosen, *Psychobabble: Fast Talk and Quick Cure in the Era of Feeling* (New York: Atheneum, 1977), 16.

for example, was a runaway best-seller in 1982.) In any event, such self-help programs can totally saturate the American market, entering millions of homes and minds, without any serious examination as to validity. Typically, by the time the academic establishment responds to these new ideas and techniques, the book that initiated them is well past its sales peak, and its sequel may already be making its way onto the best-seller lists. Many are never responded to at all, perhaps because they are considered unworthy of serious consideration. For example, *30 Days to a Better Bust* sold 359,000 copies in a single month (December) in 1982, as readers attempted to complement their newly thinned thighs. Were a serious independent evaluation of this plan attempted, it would almost certainly have taken more than a year to find appropriate subjects and controls, conduct the study, analyze the data, and write up the results; it would have been another year before the work was reported in an appropriate professional journal.

The oracle at Delphi, whose wisdom, we are assured by legend, came directly from the gods, spoke with relatively few privileged pilgrims and never offered clear-cut directions or solutions; ambiguous prophecies were the order of the day. The new oracle, on the other hand, regularly addresses a mass audience, offers exact directions for solving problems, claims competence in virtually all aspects of human concern, and is relatively free of external evaluation and regulation. It does not seem wise to ignore an agency with characteristics such as these.

SOURCES OF SUCCESS

A full examination of the new oracle must consider many factors that contribute to its power, some psychological, others social or historical. A few very pragmatic advantages of self-help over the professional variety, however, are at once obvious:

Cost—Professional helpers share certain characteristics. Foremost among these, perhaps, are their increasingly prohibitive costs. Psychologists, psychiatrists, internists, counselors, consultants, and other problem-solvers may require at least several visits at between $50 and $150 per hour. Despite the expense, they seldom offer any promises of success; most are prohibited from doing so by the ethical codes of their respective professions. The self-help book, on the other hand, requires an investment of perhaps $3.95 in paperback, or up to $16.95 in a hardbound deluxe edition. In return for this one-time-only payment it will frequently promise complete success, at least in the extravagant blurbs on front and back covers.

Accessibility—In seeking out a reputable professional helper one must make discreet inquiries, call well in advance for an appointment, travel to an office, sit in a waiting area, and negotiate fees; all are inconvenient. When multiple visits are required, this disrupts normal daily routines.

The self-help book, on the other hand, is usually available in the neighborhood supermarket or bookstore. At worst, it can be ordered with a phone call. Once acquired, it makes few demands, awaiting the pleasure of the reader. It is content to be consulted at odd hours, during coffee breaks or television commercials, or as a midnight antidote to insomnia. In an era when "house calls" are almost unheard of, the self-help book provides a medical/psychological clinic of sorts in every home.

Privacy—In seeking professional help, individuals confront the painful decision to "go public," to confide their difficulties to a relative stranger. This is a very difficult step, one that many people are unable to take until their situations have deteriorated to an alarming degree. It is as if consultation makes the difficulty, once and for all, "real"—and is therefore to be avoided at all costs. Moreover, initial discussion of personal difficulties, whether of sexuality, finances, family life, loneliness, and so on, often is experienced as acutely embarrassing, if not humiliating. There may be a brief bout of embarrassment associated with the purchase of a self-help book, but this is rather transient and mild. "After all, I could be buying this for a friend." The privacy aspect of the self-help book apparently was well understood by Dr. David Reuben, author of the bestselling *Everything You Always Wanted to Know About Sex (But Were Afraid to Ask)* (1969).

Excitement—Once a self-help book has been identified as a "best-seller," 20 as the "in" thing to read, anyone may share in the delight and excitement of belonging to the in-group by purchasing a copy. There is no embarrassment about dieting when one has joined a few million others in a fabulous new diet plan; no shame in searching for your "G-spot" along with everyone else; no stigma in trying to improve a deteriorating marriage by learning a popular new system of "fair" fighting. Rather, there is the security of belonging, the opportunity to discuss the latest trend with friends, the thrill of seeing the author on television, and the gratification of participating in a pop culture "happening."

A Quick Survey

The reading public, it seems, has given the self-help genre a ringing vote of confidence at the cash register. Are they finding whatever it is they seek?

In a preliminary survey, I asked sixty-seven volunteer hospital workers, men and women ranging from twenty-seven to eighty-six years of age, whether they believed such works to be harmful, unhelpful, rarely helpful, sometimes helpful, or often helpful. Only one person, a seventy-eight-year-old retired man who frequently read self-help books, circled "harmful" (he also circled "sometimes helpful," neatly circumventing the instructions in order to indicate his mixed feelings on the issue). Another, a twenty-seven-year-old high school dropout who reported little reading history, ignored the offered choices to write in "boring." Seven individuals circled "rarely helpful." The strongly prevailing attitude (85 percent), however, was one of optimism ("sometimes helpful" and "often helpful"), with "often helpful" the single most frequently selected category (47 percent). Aside from that one thoughtful, elderly gentleman, then, none of the participants considered the books a potential source of mischief or worse. By and large, these people viewed the self-help genre as exerting an influence for the good.

The preliminary survey also produced some brief comments on the benefits of reading self-help books. The following are representative:

— Opened new avenues to me, mapped out routines.

— Lost weight, gave me a good diet.

— More self-confidence.

— Made me understand myself and others.

— Personal growth and maturity.

— Insight into problem areas.

— Peace of mind.

— Helped to overcome grief.

— Presented a new and thought provoking perspective.

— Knowledge of hypertension and stress.

One "retired executive" noted that such works "confirmed many established concepts"; a clergyman similarly reported that they "confirmed practices already in use." One participant commented, "A person must have push and drive to follow through. Many books are read and then just put on the shelf." Another, a woman who had acquired numerous volumes on diet, exercise, personal growth, and psychological adjustment, complained, "I just can't get into them enough to read one all the way through."

The decidedly positive evaluation accorded self-help books by the respondents to my brief survey is in close agreement with parents' evaluations of popular child-care books in the Clarke-Stewart study. That is, most readers of such works felt that suggestions were effectively communicated (86 percent), that they would read another such book (85 percent) and that they would recommend the book to a friend (85 percent). Moreover, 81 percent of those questioned mentioned something specifically positive about whatever child-care book they had read, and 38 percent said there was "nothing in the book with which they disagreed."

Whether readers really benefit from their adventures in self-help reading is a matter of some interest to psychologists, physicians, counselors, educators, and sociologists. Perhaps the preoccupation with self-help books in this country is merely another aspect of that well-known American optimism, self-reliance, and determination to succeed. Perhaps it represents a contemporary "fast food" version of psychotherapy or religion, or reveals an unhealthy degree of narcissism in our society. Whatever the social or symbolic significance of this pop culture phenomenon, however, self-help books are providing *something* of value to their many dedicated readers. The overwhelming success of the self-help genre may indicate that we are on the verge of a new, slim, healthy, long-lived, creative, successful, emotionally stable, and appropriately assertive society. An alternative possibility, however, suggests that the benefits of the millions of self-help books sold each year differ from those promised on their covers.

CONCLUSION

The self-help book in America appears to occupy the social niche roughly on a par with that of the legendary oracle at Delphi. Offering wisdom and enlightenment at discount prices, it speaks to a vast audience on a variety of topics and provides specific directions for achieving love, health, wealth, peace of mind, and any number of practical skills. It is too prevalent and powerful a phenomenon to overlook, despite its belonging to "pop" culture. Inasmuch as self-help books are dispensing advice to millions on matters physical, psychological, and spiritual, they cannot responsibly be ignored by social scientists and health care practitioners. Questions regarding their relative merits and potential dangers deserve careful consideration.

▪ **CONSIDER THE SOURCE**

1. How does Starker liken self-help books to traditional sources of instruction, such as oracles and libraries? How do they differ?
2. Summarize the advantages that Starker claims self-help books have over professional sources of help. Which would you rank as most important? Why?
3. How does the learned community regard popular culture in general and self-help books in particular, according to Starker? Why do you think he includes that point in his article in *Book Research Quarterly*?
4. What is the most serious problem Starker sees with the proliferation of self-help books?

▪ **CONSIDER THE IMPLICATIONS**

5. In your journal, reflect on the self-help books you may have read. What did you seek to learn from them? What benefits did you derive? Were you satisfied or dissappointed? Why?
6. Bring a self-help book to class for examination in small groups. What promises does the book make? What credentials does the author have?

How easy is the book to read and understand? How does it demonstrate the qualities that Starker lists as "sources of success"?

7. Using Starker's methodology, survey the self-help books at your local grocery store. How many are there? What subjects do they address? What do they typically cost? Who writes them? Who are they aimed at? Write an analysis of the current market trends indicated by your research.

8. Look at a magazine you read regularly to see how many articles fall into the self-help or how-to category. What problems do the articles address? What sort of reader do the articles seem to envision? Are you that reader? To what extent do the magazine's advertisements illustrate the promised results of the how-to articles? Write an analysis of the magazine as an "oracle."

9. Compare the "excitement" Starker ascribes to self-help books with the motives for reading described by Bernard Berelson (pp. 322–30) and Joan Shelley Rubin (pp. 377–88). What kinds of books provide what Starker calls "the security of belonging"? What other cultural products promise consumers "the delight and excitement of belonging to the in-group"?

10. Starker speculates that the popularity of self-help books may demonstrate "that well-known American optimism, self-reliance, and determination to succeed." Write an essay analyzing the autobiographical narratives of Benjamin Franklin (pp. 29–37), Frederick Douglass (pp. 130–36), or Zitkala-Ša (pp. 150–56) as "self-help" books.

■ ■ ■ ■ ■ ■

LAURIE OUELLETTE

'Zines: Notes from the Underground

Just as every mainstream has its branches and tributaries, so every culture has its subcultures. And every subculture has its publications—small, localized, often surreptitious pamphlets, newsletters, and journals that serve a specialized audience. One of the most fertile areas of alternative publishing began with the science fiction fan magazines of the 1940s. Soon "fanzines" cropped up to satisfy all sorts of interests, and today, "'zines," as they're now known, treat every conceivable facet of popular culture. Laurie Ouellette (b. 1966) takes us on a tour of this amazing underground that exists beyond the border—and beneath the notice—of the conventional publishing world. She defines and classifies a remarkable array of 'zines and speculates about why they have proliferated in the past decade. Ouellette is a freelance journalist and critic currently working toward a Ph.D.

From *Utne Reader* (November/December 1991), pp. 139–42.

in communications at the University of Massachusetts, Amherst. Her work has appeared in the Utne Reader *(for which she once served as librarian), the feminist magazine* On the Issues, *and* The Women's Review of Books.

You're as likely to find copies of *Profane Existence, Holy Titclamps,* or *Twisted Image* at the local newsstand as you are to find their respective subject matter (anarchist politics and punk music, Queer culture, radical comics) in the latest issue of *Women's Day* or *U.S. News & World Report.* Cantankerous, outrageous, and completely uncensored, these publications are radically removed from the established press and even from the alternative press. Virtually invisible to mainstream America, they belong to a growing genre of do-it-yourself publishing that is integral to today's counterculture. Within subcultures that are most alienated and marginalized by conventional society—radical youth, gays and lesbians, political and social nonconformists—you'll find thousands of similar underground publications: homemade, self-published musings known as fanzines, or more often just as 'zines.

Embodying grass-roots democracy, mailbox comradeship, and flagrant freedom of expression, 'zines are a product of the recent communications revolution. Ever since the printing press was invented, independent thinkers have struggled to publish their own alternatives to mainstream viewpoints. Today, anyone with something to say and access to a photocopy machine can publish a 'zine on any topic, no matter how unconventional or obscure.

And they do. It's impossible to know exactly how many 'zines are currently being published, but estimates range into the tens of thousands. For every passion there is at least one 'zine circulating somewhere for like-minded aficionados: Alternative bowling (*Baby Split Bowling News*), urban witchcraft (*Enchanté*), cross dressing (*Girlfriends*), *Twin Peaks* (*Coffee & Donuts*), punk gender issues (*Girl Germs*), and working-class biography (*People's Culture*) are but a few examples.

'Zines are unpredictable and individualistic by definition, but there are certain characteristics that define 'zine publishing as a genre. Most 'zines are produced by one person in his or her spare time, using a pen-and-typewriter, cut-and-paste, photocopy-and-staple method. Most have a rough, crowded, amateur look that can be visually interesting and highly creative. 'Zines are written in a voice that suggests personal correspondence more often than journalism and that cares less about grammar and spelling than it does about honesty and spontaneity. Many 'zines defy a regular schedule, but are published whenever time, energy, and cash allow. And almost all 'zines are distributed free or for the cost of postage—or in exchange for other 'zines—to a readership that numbers from the low thousands to the hundreds and even the teens.

'Zines tend to cover a diverse range of subjects that are usually ignored by (or sometimes unknown to) the mainstream media. Since 'zines are not controlled by advertising, they are free to be as shocking, accusatory, or nasty as they like. According to Mike Gunderloy, a 'zine expert who publishes an authoritative 'zine on 'zines, 'zines often cover controversial topics—HIV as a cause of AIDS and U.S. dealings in the Middle East are two examples—long before the mainstream media. Since they're on the fringes of society, where trends are often conceived, 'zines can be trendsetters themselves. Recycling was a popular 'zine topic years before the mainstream caught on. But there is a flip side to all of this. While 'zines do provide an alternative, they should be viewed as passionately opinionated rather than objective. 'Zines can't always be counted on as a reliable source of information, and many have lost credibility by printing wild conspiracy theories and unresearched stories, Gunderloy explains.

Some of the most quirky 'zines are one-of-a-kind publications that focus on offbeat subjects: *Frostbite Falls Far-Flung Flier* is devoted to the Rocky and Bullwinkle cartoon characters, and *Three Twenty-Seven* is "by and for people born on 3/27." Most 'zines, however, can be classified into loosely defined subgenres that sometimes overlap.

Alternative music, mainly punk music, inspires more 'zines than any other subject. *Ben Is Dead, Breakfast Without Meat,* and *Yoko Only,* a 'zine devoted to Yoko Ono, are just a few of many 'zines in this category. Comics 'zines, such as the popular *Twisted Image,* are often political, but some are sexually explicit at the expense of women. Radical politics is another impetus behind many 'zines. Appropriate to the do-it-yourself 'zine philosophy, anarchist views—promoted by the feisty *Instead of a Magazine* and *Dumpster Times*—are the most popular.

Many frustrated writers and poets turn to 'zines as a vehicle of expression and a way to get published. Talent is variable, but as titles like *Shattered Wig Review* and *Poems Inspired by Poverty and Beer* suggest, these literary 'zines are not exactly out to emulate *The Paris Review*[1]. Feminist 'zines—such as *Not Your Bitch* and *Girl Germs,* two 'zines that question sex roles in male-dominated punk culture, *f/Lip,* a feminist literary 'zine, and *Femzine,* a mini *Ms.* of the micropress—constitute another subgenre of the 'zine community.

Ecology-oriented 'zines such as *The Deep Ecologist* and pagan 'zines such as *Harvest,* which is devoted to urban witchcraft, sometimes overlap. Alternative art, graphics, performance art, and mail art are featured

---

1. *The Paris Review:* Founded in 1953, the *Review* is a highly-respected journal of fiction and poetry.—ED.

in 'zines like *Art Police,* the photography-oriented *Shots,* and the beauti-fully designed *Maximum Traffic.*

Diseased Pariah News, a 'zine for HIV-positive gay men, and *Girl Jock,* 10 "for the athletic lesbian with a political consciousness," are just two of the many 'zines serving the gay and lesbian communities. TV and other types of popular culture also inspire 'zine commentators. Titles like *Pop-ular Life* and *Teenage Gang Debs,* a clever 'zine devoted to *The Brady Bunch* and other seventies television shows, can often interpret mass cul-ture better than any stuffy volume of academic theory.

Violence and dark humor are perhaps the most shocking subjects found in 'zines. *Murder Can Be Fun* (the latest issue focused on "Death at Disneyland"), *Weekly World Noose* (it pokes fun at suicide), and *Skag Rag* (a violent literary 'zine containing poetry about self-cannibalism) are 'zines that have worried some readers.

Science fiction 'zines, which began in the 1940s as the original "fanzines" and from which the current concept of 'zines was derived, keep perhaps the most insular company of any subgenre within the 'zine community. *The Fandom Directory* (Fandata Publications, 1991) de-tails a spectrum of science fiction 'zines and is an excellent resource on fandom, the organized fan groups who worship celebrities like Jack Ker-ouac (*Moody Street Irregulars*), obscure interests and hobbies like poetic lawn care (*Leaves of Grass*), and cult films and television shows such as *Star Trek* (too numerous to mention).

People usually discover 'zines through their association with an al-ternative social group. Queer culture is bursting with 'zines like *Holy Titclamps* and the militant *Bimbox.* The alternative music scene relies on 'zines just as Madison Avenue relies on *Advertising Age.*[2] Fandom cul-tures, including the group that worships Jim Morrison and publishes the 'zine *The Deadly Doorknell: The Organ of the First Church of The Doors,* would be lost without their 'zines.

In the world of 'zines, there are few distinctions between publishers and readers—everyone's an equal member of the 'zine community. Readers contribute most of the 'zines' material by sending passionate and personal letters of comment (known in 'zine lingo as LOCs). 'Zine enthusiasts often form friendships with each other through the mail, and many readers eventually start their own 'zines. Publishers regularly trade 'zines with one another. 'Zines review and encourage readers to send for samples of other 'zines, a circular process that steadily feeds the growth and furthers the reach of amateur publishing.

At the center of the 'zine network is *Factsheet Five,* a publication that 15 has earned an esteemed reputation as the 'zine of all 'zines. Started nine years ago by 'zine connoisseur Mike Gunderloy as a single photocopied sheet intended to inform friends about interesting 'zines, *Factsheet Five*

---

2. *Advertising Age:* Founded in 1930, this weekly trade magazine is a virtual bible for the advertising and marketing industries.—ED.

has evolved into the indispensable bible of the 'zine community. For the uninitiated reader, *Factsheet Five* offers an excellent way to sample 'zine culture and connect with thousands of 'zines. Each issue contains more than one hundred pages of reviews and other news for the underground publishing community.

Gunderloy, who sees more 'zines than probably anyone else in the world, believes that 'zines are a growing phenomenon. In addition to new technology, he cites the conservative climate of the 1980s and people's desire to shape their own lives instead of relying on cultural institutions as major factors in the 'zine boom over the past ten years.

For his booklet "Why Publish" (Pretzel Press, 1989), Gunderloy conducted a series of interviews with dozens of 'zine publishers, who explain their compulsion to publish:

"Well, why NOT publish? Maybe it's the only way, doing it yourself . . . it feels good knowing you have at least a semblance of a voice in the madness out there."

"Because it's fun, and you meet interesting folks, plus you get to say exactly what you want to say."

"To bring relief . . . a small 'zine brings out a new world for people 20 like me to escape to."

Troll, a twenty-year-old from Minneapolis, started the anarchist / punk music / 'zine *Profane Existence* about two years ago. He got into 'zines because he wanted to be a part of the punk music scene but wasn't in a band. Publishing a 'zine seemed another way to contribute to the punk culture. He financed his 'zine with money originally intended for college; he dropped out because he felt he wasn't learning anything. *Profane Existence* has grown quickly and is now considered one of the largest and best of its kind, distributed to about four thousand readers across the United States and even overseas.

Troll is representative of the people most frequently involved in the 'zine scene, according to Gunderloy. The same people who flocked to earlier counterculture movements like the hippies and the Beats— namely young, white, middle-class urban males who are rebelling against both liberal and conservative culture—also dominate 'zine culture. "The 'zine scene isn't real open to other groups," explains Gunderloy. There are few 'zines coming from minority or working-class communities. Gunderloy notes that proportionately fewer women publish 'zines than men, and when they do, they tend to be feminist- or pagan-oriented.

Gunderloy feels that 'zines, even though they're usually published by middle-class white males, can be an important tool in promoting social change. "Even when ['zine publishers] think they're just writing or reading about punk music, kite-flying, the revival of Asatru, or new sculpture, these people are part of a phenomenon," he wrote in *Whole Earth Review* (Fall 1990). "Presented with access to an inexpensive means to say things, people have found things to say, and, better yet, they have discovered that other people will listen."

And in an age when a very small number of corporate conglomerates own the majority of the world's media outlets, 'zines take on an even greater importance. While commercial mass media become increasingly homogenous, 'zines add new alternative views to the publishing spectrum. Along with cable-access video and computer bulletin boards, 'zines are paving the way toward media decentralization, empowering people at the grass-roots level to take media into their own hands.

■ **CONSIDER THE SOURCE**

1. What characteristics does Ouellette say define 'zines as a genre?

2. What do 'zines gain by their freedom from the conventions of mainstream media? What does Ouellette warn is the down side of that freedom?

3. What sorts of readers and writers gravitate toward the 'zine scene, according to Ouellette? What characteristics do the groups that publish 'zines seem to have in common? Why would 'zine culture appeal to such individuals and groups?

4. Why might readers of the *Utne Reader* be particularly interested in Ouellette's article?

■ **CONSIDER THE IMPLICATIONS**

5. In your journal, explore your reactions to the titles of the 'zines Ouellette lists. Did you find them amusing? Offensive? Inscrutable? How do the titles reflect the "alternative" quality of 'zines? How do they attract (or repel) readers?

6. Bring some 'zines to class and examine them in groups. (You might find them at small record stores or bookstores.) What do they look like? What effect does their appearance have on you as a reader? What is the tone of the writing in the 'zines?

7. Write an essay analyzing the relationship between producers and consumers of a particular 'zine. How do the writers address their audience? What influence do readers have on the 'zine's content or tone? How does the overall relationship differ from that in the mainstream media? What factors best explain the differences?

8. Ouellette contends that the 'zine world is dominated by people "on the fringes of society." Make a list on the board of groups that you would therefore expect to be represented in 'zine culture. Compare your list with the groups Ouellette describes. To what extent do they differ? What groups do not seem to participate in 'zine culture? Why?

9. Compare Mike Gunderloy's *Factsheet Five* with *The New York Times Book Review* or *Publishers Weekly*. What functions do these publications serve? How do they differ? (You can find *Factsheet Five* on the World Wide Web at http://www.etext.org:80/Zines/F5/.)

10. Read the essays by Gridley Minima (pp. 419–22) and M. Kadi (pp.

598–608), from the 'zine *h2so4*, paying careful attention to their tone and diction. How do their writing styles differ from that of essays in mainstream magazines, such as Richard Zoglin's piece in *Time* (pp. 97–104) or John Seabrook's article in *The New Yorker* (pp. 609–25)? Write a literary analysis comparing the style of *h2so4* with more traditional publications.

11. Based on Mark Thompson's description (pp. 188–97), would *The Advocate* ever have fit Ouellette's criteria for 'zines? If so, when did it cease to be a 'zine? If not, what distinguished it from a 'zine?

■ ■ ■ ■ ■ ■

GRIDLEY MINIMA

Other People's 'Zines

Since 'zines stand outside the main avenues of our culture, they offer an ideal vantage point for commentary on the dominant culture. Many 'zines parody the format of a conventional magazine as a way of calling attention to the arbitrariness of the features we're accustomed to, such as tables of contents, letters to the editor, and reviews. Consider the 'zine h2so4, *named for sulphuric acid and recently nominated for an Alternative Press Award by the* Utne Reader. *The masthead of a recent issue describes editor Jill Stauffer as "Control Freak" and Halliday Dresser as "Singlehandedly responsible for making No. 4 late." Someone with the pseudonym "Gridley Minima" writes a column that usually carries some variation of the title "Reviews of Books I Haven't Read, and Why I Haven't Read Them." This is hardly the stuff you'd find in the* New York Times. *The following selection by Gridley Minima (b. 1965) ostensibly "reviews" other people's 'zines, but in fact offers a philosophical meditation on 'zine readership. He ponders what makes us fork over cash for a magazine and how that cash transaction colors our perception of the publication. "When he is not traveling," according to his editor, Minima "is based in San Francisco, where he does what he can and writes what he will."*

(Although I'm not entirely sure *h2so4* is a 'zine; it may be too slick and closely reasoned . . . and not sassy enough. Maybe there's some sort of high 'zine tribunal we can appeal to and find out.)

I really wish I would read more of these, actually. I'm completely in favor of what's called the DIY[1] aesthetic (or ethic, really) and always

From *h2so4* 3 (November 1994), pp. 10–11.
1. **DIY**: "Do-it-yourself."—ED.

have been—but like most people who feel strongly about the subject I'm often too busy doing things for myself to get out and examine any of what my revolutionary brothers and sisters are doing for themselves. So you can see that the whole phenomenon highlights an interesting conflict: 'Zines lie on the cusp of two metaphors of communication, that of the letter and that of the stage.

A common criticism one hears of 'zines, and many other marginal cultural productions, including *h2so4*, is that they're "amateurish," the typical statement expressing the critic's response being (with audible quotation marks), "Let's put on a show." Now I probably don't need to remind you (but have I ever let that stop me?) that etymologically, the word "professional" means one who professes to do something (and thus gets paid for it), while an "amateur" is one who loves something (and who does it only for love).

I'll leave you to determine for yourself which of those courses of action is the nobler; all I want to point out is the interesting presupposition being made by one who criticizes a work of art, or communication, because it seems "unprofessional." Obviously one would never refuse delivery of a postcard from a vacationing friend because it was too "amateurish," nor would one ask to be dealt out of an "amateurish" poker game, or complain of an "amateurish" conversation with a neighbor; though in all these cases one might feel "bored," "left out," "uncomfortable," and so on. So at what point does one's critical vocabulary abandon the subjective "I was bored" for the quasi-objective "it was unprofessional"?

I shudder to think that this switch happens precisely when money begins to be involved.

But the conclusion seems hard to avoid. Conversations, correspondences, and card games are all more or less systems of barter; if I stop receiving letters from you, I will eventually stop sending 'em; but the minute you say to me (as JS and HD[2] effectively have said to you) "to get the latest postcard from my trip to Madagascar, send $6 American to my address blah blah," our whole relationship has changed. I no longer need feel obliged to answer your affection with affection, to mull thoughtfully over your thought—I just have to keep signing the checks. And by the same token, I no longer will ask myself, "is this letter (friendship) worth responding to, or is it just too stupid," but instead, "is this letter (friendship?) worth six clams, or is it just too amateurish?"

The funny thing about this is that something can be professional and still be very, very stupid (one need look no further than one's cable TV), and the reverse. So it is not just the vocabulary that has changed. An entirely different system of value has slipped, unnoticed, into play.

I might pick up a copy of (let's just say) *Sassy* magazine, and, while

5

---

2. **JS and HD**: Jill Stauffer and Halliday Dresser plead for subscription money on behalf of the 'zine *h2so4*.—ED.

finding nothing in it that would make *me* want to pay $6 for it, might agree that it is "worth" the $6 in some sort of absolute sense. Now what is this worthiness? Where in the magazine is it hidden? Not, certainly, in the materials; nor, given the ratio of advertising to editorial content, does it seem likely that my $6 is needed to pay the staff. Nor is it any practical usefulness; nobody (let us hope) *needs Sassy* magazine to survive.

No, I'm afraid we're all going to have to admit that the worthiness, the professional sheen that bewitches us into equating things with each other through the medium of funny-smelling green coupons, is a purely arbitrary set of criteria; it is not even the virtuosity with which these acts are performed that makes them professional, it is their presentation, their staging.

So, anyway, 'zines are a sort of hybrid of these classifications, not so much "let's put on a show" as "let's put on a letter to our friends (who we don't even know yet)." *h2so4* would be a 'zine by this definition; although it presents itself as a "literary magazine," with all the trimmings (editor's notes, reviews, poetry, fiction, even a table of contents!), stylistically, it most often refers to the letter (a much older form, both more constrained and, perhaps, organic). Even those sections of the magazine which are not either actual letters, editorial response to them, or discussion about them (like Anne Senhal's marvelous "fiction" in issue 2) reveal their status as crypto-epistles in other ways, by their use of the label "P.S." to announce addenda, by bylines "signed" "love, X," or "your uncle, Y," etc. In fact, the phrase I used above, "our friends, who we don't even know yet," would seem, on a good day, to sum up the editorial policy of this fine if somewhat amateurish magazine.

I guess (since that's the supposed purport of this column) I oughtta say something about why I *don't* read more 'zines, and the reason is simple: I'm overwhelmed. Much like navigating the internet, the primal 'zine scene is one in which you wake up one morning to find your mailbox bursting open, stuffed to the gills with correspondence from an endlessly proliferating "network" (as they say) of friends you've never met, all of whose lives are at least as interesting as your own. But I have a hard enough time dealing with the idiosyncracies of the friends I already *have* met. This one-way-mirror mode of partaking of the lives of folks the world over on the one hand is great; it's essential that people document the quotidian facts of their lives, because that's where poetry, by which I mean truth, lies—but on the other hand, in the realm of that other metaphor for communication, the stage, isn't this just another example of the prescience of the fucked Warholian vision, fifteen minutes of fame for all?[3] Are you people documenting your lives at the expense

10

---

3. **Warholian vision**: Pop artist Andy Warhol (1930?–1987) famously pronounced that in the future everyone would be guaranteed fifteen minutes of fame.—ED.

of living them? Am I consuming this documentation (a 'zine is a product that can be consumed, a life is not) all the expense of living mine? *IS THIS ALL A GOD DAMN SPECTACLE?*

Just wondering.

▪ **CONSIDER THE SOURCE**

1. What differentiates the "amateur" and the "professional," according to Minima?

2. What change does Minima say that money causes in the relationship between writer and reader?

3. Explain what Minima means by the "staging" of a publication. What is the "professional sheen that betwitches us"?

4. How does Minima's essay demonstrate the goals of *h2so4*, as they are described in the appendix (p. 640)?

▪ **CONSIDER THE IMPLICATIONS**

5. List aspects of Minima's prose that resemble a letter. How does his adoption of the letter writer's voice carry out his philosophy about 'zines?

6. In class, discuss the merits and drawbacks of "amateur" and "professional" publications, movies, plays, or concerts. What are the hallmarks of each? How does each appeal to its audience? Do the criteria by which we judge them differ according to whether they are amateur or professional? If so, how?

7. Compare Minima's definition of a 'zine with Laurie Ouellette's (pp. 413–19). What features does each writer emphasize? Why?

8. What hobby or activity have you done recently for the sheer love of it? In your journal, explore how the experience of that activity might change if you were to do it professionally. What would be the advantages and disadvantages of the change in status? How would you expect your performance and attitude to change?

9. Compare the "cultural prejudice" that John P. Dessauer deplores (pp. 372–77) with the bias toward "professionalism" that Minima discusses. Would Dessauer and Minima agree about how written works justify their existence? Write an essay analyzing what gives a book or magazine "value."

CHAPTER

5

WHAT SHOULDN'T YOU READ?

Censorship and the First Amendment

*C*ensorship. What do you envision when you read this word? Piles of books burning in the night? Personal letters defaced with a black marker? The heavy hand of government repression? Censorship didn't always have such ominous connotations. The "censor" in ancient Rome was the person responsible for keeping track of everybody's whereabouts for taxation purposes (performing the "census"). While he was at it, the censor oversaw everyone's morals and behavior to make sure they weren't up to any improprieties or doing or saying anything harmful to the state. This form of governmental control was considered appropriate in a well-governed society. As written material proliferated, the Roman censor's duties soon included inspecting documents to make sure they, too, contained nothing that would upset the social order.

As systematized censorship evolved, it developed two main functions: punishment for bad behavior and thoughts uttered (and later, for ideas written and distributed) and restraint of ideas before they were uttered or published. But what ideas, if any, should the censor suppress? Those that are "immoral, heretical, or offensive, or injurious to the state," according to the *Oxford English Dictionary*. Immoral by whose standards? Offensive to whom? And what constitutes heresy? *Heresy* is now defined as an opinion that runs counter to the established system of belief, and we usually associate it with religious beliefs. The word, however, has its roots in the Greek word for "faction," or "choice." And choice lies at the heart of the modern attitude toward censorship.

To choose, you have to have options. However, rulers have traditionally found that the best way to maintain their power is to suppress competing points of view, to eliminate options. It's pretty easy to put down dissent in an oral society: Just round up dissenters and imprison, torture, or kill them. This effectively stifles their voices, and it usually discourages others from following their examples.

The development of writing made it more difficult to punish dissidents directly, since their words could exist at some distance from their bodies. Nonetheless, it was still possible to eliminate the troubling words even if their author escaped punishment. Books and manuscripts burn quickly. A stray copy of an offending document may survive here or there, but on the whole, it was relatively easy to suppress an offensive work in the days when manuscripts were laboriously copied out by hand.

All that changed with the invention of the printing press. The press's ability to churn out hundreds of identical copies dramatically increased the amount of material that was available for people to read. Suddenly, dissenting ideas could be distributed on an unprecedented scale. Not surprisingly, Gutenberg's revolution also prompted a dramatic increase in systematic efforts to prohibit people from reading.

Now, state-sponsored censorship—even in the interest of a well-run society—wasn't wholly supported by the people. When there were only a few dishes to choose from, it may not have been so bad to be kept from the dinner table, but with a whole new smorgasbord of ideas from which to choose, people hungry for ideas began to resent that restriction. Governments in print-dominated societies throughout Europe found it increasingly difficult to control people's thoughts, so they instead tried to limit the spread of those thoughts. They tightly controlled the printing press, for until the twentieth century printing was the fastest way to spread new ideas. (Chapter 2 presents other key ways to control the spread of ideas: controlling access to printed books and to education.) Presses had to be licensed; paper suppliers and type founders faced strict regulation; books, pamphlets, and newspapers had to obtain the censor's seal of approval (the *imprimatur*—Latin for "let it be printed") before they could be distributed. In fact, repressive governments today still use some of these methods. In the past few years, newspapers in China, Kuwait, Palestine, Guatemala, and Iran have been shut down by government authorities.

MAKING US ALL ALIKE

No matter what the means, all censorship has the same purpose: to suppress objectionable material in speech, print, art, music, or whatever form it comes in. The censor aims to eliminate dissent, to make everybody else agree with "approved" thoughts and values. The censor seeks uniformity, not diversity. Thomas Jefferson questioned whether such uniformity of belief was attainable: "Millions of innocent men, women, and children, since the introduction of Christianity, have been burnt, tortured, fined, imprisoned," he declared, "yet we have not advanced one inch towards uniformity."

Many censors behave as if ideas are contagious. They act as though mere exposure to an idea will lead people to embrace and act on that idea. If certain books serve as the carriers of that contagion, then it is vital to eliminate them completely in order to stamp out any trace of the offensive idea. The censor often justifies his or her activity as a way to protect those who are vulnerable, those who would be harmed by exposure to "bad" ideas or books.

But surely you've read things that you disagree with. Surely you've come across ideas that you have rejected. We constantly use our own judgment to decide which ideas to adopt and which to discard. We choose for ourselves. The censor tries to choose for us. The fiercest battles over the First Amendment often can be reduced to the matter of who should choose what materials we may and may not read.

THE CHURCH, THE STATE, AND THE CENSOR

The earliest censorship proceeded largely on religious and political grounds. Indeed, challenges to the religious hierarchy were often indistinguishable from assaults on the political power structure. And of course, the worst assaults were those that had been printed, those that could infect the whole community.

It's no secret that seventeenth-century astronomer Galileo ran afoul of both religious and political authorities. However, he was punished not for his scientific ideas per se, but for his insistence on printing those ideas and disseminating them. The powerful Roman Catholic Church had adopted Aristotle's view of the earth as the center of the universe and decreed that the heavens were perfect. In 1610, Galileo used the newly invented telescope to observe the moon's irregular craters and seas. Three years later he published an article describing sunspots, which countered the idea of unblemished heavenly bodies. The Church reluctantly allowed him to continue his research unhindered, provided he revealed his arguments slowly so as not to shake people's faith in the Scriptures and, more importantly, in the validity of the Church hierarchy. When Galileo published a 1632 treatise supporting Copernicus's 1514 hypothesis that the earth rotated around the sun, he directly and publicly challenged the entire Aristotelian system. Now he had gone too far. Civil and religious authorities put him under house arrest, where he remained until his death in 1642, a captive forbidden to write or, more importantly, to publish ever again. Even after his death, the Church continued to suppress his treatise, placing it on the Index to Prohibited Books where it stayed until 1835.

Frequently the censor punished not just the person responsible for the ideas, but the books that carried them and even the printing press. Consider the case of Étienne Dolet, a Protestant scholar and printer in sixteenth-century Paris. Dolet's pamphlets and other printed works repeatedly attacked the powerful elite and France's ruling clerics. Efforts to silence him for his views finally succeeded when a line from his translation of Plato was used to prove that he was a "relapsed atheist." Dolet was convicted of being a heretic and sentenced to death. First, he was tortured. Then he was hanged. Finally, his corpse was burned along with his books, as an example to his fellow printers.

IT CAN'T HAPPEN HERE

In the United States we often take for granted the right to freedom of the press, but that freedom was hard won. In Europe printers had been controlled by licensing boards and strict censorship, and those same restrictions were imported when Europeans settled here in the early seventeenth century. In 1639, North America's first printing press was established in Cambridge, Massachusetts; there were about fifty presses in the British colonies by the time of the American Revolution. All operated under some regulation.

Typical of the colonial attitude toward a free press was the declaration of the governor of the Virginia colony in 1671.

> I thank God we have not free schools nor printing; and I hope we shall not have these hundred years. For learning has brought disobedience and heresy, and sects into the world; and printing has divulged them and libels against the government. God keep us from both.

Education was bad because it prompted new ideas, but the printing press was the governor's real villain, since it could "divulge" those ideas and spread them far and wide.

The first step toward freedom of the press in the North American colonies was the 1735 case of John Peter Zenger. Articles in Zenger's newspaper, *The Weekly Journal,* repeatedly attacked the governor of the colony of New York for, among other things, putting all his relatives on the payroll. Zenger was imprisoned for his criticisms and charged with "printing and publishing a false, scandalous, and seditious libel." After eight months in prison, he finally came to trial. His lawyer, Andrew Hamilton, readily admitted that Zenger had printed the offending comments, and he conceded that those comments could be considered seditious, since they could undermine the authority of the governor. However, argued an impassioned Hamilton, the printed statements were true and every free citizen had the right to speak the truth. The jury deliberated only ten minutes before finding Zenger not guilty. The spectators cheered, Zenger was unshackled, and Hamilton was given the key to the city! The John Peter Zenger Freedom of Information Award has been presented annually since 1954 to those who preserve the people's right to know and promote freedom of the press.

Free speech, free press, and the right to complain about the government proved so important to the American revolutionaries in their struggle against Britain that they officially protected those rights in the First Amendment to the United States Constitution.

> Congress shall make no law respecting an establishment of religion, or prohibiting the free exercise thereof; or abridging the freedom of speech, or of the press; or the right of the people peaceably to assemble, and to petition the Government for a redress of grievances.

This portion of the Bill of Rights fundamentally establishes your right to disagree and to make known your dissenting views. Its intent is to protect individual beliefs from being squelched by the government and to keep the majority from silencing minority views.

The First Amendment has not always deterred state-sponsored repression of dissent. Less than a decade after the Constitution was adopted, President John Adams's Federalist party passed a law that forbade criticism of the government by their opponents, Jefferson's Republican-Democratic party. In the years before the Civil War, attempts were made in both the North and the South to stifle the abolitionist press. In this century, laws were passed punishing those who advocated pacifism or socialism. The Supreme Court has repeatedly upheld the government's right to withhold some information from citizens on the basis of "national security." Today's society still bears the mark of Joseph McCarthy's efforts in the 1950s to purge the country of anyone who had ever espoused opinions associated with communism. Religious groups have tried repeatedly to ban the teaching of secular doctrines, such as evolution, that run counter to religious dogma. With their victory in the 1925 Scopes "monkey" trial, they largely kept Charles Darwin's ideas out of school textbooks until the 1960s. Since its founding, then, the United States has been no stranger to political and religious censorship, both of the press and of speech.

DIRTY BOOKS

Political and religious censorship were later joined by censorship on moral grounds. The first obscenity conviction against a bookseller was in 1821, but it wasn't until the end of the nineteenth century that America's moral censors gained a prominent voice in society. When Anthony Comstock founded the New York Society for the Suppression of Vice in 1873, he was on a mission to rid the country of "impure literature." Ally-ing himself with the U.S. Post Office, Comstock persuaded Congress to pass a law banning the mailing of any book that was "obscene, lewd, or lascivious, indecent, filthy, or vile." Acting as a special agent to the post office, Comstock seized thousands of pounds of books—especially works by such European authors as Honoré de Balzac, Gustave Flaubert, and Leo Tolstoy—solely on his own sense of decency and indecency.

Elsewhere across the country, societies modeled after Comstock's sprang up, such as the New England Watch and Ward Society and later the Boston Booksellers Committee. The Boston group set up a review board with a clever method of suppressing books they judged to be obscene. If the board disapproved of a book, booksellers wouldn't sell it, newspapers wouldn't advertise it, and book reviewers wouldn't review it. This embargo on publicity and distribution effectively banned the book, without the committee ever having to challenge the book directly in the courts. Some sixty to seventy titles were banned in Boston by the mid-1920s, but that number increased dramatically by the end of the decade. The committee ultimately banned books by Theodore Dreiser, Ernest Hemingway, Upton Sinclair, John Dos Passos, Sinclair Lewis, and William Faulkner, among others.

The tide turned for the moral censors with the case of Irish author James Joyce's novel *Ulysses*. The book had been banned in 1922 because it contained some erotic passages and plenty of four-letter words. In 1933, Random House publisher Bennett Cerf decided to test the courts once again. He had the book clumsily "smuggled" into the country so that it would be seized by U.S. Customs officials, and the case was brought to trial once more. This time, Judge John M. Woolsey handed down a landmark verdict: *Ulysses* was not obscene, he ruled, for its author was trying to make a legitimate contribution to literature. Joyce, he said, was not writing "dirt for dirt's sake." Most importantly, Woolsey's decision meant that in the future, books must be looked at in their entirety before they could be judged obscene. It was no longer possible to ban a book just by pointing to a few dirty words or a particularly steamy paragraph.

Have you noticed that none of these cases really says what obscenity is? Comstock and his followers defined obscenity as whatever was "dirty" or "impure." But such a vague standard is difficult to enforce. One hundred years after Comstock founded his society, the U.S. Supreme Court attempted to provide some guidelines for what constituted obscenity. In the case known as *Miller vs. California* (1973) the court ruled that a work must meet all three of the following criteria in order to be judged obscene:

1. The average person, applying contemporary community standards, would decide that the work, taken as a whole, predominantly appeals to a prurient interest.

2. The material, taken as a whole, lacks serious literary, artistic, political, or scientific value.

3. The material depicts or describes, in a patently offensive way, sexual conduct specifically defined by the applicable state law.

These criteria, however, still present problems. Do you consider yourself an "average person"? Can you judge "contemporary community standards"? Wouldn't those standards vary depending on the community? Could a book that's a best-seller in New York be judged obscene in Peoria, Illinois? What constitutes "serious" literary value or makes something "patently offensive"?

The same sorts of problems plague the most recent challenge to the First Amendment: censorship on social grounds, sometimes called "political correctness." It's easy to deplore words—whether spoken or printed—that perpetuate traditional forms of discrimination. But how should socially unacceptable speech be dealt with? The Roman censor's punishment of the speaker won't work in contemporary U.S. society. For one thing, our society has no single government-regulated standard for acceptable speech. What's offensive to one person for racial or ethnic reasons may be perfectly fine with another person in another place. Who is to decide what words or images are politically correct? Efforts to regulate spoken language have consistently landed in the courts, where standards for dealing with speech codes are still evolving.

But how about printed materials that offend on social grounds? It's tricky to argue that socially offensive writings should be banned, but that's just what is happening. The battle against racially and ethnically offensive books most often takes place in schools and public libraries—institutions supported by taxpayer dollars and, therefore, susceptible to taxpayers' challenges. Especially vulnerable are books on required reading lists, for they carry the implicit endorsement of the government by way of the local school board and state board of education.

According to People for the American Way, a watchdog group opposing censorship, the books most frequently targeted for removal from schools and public libraries during the decade from 1982 to 1992 were as follows: *Of Mice and Men,* John Steinbeck; *The Catcher in the Rye,* J. D. Salinger; *The Chocolate War,* Robert Cormier; *Adventures of Huckleberry Finn,* Mark Twain; *A Light in the Attic,* Shel Silverstein; *Go Ask Alice,* Anonymous; *Blubber,* Judy Blume; *The Witches,* Roald Dahl; *Ordinary People,* Judith Guest; *Forever,* Judy Blume; *Then Again, Maybe I Won't,* Judy Blume; and *Scary Stories,* Alvin Schwartz. How many of those have you read? Can you guess why each was banned? None came under fire for its political views—a sign that our society tolerates a wide range of political opinions. Instead, they were challenged on moral or religious grounds or for social offenses. As the selections in this chapter show, the boundaries of the First Amendment's protection of free speech and a free press continually shift in response to new challenges.

THE READINGS

The essays in this chapter explore some of the more interesting areas in the realm of censorship. Benjamin Franklin begins by defending himself—and by extension all printers—against disgruntled citizens who disagreed with what he printed. Then we jump 250 years ahead to Erwin Knoll, who provocatively links two recent episodes involving diametrically opposed materials—erotic gay photographs and ads for mercenaries in *Soldier of Fortune* magazine. He warns that regardless of one's attitude toward either type of material, any attempts to repress them constitute threats to freedom of the press. Noting the increased number of book-banning incidents since Ronald Reagan took office, Joan DelFattore surveys the recent rise in religious fundamentalist challenges to books in the public schools. Both DelFattore and William Noble argue that, in their attempts to control the press, conservative and liberal extremists closely resemble one another. Noble introduces us to examples of political correctness, and book banning on social grounds. The most controversial battle has been waged over Mark Twain's *Adventures of Huckleberry Finn*. John H. Wallace advocates banning this example of "racist trash," while high school teacher Dudley Barlow defends the book against charges of racism. Huntly Collins sorts out myth from fact in the mainstream press's treatment of political correctness on college campuses, and she speculates about why the press jumped on this issue (or nonissue) so eagerly. The attempt to protect people from discrimination that lies behind speech codes on campus also seems to be guiding efforts to guarantee equality in other areas of life. Nat Hentoff criticizes these actions when they infringe on First Amendment protection for publishers. After we read Hentoff's scrutiny of Andrea Dworkin and Catharine MacKinnon's recent attempts to define pornography as a civil rights issue, we'll examine MacKinnon's views on pornography and campus speech codes as she discusses them with First Amendment lawyer Floyd Abrams. Finally, we'll follow an online chat among a group of computer hackers who are claiming First Amendment protection in order to defend the free flow of information.

BENJAMIN FRANKLIN

An Apology for Printers

Benjamin Franklin (1707–1790) was first trained as a printer as he described in "A Bookish Inclination" (pp. 29–37); only later did he become a politician. As the following essay shows, however, those two occupations are not widely separated. At age twenty-four, Franklin had owned the Pennsylvania Gazette *for only a year when he came under fire for printing an advertisement that demeaned the clergy. In response to his critics, Franklin published "An Apology for Printers" (1731). His "apology" is not an expression of regret or a request for forgiveness, as we might expect. Rather, he returns to an earlier meaning of apology, the classical "apologia," which was a formal defense or justification. Not only does Franklin defend his actions, he establishes a set of ground rules for the public to use when they think about printers. His argument for circulating all ideas and opinions is intended to placate his opponents even as it makes it virtually impossible to determine which views printed in his paper were held by Franklin. No wonder, then, that he was such an adept statesman.*

Being frequently censur'd and condemn'd by different Persons for printing Things which they say ought not to be printed, I have sometimes thought it might be necessary to make a standing Apology for my self, and publish it once a Year, to be read upon all Occasions of that Nature. Much Business has hitherto hindered the execution of this Design; but having very lately given extraordinary Offence by printing an Advertisement with a certain *N.B.* at the End of it, I find an Apology more particularly requisite at this Juncture, tho' it happens when I have not yet Leisure to write such a thing in the proper Form, and can only in a loose manner throw those Considerations together which should have been the Substance of it.

I request all who are angry with me on the Account of printing things they don't like, calmly to consider these following Particulars

1. That the Opinions of Men are almost as various as their Faces; an Observation general enough to become a common Proverb, *So many Men so many Minds.*

2. That the Business of Printing has chiefly to do with Men's Opinions; most things that are printed tending to promote some, or oppose others.

3. That hence arises the peculiar Unhappiness of that Business, which   5

From *The Papers of Benjamin Franklin*, ed. Leonard Labaree (New Haven & London: Yale University Press, 1959), vol. 1, pp. 194–99; originally published in *The Pennsylvania Gazette*, 1731.

other Callings are no way liable to; they who follow Printing being scarce able to do any thing in their way of getting a Living, which shall not probably give Offence to some, and perhaps to many; whereas the Smith, the Shoemaker, the Carpenter, or the Man of any other Trade, may work indifferently for People of all Persuasions, without offending any of them: and the Merchant may buy and sell with Jews, Turks, Hereticks, and Infidels of all sorts, and get Money by every one of them, without giving Offence to the most orthodox, of any sort; or suffering the least Censure or Ill-will on the Account from any Man whatever.

4. That it is as unreasonable in any one Man or Set of Men to expect to be pleas'd with every thing that is printed, as to think that nobody ought to be pleas'd but themselves.

5. Printers are educated in the Belief, that when Men differ in Opinion, both Sides ought equally to have the Advantage of being heard by the Publick; and that when Truth and Error have fair Play, the former is always an overmatch for the latter: Hence they cheerfully serve all contending Writers that pay them well, without regarding on which side they are of the Question in Dispute.

6. Being thus continually employ'd in serving all Parties, Printers naturally acquire a vast Unconcernedness as to the right or wrong Opinions contain'd in what they print; regarding it only as the Matter of their daily labour: They print things full of Spleen[1] and Animosity, with the utmost Calmness and Indifference, and without the least Ill-will to the Persons reflected on; who nevertheless unjustly think the Printer as much their Enemy as the Author, and join both together in their Resentment.

7. That it is unreasonable to imagine Printers approve of every thing they print, and to censure them on any particular thing accordingly; since in the way of their Business they print such great variety of things opposite and contradictory. It is likewise as unreasonable what some assert, *That Printers ought not to print any Thing but what they approve;* since if all of that Business should make such a Resolution, and abide by it, an End would thereby be put to Free Writing, and the World would afterwards have nothing to read but what happen'd to be the Opinions of Printers.

8. That if all Printers were determin'd not to print any thing till they were sure it would offend no body, there would be very little printed. 10

9. That if they sometimes print vicious or silly things not worth read-

---

1. **Spleen:** In Franklin's day, the spleen was considered the organ that produced ill temper and melancholy in people; hence, the term "spleen" was used to denote ill temper itself.—ED.

ing, it may not be because they approve such things themselves, but because the People are so viciously and corruptly educated that good things are not encouraged. I have known a very numerous Impression of *Robin Hood's Songs* go off in this Province at 2s. [two shillings] per Book, in less than a Twelvemonth; when a small Quantity of *David's Psalms* (an excellent Version) have lain upon my Hands above twice the Time.

10. That notwithstanding what might be urg'd in behalf of a Man's being allow'd to do in the Way of his Business whatever he is paid for, yet Printers do continually discourage the Printing of great Numbers of bad things, and stifle them in the Birth. I my self have constantly refused to print any thing that might countenance Vice, or promote Immorality; tho' by complying in such Cases with the corrupt Taste of the Majority, I might have got much Money. I have also always refus'd to print such things as might do real Injury to any Person, how much soever I have been solicited, and tempted with Offers of great Pay; and how much soever I have by refusing got the Ill-will of those who would have employ'd me. I have heretofore fallen under the Resentment of large Bodies of Men, for refusing absolutely to print any of their Party or Personal Reflections. In this Manner I have made my self many Enemies, and the constant Fatigue of denying is almost insupportable. But the Publick being unacquainted with all this, whenever the poor Printer happens either through Ignorance or much Persuasion, to do any thing that is generally thought worthy of Blame, he meets with no more Friendship or Favour on the above Account, than if there were no Merit in't at all. Thus, as Waller says,[2]

> *Poets loose half the Praise they would have got*
> *Were it but known what they discreetly blot;*

Yet are censur'd for every bad Line found in their Works with the utmost Severity.

I come now to the particular Case of the *N.B.* above-mention'd, about which there has been more Clamour against me, than ever before on any other Account. In the Hurry of other Business an Advertisement was brought to me to be printed; it signified that such a Ship lying at such a Wharff, would sail for Barbadoes in such a Time, and that Freighters and Passengers might agree with the Captain at such a Place; so far is what's common: But at the Bottom this odd Thing was added, N.B. *No Sea Hens nor Black Gowns will be admitted on any Terms.* I printed it, and receiv'd my Money; and the Advertisement was stuck up round the Town as usual. I had not so much Curiosity at that time as to enquire the Meaning of it, nor did I in the least imagine it would give so much

---

2. Edmund **Waller** (1606–1687): English poet and politician.—ED.

Offence. Several good Men are very angry with me on this Occasion; they are pleas'd to say I have too much Sense to do such things ignorantly; that if they were Printers they would not have done such a thing on any Consideration; that it could proceed from nothing but my abundant Malice against Religion and the Clergy: They therefore declare they will not take any more of my Papers, nor have any farther Dealings with me; but will hinder me of all the Custom they can. All this is very hard!

I believe it had been better if I had refused to print the said Advertisement. However, 'tis done and cannot be revok'd. I have only the following few Particulars to offer, some of them in my Behalf, by way of Mitigation, and some not much to the Purpose; but I desire none of them may be read when the Reader is not in a very good Humour.

1. That I really did it without the least Malice, and imagin'd the *N.B.* was plac'd there only to make the Advertisement star'd at, and more generally read.

2. That I never saw the Word *Sea-Hens* before in my Life; nor have I yet ask'd the meaning of it; and tho' I had certainly known that *Black Gowns* in that Place signified the Clergy of the Church of England, yet I have that confidence in the generous good Temper of such of them as I know, as to be well satisfied such a trifling mention of their Habit gives them no Disturbance.

3. That most of the Clergy in this and the neighbouring Provinces, are my Customers, and some of them my very good Friends; and I must be very malicious indeed, or very stupid, to print this thing for a small Profit, if I had thought it would have given them just Cause of Offence.

4. That if I have much Malice against the Clergy, and withal much Sense; 'tis strange I never write or talk against the Clergy my self. Some have observed that 'tis a fruitful Topic, and the easiest to be witty upon of all others. I can print any thing I write at less Charge than others; yet I appeal to the Publick that I am never guilty this way, and to all my Acquaintance as to my Conversation.

5. That if a Man of Sense had Malice enough to desire to injure the Clergy, this is the foolishest Thing he could possibly contrive for that Purpose.

6. That I got Five Shillings by it.

7. That none who are angry with me would have given me so much to let it alone.

8. That if all the People of different Opinions in this Province would engage to give me as much for not printing things they don't like, as I can get by printing them, I should probably live a very easy Life; and if all Printers were every where so dealt by, there would be very little printed.

9. That I am oblig'd to all who take my Paper, and am willing to think they do it out of mere Friendship. I only desire they would think the same when I deal with them. I thank those who leave off, that they have taken it so long. But I beg they would not endeavour to dissuade others, for that will look like Malice.

10. That 'tis impossible any Man should know what he would do if he was a Printer.

11. That notwithstanding the Rashness and Inexperience of Youth, 25 which is most likely to be prevail'd with to do things that ought not to be done; yet I have avoided printing such Things as usually give Offence either to Church or State, more than any Printer that has followed the Business in this Province before.

12. And lastly, That I have printed above a Thousand Advertisements which made not the least mention of *Sea-Hens* or *Black Gowns;* and this being the first Offence, I have the more Reason to expect Forgiveness.

I take leave to conclude with an old Fable, which some of my Readers have heard before, and some have not.

"A certain well-meaning Man and his Son, were travelling towards a Market Town, with an Ass which they had to sell. The Road was bad; and the old Man therefore rid,[3] but the Son went a-foot. The first Passenger they met, asked the Father if he was not ashamed to ride by himself, and suffer the poor Lad to wade along thro' the Mire; this induced him to take up his Son behind him: He had not travelled far, when he met others, who said, they were two unmerciful Lubbers to get both on the Back of that poor Ass, in such a deep Road. Upon this the old Man gets off, and lets his Son ride alone. The next they met called the Lad a graceless, rascally young Jackanapes, to ride in that Manner thro' the Dirt, while his aged Father trudged along on Foot; and they said the old Man was a Fool, for suffering it. He then bid his Son come down, and walk with him, and they travell'd on leading the Ass by the Halter; 'till they met another Company, who called them a Couple of sensless Blockheads, for going both on Foot in such a dirty Way, when they had an empty Ass with them, which they might ride upon. The old Man could bear no longer; My Son, said he, it grieves me much that we cannot please all these People: Let us throw the Ass over the next Bridge, and be no farther troubled with him."

Had the old Man been seen acting this last Resolution, he would probably have been call'd a Fool for troubling himself about the different Opinions of all that were pleas'd to find Fault with him: Therefore, tho' I have a Temper almost as complying as his, I intend not to imitate him in this last Particular. I consider the Variety of Humours among

---

3. **rid:** Archaic past tense of "ride."—ED.

Men, and despair of pleasing every Body; yet I shall not therefore leave off Printing. I shall continue my Business. I shall not burn my Press and melt my Letters.

■ **CONSIDER THE SOURCE**

1. Explain how the proverb "So many men, so many minds" governs the stance Franklin takes in this apology.

2. How does Franklin compare printing with other occupations? What burdens do printers have that others do not?

3. How do market forces affect what gets printed, according to Franklin?

4. In your own words, summarize Franklin's main arguments in defense of printers. How does his tenth point contradict his earlier arguments?

■ **CONSIDER THE IMPLICATIONS**

5. Have you ever been offended by an advertisement printed in a newspaper or magazine? In your journal, describe why you found the ad objectionable and then apply Franklin's arguments in defense of the publication that printed it. Would his arguments persuade you to excuse the printer for printing the ad?

6. In small groups, discuss which points are most persuasive in Franklin's general defense of printers and his specific defense of himself. Which of his arguments is least convincing? Why? How does his humor contribute to his arguments?

7. Compare Franklin's position on the printer's responsibility for what he prints with Erwin Knoll's arguments (pp. 437–40). Would Franklin agree with Knoll in theory? Would Knoll approve of Franklin's practice as a printer?

8. Read or review Joe Tye's essay (pp. 268–73) on cigarette advertising in light of Franklin's views on the printer's responsibilities to the public. Write an essay analyzing the "Chinese Wall" that journalists claim exists between editorial content and advertising. How much separation should there be between the two? To what extent do market forces determine what gets printed?

ERWIN KNOLL

Don't Print That!

Setting books on fire, imprisoning controversial authors, and confiscating printing presses are some direct and effective ways to silence voices we don't agree with. In this brief editorial, Erwin Knoll (1931–1994) points to an indirect form of censorship, one that occurs prior to the publication of material. Knoll looks at two different examples and finds that they amount to much the same thing for publishers: "prior restraint," as it's known in First Amendment circles. In both instances, he argues, someone else has taken away your right to decide for yourself what you want to read. Knoll, editor of the liberal publication The Progressive *from 1973 to 1994, was firmly committed to free speech and nonviolence. In 1979 his magazine tested the country's First Amendment by publishing "The H-Bomb Secret: How We Got It—Why We're Telling It." For six months, the federal government blocked the story, which explained the physics behind the hydrogen bomb, until the courts upheld Knoll's contention that the government's prior restraint violated the First Amendment protection of freedom of the press. After his vociferous opposition to the Persian Gulf War, Knoll became, until his death, a regular commentator on the* MacNeil/Lehrer NewsHour, *a public television program devoted to report and analysis of the news.*

Richard Mohr is a professor of philosophy at the University of Illinois and the author of a book called *Gay Justice*. His new book, *Gay Ideas: Outing and Other Controversies*, is to be published in November [1992] by Beacon Press of Boston. But *Gay Ideas* almost didn't make it into print. Beacon was turned down by twenty-three printers before it found one willing to handle the book.

Beacon has never before run into censorship-by-printer, according to Director Wendy Strothman—even when it defied the Nixon administration by publishing the text of the Pentagon Papers.[1] Strothman is sure that what the printers found objectionable in Mohr's book is a chapter that analyzes erotic gay art. The chapter includes photographs and other illustrations by gay artists, among them the late Robert Mapplethorpe.[2]

From *The Progressive* 56:10 (October 1992), 4.

1. **Pentagon Papers:** A secret report about U.S. involvement in Southeast Asia from 1945 to 1968 that was published by the *New York Times* in 1971. The Supreme Court upheld the paper's right to print the report and thwarted the Nixon administration's attempt to suppress the information for reasons of "national security." —ED.

2. **Robert Mapplethorpe:** Controversial photographer whose depictions of nudity, sadomasochism, and homosexual activity survived court challenges on obscenity charges a year after his death in 1989.—ED.

"This book has been as carefully edited as any book we've ever done," Strothman recently told *Publishers Weekly*. "For printers to be able to overrule our editorial judgment is really quite frightening."

What's frightening is that a printers' veto could, in effect, stifle publication of a serious work of scholarship—or, for that matter, of a frivolous and trivial book. Who's to have the power to decide which is which?

One of the firms that found *Gay Ideas* offensive, Strothman tells me, 5 prints *Penthouse* magazine.

Soldier of Fortune, the monthly magazine for would-be mercenaries and military adventurers of sundry persuasions, has little in common with the serious and scholarly output of Beacon Press. But like Richard Mohr's *Gay Ideas,* the magazine is on the receiving end of disquieting interference with the freedom to publish.

Seven years ago, an issue of *Soldier of Fortune* contained this classified advertisement: "GUN FOR HIRE: 37-year-old professional mercenary desires jobs. Vietnam veteran. Discrete and very private. Bodyguard, courier, and other special skills. All jobs considered."

Ads of that kind appear frequently in *Soldier of Fortune.* (Often they're placed by people who don't much care about such niceties as the spelling of *discreet.*) This ad had tragic results: It led to the contract killing of an Atlanta man whose business associates hired the advertiser to do their dirty work. Two sons of the victim sued the magazine and won a $4.37 million judgment, which was upheld this August by a federal appeals court.

The ruling left us wondering, here at *The Progressive,* how closely we must scrutinize our own classified ads, lest one or another of them leave us liable for unforeseen consequences. The implications for all publishers are broad and, perhaps, incalculable.

Most readers of *Soldier of Fortune,* Is suspect, would be quite indif- 10 ferent to the refusal of twenty-three printers to touch Professor Mohr's *Gay Ideas*—and many might, indeed, applaud this attempt at suppression. And many readers of Beacon Press's solid and responsible works would cheerfully suppress all of *Soldier of Fortune*'s contents—not just its classified ads. I can already visualize the mail from irate readers of *The Progressive* who will demand to know how I can defend such dangerous trash.

The fact is that I detest *Soldier of Fortune* and, as it happens, I don't much care for Robert Mapplethorpe's homoerotic photographs. But I insist on my right to see them, so that I can make up my own mind about what I detest or dislike. And I understand that when Beacon Press finds its right to publish imperiled by narrow-minded printers, or when *Soldier of Fortune* is compelled by a federal court to pay millions of dollars in damages for publishing a classified ad, my rights, too, have been placed in jeopardy.

And yours.

One more item from the censorship front: In Irvine, California, last spring, a teacher assigned her eighth-grade students to read Ray Bradbury's *Fahrenheit 451*, a modern classic about book-burning. Bradbury's story describes a society whose leaders exercise total control by maintaining a monopoly on the flow of information. Firefighters are dispatched to burn down the homes of people guilty of the crime of possessing books.

The copies of *Fahrenheit 451* passed out in Irvine's Venado Middle School had scores of words blacked out—words like *hell* and *damn*. The teacher felt such words didn't belong in the book and weren't essential to the story.

Call the fire department.   15

■ **CONSIDER THE SOURCE**

1. What is Knoll's main argument? Where does his thesis appear?

2. Explain why Knoll believes that his rights and yours have been "placed in jeopardy" by the two cases he describes.

3. Explain the irony in Knoll's example about *Fahrenheit 451*.

4. Why does Knoll mention that one of the printers who refused to print *Gay Ideas* prints *Penthouse* magazine? How does that information contribute to his argument?

■ **CONSIDER THE IMPLICATIONS**

5. Review the court's definition of obscenity (pp. 428–29) and then apply it to Mohr's *Gay Ideas*. In your journal, explore whether the printers could have faced prosecution on obscenity charges, based on what you know from Knoll's description of the book. Find a copy of *Gay Ideas* in your library and read a chapter. Does the book meet any or all of the criteria for obscenity?

6. Knoll implies that magazines should not be held responsible for the content of their ads, nor for any actions that may ensue as a result of those ads. Review Benjamin Franklin's position on not publishing "anything that might countenance vice or promote immorality" (pp. 431–36). Write a letter from Knoll to Franklin, persuading him that readers have the right to decide for themselves what is injurious to the public good. Or, write from Franklin to Knoll, arguing that self-censorship on the part of the press is necessary.

7. Imagine yourself as the publisher of a magazine targeted at high school students. Study the advertisements in mainstream magazines to see

which would be appropriate for your publication and which might be too mature for your readers. In small groups, list criteria you would use to determine which ads to accept and which ones to reject.

8. Compare the Irvine Middle School teacher's "editing" of *Fahrenheit 451* with the opposition to *Huckleberry Finn* described by Dudley Barlow "Why We Still Need *Huckleberry Finn* (pp. 466–72) or the larger objections to school textbooks described by Joan DelFattore (pp. 440–49). Do you think certain words or concepts should be off limits to children? Who should decide when children are ready to handle those words or ideas?

9. After researching published news reports and analysis of the August 1992 appeals court ruling mentioned in Knoll's editorial, hold a class debate on the First Amendment implications of the *Soldier of Fortune* case. Then write an essay arguing your position on whether the appeals court decision threatens the First Amendment protection of the press.

10. Review Gloria Steinem's exposé of advertising practices affecting women's magazines (pp. 277–303). Would Knoll approve of *Ms.* magazine's refusal to accept certain kinds of ads? How would he regard the "complementary copy" requirements of advertisers? Write an analysis of the situation Steinem describes from Knoll's point of view as a fierce opponent of prior restraint.

▪ ▪ ▪ ▪ ▪ ▪
⋯⋯⋯⋯⋯

JOAN DELFATTORE

Romeo and Juliet Were Just Good Friends

One of the hotbeds of censorship is the public schools because they are sup-
ported by taxes and attendance is mandatory. Many people believe that
taxpayers should be allowed to determine the content of their children's ed-
ucation. Joan DelFattore (b. 1946) examines recent attempts by religious
fundamentalists and liberal extremists to mold society to their world view
by influencing the content of school texts. This introductory chapter from
DelFattore's What Johnny Shouldn't Read: Textbook Censorship in
America *(1992) sets forth the problem and defines some of the slippery*
terms frequently encountered in discussions of textbook censorship: fundamentalist, conservative, politically correct. *DelFattore restricts her*
study to elementary and secondary school textbooks. She excludes college
textbooks because, as she says, "college attendance is voluntary and most
college students are legally adults, which makes college instruction less
vulnerable to lawsuits than public education is" (pp. 8–9). Moreover, texts

From *What Johnny Shouldn't Read: Textbook Censorship in America* (New Haven: Yale University Press, 1992), 1–8.

for college courses are usually chosen by individual professors, not by school boards or textbook selection committees, as is the case for elementary and secondary school books. And yet the censorship of ideas at the lower levels affects college-bound students as they prepare for more challenging courses. DelFattore is a professor of English at the University of Delaware. Her book has won awards from the American Library Association Intellectual Freedom Round Table and the American Educational Research Association.

A few years ago, I taught a summer course in literary classics for high school English teachers. When the class began talking about *Romeo and Juliet,* two of the teachers had trouble following what the others were saying. Those two teachers were using high school literature anthologies; the rest of the class had read paperback versions of *Romeo and Juliet.* We compared the high school anthologies with the paperbacks and found more than three hundred lines missing from the play in each anthology. Neither textbook mentioned that its presentation of *Romeo and Juliet* was definitely not Shakespeare's.

In the anthologies, lines containing sexual material—even such mild words as *bosom* and *maidenhood*—were missing. Removing most of the love story shortened *Romeo and Juliet* considerably, but the publishers did not stop there; they also took out material that had nothing to do with sex. Both anthologies, for example, omitted Romeo's lines,

> When the devout religion of mine eye
> Maintains such falsehood, then turn tears to fires;
> And these who, often drown'd, could never die,
> Transparent heretics, be burnt for liars! (I, 2)

I later found that this speech is routinely removed from high school anthologies because it associates religion with falsehood and violence, thus offending people who demand that religion must always be presented favorably.

The realization that publishers can simply drop three hundred lines from a Shakespeare play was startling, and I set out to discover what other material is being deleted from textbooks, why, and by whom. I found excellent books and articles discussing various aspects of textbook censorship from the 1950s through the early 1980s. The work of Lee Burress, James Davis, Kenneth Donelson, Frances FitzGerald, Edward Jenkinson, Nicholas Karolides, Judith Krug, James Moffett, Robert O'Neil, and Diane Shugert was particularly helpful in clarifying the extent and importance of textbook censorship issues.

Along with books and articles, I was also reading newspapers. Throughout the 1980s, one censorship lawsuit after another made front-page headlines. *Mozert vs. Hawkins County Public Schools* was filed by Tennessee parents who maintained that an entire elementary school reading series, including "Cinderella," "Goldilocks," and *The Wizard of Oz*, violated their fundamentalist religious beliefs. More than half a century after the Scopes "monkey trial,"[1] *McLean vs. Arkansas Board of Education* and *Aguillard vs. Edwards* evaluated attempts to promote the teaching of creationism[2] in public schools. In *Smith vs. Board of School Commissioners of Mobile County*, a federal district court ordered the removal of forty-four history, social studies, and home economics textbooks from public school classrooms on the grounds that the books violate the First Amendment by promoting the religion of secular humanism. *Farrell vs. Hall* and *Virgil vs. Columbia County School Board* pitted parents and teachers against school boards that had banned literary classics, such as *Lysistrata, Macbeth,* and *The Autobiography of Benjamin Franklin*.

Behind each court case was a red-hot local controversy fanned by 5 national organizations that eventually funded the lawsuits they had helped to bring about. The dynamics leading up to legal action, the educational agendas of national lobbying groups, and the rulings in the lawsuits all have powerful implications for the future of education in this country. *What Johnny Shouldn't Read*, which is based on court documents, textbook adoption records, and interviews, adds to the ongoing discussion of textbook censorship in twentieth-century America by describing how these lawsuits combined with the textbook adoption process to affect textbooks sold nationwide.

All six of the federal court cases discussed in this book involve attempts by religious fundamentalists to influence the content of public education. The *American College Dictionary* defines fundamentalism as "a movement in American Protestantism which stresses the inerrancy of the Bible not only in matters of faith and morals but also as literal historical record and prophecy." Trying to decide how to use the word *fundamentalist* in a discussion of textbook censorship is, however, more problematic than the dictionary definition suggests. Over the past five years, I have given more than a hundred talks on this subject at public gatherings as well as at professional conferences. That experience has made it clear that the term *fundamentalist* does not, in practice, describe a monolithic belief system. Time after time, audience members have stood up and said something to this effect: "I am a fundamentalist, but I do not agree with what the textbook protesters are doing. I am embarrassed when extremists use the name *fundamentalist* because it makes people think we are all like that." Conversely, others proclaim that they do not

---

1. **Scopes "monkey trial":** Public school teacher John T. Scopes was convicted in 1925 of violating Tennessee law by teaching Charles Darwin's theory of evolution, which was banned in Tennessee until 1967.—ED.

2. **creationism:** Also known as "creation science," creationism rejects the theory of evolution in favor of the Biblical account of the creation of the world.—ED.

consider themselves fundamentalists but do oppose evolution or non-traditional female roles.

A similar dilemma arises with regard to the word *conservative.* Textbook protesters often describe themselves as conservatives, but when George Will and James Kilpatrick[3] write scathing columns condemning a textbook challenge, it is difficult to believe that that challenge represents mainstream conservative thought. Problems also arise when it comes to identifying the locations in which textbook controversies take place. While visiting southern states where court cases and controversial textbook adoption activities had occurred, I often met people who opposed the textbook activists and were irritated that the names of their states were associated with them. The same thing happened in California with regard to textbook protesters who call themselves liberals but represent viewpoints that mainstream liberals consider extreme and that many Californians do not endorse.

It would be inappropriate and unfair to suggest that extremist views, on either the right or the left, are more widespread than they are. On the other hand, it is necessary to call textbook protesters something that reflects what they call themselves and to acknowledge that they live somewhere. Whenever possible, I have specified particular groups, such as the *Smith* plaintiffs or health food lobbyists, rather than saying *the fundamentalists* or *the Californians.* When a more general term is necessary, my use of that term does not imply that everyone who is a fundamentalist, liberal, Texan, Californian, or whatever agrees with the protesters' views.

The reason for focusing on recent federal textbook lawsuits that involve fundamentalist ideology is simple: There is none that does not. In some cases, parents and teachers who describe themselves as fundamentalists initiate lawsuits against a school district for using books that violate their religious beliefs; in others, a school board bans books because of fundamentalist lobbying, whereupon other parents and teachers file suit.

Apart from lawsuits, there are hundreds of incidents every year in 10 which parents or teachers try to convince school boards to include or exclude certain materials. Such controversies are reflected on a wider scale in the textbook adoption process in large states. Challenges initiated by people who identify themselves as fundamentalists not only outnumber the protests of all other groups combined but also involve far more topics. The National Organization for Women (NOW), for example, advocates the depiction of women in nontraditional roles, and the National Association for the Advancement of Colored People (NAACP) lobbies for more favorable presentations of African Americans. One may agree or disagree with the stands taken by NOW and the NAACP, but neither

---

3. **George Will** (b. 1941) and **James Kilpatrick** (b. 1920): Nationally syndicated conservative newspaper columnists and television commentators.—ED.

group is likely to comment on such issues as the age of the earth, the development of language, or the probable domestication of dinosaurs. Fundamentalist textbook activists, on the other hand, lobby for geology and history books that conform to their interpretation of *Genesis* by teaching that the earth is about five thousand years old and that dinosaurs once coexisted with humans Flintstones-style. Their interpretation of the Bible also rejects biological evolution and, by extension, gradual development of any kind, such as the evolution of language over time.

The fundamentalist textbook activists discussed in this book are determined to color the education of all students with their entire world view. Their protests therefore target a wide range of subjects, including personal decision making, imagination, conservation, world unity, tolerance for cultural diversity, religious tolerance, negative portrayals of religion, unflattering depictions of the military or the police, empathy toward animals, antipollution laws, pacifism, socialism, gun control, nontraditional roles for women, minority issues, and evolution.

Because the word *fundamentalist* means different things to different people, it is impossible to tell exactly how many fundamentalists there are in the United States. Estimates generally range from 3 percent to 20 percent of the total population, with a few enthusiasts claiming that more than half of all American citizens are fundamentalists. But even if no more than three Americans out of a hundred are fundamentalists, and some of them do not support all of the textbook protesters' views, they are effective out of all proportion to their numbers because of their intense dedication to what they see as the salvation of American children from political, social, economic, and spiritual ruin. In most local elections, a very small proportion of qualified voters shows up at the polls, and few of them have paid close attention to the candidates for school board seats. Under those conditions, how many determined voters does it take to elect a sympathetic candidate to the school board? It is also important to remember the cardinal rule of any political dynamic: The number of people needed to make a difference is inversely proportionate to their level of expertise at working the system. Saying that a relatively small number of intense activists cannot have much effect on textbooks is like looking at the shape of a bumblebee and saying, "That thing can't possibly get off the ground." Maybe it can't, but it does. Far Right national organizations have become very adept at supporting grass-roots legal challenges and at influencing the state-level textbook adoption process, thus affecting the content of textbooks purchased by school districts and private schools throughout the country.

Textbook protests are nothing new to the United States. As Kenneth Donelson explains in "Obscenity and the Chill Factor," activists of one kind or another have influenced the selection of classroom materials since colonial times. Nevertheless, according to the American Library

Association, challenges to reading materials, including textbooks, have increased dramatically since 1980—the year in which Ronald Reagan was first elected president of the United States. Far Right perspectives are reflected in the vast majority of these challenges, suggesting that the increase in textbook protests is probably related to the overall upswing in ultraconservative activism surrounding the Reagan victory. Moreover, the changing content of textbooks themselves has motivated protesters to proclaim loudly—and accurately—that education is not what it was in the old days. From presenting traditional family, religious, and patriotic themes, textbooks have moved to endorsing multiculturalism, environmentalism, and globalism while discouraging militarism, stereotyping, and unbridled capitalism. The gradual change in textbooks began in the 1960s, but it was not until the 1970s and early 1980s that nationally organized campaigns were mounted against the new books.

In the Dick and Jane readers some of us remember from our childhoods, a family consisted of a married couple, two or three well-behaved children, and a dog and a cat. Father wore suits and went out to work; mother wore aprons and baked cupcakes. Little girls sat demurely watching little boys climb trees. *Home* meant a single-family house in a middle-class suburban neighborhood. Color the lawn green. Color the people white. Family life in the textbook world was idyllic: Parents did not quarrel, children did not disobey, and babies did not throw up on the dog.

With the advent of civil rights and feminism, and with the rise of pollution, overpopulation, drug use, and the threat of nuclear war, the key word in textbooks became *relevance*. People who were not white or middle-class and did not live in traditional nuclear families began to demand representation in textbooks. Textbooks also began to talk about the importance of international understanding and independent thinking in today's complex and troubled world. 15

The new books are deeply disturbing to people who do not want education to describe a changing social order or promote independent decision making. At its extreme, fundamentalist textbook activism is based on the premise that the act of creative thinking is evil in itself, regardless of content, because it might lead to thoughts that are displeasing to God. Pictures of little girls engaging in activities traditionally associated with boys, such as playing with toy cars or petting worms, threaten American family life because girls might grow up craving male roles. Pollution is a humanist myth promoting international cooperation, which could lead to world unity and thus to the reign of the Antichrist, which will signal the end of the world. Conservation is an act of human pride and an offense against God. Humans have no business worrying about the extinction of whales; if God wants whales to exist, they will exist. If not, then preserving them is an act of rebellion against God.

Textbook activism often begins at the grass-roots level, but successful drives to ban or change books require the support of powerful national groups. The Far Right organizations that are most vocal about textbook content are the American Family Association, based in Mississippi and headed by Donald Wildmon; Citizens for Excellence in Education (California, Robert L. Simonds); Concerned Women for America (Washington, D.C., Beverly LaHaye); the Eagle Forum (Illinois, Phyllis Schlafly); Focus on the Family (California, James Dobson); and the National Legal Foundation (Virginia, Pat Robertson). These well-funded, politically sophisticated national organizations supply legal representation for local textbook protesters and support efforts to lobby school boards and state legislatures.

It would be misleading to suggest that all textbook activism—conservative or liberal—is censorship, since decisions about what to teach and what not to teach are a necessary part of every educational system. Some material may be too advanced, academically or socially, for students of a particular age. Besides, human knowledge is cumulative: As scientific discoveries are made, as poems and novels are written, as historic events occur, information previously taught is pushed aside to make room for newer material. The school day has just so many minutes, and the school year has just so many days. For every fact that is put into a textbook, something else is left out. Given that some degree of selectivity is essential to education, advocacy groups will, naturally, try to influence textbook content in directions they consider appropriate. A certain amount of activism is part of the normal functioning of an educational system in a nontotalitarian state; the challenge is to determine the point at which attempts to influence textbook content shade into attempts to censor education.

The verb *to censor* operates according to its own peculiar grammatical rules. It is used almost exclusively in the second or third person: "You are censoring" or "They are censoring." It is almost never used in the first person: "We are censoring." A much more common self-perception is "We are participating in the common-sense selection of material suitable for children and adolescents." In order to make the point that even by the most rigorous definition censorship is occurring in American schools, neither conservatives nor liberals are called censors in this book unless their goal is to obliterate from the store of human knowledge all trace of ideas with which they disagree. By that stringent definition, relatively little of today's textbook activism is actually censorship, but the incidents that do fall under that heading are very serious indeed. Only two major groups thereby qualify as textbook censors: fundamentalists and politically correct extremists.

The changing image of textbooks has aroused liberal advocates who 20 are as dedicated to intensifying the new trend as their opponents are to reversing it. Some liberal protesters call for an increase in the representation of women, minorities, and non-Western cultures in textbooks without specifically targeting anything for removal. It would be naive to suggest that such inclusion does not involve exclusion; given the constraints of textbook space and classroom time, *something* that used to be covered has to be eliminated to make room for the new material. "Inclusionary" liberal textbook activists also tend to encourage the selection of facts that place previously underrepresented groups in the best possible light. By the definition of censorship given above, however, such lobbyists are not censors. Their efforts certainly contribute to the fragmentation of textbooks, but they do not tend toward the systematic elimination of any particular idea or fact.

Somewhere along the continuum of liberal textbook activists, however, "inclusionary" advocates give way to liberal censors. *Battle of the Books,* Lee Burress's study of literary censorship in the schools, describes organizations whose attempts to eliminate racism and sexism from textbooks have become so extreme that they are themselves censoring part of the truth. Since Burress's book was written before the term *politically correct* came into vogue, it is clear that the movement preceded its current label. Regardless of what liberal censors are called, the exact point at which they take over from "inclusionary" liberal activists is difficult to identify because the difference is in degree, not in kind. The noncensor leans toward additional, and favorable, representation of minorities and women. The politically correct censor is determined to eliminate all depictions of women in traditional roles, or every statement that could possibly be construed as disparaging a particular racial, ethnic, or religious group. The accuracy of a statement and the context in which it occurs are dismissed as irrelevant. Politically correct extremists, like their fundamentalist counterparts, operate on the assumption that education has two functions: to describe what should be rather than what is, and to reverse the injustices of yesterday's society by shaping the attitudes of tomorrow's. Balanced portrayals of reality—some women *are* full-time homemakers, while others *do* have careers—get lost in the shuffle.

Taken to its extreme, the term *political correctness* denotes a form of intellectual terrorism in which people who express ideas that are offensive to any group other than white males of western European heritage may be punished, *regardless of the accuracy or relevance of what they say.* Racism, sexism, and other forms of prejudice are abhorrent and cannot be tolerated by any culture that claims to be civilized. Nevertheless, if we were *trying* to perpetuate mutual hostility and suspicion, we could not find a better way to do it than by suppressing honest questions because somebody might not like the answers, or by selecting and altering facts solely to shape opinion. Politically correct censors, like fundamentalist censors, also ignore the broader implications of their activities. By what logic can people defend their own freedom of expression while denying the rights of others to state facts and express beliefs? Once a culture decides that the truth can be suppressed because it is offensive to some, all that remains is a trial of strength to determine whose sensibilities take precedence. In this regard, the only difference between fundamentalist and politically correct extremists lies in the specific truths they wish to promote or suppress; the principles on which they operate are the same.

■ **CONSIDER THE SOURCE**

1. What kind of material was removed from the high school version of *Romeo and Juliet*? Why? According to DelFattore, why do fundamentalist textbook activists object to independent decision making and creative thinking?

2. Explain why DelFattore finds the dictionary definition of *fundamentalist* inadequate for her purposes. How does she resolve the dilemma posed by group labels?

3. What material does DelFattore say "politically correct extremists" wish to eliminate from textbooks? Why?

4. What does DelFattore mean when she says that "the verb *to censor* operates according to its own peculiar grammatical rules"? Why is *to censor* rarely used in the first person? What definition of "censorship" does DelFattore use?

5. What assumptions about the function of education does DelFattore say that fundamentalists and politically correct extremists share? Summarize how those assumptions affect both groups' choices about textbook content.

■ **CONSIDER THE IMPLICATIONS**

6. What do you believe to be the most important function of education? In your journal describe the kinds of materials that you would include in a textbook in order to achieve your educational goals. Write a proposal for such a textbook.

7. Hold a debate in class on how much control parents should have over their children's education. To what extent should public schools be influenced by taxpayers' views? How much independence should educators have to determine the school curriculum?

8. Locate the offices of any of the groups DelFattore identifies on page 446 as "Far Right organizations." Contact one of these groups and obtain information—pamphlets, position papers, flyers—regarding their views on textbook content. How do they articulate their views? Do they present arguments in their favor that DelFattore ignores? Write a paper analyzing the rhetoric on both sides of the question.

9. In your library, research a recent case of bookbanning or a challenge to the use (or presence) of a particular book in the public schools. (You might begin with the books mentioned in the introduction to this chapter, p. 429.) Write a paper in which you summarize the arguments on both sides, and then analyze the implications of the case.

10. Compare Gloria Steinem's efforts to get nonsexist ads for *Ms.* magazine (pp. 277–303) with DelFattore's description of how the "politically correct censor" operates. Discuss how textbooks and magazines differ in their portrayals of women. Which do you think is more "balanced"?

11. Contact your local school district and find out what books are required reading for high school students. Familiarize yourself with the books by skimming those you haven't read. Then write an essay defending or criticizing the reading list.

12. Read or review John Wallace's essay on why *Huckleberry Finn* should be banned from the classroom (pp. 457–66). Analyze Wallace's arguments from DelFattore's point of view. Adopting DelFattore's position, write a letter to Wallace explaining why the book should not be banned. Or, write a letter from Wallace explaining to DelFattore that the book's harm overrides her concerns about censorship.

■ ■ ■ ■ ■ ■

WILLIAM NOBLE

The Newest Bookbanners

Traditional censorship for religious, political, or moral reasons has historically come from the ranks of conservatives, who have a stake in maintaining the status quo. In this essay, William Noble (b. 1932) discusses censorship on the basis of social concerns, a new type of censorship that has emerged in the last few decades in the United States. Noble analyzes challenges to freedom of expression coming from liberals dedicated to social change. Attacks from this quarter often focus on banishing ethnic or racial stereotypes, a goal that many of us would certainly applaud. But as we will see in the case of feminism and pornography, not every member of the victimized group agrees with the method being used for its protection. William Noble was a practicing attorney in Pennsylvania before he moved to Vermont to become a full-time writer. In addition to Bookbanning in America: Who Bans Books?—And Why *(1990), from which this chapter is taken, he's written several books for writers, including* "Shut Up!" He Explained *(1987) and* Conflict, Action, and Suspense *(1994), a guide for fiction writers.*

When he wrote *The Adventures of Huckleberry Finn* in 1885, Mark Twain knew he would be tweaking Victorian morality. His characters

From *Bookbanning in America: Who Bans Books?—And Why* (Middlebury, VT: Paul S. Eriksson, 1990), 268–81.

and situations repelled a conventional work ethic and wisdom gained through formal education. His heroes were not high born, yet they tantalized with their sense of adventure and their underdog role in a life harsher than most readers could know.

Many were attractive rogues and criminals, often speaking with fractured syntax and in street vernacular; others—particularly the runaway slave, Jim—spoke in crude misstatement but offered insights and judgments both accurate and humorous. Mark Twain knew his characters would offend because he understood the conventional morality that would judge his book.

But, of course, he had made a career of poking fun at that morality, so he never really hesitated to write the book. And when the Concord, Massachusetts, Public Library banned his book shortly after its publication, he was not surprised.

That was more than one hundred years ago, and conventional morality has certainly changed; so much so, in fact, that what the blue-nosed set in Concord found objectionable in 1885 would cause nary a stir today. The troika of bookbanning categories—political, religious, sexual—that has blanketed the field for so long would find no home for *The Adventures of Huckleberry Finn*.

But the book continues to be banned. In fact, since the late 1950s it 5 has been condemned in a number of states and by a number of organizations. The reason is not one Mark Twain could have imagined.

To some, *The Adventures of Huckleberry Finn* is racist.

The first inklings came in New York City. In 1957, the National Association for the Advancement of Colored People [NAACP] brought pressure on a local high school to remove the book from its shelves. To those who sought answers from past bannings of the book, this challenge was unforeseen. For almost three-quarters of a century (and in this time the book had reached that zenith of literary longevity—the "classic") no one had muttered an objection like this.

Black author Ralph Ellison helped to explain: "Jim's friendship with Huck comes across as that of a boy for another boy rather than as the friendship of an adult for a junior; thus there is implicit in it not only a violation of the manners sanctioned for relations between Negroes and whites, there is a violation of our conception of adult maleness. . . ."

In short, *The Adventures of Huckleberry Finn* demeaned the stature of a black man, portrayed as something less than he actually was. This was racism because only the black man was singled out for this treatment and because the effect was to force the reader to lose respect for the character, not because of what he said or did, but because of his skin color.

This was a new approach to bookbanning. Usually, challenges to 10 books galvanized from the Right where established ideas and doctrines had girded to fight off change-provoking threats. From the sputterings of the colonial government in John Peter Zenger's 1734 case[1] to the shouts of obscenity in Boston in the 1920s to the accusations of secular humanism in 1987 Alabama, the bookbanner had seemed to materialize from the conservative side of a controversy.

Now all of a sudden the bookbanner came from a different direction. The NAACP, and other groups which had joined them, were not mired in stereotypical value judgments. They desired change; in fact they were beginning to *insist* on change. They did not have an established political base to protect, nor were they concerned with the religious or sexual aspects of the book. They saw it in altogether different terms: As a slur upon their sense of being, and in this regard no conservative bookbanner could find quite so emphatic a likeness. Banning a book because it offends one's sensibilities is strong enough; but banning a book because it slurs one's very nature is something else again.

And so the people who thrive on categorizing things began to sift through this new bookbanning sortee. In the meantime *The Adventures of Huckleberry Finn* continued to be attacked, every year or two bringing a fresh challenge because of its perceived racist cast. And sometimes the attacks succeeded: In 1984, for example, the book was removed from a public high school reading list in Waukegan, Illinois, because a black alderman found the language offensive. By this time it was clear bookbanning was no longer the purview of the conservative right; those who sought equality and freedom from discrimination also felt the urge to bookban.

And from the categorizers came the word: A new bookbanning category was born.

Social issues, they called it.

And now there were four.   15

This one is less definable than the others, mainly because its victims pass across the behavioral and cultural spectrum. Its broader reach makes it more encompassing. Look at the trials of Raymond English who worked with an educational research organization some years ago as a writer for social science textbooks. As a political science professor he had publicly bemoaned the political ignorance of college freshmen, and he thought the problem lay in what these freshmen had been exposed to earlier in their academic lives. They had been reared on pap; they had not been forced to take a stand; they had absorbed light-hitting accounts which avoided controversy and offense. He wanted to change all that.

He and several others began work on a world history text, and for awhile things seemed to go well. They had their problems with religious depiction, at first, because of objections to differing accounts of the Re-

---

1. For a discussion of the Zenger case, see pp. 426–27.—ED.

formation (the Catholics and Lutherans saw it one way, the Baptists another) but it seemed to work itself out. A little later there was a problem with political portrayals because the conservative right objected to certain economic designations (such as calling the United States a "mixed economy" and mentioning farm supports with some favor). But these objections, too, were worked out.

Then, in the 1970s Raymond English came face to face with a different, less malleable set of objections. Work on the history textbooks had continued, and suddenly there were new confrontations. First it was the Filipinos who objected to the account of the annexation of the Philippines at the end of the nineteenth century.

This must be rewritten, they demanded. You must show that the sugar interests in the United States controlled President McKinley and insisted he take over the islands in order to thwart the growing independence movement. It was not the product of imperialistic rivalries, as you suggest, they said.

No sooner did Raymond English and the other writers catch their 20 breath, than it was the Zionists who came after them. You must change the text concerning the ethnic make-up of Palestine before 1947, they said. It was not predominantly Arab as you write (even though reliable statistics would have had it so). Better you remove any reference to population levels before 1947.

Then, before long, came still another complaint—this time from a state committee on ethnic and sex discrimination. You are wrong in your account of the rise of feminism, they declared. It did not begin in the 1860s and '70s with certain economic and technological advances (such as ready-made clothes and bulk canned food). It was not the fact that industrialization had made it easier for them to work outside the home. Instead, it was women's "character and self-assertion" that brought about their emancipation.

Finally, Raymond English and his group heard from a Japanese American critic who objected to the portrayal of the Japanese American in the history textbook. English had written that on a proportionate basis, there were more Japanese Americans than any other ethnic group in executive and professional positions. Take this out! demanded the critic. It must come out!

But why? asked Raymond English.

"It reinforces the myth of success," came the answer. For this Japanese American, at least, it was more important to remain modest and self-effacing, and he was willing to do it, even if it meant twisting the words in the text.

In these examples of "social issues" there are no political, religious, or 25 sexual overtones, but there certainly are sensibilities that appear offended. This is clearly a product of the last third of the twentieth century. People who find offense in the books they read grasp a ready outlet in bookbanning. Better to ban the book, they say, than to propagate the poison.

But, of course, the same argument was used in the 1920s in Boston and New York when obscenity was the dragon, and in the 1950s when communism was the monster and loyalty oaths were in flower, and throughout recorded history when orthodox religion faced the heretics. It is not enough to feel offense and simply turn away; one must act to save others. Here is where bookbanners on the left have joined bookbanners on the right in lockstep. Bookbanning becomes the only acceptable remedy. . . .

Since the middle 1960s various groups and philosophies have grown more assertive as they have seen others acquire respectability, even deference, in the literary marketplace. It isn't only African Americans, or American Indians or Jews who have spoken out about their portrayals in books and films; it is the elderly who now complain about age-discrimination; the homosexuals who complain about antigay writing; the poor who complain about the "welfare" stereotype. The category may be new, but that doesn't change the remedy. Parents who are offended by sexually explicit materials in the schools seek the same thing as do gay men who see themselves victims of "gay-bashing."

Ban that book!

Initial reactions might seem most appropriate, at first. If a book treats us unfairly, if it denigrates us or demeans us because of our race, color, nationality, sex, age, or sexual preference, there would seem little reason it should occupy shelf space. It is deeply offensive, and it serves no purpose other than to perpetuate long-held prejudices. Out it must go.

But . . . is there any more justification for censoring books than for censoring what offends us in the sexual or religious or political areas? The social-issues category may have developed a new area of potential harm and injury, but censorship, even though it might solve an immediate problem, may not be the answer.

No better arena for judging this exists than with feminism. As with other victims of discrimination, women have long pointed to certain books and authors as having treated them unfairly, unequally, and with conscious disdain. It was only in 1964, with passage of the Civil Rights Act, that "sex" discrimination was declared illegal. It was a breakthrough on the federal level that enabled women to assert their right to equal treatment and equal opportunity, and it spurred an already burgeoning feminist movement. It blossomed just as the barriers to literary censorship seemed to come tumbling down, with decisions involving *Lady Chatterley's Lover, Memoirs of a Woman of Pleasure,* and *Tropic of Cancer* finally opening the door.[2] We should be able to write whatever we want, and we should be able to *do* whatever we want. No discrimination, no censorship.

---

2. D. H. Lawrence's *Lady Chatterley's Lover* (1928), John Cleland's *Memoirs of a Woman of Pleasure* (1748), and Henry Miller's *Tropic of Cancer* (1934) survived challenges on obscenity charges in the 1960s.—ED.

The problem was that these two freedoms seemed to go together, but actually, they didn't. There came a time when they headed right at one another, becoming adversaries.

The culprit was pornography, or more particularly, *sexually explicit material which subordinates women*. Feminists saw themselves as victims of this type of writing, and some could imagine no more appropriate solution than to have pornography banned.

Pornography *demeans us, it insults us, it puts us in an inferior position*. To certain feminists it violated women's civil rights because it perpetuated sex discrimination.

And *that* was a violation of the law.   35

Leading the fight were the radical feminists, and heading the charge were writer Andrea Dworkin and lawyer Catharine MacKinnon. Dworkin, a novelist, political pamphleteer, and harshly critical essayist, believed that pornography created "bigotry and hostility and aggression toward all women," and that it only served to confirm the fact that "[t]he hurting of women is . . . basic to the sexual pleasure of men." For her the idea of using the obscenity laws to ban pornography could never work because the "community standards" yardstick also includes ubiquitous sentiments approving violence against women. Instead, pornography had to be recognized as a pernicious form of sex discrimination . . . and then it could be controlled by the civil rights laws.

And the only effective remedy she saw was for the civil rights laws to ban pornography altogether, as they did racism.

Dworkin and MacKinnon drafted a model ordinance and proposed it to city councils in Minneapolis and Indianapolis and Bellingham, Washington. The legislation would have allowed a woman who believed herself victimized by pornography to sue bookstore owners for civil damages, and, of course, to have the offending books removed from the shelves. It was not a complicated ordinance:

> Pornography is the sexually explicit subordination of women, graphically depicted whether in pictures or words.

It then listed nine separate situations where this might happen, including when:

> Women are presented as dehumanized sexual objects, things, or commodities.

The ordinance specifically stated that even if a woman had given   40
her consent to this depiction it was no defense. It was irrelevant because consent under these circumstances is a sham. The male had total control and power.

These were hard-hitting proposals, but Dworkin and MacKinnon almost succeeded. In Minneapolis the legislation passed twice, only to be vetoed by the mayor; in Indianapolis, it was passed and signed, only to be challenged and overturned in court; in Bellingham, Washington, it had added support from writers Susan Brownmiller and Gloria Steinem,[3] but a court proceeding brought everything to a halt.

A troubling question surfaced early: Did Dworkin and MacKinnon speak for the feminist movement when they urged banning of pornographic material? The answer came quickly, and it was a resounding NO! Feminists, generally, had little use for books and stories which extolled violence, and they were quick to criticize material which tended to dehumanize women and to turn them into sex objects.

But ban such books and stories? For many feminists the cure was worse than the disease. As one feminist newsletter stated: "These [banning] laws can be used to attack and limit feminist self-expression, including women's writing about sexuality, abortion, birth control and medical self-help. Once these laws are on the books, feminists have minimal control over their interpretation and enforcement by the courts."

To these anti-bookbanning feminists the question of what really constituted "pornography" was unsettling because of its vagueness. If "sexually explicit" was used as a standard, then there were bound to be those who saw this as simple erotica and not pornography; if "sexual submission or subordination" was used, then some would see submission or subordination where others didn't, and some might even see the woman in control. Uncertainty like this could have only one result: Bookbanning was not the answer.

But the voices of censorship in the feminist movement are not 45 stilled, and there remains a wellspring of feeling that pornography is best done away with completely, that its degradation of women has canceled its right to protection under the First Amendment's guarantees of free expression. As a social issue in the realm of bookbanning, it will not go away. But for the moment, anyway, feminists who seek to continue the bookbanning battle will have to contend with the forceful logic of Federal Judge Sarah Barker who overturned the Indianapolis ordinance, after it had been passed and signed into law:

> To deny free speech in order to engineer social change in the name of accomplishing a greater good for one sector of our society erodes the freedoms of all and, as such, threatens tyranny and injustice for those subjected to the rule of such laws.

▪ CONSIDER THE SOURCE

1. How does the social category of bookbanning differ from the religious, political, or sexual categories, according to Noble?

2. Summarize the reasons some people find *Adventures of Huckleberry Finn* a

---

3. **Susan Brownmiller** (b. 1935): Author of *Against Our Will: Men, Women, and Rape* (1975); **Gloria Steinem** (b. 1934) Founding editor of *Ms.* magazine. Both women have been leaders in the feminist movement since the 1970s.—ED.

racist book, according to Noble. What other examples does Noble offer of "social" objections to texts?

3. In your own words, explain how the fight against pornography pits the First Amendment's protection of free speech against the Civil Rights Act's guarantee of freedom from discrimination.

■ **CONSIDER THE IMPLICATIONS**

4. How would Joan DelFattore (pp. 440–49) explain the challenges to Raymond English's history textbook that Noble describes? Discuss how these challenges demonstrate the philosophy of education DelFattore attributes to extremists from both ends of the political spectrum.

5. Noble says that people often turn to bookbanning in order to protect others from the "poison" of unacceptable ideas. In a journal entry, explore this notion of ideas as poison. How does the poison spread? What might be the antidotes to such poison? Can you think of a better image to describe objectionable ideas?

6. In small groups, imagine you are preparing a new history textbook. Read or review Malcolm X's discussion of how history has been "whitened" ("A Homemade Education," pp. 164–72). Keeping in mind Noble's and DelFattore's discussions of textbook censorship, discuss how you would accommodate his objections.

7. Review the criteria for obscenity established in *Miller vs. California* (p. 428). Then hold a class debate on Andrea Dworkin's contention that the reliance on "community standards" renders obscenity laws inadequate to protect women against pornography.

8. Dworkin and MacKinnon argue that pornography is so degrading to women that it forfeits its right to First Amendment protection. Research news reports about racist pamphlets, antisemitic writings, gay-bashing texts, or any other publications targeted against a particular group of people. Based on your research—or, if possible, actual copies of such writings—write an essay in which you apply Dworkin's argument to that class of publications. Have they crossed the line that Dworkin and MacKinnon seem to describe? Or do they still deserve First Amendment protection?

9. Read the essays on *Huckleberry Finn* by John H. Wallace (pp. 457–66) and Dudley Barlow (pp. 466–72) and compare their arguments to Noble's. In class, stage a debate among the three writers on the question of what role literature should play in the classroom.

John H. Wallace

The Case against Huck Finn

One of the most strenuous opponents to including Mark Twain's 1885 novel Adventures of Huckleberry Finn *in the public school curriculum is John H. Wallace. Wallace was an official at Mark Twain Intermediate School in Virginia when he sued to have the book removed from the classroom. Wallace, now a consultant for the Chicago public schools, contends that the book is "racist trash" and owes its status as an American literary classic precisely to its racist ideology. His essay originally appeared in a collection of essays by African American critics and scholars,* Satire or Evasion? Black Perspectives on Huckleberry Finn *(1992). As the editors of that anthology note, "Wallace's analyses of various episodes differ noticeably from most critical evaluations, including those of other contributors to this volume, by emphasizing the literal content of passages without recourse to the irony usually seen as crucial to Twain's intention" (p. 14). Whether or not you've read* Huck Finn, *Wallace's essay raises once more the questions of who should judge what others may or may not read and on what basis those judgments should be made.*

THE ISSUE

The *Adventures of Huckleberry Finn,* by Mark Twain, is the most grotesque example of racist trash ever written. During the 1981–1982 school year, the media carried reports that it was challenged in Davenport, Iowa; Houston, Texas; Bucks County, Pennsylvania; and, of all places, Mark Twain Intermediate School in Fairfax County, Virginia. Parents in Waukegan, Illinois, in 1983 and in Springfield, Illinois, in 1984 asked that the book be removed from the classroom—and there are many challenges to this book that go unnoticed by the press. All of these are coming from black parents and teachers after complaints from their children or students, and frequently they are supported by white teachers, as in the case of Mark Twain Intermediate School.

For the past forty years, black families have trekked to schools in numerous districts throughout the country to say, "This book is not good for our children," only to be turned away by insensitive and often unwittingly racist teachers and administrators who respond, "This book is a classic." Classic or not, it should not be allowed to continue to cause our children embarrassment about their heritage.

From *Satire or Evasion? Black Perspectives on* Huckleberry Finn, ed. James S. Leonard, Thomas A. Tenney, and Thadious M. Davis (Durham, N.C.: Duke University Press, 1992), pp. 16–24.

Louisa May Alcott, the Concord Public Library, and others condemned the book as trash when it was published in 1885. The NAACP [National Association for the Advancement of Colored People] and the National Urban League successfully collaborated to have *Huckleberry Finn* removed from the classrooms of the public schools of New York City in 1957 because it uses the term "nigger." In 1969 Miami-Dade Junior College removed the book from its classrooms because the administration believed that the book creates an emotional block for black students which inhibits learning. It was excluded from the classrooms of the New Trier High School in Winnetka, Illinois, and removed from the required reading list in the state of Illinois in 1976.

My own research indicates that the assignment and reading aloud of *Huckleberry Finn* in our classrooms is humiliating and insulting to black students. It contributes to their feelings of low self-esteem and to the white students' disrespect for black people. It constitutes mental cruelty, harassment, and outright racial intimidation to force black students to sit in the classroom with their white peers and read *Huckleberry Finn*. The attitudes developed by the reading of such literature can lead to tensions, discontent, and even fighting. If this book is removed from the required reading lists of our schools, there should be improved student-to-student, student-to-teacher, and teacher-to-teacher relationships.

"Nigger"

According to *Webster's Dictionary,* the word "nigger" means a Negro   5
or a member of any dark-skinned race of people and is *offensive.* Black people have never accepted "nigger" as a proper term—not in George Washington's time, Mark Twain's time, or William Faulkner's time. A few white authors, thriving on making blacks objects of ridicule and scorn by having blacks use this word as they, the white authors, were writing and speaking for blacks in a dialect they perceived to be peculiar to black people, may have given the impression that blacks accepted the term. Nothing could be further from the truth.

Some black authors have used "nigger," but not in literature to be consumed by children in the classroom. Black authors know as well as whites that there is money to be made selling books that ridicule black people. As a matter of fact, the white child learns early in life that his or her black peer makes a good butt for a joke. Much of what goes on in the classroom reinforces this behavior. Often the last word uttered before a fight is "nigger." Educators must discourage the ridicule of "different" children.

IN THE CLASSROOM

Russell Baker, of the *New York Times* (14 April 1982), has said (and Jonathan Yardley, of the *Washington Post* [10 May 1982], concurred),

> Kids are often exposed to books long before they are ready for them or exposed to them in a manner that seems almost calculated to evaporate whatever enthusiasm the students may bring to them. . . . Very few youngsters of high school age are ready for *Huckleberry Finn.* Leaving aside its subtle depiction of racial attitudes and its complex view of American society, the book is written in a language that will seem baroque, obscure and antiquated to many young people today. The vastly sunnier *Tom Sawyer* is a book for kids, but *Huckleberry Finn most emphatically is not.*

The milieu of the classroom is highly charged with emotions. There are twenty to thirty unique personalities with hundreds of needs to be met simultaneously. Each student wants to be accepted and to be like the white, middle-class child whom he perceives to be favored by the teacher. Since students do not want their differences highlighted, it is best to accentuate their similarities; but the reading of *Huck Finn* in class accentuates the one difference that is always apparent—color.

My research suggests that the black child is offended by the use of the word "nigger" anywhere, no matter what rationale the teacher may use to justify it. If the teacher permits its use, the black child tends to reject the teacher because the student is confident that the teacher is prejudiced. Communications are effectively severed, thwarting the child's education. Pejorative terms should not be granted any legitimacy by their use in the classroom under the guise of teaching books of great literary merit, nor for any other reason.

EQUAL PROTECTION AND OPPORTUNITY IN THE CLASSROOM

To paraphrase Irwin Katz,[1] the use of the word "nigger" by a prestigious adult like a teacher poses a strong *social* threat to the black child. Any expression by a white or black teacher of dislike or devaluation, whether through harsh, indifferent, or patronizing behavior, would tend to have an unfavorable effect on the performance of black children in their school work. This is so because *various psychological theories suggest that the black students' covert reactions to the social threat would constitute an important source of intellectual impairment.*

Dorothy Gilliam, writing in the *Washington Post* of 12 April 1982,

---

1. Martin Deutsch, Irwin Katz, and Arthur R. Jensen, *Social Class, Race, and Psychological Development* (New York: Holt, Rinehart, and Winston, 1968), pp. 256–57.

said, "First Amendment rights are crucial to a healthy society. No less crucial is the Fourteenth Amendment and its guarantee of equal protection under the law." *The use of the word "nigger" in the classroom does not provide black students with equal protection and is in violation of their constitutional rights. Without equal protection, they have neither equal access nor equal opportunity for an education.*

One group of citizens deeply committed to effecting change and to retaining certain religious beliefs sacred to themselves are members of the Jewish religion. In a publication issued by the Jewish Community Council (November 1981), the following guidelines were enunciated regarding the role of religious practices in public schools: "In no event should any student, teacher, or public school staff member feel that his or her own beliefs or practices are being questioned, infringed upon, or compromised by programs taking place in or sponsored by the public school." Further, "schools should avoid practices which operate to single out and isolate 'different' pupils and thereby [cause] embarrassment."[2]

I endorse these statements without reservation, for I believe the rationale of the Jewish Community Council is consistent with my position. I find it incongruent to contend that it is fitting and proper to shelter children from isolation, embarrassment, and ridicule due to their religious beliefs and then deny the same protection to other children because of the color of their skin. The basic issue is the same. It is our purpose to spare children from scorn, to increase personal pride, and to foster the American belief of acceptance on merit, not color, sex, religion, or origin.

THE TEACHER

Many "authorities" say *Huckleberry Finn* can be used in our intermediate and high school classrooms. They consistently put stipulations on its use like the following: It must be used with appropriate planning. It is the responsibility of the teacher to assist students in the understanding of the historical setting of the novel, the characters being depicted, the social context, including prejudice, which existed at the time depicted in the book. Balanced judgment on the part of the classroom teacher must be used prior to making a decision to utilize this book in an intermediate or high school program. Such judgment would include taking into account the age and maturity of the students, their ability to comprehend abstract concepts, and the methodology of presentation.

Any material that requires such conditions could be dangerous 15 racist propaganda in the hands of even our best teachers. And "some,

---

2. Jewish Community Council of Greater Washington, *Guidelines on Religion and the Public School* (Washington, D.C., 1981).

not all, teachers are hostile, racist, vindictive, inept, or even neurotic," though "many are compassionate and skillful."[3] Teacher attitudes are important to students. Some teachers are marginal at best, yet many school administrators are willing to trust them with a book that maligns blacks. *Huckleberry Finn* would have been out of the classroom ages ago if it used "dago," "wop," or "spic."

When "authorities" mention the "historical setting" of *Huckleberry Finn*, they suggest that it is an accurate, factual portrayal of the way things were in slavery days. In fact, the book is the outgrowth of Mark Twain's memory and imagination, written twenty years after the end of slavery. Of the two main characters depicted, one is a thief, a liar, a sacrilegious corn-cob-pipe-smoking truant; the other is a self-deprecating slave. No one would want his children to emulate this pair. Yet some "authorities" speak of Huck as a boyhood hero. Twain warns us in the beginning of *Huckleberry Finn*, "Persons attempting to find a motive in this narrative will be prosecuted; persons attempting to find a moral in it will be banished; persons attempting to find a plot in it will be shot." I think we ought to listen to Twain and stop feeding this trash to our children. It does absolutely nothing to enhance racial harmony. The prejudice that existed then is still very much apparent today. Racism against blacks is deeply rooted in the American culture and is continually reinforced by the schools, by concern for socioeconomic gain, and by the vicarious ego enhancement it brings to those who manifest it.

Huckleberry Finn is racist, whether its author intended it to be or not. The book implies that black people are not honest. For example, Huck says about Jim: "It most froze me to hear such talk. He wouldn't ever dared to talk such talk in his life before. Just see what a difference it made in him the minute he judged he was about free. It was according to the old saying, 'give a nigger an inch and he'll take an ell.' Thinks I, this is what comes of my not thinking" (chap. 16). And in another section of the book, the Duke, in reply to a question from the King, says: "Mary Jane'll be in mourning from this out; and the first you know the nigger that does up the rooms will get an order to box these duds up and put 'em away; and do you reckon a nigger can run across money and not borrow some of it?" (chap. 26).

Huckleberry Finn also insinuates that black people are less intelligent than whites. In a passage where Huck and Tom are trying to get the chains off Jim, Tom says: "They couldn't get the chain off, so they just cut their hand off and shoved. And a leg would be better still. But we got to let that go. There ain't necessity enough in this case; and, besides, Jim's a nigger, and wouldn't understand the reason for it" (chap. 35). On another occasion, when Tom and Huck are making plans to get Jim out of the barn where he is held captive, Huck says: "He told him every-

---

3. Robert D. Strom, *The Innercity Classroom* (Columbus, Ohio: Charles E. Merrill, 1966) 104.

equate, Huck
w/ Twain

thing. Jim, he couldn't see no sense in most of it, but he allowed we was white folks and knowed better than him; so he was satisfied, and said he would do it all just as Tom said" (chap. 36).

Twain said in *Huckleberry Finn* more than one hundred years ago, what Dr. W. B. Shockley and A. R. Jensen are trying to prove through empirical study today.[4] This tells us something about the power of the printed word when it is taught to children by a formidable institution such as the school.

Huckleberry Finn even suggests that blacks are not human beings. 20 When Huck arrives at Aunt Sally's house, she asks him why he is late:

> "We blowed a cylinder head."
> "Good gracious! anybody hurt?"
> "No'm. Killed a nigger."
> "Well, it's lucky; because sometimes people do get hurt" (chap. 32).

There are indications that the racist views and attitudes implicit in the preceding quotations are as prevalent in America today as they were over one hundred years ago. *Huckleberry Finn* has not been successful in fighting race hate and prejudice, as its proponents maintain, but has helped to retain the status quo.

THE BLACK STUDENT

In 1963 John Fisher, former president of Columbia Teachers College, stated:

> The black American youngster happens to be a member of a large and distinctive group that for a very long time has been the object of special political, legal, and social action. . . . To act as though any child is separable from his history is indefensible. In terms of educational planning, it is *irresponsible*.
>
> Every black child is the victim of the history of his race in this country. On the day he enters kindergarten, he carries a burden *no white child* can ever know, no matter what other handicaps or disabilities he may suffer.[5]

The primary school child learns, almost the minute he enters school, that black is associated with dirtiness, ugliness, and wickedness. Much of what teachers and students think of the black child is color based. As a result, the black pupil knows his pigmentation is an impediment to his progress.

---

4. Wallace's reference here is to doctrines of biological determinism, especially to the notion that some racial groups are genetically superior, in certain ways, to other groups.—James S. Leonard, Thomas A. Tenney, and Thadious M. Davis.

5. Harry A. Passow, *Education in Depressed Areas* (New York: Teachers College P [Columbia U], 1963) 265.

As early as the fifth grade, the black student studies American history and must accept his ancestors in the role of slaves. This frustrating and painful experience leaves scars that very few educators, writers, and especially English teachers can understand. We compound these problems for black children when we force them to read aloud the message of *Huckleberry Finn*. It is so devastatingly traumatic that the student may never recover. How much pain must a black child endure to secure an education? No other child is asked to suffer so much embarrassment, humiliation, and racial intimidation at the hands of so powerful an institution as the school. The vast majority of black students have no tolerance for either "ironic" or "satirical" reminders of the insults and degradation heaped upon their ancestors in slavery and postslavery times.

Dorothy Gilliam (*Washington Post*, 12 April 1982) makes a good case for protecting the rights of students when she says, "Where rights conflict, one must sometimes supersede the other. Freedom of speech does not, for example, allow words to be deliberately used in a way that would cause someone to suffer a heart attack. By the same token, the use of words in ways that cause psychological and emotional damage is an unacceptable exercise of free speech." 25

RACISM

If indeed, as *Huckleberry Finn*'s proponents claim, the book gives a positive view of blacks and has an antislavery, antiracist message, then the Nazi party, the Ku Klux Klan, and the White Citizens Council must see something different. Most of the hate mail received when a school in northern Virginia restricted the use of the book was from these groups.

It is difficult to believe that Samuel Clemens would write a book against the institution of slavery; he did, after all, join a Confederate army bent on preserving that peculiar institution. Also, he could not allow Huck to help Jim to his freedom. It seems he was a hodgepodge of contradictions.

Huckleberry Finn is an American classic for no other reason than that it ridicules blacks to a greater extent than any other book given our children to read. The book and racism feed on each other and have withstood the test of time because many Americans insist on preserving our racist heritage.

Marguerite Barnett (1982) points out:

By ridiculing blacks, exaggerating their facial features, and denying their humanity, the popular art of the Post-Civil-War period represented the political culture's attempt to deny blacks the equal status and rights awarded them in the Emancipation Proclamation. By making blacks inhuman, American whites could destroy their claim to equal treatment. Blacks as slaves posed no problem because they were under complete domination, but blacks as free men created political problems. The popular culture of the day supplied the answer by dehumanizing blacks and picturing them as childlike and inferior.[6]

In this day of enlightenment, teachers should not rely on a book that teaches the subtle sickness of racism to our young and causes so much psychological damage to a large segment of our population. We are a multicultural, pluralistic nation. We must teach our young to respect all races, ethnic groups, and religious groups in the most positive terms conceivable.

RECOMMENDATIONS

This book should not be used with children. It is permissible to use the original *Huckleberry Finn* with students in graduate courses of history, English, and social science if one wants to study the perpetration and perpetuation of racism. The caustic, abrasive language is less likely to offend students of that age group because they tend to be mature enough to understand and discuss issues without feeling intimidated by the instructor, fellow students, or racism.

My research relating to *Huckleberry Finn* indicates that black parents and teachers, and their children and students, have complained about books that use the word "nigger" being read aloud in class. Therefore, I recommend that books such as *Huckleberry Finn, The Slave Dancer,* and *To Kill a Mockingbird*[7] be *listed as racist* and excluded from the classroom.

If an educator feels he or she must use *Huckleberry Finn* in the classroom, I would suggest my revised version, *The Adventures of Huckleberry Finn Adapted,* by John H. Wallace. The story is the same, but the words "nigger" and "hell" are eradicated. It no longer depicts blacks as inhuman, dishonest, or unintelligent, and it contains a glossary of Twainisms. Most adolescents will enjoy laughing at Jim and Huck in this adaptation.[8]

---

6. Documentation on this statement by Marguerite Barnett (possibly from a dissertation) is not currently available.

7. *The Slave Dancer* (1973): A novel by Paula Fox, set on a slave-trading ship; *To Kill a Mockingbird* (1960), Harper Lee's novel about the trial of a black man unjustly accused of raping a white woman.—ED.

8. For additional reading on the subject of racial considerations in education, see James A. Banks and Jean D. Grambs, *Black Self-Concept: Implications for Education and Social Science* (New York: McGraw-Hill, 1972); Robert F. Biehler, *Psychology Applied to Teaching* (Boston: Houghton Mifflin, 1971); Gary A. Davis and Thomas F. Warren, *Psychology of Education: New Looks* (Lexington, Mass.: Heath, 1974); Marcel L. Goldschmid, *Black Americans and White Racism* (New York: Holt, Rinehart, and Winston, 1970); Donnarae MacCann and Gloria Woodard, *The Black American in Children's Books* (Metuchen, N.J.: Scarecrow, 1972).

- **CONSIDER THE SOURCE**

1. What harm does Wallace claim arises from requiring students to read *Huckleberry Finn*? What benefits would result from banning the book? What evidence does he give to substantiate these claims?

2. According to Wallace, how does the classroom environment enhance the power of *Huckleberry Finn*? What role does he believe teachers and peers play in legitimizing the the racism of Twain's novel?

3. What age group does Wallace feel can handle *Huckleberry Finn*? Why? Why must other students be protected from the book? Which category do you fall into, according to Wallace?

4. Examine Wallace's analogy with the Jewish Community Council's recommendations regarding "religious practices" and school-sponsored programs. What "practices" and "programs" do you think the council was referring to? How does Wallace connect their arguments with his own position?

- **CONSIDER THE IMPLICATIONS**

5. Both Wallace and Catharine MacKinnon (pp. 492–508) argue that the First Amendment right to free speech conflicts with the Fourteenth Amendment's guarantee of freedom from discrimination. Compare Wallace's argument for banning *Huck Finn* with MacKinnon's position regarding pornography. When should one right supersede the other? Under what circumstances is equal opportunity more important than free speech?

6. Consider the books you read in high school and middle school. Did any contain language that you found objectionable? Did any portray groups or individuals in ways that could embarrass them? In your journal, explore the impact of those books on you and consider how your education would have benefited or suffered if those books had been omitted.

7. In Wallace's edited version of *Huckleberry Finn,* the conversation between Huck and Aunt Sally that he quotes on page 462 omits the words "Killed a nigger," but remains otherwise the same. How does the omission affect the meaning of the passage from chapter 32 of Twain's novel? What view of Aunt Sally do you get from each version? Write an essay comparing the two versions of the dialogue and exploring the social or moral implications of each.

8. Wallace claims that "*Huckleberry Finn* is an American classic for no other reason than that it ridicules blacks to a greater extent than any other book given our children to read." Review E. D. Hirsch's argument about how literary classics "transmit the mythology and values" of the nation ("The Formation of Modern National Cultures," pp. 331–42). Write an essay examining the status of *Huckleberry Finn* and defending your own view of its proper place in our national culture.

9. Assuming Wallace's position with regard to *Huckleberry Finn*, write a let-

ter to William Noble (pp. 449–56) or Dudley Barlow (pp. 466–72) persuading him to change his position. Be sure to address Noble's or Barlow's arguments in favor of the book.

▪ ▪ ▪ ▪ ▪ ▪
⋮⋯⋯⋯⋯⋯⋯

DUDLEY BARLOW

Why We Still Need Huckleberry Finn

Joan DelFattore (pp. 440–49), William Noble (pp. 449–56), and John H. Wallace (pp. 457–66) present differing views on censoring school textbooks, but all speak from positions outside the classroom. Dudley Barlow (b. 1942), a high school English teacher in Plymouth, Michigan, speaks from within the public school classroom. In this 1992 essay for Education Digest, *Barlow responds to arguments in favor of banning Mark Twain's novel* Adventures of Huckleberry Finn. *Addressing his remarks to other schoolteachers, he defends Twain's use of language that many people today find offensive, and he discusses appropriate ways to introduce young students to controversial language and issues. Indeed, Barlow implies that the book should be taught precisely because it raises the difficult issues of racism and stereotyping. At least one commentator on this subject has suggested that the best way to get students to read* Huckleberry Finn *is to ban it; that way students will seek out the book on their own, unhampered by all the adult fuss about language and politics.*

In a syndicated column in the *Detroit Free Press* on April 5, 1992, James J. Kilpatrick[1] reports, "A school superintendent in North Carolina last month threw *Huck Finn* out of his classrooms. I think the gentleman acted properly." He goes on to say, "because I have spent my life fighting censorship by the state, I want to brood aloud about the affair."

The book was ordered out of middle school classrooms by Harold Fleming, interim superintendent of schools, because, as Kilpatrick explains it, "the novel contains language that is offensive to blacks." Fleming, Kilpatrick notes, is black. Kilpatrick further informs us that "the school principal, Earl Heath, also black, said there are words 'we may not want to deal with' at the seventh- and eighth-grade level." The offensive language, of course, is the word *nigger*, and, of course, Fleming is correct in saying it is offensive to blacks. It is also legitimate to press

From *Education Digest* 58:1 (Sept. 1992), 31–35.

1. **James J. Kilpatrick** (b. 1920): Conservative commentator and author.—ED.

teachers for a justification of a book that is a racial affront to some of our students.

Remember, first of all, that "nigger" is Huck's, not Twain's, label for blacks. And Huck uses this word for the same reason that, thirty years ago, we all used the label "Indians" to identify the various groups we now know as Native Americans. Unpleasant as the word *nigger* is, and that is why Twain keeps lashing us with it, it is the only word Huck knows for black Americans. This is Twain's point: The word grows out of Huck's paradigm, his system of viewing things, and this limits his ability to think about blacks. We see this again and again when Huck says such things as: "He was right; he was most always right; he had an uncommon level head for a nigger" and "You can't teach a nigger to argue" and "I do believe he [Jim] cared just as much for his people as white folks does for their'n. It don't seem natural, but I reckon it's so." Huck's provincial life in antebellum Missouri has defined for him what a "nigger" is. It is only his personal experience with Jim in their flight down the Mississippi that forces him to see beyond the inaccurate assumptions that come packaged with the epithet.

In defense of the book's removal from Kinston, North Carolina, classrooms, Kilpatrick tells us that in 1885, the Boston library committee found *Huckleberry Finn* "more suited to the slums than to intelligent, respectable people." My guess is that the library committee also found Whitman's *Leaves of Grass* only "suited to the slums." Nor would they have approved of Ralph Ellison's *Invisible Man*, Toni Morrison's *Tar Baby*, or Claude Brown's *Manchild in the Promised Land*. The point here is that what the Boston library committee had to say 107 years ago is neither particularly instructive nor helpful today. We can be sure that *Huckleberry Finn* is available in Boston libraries today. After all, Harold Fleming may have directed an English teacher not to assign the book in Kinston, North Carolina, but he still permitted it to stay in the school library.

Kilpatrick also reports that Fleming said the teacher was not adequately prepared to teach *Huckleberry Finn*, seeming to imply that Fleming might let an adequately prepared teacher proceed with the book. We are never told, though, what adequate preparation might be. What qualifies teachers to teach this book? Must they be black, and, if so, why? I think, to be qualified, they must be: aware of (and able to make clear) what Twain was doing, sensitive to the emotional impact of the material, and responsive to the emotional needs of their students.

Just as Huck's concept of "nigger" limits his ability to understand Jim fully, our students are also victimized by the intellectual blinders imposed by racial, ethnic, and sexual epithets. Many of our students cannot get beyond the words "Arab" and "Japanese" and "fag." Qualified teachers understand how all these labels are powerful, limiting, and sometimes painful, and understand how to help their students see what Huck came to see only after he had come to know and love the man obscured by the word *nigger*.

Kilpatrick says he first read and loved the book when he was "a white boy growing up in a segregated city." He adds, "This is a fun book for white boys to read. . . . For black children, I have come to realize, it is a brutal slap in the face." That is exactly why the book needs to be taught by qualified teachers: to help all our students see the limitations imposed on them by their surroundings and to help them see how Mark Twain and Spike Lee (whose films many high school students know) attack many of the same targets with some of the same weapons.

Kilpatrick also thinks the book's irony disqualifies it from use in schools. He says, "One of the essayists [represented in *Satire or Evasion?*, a collection of fifteen essays by black scholars on *Huckleberry Finn*] . . . comments upon Twain's point—that a close friendship between black and white could develop 'only on a socially isolated raft in the middle of the nation's biggest and longest river.'"

Let's be fair. This kind of isolation away from contaminating influences is a common literary device. Think back to *The Defiant Ones,* the Sidney Poitier-Tony Curtis film in which two convicts, one black and one white, escape from prison chained together. They share a mutual, racial animosity, and it is only because they are forcibly linked that they learn to respect and care about each other. In *Moby-Dick,* Herman Melville has his protagonist, Ishmael, head out to sea when he can no longer stand the company of his fellow men. It is only through the isolation at sea that Ishmael rediscovers through Queequeg, the harpooner/cannibal, his links to the rest of humanity. In Erich Maria Remarque's *All Quiet On the Western Front,* it is only because he is isolated in a shell crater with a French soldier whom he has mortally wounded that Paul, the German protagonist, discovers a brotherhood that transcends nationalities.

It is true that the raft isolates Huck from the rest of society, but this 10 very isolation forces Huck to come face to face with the real Jim and with his own limited views. Huck never does get beyond the label "nigger," but he does get beyond his original perception that Jim is simply an unthinking, unfeeling piece of property. In the course of the novel, he plays several tricks on Jim. In the last one, Huck, who is in a canoe, gets separated from Jim and the raft in a fog. When he manages to return to the raft (now littered with trash from ramming into towheads and islands), he tricks Jim into thinking he has been there all along. Jim finally realizes he has been tricked and says:

"When I got all wore out wid work, en wid de callin' for you, en went to sleep, my heart wuz mos' broke becase you wuz los', en I didn' k'yer no' mo' what become er me en de raf'. En when I wake up en fine you back ag'in, all safe en soun', de tears come, en I could 'a' got down on my knees en kiss yo' foot, I's so thankful. En all you wuz thinkin' 'bout wuz how you could make a fool uv ole Jim wid a lie. Dat truck dah is *trash;* en trash is what people is dat puts dirt on de head er day fren's en makes 'em ashamed."

Huck says, "It made me feel so mean I could almost have kissed *his* foot to get him to take it back. It was fifteen minutes before I could work myself up to go and humble myself to a nigger; but I done it, and I warn't ever sorry for it afterward, neither. I didn't do him no more mean tricks, and I wouldn't done that one if I'd 'a' knowed it would make him feel that way." The word is still there, but Huck is changing.

If the raft is a sanctuary, it is also a crucible. It separates the dross of the racial views Huck has been steeped in from the truths he discovers in his daily experiences with Jim. The raft is where Huck is forced to look unflinchingly at a black man and at his own assumptions about race and about what is right and wrong. Huck and Jim eventually leave the raft, but Huck at the end of the book is a different person from Huck at the beginning. He is never able to abandon the only word he knows for blacks, but his experience teaches him that his lifelong assumptions represented by the word *nigger* have been terribly wrong. The friendship may begin on the raft, but it endures beyond it.

Kilpatrick complains that the end of the novel is "facile." I think most critics will agree that perhaps the last fourth of the book is flawed. Tom Sawyer's and Huck's "rescue" of Jim even though Jim is actually free, and only Tom knows it, seems too drawn out. Most readers will feel that since Huck's moral struggle (caused by the clash between his assumptions about blacks and his experiences with Jim) has been resolved, the book needs to end earlier. Twain tried to end the book in a burlesque echoing events that had occurred between Tom and Huck early in the novel. That just won't do at this point in the book. Huck has grown too much, and his behavior here seems forced. After all, at this point in the book, he and Tom are not planning another raid on a Sunday school picnic; Jim's freedom is at stake. Also, the final resolution of Huck's domestic problems (his father is dead and Huck still has $6,000 in the bank) and the announcement of Jim's freedom are just too neat and rushed.

Huckleberry Finn may not be a perfect novel, but it is a wonderful | 15 achievement. First, as a literary creation, Huck is a fully realized character. We absolutely believe in him. He is so completely limned that we know him better than we know most of the real people in our lives. He is also involved in a serious and genuine human problem, and Twain has not flinched; he has told the truth. That is, he hasn't minimized the situation and settled for easy solutions. Huck is completely unaware of, and therefore insensitive to, Jim's humanity early in the book, and Twain does not sugarcoat it. Nor does Huck discover the real Jim (and thereby the real Huck) through inadequately motivated and painless means. Twain allows Huck to be cruel to Jim, and when Huck discovers what is best in Jim he also sees what is worst in himself. Not once as

Huck's journey of self-discovery progresses do we say, "Oh, come on, I don't buy that!" Huck's story is what Ezra Pound[2] called "news that stays news." It explores a universal and timeless human problem, and therefore, it is the truth, even if it didn't happen.

Huckleberry Finn can be a painful book to teach. Kilpatrick says, "It is a formidably difficult work for any teacher to teach." I think that overstates it. I always work to make my students see the savagery that is the target of Twain's often brutal satire, to get them to understand how this book is a broadside against stupidity and intolerance. It isn't just about racial intolerance, after all. Huck's experience with the Grangerfords is the corollary to his experience with Jim. The Grangerfords are a family involved in a feud with the Shepherdsons. The Grangerfords take Huck in, and he thinks they are the grandest people he has ever seen. They are the epitome of southern gentility, handsome and well mannered. But, if Huck is initially deceived by Jim's dark skin and by the label "nigger," he is equally deceived by the Grangerford's genteel appearance. He quickly learns, though, that these fine-looking people and their neighbors are methodically killing each other over an ancient wrong that no one can even recall. Twain absolutely distrusted any opinion, whether it involved race or politics or religion or fashion, that grew out of a group consensus. (For an extended discussion of this idea, see Twain's essay, "Corn Pone Opinions.")

It is a mistake, therefore, for a teacher to present this novel as an adventure story. It is satire, and if students are to understand it, they must first understand the nature of satire. I begin by telling my students about Voltaire's *Candide*. Voltaire wrote this work to ridicule Gottfried Wilhelm Von Leibniz's carefully constructed view that this is "the best of all possible worlds." In order to destroy Leibniz's view, Voltaire created the young and credulous protagonist, Candide. His teacher is Dr. Pangloss, who proclaims the Leibniz dictum. The gullible Candide believes his teacher and continually recites his "best of all possible worlds" catechism in spite of the outrageous catastrophes that befall him and the people around him. The more mayhem we see, the dumber Pangloss (and Leibniz) appear.

This is how Twain blasts the "nigger" view. Everything Huck experiences with Jim contrasts jarringly with his view of Jim as "nigger." Jim is the most noble character in the book, and eventually his goodness forces Huck to abandon what he "knows" is right. Huck can't reason himself to this new position, but his heart leads him there. He knows he is bound by honor, by the law, and by religion to turn in this runaway slave. There is that pivotal moment in the book, though, when he decides to follow his heart and not to betray Jim. He says, "All right, then, I'll go to hell." That simple declaration of love and faithfulness blasts away that phony but time-honored racial hierarchy that Huck has struggled with throughout the book.

---

2. **Ezra Pound** (1885–1972): Influential American poet and translator.—ED.

Still, the awfulness of that word will not go away. But the awfulness refuses to go away because we are still stuck with the problem Huck struggled with. If racial and sexual and ethnic intolerance were to disappear, then I suppose *Huckleberry Finn* would become to American literature what the works of John Dryden and Alexander Pope are to English literature: dusty literary gems about quaint and forgotten problems. Consequently, the book would lose its sting for black students. In the meantime, though, Huck reminds us again and again of that old Pogo cartoon: "We have met the enemy, and he is us."[3]

Maybe the current furor over *Huckleberry Finn* is a sign that we have [20] made some progress. Are we less tolerant of the word *nigger* than people were fifty or thirty or even twenty years ago? I hope so. It strikes me as ironic, though, that in this 107-year-old novel, we have Huck Finn, who never abandons the epithet but does learn to reject his preconceived notion of what Jim, the "nigger," is. We, on the other hand, have at least learned the social grace to disapprove of the word, but our treatment of blacks and Native Americans (and other groups we could name), in political and economic terms, flags way behind the moral growth Huck Finn managed. And even if race should ever cease to be an issue in this country, bigotry and intolerance always seem to find their way into the human experience. As long as this is true, *Huckleberry Finn* will be there to goad us and help bring us back to our better selves. As Huck says, "It shows how a body can see and don't see at the same time." This is a great book, and it still deserves to be read and taught.

▪ CONSIDER THE SOURCE

1. What concession does Barlow make to those who oppose *Huckleberry Finn* because it contains the word *nigger*? According to Barlow, why did Twain use the word in his story?

2. What kind of preparation does Barlow feel teachers must have to teach *Huckleberry Finn*? How should they prepare students to read the novel?

3. How does Barlow believe *Candide* can help students understand *Huckleberry Finn*? Why does he feel *Huckleberry Finn* should be taught as satire, not as an adventure story?

4. Explain the irony Barlow sees when he compares Huck Finn's moral growth with the treatment of minorities in today's society.

▪ CONSIDER THE IMPLICATIONS

5. The extent to which people object to the word *nigger* gives an indication of the power of language. In a journal entry, explore other words that have such power. Think about whether those words gain greater power by

---

3. **Pogo:** Comic strip (begun in 1949) by Walt Kelly (1913–1973) that often ventured into political satire.—ED.

being put into print than they would have if they just remained in the oral realm. What effect does print have on such words?

6. List the reasons Barlow cites for banning *Huckleberry Finn* alongside those given by John Wallace (pp. 457–66). How are they similar or different? Which reasons present the most substantial objections to the book? Write an essay defending or opposing the three strongest arguments in favor of banning *Huck Finn*.

7. Barlow and Wallace discuss how a teacher could prepare students to read *Huckleberry Finn,* but they focus on different prerequisites for reading the novel. In small groups, closely compare their discussions. What issues, according to the authors, should a teacher make clear to a class reading *Huck Finn*? Would you want to add any items? What, if anything, would make a student "adequately prepared" to read the book?

8. Hold an in-class debate on whether or not to ban *Huckleberry Finn* from high school classrooms. Supplement the arguments given by Barlow and John Wallace (pp. 457–66) with your own positions.

9. Review C. H. Knoblauch's essay on "Literacy and the Politics of Education" (pp. 122–30). What political position underlies Barlow's arguments in favor of including *Huckleberry Finn* in the curriculum? Write an essay analyzing Barlow's educational goals using the terms Knoblauch employs.

▪ ▪ ▪ ▪ ▪ ▪

HUNTLY COLLINS

PC and the Press

A regular reader of mainstream American magazines and newspapers might easily conclude that the thought police have been patrolling college campuses with increasing vigilance this past decade, busily enforcing "political correctness" and campus speech codes. Huntly Collins (b. 1946), a reporter who has covered the higher education beat for the Philadelphia Inquirer, *takes issue with this picture of Big Brother on campus. She carefully scrutinizes the "facts" and concludes that the mainstream media have exaggerated the influence of political correctness in the country's universities. In spite of the headlines and scare stories, Collins finds that traditional Western culture is still firmly entrenched in the curriculum, and the ominous speech codes that we hear about are few and far between. She offers an explanation for the press's treatment of the PC debate, suggesting that it is a response to the increasing numbers of minorities and women within the news media. Collins's piece originally appeared in* Change, *a*

From *Change* 24:1 (Jan.– Feb. 1992), 12–16.

journal for faculty and administrators in higher education. Hers was one in a group of essays examining the ramifications of multiculturalism on campus. Collins continues as a reporter for the Philadelphia Inquirer, *now covering health issues, especially AIDS.*

As a higher education reporter at *The Philadelphia Inquirer,* I seem to have missed the biggest story on my beat last year: the rise of the "political correctness" movement on American college campuses. Somehow, I got caught up in less weighty matters like massive budget cuts at state-funded schools, the effort to improve undergraduate teaching at major research universities, and a month-long faculty strike at Temple University, the largest school in the Philadelphia area.

It wasn't until I read *Newsweek's* cover story of December 24, 1990 (entitled "Thought Police: There's a 'Politically Correct' Way to Talk About Race, Sex and Ideas. Is This the New Enlightenment—or the New McCarthyism?") that I began to realize what was really happening in academe.

The big news on campus had nothing to do with budget cuts, or the competing interests of undergraduate teaching and university research, or the faculty's role in academic decision making. The big news was a left-wing conspiracy by college administrators and 1960s-era professors to stifle dissent and impose a "liberal orthodoxy" about race and gender. The goal: to capture the hearts and minds of the nation's thirteen million college students.

Such is the alarmist picture that has emerged from a significant segment of the popular press—especially magazines—over the past year. One need look only as far as the headlines and graphics to get the message.

Following *Newsweek's* lead, *New York* magazine weighed in with 5 John Taylor's January 21, 1991 story entitled "Are You Politically Correct?" It ran with a photograph of Red Guards jeering at Chinese academics in dunce caps; another photo showed a public book burning by Hitler youth in Nazi Germany. The headline superimposed on the photos read: "Am I Misogynistic, Patriarchal, Gynophobic, Phallocentric, Logocentric? Am I Guilty of Racism, Sexism, Classism? Do I say 'Indian' Instead of 'Native American'? 'Pet' Instead of 'Animal Companion'?"

Then in March came the *Atlantic's* excerpts from Dinesh D'Souza's book, *Illiberal Education.* The cartoon-like cover illustration showed an aging white male professor about to be set afire as he lay sandwiched between the cracking covers of a Western classic. Hands representing different minority groups were shown tugging the professor in different directions by the arms and legs. In the foreground was an even more ominous image: a pile of books being doused with gasoline. The hand holding the gas canister was dark-skinned.

By April 1, *Time* magazine had jumped on the PC bandwagon. "U.S.

Campuses: The New Intolerance," said the teaser headline on the cover. Inside, readers were treated to "Upside Down in the Groves of Academe," an essay by William A. Henry III. "Imagine a place where it is considered racist to speak of the rights of the individual when they conflict with the community's prevailing opinion," Henry began.

Magazine journalism, of course, isn't the only popular medium where the nation's colleges and universities have been depicted as captive to a left-wing orthodoxy. Syndicated columnists like George Will[1] have had a heyday with PC, as have editorial writers and cartoonists at newspapers across the country.

In an April 23rd editorial about the controversy over the diversity standards of the Middle States Association of Colleges and Schools, the *Wall Street Journal* declared: "The truth is that we are far worse off now as regards the threat to intellectual freedom, the pressures to conform ideologically, than during the McCarthy era. . . . Today the most serious assault on that freedom comes from within the universities themselves."

The tale being told by these and other publications reads the same 10 from one to another. It is a tale of how colleges and universities have adopted student conduct codes restricting free speech. A tale of how Third World and women's literature has supplanted the Western classics as requirements in the college curriculum. A tale of how conservative faculty members are being silenced and hounded out of their jobs by liberal colleagues and administrators. A tale of how unqualified black students are being admitted to elite private schools. A tale of how English professors have fallen captive to a strange brand of literary criticism known as deconstructionism,[2] which challenges the existence of "truth itself."

No matter that each of these topics is a complicated story, with its own history, its own context at various schools, its own lineup of players on one side or another. Much of the popular press, taking a cue from D'Souza and others, has lumped the issues together to prove that "politically correct" thinking has gained a hammerlock on academic life. As *Newsweek* put it: "PC [political correctness] is, strictly speaking, a totalitarian philosophy. No aspect of university life is too obscure to come under its scrutiny."

There is one problem with the portrait that has dominated the mainstream media: It grossly exaggerates the influence of PC, and badly distorts reality on the vast majority of American campuses. A recent survey by the American Council on Education (ACE), for instance, asked ad-

---

1. **George Will** (b. 1941): Conservative newspaper columnist for the *Washington Post.*—ED.

2. **deconstructionism:** A movement in philosophy and literary criticism initiated by French philosopher Jacques Derrida. Deconstructionists seek to reveal logical or rhetorical tensions and oppositions within a text that undermine the possibility of any single "correct" reading or meaning.—ED.

ministrators on a representative sample of 444 campuses whether their schools had experienced controversy over the "political correctness" of courses, speeches, or faculty lectures. Ten percent or less of the 359 schools responding to the survey said "yes."

A reporter who visits almost any campus today would have to deny his or her senses to conclude that women and minorities are in control of the curriculum. Even a cursory look at college catalogs shows that Western culture, including science and technology, is still the centerpiece.

While much ado has been made of deconstructionism, the debate has generally failed to reach beyond English departments. The only segment of higher education where much heat has been generated by it is the highly selective private schools and the so-called public Ivys.

And while the raw number of black students on college campuses 15 has risen, that's primarily because of demographic changes, not skewed admissions policies. In fact, the percentage of black high school graduates attending college has declined, from 33.5 percent in 1976 to 30.8 percent in 1989—this, during a period when the proportion of blacks graduating from high school rose from 67.5 percent to 76.1 percent.

Even if there had been a left-wing conspiracy on campus, one would have to conclude that it has been a monumental failure, at least judging by the predilections of students themselves. Business administration remains the most popular major among undergraduates. Surveys show that college graduates today are more concerned with landing a good job than changing the world. And, in recent years, the GOP has enjoyed new-found popularity among college-age students.

The number of campus Republican clubs went from several hundred in the early 1980s to about 1,100 today. A recent poll by the Wirthin Group found that Republicans enjoyed their greatest strength among people aged eighteen to twenty-four. Forty-two percent—more than any other age group—said they thought of themselves as Republicans. Thirty-five percent identified themselves as Democrats, and 23 percent as independents.

Nonetheless, the press has made a case for a PC conspiracy by relying almost exclusively on a litany of by-now-familiar anecdotes, recycled from one publication to another. Often, the yarns are oversimplified and incompletely reported. Sometimes they are simply false.

Many stories, for instance, cite the catchy chant of student protesters at Stanford University: "Hey, hey, ho, ho, Western culture's got to go." The impression left is that the students were opposed to Western culture itself; in fact, they were referring to the school's Western culture requirement. As it turns out, Stanford's new "Culture, Ideas, and Values" (CIV) course, which replaced the Western culture course, retains the Western classics in seven of eight tracks. And even in the less traditional eighth track, "Europe and the Americas," students are required to read selections from the Bible and other works in the Western tradition.

"In fact, the West was not being 'phased out' at Stanford," wrote 20
Anthony Day, in a page-one piece for the *Los Angeles Times* on May 3,
1990. "In addition to 'Europe and the Americas,' which this year has
about 100 students, the other seven CIV courses offered to freshmen remained much as they were."

Day's piece, which took an in-depth look at Stanford a year after the
curricular reform went into effect, is a fine example of on-site reporting,
the kind of coverage that has been missing elsewhere. Unlike other reporters, Day actually spent time on campus, sat in classes, and interviewed a large number of faculty members and students.

Apart from anecdotes, statistical evidence of PC's reign on campus
is hard to find in most of the stories. And when numbers are cited, they
are often cited inaccurately. For instance, many editorials—rightly concerned about First Amendment violations in student conduct codes—assert that 70 percent of the nation's colleges and universities have
adopted such restrictive codes. The number, widely disseminated to the
press by the American Civil Liberties Union, comes from a 1989 survey
of student affairs officers that was published by the Carnegie Foundation for the Advancement of Teaching as part of its 1990 report, "Campus Life: In Search of Community."

In fact, the survey did not ask a single question about campus
speech codes. But it did ask whether schools had a "written policy on
bigotry, racial harassment, or intimidation." The response: 60 percent
had such a policy, 11 percent were developing one, and 29 percent had
no policy. Of course, such policies could run the gamut from something
as innocuous as a statement condemning racial bigotry to something as
troubling as speech codes that infringe on First Amendment rights. The
survey, however, did not ask about the content of the policies, so any
conclusions about that are shaky at best. The point was totally missed by
the mainstream press.

"I sent out a correction and clarification saying 'Buyer Beware,'"
said David Merkowitz, spokesman for the ACE, which co-sponsored the
original survey. "But, as usual, the correction never catches up with the
original story. We keep seeing this figure repeated everywhere."

To be sure, there are some campuses, such as the University of 25
Michigan, where speech codes have been found unconstitutional by the
courts. There are also legitimate differences of opinion on every campus
about affirmative action, curricular reform, and new forms of faculty
scholarship. To write about each of these issues in separate stories is one
thing; to mix them all together into catch-all pieces on political correctness is something else.

The best of the country's education reporters, including Kenneth J.
Cooper of the *Washington Post*, have picked off the issues one by one and
attempted to take a careful and balanced look at how they have played
out. In a May 27, 1991 page-one story, for instance, Cooper examined the
new "American cultures" requirement for freshmen at the University

of California, Berkeley. Although the controversial new requirement wasn't scheduled to take effect until this fall, Cooper sat in on three pilot courses taught last spring. There, he found "a range of lessons" being taught, not the politically correct line suggested by critics.

One of the lessons: "In a journalism course, 'News and the Underdog in American Society,' a dozen students discussed sympathetic photographs of migrant 'Okies' published during the Depression.[3] One theme was that white folks can be victims too," Cooper wrote.

Although he interviewed scores of students, Cooper found few who believed that the Berkeley faculty had caved in to left-wing ideology— quite the contrary. A number of students complained that the university was too conservative.

Other education reporters who have gone out to find the stifling campus atmosphere described by *Newsweek* and others have come away dumbfounded. "When you are out there on the campuses and you don't see it, you wonder, am I crazy or are they?" said an education writer at a large West Coast newspaper.

The very debate over PC on college campuses would seem to signal 30 that a spirit of free inquiry is alive and well. And although some conservative faculty members and students may feel uncomfortable with multiculturalism, even Lynne V. Cheney, chairwoman of the National Endowment for the Humanities and one of the country's most strident critics of PC, admitted in a September 25th speech before the National Press Club that, to her knowledge, no professor had actually been fired over PC, though some, she asserted, had not been hired. While that may be true, it's a far cry from the Congressional investigations and loyalty oaths of the McCarthy era that Cheney and many in the media continue to invoke.

What explains the abysmal performance of the press in covering the controversies that have arisen over issues of race and gender on campus? To some extent, schools themselves are to blame. There are at least two things dear to every journalist's heart—the First Amendment and the English language. When colleges and universities start pushing the boundaries of either, they are, rightly or wrongly, inviting criticism.

What journalist could resist poking fun at mangled language like "lookism," "vertically challenged," and "differently abled"? The phrases are typical of the twisted rhetoric that has worked its way into official policy on many campuses.

By contrast, the conservative critics of multiculturalism have spoken with a less tortured tongue, a language that is readily accessible to the media as well as to the average reader. What's more, the conservatives

---

3. **Okies:** A disparaging term for the poor migrant farm workers who fled Oklahoma during the Depression, after years of drought had turned the area into a dust bowl.—ED.

have organized—an occurrence that was duly noted by the reporters who followed the formation of the National Association of Scholars, a vocal critic of PC.

Beyond that, however, the distorted coverage of PC is part of a long tradition of anti-intellectualism in the popular press, which has tended to put down what it doesn't understand. The annual meeting of the Modern Language Association, for instance, produces a predictable string of stories spanning the seemingly esoteric topics discussed in scholarly papers.

When the press belatedly discovered deconstructionism, which has 35 formed the philosophical underpinnings for at least some of the campus debate over multiculturalism, it is not surprising that most reporters didn't take the time to understand what the critique was all about.

"Journalists have sort of given up knowing what's going on (in scholarship)," says Mitchell Stephens, an associate professor of journalism at New York University. "The scholarship itself has gotten more complicated. If we are talking about the latest Saul Bellow novel, journalists can read it, too. But if we are talking about deconstructing Heidegger,[4] that's too much work."

Although a few papers, like the *New York Times* and the *Boston Globe*, have assigned specialists to cover "the egghead beat," as it's known in the trade, those whose job it is to cover ideas are few and far between. So are those assigned to cover higher education full time. Of the 369 members of the Education Writers Association, just thirteen identify themselves as higher education writers. The dearth of beat reporters in higher education has undoubtedly contributed to the lackluster coverage of multiculturalism and has allowed distortion of the PC issue to go unchallenged.

One of the nation's few full-time higher education writers is Anthony Flint of the *Boston Globe*. In a thoughtful piece on July 8, Flint catalogued the growing number of educators who were speaking out against the conservative critics of PC.

"Those who have been labeled politically correct—advocates of greater sensitivity about race and gender awareness, for example—say they have been the victims of a right-wing smear campaign, exaggerated by a pack-mentality media using a handful of damning anecdotes," Flint wrote. More than two months later, on September 25, the *New York Times*'s Anthony DePalma wrote the same piece. The news peg was the formation of Teachers for a Democratic Culture, a group of thirty scholars waging a counteroffensive against their conservative critics.

These two stories were among the first in the mainstream press to 40

---

4. **Saul Bellow** (b. 1915): American novelist, author of *Henderson the Rain King* (1959), *Herzog* (1964), and *Humboldt's Gift* (1975); Martin **Heidegger** (1889–1976) German philosopher whose writings on art emphasized its essential resistance to rational understanding.—ED.

devote considerable space to telling the other side of the PC story. In the view of some media experts, the skewed reporting of PC and the belated effort to right the balance stem from the rightward drift of the press in recent years. As the country has moved to the Right, so has much of the media. Ever since the Reagan years, the press has been extremely sensitive to charges of a liberal bias; to compensate, many publications, including the *Philadelphia Inquirer,* have added strong conservative voices to their editorial pages.

More fundamentally, however, the press, like other institutions of American society, is undergoing fundamental change as more women and minorities enter the journalism profession. Though minorities and women are still underrepresented, especially at the top (minorities now constitute 8.72 percent of the supervisors, editors, copyeditors, reporters, and photographers on the nation's newspapers, according to a 1991 survey by the American Society of Newspaper Editors), they have forced news organizations to confront their own racism and sexism.

For some of the white men whose world view is being challenged, the change has proved discomfiting. "News executives are experiencing many of the same pressures within their own organizations as the universities have felt," says Larry Gross, a professor of communications at the University of Pennsylvania's Annenberg School. "By jumping on the bash-academia bandwagon, they are putting down the forces of uppity groups within their own circles."

At a time of declining readership, the alleged PC conspiracy has also provided an irresistible opportunity to attract more readers with sensationalized headlines, graphics, and stories that play on the deepest fears of white, middle-class Americans—the very segment of the population that newspapers and magazines must attract if they are to remain economically viable.

"We have begun to define success in the press the same way it would be defined by Nike—profits before social obligation," laments Mercedes Lynn de Uriarte, an associate professor of journalism at the University of Texas, Austin. "Why do you need the protection of the First Amendment when you are basically selling sneakers?"

Enough. I have to go write my first story about the PC conspiracy. 45 Make that my second.

▪ **CONSIDER THE SOURCE**

1. Summarize the "tale" Collins says the mainstream media have told about political correctness.

2. What evidence does Collins offer to demonstrate her claim that the popular press has exaggerated and distorted the image of PC on campus? Locate two instances in the essay where she corrects (or adds details to) an overly simplified version of college policies.

3. How have concerns over the First Amendment and the English language

contributed to the press's distortion of the PC issue, according to Collins? What other factors does she cite?

4. What relation does Collins see between the "alleged PC conspiracy" and the social changes experienced by the press and the nation's newspaper and magazine readers?

▪ **CONSIDER THE IMPLICATIONS**

5. Collins claims that "mangled language" has accompanied the phenomenon that is being labeled "political correctness." In your journal, explore the extent to which the language you hear and speak has been influenced by an awareness of race and gender issues. Have you heard "Native American" substituted for "Indian," "Asian" for "Oriental"? How have such linguistic shifts been regarded by you, your peers, the media?

6. In small groups, carefully review your college or university catalog to see how "politically correct" your own institution is. To what extent do traditional Western culture courses dominate the curriculum? How many multicultural course offerings are there? Is there an explicit speech code at your institution? Is there an antidiscrimination policy? Is there any requirement that students take courses in non-Western cultures? Compare your findings with those of other groups.

7. Is PC a real issue or a nonissue? Collins's essay seems to suggest it is a phenomenon largely invented by the press and heavily dependent on anecdotal evidence. In class discussion, provide evidence from your own experience to support or refute the position that "the nation's colleges and universities . . . [are] captive to a left-wing orthodoxy."

8. In your college library, track down articles in the mainstream media about the annual meeting of the Modern Language Association that Collins cites as part of "a long tradition of anti-intellectualism in the popular press." Compare the coverage of the MLA convention, held December 27–30 each year, with the full listing of papers delivered at the conference, published as the November issue of the scholarly journal *PMLA*. (If you can't find it in your library, your instructor may have a copy.) Do you find a predominance of PC topics or are traditional authors and books well represented? Have reporters fairly characterized the scholarly papers or have they lampooned a few esoteric topics they didn't understand, as Collins claims? Write a paper summarizing your findings.

9. Compare Collins's summary of the press's coverage of PC on campus with Susan Faludi's profile of press coverage of "trends" among women (pp. 248–62). What faults do they find in the mainstream media's coverage? What sort of reporting do they praise? Based on their analyses, draw up a list of guidelines that consumers of mainstream media should use when reading "trend" stories.

NAT HENTOFF

The Gospel According to Catharine MacKinnon

Just as the popular press characterizes universities as bastions of liberalism and political correctness, it often portrays feminism as if it were a single philosophy to which all feminists adhere without reservation. Nat Hentoff (b. 1925) shows us in this essay how deeply divided feminists are on pornography and censorship, among other issues. His focus is the proposal by Andrea Dworkin and Catharine MacKinnon to move pornography out from under protection of the First Amendment and instead consider it a violation of the civil rights of women. Hentoff says the proposal would lead to "the most direct and destructive suppression of speech that can be perpetrated by the state." Nonetheless, Dworkin and MacKinnon have the backing of such prominent feminists as Gloria Steinem. Their cause is also, ironically, supported by the Religious Right, even though one fundamentalist minister said he would consider Dworkin's own work pornographic, and he "would most certainly ban such ungodly writings." Hentoff's columns for the Progressive *magazine, the* Village Voice, *the* Washington Post, *and* The New Yorker *frequently wrestle with First Amendment issues. His books on this subject include* The First Freedom: The Tumultuous History of Free Speech in America *(1980), and* Free Speech for Me—But Not for Thee: How the American Left and Right Relentlessly Censor Each Other *(1992), from which this essay is taken.*

Madison, Wisconsin, is one of my favorite college towns. In the bars and restaurants, the college paper and the classrooms, ideas still matter, even if they don't have a direct connection to a job down the line. It's a lively, often contentious place, with some of the flavor, if not the exalted desperation, of the sixties.

As far as I can tell, most of the folks there, if you ask them, are opposed to censoring anything.

Censors do exist in Madison, though. In the 1980s, a brave bunch of radicals shouted down born-again Christian minister Eldridge Cleaver when he tried to give a scheduled talk at the university. The ex-radical and former Black Panther leader was too corrupt to be heard, they said. And if you wanted to hear him anyway, then clearly you were also full of bourgeois corruption.

Then there was the attempt by a feminist group to shut down an art exhibit at the university. They said it was sexist. I questioned whether it was art, but it sure was sexist. During a lecture there, I pointed out that

From *Free Speech for Me—But Not for Thee: How the American Left and Right Relentlessly Censor Each Other* (New York: HarperCollins, 1992), 336–55.

picketing and counterexhibits were the way to deal with the provocation. Censoring it would just establish the precedent of shutting down controversial exhibits, and the university would eventually use that precedent to shut down some "offensive" feminist exhibition. In response, it was suggested that it was long past time for me to be shut down.

Feminists on campus were split on the matter of that exhibit. Feminists often are divided, though you'd hardly know it from the press, which views that movement as being conveniently monolithic.

Despite these exceptions to the free flow of ideas, the town had had the feeling of a good bar. You could get into a reasonably interesting argument almost any place, and nobody would call the law on you, no matter how outrageous your ideas and language.

Then, on Ted Koppel's *Nightline,* I saw a march in Madison. The program was entitled "Women and Pornography," and near the top of the half hour, there was footage of Madison's annual "Take Back the Night" demonstration. The focus of the march that year was pornography and the overwhelming need to get rid of it because, as county supervisor Kathleen Nichols had told a rally earlier that evening, pornography is now 70 percent more violent than it was a decade ago, thereby being all the more dangerous to women.

Nichols had proposed a new law for the county that would make pornography into a civil rights, not a First Amendment, violation. Perpetrators would be guilty of sex discrimination. This approach is based on a theory developed by Catharine MacKinnon, professor of law at the University of Michigan, and Andrea Dworkin.

Professor MacKinnon had taken part in a symposium in Madison on the day of the march, and Andrea Dworkin was also in town.

On *Nightline,* the marchers looked as if they had stepped off the canvas of a latter-day Norman Rockwell[1] devoted to portraying the diversity of good, caring citizens. Students, elderly people, professionals, union organizers, bohemians, teachers, musicians. You could tell (and friends of mine in Madison later confirmed) that most of them were liberal, antiracist, and regular listeners to *Morning Edition* and *All Things Considered* on National Public Radio.[2]

Their faces were lit by street lamps, and by lighting crews. But there was also an inner illumination—the light of faith, the fire of conviction that you are part of a true solidarity of will that must triumph because it is so right. Had there been a plebiscite during the march that night on a

---

1. **Norman Rockwell** (1894–1978): American artist known for his folksy paintings of domestic life, many of which were featured on the cover of the *Saturday Evening Post.*—ED.

2. *Morning Edition* and *All Things Considered:* Morning and afternoon news shows, respectively, on NPR (National Public Radio), which has been accused of a liberal bias.—ED.

civil rights statute that would censor pornography, that bill would have passed by acclamation.

Watching the zeal in those eyes, I wondered what would have happened if, in Madison—with its lively, free marketplace of ideas—a few of the marchers had been swept by their feelings to break into some of those pornographic bookstores en route and, well, reduce the vileness in them to ashes. Provided no clerks or customers had been injured, would those still in the line of march have cheered?

In a subsequent year, an "adult" bookstore was indeed largely destroyed in Madison. And there were cheers from the true believers in suppression of vile-free expression.

Meanwhile, the MacKinnon-Dworkin jihad against pornography and the First Amendment has had a greater impact throughout the nation than I first thought possible. While their followers do not burn down "adult" bookstores, except perhaps in their dreams, they are busy lobbying legislators, lecturing, and otherwise resembling latter-day Anthony Comstocks.[3] And the spectrum of support for MacKinnon and Dworkin reveals, once more, that the Right is hardly the only force for censorship.

The history of this strategy also indicates that the growing division among feminists about whether the state should decide what we read and see can deeply affect the nature and future of feminism. As Cryss Farley, a feminist and executive director of the Iowa Civil Liberties Union, says of the spread of the MacKinnon-Dworkin credo: "Does the women's movement really want to lend its name to such repression?" Gloria Steinem already has.

First, the theory of this censorship in the name of civil rights—as it has been embodied in an actual law, the first MacKinnon-Dworkin statute to be passed. It was signed by the mayor of Indianapolis on May 1, 1984.

After holding hearings on women and pornography, the Indianapolis City Council declared that pornography "discriminates against women by exploiting and degrading them, thereby restricting their full exercise of citizenship and participation in public life."

The ordinance followed, and it further underlined the civil rights rationale first developed by MacKinnon and Dworkin:

> Pornography is a discriminatory practice based on sex because its effect is to deny women equal opportunities in society. . . . The bigotry and contempt it promotes, with the acts of aggression it fosters, harm women's opportunities for equality of rights in employment, education, access to and use of public accommodations, and acquisition of real property, and contribute significantly to restricting women in particular from full exercise of citizenship and participation in public life, including in neighborhoods.

---

3. For a discussion of **Anthony Comstock,** see pp. 427–28.—ED.

What, then, *is* pornography? Under the MacKinnon-Dworkin law in Indianapolis—and ten cities or more were waiting to enact similar laws if Indianapolis's held up in court—the core definition is "the graphic sexually explicit subordination of women, whether in pictures or in words."

Off the drawing board and into real life: A woman walks into a 20 bookstore or a movie house or past a newsstand and finds herself offended by some material that meets the minimal triggering criteria. She then files a complaint with Indianapolis's Office of Equal Opportunity, which thereupon sends out its investigators. A hearing is then held and if the agency finds the material is pornographic—and is upheld by a court—the material is removed and fines are levied. Moreover, the court would be asked to issue in injunction forbidding the further dissemination of the given book, magazine, or movie in Indianapolis.

This injunction is what is called in the First Amendment trade a "prior restraint." Pure censorship. The most direct and destructive suppression of speech that can be perpetrated by the state, short of what happened at Kent State.[4]

There's more. A woman in Indianapolis is raped, and claims that a particular movie or television news report about a rape had incited her assailant. Under the ordinance, she can sue the film distributor, the owner of the movie house, or the television station for damages. Indeed, in this and other claims for damages allowed by this law, the plaintiff can go after the writer of a script, the publisher of a book—anyone in the production chain.

To win money damages, the plaintiff must prove "intent"—knowledge on the part of the person being sued that the material is pornographic under the MacKinnon law. As we shall see, that law is so broad and vague that God could be in the dock for passages in the Old Testament.

This "civil rights" approach to eradicating pornography was first introduced in Minneapolis. A bill similar to the Indianapolis statute twice passed the city council there, and was twice vetoed by Mayor Donald Fraser because he would not defect from "our cherished tradition and constitutionally protected right of free speech."

Perhaps the most bizarre turn in the tumultuous history of the 25 MacKinnon-Dworkin countertradition was a letter sent to the president of the Minneapolis City Council on the occasion of Donald Fraser's first veto of the MacKinnon-Dworkin bill. The letter was written—"in dissent and dismay" at Fraser's veto—by the justly celebrated First Amendment gladiator, Professor Laurence Tribe of Harvard Law School.

---

4. **Kent State:** National Guardsmen fired on protesting students on the campus of Kent State University in 1970, killing four students and injuring nine.—ED.

In the letter, Tribe chastised the mayor for "hiding behind the First Amendment" by not letting the courts decide, instead of unilaterally killing the bill by veto. The Dworkin-MacKinnon legislation, said Tribe, "is not obviously unconstitutional" and its supposed invalidity "follows surely from no clear precedent." Tribe added that while he is uncertain as to how a judicial test will come out, he felt the MacKinnon-Dworkin creation "may eventually be found to be the first sensible approach to an area which has vexed some of the best legal minds for decades."

Professor Tribe later acknowledged error and resumed his support of the First Amendment.

During that period in Minneapolis, a feminist member of the city council, Kathy O'Brien, opposed the statute. "The status of women," she said, "is better in open societies than in closed, restrictive societies. This is censorship."

The woman with whom he had been living left in anger, and returned to her father's house—a long journey away. After four months, the man she had left went to visit her, hoping to persuade his former companion to go back with him. He succeeded.

They left her father's house, and on the road, as evening came, they 30 stopped in a small town. There was no hotel, and no one offered to take them in for the night until an old man finally said they could stay with him.

During dinner, there was much pounding on the door and when the old man opened it, a group of men ordered him to send out his male guest, because they wanted to sodomize him. The guest preferred not to accommodate them, and instead offered to lend the men the woman he had just convinced to return to him. She had no voice in the matter.

The deal was struck; a lengthy gang rape took place. In the morning the traveler found the woman lying at the door of the house with her hands on the threshold. "Stand up," he said. "It's time to leave." There was no answer. The woman was dead.

He placed the woman across his horse and continued on the way home. Once he got there, he took a knife and cut the woman's corpse into twelve pieces. He sent one piece to each of the twelve family branches with which he, and his father before him, had nurtured close relations. With each piece of the corpse was a message. It can be distilled into a single word: "Vengeance!" And vengeance was taken on all the men who had raped the woman.

That story, and therefore the book containing it, was in violation of the letter and spirit of the antipornography law in Indianapolis designed by Catharine MacKinnon and Andrea Dworkin.

The Indianapolis ordinance, after all, defines pornography as "the 35 sexually explicit subordination of women, graphically depicted whether in pictures or in words, that includes one or more of the following":

— "Women are presented as sexual objects who enjoy pain or humiliation; or

— "Women are presented as sexual objects who experience sexual pleasure in being raped; or

— "Women are presented being penetrated by objects or animals; or

— "Women are presented in scenarios of degradation, injury, abasement, torture, shown as filthy and inferior, bleeding, bruised, or hurt in a context that makes these conditions sexual;

— "Women are presented as sexual objects for domination, conquest, violation, exploitation, possession or use through postures or positions of servility or submission or display; or

— *"Women are presented as sexual objects tied up or mutilated or bruised or physically hurt, or as dismembered or truncated or fragmented or severed into body parts."* (Emphasis added.)

The story I've just told you was clearly guilty of being pornographic under the Indianapolis ordinance, a civil rights statute aimed at material that cannot be prosecuted under obscenity statutes.

Any woman in Indianapolis, if the courts had allowed the law to be enforced, could sue to have the book containing this story removed from the city. She could also ask the court to issue an injunction forbidding the appearance of this material in the city forevermore. And she could sue the publisher, the editor, the writer—anyone in the chain of production—for damages if she could prove that they knew this stuff was pornographic under the city statute.

A plaintiff could have some trouble collecting from the writer because the story is from Chapter 19 of the Book of Judges in the Old Testament.

The scope of the material—in all forms of expression—that the MacKinnon-Dworkin guillotine would remove from all eyes was, as Thomas Emerson of Yale Law School put it, "breathtaking."

During his years at Yale, Emerson became the nation's most lucid 40 and challenging analyst of the First Amendment. (See *The System of Freedom of Free Expression,* Vintage paperback.) In his commentary on the new censorship, Emerson noted that he agreed with MacKinnon that "pornography plays a major part in establishing and maintaining male supremacy in our society."

But, Emerson asks, is the solution to the harm done by pornography a law so "nearly limitless" in its scope that it "would outlaw a substantial portion of the world's literature"?

Among the works Emerson cites as being tossed into the tumbrils if the courts were to affirm the Indianapolis ordinance were William Faulkner's *Sanctuary* and those two venerable novels whose court appearances we thought were finally over, Henry Miller's *Tropic of Cancer* and D. H. Lawrence's *Lady Chatterley's Lover.*

But there were many more books, sculptures, movies, magazines, videocassettes, television programs, and newspapers that could be banished from Indianapolis and any other city persuaded by MacKinnon and Dworkin to protect their inhabitants from the pornography plague.

During the court battle in the U.S. District Court for the Southern District of Indiana, the American Civil Liberties Union and the Indiana ACLU filed a joint *amicus* brief.[5] It included a very small sampling of what works would be banned under the Indianapolis ordinance. Among them: Nabokov's *Lolita*, Petronius's *Satyricon*, Fielding's *Tom Jones,* and Géricault's *A Nude Being Tortured.* The *amicus* brief also spoke of film scenes that would be stopped at the borders of any cities adopting this legislation: ". . . the shower scene in *Psycho,* the sexual subordination and debasement in *Seven Beauties,* the dramatization of Jack the Ripper in *The Ruling Class* and *Time After Time,* the rape scenes in *Looking for Mr. Goodbar* . . . domestic violation and domination in *The Godfather.* . . ."

The ACLU court papers went on to point out that "on its face, the ordinance would prohibit much clinical sexual literature, from medical texts and scholarly studies to popularized works of sociology. . . ."

Farfetched? Well, said the ACLU, "Since the key operative term, 'sexual subordination,' is inherently vague, . . . individuals who object simply to the neutral scholarly presentation of such material as inevitably perpetuating a climate of subordination will be empowered to object to such material."

The "linchpin of the ordinance," as the ACLU describes it, is the term, "subordination of women." To the writer of a book, the maker of a movie or a piece of sculpture who doesn't want to get banned in MacKinnon-Dworkin model cities, what kind of guideline is that term? What does it mean?

When a statute is made out of fog, it fails to give, as the Supreme Court has said, "the person of ordinary intelligence a reasonable opportunity to know what is prohibited, so that he may act accordingly." That's not all the destructive mischief that can be caused by vagueness in a law. There are no reasonably clear guidelines for the police and judges who have to enforce the law. The result is drumhead justice. Police and judges decide arbitrarily who gets taught a lesson.

Moreover, the MacKinnon-Dworkin way of strangling pornography leads to epidemic self-censorship, should their standards ever be adopted. If you're unclear as to what you're forbidden to write or paint or film, you—in the language of the Supreme Court—"steer far wider of the unlawful zone . . . than if the boundaries of the forbidden areas were clearly marked."

Keeping the boundaries of the forbidden areas imprecise has long been the delight of censors. Anthony Comstock, for instance, was re-

---

5. *amicus* **brief:** A report filed in a legal case by someone not involved in that case, but acting as an *amicus curiae,* a "friend of the court."—ED.

sponsible for the 1873 laws that bore his name and banned from the federal mails all publications of an "obscene" or otherwise indecent character. What did those terms mean? The Comstock laws did not say.

Later amendments made the Comstock laws even vaguer by prohibiting from the mails any "lewd and lascivious" or "filthy" stuff or anything with an "indecent or immoral purpose."

"The definition," historian William Preston has pointed out, "was broad enough to exclude discussion of birth control, marriage counseling, and abortion for years."

It is one of the marvels of censorship that its architects, no matter how disparate their intentions and their backgrounds, end up uncannily resembling each other. So it is that if Catharine MacKinnon looks into a mirror one day, she may see, staring sternly at her, Anthony Comstock.

In Des Moines, Iowa, every member of the city council, I was told, would have considered it an honor and a privilege to vote for a MacKinnon-Dworkin bill. The then-mayor of that city, Pete Crivaro, admitted that there were people who would view such an ordinance as "censorship" and would contest it. But the mayor of Des Moines was unafraid. He says: "We must do what is in the best interest of the majority."

In a letter to Thomas Jefferson, James Madison warned of majoritarianism as the insatiable enemy of the Bill of Rights: 55

> The invasion of private rights is chiefly to be apprehended not from acts of Government contrary to the sense of its Constituents, but from acts in which the Government is the mere instrument of the major number of the Constituents.

James Madison, however, did not have the right stuff for Des Moines. Patrice Sayre, president of the city's chapter of the National Organization for Women, understands America better than that Virginian ever did. She said of the gospel according to MacKinnon and Dworkin: "It is a civil rights issue when a group of citizens are being degraded. This is an issue where civil rights should supersede First Amendment rights."

Among the cities that agreed and were willing to pass the MacKinnon ordinance were Detroit, Des Moines, Omaha, Columbus, St. Louis, Cincinnati, and Madison, Wisconsin.

What the smiters of pornography ignore is that this kind of "civil rights" relief cannot be limited to only one group. If the courts do eventually approve the MacKinnon-Dworkin theory, then many other groups with strong claims of being harmfully discriminated against in books, films, and television will also start using these statutes. They will sue for an injunction to have certain offensive material forever banned from a town or a city. They will bring suit for damages against anyone involved in the making and production of that material.

As Cryss Farley, executive director of the Iowa Civil Liberties Union, says—with crunching logic—"Few would argue that sex discrimination, brutality against women, and oppression of women do not exist. Much in our culture also oppresses Indians, Hispanics, Asians, homosexuals, and others. Anti-Semitic literature is unarguably harmful to Jews, as is racist literature to blacks. Are we going to afford racial and ethnic minorities and religious minorities a similar civil right to suppress speech which denigrates these groups?"

I know of black educators who would surely go after an injunction 60 to ban *Huckleberry Finn*. I can think of some Jews who would finally take care of *The Merchant of Venice* and *Oliver Twist*.

For the first time, books and movies and television will be as pure as country water. To maintain the peaceable kingdom, publishers and filmmakers will hire consultants trained by every group that has been offended by "pornographic" material, and those consultants will keep towns, cities, and minds clean.

And won't a result of this cleaning of the air be a marked decrease in crimes of rape and other violence against women? That's what the procensorship feminists have aggressively maintained.

A particularly useful analytical survey of the research in this field has been written by Marcia Pally and published by the Freedom to Read Foundation and the Americans for Constitutional Freedom. (Executive director of the Freedom to Read Foundation is Judith Krug, who is in charge of the Office of Intellectual Freedom of the American Library Association.)

In 1986, then-Surgeon General C. Everett Koop convened a Workshop on Pornography and Public Health, and the researchers reported— as Marcia Pally notes—that there is "no evidence that exposure to sexual material leads to sex crimes."

Pally also quotes Drs. Edward Donnerstein, Daniel Linz (University 65 of California), and Steven Penrod (University of Wisconsin) in a 1987 book, *The Question of Pornography: Research Findings and Policy Implications:*

> Should harsher penalties be leveled against persons who traffic in pornography, particularly violent pornography? We do not believe so. Rather, it is our opinion that the most prudent course of action would be the development of educational programs that would teach viewers to become more critical consumers of the mass media. . . . The legal [punitive] course of action is more restrictive of personal freedoms than an educational approach.

In 1990, Donnerstein and Linz added:

> Despite the Attorney General's Commission's report [the Meese Commission] that most forms of pornography have a causal relationship to sexually aggressive behavior, we find it difficult to understand how this conclusion was reached. . . .
> Most social scientists who testified before the commission were also cautious . . . when making statements about causal links between pornog-

raphy and sexually aggressive behavior. *Any reasonable view of the research would not come to the conclusion that . . . pornography conclusively results in antisocial effects.* (Emphasis added.)

And in 1986, Drs. Neil Malamuth and Joseph Ceniti (University of California) found (Pally reports) "no increase in aggression toward women in men who had watched sexually violent material."

The causes of rape and other violence against women are deeply rooted. Those women who believe that outlawing pornography will lessen violence against women might focus more on the family backgrounds and childhood experiences of violent males.

Roland Johnson, a social worker at a Minnesota treatment center for adolescent rapists, pointed out (*New York Times,* August 28, 1984) that most of them "have had no exposure, or very little, to pornography." More than 90 percent, however, were sexually abused as children. "I don't think pornography has that much influence on those who rape," Johnson said. "More important is what's happened to them in their past."

Still, it is possible, some would say, that along with a number of 70 other influences that shaped the man, pornography might have had something to do with an act of violence against a woman. In that event, if the rapist were caught and it was alleged that a particular magazine, movie, or book had incited him to commit the rape, should that magazine, movie, or book be banned lest it be culpable, in some way, for another rape by some other perpetrator later on?

The assumption, then, would be that many men with certain propensities would react to the material the same violent way. Yet, as Dr. Edward Donnerstein emphasizes, it is impossible to determine, with any accuracy, what will actually trigger someone to violence.

"Certain people," says Donnerstein, "are influenced by who knows what. . . . It is very difficult to say what type of stimuli are going to take those individuals on the fringe . . . and cause them to act in a certain way."

In 1966, William O. Douglas, during a concurring opinion in *A Book Named "John Cleland's Memoirs of a Woman of Pleasure"* vs. *Attorney General of the Commonwealth of Massachusetts,* observed in a footnote that "it would be a futile effort even for a censor to attempt to remove all that might possibly stimulate antisocial conduct."

Everything, and anything, said Douglas, is capable of triggering violence, and he quoted from a study on the subject in the *Wayne Law Review* (1964):

> Heinrich Pommerenke, who was a rapist, abuser, and mass slayer of women in Germany, was prompted to his series of ghastly deeds by Cecil B. DeMille's *The Ten Commandments.* During the scene of the Jewish women dancing about the Golden Calf, all the doubts of his life came clear: Women were the source of the world's trouble and it was his mis-

sion to both punish them for this and to execute them.

John George Haigh, the British vampire who sucked his victims' 75 blood through soda straws and dissolved their drained bodies in acid baths, first had his murder-inciting dreams and vampire-longings from watching the "voluptuous" procedure of—an Anglican High Church service.

■ CONSIDER THE SOURCE

1. What words, phrases, or examples reveal Hentoff's attitudes toward censorship, even before he mentions Dworkin or MacKinnon?

2. What does Hentoff believe is the most effective way to combat ideas you disagree with?

3. Summarize the key points of the MacKinnon-Dworkin argument defining pornography as a civil rights issue.

4. Why does Hentoff object to what he terms the "vagueness" and "imprecision" of the MacKinnon-Dworkin ordinance? What consequences does he foresee from the law's vagueness?

5. List the strategies Hentoff uses to counter the contention that there is a causal connection between pornography and rape. Can you discern any particular order to his arguments? Which strategies are most effective? Why do you think Hentoff structured his refutation this way?

■ CONSIDER THE IMPLICATIONS

6. Hentoff's and MacKinnon's positions depend on their interpretation and valuation of the First Amendment to the Constitution. In your journal, consider what Benjamin Franklin, who was around when that amendment was written, might say about this dispute if he were alive today. To help determine his position on freedom of the press, review the selections by Franklin (pp. 29–37 and 431–36) as well as Larzer Ziff's essay about Franklin (pp. 37–51).

7. In her discussion with Floyd Abrams, Catharine MacKinnon disagrees with the conclusion that her statute would apply to such works as James Joyce's *Ulysses* or D. H. Lawrence's novels (pp. 492–508). Write a letter from MacKinnon to Hentoff, responding to his Biblical example.

8. Just as MacKinnon and Dworkin hope to protect women from discrimination, John Wallace has argued (pp. 457–66) that African Americans must also be protected from discrimination even if it means sacrificing some First Amendment rights. Working in groups and using the MacKinnon-Dworkin ordinance as a guide, draft a similar ordinance protecting the civil rights of African Americans from discriminatory and degrading books and/or movies. What works would your ordinance ban?

9. James Madison's concern about "majoritarianism" may seem at odds with the rationale for a democracy—government by the majority. Hold a class debate on using "community standards" to determine what constitutes pornography, with half of the class supporting the dictum "Majority

Rules" and the other half arguing against the tyranny of the majority. How are First Amendment freedoms affected by each position?

10. Some feminists and civil libertarians worry that a measure such as the MacKinnon-Dworkin statute would grant too much power to state and local authorities to decide what should be published and what should be banned. Joan DelFattore ("Romeo and Juliet Were Just Good Friends, pp. 440–49) writes similarly of the dangers of allowing local school boards to decide the content of textbooks. Write a response to Dworkin and Mac-Kinnon's proposal from DelFattore's point of view.

▪ ▪ ▪ ▪ ▪ ▪

CATHARINE A. MACKINNON, FLOYD ABRAMS, AND ANTHONY LEWIS

A Conversation on the First Amendment

Threats to the First Amendment naturally upset members of the media, who depend on freedom of the press. The recent challenges to that freedom from the political left—from the antipornography movement and the on-campus forces for political correctness—caused the New York Times *to wonder whether the First Amendment was in more serious trouble now than it had been when the threats came from conservatives. The newspaper brought together two important and articulate spokespeople for opposing sides of the debate: Floyd Abrams (b. 1936), a lawyer who has spent his career defending challenges to the First Amendment and who has taught at Columbia University's Law School as well as its Graduate School of Journalism; and Catharine MacKinnon (b. 1946), professor of law at the University of Michigan, Ann Arbor, and co-author of the MacKinnon-Dworkin statute defining pornography as a civil rights violation. Moderating their dialogue is Anthony Lewis (b. 1927), a columnist for the* Times *and author of* Make No Law: The Sullivan Case and the First Amendment *(1991). Their conversation ranges over several topics related to the First Amendment, including speech codes on campus, advertising in campus newspapers, sexual harassment, and pornography.*

"Congress shall make no law . . . abridging the freedom of speech, or of the press." The late Justice Hugo L. Black wrote memorably about

From *The New York Times Magazine*, 13 March 1994, pp. 40–45, 56–57, 68, 71, and 81.

that proposition: "First in the catalogue of human liberties essential to the life and growth of a government of, for and by the people are those liberties written into the First Amendment to our Constitution."

Are those guarantees in trouble? That is the question put by the *Times Magazine* to two quite different authorities: Floyd Abrams, the prominent First Amendment lawyer, and Professor Catharine A. MacKinnon, the author of *Only Words* and an advocate of legal measures to curb pornography. They met at the *New York Times* for the discussion excerpted here. Anthony Lewis, a columnist for the *New York Times*, was the moderator.

ANTHONY LEWIS: Repression in this country, repression of speech, has historically come from the right. It was so with the Sedition Act of 1798; it was so when Attorney General A. Mitchell Palmer arrested thousands of supposed radicals in 1920; it was so when Senator Joseph McCarthy tyrannized the nation. Now I think there is a significant movement for repression from the political left. There have been calls, especially on campus, to repress certain kinds of expression—speech demeaning to minorities and disadvantaged groups, pornography. Mr. Abrams, could you comment on this phenomenon?

FLOYD ABRAMS: Well, I think there is a significant effort to restrict First Amendment values, if not legally defined First Amendment rights, which comes from the liberal community or the left-liberal community. Why is that so? It is human nature. People don't like to permit speech of which they thoroughly disapprove, and liberals are no more able to disassociate themselves from trying to impose into law what they wish people would say than conservatives are. It's true that most of the efforts, historically speaking, that have posed direct threats to the First Amendment have come from the right. Now we see on campuses around the country in a wide range of circumstances things being done, limitations on speech being imposed, that if they came from the right we would call McCarthyism.[1] And so they are.

LEWIS: Professor MacKinnon, has anything been said so far that you take exception to?

CATHARINE MACKINNON: I agree that First Amendment values are in trouble on the ground. But the trouble I see is different from what Professor Abrams sees. It seems to me that the lack of access to speech by those with dissident views—views not allowed to be expressed in the media, by a publishing world that excludes these, as well as by systematic forms of exclusion like lousy educational systems that promote illit-

---

1. **McCarthyism:** Named for Communist-hunting Senator Joseph McCarthy (1909–1957), McCarthyism refers to the practice of investigating and accusing individuals of disloyalty, subversion, or criminal activity with only superficial regard for the evidence.—ED.

eracy—are all forms of trouble for the First Amendment. But there are other distortions of the First Amendment, where it protects direct harm: I refer to the pornography industry, as well as cross-burning, an act of terrorism that's defended as an act of speech. As for limitations on speech on campus, I'm not sure what Mr. Abrams was referring to. There have been grievance procedures on campuses to restrict sexual harassment for over a decade. Is that what you mean by limits on speech on campus? Are you saying that when a teacher says to a student, "Sleep with me and I will give you an 'A'?" that is protected speech so long as it is done on a campus? Procedures to allow students to bring complaints about that kind of activity have been recognized as necessary for equal access to the benefits of an education for some time. That's just one example of an abuse that can hide behind freedom of speech when in fact it is an act of inequality.

LEWIS: Let me test your proposition by citing one much-advertised example of campus speech problems—the seizure of student newspapers at the University of Pennsylvania. It's happened elsewhere; it happened at Brandeis when a student newspaper carried a paid ad from one of those Holocaust revisionist outfits,[2] and students who didn't like the ad trashed the newspaper.

MACKINNON: That is, they engaged in a demonstration.

LEWIS: Well, that's my question. Is it your notion that nothing should be done about that? Is it permissible to trash newspapers if you don't like something that's in them?

MACKINNON: There is expressive value in what the students did, and there is also expressive value in letting the paper publish.   10

ABRAMS: I am prepared to make a somewhat stronger value judgment than that. I think that the students who seized and destroyed newspapers at Penn, at Brandeis, and elsewhere were doing something profoundly antithetical to First Amendment values, and I think they are the product of bad teaching. They justify what they have done either because they think it's right politically or because they think they are engaging in expressive conduct, and therefore "anything goes." But anything can be said to fall within the rubric of expressive conduct, including murder and rape. It seems to me that burning newspapers is something that should be beyond the pale in our society—that there should be far more agreement around this table that it is wrong to do and contrary to First Amendment values to do.

MACKINNON: What I think about it would depend on the position I was in or in whose shoes I was acting. It would seem to me to have been

---

2. **Holocaust revisionist:** One who contends that the Nazi extermination of millions of Jews, Catholics, gays, gypsies, and others did not occur.—ED.

preferable for the people who ran the ad to have decided not to run it—for reasons of not promoting lies, or not endangering or targeting specific groups for abuse.

LEWIS: In 1919, Justice Holmes[3] wrote an opinion in which he said that the First Amendment envisaged freedom for ideas "that we loathe and believe to be fraught with death." You can't get any stronger or more poetic language than that. I take it that you don't agree with it.

MACKINNON: I do agree with that, but one thing freedom of speech gives editors is the right to make decisions not to run lies. If it's false, you don't have to run it just because you disagree with it, to respect Holmes.

ABRAMS: But even someone living on a university campus, it seems to me, should know that newspapers may not be destroyed. That seems to me self-evident.

MACKINNON: But what about the idea that newspapers should not publish lies, including lies that target groups of people for abuse and aggression in that community?

ABRAMS: Newspapers are permitted—as you just said—to publish what they choose. It is an editorial decision, as you just said, whether to publish an advertisement like this. Once the student newspaper has decided to publish it, it is unacceptable for other students to respond by seizing the papers and taking that topic out of the realm of public debate.

MACKINNON: But is it acceptable to you that the newspaper chose to publish it?

ABRAMS: Yes, I think that it's important that there be public debate even about statements that I think are lies and in some cases that I am sure are lies.

MACKINNON: If you had been in a position to have a discussion with those students, would you have urged them to publish such material or not to publish it?

ABRAMS: I have had that discussion with some college newspapers, and I have urged them to publish it and to run editorials denouncing it. And that is the way I think the First Amendment should work on campus.

LEWIS: Another area: speech codes. One speech code—it was at the University of Connecticut—prohibited inappropriately directed laughter. That's perhaps an extreme example; but a good many of them go very

---

3. **Justice Holmes:** Oliver Wendell Holmes, Jr. (1841–1935), justice of the Supreme Court (1902–1932), staunchly defended free speech except in the face of "a clear and present danger."—ED.

far in prohibiting bad manners. How do you two feel about speech codes, university speech codes in particular?

MACKINNON: I found that sexual-harassment prohibitions or policies that allow students to complain about acts of harassment that are actionable under federal law have been included under the rubric of speech code. So I don't frankly know what you are talking about. Title VI of the Civil Rights Act promotes equal access to the benefits of an education on the basis of race; it's a federally guaranteed right. So, one could say that if you have epithets, invective, harassment and abuse on the basis of race or religion or sexual orientation, you have an environment in which the equal ability of students to learn is obstructed. These grievance procedures arise under federal equality guarantees.

ABRAMS: In my view, they threaten the values and sometimes the text of the First Amendment itself.

MACKINNON: I'm not defending every one of these codes in each of 25 their particulars. I want to make clear that many of them include procedures that make it possible to bring complaints about sexual harassment in education. The litigation that has attacked these codes on First Amendment grounds has also attacked these complaint procedures, although the results on that are inconclusive.

ABRAMS: I think it's important to distinguish between different forms of speech. First, I agree with Professor MacKinnon that a professor who says, "Sleep with me and I'll give you an 'A'," not only violates the law but should be fired. There was too much of that and too little was done about it for too long. I think that is very different from the situation of a professor now challenging sanctions imposed upon him by the University of New Hampshire, Professor J. Donald Silva, who during a lecture to his students made some references to sex. He was brought up on charges, suspended for a year and directed to get counseling to cure him of what the university thus far has found to be sexual harassment. I think that example—and there are a number of others—is one in which what is wrong is not the procedure. Professor MacKinnon is quite right in my view that there have to be procedures to implement our abhorrence of sexual harassment. But on more than one campus, charges have been made by students about words not proposing sexual conduct or suggesting any harm to a student but words used in a lecture and other statements made that have been accused of constituting sexual harassment. There at least First Amendment values are implicated, and I think it's very important for the university community to look very, very hard before they find violations of sexual-harassment codes or law in such situations.

MACKINNON: I certainly agree with the hard look, but I do have a question about what you said. Is it possible for sexual harassment to occur in a setting in which a teacher uses words in a classroom to a group of students?

ABRAMS: Yes, I suppose, but it would have to be very direct. It would have to be something that simply leaps off the page as constituting harassment and not just a reference to sex. There are people who are offended, for reasons I understand full well, but who are offended at sexual references. It's very important that we not engage in a sort of puritanical cleansing effort on campus to strike such references from the vocabulary of faculty and students.

MACKINNON: I agree with that. There's no problem between us on that. Nothing I have been involved in has had anything to do with being offended, with clean language, or with restricting ideas I don't like, for that matter.

LEWIS: Sometime not so long ago, if I remember it correctly, a professor at a major law school quoted an opinion of Justice Robert Jackson's.[4] Jackson in turn quoted Byron's Julia, a character in his poem "Don Juan" who—I think I have this right—"whispering 'I will ne'er consent,' consented." I've forgotten what the context was, but charges were pressed quite vigorously against the professor. What do you think of that rather marginal sexual reference passing through two learned authors, Byron and Justice Jackson? Does it bother you? Should it be ground for a complaint?

MACKINNON: I guess what is being raised there is a positive-outcome rape scenario.

LEWIS: What do you mean by that? I'm sorry, I don't understand.

MACKINNON: A positive-outcome rape scenario—it's one of the most common in pornography—is one in which the woman is shown being subjected to sexual aggression. She resists; she's further aggressed against. She further resists; the more she's aggressed against, the more she begins to get into it. Finally she is shown to be ecstatically consenting and having a wonderful time—in other words, it could be described as "whispering that she would ne'er consent, consented." Not consenting is itself the turn-on, saying no is part of meaning yes.

LEWIS: What do you think about professors who have made sexually oriented comments in class that students have found offensive or even to constitute harassment? Is it your view that professors ought [to] be free to do that?

---

4. **Justice Robert Jackson** (1892–1954): Supreme Court justice (1941–1954) who also served as chief counsel for the United States in the prosecution of Nazi war criminals at Nuremburg.—ED.

MacKinnon: The campus is different from the workplace, but in both 35
we have equality guarantees, and an analogy between work and school
has been a helpful starting place. Students are guaranteed equal access
to the benefits of an education without discrimination on the basis of
race or sex. So the question is: Does what you are asking about interfere
with this, together with rights to academic freedom and freedom of
speech? In the workplace, harassment has to be sufficiently severe or
pervasive as to change the conditions of work. Just as a beginning, think
by analogy of a hostile learning environment—one in which sexualized,
demeaning, denigrating comments, subordinating comments, or materials were sufficiently pervasive or severe as to alter the learning environment so it was discriminatory. I don't think professors should be free to
do that.

Abrams: I start not with federal statutes as my model, but with the
proposition that a university is fundamentally a place of free expression,
that professors ought to be free to have their say and to teach their
courses as they see fit, and that students ought to be free to talk to each
other openly, candidly, and sometimes very roughly. The price tag will
inevitably be some discomfort—sometimes a lot of discomfort. That
doesn't begin to lead me to the proposition that the students who feel
bad about what has been said should have the power to prevent, to bar,
or to sanction the speech involved. It's true that at some point comments
can get to a point where the learning experience is not only altered but
nonexistent. But I am more concerned at this point about the pall of orthodoxy that I believe has descended upon our campuses, where professors are afraid to talk about certain topics. Rape is not being taught in a
lot of law schools now because it's just not worth the hassle. Anthropology students are not being taught about race because it isn't worth the
risk to professors involved. I know professors who have found themselves in a situation where the choice they have made is to teach other
things. And I think that this is the result of an explosion not only of criticism but of threats, made against faculty members by students who
have come to believe that if they are troubled by the terms in which they
are taught the remedy is to stifle their professors.

MacKinnon: But one of the things they are doing is speaking. In fact,
there is now an explosion of speech from previously silenced quarters,
including those who have been targeted by the subjects you mentioned.
If teachers are now afraid to teach rape because it's not worth the hassle
or the risk, the question is: What is the risk? It includes that their students will *speak* to them and say things that formerly they had not said.
There are a great many more women in law schools than before. They
are speaking out in opposition to the way rape has always been taught,
which frankly has often been from the standpoint of the perpetrator.
Much of the rape law is written from that standpoint, and it has implicitly been taught largely as a defendant's rights issue. A lot of women

and some men are *dissenting* from that. They won't sit quietly and take it anymore, because it affects the conditions of their lives. There's been a challenge to the power of professors to control discussions from the point of view from which they've always controlled it. Instead of taking the chance to become educated, some professors take their marbles and go home.

ABRAMS: I think dissent in class is a marvelous thing.

MACKINNON: Well, a lot of professors don't.

ABRAMS: I understand that, but what concerns me is that what is going   40
on is less dissent than students basically making charges, formal charges; charges of sexual harassment, charges of racial insensitivity, where what is involved—at worst—is a difference of opinion about how best to teach a course.

MACKINNON: Ultimately, that is also a challenge to what has been the absolute power of teachers to control the terms of discourse. You're sensitive to how professors feel about dissent. But what you're characterizing as a pall of orthodoxy I think is a breath of freedom. It's a challenge to the absolute authority of dominant groups to control the discussion from the standpoint of white male and upper-class privilege and power. It isn't cheap anymore to denigrate people's human dignity in class. It isn't free anymore. Teachers have to pay a price in terms of being challenged now in ways that they didn't before. The question is, is there *ever* a legal bottom line that gives students something they can use? Do they *ever* have legal rights in this area?

ABRAMS: But the price that is being paid is not always for denigration. Sometimes, indeed often, there is genuine disagreement about how to teach and what to teach. There is far too much censure in a formal, juridical sense, far too much use of procedures with a capital P to punish professors who don't view things the way you do.

LEWIS: You have talked repeatedly, Professor MacKinnon, about what you call "equality rights." I'd like to know precisely what you mean by this term. Analyze for us how a judge or a sensible citizen should weigh the equality concern as against free speech or freedom of the press.

MACKINNON: Well, the concern of my book *Only Words* has been that discussions like this one have been conducted as if the only ground rule were free expression, and if someone feels bad about what's been said, those are the breaks. Feeling good is not an equality right. Equal access to an education that you don't have to absorb years of abuse to get, *is*.

ABRAMS: Can I add a word about equality rights? It ought to be said   45
that there's no inherent conflict between First Amendment principles

and equality principles and indeed in most circumstances they flow together. More speech has been the savior in good part of minorities in
this country; the ability of minorities to speak out, to have their say, to
be heard, not to be punished for what they think is at the core of this
country at its best. To put in conflict equality rights and free-expression
rights is to put in conflict principles that are not in conflict at all.

LEWIS: In *Only Words* you suggest, if I read that book correctly, that
equality can trump First Amendment values. In this regard I'd like to
offer a quote from the Canadian lawyer Kathleen Mahoney, who argued
and won a landmark pornography case in which the Supreme Court of
Canada adopted Professor MacKinnon's broad view of what should be
suppressed as pornography: "The law has not treated women and other
minority groups fairly. If we truly believe in democracy in the fullest
sense of the word, then everyone should be able to participate. That
means some sort of cutting back of individual rights as we've always
known them." Is that your view?

MACKINNON: Well, freedom of expression and equality are both individual rights. The traditional model of civil liberties has been more generous to those rights that the people who set up the system wanted to
keep for themselves. And equality wasn't something they guaranteed
because they didn't need it. So equality, as much as it has always been
an important systemic value, an important formal value in the legal system, as a substantive value it's only been recently recognized. It wasn't
in the Constitution in the first place; it took a long time and a lot of
blood and grief to get it in there at all. Guarantees of equality in social
life have been even more recent. Equality guarantees conflict with individual rights that powerful groups already had—or thought they had. It
is their power, but they take it for their freedom and their rights. If you
look at the First Amendment properly, you may not ultimately have this
conflict. But because the First Amendment has not been seen properly,
we've got a conflict between equality guarantees and views of individual rights that preexist serious equality guarantees. That's what Kathleen Mahoney is referring to.

LEWIS: In your book you suggest that the First Amendment has been of
use primarily to those who hold power. But isn't it true that since the
1920s, when the First Amendment began to be seriously enforced in this
country, it has been primarily of use in protecting the free speech and
press rights of the dissident—the Seventh-Day Adventists, the commu-
nists, the Ku Klux Klan, the civil rights movement? Not the powerful.
The First Amendment is of use to the nonpowerful. Is that wrong?

MACKINNON: It's partly wrong and it's partly right. It's not that there
haven't been dissidents who have found that the First Amendment is
helpful. It's that the First Amendment only protects that speech that can
manage to get itself expressed, and often that is the speech of power.

Only that speech that can be expressed is speech that the government can attempt to silence; in the name of dissent one can then attempt to use the First Amendment to defend that speech. But what about those layers of society that have been deeply silenced, among them sexually violated women, including prostituted women, including groups who are kept illiterate and thus not given access to speech from slavery times through the present. Those groups the First Amendment doesn't help. They need equality to get access to speech—to get to the point where the First Amendment could help them by keeping the government from interfering with their speech. We have barely heard from those groups.

LEWIS: Why aren't *you* a representative of the women you say have been 50 voiceless? It seems to me that in terms of First Amendment expression, the women's movement is one of the most successful and admirable reform movements in American history.

MACKINNON: Yes, and one of our jobs is to keep talking to you about all the women you're not listening to, all the women who can't speak, instead of getting bought off by some illusion of preeminence. We are here to talk not only about all the things that haven't been said, but also about all the women who haven't been heard and are still unheard. . . . I am no substitute for them.

ABRAMS: I agree with Professor MacKinnon in so far as what she's saying is that our society rewards power and to a large extent rewards wealth. People who have money have a lot more say about how our society is run than people who don't. People who are powerful by definition have a lot more say about what happens in our society than people of the underclass. There are ways to try to deal with that if one chooses to. One way is to speak about it. Another way is to legislate about it. But one way that I would oppose trying to deal with it is to suppress speech with which we disagree.

MACKINNON: What about the film, *Deep Throat,* which Linda Lovelace was coerced into making? Is that what you call the expression of ideas I disagree with?

ABRAMS: Well, I think first of all it is the expression of ideas—

MACKINNON: So is the rape of women.   55

ABRAMS: The rape of women is handled by rape laws.

MACKINNON: And *Deep Throat*—how should that be handled?

ABRAMS: Judged by obscenity laws.

MACKINNON: It's been judged obscene in some places and not in others. You think Linda Lovelace should have no equality rights in relation to that film? How does that film give rise to a speech interest you want to protect?

ABRAMS: I don't even know what you mean in this case about equality 60 rights. She has a perfect right not to be raped.

MACKINNON: I mean that, as a woman, Linda was sexually subordinated to make it and that—as she puts it—"every time someone watches that film they are watching me be raped." She has an equality right not to have that done. And to stop the film that is doing it, and whose profit is an incentive to keep doing it.

LEWIS: Am I right in thinking that coercion as you would define it in the law you drafted with Andrea Dworkin—that is, graphic, sexually explicit materials that subordinate women through pictures and words— disallows voluntarily engaging in a pornographic film since it says that a written consent shall not be proof that there was no coercion?

MACKINNON: No, you're not. If you can force a woman to have sex with a dog, you can force her to sign a contract. The mere fact of a contract being signed doesn't in itself negate a finding of coercion. The coercion itself would have to be proven under our ordinance.

ABRAMS: Look, your statute provides in part that graphic, sexually explicit subordination of women in which women are presented as sexual objects for domination, conquest, violation, exploitation, possession or use, etc., can give rise to a private cause of action. The Court of Appeals in holding the statute unconstitutional—a decision affirmed by the Supreme Court—indicated that books like Joyce's *Ulysses*, Homer's *Iliad*, poems by Yeats, novels by D. H. Lawrence and the like could all be subject to a finding of violation of the statute that you have drafted.

MACKINNON: And that's just simply false. 65

ABRAMS: Well, I don't think it *is* false.

MACKINNON: Those materials are not even sexually explicit. They don't even get in the door.

LEWIS: Why don't you just repeat your definition of pornography?

MACKINNON: Professor Abrams just quoted the definition. Andrea Dworkin's and my approach to pornography is to define it in terms of what it does, not in terms of what it says, not by its ideas, not by whether someone is offended by it, not by whether somebody doesn't like it. None of that has anything to do with our definition. Our definition, and our legal causes of action, all have to do with what it *does* to the women in it, to the children in it and to other people who can *prove* that as a direct result of these materials they were assaulted or made second-class citizens on the basis of sex.

ABRAMS: You mean because people will think less of women on account 70 of how they're portrayed?

MACKINNON: No, because people will *do* things to them like not hiring them, like sexualizing them and not taking them seriously as students, the entire array of violent and nonviolent civil subordination, when they can prove it comes from pornography.

ABRAMS: That is why your legislation is so frontal an attack on the First Amendment. When the Court of Appeals said that the impact of your statute is such that it could apply to everything from hard-core films to the collected works of James Joyce, D. H. Lawrence, and John Cleland, it was entirely correct. It is correct because what you have drafted as a definition of actionable pornography is "graphic sexually explicit subordination of women, in which women are presented as sexual objects for domination." Lots of great art as well as cheap and vile productions have depicted women in just that way—*The Rape of the Sabine Women,* for example. And my point is not that your definition is vague, but that it is clear. It includes any art, whether it is good or bad, art or nonart, that you have concluded may do harm. That's an unacceptable basis and it should be.

MACKINNON: O.K., there are several things wrong with this. Number one, those materials are not sexually explicit. The court was told exactly what sexually explicit means in law and in ordinary use, and it should have known better. Number two, these materials have never yet been shown in any study to have produced any of the effects that pornography produces. So no one could prove that women are subordinated as a result of them. This statute does not cover those materials, period. It is false as a matter of statutory construction. The statute could potentially cover something like a film in which somebody was actually killed but claims are made that it has artistic value—an artistic snuff film—or in which someone is raped but the film has interesting camera angles. That does raise a conflict between existing law and our statute. The examples you cite do not.

LEWIS: Professor MacKinnon, we do have a concrete example of what your view of the law might result in. The Canadian Supreme Court adopted your view. Since then, there has been an intensification of gay and lesbian books being intercepted at the border. That seems to be the result of a country actually adopting your standard.

MACKINNON: That's disinformation. Canada customs has singled out 75 those materials for years, and customs law was not involved in the case I was part of in Canada. What happened was, the Supreme Court of

Canada rejected its morality-based standard for obscenity and held that when pornography hurts equality it can be stopped. Customs has not reviewed its standards since. I think that if Canada customs is still stopping materials because they are gay or lesbian, on a moral ground not a harm ground, they have lost their constitutional authority to do it under this ruling. If the materials hurt women or men or their equality, they can still stop them. But Andrea Dworkin and I do not favor addressing pornography through criminal law, especially obscenity law, so in that way Canada has not adopted our approach.

LEWIS: Professor MacKinnon, there's an assumption explicitly stated in your book that pornography as you define it results in antisocial, abusive activity by the customers.

MACKINNON: There's overwhelming documentation of it.

LEWIS: But it is a fact that in countries in which pornography is lawful and there are no legal restraints whatever on sexually explicit materials the incidence of sexual crimes is much lower than in this country.

MACKINNON: Actually, that isn't true. It's urban legend.

LEWIS: In Denmark, in Germany, in Japan—

MACKINNON: In Denmark, data on reported rape after liberalization is inconclusive. It did not drop, though. Also, the definitions and categories of sexual offenses were changed at the same time that pornography was decriminalized. Also, reporting may well have dropped. If your government supports pornography, reporting sexual abuse seems totally pointless to women. So, too, Germany and Sweden. Once pornography is legitimized throughout society, you get an explosion in sexual abuse, but women don't report it anymore because they know that nothing will be done about it. Feminists and sex educators in Denmark are beginning to say that selling twelve-year-old children on street corners is not what they mean by sexual liberation. What's happened in Japan and other places is that much of sexual abuse is just part of the way women are normally treated. If you're still essentially chattel, what is it to rape you? In Sweden there aren't any rape-crisis centers. All there are is battered-women shelters. So the battered-women's movement has been pushing the government to look at the reality of rape there, which is massive.

ABRAMS: But those countries that are harshest on what you would call pornography are also harshest on women. In China promulgation of pornography leads to capital punishment. In Iran it leads to the harshest and most outrageous physical torture. These are not good countries for women to live in. If you look at countries like Sweden and Japan and Holland and Germany, which have allowed more rather than less free expression in this area of sexually explicit speech, you'll find that these are the countries in which sexual abuse of women is not particularly prevalent. It's one thing for you to advocate a statute such as you have proposed in Sweden, but I daresay it has not been seriously suggested that Swedish women as a group have been victimized by their free press and free-speech laws.

MACKINNON: Swedish women have seriously supported our law, against the legalized victimization of pornography. But it's hard to know what the reality is. It's wrong to base how much rape there is on reported rape. It's also very hard to know how much pornography is actually available. You could look at the U.S. laws and get the impression that pornography was being taken seriously as a problem in this country.

ABRAMS: But when you cite, for example, the Balkans as a place where there's been a vast amount of rape and infer that it has something to do with the existence of sexually explicit materials, you don't tell us that in 1913 there was an orgy of rapes at a time when such material didn't exist at all. It puts into question the validity of the whole thesis.

MACKINNON: It is not an exclusive thesis. There are lots of ways of sex- 85 ualizing subordination—religion, veiling, clitoridectomies. Pornography is one way, and some of the abuses it is connected to we can do something about. In countries where women have recently got more voice, like the United States and Sweden, women are becoming more able to identify the sources of our subordination. The United States is a mass culture, media-saturated and capitalistic. In asking how women are subordinated in the United States, it would be wrong to eliminate the capitalistic mass media of the pornography industry. At other times and places, the ways in which women are subordinated are different. But now, the United States is exporting this form of subordination to the rest of the world.

ABRAMS: Didn't you say you were going to give us a few minutes to summarize?

LEWIS: Yes, we'd better do it.

MACKINNON: In looking at areas in which women are most distinctively kept unequal, surely those areas include the workplace and school. But they also include the home and the street and the public order. That's why, in Andrea Dworkin's and my approach to freedom of speech, we don't limit ourselves to the traditional equality areas. Women haven't been permitted to address the ways in which we are distinctively subordinated. And the equality interests at stake for women, for people of color, for all people who are subjected to inequality on the basis of sex or race or sexual orientation in particular—

those are interests that the First Amendment as it has been interpreted has not taken into account. It has not been a real legal concern. That doesn't mean that it couldn't be. These rights can be accommodated. A First Amendment properly understood would give everyone greater access to speech. It would also recognize that to violate someone, to subordinate someone, to abuse someone, to rape someone are not First Amendment-protected activities. They aren't what the freedom of speech is about. Trafficking in sexual slavery is not a discourse in ideas anymore than an auction block is a discourse in ideas or burning a cross is a discourse in ideas. They are activities that subordinate people. They are, of course, expressive. Rape is expressive. Murder is expressive. My punching someone in the face to express my contempt for that person's ideas is expressive. That doesn't make it protected expression. The fact that abuse is well organized and highly profitable and produces a product that produces more abuse does not make it protected speech, just because that product is picture and words. The pornographic industry does not promote speech; it silences women. It contributes to creating a context, an objectified and sexualized and denigrated context, for the deprivation of women's human rights on a mass scale.

ABRAMS: The First Amendment in my view is not at odds with, not at war with, not even in conflict with principles of equality. It is one of the great forces by which equality comes to occur in our society. We don't need a First Amendment for a lot of speech in our society. I don't think I've ever said anything that required any First Amendment protection, because no one would ever put me in jail for what I had to say or for what I suspect Professor MacKinnon or Mr. Lewis has to say. We need a First Amendment most of all to protect people who say very unpopular things, unpopular with government, unpopular with the public at large. We do not permit and should not permit the First Amendment to be overcome on the basis of some sort of continuous balancing, where we simply look at the supposed harm caused by speech as against the supposed value of what is said. I might conclude that what Professor Mac-Kinnon had to say today is harmful; maybe she'll persuade some people and in the course of persuading some people do some real harm to the First Amendment, as I perceive it, and to freedom of expression as I hope we will continue to have it in this country. I don't think we can engage in any such balancing process. She's allowed to say what she has to say; I'm allowed to say what I have to say; Mr. Lewis is allowed to say what he has to say. In only the rarest case do we even start down the road of saying, well this speech is so likely to cause harm of such extraordinary, provable, damaging nature that we won't allow it. I don't believe we ought to do that in almost any case on a university campus. There more than anywhere freedom ought to be the rule and almost the invariable rule. I don't believe we should do it in the area of sexually oriented speech beyond the law of obscenity as we now have that law. That body of law looks to whether a speech has serious artistic value. If it does, by the definition of our law, it can't be obscene. It can be outrageous, it can be pornographic in the sense that Professor MacKinnon defines it, but we protect it because we think that ideas—even disagreeable ideas—matter so much that we are unwilling to pay the price of suppression of speech. I think that at the end of the day what animates me most in this area—and what I don't think Professor MacKinnon takes sufficient account of—are the risks of suppression of speech. There's a lot of speech that isn't very helpful or useful or societally beneficial—and even some speech that may well do some harm—that I'm not at all willing to suppress or to allow lawsuits to punish. That's because I think our First Amendment is right in reflecting a profound distrust of the government telling us what we can say, what we can think, how we can express our views; and I think that to start down the road of suppressing more speech, limiting the speech that we are free to express as a people would be to strip us of what makes us so unique: a commitment to free expression that makes us one of the wonders of the world. I think we should be proud of that, and I think we should leave it the way it is.

MacKINNON: I don't think our pornography industry is one of the wonders of the world, nor is our rape rate. I've got a question . . . a rude question. You haven't ever represented a pornographer, have you? 90

ABRAMS: I've got to think of everyone you might consider a pornographer.

MacKINNON: Start where the industry starts, with *Playboy* or *Penthouse* or *Hustler.*

ABRAMS: No.

MacKINNON: I didn't think you had.

■ **CONSIDER THE SOURCE**

1. Explain what Floyd Abrams means by "First Amendment values."

2. Describe what Abrams refers to as a "pall of orthodoxy." Why does MacKinnon regard that same phenomenon as "a breath of freedom"?

3. What does MacKinnon mean by "equality rights"? How do those rights conflict or coincide with freedom of expression?

4. What evidence does MacKinnon offer to support her connection between pornography and antisocial or abusive behavior by consumers of pornography? What objections do Lewis and Abrams raise? How does MacKinnon refute those objections?

▪ **CONSIDER THE IMPLICATIONS**

5. In your journal, adopt Catharine MacKinnon's point of view and respond to the criticism leveled at her by William Noble (pp. 449–56) or Nat Hentoff (pp. 481–92).

6. Basing your arguments on Benjamin Franklin's remarks in his "Apology for Printers" (pp. 431–36), write a letter from Franklin to the editor of the student newspaper, supporting or condemning the decision to publish an ad from a Holocaust revisionist group.

7. Hold a class debate on whether the university is analogous to the workplace, as MacKinnon believes, or is "fundamentally a place of free expression," as Abrams contends.

8. MacKinnon sees a violation of the First Amendment protection of free speech in "systematic forms of exclusion like lousy educational systems that promote illiteracy." Review the essays in chapter 2 that discuss access to literacy, such as those by Frederick Douglass (pp. 130–36), Linda Kerber (pp. 136–50), Malcolm X (pp. 164–72), and Jimmy Santiago Baca (pp. 180–88). Write a letter to MacKinnon from one of those authors supporting, refuting, or modifying her position.

9. Enforcement of the MacKinnon-Dworkin antipornography statute depends on proving that discriminatory behavior was "a direct result of [pornographic] materials." Discuss in groups how you would "prove" that a pornographic book or movie resulted in such an action. What evidence would convince you of the connection between behavior and pornography?

10. Write an essay expressing your position on this debate between the guarantees of freedom of speech and freedom from discrimination. If one freedom outweighs the other, which do you think is more important to preserve, and why? If they can be made compatible, how would you reconcile them?

11. Read or review Huntly Collins's essay about press coverage of "political correctness" on campus (pp. 472–80). How would Collins assess the treatment of campus-related issues by Abrams, Lewis, and MacKinnon? How much do they rely on anecdotal evidence, exaggeration, or oversimplification?

Don't Tread on My Cursor:
Freedom of Electronic Speech

How far will the First Amendment stretch? That's one of the issues that confronts us in the electronic age, as laws and precedents that arose to govern printed materials are applied to digital technology. The nature and the potential abuses of that technology are the subject of a debate conducted by Harper's Magazine *among computer hackers, those cybernauts who roam the corridors of the digital universe as easily as most people navigate around their hometowns. With twenty participants chatting over an eleven-day period, the discussion in this selection may be difficult to follow on first reading. Topics are raised, dropped, and then picked up again by later voices—rather like any conversation you might have among twenty of your friends. The only difference is that this "conversation" took place in an electronic discussion group, with the "speakers" sitting hundreds of miles apart, typing their replies on a screen and sending them over the phone lines to a computer in Sausalito, California.*

The image of the computer hacker drifted into public awareness in the mid-seventies, when reports of Chinese-food-consuming geniuses working compulsively at keyboards began to issue from MIT [Massachusetts Institute of Technology]. Over time, several of these impresarios entered commerce, and the public's impression of hackers changed: They were no longer nerds but young, millionaire entrepreneurs.

The most recent news reports have given the term a more felonious connotation. Early this year, a graduate student named Robert Morris Jr. went on trial for releasing a computer program known as a worm into the vast Internet system, halting more than six thousand computers. The subsequent public debate ranged from the matter of proper punishment for a mischievous kid to the issue of our rapidly changing notion of what constitutes free speech—or property—in an age of modems and databases. In order to allow hackers to speak for themselves, *Harper's Magazine* recently organized an electronic discussion and asked some of the nation's best hackers to "log on," discuss the protean notions of contemporary speech, and explain what their powers and talents are.

The following forum is based on a discussion held on the WELL, a computer bulletin-board system based in Sausalito, California. The forum is the result of a gradual accretion of arguments as the participants—located throughout the country—opined and reacted over an

From *Harper's Magazine* (March 1990), pp. 45–57.

eleven-day period. *Harper's Magazine* senior editor Jack Hitt and assistant editor Paul Tough served as moderators.

ADELAIDE is a pseudonym for a former hacker who has sold his soul to the corporate state as a computer programmer.

BARLOW is John Perry Barlow, a retired cattle rancher, a former Republican county chairman, and a lyricist for the Grateful Dead, who currently is writing a book on computers and consciousness entitled *Everything We Know Is Wrong*.

BLUEFIRE is Dr. Robert Jacobson, associate director of the Human Interface Technology Laboratory at the University of Washington and a former information-policy analyst with the California legislature.

BRAND is Russell Brand, a senior computer scientist with Reasoning Systems, in Palo Alto, California.

CLIFF is Clifford Stoll, the astronomer who caught a spy in a military computer network and recently published an account of his investigation entitled *The Cuckoo's Egg*.

DAVE is Dave Hughes, a retired West Pointer who currently operates his own political bulletin board.

DRAKE is Frank Drake, a computer science student at a West Coast university and the editor of *W.O.R.M.*, a cyberpunk magazine.

EDDIE JOE HOMEBOY is a pseudonym for a professional software engineer who has worked at Lucasfilm, Pyramid Technology, Apple Computer, and Autodesk.

EMMANUEL GOLDSTEIN is the editor of *2600*, the "hacker's quarterly."

HANK is Hank Roberts, who builds mobiles, flies hang gliders, and proofreads for the *Whole Earth Catalog*.

JIMG is Jim Gasperini, the author, with TRANS Fiction Systems, of Hidden Agenda, a computer game that simulates political conflict in Central America.

JRC is Jon Carroll, daily columnist for the *San Francisco Chronicle* and writer-in-residence for the Pickle Family Circus, a national traveling circus troupe based in San Francisco.

KK is Kevin Kelly, editor of the *Whole Earth Review* and a cofounder of the Hacker's Conference.

LEE is Lee Felsenstein, who designed the Osborne-1 computer and cofounded the Homebrew Computer Club.

MANDEL is Tom Mandel, a professional futurist and an organizer of the Hacker's Conference.

RH is Robert Horvitz, Washington correspondent for the *Whole Earth Review*.

RMS is Richard Stallman, founder of the Free Software Foundation.

TENNEY is Glenn Tenney, an independent-systems architect and an organizer of the Hacker's Conference.

ACID PHREAK and PHIBER OPTIK are both pseudonyms for hackers who decline to be identified.

HARPER'S [Day 1, 9:00 A.M.]: When the computer was young, the word *hacking* was used to describe the work of brilliant students who explored and expanded the uses to which this new technology might be employed. There was even talk of a "hacker ethic." Somehow, in the succeeding years, the work has taken on dark connotations, suggesting the actions of a criminal. What is the hacker ethic, and does it survive?

ADELAIDE [Day 1, 9:25 A.M.]: The hacker ethic survives, and it is a   5
fraud. It survives in anyone excited by technology's power to turn many small, insignificant things into one vast, beautiful thing. It is a fraud because there is nothing magical about computers that causes a user to undergo religious conversion and devote himself to the public good. Early automobile inventors were hackers too. At first the elite drove in luxury. Later practically everyone had a car. Now we have traffic jams, drunk drivers, air pollution, and suburban sprawl. The old magic of an automobile occasionally surfaces, but we possess no delusions that it automatically invades the consciousness of anyone who sits behind the wheel. Computers are power, and direct contact with power can bring out the best or the worst in a person. It's tempting to think that everyone exposed to the technology will be grandly inspired, but, alas, it just ain't so.

BRAND [Day 1, 9:54 A.M.]: The hacker ethic involves several things. One is avoiding waste; insisting on using idle computer power—often hacking into a system to do so, while taking the greatest precautions not to damage the system. A second goal of many hackers is the free exchange of technical information. These hackers feel that patent and copyright restrictions slow down technological advances. A third goal is the advancement of human knowledge for its own sake. Often this approach is unconventional. People we call crackers often explore systems and do mischief. They are called hackers by the press, which doesn't understand the issues.

KK [Day 1, 11:19 A.M.]: The hacker ethic went unnoticed early on because the explorations of basement tinkerers were very local. Once we all became connected, the work of these investigators rippled through the world. Today the hacking spirit is alive and kicking in video, satellite TV, and radio. In some fields they are called chippers, because they modify and peddle altered chips. Everything that was once said about "phone phreaks" can be said about them too.

DAVE [Day 1, 11:29 A.M.]: Bah. Too academic. Hackers hack. Because they want to. Not for any higher purpose. Hacking is not dead and won't be as long as teenagers get their hands on the tools. There is a hacker born every minute.

ADELAIDE [Day 1, 11:42 A.M.]: Don't forget ego. People break into computers because it's fun and it makes them feel powerful.

BARLOW [Day 1, 11:54 A.M.]: Hackers hack. Yeah, right, but what's   10
more to the point is that humans hack and always have. Far more than just opposable thumbs, upright posture, or excess cranial capacity, human beings are set apart from all other species by an itch, a hard-wired dissatisfaction. Computer hacking is just the latest in a series of quests that started with fire hacking. Hacking is also a collective enterprise. It brings to our joint endeavors the simultaneity that other collective organisms—ant colonies, Canada geese—take for granted. This is important, because combined with our itch to probe is a need to *connect*. Humans miss the almost telepathic connectedness that I've observed in other herding mammals. And we want it back. Ironically, the solitary sociopath and his 3:00 A.M. endeavors hold the most promise for delivering species reunion.

EDDIE JOE HOMEBOY [Day 1, 4:44 P.M.]: Hacking really took hold with the advent of the personal computer, which freed programmers from having to use a big time-sharing system. A hacker could sit in the privacy of his home and hack to his heart's and head's content.

LEE [Day 1, 5:17 P.M.]: "Angelheaded hipsters burning for the ancient heavenly connection to the starry dynamo in the machinery of night" (Allen Ginsberg, "Howl").[1] I still get an endorphin rush when I go on a design run—my mind out over the edge, groping for possibilities that can be sensed when various parts are held in juxtaposition with a view toward creating a whole object: straining to get through the epsilon-wide crack between What Is and What Could Be. Somewhere there's the Dynamo of Night, the ultra-mechanism waiting to be dreamed, that we'll never get to in actuality (think what it would *weigh!*) but that's present somehow in the vicinity of those mental wrestling matches. When I reemerge into the light of another day with the design on paper—and with the knowledge that if it ever gets built, things will never be the same again—I know I've been where artists go. That's hacking to me: to transcend custom and to engage in creativity for its own sake, but also to create objective effects. I've been around long enough to see the greed

---

1. **Allen Ginsberg** (b. 1926): American poet of the Beat generation, best known for his poem "Howl" (1956).— ED.

creeps take up the unattended reins of power and shut down most of the creativity that put them where they are. But I've also seen things change, against the best efforts of a stupidly run industry. We cracked the egg out from under the Computer Priesthood, and now everyone can have omelets.

RMS [Day 1, 5:19 P.M.]: The media and the courts are spreading a certain image of hackers. It's important for us not to be shaped by that image. But there are two ways that it can happen. One way is for hackers to become part of the security-maintenance establishment. The other, more subtle, way is for a hacker to become the security-breaking phreak the media portray. By shaping ourselves into the enemy of the establishment, we uphold the establishment. But there's nothing wrong with breaking security if you're accomplishing something useful. It's like picking a lock on a tool cabinet to get a screwdriver to fix your radio. As long as you put the screwdriver back, what harm does it do?

ACID PHREAK [Day 1, 6:34 P.M.]: There is no one hacker ethic. Everyone has his own. To say that we all think the same way is preposterous. The hacker of old sought to find what the computer itself could do. There was nothing illegal about that. Today, hackers and phreaks are drawn to *specific*, often corporate, systems. It's no wonder everyone on the other side is getting mad. We're always one step ahead. We were back then, and we are now.

CLIFF [Day 1, 8:38 P.M.]: RMS said, "There's nothing wrong with break- 15
ing security if you're accomplishing something useful." Huh? How about, There's nothing wrong with entering a neighbor's house if you're accomplishing something useful, just as long as you clean up after yourself. Does my personal privacy mean anything? Should my personal letters and data be open to anyone who knows how to crack passwords? If not my property, then how about a bank's? Should my credit history be available to anyone who can find a back door to the private computers of TRW, the firm that tracks people's credit histories? How about a list of AIDS patients from a hospital's data bank? Or next week's prime interest rate from a computer at the Treasury Department?

BLUEFIRE [Day 1, 9:20 P.M.]: Computers are everywhere, and they link us together into a vast social "cybernetia." The grand skills of the hackers, formidable though they may have been, are incapable of subverting this automated social order. The networks in which we survive are more than copper wire and radio waves: They are *the* social organization. For every hacker in revolt, busting through a security code, ten thousand people are being wired up with automatic call-identification and credit-checking machines. Long live the Computer Revolution, which died aborning.

JRC [Day 1, 10:28 P.M.]: We have two different definitions here. One speaks of a tinkerer's ecstasy, an ecstasy that is hard to maintain in the corporate world but is nevertheless at the heart of Why Hackers Hack. The second is political, and it has to do with the free flow of information. Information should flow more freely (how freely is being debated), and the hacker can make it happen because the hacker knows how to undam the pipes. This makes the hacker ethic—of necessity—antiauthoritarian.

EMMANUEL GOLDSTEIN [Day 2, 2:41 A.M.]: It's meaningless what we call ourselves: hackers, crackers, techno-rats. We're individuals who happen to play with high tech. There is no *hacker community* in the traditional sense of the term. There are no leaders and no agenda. We're just individuals out exploring.

BRAND [Day 2, 9:02 A.M.]: There are two issues: invariance and privacy. Invariance is the art of leaving things as you found them. If someone used my house for the day and left everything as he found it so that there was *no way* to tell he had been there, I would see no problem. With a well-run computer system, we can assure invariance. Without this assurance we must fear that the person picking the lock to get the screwdriver will break the lock, the screwdriver, or both. Privacy is more complicated. I want my medical records, employment records, and letters to *The New Republic* private because I fear that someone will do something with the information that is against my interests. If I could trust people not to do bad things with information, I would not need to hide it. Rather than preventing the "theft" of this data, we should prohibit its collection in the first place.

HOMEBOY [Day 2, 9:37 A.M.]: Are crackers really working for the free 20 flow of information? Or are they unpaid tools of the establishment, identifying the holes in the institutional dike so that they can be plugged by the authorities, only to be tossed in jail or exiled?

DRAKE [DAY 2, 10:54 A.M.]: There is an unchallenged assumption that crackers have some political motivation. Earlier, crackers were portrayed as failed revolutionaries; now Homeboy suggests that crackers may be tools of the establishment. These ideas about crackers are based on earlier experiences with subcultures (beats, hippies, yippies). Actually, the contemporary cracker is often middle-class and doesn't really distance himself from the "establishment." While there are some anarcho-crackers, there are even more right-wing crackers. The hacker ethic crosses political boundaries.

MANDEL [Day 2, 11:01 A.M.]: The data on crackers suggests that they are either juvenile delinquents or plain criminals.

BARLOW [Day 2, 11:34 A.M.]: I would far rather have *everyone* know my most intimate secrets than to have noncontextual snippits of them "owned" by TRW and the FBI—and withheld from me! Any cracker who is entertained by peeping into my electronic window is welcome to the view. Any institution that makes money selling rumors of my peccadilloes is stealing from me. Anybody who wants to inhibit that theft with electronic mischief has my complete support. Power to the techno-rats!

EMMANUEL [Day 2, 7:09 P.M.]: Calling someone on the phone is the equivalent of knocking on that person's door, right? Wrong! When someone answers the phone, you are *inside* the home. You have already been *let in*. The same with an answering machine, or a personal computer, if it picks up the phone. It is wrong to violate a person's privacy, but electronic rummaging is not the same as breaking and entering. The key here is that most people are unaware of *how easy it is* for others to invade their electronic privacy and see credit reports, phone bills, FBI files, Social Security reports. The public is grossly underinformed, and that's what must be fixed if hackers are to be thwarted. If we had an educated public, though, perhaps the huge—and now common—data bases would never have been allowed to exist. Hackers have become scapegoats: We discover the gaping holes in the system and then get blamed for the flaws.

HOMEBOY [Day 2, 7:41 P.M.]: Large, insular, undemocratic governments and institutions need scapegoats. It's the first step down the road to fascism. *That's* where hackers play into the hands of the establishment. 25

DAVE [Day 2, 7:55 P.M.]: If the real criminals are those who leave gaping holes in their systems, then the real criminals in house burglaries are those who leave their windows unlatched. Right? Hardly. And Emmanuel's analogy to a phone being answered doesn't hold either. There is no security protection in making a phone call. A computer system has a *password*, implying a desire for security. Breaking into a poorly protected house is still burglary.

CLIFF [Day 2, 9:06 P.M.]: Was there a hacker's ethic and does it survive? More appropriately, was there a vandal's ethic and does it survive? As long as there are communities, someone will violate the trust that binds them. Once, our computers were isolated, much as eighteenth-century villages were. Little was exchanged, and each developed independently. Now we've built far-flung electronic neighborhoods. These communities are built on trust: people believing that everyone profits by sharing resources. Sure enough, vandals crept in, breaking into systems, spreading viruses, pirating software, and destroying people's work. "It's okay," they say. "I can break into a system because I'm a hacker." Give me a break!

BARLOW [Day 2, 10:41 P.M.]: I live in a small town. I don't have a key to my house. Am I asking for it? I think not. Among the juvenile delinquents in my town, there does exist a vandal's ethic. I know because I once was one. In a real community, part of a kid's rite of passage is discovering what walls can be breached. Driving 110 miles per hour on

Main Street is a common symptom of rural adolescence, publicly denounced but privately understood. Many teenagers die in this quest—two just the night before last—but it is basic to our culture. Even rebellious kids understand that risk to one's safety is one thing, wanton vandalism or theft is another. As a result, almost no one locks anything here. In fact, a security system is an affront to a teenage psyche. While a kid might be dissuaded by conscience, he will regard a barricade as an insult and a challenge. So the CEOs who are moving here (the emperor of PepsiCo and the secretary of state among them) soon discover that over the winter people break into their protected mansions just to hang out. When systems are open, the community prospers, and teenage miscreants are satisfied to risk their own lives and little else. When the social contract is enforced by security, the native freedom of the adolescent soul will rise up to challenge it in direct proportion to its imposition.

HANK [Day 2, 11:23 P.M.]: Barlow, the small town I grew up in was much like yours—until two interstate highways crossed nearby. The open-door style changed in one, hard summer because our whole *town* became unlocked. I think Cliff's community is analogous to my little town—confronted not by a new locked-up neighbor who poses a challenge to the local kids but by a sudden, permanent opening up of the community to many faceless outsiders who owe the town no allegiance.

EMMANUEL [Day 3, 1:33 A.M.]: Sorry, I don't buy Dave's unlatched- 30
window analogy. A hacker who wanders into a system with the ease that it's done today is, in my analogy, walking into a house without walls—and with a cloaking device! Any good hacker can make himself invisible. If housebreaking were this easy, people would be enraged. But we're missing the point. I'm not referring to accessing a PC in someone's bedroom but about accessing credit reports, government files, motor vehicle records, and the megabytes of data piling up on each of us. Thousands of people legally can see and use this ever-growing mountain of data, much of it erroneous. Whose rights are we violating when we peruse a file? Those of the person we look up? He doesn't even know that information exists, that it was compiled without his consent, and that it's not his property anymore! The invasion of privacy took place long before the hacker ever arrived. The only way to find out how such a system works is to break the rules. It's not what hackers do that will lead us into a state of constant surveillance; it's allowing the authorities to impose on us a state of mock crisis.

MANDEL [Day 3, 9:27 A.M.]: Note that the word *crime* has no fixed reference in our discussion. Until recently, breaking into government computer systems wasn't a crime; now it is. In fact, there is some debate, to be resolved in the courts, whether what Robert Morris Jr. did was actually a crime. . . . *Crime* gets redefined all the time. Offend enough people or institutions and, lo and behold, someone will pass a law. That is partly what is going on now: Hackers are pushing buttons, becoming more visible, and that inevitably means more laws and more crimes.

ADELAIDE [Day 3, 9:42 A.M.]: Every practitioner of these arts knows that at minimum he is trespassing. The English "country traveler ethic" applies: The hiker is always ethical enough to close the pasture gates behind him so that no sheep escape during his pastoral stroll through someone else's property. The problem is that what some see as gentle trespassing others see as theft of service, invasion of privacy, threat to national security—take your pick.

BARLOW [Day 3, 2:38 P.M.]: I regard the *existence* of proprietary data about me to be theft—not just in the legal sense but in a faintly metaphysical one, rather like the belief among aborigines that a photograph steals the soul. The crackers who maintain access to that data are, at this level, liberators. Their incursions are the only way to keep the system honest.

RMS [Day 3, 2:48 P.M.]: Recently, a tough antihacker measure was proposed in England. In *The Economist*[2] I saw a wise response, arguing that it was silly to treat an action as worse when it involves a computer than when it does not. They noted, for example, that physical trespassing was considered a civil affair, not a criminal one, and said that computer trespassing should be treated likewise. Unfortunately, the U.S. government was not so wise.

BARLOW [Day 3, 3:23 P.M.]: The idea that a crime is worse if a computer is involved relates to the gathering governmental perception that computer viruses and guns may be related. I know that sounds absurd, but they have more in common than one might think. For all its natural sociopathy, the virus is not without philosophical potency—like a gun. Here in Wyoming guns are part of the furniture. Only recently have I observed an awareness of their political content. After a lot of frothing about prying cold, dead fingers from triggers, the sentiment was finally distilled to a bumper sticker I saw on a pickup the other day: "Fear the Government That Fears Your Gun." Now I've read too much Gandhi[3] to buy that line without misgivings, but it would be hard to argue that Tiananmen Square[4] could have been inflicted on a populace capable of shooting back. I don't wholeheartedly defend computer viruses, but one

---

2. *The Economist:* Published in London since 1843, *The Economist* provides weekly coverage of trends in business, finance, and politics worldwide.—ED.

3. Mohandas K. **Gandhi** (1869–1948): Indian statesman who advocated nonviolent resistance to political oppression.—ED.

4. **Tiananmen Square:** In June 1989, the Chinese government violently suppressed popular resistance in Tiananmen Square, a huge plaza in the center of Beijing.—ED.

must consider their increasingly robust deterrent potential. Before it's over, the War on Drugs could easily turn into an Armageddon between those who love liberty and those who crave certainty, providing just the excuse the control freaks have been waiting for to rid America of all that constitutional mollycoddling called the Bill of Rights. Should that come to pass, I will want to use every available method to vex and confuse the eyes and ears of surveillance. The virus could become the necessary instrument of our freedom. At the risk of sounding like some digital *posse comitatus*,[5] I say: Fear the Government That Fears Your Computer.

TENNEY [Day 3, 4:41 P.M.]: Computer-related crimes are more feared because they are performed remotely—a crime can be committed in New York by someone in Los Angeles—and by people not normally viewed as being criminals—by teenagers who don't look like delinquents. They're very smart nerds, and they don't look like Chicago gangsters packing heat.

BARLOW [Day 4, 12:12 A.M.]: People know so little of these things that they endow computers and the people who *do* understand them with powers neither possesses. If America has a religion, its ark is the computer and its covenant is the belief that Science Knows. We are mucking around in the temple, guys. It's a good way to catch hell.

DAVE [DAY 4, 9:18 A.M.]: Computers *are* the new American religion. The public is in awe of—and fears—the mysteries and the high priests who tend them. And the public reacts just as it always has when faced with fear of the unknown—punishment, burning at the stake. Hackers are like the early Christians. When caught, they will be thrown to the lions before the Roman establishment: This year the mob will cheer madly as Robert Morris is devoured.

KK [Day 6, 11:37 A.M.]: The crackers here suggest that they crack into systems with poor security *because* the security is poor. Do more sophisticated security precautions diminish the need to crack the system or increase it?

ACID [Day 6, 1:20 P.M.]: If there was a system that we knew was un- 40
crackable, we wouldn't even try to crack it. On the other hand, if some organization boasted that its system was impenetrable and we knew that was media hype, I think it would be safe to say we'd have to "enlighten" them.

EMMANUEL [Day 2, 2:49 P.M.]: Why do we insist on cracking systems? The more people ask those kinds of questions, the more I want to get in! Forbid access and the demand for access increases. For the most part, it's

---

5. *posse comitatus:* From the Latin phrase "force of the county," a group empowered by local law enforcement to help maintain order.—ED.

simply a mission of exploration. In the words of the new captain of the starship *Enterprise*, Jean-Luc Picard,[6] "Let's see what's out there!"

BARLOW [Day 6, 4:34 P.M.]: Tell us, Acid, *is* there a system that you know to be uncrackable to the point where everyone's given up?

ACID [Day 6, 8:29 P.M.]: CICIMS is pretty tough.

PHIBER OPTIK [Day 7, 2:36 P.M.]: Really? CICIMS is a system used by Bell operating companies. The entire security system was changed after myself and a friend must have been noticed in it. For the entire United States, there is only one such system, located in Indiana. The new security scheme is flawless *in itself*, and there is no chance of "social engineering," i.e., bullshitting someone inside the system into telling you what the passwords are. The system works like this: You log on with the proper account and password; then, depending on who you are, the system asks at random three of ten questions that are unique to each user. But the system *can* be compromised by entering forwarding instructions into the phone company's switch for that exchange, thereby intercepting every phone call that comes in to the system over a designated period of time and connecting the call to your computer. If you are familiar with the security layout, you can emulate its appearance and fool the caller into giving you the answers to his questions. Then you call the system yourself and use those answers to get in. There are other ways of doing it as well.

BLUEFIRE [Day 7, 11:53 P.M.]: I can't stand it! Who do you think pays for the security that the telephone companies must maintain to fend off illegal use? I bet it costs the ratepayers around $10 million for this little extravaganza. The cracker circus isn't harmless at all, unless you don't mind paying for other people's entertainment. Hackers who have contributed to the social welfare should be recognized. But cracking is something else—namely, fun at someone else's expense—and it ain't the folks who own the phone companies who pay; it's us, me and you.

BARLOW [Day 8, 7:35 A.M.]: I am becoming increasingly irritated at this idea that you guys are exacting vengeance for the sin of openness. You seem to argue that if a system is dumb enough to be open, it is your moral duty to violate it. Does the fact that I've never locked my house—even when I was away for months at a time—mean that someone should come in and teach me a good lesson?

ACID [Day 8, 3:23 P.M.]: Barlow, you leave the door open to your house? Where do you live?

BARLOW [Day 8, 10:11 P.M.]: Acid, my house is at 372 North Franklin

---

6. **Jean-Luc Picard:** The captain of the starship *Enterprise* in the television series *Star Trek: The Next Generation* (1987–1994).—ED.

Street in Pinedale, Wyoming. Heading north on Franklin, go about two blocks off the main drag before you run into a hay meadow on the left. I'm the last house before the field. The computer is always on. But do you really mean to imply what you did with that question? Are you merely a sneak looking for easy places to violate? You disappoint me, pal. For all your James Dean-on-Silicon rhetoric, you're not a cyberpunk. You're just a punk.

EMMANUEL [Day 9, 12:55 A.M.]: No offense, Barlow, but your house analogy doesn't stand up, because your house is far less interesting than a Defense Department computer. For the most part, hackers don't mess with individuals. Maybe we feel sorry for them; maybe they're boring. Institutions are where the action is, because they are compiling this mountain of data—without your consent. Hackers are not guardian angels, but if you think we're what's wrong with the system, I'd say that's precisely what those in charge want you to believe. By the way, you left out your zip code. It's 82941.

BARLOW [Day 9, 8:34 A.M.]: Now that's more like it. There is an ethical 50 distinction between people and institutions. The law makes little distinction. We pretend that institutions are somehow human because they are made of humans. A large bureaucracy resembles a human about as much as a reef resembles a coral polyp. To expect an institution to have a conscience is like expecting a horse to have one. As with every organism, institutions are chiefly concerned with their own physical integrity and survival. To say that they have some higher purpose beyond their survival is to anthropomorphize them. You are right, Emmanuel. The house analogy breaks down here. Individuals live in houses; institutions live in mainframes. Institutions are functionally remorseless and need to be checked. Since their blood is digital, we need to be in their bloodstreams like an infection of humanity. I'm willing to extend limitless trust to other human beings. In my experience they've never failed to deserve it. But I have as much faith in institutions as they have in me. None.

OPTIK [Day 9, 10:19 A.M.]: In other words, Mr. Barlow, you say something, someone proves you wrong, and then you agree with him. I'm getting the feeling that you don't exactly chisel your views in stone.

HANK [Day 9, 11:18 A.M.]: Has Mr. Optik heard the phrase "thesis, antithesis, synthesis"?

BARLOW [Day 10, 10:48 A.M.]: Optik, I do change my mind a lot. Indeed, I often find it occupied by numerous contradictions. The last time I believed in absolutes, I was about your age. And there's not a damn thing wrong with believing in absolutes at your age either. Continue to do so, however, and you'll find yourself, at my age, carrying placards filled with nonsense and dressing in rags.

ADELAIDE [Day 10, 6:27 P.M.]: The flaw in this discussion is the distorted image the media promote of the hacker as "whiz." The problem is that the one who gets caught obviously isn't. I haven't seen a story yet on a true genius hacker. Even Robert Morris was no whiz. The genius hackers are busy doing constructive things or are so good no one's caught them yet. It takes no talent to break into something. Nobody calls subway graffiti artists geniuses for figuring out how to break into the yard. There's a difference between genius and ingenuity.

BARLOW [Day 10, 9:48 P.M.]: Let me define my terms. Using *hacker* in a 55
midspectrum sense (with crackers on one end and Leonardo da Vinci on the other), I think it does take a kind of genius to be a truly productive hacker. I'm learning PASCAL now, and I am constantly amazed that people can spin those prolix recursions into something like PageMaker. It fills me with the kind of awe I reserve for splendors such as the cathedral at Chartres. With crackers like Acid and Optik, the issue is less intelligence than alienation. Trade their modems for skateboards and only a slight conceptual shift would occur. Yet I'm glad they're wedging open the cracks. Let a thousand worms flourish.

OPTIK [Day 10, 10:11 P.M.]: You have some pair of balls comparing my talent with that of a skateboarder. Hmm . . . This was indeed boring, but nonetheless: [*Editors' Note: At this point in the discussion, Optik—apparently having hacked into TRW's computer records—posted a copy of Mr. Barlow's credit history. In the interest of Mr. Barlow's privacy—at least what is left of it—*Harper's Magazine *has not printed it.*] I'm not showing off. Any fool knowing the proper syntax and the proper passwords can look up a credit history. I just find your high-and-mighty attitude annoying and, yes, infantile.

HOMEBOY [Day 10, 10:17 P.M.]: Key here is "any fool."

ACID [Day 11, 1:37 P.M.]: For thirty-five dollars a year anyone can have access to TRW and see his or her own credit history. Optik did it for free. What's wrong with that? And why does TRW keep files on what color and religion we are? If you didn't know that they kept such files, who would have found out if it wasn't for a hacker? Barlow should be grateful that Optik has offered his services to update him on his personal credit file. Of course, I'd hate to see my credit history up in lights. But if you hadn't made our skins crawl, your info would not have been posted. Everyone gets back at someone when he's pissed; so do we. Only we do it differently. Are we punks? Yeah, I guess we are. A punk is what someone who has been made to eat his own words calls the guy who fed them to him.

HARPER'S [Day 4, 9:00 A.M.]: Suppose that a mole inside the government confirmed the existence of files on each of you, stored in the White House computer system, PROFS. Would you have the right to hack into that system to retrieve and expose the existence of such files? Could you do it?

TENNEY [Day 4, 1:42 P.M.]: The proverbial question of whether the end 60 justifies the means. This doesn't have much to do with hacking. If the file were a sheet of paper in a locked cabinet, the same question would apply. In that case you could accomplish everything without technological hacking. Consider the Pentagon Papers.[7]

EMMANUEL [Day 4, 3:55 P.M.]: Let's address the hypothetical. First, I need to find out more about PROFS. Is it accessible from off site, and if so, how? Should I update my 202–456 scan [a list of phone numbers in the White House's exchange that connect incoming calls to a computer]? I have a listing for every computer in that exchange, but the scan was done back in 1984. Is PROFS a new system? Perhaps it's in a different exchange? Does anybody know how many people have access to it? I'm also on fairly good terms with a White House operator who owes me a favor. But I don't know what to ask for. Obviously, I've already made up my mind about the *right* to examine this material. I don't want to debate the ethics of it at this point. If you're with me, let's do something about this. Otherwise, stay out of the way. There's hacking to be done.

ACID [Day 4, 5:24 P.M.]: Yes, I would try to break into the PROFS system. But first I'd have someone in the public eye, with no ties to hacking, request the info through the Freedom of Information Act.[8] Then I'd hack in to verify the information I received. . . .

EMMANUEL [Day 4, 11:27 P.M.]: The implication that a trust has been betrayed on the part of the government is certainly enough to make me want to look a little further. And I know I'm doing the right thing on behalf of others who don't have my abilities. Most people I meet see me as an ally who can help them stay ahead of an unfair system. That's what I intend to do here. I have a small core of dedicated hackers who could help. One's specialty is the UNIX system, another's is networks, and another's is phone systems. . . .

BARLOW [Day 5, 2:46 P.M.]: This scenario needs to be addressed in four parts: ethical, political, practical I (from the standpoint of the hack

---

7. **Pentagon Papers:** In 1971 the *New York Times* published a secret Pentagon report about U.S. involvement in Southeast Asia from 1945 to 1968, in spite of the Nixon administration's insistence that the report needed to remain secret in the interests of "national security."— ED.

8. **Freedom of Information Act** (1966): Provides for public access to information held by federal agencies, unless national security or rights to privacy are compromised; the Privacy Act of 1974 extends to individuals the right to obtain any records on themselves kept by the federal government.— ED.

itself), and practical II (disseminating the information without undue risk).

Ethical: Since World War II, we've been governed by a paramilitary 65 bureaucracy that believes freedom is too precious to be entrusted to the people. These are the same folks who had to destroy the village in order to save it. Thus the government has become a set of Chinese boxes. Americans who believe in democracy have little choice but to shred the barricades of secrecy at every opportunity. It isn't merely permissible to hack PROFS. It is a moral obligation.

Political: In the struggle between control and liberty, one has to avoid action that will drive either side to extreme behavior. The basis of terrorism, remember, is excess. If we hack PROFS, we must do it in a way that doesn't become a pretext for hysterical responses that might eventually include zero tolerance of personal computers. The answer is to set up a system for entry and exit that never lets on we've been there.

Practical I: Hacking the system should be a trivial undertaking.

Practical II: Having retrieved the smoking gun, it must be made public in such a way that the actual method of acquisition does not become public. Consider Watergate: The prime leaker was somebody whose identity and information-gathering technique is still unknown. So having obtained the files, we turn them over to the *Washington Post* without revealing our own identities or how we came by the files. . . .

BRAND [Day 6, 10:06 A.M.]: I have two questions: Do you believe in due process as found in our Constitution? And do you believe that this "conspiracy" is so serious that extraordinary measures need to be taken? If you believe in due process, then you shouldn't hack into the system to defend our liberties. If you don't believe in due process, you are an anarchist and potentially a terrorist. The government is justified in taking *extreme* action to protect itself and the rest of us from you. If you believe in the Constitution but also that this threat is so extreme that patriots have a duty to intercede, then you should seek one of the honest national officials who can legally demand a copy of the document. If you believe that there is no sufficiently honest politician and you steal and publish the documents, you are talking about a revolution.

ACID [Day 6, 1:30 P.M.]: This is getting too political. Who says that 70 hacking has to have a political side? Generalizing does nothing but give hackers a false image. I couldn't care less about politics, and I hack.

LEE [Day 6, 9:01 P.M.]: Sorry, Acid, but if you hack, what you do is inherently political. Here goes: Political power is exercised by control of information channels. Therefore, any action that changes the capability of someone in power to control these channels *is* politically relevant. Historically, the one in power has been not the strongest person but the one who has convinced the goon squad to do his bidding. The goons give their power to him, usually in exchange for free food, sex, and great uniforms. The turning point of most successful revolutions is when the troops ignore the orders coming from above and switch their allegiance. Information channels. Politics. These days, the cracker represents a potential for making serious political change if he coordinates with larger social and economic forces. Without this coordination, the cracker is but a techno-bandit, sharpening his weapon and chuckling about how someday. . . . Revolutions often make good use of bandits, and some of them move into high positions when they're successful. But most of them are done away with. One cracker getting in won't do much good. Working in coordination with others is another matter—called politics. . . .

HARPER'S [Day 7, 9:00 A.M.]: Suppose you hacked the files from the White House and a backlash erupted. Congressmen call for restrictions, arguing that the computer is "property" susceptible to regulation and not an instrument of "information" protected by the First Amendment. Can we craft a manifesto setting forth your views on how the computer fits into the traditions of the American Constitution?

DAVE [Day 7, 5:30 P.M.]: If Congress ever passed laws that tried to define what we do as "technology" (regulatable) and *not* "speech," I would become a rebellious criminal immediately—and as loud as Thomas Paine ever was. Although computers are part "property" and part "premises" (which suggests a need for privacy), they are supremely instruments of *speech*. I don't want any congressional King Georges treading on my cursor. We must continue to have *absolute* freedom of electronic speech!

BARLOW [Day 7, 10:07 P.M.]: Even in a court guided by my favorite oxymoron, Justice Rehnquist, this is an open-and-shut case. The computer is a printing press. Period. The only hot-lead presses left in this country are either in museums or being operated by poets in Vermont. The computer cannot fall under the kind of regulation to which radio and TV have become subject, since computer output is not broadcast. If these regulations amount to anything more than a fart in the congressional maelstrom, then we might as well scrap the whole Bill of Rights. What I am doing with my fingers right now is "speech" in the clearest sense of the word. We don't need no stinking manifestos.

JIMG [Day 8, 12:02 A.M.]: This type of congressional action is so clearly   75
unconstitutional that "law hackers"—everyone from William Kunstler to Robert Bork[9]—would be all over it. The whole idea runs so completely counter to our laws that it's hard to get worked up about it.

---

9. **William Kunstler** (1919–1995): Radical civil rights lawyer; **Robert Bork** (b. 1927) Conservative former federal judge whose 1987 nomination to the U.S. Supreme Court was denied.—ED.

ADELAIDE [DAY 8, 9:51 A.M.]: Not so fast. There used to be a right in the Constitution called "freedom from unreasonable search and seizure," but, thanks to recent Supreme Court decisions, your urine can be demanded by a lot of people. I have no faith in the present Supreme Court to uphold any of my rights of free speech. The complacent reaction here—that whatever Congress does will eventually be found unconstitutional—is the same kind of complacency that led to the current near-reversals of *Roe* vs. *Wade*.[10]

JRC [Day 8, 10:05 A.M.]: I'd forgo the manifestos and official explanations altogether: Fight brushfire wars against specific government incursions and wait for the technology to metastasize. In a hundred years, people won't have to be told about computers because they will have an instinctive understanding of them.

KK [Day 8, 2:14 P.M.]: Hackers are not sloganeers. They are doers, take-things-in-handers. They are the opposite of philosophers: They don't wait for language to catch up to them. Their arguments are their actions. You want a manifesto? The Internet worm[11] was a manifesto. It had more meaning and symbolism than any revolutionary document you could write. To those in power running the world's nervous system, it said: Wake up! To the underground of hackers, crackers, chippers, and techno-punks, it said: You have power; be careful. To the mass of citizens who find computers taking over their telephone, their TV, their toaster, and their house, it said: Welcome to Wonderland.

BARLOW [Day 8, 10:51 P.M.]: Apart from the legal futility of fixing the dam after it's been breached, I've never been comfortable with manifestos. They are based on the ideologue's delusion about the simplicity, the figure-out-ability, of the infinitely complex thing that is Life Among the Humans. Manifestos take reductionism for a long ride off a short pier. Sometimes the ride takes a very long time. Marx and Engels didn't actually crash until last year.[12] Manifestos fail because they are fixed and consciousness isn't. I'm with JRC: Deal with incursions when we need to, on our terms, like the guerrillas we are. To say that we can outmaneuver those who are against us is like saying that honeybees move quicker than Congress. The future is to the quick, not the respectable.

RH [Day 8, 11:43 P.M.]: Who thinks computers can't be regulated? The 80 Electronic Communications Privacy Act of 1986 made it a crime to own

---

10. *Roe* vs. *Wade:* The 1973 Supreme Court decision that legalized abortion in the first trimester of pregnancy.—ED.

11. **Internet worm:** A destructive program released on the Internet computer network in November 1988, disabling more than six thousand computers for two days.—ED.

12. Karl **Marx** (1818–1883) and Friedrich **Engels** (1820–1895): Co-authors of *The Communist Manifesto* (1848).—ED.

"any electronic, mechanical, or other device [whose design] renders it primarily useful for the purpose of the surreptitious interception of wire, oral, or electronic communication." Because of the way Congress defined "electronic communication," one could argue that even a modem is a surreptitious interception device (SID), banned by the ECPA and subject to confiscation. It's not that Congress intended to ban modems; it was just sloppy drafting. The courts will ultimately decide what devices are legal. Since it may not be possible to draw a clear bright line between legal and illegal interception devices, the gray area—devices with both legitimate and illegitimate uses—may be subject to regulation.

BARLOW [Day 9, 8:52 A.M.]: I admit with some chagrin that I'm not familiar with the ECPA. It seems I've fallen on the wrong side of an old tautology: Just because all saloon keepers are Democrats, it doesn't follow that all Democrats are saloon keepers. By the same token, the fact that all printing presses are computers hardly limits computers to that function. And one of the other things computers are good at is surreptitious monitoring. Maybe there's more reason for concern than I thought. Has any of this stuff been tested in the courts yet?

RH [Day 9, 10:06 P.M.]: My comments about surreptitious interception devices are not based on any court cases, since there have not been any in this area since the ECPA was enacted. It is a stretch of the imagination to think that a judge would ever find a stock, off-the-shelf personal computer to be a "surreptitious interception device." But a modem is getting a little closer to the point where a creative prosecutor could make trouble for a cracker, with fallout affecting many others. An important unknown is how the courts will apply the word *surreptitious*. There's very little case law, but taking it to mean "by stealth; hidden from view; having its true purpose physically disguised," I can spin some worrisome examples. I lobbied against the bill, pointing out the defects. Congressional staffers admitted privately that there was a problem, but they were in a rush to get the bill to the floor before Congress adjourned. They said they could patch it later, but it is a pothole waiting for a truck axle to rumble through.

JIMG [Day 10, 8:55 A.M.]: That's sobering information, RH. Yet I still think that this law, if interpreted the way you suggest, would be found unconstitutional, even by courts dominated by Reagan appointees. Also, the economic cost of prohibiting modems, or even restricting their use, would so outweigh conceivable benefits that the law would never go through. Finally, restricting modems would have no effect on the phreaks but would simply manage to slow everybody else down. If modems are outlawed, only outlaws will have modems.

RH [Day 10, 1:52 P.M.]: We're already past the time when one could wrap hacking in the First Amendment. There's a traditional distinction between words—expressions of opinions, beliefs, and information—and deeds. You can shout "Revolution!" from the rooftops all you want, and the post office will obligingly deliver your recipes for nitroglycerin. But acting on that information exposes you to criminal prosecution. The philosophical problem posed by hacking is that computer programs transcend this distinction: They are pure language that dictates action when read by the device being addressed. In that sense, a program is very different from a novel, a play, or even a recipe: Actions result automatically from the machine reading the words. A computer has no independent moral judgment, no sense of responsibility. Not yet, anyway. As we program and automate more of our lives, we undoubtedly will deal with more laws: limiting what the public can know, restricting devices that can execute certain instructions, and criminalizing the possession of "harmful" programs with "no redeeming social value." Blurring the distinction between language and action, as computer programming does, could eventually undermine the First Amendment or at least force society to limit its application. That's a very high price to pay, even for all the good things that computers make possible.

HOMEBOY [Day 10, 11:03 P.M.]: HACKING IS ART. CRACKING IS REVOLU- 85
TION. All else is noise. Cracks in the firmament are by nature threatening. Taking a crowbar to them is revolution.

- **CONSIDER THE SOURCE**

1. Define the "hacker ethic." What are some of the reasons hackers hack, according to the hackers?

2. How do hackers believe they assist the free flow of information? How do they inhibit it?

3. Explain how hackers like Barlow interpret the right to privacy. Whose privacy do they violate? Whose privacy do institutional databases violate?

4. Trace the analogy about breaking into a house. How does it apply to hacking? Where does it break down? How is Barlow's view of the analogy an example of "thesis, antithesis, synthesis"?

5. In what way is hacking a "political" act? How is politics related to the flow of information, according to Lee?

6. Compare this online "chat" with the face-to-face discussion among Floyd Abrams, Catharine MacKinnon, and Anthony Lewis (pp. 492–508), in terms of their language, tone, and level of discourse. To what extent can the differences be attributed to the difference in physical proximity of the participants? How much difference does it make that one was published in *The New York Times Magazine* and the other in *Harper's Magazine*?

▪ **CONSIDER THE IMPLICATIONS**

7. Hold a class debate on RMS's remark that it's "silly to treat an action as worse when it involves a computer than when it does not." What "crimes" do computer hackers commit that are more serious than their nondigital counterparts?

8. Do you agree with Barlow and Dave that computers are "the new American religion"? In your journal explore your relation to digital technology. How much do computers enter your life? Are they mysterious or familiar to you? What do you think are their strengths and limitations?

9. How do the media portray hackers? Are they liberators? Vandals? Punks? Geniuses? Write a profile of the hacker based on recent articles in mainstream newsmagazines.

10. Barlow claims that "The computer is a printing press. Period." On the chalkboard, list the ways that the computer resembles and differs from the printing press. Are the similarities sufficient to warrant extending First Amendment protection to computer "speech"? Are the differences great enough to justify denying those protections? Discuss in class what regulations you think should be used to control computers.

11. RH argues that because computer programs are "pure language that dictates action when read by the device being addressed," they blur the distinction between words and deeds that traditionally guides First Amendment law. Compare a computer virus—a sequence of commands that acts destructively when read by the computer that receives it—with pornography, as Catharine MacKinnon defines it in her discussion with Floyd Abrams (pp. 492–508). Write an essay arguing that the First Amendment does or does not apply to these sorts of communication, or proposing guidelines for deciding whether such "speech" deserves First Amendment protection.

12. Read John Seabrook's article on computer viruses and flaming (pp. 609–25). Would Seabrook agree with KK that "the Internet worm was a manifesto" and an exercise of free speech?

CHAPTER 6

WHAT'S NEXT?

*Communication
in the Electronic Era*

"The book is dead! Long live the computer!"

In essence, this has been the cry of those who have mastered electronic communication and who see its incredible potential to alter our world. Books, they claim, are an outmoded technology that will soon be replaced by the faster and cheaper communication offered by computers.

"Not so fast!" respond advocates of the book. The printing press can do things that the computer will never be able to replicate. All the microchips in the world cannot offer the sheer sensuous pleasure of curling up with a good book.

BETWEEN TWO REVOLUTIONS

For five hundred years Western society has been feeling the effects and exploring the ramifications of Gutenberg's revolution. As earlier chapters show, our culture is saturated in print. Control of print and access to printed matter has proven to be one of the most powerful means to control people's ideas and actions. Our tastes, goals, and opinions are influenced by what we read or don't read.

Now the electronic revolution seems likely to change society's habits as profoundly as the print revolution did. Futurists tell us that computers will bring people together like never before, allowing them to communicate across vast distances in the blink of an eye. Information will flow freely, unrestricted by censorship, unhindered by politics. No longer will researchers spend laborious hours combing printed sources for information. At the click of a mouse, the world's knowledge will be at everyone's fingertips.

Not everyone is so hopeful. Some fear that computers will change our ways of thinking and interacting for the worse. They worry that people will become alienated from one another, able to communicate across continents, but incapable of communicating across the back fence. Global community will promote local isolation. The pleasures of leisurely reading will be replaced by the frenetic pace of online scanning. Language will erode into simplified, abbreviated dullness. Our sense of history will flatten as we focus increasingly on the immediate moment. Our attention spans will shorten as we flit between endless options on the many electronic media that will bombard us.

These fears and hopes may sound familiar, for much the same rhetoric accompanied the arrival of the printing press. People lamented the decline in quality even as they celebrated the increase in the quantity of books that the printing press could provide. They worried that the ability to speak and to remember would be lost. On the other hand, they praised the press for its ability to democratize knowledge. No longer would an elite scholarly class control the world of information. With the advent of printing, knowledge would belong to everyone. Moreover, the press would make it possible to communicate ideas across great distances: All writers had to do was print up their thoughts and send them across Europe. With hundreds of copies available, new ideas would reach vast audiences, and they would be impossible to censor.

It seems that every new technology inspires equal amounts of admiration and condemnation. We cannot know now, at the outset of the electronic revolution, the full extent of the changes that the computer will wreak on our society. No doubt we presently exaggerate both the promise and the pestilence of the computer. And yet it is important to speculate on the future and to analyze the effects of past technologies. We need to know where we have been in order to assess where we are going.

COMMUNICATION AND COMMUNITY

The computer has the capacity to bring the world together by linking users in a worldwide web of connections. Geography need not be a barrier to communication. People from Calcutta to Kowloon to California will be able to "chat" online, forming a "virtual community" based on mutual interests. Indeed, this is already happening as more people subscribe every day to the Internet, a worldwide network of computer users. Hundreds of newsgroups and discussion groups have sprung up around every conceivable interest. Chat groups exist for everyone: Grateful Dead fans, nuclear physicists, cat-lovers, witches, and Shakespearean scholars.

The computer skeptic may question whether improving the speed and ease of communication necessarily improves society. In 1854, Henry David Thoreau speculated about the value of a similar "improvement" in communications technology. "We are in great haste to construct a magnetic telegraph from Maine to Texas," he wrote in *Walden*, "but Maine and Texas, it may be, have nothing important to communicate." Perhaps the same will prove true for the great network of online communications. Perhaps we will find that we have nothing of great importance to say, even though we can say it quickly, cheaply, and over great distances.

Regardless of whether what we say is momentous or trivial, *how* we say it will certainly change in the electronic era. Technology has repeatedly altered the way humans interact. Once we learned to write letters, we began to communicate in the absence of face-to-face contact, without benefit of the visual cues that accompany personal interaction. Letters are monologues, one-way messages that can take days or even weeks to reach their destinations. Responses come slowly, if at all. The telephone initiated instantaneous two-way communication that, like written speech, also lacks the cues that body language and facial expression provide. With phone calls, however, much of the meaning in words is conveyed through tone of voice. You can discern whether the friend you have called is amused or offended by your comments, just by listening to the subtle changes in tone that come across the phone line. What happens when that emotional signaling is cut off, but communication remains virtually instantaneous?

With online communication you can "chat" with total strangers, people known to you only through the words that glow on the computer screen. How can you know if those strangers understand your wry sense of humor the way your friends do? How can you be sure they will understand which remarks are sarcastic and which are serious? How can you register your comprehension of their words, their jokes, their tirades?

In only a few short years, an entire vocabulary of symbols has sprung up to overcome the dehumanizing force of faceless online communication. These shorthand symbols are called "emoticons" or "smileys," and more are invented every day. (See sidebar, p. 532.) They allow you to insert emotion into your prose without having to command the subtleties of language or even use complete sentences. It takes some effort, some control of the writing process, to convey ideas clearly and with all their emotional weight. But who has time for such craftsmanship in the age of e-mail? It is much easier to signal your sarcasm by typing <g> after a remark, shorthand for "grin." Instead of telling your online buddy that you found his remarks hilarious, why not telegraph that

EMOTICONS EXPLAINED

Electronic communication has all the speed of a telephone call, but it does not allow us to modify our remarks by using our tone of voice. A whole array of shorthand symbols—called emoticons or "smileys"—has cropped up in online messages to indicate emotions and attempts at humor.

They began with the simplest version, a colon followed by a hyphen and a righthand parenthesis. This looks like a smiling face when you turn your head sideways. :-) (Hence, the term "smiley.") Now there are emoticons to express a whole range of feelings, from laughter to tears, indecision to astonishment. Here are just a few:

:-)	Smile (used to convey sarcasm)
:-(	Frown
;-)	Wink
:'-(	Tears
:-&	Tongue-tied
:-/	Indecision
:-J	Tongue-in-cheek
:-O	Eeeek!!
:-@	Scream
:-D	Big smile; or laughing out loud
:-x	Kiss
{ }	Hug

Then there are the more elaborate (but less commonly used) variations:

=:-)	Scared smiley
O:-)	Innocent smiley (with a halo)
:-)8	Smiley wearing a bowtie
8:-)	Smiley with bow in hair
%-)	Smiley with crossed eyes
:-$	Smiley with braces
:-p	Smiley sticking out tongue
:-[	Pouting smiley

thought with the abbreviation "lol" for "laughing out loud"; better yet, send him a big smile :-D to show you got the joke.

The speed of communication enabled by the computer does not necessarily require that writers resort to simplified, abbreviated plainspeak. In practice, however, it seems that this is precisely what is happening to the prose of many people. Complex sentences give way to simple ones; nuances of emotion are replaced by smileys. If we pay attention to these changes now, we may be able to track future modulations in language that have their origins in the computer's circuitry.

ACCESS TO KNOWLEDGE

Computer advocates often claim that computers will democratize knowledge by making the whole universe of information available to anybody and everybody. Of course, the same was said about the printing press. Anyone could plumb the depths of a book, a pamphlet, a broadside. The printed object knew no social divisions; it did not discriminate by race or class. The only problem, as revealed in chapter 2, was that in order to gain access to all that printed wealth you had to be able to read. Only the literate could open the doors to the temple of knowledge.

Is the digital temple really open to everyone? The basic literacy essential in a print culture has its counterpart in "computer literacy." In our information-driven economy, only those who can get to the information will succeed. But what if you don't know how to use a computer? Maybe you can do word processing but will that be enough? What if you haven't mastered the intricacies of retrieving information from cyberspace? Will you fall by the wayside, along with the other information have-nots that LynNell Hancock describes in chapter 2 (pp. 198–202)?

Speaking of have-nots, let's not forget the economics of computer literacy. If you don't have the money for a computer, you can't become one of the cognitive elite who will control the society of the future. Computers get more affordable every year, but they still cost far more than many households can manage. Moreover, the costs of connecting to the online world are not insignificant, as M. Kadi's essay shows (pp. 598–608). Those costs will only increase as the federal government, which has subsidized the online network since its inception, hands over to the private sector the job of funding the information superhighway.

Helena Viramontes eloquently recalled how the public library provided her with cherished access to the world of books as she grew up in Los Angeles' barrio (pp. 177–80). As funding for public libraries dwindles, we might well wonder where the next generation of barrio children will go for access to the knowledge that will increasingly be dispensed through expensive electronic hardware and pay-as-you-go communications hookups. Far from democratizing society, the computer has the potential to further stratify it into haves and have-nots unless we build public access into our plans for the information superhighway.

FREE SPEECH IN FLAMES

If it's not quite true that anyone can get in on the computer revolution, at least those who are online will have complete freedom of speech. And that's a good thing, right?

The freedom available online is actually an unintentional side effect of the network's original design. The Internet grew out of ARPANET, a decentralized system designed for military command and control in the event of nuclear attack. The system can route each message in any number of ways, through any number of nodes in the network. Therefore, if any important U.S. city were destroyed, messages could bypass that city, find their way around the damaged node, and still reach their destinations. This flexibility has crucial consequences in the nonmilitary world. It virtually guarantees that messages cannot be censored or blocked. As one computer pioneer put it, "The Net interprets censorship as damage and routes around it."

The result is a freedom of speech unprecedented even in a country that prides itself on the First Amendment. Once a message is created, it can be sent anywhere, to hundreds of destinations simultaneously. It can be copied and forwarded to even more recipients. Any attempt to block the message will simply cause the system to reroute it. The only way to block undesirable communication is to deny the writer access to the Net *before* the message is sent. That, of course, amounts to a "prior restraint" of free speech that our courts have consistently deemed unconstitutional.

Why should online communication be censored? Shouldn't people be free to say anything they want? In the past, laws have been enacted to regulate undesirable speech, but those laws were predicated on speakers being identifiable: Authors could be held accountable for their writings; libels and falsehoods could be traced to their sources and prosecuted if necessary. Such is not the case in cyberspace—the nondimensional "space" in which online communication occurs—where communication is virtually anonymous. Faceless communication at a distance permits all sorts of tricks and evasions. We can create online identities for ourselves, identities that may have nothing to do with who we are in real life. We can even adopt another person's identity if we are clever enough. Crack someone else's password and you can impersonate that person online with nobody being the wiser.

Even without resorting to impersonation, individuals have little incentive to feel accountable for what they say online. What, after all, would be the consequence of verbally attacking—or "flaming"—somebody in Des Moines if you were sitting comfortably in Pittsburgh? Even if the victim of your flame got offended, he or she would be unlikely to drive hundreds of miles to confront you about it. Your physical safety is assured by the distances the Net covers. And besides, who could prove—absolutely, incontrovertibly—that you really wrote the offensive message? There is no telltale handwriting in cyberspace.

Accountability for one's speech, then, cannot be guaranteed in the online world. Neither can access to information be restricted if it is publicly posted. Anyone can post pornographic messages, for instance, without the ability to monitor who can retrieve the messages. In an effort to protect children, laws have been instituted to control the sale of *printed* pornography to minors. But how can the downloading of pornography from online sources be controlled? How can it be determined which users are underage and which are not? Currently, efforts are underway to resolve these problems, but at the time this book went to press, no adequate solution had been found. (Congress had just passed a bill banning pornography on the Internet, but it had not been signed into law, nor had its constitutionality been tested in the courts.)

NEW RULES

Over the past five hundred years, our society has evolved complex systems for dealing with the spread of information in printed form. Gutenberg's original hand press has been steadily improved with faster and more powerful machine presses that dramatically increased the volume of printed material in our daily lives. With each new technological advance, we stretched and pulled our coping mechanisms to accommodate the new onslaught of printed information. We refined our individual filters for sorting out the important texts from the unimportant ones, the trustworthy from the trashy.

It may be that the computer revolution will require us to do more than extrapolate from existing conventions for dealing with printed texts. Even if computers do not replace books, they will certainly require us to renegotiate our relationship to printed materials. We will also need to monitor closely society's relationship to knowledge and reading. As our sense of community and our notions of identity change, we will inevitably alter the ways we communicate with one another, both online and in person. Computer-mediated communication will probably necessitate new rules of engagement.

No one knows for certain what the future will look like a generation from now. The best we can do to prepare for that unknown future is to understand the past, pay attention to the rapid changes of the present, and stay as flexible as possible.

THE READINGS

The selections in this chapter try to look into the future by gazing thoughtfully at what the present has to offer and how it differs from the past. The primary concerns of the essays are how the computer builds on and departs from modes of communication that are familiar in our print-centered culture. The computer has not killed literacy, according to Umberto Eco, it's just complicated and perhaps enriched literacy. Obituaries for the printed book seem to be premature, agrees D. T. Max, who assesses the book and the multimedia computer as competing technologies. Not surprisingly, he finds that each has its strengths and its weaknesses. Paul Saffo also compares books and computers, but he addresses issues of quality, cost, and availability. Bernard Sharratt and George Melrod look at the things the computer can do that the book cannot. Sharratt describes a CD-ROM disk that puts images of an entire museum's paintings on your desktop computer for your browsing pleasure, while Melrod explores hyperfiction, a new way of writing and reading that the computer has made possible. Sven Birkerts looks at educational programs based on this same reader-governed dynamic, "hypertext" programs that blur traditional disciplinary boundaries and let students guide their own learning by jumping from one idea to another. He questions whether all forms of knowledge lend themselves to this mode of learning and asks if wisdom can be gained through the ingestion of information. Walt Crawford and Michael Gorman similarly distinguish between data, information, knowledge, and wisdom, as they scope out the best ways to organize and make available the expanding volume of information that is flooding researchers. M. Kadi challenges several of the grandest claims being made for the information superhighway: Its diversity fosters global community; it puts limitless knowledge at your fingertips; it allows instant communication anywhere on the globe. Just as Kadi uncovers some of the limitations of the infohighway, John Seabrook discovers that the relationships formed in cyberspace do not always follow the rules of social engagement that are customary in real life. Speech that would be unthinkable face to face is all too common in the virtual world of the Internet. Seabrook uses his experience with "flames" and "worms" as an occasion to investigate the social interactions made possible by computer-mediated communication. Finally, Amy Harmon reports on how white supremacists are using online communications to spread messages of racial intolerance and recruit new members. Both Seabrook and Harmon raise the specter of online censorship, with all its attendant technical and ethical complications. All of the essays invite you to think about where you would like computer technology to take you in the future.

UMBERTO ECO

The Future of Literacy

Much of the discussion about the future of communication has been con-
ducted as if there were an either/or choice to be made between books and
computers. In changing the typical terms of the debate, Umberto Eco (b.
1932) sees book literacy and computer literacy working together—in com-
pany with visual literacy. In addition, he draws attention to some problems
and possibilities that the various modes of communication hold for the
whole world, not just for the elite of Western culture. Eco, best known as a
leading theorist in the field of semiotics—the study and interpretation of
signs in language, culture, and behavior—became an international literary
figure when his novel about a medieval library, The Name of the Rose
(1980), became an unexpected best-seller and then a movie. Born in
Alessandria, Italy, Eco has been a professor of semiotics at the University
of Bologna since 1975. His most recent works include Foucault's Pendu-
lum *(1989),* The Limits of Interpretation *(1990),* Interpretation and
Overinterpretations *(1992),* Misreadings *(1993), and* Apocalypse
Postponed *(1994), from which this essay is taken.*

According to Plato (in the *Phaedrus*) Thoth, or Hermes, the alleged
inventor of writing, presents his invention to the Pharaoh Thamus,
praising this new technique which will allow human beings to remember what they would otherwise forget. But the Pharaoh is not satisfied.
My skilful Thoth, he says, memory is such a great gift that it ought to be
kept alive by training it continuously. With your invention people will
no longer be obliged to train memory. They will remember things not
because of an internal effort, but by virtue merely of an external device.

We can understand the Pharaoh's concern. Writing, like any other
new technological device, would have made sluggish the human power
which it replaced and reinforced—just as cars have made us less able to
walk. Writing was dangerous because it decreased the powers of the
mind, by offering human beings a petrified soul, a caricature of mind, a
machine memory.

Plato's text is, of course, ironic. Plato was writing his argument
about writing. But he is putting it into the mouth of Socrates, who did
not write. Therefore Plato was expressing a fear that still survived in his
day. Thinking is an internal matter; the real thinker would not allow
books to think in his place.

Nowadays nobody shares these concerns, for two very simple rea-

---

From *Apocalypse Postponed,* ed. Robert Lumley (Bloomington: Indiana Univ.
Press, 1994), pp. 64–71.

sons. First of all, we know that books are not ways of making somebody else think in our place; on the contrary they are machines which provoke further thoughts. Secondly, if once upon a time people needed to train their memory in order to remember things, after the invention of writing they had also to train their memory in order to remember books. Books challenge and improve memory. They do not narcotize it. This old debate is worth reflecting on every time one meets a new communicational tool which pretends or appears to replace books.

During the last year some worried and worrying reports have been published in the United States on the decline of literacy. One of the reasons for the recent Wall Street crash, according to some observers, has been not only an exaggerated confidence in computers but also the fact that none of the yuppies who were controlling the stock market knew enough about the 1929 crisis. They were unable to face a crisis because of their lack of historical information. If they had read some books about Black Thursday[1] they might have been able to make better decisions and avoid many well-known pitfalls.

I agree. But I wonder if books would have been the only reliable vehicle for acquiring information. Time was when the only way to acquire a foreign language (apart from traveling abroad) was to study the language from a book. Now kids frequently learn other languages by listening to records, watching movies or TV programs in original versions, or deciphering the instructions on a drink can.

The same happens with geographical information. In my childhood I got the best of my information about exotic countries not from textbooks but from adventure novels (Jules Verne, for example, or Emilio Salgari, or Karl May).[2] My children at a very early age knew more than me on the same subject by watching movies and TV.

The illiteracy of the Wall Street yuppies was due not only to an insufficient exposure to books but also to a form of visual illiteracy. Books about the 1929 Black Thursday exist, and are still regularly published (the yuppies can be blamed for not being bookstore and library-goers), while television and cinema are largely unconcerned with any rigorous reconstruction of historical events. One could learn the history of the Roman Empire very well from the movies, if only those movies were historically accurate. The fault of Hollywood is not to have set up its films as an alternative to the books of Tacitus or Gibbon, but rather to have imposed a romantic, pulp version of both Tacitus and Gibbon.[3]

---

1. **Black Thursday:** October 29, 1929, the day of the stock market crash that began the Great Depression.—ED.

2. **Jules Verne** (1828–1905): Father of modern science fiction, author of *20,000 Leagues Under the Sea* (1870) and *Around the World in Eighty Days* (1873); **Emilio Salgari** (1862–1911) Italian author of pirate stories and early science fiction; **Karl May** (1842–1912) German author of boys' adventure books.—ED.

3. **Tacitus** (A.D. ca. 55–A.D. ca. 117): Roman historian; Edward **Gibbon** (1734–1794) Author of the six-volume *History of the Decline and Fall of the Roman Empire* (1776–1788).—ED.

The yuppies' problem is not only that they watch TV instead of reading books; it is that in New York only on Channel 13[4] is there anyone who knows who Gibbon was.

I am not stressing these points in order to assert the possibility of a new literacy which would make books obsolete. God knows, every penny I ever made in my life—as publisher, as scholar, or as author—has come from books. My points are rather the following:

1. Today the concept of literacy comprises many media. An enlightened policy on literacy must take into account the possibilities of all these media. Educational concerns must be extended to the whole of the media. Responsibilities and tasks must be carefully balanced. If tapes are better than books for learning languages, look after cassettes. If a commentated presentation of Chopin on compact disc helps people to understand Chopin, don't worry if people don't buy a five-volume history of romantic music.

2. Do not fight against false enemies. Even if it were true that today visual communication has overwhelmed written communication, the problem is not one of opposing written to visual communication. The problem is rather how to improve both. In the Middle Ages visual communication was, for the masses, more important than writing. But Chartres Cathedral was not culturally inferior to the *Imago mundi* by Honorius of Autun.[5] Cathedrals were the TV of their times, and the difference with our TV was that the directors of the medieval TV read good books, had a lot of imagination, and worked for the public good.

We are regularly misled by a "mass media criticism of the mass media" which is superficial and almost always belated. The mass media are still repeating that our historical period is and will be more and more dominated by images. Mass media people have read McLuhan[6] too late. The present and the forthcoming young generation is and will be a computer-oriented generation. The main feature of a computer screen is that it hosts and displays more alphabetic letters than images. The new generations will be alphabet and not image-oriented.

Moreover, the new generation is trained to read at an incredible speed. An old-fashioned university professor today cannot read a computer screen at the same speed as a teenager. These same teenagers, if

---

4. **Channel 13:** WNET, the New York public television station.—ED.

5. *Imago mundi* was a compendium of cosmology and geography popular throughout the Middle Ages and translated into various vernaculars.

6. Marshall **McLuhan** (1911–1980): Communications theorist and educator whose writings on the impact of television in *The Gutenberg Galaxy* (1962) and *Understanding Media* (1964) predicted that the medium of communication would soon come to have more influence than the content of the messages.—ED.

they should happen to want to program their own home computer, must know, or learn, logical procedures and algorithms, and must type on a keyboard, at great speed, words and numbers.

I have said that we should not fight against false enemies. In the same vein let me say that we should not endorse false friends. To read a computer screen is not the same as to read a book. I do not know if you are familiar with the process of learning a new computer program. Usually the program is able to display on the screen all the instructions you need. But generally users who want to learn the program and to save their eyesight either print out the instructions and read them as if they were in book form, or buy a printed manual. It is possible to conceive of a visual program which explains very well how to print and bind a book, but in order to get instructions on how to write a computer program we need a book.

After spending a few hours at a computer console I feel the need to sit down comfortably in an armchair and read a newspaper, or maybe a good poem.

I think that computers are diffusing a new form of literacy but are unable to satisfy all the intellectual needs that they stimulate. I am an optimist twelve hours a day and a pessimist the remaining twelve. In my optimistic mood I dream of a computer generation which, obliged compulsively to read a computer screen, gets acquainted with reading but at a certain moment comes to feel dissatisfied and looks for a different form of reading, more relaxed and generating a different form of involvement. In Hugo's *Notre Dame de Paris*, Frollo, comparing a book with his old cathedral, says: *"Ceci tuera cela."* I think that today, speaking of computers and books, one could say: *"Ceci aidera cela."*[7]

Do not fight against false enemies. One of the most common objec- 15 tions to the pseudo-literacy of computers is that young people get more and more accustomed to speaking through cryptic short formulas: dir, help, diskopy, error 67, and so on. Is that still literacy?

I am a collector of old books and I feel delighted when I read the seventeenth-century titles which take up a whole page and sometimes more. Introductions were several pages long, started with elaborate courtesy formulae praising the ideal addressee, usually an emperor or a pope, and went on for pages and pages explaining in a very baroque style the purposes and virtues of the text to follow.

If baroque writers were to read our modern scholarly books they would be horrified. Introductions are one page long, briefly outline the subject matter of the book, thank some national or international endowment for a generous grant, briefly explain that the book has been made

---

7. Victor **Hugo** (1803–1885): French novelist best known for *Les Miserables* (1862) and *Notre Dame de Paris* (1831); *Ceci tuera cela:* "This will kill that"; *Ceci aidera cela:* "This will aid that."—ED.

possible by the love and understanding of a wife or husband or children, credit a secretary for having patiently typed the manuscript. We understand perfectly all the human and academic ordeals suggested by those few lines, the hundreds of nights spent highlighting photocopies, the innumerable frozen hamburgers eaten on the go (no caviar for the scholar) . . . I guess that in the near future three lines saying

> TWO
> SMITH
> ROCKEFELLER
> (to be read as: I thank my wife and my children, the book is due to the generous assistance of Professor Smith and was made possible by the Rockefeller Foundation)

would be as eloquent as a baroque introduction. It is a problem of rhetoric and of acquaintance with a given form of rhetoric. In years to come, I think, passionate love letters will be sent in the form of a short instruction.

There is a curious notion according to which in verbal language the more you say the more profound and perceptive you are. Mallarmé, however, told us that it is sufficient to spell out *"une fleur"* to evoke a universe of perfumes, shapes, and thoughts.[8] Frequently, for poetry, the fewer the words the more things they imply. Three lines of Pascal say more than three hundred pages of a long and boring treatise on morals and metaphysics. The quest for a new and surviving literacy ought not to be the quest for a pre-computer verbal bulimia.

The enemies of literacy are hiding elsewhere.

Let us know reconsider the debate between Toth and Thamus. Thamus assumed that the invention of writing would diminish the power of human memory. I objected that human memory has been improved by the continual exercise of remembering what books say. But to remember written words is not the same as to remember things. Probably the memory of the librarians of Alexandria was quantitatively greater than that of the illiterate savage, but the illiterate savage has a more specialized memory for things, shapes, smells, colors. In response to the invention of writing, Greek and Latin civilization invented the *artes memoriae*[9] so that orators and teachers could survive as thinkers in times when books were in short supply.

The memory of Cicero or Aquinas[10] was more flexible and powerful 20

---

8. Stéphane **Mallarmé** (1842–1898): French poet and forebear of the Symbolists.—ED.

9. *artes memoriae* ("memorial arts"): Refers to a medieval system of enhancing and developing memory, primarily through the use of mental images.—ED.

10. **Cicero** (106 B.C.–43 B.C.): Roman orator; Saint Thomas **Aquinas** (1225–1274) Italian philosopher and theologian.—ED.

than ours. Though Thoth's invention may not have, Gutenberg's has certainly weakened the mnemonic capacity of our species. To counteract the negative effects of printing, the old school insisted on training young people to learn poems, dates and lists of historical figures by heart.

Our permissive society, relying on the abundance of tapes and other forms of recording, has further rendered memory as a mental ability somewhat obsolete. The use of computers will work in the same direction. You may recall a short story by Isaac Asimov where, in a future world dominated by intelligent machines, the last human being who still knows the multiplication tables by heart is wanted by the Pentagon and by various secret services because he represents the only calculator able to function in the event of power shortages. The way our present society tends to encourage well-trained memories is through TV quiz programs and so-called trivia games.

Menaced by the growth of an image-oriented culture, our technological society has already spontaneously reacted in terms of free-market dynamics. After all, since the invention of TV the quantity of printed matter in the world has not decreased. On the contrary it has grown to an extent unprecedented in previous centuries—even though this increase has to be set against a corresponding increase in world population.

In simple terms, it seems that previously illiterate people, once exposed to television, at a certain moment start to read newspapers. I appreciate that such a merely quantitative evaluation is not very illuminating in terms of highbrow culture, since there are newspapers that are worse than TV programs. But when speaking of literacy it is better to forget the shibboleths of highbrow culture. Speaking of literacy in the world today we are not only concerned with the happy few of Bloomsbury,[11] but with the masses of the Third World.

The real question rather is how to confront a series of phenomena which are menacing the universe of books and the cultural heritage that books represent. I shall list some problems, without pretending to propose solutions. It is pretty late in the day and I have started my twelve hours of pessimism.

1. Books are menaced by books. Any excess of information produces silence. When I am in the United States I read the *New York Times* every day except on Sunday. Sunday's *Times* contains too much information and I do not have time enough to consume it. Bookstores are so crowded with books they can only afford to keep the most recent ones.

2. Books are still an expensive commodity, at least in comparison with other forms of communication such as TV. An international committee to oppose the taxation of books in the European Community

---

11. **Bloomsbury:** Fashionable and "literary" section of London, once the home of Virginia Woolf and other writers.—ED.

has just been created and since I am its president I cannot but agree with its demands. But good ideas have unfortunate side effects. Lowering the price of books will encourage their publication and circulation but will at the same time increase their number—with all the dangers referred to under 1, above.

3. New technologies are competing with each other. Books are now more widely available than in any other period of human history, but all publishers know the extent to which photocopying technology is jeopardizing their interests.

   A photocopy of a paperback is still more expensive than the original, but publication in paperback is dependent on the success of the hardcover edition and for many important scientific books only hardcover publication is possible. I am a writer. I live on my royalties, and once my American publisher told me he was thinking of suing a professor who had told his thirty students to make photocopies of one of my books, too expensive for them to buy. I asked the publisher to refrain from any legal action, since in the professor's place I would have done the same.

   The main international scientific publishers have found a way to escape this predicament. They publish a very limited number of copies, they price the book at $300, and they take it for granted that copies will be bought only for major libraries and the rest will be piracy. So prices increase and the physical act of reading scientific material becomes more and more unpleasant, since everyone knows the difference between reading a crisp original page and a xerox. Moreover, the very act of photocopying a book tends to make me feel virtuous and up-to-date in my scholarship: I have the text, and afterwards I no longer feel the need to read it. Today scholars are accumulating enormous stocks of xeroxed material that they will never read. Ironically, the technology of photocopying makes it easier to have books, not easier to read them. Thus billions of trees are killed for the sake of unread photocopies.

4. Trees, alas. Every new book reduces the quantity of oxygen. We should start thinking of ecological books. When, in the last century, the book industry stopped making books from rags and started to make them from trees, it not only menaced our survival, it jeopardized the civilization of the book. A modern book cannot survive more than seventy years. I have books from the fifties that I can no longer open. In the next fifty years the modern section of my personal library will be a handful of dust. We know that acid-free paper is expensive, and that chemical procedures for preserving already existing books can be reasonably applied only to a limited number of them. To microfilm all the books contained in a huge library will certainly save their content, but will limit the opportunity to consult them to a small number of professional students. A way

to escape this danger is to republish books every few years. But decisions of this type are regulated by the market and by public demand. According to this criterion, a thousand years from now *Gone with the Wind* will survive, and *Ulysses* will not.

The only solution would be to appoint special committees to decide which books to save (by chemical rescue, by reprint, or by microfilm). The power of such committees would be enormous. Not even Torquemada, or Big Brother in *1984*,[12] had such an authority to select.

I am an author. I want not to be saved by a special committee. I want not to be saved by mass demand. I want not to be saved in the form of a cryptic microfilm. I want to survive for centuries and centuries, unknown to everybody, in the secret of an old forgotten library, as happened to the classical authors during the Middle Ages. I cannot. I know for sure that I cannot. Should I sell myself to Gorbachev, to Reagan, to the pope, to Khomeini, in order to have as a reward an acid-free edition?

5. Finally, who will decide which books to give to the Third World? I recently attended a meeting at the Frankfurt Book Fair, organized by German publishers, about the need to send books to the young people of Nicaragua. I was sympathetic to the initiative, and I trust the group that invited me. But the problem is bigger than that. The whole of the Third World is escaping from illiteracy in the sense that the kids there will probably learn to read and write. But they will not have the economic possibility of having books. Who will choose the books for them? The American fundamentalist churches which are engaged in an economic push to spread their doctrines through Latin America? The Soviet Union? The Roman [Catholic] Church?

I suppose that three-quarters of the world population today cannot afford books. They can only accept some of them graciously. Who will decide for them? The immediate future offers the opportunity to make millions and millions of people think in one way or another, depending on the economic and organizational effort of those who decide to send them books. I feel worried by the power that somebody—I don't know who, but certainly not my university—will have in the next few decades.

■ **CONSIDER THE SOURCE**

1. Define "literacy" as Eco uses the term in his title. What is the "new form of literacy" that Eco thinks computers are diffusing? How does it differ from traditional literacy? How does he believe literacy extends to other media than print?

---

12. Tomas de **Torquemada** (1420–1498): A leading figure in the Spanish Inquisition; **Big Brother:** The name for the repressive government in George Orwell's novel *1984*.—ED.

2. What relationship does Eco see between computers and changes in modern rhetoric? How does he view the brevity of contemporary writing?

3. Summarize in your own words the threats that Eco sees menacing the traditional book world. What role do market forces play in each?

4. Why does Eco repeatedly refer to his own status as a writer who depends on print? How do those references influence your understanding of his argument?

■ **CONSIDER THE IMPLICATIONS**

5. What role has memory played in your intellectual development? In your journal, explore what sorts of information you memorized and why. Have you memorized things for fun, such as sports statistics, dialogue from movies, lyrics of songs? What role have books played in training or "narcotizing" your memory?

6. Discuss in class how technological devices have improved or weakened (or even annihilated) traditional methods of accomplishing tasks. For instance, how many people rely on a pocket calculator? How have such devices changed people's relationship to the tasks they perform?

7. Using Eco's analysis of the computer as a model, write a paper analyzing the benefits and liabilities of another technological development. How has the technology affected our lives? How has it changed the way we work or play?

8. Review Walter J. Ong's discussion of how print changed our relationship to words ("Print, Space, and Closure," pp. 52–65). Using Eco's observations about computers, write an essay analyzing how the word on the screen differs from the word on the page. How does each use space? How much "closure" is offered by each form?

9. Interview the director of a charitable book distribution program in your area. Who is sponsoring the distribution to other countries or to underprivileged people in this country? What sorts of books are they most interested in? Why? What do they see as their mission? Write a profile of the program, keeping in mind Eco's "pessimism" and worries about such projects.

10. Review C. H. Knoblauch's essay on "Literacy and the Politics of Education" (pp. 122–30). How does the "new form of literacy" that Eco describes contain a political dimension similar to the literacy programs Knoblauch discusses? Write an essay analyzing Eco's politics and the implications of the spread of new and old literacy.

From *The Atlantic Monthly* (Sept. 1994), 61–71.

D. T. MAX

The End of the Book?

Some futurists confidently predict that the computer will end the long reign of the book as the place where we store and retrieve information. Naturally such predictions scare the dust jackets off of writers, publishers, and devoted book consumers. D. T. Max (b. 1961), who writes often on issues of media and publishing, takes to the streets of Multimedia Gulch, the center for interactive media technology in San Francisco, to discover just what the competition for books looks like. His essay explores the benefits and liabilities of the interactive reading experience offered by CD-ROMs and assesses the impact that computer technology has had on the publishing world. If his conclusions seem largely hopeful for book lovers, that may be no accident: This article originally appeared in one of the nation's oldest literary magazines, The Atlantic Monthly. *Max, formerly the book editor of the* New York Observer, *is now senior features editor at* Harper's Bazaar *and a contributing editor for* The Paris Review.*

> "We'll teach you about multimedia before your kids have to."
> – Billboard on Route 101 near Silicon Valley

An office-party atmosphere pervaded the headquarters of *Wired* magazine, the newly created oracle of the computer-literate generation. *Wired* is housed on the third floor of a flat, low brick building with plain-pine interiors in an industrial section of San Francisco south of Market Street. The area is known as Multimedia Gulch, for the scores of small companies working in the neighborhood which mix sound, video, and text into experimental interactive multimedia computer products that they hope will one day sell millions of copies. *Wired* is not an ordinary computer magazine: It promises the faithful reader not mere computing power—something available from a grown-up computer magazine like *Macworld*, which happens to be across the street—but, more important, hipness, the same sense of being ahead of the curve that once attached to a new Bob Dylan album or Richard Brautigan book.

The weekday afternoon I was there, hero sandwiches lay on the table, the magazine's pet gray parrot was hanging outside its cage, and young men and women with sophisticated eyewear sat rapt before their computer screens. The reference folders and layout paraphernalia common to magazine editorial departments were scattered around. The ringing of the phones was constant. When I had first called *Wired*'s cofounder, Louis Rossetto, in the summer of 1993, I got through to him immediately, and he had, if anything, too much time to speculate about the shape of things to come. Several months later I had to go through a secretary and a publicist for my interview, and once I arrived, I was made to wait while more urgent calls were put through. What happened in the interim is that the information highway became a hot subject. Rossetto was now every media journalist's and Hollywood agent's first call.

What I wanted from Louis Rossetto was his opinion on whether the rise of the computer culture that his magazine covered would end with the elimination by CD-ROMs and networked computer databases of the hardcover, the paperback, and the world of libraries and literate culture that had grown up alongside them. Was print on its way out? And if it was, what would happen to the publishers who had for generations put out books, and to the writers who had written them? Or was there something special about the book that would ensure that no technical innovation could ever supplant it? Would the book resist the CD-ROM and the Internet just as it has resisted radio, television, and the movies?

Finally I was taken into the sunlit confines of his office. Bookshelves ran along one wall. A forty-five-year-old career journalist with shoulder-grazing gray hair, Rossetto is a late convert to computers. He spent much of the 1980s in Europe, and gives off a mild sense of disengagement—there is a touch of the sixties about him, as there is about much else in the Gulch. Now he set out his vision of a fast-changing computerized, paperless, nearly book-free society, and did so with a certainty that would frighten even someone whose sense of equilibrium, unlike mine, did not involve visits to bookstores or the belief that last year's laptop is basically good enough. "The changes going on in the world now are literally a revolution in progress, a revolution that makes political revolution seem like a game," Rossetto, who recently sold a minority interest in his magazine to Condé Nast, said. "It will revolutionize how people work, how they communicate, and how they entertain themselves, and it is the biggest engine for change in our world today. We're looking at the end of a twenty- or thirty- or forty-year process, from the invention of tubes to transistors to fiber-optic and cable to the development of cable networks, until we've reached critical mass today."

I asked if there was no downside, no tradeoff for all that informa- 5 tion in the world that was to come. "It doesn't keep me up at night, I admit," he said. "Written information is a relatively new phenomenon. Depositing it and being able to reference it centuries later is not common human experience. In some ways what is happening with online is a return to our earlier oral tradition. In other ways, it is utterly new, a direct connection of minds. Humans have always been isolated, and now we're starting to see electronic connections generating an intellectual organism of their own, literally a quantum leap beyond our experience with consciousness."

This is classic 1990s cybervisionarism, repeated up and down the halls of *Wired* and echoed throughout the Bay area, and it derives directly from the teenage-male personalities of the hackers who created the computer industry: Cyberspace will be like a better kind of school.

There are three principal articles of faith behind this vision. 1) The classroom will be huge: The linking of information worldwide will cause a democratic explosion in the accessibility of knowledge. 2) The classroom will be messy: The sense of information as an orderly and retrievable quantity will decline, and you won't necessarily be able to find what you're looking for in cyberspace at any given time. 3) There will be no teachers: The "controllers of information"—censors, editors, and studio executives—will disappear, and the gates of public discourse will swing open before everyone who can get online. Anyone can publish; anyone can read what is published; anyone can comment on what he or she has read. Rossetto had been delineating his vision for twenty minutes, but suddenly it was time to go. An assistant popped in to pull him into an editorial meeting. "I have a pretty cynical view of most of the American media," Rossetto said before leaving (read: "You'll get this wrong. You'll be hostile."). "Their jobs are at stake, because their businesses are threatened. Take *Time* magazine. What function would it have in the modern world?"

One look at *Wired* suggests a gap between message and messenger. *Wired* looks more radical than it is. It cheerleads and debunks its subjects using editorial formulas that came in with the nineteenth-century magazine—a fictional takeoff on Microsoft, written by Douglas Coupland, the author of *Generation X*; a classic star cover on Laurie Anderson, "America's multimediatrix"—rather than harnessing any global back-and-forth among literate minds. Although *Wired* communicates extensively by e-mail with its readers, conducts forums, and makes back issues available online, its much-repeated goal of creating a magazine—currently called *HotWired*—that is especially designed to exist electronically remains fuzzy. For the moment this is no open democracy, and *Wired* is no computer screen—its bright graphics would make a fashion magazine envious. *Wired* celebrates what doesn't yet exist by exploiting a format that does: It's as if a scribe copied out a manuscript extolling the beauty that would one day be print.

THE LIMITATIONS OF THE BOOK

Overhyped or not, interactive multimedia do hold vast potential for the companies that in the next decades back the right products in the right formats. Multimedia are not new—a child's pop-up book is one example, and an illustrated pre-Gutenberg Bible is another. But interactive multimedia as envisioned by the computer industry (especially if television cables or telephone wires are reconfigured to accommodate two-way high-quality video digital transmissions—technologies that may be in place on a national scale sometime around the millennium) have great potential, because they would persuade consumers to bring software into their homes as they brought it into their offices in the 1980s. Who wouldn't want a screen that accessed all currently existing forms of information, from mail to movies, and did so with great convenience and flexibility?

Even if this vision is only partly realized, the book, the newspaper, and the video will be hard-pressed to maintain their place in our culture. Look at the book without sentiment and its limitations are evident: Books can excite the imagination, but they can't literally make you see and hear. "What is the use of a book without pictures or conversations?" Lewis Carroll's Alice grouses, before tumbling down the rabbit hole into the more absorbing precincts of Wonderland, in one of the favorite texts of hackers. Interactive-multimedia designers, with their brew of sights, sounds, and words, believe that they could keep Alice (her age puts her very much in their target group) above-ground and interested. Or a multimedia designer could expand the book's plot line, giving the reader the choice of whether Alice goes down the hole or decides to stick around and read alongside her sister on the riverbank. The reader could hear Alice's voice, or ask her questions about herself, the answers to which are only implicit in the book.

When something intrigues the readers of a printed book, they have to wrestle with an index and then, perhaps, go to a library to find out more about the subject; they can't just hit a search button to log on to a database attached to the book and read something else on the same subject, as they can on a computer. "I decided books were obsolete thirty-four years ago," says Ted Nelson, an early computer hacker who coined the word *hypertext* in the early sixties to describe how knowledge would be accessed if all information were available simultaneously. "I have thousands of books and I love them. It's only intertwining I want more of."

But such intertwining—a vast linkage of electronic text across databases worldwide—would inevitably push the printed word to the margins and replace it with sleeker, more efficient text conveyers. It is not the viability of text itself that is in question. On the contrary, whether paper gives way to the computer screen or not, there is little question that words as the cornerstone of communication are safe. "*Littera scripta manet,*" an anonymous Roman wrote: "The written word endures." This is a comforting quotation—typically if erroneously attributed to the poet Horace—that writers about multimedia are fond of using. In fact, words are multiplying wildly. In the world of computers they are a bargain compared with images: cheap to transport and easy to store. Probably more words are put out in a week by the twenty million people who use the loosely strung computer networks that constitute the Internet than are published by all major American publishing companies in a year. There's a "Poetry Corner" and bulletin boards where new novels get

₁₀

posted constantly. In a recent announcement a nonprofit organization called Project Gutenberg, run out of a university in Illinois, presented as its mysteriously precise goal "To Give Away One Trillion E[lectronic] Text Files [of classic books] by December 21, 2001." When I mentioned the scope of fiction on the Internet to the novelist John Updike, he said lightly, "I imagine most of that stuff on the information highway is roadkill anyway." And of course he is right. But his is a minority opinion outside the circles of tastemakers.

VAPORWARE INTIMIDATION

Text and books are not, however, joined at the hip—words don't need print. "Books on paper are a medium unto themselves," Louis Rossetto says, "and my sense is that anything that is stand-alone is a dead end." But even to Rossetto a world completely without books seems unlikely. One view is that the book will become the equivalent of the horse after the invention of the automobile or the phonograph record after the arrival of the compact disc—a thing for eccentrics, hobbyists, and historians. It will not disappear, but it will become obsolete. Multimedia programmers themselves disagree sharply on whether this will come to pass in five years, ten years, or never. One question is whether there is money to be made in the production of multimedia. Another is how good multimedia products will ever be, for by industry admission they are not very good now. The great majority of the three thousand multimedia products launched last year were little more than rudimentary efforts. "I think that there are fewer than thirty titles with good, solid, deep information out there," Rick Fischer, the director of product development at Sony Electronic Publishing, says. "The majority of titles are kind of pseudomultimedia. People are still learning how to do this." Besides, computer companies are not as excited by books as they are by games, which represent an ever-increasing share of the market. Sony, for example, has backed an interactive game version of its movie *Bram Stoker's Dracula*—Harker races against rats, wolves, and flaming torches to slay the Prince of Darkness—rather than the book *Dracula*, three hundred pages of print that could be augmented with perhaps a moving illustration or two.

Publishers are terrified. They have read a thousand times that one day we will play games, shop, watch movies, read books, and do research all on our computer or television screens. Computer companies are skillful at bluffing one another, forever claiming that they are nearly ready to release a hot new product, which is in truth barely in prototype. This kind of nonproduct has the nickname "vaporware" within the industry. But publishers, unfamiliar with computer culture, believe the hype. In the past year *Publishers Weekly* ran six major stories on how CD-ROM and the Internet will remake publishing. The comments of Laurence Kirshbaum, the president of Warner Books, a subsidiary of Time

Warner, were not untypical: "I don't know if there's the smell of crisis in the air, but there should be. Publishers should be sleeping badly these days. They have to be prepared to compete with software giants like [Microsoft's chairman] Bill Gates." Publishers are most of all afraid of doing nothing—as hardback publishers did when they ignored the paperback explosion of the 1960s and 1970s. So they are rushing to form electronic-publishing divisions and to find partners in the software business. "Eighteen months ago no one was talking about multimedia and CD-ROMs seriously, and now everyone is deeply involved and deeply conscious of them," says Alberto Vitale, the chairman of the normally cautious Random House, Inc., which has signed a co-venture deal with Broderbund, a leading children's software developer in Novato, California, to create children's interactive multimedia. Putting Dr. Seuss on CD-ROM is one of their first efforts. The Palo Alto "media kitchen" owned by Viacom, where the company's film, television, and book divisions cooperate—at least theoretically—on interactive-multimedia research, is designing new travel guides: why actually go to San Francisco when by 1995 you will be able to take a virtual walking tour on a Frommer CD-ROM? Interest has even percolated into the last redoubt of traditional publishing, the firm of Alfred A. Knopf. Since its inception Knopf has placed great emphasis on the book as handsome object. But Knopf's president attended the first International Illustrated Book and New Media Publishing Market fair, held earlier this year, which was designed to introduce multimedia's various content providers to one another. (The fact that the fair was in Cannes probably did not hurt attendance.)

Behind the stampede into electronic publishing is doubtless a wide- 15 spread feeling among those in conventional publishing that the industry is in dire, if ill-defined, trouble. A decade-long trend among major publishers toward publishing fewer trade books recently had an impact on four imprints in just two months, most notably a near-total cutback of Harcourt, Brace's trade department (the publishers of T. S. Eliot, Virginia Woolf, and Alice Walker) and the closing of Ticknor & Fields adult books, a Houghton Mifflin imprint (which included William Gass and Robert Stone among its authors). Aggressive marketing has allowed publishers to sell more copies of their top titles, creating the illusion of pink-cheeked health in some years. But after decades of competition from radio, television, movies, videos, and Americans' increasingly long workdays, it is hard to imagine how the publishers of mainstream fiction and nonfiction in book form will ever again publish as many titles as they did in the past; after all, popular fiction magazines never recovered from the advent of radio serials. Giants like Doubleday and Putnam publish perhaps a third as many hardcover books as they did ten years ago, and McGraw-Hill, once the publisher of Vladimir Nabokov and hundreds of other authors, is out of the new-trade-book business altogether. Recently Random House sent a glass-is-half-full letter to book-review editors, letting them know that the company would be making their jobs easier by publishing fewer books. According to a 1993 survey by Dataquest, a San Jose information-technology market-research firm, most employees in the multimedia-content industry come from traditional print backgrounds. And the extremely rudimentary employment statistics that exist for the publishing industry show a decline since the late 1980s in New York–based publishing jobs, though it is hardly enough of one to confirm a sea change in publishing's fortunes, or to suggest that Armageddon is around the corner. Last year nearly fifty thousand new titles destined for bookstores were published, and total consumer-reference CD-ROM software sales amounted to only about 3 percent of trade-book sales.

Besides, the computer industry acknowledges that what most readers think of as books—that is, novels and nonfiction text—gain nothing from being on screen; the appeal of the product depends on the quality of the prose and the research, neither of which is enhanced by current screens. Whether you scroll down a screen or turn a page to read *The Bridges of Madison County* makes a great deal of difference in the quality of the reading experience. "I just don't personally believe in reading novels on a computer screen," says Olaf Olafsson, the president of Sony Electronic Publishing and the author of *Absolution*, a novel published in March by Pantheon Books. He says that he would never want to see his own work on a computer: "There's a lot of content that's now being delivered on paper that's fine on paper." The book has great advantages over the computer: It's light and it's cheap. That it has changed little in four hundred years suggests an uncommonly apt design. John Updike says, "It seems to me the book has not just aesthetic values—the charming little clothy box of the thing, the smell of the glue, even the print, which has its own beauty. But there's something about the sensation of ink on paper that is in some sense a thing, a phenomenon rather than an epiphenomenon. I can't break the association of electric trash with the computer screen. Words on the screen give the sense of being just another passing electronic wriggle." You can drop a book in the bathtub, dry it out on the radiator, and still read it. You can put it in the attic, pull it out two hundred years later, and probably decipher the words. You can curl up in bed with it or get suntan lotion on it. These are definitely not possibilities suggested by the computer. A well-thumbed paperback copy of John Grisham blowing in a beach breeze represents a technological stronghold the computer may never invade.

A SOLUTION IN SEARCH OF A PROBLEM

Lovers of literature (and schlock) may not see much change, then, but that doesn't mean publishers are in for an easy ride. Novels, nonfiction, and belles lettres are a prestige sideshow for publishers—they amount to only a few billion dollars in a roughly $18 billion book industry. Take dictionaries and encyclopedias, which are in effect databases in book form. The hand cannot match a computer chip in accessing given references, which constitutes the primary function of such works. Last year the 1989 edition of the *Oxford English Dictionary*, the flagship publication of the four hundred-year-old university press, sold four times as many copies in a new CD-ROM version as in its traditional twenty-volume book form. The company has said that the next print edition, due in a decade, may well be the last. At an October 1993 celebration at the New York Public Library in honor of the publication of the fifth edition of the *Columbia Encyclopedia* in both book form and (a year hence) on CD-ROM, one guest speaker commented that the next edition, whenever it was ready, might well not have a paper counterpart. There was barely an objection from the audience.

Publishers are divided over the fate of so-called soft reference titles—cookbooks and how-to books—and children's books. These are huge markets, and the question is whether electronic books will capture them or expand on them. "My generation may be the last . . . to have a strong visceral affection for books," Janet Wikler, a former director of advanced media at HarperCollins, told *Publishers Weekly* last year.

What publishers have not stopped to consider is whether consumers like CD-ROMs in the first place—or how comfortable they will ever be with networked, digitalized, downloaded books when they become available. It may be a question of technical proficiency: How many families possess the sophistication to use Microsoft's new CD-ROM Musical Instruments—a charming visual and audio tour of the instruments of the world which is perfect for six-year-olds? The product requires either a multimedia computer or "a Multimedia PC upgrade kit, which includes CD-ROM drive (with CD-DA outputs, sustained 150K/second transfer rate and a maximum seek time of one second while using no more than 40 percent of the CPU's processing power)." Electronic encyclopedias have all but driven print encyclopedias out of the market in large part because they are "bundled"—sold at a deep discount to computer-hardware manufacturers to be included free when the consumer buys a CD-ROM drive. This is roughly like giving the consumer a book if he will only buy a lamp. "Traditional publishers may be a Luddite[1] elite, but software publishers are arrogant sheep," says Michael Mellin, a multimedia executive who until last year was the publisher of Random House's electronic-publishing division. "One thing publishers don't realize is that there hasn't been a comparable kick in sales of CD-ROM multimedia titles given the rise in the number of CD-ROM drives installed." In other words, books on CD-ROM don't sell—at least not yet. A study of the industry last year found that of those people who had bought a CD-ROM drive, fewer than half

---

1. **Luddite:** Someone who resists technology, especially in the form of automation (named after the farm laborers, said to be followers of "Ned Ludd," who rioted against mechanization in early nineteenth-century England).—ED.

had returned to the computer store to buy new discs. Compare this with the way the compact-disc player caught on in the mid-1980s. Interactive multimedia may turn out to be the biggest bust since the paperless office. One former industry executive describes multimedia as "a solution in search of a problem, doing what other things do already, only slightly less well."

Publishers derive their impressions of the awesome potential of mul-   20
timedia from products like Microsoft's much publicized Encarta CD-ROM, a magnificent encyclopedia with text drawn from Funk & Wagnalls's twenty-nine-volume encyclopedia and augmented by hundreds of video and audio clips. Alice would have fun with this: She could listen to bird calls and African drums, or experiment with changing the moon's orbit. (She could also click on Bill Gates's name and hear his nasal assurance that Microsoft "has never wavered from the vision" of a personal computer "on every desk and in every home." This was not part of Funk & Wagnalls's original text.) But having been five years in development, employing a hundred people at its peak, and reportedly costing Microsoft well upward of $5 million, Encarta may be something of a Potemkin Village,[2] meant for credulous competitors to marvel at. The company has dropped the price from $395 to $139 to try to get consumers to buy it.

The Limitations of the Computer

Paper has limitations, but the computer may have more. As a physical object, it is hardly comforting. "Who'd want to go to bed with a Powerbook?" John Baker, a vice president at Broderbund, asks. And even if the laptop goes on shrinking, its screen, whose components represent nearly all the machine's cost, remains at best a chore to read. At the Xerox Palo Alto Research Center (where the receptionist's cubicle still houses an IBM Selectric typewriter) is a display room with half a dozen prototype six-million-pixel AMLCD screens. The quiet hum of the room, the bright white lighting, the clean, flat antiseptic surfaces, give the impression of an aspirin commercial. "It was clear to us that no reader was going to read a book off any of the current screens for more than ten minutes," says Malcolm Thompson, the chief technologist. "We hoped to change that." A large annotated poster on the wall illustrates point for point the screen's superiority to paper, as in an old-fashioned magazine ad. This flat panel display is indeed better than commercial screens, but it is neither as flexible nor as mobile as a book, and it still depends on fickle battery power. A twentysomething software marketer who began as an editorial assistant in book publishing points out, "A book requires one good eye, one good light source, and one good finger."

---

2. **Potemkin Village:** Grigori Aleksandrovich Potemkin (1739–1791) constructed elaborate fake villages to impress Russian Empress Catherine the Great when she toured the Ukraine and the Crimea.—ED.

LOST IN CYBERSPACE

In the heart of official Washington, D.C., down the street from the Capitol and at the same intersection as the Supreme Court and the Library of Congress, stands an incongruous statue of Puck, whom the *Oxford Companion to English Literature*, soon to be issued on CD-ROM, defines as "a goblin," and whom Microsoft Encarta passes over in favor of "puck," which it defines solely as a mouselike device with crosshairs printed on it, used in engineering applications. The 1930s building next to the statue is the Folger Shakespeare Library. Two flights below the reading room, designed in the style of a Tudor banquet hall, next to which librarians and scholars click quietly on laptops and log on to the Internet's Shaksper reference group for the latest scholarly chatter, is a locked bank gate. Behind it is what librarians call a "short-title catalogue vault"—in other words, a very-rare-book room. This main room—there is another—is rectangular, carpeted in red, and kept permanently at 68 degrees. Sprinkler valves are interspersed among eight evenly spaced shelves of books dating from 1475 to 1640 and lit by harsh institutional light. Of these books 180 are the only copies of their titles left in the world: You can spot them by the small blue slips reading "Unique" which modestly poke out from their tops. At the end of the room is a long shelf on which stacks of oversize volumes rest on their sides: These are nearly a third of the surviving First Folio editions of the plays of William Shakespeare. When the First Folios were printed, in the 1620s, printing was still an inexact art. Each page had to be checked by hand, and the volumes are full of mistakes: backward type, ill-cut pages, and variant lines. Several copies lack the 1602 tragedy *Troilus and Cressida*, owing to a copyright dispute. And yet, 370 years after they came off the printing press, you can still pull down these books and read them. The pages are often lightly cockled and foxed,[3] because the folio was printed on mid-priced rag paper, but the type is still bright and the volume falls open easily. You can balance it on your lap and run your finger along the page to feel the paper grain in that sensuous gesture known to centuries of book readers: Here is knowledge.

In 1620 Francis Bacon ranked printing, along with gunpowder and the compass, as one of the three inventions that had "changed the appearance and state of the whole world." Indeed, the existence of multiple identical copies of texts that are nearly indelibly recorded, permanently retrievable, and widely decipherable has determined so much of modern history that what the world would be like without printing can only be guessed at. More books likely came into existence in the fifty years after the Gutenberg Bible than in the millennium that preceded it.

---

3. **cockled and foxed:** Over time, books and manuscripts can become wrinkled or puckered (cockled) as well as discolored (foxed) from acid residues in the paper.— ED.

"Printing was a huge change for Western culture," says Paul Saffo, who studies the effect of technology on society at the Institute for the Future, in Menlo Park (where the receptionist also uses an IBM Selectric). "The dominant intellectual skill before the age of print was the art of memory." And now we may be going back.

For the question may not be whether, given enough time, CD-ROMs and the Internet can replace books, but whether they should. Ours is a culture that has made a fetish of impermanence. Paperbacks disintegrate, Polaroids fade, video images wear out. Perhaps the first novel ever written specifically to be read on a computer and to take advantage of the concept of hypertext—the structuring of written passages to allow the reader to take different paths through the story—was Rob Swigart's *Portal*, published in 1986 and designed for the Apple Macintosh, among other computers of its day. The Apple Macintosh was superseded months later by the more sophisticated Macintosh SE, which, according to Swigart, could not run his hypertext novel. Over time people threw out their old computers (fewer and fewer new programs could be run on them), and so *Portal* became for the most part unreadable. A similar fate will befall literary works of the future if they are committed not to paper but to transitional technology like diskettes, CD-ROMs, and UNIX tapes—candidates, with eight-track tapes, Betamax, and the Apple Macintosh, for rapid obscurity. "It's not clear, with fifty incompatible standards around, what will survive," says Ted Nelson, the computer pioneer, who has grown disenchanted with the forces commercializing the Internet. "The so-called information age is really the age of information lost." Software companies don't care—early moviemakers didn't worry that they were filming on volatile stock. In a graphic dramatization of this mad dash to obsolescence, in 1992 the author William Gibson, who coined the term "cyberspace," created an autobiographical story on computer disc called "Agrippa." "Agrippa" is encoded to erase itself entirely as the purchaser plays the story. Only thirty-five copies were printed, and those who bought it left it intact. One copy was somehow pirated and sent out onto the Internet, where anyone could copy it. Many users did, but who and where is not consistently indexed, nor are the copies permanent—the Internet is anarchic. "The original disc is already almost obsolete on Macintoshes," says Kevin Begos, the publisher of "Agrippa." "Within four or five years it will get very hard to find a machine that will run it." Collectors will soon find Gibson's story gone before they can destroy it themselves.

▪ **CONSIDER THE SOURCE**

1. Explain the three "articles of faith" that Max says lie behind the futurist's vision of cyberspace. How will cyberspace be a "better kind of school"? How will it differ from traditional schools?

2. What is "vaporware" and what effect does Max say it has had on the publishing industry?

3. As a class, list on the chalkboard the advantages and disadvantages of books and computers as instruments of communication. What tasks are best suited to each medium? Is there any overlap? What sort of books do computers seem most likely to replace? Why?

4. Why does Max spend so much of his essay describing the Folger Shakespeare Library and its collection? How does that discussion enhance or detract from his argument about the impermanence of information in cyberspace?

5. What authorities does Max rely on for his information? What authors does he refer to? How appropriate is his selection of evidence for his audience, given what the appendix tells you about *The Atlantic Monthly*?

▪ CONSIDER THE IMPLICATIONS

6. Visit a large bookstore in your neighborhood and survey the different kinds of books for sale. Which ones do you think would work better on computer than on paper? Assume that you have a limitless budget and unparalleled technical expertise. What kinds of enhancements could you bring to the books through computer technology? Write a paper in which you describe the future you envision for one category of books—travel books, medical self-help, sports biographies, cookbooks, action/adventure, or whatever category interests you.

7. Books clearly evoke a great deal of affection from writers such as John Updike and Sven Birkerts (pp. 21–28). In your journal, describe your favorite book from childhood. Write about it as an object, an artifact, and recall as much as you can about the "bookishness" of the book.

8. If your school computer lab has any multimedia CD-ROMs, spend some time playing around on them. Try out an encyclopedia such as Encarta. See what video and audio clips have been added to the traditional book version of the encyclopedia. Select a fairly small subject that interests you and look it up on the disc encyclopedia. Then look up the same subject in the library using traditional encyclopedias and indexes. Write a paper in which you compare the two forms of research. What advantages did each technology offer? What were the limitations of each? How much depth of coverage did each form offer?

9. Examine a recent issue of *Wired* magazine. How does it resemble other magazines? How does it differ? What contributes to its "hipness"? Write a review of the magazine in which you demonstrate or refute Max's claim that there is a "gap between message and messenger."

10. Review LynNell Hancock's essay "Computer Gap: The Haves and the Have-Nots" (pp. 198–202) in light of Louis Rossetto's claims about the computer revolution. Write a critique of the cybervisionary faith in the "democratic explosion in the accessibility of knowledge."

PAUL SAFFO

Quality in an Age of Electronic Incunabula

Those who take the long view of the technological changes occurring in our society like to remind us that the present stage of the computer's development represents only its infancy, not its maturity. Futurist Paul Saffo compares this period of electronic books with the first fifty years after the invention of the printing press. Books printed in that initial half-century are still called "incunabula" after the Latin word for cradle. *Just as it took some time for the printed book to find its proper form and function, Saffo predicts that electronic books will soon settle into their own niche, where they will become "integral and unremarkable artifacts in our lives." Instead of fretting over the fate of the traditional book, he raises questions about quality and originality in the digital environment, where low cost and wide availability may prove to be more important values for most users. Saffo writes a column for* PC/Computing *magazine and contributes articles on technology to* Fortune, Byte, *and the* Harvard Business Review. *He is a director at the Institute for the Future, a nonprofit applied research firm in Menlo Park, California, which helps government agencies and private corporations "think systematically about the future."*

A long-forecast information future is arriving late and in utterly unexpected ways. Paper and its familiars—books, magazines, and newspapers—were supposed to become obsolete, quickly replaced by new forms of electronic media. In fact, the consumption of communications paper in the United States has grown at a rate greater than the growth in gross national product for virtually every year since World War II. Electronics didn't replace paper; it enabled the production of greater volumes of print-based media than ever.

Meanwhile, the diffusion and consumption of new media—the incunabula of our time—have occurred more rapidly yet. From television to Nintendo, wave after wave of electronic novelty has invaded our homes, utterly changing our media habits and desires. Thanks to cable and global news services, consumers today have better access to information on breaking events than President Kennedy enjoyed from the situation room in the White House during the Cuban missile crisis. The average home today holds more computing power embedded in its appliances than existed in the entire District of Columbia before 1963.

The relationship between burgeoning paper and even more rapid electronic diffusion resembles an expanding sphere, in which volume increases more rapidly than surface area. The information business has

From *Liberal Education* 79:1 (Winter 1993), 18–23.

become a kind of piñata: a thin paper crust surrounding an enabling electronic core. Paper has become an artifact of electronic media, but we barely notice because the paper crust conceals the core.

For example, the *Wall Street Journal* is written and edited on computer screens, electronically typeset, and then bounced off satellites to remote printing plants across the country. It assumes its familiar paper form only hours before it appears in our mailboxes. In offices and academic departments, the same pattern explains why we merely create greater volumes of documents than ever; xerographic copiers automate what once was laboriously copied with typewriter and spirit master.

For the moment at least, the social impact of this shift remains hidden beneath the paper skin. For instance, the way we use paper changed fundamentally in the mid-1980s with desktop publishing and new storage technologies. We think of paper as a communications medium, but in fact it has been primarily a storage medium. Consider your favorite book sitting on your bookshelf: how little time it spends in your hands being read, and how much gathering dust. Even a Bible in the hands of the most devout Christian fundamentalist spends more time shut than open.

By 1985, it had become cheaper to store information electronically than on paper, while desktop publishing makes it easier than ever to produce printed copy. The result is that paper is now interface—an increasingly volatile, disposable medium for viewing information on demand. We are solidly on the way to a future where we will reduce information to paper only when we are ready to read it—the phenomenon demonstrated by the *Wall Street Journal*—and then recycle it when done.

Evidence of paper as interface is everywhere. For example, facsimile machines also promote paper as interface. One can subscribe to a growing number of daily customized fax "newspapers" containing only the stories that interest each individual subscriber. The "database publishing" technologies that make these services possible are being used by others to profitably publish everything from customized textbooks to personalized ads in weekly magazines. In four hundred years, our universities have gone from the Stationari of Bologna to the printing press, to the copier, and now the computer to serve up course material.

The forces that made paper as interface possible will have even greater impact in the 1990s. As the communications piñata continues to expand, holes and thin spots are appearing, making paper more transitory yet. Researchers in theoretical physics and other disciplines have abandoned academic journals for electronic mail to keep up with breaking events in their fields. Meanwhile, financial exchanges have traded electrons for paper as the globe's primary transaction medium. Less than a quarter of our money supply is represented by greenbacks; the rest exists only as phantom memory patterns in huge computer data banks.

The term "electronic book" has suddenly become the hottest buzzword in the media community, and everyone is getting into the act. One company is selling "expanded books"—computer versions of popular novels like *Jurassic Park*—designed to run on laptop portables. Electronic games-maker Broderbund Software is promoting "living books" on CD-ROM disks, leading with a clever children's title, *Just Grandma and Me*. Another company, Mathcad, is offering interactive technical "electronic handbooks" in partnership with academic publishers.

Software companies aren't the only would-be electronic book publishers. IBM has debuted "illuminated books," interactive educational works developed by Bob Abel. Sony is launching its "BookMan" portable CD-ROM player, and other consumer electronics players are furiously developing electronic book platforms of their own.

All of these products share an emphasis on text as their primary information delivery vehicle. Presumably this is why they have been defined as "books," but the vast penetration of these new media belies their apparent aesthetic inferiority to the best of conventional print. Nothing created on a fax, PC, or laserprinter can match letterpress for sheer sensuous quality. More importantly, the experience offered by electronic media is fundamentally different from anything offered by traditional books.

This latter aspect holds an important clue regarding the prospects for these new media. Our new media will not replace existing media directly; rather, they will penetrate by offering experiences that traditional print does poorly, or cannot do at all. A case in point is hypertext, which is simply a superior electronic alternative to the sort of tasks previously relegated to thesauri and encyclopedias.

The term "electronic book" is misleading, however, because these products are not books at all but something new: the incunabula of our own age. We are living in a moment between two revolutions: one of print, four centuries old and not quite spent, and another of electronics, two decades young and just getting underway. Today's "electronic books" amount to a bridge between these two revolutions, and the term's historic associations can help us through a mind-bending shift in much the same way that "horseless carriage" once eased our grandparents into the age of the automobile.

Of course, just as practical automobiles lay decades beyond the first horseless carriages, it will be some time before our new electronic media even begin to approach the sophistication and subtleties of traditional print. Traditionalists will howl at the vulgarity of it all, much as fans of manuscript writing shuddered at the ugly and unreliable monochrome works that came off the earliest presses.

In fact, events today are unfolding much as they did in the time of the original incunabula, between the 1450s and Aldus's publication of the first modern book in 1501.[1] Recall that the very first books off Guten-

---

1. **Aldus Manutius** (1450–1515): Venetian printer who invented a new and highly readable typeface that made books more accessible.—ED.

berg's press were slavish imitations of what scriveners produced by hand. Just as the inventors of plastic first struggled to make the stuff look like wood and tortoise shell, printing pioneers worked to conceal the novelty of their new books. Mercifully, our new electronic media seem to have passed rapidly through this phase with the first wave of CD-ROM titles.

The current crop of "electronic books" recalls what emerged once the early medieval "print nerds" tired of making simple copies of manuscript works. It takes time to turn raw, untamed information technologies into compelling media that touch user imaginations. It took fifty years in the age of printed incunabula; it is likely to take at least a decade for the first wave of electronic books to be reduced to integral and unremarkable artifacts in our lives.

This period of diffusion will mask a deeper debate about quality. Are the new electronic books inferior because they remain in their infancy? Or is there something about electronics that is intrinsically inferior to print? Though I welcome today's electronic innovations, I am beginning to suspect that the latter concern has some basis.

It is possible that the very flexibility of our new electronic media constitutes their essential flaw. Several years ago, designer Milton Glaser observed that each new print technology has been infinitely more flexible than its predecessor—and has produced new conventions that were much worse. For Glaser, the essential determinant of aesthetic quality is the "resistance" of a medium; the harder an artist or craftsperson must work, the better the final product is likely to be. Thus, desktop publishing will always tend to produce results inferior to Linotype output, and no matter how hard publishers try, they will never match the quality of letterpress[2] with digital technologies. Moreover, Glaser says, "the computer bears as close a relationship to the production of quality design as the typewriter does to the production of good poetry."

The uneasy traditionalist in me agrees, even as I enter these words into my labor- and aggravation-saving word processor. Of course, "quality" is only one measure of value when it comes to information and society. Cost and availability round out the equation, and virtually every innovation since the printing press has favored both at the expense of quality. The books printed by Aldus in the early 1500s were nothing to look at compared to the work of medieval copyists, but they made information infinitely more accessible and affordable. While a privileged intellectual minority lamented the vulgarity of books in the marketplace, a newly literate population proceeded to change the course of European history.

Today's expanding electronic technologies also serve up an un-   20

---

2. **Linotype:** A form of mechanical typesetting invented in 1884 by Ottmar Mergenthaler; **letterpress:** Refers to any method of printing from a raised, inked surface.—ED.

precedented explosion in the sheer volume of information assaulting us. A single copy of the Sunday *New York Times* contains more information than a sixteenth-century Venetian merchant was likely to read in a lifetime. Today, more information is stored digitally than on all the shelves of all the libraries in the world.

The resultant "information overload" has fascinated and infuriated us all, but it is something of a red herring; we have been coping with varying degrees of overload for centuries. We will deal with overload in new media in the same way we have always dealt with it—by creating new sense-making tools and social structures tailored to ever richer information environments. Recall that the Di Medicis built their financial empire on a tool for coping with the avalanche of numbers in their brave new world of commerce. Invented by a Benedictine monk, this critical tool was double-entry bookkeeping. Today, the traders of Wall Street are finding increasingly arcane mathematical tools to be essential to survival in what has become an electronic-age "casino of the gods." This ongoing information explosion will have direct effects on our educational structures; continued emphasis on providing students with the intellectual tool kits to cope with information overload is but the most obvious implication.

The *indirect* impacts are far more important. The effect on quality of this explosion in volume is more subtle and worrisome. Quality, by its very nature, tends to be scarce. History suggests that the total amount of quality material in all media has grown slowly over the centuries, but it seems increasingly scarce because the volume of inferior work has grown so much faster. I have little doubt that Gresham's Law[3] applies to media: All things being equal, technological advances will cause the very best to be lost in a burgeoning flow of mediocre works.

Ultimately, quality and quantity in this electronic age converge around changing notions of what constitutes an "original." When a thing is created in a digital environment, every copy made is the equal of the original. In fact, there are no "copies" at all—just multiple originals. This alone guarantees that the information explosion will continue expanding exponentially for the indefinite future. More importantly, though, it may extinguish the very notion of what constitutes an "original" to begin with.

We praise "original" works, and we scorn anything that is "merely derivative." As Picasso once observed, the first man to compare his lover's lips to a rose was quite probably a genius—but everyone to make the comparison thereafter was almost certainly an idiot. The volume of truly original works is actually miniscule; what passes as original is sim-

---

3. Sir Thomas Gresham (1519?–1579): British economist whose economic principle that "bad money drives out good" is known as **Gresham's Law**. Gresham was referring to currencies, but his law has been applied to any system where debased items circulate in greater quantity than truly valuable ones.—ED.

ply a product of our bad memories. Recall that Picasso's "original" work borrowed heavily on themes from African art he observed while a young man. This link, however, is made only by a handful of specialists, while the rest of us consider his work wildly unique.

The search and access power of the digital world will bring our 25 memories back with brutal clarity. Scholars may quickly discover that *nothing* is original and everything is derivative, bordering on plagiarism. Imagine a future electronic book with the ability to link to remote hyperbases and search for sources and content similar to what is being read. The headaches that digital sampling are causing the music industry today are about to be propagated at a much larger scale among scholars. Eventually, we will discover that originality is a myth and that what lifts the great from the merely derivative is not originality at all but passion.

We are entering an age of infinite recall; much more than our information tools are changing. We will become paperless in the same way we once became horseless: Horses are still around, but they are ridden by hobbyists, not commuters. Similarly, new electronic media will creep into our lives, gradually displacing the time we spend with print.

"Electronic books" will mature into new media forms as the age of electronic incunabula comes to a close. Eventually, we will find ourselves in a world that for all intents and purposes will be paperless. We will hardly notice the shift, though, for it will so transform our intellectual lives that comparisons with even the recent past of this century will seem quaint and pointless.

■ **CONSIDER THE SOURCE**

1. Explain what Saffo means by the phrase "paper as interface"?

2. What makes "electronic books" analogous to "horseless carriages," according to Saffo? Why does he find the term "electronic book" misleading?

3. How does Saffo define "quality"? How does it depend on the "resistance" of the medium? How is quality related to "originality"?

4. Based on the description of *Liberal Education* given in the appendix (p. 645), who is Saffo's intended audience? What aspects of his argument are geared toward that reader?

■ **CONSIDER THE IMPLICATIONS**

5. D. T. Max quotes Louis Rossetto, cofounder of *Wired* magazine, as saying, "We're looking at the end of a twenty- or thirty- or forty-year process" when we look at the multimedia "books" and the information superhighway (pp. 546–57). Saffo, by contrast, talks about the electronic revolution as "two decades young and just getting underway." Which of these two views of the revolution do you find more credible? Why? What are the

implications of each? Write a paper analyzing the "revolution" and suggesting an appropriate perspective from which to view it.

6. Saffo claims that digitizing has already replaced paper as a storage medium for every sort of information, from news to bank accounts. Write a journal entry in which you explore the roles paper and computers play in your life. How do you use each one—as a storage medium, a communications medium, a medium for viewing information stored elsewhere? How do you foresee those roles changing in future years? Can you envision a paperless future for yourself? What would be the advantages or disadvantages?

7. The core of Saffo's essay concerns the idea of "quality." In small groups, discuss what he means by that term. How do you define it? What are its hallmarks? Compare your definition with that of other groups.

8. Cost and availability go along with quality to determine how we evaluate technological improvements, according to Saffo. Write an essay in which you apply these three measures of value to the electronic information revolution. How does the computer compare with the book when all three criteria are considered?

9. Hold a class discussion on Saffo's contention that "*nothing* is original and everything is derivative, bordering on plagiarism." Why does our culture prize originality and deplore copying? How does originality relate to individuality? If Saffo is correct, what are the implications of his remarks for writers, musicians, and other artists?

▪ ▪ ▪ ▪ ▪ ▪

BERNARD SHARRATT

But Is It Art? A Review of the Microsoft Art Gallery on CD-ROM

The biggest buzz in the computer industry lately has been caused by improvements in image technology. Higher resolution monitors and new digitizing techniques have enhanced the ability to incorporate pictures, both still and moving, into texts, and CD-ROM technology has made it possible to pull up onscreen images in the blink of an eye. At first such gee-whiz technology was available only at museums and other institutions, but now it has arrived on the home computer. Here, critic Bernard Sharratt assesses what it means to have the whole collection of London's National Gallery available on his desk. Every painting is accessible at the click of a button, for about $80. Sharratt can browse at his leisure, search

From *The New York Times Book Review*, 6 March 1994, pp. 3, 18.

*the collection for particular images or motifs, even cut and paste his own
version of the paintings. It's great fun, but is it art? Sharratt teaches
English and American literature at the University of Kent in Canter-
bury, England. In addition to regular contributions, such as this one, to*
The New York Times Book Review, *he has written* Reading Relations: Structures of Literary Production *(1982) and* The Literary
Labyrinth: Contemporary Critical Discourses *(1984).*

It's a familiar inner-city scene: a queue of youngsters jostling for a
place at glowing consoles, bright colors flashing as players punch the
touch-sensitive screens, a tussle for possession each time a computer is
vacated in the narrow, overcrowded space. This is no arcade, however,
but a small room tucked between restaurant and cloakrooms in the
new wing of the National Gallery in London: the Micro Gallery, with
twelve Macintosh computer screens displaying an interactive hypertext catalogue of the entire National Gallery collection, more than two
thousand digitized pictures visible in glorious color at the touch of a
finger.

The Micro allows visitors to browse the museum's holdings, select
ten paintings, then print an itinerary through the museum to locate
them easily. A jabbing finger can leap from Cézanne to Pollaiuolo, from
Caravaggio to Titian, from Cologne in 1525 to Paris in 1850, from "Self-
Portraits" to "Nudes." The viewer navigates through several ways of organizing the collection: "Artists' Lives," "Historical Atlas," "Picture
Types," "General Reference" and so forth.

Activate the "Artists' Lives" category and an alphabetical list appears: "Aachen Master" to "Zurbarán." Curiosity chooses Zurbarán. A
well-designed page pops up, offering a brief, lucid biography (flourished between Velázquez and Murillo in Seville in the 1640s), with
thumbnail images of Zurbarán's works held in the National Gallery.
Touch one of these and a fuller picture, with explanatory text, fills the
screen. Touch a highlighted phrase and a note opens clarifying Spanish
history, or a map appears with the main buildings in seventeenth-
century Madrid. Touch a name and a quiet voice murmurs the correct
Spanish pronunciation. Touch "Velázquez" and the screen responds
with several pages of Velázquez's paintings at the National. Touch one
of those and. . . .

No wonder the daily queue gets impatient. There's now a twenty-
minute time limit on users.

When the Micro Gallery first opened in 1991 I asked, in half-hope,   5
whether the system could be installed on the University of Kent campus.
They laughed, politely. Passing through London last December I again
pleaded, jokingly, that I wanted to take the Micro Gallery home as my
Christmas present. "No problem, sir," they said. "It's in the bookshop.
£45."

The CD-ROM I bought looks like any other compact disk, a slip of silver five inches across. It requires, of course, a computer with CD-ROM (computer disk—read-only memory) drive, preferably sound speakers and, as always, the more memory the better. There are versions for both Windows and Mac. A touch screen isn't necessary (clicking on a mouse does the job) though this program, above all, justifies a high-resolution color monitor. I ran it happily, however, on a modest IBM machine with a standard screen. Installation took seconds, and I finally had the whole National Gallery on my desk.

Or rather, I had the Micro Gallery. In the real National I could go from the computer screen to the paintings themselves. Sitting in my study I have no time restriction. I can explore the full ramifications of this extraordinary labyrinth of vivid color images, soberly authoritative biographies, history, commentary and glossary. I can browse through a million words, construct a continuous slide show of every painting, gaze for however long I like at my favorites, discover works and artists I haven't registered before. I am in danger of never re-emerging, even for next Christmas.

Nevertheless, a digital depiction of a Duccio altarpiece is very different from standing in front of the object itself, of course. Though that too, as Walter Benjamin[1] argued, is a profoundly different act from taking part in the religious ritual that originally gave altarpieces their meaning.

Through successive means of reproduction, from engravings to postcards, from photographs to textbooks, from television programs to laser disks, several generations have learned to approach art as a domain of cultural information, reserving the experience itself for an actual visit to a gallery. Only there, often, they find a disappointment; the desired aura seems absent and art-historical knowledge an unfulfilling substitute. The work itself can seem just another reproduction. Well-stocked bookstores and increasingly sophisticated multimedia presentations within the galleries themselves reinforce this ambivalent attitude.

The Micro Gallery and Microsoft's digital version of it are shaped by this complex tendency. Though I can't use the CD-ROM to plan a self-guided tour of the actual gallery (that device is omitted from this version), a general "Find" facility can quickly construct a personal study agenda: to search out all instances of St. George-and-the-Dragon paintings or examine systematically the iconography of lilies. The disk also includes some worthy educational animations, showing by overlaid diagrams how a painting is composed or how perspective is created. The

10

---

1. **Walter Benjamin** (1892–1940): German philospher and cultural theorist who discussed the relationship between art and technology in his essay "The Work of Art in the Age of Mechanical Reproduction" (1936); he contended that reproducing a work of art frees it from the "fabric of tradition."—ED.

best of these nicely clarifies the neck-twisting sidelong viewpoint required to reveal that weirdly skewed skull in the foreground of Holbein's *Ambassadors.* The four guided tours of the gallery included in the program are, however, somewhat disappointing; they merely reassemble existing pages, and in any updated or new edition they need to be redesigned from scratch.

But being offered all this with such ease leaves me with a genuine cultural conundrum: What to do with it all? For this is not just another art book, though it may be the best art book I've ever bought. Admittedly, a well-produced book might (many do not) offer reproductions with finer detail and more accurate color; a monograph might guide more easily to a comprehensive grasp of a period or a surer understanding and deeper appreciation of a particular painter or painting. The CD-ROM provides no overall consecutive argument, and its several layers of texts only suggest and enable connections, and point toward received views and established interpretations. The onus of learning is on us: Using Art Gallery is rather like consulting an enormous collection of postcards (albeit cards annotated in scholarly fashion), to be variously juxtaposed and reshuffled in our own active investigation of possible relations among paintings, periods, places and styles. Few books, by their very form, can enable that openness of inquiry, that self-teaching process. Yet, ironically, faced with this extraordinary richness and extreme user-friendliness, any lingering autodidact dedication to learning more *about* art can seem almost redundant when so much expertise is instantly available. The emphasis, in practice, falls elsewhere.

The response of the youngsters at the gallery suggests an alternative: to treat the CD-ROM as akin to an arcade game with numerous exciting levels to explore. And the only alien to zap is art itself, or rather that restrained "high seriousness" still so firmly characteristic of the conscientiously gallery-trained.

After all, in the comfortable sprawl of my own armchair, I can simply rediscover the sheer pleasure of looking. For fun. Scopophilic gaze.[2] A computer screen has the same captivating brilliance as a projected transparency. I can't analyze brush technique at this resolution, but I can revel in content, the marvelous diversity of subject matter that preoccupied or entranced previous generations. In almost a pre-esthetic mood I begin to reappreciate lost functions of art, like religious devotion, triumphal military celebration, civic spectacle or proud family affirmation. Prancing horses and hats with feathers, cavalcades and cathedrals,

---

2. **scopophilic gaze:** From *scopophilia,* the joy that can be derived from the act of looking; often connected with voyeurism.—ED.

saints and seacoasts, tumble across the screen. It is almost like meditating with a postmedieval book of hours.[3]

I can even construct my own versions of the paintings. An electronic clipboard allows me to export any page or picture to other programs like Photoshop or even Wordperfect. A home printer is hardly adequate for printing the result, but in Photoshop I can cut and paste between pictures, modify their colors, crop and recompose them. I can airbrush a fluffy pink beard onto Bellini's stern Doge or cut a digitized sunflower to place in homage on Van Gogh's yellow chair. And none of this affects the images that stay pristine on the CD-ROM—though the gallery's copyright notice demurely appears on any image so manipulated. I feel like Duchamp challenged by the *Mona Lisa.*

In itself this may be a juvenile enjoyment but it nevertheless recaptures, in irreverent mode, the precise pleasure and thrill of a great art gallery: the exultation of imagination and the sheer joy of strolling through a visual splendor. The usual complaint against complex hypertext programs is that one quickly gets lost in hyperspace and drowns in data overload. But a large gallery encourages, even enforces, an almost aimless browsing, an oscillation of attention and reverie, of assimilation and concentration. No one is going to digest the Louvre on a day trip. The magnificent proliferation of pictures draws one toward both reflective stillness and pleasurable drift. So does the enormous capacity and easy navigability of the CD-ROM medium. Young gamesmasters already relish that mode.

Credit for the software of Microsoft Art Gallery should go to Cognitive Applications, an organization in Brighton, England, that engineered the original Micro Gallery system. But Microsoft has the marketing impact to make this, rightly, the exemplary multimedia product it is. Other CD-ROM art collections already exist, of course, but the authoritative professionalism apparent here might encourage more galleries to follow suit. In London the National Gallery, superb in its later medieval and Renaissance holdings, leaves the post-1900 period to the Tate. So I would love to have alongside it on my desk the collections of the Art Institute of Chicago or the Museum of Modern Art in New York. Or maybe, one day, the fabulous scholarly treasure-trove of the Warburg Institute's unrivaled iconographic collection.

The step beyond this might be even more mind-dazzling. One animation on this disk reconstructs a Renaissance palace chamber in which several paintings once hung together. Recent work in virtual reality[4] has allowed the rebuilding—in virtual reality only—of the monastery of

15

---

3. A **book of hours** was a collection of prayers, psalms, hymns, and devotional readings often elaborately produced and illuminated by medieval artists.—ED.

4. **virtual reality:** Refers to computer simulations that create the illusion that the user is within a scene and able to manipulate it.—ED.

Cluny and the digital reproduction of the Church of San Francesco in Arezzo, complete with Piero della Francesca's *Story of the True Cross*. Some future version of Microsoft Art Gallery may one day allow a virtual wander through the National Gallery itself, or it may even allow one to relocate those aura-deprived altarpieces in their one-time settings, within fully re-created virtual churches. Walter Benjamin would certainly have been intrigued.

Meanwhile, my five-year-old has organized a queue of his friends outside my study door. They all want to play with the pictures. Let them.

■ **CONSIDER THE SOURCE**

1. List the features of the CD-ROM version of London's National Gallery. Which ones does Sharratt value most? Why?

2. How does the CD-ROM differ from a well-produced art book, according to Sharratt?

3. How does Sharratt compare the experience of browsing the CD-ROM with the experience of browsing in a museum? What does the CD-ROM offer that the museum does not, and vice versa?

4. What assumptions does Sharratt make about the value of visiting museums? Why would readers of *The New York Times Book Review* be likely to share those assumptions?

■ **CONSIDER THE IMPLICATIONS**

5. Sharratt claims that "a digital depiction . . . is very different from standing in front of the object itself." As a class, discuss the differences among various ways of viewing art works, including reproductions in books or by means of slide projections.

6. Like Umberto Eco (pp. 537–45) and Paul Saffo (pp. 558–64), Sharratt discusses the "data overload" made possible by modern communications technology. Compare their ways of viewing this situation. Is it a problem? If so, what solutions or coping mechanisms do they propose? What are the advantages of overload?

7. Underlying Sharratt's discussion is the following implicit question: What is a work of art? In your journal, explore your views on this central question. Is art more than the "cultural information" residing within the frame, as Sharratt suggests? Or, is a poster or digital reproduction of a painting also art? Why or why not?

8. Based on Sharratt's description, evaluate the Microsoft Art Gallery using Paul Saffo's criteria of quality, cost, and availability. What are the benefits and drawbacks of the program? Write a letter to the chair of your school's art history program, proposing that the school purchase this CD-ROM and the computer equipment necessary to run it. Alternatively, write a

letter arguing that the same funding should go toward field trips to local museums.

9. Sharratt hints that the CD-ROM version eventually may replace the experience of going to a gallery. To what extent have other technologies encouraged such substitutions? Consider, for instance, watching baseball games on television or viewing movies on cable or on video instead of in theaters. Write an essay evaluating the effect of one such technological shift.

▪ ▪ ▪ ▪ ▪ ▪

GEORGE MELROD

Digital Unbound

Just because we can put books onto computers, does that mean we should? Is there any special advantage in doing so? Few people would sit down at a computer screen to read a novel such as Moby-Dick. *For such a reading experience, the computer offers only disadvantages: The screen strains your eyes, you can't get comfortable sitting at a desk for hours on end, and so forth.* Moby-Dick *was written for book technology, and it still works best in that format. But what if novels were written to capitalize on the special attributes of the computer and could be read only on screen? George Melrod (b. 1959) describes exactly that phenomenon. It's called "hyperfiction," and it's attracting a new breed of writers. These writers are destroying the traditional notions of beginning, middle, and end. Instead they take advantage of the computer's ability to store bits of text in any sequence, to link information from all over, and to retrieve text as the reader commands. Melrod contributes articles on contemporary art and culture to* Mirabella, Vogue, *and* Art in America, *and he writes a column for* Art & Architecture *magazine. In this essay, a version of which was published in* Details *magazine, Melrod looks into the future of fiction and finds haunting echoes of the communal story-telling that took place before the invention of the printing press.*

Let us begin at the middle.

I am sitting with Michael Joyce in his garret office in the English department at Vassar College, under a peculiarly sloping wall, sipping coffee. "None of us ever intended to be a computer nerd," he observes affably. "I came into this as a writer."

From *Details* (October 1994), 162–65, 199.

In fact, he is both. By combining his hands-on interest in information technology with his own literary background, Joyce has created a new way of writing that not only utilizes the personal computer but depends on it. We are talking about software and the future of the novel. We are talking about hyperfiction.

What is hyperfiction? It is the marriage of the storybook and the PowerBook. It is the linear narrative thread spun into the labyrinth of the microchip. Hyperfiction is, in short, nonlinear interactive electronic literature. It is also potentially the next stage of evolution for storytelling, in which text is made of light instead of ink, you help the author shape the story, and you never read the same novel the same way twice.

One name you hear a lot around hypertext circles is Johann Gutenberg, whose invention of movable type (circa 1440) marked the death knell of what we now refer to as the oral tradition. With his printing press, Gutenberg indirectly sired not only the medium of the novel, but also, some might argue, the modern ideal of individual authorship. Previously, oral storytellers would recount the same stories generation after generation. Gutenberg's modest goal was to mass produce Bibles—never would he have dreamed he was begetting Jackie Collins and John Grisham.

Today's apostles of hypertext see themselves as spearheading a communications revolution no less profound then the one launched 550 years ago. But while Gutenberg took us away from the communal author, hypertext promises, at least partly, to turn back the clock.

The word "hypertext" was coined by computer visionary Ted Nelson in the 1960s. Then still a student at Swarthmore, Nelson conceived of a way to connect all the information in the world through a giant electronic network of cross-referenced documents, which he dubbed a "docuverse." He invented hypertext to mediate the nonsequential linking between these texts. So that while reading about, say, Shakespeare, for example, you could key onto a certain word or phrase and find out more about Elizabethan cross-dressing, Danish melancholia, or male pattern baldness.

It was Michael Joyce who first came up with the idea of applying hypertext to the art of writing original fiction. Joyce is a burly, genial man with a sonorous baritone and a graying beard. In spite of his venerable reputation as the grandfather of hyperfiction, he shows a boyish excitement when he points out the empty bookshelf in his office. The gesture is just one indication of his commitment to the computer and his enthusiasm for hyperfiction. "This," he says, "is an example of how electronic culture can still rock you."

A graduate of the Iowa Writer's Workshop, Joyce published his first novel, *The War outside Ireland,* in 1982. The book garnered several awards but small sales. At the time, he was teaching at a Michigan community college. One day, while playing on his Apple word processor, he had an epiphany. Seeing the ease with which text blocks could be moved around—and how a block of text might belong equally well in various places—he got the idea of writing a story that never read the same way twice.

Since the software didn't exist, he hooked up with classicist and computer scientist Jay David Bolter and John B. Smith, another computer scientist, to create Storyspace. Storyspace is the only software designed specifically for the creation of hyperfiction. (It is currently available in either Macintosh or Windows format.) The program allows you to create boxes of text on one screen, which you then connect to other boxes with lines, establishing the various pathways for the reader. The result is a weblike electronic storyboard. Because there is no standard sequence to the text, these text panels do not have numbers; they have titles.

When the time finally came to launch their product at the Hypertext Conference in 1987, Joyce and Bolter realized they didn't have an example of what it could do. So Joyce wrote *Afternoon, A Story*. "The process was incredibly liberating," he recalls. "To that extent, I never looked back."

Written in crystalline, lyrical prose, *Afternoon* remains the most popular hypernovella. The plot—to the degree there is one—concerns an unnamed narrator who has witnessed the scene of a car accident. "I want to say I may have seen my son die this morning," he declares in one panel. As the narrator wrestles with his fears, we follow him through his circle of friends and learn about their values, relationships, and infidelities.

The story opens on a screen entitled, appropriately, "Begin." From there you must either click on a word in the text or choose a direction on the toolbar menu on the bottom of the screen to progress to another panel. Using this method, you gradually cobble together a story line. As you progress the program records which panels you have visited, allowing for a certain degree of cause and effect. The program has a built-in default that prevents you from seeing a plot resolution before you've met the characters, kind of like the way a railroad switch keeps a train off the wrong track. Even so, you can expect to be tossed between story lines to a dizzying degree.

The result is a kind of narrative collage, a textual kaleidoscope in which the story is cut into fragments and is constantly changing. If it's a bit disorienting, that's part of the idea. Instead of laying out a straight path, hyperfictions set you down in a maze, give you a compass, then let you decide where to go next.

The idea of nonlinear writing is nothing new. Laurence Sterne's *Tristram Shandy* (1759–1767) is often cited as the first novel to mess with the linear story line. In the late 1910s, Dada poet Tristan Tzara made poems from words drawn from a hat. In the early sixties, William Burroughs (along with Brion Gysin) cut up blocks of text and rearranged them, finding new meanings in the haphazard juxtapositions. He used a similar technique when he wrote *The Soft Machine*. In Julio Cortázar's novel *Hopscotch*, the chapters can be read in two ways, resulting in two different stories. Other writers now seen as harbingers of hyperfiction include Thomas Pynchon, Alain Robbe-Grillet, and Italo Calvino. But it is Jorge Luis Borges, the Argentine fantasist, who invented perhaps the most dazzling antecedent for hyperfiction. In his short story "The Garden of the Forking Paths," he writes about a supposed labyrinth which turns out to be a text with contradictory plot lines; the forking paths represent the infinite possibilities for the lives of the characters.

While hyperfictions certainly build on this heritage, they also carry their own particular set of guidelines. Number one is that the act of reading requires interaction. Your choices help shape the story line; you can't just turn the page. Also, because of its inherently fragmented structure, hyperfiction seems to encourage stories with multiple voices, viewpoints, and protagonists. Moreover, hypertexts avoid endings. Instead of propelling you from A to Z, they encourage you to meander through the story at your own pace and end when you want to.

One thing hyperfictions are *not* is games. There is no scoring, no winner or loser, no right or wrong path to take. The writers assiduously avoid you-are-there fantasy adventures. Their texts are literature, not literary fun-house rides where *you* chase Moby-Dick! *You* make love to Madame Bovary! *You* get buried alive in the House of Usher!

Navigating through a hyperfiction can be frustrating because you don't always wind up where you expect. The result is that reading the story becomes a bit like playing Chutes & Ladders across a floppy disc. Some hyperfictions even invite you to wander around the internal linkage maps that connect the text panels, allowing you to be tossed between story lines different ways.

How is it done? Simple. As you read, the text panel appears against a background web of titled boxes and crisscrossing lines (picture an intricate flow chart). To move to other frames, you double-click on words in the text or use the arrows in the toolbar. If you don't like where you've ended up, you can press the Shift key while clicking on the double arrow in the toolbar to return to the previous frame. Or you can press the Option key with the double arrow to choose an alternate link. You can also click on the map in the background, select a box directly from the network, then click onto that box's title to bring up that text frame. If you loathe technology, it's as much fun as programming a VCR. But once you figure out how to work the controls, it's easy to get hooked.

Take, for instance, J. Yellowlees Douglas's crafty, hip hyperfiction *I* 20 *Have Said Nothing*, which describes—in candid, darkly funny terms—the deaths by car accident of Sherry and Jule, two former girlfriends of the narrator's brother. (Auto fatality seems to be a special theme of hyperfiction.) Once the program plops you into the story, you may follow one of several different narrative paths, from the grief-stricken reactions of the brother, to wry commentary on the way we experience death in the movies, to ruminations on the physical aspects of death itself ("Do you know what happens to you when a Chevy Nova with a 250 engine hits you going over seventy-five miles an hour?").

But you also may get shuttled to another story line—say, to the house of one of the accident victims, where "the line of really pathetic-looking stuffed animals that always looked ready to erupt into clouds of weevils seems to be waiting for her." When you actually get to the deaths of the two women (as Jule is dying in an ambulance, we get a harrowing account from her own point of view), their story lines end, the screen shows a period on a blank screen, and you have to backtrack into the web to pick up the other stories. There is no official ending. In Douglas's view, we are all the authors of our own fictions; closure is the last thing you want. "Fiction is too much like reality," Douglas explains. "It's got one ending, it's fixed, and you're stuck with it. Why have an aesthetic that restricts you to the same things life does?"

Stuart Moulthrop's *Victory Garden* is set on a college campus in a southern city resembling Atlanta, during the Persian Gulf War. A sprawling work, it incorporates 993 different text panels, connected to each other via 2,804 links. Like other hyperfictions, the novel weaves through the lives of its cast of characters—in this case professors, friends, and students—as they seduce, console, or drink with one another. One of the protagonists, Emily Runbird, is a soldier stationed in Kuwait. In some readings she is a less important character; in others she is killed; in still others she returns home intact. Interspersed between story lines are numerous quotes about hypertext and cyberculture: a device that is educational, though somewhat self-congratulatory.

Carolyn Guyer's *Quibbling* similarly braids together several couples' stories to portray a quilt of relationships, interspersing erotic encounters, interchanges of e-mail, and musings about the teaching of art. Deena Larsen's *Marble Springs* is a feminist re-creation of the life of an 1880s Colorado town, told through prose poems about the lives of individual women. The reader accesses these stories through maps of the town or family trees that diagram the characters' connections. The men's stories are left unwritten, but Larsen invites the reader to add to the narrative as he or she likes and leaves blank space on the screen to do so.

One of the zaniest hyperfictions of all is John McDaid's joyful *Uncle Buddy's Phantom Funhouse*, which documents the life and writings of rock musician/science nerd Arthur "Buddy" Newkirk, McDaid's nom de plume.[1] Using the image of a grim-looking house as a map, the reader clicks on the windows to enter quirky realms. These include a rotating globe entitled Hyperearth, an array of bizarre tarot cards called Oracle, and an encyclopedic Fictionary of the Bezoars, in which McDaid

---

1. **nom de plume:** A "pen-name," or false name, used by an author.—ED.

defines a myriad of cyberterms. Some text links are only available if you solve the underlying Egyptian riddle. You don't have to figure it out to enjoy the work's frenetic humor; however, with its giddy multimedia approach (the disk even comes with cassette tapes of Buddy's fictional rock band), *Funhouse* transcends the boundaries of a textual hyperfiction. (Because of their complex graphics, both *Funhouse* and *Marble Springs* require HyperCard, an applications program from Apple.)

But don't look for these disks at your local Waldenbooks or B. Dalton. Still in its infancy, hyperfiction is being promoted almost solely by a single maverick company in Massachusetts called Eastgate Systems, run by a saavy, eccentric, ex-chemist named Mark Bernstein. Bernstein not only selects the works to be published but is helping Joyce and Bolter upgrade Storyspace. (Both Storyspace and the hyperfictions mentioned above can be ordered by contacting Eastgate Systems, 134 Main St., Watertown, MA 02172.) 25

Over the past seven years, Eastgate has published some fourteen hypertexts and has recently inaugurated *The Eastgate Quarterly*, a floppy-disk periodical that includes shorter works of hyperfiction, non-fiction, and poetry. With each of its titles selling in the low thousands, Eastgate is more like a university press or an underground record label than a mass-market Goliath. "A lot of people working in multimedia see a mass audience; I see us speaking very much to the book audience," Bernstein says proudly. "We are the most literary electronic publishers, and are missionaries for hypertext. We're not selling perfect works of art; we're selling the birth of a new form."

Eastgate is not just selling a new way of reading, but a new way of writing. And with hyperfiction courses being taught at a growing number of colleges across the United States (Joyce estimates there to be about forty programs), campuses are providing an active training ground for the second generation of hyperauthors. At the vanguard is Brown University, which has long been a hub of hypermedia thanks to Robert Scholes and George Landow, who pioneered the use of hypertext as a pedagogical tool. In 1991 novelist Robert Coover introduced hyperfiction as an undergraduate course at Brown. Last year, his workshop was taken over by his teaching aide, Bob Arellano.

A slender, zealous man with razor-chop sideburns, Bob Arellano puts the hyper into hyperfiction. He recently handed in Brown's first electronic graduate thesis, a hyperfictional account of the infamous murder at the Rolling Stones concert at Altamont. Arellano also edits a hypertext magazine, *LSD 50*, which he distributes over the Internet, under his pen name Bobby Rabyd. His teaching forum is "The Living Syllabus," a computerized writing space that holds all of his students' assignments. Over the course of the semester, all of the students' writings—and their comments on each other's works—become integrated into a chronicle of the class's work. "It's the paperless classroom," he explains merrily.   .

The classwork includes not only writing, but the art of creating the linking superstructures, the scaffolding on which the stories are built. Part of what makes hyperfiction so dynamic are the limitless options for these superstructures. For example, Stephanie Ansen, a twenty-two-year-old theater major, created a fiction incorporating conversations overheard at the university pool, using the layout of the pool building as an organizing architecture. Eric Witherspoon, a twenty-year-old Chinese history major, used a Chinese restaurant menu as a jumping-off point for a study on the Cultural Revolution.

Shelley Jackson, a graduate student in creative writing, is working 30 on a story called *The Patchwork Girl*, a modern-day retelling of Mary Shelley's *Frankenstein* which Jackson has illustrated with her own original drawings. Jackson's monster, however, is made from the body parts of different women. By clicking onto the Patchwork Girl's body parts (leg, arm, torso, etc.), we learn the history of the woman behind each part, spoken in that character's voice. Another pathway leads the reader to a journal written in Mary Shelley's voice, recounting an erotic tryst with the monster.

Because hyperfiction mimics the way our thoughts meander, it is a seductive writing tool. It invites you to explore links between disparate thoughts and images. While the subjective nature of these connections can make it disorienting for the reader, it can be gratifying for the writer. And although many students are frustrated with the clunkiness of the technology, they can't seem to stay away. "I hate it," Ansen says bluntly, "but I can't stop thinking in terms of it. It writes the way my brain works."

Already, competing schools of hyperfiction are emerging, with writers like Joyce favoring a more free-associative approach to the linking structures, and the Brown writers favoring navigable maps and architectural systems.

To Robert Coover, this new blood is just what the medium needs. Coover, himself a noted experimental novelist, is one of hyperfiction's staunchest promoters and most exacting critics. "I've been sold on it because of what the medium has to offer, not because of what's out there," he says. But, citing the example of *Don Quixote*—often considered the first great novel, written 150 years after the Gutenberg Bible—he admits "it takes time to attract the artists to the medium." In 1993, to help expedite the process, Coover organized the Unspeakable Practices II conference, which brought together writers from the worlds of hyperfiction and contemporary literature, such as Raymond Federman, Ronald Sukenick, Kathy Acker, and Paul Auster. But so far, for all their tinkering, it seems that none of these authors have traded in their WordPerfect for Storyspace.

If the medium has still not yet found its Cervantes—or even its Judith Krantz—that may be because the idea of collaborative authorship is still so confusing. At its most loopy—when authorship is thrown open to everyone—hyperfiction can become sort of a literary virtual reality, as in the MUDs, or multiuser domains. The epitome is Brown's Hyperfiction Hotel, a fictional architecture created for Coover's undergraduate writing class. Here, students can create fictional hotel rooms in which to write their own stories and characters, can alter each other's rooms, or, if they prefer, can add to the hotel's public areas—lobby, bar, pool, hallways.

And after Tom Meyer, a grad student in computer science, made the Hyperfiction Hotel available on the Internet via World-Wide Web, it became accessible to anyone with a modem and the urge to check in, making it the first official hostel of the information superhighway. (In techspeak, it also became a MOO, or MUD-object-oriented.) Anyone on the system can visit the hotel and explore the rooms, read the stories of the fictional characters, or even converse with other real-time visitors.

The idea of someone in Wiesbaden adding a room to a fictional hotel based in some silicon chips in Providence, Rhode Island, takes the idea of group authorship to bizarre extremes. But undermining—or augmenting—the traditional idea of the author is part of what makes hyperfiction revolutionary. Joyce is among the biggest proponents of interactive authorship. "We don't know what's coming next," he says, "but we do know it's multiple. One thing I'm sure of is that authorship as we know it is doomed. But the authorial voice isn't."

Hypernovelist Carolyn Guyer conducts a women's hyperfiction cooperative called Hi-pitched Voices. She also happens to live with Joyce (they met, fittingly, at a hypertext conference). Together with Joyce's sister, a professor of anthropology at Berkeley, they are jointly writing a text called *Sister Stories*, based on the structure of the Aztec calendar.

Coover, too, feels that the future of hyperfiction probably lies in the multivocal muse: a decidedly pre-Gutenberg idea. "The real prototypical hypertexts were medieval writings," he remarks. "The idea of marginalia becoming text was a medieval notion. We don't even know who wrote 90 percent of the stuff." Still, like Joyce, he does not write off the author's voice. "For the near future, it is still the most important thing."

Ironically, the greatest threat to hyperfiction may be the burgeoning success of its big cousin, multimedia. With new computer software such as Macromedia Director making the job of downloading images, sound effects, and even movie clips, as easy as pulling greenbacks from an ATM, the spartan allure of pure text is sure to get a lot of flashy competition. So as digital convergence brings all sorts of media together through the CPU, hypermedia may well overtake hyperfiction as the narrative paradigm of the next century. As Coover muses, "It may be that future texts will be a little like Hollywood films: made by teams of writers and artists under the direction of a single vision."

For lovers of the printed word, the idea of the literary document mutated into a multi-author, multimedia collage sounds like something out of a bad sci-fi dystopia. But already, CD-ROMs are redefining the idea of the reference book. Encyclopedias expanded to multimedia can include complete photographic libraries, computer graphics, sound effects, video and film clips, even games, all at a fraction of the mass of a multivolume bookshelf set. Scenting a new market, disk publishers are releasing other CD reference texts—from history manuals to nature guides—fast on their heels. Interactive children's books, likewise, are becoming a boom business. Of course, you don't need two thousand dollars worth of computer hardware and an electrical outlet to leaf through *Peterson's Field Guide to the Eastern Birds,* or *The Cat in the Hat.*

In the short term, however, there is no question that the way we think of "books" is changing, and that interactivity is playing a key role. Voyager, the company responsible for publishing many of the most innovative CD-ROMs, including the Residents' *Freak Show,* has released a series called Expanded Books on floppy disk. Including such sci-fi blockbusters as Michael Crichton's *Jurassic Park* and William Gibson's *Neuromancer* trilogy, they are formatted to resemble book pages, but allow all the amenities of a PC, such as scanning the text for specific words, jotting comments in the margins, even adding electronic dog-ears or paper clips to mark a page. But while you are welcome to access the chapters nonsequentially, it remains in the end a linear text. As Voyager editor Roger Devine observes, "It's not really hypertext, but halfway; it's a conservative approach mimicking the print format, so that people will feel comfortable with it."

Coover, for one, thinks that a turn toward electronic text is inevitable, and that in the not-so-distant future, a majority of college courses will be taught using it. And "if the main way we access information in the future is electronic, this means that book publishing becomes more about boutique objects." By tapping into the Internet, researchers can already access texts from libraries halfway across the globe, from the relative comfort of their own desktops.

A more mundane application of electronic text is the elimination of repetitive paperwork. Sometime in the next five years, the SAT tests required for college admissions will be administered via computer. And this year, for the first time, the Common Application Form that is used by 137 colleges will be available on computer disk. In this way, at least, the decades-old promise of the computer revolution to reduce the consumption of paper— and the depletion of forests—may finally be beginning to bear fruit.

Still, Joyce's empty bookshelf notwithstanding, no one is predicting the outright death of the bound volume. For if we have learned one lesson from previous technological shifts, it is that a new medium does not abolish its precursor, it merely alters its purpose. Photography did not mean the end of painting, although it did take over the role of portraiture, freeing artists to explore their own impressionistic visions. Nor did movies kill the stage, nor TV replace movies. And after all, you still can't slip an electronic novel into your pocket to read at the beach, and you still don't have to worry whether the new Sue Grafton thriller you just bought for your Mac can port to Windows. But, to quote the ubiquitous AT&T ads, "you will."

It's also worth remembering that hyperfiction as a medium is still 45 only seven years old. As of now, most hyperficionados are academics, whose names repeatedly crop up in the introductions of each other's works. It's not hard to imagine their interweaving web of relationships forming a hyperfiction of its own, complete with erotic encounters and exchanges of e-mail. But as the tools become more sophisticated, and new voices emerge, the medium will become less insular and more accessible.

What will it become? Who knows. Just as Gutenberg could never have predicted the proliferation of Chinese restaurant menus, nor Thomas Edison have imagined Snoop Doggy Dogg, we can't predict what hidden jack-in-the-boxes the medium holds in store. Even Joyce admits it is impossible to gauge what the legacy of hyperfiction might be. "In a way, the Gutenberg analogy is very good," he notes, as the afternoon draws to its close, and he and Guyer drive me away from the serene greens of Vassar to the still-sequential train station. "He didn't know what he was starting, and he died broke."

"Interactivity" may be the buzzword today, but whether anyone will choose to interact with this new medium in the years ahead is still unknown. It is not only the quality of the writing but the receptivity of the public which will determine whether hyperfiction becomes a part of the culture, or joins the 8-track in the museum of extinct technologies. The medium may be the message, as Marshall McLuhan wrote, but the message must be heard for it to matter.

Yet time and technology have a funny way of changing our attitudes. McLuhan's take on print media is that it *created* our sequential way of thinking. Who's to say we won't simply evolve along with our media and shed our linear bias like an old skin? Once a new, computer-bred generation becomes comfortable living in a sytemsoriented world, the idea of reading nonsequential fiction might seem as logical as 1-2-33.

▪ **CONSIDER THE SOURCE**

1. Define "hyperfiction" and summarize what Melrod sees as its advantages over traditional fiction.

2. How does hyperfiction "mimic the way our thoughts meander," according to Melrod? What examples does he give to demonstrate this claim?

3. Explain how "interactive authorship" works, according to Melrod. How does it undermine traditional notions of authorship? How does the "authorial voice" survive?

4. Based on the description of *Details* in the appendix (p. 636), consider the

original readers' of Melrod's article. To what extent would they be interested in hyperfiction? How does Melrod appeal to their interests?

■   **CONSIDER THE IMPLICATIONS**

5. Hyperfiction's fans praise it for letting the reader "help the author shape the story." In your journal, explore whether such interactivity would enhance your pleasure in reading fiction. What kinds of conventional fiction do you currently read and why? How much of your pleasure derives from the author's control of the story? To what extent do you already participate in "shaping" the fiction by the act of reading?

6. Melrod claims that hyperfiction is not just "a new way of reading, but a new way of writing." As a class, discuss your "old" ways of reading and writing and compare them to hyperfiction's methods. What are the fundamental differences? Are there any similarities?

7. "Multiple" authorship is, according to Michael Joyce, the wave of the future. In small groups, experiment with different ways of collaborating on a piece of writing. Try writing a story where each group member creates a character and then see how they interact in a common setting, or pass the story along after each person has written a page or two. What were the advantages and disadvantages of multiple authorship?

8. If your library or computer center has Michael Joyce's *Afternoon, A Story*, read the hypernovella several times, selecting different paths each time. Write an essay describing your experience and comparing it to the experience of reading conventional fiction.

9. Robert Coover predicts that soon "a majority of college courses will be taught using [electronic text]." How close is your school to Coover's future? How much of the coursework is done online? How much administrative paperwork could be done via computer? Write a proposal for a paperless future for your school, or a paperless version of a particular course, suggesting concrete ways to reduce paperwork and streamline both teaching and learning. Or, write a critique of such a plan, in which you weigh the merits and liabilities of both computers and traditional "hard copy."

10. Read Jorge Luis Borges's "The Garden of the Forking Paths" and write an analysis of how the story anticipates the hyperfiction Melrod describes. What features does Borges's story share with hypernovellas like Joyce's *Afternoon*?

SVEN BIRKERTS

Perseus Unbound

Envision the. classroom of the future: a computer on every desk, each one hooked up to the whole world of information available in cyberspace. No more poring through two-dimensional books, filled with black text on a white page, perhaps brightened by the occasional illustration. Tomorrow's students will enliven their studies with full color video clips, computer graphics, maps, charts, music, drawings. Sounds exciting, doesn't it? This ideal has already become a reality with some of the CD-ROM educational packages now available. Critic Sven Birkerts (b. 1951) however, raises a few "warning flags" about these state-of-the-art hypertext teaching tools. For cne thing, not all knowledge is used the same way: Sometimes information is acquired for its practical application, but in several disciplines, knowledge is a means to deeper understanding. Birkerts wonders whether students in the humanities will benefit from or be crippled by the new technologies. This essay is from The Gutenberg Elegies *(1994), a thoughtful exploration of the impact of emerging electronic technologies on the reader-writer interchange that has characterized our society for five hundred years.*

Like it or not, interactive video technologies have muscled their way into the formerly textbound precincts of education. The videodisc has mated with the microcomputer tò produce a juggernaut: a flexible and encompassing teaching tool that threatens to overwhelm the linearity of print with an array of option-rich multimedia packages. And although we are only in the early stages of implementation—institutions are by nature conservative—an educational revolution seems inevitable.

Several years ago in *Harvard Magazine*, writer Craig Lambert sampled some of the innovative ways in which these technologies have already been applied at Harvard. Interactive video programs at the Law School allow students to view simulated police busts or actual courtroom procedures. With a tap of a digit they can freeze images, call up case citations, and quickly zero-in on the relevant fine points of precedent. Medical simulations, offering the immediacy of video images and instant access to the mountains of data necessary for diagnostic assessment, can have the student all but performing surgery. And language classes now allow the learner to make an end run around tedious drill repetitions and engage in protoconversations with video partners.

The hot news in the classics world, meanwhile, is Perseus 1.0, an in-

From *The Gutenberg Elegies: The Fate of Reading in an Electronic Age* (Boston: Faber and Faber, 1994), 134–40.

teractive database developed and edited by Harvard associate professor Gregory Crane. Published on CD-ROM and videodisc, the program holds, according to its publicists, "the equivalent of twenty-five volumes of ancient Greek literature by ten authors (1 million Greek words), roughly four thousand glosses in the online classical encyclopedia, and a thirty-five thousand-word online Greek lexicon." Also included are an enormous photographic database (six thousand images), a short video with narration, and "hundreds of descriptions and drawings of art and archeological objects." The package is affordable, too: Perseus software can be purchased for about $350. Plugged in, the student can call up a text, read it side by side with its translation, and analyze any word using the Liddell-Scott lexicon; he can read a thumbnail sketch on any mythic figure cited in the text, or call up images from an atlas, or zoom in on color Landsat photos;[1] he can even study a particular vase through innumerable angles of vantage. The dusty library stacks have never looked dustier.

Although skepticism abounds, most of it is institutional, bound up with established procedures and the proprietorship of scholarly bailiwicks. But there are grounds for other, more philosophic sorts of debate, and we can expect to see flare-ups of controversy for some time to come. For more than any other development in recent memory, these interactive technologies throw into relief the fundamental questions about knowledge and learning. Not only what are its ends, but what are its means? And how might the means be changing the ends?

From the threshold, I think, we need to distinguish between kinds 5 of knowledge and kinds of study. Pertinent here is German philosopher Wilhelm Dilthey's distinction between the natural sciences *(Naturwissenschaften)*, which seek to explain physical events by subsuming them under casual laws, and the so-called sciences of culture *(Geisteswissenschaften)*, which can only understand events in terms of the intentions and meanings that individuals attach to them.

To the former, it would seem, belong the areas of study more hospitable to the new video and computer procedures. Expanded databases and interactive programs can be viewed as tools, pure and simple. They give access to more information, foster cross-referentiality, and by reducing time and labor allow for greater focus on the essentials of a problem. Indeed, any discipline where knowledge is sought for its application rather than for itself could only profit from the implementation of these technologies. To the natural sciences one might add the fields of language study and law.

But there is a danger with these sexy new options—and the rapture with which believers speak warrants the adjective—that we will simply

---

1. **Landsat photos:** Photographs of Earth from Landsat satellites, which survey the earth's natural resources by means of television photos and radiometric scanners.— ED.

assume that their uses and potentials extend across the educational spectrum into realms where different kinds of knowledge, and hence learning, are at issue. The realms, that is, of *Geisteswissenschaften*, which have at their center the humanities.

In the humanities, knowledge is a means, yes, but it is a means less to instrumental application than to something more nebulous: understanding. We study history or literature or classics in order to compose and refine a narrative, or a set of narratives about what the human world used to be like, about how the world came to be as it is, and about what we have been—and are—like as psychological or spiritual creatures. The data—the facts, connections, the texts themselves—matter insofar as they help us to deepen and extend that narrative. In these disciplines the *process* of study may be as vital to the understanding as are the materials studied.

Given the great excitement generated by Perseus, it is easy to imagine that in the near future a whole range of innovative electronic-based learning packages will be available and, in many places, in use. These will surely include the manifold variations on the electronic book. Special new software texts are already being developed to bring us into the world of, say, Shakespeare, not only glossing the literature, but bathing the user in multimedia supplements. The would-be historian will step into an environment rich in choices, be they visual detailing, explanatory graphs, or suggested connections and sideroads. And so on. Moreover, once the price is right, who will be the curmudgeons who would deny their students access to the state-of-the-art?

Being a curmudgeon is a dirty job, but somebody has to do it. Some- 10 one has to hoist the warning flags and raise some issues that the fast-track proselytizers might overlook. Here are a few reservations worth pondering.

1. Knowledge, certainly in the humanities, is not a straightforward matter of access, of conquest via the ingestion of data. Part of any essential understanding of the world is that it is opaque, obdurate. To me, Wittgenstein's[2] famous axiom, "The world is everything that is the case," translates into a recognition of otherness. The past is as much about the disappearance of things through time as it is about the recovery of traces and the reconstruction of vistas. Say what you will about books, they not only mark the backward trail, but they also encode this sense of obstacle, of otherness. The look of the printed page changes as we regress in time; under the orthographic changes are the changes in the language itself. Old-style textual research may feel like an unnecessarily slow burrowing, but it is itself

---

2. Ludwig **Wittgenstein** (1889–1951): Austrian philosopher whose chief concern was the relationship between language, mind, and reality.—ED.

an instruction: It confirms that time is a force as implacable as gravity.

Yet the multimedia packages would master this gravity. For opacity they substitute transparency, promoting the illusion of access. All that has been said, known, and done will yield to the dance of the fingertips on the terminal keys. Space becomes hyperspace, and time, hypertime ("hyper-" being the fashionable new prefix that invokes the nonlinear and nonsequential "space" made possible by computer technologies). One gathers the data of otherness, but through a medium which seems to level the feel—the truth—of that otherness. The field of knowledge is rendered as a lateral and synchronic enterprise susceptible to collage, not as a depth phenomenon. And if our media restructure our perceptions, as McLuhan and others have argued, then we may start producing generations who know a great deal of "information" about the past but who have no purchase on pastness itself.

Described in this way, the effects of interactive programs on users sound a good deal like the symptoms of postmodernism. And indeed, this recent cultural aesthetic, distinguished by its flat, bright, and often affectless assemblages of materials may be a consequence of a larger transformation of sensibility by information-processing technologies. After all, our arts do tend to mirror who we are and anticipate what we might be becoming. Changes of this magnitude are of course systemic, and their direction is not easily dictated. Whether the postmodern "vision" can be endorsed as a pedagogic platform, however, is another question.

2. Humanistic knowledge, as I suggested earlier, differs from the more instrumental kinds of knowledge in that it ultimately seeks to fashion a comprehensible narrative. It is, in other words, about the creation and expansion of meaningful contexts. Interactive media technologies are, at least in one sense, anticontextual. They open the field to new widths, constantly expanding relevance and reference, and they equip their user with a powerful grazing tool. One moves at great rates across subject terrains, crossing borders that were once closely guarded. The multimedia approach tends ineluctably to multidisciplinarianism. The positive effect, of course, is the creation of new levels of connection and integration; more and more variables are brought into the equation.

But the danger should be obvious: The horizon, the limit that 15 gave definition to the parts of the narrative, will disappear. The equation itself will become nonsensical through the accumulation of variables. The context will widen until it becomes, in effect, everything. On the model of Chaos science, wherein the butterfly flapping its wings in China is seen to affect the weather system over Oklahoma, all data will impinge upon all other data. The technology may be able to handle it, but will the user? Will our narratives—historical, literary, classical—be able to withstand the data explosion? If they cannot, then what will be the new face of understanding? Or will the knowledge of the world become, perforce, a map as large and intricate as the world itself?

3. We might question, too, whether there is not in learning as in physical science a principle of energy conservation. Does a gain in one area depend upon a loss in another? My guess would be that every lateral attainment is purchased with a sacrifice of depth. The student may, through a program on Shakespeare, learn an immense amount about Elizabethan politics, the construction of the Globe theater, the origins of certain plays in the writings of Plutarch, the etymology of key terms, and so on, but will this dazzled student find the concentration, the will, to live with the often burred and prickly language of the plays themselves? The play's the thing—but will it be? Wouldn't the sustained exposure to a souped-up cognitive collage not begin to affect the attention span, the ability if not willingness to sit with one text for extended periods, butting up against its cruxes, trying to excavate meaning from the original rhythms and syntax? The gurus of interaction love to say that the student learns best by doing, but let's not forget that *reading* a work is also a kind of doing.

4. As a final reservation, what about the long-term cognitive effects of these new processes of data absorption? Isn't it possible that more may be less, and that the neural networks have one speed for taking in—a speed that can be increased—and quite another rate for retention? Again, it may be that our technologies will exceed us. They will make it not only possible but irresistible to consume data at what must strike people of the book as very high rates. But what then? What will happen as our neural systems, evolved through millennia to certain capacities, modify themselves to hold ever-expanding loads? Will we simply become smarter, able to hold and process more? Or do we have to reckon with some other gain/loss formula? One possible cognitive response—call it the "SAT cram-course model"—might be an expansion of the short-term memory banks and a correlative atrophying of long-term memory.

But here our technology may well assume a new role. Once it dawns on us, as it must, that our software will hold all the information we need at ready access, we may very well let it. That is, we may choose to become the technicians of our auxiliary brains, mastering not the information but the retrieval and referencing functions. At a certain point, then, we could become the evolutionary opposites of our forebears, who, lacking external technology, committed everything to memory. If this were to happen, what would be the status of knowing, of being educated? The leader of the electronic tribe would not be the person who knew most, but the one who could execute the broadest range of technical functions. What, I hesitate to ask, would become of the already antiquated notion of wisdom?

I recently watched a public television special on the history of the computer. One of the many experts and enthusiasts interviewed took up the knowledge question. He explained how the formerly two-dimensional process of book-based learning is rapidly becoming three-dimensional. The day will come, he opined, when interactive and virtual technologies will allow us to more or less dispense with our reliance on the sequence-based print paradigm. Whatever the object of our study, our equipment will be able to get us there directly: inside the volcano or the violin-maker's studio, right up on the stage. I was enthralled, but I shuddered, too, for it struck me that when our technologies are all in place—when all databases have been refined and integrated—that will be the day when we stop living in the old hard world and take up residence in some bright new hyperworld, a kind of Disneyland of information. I have to wonder if this is what Perseus and its kindred programs might not be edging us toward. That program got its name, we learn from the brochure, from the Greek mythological hero Perseus, who was the explorer of the limits of the known world. I confess that I can't think of Perseus without also thinking of Icarus, heedless son of Daedalus,[3] who allowed his wings to carry him over the invisible line that was inscribed across the skyway.

▪ **CONSIDER THE SOURCE**

1. Explain Dilthey's distinction between the natural sciences (*Naturwissenschaften*) and the sciences of culture (*Geisteswissenschaften*)? Which sciences does Birkerts believe are "more hospitable" to computers? Why?

2. What relationship does Birkerts see between knowledge and understanding? How is knowledge related to information?

3. What is the "SAT cram-course model" Birkerts refers to? How does he use it to clarify his argument about short- and long-term memory?

4. Circle any words Birkerts uses that are unfamiliar to you, or that you rarely encounter in your reading. Why do you think he uses such wide-ranging diction to discuss education and wisdom? How does his language affect you as a reader?

---

3. **Icarus:** Son of the mythic Greek inventor **Daedalus.** The pair attempted to fly with wings made of wax and feathers, but Icarus tried to soar too high; his wings melted, and he fell to his death.—ED.

■ **CONSIDER THE IMPLICATIONS**

5. In your journal, analyze your college courses in terms of the two categories of "science" that Birkerts examines. Which of your courses this semester fit into the natural sciences and which belong to the "sciences of culture"? Which courses seem best suited to the interactive computer programs Birkerts describes? Why?

6. Birkerts worries that our sense of "depth" and "context" will suffer as we use interactive programs. In class, discuss these concerns in light of Bernard Sharratt's description of how he used the Microsoft Art Gallery (pp. 564–70).

7. Hypertext teaching tools offer students vast amounts of information and may even offer knowledge, but can they offer wisdom? In small groups try to define what wisdom means to you. What are its features? How can it be obtained? Is it even a relevant term these days?

8. Birkerts contends that "the look of the printed page changes as we regress in time." In your library, locate back issues of popular magazines—such as *Life, Time,* or *The Saturday Evening Post*—from the 1920s, the 1940s, or the 1960s. Compare them with magazines of today. Write a paper in which you discuss how the "pastness" of the past is preserved by the printed page.

9. Both Umberto Eco (pp. 537–45) and Birkerts describe a future world where computers substitute for human memory. Compare their concerns about the implications of such a development. How would each author respond to D. T. Max's description of the future as a "messy" classroom where "you won't necessarily be able to find what you're looking for in cyberspace at any given time" ("The End of the Book?," pp. 546–57)? Write an essay synthesizing these views and offering your own perspective on the relation between computers and human memory.

10. Reread Birkerts's other essay in this collection, "The Paper Chase" (pp. 21–29), to clarify his argument that reading is "a kind of doing." Write a letter from Birkerts's point of view, addressed to advocates of hypermedia or hyperfiction, such as those quoted by George Melrod (pp. 570–80), in which you argue for the interactivity of bookreading as it presently exists.

11. After reviewing the selections by Birkerts, D. T. Max, and Paul Saffo (pp. 558–64), write an essay reflecting on the status of the book in the electronic age. What will books be used for? Which of their present functions will be served by computers?

WALT CRAWFORD AND MICHAEL GORMAN

Coping with Electronic Information

We've all heard about the "information explosion," and few would question the assertion that we live in an information age. Handling this exploding information is a job we often leave to computers, implicitly trusting that their memory chips are more efficient than our brain cells. That may be so, but the human mind may still prove more adept at making something of that information than any computer yet developed. Walt Crawford (b. 1945) and Michael Gorman (b. 1941) scrutinize the information age from the vantage point of librarians, a group often thought of as "technologically retrograde" and resistant to any encroachment on the book world. Gorman and Crawford point out that librarians have always excelled at organizing, disseminating, and making sense of data, and as such are the best equipped to develop systems to handle the current (and future) flood of information. In the following excerpts from their book, Future Libraries: Dreams, Madness and Reality *(1995), they evaluate the different kinds of intellectual goods purveyed by information sources—whether books or computers—and offer models for coping with the sea of information that surrounds us. Crawford is a former president of the Library and Information Technology Association (LITA), a division of the American Library Association, and is also a senior analyst at the Research Libraries Group, Inc. He has published ten books on libraries, technology, and personal computing, including* Current Technologies in the Library *(1988),* The Online Catalog Book *(1990), and* Desktop Publishing for Librarians *(1990). Gorman, dean of library services at California State University, Fresno, has lectured widely on library automation and administration, and has authored* Technical Services Today and Tomorrow *(1990). Together these two experts in library automation have written a counterargument to the "technolust" of those who envision "virtual libraries," computerized webs of resources that some say will replace libraries as we know them today.*

We are drowning in information but starved for knowledge.
                                                                                    – John Naisbitt

Mortimer Adler has made a useful distinction between what he calls "the four goods of the mind."[1] Those four goods are *information, knowl-*

From *Future Libraries: Dreams, Madness and Reality* (Chicago and London: American Library Association, 1995), pp. 70–84.

1. Mortimer Adler, *A Guidebook to Learning* (New York: Macmillan, 1986), pp. 110–134.

edge, understanding, and *wisdom.* In defining each, Adler emphasizes that they are not equal, but "ascend in a scale of values, information having the least value, wisdom the greatest." Ours is a time in which the computer dominates and its speed is seen as its most valuable characteristic. It has been said that, when the only tool you have is a hammer, everything looks like a nail. It is understandable, therefore, that today the least valuable good—information—which also happens to be the most amenable to computerization, should be seen as the most central.

Proceeding from that premise, it is easy to see how discussion of the future of libraries should center on the digitizing of information and the use of computers to transfer information at great speed. On that basis, one can understand how unexamined labels such as "The Information Age" and unchallenged confusions such as the "Virtual Library" should have gained such a hold on the popular imagination. It sometimes seems as though Gertrude Stein's observation that "everyone has so much information that they have lost their common sense"[2] has become literally true.

Adler treats information as a single good of the mind. In our opinion, information can be further subdivided into *data* (facts and other raw material that can be processed into useful information) and *information* (data processed and rendered useful). Each of these may exist independently—that is, they do not require the human mind to provide meaning and are, thus, peculiarly suitable for processing and transmission using electronic technology. As we move higher up the "ladder of learning," the human mind becomes vital and the role of the computer is consequently diminished. *Knowledge* can be defined as information transformed into meaning. It can be recorded and transmitted but the computer is by no means the ideal medium for such transmission. *Understanding* is knowledge integrated with a world view and a personal perspective and exists entirely within the human mind, as does *wisdom,* understanding made whole and generative.

Let us state, as strongly as we can, that libraries are *not wholly or even primarily about information.* They are about the preservation, dissemination, and use of recorded knowledge in whatever form it may come so that humankind may become more knowledgeable; through knowledge reach understanding; and, as an ultimate goal, achieve wisdom. The collection and absorption of data (discrete facts, numbers, etc.) and information (organized data) is often contextless and spasmodic. It may have a utilitarian purpose (usually brief) but has no enduring meaning unless the information so acquired is fitted into an intelligible structure of knowledge.

One may, for example, learn that Josephine Smith of Chico is five ₅

---

2. Gertrude Stein, *Reflection on the Atomic Bomb,* ed. Robert Bartlett Haas, vol. 1 of *Uncollected Writings of Gertrude Stein* (Los Angeles: Black Sparrow Press, 1973), p. 161.

feet, six inches tall and that the average height of American females has increased by six inches in this century. That datum and that information have no meaning or interest beyond the trivial. The information may acquire interest if it is seen as a result of nutrition, improved public health, or other causality and fitted into an existing context of knowledge. Data and information, therefore, are building blocks for organized knowledge or they are nothing. This is no light point. If the only Adlerian "good" of the mind that can be sent down "the Information Superhighway" is the least important good, then we must look elsewhere for progress in and maintenance of our culture. Humans cannot live by information alone, and a society that is informed without being knowledgeable and wise will be a society of boorish conformity. . . .

DATA, INFORMATION, KNOWLEDGE

Many people appear unwilling to concede that data and information are not the sum of human communication. Data and small assemblages of information are readily amenable to electronic transmission and access. Complex aggregations of information and recorded knowledge are not so amenable—that is a fact with which proponents of an all-electronic future have failed to deal.

Those proponents, in hot pursuit of electronic everything, tell us that the world's information (or the world's knowledge or something like that) is doubling every five years. They go on to argue that only electronic methods can possibly keep up with such a massive increase. It may well be true that the volume of *data* in the world is doubling every five years. That is not at all the same as saying that the amount of information or knowledge is increasing at such a rate.

Thirty years ago, Yehoshua Bar-Hillel inveighed against those pushing the "flood-of-information" theory.[3] It is a pity that his trenchant analyses of the situation have not changed the tenor of the discussion, which is still pervaded by extreme statements about an "information explosion" (more exactly, a "data explosion" or even a "document explosion") requiring electronic solutions.

It is almost certainly nonsense to say that the amount of *useful* information is doubling every five years. A cynic might even suggest that the amount of knowledge is *declining*, as so many people seem caught up in pursuing more and more data, failing to turn it into either useful information or worthwhile knowledge. Libraries and human communication in general are, and should be, more concerned with knowledge and what it leads to and should not be diverted by irrelevant discussions of a supposed crisis calling for electronic, and only electronic, solutions.

---

3. Yehoshua Bar-Hillel, *Language and Information* (Reading, Mass.: Addison-Wesley, 1964).

Data overload is nothing new. For example, every day insurance 10 companies churn out immense quantities of paper containing new or modified policies and coverage descriptions; more than any person could read or evaluate. Virtually none of it is relevant to anyone but the company and its clients; virtually none of it belongs on a library's shelves or in its electronic resources; and virtually none of it contributes to the knowledge of humankind or enriches our culture. These are not value judgments. The data may very well be commercially useful and necessary, but it should be seen for what it is—unprocessed data and, as such, of little concern to libraries.

COPING WITH THE I-WAY

Electronic distribution, both of data and of information, will certainly continue to grow rapidly. There is little question that the I-way (or Information Superhighway) now being developed on the basis of the Internet will be a major conduit for, and source of, data and information in the coming years. It is obvious that more data and information will be distributed electronically than in print by the end of the century; that may well be true now. Beyond the "gee whiz" aspects of this trend lie some rather difficult questions. The most problematic is: What do we do with all that *stuff*? . . .

Bibliographic and Quality Control

There are professionals in this country who have developed very effective means of bringing huge quantities of records of information and knowledge under control and making their retrieval possible. That group was one of the earliest to use computers for everyday tasks, and has used computers with increasing effectiveness for at least three decades. Amazingly, given that the group is consistently underfunded and incredibly disparate, they managed to come up with an innovative data management design more than a quarter-century ago, a design that has supported cost-effective systems handling tens of gigabytes of data covering tens of millions of records.

Unfortunately, that group—professional librarians—tends to be ignored by the computer wizards dreaming of new and wonderful tools. Worse, some librarians seem to ignore their own achievements and assume that the new ways, even ways that exist only in the fertile brain of some futurist, are better. It is likely that librarians are the only group with the professional qualifications, experience, and track record to make them capable of bringing quality, structure, and bibliographic control to the global rats' nest that is the Internet. Librarians have the professional training and experience; many have specific training in the technological environment; and they have simply done a better job of organizing the world of knowledge and information than anyone else. Despite all this, librarians are routinely castigated for being technologically retrograde. The facts belie this accusation. Librarians have been using computers effectively to provide real, but never total or permanent, solutions to incredibly complex problems since the early 1960s. Librarians have used lower-technology solutions to make sense of multi-million-volume book collections enriched by other media. Librarians have done better at making sense of massive quantities of disparate information than any other group. It is a proud record; one to build on, not one to forget.

Authenticity

How can the user of an electronic resource be sure that the electronic text received is identical to the text requested? If the user has requested an electronic text based on a citation, how can he or she be sure that the text received is the one that was cited? How can the user be sure that the text received is in fact the text that was created by the person named as its author? How can the user be sure that the person named as author is the creator of the text? In short, how can the authenticity of the text be guaranteed in an electronic environment?

A number of people say these question do not matter—that a big   15 advantage of electronic texts is that they are mutable, constantly being updated and revised. This may be a good thing for some kinds of data and purely factual information. In order for the mutability not to be significant, the user must know that the source can be trusted and that history is irrelevant.

A user following up a citation needs to know that the article he or she is reading is the article as it was when it was cited. At the very least, if it is not exactly that article but the author's current version, or one that has been changed by another person, the fact that the article has been changed (and ideally the changes themselves) should be clearly indicated. For one thing, a well-written article is much more than a series of facts. Readers derive information from data and knowledge from information; that process is debased if the reader is presented with knowledge and information that has been "improved" by anonymous others. The situation is even worse when the reader is unaware that the deformation of the text has taken place.

There are solutions to the problem of authenticity in electronic texts. Currently, the easiest is to write the text to a read-only medium; in other words, to publish it on CD-ROM. Another is to prepare a "checksum," a digital signature that can verify that the text has almost certainly not been modified. The technology exists to create such a security measure; at this point, the will to do so is lacking.

Today, most electronic texts simply cannot claim the same validity or importance as printed texts. This must change, given the reality of modern communication and the economics of communication. Electronic distribution *must* complement print-on-paper and each must be used in the manner that yields the best results. To do that effectively, a battery of solutions must be found for the many problems of electronic distribution. A necessary precursor of these solutions is abandoning the idea that "putting it on the net" solves everything—or solves anything, for that matter.

Significance

Internetters made much of a recent *New Yorker* cartoon with the caption "On the Internet, nobody knows you're a dog."[4] The joke is based on one of the wonders of electronic communication—it has no inherent discrimination on the basis of age, creed, color, gender, physical appearance or ability, or sexual preference. That is entirely to the good.

It seems to go further than that, though. An equally relevant cartoon   20 could have the caption "On the Internet, nobody knows you're a crank." Internet users know that the Net does not exclude those who are ignorant or bigoted, cannot write a simple declarative English sentence, or have neglected to check their facts. Sadly, many electronic messages emanate from cranks and fools (they seem to have a lot more time than the rest of us.) We can only trust that the sunshine of scrutiny will enable discrimination between the wheat and the tares.

Is it possible for users of electronic texts to judge significance and quality with any assurance? How can they estimate the likelihood that a given text is either correct or useful? In the print world, those familiar with a given discipline can make first-level decisions based on the source. For example, everyone in a field knows the top-ranked journals in that field and gives more credence to articles published in those journals than to articles published in totally unknown journals. That credence and ranking may be one of the greatest problems faced by those who would reform scholarly journal publishing—how do you change the rankings?

Where are the top-ranked electronic sources? How does a user determine whether a paragraph on a given topic is important, current, or even correct? Should the history of World War II be studied in an arena in which the works of "Holocaust revisionists" appear to have the same standing as the works of mainstream historians?

These are important questions—ones that librarians must answer daily in choosing and using print materials. The questions become much more difficult (if not impossible) to answer in an electronic environment. If those questions are not answered, electronic dissemination will continue to be less significant than print, if only because it is so much more difficult to evaluate what the user is getting.

---

4. *The New Yorker*, July 5, 1993, p. 61.

DROWNING, SURFING, OR SWIMMING
IN THE SEA OF INFORMATION

As we have noted, large insurance companies generate huge quantities of data on paper. Most of that data is also in machine-readable form. Let us imagine that a scholar wishes to study the insurance industry and manages to gain access to all that machine-readable data. Let us also stipulate that the scholar has access to all the computer resources she or he can possibly use. What will the scholar's options be? Most probably, that scholar will end up drowning in data—and there's a good possibility that no useful information will ever emerge from the flood. Unless, of course, the scholar has the insight and inspiration to establish incredibly efficient ways of reducing that data to information—ways that a computer can carry out unaided. Even if that unlikely scenario were so, what if another scholar doubts the results and determines to go back to the raw materials? Good luck—we'll see you in a few decades!

That may be an extreme case but it is not unrealistic. Why is it, then, 25 that so many people today seem determined to drown in data and information, spending so much time taking it all in that they never have time to synthesize knowledge and achieve understanding?

It is very easy to drown in information even now. The rapid expansion of full-text resources—which *will* happen—will greatly increase the dangers of drowning.[5] Futurists tell us that a "knowbot" (*know*ledge *robot*—a species of electronic librarian) will handle retrieval for us, operating throughout the nets and sending us whatever is relevant to our interests. Leaving aside the whiff of the 1939 World's Fair that clings to this concept, there are two important, unanswered questions about knowbots. How can a computer program judge relevance in a meaningful, useful way? Given a reasonable breadth of interest, how can the knowbot be stopped from drowning the user in material (relevant and irrelevant)?

The Young Scholar's Peril

We are told that any reputable scholar must be up-to-date on everything in his or her field (which will, these days, be quite narrowly defined). Taking that admonition literally and using electronic tools to achieve it is a recipe for disaster. Young scholars who make it a point of pride to keep absolutely up-to-the-minute on every available piece of information in their field will find at least one of two things happening:

— They will define their field so narrowly, and build search tools that search so restrictively, that they will miss the most important work being done in the field and become irrelevant.

---

5. For a discussion of the effects of too much unstructured information, see: Richard Saul Wurman, *Information Anxiety* (New York: Doubleday, 1989).

— They will spend so much time (and money) keeping up with developments that there will never be time to organize, analyze, synthesize—in other words, *create*.

Some assert that, in the future, all scholarship will be cooperative and iterative and that this is to the good. This assertion is oversimplified to the point of inanity. Some scholarship is, and should be, cooperative. Much of the best new thinking, however, is not. Some scholarship arises out of simply massaging existing data. Much of the best, however, depends on stepping back, viewing the field anew, and bringing individual genius to bear. Those who are drowning in information will be hard-pressed to take part in the former variety of scholarship and there seems to be no way that they can do the latter. For that, they will need to learn to disconnect from the Net, recognize that they will miss some items in the field, and sit back and think. Reflection is an honorable activity, but hard to do while drowning.

Surfing

The metaphor of the sea for the Internet is pervasive and illuminating. When one thinks of the uncharted depths, the innumerable varieties of aquatic life, and the dangers to life and happiness posed by the sea, the metaphor is irresistible. Even the sunnier applications of the metaphor have resonance. Surfing, after all, consists of skimming the surface in search of superficial and transitory pleasure. The surfing analogy is nothing new and "Surfing the Internet" has been worked to death as a title for courses and articles. Surfing is skimming over the Sea of Information; maneuvering without getting in too deeply—a quite different matter from being aware of all available resources and how to find them.

Surfing is an essential for anyone who wishes to become an effective user of electronic texts. However, it is scarcely unique to the Internet or other electronic structures. We know there has always been journal surfing: skimming through vast realms of information without getting bogged down by attempting to study each item in detail. Some people are better journal surfers than others, but most learn to be fairly proficient in those areas where they have to be *somewhat* familiar with what is current but cannot afford to spend all their waking hours at it.

A literary scholar might regard two or three journals and magazines as fundamental to her or his own interests. That scholar will probably subscribe to those publications and read them cover to cover. A committed person will have wider interests and, given time and access to a good collection, may well look at twenty or more other journals. For most of those journals (say 80 percent) "looking" will consist of glancing at the contents page in the expectation that one article every three or four years might be worth reading. For a smaller number of journals (most of the remaining 20 percent), the reader will glance at the abstract or first paragraph of each article and skim through the book reviews, probably reading a significant portion of each issue. That leaves a few core journals—the ones read in full. This description is another form of the 80/20 rule—20 percent of an area represents 80 percent of the value. The key element to such surfing is knowing which 20 percent deserves extra attention. Beyond that, the journal surfer needs flexibility in recognizing that important articles may occur in the lightly skimmed majority.

Is it possible to apply print journal surfing techniques to the electronic sea? It can be, but remember that it is one thing to skim a set of article titles in an electronic source; it is quite another to request the abstract for each one (particularly as the cost of doing so will increase as we move beyond our present fully-subsidized era), and it is yet another to want to look at each article.

Surfing can take place at several levels. Skimming through tables of contents of many different journals is quite different from having a highly selective search routine running on a computer. In the first case, the reader is aware of all those paper names, thus acquiring a sense of what is being published, which in turn helps to foster awareness of trends. That process is a form of socialization. It is also one reason that so many areas have at least one key journal or bulletin, a journal that many or most people in the field actually *read* in full (every issue, more-or-less cover to cover) as part of keeping up with the field. This type of surfing adds considerably more value than most Internet surfing. It is also more time consuming and, in a way, more random. It is hard to see it as being readily transferable to the electronic domain.

Swimming

Some people seem to be full-time surfers—always aware of today's currents of information and how to find enough to keep them happy, but never deeply conversant with any particular current. Some of these electronic beach bums become deeply involved in the e-mail culture—true creatures of the network. In extreme cases, if something is not on the Net and available via one of their news groups or lists, it either does not exist or its existence is without significance.

Luckily, most people cease to surf and become swimmers, at least from time to time and place to place. Swimmers read whole articles; the more advanced even read books! They explore topics in detail, not only connecting article to article but idea to idea. As this process unfolds, the swimmer will frequently move to the next step, by adding to the topics through analysis, synthesis, further research—creation. This is when it gets good.

For the Internet user, the problem is knowing the difference between swimming, surfing, and drowning. The important factor is attitude. A swimmer who becomes obsessed with currency and completeness will soon drown. If the user finds that she or he no longer reads complete articles in an area, that is surfing—not necessarily a bad thing, but one that indicates relative priorities and relative awareness.

We envisage the successful scholar on the Net as both a swimmer and a surfer. Some surf too much—treating all books as being outdated by definition; ignoring all but the few leading journals in a specialty; or, worse, ignoring *all* journals and relying only on preprints, electronic mail, and personal communications. It is conceivable that such an approach might work in a few disciplines but it meets no present scholarly standard. A balance of surfing and swimming serves most users well in their attempts to cope with the electronic chaos of today. Unfortunately, the tools for surfing and swimming effectively do not yet exist—we have no complete and accurate charts for the Sea of Information. We hope that such tools can and will be developed, and repeat our conviction that librarians are the most competent to develop them.

■ CONSIDER THE SOURCE

1. Explain the distinctions the authors make between the four "goods of the mind": information, knowledge, understanding, and wisdom. Give an example of each "good of the mind." How does data differ from information, according to Crawford and Gorman?

2. Summarize what the authors consider to be the main purposes of a library. How do they believe computers can and cannot assist those purposes?

3. What do Crawford and Gorman mean by "authenticity" and why do they believe it's important?

4. How do Crawford and Gorman appeal to the audience most likely to read a book published by the American Library Association? Where are those appeals most obvious? How are the aims of the ALA, as described in the appendix (p. 63), addressed in this essay?

■ CONSIDER THE IMPLICATIONS

5. The distinctions between surfing, swimming, and drowning do not apply exclusively to the Internet and electronic tools. Discuss other arenas of your life—such as hobbies, sports, or entertainment—in which you are overloaded with information or options. Which ones do you surf? How does surfing contribute to your "socialization" in that field? How and why do you move from surfing to swimming?

6. If you have access to computerized bibliographies and databases, whether online or on CD-ROM, spend some time using them to search for a topic that interests you. Carefully record every instruction you give the computer, every search term you try, and how many records or "hits" you get back from each search. Bring your search record to class and compare it with those of a small group of other students. Can you see any patterns in the ways that people search? Can you see any common errors or

misunderstandings on the part of the computer? Discuss your searches and assess whether a "knowbot" could have performed them instead of a human being.

7. In your library, survey the sources available for studying a particular field, such as genetics, physical anthropology, art history, eighteenth-century literature, or any other field that interests you. Which journals are available? How many online sources? Can you determine which have the most "significance" or accuracy? What criteria might you use to make distinctions among sources? Write an annotated bibliography of the available resources in that field to help others evaluate their usefulness and authority.

8. Interview a librarian about the electronic resources that are currently used in your school's library. Which ones are for patrons and which are for the library staff? How have computers assisted the staff in managing the collection? Do the librarians see any drawbacks in the computer systems presently available? Write a paper evaluating the computer's role in one particular area of the library, such as reference, acquisition, circulation, or special collections.

9. In class discussion, compare these authors' views on the relationship between computers and the various "goods of the mind" with those of Sven Birkerts ("Perseus Unbound," pp. 581–87). What value do they assign to knowledge and information? To what extent can computers transmit or help generate knowledge? How closely do the authors agree on what constitutes understanding and wisdom?

10. Interview several professors to determine the extent to which computers have affected scholarship at your institution. How do faculty members use computers? How important to their research are word processing, online bibliographies and databases, electronic journals, and e-mail? How do they judge the "authenticity" and "significance" of materials retrieved electronically? Use the interviews as evidence in an essay supporting or refuting Crawford and Gorman's vision of computer-driven scholarship.

■ ■ ■ ■ ■ ■

M. KADI

The Internet Is Four Inches Tall

The information superhighway doesn't just carry information to your door; it also connects you with other people. You can use e-mail to send an electronic message from one person to another; you can sign onto a bulletin board service (BBS) or a forum, where all postings pertain to a single topic and anyone can log on to read them; or you can participate in a chat-group,

From *h2so4* 3 (November 1994), 26–30.

a sort of electronic cocktail party where many users logged on at the same time can "talk" to each other by typing their conversation. This high-speed communication has attracted hundreds of thousands of academic users to the government-subsidized Internet, while private users rush to subscribe to commercial services such as America Online, Prodigy, and CompuServe. All you need is a computer, a modem, and a network account, and you can enjoy the wonders of a diverse global community. Or can you? Writing for the 'zine h2so4, M. Kadi (b. 1968) takes a dollars-and-cents approach to the Internet and assesses whether the online world is really as diverse as the hype would suggest. She raises important questions about how meaningful the pure information of the info-highway is and how much real connection electronic connectivity provides. Kadi is no stranger to the computer world, nor is she a technological naysayer. A self-confessed "cyberjunkie," Kadi is a freelance computer consultant in the San Francisco area whose work provides her with the raw material for her essays about computer usage. She has written on various topics for h2so4, bOING bOING *, and* hotWired, Wired *magazine's online journal.*

"Computer networking offers the soundest basis for world peace that has yet been presented. Peace must be created on the bulwark of understanding. International computer networks will knit together the peoples of the world in bonds of mutual respect; its possibilities are vast, indeed."

> – *Scientific American*

"Cyberspace is a new medium. Every night on Prodigy, CompuServe, GEnie, and thousands of smaller computer bulletin boards, people by the hundreds of thousands are logging on to a great computer mediated gabfest, an interactive debate that allows them to leap over barriers of time, place, sex, and social status."

> – *Time* Magazine

"The Internet is really about the rise of not merely a new technology, but a new culture—a global culture where time, space, borders, and even personal identity are radically redefined."

> – *Online Access* Magazine

"When you begin to explore the online world, you'll find a wealth of publicly available resources and diverse communities."

> – A 'Zine I Actually Like—so I'm not going to tell you where I got this quote

"The first time you realize the super toy you wanted is really only four inches tall you learn a hard lesson." Q: How big is the Internet? A: Four inches tall. Blah. Blah. Blah. Everyone is equal on the Net. Race, gender, sexual orientation are invisible and, being invisible, foster communication. Barriers are broken down. The global community exists and is coming together. (Right here, right now.)

Diversity. Community. Global Culture. Information. Knowledge. Communication. Doesn't this set your nostalgia alarm off? Doesn't it sound like all that sixties love-in, utopian, narcissistic trash that we've had to listen to all our lives? Does this sound familiar to anyone but me?

Computer bulletin board services offer up the glories of e-mail, the thought provocation of newsgroups, the sharing of ideas implicit in public posting, and the interaction of real-time chats. The fabulous, wonderful, limitless world of communication is just waiting for you to log on. Sure. Yeah. Right.

I confess, I am a dedicated cyberjunkie. It's fun. It's interesting. It takes me places where I've never been before. I sign on once a day, twice a day, three times a day, more and more; I read, I post, I live. Writing an article on the ever-expanding, ever-entertaining, ever-present world of online existence would have been easy for me. But it would have been familiar, perhaps dull; and it might have been a lie. The world does not need another article on the miracle of online reality; what we need, what I need, what this whole delirious, interconnected, global community of a world needs is a little reality check.

To some extent the following scenario will be misleading. There *are* flat rate online services (Netcom for one) which offer significant connectivity for a measly seventeen dollars a month. But I'm interested in the activities and behavior of the private service users who will soon comprise a vast majority of online citizens. Furthermore, let's face facts, the U.S. government by and large foots the bill for the Internet, through maintaining the structural (hardware) backbone, including, among other things, funding to major universities. As surely as the Department of Defense started this whole thing, AT&T or Ted Turner is going to end up running it so I don't think it's too unrealistic to take a look at the Net as it exists in its commercial form[1] in order to expose some of the realities lurking behind the regurgitated media rhetoric and the religious fanaticism of net junkies.

TIME AND MONEY

The average person, the normal human, J. Individual, has an income. Big or small, how much of J. Individual's income is going to be spent on Computer Connectivity? Does 120 dollars a month sound reasonable? Well, you may find that number a bit too steep for your pocket

---

1. Techno concession: I know that the big three commercial services are not considered part of the Internet proper, but they (Prodigy, CompuServe and AOL) are rapidly adding real Net access and considering AOL just bought out Netcom . . . well, just read the article.

book, but the brutal fact is that 120 dollars is a "reasonable" amount to spend on monthly connectivity. The major online services have a monthly service charge of approximately $15. Fifteen dollars to join the global community, communicate with a diverse group of people, and access the world's largest repository of knowledge since the Alexandrian Library does not seem unreasonable, does it? But don't overlook the average per-hour connectivity rate of an additional $3 (which can skyrocket upwards of $10, depending on your modem speed and service). You might think that you are a crack whiz with your communications software—that you are rigorous and stringent and never, ever respond to e-mail or a forum while online, that you always use your capture functions and create macros, but let me tell you that no one, and I repeat, no one, is capable of logging on this efficiently every time. Thirty hours per month is a realistic estimate for online time spent by a single user engaging in activities beyond primitive e-mail. Now consider that the average, one-step-above-complete neophyte user has at least two distinct BBS accounts, and do the math: Total Monthly Cost: $120. Most likely, that's already more than the combined cost of your utility bills. How many people are prepared to double their monthly bills for the sole purpose of connectivity?

In case you think thirty hours a month is an outrageous estimate, think of it in terms of television. (OK, so you don't own a television, well, goody-for-you—imagine that you do!) Thirty hours, is, quite obviously, one hour a day. That's not so much. Thirty hours a month in front of a television is simply the evening news plus a weekly *Seinfeld/Frasier* hour. Thirty hours a month is less time than the average car-phone owner spends on the phone while commuting. Even a conscientious geek, logging on for e-mail and the up-to-the-minute news that only the net services can provide is probably going to spend thirty hours a month online. And, let's be truthful here, thirty hours a month ignores shareware downloads, computer illiteracy, real-time chatting, interactive game playing and any serious forum following, which by nature entail a significant amount of scrolling and/or downloading time.

If you are really and truly going to use the net services to connect with the global community, the hourly charges are going to add up pretty quickly. Take out a piece of paper, pretend you're writing a check, and print out "One hundred and twenty dollars—" and tell me again, how diverse is the online community?

That scenario aside, let's pretend that you're single, that you don't have children, that you rarely leave the house, that you don't have a TV and that money is not an issue. Meaning, pretend for a moment that you have as much time and as much money to spend online as you damn-well want. What do you actually do online?

Well, you download some cool shareware, you post technical ques- 10 tions in the computer user group forums, you check your stocks, you read the news and maybe some reviews—Hey, you've already passed that thirty hour limit! But, of course, since "computer networks make it easy to reach out and touch strangers who share a particular obsession or concern," you are participating in the online forums, discussion groups, and conferences.

Let's review the structure of forums. For the purposes of this essay, we will examine the smallest of the major user-friendly commercial services—America Online (AOL). There is no precise statistic available (at least none that the company will reveal—you have to do the research by Hand!!!) on exactly how many subject-specific discussion areas (folders) exist on AOL. Any online service is going to have zillions of posts pertaining to computer usage (e.g., the computer games area of AOL breaks into five hundred separate topics with over 100,000 individual posts), so let's look at a less popular area: the "Lifestyles and Interests" department.

For starters, there are fifty-seven initial categories within the Lifestyle and Interests area. One of these categories is Ham Radio. Ham Radio? How can there possibly be $5,909^2$ separate, individual posts about Ham Radio? [There are] 5,865 postings in the Biking (and that's just bicycles, not motorcycles) category. Genealogy—22,525 posts. The Gay and Lesbian category is slightly more substantial—36,333 posts. There are five separate categories for political and issue discussion. The big catch-all topic area, The Exchange, has over 100,000 posts. Basically, service wide (on the smallest service, remember) there are over a million posts.

So, you want to communicate with other people, join the online revolution, but obviously you can't wade through everything that's being discussed—you need to decide which topics interest you, which folders to browse. Within The Exchange alone (one of fifty-seven subdivisions within one of another fifty higher divisions) there are 1,492 separate topic-specific folders—each containing a rough average of fifty posts, but with many containing close to four hundred. (Note: AOL automatically empties folders when their post totals reach four hundred, so total post numbers do not reflect the overall historical totals for a given topic. Sometimes the posting is so frequent that the "shelf life" of a given post is no more than four weeks.)

So, there you are, J. Individual, ready to start interacting with folks, sharing stories and communicating. You have narrowed yourself into a single folder, three tiers down in the AOL hierarchy, and now you must choose between nearly fifteen hundred folders. Of course, once you choose a few of these folders, you will then have to read all the posts in order to catch up, be current, and not merely repeat a previous post.

A polite post is no more than two paragraphs long (a screenful of   15

---

2. Statistics obtained in June 1994. Most of these numbers have increased by at least 20 percent since that time, owing to all the Internet hoopla in the media, the consumer desire to be "wired" as painlessly as possible, and AOL's guerrilla marketing tactics.

text, which obviously has a number of intellectually negative implications). Let's say you choose ten folders (out of fifteen hundred). Each folder contains an average of fifty posts. Five hundred posts, at, say, one paragraph each, and you're now looking at the equivalent of a two hundred page book.

Enough with the stats. Let me back up a minute and present you with some very disturbing, but rational, assumptions. J. Individual wants to join the online revolution, to connect and communicate. But, J. Individual is not going to read all one million posts on AOL. (After all, J. Individual has a second online service.) Exercising choice is J. Individual's god-given right as an American, and, by gosh, J. Individual is going to make some decisions. So, J. Individual is going to ignore all the support groups—after all, J. is a normal, well-adjusted person, and all of J.'s friends are normal, well-adjusted individuals. What does J. need to know about alcoholism or incest victims? J. Individual is white. So, J. Individual is going to ignore all the multicultural folders. J. couldn't give a hoot about gender issues; does not want to discuss religion or philosophy. Ultimately, J. Individual does not engage in topics which do not interest J. Individual. So, who is J. meeting? Why, people who are *just like J.*

J. Individual has now joined the electronic community. Surfed the Net. Found some friends. *Tuned in, turned on, and geeked out.* Traveled the Information Highway and, just off to the left of that great Infobahn, J. Individual has settled into an electronic suburb.

Are any of us so very different from J. Individual? It's my time and my money and I am not going to waste any of it reading posts by disgruntled Robert-Bly drum-beating men's-movement boys who think that they should have some say over whether or not I choose to carry a child to term simply because a condom broke. I know where I stand. I'm an adult. I know what's up and I am not going to waste my money arguing with a bunch of Neanderthals.

Oh yeah; I am so connected, so enlightened, so open to the opposing viewpoint. I'm out there, meeting all kinds of people from different economic backgrounds (who have $120 a month to burn), from all religions (yeah, right, like anyone actually discusses religion anymore from a user-standpoint), from all kinds of different ethnic backgrounds and with all kinds of sexual orientations (as if any of this ever comes up outside of the appropriate topic folder).

People are drawn to topics and folders that interest them and therefore people will only meet people who are likewise interested in the same topics in the same folders. Rarely does anyone venture into a random folder just to see what others (The Others?) are talking about. This magazine being what it is, I can assume that the average reader will most likely not be as narrow-minded as the average white collar worker out in the burbs—but still, I think you and I are participating in the wide, wide world of online existence only insofar as our already existing interests and prejudices dictate.

Basically, between the monetary constraints and the sheer number of topics and individual posts, the great Information Highway is not a place where you will enter an "amazing web of new people, places, and ideas." One does not encounter people from "all walks of life" because there are too many people and too many folders. Diversity might be out there (and personally I don't think it is), but the simple fact is that the average person will not encounter it because with one brain, one job, one partner, one family, and one life, no one has the time!

Just in case these arguments based on time and money aren't completely convincing, let me bring up a historical reference. Please take another look at the opening quote of this essay from *Scientific American*. Featured in their "50 Years Ago Today" column, where you read "computer networks," the original quote contained the word *television*. Amusing, isn't it?

Moving beyond the practical obstacles mentioned above, let's assume that the Internet is the functional, incredible information tool that everyone says it is. Are we really prepared to use it?

WHO, WHAT, WHERE, WHEN, AND WHY?

School trained us to produce answers. It didn't matter if your answer was right or wrong, the fact is that you did the answering while the teacher was the one asking the questions, writing down the equations, handing out the topics. You probably think that you came up with your own questions in college. But did you? Every class had its theme, its reading list, its issues; you chose topics for papers and projects keeping within the context set by your professors and the academic environment. Again, you were given questions, perhaps more thinly disguised than the questions posed to you in fourth grade, but questions nevertheless. And you answered them. Even people focusing on independent studies and those pursuing higher degrees, still do very little asking, simply because the more you study, the more questions there seem to be, patiently waiting for you to discover and answer them.

These questions exist because any contextual reality poses questions. The context in which you exist defines the question, as much as it defines the answer. School is a limited context. Even life is a limited context. Well, life was a limited context until this Information Highway thing happened to us. Maybe you think that this Infobahn is fabulous; fabulous because all that information is out there waiting to be restructured by you into those answers. School will be easier. Life will be easier. A simple tap-tap-tap on the ol' keyboard brings those answers out of the woodwork and off the Net into the privacy of your own home.

But this Information Highway is a two-way street and as it brings the world into your home it brings you out into the world. In a world filled with a billion answers just waiting to be questioned, expect that you are rapidly losing a grip on your familiar context. This loss of context makes the task of formulating a coherent question next to impossible.

The questions aren't out there and they never will be. You must make them.

Pure information has no meaning. I would venture to assert that a pure fact has no meaning; no meaning, that is, without the context which every question implies. In less than fifteen minutes I could find out how much rain fell last year in Uzbekistan, but that fact, that answer, has no meaning for me because I don't have or imagine or know the context in which the question is meaningful.

No one ever taught me how to ask a question. I answered other people's questions, received a diploma, and now I have an education. I can tell you what I learned, and what I know. I can quantify and qualify the trivia which comprises my knowledge. But I can't do that with my ignorance. Ignorance, being traditionally "bad," is just lumped together and I have little or no skills for sorting through the vast territory of what I don't know. I have an awareness of it—but only in the sense that I am aware of what I don't know about the topics which I already know something about in the first place.

What I mean to say is, I don't know what I don't know about, say, 30 miners in China because I don't know anything about China, or what kinds of minerals they have, or where the minerals are, or the nature of mining as a whole. Worse yet, I don't have a very clear sense of whether or not these would be beneficial, useful, enlightening things for me to know. I have little sense of what questions are important enough for me to ask, so I don't know what answers, what information to seek out on the Internet.

In this light, it would seem that a massive amount of self-awareness is a prerequisite for using the Internet as an information source—and very few people are remotely prepared for this task. I believe that most people would simply panic in the face of their own ignorance and entrench themselves even more firmly into the black holes of their existing beliefs and prejudices. The information is certainly out there, but whether or not any of us can actually learn anything from it remains to be seen.

FLY, WORDS, AND BE FREE

The issues pertaining to time, money, and the fundamental usefulness of pure information are fairly straightforward when contrasted with the issues raised by e-mail. E-mail is the first hook and the last defense for the Internet and computer-mediated communication. I would like to reiterate that I am by no means a Luddite[3] when it comes to computer technology; in fact, because of this I may be unqualified to discuss, or even grasp, the dark side of electronic communication in the form of e-mail. The general quality of e-mail sent by one's three-dimensional[4] friends and family is short, usually funny, and almost completely devoid of thoughtful communication. I do not know if this is a result of the fact that your 3-D friends already "know" you, and therefore brief quips are somehow more revealing (as they reflect an immediate mental/emotional state) than long, factual exposés, or if this brevity is a result of the medium itself. I do not know if I, personally, will ever be able to sort this out, owing to the nature of my friends, the majority of whom are, when all is said and done (unlike myself, I might add), writers.

Writers have a reverence for pen and paper which does not carry over well into ASCII.[5] There is no glorified history for ASCII exchange and perhaps because of this fact my friends do not treat the medium as they would a handwritten letter. Ultimately, there is very little to romanticize about e-mail. There is decidedly a lack of sensuality, and perhaps some lack of realism. There is an undeniable connection between writers and their written (literally) words. This connection is transferred via a paper letter in a way that can never be transferable electronically. A handwritten letter is physically touched by both the sender and the receiver. When I receive an electronic missive, I receive only an impression of the mind, but when I receive a handwritten letter, I receive a piece, a moment, of another's physical (real?) existence; I possess, I own, that letter, those words, that moment.

Certainly there is a near-mystical utopianism to the lack of ownership of electronic words. There is probably even an evolution of untold consequences. Personally, I do not think, as so many do, that a great democracy of thought is upon us—but there is a change, as ownership slips away. While this is somewhat exciting, or at least intriguing, insofar as public communication goes, it is sad for private correspondence. To abuse a well-known philosopher, there is a leveling taking place: The Internet and the computer medium render a public posting on the na-

---

3. **Luddite:** Rioting laborers in the early nineteenth century trashed machines that replaced human labor; they were said to be following a leader named "Ned Ludd," and so the term "Luddite" has been associated with those who oppose mechanization and technological advances.— ED.

4. So sue me for being a nerd. Personally, I find referring to friends one has made outside of the cyber world as one's "real" friends, or one's "objective" friends, to be insulting and inaccurate. Certainly one's cyber friends are three-dimensional in a final sense, but the "3-D" adjective is about the only term I have come up with which doesn't carry the negative judgmental weight of other terms so over-used in European philosophy. Feel free to write me if you've got a better suggestion. Better yet, write me in the appropriate context: flox@netcom.com.

5. **ASCII:** American Standard Code for Information Interchange, the uniform character code that allows computer systems to exchange data directly.—ED.

ture of footwear and a private letter on the nature of one's life in the same format, and to some extent this places both on the same level. I cannot help but think that there is something negative in this.

Accessibility is another major issue in the e-mail/handwritten letter debate. Text sent via the Net is instantly accessible, but it is accessible only in a temporal sense. E-text is inaccessible in its lack of presence, in its lack of objective physicality. Even beyond this, the speed and omnipresence of the connection can blind one to the fact that the author/writer/friend is not physically accessible. We might think we are all connected, like an AT&T commercial, but on what level are we connecting? A handwritten letter reminds you of the writer's physical existence, and therefore reminds you of their physical absence; it reminds you that there is a critical, crucial component of their very nature which is not accessible to you; e-mail makes us forget the importance of physicality and plays into our modern belief in the importance of time.

Finally, for me, there is a subtle and terrible irony lurking within the Net: The Net, despite its speed, its exchange, ultimately reeks of stasis. In negating physical distance, the immediacy of electronic transfers devalues movement and the journey. In one minute a thought is in my head, and the next minute it is typed out, sent, read, and in your head. The exchange may be present, but the journey is imperceptible. The Infobahn hype would have us believe that this phenomenon is a fast-paced dynamic exchange, but the feeling, when you've been at it long enough, is that this exchange of ideas lacks movement. Lacking movement and the journey, to me it loses all value.

Maybe this is prejudice. Words are not wine, they do not necessarily require age to improve them. Furthermore, I have always hated the concept that Art comes only out of struggle and suffering. So, to say that e-mail words are weaker somehow because of the nature, or lack, of their journey, is to romanticize the struggle. I suppose I am anthropomorphizing text too much—but I somehow sense that one works harder to endow one's handwritten words with a certain strength, a certain soul, simply because those things are necessary in order to survive a journey. The ease of the e-mail journey means that your words don't need to be as well prepared, or as well equipped.

Electronic missives lack time, space, embodiment, and history (in the sense of a collection of experiences). Lacking all these things, an electronic missive is almost in complete opposition to my existence and I can't help but wonder what, if anything, I am communicating.

- ■ **CONSIDER THE SOURCE**

   1. What evidence does Kadi use to demonstrate the economic limitations of the global community? How do her comparisons with other technologies, such as television and car phones, contribute to her argument?
   2. Summarize the process by which J. Individual surfs the Net. What criteria

does Kadi say J. uses to determine which folders to read? How does she differentiate *h2so4*'s readers from J. Individual?

3. Explain Kadi's argument that "the context in which you exist defines the question, as much as it defines the answer." How does the "limited context" of this course shape the questions you are reading right now?

4. How does Kadi compare e-mail messages with handwritten letters? What does she believe accounts for the differences between them? What does she mean by the "leveling" and the "struggle" she describes?

▪ **CONSIDER THE IMPLICATIONS**

5. On the chalkboard, list the features of the online network that encourage access and those that inhibit access. Make a second pair of lists for printed material, such as books, magazines, and newspapers. On the basis of your lists, discuss the "democratizing of knowledge" that figures so prominently in descriptions of the Information Highway.

6. Review LynNell Hancock's description of the "Computer Gap" (pp. 198–202) in light of Kadi's article. Write a proposal to make the info-highway more democratic or to ensure that it remains open to all. Or, write a proposal to restrict online access to those with scholarly or business purposes.

7. Use Walt Crawford and Michael Gorman's essay (pp. 588–98) to explain Kadi's observations about the context of knowledge. Which category of "goods of the mind" best fits her examples about miners and rainfall?

8. Consider in your journal whether your schooling has taught you "how to ask a question" that would make information meaningful. Do you have the self-awareness that Kadi says is a prerequisite for using the Internet?

9. Review D. T. Max's discussion of the "cybervisionary" belief that "cyberspace will be a better kind of school" (pp. 546–57). How do Kadi's arguments about contexts for information complicate that vision of the future? Assuming Kadi's point of view, write a reply to Max explaining the role teachers and classrooms play in providing contexts.

10. Kadi claims that "people are drawn to topics and folders that interest them" when they choose among the thousands of online options. The same might be said about the millions of books and magazines available to readers. How would Bernard Berelson (pp. 322–30) respond to this argument? Write a reply to Kadi extending Berelson's discussion of books to the online world.

11. Call America Online, Prodigy, or a similar network service and obtain some of their ads and brochures. What claims do such commercial services make for the value of connectivity? Who do they seem to be appealing to, and how? Write an analysis of the advertising and promotional strategies used to encourage consumers to log onto the Net.

......
....

JOHN SEABROOK

My First Flame

*Some 100,000 new users travel the information superhighway each month,
lured by the dazzle of the network's power to connect people all over the
world. But the magic can quickly wear off, as* New Yorker *staff writer
John Seabrook (b. 1959) found the first time he got "flamed." The same
technology that allowed him to communicate freely and candidly with anyone else on the Net also permitted a disgruntled reader to send him an obscene message—and perhaps even a data-destroying worm. Every new
technology has its dark side. The lack of social barriers and inhibitions that
makes cyberspace an open and egalitarian society may also lead to anarchy
and abuse, especially when anonymity liberates people from the obligation
to be responsible for what they say. Seabrook uses the occasion of his first
flame to think seriously about the problems and prospects of online communication. He ponders the nature and power of language, the "netiquette"
that guides online behavior, the threat to authority posed by the Net's freedom, and the threat to individual freedom posed by efforts to control the
Net's anarchy. Seabrook writes regularly on technology and culture for*
The New Yorker. *The present essay is a revised version of a piece originally published in* The New Yorker's *"Brave New World Department."
It will form a part of his forthcoming personal narrative of life on the Internet, tentatively titled* E-Mail from Bill: Two Years Before the Modem
(to be published by Simon & Schuster in 1997).

I got flamed for the first time a couple of months ago. To flame, according to "Que's Computer User's Dictionary," is "to lose one's self-
control and write a message that uses derogatory, obscene, or inappropriate language." Flaming is a form of speech that is unique to online
communication, and it is one of the aspects of life on the Internet that its
promoters don't advertise, just as railroad companies around the turn of
the century didn't advertise the hardships of the Great Plains to the pioneers whom they were hoping to transport out there. My flame arrived
on a windy Friday morning. I got to work at nine, removed my coat,
plugged in my PowerBook, and, as usual, could not resist immediately
checking my e-mail. I saw I had a message from a technology writer
who does a column about personal computers for a major newspaper,
and whom I knew by name only. I had recently published a piece about
Bill Gates, the chairman of Microsoft, about whom this person has also
written, and as I opened his e-mail to me it was with the pleasant expectation of getting feedback from a colleague. Instead, I got:

From *The New Yorker* (6 June 1994), pp. 70–79.

Crave THIS, asshole:

Listen, you toadying dipshit scumbag ... remove your head from your rectum long enough to look around and notice that real reporters don't fawn over their subjects, pretend that their subjects are making some sort of special contact with them, or, worse, curry favor by TELLING their subjects how great the ass-licking profile is going to turn out and then brag in print about doing it.

Forward this to Mom. Copy Tina and tell her the mag is fast turning to compost. One good worm deserves another.

I rocked back in my chair and said out loud, "Whoa, I got flamed." I knew something bad had just happened to me, and I was waiting to find out what it would feel like. I felt cold. People whose bodies have been badly burned begin to shiver, and the flame seemed to put a chill in the center of my chest which I could feel spreading slowly outward. My shoulders began to shake. I got up and walked quickly to the soda machines for no good reason, then hurried back to my desk. There was the flame on my screen, the sound of it not dying away; it was flaming me all over again in the subjective eternity that is time in the online world. The insults, being premeditated, were more forceful than insults spoken in the heat of the moment, and the technology greased the words—the toads, scum, shit, rectums, assholes, compost, and worms—with a kind of immediacy that allowed them to slide easily into my brain.

Like many newcomers to the "Net"—which is what people call the global web that connects more than thirty thousand online networks—I had assumed, without really articulating the thought, that while talking to other people through my computer I was going to be sheltered by the same customs and laws that shelter me when I'm talking on the telephone or listening to the radio or watching TV. Now, for the first time, I understood the novelty and power of the technology I was dealing with. No one had ever said something like this to me before, and no one *could* have said this to me before: In any other medium, these words would be, literally, unspeakable. The guy couldn't have said this to me on the phone, because I would have hung up and not answered if the phone rang again, and he couldn't have said it to my face, because I wouldn't have let him finish. If this had happened to me in the street, I could have used my status as a physically large male to threaten the person, but in the online world my size didn't matter. I suppose the guy could have written me a nasty letter: He probably wouldn't have used the word "rectum," though, and he probably wouldn't have mailed the letter; he would have thought twice while he was addressing the envelope. But the nature of e-mail is that you don't think twice. You write and send.

When I got on the Net, it seemed to me like a place where all the good things about e-mail had been codified into an ideology. The first thing I fell for about the medium was the candor and the lack of cant it makes possible. Also, although the spoken word can be richer and warmer than the written word, the written word can carry precision and subtlety, and, especially online, has the power of anonymity. Crucial aspects of your identity—age, sex, race, education, all of which would be revealed involuntarily in a face-to-face meeting and in most telephone conversations—do not come through the computer unless you choose to reveal them. Many people use handles for themselves instead of their real names, and a lot of people develop personae that go along with those handles. (When they get tired of a particular persona, they invent a new handle and begin again.) On the Net, a bright twelve year old in a blighted neighborhood can exchange ideas with an Ivy League professor, and a businesswoman who is too intimidated by her male colleagues to speak up in a face-to-face meeting can say what she thinks. On the Net, people are judged primarily not by who they are but by what they write.

My flame marked the end of my honeymoon with online communication. It made me see clearly that the lack of social barriers is also what is appalling about the Net. The same anonymity that allows the twelve year old access to the professor allows a pedophile access to the twelve year old. The same lack of inhibitions that allows a woman to speak up in online meetings allows a man to ask the woman whether she's wearing any underwear. The same safe distance that allows you to unburden yourself of your true feelings allowed this guy to call me a toadying dipshit scumbag. A toadying dipshit scumbag! I sent e-mail to the people at CompuServe, which was the network that carried my flame to me, to ask whether their subscribers were allowed to talk to each other this way.

> To: John Seabrook
> Fr: Dawn
> Customer Service Representative
> Since CompuServe Mail messages are private communications, CompuServe is unable to regulate their content. We are aware of an occasional problem with unwanted mail and are investigating ways to control such occurrences. If you receive unwanted mail again, please notify us of the details so that we can continue to track this problem.

If the Net as a civilization does mature to the point where it produces a central book of wisdom, like the Bible or the Koran, the following true story might make a good parable. In 1982, a group of forty people associated with a research institute in La Jolla established a small, private online network for themselves. For about six months, the participants were caught up in the rapture of the new medium, until one day a member of the group began provoking the others with anonymous online taunts. Before long, the community was so absorbed in an attempt to identify the bad apple that constructive discourse ceased. The group posted many messages imploring whoever was doing this to stop, but the person didn't, and the community was destroyed. Stewart Brand, who is a founder of the WELL, an online service based in San Francisco, and who told me this story, said, "And not only did this break up the online community—it permanently affected the trust that those people had for each other in the face-to-face world, because they were never able to figure out who did it. To this day, they don't know which one of them it was."

What would Emily Post[1] advise me to do? Flame the dipshit scumbag right back? I did spend most of that Friday in front of the screen composing the most vile insults I could dream up—words I have never spoken to another human being, and would never speak in any other medium, but which I found easy to type into the computer. But I didn't send these messages, partly because I had no way of knowing for sure whether the person whose name was on the flame had actually sent it, and since this person was a respected author, with a reputation to consider, I thought someone might be electronically impersonating him, a practice that is known online as "spoofing." I managed to restrain myself from sending my reply until I got home and asked my wife to look at it. She had the good sense to be horrified, and suggested sending the message "Do you know where I could get a good bozo filter?" But I wasn't sure I had the stomach for a flame war, so I settled on a simple, somewhat lame acknowledgment of the flame:

> Thanks for your advice on writing and reporting. The great thing about the Internet is that a person like me can get useful knowledge from experts, and for free.

In a few days, I received a reply from the writer, asking when my new column, "Pudlicker to the Celebrated," was going to start.

I was in a quandary that many newcomers to the Net face. Newbies sometimes get flamed just because they are new, or because they use a commercial online service provider, like America Online or CompuServe, which shows up in their electronic addresses, just as Italian immigrants were jeered at because they had vowels at the ends of their names. Some people are so horrified by their first flame that they turn into "lurkers": They read other people's messages in the public spaces but are too timid to post themselves. (You see lots of evidence of the fear of getting flamed; for example, long posts that end, "Sorry so lengthy, please don't flame," and messages studded with smiley faces— :) — and grin signs— <g> —which remind you of the way that dogs have to go through elaborate displays of cringing around each other to avoid starting a fight.) For other newbies, getting flamed puts the taste of blood in their mouths, and they discover that they like it. They flame

---

1. **Emily Post** (1873–1960): Her handbook *Etiquette: The Blue Book of Social Usage* (1922) made her the authority on manners for half a century.—ED.

back, and then a flame war begins: People volley escalating rounds of insults across the wires. Now that there are an estimated twenty-three million users connected to the Internet—ten million of which have come online in the last nine months, in what amounts to a massive cultural upheaval, as though a whole generation of immigrants to the New World had come over all in one day—the "netiquette" that prevailed in its early days is breaking down. And many of the new users are not the government officials, researchers, and academics for whom the Net was designed; they're lawyers, journalists, teenagers, scam artists, lonely hearts, people in the pornography business, and the faddists who were buying CB radios in 1975.

On Saturday evening, some friends came over for dinner, and I told them about my flame. They asked to see it, so I went down the hall to print out a copy. But when I opened the electronic file where I store my e-mail I noticed that the title of my reply had turned into gibberish—where there had been letters there were little boxes and strange symbols—and that the dates for when the message was created and modified said "8/4/72" and "1/9/4." It occurred to me then to wonder briefly whether the person who flamed me had also sent some sort of virus into my computer, but I was cooking and didn't really have time to think about it, and when our guests left it was late, and I turned the computer off and went to bed. Just before six the following morning, however, I awoke abruptly and sat up in bed with a sudden understanding of what the last line in the flame—"One good worm deserves another"—might mean. A worm, in computerese, is one of the many varieties of viruses that infect computers. "One good worm deserves another": This guy had sent me a worm!

I got out of bed and went down the hall, turned on my computer, 10 opened my e-mail file, and saw with a shock that the corruption had spread to the title and dates of the message stored next to my reply. The reply itself was still corrupted, but the gibberish and weird dates had mutated slightly. I tried to delete the two corrupted messages, but the computer told me it couldn't read them. The icy feeling inside my chest was back. I copied the whole file onto a floppy disk, removed the disk from my computer, dragged the original file into the electronic trash can, emptied the trash, and then sat there regarding my computer with suspicion and fear. I had the odd sensation that my computer was my brain, and my brain was ruined, and I was standing over it looking down at the wreckage. In my excitement over the new medium, I had not considered that in going online I was placing my work and my most private musings only inches from a roaring highway of data (only the short distance, that is, between the hard disk and the internal modem of my computer), and, like most highways, it didn't care about me. After thinking about this for a while, I noticed I was sitting in the dark, so I got up and pulled the chain on the floor lamp, and the bulb blew out. I thought, Wait a second, if my computer is connected to the outlet, is it possible that the worm could have gone into the plug and through the wall circuit and come out in the light bulb?

The worm had entered my mind.

I waited for my computer to die. Even though I had removed the two corrupted messages, I was worried that the worm might have infected my hard disk. At my most paranoid, I imagined that I had received a "logic bomb," which is a virus that hides in your computer until a timing mechanism triggers it. (A few years ago, a rumor went around the Net that a lot of computers had been infected with a logic bomb that was set to go off on Bill Gates's birthday, October 28th, but the rumor turned out to be false.) I felt creepy sitting in front of my computer, as though I weren't sure whether it was my friend anymore. Every time my software did something peculiar that I couldn't remember its having done before, my heart turned over a little. I'd think, It's starting.

When I tried to explain this feeling to a noncomputer-using friend of mine, she said, "Yeah, it's like when someone breaks into your car," but actually it was more like someone had broken into my head. I sent e-mail to my computer-literate friend Craig Canine, a writer and farmer who lives in Iowa, asking what he knew about worms, and he e-mailed me back:

> Coincidentally, I just gave our goats their worm medicine. It's called Valbazen, and it seems to work pretty well for ruminants—I'm not sure about computers, though. What does this worm do? Should I be communicating with you—might your e-mail be a carrier? Jesus, I've got my book on my hard disk. If your worm zaps it, I'll kill you first, then go after the evil perp, (then plead insanity, with cause).

I was a pariah.

On the Wednesday following my flaming, I took my floppy disk to work to show it to Dan Henderson, who set up the network here at the magazine. Every office where computers are networked together has a guy like Dan around, who is usually the only person who really understands the system, and is terrifically overworked, because in addition to doing his job he has to deal with all the people like me, who are mystified by their computers. Shelley said that poets are the unacknowledged legislators of the world; system administrators are the unacknowledged legislators of the Net. Sysadmins are really the only authority figures that exist on the Net. In small electronic communities, the sysadmin often owns the equipment that the community runs on—a personal computer, a modem, and a telephone line are all you need to run your own bulletin board—and therefore he has absolute power over what goes on in the community. If a sysadmin wants to read someone's mail, he reads it. If he wants to execute someone, electronically speaking—by kicking that person off the network—he doesn't need to hold a trial. A benevolent sysadmin can make the network a utopia, and a malevolent sysadmin can quickly turn it into a police state.

I sent Dan a QuickMail, which is the brand of interoffice e-mail we use, and told him that I thought my computer might have been infected with some sort of worm. I asked if he had time to see me, expecting that maybe he'd get to me before the end of the week. I was surprised when Dan appeared in my doorway within ten minutes.

"You QuickMailed me," he said. I noticed he was looking at me strangely.

"Yes . . ."

"You sent me QuickMail."

I was slow getting his drift. "So?"

Then I got it. "Wait. You mean you think I infected *The New Yorker*'s 20 network?" Dan was just looking at me, his eyebrows up around his hairline. "But I took the worm off my hard disk and put it on here," I said defensively, holding up the floppy disk.

Dan has that intense energy you often see in guys who are really into computers; the speed at which he talks and moves always makes me think of the clatter of fingers over the keyboard. He sat down at my computer with a couple of different kinds of software that looks for worms and viruses. After about ten minutes of probing my hard disk, he announced that he couldn't find any evidence of infection. He checked the floppy and found nothing there, either. The gibberish and weird dates had gone away.

Dan explained that I could not have received a worm via e-mail, because worms are programs; most e-mail carries only text. A file containing a program can be sent over e-mail, but in order for it to infect your computer you'd almost certainly have to open the file and run the program. I could see he thought I was somewhat insane. This was not technical thinking. It was literary thinking I was applying to machines in a desperate hope to make sense of something I didn't understand.

Was it possible that my worm was just some weird software glitch I had never seen before, and that it just happened to choose my reply to the flame to make its first appearance, and that the line "One good worm deserves another" was just a coincidence? After thinking about this for a couple of days, I came up with a little experiment. My hypothesis was that perhaps the worm could have burrowed into the program I was using to set up a reply to the original message, and my experiment was to perform the reply operation again, in order to see if the worm would come back.

The next morning, my new reply and the message stored next to it 25 were corrupted again. I tried to print out the gibberish, but again the machine couldn't read the characters, so I copied them down. I also got my wife's camera and took a picture of my computer screen. Then I called Dan at home.

"Dan? This is John. Dan, my worm is back. I'm looking at it now."

Dan was polite about it, but he made a sound that suggested he did not consider himself my sysadmin right now, at ten o'clock on a Saturday morning, and said, "Could we talk about this on Monday?"

I wanted to talk about my flame with someone else who had been flamed, but I didn't know anyone in my real-world life who had been. Then it occurred to me that I could use the Net. This is one of the great things about the Net: The spaces are organized around topics, so it's easy to find people who think like you and who share your interests. People who gather on the Net to discuss a specific topic are called newsgroups, and each newsgroup has its own "site." In a literal sense a site is just a small amount of storage space in a computer somewhere in the world, which you can reach by typing its address, but it feels like an actual room. So, for example, if you think you might be a pagan, but you're still in the closet, you can go to the newsgroup "alt.pagan" for enlightenment. When you arrive there, the best thing to do first is to read the FAQ, the list of Frequently Asked Questions. FAQ files are more than the prosaic things they sound like; they are the repositories of the useful knowledge that has been exchanged and meaningful events that have occurred in that particular site since it was established. The table of contents for the alt.pagan FAQ reads:

1. What is this group for?
2. What is paganism/a pagan?
2b. What is Paganism? How is it different from paganism?
3. What are different types of paganism?
4. What is Witchcraft/Wicca?
4b. Why do some of you use the word Witch? Wiccan?
5. What are some different traditions in the Craft?
6. Are pagans Witches?
7. Are you Satanists?
8. What kinds of people are pagans?
9. What holidays do you celebrate?
9b. How do I pronounce . . . ? What does this name mean?
10. What god(s) do you believe in?
11. Can one be both Christian and pagan?
12. What were the Burning Times?
13. How many pagans/Witches are there today?
14. Why isn't it soc.religion.paganism instead of alt.pagan?
15. Is brutal honesty or polite conversation the preferred tone of conversation around here?

16. What are the related newsgroups?

17. Are there any electronic mailing lists on this subject?

18. I'm not a pagan; should I post here?

19. How does one/do I become a pagan?

20. What books/magazines should I read?

21. How do I find pagans/Witches/covens/teachers in my area?

22. What's a coven really like?

23. How do I form a coven?

24. What does Dianic mean?

25. Aren't women-only circles discriminatory?

26. Can/will you cast me a love spell/curse my enemies?

27. Is it okay if I . . . ? Will I still be a pagan if I . . . ?

28. I am a pagan and I think I am being discriminated against because of my religion. What should I do?

29. What one thing would most pagans probably want the world to know about them?

Then you can scroll through a list of hundreds of discussion topics and see what people are talking about. Some are:

14. European paganism (16 msgs)

15. Statement (6 msgs)

16. College Pagan Groups

17. PAGAN FEDERATION GIG: Thanks (3 msgs)

18. Broom Closet Pagans Hurt Us All (3 msgs)

19. Pagan funerals? (27 msgs)

20. NIGGER JOKES (18 msgs)

21. Necromancy (2 msgs)

22. Another campus Pagan group (4 msgs)

23. When the Revolution comes was Re: New Forest Service . . . (6 msgs)

24. Looking for invocations to the following . . . (4 msgs)

25. New Community Pagan Group? Need help.

I suppose you could choose not to double-click on NIGGER JOKES, but 30 it's harder than you think. This is the biggest drawback of the way newsgroups are set up: A really interesting post that enriches your understanding of a subject is next to a post that is appropriate only for the space above the urinal. There's nothing to stop someone in alt.misanthropy or alt.tasteless from coming into rec.pets.cats and posting a graphic account of what it's like to behead a cat or drink its blood, and although you can bozo-filter that person after his first post, so that you never have to read a message from him again, the horrible words tend to stay in your memory for a long time.

NIGGER JOKES turns out to be a collection of racist jokes and limericks about killing African Americans, which was posted on April 5th. The name and address on the jokes is that of a student at the University of Michigan. The post has been "spammed," as they say on the Net, which means that the student has spread it around to many different newsgroups, thus ensuring himself an audience of hundreds of thousands, and maybe millions, since the jokes are still making their way through the Net. (Some employees of Fortune 500 companies have recently reported finding the jokes on their office networks.)

When someone posts a message that offends the other participants in a newsgroup, the group metes out the only punishment at its disposal, which is to flame the offender, and in this case the student who posted the jokes has been getting flames by the thousand. Also, in typical Net fashion, there has been much soul-searching in the newsgroups about the character of the Net itself:

> The Last Viking<paalde@stud.cs.uit.no>
> We don't have to go around being racists like those fascists in the real world! PEACE ON THE NET!!!!

> Michael Halleen <halleen@MCS.COM>
> As offensive as this is, I do not believe this should put this person "under investigation." . . . He should get hate mail, censure (not censors), and universal condemnation. There should be open debate and discussion, but leave his right to speak alone. He may use the net for other constructive purposes and taking it away may hurt him, and he needs help.

> Richard Darsie<darsie@eecs.ucdavis.edu>
> Get a grip, man. Free speech is *not* and never has been an *absolute* right. There's gotta be some limits. . . . This person abused his First Amendment rights and should face some consequences for it. Can't have rights without responsibilities.

An investigation at the University of Michigan recently concluded that the student whose name was on the posts hadn't made them; someone had spoofed him. The wrongly accused and now flame-broiled student had used a university-owned computer to log on to his account, and someone had tampered with the software in that computer so that it captured his password. This person had then logged on in the student's name and posted the jokes. The day after the jokes went up, another student, who had used the same computer to log on, discovered that his identity had been used to send a message to the Islamic Circle, a campus organization, calling its members "God-forsaken terrorists."

I went to alt.flame, thinking this might be the site where people talk about flaming, but it turned out to be a place where people go to flame each other. I saw that an intrepid writer from *Wired* magazine, Amy Bruckman, had posted that she was writing an article about flaming and was getting flamed for doing it.

> Insert finger in appropriate orafice and shove off.

> Sod off bitch, we don't need your glamour here. . . .

> WHAT?!? Do you think I wanted to be publicated in your low-life-scum magazine??? . . . BTW, what kind of name is Bruckman? Are you kind of a German refugees' daughter from the 2nd world war? Kraut? a sauceage woman? Anyway go to hell.

I decided not to post in alt.flame myself.

I considered posting a query about my worm in the newsgroup comp.virus, and I lurked around there for a while, but didn't post, because I was worried that my assailant might hear that I was posting queries about him in public spaces—it's difficult to keep secrets on the Net—and devise some even more elaborate torture to inflict on my computer, or begin spoofing me in some diabolical fashion. I had already seen how the Net could be used to hurt someone's reputation. One day, as I was wandering around inside the Electronic Frontier Foundation discussion space, which is one of the most interesting newsgroups on the Net, I came upon a subject line that said, "Ralph Berkeley made homosexual advances toward me." Ralph Berkeley (I'm not using his real name) is a regular participant in discussions of Net policy, who appears, on the evidence of his posts, to be an articulate and thoughtful man, and often takes the position that completely unrestricted free speech on the net might not be such a good idea—a position that causes him to receive his share of flames. However, this post upped the ante a bit:

> Ralph Berkeley made homosexual advances toward me when I visited him at his office approximately two weeks ago. As I went there just to chat with him and he's not my employer or anything I don't think I have any grounds for any legal action or anything like that. But I must say that prior to that event I had a lot of respect for him (not necessarily his opinions, but the even-handed way in which he stated them). I am really disappointed.

This brought forth even more furious bursts of thinking and feeling over the nature of the Net:

> Dik T. Winter<dik@cwi.nl>
> I think Ralph Berkeley has enough grounds for a suit on defamation of character. Ralph, I urge you, *do* sue. I do not agree with you but please, *do* sue.

> Jim Thomas<tkOjut1@mp.cs.niu.edu>
> No. Although we all assume the original post was homophobic sleaze, a suit is even more offensive. Such a suit itself constitutes "fag

bashing," because it continues the stigmatizing of gays by suggesting that homosexuality is abnormal or pathological.

Then, in the best spirit of the Net, Dr. Berkeley posted this reply:

> Thanks to readers whose responses showed such good sense. Of course it's false.
> Ralph

Everywhere I went in the newsgroups, I found flames, and fear of flames. In the absence of rules, there is a natural tendency toward anarchy on the Net anyway, and in some stretches I'd come upon sites that were in complete chaos, where people had been flaming each other nonstop, absolutely scorching everything around them, and driving all the civilized people away. Sometimes I'd arrive at a dead site long after a flame war broke out; it was like walking through what was once a forest after a wildfire. Sometimes I came upon voices that were just howling at the world; you could feel the rage and savagery pouring out through people's fingers and into the Net. Of course, you can hear this sound on the streets of New York City, but less often than you hear it on the Net, and in the city it lasts only as long as the person who is making it has breath for it and is heard only by the people within earshot. On the Net, it can be heard by millions and reverberate for a long time.

Sometimes I returned from these trips on the Net feeling lonely, cold, and depressed. I would see the Net less from the point of view of the acrobat and more from the point of view of the fish. Ironically, the Net seemed most alive to me when I was off it and found myself using a word I had picked up in my travels. The Net is a hotbed of language, because on the Net language has to accomplish everything; the whole world is made of words, and people are constantly forced to coin new ones. And, because typing takes more effort than speaking, people are always inventing acronyms or abbreviations—"lol" for "laughed out loud," "f2f" for "face to face," "BTW" for "by the way," "RTFM" for "Read the Fucking Manual," which is a message people often send back to you when you ask them for technical help. There's something wonderful about all this, but it's also sad to go to a chat group and see the "lol"s scrolling by on the screen, sometimes with no other words attached to them, just people typing "lol" to each other. How much of the pleasure of laughter can you get sitting alone with your computer, typing "lol"?

I sent a copy of my flame to someone I know only as Jennifer, a 40 woman I met on the Net and feel I know in a strange way, although in fact I know hardly anything about her. She replied:

> I must say that I was shocked to read about your experience. . . . The magnitude of your assailant's tirade rends my heart. I have been thinking about those graphic words, unbidden, for the last two days.

Here was another good thing about the Net—that a woman I didn't even know would be so concerned for me. I wrote to Jennifer that the net seemed to me in some ways a cold place, and she replied:

> You are right about the coldness of the net. There is an air of preestablished hierarchy there—if you're new to the net, or even to a particular group on the net, you don't belong a priori. As a woman, I have encountered an additional barrier; the net is heavily male and women who want to play with the big boys either have to be ultra tough-talking—one of the boys—or else play off as coy, charming, "little-ol'ME?"-feminine. (Even geeks have fantasy lives, I suppose.) Or use a male/neutral alias with no one the wiser.
>
> So part of the boy's club, I imagine, is the smallness, the selectivity—the geek elite, if you will. For more than a decade these guys had their own secret tin-can-on-a-string way to communicate and socialize, as obscure as ham radio but no pesky FCC requirements and much, much cooler.... But then the Internet—their cool secret—started to get press.... Imagine these geeks, suddenly afraid that their magic treehouse was about to be boarded by American pop culture. It was worse than having your favorite obscure, underground album suddenly appear on the Billboard charts.

As my assailant had suggested, I also forwarded a copy of the flame to my mother, whom I had got wired for e-mail. She replied:

> I deleted that thing you sent me immediately. What a terrible man. He must have been drunk....

One day at work, I asked Dan Henderson if he knew of someone I could go to for the final word on my worm—the top worm man in the country, as it were—and he gave me the e-mail address of John Norstad, at Northwestern University. Norstad is the author of Disinfectant, a popular brand of virus-protection software for the Macintosh, and probably knows as much as anyone in the world about the viruses and worms that affect Macs. I sent him e-mail saying I would be coming out to Chicago in a couple of weeks on business and wondered if I could have him examine my PowerBook. Norstad promptly e-mailed me back to say that he was in the midst of fighting a new virus that had just broken out in Italy, and didn't have time to think about my problem now, but would be happy to see me when I came to Chicago.

We arranged, through e-mail, to meet at the Palmer House, where I was staying. Because my only contact with Norstad had been online, I had no clue what sort of man to expect, and as I waited for him in my room I tried to imagine what he would be like. I realized that I was envisioning Norstad not as a Western doctor but as a kind of tribal medicine man. Whether the corrupted messages in my computer were the result of a real worm or were caused by a software glitch, all my troubles seemed to be related to the general wizardry of software—the mysterious incantations of ones and zeros being whispered inside my computer. I felt as if someone had put a spell on my computer, and I was bringing it to John Norstad to have him heal it.

Norstad turned out to be about forty-five, not tall, with a beard that had some gray in it, glasses, and a shy, polite manner. He wore a flannel jacket over a loose gray shirt, and gray pants. He was carrying a Power-Book loaded with the dominant strains of all the nastiest viruses known to the Macintosh world; the viruses were safely corralled on his hard disk with Disinfectant, which he distributes free on the Net to anyone who wants it. Norstad set his PowerBook next to my PowerBook and showed me his collection of infected programs. He moved his cursor over and pointed it at an icon, double-clicked on it, and said, "Now, if I didn't have any protection this little guy would start erasing my hard drive right . . . now. But because we do—there, see . . . Disinfectant caught it." It was awesome.

I asked Norstad about the Italian virus he had been fighting when I first e-mailed him, and he said that it had appeared in an item of software posted on a bulletin board in late February. Because the software was copyrighted, and had been posted on the board illegally, there was some suspicion that the virus writer was trying to teach the pirates a lesson about copyright infringement. Norstad opened the e-mail log in his PowerBook and showed me the hundreds of messages he had sent and received between February 28th, when he received e-mail from three people in Italy which said that a new virus was erasing people's hard disks, and March 3d, when he and his colleagues produced vaccines. Upon hearing about the Italian outbreak, Norstad had immediately sent e-mail to a group of colleagues called the Zoo Keepers, a sort of online volunteer fire squad, to alert them to the existence of the new virus. The Zoo Keepers are a virtual community that live all over the globe—Australia, Germany, the United States—and could exist only because of the Net. Norstad received a copy of the virus from Italy, made copies, and sent the copies out over the Net to the Zoo Keepers. Keeping in touch over the Net, the scientists reverse-engineered the virus and a number of effective vaccines for it. Norstad then updated Disinfectant—version 3.3 became 3.4—and posted it around the Net, where people could download it for free. All this took fifty-six hours.

I asked whether virus writers were often motivated by politics, and Norstad said no, they were mostly relatively harmless hackers, at least in the Mac world. In the world of IBM-compatible machines, which is much larger than the Mac world, there are many more viruses, and they tend to be deadlier. They are the stuff of legend. Norstad told me of an account he had once heard from a Bulgarian virus expert, about software engineers commissioned by the Communist government to crack the security seals on Western software. When the regime fell, the story goes, the unemployed engineers were said to have whiled away their empty hours writing viruses for IBM compatibles.

I asked, "Is it possible that a terrorist could take down a large part of a country's computer systems with a virus?"

"It's possible. Of course, the problem with a virus that virulent is, How do they keep it from infecting their own system?"

I told Norstad the story of my worm, and asked whether it was possible for a technically sophisticated person such as I believed my assailant to be to send a worm through e-mail.

Norstad said it was not possible. "I will say that the kind of symptoms you describe could be a software problem."

"Like what?" I asked.

"Who knows?" Norstad said. "It's software. It's weird stuff. People are always writing and calling me because they think they have some kind of virus, and in almost every case it's a software problem, not a virus—but these people are fearful and need my help. For example, quite a few people have written me to say a shrieking death's head appears occasionally in the top of their screens. You know what it is? If you have Apple's Remote Access program, hold down the option key, and hit the shift key three times, your computer makes this funny trilling sound and an object appears in the corner of your screen that could, if you were sufficiently paranoid, look like a death's head. It's not a virus. It's just a weird software thing."

While Norstad was talking, I brought my flame up onto the screen and asked him to look at it. He leaned toward me and silently read through the litany of insults. When he had finished, he sat back and sighed and didn't speak for a couple of seconds. Then he said, "I'm just so sorry when something like this happens." He lowered his head and shook it sadly. "Gee, that's terrible."

I said, "I have to admit it was upsetting. I've been thinking about it a lot. I ask myself, Do I recognize the right of this person to flame me? Yes, I do. Do I celebrate his right to flame me? I'm not sure. Do I recognize the right of this person to send me a worm? Definitely not. But at what point does a flame become a worm? I mean, can a virus be a form of free speech? In other words, could a combination of words be so virulent and nasty that it could do a sort of property damage to your head?"

I was rambling, and I could actually feel tears coming into my eyes, so I stopped there. But Norstad seemed to understand what I was talking about, and I felt better after I had told him. I realized that I would probably never know for sure whether my worm was real or just a software glitch. We chatted for a while longer, and then he said, "Don't get discouraged. The Net is a fundamentally wonderful place. Most of this work I do could be done only on the Net. Look at the work we did on the Italian virus, working with colleagues all over the world to reverse-engineer it. Can you imagine trying to do this by fax? Phone? Fed Ex? It would not be possible." He unplugged his PowerBook and began packing it up. "Of course," he said "the Net allows people to spread viruses much more easily than before."

"But that's the thing about the Net," I said. "Each of the good things about it seems to have an evil twin."

"Yes, but you could say that about all new technology," Norstad said. "There is always going to be a dark side to it. That is why it's so important to be decent on the Net, because the dark side is always right there."

▪ CONSIDER THE SOURCE

1. What are the attractions and drawbacks of the Net's anonymity, according to Seabrook? How does the physical separation from language alter the usual relations between people?

2. How does Seabrook define "spoofing," and how does it complicate online relationships?

3. List all the words, phrases, and acronyms that Seabrook defines in his article. How does he account for the new terminology? What terms doesn't he define for his reader, and what does that tell you about who he assumes his reader to be?

▪ CONSIDER THE IMPLICATIONS

4. "On the Net," writes Seabrook, "people are judged primarily not by who they are but by what they write." In class discussion, explore the pros and cons of this aspect of online communication. Who is best served by such a leveling of social distinctions?

5. Seabrook says that his flame ended his "honeymoon" with the new technology. Have you ever had your trust in technology shattered in the way Seabrook describes? Perhaps you've received an obscene phone call. Or maybe somebody has used computer banking systems to tamper with your credit or obtain charge cards in your name. In your journal, explore your own romance with a particular kind of technology other than the computer.

6. Seabrook's friend Jennifer claims that the "geek elite" of the computer world are predominantly male, while Gloria Steinem (pp. 277–303) describes electronics manufacturers' reluctance to advertise in *Ms.* magazine. Based on your own comparison of women's and men's magazines, write an essay assessing how wide the gender gap really is with reference to computers. Which magazines contain more ads and reviews of computers and related products? Whom do the ads target? If computers are marketed more to men, what do you think is responsible for that gap and how can women join the club? If not, what do you think contributes to the prevailing impression that computers are a male domain?

7. Review M. Kadi's comparison of the relative "strength" of e-mail and handwritten words (pp. 598–608). Discuss her critique in light of Seabrook's remarks about the faceless, voiceless interaction of the Net. Do you think online communication will improve our ability to write? Why do you think emoticons or "smileys" have developed so quickly? Do they increase or decrease our ability to convey nuances of emotion?

8. Compare Seabrook's reaction to his flame to the attitude toward viruses of the hackers who participated in *Harper's* forum (pp. 509–28). Are flames and viruses invasions of privacy? Are they free speech that should be protected? Write an essay arguing your views on computers and the First Amendment.

9. In small groups, discuss the "customs and laws" that Seabrook relied on to shelter him from insults like those he received in his flame. Why did those conventions fail in the online environment? Based on Seabrook's article and any online experience you may have had, compile your own etiquette book for online communication.

▪ ▪ ▪ ▪ ▪

AMY HARMON

Bigots on the Net

It seems that everybody's getting onto the Net—including white suprema-cists. Los Angeles Times *reporter Amy Harmon (b. 1968) writes of the growing number of hate groups using inexpensive online communications to recruit members, disseminate propaganda, and raise funds. Outraged by the spread of bigotry, many people are calling for restrictions to online communication. The future of cyberspace is at stake: Should it remain a de-mocratic forum, providing open access to anyone, regardless of their politi-cal views, or should the government police the Internet to regulate poten-tially dangerous activities? Harmon has written about cyberpunk author William Gibson, the digital video format war, and the next generation in VCR technology, among other aspects of new media and technology.*

Alarmed by the growing presence of hate groups in cyberspace, the Simon Wiesenthal Center[1] Tuesday sent a letter to the Prodigy online computer service protesting the "continued use of Prodigy by bigots to promote their agendas of hate."

The Los Angeles-based center said it has tracked increasing activity over the last few months by more than fifty hate groups using online services and the popular Internet global computer network. "More and more of these groups are embracing and utilizing the information super-

---

From *Los Angeles Times,* 14 December 1994, A1, A34–35.

1. **Simon Wiesenthal Center:** Founded in 1978, the Simon Wiesenthal Center educates today's generation about the Holocaust, and fights the hatred and preju-dice that enabled the Holocaust to occur.—ED.

highway," said Rabbi Abraham Cooper, associate dean of the center. "The slurs are the same but the venue is different."

The center called on commercial online services to keep hate groups out and proposed that the government play a similar policing role on the amorphous Internet. Of particular concern, Cooper said, is that young people could be exposed to white supremacy in an environment unmediated by teachers, parents, or librarians. Much of the activity takes place on open electronic forums accessible to anyone with an Internet account or a subscription to a commercial service.

About twenty million computer users are connected to the Internet, and another five million use commercial online services, including more than two million on Prodigy.

But civil libertarians—and white supremacists themselves—say that cyberspace, like any other medium of expression, must remain open to free speech. And in an uncharted territory where the rules of engagement are still unformed, the center's offensive is sure to sharpen the ongoing debate over electronic censorship.

"It's a genuinely difficult problem," says Marc Rotenberg, director of the Electronic Privacy Information Center, an online civil liberties organization. "And there are no paradigms to turn to."

It's a problem that is quickly becoming relevant to a lot more people. All sorts of enterprises, from businesses to charity organizations, have been rushing to get hooked up to computer networks, which offer fast, convenient communication at increasingly lower prices.

But for white supremacist groups like the National Alliance and the American Renaissance, cyberspace offers benefits that are proportionately far greater.

Marginalized by traditional media and short on funds, hate groups have been learning to use low-cost online communications to gain recruits and spread propaganda across state and even national boundaries, giving them access to a far wider audience than they have historically been able to reach.

Valerie Fields, for example, a West Los Angeles resident and political junkie, signs on to her Prodigy account a few times a week to read the discussion of local politics. Last month, she clicked her way into the "News" forum to find an anti-Latino diatribe that closed with a plug for a $20 subscription to the newsletter of Louisville, Kentucky-based American Renaissance.

"Around the election the messages about [Proposition] 187[2] got pretty nasty," Fields said. "But then I saw this one that seemed to be from an organized white supremacist group, and that really freaked me out."

---

2. **Proposition 187**: A controversial California ballot measure that denied schooling, medical care, and other governmental services to illegal immigrants.—ED.

The message Fields saw, and several others, including one that referred to *The Diary of Anne Frank* as a "Jewish hoax" prompted the Wiesenthal Center to ask Prodigy to strengthen its guidelines to delete such messages from its boards.

"We're having a discussion with them," Prodigy spokesman Brian Ek said Tuesday afternoon. "Our feeling is we already have a good system in place. But we have more than 1.7 million notes on the board at any given time, and we can't read them all."

Prodigy was the focus of controversy involving antisemitic comments in 1991, and worked with the Anti-Defamation League at the time to craft a policy that forbids "blatant expressions of hatred" on its boards. All messages are also run through a computer that scans for obscenities before they are posted. But Cooper says the service should look more carefully at messages that target groups rather than individuals.

Prodigy is not the only online service to be utilized by hate groups. 15

Kevin Strom, who produces a weekly radio show for the National Alliance, and has been active online, said he was recently blocked from the "Political" and "Issues" forums on CompuServe.

"Apparently somebody complained that our articles were bashing ethnic minorities," Strom says. "So the system operator decided we didn't deserve freedom of speech."

Strom says the articles he posted on the forums were among those which users transferred most frequently to their home computers. One titled "The Wisdom of Henry Ford," which reviewed the book *The International Jew,* was downloaded 120 times one week, he said.

CompuServe leaves the decision of what to screen out to the individual "sysops" who are hired to moderate the service's discussion forums. Says Georgia Griffith, the Politics sysop: "We don't block users for what they believe or say, but how they say it. The First Amendment allows people to publish what they choose, but we are not obliged to publish it for them."

The legal issue of who is ultimately responsible for what does get 20
"published" online is a thorny one that has yet to be entirely resolved.

A federal judge ruled in 1991 that CompuServe was like a bookstore owner who could not be held accountable for the contents of books on his shelves—a precedent the online services support.

But activists say there are ethical issues at stake, which public opinion can help to enforce—at least in the private sector.

The Internet, a web of several hundred computer networks not owned by any one enterprise, is a more difficult proposition. Cooper wrote a letter to Federal Communications Chairman Reed E. Hundt last summer suggesting that it "may be time for the FCC to place a cop on the Superhighway of Information."

But such an effort would involve significant technical difficulties, and would also likely encounter vehement opposition from civil liberties groups who want to preserve the Internet as a democratic forum.

Because of its anarchic structure, the Internet has generally been 25 viewed as a "common carrier" much like the telephone company, which cannot be held liable for what passes over its lines.

"That would be a very dangerous path to go down," says EPIC's Rotenberg. "It would lead to an extraordinary amount of censorship and control that would be very inappropriate."

Discussion groups geared toward white supremacist propaganda on the Internet have labels such as "skinheads," "revisionism" and "vigilantes." The Institute for Historical Review recently set up a site on the World Wide Web portion of the Internet, where some of its literature can be obtained for free. A document called "Frequently Asked Questions about National Socialism" is available at several sites.

The computer commands used on the Internet also allow users to access information anonymously, which far-right activists say helps many to overcome the inhibitions they might have about signing up.

The National Alliance rents space on a computer at Netcom Online Communication Services, one of the largest Internet access providers in California, where texts of its radio programs are available. It has also posted flyers on the Internet promoting its radio show, urging readers to send "minority parasites packing to fend for themselves" and condemning community development funding as support for black "breeding colonies."

"We've seen a huge growth in use of the Internet by our people," 30 says Alliance Chairman William Pierce. "The major media in this country are very biased against our political point of view. They present us with ridicule or in a very distorted way. The information superhighway is much more free of censorship. It's possible for a dedicated individual to get his message out to thousands and thousands of people."

▪ CONSIDER THE SOURCE

1. How are the benefits of cyberspace greater for marginalized political groups than for other groups, according to Harmon?

2. What responsibility does Harmon say that Prodigy or CompuServe have for the messages distributed on its services? How do the analogies with bookstores and telephone companies clarify or complicate the issue of liability?

3. Look closely at how Harmon characterizes the National Alliance and similar groups and at the examples she offers of their online messages. How does she gear her article for readers of the *Los Angeles Times*?

▪ CONSIDER THE IMPLICATIONS

4. Those who advocate restricting online communications point to the problem of unmediated access to the Net by children. Racism, bigotry, and even pornography are accessible by anyone with an Internet address, and

several recent cases have been reported of young teens lured away from their homes by "friends" they met online. In small groups, discuss this problem and try to propose solutions.

5. As Joan DelFattore (pp. 440–49) and William Noble (pp. 449–56) describe in their articles about censoring school textbooks, many people worry that exposure to an idea will lead to endorsement of that idea. The same fear of exposure to ideas comes up in discussions of cyberspace. In class, debate whether the arguments about print censorship extend to the world of cyberspace. Are there significant differences that are created by the technology? Or, is the computer the equivalent of the printing press?

6. William Pierce, chairman of the National Alliance, claims that the mainstream media have been biased in their presentation of his white supremacist group. In your library, find some articles in mainstream magazines about such groups and evaluate his claim. Do you agree that the presentations are biased? Do they distort or ridicule the groups' messages?

7. John Seabrook (pp. 609–25) and Amy Harmon both raise the issue of freedom of speech on the Net. But just how far should First Amendment protection extend? Does it include hate speech? Viruses? How can we enforce responsibility for speech in an environment that easily permits not only anonymity but impersonation? Write an essay exploring some of the challenges to free speech posed by the Net and proposing guidelines for online communication.

8. According to far-right activists cited by Harmon, the anonymity offered by the Internet helps people "overcome the inhibitions they might have" about accessing information. Steven Starker makes much the same point in his article about self-help books (pp. 404–13). Using Starker's criteria for the genre's success, write an essay comparing the information superhighway with self-help books. Do you think online connectivity will replace grocery-store self-help books? Or, will they serve different audiences?

WHO PUBLISHES WHAT?

A Guide to Sources of the Selections in The Press of Ideas

This alphabetically arranged section presents brief introductions to each magazine, newspaper, and publishing house represented by the selections in this book. Information about the original site of publication can suggest important aspects of each selection's relation to its audience. Taken as a whole, this appendix also offers a glimpse of the structure and market-driven nature of the publishing world—the influence of individual editors and publishers, the intensity of competition among publications, the effect of mergers and corporate takeovers. As such, "Who Publishes What?" can serve as a kind of bridge between what's in this book and the larger world of publishing.

American Library Association, Publishing Services, 50 East Huron Street, Chicago, IL 60611; telephone 312/944–6780.

[Publisher of Walt Crawford and Michael Gorman, "Coping with Electronic Information"]

The American Library Association (ALA), the oldest and largest national library association in the world, was founded in 1876 in Philadelphia by a group of about one hundred librarians. The organization was incorporated in 1879, and in 1909 its headquarters were established in Chicago. According to the ALA Policy Manual, the association's mission is "to provide leadership for the development, promotion, and improvement of library and information services and the profession of librarianship in order to enhance learning and ensure access to information for all." The ALA has had a Publishing Services program, concerned primarily with the publication of materials for libraries and librarians, since 1886.

The Anti-Slavery Office

[Publisher of Frederick Douglass, "Learning Reading, Learning Freedom"]

The Anti-Slavery Office, publisher of Frederick Douglass's *Narrative of the Life of Frederick Douglass, An American Slave,* emerged from the nineteenth-century abolition, or anti-slavery, movement in the United States. In 1832 the forceful newspaperman and abolitionist William Lloyd Garrison joined with others to found the New England Anti-Slavery Society. The following year this New England group joined with reformers from New York and Quakers from Philadelphia to establish a national organization, the American Anti-Slavery Society, at a convention in Philadelphia.

The Anti-Slavery Society hoped to achieve its goal of the abolition of slavery through establishing state organizations, arranging public speakers, and publishing anti-slavery tracts and periodicals (such as Garrison's *Liberator,* which began publication in 1831). Thus, the eloquent escaped slave Frederick Douglass was hired as a lecturer by the Massachusetts Anti-Slavery Society; in this capacity he traveled as an abolitionist speaker throughout New York, Indiana, Ohio, Pennsylvania, Vermont, and elsewhere from 1842 to 1844. By 1844, anti-abolitionist critics had begun to attack Douglass's credibility, arguing that he did not look or sound anything like an escaped slave. Hoping to defeat charges of fraud, the leadership of the Massachusetts Anti-Slavery Society encouraged Douglass to write the story of his life.

The *Narrative of the Life of Frederick Douglass, An American Slave,* published in the spring of 1845, included prefaces by William Lloyd Garrison and another abolitionist leader, Wendell Phillips. It immediately became a best-seller, both in the United States and Europe; within five years its sales had exceeded 30,000 copies.

Atlantic Monthly, 745 Boylston Street, Boston, MA 02116; telephone 617/536–9500.

[Publisher of Zitkala-Ša, "The Civilizing Machine"; D. T. Max, "The End of the Book?"]

In 1857 abolitionist and writer Francis H. Underwood, along with writer James Russell Lowell, approached Moses Dresser Phillips of the publishing firm of Phillips, Sampson and Company in Boston about a magazine that the two wanted to found. They could count on contributions to this magazine from a strong group of New England writers, including Henry Wadsworth Longfellow, Ralph Waldo Emerson, Oliver

Wendell Holmes, John Greenleaf Whittier, and Harriet Beecher Stowe. Phillips agreed to publish the magazine, and the first issue of the *Atlantic Monthly* appeared in November 1857. The magazine was named by Oliver Wendell Holmes.

The *Atlantic Monthly* was begun as an anti-slavery magazine, and, according to its founders, "to concentrate the efforts of the best writers upon literature and politics, under the light of the highest morals." The magazine has attempted to balance both political and literary concerns throughout its history. The first issue consisted of 128 pages of double-columned text with no illustrations. The format of today's *Atlantic Monthly* is similar: generally about 100 pages of double- and triple-columned text with few illustrations; each issue contains several departments, such as Articles, Arts and Leisure, Reports and Comment, Humor, Fiction, Poetry, and Books.

James Russell Lowell was the magazine's first editor, and a great deal of the writing came from New England writers. Until 1870 the *Atlantic Monthly* had a policy of not revealing the identity of its contributors; it had a reputation, as well, for paying its contributors relatively well (during its early years). In 1859 Phillips, Sampson and Company collapsed, and the *Atlantic* was bought by the publishing company Ticknor and Fields. In 1861 James T. Fields of Ticknor and Fields took over the editorship from Lowell, who remained a regular contributor to the magazine. Fields published more light articles and fiction in an effort to increase the magazine's circulation, and he also increased the number of political articles slightly. The magazine held a consistent Republican (that is, pro-Lincoln) stand during Fields's term as editor. Fields died in December 1870, and William Dean Howells, assistant editor since 1866, became the magazine's editor in 1871.

Howells also edited the magazine for ten years, and he is credited with expanding the *Atlantic*'s range to include the Midwest, the South, and the West, while still retaining its New England roots. Subsequent editors were Thomas Bailey Aldrich (1881–1890); Horace Elisha Scudder (1890–1898); Walter Hines Page (1898–1899); Bliss Perry (1899–1909); Ellery Sedgwick (1909–1938); Edward A. Weeks, Jr. (1938–1966); Robert Manning (1966–1980); and William Whitworth (1981–present). Declining circulation led a number of the magazine's editors to move away from literature and toward a greater emphasis on social and political topics. This process began during Horace Elisha Scudder's editorship and continued afterwards; Ellery Sedgwick, however, is generally credited with making the magazine the kind of general-interest magazine that it is today. Edward Weeks, who succeeded Sedgwick, increased the number of drawings and other illustrations in the magazine and introduced the first pictorial cover in 1947.

The publishing firm of Hurd and Houghton acquired the magazine in 1873 (see Houghton Mifflin in this appendix). Ellery Sedgwick organized the Atlantic Monthly Company and purchased the magazine in 1908, the year before he took over as editor. Interest in the *Atlantic* declined in the late 1970s, and the magazine began to have financial problems; in 1980 the Atlantic Monthly Company was purchased by Boston real estate developer Mortimer Zuckerman, a self-described "newspaper and magazine junkie" who wanted to extend his professional involvement into the realm of publishing. Although he had promised to stay away from editorial decisions, a few months after purchasing the magazine Zuckerman listed himself as chairman of the editorial board on the masthead, and he eventually brought in William Whitworth to replace editor-in-chief Robert Manning.

Ballantine Books, 201 East 50th Street, New York, NY 10022; telephone 212/751–2600.

[Publisher of Franz Joseph, "Communications from Star Fleet Command"]

In February 1952 Ian Ballantine left Bantam Books (where he was president and publisher) to form Ballantine Books, Incorporated, with his wife Betty. There he began the "Ballantine Plan," the practice of offering to publish paperback editions of new books *simultaneously* with their publication in hardcover by another publishing company. (Traditionally, books are first published in hardcover form, with paperback editions sometimes published later, by either the same or another publisher.) Part of the plan was to pay authors 8 percent royalties on paperback editions (rather than the usual 2.5 percent), and to sell the books for thirty-five to fifty cents (rather than the usual twenty-five cents of the time). Other companies, such as Fawcett, had already begun original paperback publishing; but the "Ballantine Plan" enabled a small company like Ballantine Books to handle important books without a great deal of capital.

Ballantine Books became increasingly successful, and in 1954 the publisher Houghton Mifflin bought a 25 percent share of the company. Particularly successful were the company's paperback editions of science fiction books (including works by writers Arthur C. Clarke and Ray Bradbury, among others), edited by Betty Ballantine. The company's switchboard operator is said to have introduced Betty Ballantine to J.R.R. Tolkien's *Lord of the Rings* trilogy, and in 1965 Ballantine published the only paperback edition of this work authorized by Tolkien himself. Ballantine Books' all-time best-seller, Tolkien's *The Hobbit* (1966), has sold more than eight million copies.

In 1969 Ballantine Books was sold to Intext of Scranton, Pennsylvania, and in 1973 Ian Ballantine arranged the sale of the company to Random House, the large and successful publisher that was in turn bought by S. I. Newhouse's Newhouse Publications (now Advance Publications) in 1980. During the 1970s, Ballantine moved beyond paperback editions and began publishing big-money books, including William Safire's *Full Disclosure*, which was bought for over $1 million. By this time Ballantine had also established a separate science fiction imprint (a separate line of books published by the original company but under a separate name), called Del Rey Books. In 1977 CBS sold Fawcett Books to Random House, and this company became a part of Ballantine/Del Rey as well. During the 1980s, the company achieved one of the greatest commercial successes in publishing with the publication of a series of paperback editions of Jim Davis's Garfield cartoons. Today Ballantine has many subdivisions, including the imprint Ivy Books as well as Del Rey, Fawcett, and others.

Betty and Ian Ballantine left Ballantine Books to begin other ventures during the 1970s, but in 1981, while continuing to work with the Peacock Press of Bantam Books, Ian Ballantine returned as a consultant to Ballantine Books. Today Ballantine/Del Rey/Fawcett/Ivy Books continues to publish science fiction, along with general fiction and nonfiction books.

Book Research Quarterly (see *Publishing Research Quarterly*).

Change, **Heldref Publications, Helen Dwight Reid Educational Foundation, 1319 18th Street NW, Washington, DC 20036–1802; telephone 202/296–6267.**

[Publisher of Huntly Collins, "PC and the Press"]

Change (subtitled *The Magazine of Higher Learning*) is a bimonthly magazine dealing with contemporary issues in higher learning. It was founded by educator George W. Bonham in 1969, and its premier issue (January/February 1969) announced the magazine's intention "to be an irreverent foe of all that is arcane, banal, and irrelevant in higher education." Under Bonham's editorship *Change* published primarily assigned investigative pieces. By 1979 Bonham was ready to sell the magazine, and in 1980 it was taken over by Heldref Publications, a division of the nonprofit Helen Dwight Reid Educational Foundation. Reid, also an educator, had established this division of the Foundation for the purpose of taking over academic magazines and journals that were foundering; Heldref Publications now handles forty-five publications, including five magazines, primarily in the field of education.

During its early years at Heldref Publications, *Change* published articles selected by an editorial board from among submissions received from outside writers. In 1984, however, the magazine formed a partnership with the American Association of Higher Education (AAHE), and the editorial board again began assigning articles for publication in the magazine. As part of this partnership, AAHE members receive a subscription to *Change* as a benefit of their membership. The magazine is also available by subscription to nonmembers.

An editorial in *Change* described its preferred form of writing as follows:

> *Change* is a *magazine,* and the magazine *article* is a genre unto itself.
> What characterizes that genre? There's no formula, but a good article compels attention to an important matter. It shows a mind at work, one that reaches judgment and takes a stance. It is necessarily personal: It has a voice that speaks to the reader. It is credible: It knows its subject and the context. And it is concrete: It names people, places, dates, specific statements, and events—these to convey feeling for the subject and for life as it is lived, not as abstracted from an armchair.

Crown Publishing Group, 201 East 50th Street, New York, NY 10022; telephone 212/572–2100.

[Publisher of Susan Faludi, "The Media and the Backlash"]

The Crown Publishing Group was founded as Crown Publishers in 1936 by Nat Wartels and Robert Simon. The company's offices were located for many years at 449 Fifth Avenue in New York. When Crown Publishers was acquired by Random House in 1988, the company moved to its current address on East 50th Street. Its current owner, Random House, had been acquired by S. I. Newhouse's Newhouse Publications (now Advance Publications) in 1980.

Crown Publishers grew by acquiring other publishing companies, generally ones that were very small and/or struggling financially. In the 1940s Crown began publishing annual collections (such as *Best Film Plays of the Year* and *Best Cartoons of the Year*), beginning an emphasis on books about the media that has continued to the present. Wartels established a very market-oriented philosophy for Crown, maintaining that the company planned to "perceive what people in the marketplace want and find the right author, art director, and whoever else is needed to shape the book for the audience." In line with this philosophy, Crown has become known for paying extremely large advances to writers such as Judith Krantz and Jean Auel.

Today Crown publishes a range of general fiction and nonfiction books, as well as offering audio and video cassettes. The company has a number of subdivisions, including Clarkson N. Potter, Orion Books, and Harmony Books.

Details, Condé Nast Publications, Inc., 632 Broadway, 12th Floor, New York, NY 10012; telephone 212/420–0689.

[Publisher of George Melrod, "Digital Unbound"]

Details magazine (subtitled *For Men*) was founded by Annie Flanders in 1982 as a chronicle of fashion and night life in downtown Manhattan. Originally printed on black and white newsprint, it has developed into a glossy male fashion and lifestyle magazine that is geared toward a broad national audience, with a look that is strongly influenced by the American punk scene. The magazine, which is published ten times a year, covers celebrities and trends, especially in the areas of fashion, art, music, and night life. In 1988 *Details* was purchased by Condé Nast Publications, which publishes numerous other magazines including *Vanity Fair, Vogue,* and *Mademoiselle,* and is owned by S. I. Newhouse's company Advance Publications (formerly Newhouse Publications: see Ballantine Books, Crown Publishing Group, *The New Yorker,* and Random House, Inc. in this appendix). The magazine was relaunched, in its current format, in 1990.

Duke University Press, P.O. Box 90660, Durham, NC 27708; telephone 919/687–3600.

[Publisher of John H. Wallace, "The Case against Huck Finn"*]*

Duke University Press was founded in 1921 as Trinity College Press. The press publishes scholarly books in the humanities and the social sciences, as well as numerous academic journals, including *American Literature, Boundary 2,* and the *South Atlantic Quarterly.* Areas of interest at Duke University Press include British literature, American literature, East European studies, Latin American studies, and history. In recent years the Press has become particularly well known for its literary theory and cultural studies titles, such as Fredric Jameson's *Postmodernism, or the Cultural Logic of Late Capitalism,* Stanley Fish's *Doing What Comes Naturally,* and Slavoj Žižek's *Tarrying with the Negative.* Duke University Press also has a growing list in gay and lesbian studies, including the recent books *Barbie's Queer Accessories* by Erica Rand and *In the Shadow of the Epidemic: Being HIV-Negative in the Age of AIDS* by Walt Odets.

Education Digest, Prakken Publications, Inc., 275 Metty Drive, Suite 1, Box 8623, Ann Arbor, MI 48107; telephone 313/769–1211.

[Publisher of Dudley Barlow, "Why We Still Need Huckleberry Finn"*]*

The *Education Digest* is a journal that reprints condensed articles from publications focusing on policies, practices, research, and other developments in education. Founded by educator Lawrence W. Prakken in November 1935, the journal is published nine times a year (monthly from September to May) and is aimed primarily at an audience of school administrators and teachers at all levels. Among the publications from which articles are reprinted are *Educational Horizons, Principal,* the *American School Board Journal,* and the *Chronicle of Higher Education.* The *Education Digest* also includes regular columns, titled "The Teacher's Lounge," "Research Spotlight," "Washington Seen," and "In Brief," as well as a calendar of significant events and an Educational Resources section that includes listings of new books in the field.

Paul S. Eriksson, Publisher, P.O. Box 62, Forest Dale, VT 05745–0062; telephone 802/247–4210.

[Publisher of William Noble, "The Newest Bookbanners"]

In 1960 Paul S. Eriksson, who had run a bookstore and worked as an editor and a director of publicity for other publishing companies, began a company that was first called Eriksson-Taplinger. A year later the company's name was changed to Paul S. Eriksson, and it began publishing an average of five or six general fiction and nonfiction books each year, including literary translations, biographies, cartoon books, bird books, and, in 1995, a book titled *Oscar Schindler and His List* (a collection of reviews and articles on the book and film, *Schindler's List*). In 1976 Paul S. Eriksson moved from New York City to Vermont, where Paul and his wife Peggy run a two-person office, publishing "basically whatever has interested" them, including translations of Scandinavian literature. Their books have been distributed through the Independent Publishers Group since the late 1980s. Eriksson says that they have deliberately kept their company small, which has allowed them to focus their attention primarily on the editorial rather than the business side of things.

Extra!, FAIR (Fairness and Accuracy in Reporting), 130 West 25th Street, 8th Floor, New York, NY 10001; telephone 212/633–6700.

[Publisher of Jeff Cohen, "Propaganda from the Middle-of-the-Road: The Centrist Ideology of the News Media]

Extra! is a publication of FAIR (which stands for Fairness and Accuracy in Reporting), an organization that monitors the U.S. media. According to *Extra!*'s masthead, FAIR "focuses public awareness on the narrow corporate ownership of the press, the media's allegiance to official agendas and their insensitivity to women, labor, minorities, and other public interest constituencies." FAIR was founded by Jeff Cohen in 1986, and the organization began publishing the magazine *Extra!* in 1987. *Extra!* is published six times a year, alternating every other month with FAIR's newsletter, *Extra Update*.

Faber and Faber, Inc., 53 Shore Road, Winchester, MA 01890; telephone 617/721–1427.

[Publisher of Sven Birkerts, "The Paper Chase" and "Perseus Unbound"]

Faber and Faber, founded in 1976, is affiliated with Faber and Faber Publishers Ltd. of London. The American company was originally established to distribute books published by the British branch of Faber and Faber in the United States. But in the early 1980s, Tom Kelleher was appointed president and publisher of Faber and Faber, Inc., and in the mid-1980s the company began publishing a few of its own fiction and nonfiction books for adults. By 1987 the American Faber and Faber was publishing around seven books per year; by 1990 that number had risen to twelve, and an additional editor was hired. Faber and Faber publishes books in the areas of popular culture, rock music, films, and screenplays, along with its general fiction and nonfiction titles and anthologies. The company is particularly known for its film list (including screenplays and the *Directors on Directors* series), its plays (including the works of British playwright Tom Stoppard), and its anthologies (including the 1988 *Deep Down: The New Sensual Writing by Women,* one of the first anthologies of its kind). Faber and Faber launched its new and flourishing gay list in 1992, with a collection of gay short fiction edited by Edmund White.

The Free Press, 866 Third Avenue, New York, NY 10022; telephone 212/698–7000.

[Publisher of Mike Rose, "Reading My Way out of South L.A."]

The Free Press was founded in 1947 by Jeremiah Kaplan and Charles Liebman. Originally known as the Free Press of Glencoe, the company specialized in books on the social sciences and religion by such renowned scholars as Emile Durkheim, Max Weber, and Clifford Geertz. In 1960 the Crowell-Collier Publishing Company purchased the Free Press and merged it with the Macmillan Publishing Company. Cofounder Jeremiah Kaplan went on to hold a number of executive positions at Macmillan, and after retiring from there he served as president of Simon & Schuster, Inc. for several years.

The Free Press was purchased from Macmillan by Paramount Publishing in 1993 for $553 million. In 1994 Erwin Glikes, who had been the president and publisher of the Free Press since 1983, announced that he would not join Paramount Publishing, choosing instead to move to Penguin USA (where he planned to form his own division, until his unexpected death in May 1994). Glikes is credited with turning the distinguished Free Press around, changing it from a financially troubled press to one of the most profitable publishing divisions in any major company. Although the Free Press publishes a wide range of titles, Glikes is also credited with establishing the press's reputation as a publisher of conservative—and often controversial—books, such as Dinesh D'Souza's *Illiberal Education,* David Brock's *The Real Anita Hill,* and Charles Murray and Richard Herrnstein's *The Bell Curve.*

In July 1994 Adam Bellow (son of the American novelist Saul Bellow) was named vice president and editorial director of the Free Press, and in June 1995 it was announced that the Free Press would become a publishing unit of the trade division at Simon & Schuster, another company owned by Paramount (see Touchstone Books in this appendix). The Free Press continues to publish scholarly and trade nonfiction books, particularly in the areas of political and social science, business, history, and psychology. Its imprints include Martin Kessler Books, Lexington Books, and New Republic Books.

h2so4, P.O. Box 423354, San Francisco, CA 94142; telephone 415/865–0231; e-mail h2so4@igc.apc.org.

[Publisher of Gridley Minima, "Other People's 'Zines"; M. Kadi, "The Internet Is Four Inches Tall"]

h2so4, a journal of literary, political, and social commentary, was founded by editor Jill Stauffer in 1993. It appears twice a year and publishes poetry, fiction, articles, art, photographs, cartoons, interviews, criticism, reviews, music, letters, and nonfiction. Its name, *h2so4*, is the chemical symbol for sulfuric acid, which, in medieval alchemy, was considered the key to knowledge. In 1995 the magazine was nominated for an Alternative Press Award by the *Utne Reader* (see *Utne Reader* in this appendix). According to the *International Directory of Little Magazines and Small Presses*, *h2so4* "hopes to situate itself in the space between idea that is not entertainment, and entertainment with no idea."

HarperCollins, Inc., 10 East 53rd Street, New York, NY 10022; telephone 212/207–7520.

[Publisher of Nat Hentoff, "The Gospel According to Catharine MacKinnon"]

Two brothers, James and John Harper, founded the J. and J. Harper printing company in New York in 1817. The Harpers began by printing a translation of Seneca's *Morals,* and in 1818 they published, at their own expense, their first book, John Locke's *Essay Concerning Human Understanding.* Two younger brothers, Joseph Wesley Harper and Fletcher Harper, joined the firm in 1823 and 1825, respectively, after completing their printing apprenticeships. In 1825 the company moved to 82 Cliff Street in New York, its address for the next one hundred years. In 1833 the company became known as Harper and Brothers.

Harper and Brothers quickly grew to become one of the largest and most successful publishers in the United States. It is believed to have been the first U.S. publisher to use cloth for the binding of books, and it became known for the development of high-quality illustrations in its books. The four brothers operated with complete trust in one another, and it is said that for many years there was no accounting of funds or division of income among them. James was considered skillful in personal relations and supervised the company's workers; John handled finances; (Joseph) Wesley dealt with booksellers and authors; and Fletcher was the originator of several successful magazines begun by Harper and Brothers, including *Harper's New Monthly Magazine* (see *Harper's Magazine* in this appendix), *Harper's Weekly,* and *Harper's Bazar* (now spelled "Bazaar").

Much of the company's early business involved reprinting British books for American audiences—a practice for which they received some criticism. But they also published significant American writers, including Washington Irving, Henry Wadsworth Longfellow, Edgar Allan Poe, Herman Melville, and, later in the 1800s, Bret Harte, Stephen Crane, and Mark Twain. In December 1853 a fire destroyed everything in press or in stock at Harper and Brothers, but the brothers immediately began rebuilding. The company's publication of school texts and magazines helped it to survive the many financial crises of the nineteenth century, including the Civil War. Eventually, though, financial strains forced the company, which had remained in the Harper family for three generations, to incorporate as a stock company. Continued financial difficulties forced the company to reorganize under a new president, George B. M. Harvey, in 1900.

Harper and Brothers editors Cass Canfield and Eugene Saxton brought in exciting new authors in the 1920s, including James Thurber, E. B. White, Aldous Huxley, and John Dos Passos. Separate departments were established for the company's college textbooks, social and economic books, children's books, and religious books. Harper and Brothers's success continued into the thirties, forties, and fifties, and the company established several paperback reprint series, including Harper Torchbooks, Perennial Classics, and Colophon Books. In 1962 Harper and Brothers merged with the publisher Row, Peterson and Company, forming Harper and Row, Publishers, Inc. Harper and Row acquired a number of other publishers during the sixties and seventies, including Basic Books, J. B. Lippincott, and Funk and Wagnalls.

Throughout the 1980s Harper and Row maintained its position as one of the largest and most successful publishers in the United States, publishing well-known contemporary writers like Saul Bellow, Gabriel García Marquez, and Milan Kundera. Ownership of the company changed yet again in 1987 when Rupert Murdoch's News Corporation (owner of the British tabloid the *Sun,* along with many other publications and publishing interests) acquired Harper and Row for approximately $300 million. In 1989 Murdoch acquired the British publisher William Collins for roughly $566 million. The following year Harper-Collins Publishers became the worldwide company name for Harper and Row, based in New York, and Collins Publishers, based in London and Glasgow, along with their many different divisions.

Harper's Magazine, 666 Broadway, New York, NY 10012; telephone 212/614–6500.

[Publisher of Michael Massing, "Bringing the Truth Commission Back Home"; Harper's Forum, "Don't Tread on My Cursor: Freedom of Electronic Speech"]

In the mid-1800s the Harper brothers of the Harper and Brothers publishing company—particularly Fletcher Harper—became interested in publishing magazines (see HarperCollins Inc. in this appendix). *Harper's New Monthly Magazine,* founded in 1850, was the first of several magazines that the company published. Initially the magazine published mainly material that was reprinted from British books and periodicals, including work by Charles Dickens, Thomas Hardy, and Charlotte and Emily Brontë, but eventually it developed into an important voice in the development of American opinions and literary tastes. *Harper's New Monthly Magazine* published portions of Herman Melville's *Moby-Dick,* for example, and it serialized Henry James's *Washington Square.* And William Dean Howells, a contributing editor to the magazine from 1888 to 1894, wrote articles defending the new realism in American literature.

In 1900 the magazine's name was shortened to *Harper's Monthly Magazine.* During the first two decades of the twentieth century the magazine's popularity declined somewhat, and in 1925 editor Thomas B. Wells decided to make a major change in the direction of *Harper's,* opting to print more social and political commentary and less literary fiction. In addition, the magazine came to reflect, in these articles addressing social and political concerns, a consistently liberal standpoint. In 1939 the name was shortened again, this time to the current *Harper's Magazine.* By the 1950s *Harper's* was including shorter articles and more illustrations, but there was still far more nonfiction than fiction in the magazine. In 1967, Willie Morris became editor-in-chief at the age of thirty-two. Morris attempted to reestablish the magazine's earlier prestige as a literary magazine. But circulation and advertising income began to fall, particularly after Morris included Norman Mailer's "The Prisoner of Sex," an attack on feminism, in 1971.

Meanwhile, *Harper's Magazine* had been bought from the publishing company Harper and Row in 1965 by John Cowles Jr. of the Minneapolis Star-Tribune Company. In 1970 *Harper's* became an operating division of the Star-Tribune Company, and Cowles and William S. Blair, president and chief executive officer of the company, began pressuring Willie Morris to make changes in the magazine in order to raise circulation. Morris refused, choosing instead to resign in 1971. Morris recounts these events in his memoir *New York Days,* published by Little, Brown and Company in 1993; the magazine's current editor, Lewis Lapham, took issue with Morris's account in an article in *The New York Times Book Review* on October 24, 1993.

Harper's continued to lose subscribers and money after Morris's resignation, and it nearly collapsed. It was saved, however, by the John D. and Catherine T. MacArthur Foundation and the Atlantic Richfield Foundation, which purchased the magazine in 1980 and allowed it to become its own organization. Today the magazine continues as a monthly, under the editorship of Lewis Lapham. Each issue is around eighty pages long, and articles and excerpts are included within a number of "departments," including Letters, Notebook (an editorial by Lapham), the Harper's Index (a chronicle of American culture created through a listing of suggestive, and often unusual, statistics), Readings (a collection of long quotations or excerpts from a range of sources), Annotations (sample pages from published documents with added comments that illuminate the documents in a way that is both serious and comical), and the *Harper's* Forum (roundtable discussions by several authorities on topical, and often controversial, issues).

Houghton Mifflin Company, 222 Berkeley Street, Boston, MA 02116–3764; telephone 617/351–5000.

[Publisher of E. D. Hirsch, "The Formation of Modern National Cultures"]

In the 1840s a young man named Henry Oscar Houghton joined the printing firm Freeman and Bolles in Boston, and in 1849 this firm became Bolles and Houghton. The firm's printing plant was moved to property near the Charles River in Cambridge, Massachusetts, and in 1852, after Bolles's retirement, it became known as The Riverside Press—a press dedicated to doing the best printing and binding available in the United States at that time. In 1864 Houghton and Melancthon M. Hurd formed the publishing company of Hurd and Houghton. In 1868 Houghton hired George Harrison Mifflin to work in the Riverside Press counting room, and by 1872 Mifflin had been made a partner in Hurd and Houghton. The following year Hurd and Houghton acquired the *Atlantic Monthly* magazine (see *Atlantic Monthly* in this appendix).

When Hurd retired in 1878, Houghton formed Houghton, Osgood and Company with James R. Osgood, who had been a partner in the publishing company Ticknor and Fields. Osgood brought along a number of important writers from his days at Ticknor and Fields, including Nathaniel Hawthorne, Ralph Waldo Emerson, and Oliver Wendell Holmes. Houghton, Osgood and Company suffered serious financial difficulties, primarily because of Osgood's personal debts. In 1880 this partnership was dissolved, and Houghton and Mifflin formed Houghton, Mifflin and Company at 47 Franklin Street in Boston.

In 1882 Houghton and Mifflin established an Educational Department, which included the important Riverside Literature series. Through this series, famous English prose and poetry pieces were made available to schools and colleges at low costs; the first text of the series was Longfellow's *Evangeline*. The company also published series on American Commonwealths, American Men of Letters, and American Statesmen. Houghton died in 1895, and Mifflin became the head of the firm while Houghton's son, Henry Houghton Jr. was appointed the head of the Riverside Press. In 1908 Houghton, Mifflin and Company changed from a partnership to a corporation, called Houghton Mifflin Company, and the *Atlantic Monthly* was sold to Ellery Sedgwick.

During the first decades of the twentieth century, Houghton Mifflin's educational sales increased significantly, surpassing the sales of its other divisions. In the mid-1930s the company established a separate children's department, and in subsequent decades Houghton Mifflin published a number of important adult works, including James Agee's *Let Us Now Praise Famous Men* and Winston Churchill's *The Second World War* (in six volumes).

Houghton Mifflin became a publicly owned corporation in 1967, and the Riverside Press was sold in 1971. The company acquired several subsidiaries during the seventies, including a revived Ticknor and Fields and the company J. P. Tarcher, Incorporated. Houghton Mifflin declared 1980 the "Year of the Bird"; that year, Roger Tory Peterson's *A Field Guide to the Birds,* published by Houghton Mifflin, appeared on the *New York Times* best-seller lists for both hardcover and paperback books. Today Houghton Mifflin's main divisions are its General Publishing and Educational Publishing groups. Within those groups, a number of subdivisions publish general fiction and nonfiction books, as well as textbooks and educational and business software. Nader F. Darehshori is the board chair, president, and chief executive officer of Houghton Mifflin Company.

The Idler

[Source of Dr. Samuel Johnson, "On the Art of Advertising"]

The Idler was the title of a regularly appearing feature in a weekly English newspaper called *The Universal Chronicle.* This feature was a lead essay, generally humorous and often scathingly satirical, written by the eighteenth-century writer, critic, and lexicographer Samuel Johnson (1709–1784). Johnson himself created the persona, and the name, of "the Idler," the voice of these weekly essays; in one of the first of the essays he writes, "Every man is, or hopes to be, an Idler. Even those who seem to differ most from us are hastening to increase our fraternity; as peace is the end of war, so to be idle is the ultimate purpose of the busy."

Throughout his writing career, Johnson took on work as a writer and critic, producing work like *The Idler* essays in order to support himself and his pursuit of the scholarship that mattered most to him. Among his scholarly works were *A Dictionary of the English Language*

(1755), an edition of *The Plays of William Shakespeare* (1765), and a series on *The Lives of the English Poets* (1779–1781). Prior to writing his *Idler* essays, Johnson had contributed to the journals *The Rambler* (in the persona of "the Rambler"), *The Adventurer,* and the *Literary Magazine.*

Johnson wrote 104 weekly *Idler* essays, from April 15, 1758 to April 5, 1760. The topics of these essays ranged from political commentary and literary criticism to what Johnson perceived as the growing volume of publication of worthless books and the evils of newspaper advertising. Many of these essays were gathered in a collected edition of *The Idler,* published in 1761.

Indiana University Press, 601 North Morton Street, Bloomington, IN 47404; telephone 812/855–4203.

[Publisher of Umberto Eco, "The Future of Literacy"]

Indiana University Press, which was founded in 1950, has its headquarters on the Bloomington campus of the Indiana University system. The press's mandate is "to serve the world of scholarship and culture as a professional publisher and also to represent and reflect the major strengths of Indiana University." Indiana's publishing list is especially strong in the areas of the humanities, the social sciences, and regional studies; it also publishes nearly a dozen journals, including *Camera Obscura,* the *Journal of Women's History, Research in African Literatures,* and *Victorian Studies.* Subject areas for which Indiana University Press is particularly well known include African studies, Russian and East European studies, semiotics, literary criticism, women's studies, folklore, Jewish studies, history, and music.

Liberal Education, Association of American Colleges and Universities, 1818 R Street NW, Washington, DC 20009; telephone 202/387–3760.

[Publisher of Paul Saffo, "Quality in an Age of Electronic Incunabula"]

Liberal Education is the quarterly magazine of the Association of American Colleges and Universities (AAC), an organization that describes itself as "the national voice for liberal learning." The magazine began in 1915 as the *Proceedings of the First Annual Meeting of the Association of American Colleges;* in 1917 this title was shortened to the *Association of American Colleges Bulletin.* In 1959 the *Bulletin* became *Liberal Education.* This new title was chosen, not to indicate political liberalism, but, according to an "Editorial Note" in its inaugural issue, "because it is the most concise and widely accepted expression of the end to which members of the Association are dedicated—education designed to foster critical intelligence, creative imagination, and moral sensitivity." In the 1970s the AAC began publishing other periodicals and newsletters, including *On Campus with Women* and the *Forum for Liberal Education*. From 1987 to 1993, *Liberal Education* was redesigned and reconceived to include various aspects of all of AAC's periodicals, but in 1993 these publications resumed their individual status and were mailed to subscribers separately from *Liberal Education*.

Los Angeles Times, Times Mirror Company, Times Mirror Square, Los Angeles, CA 90053; telephone 213/237–4712.

. *[Publisher of Amy Harmon, "Bigots on the Net"]*

In December 1881 the founders of the *Los Angeles Daily Times* fled their mounting debts, leaving the paper in the hands of the three printers at the Mirror Book Bindery, where the paper was printed. These printers hired a man named Harrison Gray Otis as editor in 1882; at the same time Otis purchased a quarter share of the newspaper for $6,000. Otis was a newspaperman, businessman, and former government employee, a Civil War veteran who had been active in Republican politics (when the Republicans were the party of Abraham Lincoln). In 1884 Otis and a business partner, Colonel H. H. Boyce, bought out the other three partners in the newspaper and incorporated the Times Mirror Company, and within three years Otis had bought out Boyce as well.

Harry Chandler, who would become another prominent figure at the *Los Angeles Times,* began his career as a carrier. In 1887 he was promoted to circulation clerk, then circulation manager, and then business manager; in 1894 he married Otis's daughter Marian. Chandler was considered the business genius at the *Times,* Otis, the outspoken writer. Under these men's leadership, the *Los Angeles Times* became known as a politically conservative newspaper, speaking out against "liberal do-gooders" and adopting a firm anti-union stance. Harry Chandler became involved in a number of real estate ventures, including the controversial routing of water to Los Angeles from the Owens Valley, located 240 miles northeast of Los Angeles, by way of a newly built aqueduct. Chandler also encouraged the growth of the movie industry in Los Angeles; the *Times* established the first motion-picture page in American journalism, a step toward elevating movies to the level of other performing arts.

At Otis's death in 1917, the paper was willed to Harry and Marian Chandler. Their son Norman set himself to the task of handling the *Times*'s growing financial problems, and in 1934 he was made general manager of the paper. Under Norman Chandler's leadership many improvements were made in the paper's editorial quality, and its business practices were modernized. In 1960 Norman Chandler's son Otis was appointed publisher of the *Los Angeles Times.* In subsequent years the *Times* improved and expanded its equipment and its editorial efficiency; under the editorship of Nick Williams (1958–1971), the paper's editorial quality continued to improve, and its political positions began to shift as well. Richard Nixon was shocked—and frustrated—when the *Los Angeles Times* did not back him in the 1962 California gubernatorial election. In 1963 the paper was listed by *Time* as one of the nation's ten best papers, and it was praised by the *Wall Street Journal*. In June 1970 the *Los Angeles Times* called for a complete withdrawal of American troops from Vietnam, and in 1973 Otis Chandler ended the *Times*'s traditional practice of endorsing U.S. presidential candidates (endorsements that had nearly always gone to Republican candidates).

The *Los Angeles Times*'s parent company, the Times Mirror Co., operates the *Los Angeles Times-Washington Post* News Service. It also owns and operates a number of other newspapers (including New York *Newsday* and the Dallas *Times Herald*), magazines, book publishing companies, television stations, and cable television systems.

Methuen, Inc., (an imprint of) Chapman and Hall (formerly Routledge, Chapman and Hall), a subsidiary of the Thomson Corporation, 29 West 35th Street, New York, NY 10001; telephone 212/244-3336.

[Publisher of Walter J. Ong, "Print, Space, and Closure"]

Methuen and Company was founded in 1889 in Great Britain by Algernon Methuen Marshall Stedman, the proprietor of a preparatory school and a successful author of school textbooks. From its beginnings, Methuen has published both popular fiction and educational works. In 1899 the company began publishing its successful Arden Shakespeare series, and following both the first and the second world wars, Methuen expanded its educational publishing considerably. In the 1960s the company launched a successful University Paperbacks series. Methuen, Inc. opened its New York office in 1978. From the late 1970s and into the 1980s, an organization called the American Book Publishers (ABP) began acquiring a number of academic and educational publishers and imprints, including Routledge and Kegan Paul; Chapman and Hall; and Methuen, Inc. All of these publishers and imprints were subsumed under the conglomerate known as the Thomson Corporation, which bought the American Book Publishers in 1987.

Minstrel Books, (an imprint of) Pocket Books, Simon & Schuster Building, 1230 Avenue of the Americas, New York, NY 10020; telephone 212/698-7000.

[Publisher of Laurie Lawlor, "Miss March, the Famous American Authoress"]

Minstrel Books is an imprint (a separate line of books published by the parent company but under a different name) of the company Pocket

Books. Minstrel publishes books, both original and reprint editions, for children in grades two through seven; its companion imprint, Archway, publishes young adult books.

Pocket Books was founded by Robert F. de Graff, who is credited with helping to launch the paperback book in the United States. This launch was based in part out of the need for books to be shipped overseas to American GIs during World War II. De Graff knew that paperback books had become very successful in Germany and Great Britain, and in 1938 he persuaded the top executives of the publishing company Simon & Schuster to become partners in an American paperback book venture, called Pocket Books, Inc.

De Graff's plan was to publish reprints of existing hardcover books, paying a royalty of one cent per copy to be split between the book's original publisher and its author. In 1939 Pocket Books published its first list of ten books; among these were a self-help book titled *Wake Up and Live,* a reprint of Emily Brontë's *Wuthering Heights,* Agatha Christie's *The Murder of Roger Ackroyd,* and Felix Salten's *Bambi.* These first paperback books were incredibly successful. Besides distributing these books through the usual venues of bookstores and department stores, Pocket Books also used magazine and newspaper wholesalers for distribution of its books. As a result, Pocket Books were sold in places like newsstands; cigar stores; grocery stores; drugstores; and subway, train, and bus stations. While the company lost business in the 1960s to other growing paperback companies, such as Bantam and Dell, by the 1970s it had established a reputation as a publisher of best-selling fiction by writers like Herman Wouk, Bernard Malamud, Joan Didion, and John Irving.

In 1961 Pocket Books became a publicly owned company, and in 1966 it became a division of Simon & Schuster (see Touchstone Books in this appendix). In 1975 Pocket Books was acquired, along with Simon & Schuster, by the conglomerate Gulf + Western Industries; both publishing companies are now affiliated with Paramount Communications, a unit of Gulf + Western. Even though Minstrel Books was originally a publisher of paperback children's books, in 1994 it began publishing hardcover books as well.

MLA Publications, Modern Language Association, 10 Astor Place, New York, NY 10003; telephone 212/475–9500.

[Publisher of C. H. Knoblauch, "Literacy and the Politics of Education"]

MLA Publications are published by the Modern Language Association of America, a professional organization for scholars in the modern languages and literatures (as opposed to classical Latin and Greek and other ancient languages) that held its first meeting at Columbia University in New York City in 1883. The founders of the MLA wished to improve both their academic status and their esteem within the public at large, and one of their goals in establishing the association was to provide greater opportunities for the publication of scholarly work within their fields. They established a quarterly journal in 1889; this journal, named *PMLA* (*Publications of the Modern Language Association*) in 1929, is now published six times a year. The MLA began publishing a Monograph Series in 1926, and in the years following World War II the organization published a number of books, some of narrower scholarly interest and some designed to serve as guides for scholars and graduate students. In 1928 the MLA, which had been based first at Johns Hopkins University in Baltimore and then at Harvard University in Cambridge, Massachusetts, established its headquarters on Washington Square in New York City. Today the MLA publishes a number of scholarly and reference works on modern languages and literature, including the important *MLA International Bibliography,* as well as software, works on CD-ROM, and a number of periodicals.

Ms., Lang Communications, Inc., 230 Park Avenue, 7th Floor, New York, NY 10169; telephone 212/551–9595.

[Original publisher of Gloria Steinem, "Sex, Lies, and Advertising")

Ms. magazine was founded in the early 1970s by Gloria Steinem and Patricia Carbine, both of whom had worked at other magazines. Frustrated by sexist treatment and discrimination at their jobs, these two women organized a small group of women with the goal of creating a feminist magazine that would address the concerns of women. The first issue of this magazine appeared as a forty-four-page special section of *New York* magazine in December 1971. The first full-length issue of the bimonthly magazine *Ms.* appeared in the spring of 1972.

Katharine Graham (publisher of the *Washington Post*) purchased stock in *Ms.,* providing initial capital for the magazine, and in 1972 Warner Communications acquired a significant but minority interest in the magazine. In the July 1972 issue *Ms.* outlined its advertising policy, announcing that it would only run ads for products that provided a service to women and would refuse to print ads for products that insult, or are harmful to, women. The magazine came under fire for excluding nonwhite readers in the 1970s, and by the late 1980s it was seen by some people as having lost sight of its original goals, becoming instead rather predictable and boring. In 1990 it ceased publication altogether for seven months, but in July of that year it reappeared, under the editorship of Robin Morgan and with a new policy: *No* advertising would be included. The first issue under this new plan sold out within a week.

Robin Morgan remained the editor of *Ms.* for three and a half years, guiding its development into a successful and committed feminist magazine, covering such wide-ranging issues as Eastern Europe, the Gulf

War, race and women, lesbian parenting, the Anita Hill–Clarence Thomas hearings, the politics of breast cancer, and women and AIDS. The magazine was purchased by Lang Communications, Inc. in 1989.

Natural History, American Museum of Natural History, Central Park West at 79th Street, New York, NY 10024; telephone 212/769–5500.

[Publisher of Laura Bohannan, "Shakespeare in the Bush"]

Natural History is a monthly magazine published by the American Museum of Natural History for the museum's supporters. It covers subjects in the fields of natural science, anthropology, archaeology, and zoology for lay readers who have an interest in natural history. The magazine was founded in 1900 as the *American Museum Journal,* which, according to the first issue's introduction, was designed to "widen the circle of interest in this noble institution for the education of the people and the diffusion of natural science." The magazine shifted to its current larger format in 1937; through the years it has become a glossy, high-quality magazine that includes many lavish color photographs.

The New York Times Book Review and *The New York Times Magazine,* The New York Times Company, 229 West 43rd Street, New York, NY 10036; telephone 212/556–1234.

[Publisher of Caryn James, "Amy Had Golden Curls, Jo Had a Rat. Who Would You Rather Be?"; Bernard Sharratt, "But Is It Art? A Review of the Microsoft Art Gallery on CD-ROM" (Book Review); Catharine MacKinnon, Floyd Abrams, and Anthony Lewis, "A Conversation on the First Amendment" (Magazine)]

On September 18, 1851 the first issue of the *New York Daily Times* was published by Henry J. Raymond, formerly of the *New York Tribune* and the *Courier and Enquirer,* and also a part-time editor at *Harper's New Monthly Magazine* (see *Harper's* in this appendix). "Daily" was dropped from the newspaper's name in 1857. Raymond had founded the paper, along with financiers George Jones and Edward B. Wesley, as part of what was called the "cheap-for-cash movement," begun by the *New York Sun* and other papers in the 1830s; thus the paper sold, initially, for a penny a copy. Like its main competitor, the *New York Tribune,* the *Times* adopted a higher moral tone than other New York dailies at the time; it established a reputation as a well-balanced, well-edited newspaper that paid special attention to foreign affairs (which is still a feature of today's *New York Times*).

After Raymond's death in 1869, the paper was in the hands of several different editors and owners. In the 1870s its staff helped to expose the corruption of the Boss Tweed ring in New York City. By the 1890s, however, the paper was failing financially; it had been hurt by the popular sensationalism (the so-called "new journalism") practiced in newspapers owned by William Randolph Hearst and Joseph Pulitzer. In 1896 the *Times* was bought by Adolph S. Ochs of the *Chattanooga Times* of Tennessee. Ochs deliberately set the *New York Times* in opposition to the sensationalistic practices of the new journalism; in his declaration of principles for the paper he promised "to give the news impartially, without fear or favor, regardless of any party, sect, or interest involved. . . ." Under Ochs's leadership the *Times* established the practices of including no comics and few pictures, and it began including the famous front-page slogan, "All the News That's Fit to Print."

Ochs also began publishing two popular sections of the newspaper's Sunday edition, the *Book Review* and the *Magazine*. In the *Book Review* he established the practice of treating books as "news"; he expected reviews and articles in the *Book Review* to provide readers with a sense of what the books they treated were about, rather than with lengthy literary or intellectual discussions. Besides reviews and nonreview articles, today's *Book Review* includes best-seller lists for both hardcover and paperback books, as well as a Letters section in which readers often express strong reactions to pieces from prior weeks' issues. Editors at the *Book Review* determine which books will be reviewed and assign the books to various reviewers, including academics, critics, writers, and experts in various fields. Reviews of books in *The New York Times Book Review* are seldom overwhelmingly negative, and a review in the *Book Review* is considered an important sign of a new book's success.

Lester Markel, editor of the Sunday *Times* from 1923 to 1964, saw both the *Book Review* and the *Magazine* as the parts of the Sunday newspaper that could provide readers with "something of permanent value. . . ." *The New York Times Magazine* began as *The New York Times Sunday Magazine Supplement,* and it was viewed as a forum for more thorough coverage of current news stories. The *Magazine*'s high-quality photographs were of particular interest to readers; the July 4, 1897 *Magazine* contained fifty photographs of Great Britain's Queen Victoria's Jubilee. Still, the *Magazine* was not consistently successful in its early years; by the 1920s it had changed names frequently and had ceased publication altogether during three different periods. From 1920 to 1926 the *Magazine* and *Book Review* were combined in one section of the Sunday paper. From 1926 to the present, however, the *Magazine* has been a separate entity, titled simply *The New York Times Magazine.* In recent years the *Magazine*'s focus has shifted away from news and more toward entertainment, and its advertising space has increased.

The *Times*'s parent company, the New York Times Company, has expanded into a large communications organization that owns numerous other newspapers (including the Gainesville *Sun* and the Wilmington *Star*), publishing companies (including Arno Press and Times books), magazines (including *Family Circle* and *Golf Digest*), television and radio stations, and educational and library materials.

The New Yorker, Advance Publications, 20 West 43rd Street, New York, NY 10036; telephone 212/840–3800.

[Publisher of John Seabrook, "My First Flame"]

Newspaperman and editor Harold Ross founded the weekly *New Yorker* magazine in 1925, setting up offices on West 45th Street in New York (and eventually moving to West 43rd Street). The magazine's initial capital—$500,000—came from Raoul Fleischmann, whose family had made their money in the yeast business. Ross was affiliated with the writers of the famed Algonquin Roundtable; a number of these writers, including George S. Kaufman and Dorothy Parker, signed up as advisory editors at *The New Yorker.* The first issue of the magazine appeared on February 21, 1925. It featured sections called "Of All Things" and "The Talk of the Town" (a section that continues in the magazine today), as well as caricatures and cartoons. On the cover was Eustace Tilley, the well-known dandy figure with top hat and monocle created by Rea Ervin—a figure that is reproduced on the cover each year on the magazine's anniversary.

In his original prospectus, Ross described *The New Yorker* as "a reflection in word and picture of metropolitan life"; it was not intended, he maintained, "for the old lady in Dubuque." Since its founding, the magazine has been known for the quality of its writing, whether political commentary; criticism of film, theater, music, literature, and art; or fiction and poetry. It is known, as well, for its "Reporter at Large" pieces and its profiles (such as Lillian Ross's portrait of writer Ernest Hemingway). Famed writers E. B. White and James Thurber began their careers at *The New Yorker,* and fiction writers J. D. Salinger, John Cheever, John O'Hara, and John Updike were nourished there. The magazine is also known for its probing social commentary, often presented in long articles that eventually became books, such as John Hersey's *Hiroshima,* Rachel Carson's *Silent Spring,* James Baldwin's *The Fire Next Time,* and Jonathan Schell's *The Fate of the Earth.*

Harold Ross died in 1951, and the next year Wallace Shawn took over as editor. By the late 1960s the magazine had become more political, adopting clear anti-Vietnam and anti-Nixon positions, for example, particularly in articles by staff writer Jonathan Schell. Advertising sales began to drop, and by the early 1970s circulation was declining as well. In 1985 *The New Yorker* was purchased by S. I. Newhouse's company Advance Publications (formerly Newhouse Publications: see Ballantine Books; Crown Publishing Group; *Details* and Random House, Inc. in this appendix). In addition to several book publishers and a large number of newspapers, Advance Publications owns a large subsidiary, Condé Nast

Publications, which publishes many magazines, including *Vogue, Vanity Fair,* and *Details.* Although Wallace Shawn had been assured that he could stay on as editor of *The New Yorker* as long as he wished (and that when he retired his successor would be an insider at the magazine), in 1987 Shawn was fired and replaced by Robert Gottlieb, former editor-in-chief at Alfred A. Knopf (which is also owned by Newhouse's Advance Publications). Shawn's firing caused anger and dissatisfaction among many of *The New Yorker's* writers.

In 1992, Robert Gottlieb resigned as editor of the magazine and was immediately replaced by Tina Brown, the editor of *Vanity Fair* (a Condé Nast publication). S. I. Newhouse cited "conceptual differences" between Gottlieb and himself over the future of the magazine when explaining the change in leadership. At the time of Brown's hiring there was speculation within publishing circles that Newhouse hoped she would boost *The New Yorker's* sagging advertising revenues, much as she had done at *Vanity Fair.* Brown has instituted some changes at the magazine, but many of its familiar features (such as the "Talk of the Town" and the ever-popular cartoons) remain.

Newsweek, Newsweek, Inc., 251 West 57th Street, New York, NY 10019; telephone 212/445-4000.

[Publisher of LynNell Hancock, "Computer Gap: The Haves and the Have-Nots"]

Newsweek was founded by Thomas J. C. Martyn, the first foreign news editor of *Time* magazine, in 1933, and it quickly became one of the top weekly news magazines in the United States. For its first four years the magazine's name included a hyphen, and the first issue of *News-week* appeared on February 18, 1933. An advertisement in the next week's issue described the magazine's material as "action stories, sifting, selecting, and clarifying the significant news of the week." While some critics of the magazine objected to this practice of "sifting and selecting" the news, *News-week* was popular with its readers, both for its coverage and its format.

In 1937 the magazine was absorbed by the weekly magazine *Today,* which was owned by Vincent Astor. Malcolm Muir, former president of the McGraw-Hill publishing company, became editor-in-chief; Muir dropped the hyphen from the magazine's title, and the editors adopted the slogan "the magazine of news significance." *Newsweek* was praised for its coverage, and also its photography, during the war years and into the 1950s. In the 1960s the magazine covered the civil rights movement and growing racial strife in the United States; this coverage included an in-depth study titled "The Negro in America," published in the July 29, 1963 issue. *Newsweek* was also praised for its coverage of U.S. space exploration, the assassination of President John F. Kennedy, and the Vietnam War during the 1960s—a decade during which the magazine's competition with *Time* magazine intensified. By gearing its coverage toward a younger, more liberal audience, *Newsweek* maintained a strong position in that ongoing competition. In the 1970s color photography and a guest essay feature, called "My Turn," were added to the magazine, and in 1982 *Newsweek* won the National Magazine Award for General Excellence.

In 1961 *Newsweek* was purchased from the Astor Foundation by the Washington Post Company, which owns a number of newspapers (besides the Washington *Post*), magazines, book publishers, and television stations.

W. W. Norton and Company, Inc., 500 Fifth Avenue, New York, NY 10110; telephone 212/354–5500.

[Publisher of Patricia Nelson Limerick, "Making the Most of Words"]

In 1924 Warder W. Norton founded a company called the People's Institute Publishing Company to publish the lectures presented as part of an adult education series at New York's Cooper Union. The first publication, Everett Dean Martin's *Psychology*, appeared as twenty pamphlets collected in a package for subscribers, and it was followed by several other such packages on related topics. Although these publications were successful, Norton realized that booksellers preferred to sell single volumes rather than collections of pamphlets. Wishing to expand the business further, he reorganized the company in 1925 as W. W. Norton and Company, adopting the seagull as a company logo and the phrase "Books That Live" as its motto. In 1930 W. W. Norton and Company established an additional textbook division.

Norton believed that publishing should provide materials that educate as well as entertain; his goal for W. W. Norton and Company was to help "modern men and women know more about themselves and their world, and to feel they understand something of what it is all about." In keeping with this goal, the company published a series of books called the New Science series, as well as works by philosopher Bertrand Russell and studies of Greek and Roman history and mythology by Edith Hamilton. Norton's wife Mary developed the company's strong music and musicology list, and although literature was not a large part of the early Norton lists, Mary Norton was influential in acquiring the rights to works by German poet Rainer Maria Rilke, several of which she translated.

After Warder W. Norton's death in 1945, the company continued to grow steadily. Its college sales more than doubled during the 1950s; prominent college textbooks published by Norton include *The American Tradition in Literature* and *The Norton Anthology of English Literature*, as well as the popular Norton Critical Editions of literary classics and the more recent *Norton Anthology of Literature by Women*. Following World War II the company also began publishing more literature, including fiction by Anthony Burgess and Jean Rhys and poetry by A. R. Ammons and Adrienne Rich. In 1974 Norton purchased the Liveright Publishing Company. W. W. Norton and Company has resisted takeovers by larger firms and remains one of the few large independent American publishing houses.

Oxford University Press, 200 Madison Avenue, New York, NY 10016; telephone 212/726–6000.

[Publisher of Henry Louis Gates, "The Trope of the Talking Book"]

Oxford University began printing books as early as the fifteenth or sixteenth century, and Oxford University Press has become renowned for its educational and scholarly publishing, including the well-known *Oxford English Dictionary* and *Oxford Companions* (*to Literature, to Music,* etc.). The American branch of Oxford University Press was established in 1896, initially for the purpose of distributing Bibles published by Oxford University Press (which had established the right to print the King James Authorized Version of the Bible in the seventeenth century). Oxford University Press (USA) is separately incorporated as a not-for-profit corporation with local trustees, even though its operations are still tied in with Oxford University Press in Great Britain. Beginning in the 1930s, the American Oxford University Press began to expand its functions, and it has gone on to publish many significant original American publications. In addition to Bibles and scholarly and reference works, Oxford University Press (USA) publishes trade and professional books and journals in the fields of history, science, medicine, the social sciences, the humanities, and music, as well as sheet music and children's books.

Pennsylvania Gazette

[Publisher of Benjamin Franklin, "An Apology for Printers"]

The *Pennsylvania Gazette* was the newspaper of American printer, journalist, inventor, and statesman Benjamin Franklin. Franklin had worked as a journeyman printer for much of the 1720s, and in 1728, along with partner Hugh Meredith, he opened the New Printing Office in Philadelphia. During this time he was also writing for newspapers, however; he wrote letters from a fictional woman, "Silence Dogood," for his brother James Franklin's paper, the *New England Courant,* and during his early years in Philadelphia he wrote the popular "Busy-Body" sections of Andrew Bradford's newspaper, the *American Weekly Mercury.*

These sections often included thinly veiled, humorous attacks on Samuel Keimer, the publisher of Philadelphia's other newspaper, the *Universal Instructor in all Arts and Sciences; and Pennsylvania Gazette* (and Franklin's former employer). Franklin's attacks were due, at least in part, to the fact that *he* had hoped to start a second Philadelphia newspaper, but Keimer had done so first.

Eventually the success of Keimer's *Instructor* began to decline, and in 1729 its last issue announced the paper's sale to "B. Franklin and H. Meredith, at the New Printing Office." Franklin's *Pennsylvania Gazette* became known for its coverage of local news and its humorous sketches, especially its letters from readers. Many of these "letters" are assumed to have been written by Franklin himself, especially the series of letters from persons with names like Anthony Afterwit, Celia Single, and Alice Addertongue, which began appearing in 1732. During the 1730s, Franklin bought out Meredith. The *Pennsylvania Gazette* typically included a first page that addressed European news and a second page made up of local news and letters from readers; during the summer, third and fourth pages would include the proceedings of the Assembly, advertisements, news of the arrival and departure of boats, rates of money exchange, and so on.

Delivery of the *Pennsylvania Gazette* was accomplished through the postal service. Franklin's rival, Andrew Bradford, was the postmaster, however, which led to occasional problems with the delivery of the *Gazette*. To counter his newspaper's flagging subscription income, Franklin became one of the first newspaper publishers to solicit advertisements regularly and to give advertising considerable space in the *Gazette* (one column per page, as compared to a few lines per page in competing newspapers).

By the end of the 1730s, the *Gazette* was publishing fewer humorous sketches. Franklin himself was becoming more involved in business and civic affairs, and the paper reflected this change in its increased coverage of political and financial topics. In 1748, Franklin retired from active control of the New Printing Office, leaving it and the *Pennsylvania Gazette* in the hands of David Hall, with whom he remained in partnership for eighteen years.

Plume Books, (a subdivision of) Penguin USA, 375 Hudson Street, New York, NY 10014; telephone 212/366–2000.

[Publisher of Farai Chideya, "Who's Making What News?"]

Plume Books is a subdivision of the publishing company Penguin, Inc., which was founded in 1939 as an American branch of Penguin Books, Limited in Great Britain (which had been founded four years earlier by Allen Lane). Ian Ballantine (see Ballantine Books in this appendix), who held a 49 percent share of the new American company, managed the American Penguin, which published the well-known orange and white paperback versions of titles that were imported from Britain. About one-third of the stores carrying Penguin Books in the early years were college bookstores, and this college connection has remained an important source of Penguin's sales.

World War II led to a restriction in trade routes, which prompted Lane to hire Kurt Enoch to work with Ballantine to begin the process of producing American books, rather than reprinting British imports. By the end of the war, American Penguin had become a successful independent company. When Lane tried to reestablish control of the company, Ballantine left to found the paperback company Bantam Books. Enoch remained, with a new partner, Victor Weybright, and by 1948 these two had broken away from Lane, buying out his interest in American Penguin and reorganizing the company as the New American Library of World Literature. Lane reentered American publishing in 1950 with a new company, Allen Lane, Inc., in Baltimore. In 1951, as soon as the terms of his agreement with Enoch and Weybright allowed, he moved this company to New York and reincorporated it as Penguin Books, Inc. In 1975 American Penguin purchased two-thirds of Viking Press, resulting in the imprint Viking Penguin. The American and British Penguins publish separate lists of books, although some titles do appear on both. Today, besides Viking Penguin and Plume Books, other subdivisions of American Penguin include E. P. Dutton and the New American Library.

Pocket Books (see Minstrel Books.)

The Progressive, 409 East Main Street, Madison, WI 53703; telephone 608/257–4626.

[Publisher of Erwin Knoll, "Don't Print That!"]

The Progressive is a monthly magazine emphasizing peace, economic justice, and individual rights. It was founded in 1909 by Robert M. LaFollette Sr. The LaFollette family led the Progressive Movement in the United States in the early part of the twentieth century; both Robert LaFollette and his son Phil served as governor of the state of Wisconsin. In 1940 the LaFollettes turned the magazine over to the editorship of Morris H. Rubin; in 1973 Erwin Knoll took over as editor, a position he held until his death in 1994. The magazine's current editor is Matthew Rothschild. Throughout its long history *The Progressive* has taken a committed, and often daring, stand on many controversial issues; in 1954, for example, it published an exposé of Senator Joseph McCarthy, and in 1979 it was involved in a lawsuit, *The United States of America* vs. *The Progressive, Inc., et al.,* over an article the magazine planned to publish on the nuclear arms industry—an article that, according to the government, revealed restricted information.

Publishers Weekly, 249 West 17th Street, New York, NY 10011; telephone 212/463–6758.

[Publisher of Katharine Weber, "The Reviewer's Experience"]

Publishers Weekly, subtitled *The International News Magazine of Book Publishing,* was founded in 1872 by Frederick Leypoldt, a former book-seller and publisher who was particularly interested in book bibliographies. The magazine had its roots in a publication called the *Literary Bulletin,* which Leypoldt began publishing in 1868 to provide booksellers with information on new U.S. and foreign books. The *Literary Bulletin,* which appeared irregularly, gradually evolved into the monthly *Trade Circular & Publishers' Bulletin,* and on January 18, 1872, Leypoldt began publishing the journal as a weekly, called *The Publishers' & Stationers' Weekly Trade Circular.* In January 1873 the name was changed to *Publishers Weekly.* As its name indicates, the magazine is published weekly (on Mondays).

In 1873 Richard Rogers Bowker joined *Publishers Weekly* as an associate, and in 1876, along with Melvil Dewey (originator of the Dewey Decimal System of library classification), Leypoldt and Bowker founded the *Library Journal.* These three men also planned the formation of the American Library Association in Philadelphia (see American Library Association in this appendix). Bowker purchased *Publishers Weekly* in 1878; Leypoldt died in 1884. In 1914, Bowker and Leypoldt's widow, Augusta Harriet Garrigue Leypoldt, incorporated the company together as the R. R. Bowker Company. The firm was bought by the Xerox Corporation in 1967. In addition to *Publishers Weekly* and the *Library Journal,* R. R. Bowker also publishes a number of reference works, including the yearly *Books in Print* series, *Ulrich's Periodicals Directory,* and the *Literary Market Place.*

Publishing Research Quarterly, P.O. Box 2423, Bridgeport, CT 06608–0423.

[Publisher of John P. Dessauer, "Cultural Pluralism and the Book World"]

Publishing Research Quarterly—formerly *Book Research Quarterly*—is published four times a year, in spring, summer, fall, and winter issues, by the Transaction Periodicals Consortium at Rutgers University (see Transaction Publishers in this appendix). It was launched with the Spring 1985 issue (under the original name, *Book Research Quarterly*) by the Center for Book Research at the University of Scranton, in conjunction with the Transaction Periodicals Consortium. In an introduction to that first issue, editor John P. Dessauer identified the journal's subject as "the creation, publication, and distribution of books, past, present, and future"; its objective, he wrote, was "to serve the public interest," and its intended audience was "professionals and scholars—writers, publishers, printers, binders, librarians, booksellers, critics, and observers—whose lives are devoted to books." In her introduction to the Spring 1991 issue of the journal, editor Beth Luey announced the change in the journal's name to the more inclusive *Publishing Research Quarterly*, a name that "reflects a belief that publishing is best defined by its purposes and activities rather than by the specific media in which these purposes are manifested." Topics of particular interest to the editors of *Publishing Research Quarterly* include electronic publishing, literacy, censorship, copyright concerns, and publishing outside the United States.

Random House, Inc., 201 East 50th Street, New York, NY 10022; telephone 212/751–2600.

[Original publisher of Malcolm X, "A Homemade Education"]

In 1925 Bennett Cerf and Donald S. Klopfer bought The Modern Library, a line of reprints of modern classic books, for $215,000 from Horace Liveright of the Boni and Liveright publishing company. They set up offices on West 45th Street in New York and commissioned Lucien Bernhardt to design their new company's logo, the familiar running figure carrying a torch. The Modern Library line was increasingly successful, allowing Cerf and Klopfer to expand their publishing interests to include a new imprint, Random House of New York and Nonesuch Press of London. Instead of the durable and inexpensive reprints of the Modern Library, the initial Random House list was made up of elegant, limited edition books; the first book published under this joint imprint was a reprint of Herman Melville's 1855 novella *Benito Cereno*.

These expensive limited editions were so successful that they tended to sell out repeatedly, so Random House turned next to publishing less expensive trade editions of its books, beginning in 1929. Among the writers published by Random House in the thirties and forties were William Faulkner, James Joyce, Gertrude Stein, and William Saroyan, as well as British poets Stephen Spender and W. H. Auden and American playwright Eugene O'Neill (the Random House editors loved the theater and continued to publish drama, despite the standard wisdom that people preferred to see plays rather than read them).

In 1932 Random House gained attention—and a great deal of respect within the literary world—when Cerf and Klopfer fought a legal battle to allow the publication of James Joyce's novel *Ulysses*, which had been declared obscene and banned in the United States. In 1933, due to the efforts of Cerf and Klopfer, the obscenity ruling was overturned, and Random House published the first American edition of the novel in 1934. Random House also began publishing children's books in the 1930s, including those of the popular Theodor Geisel, better known as Dr. Seuss. The firm continued to expand in the fifties and sixties, publishing both best-selling authors, such as James Michener, and literary authors like Robert Penn Warren. The editors at Random House became known for their skill in attracting, and helping to develop, good writers.

In 1959 Random House offered its stock to the public for the first time. In 1960 the company acquired the publishing company Alfred A. Knopf, along with its Vintage line of quality paperback books. A year later Random House bought the highly respected Pantheon imprint. Both Knopf and Pantheon retained editorial control after being acquired by Random House (although this practice would change in the 1980s, following a change in ownership and with increasing pressure to publish profitable books). In 1966 RCA took over control of Random House, and in 1973 the company acquired Ballantine Books (see Ballantine Books in this appendix). S. I. Newhouse's company, Newhouse Publications (now known as Advance Publications) purchased Random House from RCA in 1980 for $65 million. Random House is now one of the world's largest publishers.

Red Crane Books, 826 Camino de Monte Rey, Santa Fe, NM 87501; telephone 505/988–7070.

[Publisher of Jimmy Santiago Baca, "Coming into Language"]

Marianne and Michael O'Shaughnessy founded Red Crane Books in Santa Fe, New Mexico in 1989. The O'Shaughnessys and Beverly Miller-Atwater comprise the entire staff of Red Crane Books. The O'Shaughnessys became involved in publishing through their interest in the work of the Archaeological Research Center, which in turn led them to the Taos Pueblo. Together with others, they raised enough money to match a U.S. Housing and Urban Development (HUD) grant for the restoration of the Taos Pueblo. While they were involved in this process, they learned of a book manuscript by R. C. Gordon-McCutchan, called *The Taos Indians: The Battle for Blue Lake*. The O'Shaughnessys felt that this book, which recounted the struggle of the Taos Indians in New Mexico to regain the Blue Lake Watershed (an important water source that had been taken from them during the administration of President Theodore Roosevelt), should be published, and they decided to publish it themselves. They chose the red crane as their emblem because of its significance, in Asian cultures, as a symbol of good luck. Red Crane Books publishes approximately twelve general trade books per year, particularly ones focusing on the American Southwest; the company now has over thirty titles in print.

Roberts Brothers

[Publisher of Louisa May Alcott's "Literary Lessons"]

The Roberts Brothers publishing company was founded by Lewis Augustus Roberts and Austin Roberts in Boston in 1861. The Roberts brothers began their firm in response to the rising demand for photograph albums; their company's early success prompted the brothers to expand into the realm of publishing. In 1863 Austin Roberts withdrew from the firm, and Lewis Roberts hired Thomas Niles Jr. as editor. From 1839 to 1855, Niles had worked with the well-known bookseller and publisher William D. Ticknor in Ticknor's Old Corner Bookstore—an experience that had taught him invaluable lessons about working with authors.

Niles began by publishing successful juvenile literature and religious and sentimental poetry, such as the work of English poet Jean Ingelow. Because of the success of Niles's early publishing decisions, by 1866 Roberts Brothers had become a prominent Boston publisher. Louisa May Alcott wrote *Little Women* (the full title of which was *Little Women, or Meg, Jo, Beth and Amy, the Story of Their Lives*) at Niles's urging. Although Alcott had expressed a lack of interest in the subject, Niles was convinced there was a market for such a "girls' story." The first part of *Little Women* was published in September 1868, and its first printing of 2,000 copies sold out within a month. The second part appeared in April 1869, and by the end of the year there were 38,000 copies of both parts in print, with another 32,000 appearing in 1870. Roberts Brothers continued to publish Alcott's work, which included *An Old-Fashioned Girl* in 1870, *Little Men* in 1871, and *Rose in Bloom* in 1876. *Little Women* first appeared in a single volume in 1880.

In subsequent decades Roberts Brothers published a variety of literary works, including poetry by English poets Christina Rossetti and Dante Gabriel Rossetti, translations of French novelists George Sand and Honoré de Balzac, and a series of works by English novelist George Meredith. In 1884 the firm published Robert Louis Stevenson's highly successful *Treasure Island*, and in the 1890s Roberts Brothers published several series of the *Poems* of Emily Dickinson.

Niles died at the age of sixty-nine in 1894, and at the beginning of 1898 Lewis Roberts put the firm up for sale. In June of that year Roberts Brothers was purchased by Little, Brown and Company, which added most of the company's nine hundred titles to its own list. In its thirty-seven years of operation, Roberts Brothers had published 1,300 titles, many of which came to be considered literary classics.

St. Martin's Press, Inc., 175 Fifth Avenue, New York, NY 10010; telephone 212/674–5151.

[Publisher of Mark Thompson, "The Evolution of The Advocate*"]*

St. Martin's Press was established in 1952 as an American distributor for books published by Macmillan and Company, Limited of London. Thus, the earliest books published by St. Martin's were reference works, textbooks, and trade reprints of British titles. Eventually the

American company's relationship with its British parent company became more flexible, and Ian MacKenzie, who took over as director of St. Martin's in 1956, began introducing original American titles as part of its list. But the company's greatest period of growth as an independent American publisher began in 1970, when Thomas J. McCormack became its president. Under McCormack's leadership St. Martin's expanded its output, and its profits, considerably. Among the authors published by McCormack are the novelist Fay Weldon and James Herriot, author of the best-selling *All Creatures Great and Small* series. St. Martin's has come to be known for its category fiction, including romantic novels, mysteries, and science fiction, but its reference, scholarly, and textbook publishing programs have been successful as well. Imprints of St. Martin's include Stonewall Editions, which features gay writing, particularly fiction (the imprint under which Mark Thompson's book appeared); Tor Books, a line of science fiction books; and the trade paperback Griffin and Picador imprints. One imprint of St. Martin's, Bedford Books, is the publisher of this textbook.

Saturday Review of Literature

[Publisher of Bernard Berelson, "Who Reads What, and Why?"]

In 1920 a Yale University English professor, Henry Seidel Canby, was invited to establish a literary review as a weekly supplement to the New York *Evening Post*. Canby began editing this supplement, called the *Literary Review*, with a staff of three: William Benét, Amy Loveman, and Christopher Morley. Although the *Review* was a critical and journalistic success and was considered an important source of information on serious American books, it was cut from the *Post* when the newspaper was sold by its publisher, Thomas Lamont, to the Curtis Publishing interest in 1924. Lamont was upset that the *Review* was dropped, and he approached the publishers of *Time* magazine, Henry Luce and Briton Hadden, for help in reestablishing it. With financial assistance from Lamont and publishing facilities and office space at *Time*, the *Review* began again—this time under the title the *Saturday Review of Literature*—with complete editorial control given to Canby and his staff. The first issue appeared on August 2, 1924, under the *Review*'s new symbol, a phoenix rising from the ashes.

Under Canby's editorship the *Review* established the practice of defending foreign writers who were under political pressure, along with promoting the work of these writers as well as émigré writers in the United States. After 1939 the magazine's title was shortened to the *Saturday Review*, and its focus and interests were expanded under the editorship of Norman Cousins. Besides book reviews and literary articles, the magazine published a "main events" column and included coverage of film, the broadcast media, photography, music, the publishing business, and travel. In the 1950s and 1960s the *Review* expanded its coverage of social controversies such as the dangers of atomic energy and false advertising and inadequate testing at drug companies, and it further established itself as an initiator of humanitarian projects on an international scale.

Cousins stepped down as editor in 1971, and that year the magazine was sold to owners who divided it into four separate magazines on the arts, education, science, and society. This venture failed, and by 1972 the *Review* was in bankruptcy court. In 1973 Cousins returned as editor, linking the *Saturday Review* with the *World*, the magazine he had founded after leaving the *Review*. Due to a rise in postal rates, Cousins was unable to revive the magazine financially. The *Saturday Review* had a series of different owners and editors after 1977, and in 1980 the magazine was converted into a monthly. Its last owners (prior to *Penthouse* publisher Bob Guccione, who bought the *Review* in 1987) tried to appeal to a younger audience by expanding the magazine's coverage of popular culture. But circulation continued to drop, and the last few issues of the *Saturday Review* appeared bimonthly until publication was suspended altogether in mid-1986. Now owned by Guccione's organization, Penthouse International, the *Saturday Review* appears online only, through America Online, although research is being done on the possibility of returning the magazine to print. It remains primarily a review of the arts, with some emphasis on social issues as well.

Simon & Schuster (see Touchstone Books.)

Time, Time-Warner, Inc., Timelife Building, Rockefeller Center, New York, NY 10020; telephone 212/522–1212.

[Publisher of Richard Zoglin, "Trekking Onward"]

The weekly news magazine *Time* was founded by former Yale University classmates and fellow Baltimore *News* reporters Briton Hadden and Henry R. Luce. *Time* was incorporated in November 1922, and the first issue of the magazine appeared on March 3, 1923. Hadden and Luce saw their magazine as providing a service to the American "busy man" who wanted to be informed of world events but had little time; their initial prospectus for the magazine declared that "people are uninformed because no publication has adapted itself to the time which busy men are able to spend on keeping informed."

The first issue was divided into twenty-two departments (such as Nation, Business, Education), and most of these departments remain in today's magazine, although others (such as Show Business, Music, and Computers) have been added. Other aspects of the magazine's format remain the same as well, including the large title and red border on each issue's cover, and the phrase "the weekly newsmagazine," which appeared first on the cover and then on the masthead. *Time* named Charles Lindbergh its first "Man of the Year" in 1928; since then, the first issue of each year has announced the magazine's editors' choice of the man, woman, people, or thing of the year. Hadden is credited with establishing the magazine's distinctive writing style, which came to be known as "timestyle"—a style characterized by the use of many descriptive adjectives, inverted sentences, puns, alliteration, and other features. Hadden died in 1929, but Luce remained with the magazine, as editor-in-chief and finally as editorial chairman, until his death in 1967, while also developing other projects, including the very successful *Life* magazine.

Initially *Time* made no secret of the fact that most of its articles were brief, rewritten versions of articles that had appeared in the daily newspapers, mainly in the New York *Times* and the New York *Herald Tribune*. This practice lessened when *Time* joined the Associated Press in 1936, however. But *Time*'s unique reporting method, referred to as "group journalism" (which grew out of this practice of rewriting) remained; in this method, each article is produced by a team of correspondents, researchers, writers, senior editors, the managing editor, and fact checkers, and the story can be rewritten, or challenged, by anyone at any stage of the process.

Time has been criticized for its style and for its practice of group journalism. It has also been accused of confusing its readers by bombarding them with facts, and of reflecting a conservative bias by mixing fact and opinion in its stories. But it remains an extremely popular magazine, and its competition with *Newsweek* remains intense. In 1992 *Time*'s parent company, Time, Inc.—which already owned countless newspapers and newspaper chains, publishing interests, magazines (including *Sports Illustrated, Fortune, People,* and *Life*), and television and communications interests (including Home Box Office)—purchased the entertainment conglomerate Warner Communications Inc. The result was Time-Warner, Inc., one of the world's largest news, media, and entertainment conglomerates.

Tobacco-Free Youth Reporter, Stop Teenage Addiction to Tobacco (STAT), 511 East Columbus Avenue, Springfield, MA 01105; telephone 413/732–7828.

[Publisher of Joe Tye, "Buying Silence: Self-Censorship of Smoking and Health in National Newsweeklies"]

The *Tobacco-Free Youth Reporter* (formerly the *Tobacco and Youth Reporter*) is the quarterly publication of the organization Stop Teenage Addiction to Tobacco (STAT). Founded by Joe Tye in 1985, STAT is a nonprofit, international membership organization devoted to reducing the use of tobacco by children and teens. The *Tobacco-Free Youth Reporter* provides STAT members with notices of upcoming events, calls to action, and reports on topics such as cigarette advertising and state laws on tobacco sales to minors. The first issue of the *Tobacco-Free Youth Re-*

porter was published in 1986; in 1988 STAT offices relocated from California to Springfield, Massachusetts.

Touchstone Books, (an imprint of) Simon & Schuster, Inc., Simon & Schuster Building, 1230 Avenue of the Americas, New York, NY 10020; telephone 212/698–7000.

[Publisher of Christina Hoff Sommers, "The Backlash Myth"]

Touchstone Books, an imprint of Simon & Schuster, Inc., publishes a broad range of academically oriented paperback books for adults. An original Simon & Schuster imprint, Touchstone began publishing books in 1969.

Richard Leo Simon and Max Lincoln Schuster founded a publishing company in 1924 with no definite books in mind. Schuster, who had been a journalist and had worked in advertising and as an editor of a trade magazine, and Simon, who had worked in sales, adopted a plan of creating ideas for books, then looking for authors to carry out those ideas. They published their first book, the world's first crossword puzzle book, under the name Plaza Publishing Company (a name that was intended to disguise the publishers' identities, in case the book was a failure). The book was a great success, and the firm became known as Simon & Schuster. In 1924 a seventeen-year-old named Leon Shimkin joined the company as office manager, bookkeeper, and business manager. As soon as he was legally eligible (at age twenty-one), Shimkin became the company's secretary-treasurer, and he was soon made a partner. Shimkin acquired one of Simon & Schuster's great publishing successes, Dale Carnegie's *How to Win Friends and Influence People*, which was first published in 1936.

Simon & Schuster continued its practice of attempting to determine what the public wanted to read and publishing books to match those desires, eventually mixing these popular books with a number of more serious works. The company also conducted extensive advertising campaigns and opinion polls, and it was constantly trying out new merchandising methods. In 1939, Simon, Schuster, and Shimkin joined with Robert F. de Graff to launch Pocket Books, the first successful U.S. paperback imprint in this century (see Minstrel Books, an imprint of Pocket Books, in this appendix). In 1942 the company began publishing the popular Little Golden Books line of children's books, and in the 1950s Simon & Schuster began publishing the works of a number of prominent foreign writers, as well as those of popular cartoonists and humorists, including James Thurber and P. G. Wodehouse.

In 1944 Simon & Schuster and Pocket Books were purchased by Marshall Field Enterprises, but in 1957, Simon, Schuster, and Shimkin bought the firm back. In 1966, following Simon's death and Schuster's retirement, Shimkin gained control of the entire firm. He merged Simon

& Schuster and Pocket Books, and over the following years the company founded and acquired a number of additional divisions and imprints, including Touchstone Books. In 1975 Simon & Schuster was bought by the conglomerate Gulf + Western Industries, and in 1985 Gulf + Western acquired the publishing company Prentice-Hall, which it made an important subsidiary of Simon & Schuster. Today Simon & Schuster, which is officially affiliated with Gulf + Western's Paramount Communications, is made up of nine major subdivisions (including the Simon & Schuster adult hardcover imprint, Simon & Schuster Children's Books, the Simon & Schuster Education Group, the Simon & Schuster International Group, and several others), each of which includes many separate divisions and imprints.

Transaction Publishers, Department 3095, Rutgers University, New Brunswick, NJ 08903; telephone 908/445–2280.

[Publisher of Steven Starker, "The New Oracle: Self-Help Books in American Culture"]

Transaction Publishers is an independent publisher of social scientific books, periodicals, and book series, including works in the more established fields such as anthropology, economics, and political science, as well as more recent disciplines such as urban studies and criminology. It was founded in 1962 by Alvin W. Gouldner, Lee Rainwater, and Irving Louis Horowitz, through a grant sponsored by the Ford Foundation at Washington University in St. Louis. Initially Transaction was divided into three divisions: documentary films, public education, and publications. The first project of the publications division was the magazine *Transaction* (whose name was changed to *Society* in 1970).

Transaction's book division began in 1969 with a series of books derived from work in *Society* magazine. By 1973 it had become a full-scale publisher, developing a book list that was completely independent of the magazine. Besides its book division, Transaction Publishers provides technical support to a number of journals and periodicals (including the *Publishing Research Quarterly*, which is included in this appendix) through its periodicals consortium. Transaction Publishers has been located on the campus of Rutgers University since 1969.

TV Guide, News America Publishing, Inc., 1211 Avenue of the Americas, New York, NY 10036; telephone 212/852–7500.

[Publisher of Erik Davis, "True Believers"]

TV Guide, one of the best-selling magazines (if not *the* best-selling magazine) in the United States, was launched by newspaper magnate Walter Annenberg's organization, Triangle Publications, in 1953. In 1952

Annenberg had noticed a full-page ad for a local magazine, called *TV Digest*, in the Philadelphia *Bulletin*, a competitor of Annenberg's own Philadelphia *Inquirer*. This gave Annenberg the idea of a *national* television magazine in which national feature stories about television and television-related topics would be prepared as a full-color section that would then be shipped to local distributors, who would insert their own local television listings inside this national material.

Herbert Muschel and Lee Wagner, who began their New York magazine *TeleVision Guide* (later shortened to *TV Guide*) in 1948, are credited with the idea of using print to address television and television-related topics. Muschel left the magazine shortly after its founding, however, and when Wagner was facing financial difficulties a few years later, he sold the New York *TV Guide* to Annenberg's organization, Triangle Publications, for about $1.5 million. Annenberg then went on to acquire Philadelphia's local television digest and Chicago's *TV Forecast*, each for approximately $1 million. The first issue of Triangle Publications' *TV Guide* appeared on April 3, 1953. Today *TV Guide* publishes well over 100 editions each week. The original wraparound format has been changed; now national articles appear in the front of the magazine, with local television listings following.

Annenberg had envisioned a magazine that would be "the *Time* magazine of the television industry," but the magazine's topic prevented that kind of seriousness for the most part. Serious articles have appeared in the magazine, however, including discussions of television and the family, the effects of television on children, and political coverage on television. More important than any of the magazine's articles, however—at least within the television industry—is *TV Guide*'s cover photograph, which is seen as a sure ratings builder for the program that it features. In 1989 *TV Guide* was purchased by Rupert Murdoch's News America Publications, Inc., which owns numerous newspapers, publishing interests, and so on (see HarperCollins, Inc. in this appendix, for example). Some critics maintain that the magazine has become more sensationalist and tabloid-like under Murdoch's ownership, but its success continues.

University of Georgia Press, 330 Research Drive, Suite B-100, Athens, GA 30602–4901; telephone 706/369–6130.

[Publisher of Thomas J. Roberts, "On Low Taste"]

The University of Georgia Press was founded in 1938 by the trustees of the University of Georgia to support and publish the scholarship of members of the university faculty. The press's mission has changed since that time, however, and within the last twenty years only a few of its authors have been faculty members at the University of Georgia.

While its initial focus was on scholarly works, the press now publishes general trade books (both hardcover and paperback) as well; this active trade publishing program accounts for roughly 50 percent of the Press's publishing program overall.

The University of Georgia Press has particularly strong trade lists in the areas of southern regional writing and Civil Rights studies. The press also publishes literary fiction, including the works of winners of the Flannery O'Connor Award, which is awarded twice a year to collections of short fiction by previously unpublished writers. Two recent Flannery O'Connor Award winners are Carol Lee Lorenzo's *Nervous Dancer* and Alyce Miller's *The Nature of Longing*. The press is also one of the few university presses that publish novels; recent novels include Chris Fuhrman's *The Dangerous Lives of Altar Boys* and Dr. Carl Djerassi's *The Bourbaki Gambit*. Since its founding, the University of Georgia Press has published over 1,300 trade, scholarly, and monographic (single-topic scholarly) books; over 900 of those books are still in print.

University of Illinois Press, 1325 South Oak Street, Champaign, IL 61820-6903; telephone 217/333–0950.

[Publisher of Charles Kikuchi, "Tanforan, 1942: Chronicle from an American Concentration Camp"]

The University of Illinois Press was founded in 1918 as a not-for-profit scholarly publisher based at the University of Illinois. It is now one of the larger university presses in the United States, publishing around 120 books each year, along with a dozen journals (including the *Journal of English and Germanic Philology* and the *American Journal of Psychology*).

The press's mission is "to produce significant publications that present important research, advance scholarship, and inspire ongoing reflection." Areas of particular strength at the University of Illinois Press include African American studies, American history, American music, anthropology and archaeology, ethnic and immigration history, fiction and poetry, folklore, Judaica and Holocaust studies, labor history, literature, religion, social history, and women's studies. The press is also working to develop its lists in the areas of environmental studies, Native American studies, cultural studies, and creative nonfiction.

Recent successes at the University of Illinois Press include John Dittmer's *Local People: The Struggle for Civil Rights in Mississippi*, Michael Burlingame's *The Inner World of Abraham Lincoln*, Mark Doty's poetry collection *My Alexandria*, Susan E. Cayleff's *Babe: The Life and Legend of Babe Didrikson Zaharias*, and William H. Tucker's *The Science and Politics of Racial Research*, which provided one response to Charles Murray and Richard Herrnstein's *The Bell Curve* (see The Free Press in this appendix). General information about the University of Illinois Press, including a listing of the Press's over 1,500 books in print, is available on the World Wide Web at http://www.uiuc.edu/providers/uipress.

University of North Carolina Press, 116 South Boundary Street, P.O. Box 2288, Chapel Hill, NC 27515–2288; telephone 919/966–3561.

[Publisher of Linda K. Kerber, "Why Should Girls Be Learned or Wise?"; Janice A. Radway, "The Act of Reading the Romance"; Joan Shelley Rubin, "Why Do You Disappoint Yourself? The Early History of the Book-of-the-Month Club"; Barbara Sicherman, "Reading Little Women: The Many Lives of a Text"]

The University of North Carolina Press, founded in 1922, is the oldest university press in the South and one of the oldest in the United States. The press's purpose, according to its charter, is "to promote generally, by publishing deserving works, the advancement of the arts and sciences and the development of literature." It is known for developing one of the strongest regional publishing programs in the United States, which includes both scholarly and general-interest books about the state of North Carolina and the South. One of the most famous of these books, the *Encyclopedia of Southern Culture,* was published in 1989 and now has over 50,000 copies in print. The press was also the first publisher to develop an ongoing program of books by and about African Americans. Other areas of special interest are American history, literary criticism, women's studies, European history, legal history, folklore, and Latin American and Caribbean studies.

Utne Reader, Lens Publishing Co., Inc., The Fawkes Building, 1624 Harmon Place, Suite 330, Minneapolis, MN 55403; telephone 612/338–5040.

[Publisher of Laurie Ouellette, "'Zines: Notes from the Underground"]

The *Utne Reader* is a bimonthly magazine founded in 1984 by president and editor-in-chief Eric Utne. (According to the magazine's masthead, "'UTNE' rhymes with 'chutney' and means 'far out' in Norwegian.") The *Utne Reader* reprints material from magazines and books on issues such as politics, international affairs, the arts, science, and social issues—material it terms "the best of the alternative media." Recent articles in the magazine appeared originally in *The Nation,* the *L.A. Times Magazine,* and *In These Times.* The *Utne Reader* also sponsors a community service organization called The Neighborhood Salon Association, and its editorial staff selects yearly winners of its Alternative Press Awards (see, for example, *h2so4*—a nominee for an *Utne Reader* Annual Alternative Press Award—in this appendix).

Wilson Library Bulletin, **The H. H. Wilson Company, 950 University Avenue, Bronx, NY 10452; telephone 718/588–8400, ext. 2245.**

[Publisher of Joseph Deitch, "Portrait of a Book Reviewer: Christopher Lehmann-Haupt"]

The *Wilson Library Bulletin* is a magazine for library professionals that is issued monthly (except in July and August). It began in November 1914 as the *Wilson Bulletin* and was designed "to provide timely information regarding the [H. H. Wilson Company] firm's new undertakings, and also . . . a convenient check-list of all the company's publications." Early issues appeared sporadically, essentially whenever there was enough time and material to assemble them, and in the early years of the magazine's publication there was no charge to subscribers. Through the years the magazine came to be published on a regular monthly basis, and a subscription price was set. In 1928 the name was changed to the *Wilson Bulletin: A Magazine for Librarians,* in 1930 to the *Wilson Bulletin for Librarians,* and in 1939 to the current *Wilson Library Bulletin.* Beginning with the September 1984 issue, the magazine changed from its former scholarly format to a glossier, colorful, regular magazine-size format.

Yale University Press, P.O. Box 209040, New Haven, CT 06520–9040; telephone 203/432–0960.

[Publisher of Larzer Ziff, "Writing for Print"; Joan DelFattore, "Romeo and Juliet Were Just Good Friends"]

Yale University Press, considered one of the most prestigious presses in academic publishing, was established in 1908, largely through the generosity of George Parmly Day, who provided initial capital and raised money to establish an endowment fund. At first Day used a desk in his office at a New York City financial firm to house the press. When he became treasurer of Yale University in 1910, Day moved the press to New Haven. Eventually the offices were moved to a house on Green Street that had been purchased for the press in 1919. The press moved to its current offices in 1973. Yale University Press publishes scholarly materials (including audio cassettes, video discs, and CD-ROMs for certain teaching programs), primarily in the areas of art, religion, literature, women's studies, psychology, political science, history, and Judaica. Among its best-selling books are textbooks in French and Japanese, John Dizikes's *Opera in America,* Anthony Sutcliffe's *Paris: An Architectural History,* and Eugene O'Neill's *Long Day's Journey into Night.*

Jimmy Santiago Baca, "Coming into Language," *Working in the Dark: Reflections of a Poet of the Barrio.* Copyright © 1992 by Jimmy Santiago Baca. Reprinted with the permission of Red Crane Books.

Dudley Barlow, "Why We Still Need *Huckleberry Finn*" Copyright © 1992. Reprinted from *The Education Digest*, September 1992, Ann Arbor, Michigan.

Bernard Berelson, "Who Reads What, and Why?," from the May 12, 1951 issue of *Saturday Review of Literature.* Reprinted by permission of *The Saturday Review* © 1951, S. R. Publications, Ltd.

Sven Birkerts. Selections from "The Paper Chase" and "Perseus Unbound" from *The Gutenberg Elegies: The Fate of Reading in an Electronic Age* by Sven Birkerts. Copyright © 1994 by Sven Birkerts. Reprinted by permission of Faber and Faber Publishers, Inc.

Laura Bohannan, "Shakespeare in the Bush," *Natural History*, August/September 1966. Copyright © 1966. Reprinted by permission of the author.

British Library, Title Page of *The boke named the Gouernour*, 1537, shelfmark C40636. By permission of the British Library.This image has been altered slightly for the purposes of book publication.

Farai Chideya, "Who's Making What News?" from *Don't Believe the Hype: Fighting Cultural Misinformation About African-Americans* by Farai Chideya. Copyright © 1995 by Farai Chideya. Used by permission of Dutton Signet, a division of Penguin Books, USA, Inc.

Jeff Cohen, "Propaganda from the Middle of the Road: The Centrist Bias of the U.S. Media." Copyright © 1989. This article is excerpted from the Oct./Nov. 1989 issue of *EXTRA!*, the magazine published by FAIR.

Huntly Collins, "PC and the Press," from *Change*, 24:1, pp. 12–16, Jan.–Feb., 1992. Reprinted with permission of the Helen Dwight Reid Educational Foundation. Published by Heldref Publications, 1319 Eighteenth Street, NW, Washington, D.C., 20036–1802. Copyright © 1992.

Walt Crawford and Michael Gorman, "Coping with Electronic Information." Reprinted with permission of the American Library Association, from *Future Libraries: Dreams, Madness, and Reality.* Copyright © 1995, by Walt Crawford and Michael Gorman.

Erik Davis, "True Believers," *TV Guide Special Issue* (Spring 1995). Copyright © 1995. Reprinted by permission of Erik Davis.

Joseph Deitch, "Portrait of a Book Reviewer: Christopher Lehmann-Haupt," *Wilson Library Bulletin*, December 1987. Reprinted by permission.

Joan DelFattore, "Romeo and Juliet Were Just Good Friends," from *What Johnny Shouldn't Read: Textbook Censorship in America*, Yale University Press, 1992. Copyright © 1992 by Yale University.

John P. Dessauer, "Cultural Pluralism and the Book World," originally appeared in the Fall 1986 issue of *Book Research Quarterly.* Reprinted by permission of Transaction Publishers. Copyright © 1986 by Transaction Publishers. All rights reserved.

Umberto Eco, "The Future of Literacy," *Apocalypse Postponed*, ed. Robert Lumley. Copyright © 1994 . Reprinted by permission of Indiana University Press.

Susan Faludi, "The Media and the Backlash," from *Backlash* by Susan Faludi. Copyright © 1991 by Susan Faludi. Reprinted by permission of Crown Publishers.

Benjamin Franklin, "An Apology for Printers" originally published in 1731. Reprinted from *The Papers of Benjamin Franklin*, edited by Leonard Labaree (New Haven & London: Yale University Press, 1959). Vol 1., pp. 194–199.

Henry Louis Gates Jr., "The Trope of the Talking Book." Excerpted from *The Signifying Monkey: A Theory of Afro-American Literary Criticism* by Henry Louis Gates Jr. Copyright © 1988 by Henry Louis Gates Jr. Reprinted by permission of Oxford University Press, Inc.

INDEX
OF AUTHORS
AND TITLES

THE PRESS OF IDEAS

Readings for Writers on Print Culture and the Information Age

JULIE BATES DOCK

Editor's Notes to Accompany

THE PRESS OF IDEAS

*Readings for Writers
on Print Culture
and the Information Age*

PREPARED BY

Julie Bates Dock

BEDFORD BOOKS OF ST. MARTIN'S PRESS
Boston

PREFACE

Each chapter of *The Press of Ideas* asks a specific question that provokes students to think critically about an aspect of the world of information and print that they otherwise may have taken for granted. The essays focus attention on features of the print-dominated world so pervasive that they often go unnoticed. By presenting issues in the form of questions, the book challenges students to scrutinize their culture rather than accept it uncritically. They essays in each chapter don't necessarily provide answers; instead, they present a selection of responses to and complications of the organizing question.

Chapter 1, "How Do We Read?", allows students to examine closely an activity that they have been performing almost unconsciously for most of their lives: making meaning from printed texts. Through several clusters of essays, the chapter demonstrates the range of readers' responses to texts, the many uses that we make of our reading, and the role that print plays in validating cultural activity. The selections in chapter 2, "Who Reads?", offer a variety of perspectives on the crucial issue of access to print. The essays, half of them personal narratives of literacy education, demonstrate the inexorable line between literacy and empowerment, both political and personal. Chapter 3, "What Do You Think?", helps students become more savvy consumers of some of the information and products purveyed by newspapers and magazines—hard news, lifestyle trends, advertising, and books themselves. Print guides our opinions, and it also influences or tastes, as chapter 4, "What Should You Read", makes clear. These selections look at relationships between popular culture and official (or high) culture, and how each is disseminated and validated. The final essays in the chapter examine particular genres of popular print: the romance, the self-help book, and the fanzine. The connection between knowledge and power comes to the forefront in chapter 4, "What Shouldn't You Read?" In these essays on censorship and the First Amendment, students will encounter many arguments for restricting the flow in information: religious fundamentalists' objections to secular humanism; African American's protests that *Huckleberry Finn* is racist; "politically correct" reformers lobbying for campus speech codes and changes in curricula to eliminate Western bias; radical feminists' contentions that pornography violates women's civil rights and cannot claim protection as free speech; and finally, computer hackers pushing the limits of freedom to include electronic "speech." The last selection segues to the final chapter, "What's Next?", an examination of the future of the book in the electronic age. Tributes to technology mingle with expressions of profound doubt as writers come to grips with the magnitude of the computer's impact on society and the further effects on communication that computers seem likely to inspire.

CONTENTS

INTRODUCTION

*Print Culture and
the Composition Course*

WHAT IS PRINT CULTURE STUDIES?

This book is informed by a field you may never have heard of: print culture studies. Since a big part of a composition instructor's job involves teaching students to read more critically, and since that reading is generally embodied in printed texts, the study of how print influences the dissemination of knowledge and power seems a natural for a writing class. But what, exactly, is print culture studies? What are its assumptions and its areas of interest?

Print culture studies, history of the book, *histoire du livre, Geschichte des Buchwesens*—this emerging field goes by many names and involves scholars from many disciplines. Historians, sociologists, literary scholars, librarians, psychologists, and bibliophiles have been among those whose work has converged in the past three decades to create a new interdisciplinary field that embraces all aspects of reading the printed word. Robert Darnton has described book history as "the social and cultural history of communication by print, . . . [whose] purpose is to understand how ideas were transmitted through print and how exposure to the printed word affected the thought and behavior of mankind during the last five hundred years" ("What Is the History of Books?," p. 27).

Darnton's definition is too backward-looking for my taste, for it excludes those who seek to understand the continuities between past and future uses of the book, those who view electronic communication as an extension of printed communication. Therefore, I have used the term *print culture studies* throughout this book, seeking to deemphasize the historical component and highlight the cultural basis of this approach. In this broader definition, print culture studies can encompass an analysis of the sales of Shakespeare's First Folio as well as the dissemination of fanzines on the Internet, a study of eighteenth-century broadside ballads and twentieth-century graphic novels, the protocols of reading both epistolary novels and e-mail.

The recent concern over the future of the book and the role of computers in communication makes this inclusive definition imperative. Exploring the links between the print revolution and the technological revolution can make us more conscious of the influence of the former and less anxious about the ramifications of the latter. Understanding how and why print has affected us in the past five hundred years, we can gain a better perspective on the cultural uncertainties of the electronic age. For those who find the advent of computers worrisome, comprehending the similarities between printed and electronic communication may allay some fears. Those who rush to embrace new technologies may come to understand the extent to which thought and behavior will likely remain governed by the conventions that emerged from print, even in the computer age. Historical reference points are necessary to understand the continuity of processes long established, as well as the changes that will occur in those processes as technology alters the flow of information.

Whether it examines printed or electronic communication, print culture studies can be divided into three large and sometimes overlapping areas: production, distribution, and reception of knowledge. Production encompasses not only analyses of how authors write, but also of how books (and other alphabetic products) are manufactured. Distribution considers how texts get from producer to consumer. This may include studies of shippers, booksellers, publishers, peddlers, smugglers, libraries, and e-text distributors. Reception studies include analyses of individual readers' practices, as well as the study of reviews, book clubs, salons, sales figures, and the like. Each of these broad areas influences and is in turn influenced by the others. Moreover, each must be considered in relation to prevailing economic, social, political, and intellectual climates.

One of the main assumptions of print culture studies is that ideas exist not just intellectually, but as part of material culture. This discipline keeps ever in view the concrete reality of books, magazines, newspapers, pamphlets, contracts, and other printed documents. It studies the ideas and images in their material form, as objects and not just as abstractions. Even the words on a computer screen exist, if only temporarily, in a material context.

This field touches nearly every aspect of culture, because so much of a modern society's intellectual and social life is transmitted through print. Print culture studies seeks to focus attention on the mechanisms by which knowledge and culture are transmitted in order to better understand how print influences our behavior. It also examines the power relations that are often expressed through print, especially in terms of access or lack of access to the power of the press.

The ubiquity of print has often led to its being overlooked as a source of influence over our ideas and actions. The very books we use in teaching writing often seem to disclaim their own participation in the world of print. Typically, composition textbooks present essays in terms of their intellectual content and their rhetorical value. Rarely do they focus either students' or teachers' attention on the material aspects of the essays, on their status as printed objects. Rarely do college textbooks in any discipline call attention to the power with which they invest their ideas, simply by the fact of being college textbooks.

Every alphabetic communication consists of more than disembodied ideas and words. Once an idea is concretized in print, it exists in a tangible realm and can be studied using a variety of methods. Print culture studies assumes that every book, every newspaper, every e-mail message, every magazine can be examined in terms of its participation in recognizable processes of production, distribution, and reception.

HOW DOES PRINT CULTURE STUDIES RELATE TO TEACHING WRITING?

The college composition course hits students at a crucial moment in their intellectual development. This is when they are invited, often for the first time, to enter the world of ideas. Those ideas are transmitted almost exclusively through print, with all its attendant manipulations of readers and writers. Students in a writing class work to develop the skills that will enable them to become active participants in that world by producing their own writing in addition to consuming the prose of others. There is no better time for them to begin comprehending the dynamics of written discourse.

As writing instructors, we often spend as much time teaching students how to read critically as we do teaching them how to write, for becoming a good writer involves becoming a good reader as well. Critical reading develops the critical thinking skills essential for strong writing. Print culture studies offers students a practical framework for analyzing written discourse. That framework, moreover, is immediately applicable to the students' own writing; it does not require a shift in context.

This book picks up the composition process at the point—often very early in the process—when outside forces begin to influence the writer's text in noticeable ways. It doesn't deal directly with the brainstorming, prewriting, and organizing that many writing textbooks cover, but instead concentrates on the interactions of writers, readers, and the material objects that carry messages between them. As students analyze how those interactions pertain to other people's writing, they can easily apply the same techniques of analysis to their own prose. Even though they may not yet write for print, students write with readers in mind, and they shape their prose accordingly. They can readily see how their own written messages participate in the same interactions that govern the prose they analyze in class.

Too often the writing done in composition classes seems disconnected from any purpose beyond fulfilling a required assignment and unrelated to any audience other than the teacher. Print culture studies' emphasis on the many audiences a writer addresses and on the many forces that shape written discourse keeps the interactive dynamic of writing at the forefront of the student writer's mind. It allows students to project their audience's needs and expectations before they write, helping them break away from the narcissistic notion that writing is solely a means of self-expression.

Because this field's methods and concerns apply to the whole realm of printed discourse, the materials of popular culture are as valid for study as the most scholarly academic articles. This range of materials presents several advantages for the composition instructor. First of all, it allows you and your students to have fun in the classroom. Fun is, of course, the last thing students expect from a required writing course, so it comes as a welcome surprise when they get to spend an hour flipping through surfing magazines or playing on the Internet—all in the service of intellectual analysis. From the instructor's standpoint, fun can be profitable, too. We all know how much easier it is to teach students who are interested in and enjoying the material. Letting students explore areas of print culture that intrigue them can yield greater comprehension and engagement with their subject.

On a more serious note, dealing with popular culture materials with which students are already familiar, and in some senses even expert, can build confidence that many lack at the outset of their college careers. Students are frequently adept at discussing and analyzing advertisements, fan magazines, or sci-fi novels. They often feel more comfortable with these artifacts than with examples of scholarly discourse. As they view scholarly articles alongside grocery-store self-help books or popular magazines, students can begin to recognize that academic texts share many features with texts they have already mastered. Analyzing such texts and questioning their assumptions can help students develop the assurance that they can master academic prose as well.

This method of studying prose pays careful attention to the physical embodiment of written discourse. The form of the book is as important as its content. Thus you'll find repeated references throughout *The Press of Ideas* to the materiality of the textbook the students hold in their hands. I encourage you to use this book as an object, not just as a container for ideas. It is, after all, one book you can be sure all your students have in common. This emphasis on the tangible aspects of print culture often gives the intellectually timid student a comfortable field for study.

Along with all the traditional critical thinking skills that students can derive from discussion and analysis of intellectually challenging readings on important issues, then, print culture studies offers additional resources for intellectual development. I hope you'll find, as I have, that it produces lively discussion and powerful writing from students who are interested in the materials and increasingly self-assured as they master the analytical techniques that render printed texts an open book.

FURTHER READINGS IN PRINT CULTURE STUDIES

Innumerable books and articles trace the practices of printers, publishers, booksellers, and readers. I offer here a brief list of works that study how print and literacy affected and continue to affect the way people think and communicate with one another. These works often elaborate on issues and ideas introduced in the readings in *The Press of Ideas*.

Birkerts, Sven. *The Gutenberg Elegies: The Fate of Reading in an Electronic Age.* Boston: Faber and Faber, 1994.

> Birkerts examines the changes taking place as we rush to embrace electronic technologies. I've included one of his personal essays recounting his passion for the printed word as well as an essay from the second section of the book, in which he analyzes several aspects of the emergent computer technologies. In the final section, Birkerts looks at how electronic communication is changing criticism and literary practice.

Burke, James. "Printing Transforms Knowledge," from the BBC series *The Day the Universe Changed*, 1986. Produced by John Lynch. Originally broadcast under the title "A Matter of Fact."

> Burke's entertaining and enlightening 52-minute video dramatically demonstrates the changes that came about through the invention of the press. The companion book to the public television series, also called *The Day the Universe Changed* (Boston: Little, Brown, 1985), includes a chapter presenting the same material, though in a less engaging manner. I recommend the video for classroom use.

Chartier, Roger. *Forms and Meanings: Texts, Performances, and Audiences from Codex to Computer.* Philadelphia: University of Pennsylvania Press, 1995.

> Using a wide range of examples from the early modern period through the present, Chartier examines how the form in which a text is transmitted "constrains the production of meaning [and] defines and constructs its audience." He situates electronic technologies in the context of the long history of representations of the written word. Three of the four essays in this book were given as the 1994 Rosenbach Lectures at the University of Pennsylvania.

_____. *The Order of Books: Readers, Authors, and Libraries in Europe between the Fourteenth and Eighteenth Centuries.* Translated by Lydia G. Cochrane. Stanford: Stanford University Press, 1994.

> A concise and readable analysis of how efforts to manage an increasing number of written texts, first manuscript then printed, led to the conceptual invention of the author, the library, and the book. His first chapter on "Communities of Readers" traces the theoretical relations between text, book, and reader outlined in my introduction to chapter 1.

Chaytor, H. J. *From Script to Print: An Introduction to Medieval Vernacular Literature.* Cambridge: Cambridge University Press, 1955.

> Chaytor traces the differences between listeners and readers of vernacular writing before and after the invention of printing.

Clanchy, Michael T. *From Memory to Written Record: England 1066–1307.* Cambridge, Mass.: Harvard University Press, 1979.

> This book takes a look at the late medieval transition to literacy that prepared the way for the printing press.

Darnton, Robert. "First Steps toward a History of Reading." *Australian Journal of French Studies*, v. 23, no. 1 (Jan.–Apr. 1986), pp. 5–30.

> Less readily available than Darnton's essay reprinted in Davidson's collection, this piece surveys how scholars have studied who read what books in different times and places. Darnton then suggests five approaches to the more difficult study of how and why readers read.

Davidson, Cathy. *Reading in America*. Baltimore, Md.: Johns Hopkins University Press, 1989.

> This is an anthology of essays on print culture in the United States from colonial to modern times. Especially useful is Robert Darnton's essay "What Is the History of Books?", an overview of the field of print culture studies. E. Jennifer Monaghan's essay on "Literacy Instruction and Gender in Colonial New England" offers useful material to supplement Linda Kerber's essay in this book. Janice A. Radway's "The Book-of-the-Month Club and the General Reader" builds on Joan Shelley Rubin's work, also reprinted in this book.

Eisenstein, Elizabeth L. *The Printing Revolution in Early Modern Europe*. Cambridge: Cambridge University Press, 1983. This text is ssentially the same as her earlier two-volume study, *The Printing Press as an Agent of Change: Communications and Cultural Transformation in Early Modern Europe*. Cambridge: Cambridge University Press, 1979, but does not contain the extensive footnotes and scholarly apparatus.

> Writing for the general reader, Eisenstein offers a good overview of the social implications of print, especially its impact on the religious and scientific worlds, though she overstates the extent to which she pioneered this field. Contains a useful if subjective annotated bibliography.

Febvre, Lucien, and Henri-Jean Martin. *The Coming of the Book: The Impact of Printing 1450–1500*. Translated by David Gerard. London: Verso, 1990. First edition: *L'Apparition du livre*. Paris, 1958.

> This seminal study treats the book as "one of the most potent agents at the disposal of western civilisation in bringing together the scattered ideas of representative thinkers." The authors provide a wealth of information about the spread of printing and the mechanisms of production and distribution throughout Europe. Their final chapter, "The Book as a Force for Change," offers a thoughtful overview of the social and intellectual impact of the printing press.

Gilmore-Lehne, William J. "Literacy," in *Encyclopedia of American Social History*, ed. Mary Kupiec Cayton, et al. 3 vols. New York: Scribners, 1993. Vol. 3:2413–2426.

> Gilmore-Lehne provides a readable and information-filled survey of definitions and measurements of literacy in the United States from colonial times to the present. He includes a useful bibliography of studies of literacy among African Americans, Native Americans, and Hispanic Americans.

Lanham, Richard A. *The Electronic Word: Democracy, Technology, and the Arts*. Chicago: University of Chicago Press, 1993.

> This collection of essays discusses the challenges and possibilities posed by digital technologies. Lanham sees cause for celebration in the dynamic and interactive mixtures of words and images that the computer encourages.

McLuhan, Marshall. *The Gutenberg Galaxy: The Making of Typographical Man*. Toronto: University of Toronto Press, 1962.

> This study of the effects of printing is idiosyncratic and often misleading, but always entertaining and provocative. McLuhan's bizarre "mosaic" mingling of data, quotations, and analysis makes the book difficult to use, especially in the absence of a comprehensive subject index.

USING
THE PRESS OF IDEAS

ORGANIZING YOUR SYLLABUS

The Press of Ideas follows a roughly chronological arrangement, tracing print's effects from Gutenberg to hypertext. The first chapter points to the initial shift away from scribal and oral tradition to a print-centered culture, while the final chapter looks at the shift presently under way from print to electronic communication. Much of the impact of that final chapter depends on students' understanding of the issues presented in earlier chapters, in order that they may note the fundamental similarities and appreciate the differences between the print and electronic revolutions.

Not everyone will want to teach all the readings, exactly in the order presented. In fact, you probably won't be able to fit all the essays into a single academic term. In addition to time constraints, you'll have to consider the skill level of your students as you devise your syllabus. You'll need to adapt the textbook's table of contents to suit your own interests and those of your students. You may want to eliminate one or two chapters entirely, although each of the six main thematic units presents an important facet of print culture. Another approach would be to select only a core group of readings from each chapter, addressing all the topics of the book and also allowing students to read further if they wish. Whichever tactic you choose, I strongly suggest including the general introduction to the book. It offers an overview of print culture and points to the way the book's issues affect the student as both a reader and a writer.

I would also encourage you to take advantage of the broad range of discourse offered in *The Press of Ideas*. Be sure to assign your students selections from popular *and* academic sources, belletristic essays *and* transcribed conversations, serious *and* humorous pieces. In each chapter, you'll find at least one essay from the academic world that your students will encounter in their college careers. You'll also find pieces that depart from the essay format: Franz Joseph's memos from Star Fleet Command and excerpts from novels by Louisa May Alcott and Laurie Lawlor (chapter 1); Charles Kikuchi's war diary and Helena María Viramontes's letters to me and to supporters of a local library (chapter 2); Michael Massing's annotations of a letter to the editor of the *Wall Street Journal* (chapter 3); and a transcribed conversation among Catharine MacKinnon, Floyd Abrams, and Anthony Lewis, and an online "chat" among computer hackers (chapter 5). You'll also find pieces by Benjamin Franklin, Samuel Johnson, and Louisa May Alcott that will let your students taste the flavors of written language in earlier eras, perhaps to compare them to the very contemporary language of Gridley Minima, M. Kadi, and Laurie Ouellette—twentysomething writers published in today's alternative press. The infinite diversity of the print world is one of the implicit arguments of this collection, so use it!

ALTERNATIVE THEMATIC GROUPINGS

Since all the readings in *The Press of Ideas* relate to print culture, they invariably overlap one another. I've organized them in chapters according to the dominant issue in each selection, as I perceive it. However, several thematic threads weave through the whole book, and you may wish to organize one or two units—or even your whole class—around these alternative themes. The topics and lists of readings that follow are by no means exclusive. Use them as springboards for your own ideas.

Personal Development and Change

— Birkerts, "The Paper Chase" (chapter 1)
— Franklin, "A Bookish Inclination" (chapter 1)
— James, "Amy Had Golden Curls" (chapter 1)
— Douglass, "Learning Reading, Learning Freedom" (chapter 2)
— Zitkala-Ša, "The Civilizing Machine" (chapter 2)
— Malcolm X, "A Homemade Education" (chapter 2)
— Rose, "Reading My Way out of South L.A." (chapter 2)
— Baca, "Coming into Language" (chapter 2)
— Bohannan, "Shakespeare in the Bush" (chapter 4)
— Seabrook, "My First Flame" (chapter 6)

Political Activism and Social Change

— Knoblauch, "Literacy and the Politics of Education" (chapter 2)
— Douglass, "Learning Reading, Learning Freedom" (chapter 2)
— Kerber, "Why Should Girls Be Learned or Wise?" (chapter 2)
— Malcolm X, "A Homemade Education" (chapter 2)
— Viramontes, "An Island of Flight in the Barrio" (chapter 2)
— Thompson, "The Evolution of *The Advocate*" (chapter 2)
— Hancock, "Computer Gap" (chapter 2)
— Cohen, "Propaganda from the Middle of the Road" (chapter 3)
— Chideya, "Who's Making What News?" (chapter 3)
— Massing, "Bringing the Truth Commission Back Home" (chapter 3)
— Faludi, "The Media and the Backlash" (chapter 3)
— Knoll, "Don't Print That!" (chapter 5)
— DelFattore, "Romeo and Juliet Were Just Good Friends" (chapter 5)
— Noble, "The Newest Bookbanners" (chapter 5)
— Wallace, "The Case against *Huck Finn*" (chapter 5)
— Collins, "PC and the Press" (chapter 5)
— Hentoff, "The Gospel according to Catharine MacKinnon" (chapter 5)
— *Harper's* Forum, "Don't Tread on My Cursor" (chapter 5)
— Harmon, "Bigots on the Net" (chapter 6)

Communities of Readers

— Sicherman, "Reading *Little Women*" (chapter 1)
— Zoglin, "Trekking Onward" (chapter 1)
— Davis, "True Believers" (chapter 1)
— Kikuchi, "Tanforan, 1942" (chapter 2)
— Viramontes, "An Island of Flight in the Barrio" (chapter 2)
— Thompson, "The Evolution of *The Advocate*" (chapter 2)
— Limerick, "Making the Most of Words" (chapter 3)
— Berelson, "Who Reads What, and Why?" (chapter 4)
— Hirsch, "The Formation of Modern National Cultures" (chapter 4)
— Roberts, "On Low Taste" (chapter 4)
— Rubin, "Why Do You Disappoint Yourself?" (chapter 4)
— Radway, "The Act of Reading the Romance" (chapter 4)
— Ouellette, "'Zines: Notes from the Underground" (chapter 4)
— Kadi, "The Internet Is Four Inches Tall" (chapter 6)
— Seabrook, "My First Flame" (chapter 6)

Gender

— Alcott, "Literary Lessons" (chapter 1)
— Sicherman, "Reading *Little Women*" (chapter 1)
— James, "Amy Had Golden Curls" (chapter 1)
— Lawlor, "Miss March, the Famous American Authoress" (chapter 1)
— Kerber, "Why Should Girls Be Learned or Wise?" (chapter 2)
— Faludi, "The Media and the Backlash" (chapter 3)
— Sommers, "The Backlash Myth" (chapter 3)
— Steinem, "Sex, Lies, and Advertising" (chapter 3)
— Radway, "The Act of Reading the Romance" (chapter 4)
— Hentoff, "The Gospel according to Catharine MacKinnon" (chapter 5)
— MacKinnon, Abrams, and Lewis, "A Conversation on the First Amendment" (chapter 5)

Class and the Democratizing of Information

— Franklin, "A Bookish Inclination" (chapter 1)
— Ziff, "Writing for Print" (chapter 1)
— Sicherman, "Reading *Little Women*" (chapter 1)
— Knoblauch, "Literacy and the Politics of Education" (chapter 2)
— Viramontes, "An Island of Flight in the Barrio" (chapter 2)
— Hancock, "Computer Gap" (chapter 2)
— Berelson, "Who Reads What, and Why?" (chapter 4)
— Roberts, "On Low Taste" (chapter 4)
— Dessauer, "Cultural Pluralism and the Book World" (chapter 4)
— Rubin, "Why Do You Disappoint Yourself?" (chapter 4)
— Eco, "The Future of Literacy" (chapter 6)
— Crawford and Gorman, "Coping with Electronic Information" (chapter 6)
— Kadi, "The Internet Is Four Inches Tall" (chapter 6)

Race and Ethnicity

— Douglass, "Learning Reading, Learning Freedom" (chapter 2)
— Zitkala-Ša, "The Civilizing Machine" (chapter 2)
— Kikuchi, "Tanforan, 1942" (chapter 2)
— Malcolm X, "A Homemade Education" (chapter 2)
— Viramontes, "An Island of Flight in the Barrio" (chapter 2)
— Baca, "Coming into Language" (chapter 2)
— Chideya, "Who's Making What News?" (chapter 3)

— Gates, "The Trope of the Talking Book" (chapter 4)
— Wallace, "The Case against *Huck Finn*" (chapter 5)
— Barlow, "Why We Still Need *Huckleberry Finn*" (chapter 5)
— Harmon, "Bigots on the Net" (chapter 6)

The Business of Publishing

— Ziff, "Writing for Print" (chapter 1)
— Thompson, "The Evolution of *The Advocate*" (chapter 2)
— Cohen, "Propaganda from the Middle of the Road" (chapter 3)
— Chideya, "Who's Making What News?" (chapter 3)
— Massing, "Bringing the Truth Commission Back Home" (chapter 3)
— Tye, "Buying Silence" (chapter 3)
— Johnson, "On the Art of Advertising" (chapter 3)
— Steinem, "Sex, Lies, and Advertising" (chapter 3)
— Deitch, "Portrait of a Book Reviewer" (chapter 3)
— Weber, "The Reviewer's Experience" (chapter 3)
— Rubin, "Why Do You Disappoint Yourself?" (chapter 4)
— Starker, "The New Oracle" (chapter 4)
— Franklin, "An Apology for Printers" (chapter 5)
— Collins, "PC and the Press" (chapter 5)
— Max, "The End of the Book?" (chapter 6)
— Saffo, "Quality in an Age of Electronic Incunabula" (chapter 6)
— Sharratt, "But Is It Art?" (chapter 6)
— Appendix: Who Publishes What?

Popular Culture (in addition to the readings in chapter 4)

— James, "Amy Had Golden Curls" (chapter 1)
— Zoglin, "Trekking Onward" (chapter 1)
— Davis, "True Believers" (chapter 1)
— Joseph, "Communications from Star Fleet Command" (chapter 1)

Censorship and Choice (in addition to the readings in chapter 5)

— Kikuchi, "Tanforan, 1942" (chapter 2)
— Cohen, "Propaganda from the Middle of the Road" (chapter 3)
— Chideya, "Who's Making What News?" (chapter 3)
— Massing, "Bringing the Truth Commission Back Home" (chapter 3)
— Tye, "Buying Silence" (chapter 3)

— Steinem, "Sex, Lies, and Advertising" (chapter 3)

— Dessauer, "Cultural Pluralism and the Book World" (chapter 4)

— Eco, "The Future of Literacy" (chapter 6)

Alternative (nonmainstream) Cultures

— Zoglin, "Trekking Onward" (chapter 1)

— Davis, "True Believers" (chapter 1)

— Thompson, "The Evolution of *The Advocate*" (chapter 2)

— Ouellette, "'Zines: Notes from the Underground" (chapter 4)

— Minima, "Other People's 'Zines" (chapter 4)

— *Harper's* Forum, "Don't Tread on My Cursor" (chapter 5)

APPARATUS TO ENCOURAGE STUDENT ENGAGEMENT

The Press of Ideas lets students assess their own involvement in print culture just as they are learning skills that will help them participate fully in written (and, perhaps someday, printed) discourse. The more involved they get in discussing and exploring the readings, the more they can apply the ideas to their own lives and writing. I've framed each selection with an apparatus that encourages understanding of the essays and engagement with other students, and also provokes reflection, analysis, research, and writing. Here's an overview of that apparatus, along with suggestions about how each part can be used.

Chapter Introductions

The introductions to the six chapters are an important part of the book, for they contextualize the questions that organize the chapters. They provide historical overviews of issues such as the spread of literacy, rationales and methods of censorship, or the development of the Internet. The introductions also lay out some theoretical concerns of print culture studies, including differences between orality and literacy, the criteria used in evaluating printed material, and the role of journalists as either mirrors of society or gatekeepers of information. While they may not prompt discussion in and of themselves, the introductions offer critical frameworks for understanding the essays that follow.

Headnotes

Each reading begins with a note that contextualizes the selection for students and teachers. In addition to biographical data about the author(s), the headnotes include information about where and when the piece was first published, and suggest ways of approaching the work. The information about the original site of publication can lead students to the Appendix of this book, where they can learn more about a publisher or publication before or after reading the essay.

Consider the Source Questions

After each selection, a group of questions labeled "Consider the Source" guides students back into the essays to reread and grasp key concepts. These comprehension questions help your students read carefully and accurately. Such questions typically ask students to identify and explain important points, define key terms, summarize an author's argument, or survey supporting evidence. Additionally, many selections are followed by questions that ask students to focus on the author's assumptions about his or her readers, and to analyze how the piece might have worked for its original audience. For these questions, the Appendix will prove useful; indeed, some questions explicitly guide students to the Appendix. Consider the Source questions are not directly tied to writing or discussion assignments, but you might have students answer them in their journals or use them to begin class discussion. You'll then have a way to check whether students understand the readings—especially the more difficult academic essays—and students will have some prepared responses to share with their peers. This manual usually doesn't "answer" the Consider the Source questions, since most answers can be found in a careful reading of the text, but I may point to links between author and audience that may not be immediately apparent.

Consider the Implications Questions

Each selection is followed by questions, dubbed "Consider the Implications," that invite students to connect the essay with others in the book and with their own lives outside the book. For the most part, these questions connect to critical thinking and writing activities. Some prompt students to ruminate in their journals on how their own experience resembles or differs from the issue addressed in the reading. These topics can work for individual or for team journals (see below). Such reflections can also feed into class discussion of the topic, allowing students to counter or reinforce authors' claims with their own experience.

Discussion questions ask students to perform a variety of in-class activities, including—but by no means limited to—conventional discussion. I have suggested collaborative work, team debates, as well as role-playing. Frequently, I ask students to bring in print material—magazines, flyers, ads, contracts, newspapers—that can be studied in class in small groups. The results of such activities can never be determined in advance, or controlled by the instructor. These unpredictable activities often provide the most exciting learning experiences, precisely because they encourage students to take responsibility for providing the materials of their own education.

Essay questions stimulate a range of written responses, inviting many modes of discourse (evaluation, comparison, argumentation, and so on). Some ask students to engage directly with the author of a selection, while others invite them to compare two or more authors' views on a single topic. Some elicit formal argumentative essays; others invite students to write reviews or proposals. Several questions prompt students to write letters to authors, editors, publishers, or advertisers. Urging—even requiring—your students to send their letters will enhance the assignment by making it more than an academic exercise. Require each student to submit to you a stamped, addressed envelope along with two copies of the completed letter. Then you can comment on and return one copy, and mail the other—or wait for revisions before mailing it. If replies arrive before the term ends, students can share them with their peers, and they can use the experience to evaluate the efficacy of their written prose.

For nearly every selection, I have suggested a research activity. These research topics come in many varieties, and often do not resemble traditional library research assignments. Print culture surrounds students and offers them a wealth of material that never makes it into libraries. In the context of this book, it's all fair game for analysis. Therefore, you'll see questions that send students to the grocery-store magazine rack or to their local bookstore or coffeehouse. Others invite analysis of individual magazines—from mainstream mass-market publications to underground fanzines. Research also includes interviews with peers, faculty members, librarians, and book buyers. The final chapter sends students to their computers to cruise the information superhighway, browse the Internet, and explore hypertext novels or interactive CD-ROMs. Even the assignments that direct students to the college library may have a nontraditional twist: scanning the covers of a year's worth of *Time* magazines or looking at the format of eighteenth-century newspapers, without necessarily reading the articles. The packaging of printed matter is sometimes as revealing as the content, so the research assignments allow students various opportunities for appropriate field work.

You may have to modify some of the Consider the Implications questions to suit your particular students or to accommodate the limitations or opportunities provided by your institution. Some students, for instance, may find it hard to respond to questions about their prior relation to books, for books may not have formed a significant part of their childhood or early adolescent experience. The critical scrutiny of how print affects our lives applies, of course, to other media as well, and you'll want to make that link in the classroom. If you find that many of the assignments don't register with your students, simply adapt the questions to other media, such as television, movies, or music, for many of the same principles apply. Similarly, you may find it hard to send students to large bookstores or have them read metropolitan newspapers if your institution is located in a remote area. Likewise, some research assignments won't work unless your library has back issues of popular magazines or newspapers. In these cases, you may have to bring in print material from your own collection, or adapt the questions to the material available.

By the same token, if your library is rich in early printed material, make use of it. My students have always delighted in seeing old books, manuscripts, and newspapers up close, and the experience has helped them understand some of the lyrical adorations of the printed book that they encounter. Scope out your library's rare book room in advance, and arrange for a lecture by one of the librarians. They're usually delighted to display their treasures to an appreciative audience. If possible, arrange for your students to have some hands-on experience with old books and newspapers, if only to impart to them a sense of the tactile dimension of the book world.

Similarly, you'll want to assess the computer capabilities of your institution—beyond simple word processing. See if you can arrange hands-on demonstrations of interactive computer programs, "books" on CD-ROM, and Internet and World Wide Web searching. Ask your techies to purchase and install a copy of Michael Joyce's hypertext novella, *Afternoon: A Story*, for use when your students get to chapter 6 (see p. 575 for the address of the supplier, Eastgate Systems). See what paperwork you need to complete in order to set up online journal groups for your students.

Appendix: Who Publishes What?

At the end of *The Press of Ideas* you'll find a feature unique to this textbook. The appendix, "Who Publishes What?", offers thumbnail sketches of each magazine, newspaper, and publishing house represented by the selections in the book. This information about the original site of publication can help students better understand the audience for a given essay. Additionally, the Appendix as a whole gives students a glimpse of the structure and market-driven nature of the publishing world—the influence of individual editors and publishers, the intensity of competition among publications, the effect of mergers and corporate takeovers.

By building research assignments from the materials of the Appendix, you can use it as a bridge between this textbook and the world of publishing. You can also point to the way each entry concisely conveys a great deal of information, making the Appendix entries models for reporting the results of research. Here are some research ideas that arise from the material or methodology of the Appendix and send your students beyond the confines of this book.

1. *Who owns what?* Using the Appendix as a starting point, research the holdings of a major company like Paramount Communications, Rupert Murdoch's News America Publications, or S. I. Newhouse's Advance Publications. What do they own in the various communications media? What magazines and newspapers belong to the same "family"? Then analyze the coverage that an individual publication gives to the parent company's other holdings. Is it puffery? Does it gloss over problems? Is it biased in other ways? That is, are the parent company's publications independent or not? With its emphasis on the corporate side of publishing, this assignment might appeal to business majors.

2. *What does it look like?* The Appendix frequently reports format changes by an individual magazine, such as *Details*. Ask students to compare copies of the publication before and after the change in style. What differences were visible? Why might such changes have been made? Is there a new audience being appealed to? The same topic could work for a local newspaper that has undergone changes over the decades. Artistic and style-conscious students may particularly enjoy this assignment.

3. *What do the other guys say?* The Appendix points to the rivalry between publications targeted at the same audience, such as *Time* and *Newsweek*, or *Harper's* and the *Atlantic Monthly*. Ask students to compare how rival publications (in any publishing niche) treat the same topic. Are there philosophical differ-

ences? political ones? stylistic ones? differences in emphasis? Or does it make no difference which magazines you buy?

4. *What's it really like?* Students should be encouraged to go beyond the general sketches offered in the Appendix to conduct in-depth research on a particular magazine. Begin with the masthead: Who edits and publishes the magazine? What corporation owns it? Write to the publisher and get information about the magazine's founding, its mission, its history. Also look in *Literary Market Place, Writer's Market, Publishers Weekly*, and other industry sources for information about the publication.

5. *Who's important?* Many of the same names keep cropping up in the Appendix sketches, including Ian Ballantine, Rupert Murdoch, and Bennett Cerf. Students could conduct biographical research about an individual editor or publisher mentioned in the Appendix. Or they could write a biographical summary of any interesting figure in the publishing world, such as Tina Brown, Jann Wenner, or Robert Sam Anson.

COLLABORATIVE JOURNALS

Journals have long formed an important part of the college writing course—and for good reason. They allow the student the opportunity to respond privately to readings and class discussion, as well as to conduct a whole range of prewriting activities, such as brainstorming and free writing. Because they are informal and (usually) ungraded, journals provide a nonthreatening arena in which students can experiment with ideas or voices. The assignments in this book encourage students to use their journals in a variety of ways so that the journal becomes more than just a reading log or a place to answer comprehension questions.

One of the chief drawbacks I have found with journals is that, even though they purport to be private forums for the students themselves, instructors must respond to the journals if they are to serve any pedagogical purpose. For the student, this invariably results in a journal written with the instructor envisioned as the primary (and sometimes the exclusive) audience. For the instructor, it means a stack of journals to haul home and comment on every week or two, since students need feedback on their writing.

A less labor-intensive and generally more fruitful tool is the team journal, a project I have adapted from one used by Elizabeth Renfro at California State University, Chico, and described in *Resources for Teaching THE WINCHESTER READER* (Bedford Books, 1991). Small groups of students write in the same journal every week. They address their remarks to one another, not to their instructor, as they respond to reading assignments, class discussion, and each other's journal entries. Once a week, the instructor reads *but does not write in* the journals. The journal becomes a place for dialogue, with peers providing feedback instead of the instructor. The process emphasizes the collaborative nature of writing and keeps students constantly aware of their audience. Here's how it works.

1. *Forming groups*. Once you have a sense of students' strengths, weaknesses, backgrounds, and temperaments, divide your class into groups of four or five students. Make sure each group includes diverse skills and personalities. Do not let students group themselves, for they will follow pre-existing formations. Do not put more than five students in a group, for the project will become unmanageable. Three students per group is usually too few; four seems to be the ideal number.

2. *Owning the journal*. Form the groups in class and give each group a blank sticky label. Allow them five to ten minutes to get to know each other and to devise a name for their group. Have a student write that name on the label. The name will become the title of their journal, and it usually provides some esprit de corps to the group.

3. *Locating the journals centrally*. Affix the labels to spiral-bound notebooks of lined paper, one for each group. Deposit the notebooks in some location where students can get to them easily, but not disappear with them. I have used the reserve services of my library, making sure that each journal is logged in with the title the students gave to it. You might find a campus coffeehouse or similar facility willing to give your class's journals space behind the counter, so that only the appropriate students may check out the journals.

4. *Assigning a cutoff time*. All journal entries for the week should be completed by a clearly stated deadline so you may read the journals in a single sitting, without having to track down students who are still writing.

5. *Delineating student responsibilities*. Students must read each week's entries, as well as all of the previous week's entries to catch up on what's occurred since they last wrote. They must write at least a page in the journal at least once each week, heading their entry with their name and the date.

6. *Determining the content of journals*. You may assign questions from the textbook, or let the students use the journal as they choose. I'd advise a blend of the two approaches: enough freedom so that students feel the journal belongs to them, but sufficient structure to prevent it from becoming a free-for-all. Students might respond to an issue raised in class or in the readings, or raise an idea or problem that they wish to get feedback on. They may explore topics for an upcoming paper, or ways to develop a topic already in hand. Most importantly, they should write fully developed, intelligent responses to one or more of their team members' writings. They may agree, disagree, or elaborate on something someone else has said, but they may not belittle the other person.

It's helpful for students to introduce themselves in their first entry. First-year students especially appreciate getting to know a few other students early in the term. After that, they should write on topics related to class discussion or readings, since that is the one area that all members of the group will certainly have in common. Vital issues outside those parameters may crop up, and the journal can be a place for them. (For instance, I've had students write about urgent family problems, including a parent missing in Bosnia; the group gave important and supportive feedback, and the problem put the tribulations of college into perspective for all.) On the whole, however, it's best to keep the journals focused on class-related issues.

7. *Avoiding certain topics.* Two types of journal entries are off limits because they offer too little opportunity for intelligent dialogue. The first is the "I-hate-being-the-first-person-to-write-in-the-journal" motif. It continues with "I-never-know-what-to-say" and it offers the rest of the group nothing to say either, except "Me, too." The second category is "unfocused bitching and moaning." Complaints are okay, but only if they are fully developed arguments, complete with examples.

8. *Evaluating the journals.* Once a week, as you read the journals, keep a log of who has written in each group, and briefly summarize what was said. Keep track of how well group members are interacting with and responding to one another; the journal should be more than a series of monologues. If problems arise, address them in conference or in class. Try to avoid the impulse to write in the journals so that students don't feel their journal has been usurped.

9. *Grading the group.* Participation in the journal should be required of all students, and they should feel responsible for one another. Assigning a single grade to the entire group helps students take the project more seriously and ensures that they will track down delinquent members of their group who have not written. Some latitude in grading may be required, to accommodate good-faith efforts on the part of students whose team may include a flaky member or two.

The team journal project can also be conducted online by setting up discussion groups on a campus computer network. Talk to your institution's computer support personnel and see what they suggest. A bulletin board system, where all students post their remarks to the whole class, offers a computer emulation of the classroom experience—with similar drawbacks. Quiet students may disappear from the discussion even more easily in virtual space than in the physical classroom. Some version of small groups may work better to keep everyone involved, but you will have to see what your computer network permits. Also, be aware that the bulletin boards some networks accommodate are open to the entire campus community. Your students deserve to know in advance who can and cannot read their entries.

Group projects like these emphasize the collaborative process of writing and the multitude of readers that any piece of writing may reach. You'll find many group writing assignments in this book, not only for the valuable pedagogical benefits such projects provide, but also because so many of the readings stress the nonautonomous nature of writing and publishing. The printed word requires group effort, even though only a single author's name may appear on the title page. Even the writer whose words will not see print must rely on others, for making meaning from written material is always a joint process, involving at the very minimum both a writer and a reader. Group assignments help students understand this dynamic firsthand.

CHAPTER

1

HOW DO WE READ?

Interacting with Print

The process of reading has become so habitual that most of us no longer think about how we read or how we make sense of what we read. This chapter aims to slow that process down, so that students and teachers can examine the act of making meaning from printed texts and assess the value print has in our culture. The selections are deliberately far-ranging: Ben Franklin and Louisa May Alcott join the crew of the star ship *Enterprise* by the time the chapter ends. What unites these eclectic readings is that they all point to various ways print is used and guide students to think about their own uses of print. The questions that follow each reading offer constant reminders that we are all embedded in the culture of print, however much we think of ourselves as a post-print generation.

Most of the readings fall into three clusters: two concern Benjamin Franklin as a reader and publisher; four focus on Alcott's *Little Women* and the variety of responses a text can engender; and the final three selections deal with the way print extends and validates the world of *Star Trek*. Bracketing the Franklin cluster are important essays by Sven Birkerts and Walter J. Ong. The chapter's most difficult but perhaps most crucial selection is Walter J. Ong's abstract discussion of "Print, Space, and Closure." He addresses the effects of print and contrasts them lucidly and insightfully with oral communication, as well as with chirographic or scribal communication. Rather than plunging students directly into the tricky currents that Ong swims in, you'll find it more productive to begin with Birkerts's highly readable account of how reading functioned in his adolescence and gradually turned him into a professional writer. Once students have begun to focus on how readers engage with books, they will be ready for more difficult theoretical perspectives.

In addition to raising students' awareness of key issues in print culture studies, these selections also address aspects of college culture that beginning students may not have thought about. The subject of reading leads easily to such "academic" issues as plagiarism and intellectual property rights, the form and function of textbooks, and the authority and credibility of authors. The readings and questions encourage critical thinking about the products of academe and the tools these students will use throughout their college careers. Frequent reference to their lives and practices as students, as readers, and as consumers of popular culture will help make even the most abstract readings relevant and interesting to them.

Sven Birkerts, "The Paper Chase"

Birkerts inhabits the world of books in a way that may be familiar to those of us who have gone into the business of teaching writing and literature, but that few first-year students can understand. His set of references is vast, and he assumes a reader who recognizes differences between authors, a reader who understands that reading "Hemingway or Thomas Wolfe or Ian Fleming" refutes his father's contention that reading allies him with "the feminine principle." Questions 3 and 4 direct attention to this set of references, and allow students to determine to what extent they are included in Birkerts's world. Question 9 sends students to the physical world of books to spot trends in packaging as a way to distinguish different genres and subgenres.

Unlike Franklin, who used books for self-improvement and public advancement, Birkerts describes reading for pure escape and enjoyment. His sensuous descriptions of the experience of reading contrast markedly with Franklin's pragmatic assessments of particular benefits he derived from specific books. Some students may have experienced what Birkerts describes, while others will have used books only pragmatically. This would be a good time to hold a class discussion on how books have shaped students' lives. Ask them to share their journal responses to question 6 or their recollections of the experience of reading specific books. If two students have written about the same book, you'll be able to direct class discussion to a consideration of Birkerts's contention that reading is a peculiarly individualistic act. He introduces an idea that Sicherman will discuss at greater length: "No one, not even another reader reading the same words, could know what those signs created once they traveled up the eyebeam." Questions 2 and 7 expand on this idea by asking students to consider how privacy and secrecy enhance the experience of reading. Escaping into another world removes the reader from the company of other human beings and takes him or her into a realm peopled by imaginary characters. This private world of the mind certainly cuts the reader off from other people, but the act of reading can also return the reader to the real world, changed and enriched.

Arriving from different directions, questions 1 and 8 approach the same issue: What value does contemporary society place on the intellectual activities of reading and writing? If students reject Birkerts's contention that "doing is prized over being or thinking," you might direct discussion to the relative salaries accorded to different occupations: professional athlete, teacher, pilot, miner, actor, poet, to name a few. If they've thought at all about writing as a profession, students have probably considered only best-selling novelists like Stephen King. The supporting cast that surrounds the well-known writer goes unnoticed. Question 8 directs attention to Birkerts's early assumption of a hierarchy of writing activities: Those who can, do; those who can't, write; those who can't write, write reviews. And yet, as the essays cited from chapter 3 will make clear, reviewing plays more than an incidental role in the critical success of a famous author.

Birkerts's essay explores the connection between reading and writing, and question 10 asks students to consider that link in their own lives. It also offers an occasion for students to voice their attitudes toward both reading and writing—their fears, their delights, their favorite and least favorite ways of approaching the written word. A class discussion may well allow students with writing anxiety to discover that they are not alone and to begin to address some causes of their anxieties.

Benjamin Franklin, "A Bookish Inclination"

In this excerpt from his autobiography, Franklin portrays himself as the quintessential autodidact and a model for others. His unstructured education from books differs markedly from the classroom education students today uncritically assume as the norm. Questions 5 and 8 ask students to focus on how books contribute to education, and to assess the differences between their use of books and Franklin's. Reading had some very specific functions for Franklin; he read primarily for information and instruction, or for improvement in style and argumentation. Reading helped him to better his writing, and writing helped him to better his circle of acquaintances. Noticeably absent from Franklin's purposes are amusement, escape, and entertainment, functions students will probably cite as important to them.

Franklin's didacticism and moralizing are appropriate for a work that originated as letters to his son. He fills his narrative with advice on behavior that would lead to success in the world of commerce and politics. In spite of his own preachiness, he advises his readers to cultivate the tone of "humble enquirer." Questions 2 and 3 ask students to pay attention to his tone and determine how it helps him fulfill his purposes, while question 7 allows them to try their hand at imitating Franklin's voice. Imitation can serve as a springboard for a class discussion of Franklin's old-fashioned style and a comparison of his prose with today's style. Have students read passages of the text aloud; it may help them catch the nuances of Franklin's style and tone, especially in his most self-serving moments. They can judge for themselves just how humble an enquirer Franklin proves to be. Question 9 allows them to try out the humble enquirer pose, and assess its value as an argumentative strategy.

Question 6 prepares students for Larzer Ziff's article by directing their attention to Franklin's often opportunistic behavior: his "borrowing" of books from the booksellers' apprentices and his somewhat unethical escape from his indentures to his brother. In both instances his careful language helps him to whitewash the deceptions. Students may find it useful to discuss how they would narrate their own peccadilloes, especially if they were writing to their children. How can they use language to put their actions in the best possible light?

Larzer Ziff, "Writing for Print"

Ziff offers a critical reading of Benjamin Franklin's *Autobiography* that can help students see beyond the persona Franklin creates. Though this academic essay is long and complex, it raises several important issues that concern all writers. Ziff brilliantly links Franklin's creation of a public persona to his mastery of writing and the medium of print. Students may need help understanding the concept of representation, and the idea that print creates only a version of experience. After their acquaintance with the benign, public-spirited Franklin of the *Autobiography*, students may also be startled by Ziff's rendering of Franklin's ideology, especially the opportunistic self-fashioning that Franklin seemed to think modern urban life required.

Questions 1 and 2 guide students to an understanding of the dynamic between the private, immanent self and the public self—which, as a representation, is susceptible to manipulation and dependent on observers for its validity. Question 7 expands on this notion of external validation of the self by focusing on how the printed word establishes and spreads personal fame and reputation. Students are asked to weigh the relative authority of printed and oral representations. The next question asks them to compare print and other communications media as purveyors of public images. You might focus their research on public figures by asking them to study a current scandal. (As I'm writing this, the scandal *du jour* is Hugh Grant's involvement with a prostitute; as you read this, there will surely be some other momentary public disgrace making headlines in print and on talk shows.) Discuss the "spin control" conducted by politicians and public relations experts. How much weight is given to a magazine interview or newspaper story as opposed to an appearance on Larry King or Oprah?

Ziff also points to an issue that Walter Ong later takes up in more detail: the written word's ability to sever the speaker from the spoken. Question 3 returns students to Ziff's comparison of orally delivered sermons, where the speaker addresses a physically present audience, with printed sermons, which have no such captive audience. The catalog of rhetorical figures that Franklin scoffs at can provide the starting point for a useful discussion of the aims of rhetoric. (Franklin, of course, uses many of the same figures in his own writing, but not all at once.)

This issue of distance between author and reader immediately raises two important questions for any writer: Who will be the audience for my writing? And how will I get that audience to believe me? Question 6 allows students to address these points with reference to Ziff and Franklin. Both establish credibility with logical, orderly discourse and a tone of reasonableness; Ziff provides a model for academic discourse in his use of documentary evidence. Though Ziff claims that Franklin did not use his prior reputation to establish his authority in his prose, that reputation certainly functions in our readings of Franklin. So, too, does the "prior reputation" of Ziff in academe; even those who haven't read his previous books will doubtless be swayed by the Yale University Press imprint on this book. Students may need some coaching in how publishers' imprints provide a sense of reputation and authority.

Franklin's views on intellectual property can provoke a discussion of plagiarism that goes beyond just showing students how and when to provide documentation. Students often have difficulty in conceiving of ideas as "property"— hence, their inadvertent plagiarism. Try to get them to recall projects on which they expended considerable intellectual and creative effort, and then posit a situation in which someone else built on or reproduced *their* work. Does the Franklinesque idea of common property feel right? Or is it an untenable ideal in a profit-driven economy?

Walter J. Ong, "Print, Space, and Closure"

Walter Ong is an important participant in the discussion about the development of literacy and the impact of print. His essay is not easy to read, but it's worth spending some time on. He charts the effects of a major transformation in human consciousness, the shift from orality to literacy—specifically print literacy. Several of the questions are meant to guide students to review key points of Ong's argument, such as the shift from hearing-dominance to sight-dominance (question 1) and the difference between scribal and printed texts in terms of their audience (questions 2 and 4).

One of the best ways to help students understand Ong's ideas is to connect those ideas to contemporary practices. Question 6 points to the title page of this book to demonstrate how accustomed we are to the signals that type style and layout send. Generally, the title of a book appears in larger type than the author's name, sending a clear message about the importance of authors. However, books that are sold on the basis of name recognition will reflect that on their title pages: For instance, Rush Limbaugh's name overshadows the titles of his books on their covers, spines, and title pages. You might give a historical twist to the discussion by bringing to class books—or photocopies of their title pages— from earlier centuries and asking students to analyze them in small groups. Look, too, at Umberto Eco's discussion of seventeenth-century title pages and his appreciation of what we might regard as their wordiness (pp. 540–41).

Question 7 turns students into scribes as they compare handwritten and printed versions of the same texts. With the aid of word processing, a neatly "printed" version of a journal will probably look much more official and authoritative than a handwritten one. Similarly, a scribal version of a printed text will lack the authority that the fact of print gave to the original.

Ong's discussion of closure allows students to think critically about the books that their education offers them. They may be intrigued to learn that the illusion of comprehensiveness fostered by modern textbooks derives from Peter Ramus's books of the sixteenth century. Question 8 lets students compare the sorts of textbooks that different disciplines use: Which ones invite argument and critical reading? Which invite memorization, and why? How does the book's format tell you what sort of attitude the reader is supposed to adopt toward the material?

Ever since Marshall McLuhan's *Understanding Media* was published, there has been talk about how our society is no longer literate but oral, because of the influence of television and radio. However, Ong makes an important distinction between "primary" and "secondary" orality. Any orality our society may have has been so thoroughly conditioned by the circumstances of print that it no longer constitutes true orality. The discussion of talk radio raised by question 9 can make this point clear. Talk show hosts like Limbaugh or Gordon Liddy create a seeming "community" of listeners, but that community more closely resembles the communities created by print than those of a fundamentally oral culture. Like readers, the listeners are scattered, disconnected from one another. Radio carries the speaker's words across great distances, in the same way that print distances the author from the reader. Individual callers to a radio talk show may participate in the feedback that primary orality provided, but most listeners will have to experience that aspect of orality vicariously. In spite of the resemblance, then, our technologically induced orality does not remove us from a culture and a consciousness created and maintained by print. These concerns will surface again when computers come into the picture. You may want to hold off that phase of discussion until students have read some of the essays in chapter 6, especially John Seabrook's "My First Flame" (pp. 609–24) and M. Kadi's "The Internet Is Four Inches Tall" (pp. 599–607).

Finally, Ong's discussion of how print fosters private ownership of words provides a nice contrast to Franklin's view that whatever is printed becomes public property. In addressing the issues raised in question 10, you might call students' attention to the copyright pages of this textbook with the credit lines for each selection. Every essay or excerpt that was not in the public domain (essentially anything printed after 1906) required written permission for reproduction in this book. Some fifty publishers were contacted, and the total permission and rights fees cost about $13,000. Ask students to study the credit lines to see who claims "ownership" of the printed words, the author or the publisher? How does that square with our commonsense notions of who's responsible for a given essay?

Louisa May Alcott, "Literary Lessons"

This selection from Alcott's *Little Women* provides a touchstone for the whole cluster of readings that follow it. I've chosen this piece because it concerns both writing and publishing. Jo's activities as a writer and her absorption in her intellectual labor have long provided a basis for construing her as a role model for women, especially women writers, as both Sicherman and James point out. Alcott's depiction of her, however, need not be read as entirely flattering. Jo's "vortex" and her "scribbling suit" create a comical tone that undermines her as a serious writer, even as Alcott maintains that writing was Jo's greatest happiness. Questions 1 and 8 invite students to analyze Alcott's attitude toward Jo and her writing, especially with regard to her gender. These questions will help prepare them for the essays by Sicherman and James.

This selection also concerns the commercial side of authorship: Jo tunes her writing to the popular audience in order to sell it. She knows that potboilers are a lesser form of writing than the more idealized romances she had been turning out, but she also knows she must write for the marketplace if she is to get published at all. Students may need some background to understand the hierarchies of taste that Alcott invokes here. It might help to focus on the wildly dramatic illustration that accompanies S.L.A.N.G. Northbury's story, along with Alcott's description of "that class of light literature in which the passions have a holiday." As a prelude to the discussion of categories of taste in chapter 4, questions 2, 6, and 7 ask students to focus on the distinctions between types of literature, and to consider current categories of fiction. They also enable students to begin exploring the relationship between literary and commercial value.

Alcott's description of Jo's absorption in her writing opens the way for a discussion of students' own writing processes. Question 5 lets them have fun comparing writing habits and paraphernalia—clothes, music, pens—even as it invites them to take themselves seriously as writers. You might begin the class discussion by confessing to any quirks you have as a writer. I, for example, can scarcely write without a keyboard, but if necessary I'll use a pen—never a pencil. I also rely heavily on Post-it notes during the revision process.

Barbara Sicherman, "Reading *Little Women*: The Many Lives of a Text"

Barbara Sicherman offers a feminist historian's perspective on Alcott's classic juvenile novel. She demonstrates the practices and style of discourse of the academic historian, relying heavily on interpretations of documentary evidence. Moreover, her essay originally appeared in a collection of feminist essays, and so reflects a particular ideology.

Although many of your students will not have read *Little Women* in its entirety, they can still appreciate Sicherman's argument about the cultural work of the novel, for she gives adequate contextual information for her analysis. The questions following the essay draw on the students' backgrounds without assuming more familiarity with Alcott's novel than could be derived from the various selections provided here. Sicherman puts into practice the theoretical concerns of print culture studies. She reconstructs "communities of readers" to ascertain what "cultural work" a given text performed. Her selection of communities may be restricted to those for which she has documentary evidence, but it is also limited by her own interests. In answering question 2, students should notice that she examines primarily white women: the middle class, the working class, and new immigrants. Though she makes glancing reference to black middle-class women, she offers no discussion of male readers. Ask students to speculate on why she omits these groups. Is it because of her own argument, or is it for lack of documentary evidence? How would a reader know?

Fundamental to Sicherman's argument is her reading of the "female quest plot," primarily with reference to Jo March. The constructions of female identity permitted by *Little Women* require that Jo be read as a heroic iconoclast, carving out her own independent career as a writer in the face of societal pressure to marry well. You'll want to pair Sicherman's essay with that of Caryn James, who challenges this standard reading. Questions 7 and 11 directly address the issue of gender, which is integral to understanding Sicherman's essay. Ask students if they regarded this textbook's cluster of readings on *Little Women* as a "female" topic, and the one on *Star Trek* as the corresponding "male" topic. If so, why?

Sicherman raises the issue of how reading in general and fiction in particular help readers escape their everyday selves and project themselves into different personae. Sven Birkerts (pp. 21–28) and Mike Rose (pp. 173–76) similarly describe how they identified with the subjects of their reading. Janice Radway's interviews with women who read romances (pp. 389–403) also reveal that identification with the heroine is a fundamental attraction of certain types of reading. Projections of the self into the fictional character prove particularly valuable when the persona is one who is loved for herself, regardless of her defiance of convention. Questions 3, 5, 6, and 11 prompt students to assess how such projections aid in the formation of identity—including their own.

Question 9 asks students to apply critical reading skills as they analyze Sicherman's reading of a key passage of *Little Women* (part of the selection on pp. 65–69), determining for themselves whether Alcott's tone undercuts or reinforces her message. The students should be reminded that they, too, constitute a "community of readers," and Sicherman's conclusions may not apply to them. Sicherman assumes that readers will see Jo's literary production as a positive thing, but Alcott's tone toward Jo is not so simple, as noted in question 1 following the Alcott selection.

The variation in responses from readers applies, of course, not just to *Little Women* but to all texts. Question 8 asks students to apply Sicherman's methods to books with which they are more familiar. Similarly, question 10 extends the discussion of juvenile literature to the Sweet Valley High series of girls' books, which many of your female students will have read and loved. Question 6 also expands Sicherman's essay into the more comfortable territory of contemporary cultural productions like movies and television shows.

Another way to bring home the point about how important readers are in constructing the meanings of texts is to supplement Sicherman and James with a short story that lends itself to divergent responses, such as Toni Cade Bambara's "The Lesson." Ask the class to analyze how their responses to the story differ. To what extent does gender or race influence their reactions? Are there cultural or class differences that condition which characters they'll respond to with sympathy?

Caryn James, "Amy Had Golden Curls, Jo Had a Rat. Who Would You Rather Be?"

This selection acts as a counterpoint to Sicherman's feminist emphasis on Jo as every woman's role model, and it's important that students read Sicherman first. James's argument is fairly straightforward and her prose is entertaining. This selection should pose few difficulties for students.

Like Sicherman, James uses historical materials to support her arguments, but she paints quite a different picture of Alcott and her characters. Questions 5, 8, and 9 ask students to explore those differences. By invoking the "fairy-tale" model for how she used *Little Women*, James draws attention again to the varying ways that readers apprehend texts. In guiding students through questions 6 and 7, you may wish to invoke particular fairy-tale characters as potential role models. Similarly, recent Disney movies offer models, especially for women: Consider the intrepid Little Mermaid, Ariel, who repeatedly rescues her handsome prince, or Belle, the book-reading feminist heroine of *Beauty and the Beast*, who is sure that there "must be more to life" than marriage to the village he-man.

James's discussion of the movie versions of *Little Women* offers the opportunity to explore the effects of transforming a text not just into a different "book" form, but into an entirely new medium. How does this transformation alter the audience's experience of the text? What are the trade-offs? Can the student of print culture legitimately treat movies as "readings" of a text (question 10)? In addition to promoting McLuhanesque discussion of the differences between various media, comparison of Hollywood's myths and fairy-tale traditions can play off against Sicherman's discussion of the realism of the story and Alcott's conscious avoidance of (some) romantic conventions.

Laurie Lawlor, "Miss March, the Famous American Authoress"

Laurie Lawlor's novelization creates opportunities to discuss the "dumbing down" of contemporary culture, as well as twentieth-century views of the nineteenth century. The first two questions ask students to pay attention to Lawlor's tone and characterization. The twittering birds of the opening paragraph create an atmosphere far more romanticized than anything in Alcott's rather plainspoken original. Lawlor also exaggerates Jo's tomboy antics—shimmying down the drainpipe with her skirt tied round her waist—perhaps as a means of emphasizing how unconventional her behavior is. Because of the condensation of the novelization format, the plot of Lawlor's version does not exactly parallel Alcott's original. Nonetheless, it does show Jo as an aspiring writer, though perhaps a more hesitant one than Alcott depicted. This Jo is insecure about her abilities, and she speaks longingly of going to college (which seems to be forbidden to her) and feels certain that Laurie will never care for such an uneducated, unsophisticated wretch as she when he returns from Harvard. Question 3 asks students to consider the overall image of American society Lawlor conveys with such details. In all, Lawlor seems to create an impression of the nineteenth century that simplifies the era's complexities for twentieth-century readers. After students have addressed question 6, regarding Lawlor's assumptions about today's adolescent readers, you might ask them to consider whether Sicherman similarly simplifies nineteenth-century complexities for her adult readers.

Richard Zoglin, "Trekking Onward"

Richard Zoglin's article leads off the final cluster of readings in this chapter. Together with Davis's "True Believers" and Joseph's memos from Star Fleet, this article allows students to think about the role print plays in reifying the imaginary. *Star Trek* began on the television screen, but the voluminous prose that has been devoted to *Star Trek* creates its own sort of culture even as it validates the video culture.

Zoglin writes about the *Star Trek* phenomenon from the position of an outsider, and he seems to be writing for other outsiders. His *Time* magazine audience may contain some Trekkers who are attracted by the cover photo, but they will be a minority. Zoglin therefore explains the world of *Star Trek* to the uninitiated, differentiating the various series and providing a thumbnail history of the growth of the *Star Trek* industry. This piece provides a good backdrop to the subsequent article by Davis, who writes as a fan of the series, and the excerpts from the *Star Fleet Technical Manual* that complete the cluster. It allows students (and teachers) who are not Trekkers to get a feel for *Star Trek*'s imaginary world before moving further inside it.

Several of the questions guide students to an understanding of Zoglin's relation to his subject and his audience. He seems to belong to the non-Trekker mainstream, and he gives the sense that there's something distinctly odd about die-hard *Trek* fans. This tone probably meshes well with the attitudes of his *Time* magazine audience. And yet, that audience may have been hooked by the photo of the *Enterprise*'s captains, so there is clearly interest in *Star Trek*, if not whole-hearted commitment.

Zoglin's refusal to adopt the term *Trekkers*, the label he says fans prefer for themselves, provides telling evidence of his relation to his subject. It also undercuts fans' ability to name themselves and provide their own imagery. While Zoglin and Erik Davis use the terms *Trekkie* and *Trekker* respectively to encompass all fans, some *Star Trek* devotees would argue that *Trekkie* applies to fans of the original series and *Trekker* refers to fans of *The Next Generation* and subsequent series. Question 5 points students back into Zoglin's essay to see how he uses labels, while question 7 moves the discussion of labels out into the culture at large and asks students to examine print's role in shaping our images of sections of that culture. Because they have been so inundated with politically loaded terminology, students may not be able to establish enough distance to think critically about the subject at first. You might stimulate their list-making with examples like these: Indians, Native Americans, or indigenous peoples; African American, black, or Negro; anti-abortion or pro-life; pro-abortion or pro-choice. You could also discuss why Bosnian military leaders are called *commanders*, while Somali leaders were consistently labeled *warlords* by the American press. Or you could consider why some militant gays have adopted the once pejorative label *queer*. Who decides which label to use? How does print confirm that as the "correct" label?

Zoglin's establishment of the profitability of *Star Trek*—the sheer dollar value of the trend—seems a way of convincing himself and his readers that there must be something of value in the phenomenon. Questions 8 and 9 tap into this connection between cash and popular culture, and prepare students for Thomas Roberts's later discussion of "Low Taste" (pp. 360–70). The very popularity of pop culture disqualifies it from serious consideration by the elite, and yet, as Zoglin reveals, many intellectuals enjoy the show.

The final two questions explore the effects that print has on our attitudes toward and experience of popular culture. The very fact that *Time* chose to print articles about *Star Trek* validates the show as a cultural phenomenon. It not only makes a lot of money, it's newsworthy. See, it's in *Time* magazine, right there where we're used to seeing presidents and prime ministers. Print gives its imprimatur to television, even as it tries to maintain its own cultural superiority over electronic media. Students exploring the differences between media (question 11) may agree that the reading experience is superior, or they may conclude that image-based entertainment should remain in the realms of television and movies.

Erik Davis, "True Believers"

Unlike Zoglin, Erik Davis writes as a fan and for other fans. He knows he's writing for an audience committed enough to *Star Trek* to shell out a few bucks for the Collector's Edition of *TV Guide* in the first place. But he tries to show that reader the deeper significance of his or her fandom. Davis makes it seem noble instead of odd to be a Trekker. Where Zoglin stresses the weirdness of Trekkers, Davis emphasizes their extraordinary creativity. He also argues that they form a distinct and vibrant community, committed to a shared set of ideals. Your class may include some Trekkers (perhaps you fall into this category yourself); be sure to exploit their expertise as well as their passion for the show.

Questions 4, 5, and 6 address the fan scene, first by comparing the attitudes of Davis and Zoglin toward Trekkers, and then by comparing *Star Trek* fandom with other kinds of fandom. Students' own clothing or hairstyles may be modeled after actors or musical groups they admire. Others may wear the colors or logos of sports teams, especially around playoff time. The degree to which Trekkers replicate and participate in the imaginary world of their favorite show may seem extreme, but sports or music fans can be just as obsessive.

Davis taps into the same cultural bias that Sven Birkerts isolated when he claimed that Americans value doing over being, activity over passivity. If book reading is passive, in this view, television viewing is even more so. Davis challenges this view, and questions 7 and 8 ask students to measure their own attitudes about this issue. You might begin the discussion by asking them how they respond when a phone call awakens them. Most of us tend to lie about having been asleep, even if the call comes in at an unreasonable hour. "No, no," we mutter, "I was awake"—as if sleep were a shameful pastime because it's the antithesis of activity. Students may discover that they habitually justify their "passive" television viewing, but not their "active" sports—usually those that take place out of doors. What values do they claim that passive pursuits offer? What reasons do they offer for watching daytime soaps, or *Melrose Place*, or whatever the coolest shows now are? You might later compare these "reasons" with those offered by the romance-readers in Janice Radway's essay (pp. 389–403). Question 8 may prompt students to make facile generalizations about various media, so it's important to subdivide the broad categories of books, television, radio, and movies. Some reading requires imagination (novels), and some prompts action (cookbooks). Some radio shows are call-ins, while others present no opportunity for listener interaction. Watching a game show may be less passive than watching the news, while the home shopping network depends on viewer/consumer activity.

Question 9 allows students to use the critical terminology of print culture studies to analyze a visual medium. Communities, whether of readers or viewers, use cultural commodities for discernable purposes—escape, entertainment, or education, to name a few. The viewing or reading itself helps bind people into a community with a shared set of references and attitudes. E. D. Hirsch will later use a similar argument to make his case for cultural literacy (pp. 331–41). Here students can begin to extend print-based arguments to other media, in preparation for their analysis of popular and official culture in chapter 4.

Franz Joseph, "Communications from Star Fleet Command"

After students have read about *Star Trek* fandom from the perspective of both the outsider and the insider, they'll be ready for this selection, a genuine artifact from the world of the Trekker. Joseph's *Technical Manual* appeared in 1975, but was reissued for the twentieth and twenty-fifth anniversaries of the original series. There is also a comparable manual for the *Next Generation* series, and by the time you read this there may even be manuals for *Deep Space Nine* and *Voyager*.

Joseph uses these memos to justify the existence in 1975 of a printed manual of technology that hasn't yet been invented. The fiction works fairly well. He uses the Prime Directive of the *Star Trek* series—the order that no Star Fleet crew member will interfere with the culture of any other civilization—to explain why many as yet uninvented technologies are not described in the book. He also tries to suggest in a third communiqué that the future will not have books as we know them today. Instead, future readers will rely on "data read-out stations." But the fiction breaks down when you try to puzzle out how the second memo reached earth in 1975. How did Joseph communicate with Star Fleet to get those explanatory messages? Question 4 lets students determine where the fantasy breaks down, while question 5 asks them to assess the value of the fantasy when it's in place. You might want to introduce here the concept of the suspension of disbelief that accompanies any fiction.

In spite of its inconsistencies, the manual does manage to concretize the world of *Star Trek* by moving the Federation from the video world to the print world. Print serves to validate the existence of the imaginary. We are so accustomed to manuals, diagrams, schematics, blueprints, and other forms of print that we crave such authenticity even for imaginary objects like tricorders and phasers. Question 6 reintroduces Walter Ong's arguments about print and closure, and allows students to grapple with whether print offers a sense of completion that video images cannot. Question 7 asks students to stand back from the whole cluster of selections about *Star Trek* to evaluate the effects of printed texts on the cultural products of the image-based media of film and television. Those texts fix the imaginary world in space and time, allowing us to interact with that world at our own pace. They also extend the community beyond those who have experienced the series directly, and they offer Trekkers additional touchstones to solidify their community.

Questions 1 and 3 call attention to the tone and format of the letters, and allow you to discuss bureaucratic style. These memos from the future look and sound awfully similar to the institutional communications we are accustomed to in the twentieth century. Is this because Joseph is so print-conditioned that he cannot imagine a format not based on print? Or is it because he is appealing to a print-mired audience? Whatever the reason, his memos seem to demonstrate that institutions don't change much across centuries; bureaucrats will still flourish in the future. Both memos use what Richard Lanham in *Revising Prose* (1979; second edition, New York: Macmillan, 1987) calls The Official Style; Lanham criticizes the style's wordiness and its reliance on passivity and indirection. Nonetheless, the official language helps lend credibility to the memos; it gives them weight and the authority of the military.

WHO READS?
Access to Print

 The gateway to discussions of print culture is the concept of literacy in all its forms. This chapter charts the parameters of literacy and explores the political implications of its encouragement or restriction. A useful introduction to patterns of literacy in America can be found in William Gilmore-Lehne's article on "Literacy," listed in "Further Readings in Print Culture Studies" (pp. 4–6 of this manual). Gilmore-Lehne provides more detailed discussion of the problems with defining and measuring literacy than the introduction to this chapter could accommodate. He also addresses variations in literacy rates by region, by gender, by class, and, to a lesser extent, by race.

 As the introduction to this chapter notes, "access to print" refers both to the consumer's ability to obtain and read printed material and to the producer's ability to print and disseminate his or her message. The essays that follow progress roughly from the most obvious restrictions on literacy—Frederick Douglass's account of his struggle to overcome laws banning slaves from learning to read and write—to more subtle considerations of the empowerment access to print provides, both individually (as with Jimmy Baca) and collectively (for the gay community served by *The Advocate*).

 C. H. Knoblauch's essay on "Literacy and the Politics of Education" (pp. 122–29) provides a critical framework for all the essays in the chapter. I consider it a "must-read" essay, even if time constraints force you to pick and choose among the other selections. Among the other essays, some are autobiographical narratives of literacy and access to books themselves (Douglass, Rose, Malcolm X, Baca, Viramontes); some are about limitations on what people can read (Kerber) or whether they should read (Zitkala-Ša); and some are about access to the press to disseminate ideas and images, not just receive them (Kikuchi, Thompson). Douglass, Baca, Malcolm X, and Viramontes demonstrate most clearly the political implications of education that Knoblauch points out. Knoblauch claims that the types of literacy education are nonhierarchical. However, the selections seem to demonstrate that functional literacy can quickly lead to critical literacy, as many readers—especially those who have traditionally been denied education or access—rebel against the strictures of society. The final selection in the chapter, LynNell Hancock's essay on the "Computer Gap," provides a nice setup for the issues raised in chapter 6 about electronic communication; moreover, it's easy to read and talk about.

The essays also demonstrate an array of styles, formats, and audiences. Knoblauch and Kerber write for an academic audience, while the rest of the selections aim for a broad, general readership. Douglass and Zitkala-Ša offer examples of nineteenth-century prose. Consider including Kikuchi's diary entries and Viramontes's letters if you wish to expose your students to forms of writing other than the traditional essay.

Since so many of the selections are autobiographical narratives, a natural outgrowth of this whole chapter would be for students to write their own "literacy autobiography." They could consider when they first remember encountering books, how that encounter occurred, and what books influenced them and why. Many of the questions invite them to do this in their journals, but you could easily convert such reflective assignments into a formal writing assignment.

As students read essays on literacy and power, they may need to step back from that activity to remind themselves of their own literacy. The act of reading may have become so habitual that they lose sight of its power. Use the questions in the chapter to provoke students into an awareness of their own power as members of a literate community, and of the further powers that await them as they master other forms of literacy.

C. H. Knoblauch, "Literacy and the Politics of Education"

Knoblauch's essay may not be the most engaging of the pieces in the chapter, but it is arguably the most important. It establishes the idea that "literacy" means many things, and it sets up the varying perspectives on literacy in the selections that follow. It also connects to the essays in chapter 5 on censorship by way of the notion that literacy education is used by privileged groups to maintain their privilege. The introduction of the idea of cultural literacy here will also pave the way for the discussion of official and popular culture in chapter 4.

Students may have difficulty at first in understanding (or admitting) that political aims underlie such a benevolent project as literacy education. Tracing the different kinds of literacy and the values that each promotes will help open the discussion to issues of ideology. Question 4 personalizes literacy and lets students evaluate their own biases and images of illiteracy. Allow them to share their journal entries and to discuss what illiteracy means to them. When you turn to question 5, they'll be ready to assess whether they are literates or illiterates in other forms of literacy, such as science or computers. Encourage them to explore areas of "literacy" in which they may be experts, such as popular music, fashion, sports, or movies. Why is "fashion literacy" or "sports literacy" not part of our vocabulary the way "computer literacy" is? Who decides what sort of literacy is most important?

Preparing the way for Hirsch's essay in chapter 4, question 6 sends students to the library to research the "crisis" in American literacy. Questions 7 and 8 focus students' attention on their own schooling: Building on their understanding of what sort of literacy education they received, they can advise educators about education. Students will probably welcome the opportunity to critique their high schools (and earlier education). Question 8 makes sure they turn that criticism into effective advice.

Frederick Douglass, "Learning Reading, Learning Freedom"

Frederick Douglass's account of his education is deservedly famous. His experience demonstrates the value of education in the clearest of terms. But there are other levels to be explored in this familiar selection. Literacy is fundamentally political for Douglass, for it gives whites power over blacks (though he never explicitly says how). He makes clear the link between knowledge and power as he uses literacy to attain his freedom.

Despite the joy he finds in educating himself, Douglass says he reaps discontent—for a while. Like Franklin, Malcolm X, and Baca, he finds that a taste of education inspires him to want more out of life. Question 6 asks students to compare these autodidacts, and to discuss how education stimulates the desire for a better life.

Douglass's narrative also demonstrates literacy of the sort that Knoblauch (pp. 122–29) calls "critical literacy"—to promote consciousness of social conditions. Douglass first aimed for functional literacy, but his reading of books like *The Columbian Orator* gave him access to radical ideas that challenged the status quo. Questions 8 and 9 ask students to explore the value of these types of literacy. Douglass's experience calls into question Knoblauch's categories, for it suggests that functional literacy cannot be contained. Mrs. Auld aimed to teach young Frederick basic reading skills, but Mr. Auld recognized that such skills are transferable—and hence dangerous.

Linda K. Kerber, "Why Should Girls Be Learned or Wise?"

In this fairly long essay, students will find another example of the scholarly prose that they may encounter in their college coursework. Linda Kerber's study of women's education in the early years of the American republic lays the groundwork for many of the other gender-related selections in this book. Though women were not denied access to literacy as fiercely as slaves were, Kerber shows that the limitations on their education were nonetheless crippling, both intellectually and socially.

Have women "come a long way, baby"? Students should find it stimulating to measure the progress women have made, and to debate whether gender gaps in education still exist. You can provoke responses to questions 5 and 6 by asking about specific well-educated, influential women, such as Hillary Rodham Clinton, Janet Reno, or Anita Hill, and asking students to name others. Encourage students to examine whether gaps in knowledge or education between men and women have affected their own lives. Were women channeled away from math, science, or business majors? Were men discouraged from pursuing careers in literature, art, and early childhood education? How are our senses of our identities and roles in society influenced by what we read and what we are validated for reading?

Kerber's essay opens up the subject of just what we expect education to provide. Question 8 puts the emphasis on educating a "citizen" of the United States. Students must first decide what constitutes effective citizenship if they are to decide how to educate the model American. Questions 9 and 10 address the differences between a liberal education and a vocational one. Students at liberal arts institutions frequently object that their education doesn't equip them well enough for the job market, and they often select majors they think will help them get jobs. And yet, if you ask them why they did not select a trade school— a place geared specifically to train people for employment—most will evince some consciousness of the traditional cachet attached to the genteel education. Debating the relative merits of the two brands of schooling, they can begin to address the political implications underlying each, especially after reviewing Knoblauch's essay.

The final question asks students to make the analogy between restrictions on women's education and prohibitions against educating slaves in the pre-Civil War South. In a later essay, Gloria Steinem will have repeated recourse to the same analogy between women and slaves as she discusses advertising and media images of women (pp. 277–302). Using Frederick Douglass's narrative, students can anticipate and work through that analogy here.

Zitkala-Ša (Gertrude Bonnin), "The Civilizing Machine"

Indian activist Zitkala-Ša offers a moving and accessible account of her transition from an oral tradition to a written one. Earlier sections of the memoir describe how she begged her mother to permit her to attend school in the East, how she ached to learn the wonderful things the white missionaries described. In the selections included here, she narrates how her long-sought education leaves her caught between two worlds, unable to fit into either one.

Reading and writing figure in each section of the memoir, and books are consistently connected to power: The devil pictured in the Bible punishes delinquent students; the teacher relentlessly records her pupils' failings in her roll book; Zitkala-Ša's mother feels the Bible has power to console her distraught daughter. Recognizing the connection, Zitkala-Ša vents her rage at the white man by attacking his books—especially the Bible, which represents all of the "white man's papers," and seems to typify the whole of white society.

Questions 4 and 8 ask students to assess how literacy education alienates the author from her Indian tradition and from her family. She is too educated to communicate with her mother, not educated enough to join her brother and his "civilized" friends. The solution to her dilemma seems to be more education, as she returns to school in the East. Students may enjoy role-playing a dialogue between Zitkala-Ša and her mother to see whether such a solution could work, or whether further education would result in deeper alienation.

Zitkala-Ša's narrative presents a complex relationship between author and reader, addressed in question 7. She writes as an activist, deploring many of the conditions she describes, but also trying to engage her audience in her cause. Therefore she tries to avoid antagonizing her white reading audience, even as she details the cruelty of her teachers. For instance, the description of her teacher as "the hard-working, well-meaning, ignorant woman," both condemns and exonerates the white missionary. Readers can sympathize with Zitkala-Ša and at the same time distance themselves from the "ignorance" of her teachers. They can position themselves as the ideal audience that Zitkala-Ša describes at the close of the second section: "those [with] ears that are bent with compassion."

Charles Kikuchi, "Tanforan, 1942: Chronicle from an American Concentration Camp"

The fragmentary nature of Charles Kikuchi's diary entries excerpted here may present initial difficulties for students. The selection does not flow like an essay, but there are persistent threads that run throughout: the newspaper as a disseminator of information and a community-builder; government censorship and self-censorship; and the readers' uses of the newspaper.

Like Mark Thompson in his discussion of *The Advocate* (pp. 188–96), Kikuchi raises the issue of how a publication represents a community to itself and to others (questions 1, 5, and 9). The very existence of the paper helps individuals become a community and raises their consciousness of themselves as a group. Public representation of their concerns raises morale within the group and prevents outsiders from overlooking the group. Kikuchi is very concerned that the paper not misrepresent camp life by glossing over injustices and restrictions; at the same time, he feels that the publication's existence is more important than its role as gadfly to the U.S. government. He participates in Army publicity photos showing the Japanese as happy campers, even as he records his unhappiness and anger in his journal.

Various kinds of censorship show up throughout Kikuchi's account of the newspaper, and questions 4, 6, and 7 focus attention on this crucial issue. The *Tanforan Totalizer* underwent several levels of government scrutiny, acknowledged by writers, editors, and readers. At times, the writers and editors tried to push the limits of censorship; other times, they monitored themselves before they could be censored by officials. Kikuchi and his colleagues deliberately limited their coverage of traditional Japanese cultural activities, preferring to present a more Americanized image of themselves to their fellow internees and to the overseeing army officials. Was that a form of self-censorship, or was it a political self-fashioning? Question 7 links the discussion of censorship to the essays in chapter 5, especially Erwin Knoll's discussion of prior restraint (pp. 437–39).

The existence of censors can produce a chilling effect on writers, which may amount to prior restraint. And yet, some circumstances may warrant such restraint.

The final question focuses attention on diary writing and the diarist's many audiences. Even the most private diaries are written to be read, if only by the writer at a later date. That imagined future self also constitutes an audience. Kikuchi's case is somewhat different, for he writes with the knowledge that others will read his words. Ask students who keep diaries whether they ever imagine their words being read by outsiders—perhaps some day in the future, when they have become famous. If your class is participating in the group journal project described earlier in this manual, students will have much to say about their sense of audience. How often do they write without thinking about the instructor as reader? How do their peers function to shape their texts? If they have ever read a published diary besides Kikuchi's, how did they react to the presumed private-ness of the text? Is there a voyeuristic quality to reading a diary that other forms of text do not provide? Question 2 addresses the heightened authenticity a diary automatically seems to possess. If you are teaching any fiction in your course, you might introduce here a first-person narrative and compare the two forms of writing.

Malcolm X, "A Homemade Education"

Students may already be familiar with Malcolm X's classic account of his education while in prison, or they may have seen Spike Lee's movie *Malcolm X* (1992). The context of this textbook freshens up a familiar piece by focusing on the politically and personally empowering nature of print and reading in particular instead of education in general.

Both Malcolm X and Benjamin Franklin use print in specific, goal-oriented ways—Franklin for social advancement and Malcolm X for greater political efficacy. Neither one seems ever to have dabbled or read for pure enjoyment. Question 5 asks students to make this connection, while question 6 lets them link Malcolm X with Jimmy Santiago Baca, another self-educated prisoner. Baca makes discoveries about his heritage similar to Malcolm X's, but his reading leads him first to personal revelations and expression, and only later to a political struggle. For both prisoners, reading becomes a liberating and subversive activity.

In his analysis of various history books, Malcolm X provides some justifi-cation for recent multicultural textbooks. You'll want to link his narrative with the issues raised by DelFattore and Noble, either here (with question 7) or when you discuss censorship and "political correctness" in chapter 5. If your library has a good collection of general history books, students will be able to find a range of books to bring into class for the discussion suggested by question 8. This exercise presents a good opportunity to teach students how to survey a scholarly book: Read the table of contents, skim the introduction, scan the index for key headings, and so forth. They can also compare the books as objects, examining the look and feel of the different books and weighing the relative authority each provides. While the students are examining the history books, be sure they take note of how Chicanos, Native Americans, and immigrants are depicted in the texts. They'll want to use their observations when they compare Malcolm X's reading with Jimmy Baca's (pp. 181–87).

Spike Lee's movie depicts Malcolm X's prison education in somewhat different terms than does the autobiography. Brother Baines, who converts Malcolm to Islam, is also his mentor in the prison library. He explains to Malcolm about the "whitening" of history, and he starts Malcolm on his project of copying the dictionary. Malcolm is the passive recipient of Baines's observations, though he is later shown reading in his cell and writing letters to Elijah Muhammad.

Mike Rose, "Reading My Way out of South L.A."

Mike Rose provides a humorous look at how reading can remove a young boy from the quotidian world of his immigrant home and transport him to other realms. Like Birkerts, Rose escapes his parents (and his teachers) through the pages of a book.

Students may enjoy comparing their own fantasy worlds with Rose's. Which fantasies were the most effective in escaping the everyday world? What did the fantasies offer that real life could not? Why were they necessary? Less book-oriented students will be able to participate if you broaden the discussion to include television and movies. After letting students explore the nature of fantasy, you can introduce the media comparison of question 7. Print differs from image-based media in that it requires its audience to use their visual imagination (as does radio). Television and movies provide images that may be so indelible that they overpower imagination. Computer images come in several forms: One type of computer fantasy game is text-based, asking questions and providing descriptions of scenes, objects, and events; the other type is graphics-based, essentially allowing the player to interact with a video image. Ask students if they've played either kind of game, which they prefer, and why.

Rose's autobiographical narrative is laced with object lessons for educators. You might ask students to compare Franklin's didacticism with Rose's. Which more subtly conveys its message? Did they even notice Rose's arguments about education? In responding to question 8, it may help students to outline the stages of Rose's recollections, noting the transitions and highlighting the key points of his argument.

Helena María Viramontes, "An Island of Flight in the Barrio"

Viramontes's letters move the literacy debate to more recent times with a different population as its focus. According to Viramontes, barrio children are routinely denied literacy, access to print, and thereby power. Closing the neighborhood branch library, The Friendly Stop, is merely another example of this familiar process. Viramontes protests the library closing because it locks barrio kids out of literate society, and she calls for a letter-writing campaign to remedy the problem. Clearly she is addressing literates, those already empowered by reading and writing. Her recollection of the value of the library in her own life adds a personal dimension to her plea, and she expects it to tap into similar recollections on the part of her readers.

Viramontes explicitly connects literacy, libraries, and power. Questions 2, 4, and 8 address the politics of literacy, allowing students to apply Knoblauch's terminology of "critical literacy" (pp. 122–29) to the situation in the barrio. Libraries may not seem to be hotbeds of radical political activity, but Viramontes suggests that libraries serve the cause of literacy, which gives voice to the silenced. Students may wish to discuss whether reading is a "right" before they try to respond to question 8. Divide the class into teams and hold a formal debate. You could particularize the issue by asking students to consider whether public funding ought to support libraries, especially given the present rhetoric about smaller government and lower taxes.

Like so many writers, Viramontes connects reading to a particular place. For her, escape into books happened in the library; Birkerts retreated to his room, and Rose to the chaise longue in the living room; Baca and Malcolm X freed their minds as they read behind bars. Questions 5 and 6 allow students to explore the connection between reading and refuge. This may fuel the letters they write in response to question 9, either arguing for or against neighborhood libraries like The Friendly Stop.

Jimmy Santiago Baca, "Coming into Language"

This selection from Jimmy Santiago Baca's autobiographical narrative offers a poet's view of the power of language. As he moves between straightforward narrative and the evocative language of poetry, he touches on major themes of the chapter: illiteracy as incoherence, even danger; literacy as empowerment; the ability of books to connect him to his identity; and language's power to create liberating imaginative space.

Question 5 asks students to attend to Baca's examples of the various powers of language, and to explore how they use language in their own lives. Baca uses writing as a means of self-definition and self-expression. Much of his poetry concerns the struggles of Chicanos in an Anglo-dominated society. "Immigrants in Our Own Land" speaks powerfully about the hopes and frustrations of his prison experience. The present essay provides an eloquent statement about what Knoblauch (pp. 122–29) calls "literacy-for-personal-growth" (question 7). Remind students of the political agenda that Knoblauch sees behind educational programs emphasizing this form of literacy. Would Baca agree that educating him in reading and writing would be an example of "allowing modest symbols of self-determination to release built-up pressures of dissatisfaction"?

Questions 8 and 9 compare Baca's essay with several others in the chapter. If your students examined history books in response to question 8 following the Malcolm X selection, then ask them to apply their observations to the discussion of Latino representation in history textbooks. Both Malcolm X and Baca find that books validate and illuminate their identities as nonwhites, but while Malcolm X angrily denounces white historians for excluding or misrepresenting the black man, Baca turns inward to explore facets of his identity revealed to him by the books he reads.

Baca's skill with language allows him to present his imprisonment to his reader in a way that enhances our sympathy for him. Ask students to list instances where he presents himself as unjustly imprisoned or otherwise wronged. How do those examples play on readers' sympathies? Given the description of the interests of the founding publishers of Red Crane Books (Appendix, p. 660), how might Baca have shaped his case to appeal to the sympathies of his audience?

The last question sends students directly to the environment that Baca describes. They may call, write, or visit a prison in the area to research literacy education programs. You might also ask them to inquire about rates of illiteracy in the prison, the level of education of the prisoners, the types of books and magazines available in the prison library (if there is a library), and the reading materials most prisoners seem to favor. Other twists on this assignment might be to encourage them to correspond with a prisoner, or to collect books to donate to the prison library. What publications would students want to send and why? What would prisoners want to receive and why?

Mark Thompson, "The Evolution of *The Advocate*"

Sometimes access to literacy means access to the printing press itself, as Mark Thompson demonstrates in this essay. Print functions here as a means of establishing identity—it reflects the identity of its audience and also helps readers construct that identity within themselves.

Thompson spends a good deal of time describing changes in the physical format of the publication. Question 4 asks students to consider how format influences their attitudes toward publications. Do glossy pages and an abundance of ads enhance the authority of a magazine? Thompson describes how the mainstreaming of the gay movement was reflected in the design of *The Advocate*. As the publication increasingly resembled and was marketed alongside more familiar journals, it represented the gay community as a variation of the familiar, instead of as an aberrant "other." Questions 5 and 6 send students to the magazine racks to see where and how gay publications are marketed, and to discern differences among them.

The Advocate provides an obvious example of how print helps build community. Questions 7, 8, and 9 allow students to approach this issue from a variety of angles. The first approach asks them to survey existing publications targeted to distinct market segments. The discussion may range from hobby magazines, such as *Runner's World* or *HotRod*, to magazines that serve particular ethnic, racial, or religious groups, such as *Latin Style*, *Ebony*, or *Tikkun*. Question 8 narrows the discussion to on-campus publications, letting students conduct field research through interviews. If your campus has few or no such special-interest publications, question 9 will allow your students to address the same issues, but they'll have to generate the connections between publication and audience.

To drive home some key points in this chapter and prepare students for the essays on freedom of the press in chapter 5, question 10 casts a net back through the whole of chapter 2. Students should have ample evidence—especially from

Thompson and Kikuchi (pp. 157–63)—as to the importance of access to the press. Printing enables any group to control the imagery that is used to represent them. As Thompson pointed out, *The Advocate* represented gays to themselves as okay, not as deviants; moreover, it increasingly represented them to mainstream heterosexuals as a legitimate group, with rights and dignity. Without print, or with only underground print, such recognition would have been nearly impossible.

LynNell Hancock, "Computer Gap: The Haves and the Have-Nots"

Hancock's article extends the discussion of access to literacy into the digital arena and sets up many of the comparisons that will be addressed more fully in chapter 6. Once students have read several of the other essays in the present chapter, they will readily see the similarities between discussions of books and computers. Computers are now hailed for democratizing knowledge, just as the printing press once was, but the same inequities of access persist into cyberspace. Students can compare their own access to computers among themselves (question 4) and in relationship to the examples that Hancock offers. Question 5 lets them assess whether they will be haves or have-nots in the digital world.

Because the consequences of illiteracy are just as great (some would say greater) in the computer world as in the print world, it's important to chart the lines along which computer literacy is presently divided. Questions 6 and 7 allow students to do this, both in the classroom and through field work. Encourage students to share their experiences in a computer store with the whole class, perhaps as a contribution to the discussion of gender bias prompted by question 6. You may wish to refer to their experience when discussing Gloria Steinem's essay "Sex, Lies, and Advertising" (pp. 277–302), particularly her discussion of how personal electronics are marketed almost exclusively to men.

CHAPTER

3

WHAT DO YOU THINK?

Print and Opinion Making

It's probably preaching to the converted to inform instructors of writing that language can be a powerful shaper of opinions. This chapter aims to let students in on that secret by guiding them to an understanding of how language, especially when it appears in print, manipulates their emotions and intellects every day. The readings guide students through various types of printed material—historical documents, newspapers, magazines, advertisements, book reviews—to see what strategies such materials use to shape the reader's opinions.

While working through this unit, you might wish to include a discussion of propaganda. On some level, all persuasive writing can be considered a form of propaganda, but students should learn to distinguish reasonable argument from egregious appeals to emotion and illogic. Spend some time going over various cheap tricks and logical fallacies so students can recognize and avoid them. If you are using a handbook, rhetoric, or critical thinking guide along with this reader, you will probably find a section describing such things as *ad hominem* attacks, guilt or glory by association, faulty causality, and so forth.

Several of the essays in the chapter rely on documentary or statistical evidence. Use these selections as an occasion to teach students to pay attention to the way evidence is used. The questions following the essays often point students to instances of dubious interpretation of evidence (see, in particular, the readings by Michael Massing, Susan Faludi, and Christina Hoff Sommers). Often the evidence tendered does not necessarily prove the author's point. Ask students which evidence they find persuasive and why. Let them scrutinize the statistics and the authors' interpretations. As the saying goes, "Statistics don't lie, but liars use statistics."

The three selections by Farai Chideya, Michael Massing, and Joe Tye present the core issues of how our opinions are shaped by the news we see. Each author focuses on a different force that influences the news: for Chideya, it's race; for Massing, politics; and for Tye, money. Several of the other essays work well in pairs. Samuel Johnson's brief assessment of advertising in his day paves the way for Gloria Steinem's remarkable account of advertisers' attempts to influence the content of *Ms.* magazine. Christina Hoff Sommers responds directly to Susan Faludi's critique of the media. Joseph Deitch and Katharine Weber present complementary views of book reviewing.

Many of the topics in this chapter apply equally well to nonprint media, such as television, movies, and radio, so feel free to move the discussion to those arenas, especially if your students seem uncomfortable with print. I've kept the focus on print not only because that's the subject of this book, but also because it's often the source of the other media's coverage. Look at how many television news stories rely on newspaper coverage—the *New York Times*, the *Wall Street Journal*, the *Washington Post*, the *Los Angeles Times*, and *USA Today*, especially. Or the number of scholarly journals that become the basis for news stories, especially medical stories: *JAMA*, *The New England Journal of Medicine*, and *Lancet*. Print reviews also appear regularly in television and movie ads: Automobile ads constantly use quotations from *Road and Track*, *Car & Driver*, even *Consumer Reports*. Movie previews and ads contain quotations from reviewers in various media, but even there print predominates. Cyberspace, too, depends on print: A recent television commercial for America Online markets the glories of computer connectivity by showing the glossy covers of the many printed magazines now available online.

Patricia Nelson Limerick, "Making the Most of Words: Verbal Activity and Western America"

Patricia Nelson Limerick's important essay may be the most difficult piece in the chapter. Limerick's lively prose makes for engaging reading, but students may not immediately see the connection between her essay and those that follow it. She focuses on how words, in effect, created the images of the American West that we believe in and act on. Her essay gives a historical foundation for the treatment of language and newspapers that follows. Spend some time on Limerick so that students can expand on her observations when they apply the same scrutiny to today's publications.

Limerick also demonstrates how a critical reader approaches texts. She regards words skeptically and looks at the power relations behind them. Though she writes for historians, her critical reading techniques apply in any discipline.

This essay looks at an unusual combination of issues: languages, newspapers, and legal documents. Limerick brings them together under the heading "verbal activity" to examine the mingling of orality and literacy that takes place on the frontier. The Consider the Source questions help students trace her different arguments and understand the relationships between the various types of verbal activity.

The Consider the Implications questions let students test Limerick's ideas using present-day examples. Question 5 asks students to scrutinize their own conception of the West and discover where it comes from. Movies and television will play a big part in their answers, as will such images as the Marlboro Man. You might get them to compare their recollections of high school history lessons with such recent revisionist versions of western history as *Dances with Wolves* and *Unforgiven*. What versions of the West did their schools authorize as "official"?

Questions 6 and 7 focus on the multilingualism of the historical West and the contemporary United States. Students in some regions of the country will be less familiar with the English-only debates than those in states with a large immigrant population. You may wish to turn question 7 into a research assignment, sending students to recent newspapers and magazines for information about attempts to legislate English as the official language of the United States.

The questions on newspapers (questions 8 and 9) and those on legal documents (questions 10 and 11) give students hands-on experience in analyzing printed texts. Encourage them to treat the various documents as "literature," in the way that Limerick does, applying critical reading techniques and looking for the ideologies that underlie the texts. In discussing question 11, see how many of your students plan to attend law school. Ask them to discuss what role they imagine interpretation of texts will play in their lives as lawyers.

Question 9 lends itself to an interesting research assignment if your community library or historical society has copies of early regional newspapers. Ask students to compare a newspaper published during the time their city or county was settled with one published there today. How have the cultural assumptions and interests of the publication changed? How might its audience have changed?

An interesting class discussion could center on whether Limerick's writing reads like conventional historical prose. Students could compare her style with that of their other history texts. They might also read the Appendix entry on W. W. Norton and assess how well Limerick's style and substance fit with the Norton policy of publishing books that educate as well as entertain, and help people "know more about themselves and their world."

Jeff Cohen, "Propaganda from the Middle of the Road: The Centrist Ideology of the News Media"

What is propaganda and what is news? How can you tell which is which? Jeff Cohen's essay asks students to examine their news coverage with a critical eye. Instead of focusing on the usual left versus right debate, Cohen considers the whole mainstream press as representative of a single point of view: the center. At first students may have trouble understanding what Cohen means by an *ideology*. Focus on the "values and opinions, beliefs about the past, goals for the future" that constitute the centrist ideology for Cohen.

The first three Consider the Implications questions allow students to test Cohen's assertions in current publications. Try to make sure students have access to a variety of mainstream newspapers and magazines so that they can compare so-called "different" sources. See if the sameness that Cohen laments shows up.

Question 7 lets students scrutinize their own political bent. Many may not have examined their politics before, or they may have simply adopted their parents' beliefs unquestioningly. Allow them to share their discoveries about their own ideologies in a nonthreatening class forum. To diffuse potential political conflicts among students, focus on where their beliefs come from: parents, peers, and especially the press. Our political views are conditioned by what we read—and what we don't read, either because we choose not to or because we were not given the choice.

The final question was written in the same week that Walt Disney Co. took over Capital Cities/ABC, Westinghouse Electric Corp. purchased CBS Inc., and Congress passed the Telecommunications Act permitting further mergers and takeovers. It is hard to tell what the ramifications of these actions will be, but there has already been some discussion of the potential conflicts of interest that will face members of the press. The *Los Angeles Times* carried an editorial on August 8, 1995, entitled "Will TV News Bite Its Corporate Hand?" and an article that same week about Robert Sam Anson, the controversial editor of *Los Angeles Magazine*, who has written critically of Disney chairman Michael Eisner and whose magazine will now be owned by Disney. Anson's case could yield a useful research assignment relating to corporate control of the press: Simon & Schuster was initially slated to print Anson's book, but backed out of their contract; some publishing insiders speculate that Simon & Schuster bowed to pressure from Paramount, its parent company, which was uncomfortable with Anson's criticism of Paramount executives. Students could research the claims and counterclaims, and then summarize the case and evaluate the impact of consolidated ownership that Cohen criticizes. Use the Appendix as a springboard for additional assignments that guide students to investigations of corporate ownership of the press. You might start with the Appendix entries on HarperCollins and Minstrel Books.

Farai Chideya, "Who's Making What News?"

Farai Chideya's essay provides a strongly argued critique of the media from the perspective of an African American. Her statistics about the scarcity of blacks in the newsroom bolster her central argument about how the media portray minorities. You may wish to have your students extend her criticisms to apply to other minorities and to women. Compare, for instance, Steinem's discussion of the effects of the scarcity of women in top positions in publishing or advertising (pp. 277–302).

The selection of news stories profoundly affects our understanding of what issues are important in our culture. Questions 4, 5, and 6 ask students to assess their views of particular communities and scrutinize how the media—both print and television—cover those communities. Chideya charges that the omission of good news about African Americans changes the way we regard whole communities. Mark Thompson (pp. 188–96) implied a similar thesis with regard to the homosexual community. Both authors seem to argue that groups need to complain loudly, and/or take control of their own media images; otherwise they'll be misrepresented by the predominantly white, middle-class, heterosexual mainstream.

Chideya addresses the power of the status quo that Jeff Cohen (pp. 222–27) writes about. In the centrist ideology, as he defines it, social criticism is limited. White reportage of black community issues may focus on "minor glitches, problems, or inequities," which are on their way to being fixed by a basically equitable system. Let students freely test this view with reference to current newspapers and television reports.

Michael Massing, "Bringing the Truth Commission Back Home"

Michael Massing's annotations of A. M. Rosenthal's letter create a complex web that students may find difficult to untangle. Spend some time going over the various positions, and you'll find that the selection is worth the effort for the important questions it raises. Where does truth reside? How much can we trust newspapers? Is there such a thing as journalistic objectivity?

Summarizing the various versions of the truth (questions 1 and 2) will help students see how the truth changes and can be determined by a publication's interests and political bent. We like to believe in journalistic objectivity, but there may be no such thing, in spite of the methodology followed by journalists. All reporting may be invested with motives; to some extent all journalism is "advocacy journalism."

As newspaper readers, we cannot determine the truth for ourselves. We must trust the reporter and our own sense of the author's and publication's credibility, both of which are subjectively determined. Questions 4, 5, and 7 focus student attention on the various participants' tone and use of evidence. Massing's snide characterizations of Rosenthal tend to undercut his own credibility. He also goes beyond the boundaries of his own evidence, as when he seems to be inside Bonner's head on p. 246, telling his reader that Bonner was "discouraged," felt demoted, and "reluctantly left the paper." How does he know this? Though he concedes Bonner's inexperience and fallibility, he fails to point out that the El Mozote story came out in the very same month that Bonner's story on the torture sessions appeared, and that the story had left egg on the *Times*'s face. Rosenthal, on the other hand, plays an us-versus-them game that works fairly well. He repeatedly praises the *Journal* as a respectable paper, while castigating other publications as unprofessional and beneath notice. The class debate on reputation (question 6) should bring the subjective side of journalism to the forefront. You may wish to supplement the debate by asking students to conduct further research on the various players and their reputations through such sources as *Publishers Weekly* and *Editor & Publisher*.

Question 11 asks students to focus on the reading experience that the Massing annotation prompted, and it can lead to a useful discussion of intertextuality.

In a piece like this selection, the foreground and background texts must both be held in mind as the reader moves between them. This may create difficulties of comprehension, but it also leads to an enriched reading of both texts. Use students' reports on their experience to guide them to an understanding of the density of intertextual references in scholarly prose.

Susan Faludi, "The Media and the Backlash"

Whether or not students agree with Susan Faludi's interpretation of media attitudes toward women, her article should provoke examination of the trend stories that figure so prominently in today's newspapers and magazines. Faludi points to journalistic practices that students may not be aware of, and reveals the often alarming extent to which journalists build on each other's stories. The selection demonstrates extensive use of sources, both primary and secondary. In order for students to assess Christina Hoff Sommers's critique of Faludi (pp. 262–67) they will need to pay close attention to the evidence on which the original argument is built.

Faludi seems to assume that journalism should consist only of objective reporting, free of any attempt to shape public opinion. After reading the selections by Jeff Cohen (pp. 222–27) and Michael Massing (pp. 241–47), students may find Faludi somewhat naive in this assumption. "Facts" are always subjectively selected and interpreted. Question 9 lets students address Faludi directly and bring to bear on their arguments their understanding of the role of the press in shaping opinion.

In response to Faludi's criticisms of the press's behavior, question 5 asks students to assemble their own code of journalistic ethics. They should be able to synthesize the various criticisms leveled at journalists by Massing and Rosenthal, Cohen, and Chideya (pp. 229–38). Even if your students haven't read those selections, they may rely on their own ideas about what constitutes fair practice and responsible reporting. They may even draw on images of journalists in popular culture, such as television's Murphy Brown.

Several of the questions let students test Faludi's generalizations against the current crop of trend stories. You might hold a class brainstorming session, listing on the board as many trends as you can think of, such as the "retrotrends" involving SPAM, the *Brady Bunch*, *Casper*, and disco music. Your students will be the experts on the trends that affect their generation. Ask them to research the media's portrayal of their generation and compare it to their own experiences. Do they agree with the trends predicted? Or do they believe, as Faludi does, that the media create the trends instead of just reporting them?

Christina Hoff Sommers, "The Backlash Myth"

Christina Hoff Sommers's refutation of Susan Faludi's arguments about the media demonstrates the dialogue among readers and writers that is conducted in print. Publication is, by definition, public. It always leaves an author open to challenge, and reviews are a primary site where such challenge takes place.

Thus, Sommers relies heavily on reviewers' comments in her own challenge to Faludi.

The quote from St. Augustine sets up Sommers's main premise: Even the slightest error renders an entire argument untenable. Sommers proceeds to point out errors and inconsistencies in Faludi's argument that she considers so "serious" or "egregious" that they undermine Faludi's entire point. Question 5 allows students to discuss whether they agree that Faludi has so seriously violated principles of truth that her whole argument is suspect. Many of the errors seem quite slight when compared with the weight of the many sources Faludi adduces in her own essay. Moreover, if students compare Sommers's essay with Faludi's, they'll find that Sommers herself doesn't always quote accurately.

Not all of Sommers's "refutations" hold up. Question 4 points to an instance where one statistic—graduates of business school—is used to refute Faludi's claim about a decline in another statistic—*applications* to business school. Those two figures do not necessarily correspond. You might have students test the correspondence by investigating your own school's proportion of minority or women *applicants* compared with its proportion of minority or women *graduates*. The evidence is oblique, at best, and doesn't really show Faludi in error, though Sommers makes much of her source's objections.

Since both Sommers and Faludi rely so heavily on secondhand sources, several questions send students directly to those sources to evaluate how well or poorly the authors used them. Questions 6, 8, and 9 allow students to compare whole essays with the snippets that are quoted by Faludi and Sommers. They can then evaluate how each author uses her sources, and perhaps gain some skepticism about sources that will be useful in their own writing. Question 9 lets students see firsthand how Sommers's own book was received, so they can measure their own response to her against that of other thinkers.

Sommers's characterization of the two types of feminism is, of course, highly controversial. Questions 7 and 10 address her categorizations, and permit students to debate their own views of feminism. The final question also points to Simon & Schuster's motives in publishing both Steinem and Sommers. Corporations don't always have ideologies, it would seem, so perhaps media conglomeration won't result in a stifling of dissenting voices—so long as those dissenting voices can still turn a profit.

Joe Tye, "Buying Silence: Self-Censorship of Smoking and Health in National Newsweeklies"

Joe Tye's essay presents a clear example of advocacy journalism. Tye makes his case against the newsmagazines by relying on lucidly presented statistical evidence. Moreover, he makes few concessions to his opponents. He raises their arguments just enough to make his own voice seem reasonable. Encourage students to look critically at his statistics: If one-third of *Time*'s stories covered the business aspects of cigarettes, what did the other two-thirds cover? Perhaps there were more critical stories than Tye would have us believe.

Most of the questions send students directly to magazines to research the accuracy of Tye's claims. Question 4 asks them to update Tye's study to discover whether the situation has improved or worsened. Questions 5 and 6 look directly at the cigarette companies' ads to see which audiences they are targeting and how well they conform to the industry's own ethical standards. You might combine these two questions into a single class day, letting students work in groups and pore over a variety of magazines that they bring into the classroom.

Question 8 extends the discussion from cigarettes to other industries to see how advertisers might control our news. You'll want to make the connection with Gloria Steinem's discussion of ads, if only to demonstrate that the problems she describes are not necessarily limited to women's magazines, as she seems to think. Advertisers have the potential to control editorial content in any magazine that depends on ad revenues for its success. Consider how these news stories might offend particular advertisers: rising rates and consequences of alcoholism; medical reports about fetal alcohol syndrome; automobile safety issues; Clinton's tariff on Japanese cars; airline safety records; airline price wars or price-fixing scandals. Would an editor be likely to practice "self-censorship" of such stories if there were a likelihood of losing advertising dollars?

Question 11 relates Tye's essay to chapter 5's discussion of censorship by invoking the term "prior restraint." Is it prior restraint if an editor *chooses* to censor material? Students may feel that the editors bear the responsibility for selecting material, and that advertisers cannot be charged with censorship or undue influence for simply doing their job. Others may argue that ad dollars represent a silent stranglehold that corporations have over editors, so even if an editor assumes responsibility for choosing the news, the advertiser's interests color all editorial decisions.

How can a magazine escape such problems? The magazines listed in *JAMA* simply refuse to carry tobacco ads (question 9). Students can see how that decision relates to the magazines' focus—youth, sports, health, and so forth. They can also formulate their own views on the proper relation between ads and editorial content, and express those views by answering question 10.

Dr. Samuel Johnson, "On the Art of Advertising"

Despite the difficulties students may have with Samuel Johnson's archaic style, this brief essay should amuse them, for Johnson's complaints about advertising sound remarkably contemporary. The problems he bemoans still exist, perhaps to an even greater degree in our own day. Question 6 lets students look for current ads that rely on the same tricks Johnson described. They can also see how unabashedly sex is used today, almost to the exclusion of other appeals.

Most of the questions focus on the physical placement of ads rather than their content. Students may have had practice analyzing advertising content, but they are rarely asked to look at ads in relation to editorial copy. Comparing Steinem's essay with Johnson's (question 7) will point up key attitudes that can guide further discussion. Steinem and Johnson both believe that the credibility of ads can only be enhanced by their placement amid editorial content known for its independence from outside influence. Johnson even reminds advertisers that their products will appear alongside the great news of the day; they should be honored by any juxtaposition, and should elevate their ads to match the tenor of the news. Advertisers, on the other hand, seem to believe that independent editorial copy can only damage the status of the product advertised. Negative news will seep into the adjacent ad, rendering the product unattractive.

Question 8 allows students to test these beliefs by looking at today's magazines, while question 9 sends them to publications of an earlier period. You may need to prepare a list of sources for older periodicals that will be available in your own institution's library. Not all schools will be able to supply eighteenth- or nineteenth-century newspapers for students to peruse. However, many may have early American or British newspapers available on microfilm. Although it is preferable for students to handle the actual newspapers, they can still learn a great deal from viewing microfilm. They can see, for instance, that it was not uncommon to find ads on the front page of a newspaper—a practice rare today. They can also look at the extravagance of advertisers' claims for patent medicines, for instance, and compare such practices to today's appeals. Make the microfilm research fun by asking students to photocopy and bring to class the most outrageous ads they find. While you discuss the ads, remind students of Johnson's regard for future generations. We are looking at newspapers now exactly as he had predicted; we're using them to give us a glimpse of the past. What will our ads tell future generations about us?

Gloria Steinem, "Sex, Lies, and Advertising"

If Joe Tye's findings about the impact of cigarette advertisers are alarming, Gloria Steinem's well-known exposé about advertisers' influence over women's magazines will terrify anyone who cares about the First Amendment. The appalling practices she claims are business as usual for women's magazines may be becoming standard practice in other sources of information as well. Thus her essay should not be regarded just as a piece that emphasizes gender inequities. It also raises important issues about credibility and the independent press.

Several questions let students address the gender issues that clamor for discussion. Question 5 points to how magazines are marketed. Analyzing the arrangement on shelves at a bookstore will show distinct categories for many magazines, while others will seem to overlap categories. Question 7 asks students to compare two categories directly to see how aptly Steinem characterizes the double standard in magazines. Some typical "men's" magazines might be *GQ*, *Esquire*, or *Details*. Perhaps these magazines' editors face the same problems that Steinem faced as editor of *Ms.* Susan Faludi would certainly agree with Steinem about the double standard applied to women's magazines (question 6). She would see more evidence of media backlash in Steinem's fears that the media would criticize the entire feminist movement if *Ms.* failed financially.

One of Steinem's arguments is that the scarcity of women in advertising and publishing makes possible the inequities she witnessed. Question 8 lets students compare Steinem's claim with Farai Chideya's quite similar contention regarding African American journalists. Both Steinem and Chideya believe that what does or does not get published influences public perception in vital ways.

The final two questions relate Steinem's essay to the censorship issues that are examined in greater detail in chapter 5. Question 10 lets students examine the capitulation of *Sassy* magazine's editors in the broader context of pressure from the religious right. Joan DelFattore's discussion of religious fundamentalists and their efforts to control the content of school textbooks (pp. 441–48) makes the *Sassy* decision seem part of a larger effort by certain groups to control the media. Students may disagree about whether there should be a "Chinese wall" between advertising and editorial content. Question 11 lets them address their views to an advertiser or editor, or respond directly to Steinem or Tye in the interests of advertising's right to free trade. In either case, they will have had to formulate a coherent position about the degree to which advertisers should influence the media.

In the context of your discussions of Steinem's essay, you might wish to raise the analogy with public broadcasting's longstanding policy against accepting advertising. *Ms.* magazine tried to gain its independence in exactly the same way that public broadcasting did. Recent challenges to public funding of such broadcasting may put the advertiser back into the picture—quite literally, in the case of television. Students should consider how advertisers' invasiveness might already extend to television and radio.

Joseph Deitch, "Portrait of a Book Reviewer: Christopher Lehmann-Haupt"

Book reviewing may not immediately intrigue students, but they will quickly see how the review process colors our opinions of nearly all consumer items, especially those having to do with "culture." Students may be more comfortable talking about reviews of movies, concerts, or CDs than of books, and they may be more familiar with TV "reviewers" like Siskel and Ebert than with print reviewers. Lehmann-Haupt's observations about books apply to other media as well. You can therefore conduct the discussion on whatever plane suits your students, and the same issues of power and influence will arise.

Though Joseph Deitch is the author of this selection, Christopher Lehmann-Haupt really controls the flow of information. Question 3 points students to Deitch's lack of critical distance from his subject. He fawns over Lehmann-Haupt, perhaps because of the reviewer's presumed power. Deitch seems thrilled to be seen hobnobbing with the great man, swapping Thomas Wolfe stories. If Lehmann-Haupt were a book, Deitch would be the uncritical reviewer. You might spend some time assessing whether Deitch's admiration gets in the way of his credibility with his readers.

Questions 4 and 5 address the process of reviewing from opposite perspectives. First, students are asked to replicate the reviewer's activities; then they look at how a reader approaches a review. The motives of reviewer and reader may not be the same; that difference may determine the impact the review will have.

Questions 6 and 7 address the power and use of reviews as marketing devices. Even if nobody reads a newspaper review, its effects linger. Frequently, the little snippets of a review reprinted in ads carry more weight than the original review. Moreover, the legitimizing function of a review extends beyond the realm of books. Print reviews often show up in ads for nonprint items, such as cars and movies. For other products, *Consumer Reports* is often cited as the reviewing authority. Question 7 extends the issue of marketing techniques to consider how reviews sell the newspapers they appear in, not just the books they discuss. Is there an ethical conflict in linking news stories to book reviews, as in the case of Woodward's *Veil?* The link helps sell newspapers, but does the news story risk becoming a mere puff piece for the review, or vice versa? How about when a television news show runs a "story" about the filming of that same station's movie of the week? or an interview with a star of a network show? Should there be a "Chinese wall" between news and reviewing?

Finally, the last two questions send students to actual reviews. Question 8 asks students to look critically at a single review, evaluating it for content, credibility, and purpose. If your local paper doesn't carry any reviews, send students to a larger regional paper for this assignment, especially the Sunday edition. Question 9 allows students to compare their own experience with that of several reviewers. We've probably all had the experience of reading a review and wondering if the reviewer attended the same play, movie, or concert we saw, so widely did our opinions vary. Sampling a variety of reviews should give students a range of opinions to compare to their own. You may have to show them how to track down reviews, using the *Reader's Guide to Periodical Literature*, *Book Review Digest*, or online indexes by title of the book or movie.

Katharine Weber, "The Reviewer's Experience"

Just as Christopher Lehmann-Haupt describes the hidden process of reviewing, Katharine Weber calls attention to marketing strategies for new books that may be unimagined by students. She also attunes students to the physical properties of books, and may help them learn how to assess a book before (or without) reading it. For discussion purposes, bring into class some of the promotional brochures, flyers, or order forms—the academic *bumph*—that you as a writing teacher may have received for this book or another textbook that publishers are enticing you to order. Let the class analyze it. What claims are made? What authorities are invoked? Help them see that the content of the book isn't always the most important factor in book sales.

After they've looked at the marketing strategies publishers use for textbooks, students can apply the same analytical techniques to popular books. Questions 4 and 5 send them to bookstores to examine books as objects that are being marketed to consumers. They can assess critically the ploys and the packaging that are used to gain their attention and their dollars. Question 6 lets them examine how the publishing industry believes reviews are regarded by the public. The predominance of certain reviewers' or publications' quotations will show students the hierarchy of reviewing publications that the book industry puts faith in. Their findings will probably reinforce the observations made by Christopher Lehmann-Haupt and Joseph Deitch about the power of the *New York Times* in book review circles.

The final question allows students to pen their own reviews, designed specifically for their peers. They can see for themselves the difficulties reviewers face in evaluating their audience and supplying the right amount of information for their readers. They may also find themselves verging on hyping a book they like, rather than reviewing it; if so, they will be better able to appreciate the gray areas between reviewing and advertising that these selections address.

CHAPTER

4

WHAT SHOULD YOU READ?

Popular versus Official Culture

This chapter focuses attention on the various definitions of culture, and asks students to think about who decides which cultural artifacts have value. As you work through the chapter, ask your students to keep their own reading preferences in view. What do they read? How highly do they value such reading? Where does their sense of its value or lack of value come from? I frequently begin by asking how many students read a book last summer. Then I ask how many read a *good* book. Typically, more than half the students who raised their hand in answer to the first question will lower it after I ask the second question. When I press them on what they read and why it's not "good," they'll sheepishly admit to devouring a Barbara Cartland romance or a Stephen King thriller, and then dismiss such reading as trash. Many students have so internalized the standards of high culture that they discount their own tastes and preferences. Moreover, they often expect that their college education will help civilize them and turn them into "cultured" human beings. Just how that process is supposed to occur they don't quite know, but they are sure that their own popular tastes are somehow deficient.

You may find students with similar assumptions, or you may discover that your students quite happily embrace popular culture with no aspirations toward elite culture. In either case, you can discuss what stereotype students have of the "cultured" individual and compare it with the stereotype of the "cool" person. Once students have listed the images they associate with high culture and with pop culture, they can critique those images. Most importantly, they can begin to consider where their images come from, and whether different types of culture are mutually exclusive. Books, movies, and television shows are filled with models of people moving from one cultural domain to another. *Pretty Woman* and *Moonstruck*, for instance, both feature opera scenes, where a plebian woman is introduced to the glories of high culture. Other common plots involve a stuffy, uptight, rich man or woman experiencing the liberating influence of pop culture. Why is high culture so often associated with stiffness? Why is pop culture linked to spontaneity? To some extent, the answer lies in the fixity of the print in which high culture is often embodied, as compared to the fluidity of oral forms of cultural expression. (Even though opera should fall into the fluid/oral category, it resides in a written score and libretto that follow strict formal conventions.)

The first two essays set the stage for the rest of the chapter. Bernard Berelson surveys assumptions about America's reading habits, and suggests a more complicated picture of American culture than the usual generalizations would permit. E. D. Hirsch looks at what binds a nation together as a distinct culture, and lays the groundwork for future discussions of the canon and popular culture. Laura Bohannan and Henry Louis Gates both offer counterpoints to the idea that high culture has universal applicability. Bohannan tests *Hamlet* on an African tribe with non-Western cultural expectations, while Gates examines how literate society imposed its own criteria on what constituted culture or even humanity. Thomas J. Roberts explores the notion of taste, and finds that good taste doesn't always mean "good" reading. The marketing and dissemination of culture are the subject of the essays by John P. Dessauer and Joan Shelley Rubin. The final four essays offer views of often read but little studied segments of print culture: romances, self-help books, and fanzines.

Bernard Berelson, "Who Reads What, and Why?"

Though this piece is somewhat dated in its references, many of the assumptions about American reading that Bernard Berelson lists are still in circulation. You should have no trouble coming up with examples of the practice of "Viewing with Alarm the state of popular culture." Bob Dole's campaign speeches about Hollywood certainly fall into this category, as do many other diatribes against movies, television, or rap music. Books per se have come in for less criticism, perhaps because their very status as books gives them more cachet than other forms of culture.

Berelson's own implicit assumptions deserve some scrutiny. Questions 4 and 5 ask students to think about the precise segment of "American people" he's writing about and for. He writes as an elite reader for others who are of the elite, or at least near enough to endorse elite values. Berelson talks about the differentiation among the American public, but he seems to be differentiating *within* the category of white, middle-class readers. He also seems to envision largely suburban patterns of life—keeping up with the neighbors and other mothers.

Today's assumptions about book reading have definite affinities with those of Berelson's day. Question 6 lets students update Berelson's assumptions and evaluate the place book reading has in our intellectual life. Link it with question 7, regarding television's effect on book reading, for many of our most cherished assumptions have to do with the way TV has replaced books in our cultural life.

We certainly watch more television as a society than people did in the 1950s, but we are also buying books at record rates. Book groups are gaining in popularity, and the past decade has seen the success of megabookstores such as Borders, Bookstar, and Barnes & Noble in many cities.

Spend some time in class assessing Berelson's rhetorical strategy of putting forth an assumption and then refuting or complicating it. It's a nice technique for getting across lots of information and demonstrating subtleties of evaluation. Question 9 lets students try their hand at the same strategy, using an activity they know well. The easy part of the essay will be generating a list of stereotypes for the activity. Push students to do the hard work of looking at the assumptions that underlie the stereotypes, analyzing where the images come from, and regarding the stereotypes critically.

E. D. Hirsch Jr., "The Formation of Modern National Cultures"

E. D. Hirsch's book *Cultural Literacy* laid the groundwork for attacks on multiculturalism and for a conservative pedagogical emphasis on "back to basics" programs. One of Newt Gingrich's current platform planks, for instance, is an emphasis on "American culture," though he doesn't define precisely what that is. This essay should encourage students to debate the origins and applicability of that culture.

By applying C. H. Knoblauch's essay on literacy, students can begin to assess the politics that underlie cultural nationalism (question 6). This will better prepare them to conduct the class debate in response to question 7. You may wish to have students refer to the essay by Huntly Collins (pp. 473–79) to defuse any glib stereotypes about multiculturalism or political correctness.

Hirsch's idea that cultural literacy is a "socially progressive" notion deserves some scrutiny. Though he asserts the malleability of national culture, Hirsch says it can't be changed by fiat. Ask students to consider what changes, if any, have arisen recently. You might want to compare sections of the list of "What Literate Americans Know," printed at the back of Hirsch's book, with "The Beginnings of an Expanded List of Essential Names, Phrases, Dates, and Concepts" compiled by Rick Simonson and Scott Walker, editors of *The Greywolf Annual 5: Multi-Cultural Literacy* (1988), which provides a less Eurocentric, male perspective than Hirsch's. Or you could compare Hirsch's *Dictionary of Cultural Literacy* with the *Dictionary of Global Culture* (1995), coedited by Henry Louis Gates and Kwame Anthony Appiah. What values do each of the compilations promote? Have American values changed? Questions 8 and 9 follow up on such a discussion by letting students create their own lists and explore whether such lists make any sense in a culture as diverse as ours.

Laura Bohannan, "Shakespeare in the Bush"

Students unfamiliar with *Hamlet* may have difficulty with this essay, primarily because they won't get the jokes. Others may have difficulty allowing themselves to laugh at the jokes. Shakespeare often induces deadly seriousness in students, but Bohannan's essay involves a great deal of self-deprecating humor. Questions 1 and 2 aim to help students understand the comedy of Bohannan's characterizations of herself and her naive and even arrogant attitudes toward the Tiv. Encourage them to have fun with this essay.

Bohannan begins with the assumption that one's cultural superiority is indicated by one's understanding of *Hamlet*. To help students with question 5, you may have to explain why her British friend pulls rank on Bohannan, the ignorant American. In the same way, Bohannan assumes her own superiority to the Tiv: She is elated that the rainy season will allow the tribespeople to explain their rituals to her, as if that's what rituals are for. For their part, the Tiv assume they are superior to Bohannan, for they understand her story better than she does. Question 8 allows students to reflect on their own standing in this hierarchy.

Bohannan's experience strikes at the heart of the notion that the artifacts of high culture have universal appeal. Human nature isn't the same everywhere: It's culturally mediated, more like human "nurture." Question 6 lets students use Bohannan to counter E. D. Hirsch, while question 7 frames the same contrast in terms of the college curriculum.

Beyond the question of *Hamlet*'s universality, there is much in Bohannan's essay about the value of writing versus oral storytelling. Questions 3 and 9 focus attention on these features of the essay, and highlight the literate society's implicit assumption that literacy and civilization are congruent. It is important to remind students that the Tiv are not illiterate: That is, they are not members of a literate society who for some reason have not mastered basic literacy. Rather, they are nonliterate. They belong to an oral society in which literacy is not a valid yardstick for measuring intelligence or achievement.

Henry Louis Gates Jr., "The Trope of the Talking Book"

Because of its elevated level of discourse, this essay may prove troublesome for many students. Gates's language is abstract, and his arguments are difficult to grasp. Question 5 lets you confront this difficulty directly with students.

Despite its toughness, Gates's essay provides a useful analytical framework for assessing the contact between oral and literate cultures. The questions and writing assignments use a variety of tactics to help students address the differences between orality and literacy. These include a practical demonstration of the differences between the spoken and written word (question 6), comparison of African slaves with another oral society, Zitkala-Ša's Sioux culture (question 7), and applications of the oral/written distinction within contemporary American culture (question 8) and Western culture at large (question 9). In all these questions, students should be encouraged to examine their own assumptions regarding the relative value of oral and written cultures. Challenge them to articulate their own sense of cultural hierarchies, to see whether it is influenced by the same biases that Gates examines. If so, is that necessarily a bad thing?

The final question addresses the reasons that writers write, and lets students extend Gates's arguments to groups other than African Americans. Writing functions to include writers of all sorts in the human community. Just as Zitkala-Ša could prove the Sioux's humanity to the readers of *The Atlantic* in 1903, Charles

Kikuchi could use writing to prove the humanity of Japanese Americans in the 1940s and *The Advocate* could do the same for the gay community in the 1970s and 1980s. Print gives individuals and groups a voice in the conversation that counts the most in a literate society.

As students come to a fuller understanding of Gates's argument, you might return to the matter of Gates's own difficult language and style to ask whether Gates himself reenacts the trope of the talking book: Is he trying somehow to prove that African Americans belong in the intellectual realm of whites by taking on board the whole range of intellectual abstractions that written discourse promotes? If the act of writing is somehow a way of being coopted by the dominant culture, as he implies, has he been so coopted? Is Gates himself reinforcing the idea that white literate tradition is the sign of civilization, even as he criticizes that notion?

Thomas J. Roberts, "On Low Taste"

Thomas J. Roberts's observations complicate the hierarchies of taste and culture that other writers in this chapter have alluded to. Spend some time going over his classifications of types of readers and reading matter so that students understand what he means when he describes readers who cross those boundaries (questions 5 and 6). If your students seem better able to talk about taste in movies or music than taste in books, feel free to adapt the questions accordingly. The same crossing of boundaries applies. Serious filmgoers are often found sampling what Roberts would call "vernacular" films.

Many students will identify easily with Roberts's description of the "aesthetic pretender." Question 4 lets them explore why and for whom they pretended to like something they thought ranked high on the cultural ladder. This pretense taps into the sense of hierarchies that our education often instills in us. Question 8 addresses the matter of taste education. See how many of your students expect college to be the place where they acquire good taste. Especially at liberal arts institutions, Culture (with a capital C) seems to be one of the main commodities students expect to purchase with their tuition dollars. Question 10 lets students see how many of their peers or professors engage in the same aesthetic pretense Roberts describes. Poll results may be skewed by the fact that serious readers tend to hide their slumming, as Roberts notes. Ask students as a group to design a questionnaire, or a series of oral questions, that will define "vernacular fiction" for the recipient, and also make the person being polled feel comfortable enough to answer honestly. Anonymity may be required.

Since Roberts raises the issue of clichés with a list of science fiction plot clichés, you have a good opportunity to examine how clichés work for and against writers. Question 7 should be a fun assignment, letting students demonstrate their thorough knowledge of hackneyed devices and expressions associated with a particular genre. Once they've generated their lists, discuss what makes a cliché in the first place. The predictability of a cliché both comforts us and bores us. Students may wonder how to identify a cliché. I use a fill-in-the-blank exercise: Write the first half of a few trite phrases on the board. "As easy as falling off _____." "No pain, _____." If students can fill in the second half of the phrase, it's probably worn out. Good writers, however, can often freshen up a cliché and turn it to good rhetorical use. Survey some advertising copy for examples of clichés with a clever twist put on them.

Roberts raises an important counterpoint to E. D. Hirsch's ideas about a common culture. Question 9 sends students back to Hirsch with Roberts's arguments about the ubiquity of popular culture in mind. It could be argued that pop culture forms the biggest part of our national culture, despite insistence on educating people in the touchstones of elite culture. In fact, Roberts's final paragraph suggests an explanation for the alienation often associated with those who only value high culture.

John P. Dessauer, "Cultural Pluralism and the Book World"

John Dessauer is a publishing insider, writing for others in the book world. He takes for granted the longstanding publishing practice of using potboilers and hot-selling popular writing to underwrite the costs of producing a few "serious" books that will garner critical attention but little revenue. Dessauer criticizes the elitist attitudes of a broad range of people: publishers, booksellers, reviewers, academics, librarians, and teachers. His tendency to generalize about these categories of people may weaken his argument. Ask students to fill in particular instances that may come to mind when they read Dessauer's condemnation of teachers or librarians, for instance, who push only the classics, ignoring readers' preferences.

Dessauer effectively uses definitions and analogies to make his point. However, his assumption about political pluralism in the first paragraph may not be accepted by all students. Not everyone is as committed to openness and tolerance as he might think. Even if multiculturalism were adopted by everyone, it still smacks of the elitism that Dessauer criticizes: Multiculturalism moves horizontally across cultures, picking the "best" of all cultures; it rarely descends vertically, if you will, into popular culture.

There are several ways to test Dessauer's claims of elitism on the part of the book world. Question 6 asks for individual reflection on cultural snobbery, while question 8 sends students to book review pages for evidence of the accuracy of Dessauer's observations. If your institution is located in an area with several bookstores, you might also have students study reviewing and marketing practices in your area. Look up bookstores in the phone book: How many "good" bookstores are there compared to the chains and megastores, such as Borders or Barnes & Noble? Visit some stores to see if the big discounters are underpricing and so driving out the small stores, as the elitists claim; or, are they selling the books that people really want to read instead of the ones booksellers and reviewers think they should read?

Dessauer calls for a revision of the priorities of the book world, which were well articulated by Christopher Lehmann-Haupt (pp. 305–6). Question 10 allows students to frame a response to the *New York Times* reviewer that establishes a new set of criteria for evaluating culture. Those criteria include paying more attention to which books people actually read, rather than judging books against some abstract cultural standard. Priority would not necessarily be given to familiar, big-name authors of what Lehmann-Haupt calls "important" books, unless there is demonstrable evidence that many people really read such books.

Joan Shelley Rubin, "Why Do You Disappoint Yourself? The Early History of the Book-of-the-Month Club"

Joan Shelley Rubin studies an institution that accounts for a hefty chunk of a book's sales, if the book is lucky enough to be chosen by the Book-of-the-Month Club. The club wields a great deal of cultural clout. It also, as Rubin points out, commodifies culture. The BOMC promises a monthly dose of good taste, delivered right to your door.

Most of the questions following this selection focus on the way readers' needs are met by this institutionalization of culture. Question 6 asks students to reflect on their own need to feel "in the know," whether about books or other cultural commodities. Understanding their own desire to feel current will help them grasp the function that Rubin says the BOMC aims to fulfill. They can compare that use of books with the motives for reading described by other authors in this book (question 11). Rubin, like Berelson, believes people often read books to keep up with others in their social set, rather than from intrinsic interest.

The passivity engendered by the club's selection process may be only an extension of what happens when readers rely on reviewers to tell them which books to buy. Questions 8 and 9 let students discuss how reviews function in general, and also explore their own particular use of reviews. You might ask them to consider how else they might evaluate books, if not through reviews. Do readers generally have the time or inclination to evaluate new books on their own? Do we generally trust our own taste? Or do we derive some comfort from having our choices made for us by certified experts?

Questions 7 and 10 send students to current marketing materials to see whether the club's strategies persist today. The BOMC review board that Rubin describes was disbanded in 1994, and Clifton Fadiman, on the board since 1944, was appointed Chief Editorial Advisor. The panel of experts was replaced by "staff" so that selections can be made in a more timely manner. That is, the club now aims for more currency than before, and relies less on named experts to validate its decisions. Other clubs have copied BOMC's format, and many of your students may belong to such a club. Especially prevalent among college students is the Columbia House Music club, which delivers current CDs on a monthly schedule. It offers convenience, but often frustration as well. Selections are sent on a system of tacit approval—silence means assent—so that members often receive items they didn't know they had ordered, simply by not responding to mailings. The marketing strategy relies on the consumer's passivity and desire for convenience.

Janice A. Radway, "The Act of Reading the Romance"

Janice Radway's long essay on romance readers presents a wide range of issues that intersect with other readings in this book. She traces readers' motivations for reading, deals with a genre of fiction often dismissed as beneath critical notice, raises questions of gender, and discusses publishers' marketing strategies. In addition, her interesting methodology deserves to be pointed out. She bases her study of romance readers on interviews and questionnaires, rather than on the secondary sources so often encountered in historical scholarship. Moreover, she describes how she began with certain assumptions that her data forced her to modify. Radway clearly wanted the women of Smithton to complain about their lives as housewives, but they were proud of their lives. This essay offers a good opportunity to discuss how a writer's or a researcher's biases often guide the research process and can skew the data and conclusions if the researcher is not flexible and self-aware.

The women Radway interviewed returned again and again to several motivations for reading—particularly escape and education. Question 6 lets students examine escape in the context of identification with a main character, something other writers have discussed and students may have experienced. You'll also want to explore the connection between escape and addiction that the women mention. How does reading differ from drugs or alcohol? Why is a reading parent a positive role model, as these women seem to feel? Ask students how many of them had reading parents, and how reading figured in their family dynamic. The educational function of reading is addressed by question 7, in which students compare Franklin's autodidacticism with the education the romance readers claim they derive from their books. Question 11 allows industrious students to see just what sort of "information" they can obtain from a Harlequin romance. Chances are that information differs significantly from the kinds of knowledge Franklin gleaned from his reading.

Question 8 directly raises the gender issue, and question 9 expands on it. Allow students to compare in class the results of their interviews with readers of genre fiction. See how many male readers were attracted to spy thrillers or similar adventure novels, perhaps as a way to escape from their lives as accountants or lawyers. Men's and women's escapist fantasies may differ, but there is probably a genre of fiction that fulfills every sort of fantasy.

Marketing strategies for genre fiction often play up the formulaic aspects of the stories that are deplored by critics, but cherished by readers. Novels that violate the formula don't succeed in giving the reader the experience he or she sought. Therefore, packaging by publishers assures readers of the formulaic qualities by using similar designs and typefaces on book jackets. Question 10 lets students see how easy it is to judge such books by their covers, and judge them accurately.

Though romances serve millions of readers and generate high sales volumes, they are ignored by "serious" readers and critics. Question 12 lets students return to the debate over cultural hierarchies that forms the core of this chapter. They can use romances to compare the cultural landscape envisioned by E. D. Hirsch with that extolled by Thomas Roberts and John Dessauer.

The final question directs students' attention to the features of scholarly writing that they are likely to encounter in their college careers. In particular, this question focuses on the variety of evidence used by four academic historians. In addition to standard "secondary sources" (that is, other scholars), these authors use interviews and questionnaires (Radway); memoirs, letters, and diaries (Sicherman); contemporary essays (Kerber); and advertising material (Rubin).

The richness of their sources may give your students a fuller notion of the range of materials available to them as researchers. More important, you can use this question as an occasion to examine academic techniques of quotation, paraphrase, summary, and documentation.

Steven Starker, "The New Oracle: Self-Help Books in American Culture"

Like Janice Radway, Steven Starker examines a segment of the book industry that generates millions of dollars in annual revenue, but falls outside the usual boundaries of the book reviewer's notice. The main problem Starker sees with these books is the lack of authority of the authors. "Apparent expertise" is no guarantee of any sort of competence, and yet we willingly grant authority to authors if their words are validated by print. You might compare the reader's need for instruction on aspects of complex modern life with Joan Shelley Rubin's discussion of the ad campaigns mounted by the Book-of-the-Month Club. Just as those ads of the 1920s promised expert advice to cope with the chaotic proliferation of choices in the book world, self-help books offer the same guidance for the bewildered—cheaply, easily, and privately—on any topic you can imagine.

The questions ask students to look closely at self-help books from a variety of perspectives, beginning with their own past experience with the genre (question 5). In class, students can examine the books that they or their roommates or family members may own (question 6). They should scrutinize the book in terms of Starker's critique and read the author blurbs critically: What real credentials does he or she have, as opposed to "apparent" expertise? Question 7 is similar, but it sends students to the store to look at an array of current self-help books. Here the emphasis is on marketing trends, rather than particular books. Question 8 allows students to see how the self-help genre has permeated the magazine industry. Even students who claim never to have read a self-help book probably cannot claim to have avoided all such "expert" advice.

In class discussion, you might ask students to compare Ben Franklin's trio of "healthy, wealthy, and wise" with Starker's "health, wealth, and happiness." Have we substituted happiness for wisdom? These books surely can't promise wisdom; can they assure happiness? What's the difference? Does the self-help genre spring from the self-reliance that Franklin exemplified? Question 10 lets students explore these connections.

Laurie Ouellette, "'Zines: Notes from the Underground"

Laurie Ouellette's rundown of 'zines provides a nice rhetorical model of definition and classification. Students should have no trouble tracing her argument, or outlining her essay to see its structure, even as they can be amused by the subject she discusses. Question 11 lets them test her definition of a 'zine against a description of *The Advocate*, an alternative publication that addresses one of the main topic areas of 'zines—gay life—but that may not meet all her criteria.

Your students may not have encountered 'zines before, and they may have difficulty tracking down current examples. Even so, they can register their own reactions to the 'zines Ouellette describes (question 5). She seems to have picked especially outrageous titles and topics, many of which might offend your students. The publications reveal an underground that many students may prefer remained hidden from view. If 'zines are available in your area, question 6 will let students see how 'zines physically resemble and differ from conventional publications, while question 7 will allow them to examine the writer/reader dynamic of 'zines. If 'zines are not available, question 10 picks up on the comparison between 'zines and mainstream magazines by using examples reprinted elsewhere in this book. Gridley Minima and M. Kadi write regularly for the 'zine *h2so4*, and their prose differs markedly from that of writers for *Time*, *Newsweek*, or *The New Yorker*.

Questions 3, 4, and 8 focus on 'zines as "alternative culture." They may not be mainstream, but they still seem to be dominated by white, middle-class participants. They appeal to white, middle-class disaffected people (such as the *Utne Reader*'s subscribers), because that's largely who writes them. 'Zines are part of literate culture, by and for people who grew up in a reading world. Non-readers wouldn't think to publish their views in formats self-consciously designed to disconnect from mainstream publishing, for they would not have been steeped in mainstream conventions to begin with. Only readers who understand the power of the press can begin to play with that power and manipulate the press for their own purposes.

Gridley Minima, "Other People's 'Zines"

After students have read about 'zines from Laurie Ouellette's perspective as an analytical outsider, they can appreciate Gridley Minima's status as a genuine 'zine author. He's conversational and brash, and he aims to shake up his reader. His style and rhetoric are worth pointing out, especially as they exemplify his philosophy about 'zines as letters to friends we've never met (question 5).

The core of Minima's essay is the philosophical debate about the difference between amateurs and professionals. Question 6 asks for class discussion of the distinction, while question 8 lets students reflect on their own amateur activities. Minima locates the distinction in the arena of how we evaluate printed publications. Do we use different criteria when money enters the picture? Of course we do. We expect more bang for the buck, but the only bang that we recognize is the one that we've become accustomed to: the bang provided by polished, glossy, "professional" magazines. Here students can draw on the discussions of books as material objects that have cropped up throughout this book. The material form of a 'zine conveys as much information about its status as the content of the publication does.

CHAPTER

5

WHAT SHOULDN'T YOU READ?

*Censorship and
the First Amendment*

Any restriction on the distribution of ideas can be considered a form of censorship. The essays in this chapter largely deal with institutionalized censorship—that is, restrictions sanctioned or carried out by governmental authority. They also focus on censorship of printed materials, though the subject naturally spills over to restrictions of broadcast ideas as well as speech. Personal objections to a book or individual attacks on a form of print may seem to be matters of taste, not censorship. However, if they involve court-enforced bans or legislated guidelines for taste, they fall into the enormous territory covered by the First Amendment.

The first two selections—Benjamin Franklin's "Apology for Printers" and Erwin Knoll's "Don't Print That!"—are essential to an understanding of the more subtle aspects of censorship. Franklin presents a good look at the market forces that govern the press, while Knoll introduces the fundamental concept of "prior restraint." Neither essay is very long, and they could usefully be taught together. The rest of the selections deal with particular types of bookbanning or restraint, falling into several clusters. Joan DelFattore offers an overview of bookbanning efforts that affect school textbooks, and she provides a larger context for the debate over *Huckleberry Finn* articulated in greater detail by John Wallace and Dudley Barlow. Nat Hentoff and Catharine MacKinnon serve as the main opponents in the discussion of the effort to redefine pornography as a civil rights issue. Hentoff's piece is a straightforward essay, while MacKinnon voices her views in conversation with another opponent, First Amendment lawyer Floyd Abrams. William Noble touches on both the *Huck Finn* and pornography controversies, acting as a bridge between the two clusters, or a substitution for one entire cluster. MacKinnon's conversation covers more ground than just the pornography debate. She and Abrams address campus speech codes and regulatory efforts coming from the liberal left. If you wish to focus on this aspect of the discussion, Huntly Collins's "PC and the Press" will be mandatory reading, for she shows that many of the wildest stories about leftist ideology on campus have little basis in fact. The final conversation among computer hackers moves the censorship debate into cyberspace, and will pave the way for the following chapter on "Communication in the Electronic Era."

The issues in this chapter cry out for in-class debates, and you'll find questions throughout the section that suggest such debates. Students should be encouraged to express their objections and convictions regarding the spread of ideas that may be considered offensive. Vigorous debate guarantees a healthy First Amendment.

Benjamin Franklin, "An Apology for Printers"

Benjamin Franklin's defense of printers appeared more than half a century before the First Amendment was ratified. He cannot, therefore, appeal to the law to back him up. Instead he appeals to common sense and the laws of commerce: Knowing that they can't please everybody, printers remain philosophically neutral, and print whatever pays. His argument for market-driven decisions sounds remarkably modern, especially when compared with the situations described by Joe Tye (pp. 269–72) and Gloria Steinem (pp. 277–302).

The complexity in Franklin's essay arises from his sense of the printer's responsibility to the public. Question 4 points to the passage that undermines the previous arguments, and question 7 calls for further exploration of that responsibility. By claiming that printers really do weed out the most offensive stuff before it gets printed, and that he himself has printed only what would serve the public good, Franklin condones a degree of censorship that Erwin Knoll would probably describe as "prior restraint."

Franklin touches on the matter of popular taste, claiming that he has printed high-minded moral works that remain unsold while less worthy works of "low taste" sell so quickly he can't keep them in stock. Remind students how this argument connects to the discussions of popular and official culture in chapter 4. If Franklin believes that market forces should determine what gets printed, ask students to speculate on whether he would condone all that gets printed today. How would he feel about pulp fiction and tabloid journalism?

Spend some time looking at Franklin's humor, for it contributes greatly to the success of his apology. You could ask students to review Larzer Ziff's essay on "Writing for Print" (pp. 38–50) to see how the persona that Franklin creates fits with his beliefs about the public function of printing. He appears reasonable, likable, and noncombative, even as he stands his ground against his opponents.

Erwin Knoll, "Don't Print That!"

The issue of "prior restraint" is fundamental to an understanding of the First Amendment. Erwin Knoll's essay provides an opportunity to look at the chilling effects of court decisions on the press's right to print and on the individual's right to speak freely. Knoll and Nat Hentoff believe in strict construction of the First Amendment freedoms: They brook no interference with the individual's right to decide what to read or say, and they believe that counterargument is the best way to deal with objectionable ideas.

The questions dealing with Mohr's book (questions 4 and 5) raise the issue of the double standard we apply to portrayals of homosexual and heterosexual acts. You might want to discuss the inherent subjectiveness of the Miller obscenity definition which relies on "community standards." It may be interesting to revisit this piece after the students read about the Dworkin-MacKinnon definition of pornography as a violation of women's civil rights.

Another important issue, raised by the *Soldier of Fortune* example, is that of the responsibility that goes along with freedom of the press. Question 6 lets students compare Franklin and Knoll on this issue, while question 10 allows them to assess Gloria Steinem's practices as an editor in light of Knoll's position. Knoll's discussion is necessarily brief so question 9 invites further research and analysis of the complexities of the case. The ad for a hit man is a dramatic example of print that most people would find objectionable, and the consequence of the court's ruling was equally extreme: Such huge damages were assessed that *Soldier of Fortune* ceased publishing altogether.

Students may feel that censorship is justified in certain cases, especially with regard to children. Question 8 raises the censorship issue in the context of school textbooks, and links Knoll's discussion to the cluster of readings about *Huckleberry Finn*. The boundaries of censorship are continually being challenged and redefined; students should be encouraged to try to draw their own boundaries and defend them. Question 7 puts students in the place of the publisher to see how freedom of the press plays out from the producer's vantage point.

Spend some time going over the crisp structure of Knoll's argument: He offers two main examples and then presents his thesis, followed by one final example. The last example also gives you the opportunity to guide students to an understanding of irony, which will be particularly useful when they read the selections about *Huckleberry Finn*.

Joan DelFattore, "Romeo and Juliet Were Just Good Friends"

Students may need some background information to understand fully the implications of the textbook censorship that Joan DelFattore describes. In the course of her book, DelFattore demonstrates convincingly how challenges to textbooks affect publishers and consumers, even when those challenges do not succeed. The publicity of a challenge—even an unsuccessful one—can adversely affect sales, and publishers depend on textbook sales. As a result, they become more cautious and try to remove in advance any material that might offend. Thus, even if the extremists on either side of the political spectrum fail in their efforts to ban books, they have succeeded in influencing the content of future textbooks. This, of course, affects all schools, not just the ones where the challenge occurred. Even private schools, not subject to state board recommendations, will feel the impact, for they can only order books that publishers make available.

Students may want to know why fundamentalist parents don't send their children to private schools, if they feel so strongly that public schools are harming their kids. It's important to make students understand that even parents who do send their kids to private schools still pay taxes to support public education. As taxpayers, they feel entitled to have public education support their beliefs. Question 7 addresses this issue of parental and taxpayer control over the content of education.

To understand the textbook censor's arguments, it's important to explore whether the presence of an idea equals advocacy of that idea. There is a crucial distinction between knowing about the existence of a belief or way of life and promoting that belief. Does the mention of homosexuality constitute approval of it? Does a depiction of a housewife imply that women are suited to no other roles? Students may want to argue for inclusion of all ideas and points of view as a way to resolve such issues. Remind them of the practical constraints that DelFattore mentions: textbook space, class time, and so forth.

Questions 5 and 6 about the goals of education strike at the heart of the censorship debate. Let students explore their own concepts of what education should do and see if they immediately identify critical thinking and independent judgment as important goals. I often play devil's advocate, posing as a thoroughgoing fundamentalist parent, opposed to any sort of independent thinking on the part of children; I reply to their arguments about critical thinking by insisting that I don't *want* my kids thinking for themselves. Children should obey their parents, not think for themselves. Those students who have come to college straight from high school take this issue most to heart. From their own response to parental control they can extrapolate a deeper understanding of the basis of the First Amendment.

Several of the questions invite students to research different facets of the textbook debate. Question 8 lets the organizations that DelFattore criticizes speak for themselves in their own publications. Students can then assess the rhetoric of those positions and evaluate the arguments critically. Question 9 allows them to research a particular case of bookbanning. The chapter introduction lists frequently challenged books, many of which your students will be familiar with already (especially the Judy Blume books). They are often intrigued to discover why a book they read and enjoyed provokes intense opposition from some quarters. Question 11 sends students to the local school district to see what books high school students are required to read. Be sure your students understand the issues targeted by fundamentalists and liberal extremists, as DelFattore describes them. They can then assess the reading lists with an eye to any moral or social issues that the required readings may present or avoid.

William Noble, "The Newest Bookbanners"

William Noble's very accessible discussion of censorship works well as a backdrop to the debate over *Huckleberry Finn* as well as the discussion of pornography and feminism. He establishes a broad context for considering censorship on social grounds. This essay could stand in for either the cluster on *Huck Finn* or the cluster on pornography, if you wish to skip some of the readings in this chapter.

Several of the questions invite students to think about how ideas should be controlled, if at all. The notion of ideas as poison (question 5) resonates throughout this chapter on censorship, and deserves serious consideration. Individual determinations of what constitutes poison send the discussion right back to Benjamin Franklin's "Apology for Printers": "so many men, so many minds" might also read "one man's meat is another man's poison." Question 6 lets students decide what meat to serve in a textbook, or how to present an adequate smorgasbord.

The notion of "community standards" offers a guideline for restricting certain kinds of material, but students may agree with Dworkin's objections to that notion (question 7). The same variability of opinion that Franklin relied on in his apology may protect the pornographer equally well. The solution Dworkin proposes, however, is controversial. If civil rights supersede First Amendment rights in the case of pornography, the same argument could be made about publications that demean groups other than women. In fact, John Wallace raises the same issue in his discussion of racist literature. Question 8 lets students research writing that degrades various groups to see whether Dworkin's argument would apply. If possible, they should try to obtain actual examples of such publications, either in print or on the Internet. Otherwise, news reports will have to suffice.

Question 9 sets up a debate among Noble, John Wallace, and Dudley Barlow on *Huckleberry Finn*'s role in the classroom. Wallace implies that required literary texts should reinforce positive self-images for students, while Barlow wants literature to prompt critical thinking in his students. Noble thinks students should read acknowledged classics, racist or not. If *Huck Finn* is racist, it would not perform the role Wallace's view assigns to literature and should therefore be banned; however, any racism would be irrelevant to Barlow's view—it would just prompt more critical thinking.

John H. Wallace, "The Case against *Huck Finn*"

John Wallace presents the most often quoted and staunchest opposition to *Huckleberry Finn* in recent years. Wallace has appeared on *Nightline* and other news shows to argue his case. This essay appeared in a collection of scholarly essays on Twain's novel, and has been reprinted in anthologies for students wishing to debate the merits of the book.

However, the essay presents numerous occasions to point out logical fallacies and argumentative slipperiness. Wallace repeatedly refers to "my own research" but offers no details or citations of that "research." He quotes out of context and applies arguments made in one sphere to an entirely different arena. Question 4 directs attention to one such instance: The Jewish Community Council was arguing against Christian prayer in schools—"religious practices and programs"—not arguing to eliminate any references to Christianity in classroom materials. Ask students to consider the difference between "religious practices" and "programs," and textbooks. Wallace invokes authorities in ways that are similarly misleading. He inserts the quotation from Robert Strom among paragraphs about unnamed authorities discussing *Huck Finn* in particular. It is not clear, however, whether Strom was referring to *Huckleberry Finn* when he made his remarks about "hostile, racist, vindictive, inept, or even neurotic" teachers—though Wallace's use of Strom implies that he was.

Question 6 allows students to review their own prior education to see if they were negatively influenced by the literature they read. They may have had no such experiences, having read only books that would be approved by every group. If that is the case, you might ask them whether, after reading Wallace and DelFattore, they feel that their education was sanitized or simplified for them. What values did their reading promote? How accurate or complex a picture of the modern world did the books present? Question 8 approaches this same notion of literature as being reflective of the values of a national culture.

Even if students have never read *Huckleberry Finn*, they should be able to follow the debate about it. They should even be able to perform the literary analysis prompted by question 7, for they need only look at the limited section of dialogue between Huck and Aunt Sally. Ambitious students who have already read *Huck Finn* may wish to track down Wallace's edited version that he mentions at the close of his essay and conduct a more extensive comparison. Wallace offers no explanation as to why he eliminates *hell* from his edited version, though his own evangelical background could be the reason. Nonetheless, he implies that there are other words besides *nigger* that disqualify *Huckleberry Finn* from the school classroom.

At the core of Wallace's argument is the word *nigger*, a word thrust into the limelight by the recent O. J. Simpson trial. Is Wallace right in saying no black would ever use such a term, or only use it to make money from a white audience? Is that why Ralph Ellison (who also contends that *Huckleberry Finn* is racist) uses the refrain "Keep this nigger boy running" in his novel *Invisible Man*? You might ask students to think about how African Americans use *nigger* among themselves, or in rap music. Is it okay to use pejorative terms on one's own group, but not okay if someone else applies the label? Compare *nigger* with *queer* or *kike*. Do the same rules apply to other words? or other groups?

Dudley Barlow, "Why We Still Need *Huckleberry Finn*"

Dudley Barlow's essay completes the cluster on *Huckleberry Finn*, countering the arguments of Wallace and others who oppose the novel. He offers a carefully reasoned defense of Twain's language, conceding that *nigger* is an offensive term but justifying its use in the context of the novel. Ask how many students have read *Huckleberry Finn* and whether they found it "racist" when they read it.

Barlow focuses on the classroom presentation of Twain's novel, offering strategies to his audience of educators. Students should think about themselves as the recipients of these teaching strategies (question 7) and determine what preparation a controversial book requires for both teacher and student. They should keep in mind the philosophies of education that are implicit in the arguments for or against *Huckleberry Finn*, as well as the politics behind those philosophies (question 9). Barlow's philosophy favors critical thinking, rendering controversial works like Twain's important to the learning process. He insists on the value of Twain's work to today's society, not because it's a "classic" but because it provokes discussion of important societal issues.

Question 5 asks students to revisit the notion that words have power, but this time to concentrate on how print affects that power. Ask students how they might react to seeing other racial or ethnic epithets—such as *kike, mick, spic, fag, greaser*—in print. They might research how Mark Fuhrman's racial slurs were reported in the print media at the time of the O. J. Simpson trial (especially July and August 1995) as compared to slurs against other groups. In Los Angeles, some news outlets referred to "the N-word," rather than *nigger*, though that scruple was more common in television news than in print sources. Does saying a word carry more or less weight than printing or reading it? Wallace refers to the trauma experienced by African American students who must listen to *Huckleberry Finn* being read aloud, but says little of the effects of reading the story silently.

Huntly Collins, "PC and the Press"

Political correctness may seem only marginally related to print culture studies, having more to do with speech than with print. However, as essays such as Joan DelFattore's and William Noble's have shown, PC extremists have attempted to influence textbook content by banning certain words or images in favor of others. Moreover, Huntly Collins's essay powerfully documents the way that print contributes to bringing such an issue before the public—even when there is no real issue.

Even if Collins is correct in her analysis of PC as a nonissue, the press's coverage of it has made it into a force to be reckoned with. Questions 5 and 6 allow students to assess the impact of political correctness in their own lives and on their own campus. The fear of the PC police may have inspired preemptive measures in terms of curriculum decisions. However, Collins contends that such measures do not indicate a wholesale movement away from traditional Western culture, but only a moderate broadening of the base of cultures included in the college curriculum. Question 6 offers a reality check using your own institution. Let the groups compare their findings. Even though they will all be examining the same document, their own sensitivity to PC issues will probably lead the various groups to somewhat different conclusions. Question 8 lets students check up on the press's coverage of the MLA convention, coverage which Collins cites as particularly prone to anti-intellectualism. They might also research press coverage of other academic conventions, such as scientific conferences, to see if the humanities bear the brunt of such anti-intellectualism. You might have them go back a few years to look up William Proxmire's notorious "Golden Fleece Awards," in which the Wisconsin senator derided funding for particular scientific projects, often based on an oversimplified description of such projects.

Like Susan Faludi, Collins tracks the journalists' tendency to oversimplify and to build on one another's stories. Question 9 lets students compare the "trend" stories Faludi criticizes with the PC scare stories Collins examines. In both cases, anecdotal evidence often fills in for more solid research. Question 7 lets students supply their own anecdotes, offering the same sort of verbal testimony on which so many of the news stories rely. After they have had a chance to supply some anecdotes, allow students to scrutinize them and consider whether their experiences set a trend or follow one indicated by the press.

Collins's essay criticizes other journalists for their use of evidence and their oversimplification. Her own work, by contrast, provides a model for the use of evidence. She refutes other arguments by clarifying statistics and "facts" that have been misrepresented by others. Spend some time tracing her techniques so students can compare them to less thorough journalism.

Nat Hentoff, "The Gospel according to Catharine MacKinnon"

Nat Hentoff's spirited defense of the First Amendment against the Dworkin-MacKinnon ordinance must be paired with Catharine MacKinnon's conversation with Floyd Abrams in order to give both sides of the issue a fair hearing. Once students hear from MacKinnon, they'll be able to use her position to counter Hentoff in question 7.

Hentoff raises the issue of "majoritarianism," and argues that the First Amendment exists to protect the minority from the will of the majority. Question 9 lets students explore this notion and debate the consequences of majority rule. Try to raise concrete examples of the "tyranny of the majority." For instance, should all schools close on Christmas and Easter because most students are Christian? What about neighborhoods where most students are Muslim or Jewish or Buddhist? Should their holidays be honored instead? Question 10 addresses the related issue of local enforcement of such statutes as Dworkin and MacKinnon's, which would put great power in the hands of a few officials, not always those elected by the people. Like DelFattore, many critics of Dworkin and MacKinnon worry that the decisions of the few will affect the rights of the many.

Spend some time looking at Hentoff's tone and strategies. His examples are dramatic, but his prose is often condescending or snide, which may work against him. Hentoff makes his living as a journalist, and he is wholly committed to free speech. Moreover, as he points out in his essay, he believes that the best way to counter offensive speech is with better speech. Perhaps this philosophy explains his confrontational style and his willingness to provoke controversy: Both tactics invite the sort of dialogue he encourages.

Catharine MacKinnon, Floyd Abrams, and Anthony Lewis, "A Conversation on the First Amendment"

This selection may initially be difficult for students because it is a conversation and not a straightforward essay. Instead of a single authorial voice articulating arguments and rebuttals, MacKinnon, Abrams, and Lewis weave their way among many issues. Moreover, the participants in the conversation do not always address or understand one another's questions. You might wish to spend some time analyzing the differences between a conversation and an essay, letting students assess the effect of the format on their comprehension of the various arguments.

MacKinnon here speaks in her own voice, countering the criticisms of her position on pornography. She seems rather narrowly focused and remarkably uninformed about other issues. For instance, she doesn't seem aware of the campus speech codes Huntly Collins discussed, but responds to a question about them as if it were a question about sexual harassment in the classroom. Abrams seems more informed about various threats to the First Amendment, as befits a lawyer who specializes in that field. He takes much the same position as Nat Hentoff, but his style of argumentation is more measured, perhaps because he's a lawyer and not a writer.

Some of the discussion addresses issues specifically related to free speech on campus. Question 7 asks students to consider the nature of the university: Is it like any other workplace, or does its status as an intellectual institution grant it special privileges and responsibilities? You might explain to students how the tenure system ties into this conception of the university as a place of free expression. Question 6 positions the school newspaper in the same realm as Benjamin Franklin's *Pennsylvania Gazette*, but you might ask students to consider whether school papers partake of the same latitude for free expression that the rest of the university often receives.

MacKinnon raises an interesting point in describing inadequate education as a violation of the First Amendment right to free speech. Question 8 sends students to writers in chapter 2 who describe the effects of being denied access to literacy. The newly literate frequently describe literacy education as giving them words for thoughts that they didn't know they had. Illiteracy left them unable to formulate or articulate their own ideas; literacy made those thoughts coalesce into meaning and gave them a voice. Education, then, can be said to enable free speech. But can lack of education truly be described as violating the protection of free speech?

The weakest link in the MacKinnon-Dworkin statute is its dependence on proving that behavior resulted from pornography. Hentoff and other critics repeatedly cite studies of pornography that fail to demonstrate that link, and Hentoff gives a dramatic example of violent behavior prompted by the benign rituals of the Anglican church. Question 9 asks students to decide how one could adequately demonstrate the link that the statute requires. You might ask them to assume the roles of prosecutor or jury; based on their knowledge of courtroom proceedings, what evidence would convince a jury enough to convict?

Harper's Forum, "Don't Tread on My Cursor: Freedom of Electronic Speech"

The forum among computer hackers presents many arguments through many voices, and it may seem to ramble at times. As such, it offers opportunities for confusion, but also opportunities to see how argumentative dialogue works. The verbal free-for-all transcribed here should give students some sense of the liberating effects of online communication, which are discussed frequently in chapter 6. The participants are protected by distance and by anonymity, and so they can say and do things that would ordinarily be taboo.

In this discussion you'll be able to point out many fine examples of argument by analogy—especially the extended link between housebreaking and hacking. You can also call attention to how individuals such as Barlow clarify and modify their positions in response to challenges from others. Ask students to assess which argumentative strategies are most effective. For instance, does Optik's posting of Barlow's credit history constitute a valid argument, or does it diminish his credibility by violating rules of civil engagement? How about all the name calling that the participants engage in? Are these *ad hominem* attacks legitimate?

The reason for all the analogies seems to be that the participants are attempting to apply old rules to a new technology. Questions 6 and 7 focus student attention on whether computers really are different from other technologies. This paves the way for fuller discussion of the same idea in chapter 6. At this point, you might just ask students to consider whether the differences are in kind or in degree. Are computers like printing presses, only more so? Or are they different altogether? Question 10 allows you to hold a class discussion on this issue, listing all the similarities and differences that apply and then exploring their consequences for First Amendment protection.

The computer hackers often present themselves as civil libertarians, keeping cyberspace safe for democracy. They express profound reservations about the data-gathering that intrudes on private lives, and they consider it a moral obligation to hack into the systems that store such personal information. Question 9 asks students to think about images of hackers to see whether the mainstream media usually portray them as flatteringly as they portray themselves. You may have some students who hack or know hackers. Draw on their personal experiences to see whether they think the media portrayals or the self-portrayals are more accurate.

Computer worms and viruses constitute some of the scariest differences between computer speech and other speech. Questions 11 and 12 look at how viruses differ from other speech, first by making the analogy with pornography as MacKinnon describes it, and then by looking at the effects of a computer virus described by John Seabrook. Students may wish to argue that the destructive quality of viruses disqualifies them from free speech protection. However, many people would regard hate speech as equally destructive, yet it is fully protected by the First Amendment. Perhaps the more important distinction is whether the speech requires interpretation and an act of human will in order to be translated into deeds: Viruses work automatically, hate speech and pornography do not.

CHAPTER

6

WHAT'S NEXT?

Communication in the Electronic Era

Print culture studies does not limit itself to print anymore. With the advent of digital communication, those who are interested in the dissemination and reception of information have turned their attention to computers. Many of the same techniques used to study printed matter can be applied to electronic communication. Moreover, many of the same debates that attended the development of the printing press reappear today in the context of computer technology.

This chapter explores only a few of the many interesting issues and connections that computer communication engenders. Umberto Eco's analysis of new kinds of literacy propels forward the discussion of literacy begun in chapter 2. D. T. Max and Paul Saffo provide basic comparisons of books and computers that lay the groundwork for an understanding of the complexities of the digital future. Together, these three essays give a good overview of the advantages and disadvantages of computer technology. Some of the computer's most heralded skills are its multimedia capacities and its ability to link information nonsequentially. The cluster of selections by Sharratt, Melrod, and Birkerts addresses these aspects of computer technology, in terms of both its promises and its limitations. Birkerts also introduces a set of readings that focus on the status of information. Crawford and Gorman differentiate between information and knowledge, and M. Kadi discusses the contexts that make information meaningful. Kadi's essay also acts as a bridge to the final two readings that concern communication over the Internet and other networks.

Ideally, you should accompany the readings in this chapter with hands-on experience with computers. The essays provide sufficient description of the technologies for students to understand the readings, even if computers are not available at your institution. However, you and your students will have more fun and more thorough understanding of the issues if computers can be integrated into the curriculum. While reading about multimedia CD-ROMs and hypertext, have your students sample some such programs. While discussing the Internet, let your students surf online. The following discussions of individual essays suggest many other ways to incorporate computers into your course.

Umberto Eco, "The Future of Literacy"

Umberto Eco's essay is somewhat difficult, since he covers so much terrain so quickly. His is not a straightforward argumentative piece, but rather a meditation on various aspects of technology, both new and old. He draws on a wide knowledge of the impacts of various technologies on human communication, rhetoric, and recall.

The discussion of memory links computers to the ancient development of writing and the later invention of printing. Question 5 lets students analyze the role of memory in their own education. Typically, we memorize things that brook no argument: the alphabet, the multiplication tables, the Pledge of Allegiance. Memorization discourages critical thinking. But we also use memorization for fun, as with batting averages or song lyrics.

Technology invariably changes behavior, but those changes may not necessarily be bad. Questions 6 and 7 address the positive and negative effects of such changes. You might ask students whether they multiply in their heads, on paper, or with a calculator. Does the existence of the calculator precipitate a change in our behavior? Or do we choose to relinquish some tasks to technology in order to free our minds for other tasks? Does technology distance us from work and so diminish the value of the product of technological labor? Ask students to consider, for instance, their clothes. How many have owned a hand-knit sweater or sewn their own garments? How do those products compare to machine-made or factory-produced articles?

Question 8 may seem somewhat abstract, but it allows students to connect computer words to printed ones. The ephemeral light that makes up a computer screenful of words differs markedly from the solid black on white of the printed page. As so many of the selections in this book have shown, material properties of texts have everything to do with how we absorb and regard those texts.

The politics of future literacy will certainly exacerbate the disparity between haves and have-nots. Eco takes note of this difference, but in an unexpected way. By focusing on the preservation of books and their distribution to nonindustrialized countries, he raises new implications for the politicization of literacy. Often charitable distribution programs select books that disseminate the values they wish to perpetuate. Other times, they indiscriminately forward whatever books are donated—thus passing along those items that are no longer valued by donors. Question 9 lets students research the book distribution programs Eco describes. These are usually, but not necessarily, connected to religious institutions and their missionary work in other countries. Futures for Children, for instance, is a nonsectarian organization that arranges for books to reach Native American children on reservations in the southwestern United States.

D. T. Max, "The End of the Book?"

D. T. Max's essay addresses the fundamental differences between books and computers as forms of technology that can store and deliver information. He introduces students to the terminology of the field, and analyzes how slight the impact of CD-ROMs has been on the publishing business so far, in spite of all the hoopla about multimedia.

Questions 6, 8, and 9 prompt more thorough consideration of the two technologies. Question 6 asks students to think first about what functions books and computers are presently best suited for, and then to imagine future applications of computer technology to certain kinds of books. It can lead the imaginative student to discover the excitement that drives much of the work done in Multimedia Gulch, the thrill of "What if?" Question 8 lets students compare books and CD-ROMs as research tools, assessing the strengths and limitations of each. This activity should provide a measure of skepticism about the glories of computer research—skepticism that is necessary in the face of all the hype about computers as storehouses of information. The success of this assignment will, of course, depend on the resources available at your institution. However, it can be as enlightening for the student to find out what is *not* on the CD-ROM as it can be for the traditionalist to discover what *is* on CD. Question 9 lets students see how indebted computers are to the print culture that preceded them. Even the most forward-looking computer publications still rely on the conventions of printed communication that have evolved over the last five hundred years.

Question 7 asks students to recall a favorite childhood artifact, but this question may be applicable only to a few students. Many will not have this nostalgic affection for books as objects. They may never have owned or even held a really fine piece of printing. You may want to bring in a simply beautiful book in order to help students understand what writers like Updike mean when they talk about the "aesthetic values" of the book, and its sensuous appeal.

On the other hand, college students may well understand how the march of technology makes computers obsolete. Ask them to recall their first computer games. Were those games played on an Atari? How sophisticated were they? Students will have no trouble discussing the dizzying speed of technological change with reference to games, and you can build on that awareness to move back into Max's discussion of "transitional technology" and literary works.

Max's interview with Louis Rossetto offers the first of many discussions of the computer's ability to democratize knowledge. Question 10 sends students back to LynNell Hancock's overview of computer haves and have-nots in chapter 2. Other selections in this chapter will expand on the disparities of access that make Rossetto's claim ring false. See especially M. Kadi's assessment of the diversity of the Internet (pp. 599–607).

Paul Saffo, "Quality in an Age of Electronic Incunabula"

Paul Saffo's essay offers an approach to the question of the book's future that is informed by the long view of history. He neither frets nostalgically about the book's demise nor crows ecstatically about multimedia and hypertext. Indeed, Saffo's matter-of-fact tone about technology may seem rather dull by comparison to the enthusiasm of *Wired* co-founder Louis Rossetto in Max's article "The End of the Book?" Question 5 asks students to compare these two ways of looking at the future.

Not all students have long relationships with the book as an object, but virtually all will be able to discuss their relationship with paper, as question 6 asks them to do. It may seem utopian to imagine a paperless office or a paperless classroom. Think of the trees that would be saved! But so much of our relationship to information has involved paper that many of us are unable to process ideas without printing them out. (I know I am one of the paper-addicted.) This question asks students to think long and hard about whether they can break free from their ties to paper, or whether that will have to wait for future generations.

Questions 7 and 8 focus on Saffo's notions about quality, cost, and availability as criteria for measuring the value of technological innovation. Booklovers bemoan the loss of quality, while computer aficionados stress the increased availability of information. Perhaps they're both wrong. Quality may increase as technology improves—already visual images on screen are vastly superior to those of a few years ago. By the same token, digitizing information does not guarantee its availability. Already many people are left out of the information loop because they cannot afford the technology necessary to retrieve that information.

The final question addresses Saffo's ideas about originality and plagiarism. Our culture so values originality that we even scorn "copycat killers" who aren't as inventive as original serial murderers. Students may wish to discuss originality in light of their fears about academic plagiarism. They have so often been warned against plagiarism that many students hesitate to use any secondary sources. Saffo's argument may suggest that no thoughts are original anyway, so why not plagiarize? That idea tends to undermine cherished notions of our own individuality and specialness, so students may reject it. You might ask them to focus on whether originality might consist in fresh combinations of borrowed materials. You could also refer them back to Benjamin Franklin's attitudes toward plagiarism, as described by Larzer Ziff (pp. 38–50).

Bernard Sharratt, "But Is It Art? A Review of the Microsoft Art Gallery on CD-ROM"

Bernard Sharratt describes one enticing example of what new computer technologies can accomplish that differentiates them from books. His review of the multimedia Microsoft Art Gallery highlights many of the features that computer aficionados praise, but also raises many of the fears that booklovers voice.

Question 4 lets students consider how Sharratt's review might have differed if it had not been written for *The New York Times Book Review*, whose readers have ready access to some of the greatest museums in the world. He assumes his readers will share his beliefs about the value of firsthand viewing. Readers in other parts of the country without such ready access to paintings and sculptures may not share his implicit belief in the diminished quality of reproductions. Question 5 challenges this same set of assumptions, and should prompt a lively class discussion, especially if your students come from diverse backgrounds. Students who have had the advantage of visiting art museums will be able to describe the experience of viewing a painting in person: the ambiance of the museum, the special quality of time spent viewing, the sheer difference in scale of a full-sized painting and an onscreen reproduction. Those who have not been so privileged will doubtless point out that a reproduction of a painting is better than no painting at all.

Computer advocates point to the microchip's ability to store and give back massive quantities of data. In the face of the "data overload" that so many commentators describe, this feature seems worth attending to. Question 6 asks students to compare how Sharratt, Umberto Eco, and Paul Saffo address the issue. Sharratt recognizes that there is more in the Art Gallery than he could ever absorb. However, that very superabundance encourages him to browse and reassemble information in patterns that he would not otherwise hit on. The random access that computers encourage can lead to liberation from previous modes of thinking and stale patterns of interpretation. Or it can lead to aimless wandering, as Sharratt also notes.

Sharratt's essay addresses one of the central debates about multimedia technology: Is a CD-ROM version of a thing equivalent to the thing itself? Several of the questions ask students to engage this issue. Based on Sharratt's description, students should be able to judge the merits of the Microsoft Art Gallery program (question 8). The advantage of such technology is clear: It economically makes artworks available to people who otherwise would not be able to see them, thereby scoring high in Saffo's categories of cost and availability. But is a painting something more than the information contained within the frame? Is there some other factor that makes a work of art, besides digitizable bits of color? Finally, we get to the $64,000 question: What is art? Computer technology increasingly lets us treat art as information, but many people balk at this attitude. It may be interesting for students to explore their own definitions of art in answer to question 7, and then share them with the class.

Sharratt also raises the fear that the digitized image will come to substitute for the painting itself. Question 9 lets students examine whether other technological innovations have encouraged the same sort of substitution of secondhand for firsthand experience. If they have, is that necessarily a bad thing? Is the diminishment of quality offset by the increase in availability, as Saffo would put it?

George Melrod, "Digital Unbound"

Some students may find it hard to grasp just what George Melrod means when he discusses hyperfiction. Questions 1, 2, and 3 try to guide them to an understanding of the fundamental qualities of hypertext: nonsequential narrative; multiple plot lines and narrative points of view; and participation of the reader in shaping the story anew each time it's read.

Proponents of hyperfiction hail it most of all for changing the way we think about reading and writing. Questions 5, 6, and 7 ask students to pay attention to how they read and write now, and then to try to break free of the conventional ways of writing. Sequential, linear thinking is not the only "right" way, and hypertext webs make that point graphically clear. Thinking of alternatives may be especially liberating for students who have had trouble arranging their thoughts linearly.

Students will be able to understand hyperfiction more thoroughly if they can experience it for themselves, as they are asked to do in question 8. The modest cost of Michael Joyce's *Afternoon, A Story* ($20 directly from Eastgate systems) ought not to strain any library budgets, provided your institution has the computers to support it. You may even find students interested in writing their own hyperfictions, using Storyspace, also available from Eastgate. After spending some time playing with Joyce's story yourself, you may enjoy reading Sven Birkerts's critique of hypertext in his essay "Hypertext: Of Mouse and Man," in *The Gutenberg Elegies* (1994).

Computer advocates repeatedly point to the "paperless office" as the ideal for the future. Question 9 asks students to envision such a future for their own campus or classroom. It encourages them to develop innovative ways to teach and learn, and to free themselves from business as usual. Let the students know that their ideas will be taken seriously. Share their innovations with the class as a whole. Consider implementing some of the best ideas for the latter part of the semester.

If you wish to incorporate fiction into your writing class, question 10 offers a chance to do so. Reading Borges's story can lead to literary analysis assignments, but it also links nicely with Melrod's discussion of hypertext. This assignment will work especially well if students have access to Joyce's hypernovella, instead of relying on Melrod's description of it. Then they can compare the experience of reading the two texts and can trace the mental and imaginative efforts required by each.

Sven Birkerts, "Perseus Unbound"

Sven Birkerts happily plays the role of skeptic in the face of the hype about computers. Here he looks at the same hypertext capabilities that George Melrod examines, and asks important questions relative to the value of information and knowledge. Birkerts introduces epistemological distinctions that reappear in the essays by Walt Crawford and Michael Gorman, and by M. Kadi.

Hypertext's power to connect texts from disparate disciplines has been one of its strongest selling points. Students can follow their own interests, jumping from one way of knowing to the next as their inclination takes them. But the flip side of this intellectual flexibility and laudable cross-disciplinarity is a lack of context, according to Birkerts. Question 6 points students back to Bernard Sharratt's description of how he used the Microsoft Art Gallery as a way to demonstrate Birkerts's point. Because the program "provides no overall consecutive argument," but instead suggests and makes possible all sorts of connections, "the onus of learning is on us," says Sharratt. While this sounds like a potentially valuable pedagogy, Sharratt suggests that the actual effect is quite different: The user relies on the received opinions and expert interpretations made so readily available, and then dashes on to the next interesting bit of information.

Many students (and others) equate knowledge with information, a commodity that CD-ROMs can certainly supply. But Birkerts's objections to interactive teaching programs focus on the idea of knowledge as something quite distinct from mere data. He looks at how knowledge is used, how it is acquired and retained, and most importantly how it is made meaningful. Questions 1 and 5 enable students to explore how different disciplines define, use, and transmit knowledge. A fruitful discussion of the aims of education could arise from these distinctions. Question 7 follows up on this idea and asks students to formulate their own definition of wisdom.

Question 4 focuses on Birkerts's diction, especially his use of such words as *juggernaut, bailiwick, nebulous, curmudgeon, proselytizers, obdurate, orthographic, synchronic, ineluctably,* and *cruxes.* Is he just showing off, or is he trying to make a point by steeping the reader in "learned" diction? Can interactive multimedia offer the density of language that books can? Perhaps Birkerts uses this difficult language to "encode this sense of obstacle" that he values. You might connect this question to question 8 about the "pastness" of the printed page, and to Paul Saffo's notions about quality's connection to the resistance of the material. The Perseus program can make ancient history readily accessible, but it may also sacrifice valuable texture and depth that lead to knowledge.

Questions 9, 10, and 11 allow students to synthesize various views on computers that have been offered by several essays. Any of these questions could form the basis of an assignment that would serve as a culmination of this unit on electronic communication. Question 11 on the future of the book could even work as a final topic for the semester, allowing students to reflect on all the uses of the book that preceded the electronic age.

Walt Crawford and Michael Gorman, "Coping with Electronic Information"

This essay turns the students' attention to libraries and their function as repositories of information and aids to scholarship. Students may not find libraries inherently interesting, but they should recognize the important role libraries play in education. Crawford and Gorman write with humor and clarity; they make their subject interesting and accessible to the nonlibrarian.

Crawford and Gorman begin by making distinctions among "goods of the mind" (question 1). Their discussion resembles Birkerts's, and question 9 lets students explore the resemblance. It also asks them to assess the relationship between information and knowledge, and to evaluate the computer's ability to disseminate either. Ask students to go over the list of goods of the mind and determine which ones books can disseminate.

This selection gives students the opportunity to familiarize themselves with the various resources offered by a modern library. Questions 6, 7, and 8 send students to the library to evaluate computerized bibliographies and other electronic sources of information. Question 6 requires rigorous attention on the part of students. They must record every instruction and search term in order to have valid data for evaluation. This assignment may work best if students work in pairs: one student to search and the other to record. Once they've gathered their data, they can begin to see patterns in how human minds search, and how computers can and cannot respond to those inquiries. As students become more familiar with online searching, they usually find themselves adapting their mental patterns to fit the patterns recognized by the computer program. Question 7 asks students to compare online sources with traditional printed sources, devising their own criteria for judging the various sources. Online sources may be quicker to use, but they may also lack authority. Interviews with librarians (question 8) will help students see how actual users fare with different computerized resources. Librarians may offer new views of the management of information that complement the perspectives of students and teachers.

Question 10 lets students extend their own experience as novice researchers by interviewing professors about their scholarship. Students should be able to see the continuities between their own research and that of their professors, even as they appreciate the differences. You might ask students to share their interview results in class and then hold a discussion on how different disciplines use computers. This could fruitfully refer back to Birkerts's distinction between the natural sciences and the sciences of culture.

M. Kadi, "The Internet Is Four Inches Tall"

This essay from the 'zine *h2so4* raises important points about the information superhighway, and does so in a manner that is refreshing and provocative. M. Kadi's humorous and direct prose contrasts markedly with some of the academic considerations of computers. She makes her points with intellectual rigor but certainly without academic rigor mortis. Kadi's essay covers a lot of ground: She discusses epistemology and contexts for knowledge, the economics of access to the information highway, and the limitations of online communication.

Questions 1, 5, and 6 focus on Kadi's demonstration of how undemocratic the information highway really is. Spend some time evaluating her use of statistics to make her point. Kadi humanizes the statistics by offering analogies with more familiar realms, such as television viewing. She thereby makes the raw numbers more comprehensible to her readers.

Kadi argues that information can only be meaningful if it occurs in a context. Questions 3, 7, 8, and 9 address this notion of context from different vantage points. Question 3 lets students step back from the act of reading this textbook to determine how the context of a writing class guides the questions printed after Kadi's essay. Would these be the questions students would ask of the essay if they were reading it in the fanzine it originally appeared in? Question 9 lets them use that exploration to reply to D. T. Max's cybervisionaries with an understanding of the role that traditional school contexts play in our education. Students who have examined their own ability to create contexts (question 8) may agree with Max's elation at a school without teachers, for they may already find themselves adept at asking questions. Others may see the need for mentors and conceptual frameworks.

Question 2 asks students to examine Kadi's extended example of how J. Individual surfs the Internet. Kadi's demonstration casts serious doubt on the idealistic claims for the diversity of the online environment. Combine this analysis with question 10 to explore how any reader "surfs" the overwhelming sea of publications that are available. Despite the variety of perspectives and ideas that print and computers make available, do most people gravitate toward what they already know? Do we use information only to reinforce our own ideas, not to challenge or enlarge them?

The final question lets students scrutinize how online services are marketed. Once they have read Kadi's criticisms of the diversity and usefulness of online information, they can think more critically about the promotional strategies used to encourage connectivity.

John Seabrook, "My First Flame"

Many of the problems of online communication arise from the anonymity that the computer makes possible, as John Seabrook explains in this essay. Several of the study questions ask students to explore this aspect of the Net. If we are known only by what we type onto a screen, many of our social barriers and long-held prejudices will finally come crashing down. However, that same anonymity allows us to create personae for ourselves that may not match who we are in real life. We can change our age, sex, race, and ethnicity—and nobody will be the wiser. Which of us can resist the temptation to become the person we've always wanted to be? Question 4 invites students to explore the anonymity of the Net, while question 9 lets them devise guidelines to prevent the abuses Seabrook describes.

Some students may feel that Seabrook overreacted to his flame. They may wonder why he didn't just erase the message and "get over it." Question 5 tries to address the underlying issue of how the flame destroyed Seabrook's faith in the new technology. You might point to other instances in modern history in which society suddenly glimpsed the dark side of a wonderful technology. When D. B. Cooper skyjacked an airliner, for example, Americans saw their gleaming passenger jets as potential sites of crime and extortion for the first time. Students will probably relate best to the obscene phone call analogy, with its sense of violation and vulnerability. Try to get them to analyze their relationship to new inventions. Do they trust progress implicitly, or are they wary?

There are many ways to approach question 6, which addresses the gender gap that seems to exist with regard to computers. Call students' attention to the young, white, suburban male LynNell Hancock uses to exemplify a fully participating member of the cyberculture (p. 198). Or ask them to notice that George Melrod's essay on hypertext appeared in *Details: For Men*, not in *Elle*. See if they can find similar articles in women's magazines. Or you might have students bring to class a variety of computer magazines to examine the advertising and the roster of writers. How many ads depict women (or minorities, for that matter)? What proportion of the writers are male? How many of the students in class have had online experience? Of those, what was the ratio of men to women?

Seabrook's article raises the key issue of the extent to which freedom of speech exists and should continue to exist in the online environment. Question 8 sends students back to the hackers' forum in the preceding chapter for more views on this fundamental freedom. You'll want to continue the discussion after students have read Amy Harmon's essay on hate speech and the Internet.

Amy Harmon, "Bigots on the Net"

This selection amplifies the debate over free speech on the Net begun by the *Harper's* magazine forum among hackers and continued by John Seabrook's article "My First Flame." Here the focus is on organized hate speech, as compared to individually offensive messages or viruses. Legal policy regarding computer technology is still evolving, but so far the courts have tended to treat e-mail messages as private communications. The online services are likened to telephone companies: They are the carriers of the messages, but they are not responsible for regulating the content of the messages. Similarly, government agencies may not monitor communications without a court order, obtained only after producing evidence that suspected criminal activity is being conducted. These regulations, however, are in the midst of change. You may want to ask students to research the most current policies as they address question 7, to see whether recent legislation takes into consideration the complexities that Harmon and Seabrook describe.

Questions 4 and 5 revisit the censorship issues that were discussed in chapter 4 with respect to the print media. Students are usually in favor of complete freedom of speech, until they start to consider the problems posed by this ideal. The accessibility of computer communication by unsupervised children will usually hit a nerve with students (question 4). They vehemently oppose censorship that deprives mature adults of the right to decide what is in their own best interest, but when it comes to protecting younger readers from potentially harmful communications, they often modify their positions. It's important to have students consider the practical, everyday situations that often prevail over the ideal. How are computers really used? Do parents really supervise their kids when they are online (for that matter, do they supervise their kids when they watch TV)?

Question 6 lets students look more closely at the groups that Harmon's article concerns by asking them to test William Pierce's claim about media portrayals of his organization. Harmon's article appeared before the bombing of the federal building in Oklahoma and the ensuing spate of articles about the spread of right-wing militia movements and white supremacist organizations. Students should therefore have no trouble finding articles about such groups. Coverage of those groups, however, may have been changed by the events in Oklahoma.

Media portrayals may be more balanced and careful now, given the recent discoveries about how widespread such organizations are.

Many people laud the Internet for the ease with which they can find information on any subject. Question 8 asks students to consider whether the Internet could become analogous to the grocery-store self-help books described by Steven Starker (pp. 405–12). The Net offers the same privacy, availability, and cost-effectiveness that Starker claims are keys to the success of self-help books. It also offers the same lack of authority, the same ability for charlatans and legitimate experts to appear side by side.

BEDFORD BOOKS *of* St. Martin's Press